JUSTICE STATISTICS

JUSTICE STATISTICS

AN EXTENDED LOOK AT CRIME IN THE UNITED STATES

Fourth Edition
2018

Edited by
Shana Hertz Hattis

Lanham, MD

Bernan Press

Published by Bernan Press
An imprint of The Rowman & Littlefield Publishing Group, Inc.
4501 Forbes Boulevard, Suite 200, Lanham, Maryland 20706
www.rowman.com
800-865-3457

6 Tinworth Street, London SE11 5AL, United Kingdom

 ISBN: 978-1-64143-267-2
eISBN: 978-1-64143-268-9

∞™ The paper used in this publication meets the minimum requirements of
American National Standard for Information Sciences—Permanence of
Paper for Printed Library Materials, ANSI/NISO Z39.48-1992.

Printed in the United States of America.

Contents

INTRODUCTION

Bernan Press is pleased to present the fourth edition of its comprehensive collection of justice statistics in the United States. This volume provides valuable information compiled by the Department of Justice, including its subsidiaries, the Bureau of Justice Statistics (BJS) and the Federal Bureau of Investigation (FBI).

This volume brings together 11 key reports that fall under this category. Topics covered include criminal victimization, correctional populations, crime in the United States, hate crimes, probation, parole, school violence, and law enforcement officers killed and assaulted. Tables in this volume provide a comprehensive account of each of these subjects; for more information, including full-scope methodologies and information about standard errors for each table, please see the full reports at the URLs listed below.

Each section contains statistical tables and figures highlighting the data, as well as a brief summary of the report's methodology and at-a-glance highlights of the most compelling information.

The reports:

Capital Punishment, 2016, https://www.bjs.gov/index.cfm?ty=pbdetail&iid=6246.

Correctional Populations in the United States, 2016, discusses the trends and changes in the incarcerated populations of the country's prisons. The full report can be found at https://www.bjs.gov/index.cfm?ty=pbdetail&iid=6226.

Crime Against Persons with Disabilities, 2009–2015, presents estimates of nonfatal violent crime (rape or sexual assault, robbery, aggravated assault, and simple assault) against persons age 12 or older with disabilities. Disabilities are classified according to six limitations: hearing, vision, cognitive, ambulatory, self-care, and independent living. The full report can be found at https://www.bjs.gov/index.cfm?ty=pbdetail&iid=5986.

Crime in the United States, 2016, provides an introduction to overall crime trends. This report is more fully presented in Bernan Press's companion volume, *Crime in the United States.* However, given the importance of the report in the understanding of justice and crime trends in the United States, its most relevant tables have been included in this volume. Once again appearing in this book, and not contained in the complementary *Crime* volume, is the full range of the UCR's

expanded offense tables. Also included are three supplementary reports: Federal Crime Data, Human Trafficking, and Cargo Theft. The full report can be accessed at https://ucr.fbi.gov/crime-in-the-u.s/2016/crime-in-the-u.s.-2016/cius-2016.

Criminal Victimization, 2016, takes a close look at the victims of violent and property crime in the United States. The full report is accessible at https://www.bjs.gov/content/pub/pdf/cv16.pdf.

Hate Crime Statistics, 2016, details the hate crimes committed in the United States throughout 2015. It can be accessed at https://ucr.fbi.gov/crime-in-the-u.s/2016/crime-in-the-u.s.-2016/resource-pages/hate-crime-statistics.

Indicators of School Crime and Safety, 2016, is an annual report that presents data on crime and safety at school from the perspectives of students, teachers, and principals. Conducted jointly by the Bureau of Justice Statistics and the National Center for Education Statistics, the report's data sources include the National Crime Victimization Survey (NCVS), the School Crime Supplement to the NCVS, the Youth Risk Behavior Survey, and the School Survey on Crime and Safety. The full report can be accessed at http://www.bjs.gov/index.cfm?ty=pbdetail&iid=5926.

Jail Inmates in 2016 presents estimates of the inmate populations of jails based on various demographic characteristics. The full report can be accesses at https://www.bjs.gov/content/pub/pdf/ji16.pdf.

Law Enforcement Officers Killed and Assaulted, 2017 (LEOKA), is the primary resource for data about harm done to law enforcement officers. This volume provides a comprehensive sample of the report; further information can be obtained at https://ucr.fbi.gov/leoka/2017.

Probation and Parole in the United States, 2016, details data about post-release inmates still in the legal system. The report can be accessed at https://www.bjs.gov/content/pub/pdf/ppus16.pdf.

2018 Update on Prisoner Recidivism: A 9-Year Follow-Up Period (2005–2014) is new to this edition. It examines the rate, number, and percent of prisoners who were arrested at least once during the nine years following their release. It can be found at https://www.bjs.gov/content/pub/pdf/18upr9yfup0514.pdf.

ABOUT THE EDITOR

Shana Hertz Hattis is an editor with over a decade of experience in statistical and government research publications. Past titles include *State Profiles: The Population and Economy of Each U.S. State*, *Crime in the United States*, and *The Almanac of American Education*. She earned her bachelor of science in journalism and master of science in education degrees from Northwestern University.

PART 1

Capital Punishment, 2016

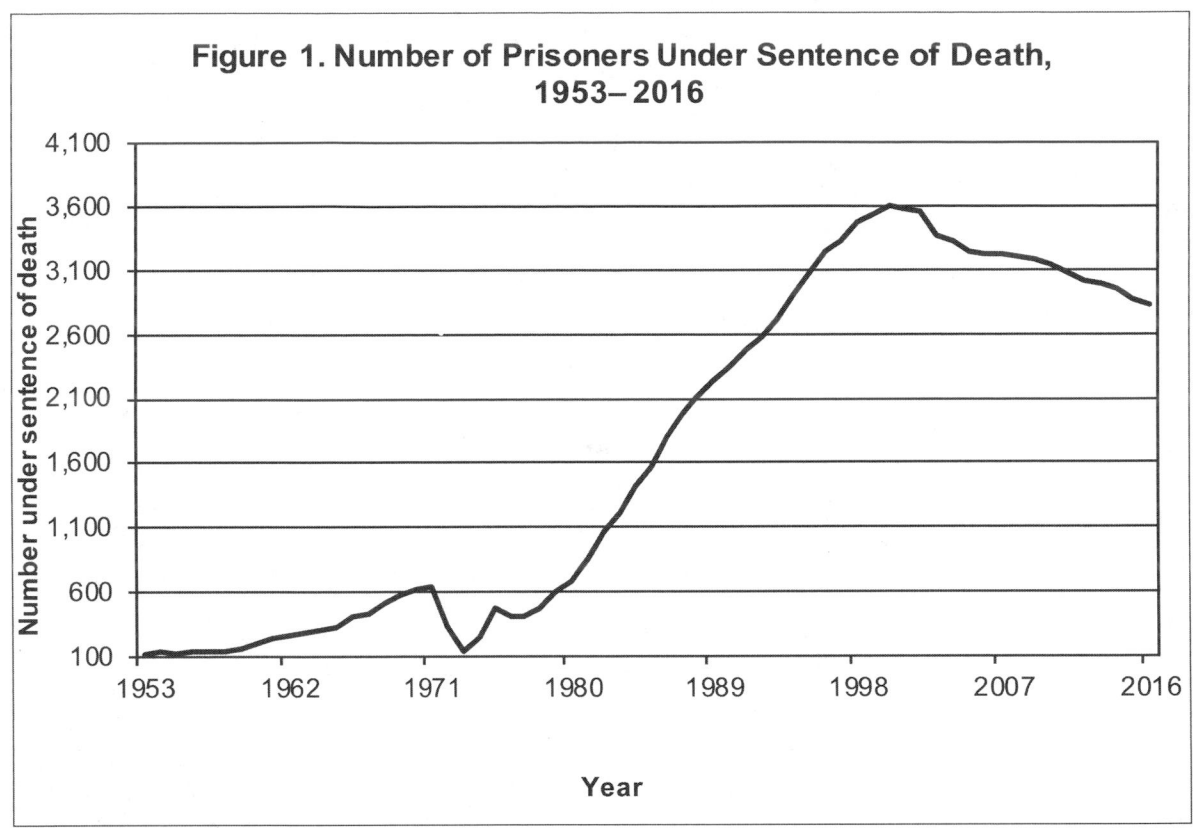

Figure 1. Number of Prisoners Under Sentence of Death, 1953–2016

- At yearend 2016, 32 states and the Federal Bureau of Prisons (BOP) held 2,814 prisoners under sentence of death, 58 persons (2 percent) fewer than at yearend 2015. This was the 16th consecutive year in which this number has decreased.

- Twenty prisoners were executed in the United States in 2016; 18 were White and 2 were Black. Two prisoners were of Hispanic/Latino origin.

- The number of prisoners executed in 2016 represented the smallest number of executions since 1991, when 14 prisoners were executed.

- Thirteen states and the BOP held fewer prisoners under sentence of death at yearend 2016 than at yearend 2015, while 4 states held more prisoners and 16 states held the same number of prisoners.

- Approximately 55 percent of prisoners under sentence of death at yearend 2016 were White, while approximately 42 percent were Black and approximately 15 percent of were of Hispanic or Latino origin (in cases in which origin was known). Approximately 98 percent of prisoners under sentence of death were male.

- Nearly half (49 percent) of prisoners held under sentence of death were located in California (26 percent), Florida (14 percent), and Texas (9 percent). In 2016, Texas executed 7 prisoners; Florida, 1 prisoner; and California, no prisoners.

- Twelve states received a total of 32 prisoners under sentence of death in 2016; 17 states and the BOP removed 70 prisoners from under sentence of death by means other than execution.

Table 1. Status of the Death Penalty, 2015–2016

(Number.)

State	Executions		Number of prisoners under sentence of death on 12/31	
	2015	2016	2015	2016
Total	28	20	2,881	2,814
Alabama..	0	2	187	183
Arizona...	0	0	119	118
California..	0	0	739	742
Federal Bureau of Prisons.....................................	0	0	59	58
Florida	2	1	390	382
Georgia	5	9	71	58
Louisiana	0	0	82	73
Mississippi..	0	0	47	47
Missouri..	6	1	NA	NA
Nevada	0	0	82	83
North Carolina..	0	0	147	150
Ohio...	0	0	137	140
Oklahoma...	1	0	47	46
Pennsylvania...	0	0	181	174
Tennessee	0	0	67	63
Texas..	13	7	254	244
Virginia...	1	0	NA	NA
Other jurisdictions..	0	0	272 (19 jurisdictions)	253 (18 jurisdictions)

Note: Jurisdictions without the death penalty in 2016 include Alaska, Connecticut, District of Columbia, Hawaii, Illinois, Iowa, Maine, Maryland, Massachusetts, Michigan, Minnesota, New Jersey, North Dakota, Rhode Island, Vermont, and West Virginia. New Mexico repealed the death penalty for offenses committed after July 1, 2009. As of December 31, 2016, two males in New Mexico were under previously imposed death sentences.

Table 2. Prisoners Under Sentence of Death, by Region, Jurisdiction, and Race, 2015 and 2016

(Number.)

Region and jurisdiction	Prisoners under sentence of death, 12/31/15			Received under sentence of death, 2016			Removed from death row (excluding executions), 2016			Executed, 2016			Prisoners under sentence of death, 12/31/16		
	Total[1]	White[2,3]	Black[2]	Total[1]	White[2]	Black[2]	Total[1]	White[2]	Black[2]	Total[1]	White[2]	Black[2]	Total[1]	White[2]	Black[2]
U.S. Total	2,872	1,606	1,202	32	8	20	70	36	31	20	18	2	2,814	1,560	1,189
Federal[4]	59	30	28	0	0	0	1	0	1	0	0	0	58	30	27
State	2,813	1,576	1,174	32	8	20	69	36	30	20	18	2	2,756	1,530	1,162
Northeast	193	87	104	1	0	0	19	8	11	0	0	0	175	79	93
Connecticut[5]	11	5	6	0	0	0	11	5	6	0	0	0	0	0	0
New Hampshire	1	0	1	0	0	0	0	0	0	0	0	0	1	0	1
New York	0	0	0	0	0	0	0	0	0	0	0	0	0	0	0
Pennsylvania	181	82	97	1	0	0	8	3	5	0	0	0	174	79	92
Midwest	200	109	90	5	2	3	3	2	1	1	1	0	201	108	92
Indiana	13	10	3	0	0	0	0	0	0	0	0	0	13	10	3
Kansas	10	7	3	1	1	0	1	1	0	0	0	0	10	7	3
Missouri	26	18	8	0	0	0	0	0	0	1	1	0	25	17	8
Nebraska[3]	10	8	2	0	0	0	0	0	0	0	0	0	10	8	2
Ohio	138	63	74	4	1	3	2	1	1	0	0	0	140	63	76
South Dakota	3	3	0	0	0	0	0	0	0	0	0	0	3	3	0
South	1,413	742	651	17	4	12	41	21	17	19	17	2	1,370	708	644
Alabama	187	92	94	3	1	2	5	3	2	2	2	0	183	88	94
Arkansas[6]	35	16	19	1	1	0	1	1	0	0	0	0	35	16	19
Delaware	14	6	8	0	0	0	1	1	0	0	0	0	13	5	8
Florida[7]	389	235	153	3	1	2	9	3	6	1	1	0	382	232	149
Georgia	68	35	33	0	0	0	1	1	0	9	7	2	58	27	31
Kentucky	32	27	5	0	0	0	0	0	0	0	0	0	32	27	5
Louisiana	82	26	55	0	0	0	9	2	6	0	0	0	73	24	49
Mississippi	47	20	26	0	0	0	0	0	0	0	0	0	47	20	26
North Carolina	147	64	76	5	0	4	2	1	0	0	0	0	150	63	80
Oklahoma	47	23	20	1	0	1	2	1	0	0	0	0	46	22	21
South Carolina	40	17	23	0	0	0	3	1	2	0	0	0	37	16	21
Tennessee[7]	67	36	30	0	0	0	4	4	0	0	0	0	63	32	30
Texas[8]	251	141	106	4	1	3	4	3	1	7	7	0	244	132	108
Virginia	7	4	3	0	0	0	0	0	0	0	0	0	7	4	3
West	1,007	638	329	9	2	5	6	5	1	0	0	0	1,010	635	333
Arizona	119	96	18	1	0	0	2	2	0	0	0	0	118	94	18
California[3,6]	739	439	269	7	2	4	4	3	1	0	0	0	742	438	272
Colorado	3	0	3	0	0	0	0	0	0	0	0	0	3	0	3
Idaho	9	9	0	0	0	0	0	0	0	0	0	0	9	9	0
Montana	2	2	0	0	0	0	0	0	0	0	0	0	2	2	0
Nevada	82	49	31	1	0	1	0	0	0	0	0	0	83	49	32
New Mexico	2	2	0	0	0	0	0	0	0	0	0	0	2	2	0
Oregon[3]	33	29	3	0	0	0	0	0	0	0	0	0	33	29	3
Utah	9	7	1	0	0	0	0	0	0	0	0	0	9	7	1
Washington	9	5	4	0	0	0	0	0	0	0	0	0	9	5	4
Wyoming	0	0	0	0	0	0	0	0	0	0	0	0	0	0	0

Note: Some figures shown for yearend 2015 are revised from those reported in *Capital Punishment, 2014–2015 Statistical Brief* (NCJ 250638, BJS web, May 2017). The revised figures include 5 inmates who were either reported late to the National Prisoner Statistics program or were not in custody of state correctional authorities on December 31, 2015 (1 each in Ohio, Mississippi, Oklahoma, California, and Nevada), and exclude 14 inmates who were relieved of a death sentence before December 31, 2015 (3 each in Georgia and Texas; 2 in California; and 1 each in Missouri, Mississippi, Oklahoma, South Carolina, Tennessee, and Nevada).

[1]Includes American Indians and Alaska Natives, Asians, Native Hawaiians and Other Pacific Islanders, and persons of Hispanic/Latino origin for whom no other race was identified.
[2]Counts of White and Black inmates include persons of Hispanic/Latino origin.
[3]The race reported for 5 inmates has been revised from Hispanic to White (2 each in Nebraska and California and 1 in Oregon). The Hispanic/Latino origin for these inmates remains unchanged.
[4]Excludes persons held under Armed Forces jurisdiction with a military death sentence for murder.
[5]The Connecticut Supreme Court upheld a previous ruling that extended the repeal of the capital statute to include 11 males under a previously imposed death sentence. These prisoners will be resentenced to life in prison without the possibility of parole (State v. Peeler, 321 CONN. 375 (2016)).
[6]One inmate under sentence of death in Arkansas was erroneously reported as being under sentence of death in California in the 2014–2015 report.
[7]One inmate who was previously in the custody of Florida is now being reported in Tennessee where he is under a separate sentence of death.
[8]Two of the White prisoners executed were of Hispanic origin.

Table 3. Prisoners Removed from Under Sentence of Death, by Region, Jurisdiction, and Method of Removal, 2016

(Number.)

Region and jurisdiction	Not overturned by appeals court or higher court			Overturned by appeals court or higher court		
	Total	Execution	Other death[1]	Capital statute	Capital conviction[2]	Death sentence
U.S. Total..	90	20	19	11	15	25
Federal...	1	0	0	0	0	1
State..	89	20	19	11	15	24
Northeast....................................	19	0	0	11	3	5
Connecticut....................................	11	0	0	11	0	0
Pennsylvania..................................	8	0	0	0	3	5
Midwest.......................................	4	1	1	0	1	1
Kansas...	1	0	1	0	0	0
Missouri..	1	1	0	0	0	0
Ohio...	2	0	0	0	1	1
South..	60	19	14	0	10	17
Alabama..	7	2	1	0	2	2
Arkansas...	1	0	0	0	1	0
Delaware...	1	0	0	0	1	0
Florida...	10	1	2	0	3	4
Georgia...	10	9	0	0	0	1
Louisiana...	9	0	3	0	3	3
North Carolina................................	2	0	2	0	0	0
Oklahoma.......................................	2	0	1	0	0	1
South Carolina................................	3	0	0	0	0	3
Tennessee.......................................	4	0	3	0	0	1
Texas...	11	7	2	0	0	2
West...	6	0	4	0	1	1
Arizona...	2	0	1	0	0	1
California...	4	0	3	0	1	0

[1]In 2016, all other deaths were due to natural causes.
[2]Includes capital conviction and sentence.

Table 4. Demographic Characteristics for Prisoners Under Sentence of Death, 2016

(Percent; number.)

Characteristic	Total yearend		Admissions		Removals	
	Number	Percent	Number	Percent	Number	Percent
Total	2,814	100.0	32	100.0	90	100.0
Sex...						
Male...	2,762	98.2	31	96.9	87	96.7
Female...	52	'1.8	1	3.1	3	3.3
Race[1,2]						
White	1,560	55.4	8	25.0	54	60.0
Black...	1,189	42.3	20	62.5	33	36.7
Other[3]...	65	2.3	4	12.5	3	3.3
Hispanic/Latino Origin[3]................................						
Hispanic/Latino	378	13.4	3	9.4	10	11.1
Non-Hispanic/Latino................................	2,175	77.3	24	75.0	68	75.6
Unknown...	261	9.3	5	15.6	12	13.3
Age...						
18 to 19 years...................................	1	-	1	3.1	0	0.0
20 to 24 years...................................	8	0.3	0	0.0	0	0.0
25 to 29 years...................................	67	2.4	4	12.5	2	2.2
30 to 34 years...................................	167	5.9	9	28.1	3	3.3
35 to 39 years...................................	334	11.9	8	25.0	14	15.6
40 to 44 years...................................	441	15.7	4	12.5	14	15.6
45 to 49 years...................................	509	18.1	3	9.4	13	14.4
50 to 54 years...................................	448	15.9	1	3.1	9	10.0
55 to 59 years...................................	380	13.5	1	3.1	10	11.1
60 to 64 years...................................	233	8.3	1	3.1	9	10.0
65 years and older	226	8.0	0	0.0	16	17.8
Average Age (Years)						
Mean...	49	X	38	X	51	X
Median...	48	X	38	X	49	X
Education[4]...						
8th grade or less................................	275	9.8	3	9.7	20	22.2
9th to 11th grade	784	27.9	8	25.8	19	21.1
High school graduate/GED	983	34.9	6	19.4	33	36.7
Any college...................................	203	7.2	2	6.4	4	4.4
Unknown...	569	20.2	12	38.7	14	15.6
Median Education Level						
Grade...	12th	X	11th	X	11th	X
Marital Status[5]...................................						
Total	2,814	100.0	32	100.0	90	100.0
Married	515	18.3	2	6.3	15	16.7
Divorced/separated	477	17.0	2	6.3	21	23.3
Widowed	86	3.1	0	0.0	2	2.2
Never married...................................	1,357	48.2	15	46.9	41	45.6
Unknown...	379	13.5	13	40.6	11	12.2

Note: Detail may not sum to total due to rounding.
X = Not applicable.
- = Less than 0.05 percent.
[1]Percentages for White, Black, and all other races include persons of Hispanic/Latino origin.
[2]At yearend 2016, prisoners of all other races consisted of 19 American Indians or Alaska Natives (AIANs), 40 Asians, and 6 Native Hawaiian or Other Pacific Islanders. During 2016, one AIAN prisoner and three Asian prisoners were admitted, while two AIAN prisoners and one Asian prisoner were removed.
[3]Excludes prisoners with unknown origin: 261 at yearend, 5 admissions, and 12 removals.
[4]Excludes prisoners with unknown education level: 569 at yearend, 13 admissions, and 14 removals.
[5]Excludes prisoners with unknown marital status: 379 at yearend, 13 admissions, and 11 removals.

Table 5. Advance Count of Executions, January 1–December 31, 2017

(Number.)

Year	Number of executions
Total	23
Texas..	7
Arkansas..	4
Alabama...	3
Florida	3
Ohio	2
Virginia	2
Missouri	1
Georgia	1

Table 6. Authorized Method of Execution, by State, 2016

(Percent; number.)

State	Lethal injection	Electrocution	Lethal gas	Hanging	Firing squad	Nitrogen hypoxia
Total	34	8	3	3	2	1
Alabama............................	√	√				
Arizona[1]...........................	√		√			
Arkansas[2]..........................	√	√				
California...........................	√					
Colorado............................	√					
Delaware[3]..........................	√			√		
Florida	√	√				
Georgia..............................	√					
Idaho.................................	√					
Indiana..............................	√					
Kansas...............................	√					
Kentucky[4]..........................	√	√				
Louisiana...........................	√					
Mississippi.........................	√					
Missouri.............................	√		√			
Montana............................	√					
Nebraska...........................	√					
Nevada..............................	√					
New Hampshire[5]................	√			√		
New Mexico[6]......................	√					
New York............................	√					
North Carolina...................	√					
Ohio..................................	√					
Oklahoma[7]........................	√	√			√	√
Oregon...............................	√					
Pennsylvania......................	√					
South Carolina...................	√	√				
South Dakota......................	√					
Tennessee[8]........................	√	√				
Texas.................................	√					
Utah[9]................................	√				√	
Virginia..............................	√	√				
Washington	√			√		
Wyoming[9].........................	√		√			√

Note: The method of execution of federal prisoners is lethal injection, pursuant to 28 C.F.R. Part 26. For offenses prosecuted under the Violent Crime Control and Law Enforcement Act of 1994, the execution method is that of the state in which the conviction took place (18 U.S.C. 3596).
[1]Authorizes lethal injection for persons sentenced after November 23, 1992; inmates sentenced before that date may select lethal injection or gas.
[2]Authorizes lethal injection for those whose offense occurred on or after July 4, 1983; inmates whose offense occurred before that date may select lethal injection or electrocution. Electrocution is the authorized method of use if lethal injection is invalidated by an unappealable court order.
[3]Authorizes hanging if lethal injection is held to be unconstitutional by a court of competent jurisdiction.
[4]Authorizes lethal injection for persons sentenced on or after March 31, 1998; inmates sentenced before that date may select lethal injection or electrocution.
[5]Authorizes hanging only if lethal injection cannot be given.
[6]Authorizes lethal injection for those whose capital offense occurred prior to July 1, 2009.
[7]Authorizes nitrogen hypoxia if lethal injection is held to be unconstitutional, electrocution if both lethal injection and nitrogen hypoxia are held to be unconstitutional, and firing squad if all other methods are held to be unconstitutional.
[8]Authorizes lethal injection for those whose capital offense occurred after December 31, 1998; inmates whose offense occurred before that date may select electrocution by written waiver. Electrocution is the authorized method if a court or the commissioner of corrections determines that lethal injection cannot be given.
[9]Authorizes firing squad if lethal injection is held unconstitutional. Inmates who selected execution by firing squad prior to May 3, 2004, may still be entitled to execution by that method.

Table 7. Number of Persons Executed Under Civil Authority in the United States, 1930–2016

(Number.)

Year	Executions
1930	155
1931	153
1932	140
1933	160
1934	168
1935	199
1936	195
1937	147
1938	190
1939	160
1940	124
1941	123
1942	147
1943	131
1944	120
1945	117
1946	131
1947	153
1948	119
1949	119
1950	82
1951	105
1952	83
1953	62
1954	81
1955	76
1956	65
1957	65
1958	49
1959	49
1960	56
1961	42
1962	47
1963	21
1964	15
1965	7
1966	1
1967	2
1968	0
1969	0
1970	0
1971	0
1972	0
1973	0
1974	0

(Number.)

Year	Executions
1975	0
1976	0
1977	1
1978	0
1979	2
1980	0
1981	1
1982	2
1983	5
1984	21
1985	18
1986	18
1987	25
1988	11
1989	16
1990	23
1991	14
1992	31
1993	38
1994	31
1995	56
1996	45
1997	74
1998	68
1999	98
2000	85
2001	66
2002	71
2003	65
2004	59
2005	60
2006	53
2007	42
2008	37
2009	52
2010	46
2011	43
2012	43
2013	39
2014	35
2015	28
2016	20

Table 8. Number of Persons Under Sentence of Death, 1953–2016

(Number.)

Year	Number of prisoners under sentence of death
1953	131
1954	147
1955	125
1956	146
1957	151
1958	147
1959	164
1960	212
1961	257
1962	267
1963	297
1964	315
1965	331
1966	406
1967	435
1968	517
1969	575
1970	631
1971	642
1972	334
1973	134
1974	244
1975	488
1976	420
1977	423
1978	482
1979	593
1980	692
1981	860
1982	1,066
1983	1,209
1984	1,420
1985	1,575
1986	1,800
1987	1,967
1988	2,117
1989	2,243
1990	2,346
1991	2,465
1992	2,580
1993	2,727
1994	2,905
1995	3,064
1996	3,242
1997	3,328
1998	3,465
1999	3,527
2000	3,601
2001	3,577
2002	3,562
2003	3,377
2004	3,320
2005	3,245
2006	3,228
2007	3,215
2008	3,210
2009	3,173
2010	3,139
2011	3,065
2012	3,011
2013	2,983
2014	2,942
2015	2,881
2016	2,814

Table 9. Admissions to and Removal from Under Sentence of Death, 1973–2016

(Number.)

Year	Admissions	Removals
1973	44	240
1974	161	55
1975	318	67
1976	249	317
1977	159	156
1978	211	150
1979	172	61
1980	202	101
1981	249	84
1982	287	79
1983	266	123
1984	305	90
1985	291	130
1986	320	109
1987	311	142
1988	317	165
1989	275	149
1990	270	152
1991	285	159
1992	300	173
1993	299	162
1994	330	153
1995	325	171
1996	323	155
1997	283	187
1998	310	174
1999	287	221
2000	235	173
2001	164	194
2002	172	191
2003	156	346
2004	140	198
2005	143	216
2006	125	145
2007	129	140
2008	122	136
2009	118	166
2010	116	143
2011	84	153
2012	85	128
2013	85	115
2014	68	111
2015	54	120
2016	32	90

Table 10. Number of Prisoners Under Sentence of Death, by Race, 1968–2016

(Percent; number.)

Year	White	Black	All other races
1968	243	271	3
1969	263	310	2
1970	293	335	3
1971	306	332	4
1972	167	166	1
1973	64	68	2
1974	110	128	6
1975	218	262	8
1976	225	195	0
1977	229	192	2
1978	281	197	4
1979	354	236	3
1980	424	264	4
1981	499	353	8
1982	613	441	12
1983	692	505	12
1984	806	598	16
1985	896	664	15
1986	1,013	762	25
1987	1,128	813	26
1988	1,235	848	34
1989	1,308	898	37
1990	1,368	940	38
1991	1,449	979	37
1992	1,511	1,031	38
1993	1,575	1,111	41
1994	1,653	1,203	49
1995	1,732	1,284	48
1996	1,833	1,358	51
1997	1,864	1,408	56
1998	1,917	1,489	59
1999	1,960	1,515	65
2000	1,989	1,541	71
2001	1,968	1,538	71
2002	1,931	1,554	72
2003	1,883	1,417	78
2004	1,856	1,390	74
2005	1,802	1,366	77
2006	1,806	1,353	74
2007	1,806	1,338	71
2008	1,795	1,343	72
2009	1,779	1,318	76
2010	1,743	1,309	87
2011	1,721	1,274	70
2012	1,684	1,258	69
2013	1,670	1,251	62
2014	1,647	1,233	62
2015	1,606	1,202	64
2016	1,560	1,189	65

METHODOLOGY

Capital punishment information is collected annually as part of the Bureau of Justice Statistics' (BJS) National Prisoner Statistics program (NPS-8). This data series is collected in two parts:

- Data on persons under sentence of death are obtained from the department of corrections in each jurisdiction currently authorizing capital punishment.

- The status of death penalty statutes is obtained from the Office of the Attorney General in each of the 50 states, the U.S. Attorney's Office in the District of Columbia, and Federal Bureau of Prisons for the federal government.

Data collection forms are available on the BJS website at www.bjs.gov.

The NPS-8 covers all persons under a state or federal civil sentence of death at any time during the year. This incudes capital offenders transferred from prison to mental hospitals and those who may have escaped from custody. It excludes persons sentenced to death under the Uniform Code of Military Justice and those whose death sentences have been overturned by a court or executive action, regardless of their current incarceration status.

Statistics in this report may differ from data collected by other organizations for various reasons:

- The NPS-8 adds prisoners to the population under sentence of death not at sentencing, but at the time they are admitted to a state or federal correctional facility.

- If prisoners entered prison under a death sentence or were reported as being relieved of a death sentence in one year but the admission or removal had occurred in a previous year, counts are adjusted to reflect the actual dates of sentence or removal.

- NPS-8 counts are for the last day of the calendar year and will differ from counts for more recent periods.

Definitions

Aggravating factor—Specific elements of a crime defined by statute. When present, these factors may allow a jury to impose a death sentence for a person convicted of a capital offense. Sometimes these are also called aggravating circumstances.

Capital conviction—A formal declaration that a defendant is guilty of a capital offense, made by the verdict of a jury, the decision of a judge, or a guilty plea by the defendant in a court of law.

Capital offense—A criminal offense punishable by death. Offenses that are eligible for a death sentence are defined by statute in each jurisdiction that authorizes capital punishment. The most common is first-degree murder accompanied by at least one aggravating factor.

Lists of capital offenses by state and by federal can be found at the end of this section.

Capital punishment—The process of sentencing convicted offenders to death for the most serious crimes and carrying out that sentence. The specific offenses and circumstances which determine if a crime is eligible for a death sentence are defined by statute and are prescribed by Congress or a state legislature.

Capital statute—State or federal laws dictating specific crimes that are eligible for a death sentence and specific procedures to be followed in carrying out such sentences.

Civil authority— For the purposes of this report, the state or federal entities responsible for implementation and enforcement of capital punishment laws, excluding military authorities.

Commutation—Reduction of a death sentence by a governor or a board of advisors empaneled to review sentences. Criteria for granting a commutation vary by state. The new sentence can be to life or a term of years.

Death row—A slang term referring to the area of a prison in which prisoners under sentence of death are housed. Usage of the term "death row" continues despite the fact that many states do not maintain a separate unit or facility for prisoners under sentence of death.

Received under sentence of death—Persons admitted to prison after being sentenced to death by a court.

Removal from under sentence of death—A prisoner who was previously under sentence of death and is no longer included in the count of persons under sentence of death. An inmate can be relieved of a death sentence by several methods: execution, death by causes other than execution, commutation, or an overturned capital conviction or sentence.

Sentence of death—A sentence imposed by a court for a capital offense which authorizes the state to execute a convicted offender.

Yearend—As of December 31 of the calendar year.

Capital Offenses, by State, 2016

State	Offenses
Alabama	Intentional murder (Ala. Stat. Ann. 13A-5-40(a)(1)-(18)) with 10 aggravating factors (Ala. Stat. Ann. 13A-5-49).
Arizona	First-degree murder, including premeditated murder and felony murder, accompanied by at least 1 of 14 aggravating factors (A.R.S. ß 13-703(F)).
Arkansas	Capital murder (Ark. Code Ann. ß 5-10-101) with a finding of at least 1 of 10 aggravating circumstances; treason (Ark. Code Ann. ß 5-51-201).
California	First-degree murder with special circumstances; military sabotage; death in the course of train wrecking; treason; perjury resulting in execution of an innocent person; fatal assault by a prisoner serving a life sentence.
Colorado	First-degree murder with at least 1 of 17 aggravating factors; first-degree kidnapping resulting in death; treason.
Delaware	First-degree murder (11 Del. C. ß 636) with at least one statutory aggravating circumstance (11 Del. C. ß 4209).
Florida	First-degree murder with aggravating factors; felony murder.
Georgia	Murder with aggravating circumstances; rape, armed robbery, or kidnapping with bodily injury or ransom when the victim dies; aircraft hijacking; treason (O.C.G.A. ß 17-10-30).
Idaho	First-degree murder with aggravating factors; first-degree kidnapping; perjury resulting in the execution of an innocent person.
Indiana	Murder with 18 aggravating circumstances (I.C. 35-50-2-9).
Kansas	Intentional and premeditated killing of a person in one or more of seven different circumstances (K.S.A. 21-5401).
Kentucky	Capital murder with the presence of at least one statutory aggravating circumstance; capital kidnapping (K.R.S. 532.025).
Louisiana	First-degree murder with aggravating circumstances (La. R.S. 14:30); treason (La. R.S. 14:113).
Mississippi	Capital murder with aggravating circumstances (Miss. Code Ann. ß 97-3-19(2)); aircraft piracy (Miss. Code Ann. ß 97-25-55(1)).
Missouri	First-degree murder with at least 1 statutory aggravating circumstance (565.020 R.S.M.O. 2000).
Montana	Capital murder with one of nine aggravating circumstances (Mont. Code Ann. ß 46-18-303); aggravated kidnapping; felony murder; capital sexual intercourse without consent (Mont. Code Ann. ß 45-5-503).
Nebraska	First-degree murder with a finding of one or more statutory aggravating circumstances.
Nevada	First-degree murder with at least 1 of 15 aggravating circumstances (N.R.S. 200.030, 200.033, 200.035).
New Hampshire	Murder committed in the course of rape, kidnapping, drug crimes, or home invasion; killing of a police officer, judge, or prosecutor; murder for hire; murder by an inmate while serving a sentence of life without parole (R.S.A. 630:1, R.S.A. 630:5).
New Mexico	First-degree murder with at least one of seven aggravating factors (N.M.S.A. 1978 ß 31-20A-5). New Mexico enacted a prospective appeal of its capital statute as of July 1, 2009. Offenders who committed capital offenses prior to that date are eligible for the death penalty.
New York	First-degree murder with 1 of 13 aggravating factors (NY Penal Law ß125.27). The New York Court of Appeals has held that a portion of New York's death penalty sentencing statute (C.P.L. 400.27) was unconstitutional (People v. Taylor, 9 N.Y.3d 129 (2007)). No legislative action has been taken to amend the statute. As a result, capital cases are no longer pursued in New York.
North Carolina	First-degree murder (N.C.G.S. ß14-17) with the finding of at least 1 of 11 statutory aggravating circumstances (N.C.G.S. ß 15A-2000).
Ohio	Aggravated murder with at least 1 of 10 aggravating circumstances (O.R.C. 2903.01, 2929.02, and 2929.04).
Oklahoma	First-degree murder in conjunction with a finding of at least one of eight statutorily defined aggravating circumstances.
Oregon	Aggravated murder (O.R.S. 163.095).
Pennsylvania	First-degree murder with 18 aggravating circumstances.
South Carolina	Murder with at least 1 of 12 aggravating circumstances (ß 16-3-20(C)(a)).

South Dakota	First-degree murder with 1 of 10 aggravating circumstances (S.D.C.L. 23A-27A-1).
Tennessee	First-degree murder (Tenn. Code Ann. ß 39-13-202) with 1 of 15 aggravating circumstances (Tenn. Code Ann. ß 39-13-204).
Texas	Criminal homicide with one of nine aggravating circumstances (Tex. Penal Code ß 19.03).
Utah	Aggravated murder (Utah Code Ann. ß 76-5-202).
Virginia	Premeditated murder with 1 of 15 aggravating circumstances (VA Code ß 18.2-31(1-15)).
Washington	Aggravated first-degree murder.
Wyoming	First-degree murder; murder during the commission of sexual assault, sexual abuse of a minor, arson, robbery, burglary, escape, resisting arrest, kidnapping, or abuse of a minor under 16 (W.S.A. ß 6-2-101(a)).

Federal Capital Offenses, 2016

Statute	Description
8 U.S.C. 1342	Murder related to the smuggling of aliens.
18 U.S.C. 32-34	Destruction of aircraft, motor vehicles, or related facilities resulting in death.
18 U.S.C. 36	Murder committed during a drug-related drive-by shooting.
18 U.S.C. 37	Murder committed at an airport serving international civil aviation.
18 U.S.C. 115(b)(3) [by cross-reference to 18 U.S.C. 1111]	Retaliatory murder of a member of the immediate family of law enforcement officials.
18 U.S.C. 241, 242, 245, 247	Civil rights offenses resulting in death.
18 U.S.C. 351 [by cross-reference to 18 U.S.C. 1111]	Murder of a member of Congress, an important executive official, or a Supreme Court Justice.
18 U.S.C. 794	Espionage.
18 U.S.C. 844(d), (f), (i)	Death resulting from offenses involving transportation of explosives, destruction of government property, or destruction of property related to foreign or interstate commerce.
18 U.S.C. 924(i)	Murder committed by the use of a firearm during a crime of violence or a drug-trafficking crime.
18 U.S.C. 930	Murder committed in a federal government facility.
18 U.S.C. 1091	Genocide.
18 U.S.C. 1111	First-degree murder.
18 U.S.C. 1114	Murder of a federal judge or law enforcement official.
18 U.S.C. 1116	Murder of a foreign official.
18 U.S.C. 1118	Murder by a federal prisoner.
18 U.S.C. 1119	Murder of a U.S. national in a foreign country.
18 U.S.C. 1120	Murder by an escaped federal prisoner already sentenced to life imprisonment.
18 U.S.C. 1121	Murder of a state or local law enforcement official or other person aiding in a federal investigation; murder of a state correctional officer.
18 U.S.C. 1201	Murder during a kidnapping.
18 U.S.C. 1203	Murder during a hostage taking.
18 U.S.C. 1503	Murder of a court officer or juror.
18 U.S.C. 1512	Murder with the intent of preventing testimony by a witness, victim, or informant.
18 U.S.C. 1513	Retaliatory murder of a witness, victim, or informant.
18 U.S.C. 1716	Mailing of injurious articles with intent to kill or resulting in death.
18 U.S.C. 1751 [by cross-reference to 18 U.S.C. 1111]	Assassination or kidnapping resulting in the death of the President or Vice President.
18 U.S.C. 1958	Murder for hire.
18 U.S.C. 1959	Murder involved in a racketeering offense.
18 U.S.C. 1992	Willful wrecking of a train resulting in death.
18 U.S.C. 2113	Bank robbery-related murder or kidnapping.
18 U.S.C. 2119	Murder related to a carjacking.
18 U.S.C. 2245	Murder related to rape or child molestation.
18 U.S.C. 2251	Murder related to sexual exploitation of children.

18 U.S.C. 2280	Murder committed during an offense against maritime navigation.
18 U.S.C. 2281	Murder committed during an offense against a maritime fixed platform.
18 U.S.C. 2332	Terrorist murder of a U.S. national in another country.
18 U.S.C. 2332a	Murder by the use of a weapon of mass destruction.
18 U.S.C. 2340	Murder involving torture.
18 U.S.C. 2381	Treason.
21 U.S.C. 848(e)	Murder related to a continuing criminal enterprise or related murder of a federal, state, or local law enforcement officer.
49 U.S.C. 1472-1473	Death resulting from aircraft hijacking.

PART 2

Correctional Populations in the United States, 2016

HIGHLIGHTS

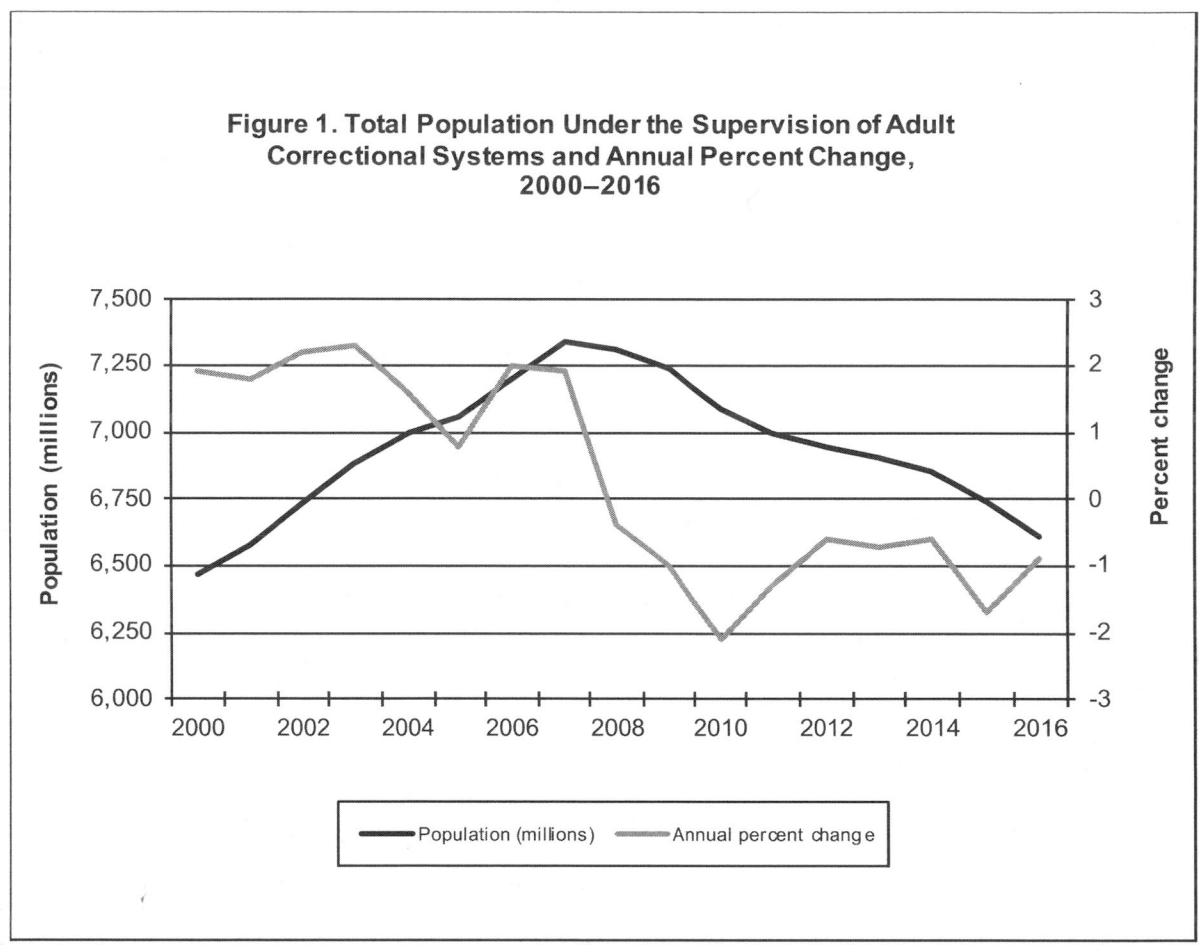

Figure 1. Total Population Under the Supervision of Adult Correctional Systems and Annual Percent Change, 2000–2016

- In 2016, the number of persons supervised by U.S. adult correctional systems dropped for the ninth consecutive year. At yearend, an estimated 6,613,500 persons were under supervision, about 126,800 persons less than at yearend 2015.

- From 2007 to 2016, the portion of the adult population under supervision of U.S. correctional systems decreased by 18 percent, from 3,210 to 2,640 per 100,000 adult residents.

- About 1 in 38 adults (or 2.6 percent of adults in the United States) had some form of correctional supervision at yearend 2016, the lowest rate since 1993.

- The community supervision population (4,537,100) dropped to its lowest point in the 21st century, and the incarcerated population (2,162,400) fell to its lowest level in a decade (2,136,600)

Data in this section have been derived from *Correctional Populations in the United States, 2016.*

Table 1. Number of Persons Supervised by Adult Correctional Systems, by Correctional Status, Selected Years, 2000 and 2006–2016

(Number; percent.)

Year	Total correctional population[1]	Community supervision			Incarcerated[2]		
		Total[1,3]	Probation	Parole	Total[1]	Local jail[4]	Prison
2000..	6,467,800	4,564,900	3,839,400	725,500	1,945,400	621,100	1,394,200
2006..	7,199,600	5,035,000	4,236,800	798,200	2,256,600	765,800	1,568,700
2007..	7,339,600	5,119,000	4,293,000	826,100	2,296,400	780,200	1,596,800
2008..	7,312,600	5,093,400	4,271,200	826,100	2,310,300	785,500	1,608,300
2009..	7,239,100	5,019,900	4,199,800	824,600	2,297,700	767,400	1,615,500
2010..	7,089,000	4,888,500	4,055,900	840,800	2,279,100	748,700	1,613,800
2011..	6,994,500	4,818,300	3,973,800	855,500	2,252,500	735,600	1,599,000
2012..	6,949,800	4,790,700	3,944,900	858,400	2,231,300	744,500	1,570,400
2013..	6,899,700	4,749,800	3,912,900	849,500	2,222,500	731,200	1,577,000
2014..	6,856,900	4,713,200	3,868,400	857,700	2,225,100	744,600	1,562,300
2015..	6,740,300	4,650,900	3,789,800	870,500	2,172,800	727,400	1,526,600
2016..							
January 1[5].................................	6,676,200	4,586,900	3,725,600	870,700	NA	NA	NA
December 31...............................	6,613,500	4,537,100	3,673,100	874,800	2,162,400	740,700	1,505,400
Average annual percent change, 2007–2016.....	-1.2	-1.3	-1.7	0.6	-0.7	-0.6	-0.7
Percent change, 1/1/16 to 12/31/16[6]..................	-0.9	-1.1	-1.4	0.5	-0.5	1.8	-1.4

Note: Estimates are rounded to the nearest 100 and may not be comparable to previously published BJS reports due to updated information or rounding. Counts include estimates for nonresponding jurisdictions. All probation, parole, and prison counts are for December 31, except where noted; jail counts are for the last weekday in June. Detail may not sum to total due to rounding and adjustments made to account for offenders with dual correctional statuses. 2016 is considered a comparison year by BJS.
NA = Not applicable.
[1]Total was adjusted to account for offenders with dual correctional statuses.
[2]Includes offenders held in local jails or under the jurisdiction of state or federal prisons.
[3]Includes some offenders held in a prison or jail but who remained under the jurisdiction of a probation or parole agency.
[4]The Annual Survey of Jails is a nationally representative sample of jails rather than a full census.
[5]The total correctional population for January 1, 2016, is the sum of the total community supervision population for January 1, 2016, and the total incarcerated population for December 31, 2015, adjusted for the number of persons in 2015 on dual correctional statuses.
[6]Within-year change for the prison population is calculated as the difference between December 31, 2015, and 2016, while change for the jail population is calculated as the difference between the last weekday of June 2015 and June 2016.

Table 2. Rate of Persons Supervised by U.S. Adult Correctional Systems, by Correctional Status, Selected Years, 2000 and 2006–2016

(Number; rate per 100,000 U.S. residents.)

Year	Total correctional population[1]			Community supervision population		Incarcerated population[2]	
	Number supervised per 100,000 U.S. adult residents[3]	U.S. adult residents under correctional supervision	Number supervised per 100,000 U.S. residents of all ages[4]	Number on probation or parole per 100,000 U.S. adult residents[3]	Number on probation or parole per 100,000 U.S. residents of all ages[4]	Number in prison or local jail per 100,000 U.S. adult residents[3]	Number in prison or local jail per 100,000 U.S. residents of all ages[4]
2000......................................	3,060	1 in 33	2,280	2,160	1,610	920	690
2006......................................	3,190	1 in 31	2,400	2,230	1,680	1,000	750
2007......................................	3,210	1 in 31	2,420	2,240	1,690	1,000	760
2008......................................	3,160	1 in 32	2,390	2,200	1,670	1,000	760
2009......................................	3,100	1 in 32	2,350	2,150	1,630	980	750
2010......................................	3,000	1 in 33	2,280	2,070	1,570	960	730
2011......................................	2,930	1 in 34	2,240	2,020	1,540	940	720
2012......................................	2,880	1 in 35	2,210	1,980	1,520	920	710
2013......................................	2,830	1 in 35	2,170	1,950	1,490	910	700
2014......................................	2,780	1 in 36	2,140	1,910	1,470	900	690
2015......................................	2,710	1 in 37	2,090	1,870	1,440	870	680
2016......................................	2,640	1 in 38	2,040	1,810	1,400	860	670

Note: Rates were estimated to the nearest 10. Estimates may not be comparable to previously published BJS reports due to updated information or rounding.
[1]Includes offenders in the community under the jurisdiction of probation or parole agencies, under the jurisdiction of state or federal prisons, or in the custody of local jails.
[2]Includes offenders under the jurisdiction of state or federal prisons or held in local jails.
[3]Rates were computed using estimates of the U.S. resident population for persons age 18 or older from the U.S. Census Bureau for January 1 of the following year.
[4]Rates were computed using estimates of the U.S. resident population for persons of all ages from the U.S. Census Bureau for January 1 of the following year..

Table 3. Number of Persons Supervised by U.S. Adult Correctional Systems, by Correctional Status, 2007 and 2016

(Number; percent.)

Correctional populations	2007		2016	
	Population	Percent of total population	Population	Percent of total population
Total[1]	7,339,600	100.0	6,613,500	100.0
Probation[2]	4,293,000	58.5	3,673,100	55.5
Prison[2]	1,596,800	21.8	1,505,400	22.8
Parole[2]	826,100	11.3	874,800	13.2
Local jail[3]	780,200	10.6	740,700	11.2
Offenders with dual correctional statuses[4]	156,400	:	180,500	:

Note: Counts were rounded to the nearest 100 and include estimates for nonresponding jurisdictions. Detail may not sum to total due to rounding and because offenders with dual correctional statuses were excluded from the total correctional population.
: = Not calculated.
[1]Adjusted to exclude offenders with dual correctional statuses to avoid double counting.
[2]Population as of December 31.
[3]Population as of the last weekday in June.
[4]Some probationers and parolees on December 31 were held in a prison or jail but still remained under the jurisdiction of a probation or parole agency, and, also, some parolees were also on probation. In addition, some prisoners were being held in jail. See Table 6.

Table 4. Change in the Number of Persons Supervised by U.S. Adult Correctional Systems, 2007–2016

(Number; percent.)

Correctional population	2017–2016	
	Change in population	Percent of total change
Total Change[1]	-726,200	100.0
Probation[2]	-619,800	85.3
Prison[2]	-91,400	12.6
Local jail[3]	48,700	-6.7
Parole[2]	-39,500	5.4
Offenders with mulitple correction statuses[4]	24,100	:

Note: Estimates are rounded to the nearest 100 and include adjustments for nonresponding jurisdictions. Detail may not sum to total due to adjustments to exclude offenders with dual correctional statuses from the total to avoid double counting.
: = Not calculated.
[1]To avoid double counting, the total represents the combined probation, prison, parole, and jail counts minus those who have dual correctional statuses.
[2]Population as of December 31.
[3]Population as of the last weekday in June.
[4]Some probationers and parolees on December 31 were held in a prison or jail but still remained under the jurisdiction of a probation or parole agency, and some parolees were also on probation. In addition, some prisoners were held in a jail on December 31. See Table 6.

Table 5. Number and Rate of Persons Supervised by U.S. Adult Correctional Systems, by Jurisdiction and Correctional Status, 2014 and 2015

(Number; rate per 100,000 U.S. residents of all ages.)

	Total correctional population, 12/31/14					Total correctional population, 12/31/15				
	Number			Rate[1]		Number			Rate[1]	
Jurisdiction	Total[2]	Male	Female	Male	Female	Total[2]	Male	Female	Male	Female
U.S. Total[3]............	6,810,800	5,560,100	1,250,600	3,530	770	6,712,600	5,462,700	1,249,900	3,440	760
Federal............	338,000	300,600	37,400	190	20	328,500	292,000	36,500	180	20
State............	6,472,700	5,259,500	1,213,200	3,340	750	6,384,100	5,170,700	1,213,400	3,250	740
Alabama............	103,400	86,400	17,100	3,670	680	107,500	89,200	18,300	3,780	730
Alaska[4]............	14,600	12,100	2,400	3,120	700	13,900	11,400	2,500	2,930	720
Arizona............	133,600	111,900	21,700	3,320	640	136,300	114,100	22,200	3,340	640
Arkansas............	69,400	55,800	13,600	3,820	900	73,200	58,300	14,900	3,980	980
California[4]............	592,500	497,900	94,600	2,570	480	550,600	463,400	87,200	2,370	440
Colorado............	119,800	94,000	25,800	3,460	960	120,000	93,900	26,000	3,390	950
Connecticut............	62,300	51,500	10,700	2,940	580	61,000	50,300	10,700	2,870	580
Delaware............	23,300	18,800	4,500	4,130	920	22,700	18,500	4,200	4,020	870
District of Columbia............	11,900	10,200	1,800	3,210	500	10,600	9,800	800	3,050	230
Florida............	382,800	308,900	73,900	3,150	720	375,800	302,600	73,200	3,030	700
Georgia[5]............	578,000	462,300	115,800	9,330	2,220	540,000	432,900	107,100	8,650	2,030
Hawaii............	28,300	22,300	6,000	3,090	860	28,300	22,400	6,000	3,070	840
Idaho............	48,700	37,700	10,900	4,580	1,330	48,700	37,400	11,200	4,490	1,350
Illinois............	219,000	181,000	38,000	2,860	580	215,100	177,700	37,500	2,810	570
Indiana[4]............	172,500	136,900	35,600	4,200	1,060	166,000	131,300	34,700	4,020	1,030
Iowa............	46,500	36,600	9,900	2,360	630	46,700	36,900	9,900	2,370	630
Kansas[4]............	37,200	31,000	6,200	2,130	420	37,400	31,000	6,400	2,130	440
Kentucky............	103,600	77,900	25,800	3,580	1,150	103,700	77,500	26,200	3,550	1,160
Louisiana............	113,700	96,300	17,400	4,220	730	114,600	97,100	17,500	4,240	730
Maine............	10,100	8,400	1,700	1,290	250	10,100	8,400	1,700	1,290	260
Maryland............	109,700	92,100	17,700	3,170	570	104,500	87,600	16,900	3,000	550
Massachusetts............	90,300	75,900	14,400	2,310	410	86,900	71,400	15,500	2,160	440
Michigan............	256,700	203,200	53,400	4,170	1,060	250,200	199,600	50,600	4,090	1,000
Minnesota............	120,500	95,500	25,000	3,510	910	121,600	95,900	25,700	3,500	930
Mississippi............	69,700	58,200	11,500	4,000	750	71,900	60,400	11,500	4,160	740
Missouri............	108,500	88,700	19,800	2,980	640	106,000	86,100	19,900	2,880	640
Montana............	14,600	11,700	2,800	2,270	550	14,700	11,700	3,000	2,240	570
Nebraska............	22,500	17,800	4,700	1,890	490	22,300	17,600	4,600	1,860	480
Nevada............	37,200	31,200	6,000	2,170	420	38,300	32,100	6,200	2,190	430
New Hampshire............	11,200	9,300	1,900	1,420	280	10,900	9,000	1,900	1,370	280
New Jersey............	164,500	137,300	27,200	3,140	590	183,500	147,800	35,700	3,370	780
New Mexico............	32,400	25,900	6,500	2,510	620	25,000	19,800	5,200	1,910	490
New York............	222,100	192,200	29,800	2,000	290	216,700	187,300	29,400	1,940	290
North Carolina............	153,300	123,800	29,500	2,540	580	151,200	122,200	29,000	2,490	560
North Dakota............	9,300	7,300	2,000	1,900	560	10,100	7,800	2,300	1,990	610
Ohio............	324,200	249,400	74,800	4,390	1,260	331,500	251,500	80,000	4,420	1,350
Oklahoma............	69,500	57,600	11,900	2,990	600	73,100	60,200	12,900	3,090	650
Oregon............	82,700	68,200	14,500	3,450	720	82,900	68,200	14,700	3,400	720
Pennsylvania............	360,900	284,800	76,100	4,550	1,160	374,200	294,300	79,900	4,690	1,220
Rhode Island............	25,100	21,300	3,800	4,160	700	25,300	21,500	3,800	4,190	700
South Carolina............	71,800	61,000	10,900	2,580	430	70,100	59,400	10,800	2,480	430
South Dakota[4]............	14,500	11,600	2,800	2,700	660	15,000	11,900	3,100	2,750	720
Tennessee............	119,800	95,800	24,000	2,990	710	119,900	95,700	24,200	2,960	710
Texas............	697,100	562,300	134,900	4,160	980	687,300	553,500	133,800	4,020	960
Utah............	25,800	20,700	5,100	1,390	340	25,500	20,500	5,000	1,350	330
Vermont............	8,400	6,700	1,700	2,180	530	8,000	6,400	1,600	2,070	520
Virginia............	115,300	95,900	19,400	2,330	460	114,400	94,800	19,600	2,290	460
Washington............	137,200	110,500	26,700	3,100	750	130,600	104,500	26,100	2,890	720
West Virginia............	19,600	15,500	4,100	1,700	440	20,100	15,900	4,200	1,740	450
Wisconsin[4]............	97,300	82,300	15,000	2,870	520	100,600	84,500	16,100	2,940	550
Wyoming............	9,700	7,700	2,000	2,570	710	9,900	7,700	2,100	2,580	750

Note: Counts were rounded to the nearest 100, and rates were rounded to the nearest 10. Detail may not sum to total due to rounding and because offenders with multiple correctional statuses were excluded from totals. Counts include estimates for nonresponding jurisdictions.
[1]Rates were computed using the U.S state resident population of all ages, by sex. U.S. resident populations of persons age 18 or older were not available by sex at the time this report was published. For this reason, jurisdiction-level rates in other tables of this report may not be comparable to this table.
[2]Excludes, by jurisdiction, an estimated 155,100 males and 18,900 females in 2015 and an estimated 154,100 males and 16,700 females in 2014 with multiple correctional statuses.
[3]Includes local jail counts that are based on December 31, 2015, to produce jurisdiction-level estimates. For this reason, the estimates in this table differ from a significant number f the national estimates presented in other tables and figures.
[4]Excludes about 11,000 inmates that were not held in locally operated jails but rather facilities that were operated by the Federal Bureau of Prisons and functioned as jails.
[5]Includes estimates due to nonresponse for sex.

Table 6. Number of Offenders with Dual Correctional Statuses at Yearend, by Correctional Status, 2000–2016

(Number.)

Year	Total	Prisoners held in local jail	Probationers		Parolees		On probation
			Local jail	State or federal prison	Local jail	State or federal prison	
2000	112,500	70,000	20,400	22,100	:	:	:
2001	116,100	72,500	23,400	20,200	:	:	:
2002	122,800	72,600	29,300	20,900	:	:	:
2003	120,400	73,400	25,500	21,500	:	:	:
2004	130,400	74,400	34,400	21,600	:	:	:
2005	164,500	73,100	32,600	22,100	18,300	18,400	:
2006	169,900	77,900	33,900	21,700	20,700	15,700	:
2007	156,400	80,600	19,300	23,100	18,800	14,600	:
2008	178,500	83,500	23,800	32,400	19,300	15,600	3,900
2009	168,100	85,200	21,400	23,100	19,100	14,300	5,000
2010	170,300	83,400	21,300	21,500	21,400	14,400	8,300
2011	169,300	82,100	21,100	22,300	18,000	14,900	11,000
2012	168,400	83,600	21,200	21,700	18,500	10,700	12,700
2013	170,800	85,700	22,400	16,700	21,800	11,800	12,500
2014	176,100	81,800	23,500	24,600	21,800	11,600	12,900
2015	174,000	81,200	24,400	28,200	19,600	11,200	9,400
2016	180,500	83,700	24,400	24,000	24,500	13,000	10,800

Note: Estimates were rounded to the nearest 100 and may not be comparable to previously published BJS reports due to updated information. Detail may not sum to total due to rounding.
: = Not collected or excluded from total correctional population.

Table 7. Estimated Number and Rate of Persons Supervised by U.S. Adult Correctional Systems, by Jurisdiction and Correctional Status, 2016

(Number as of 12/31/16; rate per 100,000 adults.)

Jurisdiction	Total correctional population			Community supervision			Incarcerated		
	Total correctional population[1]	Correctional supervision rate, 18 years and over[2]	Correctional supervision rate, all ages[2]	Number on probation or parole[3]	Correctional supervision rate, 18 years and over[2]	Correctional supervision rate, all ages[2]	Number in prison or local jail[4]	Incarceration rate, 18 years and over[2]	Incarceration rate, all ages[2]
U.S. Total[5].............................	6,582,100	2,630	2,030	4,537,100	1,810	1,400	2,131,000	850	660
Federal[6].................................	320,000	130	100	131,700	50	40	188,400	80	60
State.......................................	6,262,000	2,500	1,930	4,405,400	1,760	1,360	1,942,600	780	600
Alabama...................................	99,800	2,640	2,050	60,700	1,610	1,250	40,900	1,080	840
Alaska......................................	12,900	2,320	1,730	8,400	1,520	1,140	4,400	800	600
Arizona....................................	137,500	2,570	1,970	84,800	1,590	1,220	55,000	1,030	790
Arkansas..................................	72,100	3,150	2,410	51,500	2,250	1,720	24,000	1,050	800
California.................................	536,100	1,770	1,360	333,300	1,100	850	202,700	670	510
Colorado	121,900	2,820	2,180	90,900	2,110	1,630	32,100	740	580
Connecticut..............................	59,600	2,110	1,670	44,700	1,580	1,250	15,000	530	420
Delaware..................................	22,400	2,980	2,340	15,800	2,100	1,650	6,600	880	690
District of Columbia..................	10,400	1,840	1,510	9,600	1,710	1,400	1,800	320	270
Florida	366,000	2,200	1,760	218,600	1,320	1,050	149,800	900	720
Georgia[7]	..	..	..	..	..	..	91,400	1,160	880
Hawaii.....................................	27,500	2,450	1,920	21,900	1,950	1,530	5,600	500	390
Idaho.......................................	48,800	3,880	2,870	37,500	2,980	2,210	11,300	900	670
Illinois.....................................	204,200	2,070	1,600	143,400	1,450	1,120	60,800	620	480
Indiana....................................	159,900	3,150	2,400	116,700	2,300	1,760	43,200	850	650
Iowa..	46,700	1,940	1,490	35,100	1,460	1,120	13,400	560	430
Kansas.....................................	38,500	1,750	1,320	21,500	980	740	17,200	780	590
Kentucky	97,900	2,850	2,200	63,800	1,860	1,440	34,700	1,010	780
Louisiana.................................	111,000	3,110	2,370	71,000	1,980	1,510	45,400	1,270	970
Maine......................................	10,300	960	780	6,800	630	510	4,100	380	300
Maryland..................................	99,000	2,120	1,640	82,800	1,770	1,370	28,400	610	470
Massachusetts	82,900	1,520	1,210	63,600	1,170	930	19,400	360	280
Michigan..................................	..	..	..	..	..	..	56,500	730	570
Minnesota................................	119,500	2,810	2,160	103,900	2,450	1,880	16,300	380	290
Mississippi...............................	65,300	2,880	2,180	37,700	1,660	1,260	28,700	1,260	960
Missouri...................................	105,900	2,240	1,730	61,600	1,300	1,010	44,300	940	730
Montana...................................	15,200	1,860	1,460	10,200	1,250	970	5,700	700	550
Nebraska..................................	23,300	1,620	1,220	14,600	1,010	760	8,800	610	460
Nevada.....................................	39,200	1,720	1,320	19,000	830	640	20,200	890	680
New Hampshire........................	10,800	1,010	810	6,400	590	480	4,500	410	330
New Jersey................................	186,300	2,670	2,080	155,700	2,230	1,740	32,000	460	360
New Mexico..............................	30,200	1,900	1,450	15,500	970	740	14,700	930	710
New York..................................	212,100	1,360	1,070	142,400	910	720	74,400	480	380
North Carolina..........................	149,300	1,890	1,460	95,200	1,210	930	54,100	680	530
North Dakota............................	10,300	1,770	1,350	7,100	1,230	940	3,100	540	410
Ohio..	326,200	3,620	2,810	256,400	2,840	2,200	71,000	790	610
Oklahoma[7]..............................	74,500	2,510	1,890	35,500	1,190	900	39,000	1,310	990
Oregon.....................................	82,000	2,520	1,990	61,400	1,890	1,490	20,700	640	500
Pennsylvania............................	368,100	3,640	2,880	291,600	2,880	2,280	82,400	810	640
Rhode Island............................	24,300	2,850	2,290	23,200	2,730	2,200	3,100	370	290
South Carolina..........................	68,800	1,770	1,380	36,700	940	740	32,100	820	640
South Dakota............................	15,000	2,290	1,720	9,300	1,420	1,070	5,800	880	670
Tennessee................................	119,400	2,310	1,790	74,700	1,440	1,120	48,400	930	720
Texas.......................................	681,900	3,290	2,430	482,900	2,330	1,720	218,500	1,050	780
Utah..	25,400	1,180	820	15,900	740	520	11,700	540	380
Vermont	7,400	1,450	1,180	5,800	1,150	940	1,700	340	280
Virginia....................................	120,000	1,830	1,420	62,500	950	740	57,500	880	680
Washington..............................	127,000	2,230	1,730	100,600	1,760	1,370	30,400	530	410
West Virginia	20,100	1,380	1,100	10,100	690	550	10,100	690	550
Wisconsin................................	100,500	2,230	1,740	64,900	1,440	1,120	35,600	790	620
Wyoming..................................	9,400	2,100	1,600	5,500	1,230	940	3,900	870	660

Note: Counts are rounded to the nearest 100, and rates are rounded to the nearest 10. Detail may not sum to total due to rounding and because offenders with dual correctional statuses are excluded from totals. Counts include estimates for nonresponding jurisdictions.
[1]Excludes, by jurisdiction, an estimated 83,700 prisoners held in jail, 24,000 probationers in prison, 24,400 probationers in jail, 24,500 parolees in jail, 13,000 parolees in prison, and 10,800 parolees on probation. See Table 6.
[2]Rates are computed using estimates of the U.S adult resident population of persons age 18 or older and persons of all ages on January 1, 2017, within jurisdiction.
[3]Excludes, by jurisdiction, an estimated 10,800 parolees on probation. See Table 6.
[4]Excludes, by jurisdiction, an estimated 83,700 prisoners held in local jails. See Table 6.
[5]Total correctional population and total number in prison and jail include local jail counts that are based on December 31, 2016, to produce jurisdiction-level estimates. For this reason, estimates in this table differ from national estimates presented in other tables and figures in this report.
[6]Excludes about 11,000 inmates who were not held in locally operated jails but rather facilities operated by the Federal Bureau of Prisons and functioned as jails.
[7]Total correctional population and community supervision population estimates include misdemeanant probation cases, not individuals, supervised by private companies, and may overstate the number of offenders under supervision.

Table 8. Persons Held in Custody in State or Federal Prisons or in Local Jails, 2000, 2010, and 2015–2016

(Number; percent.)

Characteristic	Number of inmates				Average annual change, 2000–2015	Percent change, 2015–2016
	2000	2010	2015	2016		
Persons in Custody...................................	1,938,500	1,517,800	2,166,600	2,157,800	0.7	-0.4
Federal prisoners[1]................................	140,100	207,000	195,600	188,300	1.8	-3.7
Prisons..	133,900	198,300	186,500	179,100	1.8	-4.0
Federal facilities	124,500	173,100	160,700	154,200	1.3	-4.0
Privately operated facilities.................	9,400	25,200	25,800	24,900	6.1	-3.5
Community corrections centers[2]...........	6,100	8,600	9,200	9,200	2.6	0.0
State prisoners.....................................	1,177,200	1,310,800	1,243,500	1,228,800	0.3	-1.2
State facilities[3]	1,101,200	1,216,700	1,152,200	1,134,700	0.2	-1.5
Privately operated facilities..................	76,100	94,100	91,300	94,200	1.3	3.2
Local jails..	621,100**	748,700	727,400	740,700*	1.1	1.8
Incarceration rate[4]..............................	690	700	680	670	-0.2	-1.5
Adult incarceration rate[5]	920	910	870	860	-0.4	-1.1

Note: Estimates may not be comparable to previously published BJS reports due to updated information. Counts are rounded to the nearest 100 and include estimates for nonresponding jurisdictions. Rates are rounded to the nearest 10. Detail may not to sum to total due to rounding. Prison counts are for December 31, and jail counts are for the last weekday in June. Total includes all persons held in local jails, state or federal prisons, or privately operated facilities. Excludes persons held in U.S. territories, military facilities, U.S. Immigration and Customs Enforcement facilities, jails in Indian country, or juvenile facilities.
* = Comparison year.
** = Difference from comparison year is significant at the 95% confidence level.
... = Less than 0.05 percent.
[1]After 2001, responsibility for sentenced prisoners from the District of Columbia was transferred to the Federal Bureau of Prisons.
[2]Nonsecure, privately operated community corrections centers.
[3]Excludes prisoners held in local jails in Georgia for 2010, 2015, and 2016 to avoid double counting.
[4]Total number in the custody of local jails, state or federal prisons, or privately operated facilities within the year per 100,000 U.S. residents of all ages.
[5]The total number in custody per 100,000 U.S. residents age 18 or older.

Table 9. Number of Persons Incarcerated by Other Adult Correctional Systems, 2000, 2010, and 2015–2016

(Number; percent.)

Characteristic	Number of inmates				Average annual change, 2000–2015	Percent change, 2015–2016
	2000	2010	2015	2016		
Other Adult Correctional Systems	20,400	17,600	16,800	16,100	-1.5	-4.0
Territorial prisons[1]	16,200	13,800	12,900	12,300	-1.7	-5.0
Military facilties[2]...	2,400	1,400	1,400	1,300	-3.7	-4.3
Jails in Indian country[3]...................................	1,800	2,400	2,500	2,540	2.2	1.2

Note: Estimates were rounded to the nearest 100 and are for December 31. Total excludes persons in local jails, under the jurisdiction of state or federal prisons, in U.S. Immigration and Customs Enforcement facilities, or in juvenile facilities.
[1]The 2015 and 2016 totals include population counts that were estimated for some territories due to nonresponse. See Prisoners in 2016 (NCJ 251149, BJS web, January 2018) for detailed statistics of this population.
[2]See Prisoners in 2016 (NCJ 251149, BJS web, January 2018) for detailed statistics of this population.
[3]Population counts are for the last weekday in June of each year. See Jails in Indian Country, 2016 (NCJ 250981, BJS web, December 2017) for detailed statistics of this population.

Methodology

About the Data

The statistics presented in this chapter include data from *Correctional Populations in the United States, 2016*, which itself relies on various Bureau of Justice Statistics (BJS) data collections, each relying on the voluntary participation of federal, state, and local respondents. This report presents statistics on offenders supervised by adult correctional systems in the United States at yearend 2016, including offenders supervised in the community on probation or parole and those incarcerated in prison or local jail. The report provides the size and change in the total correctional population during 2016. It details the slowing rate of decline in the population and the downward trend in the correctional supervision rate. It also examines the impact of changes in the community supervision and incarcerated populations on the total correctional population in recent years. Other information comprises correctional populations, including prisoners under military jurisdiction, inmates held by correctional authorities in the U.S. territories and commonwealths, and jail inmates held in Indian country facilities.

For more information about any of the following data collections, or to see the full report, please see https://www.bjs.gov/index.cfm?ty=pbdetail&iid=6226.

Annual Probation Survey and Annual Parole Survey

These surveys collect administrative data from probation and parole agencies in the U.S. Data collected include the total number of adults on state and federal probation and parole on January 1 and December 31 of each year, the number of adults entering and exiting probation and parole supervision each year, and the characteristics of adults under the supervision of probation and parole agencies. Published data include both national and state-level data. The surveys cover all 50 states, the federal system, and the District of Columbia. They began in 1980 and are conducted annually (except for the year 1991). Probation data are also available dating back to 1977. Through BJS's National Probation Reports, probation data were collected from 1977 to 1979. Parole data are available dating back to 1975. The parole data from 1975 to 1979 were collected through BJS's Uniform Parole Reports.

Annual Survey of Jails

This survey collects data from a nationally representative sample of local jails on jail inmate populations, jail capacity, and related information. The collection began in 1982 and has been conducted annually, except for years 1983, 1988, 1993, 1999, and 2005, during which a complete census of U.S. local jails was conducted.

Census of Jails

The Census of Jail Facilities is part of a series of data collections that study the nation's local jails. To reduce respondent burden and improve data quality and timeliness, the original jail census was split into two parts in 2005: the Census of Jail Inmates (2005) and the Census of Jail Facilities (2006). In 2013, BJS expanded the 2013 Deaths in Custody Reporting Program—Annual Summary on Inmates under Jail Jurisdiction to act as the 2013 Census of Jails. The Census of Jail Facilities collects information on each facility, including admissions and releases, court orders, programs that offer alternatives to incarceration, counts of inmates on hold for other jurisdictions, use of space and crowding, staffing, inmate work assignments, and education and counseling programs. The census provides the sampling frame for the nationwide Survey of Inmates in Local Jails (SILJ) and the Annual Survey of Jails (ASJ).

Deaths in Custody Reporting Program (DCRP)

This program collects inmate death records from each of the nation's 50 state prison systems and approximately 2,800 local jail jurisdictions. In addition, this program collects records of all deaths occurring during the process of arrest. Data are collected directly from state and local law enforcement agencies. Due to concerns regarding data quality and coverage issues, BJS temporarily suspended the arrest-related death portion (ARD) of the DCRP in 2014.

Death records include information on decedent personal characteristics (age, race or Hispanic origin, and sex), decedent criminal background (legal status, offense type, and time served), and the death itself (date, time, location, and cause of death, as well as information on the autopsy and medical treatment provided for any illness or disease).

Data collections covering these populations were developed in annual phases: Annual collection of individual death records from local jail facilities began in 2000, followed by a separate collection for state prison facilities in 2001. Collection of state juvenile correctional agencies began in 2002 but was discontinued in 2006, and collection of arrest-related death records began in 2003. Datasets are produced in an annual format.

National Prisoner Statistics (NPS) Program

This program produces annual national and state-level data on the number of prisoners in state and federal prison facilities. Aggregate data are collected on race and sex of prison inmates, inmates held in private facilities and local jails, system capacity, noncitizens, and persons under age 18. Findings are released in the Prisoners series. Data are from the 50 state departments of corrections, the Federal Bureau of Prisons, and until 2001, from the District of Columbia (after 2001, felons sentenced under the District of Columbia criminal code were housed in federal facilities).

Survey of Jails in Indian Country

This survey collects detailed information on confinement facilities, detention centers, jails, and other facilities operated by tribal authorities or the Bureau of Indian Affairs (BIA). Information is gathered on inmate counts, movements, facility operations, and staff. In selected years (1998, 2004, 2007, and 2011), additional information is collected on facility programs and services, such as medical assessments and mental health screening procedures, inmate work assignments, counseling, and educational programs.

Additional Information

Counts Adjusted for Offenders with Multiple Correctional Statuses

Offenders under correctional supervision may have multiple correctional statuses for several reasons. For example, probation and parole agencies may not always be notified immediately of new arrests, jail admissions, or prison admissions; absconders included in a probation or parole agency's population in one jurisdiction may actually be incarcerated in another jurisdiction; persons may be admitted to jail or prison before formal revocation hearings and potential discharge by a probation or parole agency; and persons may be serving separate probation and parole sentences concurrently. In addition, state and federal prisons may hold inmates in county facilities or local jails to reduce crowding in their prisons.

In 1998, through the ASPP, BJS began collecting data on the number of probationers and parolees with multiple correctional statuses and has since expanded on the information collected. In 1999, through the NPS, BJS began collecting data on the number of prisoners under the jurisdiction of state or federal prisons that were held in county facilities or local jails. Table 6 includes adjustments that were made to the total correctional population, total community supervision population, and total incarcerated population estimates presented in this report to exclude offenders with multiple correctional statuses to avoid double counting offenders. The estimates from the ASPP are

based on data reported by the probation and parole agencies that were able to provide the information within the specific reporting year. Because some probation and parole agencies did not provide these data each year, the numbers may underestimate the total number of offenders who had multiple correctional statuses between 2000 and 2013. Due to these adjustments, the sum of correctional statuses in Tables 1, 2, 3, 4, 5 and appendix table 1 will not equal the total correctional population. In addition, the sum of the probation and parole populations for 2008 through 2013 will not yield the total community supervision population because the total was adjusted for parolees who were also on probation. In addition, the sum of the prison and local jail populations for 2000 through 2016 will not equal the total incarcerated population because prisoners held in local jails were excluded from the total.

Adjustments for Nonresponse

Probation, parole, jail, and prison population counts were adjusted to account for nonresponse across the data collections. The methods varied and depended on the type of collection, type of respondent, and availability of information. The 2013 Census of Jails gathered data from all jail detention facilities holding inmates beyond arraignment, a period normally exceeding 72 hours. Included in the census were 2,872 local jail jurisdictions (including 77 regional jails with 2 or more jail jurisdictions having a formal agreement to operate) made up of 3,163 city, county, or privately operated (39 facilities) jail facilities and 12 BOP facilities that functioned as jails. Excluded were combined jail and prison systems in Alaska, Connecticut, Delaware, Hawaii, Rhode Island, and Vermont. The Census included 15 locally operated jails in Alaska.

Estimates of Males and Females Under Correctional Supervision

The number of males and the number of females on probation or parole were adjusted to account for nonresponse using a ratio adjustment method. For jurisdictions that did not provide data on sex for a portion of their population, the sex distribution of the known portion of the population was used to impute for the unknown portion because it was assumed that the distributions were the same. For states that were unable to provide any data on sex, the state national average was used to impute the number of males and females supervised in those states. Adjusted jurisdiction totals were then aggregated to produce national estimates of the number of males and females on probation and parole. The number of prisoners by sex represents the reported number of males and females under the jurisdiction of state or federal prisons within the reference year. The number of local jail inmates by sex represents the adjusted number of males and females in the custody of local jails within the reference year.

Definitions

Adult—persons subject to the jurisdiction of an adult criminal court or correctional agency. Adults are age 18 or older in most jurisdictions. Persons age 17 or younger who were prosecuted in criminal court as if they were adults are considered adults, but persons age 17 or younger who were under the jurisdiction of a juvenile court or agency are excluded.

Annual change—change in a population between two consecutive years.

Average annual change—average (mean) annual change in a population across a specific period.

Community supervision population—estimated number of persons living in the community while supervised on probation or parole.

Community supervision rate—estimated number of persons supervised in the community on probation or parole per 100,000 U.S. residents of all ages (i.e., total community supervision rate) or U.S. residents age 18 or older (i.e., adult community supervision rate).

Correctional population—estimated number of persons living in the community while supervised on probation or parole and persons under the jurisdiction of state or federal prisons or held in local jails.

Correctional supervision rate—estimated number of persons supervised in the community on probation or parole and persons under the jurisdiction of state or federal prisons or held in local jails per 100,000 U.S. residents of all ages (i.e., total correctional supervision rate) or U.S. residents age 18 or older (i.e., adult correctional supervision rate).

Imprisonment rate—estimated number of prisoners under state or federal jurisdiction sentenced to more than 1 year per 100,000 U.S. residents of all ages (i.e., total imprisonment rate) or U.S. residents age 18 or older (i.e., adult imprisonment rate). This statistic does not appear in this report; see *Prisoners in 2016*.

Incarcerated population—estimated number of persons under the jurisdiction of state or federal prisons or held in local jails.

Incarceration rate—estimated number of persons under the jurisdiction of state or federal prisons or held in local jails per 100,000 U.S. residents of all ages (i.e., total incarceration rate) or U.S. residents age 18 or older (i.e., adult incarceration rate).

Indian country jail population—estimated number of inmates held in correctional facilities operated by tribal authorities or the Bureau of Indian Affairs (BIA), U.S. Department of the Interior. These facilities include confinement facilities, detention centers, jails, and other facilities operated by tribal authorities or the BIA.

Local jail population—estimated number of inmates held in a confinement facility usually administered by a local law enforcement agency that is intended for adults, but sometimes holds juveniles, for confinement before and after adjudication. These facilities include jails and city or county correctional centers; special jail facilities, such as medical treatment or release centers; halfway houses; work farms; and temporary holding or lockup facilities that are part of the jail's combined function. Inmates sentenced to jail facilities usually have a sentence of 1 year or less.

Military prison population—estimated number of service personnel incarcerated under the jurisdiction of U.S. military correctional authorities.

Parole population—estimated number of persons who are on conditional release in the community following a prison term while under the control, supervision, or care of a correctional agency. Violations of the conditions of supervision during this period may result in a new sentence to confinement or a return to confinement for a technical violation. This population includes parolees released through discretionary (i.e., parole board decision) or mandatory (i.e., provisions of a statute) supervised release from prison, those released through other types of post-custody conditional supervision, and those sentenced to a term of supervised release.

Prison population—estimated number of prisoners incarcerated in a long-term confinement facility, run by a state or the federal government, which typically holds felons and offenders with sentences of more than 1 year, although sentence length may vary by jurisdiction.

Prison jurisdiction population—estimated number of prisoners under the jurisdiction or legal authority of state or federal correctional officials, regardless of where the prisoner is held. This population represents BJS's official measure of the prison population and includes prisoners held in prisons, penitentiaries, correctional facilities, halfway houses, boot camps, farms, training or treatment centers, and hospitals. Counts also include prisoners who were temporarily absent (fewer than 30 days), in court or on work release, housed in privately operated facilities, local jails, or other state or federal facilities, and serving concurrent sentences for more than one correctional authority.

Prison custody population—estimated number of prisoners held in the physical custody of state or federal prisons regardless of sentence length or the authority having jurisdiction. This population includes prisoners housed for other correctional facilities but excludes those in the custody of local jails, those held in other jurisdictions, those out to court, and those in transit from one jurisdiction of legal authority to the custody of a confinement facility outside that jurisdiction.

Probation population—estimated number of persons who are on a court-ordered period of supervision in the community while under the control, supervision, or care of a correctional agency. The probation conditions form a contract with the court by which the person must abide in order to remain in the community, generally in lieu of incarceration. In some cases, probation can be a combined sentence of incarceration followed by a period of community supervision. Often, probation entails monitoring or surveillance by a correctional agency. In some instances, probation may not involve any reporting requirements.

Territorial prison population—estimated number of prisoners in the custody of correctional facilities operated by departments of corrections in U.S. territories (American Samoa, Guam, and the U.S. Virgin Islands) and U.S. commonwealths (Northern Mariana Islands and Puerto Rico).

PART 3

Crime Against Persons with Disabilities, 2009–2015

HIGHLIGHTS

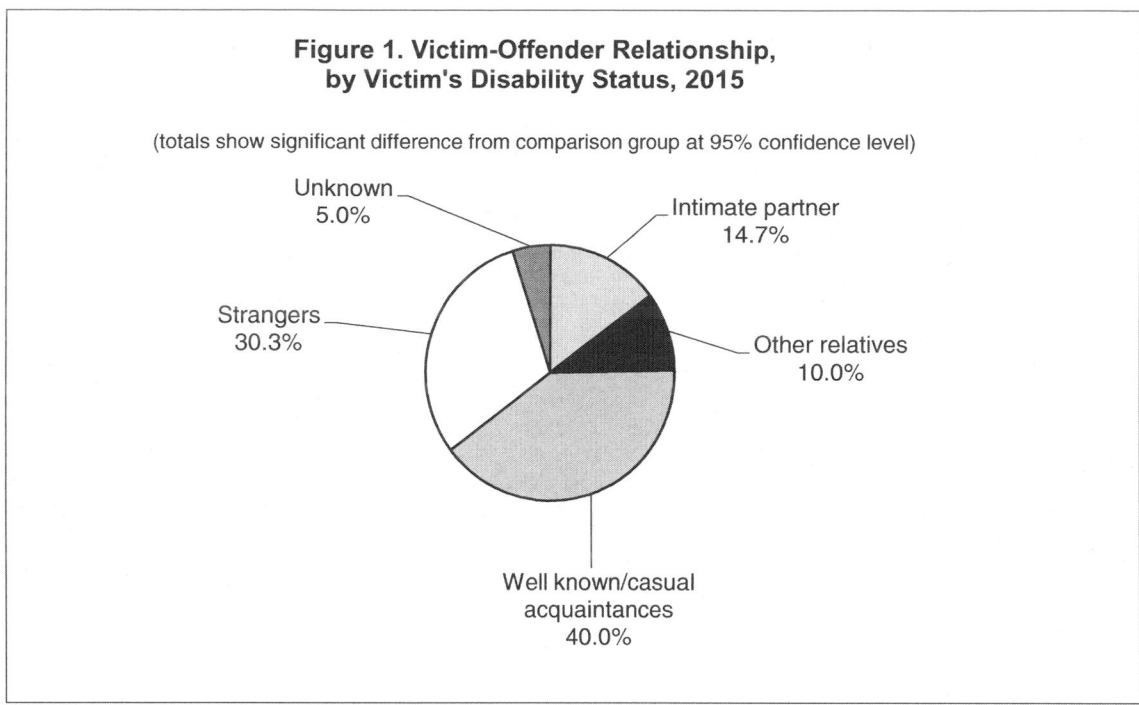

Figure 1. Victim-Offender Relationship, by Victim's Disability Status, 2015

(totals show significant difference from comparison group at 95% confidence level)

Unknown 5.0%
Intimate partner 14.7%
Strangers 30.3%
Other relatives 10.0%
Well known/casual acquaintances 40.0%

- In 2015, the rate of violent victimization against persons with disabilities (29.5 victimizations per 1,000 persons age 12 years or over) was 2.5 times the unadjusted rate for persons without disabilities. The rate for persons with disabilities has been at least double the rate for persons without disabilities for every year since 2009.

- Among those with disabilities, persons age 12 to 15 years (144.1 per 1,000 persons age 12 or older) had the highest rate of violent victimization among all age groups measured, while those age 65 years and over had no statistically significant difference between the rates of violent victimization by disability status.

- During the period from 2011 to 2015, persons with cognitive disabilities had the highest rates of total violent crime (57.9 per 1,000), serious violent crime (22.3 per 1,000), and simple assault (35.6 per 1,000) among the disability types measured. Persons with hearing disabilities (15.7 per 1,000) had the lowest rates of total violent victimization among the disability types examined.

- For each racial and ethnic group measured, persons with disabilities had higher violent victimization rates than persons without disabilities during the period from 2011 to 2015. Persons of two or more races had the highest rates of violent victimization among persons with disabilities (128.5 per 1,000) and without disabilities (33.6 per 1,000).

- The rate of violent victimization against males with disabilities was 31.8 per 1,000 males, compared to 14.1 per 1,000 males without disabilities. For females, the rate of violent victimization was 32.8 per 1,000, compared to 11.4 per 1,000 females without disabilities.

- A higher percentage of violence against persons with disabilities (40 percent) was committed by persons who knew the victims knew well or were casual acquaintances than against persons without disabilities (32 percent).

- Approximately 20 percent of violent crime victims with disabilities believed they were targeted due to their disability.

Table 1. Rate of Violent Victimization and Average Annual Number of Persons, by Victim's Disability Status and Age, 2011–2015

(Rate per 1,000 persons.)

Age of victim	Persons with disabilities		Persons without disabilities	
	Average annual number	Rate per 1,000 persons with disabilities[1]	Average annual number	Rate per 1,000 persons without disabilities*
Total	37,157,340	32.3	226,696,790	20.4
12–15..	938,300	144.1	15,682,970	38.8
16–19..	966,680	86.6	16,097,530	31.4
20–24..	1,276,180	83.4	20,982,730	29.6
25–34..	2,493,140	64.5	39,370,470	26.3
35–49..	5,387,430	58.2	56,038,570	19.7
50–64..	10,482,880	31.2	50,818,180	12.7
65 or older.......................................	15,612,740	4.8	27,706,350	4.0

Note: Based on the noninstitutionalized U.S. residential population age 12 or older.
* = Comparison group.
[1]Significant difference from comparison group at 95% confidence level for all of the values in this column.

Table 2. Rate of Violent Victimization Against Persons with and without Disabilities, by Type of Crime, 2011–2015

(Rate per 1,000 persons.)

Type of crime	Persons with disabilities[1]	Persons without disabilities*
Total crime	32.3	12.7
Serious violent crime	12.7	4.0
Rape/sexual assault	2.1	0.6
Robbery	4.7	1.3
Aggravated assault	5.9	2.1
Simple assault	19.6	8.7

Note: Based on the noninstitutionalized U.S. residential population age 12 or older. Rates for persons without disabilities were adjusted using direct standardization with the population with disabilities as the standard population.
* = Comparison group.
[1]Significant difference from comparison group at 95% confidence level for values in this column.

Table 3. Rate of Violent Victimization Against Persons with and without Disabilities, by Victim Characteristics, 2010–2014

(Rate per 1,000 persons.)

Victim characteristic	Persons with disabilities[1]	Persons without disabilities[2]*
Total crime	32.3	12.7
Sex		
Male..	31.8	14.1
Female...	32.8	11.4
Race/Hispanic Origin[3]		
White	30.8	12.0
Black	31.0	18.2
Hispanic..	29.0	13.0
Other[4]	28.0	6.4
Two or more races	128.5	33.6

Note: Based on the noninstitutionalized U.S. residential population age 12 or older.
* = Comparison group.
[1]Significant difference from comparison group at 95% confidence level.
[2]Rates for persons without disabilities were adjusted using direct standardization with the population with disabilities as the standard population.
[3]Excludes persons of Hispanic or Latino origin, unless specified.
[4]Includes persons identified as American Indian or Alaska Native and Asian, Native Hawaiian, or Other Pacific Islander.

Table 4. Rate of Violent Victimization Against Persons with Disabilities, by Disability Type and Type of Crime, 2011–2015

(Rate per 1,000 persons age 12 or older, except for independent living disabilities, which is per 1,000 persons age 15 or older.)

Disability type	Total violent crime	Serious violent crime	Simple assault
Hearing*	15.7	7.8	7.9
Vision	28.8 A	11.3 A	17.6 A
Ambulatory	29.4 A	13.1 A	16.3 A
Cognitive	57.9 A	22.3 A	35.6 A
Self-care	25.9 A	9.9	16.0 A
Independent living	30.8 A	12.1 A	18.8 A

Note: Based on the noninstitutionalized U.S. residential population age 12 or older. Includes persons with multiple disability types. Serious violent crime includes rape, sexual assault, robbery, and aggravated assault.
* = Comparison group.
A = Significant difference from comparison group at 95% confidence level.

Table 5. Rate of Violent Victimization, by Victim's Sex and Disability Type, 2011–2015

(Rate per 1,000 persons age 12 or older, except for independent living disability, which is per 1,000 persons age 15 or older.)

Disability type	Male*	Female
Hearing	15.0	16.8
Vision	24.6	32.3
Ambulatory	29.6	29.3
Cognitive	55.4	60.3
Self-care	24.7	26.8
Independent living	26.5	33.8 B

Note: Based on the noninstitutionalized U.S. residential population age 12 or older. Includes persons with multiple disability types.
* = Comparison group.
B = Significant difference from comparison group at 90% confidence level.

Table 6. Percent of Violence Against Persons with Disabilities, by Type of Crime and Number of Disability Types, 2011–2015

(Percent.)

Type of crime	Total	Single disability type*	Multiple disability types
Total	100.0	46.4	53.6 A
Serious violent crime	100.0	45.4	54.6 A
Rape/sexual assault	100.0	34.6	65.4
Robbery	100.0	48.4	51.6
Aggravated assault	100.0	46.7	53.3
Simple assault	100.0	47.0	53.0 B

Note: Based on the noninstitutionalized U.S. residential population age 12 or older. For persons age 12 to 14, independent living disabilities is not included as a disability type.
A = Significant difference from comparison group at 95% confidence level.
B = Significant difference from comparison group at 90% confidence level.

Table 7. Rate of Violent Victimization, by Number of Disability Types and Type of Crime, 2011–2015

(Rate per 1,000 persons.)

Type of crime	Single disability type*	Multiple disability types
Total	29.6	35.2 A
Serious violent crime	11.4	14.1 A
Rape/sexual assault	1.4	2.8 A
Robbery	4.5	5.0
Aggravated assault	5.5	6.4
Simple assault	18.2	21.1 B

Note: Based on the noninstitutionalized U.S. residential population age 12 or older. For persons age 12 to 14, independent living disabilities is not included as a disability type.
* = Comparison group.
A = Significant difference from comparison group at 95% confidence level.
B = Significant difference from comparison group at 90% confidence level.

Table 8. Victim-Offender Relationship, by Victim's Disability Status, 2011–2015

(Percent.)

Type of crime	Persons with disabilities	Persons without disabilities[1]*
Total	100.0	100.0
Intimate partner[1]..	14.7	12.8
Other relatives[2]	10.0 A	6.4
Well known/casual acquaintances	40.0 A	32.5
Strangers..	30.3 A	39.4
Unknown..	5.0 A	8.8

Note: Based on the noninstitutionalized U.S. residential population age 12 or older.
* = Comparison group.
A = Significant difference from comparison group at 95% confidence level.
[1]Includes spouses, ex-spouses, boyfriends, and girlfriends.
[2]Includes parents, children, and other relatives.

Table 9. Time Violent Crime Occurred, by Victim's Disability Status, 2011–2015

(Percent.)

Type of crime	Persons with disabilities	Persons without disabilities*
Total	100.0	100.0
Daytime (6 a.m.–6 p.m.)	57.1	53.6
Nighttime (6 p.m.–6 a.m.)..	38.2 B	42.7
Unknown..	4.8	3.7

Note: Based on the noninstitutionalized U.S. residential population age 12 or older.
* = Comparison group.
B = Significant difference from comparison group at 90% confidence level.

Table 10. Percent of Violent Crime Reported to Police, by Victim's Disability Status and Disability Type, 2011–2015

(Percent.)

Disability status and type	Reported to police
Persons without disabilities*	45.5
Persons with disabilities[1]	48.9
Single disability type	45.4
Multiple disability types...	51.9 A
Disability type[2]	
Hearing	51.1
Vision	42.3
Ambulatory	58.4 A
Cognitive..	47.4
Self-care...	53.6 B
Independent living..	53.9 A

Note: Based on the noninstitutionalized U.S. residential population age 12 or older.
* = Comparison group.
A = Significant difference from comparison group at 95% confidence level.
B = Significant difference from comparison group at 90% confidence level.
[1]For persons ages 12 to 14, independent living disabilities are not included as a disability type.
[2]Includes persons with multiple disability types.

Table 11. Person Who Notified Police of Violent Crime, by Victim's Disability Status, 2011–2015

(Percent.)

Person who notified police	Persons with disabilities	Persons without disabilities*
Total	100.0	100.0
Victim...	64.0	61.7
Other household member..	6.2 A	10.4
Someone official..	5.6 A	8.3
Someone else..	19.6 A	10.7
Police were at the scene..	2.5 A	6.0
Offender was a police officer......................................	0.2 C	0.3
Police notified some other way..................................	1.8	2.1

Note: Based on the noninstitutionalized U.S. residential population age 12 or older. Someone official includes a guard, apartment manager, school official, and other officials. In less than 1% of cases, the person who contacted police was unknown.
* = Comparison group.
A = Significant difference from comparison group at 95% confidence level.
C = Interpret with caution. Estimate is based on 10 or fewer sample cases or coefficient of variation is greater than 50%.

Table 12. Reasons for Not Reporting Violent Crime to Police, by Victim's Disability Status, 2011–2015

(Percent.)

Reason for not reporting crime to police	Persons with disabilities	Persons without disabilities*
Dealt with another way[1]	40.0	42.9
Other[2]..	36.8	33.1
Police would not help[3]	20.8	18.8
Was not important enough to victim[4]........................	20.4	24.2
Police could not do anything[5]...................................	3.0	3.3
Insurance would not cover..	0.1 C	0.2 C

Note: Based on the noninstitutionalized U.S. residential population age 12 or older. Detail may sum to more than 100% because more than one response was allowed.
* = Comparison group.
! = Interpret with caution. Estimate is based on 10 or fewer sample cases, or coefficient of variation is greater than 50%.
[1]Includes reported to another official and private or personal matter.
[2]Includes did not want to get offender in trouble with the law, was advised not to report to police, was afraid of reprisal, reporting was too inconvenient, did not know why it was not reported, and other reasons.
[3]Includes police would not think it was important enough, police would be inefficient, police would be biased, and offender was a police officer.
[4]Includes minor or unsuccessful crime, offender was a child, and not clear if a crime occurred.
[5]Includes did not find out until too late, could not recover or identify property, and could not find or identify offender.

Table 13. Percent of Violent Crime Victims in Which Assistance from a Nonpolice Victim Service Agency Was Received, by Victim's Disability Status, 2011–2015

(Percent.)

Disability status of victim	Percent of violent victimizations
Persons with disabilities	12.3 A
Persons without disabilities*	8.3

Note: Based on the noninstitutionalized U.S. residential population age 12 or older.
* = Comparison group.
A = Significant difference from comparison group at 95% confidence level.

Methodology

About the Data

The use of age-adjusted rates: The differences in age distributions between the two populations must be taken into account when making direct comparisons of the violent victimization rate between persons with and without disabilities. The age distribution of persons with disabilities differs considerably from that of persons without disabilities, and violent crime victimization rates vary significantly with age. According to the U.S. Census Bureau's American Community Survey (ACS), persons with disabilities are generally older than persons without disabilities. The age adjustment standardizes the rate of violence to show what the rate would be if persons without disabilities had the same age distribution as persons with disabilities.

Survey Coverage

The National Crime Victimization Survey (NCVS) is an ongoing data collection conducted by the U.S. Census Bureau for the Bureau of Justice Statistics (BJS). The NCVS is a self-report survey in which interviewed persons are asked about the number and characteristics of victimizations they experienced during the prior 6 months. The NCVS collects information on nonfatal personal crimes (rape or sexual assault, robbery, aggravated and simple assault, and personal larceny) and household property crimes (burglary, motor vehicle theft, and other theft) both reported and not reported to police. In addition to providing annual level and change estimates on criminal victimization, the NCVS is the primary source of information on the nature of criminal victimization incidents. Survey respondents provide information about themselves (e.g., age, sex, race and Hispanic origin, marital status, education level, and income) and whether they experienced a victimization.

The NCVS collects information for each victimization incident about the offender (e.g., age, race and Hispanic origin, sex, and victim–offender relationship), characteristics of the crime (including time and place of occurrence, use of weapons, nature of injury, and economic consequences), whether the crime was reported to police, reasons the crime was or was not reported, and victims' experiences with the criminal justice system. The NCVS is administered to persons age 12 or older from a nationally representative sample of households in the United States. The NCVS defines a household as a group of members who all reside at a sampled address. Persons are considered household members when the sampled address is their usual place of residence at the time of the interview and when they have no usual place of residence elsewhere. Once selected, households remain in the sample for 3 years, and

eligible persons in these households are interviewed every 6 months either in person or over the phone, for a total of seven interviews. All first interviews are conducted in person with subsequent interviews conducted either in person or by phone. New households rotate into the sample on an ongoing basis to replace outgoing households that have been in the sample for the 3-year period. The sample includes persons living in group quarters (such as dormitories, rooming houses, and religious group dwellings) and excludes persons living in military barracks and institutional settings (such as correctional or hospital facilities) and persons who are homeless.

In 2007, the NCVS adopted questions from the U.S. Census Bureau's American Community Survey (ACS) to measure the rate of victimization against people with disabilities. The NCVS does not identify persons in the general population with disabilities. The ACS Subcommittee on Disability Questions developed the disability questions based on questions used in the 2000 Decennial Census and earlier versions of the ACS. The questions identify persons who may require assistance to maintain their independence, be at risk for discrimination, or lack opportunities available to the general population because of limitations related to a prolonged (i.e., 6 months or longer) sensory, physical, mental, or emotional condition. More information about the ACS and the disability questions is available on the U.S. Census Bureau website at http://www.census.gov/acs/www/.

Definitions of Disability Type

Disabilities are classified according to six limitations: hearing, vision, cognitive, ambulatory, self-care, and independent living.

Hearing limitation entails deafness or serious difficulty hearing.

Vision limitation is blindness or serious difficulty seeing, even when wearing glasses.

Cognitive limitation includes serious difficulty in concentrating, remembering, or making decisions because of a physical, mental, or emotional condition.

Ambulatory limitation is difficulty walking or climbing stairs.

Self-care limitation is a condition that causes difficulty dressing or bathing.

Independent living limitation is a physical, mental, or emotional condition that impedes doing errands alone, such as visiting a doctor or shopping.

Crime in the United States, 2016

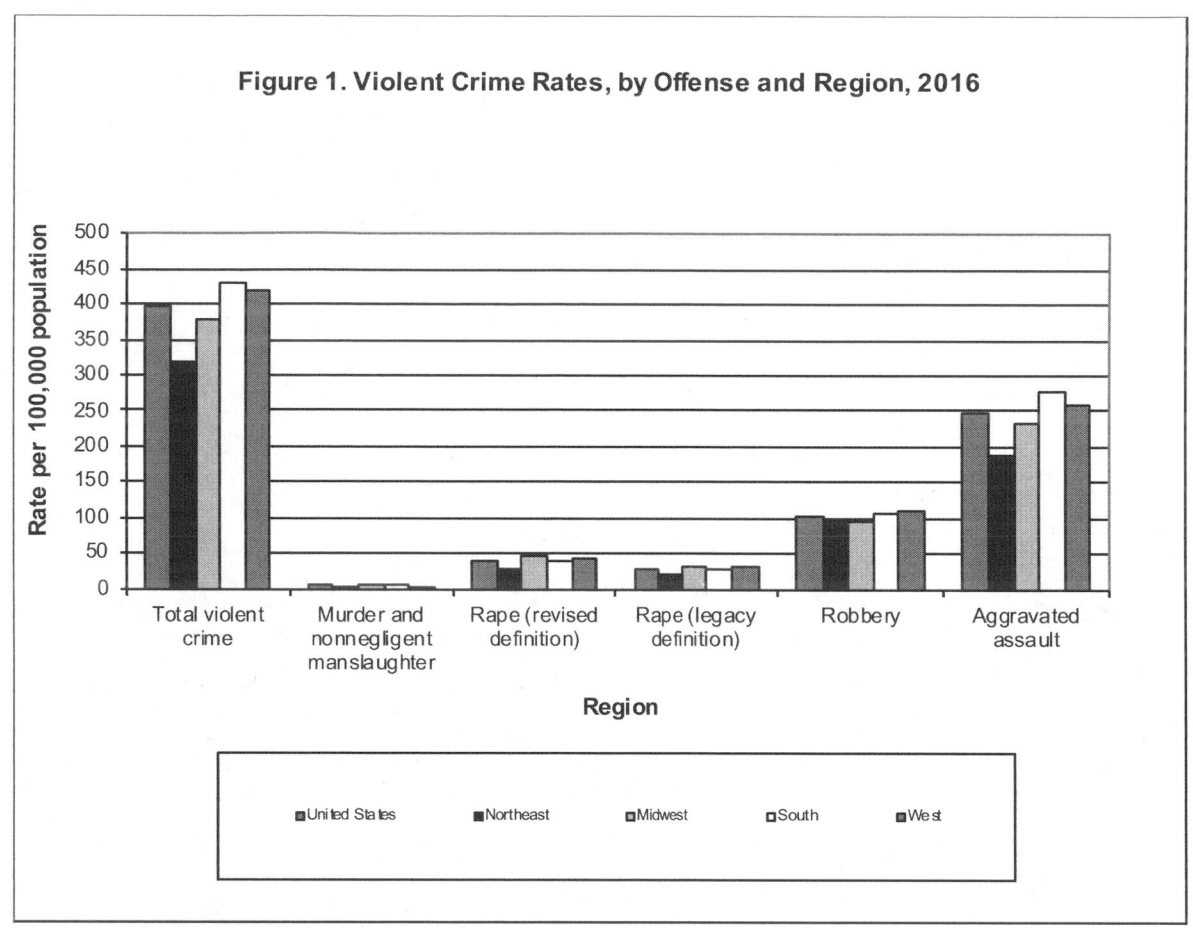

Figure 1. Violent Crime Rates, by Offense and Region, 2016

- An estimated 1,248,185 violent crimes occurred nationwide in 2016, an increase of 4.1 percent from the 2015 estimate. Aggravated assaults accounted for 64.3 percent of violent crimes reported to law.

- The 2-year trend showed that property crime offenses (an estimated total of 7,919,035) declined 1.3 percent in 2016 when compared with the 2015 estimate. Larceny-theft accounted for 71.2 percent of all property crimes in 2016.

- In 2016, 45.6 percent of violent crimes and 18.3 percent of property crimes were cleared by arrest or exceptional means.

- Law enforcement made an estimated 10,662,252 arrests nationwide in 2016. Of these arrests, 515,151 were for

violent crimes, and 1,353,283 were for property crimes. The highest number of arrests were for drug abuse violations (estimated at 1,572,579 arrests), other assaults (estimated at 1,078,808), and larceny-thefts (estimated at 1,050,058).

- Nationwide, the rate of sworn officers was 2.4 per 1,000 inhabitants. The rate of full-time law enforcement employees (civilian and sworn) per 1,000 inhabitants was 3.4.

- There were 234 violent crimes and 3,334 property crimes known to law enforcement at federal agencies in 2016.

- Of participating states, Texas had the most human trafficking violations in 2016, with 257.

- In 2016, 147 cargo theft incidents were reported among participating states. 31.4 percent of these thefts were recovered.

Table 1. Crime in the United States, by Volume and Rate Per 100,000 Inhabitants, 1996–2016

(Number, rate per 100,000 population.)

Year	Population[1]	Violent crime[2]		Murder and nonnegligent manslaughter		Rape (revised definition)[3]		Rape (legacy definition)[4]		Robbery		Aggravated assault	
		Number	Rate	Number	Rate	Number	Rate	Number	Rate	Number	Rate	Number	Rate
1996	265,228,572	1,688,540	636.6	19,645	7.4	X	X	96,252	36.3	535,594	201.9	1,037,049	391.0
1997	267,783,607	1,636,096	611.0	18,208	6.8	X	X	96,153	35.9	498,534	186.2	1,023,201	382.1
1998	270,248,003	1,533,887	567.6	16,974	6.3	X	X	93,144	34.5	447,186	165.5	976,583	361.4
1999	272,690,813	1,426,044	523.0	15,522	5.7	X	X	89,411	32.8	409,371	150.1	911,740	334.3
2000	281,421,906	1,425,486	506.5	15,586	5.5	X	X	90,178	32.0	408,016	145.0	911,706	324.0
2001[5]	285,317,559	1,439,480	504.5	16,037	5.6	X	X	90,863	31.8	423,557	148.5	909,023	318.6
2002	287,973,924	1,423,677	494.4	16,229	5.6	X	X	95,235	33.1	420,806	146.1	891,407	309.5
2003	290,788,976	1,383,676	475.8	16,528	5.7	X	X	93,883	32.3	414,235	142.5	859,030	295.4
2004	293,656,842	1,360,088	463.2	16,148	5.5	X	X	95,089	32.4	401,470	136.7	847,381	288.6
2005	296,507,061	1,390,745	469.0	16,740	5.6	X	X	94,347	31.8	417,438	140.8	862,220	290.8
2006	299,398,484	1,435,123	479.3	17,309	5.8	X	X	94,472	31.6	449,246	150.0	874,096	292.0
2007	301,621,157	1,422,970	471.8	17,128	5.7	X	X	92,160	30.6	447,324	148.3	866,358	287.2
2008	304,059,724	1,394,461	458.6	16,465	5.4	X	X	90,750	29.8	443,563	145.9	843,683	277.5
2009	307,006,550	1,325,896	431.9	15,399	5.0	X	X	89,241	29.1	408,742	133.1	812,514	264.7
2010	309,330,219	1,251,248	404.5	14,722	4.8	X	X	85,593	27.7	369,089	119.3	781,844	252.8
2011	311,587,816	1,206,005	387.1	14,661	4.7	X	X	84,175	27.0	354,746	113.9	752,423	241.5
2012	313,873,685	1,217,057	387.8	14,856	4.7	X	X	85,141	27.1	355,051	113.1	762,009	242.8
2013	316,497,531	1,168,298	369.1	14,319	4.5	113,695	35.9	82,109	25.9	345,093	109.0	726,777	229.6
2014	318,907,401	1,153,022	361.6	14,164	4.4	118,027	37.0	84,864	26.6	322,905	101.3	731,089	229.2
2015[6]	320,896,618	1,199,310	373.7	15,883	4.9	126,134	39.3	91,261	28.4	328,109	102.2	764,057	238.1
2016	323,127,513	1,248,185	386.3	17,250	5.3	130,623	40.4	95,730	29.6	332,198	102.8	803,007	248.5

Year	Property crime		Burglary		Larceny-theft		Motor vehicle theft	
	Number	Rate	Number	Rate	Number	Rate	Number	Rate
1996	11,805,323	4,451.0	2,506,400	945.0	7,904,685	2,980.3	1,394,238	525.7
1997	11,558,475	4,316.3	2,460,526	918.8	7,743,760	2,891.8	1,354,189	505.7
1998	10,951,827	4,052.5	2,332,735	863.2	7,376,311	2,729.5	1,242,781	459.9
1999	10,208,334	3,743.6	2,100,739	770.4	6,955,520	2,550.7	1,152,075	422.5
2000	10,182,584	3,618.3	2,050,992	728.8	6,971,590	2,477.3	1,160,002	412.2
2001[5]	10,437,189	3,658.1	2,116,531	741.8	7,092,267	2,485.7	1,228,391	430.5
2002	10,455,277	3,630.6	2,151,252	747.0	7,057,379	2,450.7	1,246,646	432.9
2003	10,442,862	3,591.2	2,154,834	741.0	7,026,802	2,416.5	1,261,226	433.7
2004	10,319,386	3,514.1	2,144,446	730.3	6,937,089	2,362.3	1,237,851	421.5
2005	10,174,754	3,431.5	2,155,448	726.9	6,783,447	2,287.8	1,235,859	416.8
2006	10,019,601	3,346.6	2,194,993	733.1	6,626,363	2,213.2	1,198,245	400.2
2007	9,882,212	3,276.4	2,190,198	726.1	6,591,542	2,185.4	1,100,472	364.9
2008	9,774,152	3,214.6	2,228,887	733.0	6,586,206	2,166.1	959,059	315.4
2009	9,337,060	3,041.3	2,203,313	717.7	6,338,095	2,064.5	795,652	259.2
2010	9,112,625	2,945.9	2,168,459	701.0	6,204,601	2,005.8	739,565	239.1
2011	9,052,743	2,905.4	2,185,140	701.3	6,151,095	1,974.1	716,508	230.0
2012	9,001,992	2,868.0	2,109,932	672.2	6,168,874	1,965.4	723,186	230.4
2013	8,651,892	2,733.6	1,932,139	610.5	6,019,465	1,901.9	700,288	221.3
2014	8,209,010	2,574.1	1,713,153	537.2	5,809,054	1,821.5	686,803	215.4
2015[6]	8,024,115	2,500.5	1,587,564	494.7	5,723,488	1,783.6	713,063	222.2
2016	7,919,035	2,450.7	1,515,096	468.9	5,638,455	1,745.0	765,484	236.9

Note: Although arson data are included in the trend and clearance tables, sufficient data are not available to estimate totals for this offense. Therefore, no arson data are published in this table.
X = Not applicable.
[1] Populations are U.S. Census Bureau provisional estimates as of July 1 for each year except 2000 and 2010, which are decennial census counts.
[2] The violent crime figures include the offenses of murder, rape (legacy definition), robbery, and aggravated assault.
[3] The figures shown in this column for the offense of rape were estimated using the revised UCR definition of rape.
[4] The figures shown in this column for the offense of rape were estimated using the legacy UCR definition of rape.
[5] The murder and nonnegligent homicides that occurred as a result of the events of September 11, 2001, are not included in this table.
[6] The crime figures have been adjusted.

Table 1A. Crime in the United States, Percent Change in Volume and Rate Per 100,000 Inhabitants for 2 Years, 5 Years, and 10 Years, 2007–2016

(Percent change.)

Year	Violent crime[1] Number	Rate	Murder and nonnegligent manslaughter Number	Rate	Rape (revised definition)[2] Number	Rate	Rape (legacy definition)[3] Number	Rate	Robbery Number	Rate
2007–2016	-12.3	-18.1	+0.7	-6.0	X	X	+3.9	-3.0	-25.7	-30.7
2012–2016	+2.6	-0.4	+16.1	+12.8	X	X	+12.4	+9.2	-6.4	-9.1
2015–2016	+4.1	+3.4	+8.6	+7.9	+3.5	+2.8	+4.9	+4.2	+1.2	+0.5

Table 2. Crime,[1] by Region, Geographic Division, and State, 2015–2016

(Number, rate per 100,000 population, percent.)

Area	Population[2]	Violent crime[3] Number	Rate	Murder and nonnegligent manslaughter Number	Rate	Rape (revised definition)[4] Number	Rate	Rape (legacy definition)[5] Number	Rate	Robbery Number	Rate
United States[6,7,8,9]											
2015	320,896,618	1,234,183	384.6	15,883	4.9	126,134	39.3	91,261	28.4	328,109	102.2
2016	323,127,513	1,283,058	397.1	17,250	5.3	130,603	40.4	95,730	29.6	332,198	102.8
Percent change		+4.0	+3.2	+8.6	+7.9	+3.5	+2.8	+4.9	+4.2	+1.2	+0.5
Northeast[6]											
2015	56,184,737	180,474	321.2	1,967	3.5	16,415	29.2	11,912	21.2	56,202	100.0
2016	56,209,510	178,244	317.1	1,955	3.5	16,651	29.6	12,219	21.7	53,033	94.3
Percent change		-1.2	-1.3	-0.6	-0.7	+1.4	+1.4	+2.6	+2.5	-5.6	-5.7
New England[6]											
2015	14,710,229	42,121	286.3	326	2.2	4,602	31.3	3,374	22.9	9,629	65.5
2016	14,735,525	41,598	282.3	292	2.0	4,505	30.6	3,328	22.6	9,407	63.8
Percent change		-1.2	-1.4	-10.4	-10.6	-2.1	-2.3	-1.4	-1.5	-2.3	-2.5
Connecticut											
2015	3,584,730	7,938	221.4	116	3.2	798	22.3	585	16.3	2,925	81.6
2016	3,576,452	8,123	227.1	78	2.2	763	21.3	561	15.7	2,703	75.6
Percent change		+2.3	+2.6	-32.8	-32.6	-4.4	-4.2	-4.1	-3.9	-7.6	-7.4
Maine											
2015	1,329,453	1,726	129.8	23	1.7	461	34.7	337	25.3	311	23.4
2016	1,331,479	1,648	123.8	20	1.5	412	30.9	300	22.5	266	20.0
Percent change		-4.5	-4.7	-13.0	-13.2	-10.6	-10.8	-11.0	-11.1	-14.5	-14.6
Massachusetts											
2015	6,784,240	26,453	389.9	131	1.9	2,082	30.7	1,538	22.7	5,266	77.6
2016	6,811,779	25,677	376.9	134	2.0	2,128	31.2	1,592	23.4	5,365	78.8
Percent change		-2.9	-3.3	+2.3	+1.9	+2.2	+1.8	+3.5	+3.1	+1.9	+1.5
New Hampshire											
2015	1,330,111	2,692	202.4	15	1.1	644	48.4	468	35.2	475	35.7
2016	1,334,795	2,637	197.6	17	1.3	582	43.6	423	31.7	427	32.0
Percent change		-2.0	-2.4	+13.3	+12.9	-9.6	-9.9	-9.6	-9.9	-10.1	-10.4
Rhode Island[6]											
2015	1,055,607	2,565	243.0	31	2.9	467	44.2	342	32.4	547	51.8
2016	1,056,426	2,524	238.9	29	2.7	442	41.8	328	31.0	540	51.1
Percent change		-1.6	-1.7	-6.5	-6.5	-5.4	-5.4	-4.1	-4.2	-1.3	-1.4
Vermont											
2015	626,088	747	119.3	10	1.6	150	24.0	104	16.6	105	16.8
2016	624,594	989	158.3	14	2.2	178	28.5	124	19.9	106	17.0
Percent change		+32.4	+32.7	+40.0	+40.3	18.7	+19.0	+19.2	+19.5	+1.0	+1.2
Middle Atlantic[6]											
2015	41,474,508	138,353	333.6	1,641	4.0	11,813	28.5	8,538	20.6	46,573	112.3
2016	41,473,985	136,646	329.5	1,663	4.0	12,146	29.3	8,891	21.4	43,626	105.2
Percent change		-1.2	-1.2	+1.3	+1.3	+2.8	+2.8	+4.1	+4.1	-6.3	-6.3
New Jersey											
2015	8,935,421	22,879	256.0	363	4.1	1,373	15.4	1,019	11.4	9,729	108.9
2016	8,944,469	21,914	245.0	372	4.2	1,453	16.2	1,089	12.2	8,984	100.4
Percent change		-4.2	-4.3	+2.5	+2.4	+5.8	+5.7	+6.9	+6.8	-7.7	-7.8

Table 1A. Crime in the United States, Percent Change in Volume and Rate Per 100,000 Inhabitants for 2 Years, 5 Years, and 10 Years, 2007–2016—*Continued*

(Percent change.)

Year	Aggravated assault		Property crime		Burglary		Larceny-theft		Motor vehicle theft	
	Number	Rate	Number	Rate	Number	Rate	Number	Rate	Number	Rate
2007–2016...	-7.3	-13.5	-19.9	-25.2	-30.8	-35.4	-14.5	-20.2	-30.4	-35.1
2012–2016...	+5.4	+2.4	-12.0	-14.5	-28.2	-30.2	-8.6	-11.2	+5.8	+2.8
2015–2016...	+5.1	+4.4	-1.3	-2.0	-4.6	-5.2	-1.5	-2.2	+7.4	+6.6

X = Not applicable.
[1] The violent crime figures include the offenses of murder, rape (legacy definition), robbery, and aggravated assault.
[2] The figures shown in this column for the offense of rape were estimated using the revised UCR definition of rape.
[3] The figures shown in this column for the offense of rape were estimated using the legacy UCR definition of rape.

Table 2. Crime,[1] by Region, Geographic Division, and State, 2015–2016—*Continued*

(Number, rate per 100,000 population, percent.)

Area	Population[2]	Aggravated assault		Property crime		Burglary		Larceny-theft		Motor vehicle theft	
		Number	Rate	Number	Rate	Number	Rate	Number	Rate	Number	Rate
United States[6,7,8,9]											
2015.....................................	320,896,618	764,057	238.1	8,024,115	2,500.5	1,587,564	494.7	5,723,488	1,783.6	713,063	222.2
2016.....................................	323,127,513	803,007	248.5	7,919,035	2,450.7	1,515,096	468.9	5,638,455	1,745.0	765,484	236.9
Percent change................		+5.1	+4.4	-1.3	-2.0	-4.6	-5.2	-1.5	-2.2	+7.4	+6.6
Northeast[6]..........................											
2015.....................................	56,184,737	105,890	188.5	951,940	1,694.3	157,910	281.1	737,087	1,311.9	56,943	101.3
2016.....................................	56,209,510	106,605	189.7	909,897	1,618.8	142,720	253.9	709,721	1,262.6	57,456	102.2
Percent change................		+0.7	+0.6	-4.4	-4.5	-9.6	-9.7	-3.7	-3.8	+0.9	+0.9
New England[6].....................											
2015.....................................	14,710,229	27,564	187.4	257,073	1,747.6	46,260	314.5	193,051	1,312.4	17,762	120.7
2016.....................................	14,735,525	27,394	185.9	243,769	1,654.3	42,095	285.7	182,985	1,241.8	18,689	126.8
Percent change................		-0.6	-0.8	-5.2	-5.3	-9.0	-9.2	-5.2	-5.4	+5.2	+5.0
Connecticut.....................											
2015	3,584,730	4,099	114.3	65,610	1,830.3	10,286	286.9	48,898	1,364.1	6,426	179.3
2016	3,576,452	4,579	128.0	64,664	1,808.0	10,045	280.9	47,512	1,328.5	7,107	198.7
Percent change		+11.7	+12.0	-1.4	-1.2	-2.3	-2.1	-2.8	-2.6	+10.6	+10.9
Maine..............................											
2015	1,329,453	931	70.0	24,361	1,832.4	4,694	353.1	18,853	1,418.1	814	61.2
2016	1,331,479	950	71.3	21,912	1,645.7	4,003	300.6	17,134	1,286.8	775	58.2
Percent change		+2.0	+1.9	-10.1	-10.2	-14.7	-14.9	-9.1	-9.3	-4.8	-4.9
Massachusetts											
2015	6,784,240	18,974	279.7	114,547	1,688.4	21,826	321.7	84,676	1,248.1	8,045	118.6
2016	6,811,779	18,050	265.0	106,339	1,561.1	19,193	281.8	79,088	1,161.0	8,058	118.3
Percent change		-4.9	-5.3	-7.2	-7.5	-12.1	-12.4	-6.6	-7.0	+0.2	-0.2
New Hampshire											
2015	1,330,111	1,558	117.1	23,453	1,763.2	3,482	261.8	19,076	1,434.2	895	67.3
2016	1,334,795	1,611	120.7	20,194	1,512.9	2,963	222.0	16,360	1,225.7	871	65.3
Percent change		+3.4	+3.0	-13.9	-14.2	-14.9	-15.2	-14.2	-14.5	-2.7	-3.0
Rhode Island[6]..................											
2015	1,055,607	1,520	144.0	20,038	1,898.2	3,938	373.1	14,714	1,393.9	1,386	131.3
2016	1,056,426	1,513	143.2	20,058	1,898.7	3,788	358.6	14,674	1,389.0	1,596	151.1
Percent change		-0.5	-0.5	+0.1	*	-3.8	-3.9	-0.3	-0.3	+15.2	+15.1
Vermont.........................											
2015	626,088	482	77.0	9,064	1,447.7	2,034	324.9	6,834	1,091.5	196	31.3
2016	624,594	691	110.6	10,602	1,697.4	2,103	336.7	8,217	1,315.6	282	45.1
Percent change		+43.4	+43.7	+17.0	+17.2	+3.4	+3.6	+20.2	+20.5	+43.9	+44.2
Middle Atlantic[6]..................											
2015.....................................	41,474,508	78,326	188.9	694,867	1,675.4	111,650	269.2	544,036	1,311.7	39,181	94.5
2016.....................................	41,473,985	79,211	191.0	666,128	1,606.1	100,625	242.6	526,736	1,270.0	38,767	93.5
Percent change................		+1.1	+1.1	-4.1	-4.1	-9.9	-9.9	-3.2	-3.2	-1.1	-1.1
New Jersey											
2015	8,935,421	11,414	127.7	145,701	1,630.6	27,960	312.9	105,963	1,185.9	11,778	131.8
2016	8,944,469	11,105	124.2	138,152	1,544.6	25,284	282.7	101,540	1,135.2	11,328	126.6
Percent change		-2.7	-2.8	-5.2	-5.3	-9.6	-9.7	-4.2	-4.3	-3.8	-3.9

(Number, rate per 100,000 population, percent.)

Area	Population[2]	Violent crime[3]		Murder and nonnegligent manslaughter		Rape (revised definition)[4]		Rape (legacy definition)[5]		Robbery	
		Number	Rate	Number	Rate	Number	Rate	Number	Rate	Number	Rate
New York[6]											
2015	19,747,183	75,126	380.4	613	3.1	6,141	31.1	4,414	22.4	23,879	120.9
2016	19,745,289	74,285	376.2	630	3.2	6,260	31.7	4,569	23.1	22,316	113.0
Percent change		-1.1	-1.1	+2.8	+2.8	+1.9	+1.9	+3.5	+3.5	-6.5	-6.5
Pennsylvania											
2015	12,791,904	40,348	315.4	665	5.2	4,299	33.6	3,105	24.3	12,965	101.4
2016	12,784,227	40,447	316.4	661	5.2	4,433	34.7	3,233	25.3	12,326	96.4
Percent change		+0.2	+0.3	-0.6	-0.5	+3.1	+3.2	+4.1	+4.2	-4.9	-4.9
Midwest[6]											
2015	67,838,387	242,893	358.0	3,422	5.0	30,827	45.4	22,395	33.0	62,201	91.7
2016	67,941,429	257,109	378.4	3,885	5.7	31,408	46.2	23,080	34.0	64,022	94.2
Percent change		+5.9	+5.7	+13.5	+13.4	+1.9	+1.7	+3.1	+2.9	+2.9	+2.8
East North Central[6]											
2015	46,742,511	168,762	361.0	2,471	5.3	21,268	45.5	15,455	33.1	47,806	102.3
2016	46,755,973	180,827	386.7	2,974	6.4	22,102	47.3	16,199	34.6	49,506	105.9
Percent change		+7.1	+7.1	+20.4	+20.3	+3.9	+3.9	+4.8	+4.8	+3.6	+3.5
Illinois											
2015	12,839,047	49,755	387.5	754	5.9	4,926	38.4	3,602	28.1	15,056	117.3
2016	12,801,539	55,854	436.3	1,054	8.2	4,908	38.3	3,635	28.4	17,827	139.3
Percent change		+12.3	+12.6	+39.8	+40.2	-0.4	-0.1	+0.9	+1.2	+18.4	+18.8
Indiana[6]											
2015	6,612,768	25,373	383.7	370	5.6	2,386	36.1	1,757	26.6	7,081	107.1
2016	6,633,053	26,845	404.7	439	6.6	2,501	37.7	1,851	27.9	7,330	110.5
Percent change		+5.8	+5.5	+18.6	+18.3	+4.8	+4.5	+5.4	+5.0	+3.5	+3.2
Michigan											
2015	9,917,715	41,712	420.6	585	5.9	6,710	67.7	4,782	48.2	7,818	78.8
2016	9,928,300	45,572	459.0	598	6.0	7,125	71.8	5,114	51.5	7,120	71.7
Percent change		+9.3	+9.1	+2.2	+2.1	+6.2	+6.1	+6.9	+6.8	-8.9	-9.0
Ohio[6]											
2015	11,605,090	34,373	296.2	522	4.5	5,441	46.9	3,990	34.4	12,617	108.7
2016	11,614,373	34,877	300.3	654	5.6	5,589	48.1	4,141	35.7	12,523	107.8
Percent change		+1.5	+1.4	+25.3	+25.2	+2.7	+2.6	+3.8	+3.7	-0.7	-0.8
Wisconsin[6]											
2015	5,767,891	17,549	304.3	240	4.2	1,805	31.3	1,324	23.0	5,234	90.7
2016	5,778,708	17,679	305.9	229	4.0	1,979	34.2	1,458	25.2	4,706	81.4
Percent change		+0.7	+0.6	-4.6	-4.8	+9.6	+9.4	+10.1	+9.9	-10.1	-10.3
West North Central[6]											
2015	21,095,876	74,131	351.4	951	4.5	9,559	45.3	6,940	32.9	14,395	68.2
2016	21,185,456	76,282	360.1	911	4.3	9,306	43.9	6,881	32.5	14,516	68.5
Percent change		+2.9	+2.5	-4.2	-4.6	-2.6	-3.1	-0.9	-1.3	+0.8	+0.4
Iowa											
2015	3,121,997	8,619	276.1	73	2.3	1,205	38.6	877	28.1	1,050	33.6
2016	3,134,693	9,110	290.6	71	2.3	1,247	39.8	922	29.4	1,148	36.6
Percent change		+5.7	+5.3	-2.7	-3.1	+3.5	+3.1	+5.1	+4.7	+9.3	+8.9
Kansas											
2015	2,906,721	11,483	395.0	126	4.3	1,684	57.9	1,226	42.2	1,823	62.7
2016	2,907,289	11,060	380.4	111	3.8	1,312	45.1	971	33.4	1,671	57.5
Percent change		-3.7	-3.7	-11.9	-11.9	-22.1	-22.1	-20.8	-20.8	-8.3	-8.4
Minnesota											
2015	5,482,435	13,319	242.9	133	2.4	2,321	42.3	1,679	30.6	3,771	68.8
2016	5,519,952	13,394	242.6	101	1.8	2,348	42.5	1,731	31.4	3,728	67.5
Percent change		+0.6	-0.1	-24.1	-24.6	+1.2	+0.5	+3.1	+2.4	-1.1	-1.8
Missouri											
2015	6,076,204	30,292	498.5	503	8.3	2,573	42.3	1,858	30.6	6,383	105.0
2016	6,093,000	31,644	519.4	537	8.8	2,554	41.9	1,884	30.9	6,570	107.8
Percent change		+4.5	+4.2	+6.8	+6.5	-0.7	-1.0	+1.4	+1.1	+2.9	+2.6
Nebraska[6]											
2015	1,893,765	5,167	272.8	62	3.3	885	46.7	648	34.2	994	52.5
2016	1,907,116	5,550	291.0	49	2.6	994	52.1	738	38.7	946	49.6
Percent change		+7.4	+6.7	-21.0	-21.5	+12.3	+11.5	+13.9	+13.1	-4.8	-5.5
North Dakota											
2015	756,835	1,949	257.5	21	2.8	391	51.7	285	37.7	159	21.0
2016	757,952	1,903	251.1	15	2.0	342	45.1	256	33.8	181	23.9
Percent change		-2.4	-2.5	-28.6	-28.7	-12.5	-12.7	-10.2	-10.3	+13.8	+13.7
South Dakota[6]											
2015	857,919	3,302	384.9	33	3.8	500	58.3	367	42.8	215	25.1

Table 2. Crime,[1] by Region, Geographic Division, and State, 2015–2016—*Continued*

(Number, rate per 100,000 population, percent.)

Area	Population[2]	Aggravated assault		Property crime		Burglary		Larceny-theft		Motor vehicle theft	
		Number	Rate	Number	Rate	Number	Rate	Number	Rate	Number	Rate
New York[6]											
2015	19,747,183	44,493	225.3	317,225	1,606.4	44,117	223.4	257,837	1,305.7	15,271	77.3
2016	19,745,289	45,079	228.3	305,181	1,545.6	39,821	201.7	250,968	1,271.0	14,392	72.9
Percent change		+1.3	+1.3	-3.8	-3.8	-9.7	-9.7	-2.7	-2.7	-5.8	-5.7
Pennsylvania											
2015	12,791,904	22,419	175.3	231,941	1,813.2	39,573	309.4	180,236	1,409.0	12,132	94.8
2016	12,784,227	23,027	180.1	222,795	1,742.7	35,520	277.8	174,228	1,362.8	13,047	102.1
Percent change		+2.7	+2.8	-3.9	-3.9	-10.2	-10.2	-3.3	-3.3	+7.5	+7.6
Midwest[6]											
2015	67,838,387	146,443	215.9	1,555,516	2,293.0	307,853	453.8	1,125,935	1,659.7	121,728	179.4
2016	67,941,429	157,794	232.3	1,544,531	2,273.3	300,359	442.1	1,112,596	1,637.6	131,576	193.7
Percent change		+7.8	+7.6	-0.7	-0.9	-2.4	-2.6	-1.2	-1.3	+8.1	+7.9
East North Central[6]											
2015	46,742,511	97,217	208.0	1,037,945	2,220.6	211,221	451.9	748,309	1,600.9	78,415	167.8
2016	46,755,973	106,245	227.2	1,034,762	2,213.1	207,962	444.8	742,358	1,587.7	84,442	180.6
Percent change		+9.3	+9.3	-0.3	-0.3	-1.5	-1.6	-0.8	-0.8	+7.7	+7.7
Illinois											
2015	12,839,047	29,019	226.0	256,962	2,001.4	46,846	364.9	192,424	1,498.7	17,692	137.8
2016	12,801,539	32,065	250.5	262,306	2,049.0	47,989	374.9	194,407	1,518.6	19,910	155.5
Percent change		+10.5	+10.8	+2.1	+2.4	+2.4	+2.7	+1.0	+1.3	+12.5	+12.9
Indiana[6]											
2015	6,612,768	15,536	234.9	171,878	2,599.2	34,404	520.3	123,940	1,874.3	13,534	204.7
2016	6,633,053	16,575	249.9	171,759	2,589.4	34,097	514.0	122,931	1,853.3	14,731	222.1
Percent change		+6.7	+6.4	-0.1	-0.4	-0.9	-1.2	-0.8	-1.1	+8.8	+8.5
Michigan											
2015	9,917,715	26,599	268.2	191,191	1,927.8	40,375	407.1	132,019	1,331.1	18,797	189.5
2016	9,928,300	30,729	309.5	189,620	1,909.9	39,568	398.5	129,876	1,308.1	20,176	203.2
Percent change		+15.5	+15.4	-0.8	-0.9	-2.0	-2.1	-1.6	-1.7	+7.3	+7.2
Ohio[6]											
2015	11,605,090	15,793	136.1	303,743	2,617.3	69,994	603.1	216,354	1,864.3	17,395	149.9
2016	11,614,373	16,111	138.7	299,357	2,577.5	66,883	575.9	212,807	1,832.3	19,667	169.3
Percent change		+2.0	+1.9	-1.4	-1.5	-4.4	-4.5	-1.6	-1.7	+13.1	+13.0
Wisconsin[6]											
2015	5,767,891	10,270	178.1	114,171	1,979.4	19,602	339.8	83,572	1,448.9	10,997	190.7
2016	5,778,708	10,765	186.3	111,720	1,933.3	19,425	336.1	82,337	1,424.8	9,958	172.3
Percent change		+4.8	+4.6	-2.1	-2.3	-0.9	-1.1	-1.5	-1.7	-9.4	-9.6
West North Central[6]											
2015	21,095,876	49,226	233.3	517,571	2,453.4	96,632	458.1	377,626	1,790.0	43,313	205.3
2016	21,185,456	51,549	243.3	509,769	2,406.2	92,397	436.1	370,238	1,747.6	47,134	222.5
Percent change		+4.7	+4.3	-1.5	-1.9	-4.4	-4.8	-2.0	-2.4	+8.8	+8.4
Iowa											
2015	3,121,997	6,291	201.5	64,688	2,072.0	14,977	479.7	45,328	1,451.9	4,383	140.4
2016	3,134,693	6,644	212.0	65,391	2,086.0	15,030	479.5	45,378	1,447.6	4,983	159.0
Percent change		+5.6	+5.2	+1.1	+0.7	+0.4	-0.1	+0.1	-0.3	+13.7	+13.2
Kansas											
2015	2,906,721	7,850	270.1	80,059	2,754.3	15,619	537.3	57,435	1,975.9	7,005	241.0
2016	2,907,289	7,966	274.0	78,367	2,695.5	14,364	494.1	57,066	1,962.9	6,937	238.6
Percent change		+1.5	+1.5	-2.1	-2.1	-8.0	-8.1	-0.6	-0.7	-1.0	-1.0
Minnesota											
2015	5,482,435	7,094	129.4	121,984	2,225.0	19,299	352.0	94,704	1,727.4	7,981	145.6
2016	5,519,952	7,217	130.7	117,756	2,133.3	18,606	337.1	90,422	1,638.1	8,728	158.1
Percent change		+1.7	+1.0	-3.5	-4.1	-3.6	-4.2	-4.5	-5.2	+9.4	+8.6
Missouri											
2015	6,076,204	20,833	342.9	173,788	2,860.1	34,029	560.0	122,749	2,020.2	17,010	279.9
2016	6,093,000	21,983	360.8	170,549	2,799.1	31,710	520.4	120,544	1,978.4	18,295	300.3
Percent change		+5.5	+5.2	-1.9	-2.1	-6.8	-7.1	-1.8	-2.1	+7.6	+7.3
Nebraska[6]											
2015	1,893,765	3,226	170.3	42,597	2,249.3	6,443	340.2	32,148	1,697.6	4,006	211.5
2016	1,907,116	3,561	186.7	43,163	2,263.3	6,444	337.9	31,994	1,677.6	4,725	247.8
Percent change		+10.4	+9.6	+1.3	+0.6	*	-0.7	-0.5	-1.2	+17.9	+17.1
North Dakota											
2015	756,835	1,378	182.1	17,716	2,340.8	3,296	435.5	12,686	1,676.2	1,734	229.1
2016	757,952	1,365	180.1	17,402	2,295.9	3,243	427.9	12,195	1,608.9	1,964	259.1
Percent change		-0.9	-1.1	-1.8	-1.9	-1.6	-1.8	-3.9	-4.0	+13.3	+13.1
South Dakota[6]											
2015	857,919	2,554	297.7	16,739	1,951.1	2,969	346.1	12,576	1,465.9	1,194	139.2

Table 2. Crime,[1] by Region, Geographic Division, and State, 2015–2016—*Continued*

(Number, rate per 100,000 population, percent.)

Area	Population[2]	Violent crime[3]		Murder and nonnegligent manslaughter		Rape (revised definition)[4]		Rape (legacy definition)[5]		Robbery	
		Number	Rate	Number	Rate	Number	Rate	Number	Rate	Number	Rate
2016	865,454	3,621	418.4	27	3.1	509	58.8	379	43.8	272	31.4
Percent change		+9.7	+8.7	-18.2	-18.9	+1.8	+0.9	+3.3	+2.4	+26.5	+25.4
South[6,7,8]											
2015	121,039,206	509,043	420.6	7,300	6.0	47,277	39.1	33,960	28.1	127,149	105.0
2016	122,319,574	526,999	430.8	7,961	6.5	49,246	40.3	35,869	29.3	128,842	105.3
Percent change		+3.5	+2.4	+9.1	+7.9	+4.2	+3.1	+5.6	+4.5	+1.3	+0.3
South Atlantic[6,7,8]											
2015	63,192,408	256,283	405.6	3,824	6.1	21,620	34.2	15,433	24.4	66,792	105.7
2016	63,923,309	258,672	404.7	4,077	6.4	22,333	34.9	16,174	25.3	66,402	103.9
Percent change		+0.9	-0.2	+6.6	+5.4	+3.3	+2.1	+4.8	+3.6	-0.6	-1.7
Delaware											
2015	944,076	4,760	504.2	62	6.6	361	38.2	257	27.2	1,240	131.3
2016	952,065	4,844	508.8	56	5.9	308	32.4	221	23.2	1,359	142.7
Percent change		+1.8	+0.9	-9.7	-10.4	-14.7	-15.4	-14.0	-14.7	+9.6	+8.7
District of Columbia[7]											
2015	670,377	8,538	1,273.6	162	24.2	494	73.7	365	54.4	3,746	558.8
2016	681,170	8,214	1,205.9	139	20.4	532	78.1	401	58.9	3,480	510.9
Percent change		-3.8	-5.3	-14.2	-15.6	+7.7	+6.0	+9.9	+8.1	-7.1	-8.6
Florida											
2015	20,244,914	93,625	462.5	1,041	5.1	7,552	37.3	5,396	26.7	21,137	104.4
2016	20,612,439	88,700	430.3	1,111	5.4	7,598	36.9	5,528	26.8	20,175	97.9
Percent change		-5.3	-6.9	+6.7	+4.8	+0.6	-1.2	+2.4	+0.6	-4.6	-6.3
Georgia[8]											
2015	10,199,398	38,891	381.3	622	6.1	3,257	31.9	2,343	23.0	12,545	123.0
2016	10,310,371	40,990	397.6	681	6.6	3,509	34.0	2,528	24.5	12,205	118.4
Percent change		+5.4	+4.3	+9.5	+8.3	+7.7	+6.6	+7.9	+6.7	-2.7	-3.8
Maryland											
2015	5,994,983	28,185	470.1	538	9.0	1,717	28.6	1,209	20.2	10,111	168.7
2016	6,016,447	28,400	472.0	481	8.0	1,756	29.2	1,266	21.0	10,289	171.0
Percent change		+0.8	+0.4	-10.6	-10.9	+2.3	+1.9	+4.7	+4.3	+1.8	+1.4
North Carolina[6]											
2015	10,035,186	34,734	346.1	517	5.2	2,591	25.8	1,886	18.8	8,821	87.9
2016	10,146,788	37,769	372.2	678	6.7	2,849	28.1	2,086	20.6	9,336	92.0
Percent change		+8.7	+7.5	+31.1	+29.7	+10.0	+8.7	+10.6	+9.4	+5.8	+4.7
South Carolina											
2015	4,894,834	24,448	499.5	407	8.3	2,439	49.8	1,717	35.1	3,950	80.7
2016	4,961,119	24,896	501.8	366	7.4	2,387	48.1	1,711	34.5	4,035	81.3
Percent change		+1.8	+0.5	-10.1	-11.3	-2.1	-3.4	-0.3	-1.7	+2.2	+0.8
Virginia											
2015	8,367,587	16,705	199.6	390	4.7	2,499	29.9	1,767	21.1	4,459	53.3
2016	8,411,808	18,302	217.6	484	5.8	2,737	32.5	1,965	23.4	4,803	57.1
Percent change		+9.6	+9.0	+24.1	+23.5	+9.5	+8.9	+11.2	+10.6	+7.7	+7.1
West Virginia											
2015	1,841,053	6,397	347.5	85	4.6	710	38.6	493	26.8	783	42.5
2016	1,831,102	6,557	358.1	81	4.4	657	35.9	468	25.6	720	39.3
Percent change		+2.5	+3.1	-4.7	-4.2	-7.5	-7.0	-5.1	-4.6	-8.0	-7.5
East South Central[6]											
2015	18,862,932	81,850	433.9	1,238	6.6	7,640	40.5	5,497	29.1	17,737	94.0
2016	18,940,194	86,674	457.6	1,391	7.3	7,548	39.9	5,455	28.8	18,265	96.4
Percent change		+5.9	+5.5	+12.4	+11.9	-1.2	-1.6	-0.8	-1.2	+3.0	+2.6
Alabama											
2015	4,853,875	22,957	473.0	348	7.2	2,037	42.0	1,449	29.9	4,612	95.0
2016	4,863,300	25,886	532.3	407	8.4	1,916	39.4	1,385	28.5	4,686	96.4
Percent change		+12.8	+12.5	+17.0	+16.7	-5.9	-6.1	-4.4	-4.6	+1.6	+1.4
Kentucky											
2015	4,424,611	9,887	223.5	219	4.9	1,644	37.2	1,165	26.3	3,314	74.9
2016	4,436,974	10,308	232.3	260	5.9	1,641	37.0	1,174	26.5	3,369	75.9
Percent change		+4.3	+4.0	+18.7	+18.4	-0.2	-0.5	+0.8	+0.5	+1.7	+1.4
Mississippi[6]											
2015	2,989,390	8,190	274.0	253	8.5	1,158	38.7	851	28.5	2,312	77.3
2016	2,988,726	8,383	280.5	238	8.0	1,277	42.7	905	30.3	2,397	80.2
Percent change		+2.4	+2.4	-5.9	-5.9	+10.3	+10.3	+6.3	+6.4	+3.7	+3.7
Tennessee											
2015	6,595,056	40,816	618.9	418	6.3	2,801	42.5	2,032	30.8	7,499	113.7
2016	6,651,194	42,097	632.9	486	7.3	2,714	40.8	1,991	29.9	7,813	117.5
Percent change		+3.1	+2.3	+16.3	+15.3	-3.1	-3.9	-2.0	-2.8	+4.2	+3.3

(Number, rate per 100,000 population, percent.)

Area	Population[2]	Aggravated assault		Property crime		Burglary		Larceny-theft		Motor vehicle theft	
		Number	Rate	Number	Rate	Number	Rate	Number	Rate	Number	Rate
2016	865,454	2,813	325.0	17,141	1,980.6	3,000	346.6	12,639	1,460.4	1,502	173.6
Percent change		+10.1	+9.2	+2.4	+1.5	+1.0	+0.2	+0.5	-0.4	+25.8	+24.7
South[6,7,8]											
2015	121,039,206	327,317	270.4	3,393,611	2,803.7	719,098	594.1	2,422,679	2,001.6	251,834	208.1
2016	122,319,574	340,950	278.7	3,343,799	2,733.7	684,968	560.0	2,391,288	1,955.0	267,543	218.7
Percent change		+4.2	+3.1	-1.5	-2.5	-4.7	-5.7	-1.3	-2.3	+6.2	+5.1
South Atlantic[6,7,8]											
2015	63,192,408	164,047	259.6	1,721,061	2,723.5	352,328	557.5	1,246,078	1,971.9	122,655	194.1
2016	63,923,309	165,860	259.5	1,692,669	2,648.0	330,122	516.4	1,234,761	1,931.6	127,786	199.9
Percent change		+1.1	-0.1	-1.6	-2.8	-6.3	-7.4	-0.9	-2.0	+4.2	+3.0
Delaware											
2015	944,076	3,097	328.0	25,545	2,705.8	4,797	508.1	19,555	2,071.3	1,193	126.4
2016	952,065	3,121	327.8	26,334	2,766.0	5,023	527.6	19,791	2,078.7	1,520	159.7
Percent change		+0.8	-0.1	+3.1	+2.2	+4.7	+3.8	+1.2	+0.4	+27.4	+26.3
District of Columbia[7]											
2015	670,377	4,136	617.0	31,444	4,690.5	2,971	443.2	25,208	3,760.3	3,265	487.0
2016	681,170	4,063	596.5	32,716	4,802.9	2,361	346.6	27,382	4,019.8	2,973	436.5
Percent change		-1.8	-3.3	+4.0	+2.4	-20.5	-21.8	+8.6	+6.9	-8.9	-10.4
Florida											
2015	20,244,914	63,895	315.6	570,270	2,816.9	109,268	539.7	420,341	2,076.3	40,661	200.8
2016	20,612,439	59,816	290.2	553,812	2,686.8	100,325	486.7	410,352	1,990.8	43,135	209.3
Percent change		-6.4	-8.1	-2.9	-4.6	-8.2	-9.8	-2.4	-4.1	+6.1	+4.2
Georgia[8]											
2015	10,199,398	22,467	220.3	316,013	3,098.3	68,149	668.2	220,715	2,164.0	27,149	266.2
2016	10,310,371	24,595	238.5	309,770	3,004.5	63,344	614.4	219,625	2,130.1	26,801	259.9
Percent change		+9.5	+8.3	-2.0	-3.0	-7.1	-8.1	-0.5	-1.6	-1.3	-2.3
Maryland											
2015	5,994,983	15,819	263.9	142,547	2,377.8	26,432	440.9	102,701	1,713.1	13,414	223.8
2016	6,016,447	15,874	263.8	137,445	2,284.5	24,692	410.4	100,919	1,677.4	11,834	196.7
Percent change		+0.3	*	-3.6	-3.9	-6.6	-6.9	-1.7	-2.1	-11.8	-12.1
North Carolina[6]											
2015	10,035,186	22,805	227.3	275,915	2,749.5	74,760	745.0	187,732	1,870.7	13,423	133.8
2016	10,146,788	24,906	245.5	277,765	2,737.5	72,082	710.4	190,377	1,876.2	15,306	150.8
Percent change		+9.2	+8.0	+0.7	-0.4	-3.6	-4.6	+1.4	+0.3	+14.0	+12.8
South Carolina											
2015	4,894,834	17,652	360.6	162,830	3,326.6	34,942	713.9	114,778	2,344.9	13,110	267.8
2016	4,961,119	18,108	365.0	160,928	3,243.8	32,976	664.7	114,032	2,298.5	13,920	280.6
Percent change		+2.6	+1.2	-1.2	-2.5	-5.6	-6.9	-0.6	-2.0	+6.2	+4.8
Virginia											
2015	8,367,587	9,357	111.8	157,803	1,885.9	21,542	257.4	128,064	1,530.5	8,197	98.0
2016	8,411,808	10,278	122.2	156,412	1,859.4	20,018	238.0	126,606	1,505.1	9,788	116.4
Percent change		+9.8	+9.3	-0.9	-1.4	-7.1	-7.6	-1.1	-1.7	+19.4	+18.8
West Virginia											
2015	1,841,053	4,819	261.8	38,694	2,101.7	9,467	514.2	26,984	1,465.7	2,243	121.8
2016	1,831,102	5,099	278.5	37,487	2,047.2	9,301	507.9	25,677	1,402.3	2,509	137.0
Percent change		+5.8	+6.4	-3.1	-2.6	-1.8	-1.2	-4.8	-4.3	+11.9	+12.5
East South Central[6]											
2015	18,862,932	55,235	292.8	524,162	2,778.8	126,612	671.2	362,030	1,919.3	35,520	188.3
2016	18,940,194	59,470	314.0	513,087	2,709.0	118,565	626.0	353,470	1,866.2	41,052	216.7
Percent change		+7.7	+7.2	-2.1	-2.5	-6.4	-6.7	-2.4	-2.8	+15.6	+15.1
Alabama											
2015	4,853,875	15,960	328.8	144,785	2,982.9	35,265	726.5	99,182	2,043.4	10,338	213.0
2016	4,863,300	18,877	388.2	143,362	2,947.8	34,065	700.5	97,574	2,006.3	11,723	241.1
Percent change		+18.3	+18.0	-1.0	-1.2	-3.4	-3.6	-1.6	-1.8	+13.4	+13.2
Kentucky											
2015	4,424,611	4,710	106.5	97,545	2,204.6	22,526	509.1	67,143	1,517.5	7,876	178.0
2016	4,436,974	5,038	113.5	97,158	2,189.7	20,834	469.6	66,438	1,497.4	9,886	222.8
Percent change		+7.0	+6.7	-0.4	-0.7	-7.5	-7.8	-1.0	-1.3	+25.5	+25.2
Mississippi[6]											
2015	2,989,390	4,467	149.4	85,785	2,869.6	25,068	838.6	56,446	1,888.2	4,271	142.9
2016	2,988,726	4,471	149.6	82,732	2,768.1	23,354	781.4	55,054	1,842.1	4,324	144.7
Percent change		+0.1	+0.1	-3.6	-3.5	-6.8	-6.8	-2.5	-2.4	+1.2	+1.3
Tennessee											
2015	6,595,056	30,098	456.4	196,047	2,972.6	43,753	663.4	139,259	2,111.6	13,035	197.6
2016	6,651,194	31,084	467.3	189,835	2,854.1	40,312	606.1	134,404	2,020.7	15,119	227.3
Percent change		+3.3	+2.4	-3.2	-4.0	-7.9	-8.6	-3.5	-4.3	+16.0	+15.0

Table 2. Crime,[1] by Region, Geographic Division, and State, 2015–2016—*Continued*

(Number, rate per 100,000 population, percent.)

Area	Population[2]	Violent crime[3]		Murder and nonnegligent manslaughter		Rape (revised definition)[4]		Rape (legacy definition)[5]		Robbery	
		Number	Rate	Number	Rate	Number	Rate	Number	Rate	Number	Rate
West South Central[6].........											
2015................................	38,983,866	170,910	438.4	2,238	5.7	18,017	46.2	13,030	33.4	42,620	109.3
2016................................	39,456,071	181,653	460.4	2,493	6.3	19,365	49.1	14,240	36.1	44,175	112.0
Percent change...............		+6.3	+5.0	+11.4	+10.1	+7.5	+6.2	+9.3	+8.0	+3.6	+2.4
Arkansas.........................											
2015.........................	2,977,853	15,769	529.5	189	6.3	2,008	67.4	1,425	47.9	2,117	71.1
2016.........................	2,988,248	16,461	550.9	216	7.2	2,143	71.7	1,545	51.7	2,120	70.9
Percent change.......		+4.4	+4.0	+14.3	+13.9	+6.7	+6.4	+8.4	+8.0	+0.1	-0.2
Louisiana.........................											
2015.........................	4,668,960	25,202	539.8	492	10.5	1,733	37.1	1,246	26.7	5,561	119.1
2016.........................	4,681,666	26,502	566.1	554	11.8	1,816	38.8	1,328	28.4	5,576	119.1
Percent change.......		+5.2	+4.9	+12.6	+12.3	+4.8	+4.5	+6.6	+6.3	+0.3	*
Oklahoma[6].....................											
2015.........................	3,907,414	16,746	428.6	240	6.1	1,953	50.0	1,418	36.3	3,018	77.2
2016.........................	3,923,561	17,648	449.8	245	6.2	2,039	52.0	1,509	38.5	3,162	80.6
Percent change.......		+5.4	+5.0	+2.1	+1.7	+4.4	+4.0	+6.4	+6.0	+4.8	+4.3
Texas.............................											
2015.........................	27,429,639	113,193	412.7	1,317	4.8	12,323	44.9	8,941	32.6	31,924	116.4
2016.........................	27,862,596	121,042	434.4	1,478	5.3	13,367	48.0	9,858	35.4	33,317	119.6
Percent change.......		+6.9	+5.3	+12.2	+10.5	+8.5	+6.8	+10.3	+8.5	+4.4	+2.7
West[6].............................											
2015................................	75,834,288	301,773	397.9	3,194	4.2	31,615	41.7	22,994	30.3	82,557	108.9
2016................................	76,657,000	320,706	418.4	3,449	4.5	33,298	43.4	24,562	32.0	86,301	112.6
Percent change...............		+6.3	+5.1	+8.0	+6.8	+5.3	+4.2	+6.8	+5.7	+4.5	+3.4
Mountain[6]......................											
2015................................	23,492,558	94,784	403.5	917	3.9	12,938	55.1	9,424	40.1	20,236	86.1
2016................................	23,855,067	102,674	430.4	1,124	4.7	13,126	55.0	9,689	40.6	21,739	91.1
Percent change...............		+8.3	+6.7	+22.6	+20.7	+1.5	-0.1	+2.8	+1.2	+7.4	+5.8
Arizona.............................											
2015.........................	6,817,565	27,968	410.2	306	4.5	3,109	45.6	2,268	33.3	6,360	93.3
2016.........................	6,931,071	32,583	470.1	380	5.5	3,290	47.5	2,452	35.4	7,055	101.8
Percent change.......		+16.5	+14.6	+24.2	+22.1	+5.8	+4.1	+8.1	+6.3	+10.9	+9.1
Colorado.........................											
2015.........................	5,448,819	17,348	318.4	173	3.2	3,328	61.1	2,422	44.4	3,315	60.8
2016.........................	5,540,545	18,983	342.6	204	3.7	3,555	64.2	2,619	47.3	3,528	63.7
Percent change.......		+9.4	+7.6	+17.9	+16.0	+6.8	+5.1	+8.1	+6.3	+6.4	+4.7
Idaho.............................											
2015.........................	1,652,828	3,593	217.4	32	1.9	703	42.5	508	30.7	191	11.6
2016.........................	1,683,140	3,876	230.3	49	2.9	719	42.7	529	31.4	213	12.7
Percent change.......		+7.9	+5.9	+53.1	+50.4	+2.3	+0.4	+4.1	+2.3	+11.5	+9.5
Montana.........................											
2015.........................	1,032,073	3,647	353.4	38	3.7	572	55.4	405	39.2	210	20.3
2016.........................	1,042,520	3,840	368.3	36	3.5	578	55.4	414	39.7	266	25.5
Percent change.......		+5.3	+4.2	-5.3	-6.2	+1.0	*	+2.2	+1.2	+26.7	+25.4
Nevada.............................											
2015.........................	2,883,758	20,118	697.6	178	6.2	1,688	58.5	1,232	42.7	6,287	218.0
2016.........................	2,940,058	19,936	678.1	224	7.6	1,733	58.9	1,292	43.9	6,340	215.6
Percent change.......		-0.9	-2.8	+25.8	+23.4	+2.7	+0.7	+4.9	+2.9	+0.8	-1.1
New Mexico[8].................											
2015.........................	2,080,328	13,672	657.2	117	5.6	1,663	79.9	1,218	58.5	2,485	119.5
2016.........................	2,081,015	14,619	702.5	139	6.7	1,526	73.3	1,117	53.7	2,737	131.5
Percent change.......		+6.9	+6.9	+18.8	+18.8	-8.2	-8.3	-8.3	-8.3	+10.1	+10.1
Utah.............................											
2015.........................	2,990,632	7,138	238.7	57	1.9	1,704	57.0	1,247	41.7	1,329	44.4
2016.........................	3,051,217	7,407	242.8	72	2.4	1,520	49.8	1,116	36.6	1,541	50.5
Percent change.......		+3.8	+1.7	+26.3	+23.8	-10.8	-12.6	-10.5	-12.3	+16.0	+13.6
Wyoming.........................											
2015.........................	586,555	1,300	221.6	16	2.7	171	29.2	124	21.1	59	10.1
2016.........................	585,501	1,430	244.2	20	3.4	205	35.0	150	25.6	59	10.1
Percent change.......		+10.0	+10.2	+25.0	+25.2	+19.9	+20.1	+21.0	+21.2	0.0	+0.2
Pacific[6]...........................											
2015................................	52,341,730	206,989	395.5	2,277	4.4	18,677	35.7	13,570	25.9	62,321	119.1
2016................................	52,801,933	218,032	412.9	2,325	4.4	20,172	38.2	14,873	28.2	64,562	122.3
Percent change...............		+5.3	+4.4	+2.1	+1.2	+8.0	+7.1	+9.6	+8.6	+3.6	+2.7
Alaska.............................											

(Number, rate per 100,000 population, percent.)

Area	Population[2]	Aggravated assault		Property crime		Burglary		Larceny-theft		Motor vehicle theft	
		Number	Rate	Number	Rate	Number	Rate	Number	Rate	Number	Rate
West South Central[6].........											
2015..................................	38,983,866	108,035	277.1	1,148,388	2,945.8	240,158	616.0	814,571	2,089.5	93,659	240.3
2016..................................	39,456,071	115,620	293.0	1,138,043	2,884.3	236,281	598.8	803,057	2,035.3	98,705	250.2
Percent change...............		+7.0	+5.7	-0.9	-2.1	-1.6	-2.8	-1.4	-2.6	+5.4	+4.1
Arkansas.........................											
2015..........................	2,977,853	11,455	384.7	97,391	3,270.5	22,851	767.4	68,720	2,307.7	5,820	195.4
2016..........................	2,988,248	11,982	401.0	97,673	3,268.6	23,771	795.5	66,747	2,233.6	7,155	239.4
Percent change.......		+4.6	+4.2	+0.3	-0.1	+4.0	+3.7	-2.9	-3.2	+22.9	+22.5
Louisiana........................											
2015..........................	4,668,960	17,416	373.0	157,708	3,377.8	35,457	759.4	112,520	2,410.0	9,731	208.4
2016..........................	4,681,666	18,556	396.4	154,386	3,297.7	34,667	740.5	109,380	2,336.3	10,339	220.8
Percent change.......		+6.5	+6.3	-2.1	-2.4	-2.2	-2.5	-2.8	-3.1	+6.2	+6.0
Oklahoma[6].....................											
2015..........................	3,907,414	11,535	295.2	114,055	2,918.9	28,783	736.6	74,678	1,911.2	10,594	271.1
2016..........................	3,923,561	12,202	311.0	117,037	2,982.9	29,103	741.7	75,779	1,931.4	12,155	309.8
Percent change.......		+5.8	+5.3	+2.6	+2.2	+1.1	+0.7	+1.5	+1.1	+14.7	+14.3
Texas.............................											
2015..........................	27,429,639	67,629	246.6	779,234	2,840.8	153,067	558.0	558,653	2,036.7	67,514	246.1
2016..........................	27,862,596	72,880	261.6	768,947	2,759.8	148,740	533.8	551,151	1,978.1	69,056	247.8
Percent change.......		+7.8	+6.1	-1.3	-2.9	-2.8	-4.3	-1.3	-2.9	+2.3	+0.7
West[6]..............................											
2015..................................	75,834,288	184,407	243.2	2,123,048	2,799.6	402,703	531.0	1,437,787	1,896.0	282,558	372.6
2016..................................	76,657,000	197,658	257.8	2,120,808	2,766.6	387,049	504.9	1,424,850	1,858.7	308,909	403.0
Percent change...............		+7.2	+6.0	-0.1	-1.2	-3.9	-4.9	-0.9	-2.0	+9.3	+8.2
Mountain[6]......................											
2015..................................	23,492,558	60,693	258.3	662,713	2,820.9	125,323	533.5	470,974	2,004.8	66,416	282.7
2016..................................	23,855,067	66,685	279.5	675,111	2,830.1	122,629	514.1	474,519	1,989.2	77,963	326.8
Percent change...............		+9.9	+8.2	+1.9	+0.3	-2.1	-3.6	+0.8	-0.8	+17.4	+15.6
Arizona..........................											
2015..........................	6,817,565	18,193	266.9	207,184	3,039.0	38,010	557.5	152,388	2,235.2	16,786	246.2
2016..........................	6,931,071	21,858	315.4	206,432	2,978.4	37,736	544.4	150,275	2,168.1	18,421	265.8
Percent change.......		+20.1	+18.2	-0.4	-2.0	-0.7	-2.3	-1.4	-3.0	+9.7	+7.9
Colorado........................											
2015..........................	5,448,819	10,532	193.3	144,044	2,643.6	23,490	431.1	104,532	1,918.4	16,022	294.0
2016..........................	5,540,545	11,696	211.1	151,850	2,740.7	23,903	431.4	108,336	1,955.3	19,611	354.0
Percent change.......		+11.1	+9.2	+5.4	+3.7	+1.8	+0.1	+3.6	+1.9	+22.4	+20.4
Idaho............................											
2015..........................	1,652,828	2,667	161.4	28,912	1,749.2	6,124	370.5	20,916	1,265.5	1,872	113.3
2016..........................	1,683,140	2,895	172.0	29,357	1,744.2	6,318	375.4	20,962	1,245.4	2,077	123.4
Percent change.......		+8.5	+6.6	+1.5	-0.3	+3.2	+1.3	+0.2	-1.6	+11.0	+9.0
Montana.........................											
2015..........................	1,032,073	2,827	273.9	27,276	2,642.8	3,887	376.6	20,966	2,031.4	2,423	234.8
2016..........................	1,042,520	2,960	283.9	27,976	2,683.5	3,934	377.4	21,299	2,043.0	2,743	263.1
Percent change.......		+4.7	+3.7	+2.6	+1.5	+1.2	+0.2	+1.6	+0.6	+13.2	+12.1
Nevada..........................											
2015..........................	2,883,758	11,965	414.9	77,137	2,674.9	22,360	775.4	43,426	1,505.9	11,351	393.6
2016..........................	2,940,058	11,639	395.9	76,047	2,586.6	18,850	641.1	44,017	1,497.1	13,180	448.3
Percent change.......		-2.7	-4.6	-1.4	-3.3	-15.7	-17.3	+1.4	-0.6	+16.1	+13.9
New Mexico[8].................											
2015..........................	2,080,328	9,407	452.2	77,212	3,711.5	17,084	821.2	51,485	2,474.9	8,643	415.5
2016..........................	2,081,015	10,217	491.0	81,931	3,937.1	17,281	830.4	52,907	2,542.4	11,743	564.3
Percent change.......		+8.6	+8.6	+6.1	+6.1	+1.2	+1.1	+2.8	+2.7	+35.9	+35.8
Utah.............................											
2015..........................	2,990,632	4,048	135.4	89,797	3,002.6	12,606	421.5	68,464	2,289.3	8,727	291.8
2016..........................	3,051,217	4,274	140.1	90,058	2,951.5	12,836	420.7	67,834	2,223.2	9,388	307.7
Percent change.......		+5.6	+3.5	+0.3	-1.7	+1.8	-0.2	-0.9	-2.9	+7.6	+5.4
Wyoming........................											
2015..........................	586,555	1,054	179.7	11,151	1,901.1	1,762	300.4	8,797	1,499.8	592	100.9
2016..........................	585,501	1,146	195.7	11,460	1,957.3	1,771	302.5	8,889	1,518.2	800	136.6
Percent change.......		+8.7	+8.9	+2.8	+3.0	+0.5	+0.7	+1.0	+1.2	+35.1	+35.4
Pacific[6]..........................											
2015..................................	52,341,730	123,714	236.4	1,460,335	2,790.0	277,380	529.9	966,813	1,847.1	216,142	412.9
2016..................................	52,801,933	130,973	248.0	1,445,697	2,738.0	264,420	500.8	950,331	1,799.8	230,946	437.4
Percent change...............		+5.9	+4.9	-1.0	-1.9	-4.7	-5.5	-1.7	-2.6	+6.8	+5.9
Alaska...........................											

Table 2. Crime,[1] by Region, Geographic Division, and State, 2015–2016—*Continued*

(Number, rate per 100,000 population, percent.)

Area	Population[2]	Violent crime[3]		Murder and nonnegligent manslaughter		Rape (revised definition)[4]		Rape (legacy definition)[5]		Robbery	
		Number	Rate	Number	Rate	Number	Rate	Number	Rate	Number	Rate
2015.........................	737,709	5,391	730.8	59	8.0	900	122.0	648	87.8	761	103.2
2016.........................	741,894	5,966	804.2	52	7.0	1,053	141.9	757	102.0	850	114.6
Percent change		+10.7	+10.0	-11.9	-12.4	+17.0	+16.3	+16.8	+16.2	+11.7	+11.1
California........................											
2015	38,993,940	166,883	428.0	1,861	4.8	12,811	32.9	9,341	24.0	52,862	135.6
2016	39,250,017	174,796	445.3	1,930	4.9	13,702	34.9	10,149	25.9	54,789	139.6
Percent change		+4.7	+4.1	+3.7	+3.0	+7.0	+6.3	+8.7	+7.9	+3.6	+3.0
Hawaii..............................											
2015	1,425,157	3,530	247.7	29	2.0	538	37.8	382	26.8	1,085	76.1
2016	1,428,557	4,417	309.2	35	2.5	619	43.3	447	31.3	994	69.6
Percent change		+25.1	+24.8	+20.7	+20.4	+15.1	+14.8	+17.0	+16.7	-8.4	-8.6
Oregon[6].........................											
2015	4,024,634	10,680	265.4	110	2.7	1,650	41.0	1,193	29.6	2,163	53.7
2016	4,093,465	10,830	264.6	113	2.8	1,721	42.0	1,261	30.8	2,278	55.6
Percent change		+1.4	-0.3	+2.7	+1.0	+4.3	+2.5	+5.7	+3.9	+5.3	+3.5
Washington[6]...................											
2015	7,160,290	20,505	286.4	218	3.0	2,778	38.8	2,006	28.0	5,450	76.1
2016	7,288,000	22,023	302.2	195	2.7	3,077	42.2	2,259	31.0	5,651	77.5
Percent change		+7.4	+5.5	-10.6	-12.1	+10.8	+8.8	+12.6	+10.6	+3.7	+1.9
Puerto Rico[9]											
2015.................................	3,473,181	7,629	219.7	584	16.8	165	4.8	123	3.5	4,070	117.2
2016.................................	3,411,307	7,643	224.0	679	19.9	169	5.0	128	3.8	3,201	93.8
Percent change................		+0.2	+2.0	+16.3	+18.4	+2.4	+4.3	+4.1	+6.0	-21.4	-19.9

Table 2. Crime,[1] by Region, Geographic Division, and State, 2015–2016—*Continued*

(Number, rate per 100,000 population, percent.)

Area	Population[2]	Aggravated assault		Property crime		Burglary		Larceny-theft		Motor vehicle theft	
		Number	Rate	Number	Rate	Number	Rate	Number	Rate	Number	Rate
2015	737,709	3,671	497.6	20,806	2,820.4	3,511	475.9	15,249	2,067.1	2,046	277.3
2016	741,894	4,011	540.6	24,876	3,353.0	4,053	546.3	17,766	2,394.7	3,057	412.1
Percent change		+9.3	+8.6	+19.6	+18.9	+15.4	+14.8	+16.5	+15.8	+49.4	+48.6
California........................											
2015	38,993,940	99,349	254.8	1,024,914	2,628.4	197,404	506.2	656,517	1,683.6	170,993	438.5
2016	39,250,017	104,375	265.9	1,002,070	2,553.0	188,304	479.8	637,010	1,623.0	176,756	450.3
Percent change		+5.1	+4.4	-2.2	-2.9	-4.6	-5.2	-3.0	-3.6	+3.4	+2.7
Hawaii											
2015	1,425,157	1,878	131.8	45,389	3,184.8	6,810	477.8	33,140	2,325.4	5,439	381.6
2016	1,428,557	2,769	193.8	42,753	2,992.7	6,017	421.2	31,082	2,175.8	5,654	395.8
Percent change		+47.4	+47.1	-5.8	-6.0	-11.6	-11.9	-6.2	-6.4	+4.0	+3.7
Oregon[6]............................											
2015	4,024,634	6,757	167.9	119,752	2,975.5	18,541	460.7	90,514	2,249.0	10,697	265.8
2016	4,093,465	6,718	164.1	121,345	2,964.4	16,866	412.0	91,286	2,230.0	13,193	322.3
Percent change		-0.6	-2.2	+1.3	-0.4	-9.0	-10.6	+0.9	-0.8	+23.3	+21.3
Washington[6].....................											
2015	7,160,290	12,059	168.4	249,474	3,484.1	51,114	713.9	171,393	2,393.7	26,967	376.6
2016	7,288,000	13,100	179.7	254,653	3,494.1	49,180	674.8	173,187	2,376.3	32,286	443.0
Percent change		+8.6	+6.7	+2.1	+0.3	-3.8	-5.5	+1.0	-0.7	+19.7	+17.6
Puerto Rico[9]											
2015.................................	3,473,181	2,810	80.9	37,717	1,085.9	9,150	263.4	24,493	705.2	4,074	117.3
2016.................................	3,411,307	3,594	105.4	35,201	1,031.9	8,251	241.9	23,163	679.0	3,787	111.0
Percent change................		+27.9	+30.2	-6.7	-5.0	-9.8	-8.2	-5.4	-3.7	-7.0	-5.4

Note: Although arson data are included in the trend and clearance tables, sufficient data are not available to estimate totals for this offense. Therefore, no arson data are published in this table.
X = Not applicable.
* = Less than one-tenth of 1 percent.
[1] The previous year's crime figures have been adjusted.
[2] Population figures are U.S. Census Bureau provisional estimates as of July 1, 2016.
[3] The violent crime figures include the offenses of murder, rape (revised definition), robbery, and aggravated assault.
[4] The figures shown in this column for the offense of rape were estimated using the revised Uniform Crime Reporting (UCR) definition of rape. See chapter notes for more detail.
[5] The figures shown in this column for the offense of rape were estimated using the legacy Uniform Crime Reporting (UCR) definition of rape. See chapter notes for more detail.
[6] Agencies within this state submitted rape data according to both the revised UCR definition of rape and the legacy UCR definition of rape.
[7] Includes offenses reported by the Metro Transit Police and the District of Columbia Fire and Emergency Services Fire Investigation Unit.
[8] This state's agencies submitted rape data according to the legacy UCR definition of rape.
[9] The figures submitted by Puerto Rico for rape were not verified and may not be comparable to previous years' data.

Table 3. Crime, by State and Area, 2016

(Number, percent, rate per 100,000 population.)

Area	Population	Violent crime[1]	Murder and nonnegligent manslaughter	Rape (revised definition)[2]	Rape (legacy definition)[3]	Robbery	Aggravated assault	Property crime	Burglary	Larceny-theft	Motor vehicle theft
Alabama..											
Metropolitan statistical area..............	3,716,889										
Area actually reporting......................	99.2%	20,793	331	1,489	1,084	4,174	14,799	114,605	26,966	78,072	9,567
Estimated total	100.0%	20,949	332	1,498	1,091	4,200	14,919	115,564	27,156	78,771	9,637
Cities outside metropolitan areas........	520,422										
Area actually reporting......................	96.6%	3,551	41	263	187	410	2,837	19,841	4,173	14,332	1,336
Estimated total	100.0%	3,646	42	269	193	421	2,914	20,291	4,275	14,641	1,375
Nonmetropolitan counties	625,989										
Area actually reporting......................	94.5%	1,220	31	141	95	61	987	7,096	2,490	3,934	672
Estimated total	100.0%	1,291	33	149	101	65	1,044	7,507	2,634	4,162	711
State total...	4,863,300	25,886	407	1,916	1,385	4,686	18,877	143,362	34,065	97,574	11,723
Rate per 100,000 inhabitants...............		532.3	8.4	39.4	28.5	96.4	388.2	2,947.8	700.5	2,006.3	241.1
Alaska											
Metropolitan statistical area..............	350,298										
Area actually reporting......................	100.0%	3,751	35	583	439	741	2,392	17,143	2,243	12,620	2,280
Cities outside metropolitan areas........	128,053										
Area actually reporting......................	97.4%	964	2	165	119	71	726	4,069	655	3,101	313
Estimated total	100.0%	989	2	169	123	73	745	4,177	672	3,184	321
Nonmetropolitan counties	263,543										
Area actually reporting......................	100.0%	1,226	15	301	195	36	874	3,556	1,138	1,962	456
State total...	741,894	5,966	52	1,053	757	850	4,011	24,876	4,053	17,766	3,057
Rate per 100,000 inhabitants...............		804.2	7.0	141.9	102.0	114.6	540.6	3,353.0	546.3	2,394.7	412.1
Arizona											
Metropolitan statistical area..............	6,583,506										
Area actually reporting......................	98.3%	27,522	334	2,997	2,238	6,931	17,260	196,398	35,424	143,602	17,372
Estimated total	100.0%	27,789	338	3,025	2,258	6,971	17,455	198,543	35,844	145,152	17,547
Cities outside metropolitan areas........	124,210										
Area actually reporting......................	100.0%	4,342	32	250	184	65	3,995	5,937	1,199	4,069	669
Nonmetropolitan counties	223,355										
Area actually reporting......................	100.0%	452	10	15	10	19	408	1,952	693	1,054	205
State total...	6,931,071	32,583	380	3,290	2,452	7,055	21,858	206,432	37,736	150,275	18,421
Rate per 100,000 inhabitants...............		470.1	5.5	47.5	35.4	101.8	315.4	2,978.4	544.4	2,168.1	265.8
Arkansas											
Metropolitan statistical area..............	1,851,896										
Area actually reporting......................	99.9%	11,573	144	1,315	967	1,711	8,403	68,739	15,650	47,839	5,250
Estimated total	100.0%	11,576	144	1,316	968	1,711	8,405	68,762	15,655	47,856	5,251
Cities outside metropolitan areas........	515,688										
Area actually reporting......................	94.1%	2,925	44	471	343	347	2,063	18,438	4,926	12,537	975
Estimated total	100.0%	3,109	47	500	364	369	2,193	19,599	5,236	13,327	1,036
Nonmetropolitan counties	620,664										
Area actually reporting......................	96.1%	1,704	24	313	204	38	1,329	8,944	2,766	5,344	834
Estimated total	100.0%	1,776	25	327	213	40	1,384	9,312	2,880	5,564	868
State total...	2,988,248	16,461	216	2,143	1,545	2,120	11,982	97,673	23,771	66,747	7,155
Rate per 100,000 inhabitants...............		550.9	7.2	71.7	51.7	70.9	401.0	3,268.6	795.5	2,233.6	239.4
California											
Metropolitan statistical area..............	38,426,705										
Area actually reporting......................	99.9%	170,862	1,880	13,290	9,871	54,288	101,404	983,750	182,895	626,742	174,113
Estimated total	100.0%	170,887	1,880	13,292	9,872	54,296	101,419	983,927	182,929	626,856	174,142
Cities outside metropolitan areas........	268,891										
Area actually reporting......................	100.0%	1,805	8	164	118	310	1,323	9,604	2,243	6,260	1,101
Nonmetropolitan counties	554,421										
Area actually reporting......................	100.0%	2,104	42	246	159	183	1,633	8,539	3,132	3,894	1,513
State total...	39,250,017	174,796	1,930	13,702	10,149	54,789	104,375	1,002,070	188,304	637,010	176,756
Rate per 100,000 inhabitants...............		445.3	4.9	34.9	25.9	139.6	265.9	2,553.0	479.8	1,623.0	450.3
Colorado											
Metropolitan statistical area..............	4,845,078										
Area actually reporting......................	99.9%	17,870	190	3,233	2,391	3,458	10,989	138,992	21,523	98,615	18,854
Estimated total	100.0%	17,882	190	3,235	2,393	3,459	10,998	139,156	21,542	98,740	18,874
Cities outside metropolitan areas........	337,897										
Area actually reporting......................	91.9%	641	10	167	121	48	416	8,641	1,294	6,943	404
Estimated total	100.0%	697	11	181	133	52	453	9,405	1,408	7,557	440
Nonmetropolitan counties	357,570										
Area actually reporting......................	98.6%	399	3	137	91	17	242	3,243	940	2,010	293
Estimated total	100.0%	404	3	139	93	17	245	3,289	953	2,039	297

Table 3. Crime, by State and Area, 2016—*Continued*

(Number, percent, rate per 100,000 population.)

Area	Population	Violent crime[1]	Murder and nonnegligent manslaughter	Rape (revised definition)[2]	Rape (legacy definition)[3]	Robbery	Aggravated assault	Property crime	Burglary	Larceny-theft	Motor vehicle theft
State total............................	5,540,545	18,983	204	3,555	2,619	3,528	11,696	151,850	23,903	108,336	19,611
Rate per 100,000 inhabitants..............		342.6	3.7	64.2	47.3	63.7	211.1	2,740.7	431.4	1,955.3	354.0
Connecticut...........................											
Metropolitan statistical area...............	2,961,626										
Area actually reporting.......................	100.0%	7,706	70	685	509	2,629	4,322	60,060	9,054	44,302	6,704
Cities outside metropolitan areas........	113,580										
Area actually reporting....................	100.0%	135	1	21	15	37	76	1,756	248	1,417	91
Nonmetropolitan counties	501,246										
Area actually reporting....................	100.0%	282	7	57	37	37	181	2,848	743	1,793	312
State total............................	3,576,452	8,123	78	763	561	2,703	4,579	64,664	10,045	47,512	7,107
Rate per 100,000 inhabitants..............		227.1	2.2	21.3	15.7	75.6	128.0	1,808.0	280.9	1,328.5	198.7
Delaware											
Metropolitan statistical area...............	952,065										
Area actually reporting.......................	100.0%	4,843	56	307	220	1,359	3,121	26,333	5,023	19,790	1,520
Cities outside metropolitan areas........	None										
Nonmetropolitan counties	None										
Area actually reporting....................	100.0%	1	0	1	1	0	0	1	0	1	0
State total............................	952,065	4,844	56	308	221	1,359	3,121	26,334	5,023	19,791	1,520
Rate per 100,000 inhabitants..............		508.8	5.9	32.4	23.2	142.7	327.8	2,766.0	527.6	2,078.7	159.7
District of Columbia[4]..........................											
Metropolitan statistical area...............	681,170										
Area actually reporting.......................	100.0%	8,214	139	532	401	3,480	4,063	32,716	2,361	27,382	2,973
Cities outside metropolitan areas........	None										
Nonmetropolitan counties	None										
District total............................	681,170	8,214	139	532	401	3,480	4,063	32,716	2,361	27,382	2,973
Rate per 100,000 inhabitants..............		1,205.9	20.4	78.1	58.9	510.9	596.5	4,802.9	346.6	4,019.8	436.5
Florida											
Metropolitan statistical area...............	19,905,117										
Area actually reporting.......................	99.8%	85,184	1,069	7,340	5,356	19,854	56,921	537,956	95,945	399,765	42,246
Estimated total	100.0%	85,327	1,071	7,352	5,365	19,889	57,015	538,945	96,110	400,513	42,322
Cities outside metropolitan areas........	146,572										
Area actually reporting.......................	94.3%	929	10	41	29	141	737	5,149	1,159	3,742	248
Estimated total	100.0%	985	11	44	32	149	781	5,459	1,229	3,967	263
Nonmetropolitan counties	560,750										
Area actually reporting....................	100.0%	2,388	29	202	131	137	2,020	9,408	2,986	5,872	550
State total............................	20,612,439	88,700	1,111	7,598	5,528	20,175	59,816	553,812	100,325	410,352	43,135
Rate per 100,000 inhabitants..............		430.3	5.4	36.9	26.8	97.9	290.2	2,686.8	486.7	1,990.8	209.3
Georgia[5].............................											
Metropolitan statistical area...............	8,537,584										
Area actually reporting.......................	99.5%	35,058	586	2,975	2,159	11,252	20,245	261,232	52,059	184,537	24,636
Estimated total	100.0%	35,206	588	2,986	2,168	11,297	20,335	262,449	52,298	185,405	24,746
Cities outside metropolitan areas........	644,378										
Area actually reporting.......................	89.4%	2,807	53	219	166	641	1,894	24,709	4,962	18,977	770
Estimated total	100.0%	3,132	59	238	182	717	2,118	27,637	5,550	21,226	861
Nonmetropolitan counties	1,128,409										
Area actually reporting....................	93.0%	2,464	32	262	165	178	1,992	18,309	5,112	12,086	1,111
Estimated total	100.0%	2,652	34	285	178	191	2,142	19,684	5,496	12,994	1,194
State total............................	10,310,371	40,990	681	3,509	2,528	12,205	24,595	309,770	63,344	219,625	26,801
Rate per 100,000 inhabitants..............		397.6	6.6	34.0	24.5	118.4	238.5	3,004.5	614.4	2,130.1	259.9
Hawaii.................................											
Metropolitan statistical area...............	1,160,343										
Area actually reporting.......................	100.0%	3,781	21	459	343	904	2,397	36,333	4,736	26,534	5,063
Cities outside metropolitan areas........	None										
Nonmetropolitan counties	268,214										
Estimated total	100.0%	636	14	160	104	90	372	6,420	1,281	4,548	591
State total............................	1,428,557	4,417	35	619	447	994	2,769	42,753	6,017	31,082	5,654
Rate per 100,000 inhabitants..............		309.2	2.5	43.3	31.3	69.6	193.8	2,992.7	421.2	2,175.8	395.8
Idaho.................................											
Metropolitan statistical area...............	1,127,333										
Area actually reporting.......................	100.0%	2,775	28	507	378	170	2,070	21,858	4,307	16,026	1,525
Estimated total	255,530										

Table 3. Crime, by State and Area, 2016—*Continued*

(Number, percent, rate per 100,000 population.)

Area	Population	Violent crime[1]	Murder and nonnegligent manslaughter	Rape (revised definition)[2]	Rape (legacy definition)[3]	Robbery	Aggravated assault	Property crime	Burglary	Larceny-theft	Motor vehicle theft
Cities outside metropolitan areas........	99.1%	587	11	116	85	32	428	4,583	984	3,310	289
Area actually reporting.........................	100.0%	592	11	117	86	32	432	4,625	993	3,340	292
Nonmetropolitan counties	300,277										
Area actually reporting.........................	100.0%	509	10	95	65	11	393	2,874	1,018	1,596	260
State total..................................	1,683,140	3,876	49	719	529	213	2,895	29,357	6,318	20,962	2,077
Rate per 100,000 inhabitants...............		230.3	2.9	42.7	31.4	12.7	172.0	1,744.2	375.4	1,245.4	123.4
Illinois...................................	11,329,203										
Metropolitan statistical area................											
Area actually reporting.........................	97.4%	51,812	1,016	4,262	3,172	17,372	29,162	234,747	41,931	173,922	18,894
Estimated total	100.0%	52,414	1,022	4,340	3,231	17,544	29,508	239,672	42,707	177,817	19,148
Cities outside metropolitan areas........	829,170										
Area actually reporting.........................	84.2%	2,032	6	311	226	198	1,517	14,538	2,946	11,189	403
Estimated total	100.0%	2,399	7	355	264	235	1,802	17,269	3,499	13,291	479
Nonmetropolitan counties	643,166										
Area actually reporting.........................	88.6%	923	22	189	125	43	669	4,755	1,580	2,924	251
Estimated total	100.0%	1,041	25	213	140	48	755	5,365	1,783	3,299	283
State total..................................	12,801,539	55,854	1,054	4,908	3,635	17,827	32,065	262,306	47,989	194,407	19,910
Rate per 100,000 inhabitants...............		436.3	8.2	38.3	28.4	139.3	250.5	2,049.0	374.9	1,518.6	155.5
Indiana[6]................................	5,169,542										
Metropolitan statistical area................											
Area actually reporting.........................	84.0%	22,873	370	1,868	1,400	6,857	13,778	134,126	26,691	95,363	12,072
Estimated total	100.0%	24,435	396	2,068	1,546	7,126	14,845	148,420	29,206	105,936	13,278
Cities outside metropolitan areas........	522,889										
Area actually reporting.........................	62.7%	774	7	110	81	100	557	9,245	1,381	7,357	507
Estimated total	100.0%	1,236	11	178	134	159	888	14,740	2,202	11,730	808
Nonmetropolitan counties	940,622										
Area actually reporting.........................	60.0%	694	19	143	98	27	505	5,158	1,613	3,158	387
Estimated total	100.0%	1,174	32	255	171	45	842	8,599	2,689	5,265	645
State total..................................	6,633,053	26,845	439	2,501	1,851	7,330	16,575	171,759	34,097	122,931	14,731
Rate per 100,000 inhabitants...............		404.7	6.6	37.7	27.9	110.5	249.9	2,589.4	514.0	1,853.3	222.1
Iowa	1,857,824										
Metropolitan statistical area................											
Area actually reporting.........................	98.8%	6,150	50	884	658	969	4,247	46,230	9,808	32,675	3,747
Estimated total	100.0%	6,192	50	891	663	971	4,280	46,504	9,882	32,856	3,766
Cities outside metropolitan areas........	595,688										
Area actually reporting.........................	97.4%	2,094	13	239	175	162	1,680	14,370	3,350	10,238	782
Estimated total	100.0%	2,151	13	246	181	166	1,726	14,760	3,441	10,516	803
Nonmetropolitan counties	681,181										
Area actually reporting.........................	97.5%	748	8	107	75	11	622	4,026	1,665	1,957	404
Estimated total	100.0%	767	8	110	78	11	638	4,127	1,707	2,006	414
State total..................................	3,134,693	9,110	71	1,247	922	1,148	6,644	65,391	15,030	45,378	4,983
Rate per 100,000 inhabitants...............		290.6	2.3	39.8	29.4	36.6	212.0	2,086.0	479.5	1,447.6	159.0
Kansas....................................	1,970,971										
Metropolitan statistical area................											
Area actually reporting.........................	97.9%	8,227	85	887	659	1,451	5,804	56,252	9,453	41,266	5,533
Estimated total	100.0%	8,310	86	898	666	1,460	5,866	57,021	9,579	41,845	5,597
Cities outside metropolitan areas........	605,300										
Area actually reporting.........................	95.3%	1,973	11	328	239	178	1,456	16,659	3,234	12,498	927
Estimated total	100.0%	2,068	12	341	251	187	1,528	17,483	3,394	13,116	973
Nonmetropolitan counties	331,018										
Area actually reporting.........................	92.8%	633	12	68	50	22	531	3,583	1,290	1,953	340
Estimated total	100.0%	682	13	73	54	24	572	3,863	1,391	2,105	367
State total..................................	2,907,289	11,060	111	1,312	971	1,671	7,966	78,367	14,364	57,066	6,937
Rate per 100,000 inhabitants...............		380.4	3.8	45.1	33.4	57.5	274.0	2,695.5	494.1	1,962.9	238.6
Kentucky..................................	2,604,116										
Metropolitan statistical area................											
Area actually reporting.........................	100.0%	7,859	176	879	659	2,911	3,893	73,569	14,192	51,591	7,786
Cities outside metropolitan areas........	538,773										
Area actually reporting.........................	100.0%	959	14	195	141	298	452	13,676	2,835	9,932	909
Nonmetropolitan counties	1,294,085										
Area actually reporting.........................	100.0%	1,490	70	567	374	160	693	9,913	3,807	4,915	1,191
State total..................................	4,436,974	10,308	260	1,641	1,174	3,369	5,038	97,158	20,834	66,438	9,886
Rate per 100,000 inhabitants...............		232.3	5.9	37.0	26.5	75.9	113.5	2,189.7	469.6	1,497.4	222.8
Louisiana.................................											
Metropolitan statistical area................	3,923,928										

Table 3. Crime, by State and Area, 2016—*Continued*

(Number, percent, rate per 100,000 population.)

Area	Population	Violent crime[1]	Murder and nonnegligent manslaughter	Rape (revised definition)[2]	Rape (legacy definition)[3]	Robbery	Aggravated assault	Property crime	Burglary	Larceny-theft	Motor vehicle theft
Area actually reporting.........	99.1%	22,991	497	1,631	1,198	5,198	15,665	134,283	29,366	95,483	9,434
Estimated total	100.0%	23,135	499	1,639	1,205	5,220	15,777	135,537	29,581	96,462	9,494
Cities outside metropolitan areas........	248,647										
Area actually reporting.........	91.6%	1,611	19	75	54	246	1,271	10,561	2,695	7,523	343
Estimated total	100.0%	1,758	21	82	61	268	1,387	11,525	2,941	8,210	374
Nonmetropolitan counties	509,091										
Area actually reporting.........	97.0%	1,560	33	92	60	85	1,350	7,106	2,081	4,568	457
Estimated total	100.0%	1,609	34	95	62	88	1,392	7,324	2,145	4,708	471
State total...............................	4,681,666	26,502	554	1,816	1,328	5,576	18,556	154,386	34,667	109,380	10,339
Rate per 100,000 inhabitants..............		566.1	11.8	38.8	28.4	119.1	396.4	3,297.7	740.5	2,336.3	220.8
Maine......................................											
Metropolitan statistical area..............	789,447										
Area actually reporting.........	100.0%	1,003	8	225	171	198	572	13,743	2,404	10,881	458
Cities outside metropolitan areas........	258,813										
Area actually reporting.........	100.0%	396	7	116	82	53	220	5,404	839	4,416	149
Nonmetropolitan counties	283,219										
Area actually reporting.........	100.0%	249	5	71	47	15	158	2,765	760	1,837	168
State total...............................	1,331,479	1,648	20	412	300	266	950	21,912	4,003	17,134	775
Rate per 100,000 inhabitants..............		123.8	1.5	30.9	22.5	20.0	71.3	1,645.7	300.6	1,286.8	58.2
Maryland											
Metropolitan statistical area..............	5,866,031										
Area actually reporting.........	88.1%	25,972	459	1,525	1,103	9,635	14,353	121,542	21,943	88,677	10,922
Estimated total	100.0%	28,003	477	1,711	1,235	10,222	15,593	134,419	24,001	98,686	11,732
Cities outside metropolitan areas........	52,622										
Area actually reporting.........	100.0%	246	3	24	17	58	161	1,823	325	1,451	47
Nonmetropolitan counties	97,794										
Area actually reporting.........	100.0%	151	1	21	14	9	120	1,203	366	782	55
State total...............................	6,016,447	28,400	481	1,756	1,266	10,289	15,874	137,445	24,692	100,919	11,834
Rate per 100,000 inhabitants..............		472.0	8.0	29.2	21.0	171.0	263.8	2,284.5	410.4	1,677.4	196.7
Massachusetts											
Metropolitan statistical area..............	6,713,214										
Area actually reporting.........	97.6%	24,834	128	2,026	1,512	5,265	17,415	102,464	18,439	76,183	7,842
Estimated total	100.0%	25,319	129	2,070	1,547	5,344	17,776	104,725	18,841	77,877	8,007
Cities outside metropolitan areas........	91,574										
Area actually reporting.........	84.9%	300	4	49	37	18	229	1,370	299	1,028	43
Estimated total	100.0%	353	5	57	44	21	270	1,614	352	1,211	51
Nonmetropolitan counties	6,991										
Area actually reporting.........	100.0%	5	0	1	1	0	4	0	0	0	0
State total...............................	6,811,779	25,677	134	2,128	1,592	5,365	18,050	106,339	19,193	79,088	8,058
Rate per 100,000 inhabitants..............		376.9	2.0	31.2	23.4	78.8	265.0	1,561.1	281.8	1,161.0	118.3
Michigan											
Metropolitan statistical area..............	8,132,404										
Area actually reporting.........	99.8%	40,537	568	5,310	3,900	6,971	27,688	165,035	34,569	111,303	19,163
Estimated total	100.0%	40,579	568	5,317	3,905	6,979	27,715	165,307	34,612	111,510	19,185
Cities outside metropolitan areas........	596,485										
Area actually reporting.........	91.6%	1,474	7	501	356	71	895	10,647	1,272	9,051	324
Estimated total	100.0%	1,611	8	548	390	78	977	11,623	1,389	9,880	354
Nonmetropolitan counties	1,199,411										
Area actually reporting.........	98.7%	3,339	22	1,244	809	62	2,011	12,526	3,521	8,376	629
Estimated total	100.0%	3,382	22	1,260	819	63	2,037	12,690	3,567	8,486	637
State total...............................	9,928,300	45,572	598	7,125	5,114	7,120	30,729	189,620	39,568	129,876	20,176
Rate per 100,000 inhabitants..............		459.0	6.0	71.8	51.5	71.7	309.5	1,909.9	398.5	1,308.1	203.2
Minnesota.............................											
Metropolitan statistical area..............	4,285,006										
Area actually reporting.........	100.0%	11,636	84	1,891	1,409	3,610	6,051	99,694	15,244	76,823	7,627
Cities outside metropolitan areas........	536,351										
Area actually reporting.........	100.0%	1,071	9	265	194	93	704	11,809	1,529	9,732	548
Nonmetropolitan counties	698,595										
Area actually reporting.........	100.0%	687	8	192	128	25	462	6,253	1,833	3,867	553
State total...............................	5,519,952	13,394	101	2,348	1,731	3,728	7,217	117,756	18,606	90,422	8,728
Rate per 100,000 inhabitants..............		242.6	1.8	42.5	31.4	67.5	130.7	2,133.3	337.1	1,638.1	158.1
Mississippi[6]											
Metropolitan statistical area..............	1,377,735										
Area actually reporting.........	81.7%	3,304	103	382	280	1,188	1,631	33,547	7,390	23,892	2,265

Table 3. Crime, by State and Area, 2016—*Continued*

(Number, percent, rate per 100,000 population.)

Area	Population	Violent crime[1]	Murder and nonnegligent manslaughter	Rape (revised definition)[2]	Rape (legacy definition)[3]	Robbery	Aggravated assault	Property crime	Burglary	Larceny-theft	Motor vehicle theft
Estimated total	100.0%	3,732	111	431	316	1,298	1,892	39,162	8,556	28,063	2,543
Cities outside metropolitan areas........	582,351										
Area actually reporting....................	45.4%	1,171	34	154	115	376	607	12,437	3,562	8,431	444
Estimated total	100.0%	2,602	75	360	273	829	1,338	27,419	7,853	18,587	979
Nonmetropolitan counties	1,028,640										
Area actually reporting....................	36.3%	718	19	151	99	98	450	5,856	2,518	3,047	291
Estimated total	100.0%	2,049	52	486	316	270	1,241	16,151	6,945	8,404	802
State total..............................	2,988,726	8,383	238	1,277	905	2,397	4,471	82,732	23,354	55,054	4,324
Rate per 100,000 inhabitants..............		280.5	8.0	42.7	30.3	80.2	149.6	2,768.1	781.4	1,842.1	144.7
Missouri											
Metropolitan statistical area...............	4,549,686										
Area actually reporting....................	99.9%	26,940	474	2,151	1,593	6,269	18,046	138,969	24,543	98,114	16,312
Cities outside metropolitan areas........	100.0%	26,941	474	2,151	1,593	6,269	18,047	138,978	24,544	98,121	16,313
Area actually reporting....................	660,363										
Estimated total	99.3%	2,434	32	239	177	240	1,923	21,155	3,641	16,533	981
Nonmetropolitan counties	100.0%	2,450	32	240	178	242	1,936	21,296	3,665	16,643	988
Area actually reporting....................	882,951										
Estimated total	100.0%	2,253	31	163	113	59	2,000	10,275	3,501	5,780	994
State total..............................	6,093,000	31,644	537	2,554	1,884	6,570	21,983	170,549	31,710	120,544	18,295
Rate per 100,000 inhabitants..............		519.4	8.8	41.9	30.9	107.8	360.8	2,799.1	520.4	1,978.4	300.3
Montana											
Metropolitan statistical area...............											
Area actually reporting....................	367,953										
Estimated total	99.9%	1,306	7	185	137	172	942	13,377	1,823	10,180	1,374
Cities outside metropolitan areas........	100.0%	1,307	7	185	137	172	943	13,392	1,824	10,193	1,375
Area actually reporting....................	100.0%	1,335	11	242	177	68	1,014	7,694	938	6,096	660
Nonmetropolitan counties	453,774										
Area actually reporting....................	98.9%	1,186	18	150	99	26	992	6,818	1,160	4,957	701
Estimated total	100.0%	1,198	18	151	100	26	1,003	6,890	1,172	5,010	708
State total..............................	1,042,520	3,840	36	578	414	266	2,960	27,976	3,934	21,299	2,743
Rate per 100,000 inhabitants..............		368.3	3.5	55.4	39.7	25.5	283.9	2,683.5	377.4	2,043.0	263.1
Nebraska[6]..............................	1,240,589										
Metropolitan statistical area...............	99.2%	4,383	43	719	539	877	2,744	32,557	4,432	24,021	4,104
Area actually reporting....................	100.0%	4,398	43	723	543	878	2,754	32,713	4,451	24,143	4,119
Estimated total	338,960										
Cities outside metropolitan areas........	93.5%	794	4	188	135	55	547	7,716	1,329	6,011	376
Area actually reporting....................	100.0%	848	4	200	145	59	585	8,249	1,421	6,426	402
Estimated total	327,567										
Nonmetropolitan counties	90.5%	275	2	64	43	8	201	1,992	518	1,289	185
Area actually reporting....................	100.0%	304	2	71	50	9	222	2,201	572	1,425	204
State total..............................	1,907,116	5,550	49	994	738	946	3,561	43,163	6,444	31,994	4,725
Rate per 100,000 inhabitants..............		291.0	2.6	52.1	38.7	49.6	186.7	2,263.3	337.9	1,677.6	247.8
Nevada..............................											
Metropolitan statistical area...............	2,668,109										
Area actually reporting....................	100.0%	19,133	209	1,616	1,211	6,292	11,016	71,672	17,652	41,249	12,771
Cities outside metropolitan areas........	48,603										
Area actually reporting....................	100.0%	311	5	49	35	21	236	1,308	327	875	106
Nonmetropolitan counties	223,346										
Area actually reporting....................	100.0%	492	10	68	46	27	387	3,067	871	1,893	303
State total..............................	2,940,058	19,936	224	1,733	1,292	6,340	11,639	76,047	18,850	44,017	13,180
Rate per 100,000 inhabitants..............		678.1	7.6	58.9	43.9	215.6	395.9	2,586.6	641.1	1,497.1	448.3
New Hampshire..............................											
Metropolitan statistical area...............	839,311										
Area actually reporting....................	99.0%	1,721	10	340	249	327	1,044	11,923	1,580	9,793	550
Estimated total	100.0%	1,733	10	343	252	329	1,051	12,030	1,594	9,881	555
Cities outside metropolitan areas........	452,615										
Area actually reporting....................	89.4%	749	5	200	143	85	459	6,996	1,117	5,624	255
Estimated total	100.0%	839	6	224	161	95	514	7,829	1,250	6,294	285
Nonmetropolitan counties	42,869										
Area actually reporting....................	93.6%	61	1	14	9	3	43	313	111	173	29
Estimated total	100.0%	65	1	15	10	3	46	335	119	185	31
State total..............................	1,334,795	2,637	17	582	423	427	1,611	20,194	2,963	16,360	871
Rate per 100,000 inhabitants..............		197.6	1.3	43.6	31.7	32.0	120.7	1,512.9	222.0	1,225.7	65.3
New Jersey											
Metropolitan statistical area...............	8,944,469										

Table 3. Crime, by State and Area, 2016—*Continued*

(Number, percent, rate per 100,000 population.)

Area	Population	Violent crime[1]	Murder and nonnegligent manslaughter	Rape (revised definition)[2]	Rape (legacy definition)[3]	Robbery	Aggravated assault	Property crime	Burglary	Larceny-theft	Motor vehicle theft
Area actually reporting	100.0%	21,914	372	1,453	1,089	8,984	11,105	138,152	25,284	101,540	11,328
Cities outside metropolitan areas	None										
Nonmetropolitan counties	None										
State total	8,944,469	21,914	372	1,453	1,089	8,984	11,105	138,152	25,284	101,540	11,328
Rate per 100,000 inhabitants		245.0	4.2	16.2	12.2	100.4	124.2	1,544.6	282.7	1,135.2	126.6
New Mexico[6]											
Metropolitan statistical area	1,386,406										
Area actually reporting	99.3%	10,595	90	1,053	782	2,402	7,050	61,466	12,212	39,082	10,172
Estimated total	100.0%	10,643	90	1,059	786	2,406	7,088	61,774	12,273	39,287	10,214
Cities outside metropolitan areas	399,862										
Area actually reporting	96.9%	2,628	34	273	205	290	2,031	16,171	3,615	11,494	1,062
Estimated total	100.0%	2,710	35	281	211	299	2,095	16,682	3,729	11,857	1,096
Nonmetropolitan counties	294,747										
Area actually reporting	92.9%	1,177	13	173	112	30	961	3,228	1,188	1,638	402
Estimated total	100.0%	1,266	14	186	120	32	1,034	3,475	1,279	1,763	433
State total	2,081,015	14,619	139	1,526	1,117	2,737	10,217	81,931	17,281	52,907	11,743
Rate per 100,000 inhabitants		702.5	6.7	73.3	53.7	131.5	491.0	3,937.1	830.4	2,542.4	564.3
New York[6]											
Metropolitan statistical area	18,370,635										
Area actually reporting	99.4%	71,419	610	5,218	3,864	22,032	43,559	283,107	35,538	233,778	13,791
Estimated total	100.0%	71,584	612	5,246	3,884	22,074	43,652	284,602	35,733	235,018	13,851
Cities outside metropolitan areas	506,786										
Area actually reporting	98.1%	1,297	13	311	227	180	793	11,126	1,927	8,971	228
Estimated total	100.0%	1,324	13	318	233	184	809	11,344	1,965	9,147	232
Nonmetropolitan counties	867,868										
Area actually reporting	100.0%	1,377	5	696	452	58	618	9,235	2,123	6,803	309
State total	19,745,289	74,285	630	6,260	4,569	22,316	45,079	305,181	39,821	250,968	14,392
Rate per 100,000 inhabitants		376.2	3.2	31.7	23.1	113.0	228.3	1,545.6	201.7	1,271.0	72.9
North Carolina[6]											
Metropolitan statistical area	7,938,934										
Area actually reporting	97.6%	30,341	486	2,259	1,673	8,030	19,566	216,973	51,738	152,826	12,409
Estimated total	100.0%	30,715	492	2,290	1,699	8,110	19,823	220,854	52,773	155,488	12,593
Cities outside metropolitan areas	649,752										
Area actually reporting	88.0%	3,418	67	240	179	771	2,340	26,745	7,093	18,539	1,113
Estimated total	100.0%	3,870	76	258	196	876	2,660	30,403	8,063	21,075	1,265
Nonmetropolitan counties	1,558,102										
Area actually reporting	95.3%	3,032	105	286	182	333	2,308	25,253	10,714	13,160	1,379
Estimated total	100.0%	3,184	110	301	191	350	2,423	26,508	11,246	13,814	1,448
State total	10,146,788	37,769	678	2,849	2,086	9,336	24,906	277,765	72,082	190,377	15,306
Rate per 100,000 inhabitants		372.2	6.7	28.1	20.6	92.0	245.5	2,737.5	710.4	1,876.2	150.8
North Dakota											
Metropolitan statistical area	371,557									7,562	981
Area actually reporting	100.0%	1,119	8	214	160	136	761	10,363	1,820		
Cities outside metropolitan areas	201,068									3,441	647
Area actually reporting	99.8%	591	5	86	64	36	464	5,022	934	3,449	648
Estimated total	100.0%	592	5	86	64	36	465	5,033	936		
Nonmetropolitan counties	185,327										
Area actually reporting	100.0%	192	2	42	32	9	139	2,006	487	1,184	335
State total	757,952	1,903	15	342	256	181	1,365	17,402	3,243	12,195	1,964
Rate per 100,000 inhabitants		251.1	2.0	45.1	33.8	23.9	180.1	2,295.9	427.9	1,608.9	259.1
Ohio[6]											
Metropolitan statistical area	9,255,325										
Area actually reporting	91.6%	30,462	574	4,474	3,337	11,543	13,871	237,037	53,589	165,991	17,457
Estimated total	100.0%	31,626	592	4,731	3,534	11,914	14,389	253,645	56,493	178,994	18,158
Cities outside metropolitan areas	1,046,316										
Area actually reporting	81.1%	1,463	25	381	282	334	723	24,090	4,632	18,826	632
Estimated total	100.0%	1,806	31	471	353	412	892	29,716	5,714	23,222	780
Nonmetropolitan counties	1,312,732										
Area actually reporting	94.7%	1,365	29	363	238	187	786	15,145	4,427	10,028	690
Estimated total	100.0%	1,445	31	387	254	197	830	15,996	4,676	10,591	729
State total	11,614,373	34,877	654	5,589	4,141	12,523	16,111	299,357	66,883	212,807	19,667
Rate per 100,000 inhabitants		300.3	5.6	48.1	35.7	107.8	138.7	2,577.5	575.9	1,832.3	169.3
Oklahoma[6]											
Metropolitan statistical area	2,640,800										

Table 3. Crime, by State and Area, 2016—*Continued*

(Number, percent, rate per 100,000 population.)

Area	Population	Violent crime[1]	Murder and nonnegligent manslaughter	Rape (revised definition)[2]	Rape (legacy definition)[3]	Robbery	Aggravated assault	Property crime	Burglary	Larceny-theft	Motor vehicle theft
Area actually reporting.........	99.9%	13,864	196	1,577	1,179	2,824	9,267	86,883	20,696	56,351	9,836
Estimated total	100.0%	13,866	196	1,577	1,179	2,824	9,269	86,913	20,702	56,372	9,839
Cities outside metropolitan areas........	682,233										
Area actually reporting.........	99.9%	2,714	28	324	238	311	2,051	22,843	5,563	15,775	1,505
Estimated total	100.0%	2,716	28	324	238	311	2,053	22,863	5,568	15,789	1,506
Nonmetropolitan counties	600,528										
Area actually reporting.........	91.3%	974	19	126	84	25	804	6,631	2,587	3,304	740
Estimated total	100.0%	1,066	21	138	92	27	880	7,261	2,833	3,618	810
State total.............................	3,923,561	17,648	245	2,039	1,509	3,162	12,202	117,037	29,103	75,779	12,155
Rate per 100,000 inhabitants..............		449.8	6.2	52.0	38.5	80.6	311.0	2,982.9	741.7	1,931.4	309.8
Oregon[6]..............................	3,431,824										
Metropolitan statistical area...............	3,431,824										
Area actually reporting.........	98.7%	9,177	71	1,459	1,076	2,110	5,537	102,894	13,568	77,779	11,547
Estimated total	100.0%	9,278	72	1,483	1,095	2,129	5,594	104,098	13,706	78,729	11,663
Cities outside metropolitan areas........	308,081										
Area actually reporting.........	94.6%	730	10	131	95	113	476	11,246	1,732	8,766	748
Estimated total	100.0%	770	11	137	100	119	503	11,884	1,830	9,264	790
Nonmetropolitan counties	353,560										
Area actually reporting.........	73.3%	567	22	68	45	22	455	3,930	975	2,413	542
Estimated total	100.0%	782	30	101	66	30	621	5,363	1,330	3,293	740
State total.............................	4,093,465	10,830	113	1,721	1,261	2,278	6,718	121,345	16,866	91,286	13,193
Rate per 100,000 inhabitants..............		264.6	2.8	42.0	30.8	55.6	164.1	2,964.4	412.0	2,230.0	322.3
Pennsylvania	11,313,467										
Metropolitan statistical area...............	11,313,467										
Area actually reporting.........	99.1%	37,232	626	3,535	2,632	11,996	21,075	203,086	31,518	159,219	12,349
Estimated total	100.0%	37,394	627	3,543	2,639	12,038	21,186	204,598	31,708	160,485	12,405
Cities outside metropolitan areas........	681,636										
Area actually reporting.........	95.9%	1,552	10	140	106	162	1,240	9,060	1,378	7,434	248
Estimated total	100.0%	1,609	10	137	103	169	1,293	9,449	1,437	7,753	259
Nonmetropolitan counties	789,124										
Area actually reporting.........	100.0%	1,444	24	753	491	119	548	8,748	2,375	5,990	383
State total.............................	12,784,227	40,447	661	4,433	3,233	12,326	23,027	222,795	35,520	174,228	13,047
Rate per 100,000 inhabitants..............		316.4	5.2	34.7	25.3	96.4	180.1	1,742.7	277.8	1,362.8	102.1
Puerto Rico[7]	3,262,275										
Metropolitan statistical area...............	3,262,275										
Area actually reporting.........	100.0%	7,362	650	160	121	3,155	3,397	34,107	7,907	22,453	3,747
Cities outside metropolitan areas........	149,032										
Area actually reporting.........	100.0%	281	29	9	7	46	197	1,094	344	710	40
Total	3,411,307	7,643	679	169	128	3,201	3,594	35,201	8,251	23,163	3,787
Rate per 100,000 inhabitants..............		224.0	19.9	5.0	3.8	93.8	105.4	1,031.9	241.9	679.0	111.0
Rhode Island[6]	1,056,426										
Metropolitan statistical area...............	1,056,426										
Area actually reporting.........	100.0%	2,489	28	420	314	539	1,502	19,978	3,787	14,611	1,580
Cities outside metropolitan areas........	None										
Nonmetropolitan counties	None										
Area actually reporting.........	100.0%	35	1	22	14	1	11	80	1	63	16
State total.............................	1,056,426	2,524	29	442	328	540	1,513	20,058	3,788	14,674	1,596
Rate per 100,000 inhabitants..............		238.9	2.7	41.8	31.0	51.1	143.2	1,898.7	358.6	1,389.0	151.1
South Carolina...............................	4,212,891										
Metropolitan statistical area...............	4,212,891										
Area actually reporting.........	99.7%	20,864	303	2,009	1,453	3,488	15,064	135,853	26,498	97,150	12,205
Estimated total	100.0%	20,933	303	2,016	1,459	3,500	15,114	136,379	26,574	97,566	12,239
Cities outside metropolitan areas........	205,750										
Area actually reporting.........	97.2%	1,737	33	147	106	300	1,257	10,856	2,309	8,097	450
Estimated total	100.0%	1,787	34	151	109	309	1,293	11,166	2,375	8,328	463
Nonmetropolitan counties	542,478										
Area actually reporting.........	99.2%	2,158	29	218	142	224	1,687	13,274	3,994	8,072	1,208
Estimated total	100.0%	2,176	29	220	143	226	1,701	13,383	4,027	8,138	1,218
State total.............................	4,961,119	24,896	366	2,387	1,711	4,035	18,108	160,928	32,976	114,032	13,920
Rate per 100,000 inhabitants..............		501.8	7.4	48.1	34.5	81.3	365.0	3,243.8	664.7	2,298.5	280.6
South Dakota[6]	416,782										
Metropolitan statistical area...............	416,782										
Area actually reporting.........	99.3%	1,732	15	309	228	211	1,197	10,354	1,798	7,560	996
Estimated total	100.0%	1,735	15	309	228	211	1,200	10,384	1,802	7,584	998

Table 3. Crime, by State and Area, 2016—*Continued*

(Number, percent, rate per 100,000 population.)

Area	Population	Violent crime[1]	Murder and nonnegligent manslaughter	Rape (revised definition)[2]	Rape (legacy definition)[3]	Robbery	Aggravated assault	Property crime	Burglary	Larceny-theft	Motor vehicle theft
Cities outside metropolitan areas........	219,496										
Area actually reporting.........................	94.6%	1,584	6	152	113	52	1,374	5,254	839	4,042	373
Estimated total	100.0%	1,673	6	159	119	55	1,453	5,554	887	4,273	394
Nonmetropolitan counties	229,176										
Area actually reporting.........................	78.2%	168	5	33	25	5	125	940	243	611	86
Estimated total	100.0%	213	6	41	32	6	160	1,203	311	782	110
State total..	865,454	3,621	27	509	379	272	2,813	17,141	3,000	12,639	1,502
Rate per 100,000 inhabitants..............		418.4	3.1	58.8	43.8	31.4	325.0	1,980.6	346.6	1,460.4	173.6
Tennessee	5,151,809										
Metropolitan statistical area	5,151,809										
Area actually reporting.........................	100.0%	36,002	435	2,261	1,679	7,403	25,903	154,421	31,772	110,354	12,295
Cities outside metropolitan areas........	513,895										
Area actually reporting.........................	100.0%	3,326	25	244	177	290	2,767	20,509	3,890	15,469	1,150
Nonmetropolitan counties	985,490										
Area actually reporting.........................	100.0%	2,769	26	209	135	120	2,414	14,905	4,650	8,581	1,674
State total..	6,651,194	42,097	486	2,714	1,991	7,813	31,084	189,835	40,312	134,404	15,119
Rate per 100,000 inhabitants..............		632.9	7.3	40.8	29.9	117.5	467.3	2,854.1	606.1	2,020.7	227.3
Texas	24,814,265										
Metropolitan statistical area	24,814,265										
Area actually reporting.........................	99.7%	112,094	1,382	12,022	8,912	32,508	66,182	708,595	132,040	511,044	65,511
Estimated total	100.0%	112,275	1,382	12,049	8,935	32,551	66,293	710,123	132,303	512,191	65,629
Cities outside metropolitan areas........	1,439,521										
Area actually reporting.........................	96.6%	5,470	44	682	497	596	4,148	38,585	8,950	27,759	1,876
Estimated total	100.0%	5,656	46	708	519	614	4,288	39,863	9,250	28,677	1,936
Nonmetropolitan counties	1,608,810										
Area actually reporting.........................	98.9%	3,077	49	604	400	150	2,274	18,758	7,110	10,173	1,475
Estimated total	100.0%	3,111	50	610	404	152	2,299	18,961	7,187	10,283	1,491
State total..	27,862,596	121,042	1,478	13,367	9,858	33,317	72,880	768,947	148,740	551,151	69,056
Rate per 100,000 inhabitants..............		434.4	5.3	48.0	35.4	119.6	261.6	2,759.8	533.8	1,978.1	247.8
Utah	3,051,217										
Metropolitan statistical area	2,725,548										
Area actually reporting.........................	99.4%	6,695	63	1,370	1,010	1,499	3,763	83,517	11,726	62,970	8,821
Estimated total	100.0%	6,721	63	1,375	1,014	1,505	3,778	83,912	11,789	63,255	8,868
Cities outside metropolitan areas........	149,141										
Area actually reporting.........................	90.3%	320	2	81	59	20	217	3,185	483	2,508	194
Estimated total	100.0%	354	2	90	66	22	240	3,529	535	2,779	215
Nonmetropolitan counties	176,528										
Area actually reporting.........................	95.5%	317	7	53	34	13	244	2,498	489	1,718	291
Estimated total	100.0%	332	7	55	36	14	256	2,617	512	1,800	305
State total..	3,051,217	7,407	72	1,520	1,116	1,541	4,274	90,058	12,836	67,834	9,388
Rate per 100,000 inhabitants..............		242.8	2.4	49.8	36.6	50.5	140.1	2,951.5	420.7	2,223.2	307.7
Vermont...	624,594										
Metropolitan statistical area	217,636										
Area actually reporting.........................	100.0%	439	7	74	53	54	304	4,894	747	4,058	89
Cities outside metropolitan areas........	203,654										
Area actually reporting.........................	100.0%	322	1	62	42	40	219	3,607	585	2,937	85
Nonmetropolitan counties	203,304										
Area actually reporting.........................	100.0%	228	6	42	29	12	168	2,101	771	1,222	108
State total..	624,594	989	14	178	124	106	691	10,602	2,103	8,217	282
Rate per 100,000 inhabitants..............		158.3	2.2	28.5	19.9	17.0	110.6	1,697.4	336.7	1,315.6	45.1
Virginia	8,411,808										
Metropolitan statistical area	7,366,234										
Area actually reporting.........................	100.0%	16,236	406	2,236	1,628	4,572	9,022	141,037	17,122	114,954	8,961
Cities outside metropolitan areas........	259,405										
Area actually reporting.........................	99.9%	848	23	147	104	140	538	6,736	918	5,560	258
Estimated total	100.0%	849	23	147	104	140	539	6,745	919	5,568	258
Nonmetropolitan counties	786,169										
Area actually reporting.........................	100.0%	1,217	55	354	233	91	717	8,630	1,977	6,084	569
State total..	8,411,808	18,302	484	2,737	1,965	4,803	10,278	156,412	20,018	126,606	9,788
Rate per 100,000 inhabitants..............		217.6	5.8	32.5	23.4	57.1	122.2	1,859.4	238.0	1,505.1	116.4
Washington[6]....................................	6,561,914										
Metropolitan statistical area	6,561,914										
Area actually reporting.........................	99.9%	20,475	172	2,786	2,054	5,467	12,050	235,805	44,545	160,783	30,477
Estimated total	100.0%	20,475	172	2,786	2,054	5,467	12,050	235,814	44,546	160,790	30,478

Table 3. Crime, by State and Area, 2016—*Continued*

(Number, percent, rate per 100,000 population.)

Area	Population	Violent crime[1]	Murder and nonnegligent manslaughter	Rape (revised definition)[2]	Rape (legacy definition)[3]	Robbery	Aggravated assault	Property crime	Burglary	Larceny-theft	Motor vehicle theft
Cities outside metropolitan areas........	299,860										
Area actually reporting.........................	97.8%	983	7	195	140	151	630	12,608	2,593	8,804	1,211
Estimated total	100.0%	1,004	7	199	144	154	644	12,894	2,652	9,004	1,238
Nonmetropolitan counties	426,226										
Area actually reporting.........................	100.0%	544	16	92	61	30	406	5,945	1,982	3,393	570
State total..	7,288,000	22,023	195	3,077	2,259	5,651	13,100	254,653	49,180	173,187	32,286
Rate per 100,000 inhabitants...............		302.2	2.7	42.2	31.0	77.5	179.7	3,494.1	674.8	2,376.3	443.0
West Virginia.................................	1,131,010										
Metropolitan statistical area................											
Area actually reporting.........................	89.9%	4,030	50	427	309	564	2,989	26,592	6,775	18,050	1,767
Estimated total	100.0%	4,334	52	460	335	597	3,225	29,486	7,377	20,151	1,958
Cities outside metropolitan areas........	187,738										
Area actually reporting.........................	59.0%	388	2	28	21	34	324	1,898	314	1,491	93
Estimated total	100.0%	648	3	37	28	58	550	3,220	533	2,529	158
Nonmetropolitan counties	512,354										
Area actually reporting.........................	93.7%	1,476	24	150	99	61	1,241	4,481	1,304	2,809	368
Estimated total	100.0%	1,575	26	160	105	65	1,324	4,781	1,391	2,997	393
State total..	1,831,102	6,557	81	657	468	720	5,099	37,487	9,301	25,677	2,509
Rate per 100,000 inhabitants...............		358.1	4.4	35.9	25.6	39.3	278.5	2,047.2	507.9	1,402.3	137.0
Wisconsin[6]	4,281,462										
Metropolitan statistical area................											
Area actually reporting.........................	99.0%	15,475	205	1,532	1,145	4,603	9,135	89,637	15,331	65,137	9,169
Estimated total	100.0%	15,515	205	1,541	1,152	4,608	9,161	90,113	15,411	65,509	9,193
Cities outside metropolitan areas........	648,096										
Area actually reporting.........................	99.6%	1,250	14	251	184	66	919	14,410	1,741	12,298	371
Estimated total	100.0%	1,254	14	251	184	66	923	14,471	1,748	12,350	373
Nonmetropolitan counties	849,150										
Area actually reporting.........................	100.0%	910	10	187	122	32	681	7,136	2,266	4,478	392
State total..	5,778,708	17,679	229	1,979	1,458	4,706	10,765	111,720	19,425	82,337	9,958
Rate per 100,000 inhabitants...............		305.9	4.0	34.2	25.2	81.4	186.3	1,933.3	336.1	1,424.8	172.3
Wyoming	180,145										
Metropolitan statistical area................											
Area actually reporting.........................	100.0%	413	8	59	43	30	316	5,020	866	3,739	415
Cities outside metropolitan areas........	245,821										
Area actually reporting.........................	95.7%	635	10	112	81	26	487	5,091	645	4,167	279
Estimated total	100.0%	663	10	117	86	27	509	5,321	674	4,355	292
Nonmetropolitan counties	159,535										
Area actually reporting.........................	88.4%	314	2	26	19	2	284	989	204	703	82
Estimated total	100.0%	354	2	29	21	2	321	1,119	231	795	93
State total..	585,501	1,430	20	205	150	59	1,146	11,460	1,771	8,889	800
Rate per 100,000 inhabitants...............		244.2	3.4	35.0	25.6	10.1	195.7	1,957.3	302.5	1,518.2	136.6

Note: Although arson data are included in the trend and clearance tables, sufficient data are not available to estimate totals for this offense. Therefore, no arson data are published in this table.
[1] The violent crime figures include the offenses of murder, rape (revised definition), robbery, and aggravated assault.
[2] The figures shown in this column for the offense of rape were estimated using the revised Uniform Crime Reporting (UCR) definition of rape. See chapter notes for more detail.
[3] The figures shown in this column for the offense of rape were estimated using the legacy Uniform Crime Reporting (UCR) definition of rape. See chapter notes for more detail.
[4] Includes offenses reported by the Metro Transit Police and the Arson Investigation Unit of the District of Columbia Fire and Emergency Medical Services.
[5] This state's agencies submitted rape data according to the legacy UCR definition of rape.
[6] Agencies within this state submitted rape data according to both the revised UCR definition of rape and the legacy UCR definition of rape.

Table 4. Crime, by Selected Metropolitan Statistical Area, 2016

(Number, percent, rate per 100,000 population.)

Area	Population	Violent crime	Murder and nonnegligent manslaughter	Rape[1]	Robbery	Aggravated assault	Property crime	Burglary	Larceny-theft	Motor vehicle theft
Abilene, TX M.S.A.	169,885									
Includes Callahan, Jones, and Taylor Counties										
City of Abilene..........	122,523	546	8	70	133	335	4,269	905	3,113	251
Total area actually reporting	100.0%	614	11	79	137	387	4,932	1,104	3,530	298
Rate per 100,000 inhabitants..........		361.4	6.5	46.5	80.6	227.8	2,903.1	649.9	2,077.9	175.4
Akron, OH M.S.A.[2]..........	703,561									
Includes Portage and Summit Counties										
City of Akron..........	197,257	1,216	34	212	415	555	8,646	2,483	5,483	680
Total area actually reporting	96.2%	1,739	41	335	530	833	17,453	3,865	12,599	989
Estimated total..........	100.0%	1,781	42	344	544	851	18,043	3,963	13,067	1,013
Rate per 100,000 inhabitants..........		253.1	6.0	48.9	77.3	121.0	2,564.5	563.3	1,857.3	144.0
Albany, GA M.S.A...........	152,566									
Includes Baker, Dougherty, Lee, Terrell, and Worth Counties										
City of Albany..........	74,330	873	16	28	204	625	3,620	888	2,585	147
Total area actually reporting	96.0%	1,098	18	41	237	802	5,553	1,415	3,934	204
Estimated total..........	100.0%	1,121	18	43	244	816	5,753	1,449	4,084	220
Rate per 100,000 inhabitants..........		734.8	11.8	28.2	159.9	534.9	3,770.8	949.8	2,676.9	144.2
Albany, OR M.S.A...........	122,030									
Includes Linn County										
City of Albany..........	52,544	43	0	12	21	10	1,512	146	1,256	110
Total area actually reporting	100.0%	139	0	34	33	72	3,283	462	2,564	257
Rate per 100,000 inhabitants..........		113.9	0.0	27.9	27.0	59.0	2,690.3	378.6	2,101.1	210.6
Albany-Schenectady-Troy, NY M.S.A.	878,166									
Includes Albany, Rensselaer, Saratoga, Schenectady, and Schoharie Counties										
City of Albany..........	98,617	848	2	59	250	537	3,461	491	2,858	112
City of Schenectady..........	65,138	595	6	58	146	385	2,100	378	1,525	197
City of Troy..........	49,876	362	3	25	102	232	1,792	394	1,308	90
Total area actually reporting	100.0%	2,544	18	342	603	1,581	17,647	2,472	14,455	720
Rate per 100,000 inhabitants..........		289.7	2.0	38.9	68.7	180.0	2,009.5	281.5	1,646.0	82.0
Albuquerque, NM M.S.A.	907,140									
Includes Bernalillo, Sandoval, Torrance, and Valencia Counties										
City of Albuquerque	561,560	6,245	61	381	1,957	3,846	38,528	6,236	24,582	7,710
Total area actually reporting	100.0%	8,173	75	520	2,165	5,413	47,976	8,628	30,113	9,235
Rate per 100,000 inhabitants..........		901.0	8.3	57.3	238.7	596.7	5,288.7	951.1	3,319.6	1,018.0
Alexandria, LA M.S.A...........	154,032									
Includes Grant and Rapides Parishes										
City of Alexandria	47,936	883	11	25	154	693	4,091	1,057	2,765	269
Total area actually reporting	98.8%	1,414	12	76	179	1,147	7,168	1,946	4,740	482
Estimated total..........	100.0%	1,422	12	77	180	1,153	7,236	1,958	4,793	485
Rate per 100,000 inhabitants..........		923.2	7.8	50.0	116.9	748.5	4,697.7	1,271.2	3,111.7	314.9
Allentown-Bethlehem-Easton, PA-NJ M.S.A.[3]	831,770									
Includes Warren County, NJ and Carbon, Lehigh, and Northampton Counties, PA										
City of Allentown, PA..........	120,615	552	10	55	274	213	3,337	668	2,387	282
City of Bethlehem, PA[3]..........	74,869		4	21	58		1,487	213	1,226	48
Total area actually reporting	99.6%		22	160	483			2,195		739
Estimated total..........	100.0%		22	161	485			2,202		741
Rate per 100,000 inhabitants..........			2.6	19.4	58.3			264.7		89.1
Altoona, PA M.S.A...........	124,942									
Includes Blair County										
City of Altoona	45,158	156	1	23	37	95	821	169	619	33
Total area actually reporting	100.0%	266	1	40	46	179	1,698	238	1,405	55
Rate per 100,000 inhabitants..........		212.9	0.8	32.0	36.8	143.3	1,359.0	190.5	1,124.5	44.0
Amarillo, TX M.S.A.[3]..........	263,223									
Includes Armstrong, Carson, Oldham, Potter, and Randall Counties										
City of Amarillo..........	200,141	1,414	11	162	260	981	9,472	1,797	6,756	919

Table 4. Crime, by Selected Metropolitan Statistical Area, 2016—*Continued*

(Number, percent, rate per 100,000 population.)

Area	Population	Violent crime	Murder and nonnegligent manslaughter	Rape[1]	Robbery	Aggravated assault	Property crime	Burglary	Larceny-theft	Motor vehicle theft
Total area actually reporting	100.0%	1,560	14	188	269	1,089	10,352	2,004	7,321	1,027
Rate per 100,000 inhabitants		592.7	5.3	71.4	102.2	413.7	3,932.8	761.3	2,781.3	390.2
Ames, IA M.S.A.	97,202									
Includes Story County										
City of Ames	66,333	107	1	39	15	52	1,077	164	867	46
Total area actually reporting	93.0%	141	1	51	16	73	1,517	235	1,203	79
Estimated total	100.0%	158	1	54	17	86	1,640	262	1,293	85
Rate per 100,000 inhabitants		162.5	1.0	55.6	17.5	88.5	1,687.2	269.5	1,330.2	87.4
Anchorage, AK M.S.A.	315,641									
Includes Anchorage Municipality and Matanuska-Susitna Borough										
City of Anchorage	299,097	3,422	28	542	695	2,157	14,649	2,008	10,599	2,042
Total area actually reporting	100.0%	3,519	28	548	709	2,234	15,626	2,070	11,413	2,143
Rate per 100,000 inhabitants		1,114.9	8.9	173.6	224.6	707.8	4,950.6	655.8	3,615.8	678.9
Ann Arbor, MI M.S.A.	361,440									
Includes Washtenaw County										
City of Ann Arbor	117,688	213	1	44	43	125	2,051	242	1,697	112
Total area actually reporting	100.0%	1,147	2	190	186	769	5,956	921	4,597	438
Rate per 100,000 inhabitants		317.3	0.6	52.6	51.5	212.8	1,647.9	254.8	1,271.9	121.2
Anniston-Oxford-Jacksonville, AL M.S.A.	114,790									
Includes Calhoun County										
City of Anniston	22,205	735	7	39	87	602	1,712	712	888	112
City of Oxford	17,066	63	0	0	7	56	763	127	615	21
City of Jacksonville	12,150	123	0	6	16	101	501	140	335	26
Total area actually reporting	99.3%	1,023	8	59	123	833	3,743	1,263	2,298	182
Estimated total	100.0%	1,027	8	59	124	836	3,768	1,268	2,316	184
Rate per 100,000 inhabitants		894.7	7.0	51.4	108.0	728.3	3,282.5	1,104.6	2,017.6	160.3
Appleton, WI M.S.A.	234,069									
Includes Calumet and Outagamie Counties										
City of Appleton	74,439	208	2	30	20	156	1,294	175	1,080	39
Total area actually reporting	100.0%	354	4	60	31	259	3,110	404	2,605	101
Rate per 100,000 inhabitants		151.2	1.7	25.6	13.2	110.7	1,328.7	172.6	1,112.9	43.1
Asheville, NC M.S.A.[4]	451,305									
Includes Buncombe, Haywood, Henderson, and Madison Counties										
City of Asheville	89,546	537	10	48	144	335	4,357	752	3,345	260
Total area actually reporting	99.5%	1,079	23	98	245	713			6,866	722
Estimated total	100.0%	1,085	23	98	247	717			6,918	725
Rate per 100,000 inhabitants		240.4	5.1	21.7	54.7	158.9			1,532.9	160.6
Athens-Clarke County, GA M.S.A.	205,004									
Includes Clarke, Madison, Oconee, and Oglethorpe Counties										
City of Athens-Clarke County	123,934	533	4	53	163	313	4,100	822	3,054	224
Total area actually reporting	100.0%	700	6	78	176	440	5,757	1,145	4,301	311
Rate per 100,000 inhabitants		341.5	2.9	38.0	85.9	214.6	2,808.2	558.5	2,098.0	151.7
Atlanta-Sandy Springs-Roswell, GA M.S.A.	5,790,619									
Includes Barrow, Bartow, Butts, Carroll, Cherokee, Clayton, Cobb, Coweta, Dawson, DeKalb, Douglas, Fayette, Forsyth, Fulton, Gwinnett, Haralson, Heard, Henry, Jasper, Lamar, Meriwether, Morgan, Newton, Paulding, Pickens, Pike, Rockdale, Spalding, and Walton Counties										
City of Atlanta	472,579	5,121	111	136	2,070	2,804	24,804	4,411	16,400	3,993
City of Sandy Springs	107,685	117	3	14	66	34	2,837	532	2,091	214
City of Roswell	95,684	143	2	23	42	76	1,702	228	1,391	83
City of Alpharetta	64,943	35	1	5	20	9	1,308	135	1,129	44
City of Marietta	59,516	233	1	12	117	103	2,282	307	1,825	150
Total area actually reporting	99.7%	23,275	395	1,385	8,324	13,171	173,043	33,252	121,238	18,553
Estimated total	100.0%	23,345	396	1,390	8,346	13,213	173,620	33,364	121,651	18,605
Rate per 100,000 inhabitants		403.2	6.8	24.0	144.1	228.2	2,998.3	576.2	2,100.8	321.3
Auburn-Opelika, AL M.S.A	160,071									
Includes Lee County										

(Number, percent, rate per 100,000 population.)

Area	Population	Violent crime	Murder and nonnegligent manslaughter	Rape[1]	Robbery	Aggravated assault	Property crime	Burglary	Larceny-theft	Motor vehicle theft
City of Auburn	63,871	210	4	12	31	163	1,125	203	844	78
City of Opelika	30,180	221	7	18	35	161	1,476	233	1,158	85
Total area actually reporting	100.0%	916	22	56	94	744	4,137	885	2,959	293
Rate per 100,000 inhabitants		572.2	13.7	35.0	58.7	464.8	2,584.5	552.9	1,848.6	183.0
Augusta-Richmond County, GA-SC M.S.A.	595,180									
Includes Burke, Columbia, Lincoln, McDuffie, and Richmond Counties, GA and Aiken and Edgefield Counties, SC										
Total area actually reporting	99.9%	2,039	44	214	503	1,278	18,754	3,644	13,931	1,179
Estimated total	100.0%	2,040	44	214	503	1,279	18,761	3,645	13,937	1,179
Rate per 100,000 inhabitants		342.8	7.4	36.0	84.5	214.9	3,152.2	612.4	2,341.6	198.1
Austin-Round Rock, TX M.S.A.	2,054,651									
Includes Bastrop, Caldwell, Hays, Travis, and Williamson Counties										
City of Austin	956,911	3,903	39	751	1,048	2,065	33,545	5,232	26,125	2,188
City of Round Rock	119,308	173	0	31	44	98	2,653	303	2,270	80
Total area actually reporting	99.9%	6,510	70	1,180	1,411	3,849	52,484	8,665	40,428	3,391
Estimated total	100.0%	6,511	70	1,180	1,411	3,850	52,501	8,668	40,441	3,392
Rate per 100,000 inhabitants		316.9	3.4	57.4	68.7	187.4	2,555.2	421.9	1,968.3	165.1
Bakersfield, CA M.S.A.	884,443									
Includes Kern County										
City of Bakersfield	378,788	1,821	32	67	614	1,108	17,138	3,887	10,203	3,048
Total area actually reporting	100.0%	5,128	88	307	1,166	3,567	32,570	8,351	17,742	6,477
Rate per 100,000 inhabitants		579.8	9.9	34.7	131.8	403.3	3,682.5	944.2	2,006.0	732.3
Baltimore-Columbia-Towson, MD M.S.A.	2,797,991									
Includes Anne Arundel, Baltimore, Carroll, Harford, Howard, and Queen Anne's Counties and Baltimore City										
City of Baltimore	618,385	11,010	318	299	5,236	5,157	29,547	7,375	16,855	5,317
Total area actually reporting	100.0%	19,873	395	909	7,743	10,826	78,076	14,986	54,549	8,541
Rate per 100,000 inhabitants		710.3	14.1	32.5	276.7	386.9	2,790.4	535.6	1,949.6	305.3
Bangor, ME M.S.A.	152,658									
Includes Penobscot County										
City of Bangor	32,264	75	0	15	30	30	1,340	180	1,123	37
Total area actually reporting	100.0%	146	0	43	41	62	2,964	584	2,296	84
Rate per 100,000 inhabitants		95.6	0.0	28.2	26.9	40.6	1,941.6	382.6	1,504.0	55.0
Barnstable Town, MA M.S.A.[5]	213,081									
Includes Barnstable County										
City of Barnstable	43,974	199	1	16	15	167	711	133	558	20
Total area actually reporting	100.0%		1	73	35		3,329	850	2,346	133
Rate per 100,000 inhabitants			0.5	34.3	16.4		1,562.3	398.9	1,101.0	62.4
Baton Rouge, LA M.S.A.	833,146									
Includes Ascension, East Baton Rouge, East Feliciana, Iberville, Livingston, Pointe Coupee, St. Helena, West Baton Rouge, and West Feliciana Parishes										
City of Baton Rouge	228,389	2,143	47	123	824	1,149	9,934	2,364	6,907	663
Total area actually reporting	99.7%	4,198	79	278	1,166	2,675	28,229	5,994	20,831	1,404
Estimated total	100.0%	4,207	79	279	1,167	2,682	28,310	6,008	20,894	1,408
Rate per 100,000 inhabitants		505.0	9.5	33.5	140.1	321.9	3,398.0	721.1	2,507.8	169.0
Battle Creek, MI M.S.A.	133,914									
Includes Calhoun County										
City of Battle Creek	60,904	594	3	83	64	444	2,325	607	1,629	89
Total area actually reporting	100.0%	1,000	7	178	89	726	4,205	1,065	2,979	161
Rate per 100,000 inhabitants		746.7	5.2	132.9	66.5	542.1	3,140.1	795.3	2,224.6	120.2
Bay City, MI M.S.A.	105,209									
Includes Bay County										
City of Bay City	33,725	205	1	50	25	129	925	291	600	34
Total area actually reporting	100.0%	389	3	109	32	245	1,950	505	1,358	87
Rate per 100,000 inhabitants		369.7	2.9	103.6	30.4	232.9	1,853.5	480.0	1,290.8	82.7
Beaumont-Port Arthur, TX M.S.A.[3]	408,167									
Includes Hardin, Jefferson, Newton, and Orange Counties										
City of Beaumont	118,283	1,316	14	86	379	837	5,065	1,460	3,299	306

Table 4. Crime, by Selected Metropolitan Statistical Area, 2016—*Continued*

(Number, percent, rate per 100,000 population.)

Area	Population	Violent crime	Murder and nonnegligent manslaughter	Rape[1]	Robbery	Aggravated assault	Property crime	Burglary	Larceny-theft	Motor vehicle theft
City of Port Arthur	55,510	362	5	18	105	234	1,829	580	1,123	126
Total area actually reporting	97.1%	2,308	27	167	573	1,541	10,979	3,034	7,111	834
Estimated total...............	100.0%	2,342	27	171	581	1,563	11,185	3,083	7,246	856
Rate per 100,000 inhabitants...............		573.8	6.6	41.9	142.3	382.9	2,740.3	755.3	1,775.3	209.7
Beckley, WV M.S.A	121,287									
Includes Fayette and Raleigh Counties										
City of Beckley...............	16,940	214	3	14	38	159	1,278	246	984	48
Total area actually reporting	95.7%	491	12	34	57	388	3,144	836	2,161	147
Estimated total...............	100.0%	506	12	36	59	399	3,323	865	2,301	157
Rate per 100,000 inhabitants...............		417.2	9.9	29.7	48.6	329.0	2,739.8	713.2	1,897.2	129.4
Bellingham, WA M.S.A...............	215,331									
Includes Whatcom County										
City of Bellingham	86,005	224	0	61	47	116	4,743	751	3,709	283
Total area actually reporting	100.0%	483	4	124	69	286	6,997	1,388	5,182	427
Rate per 100,000 inhabitants...............		224.3	1.9	57.6	32.0	132.8	3,249.4	644.6	2,406.5	198.3
Bend-Redmond, OR M.S.A................	180,071									
Includes Deschutes County										
City of Bend...............	89,244	96	0	17	20	59	2,010	178	1,740	92
City of Redmond...............	29,164	80	1	13	9	57	973	84	801	88
Total area actually reporting	100.0%	273	2	47	30	194	3,909	438	3,229	242
Rate per 100,000 inhabitants...............		151.6	1.1	26.1	16.7	107.7	2,170.8	243.2	1,793.2	134.4
Billings, MT M.S.A.	170,245									
Includes Carbon, Golden Valley, and Yellowstone Counties										
City of Billings...............	111,447	514	0	61	81	372	5,216	723	3,698	795
Total area actually reporting	99.7%	641	3	79	92	467	6,141	912	4,316	913
Estimated total...............	100.0%	642	3	79	92	468	6,156	913	4,329	914
Rate per 100,000 inhabitants...............		377.1	1.8	46.4	54.0	274.9	3,616.0	536.3	2,542.8	536.9
Binghamton, NY M.S.A................	243,328									
Includes Broome and Tioga Counties										
City of Binghamton...............	45,780	353	4	41	93	215	1,844	436	1,306	102
Total area actually reporting	99.7%	703	6	153	146	398	5,165	1,066	3,890	209
Estimated total...............	100.0%	704	6	153	146	399	5,177	1,068	3,900	209
Rate per 100,000 inhabitants...............		289.3	2.5	62.9	60.0	164.0	2,127.6	438.9	1,602.8	85.9
Bismarck, ND M.S.A.	129,489									
Includes Burleigh, Morton, Oliver, and Sioux Counties										
City of Bismarck...............	73,248	212	2	35	29	146	2,472	468	1,715	289
Total area actually reporting	100.0%	380	3	62	34	281	3,676	704	2,523	449
Rate per 100,000 inhabitants...............		293.5	2.3	47.9	26.3	217.0	2,838.9	543.7	1,948.4	346.7
Blacksburg-Christiansburg-Radford, VA M.S.A................	181,407									
Includes Floyd, Giles, Montgomery, and Pulaski Counties and Radford City										
City of Blacksburg...............	44,528	43	0	19	3	21	409	62	333	14
City of Christiansburg...............	22,134	35	0	12	3	20	575	62	505	8
City of Radford...............	17,504	83	1	22	8	52	316	60	244	12
Total area actually reporting	100.0%	359	5	115	27	212	3,051	470	2,474	107
Rate per 100,000 inhabitants...............		197.9	2.8	63.4	14.9	116.9	1,681.9	259.1	1,363.8	59.0
Bloomington, IL M.S.A................	189,092									
Includes DeWitt and McLean Counties										
City of Bloomington...............	78,604	307	0	42	59	206	1,347	224	1,064	59
Total area actually reporting	94.7%	503	3	89	91	320	2,720	464	2,163	93
Estimated total...............	100.0%	524	3	92	97	332	2,890	491	2,297	102
Rate per 100,000 inhabitants...............		277.1	1.6	48.7	51.3	175.6	1,528.4	259.7	1,214.8	53.9
Bloomington, IN M.S.A................	166,354									
Includes Monroe and Owen Counties										
City of Bloomington...............	84,772	378	2	46	70	260	2,703	546	2,011	146
Total area actually reporting	87.6%	491	4	71	81	335	3,967	773	2,950	244
Estimated total...............	100.0%	520	5	75	85	355	4,207	833	3,106	268
Rate per 100,000 inhabitants...............		312.6	3.0	45.1	51.1	213.4	2,528.9	500.7	1,867.1	161.1
Boise City, ID M.S.A................	693,703									
Includes Ada, Boise, Canyon, Gem, and Owyhee Counties										

Table 4. Crime, by Selected Metropolitan Statistical Area, 2016—*Continued*

(Number, percent, rate per 100,000 population.)

Area	Population	Violent crime	Murder and nonnegligent manslaughter	Rape[1]	Robbery	Aggravated assault	Property crime	Burglary	Larceny-theft	Motor vehicle theft
City of Boise	220,749	657	6	143	51	457	5,134	732	4,066	336
Total area actually reporting	100.0%	1,693	17	349	103	1,224	12,282	2,193	9,139	950
Rate per 100,000 inhabitants		244.1	2.5	50.3	14.8	176.4	1,770.5	316.1	1,317.4	136.9
Boston-Cambridge-Newton, MA-NH M.S.A.[5]	4,798,657									
Includes the Metropolitan Divisions of Boston, MA;										
Cambridge-Newton-Framingham, MA; and Rockingham										
County-Strafford County, NH										
City of Boston, MA	673,880	4,767	49	278	1,530	2,910	14,489	1,837	11,429	1,223
City of Cambridge, MA	111,030	294	2	28	76	188	2,369	326	1,924	119
City of Newton, MA	89,116	46	0	3	11	32	642	80	544	18
City of Framingham, MA	71,422	211	0	8	18	185	831	122	655	54
City of Waltham, MA	63,613	99	1	12	8	78	688	109	550	29
Total area actually reporting	98.0%		88	1,263	3,399		65,828	9,496	51,258	5,074
Estimated total	100.0%		89	1,291	3,445		67,153	9,729	52,254	5,170
Rate per 100,000 inhabitants			1.9	26.9	71.8		1,399.4	202.7	1,088.9	107.7
Boston, MA M.D.[5]	1,994,514									
Includes Norfolk, Plymouth, and Suffolk Counties										
Total area actually reporting	95.7%		58	632	2,260		30,970	4,471	24,142	2,357
Estimated total	100.0%		59	657	2,302		32,158	4,682	25,032	2,444
Rate per 100,000 inhabitants			3.0	32.9	115.4		1,612.3	234.7	1,255.0	122.5
Cambridge-Newton-Framingham, MA M.D.	2,373,065									
Includes Essex and Middlesex Counties										
Total area actually reporting	99.7%	5,562	25	451	1,060	4,026	29,097	4,291	22,354	2,452
Estimated total	100.0%	5,582	25	453	1,063	4,041	29,193	4,308	22,426	2,459
Rate per 100,000 inhabitants		235.2	1.1	19.1	44.8	170.3	1,230.2	181.5	945.0	103.6
Rockingham County-Strafford County, NH M.D.	431,078									
Includes Rockingham and Strafford Counties										
Total area actually reporting	99.2%	632	5	180	79	368	5,761	734	4,762	265
Estimated total	100.0%	637	5	181	80	371	5,802	739	4,796	267
Rate per 100,000 inhabitants		147.8	1.2	42.0	18.6	86.1	1,345.9	171.4	1,112.6	61.9
Boulder, CO M.S.A.	324,108									
Includes Boulder County										
City of Boulder	109,189	258	0	52	30	176	3,275	559	2,497	219
Total area actually reporting	100.0%	766	1	222	82	461	7,501	1,128	5,875	498
Rate per 100,000 inhabitants		236.3	0.3	68.5	25.3	142.2	2,314.4	348.0	1,812.7	153.7
Bowling Green, KY M.S.A.	170,204									
Includes Allen, Butler, Edmonson, and Warren Counties										
City of Bowling Green	64,561	204	4	51	85	64	2,773	379	2,236	158
Total area actually reporting	100.0%	280	6	74	91	109	3,664	691	2,740	233
Rate per 100,000 inhabitants		164.5	3.5	43.5	53.5	64.0	2,152.7	406.0	1,609.8	136.9
Bremerton-Silverdale, WA M.S.A.	262,877									
Includes Kitsap County										
City of Bremerton	39,862	198	0	29	38	131	1,576	257	1,159	160
Total area actually reporting	100.0%	680	1	112	93	474	6,993	1,458	5,000	535
Rate per 100,000 inhabitants		258.7	0.4	42.6	35.4	180.3	2,660.2	554.6	1,902.0	203.5
Bridgeport-Stamford-Norwalk, CT M.S.A.	935,988									
Includes Fairfield County										
City of Bridgeport	148,180	1,115	10	69	441	595	3,258	667	1,857	734
City of Stamford	130,116	351	2	29	119	201	2,073	268	1,613	192
City of Norwalk	88,989	295	1	18	65	211	1,427	239	1,034	154
City of Danbury	85,335	161	0	30	75	56	1,363	168	1,056	139
City of Stratford	52,841	67	0	6	34	27	1,160	177	867	116
Total area actually reporting	100.0%	2,151	14	175	801	1,161	13,423	2,137	9,686	1,600
Rate per 100,000 inhabitants		229.8	1.5	18.7	85.6	124.0	1,434.1	228.3	1,034.8	170.9
Brownsville-Harlingen, TX M.S.A.	423,865									
Includes Cameron County										
City of Brownsville	185,583	448	4	50	130	264	6,028	917	4,960	151
City of Harlingen	65,913	281	2	35	58	186	2,590	503	2,018	69

Table 4. Crime, by Selected Metropolitan Statistical Area, 2016—*Continued*

(Number, percent, rate per 100,000 population.)

Area	Population	Violent crime	Murder and nonnegligent manslaughter	Rape[1]	Robbery	Aggravated assault	Property crime	Burglary	Larceny-theft	Motor vehicle theft
Total area actually reporting	100.0%	1,607	8	201	224	1,174	12,101	2,116	9,654	331
Rate per 100,000 inhabitants		379.1	1.9	47.4	52.8	277.0	2,854.9	499.2	2,277.6	78.1
Brunswick, GA M.S.A.	116,597									
Includes Brantley, Glynn, and McIntosh Counties										
City of Brunswick	16,309	164	3	5	36	120	775	196	528	51
Total area actually reporting	100.0%	434	5	27	85	317	3,520	850	2,470	200
Rate per 100,000 inhabitants		372.2	4.3	23.2	72.9	271.9	3,018.9	729.0	2,118.4	171.5
Buffalo-Cheektowaga-Niagara Falls, NY M.S.A.	1,127,663									
Includes Erie and Niagara Counties										
City of Buffalo	257,446	2,857	44	153	1,049	1,611	10,599	2,631	7,133	835
City of Cheektowaga Town	78,100	181	2	22	68	89	2,523	280	2,128	115
City of Niagara Falls	48,675	565	3	14	199	349	2,402	551	1,665	186
Total area actually reporting	100.0%	4,635	55	373	1,566	2,641	27,260	5,206	20,555	1,499
Rate per 100,000 inhabitants		411.0	4.9	33.1	138.9	234.2	2,417.4	461.7	1,822.8	132.9
Burlington, NC M.S.A.	159,667									
Includes Alamance County										
City of Burlington	52,760	392	6	15	71	300	1,833	430	1,309	94
Total area actually reporting	100.0%	625	11	28	99	487	3,744	985	2,570	189
Rate per 100,000 inhabitants		391.4	6.9	17.5	62.0	305.0	2,344.9	616.9	1,609.6	118.4
California-Lexington Park, MD M.S.A.	111,930									
Includes St. Mary's County										
Total area actually reporting	100.0%	227	2	28	31	166	2,075	413	1,591	71
Rate per 100,000 inhabitants		202.8	1.8	25.0	27.7	148.3	1,853.8	369.0	1,421.4	63.4
Cape Coral-Fort Myers, FL M.S.A.	720,949									
Includes Lee County										
City of Cape Coral	179,631	224	5	16	31	172	3,081	632	2,286	163
City of Fort Myers	76,579	947	15	55	161	716	2,163	354	1,589	220
Total area actually reporting	100.0%	2,562	41	249	445	1,827	11,637	2,459	8,359	819
Rate per 100,000 inhabitants		355.4	5.7	34.5	61.7	253.4	1,614.1	341.1	1,159.4	113.6
Cape Girardeau, MO-IL M.S.A.	97,631									
Includes Alexander County, IL and Bollinger and Cape Girardeau Counties, MO										
City of Cape Girardeau, MO	39,738	236	5	10	54	167	1,628	227	1,332	69
Total area actually reporting	100.0%	469	6	21	72	370	2,342	396	1,841	105
Rate per 100,000 inhabitants		480.4	6.1	21.5	73.7	379.0	2,398.8	405.6	1,885.7	107.5
Carson City, NV M.S.A.	54,605									
Includes Carson City										
Total area actually reporting	100.0%	157	1	3	20	133	995	211	698	86
Rate per 100,000 inhabitants		287.5	1.8	5.5	36.6	243.6	1,822.2	386.4	1,278.3	157.5
Casper, WY M.S.A.	82,870									
Includes Natrona County										
City of Casper	61,343	70	0	2	7	61	1,669	255	1,297	117
Total area actually reporting	100.0%	168	0	23	12	133	2,081	389	1,535	157
Rate per 100,000 inhabitants		202.7	0.0	27.8	14.5	160.5	2,511.2	469.4	1,852.3	189.5
Cedar Rapids, IA M.S.A.[5]	267,187									
Includes Benton, Jones, and Linn Counties										
City of Cedar Rapids	131,181	387	4	67	100	216	5,019	995	3,670	354
Total area actually reporting	94.9%	566	5	96	114	351			4,512	456
Estimated total	100.0%	589	5	100	115	369			4,587	468
Rate per 100,000 inhabitants		220.4	1.9	37.4	43.0	138.1			1,716.8	175.2
Chambersburg-Waynesboro, PA M.S.A.	153,940									
Includes Franklin County										
City of Chambersburg	20,770	87	2	14	27	44	630	83	527	20
City of Waynesboro	10,902	29	6	6	6	11	266	43	211	12
Total area actually reporting	100.0%	221	13	52	56	100	2,281	444	1,763	74
Rate per 100,000 inhabitants		143.6	8.4	33.8	36.4	65.0	1,481.7	288.4	1,145.3	48.1
Champaign-Urbana, IL M.S.A.	239,184									
Includes Champaign, Ford, and Piatt Counties										

Table 4. Crime, by Selected Metropolitan Statistical Area, 2016—*Continued*

(Number, percent, rate per 100,000 population.)

Area	Population	Violent crime	Murder and nonnegligent manslaughter	Rape[1]	Robbery	Aggravated assault	Property crime	Burglary	Larceny-theft	Motor vehicle theft
City of Champaign......	87,071	625	3	41	124	457	2,838	728	1,979	131
City of Urbana	42,461	162	4	25	54	79	1,543	327	1,185	31
Total area actually reporting	99.0%	1,048	11	125	214	698	6,108	1,506	4,367	235
Estimated total......	100.0%	1,053	11	126	215	701	6,147	1,512	4,398	237
Rate per 100,000 inhabitants......		440.2	4.6	52.7	89.9	293.1	2,570.0	632.1	1,838.8	99.1
Charleston, WV M.S.A.	218,036									
Includes Boone, Clay, and Kanawha Counties										
City of Charleston......	49,429	767	13	36	152	566	3,939	947	2,694	298
Total area actually reporting	91.6%	1,293	17	90	205	981	8,585	2,061	5,708	816
Estimated total......	100.0%	1,341	17	96	210	1,018	9,056	2,157	6,052	847
Rate per 100,000 inhabitants......		615.0	7.8	44.0	96.3	466.9	4,153.4	989.3	2,775.7	388.5
Charleston-North Charleston, SC M.S.A.	762,454									
Includes Berkeley, Charleston, and Dorchester Counties										
City of Charleston......	135,153	408	11	44	107	246	3,359	417	2,681	261
City of North Charleston......	110,490	993	32	89	293	579	6,218	918	4,655	645
Total area actually reporting	99.5%	3,170	72	250	667	2,181	21,566	3,651	15,963	1,952
Estimated total......	100.0%	3,188	72	252	670	2,194	21,699	3,670	16,068	1,961
Rate per 100,000 inhabitants......		418.1	9.4	33.1	87.9	287.8	2,845.9	481.3	2,107.4	257.2
Charlottesville, VA M.S.A.	230,398									
Includes Albemarle, Buckingham, Fluvanna, Greene, and Nelson Counties and Charlottesville City										
City of Charlottesville......	46,979	245	1	36	43	165	1,228	170	983	75
Total area actually reporting	100.0%	457	3	89	80	285	3,369	446	2,738	185
Rate per 100,000 inhabitants......		198.4	1.3	38.6	34.7	123.7	1,462.3	193.6	1,188.4	80.3
Chattanooga, TN-GA M.S.A.	551,407									
Includes Catoosa, Dade, and Walker Counties, GA and Hamilton, Marion, and Sequatchie Counties, TN										
City of Chattanooga, TN......	177,801	1,819	26	111	375	1,307	9,752	1,570	7,122	1,060
Total area actually reporting	97.5%	2,938	32	208	493	2,205	17,576	3,081	12,685	1,810
Estimated total......	100.0%	2,982	33	211	506	2,232	17,926	3,160	12,921	1,845
Rate per 100,000 inhabitants......		540.8	6.0	38.3	91.8	404.8	3,251.0	573.1	2,343.3	334.6
Cheyenne, WY M.S.A.	97,275									
Includes Laramie County										
City of Cheyenne......	64,046	172	5	26	15	126	2,427	356	1,873	198
Total area actually reporting	100.0%	245	8	36	18	183	2,939	477	2,204	258
Rate per 100,000 inhabitants......		251.9	8.2	37.0	18.5	188.1	3,021.3	490.4	2,265.7	265.2
Chicago-Naperville-Elgin, IL-IN-WI M.S.A.[3]	9,523,022									
Includes the Metropolitan Divisions of Chicago-Naperville-Arlington Heights, IL; Elgin, IL; Gary, IN; and Lake County-Kenosha County, IL-WI										
City of Chicago, IL......	2,725,153	30,126	765	1,589	11,957	15,815	86,960	14,258	61,229	11,473
City of Naperville, IL......	148,070	92	0	15	34	43	1,587	141	1,401	45
City of Elgin, IL......	112,886	236	2	34	63	137	1,565	218	1,279	68
City of Gary, IN......	76,556	460	46	32	212	170	3,617	990	2,229	398
City of Arlington Heights, IL......	76,077	58	0	8	14	36	722	79	624	19
City of Evanston, IL......	75,716	130	2	6	38	84	1,671	329	1,269	73
City of Schaumburg, IL......	74,774	74	0	23	21	30	1,685	108	1,526	51
City of Skokie, IL......	64,819	158	1	15	45	97	1,557	228	1,283	46
City of Des Plaines, IL......	58,726	45	0	6	11	28	537	91	423	23
City of Hoffman Estates, IL......	52,177	55	0	11	15	29	429	52	353	24
Total area actually reporting	96.9%	41,539	958	3,088	15,723	21,770	192,468	30,652	144,323	17,493
Estimated total......	100.0%	42,187	967	3,162	15,887	22,171	198,228	31,492	148,887	17,849
Rate per 100,000 inhabitants......		443.0	10.2	33.2	166.8	232.8	2,081.6	330.7	1,563.4	187.4
Chicago-Naperville-Arlington Heights, IL M.D.[3]	7,318,619									
Includes Cook, DuPage, Grundy, Kendall, McHenry, and Will Counties										
Total area actually reporting	98.0%	37,221	867	2,546	14,474	19,334	156,027	24,872	115,796	15,359
Estimated total......	100.0%	37,530	871	2,588	14,561	19,510	158,528	25,263	117,778	15,487
Rate per 100,000 inhabitants......		512.8	11.9	35.4	199.0	266.6	2,166.1	345.2	1,609.3	211.6
Elgin, IL M.D.	634,927									
Includes DeKalb and Kane Counties										
Total area actually reporting	98.3%	1,202	14	215	218	755	8,755	1,214	7,232	309

Table 4. Crime, by Selected Metropolitan Statistical Area, 2016—*Continued*

(Number, percent, rate per 100,000 population.)

Area	Population	Violent crime	Murder and nonnegligent manslaughter	Rape[1]	Robbery	Aggravated assault	Property crime	Burglary	Larceny-theft	Motor vehicle theft
Estimated total............................	100.0%	1,225	14	218	225	768	8,943	1,243	7,381	319
Rate per 100,000 inhabitants.........................		192.9	2.2	34.3	35.4	121.0	1,408.5	195.8	1,162.5	50.2
Gary, IN M.D.	700,547									
Includes Jasper, Lake, Newton, and Porter Counties										
Total area actually reporting	84.6%	1,652	70	135	605	842	15,338	2,597	11,388	1,353
Estimated total............................	100.0%	1,908	74	156	658	1,020	17,918	2,940	13,432	1,546
Rate per 100,000 inhabitants.........................		272.4	10.6	22.3	93.9	145.6	2,557.7	419.7	1,917.4	220.7
Lake County-Kenosha County, IL-WI M.D.	868,929									
Includes Lake County, IL and Kenosha County, WI										
Total area actually reporting	96.7%	1,464	7	192	426	839	12,348	1,969	9,907	472
Estimated total............................	100.0%	1,524	8	200	443	873	12,839	2,046	10,296	497
Rate per 100,000 inhabitants.........................		175.4	0.9	23.0	51.0	100.5	1,477.6	235.5	1,184.9	57.2
Chico, CA M.S.A.	224,973									
Includes Butte County										
City of Chico................................	91,122	293	0	66	57	170	3,290	499	2,336	455
Total area actually reporting	100.0%	790	4	133	138	515	7,307	1,755	4,531	1,021
Rate per 100,000 inhabitants.........................		351.2	1.8	59.1	61.3	228.9	3,247.9	780.1	2,014.0	453.8
Cincinnati, OH-KY-IN M.S.A.	2,163,182									
Includes Dearborn, Ohio, and Union Counties, IN; Boone, Bracken, Campbell, Gallatin, Grant, Kenton, and Pendleton Counties, KY; and Brown, Butler, Clermont, Hamilton, and Warren Counties, OH										
City of Cincinnati, OH	298,880	2,720	57	249	1,278	1,136	15,382	3,929	10,216	1,237
Total area actually reporting	94.2%	5,377	98	856	2,164	2,259	54,312	10,956	40,542	2,814
Estimated total............................	100.0%	5,566	101	889	2,213	2,363	56,602	11,377	42,278	2,947
Rate per 100,000 inhabitants.........................		257.3	4.7	41.1	102.3	109.2	2,616.6	525.9	1,954.4	136.2
Clarksville, TN-KY M.S.A.	285,097									
Includes Christian and Trigg Counties, KY and Montgomery County, TN										
City of Clarksville, TN.....................	152,526	935	12	74	131	718	3,853	711	2,960	182
Total area actually reporting	100.0%	1,219	19	115	202	883	6,311	1,283	4,689	339
Rate per 100,000 inhabitants.........................		427.6	6.7	40.3	70.9	309.7	2,213.6	450.0	1,644.7	118.9
Cleveland, TN M.S.A.	121,862									
Includes Bradley and Polk Counties										
City of Cleveland	44,423	384	2	14	50	318	2,704	406	2,044	254
Total area actually reporting	100.0%	624	3	24	64	533	4,102	811	2,867	424
Rate per 100,000 inhabitants.........................		512.1	2.5	19.7	52.5	437.4	3,366.1	665.5	2,352.7	347.9
Cleveland-Elyria, OH M.S.A.	2,055,254									
Includes Cuyahoga, Geauga, Lake, Lorain, and Medina Counties										
City of Cleveland	386,227	6,299	135	488	2,980	2,696	20,533	6,333	10,001	4,199
City of Elyria	53,633	161	4	26	71	60	1,483	344	1,042	97
Total area actually reporting	85.3%	8,691	181	803	3,852	3,855	42,264	10,504	26,216	5,544
Estimated total............................	100.0%	9,156	189	900	4,009	4,058	48,994	11,617	31,555	5,822
Rate per 100,000 inhabitants.........................		445.5	9.2	43.8	195.1	197.4	2,383.8	565.2	1,535.3	283.3
Coeur d'Alene, ID M.S.A.	153,701									
Includes Kootenai County										
City of Coeur d'Alene	50,155	173	1	48	13	111	1,418	200	1,129	89
Total area actually reporting	100.0%	356	7	74	27	248	3,568	724	2,641	203
Rate per 100,000 inhabitants.........................		231.6	4.6	48.1	17.6	161.4	2,321.4	471.0	1,718.3	132.1
College Station-Bryan, TX M.S.A.	252,572									
Includes Brazos, Burleson, and Robertson Counties										
City of College Station	110,785	245	3	52	50	140	2,290	342	1,840	108
City of Bryan	83,286	420	1	59	96	264	2,552	511	1,899	142
Total area actually reporting	99.5%	833	5	149	162	517	5,969	1,108	4,557	304
Estimated total............................	100.0%	837	5	150	163	519	6,002	1,113	4,583	306
Rate per 100,000 inhabitants.........................		331.4	2.0	59.4	64.5	205.5	2,376.4	440.7	1,814.5	121.2
Colorado Springs, CO M.S.A.	707,431									
Includes El Paso and Teller Counties										
City of Colorado Springs.................	464,113	2,301	24	446	437	1,394	16,526	2,677	11,776	2,073
Total area actually reporting	99.9%	2,861	32	575	483	1,771	20,132	3,248	14,421	2,463

Table 4. Crime, by Selected Metropolitan Statistical Area, 2016—*Continued*

(Number, percent, rate per 100,000 population.)

Area	Population	Violent crime	Murder and nonnegligent manslaughter	Rape[1]	Robbery	Aggravated assault	Property crime	Burglary	Larceny-theft	Motor vehicle theft
Estimated total..........................	100.0%	2,862	32	575	483	1,772	20,150	3,250	14,435	2,465
Rate per 100,000 inhabitants..................		404.6	4.5	81.3	68.3	250.5	2,848.3	459.4	2,040.5	348.4
Columbia, MO M.S.A.	177,168									
Includes Boone County										
City of Columbia..............................	121,143	517	6	111	127	273	3,245	530	2,469	246
Total area actually reporting	100.0%	674	6	132	138	398	4,230	693	3,217	320
Rate per 100,000 inhabitants..................		380.4	3.4	74.5	77.9	224.6	2,387.6	391.2	1,815.8	180.6
Columbia, SC M.S.A.	820,037									
Includes Calhoun, Fairfield, Kershaw, Lexington, Richland, and Saluda Counties										
City of Columbia..............................	134,489	1,116	10	99	286	721	7,374	1,114	5,357	903
Total area actually reporting	100.0%	4,834	58	399	849	3,528	28,907	5,013	20,633	3,261
Rate per 100,000 inhabitants..................		589.5	7.1	48.7	103.5	430.2	3,525.1	611.3	2,516.1	397.7
Columbus, GA-AL M.S.A.	316,990									
Includes Russell County, AL and Chattahoochee, Harris, Marion, and Muscogee Counties, GA										
City of Columbus, GA........................	202,338	1,218	24	62	523	609	9,625	2,273	6,500	852
Total area actually reporting	99.8%	1,639	33	123	601	882	12,060	2,940	7,996	1,124
Estimated total..........................	100.0%	1,643	33	123	602	885	12,080	2,944	8,011	1,125
Rate per 100,000 inhabitants..................		518.3	10.4	38.8	189.9	279.2	3,810.8	928.7	2,527.2	354.9
Columbus, IN M.S.A.	81,884									
Includes Bartholomew County										
City of Columbus..............................	47,222	34	0	15	17	2	1,943	180	1,657	106
Total area actually reporting	100.0%	67	0	21	20	26	2,511	326	2,010	175
Rate per 100,000 inhabitants..................		81.8	0.0	25.6	24.4	31.8	3,066.5	398.1	2,454.7	213.7
Columbus, OH M.S.A.[3]	2,043,036									
Includes Delaware, Fairfield, Franklin, Hocking, Licking, Madison, Morrow, Perry, Pickaway, and Union Counties										
City of Columbus..............................	862,515	4,500	91	867	2,144	1,398	35,106	7,756	23,800	3,550
Total area actually reporting	91.3%	5,585	104	1,166	2,489	1,826	56,162	11,472	40,424	4,266
Estimated total..........................	100.0%	5,820	107	1,219	2,555	1,939	59,476	12,144	42,917	4,415
Rate per 100,000 inhabitants..................		284.9	5.2	59.7	125.1	94.9	2,911.2	594.4	2,100.6	216.1
Corpus Christi, TX M.S.A.....................	456,121									
Includes Aransas, Nueces, and San Patricio Counties										
City of Corpus Christi........................	327,948	2,328	24	259	424	1,621	12,198	2,296	9,246	656
Total area actually reporting	97.9%	2,981	35	306	458	2,182	16,035	3,264	11,933	838
Estimated total..........................	100.0%	3,007	35	310	464	2,198	16,273	3,302	12,116	855
Rate per 100,000 inhabitants..................		659.3	7.7	68.0	101.7	481.9	3,567.7	723.9	2,656.3	187.5
Corvallis, OR M.S.A.	88,515									
Includes Benton County										
City of Corvallis..............................	56,061	75	1	25	11	38	1,557	207	1,283	67
Total area actually reporting	100.0%	113	1	35	14	63	2,256	287	1,869	100
Rate per 100,000 inhabitants..................		127.7	1.1	39.5	15.8	71.2	2,548.7	324.2	2,111.5	113.0
Crestview-Fort Walton Beach-Destin, FL M.S.A.	268,298									
Includes Okaloosa and Walton Counties										
City of Crestview	23,749	121	3	20	19	79	897	157	678	62
City of Fort Walton Beach	22,314	67	3	12	10	42	611	72	490	49
Total area actually reporting	99.7%	1,023	14	126	96	787	6,303	1,184	4,759	360
Estimated total..........................	100.0%	1,026	14	126	97	789	6,328	1,188	4,778	362
Rate per 100,000 inhabitants..................		382.4	5.2	47.0	36.2	294.1	2,358.6	442.8	1,780.9	134.9
Cumberland, MD-WV M.S.A..............................	98,752									
Includes Allegany County, MD and Mineral County, WV										
City of Cumberland, MD....................	19,995	177	1	13	53	110	1,218	247	949	22
Total area actually reporting	94.7%	299	6	23	70	200	2,333	457	1,821	55
Estimated total..........................	100.0%	314	6	25	72	211	2,514	487	1,962	65
Rate per 100,000 inhabitants..................		318.0	6.1	25.3	72.9	213.7	2,545.8	493.2	1,986.8	65.8
Dallas-Fort Worth-Arlington, TX M.S.A.[3].........................	7,219,989									
Includes the Metropolitan Divisions of Dallas-Plano-Irving and Fort Worth-Arlington										
City of Dallas.................................	1,320,939	10,071	171	767	4,604	4,529	44,910	10,948	26,370	7,592

Table 4. Crime, by Selected Metropolitan Statistical Area, 2016—*Continued*

(Number, percent, rate per 100,000 population.)

Area	Population	Violent crime	Murder and nonnegligent manslaughter	Rape[1]	Robbery	Aggravated assault	Property crime	Burglary	Larceny-theft	Motor vehicle theft
City of Fort Worth	851,849	4,483	66	499	1,165	2,753	28,124	5,316	20,422	2,386
City of Arlington	392,666	2,188	21	307	557	1,303	12,383	2,115	9,189	1,079
City of Plano	288,242	399	5	77	109	208	5,479	903	4,181	395
City of Irving	240,765	521	5	37	213	266	6,490	1,183	4,674	633
City of Denton	134,054	349	5	95	73	176	3,025	543	2,313	169
City of Richardson	113,216	156	5	16	71	64	2,473	389	1,874	210
Total area actually reporting	99.8%	25,941	368	3,156	8,962	13,455	178,513	34,697	124,766	19,050
Estimated total	100.0%	25,971	368	3,160	8,970	13,473	178,781	34,740	124,971	19,070
Rate per 100,000 inhabitants		359.7	5.1	43.8	124.2	186.6	2,476.2	481.2	1,730.9	264.1
Dallas-Plano-Irving, TX M.D.	4,791,249									
Includes Collin, Dallas, Denton, Ellis, Hunt, Kaufman, and Rockwall Counties										
Total area actually reporting	99.8%	17,064	250	1,922	6,762	8,130	115,705	23,345	78,386	13,974
Estimated total	100.0%	17,092	250	1,926	6,769	8,147	115,952	23,385	78,575	13,992
Rate per 100,000 inhabitants		356.7	5.2	40.2	141.3	170.0	2,420.1	488.1	1,640.0	292.0
Fort Worth-Arlington, TX M.D.[3]	2,428,740									
Includes Hood, Johnson, Parker, Somervell, Tarrant, and Wise Counties										
Total area actually reporting	99.9%	8,877	118	1,234	2,200	5,325	62,808	11,352	46,380	5,076
Estimated total	100.0%	8,879	118	1,234	2,201	5,326	62,829	11,355	46,396	5,078
Rate per 100,000 inhabitants		365.6	4.9	50.8	90.6	219.3	2,586.9	467.5	1,910.3	209.1
Dalton, GA M.S.A.	143,925									
Includes Murray and Whitfield Counties										
City of Dalton	33,989	113	0	17	22	74	1,103	209	834	60
Total area actually reporting	99.6%	988	0	158	67	763	4,880	1,178	3,176	526
Estimated total	100.0%	991	0	158	68	765	4,905	1,182	3,195	528
Rate per 100,000 inhabitants		688.6	0.0	109.8	47.2	531.5	3,408.0	821.3	2,219.9	366.9
Danville, IL M.S.A.	78,439									
Includes Vermilion County										
City of Danville	31,931	502	0	47	88	367	1,894	646	1,185	63
Total area actually reporting	98.4%	631	0	74	98	459	2,720	913	1,711	96
Estimated total	100.0%	634	0	74	99	461	2,741	916	1,728	97
Rate per 100,000 inhabitants		808.3	0.0	94.3	126.2	587.7	3,494.4	1,167.8	2,203.0	123.7
Davenport-Moline-Rock Island, IA-IL M.S.A.[5]	383,016									
Includes Henry, Mercer, and Rock Island Counties, IL and Scott County, IA										
City of Davenport, IA	103,118	750	7	88	155	500	5,001	1,155	3,436	410
City of Moline, IL	42,517	196	0	26	19	151	1,459	227	1,205	27
City of Rock Island, IL	38,543	158	4	6	23	125	1,042	175	782	85
Total area actually reporting	98.6%	1,496	12	185	238	1,061			7,660	602
Estimated total	100.0%	1,506	12	186	240	1,068			7,733	607
Rate per 100,000 inhabitants		393.2	3.1	48.6	62.7	278.8			2,019.0	158.5
Dayton, OH M.S.A.[3]	800,013									
Includes Greene, Miami, and Montgomery Counties										
City of Dayton	140,260	1,402	36	133	496	737	7,235	2,269	4,252	714
Total area actually reporting	96.9%	2,453	62	443	847	1,101	22,891	5,289	15,936	1,666
Estimated total	100.0%	2,491	63	451	860	1,117	23,434	5,379	16,367	1,688
Rate per 100,000 inhabitants		311.4	7.9	56.4	107.5	139.6	2,929.2	672.4	2,045.8	211.0
Decatur, AL M.S.A.	152,077									
Includes Lawrence and Morgan Counties										
City of Decatur	55,374	154	5	9	43	97	2,600	526	1,918	156
Total area actually reporting	99.3%	346	5	29	53	259	3,812	909	2,660	243
Estimated total	100.0%	352	5	29	54	264	3,848	916	2,686	246
Rate per 100,000 inhabitants		231.5	3.3	19.1	35.5	173.6	2,530.3	602.3	1,766.2	161.8
Decatur, IL M.S.A.	106,100									
Includes Macon County										
City of Decatur	72,694	392	3	45	97	247	2,657	859	1,700	98
Total area actually reporting	99.0%	434	3	52	103	276	2,954	926	1,928	100

Table 4. Crime, by Selected Metropolitan Statistical Area, 2016—*Continued*

(Number, percent, rate per 100,000 population.)

Area	Population	Violent crime	Murder and nonnegligent manslaughter	Rape[1]	Robbery	Aggravated assault	Property crime	Burglary	Larceny-theft	Motor vehicle theft
Estimated total..............................	100.0%	436	3	52	104	277	2,973	929	1,943	101
Rate per 100,000 inhabitants......................		410.9	2.8	49.0	98.0	261.1	2,802.1	875.6	1,831.3	95.2
Deltona-Daytona Beach-Ormond Beach, FL M.S.A...........	631,296									
Includes Flagler and Volusia Counties										
City of Daytona Beach	65,495	814	9	26	94	685	4,197	572	3,234	391
City of Ormond Beach	41,325	202	0	17	40	145	1,602	312	1,158	132
Total area actually reporting	100.0%	2,471	19	168	369	1,915	18,058	3,102	13,650	1,306
Rate per 100,000 inhabitants......................		391.4	3.0	26.6	58.5	303.3	2,860.5	491.4	2,162.2	206.9
Denver-Aurora-Lakewood, CO M.S.A...............	2,868,232									
Includes Adams, Arapahoe, Broomfield, Clear Creek, Denver, Douglas, Elbert, Gilpin, Jefferson, and Park Counties										
City of Denver..................................	699,259	4,597	57	567	1,160	2,813	25,101	4,675	15,638	4,788
City of Aurora.................................	366,477	1,939	22	289	576	1,052	11,213	1,698	7,977	1,538
City of Lakewood............................	154,553	875	4	144	174	553	8,455	1,014	6,429	1,012
City of Broomfield..........................	66,953	36	0	16	2	18	1,610	216	1,236	158
Total area actually reporting	99.9%	11,149	124	1,919	2,470	6,636	84,650	12,492	58,890	13,268
Estimated total..............................	100.0%	11,156	124	1,921	2,471	6,640	84,729	12,501	58,950	13,278
Rate per 100,000 inhabitants......................		389.0	4.3	67.0	86.2	231.5	2,954.0	435.8	2,055.3	462.9
Des Moines-West Des Moines, IA M.S.A.[4]........	632,763									
Includes Dallas, Guthrie, Madison, Polk, and Warren Counties										
City of Des Moines..........................	211,501	1,497	13	140	318	1,026	8,881	1,944	5,920	1,017
City of West Des Moines.................	65,631	149	1	24	19	105	1,513	147	1,296	70
Total area actually reporting	100.0%	2,352	25	267	386	1,674		3,458		1,442
Rate per 100,000 inhabitants......................		371.7	4.0	42.2	61.0	264.6		546.5		227.9
Detroit-Warren-Dearborn, MI M.S.A.	4,302,722									
Includes the Metropolitan Divisions of Detroit-Dearborn-Livonia and Warren-Troy-Farmington Hills										
City of Detroit.................................	669,673	13,705	303	579	2,941	9,882	31,630	8,787	13,938	8,905
City of Warren................................	135,620	691	6	118	125	442	3,521	927	2,082	512
City of Dearborn............................	94,646	348	1	30	80	237	2,791	297	2,167	327
City of Livonia...............................	94,226	141	0	18	28	95	1,694	295	1,250	149
City of Troy....................................	83,743	78	1	12	16	49	1,336	94	1,183	59
City of Farmington Hills.................	81,649	77	0	18	9	50	1,050	145	834	71
City of Southfield...........................	73,438	195	3	44	52	96	2,158	353	1,514	291
City of Taylor.................................	61,290	372	2	37	83	250	1,495	290	1,042	163
City of Pontiac...............................	60,003	749	15	66	121	547	1,425	520	771	134
City of Novi...................................	59,441	32	0	6	2	24	661	56	586	19
Total area actually reporting	99.9%	23,903	389	2,141	4,653	16,720	89,693	18,887	56,067	14,739
Estimated total..............................	100.0%	23,907	389	2,142	4,654	16,722	89,714	18,890	56,083	14,741
Rate per 100,000 inhabitants......................		555.6	9.0	49.8	108.2	388.6	2,085.1	439.0	1,303.4	342.6
Detroit-Dearborn-Livonia, MI M.D...................	1,747,582									
Includes Wayne County										
Total area actually reporting	100.0%	18,073	339	1,104	3,860	12,770	54,744	12,845	30,153	11,746
Rate per 100,000 inhabitants......................		1,034.2	19.4	63.2	220.9	730.7	3,132.6	735.0	1,725.4	672.1
Warren-Troy-Farmington Hills, MI M.D.	2,555,140									
Includes Lapeer, Livingston, Macomb, Oakland, and St. Clair Counties										
Total area actually reporting	99.9%	5,830	50	1,037	793	3,950	34,949	6,042	25,914	2,993
Estimated total..............................	100.0%	5,834	50	1,038	794	3,952	34,970	6,045	25,930	2,995
Rate per 100,000 inhabitants......................		228.3	2.0	40.6	31.1	154.7	1,368.6	236.6	1,014.8	117.2
Dothan, AL M.S.A.[5]	148,284									
Includes Geneva, Henry, and Houston Counties										
City of Dothan4...............................	67,835		5	35	79		2,758	669	1,928	161
Total area actually reporting	99.4%		10	74	95		4,221	1,072	2,869	280
Estimated total..............................	100.0%		10	74	96		4,248	1,077	2,889	282
Rate per 100,000 inhabitants......................			6.7	49.9	64.7		2,864.8	726.3	1,948.3	190.2
Dover, DE M.S.A.	175,090									
Includes Kent County										

Table 4. Crime, by Selected Metropolitan Statistical Area, 2016—*Continued*

(Number, percent, rate per 100,000 population.)

Area	Population	Violent crime	Murder and nonnegligent manslaughter	Rape[1]	Robbery	Aggravated assault	Property crime	Burglary	Larceny-theft	Motor vehicle theft
City of Dover	37,824	307	2	12	57	236	1,880	100	1,699	81
Total area actually reporting	100.0%	829	6	64	156	603	4,399	652	3,579	168
Rate per 100,000 inhabitants..................		473.5	3.4	36.6	89.1	344.4	2,512.4	372.4	2,044.1	96.0
Dubuque, IA M.S.A.	97,625									
Includes Dubuque County										
City of Dubuque	59,026	210	1	52	26	131	1,832	408	1,349	75
Total area actually reporting	100.0%	237	2	58	28	149	2,054	485	1,477	92
Rate per 100,000 inhabitants..................		242.8	2.0	59.4	28.7	152.6	2,104.0	496.8	1,512.9	94.2
Duluth, MN-WI M.S.A.	279,220									
Includes Carlton and St. Louis Counties, MN and Douglas County, WI										
City of Duluth, MN	86,090	312	1	51	64	196	3,827	529	3,162	136
Total area actually reporting	100.0%	642	3	126	92	421	8,915	1,374	7,124	417
Rate per 100,000 inhabitants..................		229.9	1.1	45.1	32.9	150.8	3,192.8	492.1	2,551.4	149.3
East Stroudsburg, PA M.S.A.	165,226									
Includes Monroe County										
Total area actually reporting	100.0%	416	10	73	80	253	3,130	632	2,403	95
Rate per 100,000 inhabitants..................		251.8	6.1	44.2	48.4	153.1	1,894.4	382.5	1,454.4	57.5
Eau Claire, WI M.S.A.[3]	166,178									
Includes Chippewa and Eau Claire Counties										
City of Eau Claire	68,084	141	1	18	17	105	1,818	277	1,481	60
Total area actually reporting	100.0%	230	5	38	20	167	2,788	493	2,187	108
Rate per 100,000 inhabitants..................		138.4	3.0	22.9	12.0	100.5	1,677.7	296.7	1,316.1	65.0
El Centro, CA M.S.A.	180,066									
Includes Imperial County										
City of El Centro	44,213	205	1	19	55	130	2,314	506	1,669	139
Total area actually reporting	95.9%	676	3	34	118	521	5,195	1,165	3,483	547
Estimated total..........................	100.0%	701	3	36	126	536	5,372	1,199	3,597	576
Rate per 100,000 inhabitants..................		389.3	1.7	20.0	70.0	297.7	2,983.4	665.9	1,997.6	319.9
Elizabethtown-Fort Knox, KY M.S.A.	148,206									
Includes Hardin, Larue, and Meade Counties										
City of Elizabethtown......................	29,821	68	2	15	17	34	476	107	329	40
Total area actually reporting	100.0%	181	3	40	52	86	1,479	406	945	128
Rate per 100,000 inhabitants..................		122.1	2.0	27.0	35.1	58.0	997.9	273.9	637.6	86.4
Elmira, NY M.S.A.	86,124									
Includes Chemung County										
City of Elmira	27,995	97	2	2	34	59	1,074	172	875	27
Total area actually reporting	100.0%	172	3	28	38	103	1,892	270	1,577	45
Rate per 100,000 inhabitants..................		199.7	3.5	32.5	44.1	119.6	2,196.8	313.5	1,831.1	52.3
El Paso, TX M.S.A.	843,018									
Includes El Paso and Hudspeth Counties										
City of El Paso...........................	687,193	2,682	17	314	476	1,875	12,357	1,410	10,135	812
Total area actually reporting	99.9%	3,076	23	378	520	2,155	14,413	1,784	11,696	933
Estimated total..........................	100.0%	3,080	23	379	521	2,157	14,442	1,789	11,718	935
Rate per 100,000 inhabitants..................		365.4	2.7	45.0	61.8	255.9	1,713.1	212.2	1,390.0	110.9
Enid, OK M.S.A.	63,828									
Includes Garfield County										
City of Enid.............................	52,240	214	2	29	27	156	2,041	474	1,489	78
Total area actually reporting	100.0%	233	2	35	27	169	2,220	533	1,590	97
Rate per 100,000 inhabitants..................		365.0	3.1	54.8	42.3	264.8	3,478.1	835.1	2,491.1	152.0
Erie, PA M.S.A.	276,700									
Includes Erie County										
City of Erie..............................	99,019	353	10	46	115	182	2,278	567	1,607	104
Total area actually reporting	100.0%	594	11	100	157	326	5,307	1,077	4,052	178
Rate per 100,000 inhabitants..................		214.7	4.0	36.1	56.7	117.8	1,918.0	389.2	1,464.4	64.3
Eugene, OR M.S.A.[3]	367,343									
Includes Lane County										
City of Eugene...........................	164,883	602	6	95	137	364	6,317	1,062	4,622	633
Total area actually reporting	99.1%	1,172	7	174	208	783	12,137	1,994	9,114	1,029

(Number, percent, rate per 100,000 population.)

Area	Population	Violent crime	Murder and nonnegligent manslaughter	Rape[1]	Robbery	Aggravated assault	Property crime	Burglary	Larceny-theft	Motor vehicle theft
Estimated total..	100.0%	1,178	7	175	209	787	12,222	2,004	9,181	1,037
Rate per 100,000 inhabitants...........................		320.7	1.9	47.6	56.9	214.2	3,327.1	545.5	2,499.3	282.3
Evansville, IN-KY M.S.A.	315,875									
Includes Posey, Vanderburgh, and Warrick Counties, IN and										
Henderson County, KY										
City of Evansville..	119,908	762	8	75	210	469	5,881	1,008	4,490	383
Total area actually reporting	97.9%	1,127	11	106	253	757	8,462	1,556	6,375	531
Estimated total...	100.0%	1,144	11	107	257	769	8,644	1,577	6,523	544
Rate per 100,000 inhabitants...........................		362.2	3.5	33.9	81.4	243.5	2,736.5	499.2	2,065.1	172.2
Fairbanks, AK M.S.A.	34,657									
Includes Fairbanks North Star Borough										
City of Fairbanks..	32,456	223	7	31	31	154	1,350	157	1,069	124
Total area actually reporting	100.0%	232	7	35	32	158	1,517	173	1,207	137
Rate per 100,000 inhabitants...........................		669.4	20.2	101.0	92.3	455.9	4,377.2	499.2	3,482.7	395.3
Fargo, ND-MN M.S.A.......................................	234,910									
Includes Clay County, MN and Cass County, ND										
City of Fargo, ND..	121,217	467	3	79	68	317	3,843	566	2,962	315
Total area actually reporting	100.0%	635	5	135	91	404	5,807	974	4,337	496
Rate per 100,000 inhabitants...........................		270.3	2.1	57.5	38.7	172.0	2,472.0	414.6	1,846.2	211.1
Farmington, NM M.S.A....................................	116,108									
Includes San Juan County										
City of Farmington..	42,270	293	1	70	52	170	1,857	332	1,354	171
Total area actually reporting	100.0%	1,100	2	128	68	902	3,174	729	2,168	277
Rate per 100,000 inhabitants...........................		947.4	1.7	110.2	58.6	776.9	2,733.7	627.9	1,867.2	238.6
Fayetteville, NC M.S.A.	378,409									
Includes Cumberland and Hoke Counties										
City of Fayetteville..	202,200	1,531	33	99	316	1,083	9,201	1,868	6,942	391
Total area actually reporting	100.0%	1,982	44	123	415	1,400	13,168	3,052	9,577	539
Rate per 100,000 inhabitants...........................		523.8	11.6	32.5	109.7	370.0	3,479.8	806.5	2,530.9	142.4
Flagstaff, AZ M.S.A........................................	140,312									
Includes Coconino County										
City of Flagstaff	71,179	265	0	26	30	209	2,856	255	2,542	59
Total area actually reporting	100.0%	512	3	72	43	394	4,197	478	3,614	105
Rate per 100,000 inhabitants...........................		364.9	2.1	51.3	30.6	280.8	2,991.2	340.7	2,575.7	74.8
Flint, MI M.S.A....	407,879									
Includes Genesee County..................................										
City of Flint..	97,548	1,545	45	96	249	1,155	3,323	1,213	1,867	243
Total area actually reporting	100.0%	2,562	54	299	391	1,818	9,083	2,420	6,047	616
Rate per 100,000 inhabitants...........................		628.1	13.2	73.3	95.9	445.7	2,226.9	593.3	1,482.5	151.0
Florence, SC M.S.A.	207,007									
Includes Darlington and Florence Counties										
City of Florence..	38,382	408	1	20	73	314	2,563	407	2,026	130
Total area actually reporting	99.4%	1,320	14	102	222	982	8,787	2,207	6,028	552
Estimated total...	100.0%	1,326	14	103	223	986	8,834	2,214	6,065	555
Rate per 100,000 inhabitants...........................		640.6	6.8	49.8	107.7	476.3	4,267.5	1,069.5	2,929.9	268.1
Florence-Muscle Shoals, AL M.S.A.	146,537									
Includes Colbert and Lauderdale Counties										
City of Florence..	40,160	196	2	19	46	129	1,400	242	1,052	106
City of Muscle Shoals.......................................	13,810	54	0	5	6	43	588	108	443	37
Total area actually reporting	99.8%	428	4	42	72	310	3,197	640	2,275	282
Estimated total...	100.0%	429	4	42	72	311	3,207	642	2,282	283
Rate per 100,000 inhabitants...........................		292.8	2.7	28.7	49.1	212.2	2,188.5	438.1	1,557.3	193.1
Fond du Lac, WI M.S.A.	101,860									
Includes Fond du Lac County										
City of Fond du Lac...	42,907	136	1	38	12	85	957	75	858	24
Total area actually reporting	100.0%	184	1	52	13	118	1,377	149	1,180	48
Rate per 100,000 inhabitants...........................		180.6	1.0	51.1	12.8	115.8	1,351.9	146.3	1,158.5	47.1
Fort Collins, CO M.S.A....................................	340,447									
Includes Larimer County										

Table 4. Crime, by Selected Metropolitan Statistical Area, 2016—*Continued*

(Number, percent, rate per 100,000 population.)

Area	Population	Violent crime	Murder and nonnegligent manslaughter	Rape[1]	Robbery	Aggravated assault	Property crime	Burglary	Larceny-theft	Motor vehicle theft
City of Fort Collins	164,670	342	5	33	40	264	4,036	451	3,384	201
Total area actually reporting	100.0%	712	9	103	71	529	7,524	909	6,229	386
Rate per 100,000 inhabitants		209.1	2.6	30.3	20.9	155.4	2,210.0	267.0	1,829.7	113.4
Fort Smith, AR-OK M.S.A.	279,567									
Includes Crawford and Sebastian Counties, AR and Le Flore and Sequoyah Counties, OK										
City of Fort Smith, AR	88,573	712	4	70	97	541	5,229	888	4,008	333
Total area actually reporting	99.7%	1,388	14	191	117	1,066	9,605	2,150	6,823	632
Estimated total	100.0%	1,391	14	192	117	1,068	9,628	2,155	6,840	633
Rate per 100,000 inhabitants		497.6	5.0	68.7	41.9	382.0	3,443.9	770.8	2,446.6	226.4
Fort Wayne, IN M.S.A.	431,558									
Includes Allen, Wells, and Whitley Counties										
City of Fort Wayne	261,642	1,040	43	95	410	492	8,924	1,698	6,812	414
Total area actually reporting	94.7%	1,257	48	125	446	638	10,858	2,069	8,297	492
Estimated total	100.0%	1,288	49	129	450	660	11,122	2,135	8,468	519
Rate per 100,000 inhabitants		298.5	11.4	29.9	104.3	152.9	2,577.2	494.7	1,962.2	120.3
Fresno, CA M.S.A.	976,874									
Includes Fresno County										
City of Fresno	524,796	3,206	39	158	1,122	1,887	20,523	3,697	13,542	3,284
Total area actually reporting	100.0%	5,983	63	314	1,414	4,192	31,875	6,883	19,806	5,186
Rate per 100,000 inhabitants		612.5	6.4	32.1	144.7	429.1	3,263.0	704.6	2,027.5	530.9
Gadsden, AL M.S.A.	102,537									
Includes Etowah County										
City of Gadsden	35,927	464	4	27	56	377	2,521	401	1,893	227
Total area actually reporting	98.5%	722	6	62	77	577	3,651	700	2,584	367
Estimated total	100.0%	730	6	63	78	583	3,702	710	2,621	371
Rate per 100,000 inhabitants		711.9	5.9	61.4	76.1	568.6	3,610.4	692.4	2,556.2	361.8
Gainesville, FL M.S.A.	280,301									
Includes Alachua and Gilchrist Counties										
City of Gainesville	131,242	870	3	142	189	536	4,908	590	3,951	367
Total area actually reporting	94.6%	1,460	4	216	271	969	7,764	1,258	5,972	534
Estimated total	100.0%	1,513	5	221	280	1,007	8,068	1,320	6,191	557
Rate per 100,000 inhabitants		539.8	1.8	78.8	99.9	359.3	2,878.3	470.9	2,208.7	198.7
Gainesville, GA M.S.A.	196,154									
Includes Hall County										
City of Gainesville	39,425	162	3	14	56	89	1,405	202	1,107	96
Total area actually reporting	100.0%	512	8	39	121	344	5,026	766	3,871	389
Rate per 100,000 inhabitants		261.0	4.1	19.9	61.7	175.4	2,562.3	390.5	1,973.4	198.3
Gettysburg, PA M.S.A.	102,165									
Includes Adams County										
City of Gettysburg	7,608	31	0	4	1	26	106	14	90	2
Total area actually reporting	100.0%	166	2	42	11	111	817	155	636	26
Rate per 100,000 inhabitants		162.5	2.0	41.1	10.8	108.6	799.7	151.7	622.5	25.4
Glens Falls, NY M.S.A.	125,674									
Includes Warren and Washington Counties										
City of Glens Falls	14,212	33	1	5	3	24	220	32	187	1
Total area actually reporting	100.0%	207	2	91	14	100	1,565	227	1,317	21
Rate per 100,000 inhabitants		164.7	1.6	72.4	11.1	79.6	1,245.3	180.6	1,047.9	16.7
Goldsboro, NC M.S.A.	124,396									
Includes Wayne County										
City of Goldsboro	35,871	389	11	3	84	291	1,999	484	1,416	99
Total area actually reporting	97.7%	538	11	7	119	401	3,801	1,212	2,362	227
Estimated total	100.0%	546	11	8	121	406	3,889	1,229	2,430	230
Rate per 100,000 inhabitants		438.9	8.8	6.4	97.3	326.4	3,126.3	988.0	1,953.4	184.9
Grand Forks, ND-MN M.S.A.	101,537									
Includes Polk County, MN and Grand Forks County, ND										
City of Grand Forks, ND	57,853	177	1	36	27	113	1,783	303	1,345	135

Table 4. Crime, by Selected Metropolitan Statistical Area, 2016—*Continued*

(Number, percent, rate per 100,000 population.)

Area	Population	Violent crime	Murder and nonnegligent manslaughter	Rape[1]	Robbery	Aggravated assault	Property crime	Burglary	Larceny-theft	Motor vehicle theft
Total area actually reporting	100.0%	244	1	60	27	156	2,550	467	1,912	171
Rate per 100,000 inhabitants		240.3	1.0	59.1	26.6	153.6	2,511.4	459.9	1,883.1	168.4
Grand Island, NE M.S.A.	85,552									
Includes Hall, Hamilton, Howard, and Merrick Counties										
City of Grand Island	51,980	173	1	34	20	118	1,620	236	1,297	87
Total area actually reporting	92.5%	236	1	41	20	174	1,893	308	1,467	118
Estimated total	100.0%	245	1	43	21	180	1,973	320	1,527	126
Rate per 100,000 inhabitants		286.4	1.2	50.3	24.5	210.4	2,306.2	374.0	1,784.9	147.3
Grand Junction, CO M.S.A.	148,848									
Includes Mesa County										
City of Grand Junction	60,628	314	4	63	35	212	3,060	362	2,537	161
Total area actually reporting	99.2%	516	9	119	46	342	4,540	656	3,622	262
Estimated total	100.0%	519	9	120	46	344	4,573	660	3,647	266
Rate per 100,000 inhabitants		348.7	6.0	80.6	30.9	231.1	3,072.3	443.4	2,450.2	178.7
Grand Rapids-Wyoming, MI M.S.A.	1,048,249									
Includes Barry, Kent, Montcalm, and Ottawa Counties										
City of Grand Rapids	196,538	1,327	10	142	321	854	4,334	822	3,208	304
City of Wyoming	75,917	352	4	69	62	217	1,758	297	1,273	188
Total area actually reporting	99.8%	3,529	22	825	529	2,153	16,906	2,933	13,028	945
Estimated total	100.0%	3,534	22	826	530	2,156	16,939	2,938	13,053	948
Rate per 100,000 inhabitants		337.1	2.1	78.8	50.6	205.7	1,615.9	280.3	1,245.2	90.4
Grants Pass, OR M.S.A.	85,644									
Includes Josephine County										
City of Grants Pass	37,317	96	0	17	29	50	2,010	249	1,554	207
Total area actually reporting	100.0%	190	2	22	35	131	2,417	385	1,687	345
Rate per 100,000 inhabitants		221.8	2.3	25.7	40.9	153.0	2,822.1	449.5	1,969.8	402.8
Great Falls, MT M.S.A.	82,482									
Includes Cascade County										
City of Great Falls	59,717	162	3	21	15	123	2,944	365	2,364	215
Total area actually reporting	100.0%	189	4	24	16	145	3,149	407	2,508	234
Rate per 100,000 inhabitants		229.1	4.8	29.1	19.4	175.8	3,817.8	493.4	3,040.7	283.7
Greeley, CO M.S.A.	291,675									
Includes Weld County										
City of Greeley	102,491	468	3	85	51	329	3,275	506	2,447	322
Total area actually reporting	99.6%	749	4	123	76	546	5,861	1,001	4,214	646
Estimated total	100.0%	752	4	124	76	548	5,895	1,005	4,240	650
Rate per 100,000 inhabitants		257.8	1.4	42.5	26.1	187.9	2,021.1	344.6	1,453.7	222.9
Green Bay, WI M.S.A.[3]	318,010									
Includes Brown,[2] Kewaunee, and Oconto Counties										
City of Green Bay[2]	105,452	505	4	77	73	351	2,306	424	1,795	87
Total area actually reporting	91.0%	662	8	115	80	459	4,418	724	3,506	188
Estimated total	100.0%	681	8	119	81	473	4,618	773	3,645	200
Rate per 100,000 inhabitants		214.1	2.5	37.4	25.5	148.7	1,452.2	243.1	1,146.2	62.9
Hagerstown-Martinsburg, MD-WV M.S.A.	261,805									
Includes Washington County, MD and Berkeley County, WV										
City of Hagerstown, MD	40,567	231	0	19	105	107	1,262	374	775	113
City of Martinsburg, WV	17,789	81	0	13	25	43	882	117	740	25
Total area actually reporting	100.0%	650	7	61	193	389	5,556	1,350	3,871	335
Rate per 100,000 inhabitants		248.3	2.7	23.3	73.7	148.6	2,122.2	515.7	1,478.6	128.0
Hammond, LA M.S.A.	129,819									
Includes Tangipahoa Parish										
City of Hammond	20,576	286	7	12	59	208	2,131	627	1,412	92
Total area actually reporting	96.6%	1,170	17	72	195	886	5,470	1,646	3,459	365
Estimated total	100.0%	1,189	17	73	198	901	5,635	1,674	3,588	373
Rate per 100,000 inhabitants		915.9	13.1	56.2	152.5	694.0	4,340.7	1,289.5	2,763.8	287.3
Hanford-Corcoran, CA M.S.A.	149,661									
Includes Kings County										
City of Hanford	55,973	266	2	21	44	199	1,496	222	1,059	215
City of Corcoran	22,111	68	2	10	7	49	404	114	216	74

Table 4. Crime, by Selected Metropolitan Statistical Area, 2016—*Continued*

(Number, percent, rate per 100,000 population.)

Area	Population	Violent crime	Murder and nonnegligent manslaughter	Rape[1]	Robbery	Aggravated assault	Property crime	Burglary	Larceny-theft	Motor vehicle theft
Total area actually reporting	100.0%	639	11	72	80	476	3,167	699	1,931	537
Rate per 100,000 inhabitants.............................		427.0	7.3	48.1	53.5	318.1	2,116.1	467.1	1,290.2	358.8
Harrisburg-Carlisle, PA M.S.A..................................	566,382									
Includes Cumberland, Dauphin, and Perry Counties										
City of Harrisburg	48,996	526	13	54	160	299	1,342	404	803	135
City of Carlisle	19,225	25	1	7	11	6	400	44	345	11
Total area actually reporting	99.4%	1,439	19	214	309	897	8,326	1,536	6,440	350
Estimated total........................	100.0%	1,445	19	215	310	901	8,379	1,543	6,484	352
Rate per 100,000 inhabitants.............................		255.1	3.4	38.0	54.7	159.1	1,479.4	272.4	1,144.8	62.1
Harrisonburg, VA M.S.A.	131,581									
Includes Rockingham County and Harrisonburg City										
City of Harrisonburg	52,972	117	2	25	29	61	1,099	165	894	40
Total area actually reporting	100.0%	214	3	59	35	117	1,794	328	1,391	75
Rate per 100,000 inhabitants.............................		162.6	2.3	44.8	26.6	88.9	1,363.4	249.3	1,057.1	57.0
Hartford-West Hartford-East Hartford, CT M.S.A.[3]..........	1,019,846									
Includes Hartford, Middlesex, and Tolland Counties										
City of Hartford.......................................	123,736	1,353	14	65	476	798	5,197	808	3,616	773
City of West Hartford........................	62,979	40	0	2	38	0	1,589	131	1,351	107
City of East Hartford..................................	50,733	147	4	26	51	66	1,312	247	922	143
City of Middletown..................................	46,580	70	0	5	23	42	927	109	731	87
Total area actually reporting	100.0%	2,430	23	257	854	1,296	22,566	3,050	17,098	2,418
Rate per 100,000 inhabitants.............................		238.3	2.3	25.2	83.7	127.1	2,212.7	299.1	1,676.5	237.1
Hattiesburg, MS M.S.A.	149,558									
Includes Forrest, Lamar, and Perry Counties										
City of Hattiesburg....................................	47,006	147	8	10	52	77	2,752	374	2,292	86
Total area actually reporting	90.2%	279	9	23	66	181	3,822	819	2,872	131
Estimated total........................	100.0%	298	9	25	70	194	4,068	881	3,037	150
Rate per 100,000 inhabitants.............................		199.3	6.0	16.7	46.8	129.7	2,720.0	589.1	2,030.7	100.3
Hilton Head Island-Bluffton-Beaufort, SC M.S.A.	211,983									
Includes Beaufort and Jasper Counties										
City of Bluffton.....................................	17,498	25	2	6	5	12	267	39	217	11
City of Beaufort.....................................	13,477	85	1	3	21	60	857	100	729	28
Total area actually reporting	100.0%	668	17	76	144	431	4,634	900	3,399	335
Rate per 100,000 inhabitants.............................		315.1	8.0	35.9	67.9	203.3	2,186.0	424.6	1,603.4	158.0
Hinesville, GA M.S.A.	80,776									
Includes Liberty and Long Counties										
City of Hinesville....................................	33,477	215	2	14	49	150	1,252	210	1,011	31
Total area actually reporting	100.0%	344	3	16	65	260	1,850	401	1,372	77
Rate per 100,000 inhabitants.............................		425.9	3.7	19.8	80.5	321.9	2,290.3	496.4	1,698.5	95.3
Homosassa Springs, FL M.S.A.	141,300									
Includes Citrus County										
Total area actually reporting	100.0%	338	4	40	39	255	1,979	426	1,443	110
Rate per 100,000 inhabitants.............................		239.2	2.8	28.3	27.6	180.5	1,400.6	301.5	1,021.2	77.8
Hot Springs, AR M.S.A.	97,312									
Includes Garland County										
City of Hot Springs....................................	35,716	277	4	26	62	185	2,882	1,059	1,586	237
Total area actually reporting	100.0%	634	4	73	82	475	4,605	1,890	2,349	366
Rate per 100,000 inhabitants.............................		651.5	4.1	75.0	84.3	488.1	4,732.2	1,942.2	2,413.9	376.1
Houma-Thibodaux, LA M.S.A.	212,402									
Includes Lafourche and Terrebonne Parishes										
City of Houma	34,410	167	4	17	42	104	1,411	196	1,159	56
City of Thibodaux	14,588	90	0	3	10	77	593	142	443	8
Total area actually reporting	100.0%	954	19	61	114	760	6,693	1,591	4,871	231
Rate per 100,000 inhabitants.............................		449.1	8.9	28.7	53.7	357.8	3,151.1	749.1	2,293.3	108.8
Houston-The Woodlands-Sugar Land, TX M.S.A.	6,789,215									
Includes Austin, Brazoria, Chambers, Fort Bend, Galveston, Harris, Liberty, Montgomery, and Waller Counties										
City of Houston	2,334,348	23,960	301	1,210	9,962	12,487	100,856	18,488	69,630	12,738
City of Sugar Land	90,088	77	0	16	43	18	1,460	250	1,162	48
City of Baytown	77,224	302	9	25	98	170	2,858	525	1,960	373

Table 4. Crime, by Selected Metropolitan Statistical Area, 2016—*Continued*

(Number, percent, rate per 100,000 population.)

Area	Population	Violent crime	Murder and nonnegligent manslaughter	Rape[1]	Robbery	Aggravated assault	Property crime	Burglary	Larceny-theft	Motor vehicle theft
City of Conroe...............................	71,111	252	1	39	86	126	2,199	376	1,639	184
Total area actually reporting	99.9%	39,255	487	2,710	14,633	21,425	198,490	37,216	138,158	23,116
Estimated total.................................	100.0%	39,256	487	2,710	14,633	21,426	198,500	37,218	138,165	23,117
Rate per 100,000 inhabitants.............		578.2	7.2	39.9	215.5	315.6	2,923.8	548.2	2,035.1	340.5
Huntington-Ashland, WV-KY-OH M.S.A.[3,5]	359,412									
Includes Boyd and Greenup Counties, KY; Lawrence County OH; and Cabell, Lincoln, Putnam, and Wayne Counties, WV										
City of Huntington, WV[3].....................	48,540	378	3	33	125	217			1,497	115
City of Ashland, KY............................	20,987	51	1	16	11	23	885	146	704	35
Total area actually reporting	83.7%	900	6	137	169	588			5,159	
Estimated total.................................	100.0%	1,048	8	158	180	702			5,867	
Rate per 100,000 inhabitants.............		291.6	2.2	44.0	50.1	195.3			1,632.4	
Huntsville, AL M.S.A.	448,973									
Includes Limestone and Madison Counties										
City of Huntsville..............................	192,587	1,787	18	152	414	1,203	9,398	1,692	6,812	894
Total area actually reporting	100.0%	2,501	22	239	505	1,735	14,340	2,733	10,350	1,257
Rate per 100,000 inhabitants.............		557.0	4.9	53.2	112.5	386.4	3,194.0	608.7	2,305.3	280.0
Idaho Falls, ID M.S.A.	141,859									
Includes Bonneville, Butte, and Jefferson Counties										
City of Idaho Falls	59,615	253	1	33	13	206	1,367	370	904	93
Total area actually reporting	100.0%	425	1	48	18	358	2,226	599	1,491	136
Rate per 100,000 inhabitants.............		299.6	0.7	33.8	12.7	252.4	1,569.2	422.3	1,051.0	95.9
Indianapolis-Carmel-Anderson, IN M.S.A...................	2,004,800									
Includes Boone, Brown, Hamilton, Hancock, Hendricks, Johnson, Madison, Marion, Morgan, Putnam, and Shelby Counties										
City of Indianapolis	866,351	11,907	148	684	3,976	7,099	41,540	10,209	26,335	4,996
City of Carmel..................................	90,619	25	0	13	7	5	803	58	706	39
City of Anderson...............................	55,134	240	6	63	92	79	2,294	497	1,614	183
Total area actually reporting	82.4%	13,615	173	871	4,261	8,310	57,721	12,253	39,210	6,258
Estimated total.................................	100.0%	14,302	184	939	4,388	8,791	64,291	13,334	44,161	6,796
Rate per 100,000 inhabitants.............		713.4	9.2	46.8	218.9	438.5	3,206.9	665.1	2,202.8	339.0
Iowa City, IA M.S.A.	169,088									
Includes Johnson and Washington Counties										
City of Iowa City...............................	75,527	197	0	39	43	115	1,551	294	1,169	88
Total area actually reporting	100.0%	493	0	123	71	299	2,921	528	2,261	132
Rate per 100,000 inhabitants.............		291.6	0.0	72.7	42.0	176.8	1,727.5	312.3	1,337.2	78.1
Jackson, MI M.S.A.	159,287									
Includes Jackson County										
City of Jackson.................................	33,060	409	4	65	49	291	1,504	287	1,159	58
Total area actually reporting	98.7%	843	9	142	74	618	3,489	642	2,678	169
Estimated total.................................	100.0%	849	9	143	75	622	3,528	648	2,708	172
Rate per 100,000 inhabitants.............		533.0	5.7	89.8	47.1	390.5	2,214.9	406.8	1,700.1	108.0
Jackson, TN M.S.A.	129,606									
Includes Chester, Crockett, and Madison Counties										
City of Jackson.................................	66,990	628	7	36	108	477	2,947	650	2,170	127
Total area actually reporting	100.0%	843	7	45	114	677	3,939	1,028	2,709	202
Rate per 100,000 inhabitants.............		650.4	5.4	34.7	88.0	522.4	3,039.2	793.2	2,090.2	155.9
Jacksonville, FL M.S.A.	1,473,678									
Includes Baker, Clay, Duval, Nassau, and St. Johns Counties ...										
City of Jacksonville............................	880,557	5,504	106	517	1,463	3,418	31,538	5,851	22,660	3,027
Total area actually reporting	100.0%	7,058	125	697	1,681	4,555	42,653	8,196	30,834	3,623
Rate per 100,000 inhabitants.............		478.9	8.5	47.3	114.1	309.1	2,894.3	556.2	2,092.3	245.8
Janesville-Beloit, WI M.S.A.	161,430									
Includes Rock County										
City of Janesville	64,234	145	0	28	31	86	1,763	238	1,474	51
City of Beloit...................................	36,878	175	2	17	57	99	1,124	149	940	35
Total area actually reporting	100.0%	370	3	57	90	220	3,570	558	2,885	127
Rate per 100,000 inhabitants.............		229.2	1.9	35.3	55.8	136.3	2,211.5	345.7	1,787.2	78.7
Jefferson City, MO M.S.A....................	151,164									
Includes Callaway, Cole, Moniteau, and Osage Counties										

Table 4. Crime, by Selected Metropolitan Statistical Area, 2016—*Continued*

(Number, percent, rate per 100,000 population.)

Area	Population	Violent crime	Murder and nonnegligent manslaughter	Rape[1]	Robbery	Aggravated assault	Property crime	Burglary	Larceny-theft	Motor vehicle theft
City of Jefferson City................	43,171	174	4	9	35	126	1,318	179	1,085	54
Total area actually reporting................	100.0%	445	7	33	60	345	2,855	604	2,094	157
Rate per 100,000 inhabitants................		294.4	4.6	21.8	39.7	228.2	1,888.7	399.6	1,385.3	103.9
Johnson City, TN M.S.A.................	200,977									
Includes Carter, Unicoi, and Washington Counties										
City of Johnson City................	66,511	263	4	25	38	196	2,488	392	1,977	119
Total area actually reporting................	100.0%	585	5	48	65	467	4,662	846	3,557	259
Rate per 100,000 inhabitants................		291.1	2.5	23.9	32.3	232.4	2,319.7	420.9	1,769.9	128.9
Johnstown, PA M.S.A.................	134,652									
Includes Cambria County										
City of Johnstown................	21,227	100	5	2	20	73	633	198	416	19
Total area actually reporting................	98.0%	210	7	15	31	157	1,807	383	1,379	45
Estimated total................	100.0%	214	7	15	32	160	1,848	388	1,413	47
Rate per 100,000 inhabitants................		158.9	5.2	11.1	23.8	118.8	1,372.4	288.2	1,049.4	34.9
Jonesboro, AR M.S.A.	129,793									
Includes Craighead and Poinsett Counties										
City of Jonesboro................	75,230	387	5	35	72	275	3,369	1,528	1,727	114
Total area actually reporting................	100.0%	541	7	87	80	367	4,662	1,849	2,626	187
Rate per 100,000 inhabitants................		416.8	5.4	67.0	61.6	282.8	3,591.9	1,424.6	2,023.2	144.1
Joplin, MO M.S.A.[5]	177,228									
Includes Jasper and Newton[4] Counties										
City of Joplin................	52,001	329	2	52	72	203	3,779	569	2,895	315
Total area actually reporting................	100.0%		7	94	100		7,163	1,148	5,400	615
Rate per 100,000 inhabitants................			3.9	53.0	56.4		4,041.7	647.8	3,046.9	347.0
Kahului-Wailuku-Lahaina, HI M.S.A.................	164,771									
Includes Kalawao and Maui Counties										
Total area actually reporting................	100.0%	450	5	77	68	300	5,741	978	4,046	717
Rate per 100,000 inhabitants................		273.1	3.0	46.7	41.3	182.1	3,484.2	593.6	2,455.5	435.1
Kalamazoo-Portage, MI M.S.A.	336,919									
Includes Kalamazoo and Van Buren Counties										
City of Kalamazoo................	76,389	925	7	125	182	611	3,221	755	2,228	238
City of Portage................	48,550	103	0	31	15	57	1,289	149	1,117	23
Total area actually reporting................	100.0%	1,776	22	368	264	1,122	9,038	1,966	6,579	493
Rate per 100,000 inhabitants................		527.1	6.5	109.2	78.4	333.0	2,682.5	583.5	1,952.7	146.3
Kankakee, IL M.S.A.	109,833									
Includes Kankakee County										
City of Kankakee	26,509	203	5	26	74	98	1,098	251	786	61
Total area actually reporting................	86.7%	311	10	33	97	171	2,382	509	1,768	105
Estimated total................	100.0%	341	10	37	106	188	2,630	548	1,964	118
Rate per 100,000 inhabitants................		310.5	9.1	33.7	96.5	171.2	2,394.5	498.9	1,788.2	107.4
Kennewick-Richland, WA M.S.A.	285,194									
Includes Benton and Franklin Counties										
City of Kennewick................	79,837	183	1	31	37	114	2,254	295	1,772	187
City of Richland	55,475	101	1	20	11	69	1,344	174	1,092	78
Total area actually reporting................	100.0%	551	5	99	91	356	6,202	1,069	4,602	531
Rate per 100,000 inhabitants................		193.2	1.8	34.7	31.9	124.8	2,174.7	374.8	1,613.6	186.2
Killeen-Temple, TX M.S.A.[3]	434,470									
Includes Bell, Coryell, and Lampasas Counties										
City of Killeen................	143,248	996	16	129	234	617	3,946	1,124	2,471	351
City of Temple................	73,411	226	7	34	89	96	2,298	493	1,620	185
Total area actually reporting................	99.3%	1,673	27	242	410	994	10,468	2,458	7,290	720
Estimated total................	100.0%	1,681	27	243	412	999	10,542	2,470	7,347	725
Rate per 100,000 inhabitants................		386.9	6.2	55.9	94.8	229.9	2,426.4	568.5	1,691.0	166.9
Kingsport-Bristol-Bristol, TN-VA M.S.A.	306,101									
Includes Hawkins and Sullivan Counties, TN and Scott and Washington Counties and Bristol City, VA										
City of Kingsport, TN	53,059	369	1	18	71	279	2,501	374	1,973	154
City of Bristol, TN................	26,656	158	1	14	14	129	900	134	670	96

(Number, percent, rate per 100,000 population.)

Area	Population	Violent crime	Murder and nonnegligent manslaughter	Rape[1]	Robbery	Aggravated assault	Property crime	Burglary	Larceny-theft	Motor vehicle theft
City of Bristol, VA............................	16,908	37	1	9	7	20	432	56	338	38
Total area actually reporting	100.0%	1,124	8	125	119	872	7,135	1,294	5,236	605
Rate per 100,000 inhabitants.............		367.2	2.6	40.8	38.9	284.9	2,330.9	422.7	1,710.5	197.6
Kingston, NY M.S.A.	178,502									
Includes Ulster County										
City of Kingston..............................	23,360	76	0	10	23	43	484	57	418	9
Total area actually reporting	100.0%	292	4	72	36	180	2,336	393	1,878	65
Rate per 100,000 inhabitants.............		163.6	2.2	40.3	20.2	100.8	1,308.7	220.2	1,052.1	36.4
Knoxville, TN M.S.A.	866,010									
Includes Anderson, Blount, Campbell, Grainger, Knox, Loudon, Morgan, Roane, and Union Counties										
City of Knoxville..............................	186,583	1,672	18	157	404	1,093	10,324	1,840	7,620	864
Total area actually reporting	100.0%	3,892	37	296	610	2,949	23,900	5,043	16,881	1,976
Rate per 100,000 inhabitants.............		449.4	4.3	34.2	70.4	340.5	2,759.8	582.3	1,949.3	228.2
Kokomo, IN M.S.A.	82,350									
Includes Howard County										
City of Kokomo...............................	57,984	441	4	30	84	323	1,760	476	1,196	88
Total area actually reporting	98.7%	519	6	36	92	385	2,046	587	1,350	109
Estimated total...............................	100.0%	522	6	36	93	387	2,077	591	1,375	111
Rate per 100,000 inhabitants.............		633.9	7.3	43.7	112.9	469.9	2,522.2	717.7	1,669.7	134.8
La Crosse-Onalaska, WI-MN M.S.A. ...	137,403									
Includes Houston County, MN and La Crosse County, WI										
City of La Crosse, WI........................	52,498	131	1	32	23	75	2,290	319	1,905	66
City of Onalaska, WI........................	18,600	13	0	6	0	7	508	60	443	5
Total area actually reporting	100.0%	186	1	41	23	121	3,374	482	2,800	92
Rate per 100,000 inhabitants.............		135.4	0.7	29.8	16.7	88.1	2,455.6	350.8	2,037.8	67.0
Lafayette, LA M.S.A.[4]	493,575									
Includes Acadia, Iberia,[3] Lafayette, St. Martin, and Vermilion Parishes										
City of Lafayette.............................	128,923	641	11	19	148	463	6,417	1,025	5,013	379
Total area actually reporting	97.4%	1,830	45	58	351	1,376		3,299	10,056	
Estimated total...............................	100.0%	1,887	46	62	360	1,419		3,382	10,432	
Rate per 100,000 inhabitants.............		382.3	9.3	12.6	72.9	287.5		685.2	2,113.6	
Lafayette-West Lafayette, IN M.S.A. ...	216,480									
Includes Benton, Carroll, and Tippecanoe Counties										
City of Lafayette.............................	71,562	360	2	35	109	214	3,016	612	2,217	187
City of West Lafayette.......................	46,284	57	0	10	10	37	452	71	360	21
Total area actually reporting	87.1%	491	2	65	127	297	4,401	897	3,253	251
Estimated total...............................	100.0%	536	3	70	134	329	4,799	980	3,532	287
Rate per 100,000 inhabitants.............		247.6	1.4	32.3	61.9	152.0	2,216.8	452.7	1,631.6	132.6
Lake Charles, LA M.S.A.	206,047									
Includes Calcasieu and Cameron Parishes										
City of Lake Charles.........................	76,864	654	8	40	143	463	3,153	1,626	1,320	207
Total area actually reporting	100.0%	1,357	14	103	192	1,048	8,754	3,142	5,063	549
Rate per 100,000 inhabitants.............		658.6	6.8	50.0	93.2	508.6	4,248.5	1,524.9	2,457.2	266.4
Lakeland-Winter Haven, FL M.S.A. ...	661,218									
Includes Polk County										
City of Lakeland..............................	105,766	337	4	89	104	140	5,111	751	4,050	310
City of Winter Haven........................	38,488	196	2	10	33	151	1,339	238	1,021	80
Total area actually reporting	100.0%	2,199	26	258	350	1,565	15,567	3,214	11,201	1,152
Rate per 100,000 inhabitants.............		332.6	3.9	39.0	52.9	236.7	2,354.3	486.1	1,694.0	174.2
Lancaster, PA M.S.A.	538,376									
Includes Lancaster County										
City of Lancaster.............................	59,340	487	4	92	164	227	2,164	255	1,828	81
Total area actually reporting	100.0%	944	8	180	270	486	7,411	1,029	6,143	239
Rate per 100,000 inhabitants.............		175.3	1.5	33.4	50.2	90.3	1,376.5	191.1	1,141.0	44.4
Lansing-East Lansing, MI M.S.A.	473,685									
Includes Clinton, Eaton, and Ingham Counties										
City of Lansing...............................	115,199	1,341	9	142	260	930	3,325	897	2,053	375

Table 4. Crime, by Selected Metropolitan Statistical Area, 2016—*Continued*

(Number, percent, rate per 100,000 population.)

Area	Population	Violent crime	Murder and nonnegligent manslaughter	Rape[1]	Robbery	Aggravated assault	Property crime	Burglary	Larceny-theft	Motor vehicle theft
City of East Lansing........................	48,451	115	0	43	24	48	719	124	488	107
Total area actually reporting	100.0%	2,172	16	432	354	1,370	8,730	1,791	6,232	707
Rate per 100,000 inhabitants................		458.5	3.4	91.2	74.7	289.2	1,843.0	378.1	1,315.6	149.3
Laredo, TX M.S.A...........................	272,746									
Includes Webb County										
City of Laredo...........................	259,325	940	12	148	160	620	7,890	1,015	6,646	229
Total area actually reporting	100.0%	986	12	153	165	656	8,188	1,116	6,837	235
Rate per 100,000 inhabitants................		361.5	4.4	56.1	60.5	240.5	3,002.1	409.2	2,506.7	86.2
Las Cruces, NM M.S.A.	214,233									
Includes Dona Ana County										
City of Las Cruces	102,349	251	5	41	51	154	4,788	830	3,697	261
Total area actually reporting	95.7%	496	11	92	62	331	6,049	1,226	4,447	376
Estimated total.............................	100.0%	542	11	96	66	369	6,357	1,287	4,652	418
Rate per 100,000 inhabitants................		253.0	5.1	44.8	30.8	172.2	2,967.3	600.7	2,171.5	195.1
Las Vegas-Henderson-Paradise, NV M.S.A.	2,155,946									
Includes Clark County										
City of Las Vegas Metropolitan Police Department	1,592,178	13,520	158	1,200	4,974	7,188	46,000	12,500	24,645	8,855
City of Henderson.........................	291,584	617	10	94	235	278	5,484	1,237	3,617	630
Total area actually reporting	100.0%	16,622	194	1,420	5,781	9,227	58,811	15,522	32,417	10,872
Rate per 100,000 inhabitants................		771.0	9.0	65.9	268.1	428.0	2,727.9	720.0	1,503.6	504.3
Lawton, OK M.S.A.........................	129,814									
Includes Comanche and Cotton Counties										
City of Lawton...........................	96,420	781	4	69	110	598	3,691	1,151	2,318	222
Total area actually reporting	99.1%	813	4	75	112	622	4,125	1,303	2,556	266
Estimated total.............................	100.0%	815	4	75	112	624	4,155	1,309	2,577	269
Rate per 100,000 inhabitants................		627.8	3.1	57.8	86.3	480.7	3,200.7	1,008.4	1,985.1	207.2
Lebanon, PA M.S.A.........................	137,357									
Includes Lebanon County										
City of Lebanon...........................	25,549	60	1	3	16	40	619	129	441	49
Total area actually reporting	95.9%	203	3	13	36	151	1,942	307	1,546	89
Estimated total.............................	100.0%	212	3	14	38	157	2,028	318	1,618	92
Rate per 100,000 inhabitants................		154.3	2.2	10.2	27.7	114.3	1,476.4	231.5	1,178.0	67.0
Lewiston, ID-WA M.S.A.	62,714									
Includes Nez Perce County, ID and Asotin County, WA										
City of Lewiston, ID........................	32,665	46	0	14	3	29	1,330	366	883	81
Total area actually reporting	100.0%	95	1	25	6	63	2,189	507	1,562	120
Rate per 100,000 inhabitants................		151.5	1.6	39.9	9.6	100.5	3,490.4	808.4	2,490.7	191.3
Lewiston-Auburn, ME M.S.A............................	107,279									
Includes Androscoggin County										
City of Lewiston...........................	36,126	64	0	14	18	32	718	140	529	49
City of Auburn.............................	22,836	43	0	14	7	22	730	66	649	15
Total area actually reporting	100.0%	146	0	37	30	79	1,825	308	1,437	80
Rate per 100,000 inhabitants................		136.1	0.0	34.5	28.0	73.6	1,701.2	287.1	1,339.5	74.6
Lexington-Fayette, KY M.S.A.	505,664									
Includes Bourbon, Clark, Fayette, Jessamine, Scott, and Woodford Counties										
City of Lexington	317,853	1,079	24	200	575	280	13,058	2,435	9,465	1,158
Total area actually reporting	100.0%	1,335	25	262	667	381	18,168	3,439	13,293	1,436
Rate per 100,000 inhabitants................		264.0	4.9	51.8	131.9	75.3	3,592.9	680.1	2,628.8	284.0
Lima, OH M.S.A.	103,900									
Includes Allen County										
City of Lima...............................	37,715	356	8	44	123	181	2,259	602	1,540	117
Total area actually reporting	96.7%	400	8	55	141	196	3,652	894	2,599	159
Estimated total.............................	100.0%	405	8	56	143	198	3,729	907	2,660	162
Rate per 100,000 inhabitants................		389.8	7.7	53.9	137.6	190.6	3,589.0	873.0	2,560.2	155.9
Lincoln, NE M.S.A.	327,353									
Includes Lancaster and Seward Counties										
City of Lincoln............................	281,138	1,006	10	222	191	583	8,730	1,261	7,117	352
Total area actually reporting	99.4%	1,052	10	244	192	606	9,202	1,345	7,477	380

Table 4. Crime, by Selected Metropolitan Statistical Area, 2016—*Continued*

(Number, percent, rate per 100,000 population.)

Area	Population	Violent crime	Murder and nonnegligent manslaughter	Rape[1]	Robbery	Aggravated assault	Property crime	Burglary	Larceny-theft	Motor vehicle theft
Estimated total..	100.0%	1,055	10	245	192	608	9,244	1,349	7,511	384
Rate per 100,000 inhabitants..		322.3	3.1	74.8	58.7	185.7	2,823.9	412.1	2,294.5	117.3
Little Rock-North Little Rock-Conway, AR M.S.A.[5]............	737,086									
Includes Faulkner, Grant, Lonoke, Perry, Pulaski, and Saline Counties										
City of Little Rock..	198,800	3,044	42	159	657	2,186	13,714	2,348	10,223	1,143
City of North Little Rock..	67,344	503	11	11	115	366	2,926	523	2,016	387
City of Conway..	66,104	335	5	43	84	203	2,970	343	2,429	198
Total area actually reporting	100.0%	5,602	74	437	1,008	4,083			22,971	2,798
Rate per 100,000 inhabitants..		760.0	10.0	59.3	136.8	553.9			3,116.5	379.6
Logan, UT-ID M.S.A.	135,889									
Includes Franklin County, ID and Cache County, UT										
City of Logan, UT..	50,767	50	1	12	5	32	844	120	685	39
Total area actually reporting	100.0%	90	2	35	8	45	1,481	243	1,155	83
Rate per 100,000 inhabitants..		66.2	1.5	25.8	5.9	33.1	1,089.9	178.8	850.0	61.1
Longview, WA M.S.A.	104,085									
Includes Cowlitz County										
City of Longview..	36,854	142	0	41	40	61	1,927	409	1,314	204
Total area actually reporting	100.0%	279	2	68	58	151	3,448	712	2,376	360
Rate per 100,000 inhabitants..		268.1	1.9	65.3	55.7	145.1	3,312.7	684.1	2,282.7	345.9
Los Angeles-Long Beach-Anaheim, CA M.S.A...................	13,350,144									
Includes the Metropolitan Divisions of Anaheim-Santa Ana-Irvine and Los Angeles-Long Beach-Glendale										
City of Los Angeles..	4,007,905	28,817	293	2,343	10,307	15,874	99,151	15,821	64,739	18,591
City of Long Beach...	476,476	2,846	33	197	1,138	1,478	14,224	2,988	8,377	2,859
City of Anaheim...	353,504	1,209	7	123	390	689	9,617	1,469	6,764	1,384
City of Santa Ana..	337,419	1,612	23	142	511	936	6,980	1,119	3,913	1,948
City of Irvine...	266,663	152	3	41	52	56	3,737	640	2,918	179
City of Glendale..	202,903	227	1	38	84	104	3,450	596	2,491	363
City of Torrance..	149,078	258	1	28	119	110	3,221	458	2,326	437
City of Pasadena...	143,288	477	2	46	164	265	3,446	861	2,261	324
City of Orange...	141,841	228	1	25	57	145	2,608	464	1,783	361
City of Costa Mesa..	113,816	412	1	60	145	206	4,610	735	3,296	579
City of Burbank...	105,720	210	0	24	50	136	2,927	392	2,269	266
City of Carson...	93,613	505	10	23	165	307	2,424	439	1,463	522
City of Santa Monica	93,921	475	2	40	189	244	4,039	623	3,180	236
City of Newport Beach	87,482	110	1	34	17	58	2,241	437	1,644	160
City of Tustin..	81,642	120	2	13	34	71	1,806	229	1,412	165
City of Monterey Park..	61,710	131	1	8	59	63	1,704	460	998	246
City of Gardena	60,770	338	3	24	160	151	1,482	355	772	355
City of Arcadia..	58,816	83	2	4	44	33	1,642	520	1,045	77
City of Fountain Valley	57,291	63	0	0	21	42	1,443	246	1,072	125
Total area actually reporting	100.0%	63,646	679	4,968	22,288	35,711	318,559	58,004	204,522	56,033
Rate per 100,000 inhabitants..		476.7	5.1	37.2	166.9	267.5	2,386.2	434.5	1,532.0	419.7
Anaheim-Santa Ana-Irvine, CA M.D.	3,179,276									
Includes Orange County										
Total area actually reporting	100.0%	7,275	57	810	2,136	4,272	66,054	11,025	46,507	8,522
Rate per 100,000 inhabitants..		228.8	1.8	25.5	67.2	134.4	2,077.6	346.8	1,462.8	268.0
Los Angeles-Long Beach-Glendale, CA M.D.....................	10,170,868									
Includes Los Angeles County										
Total area actually reporting	100.0%	56,371	622	4,158	20,152	31,439	252,505	46,979	158,015	47,511
Rate per 100,000 inhabitants..		554.2	6.1	40.9	198.1	309.1	2,482.6	461.9	1,553.6	467.1
Louisville/Jefferson County, KY-IN M.S.A...........................	1,285,169									
Includes Clark, Floyd, Harrison, Scott, and Washington Counties, IN and Bullitt, Henry, Jefferson, Oldham, Shelby, Spencer, and Trimble Counties, KY										
City of Louisville Metro, KY	683,825	4,621	119	196	1,514	2,792	30,254	5,907	19,983	4,364
Total area actually reporting	94.2%	5,502	131	291	1,787	3,293	42,026	7,908	28,544	5,574
Estimated total..	100.0%	5,627	134	305	1,807	3,381	43,168	8,132	29,361	5,675
Rate per 100,000 inhabitants..		437.8	10.4	23.7	140.6	263.1	3,358.9	632.8	2,284.6	441.6
Lubbock, TX M.S.A.[3]..	314,167									
Includes Crosby, Lubbock, and Lynn Counties										

Table 4. Crime, by Selected Metropolitan Statistical Area, 2016—*Continued*

(Number, percent, rate per 100,000 population.)

Area	Population	Violent crime	Murder and nonnegligent manslaughter	Rape[1]	Robbery	Aggravated assault	Property crime	Burglary	Larceny-theft	Motor vehicle theft
City of Lubbock	252,900	2,741	6	177	471	2,087	12,661	2,678	8,933	1,050
Total area actually reporting	98.8%	2,894	9	200	488	2,197	14,117	2,983	9,980	1,154
Estimated total	100.0%	2,904	9	202	490	2,203	14,210	2,998	10,051	1,161
Rate per 100,000 inhabitants		924.3	2.9	64.3	156.0	701.2	4,523.1	954.3	3,199.3	369.5
Lynchburg, VA M.S.A.	259,926									
Includes Amherst, Appomattox, Bedford, and Campbell Counties and Bedford and Lynchburg Cities										
City of Lynchburg	80,215	298	2	33	57	206	1,802	262	1,428	112
Total area actually reporting	100.0%	530	12	83	78	357	3,739	546	2,995	198
Rate per 100,000 inhabitants		203.9	4.6	31.9	30.0	137.3	1,438.5	210.1	1,152.3	76.2
Macon-Bibb County, GA M.S.A.	229,434									
Includes Bibb, Crawford, Jones, Monroe, and Twiggs Counties										
Total area actually reporting	99.6%	872	18	61	279	514	9,457	2,289	6,452	716
Estimated total	100.0%	876	18	61	280	517	9,496	2,295	6,482	719
Rate per 100,000 inhabitants		381.8	7.8	26.6	122.0	225.3	4,138.9	1,000.3	2,825.2	313.4
Madera, CA M.S.A.	154,726									
Includes Madera County										
City of Madera	64,753	505	3	22	98	382	1,859	297	1,262	300
Total area actually reporting	100.0%	1,024	7	51	124	842	3,705	978	2,155	572
Rate per 100,000 inhabitants		661.8	4.5	33.0	80.1	544.2	2,394.6	632.1	1,392.8	369.7
Madison, WI M.S.A.[3]	647,587									
Includes Columbia, Dane, Green, and Iowa Counties										
City of Madison	252,136	832	8	125	235	464	6,932	1,014	5,544	374
Total area actually reporting	98.8%	1,304	13	198	309	784	12,263	1,720	9,959	584
Estimated total	100.0%	1,313	13	199	311	790	12,406	1,736	10,080	590
Rate per 100,000 inhabitants		202.8	2.0	30.7	48.0	122.0	1,915.7	268.1	1,556.5	91.1
Manchester-Nashua, NH M.S.A.	408,233									
Includes Hillsborough County										
City of Manchester	110,353	742	5	69	205	463	3,010	456	2,408	146
City of Nashua	88,252	151	0	48	26	77	1,218	122	1,039	57
Total area actually reporting	98.7%	1,089	5	160	248	676	6,162	846	5,031	285
Estimated total	100.0%	1,096	5	162	249	680	6,228	855	5,085	288
Rate per 100,000 inhabitants		268.5	1.2	39.7	61.0	166.6	1,525.6	209.4	1,245.6	70.5
Manhattan, KS M.S.A.	99,113									
Includes Pottawatomie and Riley Counties										
Total area actually reporting	100.0%	257	1	49	22	185	1,607	250	1,268	89
Rate per 100,000 inhabitants		259.3	1.0	49.4	22.2	186.7	1,621.4	252.2	1,279.3	89.8
Mankato-North Mankato, MN M.S.A.	99,481									
Includes Blue Earth and Nicollet Counties										
City of Mankato	41,300	112	1	27	23	61	1,329	223	1,057	49
City of North Mankato	13,553	7	0	0	0	7	149	30	116	3
Total area actually reporting	100.0%	153	2	37	26	88	1,878	368	1,432	78
Rate per 100,000 inhabitants		153.8	2.0	37.2	26.1	88.5	1,887.8	369.9	1,439.5	78.4
Mansfield, OH M.S.A.	121,064									
Includes Richland County										
City of Mansfield	46,656	209	3	58	63	85	2,605	679	1,805	121
Total area actually reporting	99.3%	290	6	90	73	121	4,437	1,205	3,084	148
Estimated total	100.0%	291	6	90	73	122	4,457	1,208	3,100	149
Rate per 100,000 inhabitants		240.4	5.0	74.3	60.3	100.8	3,681.5	997.8	2,560.6	123.1
McAllen-Edinburg-Mission, TX M.S.A.[3]	853,003									
Includes Hidalgo County										
City of McAllen	142,227	215	3	40	65	107	4,470	331	4,022	117
City of Edinburg	86,535	354	3	61	51	239	4,183	545	3,481	157
City of Mission	84,380	120	0	36	40	44	2,179	358	1,707	114
Total area actually reporting	99.3%	2,505	22	417	444	1,622	24,130	3,939	19,095	1,096
Estimated total	100.0%	2,522	22	420	448	1,632	24,276	3,962	19,207	1,107
Rate per 100,000 inhabitants		295.7	2.6	49.2	52.5	191.3	2,845.9	464.5	2,251.7	129.8
Medford, OR M.S.A.	215,751									
Includes Jackson County										

Table 4. Crime, by Selected Metropolitan Statistical Area, 2016—*Continued*

(Number, percent, rate per 100,000 population.)

Area	Population	Violent crime	Murder and nonnegligent manslaughter	Rape[1]	Robbery	Aggravated assault	Property crime	Burglary	Larceny-theft	Motor vehicle theft
City of Medford	80,794	407	1	31	115	260	5,688	486	4,793	409
Total area actually reporting	100.0%	772	5	73	150	544	9,339	1,067	7,602	670
Rate per 100,000 inhabitants		357.8	2.3	33.8	69.5	252.1	4,328.6	494.6	3,523.5	310.5
Memphis, TN-MS-AR M.S.A.	1,346,931									
Includes Crittenden County, AR; Benton, DeSoto, Marshall, Tate, and Tunica Counties, MS; and Fayette, Shelby, and Tipton Counties, TN										
City of Memphis, TN	656,434	11,947	196	534	3,188	8,029	36,988	9,150	24,604	3,234
Total area actually reporting	97.3%	14,524	248	730	3,618	9,928	51,468	12,430	34,899	4,139
Estimated total	100.0%	14,575	249	736	3,628	9,962	52,102	12,585	35,333	4,184
Rate per 100,000 inhabitants		1,082.1	18.5	54.6	269.4	739.6	3,868.2	934.3	2,623.2	310.6
Merced, CA M.S.A.	268,999									
Includes Merced County										
City of Merced	83,106	489	1	35	134	319	2,774	558	1,617	599
Total area actually reporting	100.0%	1,488	6	79	238	1,165	7,658	1,830	4,395	1,433
Rate per 100,000 inhabitants		553.2	2.2	29.4	88.5	433.1	2,846.9	680.3	1,633.8	532.7
Miami-Fort Lauderdale-West Palm Beach, FL M.S.A.	6,113,688									
Includes the Metropolitan Divisions of Fort Lauderdale-Pompano Beach-Deerfield Beach, Miami-Miami Beach-Kendall, and West Palm Beach-Boca Raton-Delray Beach										
City of Miami	449,469	3,989	55	90	1,443	2,401	18,974	2,643	14,335	1,996
City of Fort Lauderdale	181,218	1,144	18	71	483	572	10,630	1,856	7,856	918
City of West Palm Beach	108,074	954	10	71	333	540	5,599	946	4,100	553
City of Pompano Beach	109,362	931	7	77	344	503	5,205	903	3,738	564
City of Miami Beach	93,165	940	7	57	345	531	8,419	603	7,251	565
City of Boca Raton	94,931	239	1	22	105	111	2,495	507	1,831	157
City of Deerfield Beach	80,713	277	2	33	93	149	2,193	376	1,597	220
City of Delray Beach	67,400	387	5	31	125	226	2,842	385	2,218	239
City of Jupiter	64,273	147	0	15	40	92	1,261	163	1,038	60
Total area actually reporting	100.0%	29,720	355	1,866	9,299	18,200	196,533	28,357	150,604	17,572
Rate per 100,000 inhabitants		486.1	5.8	30.5	152.1	297.7	3,214.6	463.8	2,463.4	287.4
Fort Lauderdale-Pompano Beach-Deerfield Beach, FL M.D.	1,930,253									
Includes Broward County										
Total area actually reporting	100.0%	7,550	81	559	2,715	4,195	58,871	8,813	44,436	5,622
Rate per 100,000 inhabitants		391.1	4.2	29.0	140.7	217.3	3,049.9	456.6	2,302.1	291.3
Miami-Miami Beach-Kendall, FL M.D.	2,737,194									
Includes Miami-Dade County										
Total area actually reporting	100.0%	15,635	198	796	4,831	9,810	95,584	11,774	75,242	8,568
Rate per 100,000 inhabitants		571.2	7.2	29.1	176.5	358.4	3,492.0	430.1	2,748.9	313.0
West Palm Beach-Boca Raton-Delray Beach, FL M.D.	1,446,241									
Includes Palm Beach County										
Total area actually reporting	100.0%	6,535	76	511	1,753	4,195	42,078	7,770	30,926	3,382
Rate per 100,000 inhabitants		451.9	5.3	35.3	121.2	290.1	2,909.5	537.3	2,138.4	233.8
Michigan City-La Porte, IN M.S.A.	110,541									
Includes La Porte County										
City of Michigan City	31,459	186	2	19	50	115	1,444	213	1,131	100
City of La Porte	21,891	93	0	9	20	64	765	145	576	44
Total area actually reporting	95.8%	320	2	34	76	208	2,814	608	2,021	185
Estimated total	100.0%	333	2	35	79	217	2,943	623	2,126	194
Rate per 100,000 inhabitants		301.2	1.8	31.7	71.5	196.3	2,662.4	563.6	1,923.3	175.5
Midland, MI M.S.A.	83,588									
Includes Midland County										
City of Midland	42,263	48	0	17	5	26	511	77	424	10
Total area actually reporting	100.0%	107	1	44	6	56	887	203	654	30
Rate per 100,000 inhabitants		128.0	1.2	52.6	7.2	67.0	1,061.2	242.9	782.4	35.9
Midland, TX M.S.A.	171,699									
Includes Martin and Midland Counties										
City of Midland	137,780	412	3	24	93	292	3,352	604	2,563	185

Table 4. Crime, by Selected Metropolitan Statistical Area, 2016—*Continued*

(Number, percent, rate per 100,000 population.)

Area	Population	Violent crime	Murder and nonnegligent manslaughter	Rape[1]	Robbery	Aggravated assault	Property crime	Burglary	Larceny-theft	Motor vehicle theft
Total area actually reporting	100.0%	511	3	29	102	377	4,285	777	3,222	286
Rate per 100,000 inhabitants		297.6	1.7	16.9	59.4	219.6	2,495.6	452.5	1,876.5	166.6
Milwaukee-Waukesha-West Allis, WI M.S.A.[3]	1,577,025									
Includes Milwaukee, Ozaukee, Washington, and Waukesha Counties										
City of Milwaukee...	600,193	9,201	141	477	3,283	5,300	24,392	5,862	12,356	6,174
City of Waukesha..	72,223	92	0	31	14	47	1,117	182	891	44
City of West Allis[2]	60,558	200	6	20	76	98	2,262	451	1,609	202
Total area actually reporting	100.0%	10,345	156	638	3,661	5,890	42,858	8,074	27,545	7,239
Rate per 100,000 inhabitants		656.0	9.9	40.5	232.1	373.5	2,717.6	512.0	1,746.6	459.0
Minneapolis-St. Paul-Bloomington, MN-WI M.S.A.[3]........	3,555,186									
Includes Anoka, Carver,2 Chisago, Dakota, Hennepin, Isanti, Le Sueur, Mille Lacs, Ramsey, Scott, Sherburne, Sibley, Washington, and Wright Counties, MN and Pierce and St. Croix Counties, WI										
City of Minneapolis, MN	416,751	4,622	35	455	1,844	2,288	17,594	3,424	12,183	1,987
City of St. Paul, MN	303,920	1,970	19	184	700	1,067	9,811	2,278	5,659	1,874
City of Bloomington, MN	87,134	177	0	49	62	66	2,810	181	2,514	115
City of Plymouth, MN	76,996	48	1	12	14	21	1,009	215	759	35
City of Eagan, MN	66,698	40	0	11	13	16	1,144	106	995	43
City of Eden Prairie, MN.......................................	64,037	36	2	15	8	11	729	75	627	27
Total area actually reporting	99.8%	10,218	77	1,532	3,372	5,237	82,192	12,585	62,870	6,737
Estimated total..	100.0%	10,227	77	1,533	3,374	5,243	82,325	12,600	62,982	6,743
Rate per 100,000 inhabitants		287.7	2.2	43.1	94.9	147.5	2,315.6	354.4	1,771.6	189.7
Missoula, MT M.S.A.	115,226									
Includes Missoula County										
City of Missoula	71,860	377	0	65	60	252	3,761	401	3,156	204
Total area actually reporting	100.0%	476	0	82	64	330	4,087	504	3,356	227
Rate per 100,000 inhabitants		413.1	0.0	71.2	55.5	286.4	3,546.9	437.4	2,912.5	197.0
Mobile, AL M.S.A.[5]	414,817									
Includes Mobile County										
City of Mobile5...	249,921	1,709	44	89	438	1,138	11,769	2,628	8,261	880
Total area actually reporting	100.0%	2,426	61	137	604	1,624	16,688	4,005	11,299	1,384
Rate per 100,000 inhabitants		584.8	14.7	33.0	145.6	391.5	4,023.0	965.5	2,723.9	333.6
Modesto, CA M.S.A...	539,425									
Includes Stanislaus County										
City of Modesto..	212,880	2,104	13	103	481	1,507	9,324	1,421	6,350	1,553
Total area actually reporting	100.0%	3,366	34	199	835	2,298	17,918	3,303	11,119	3,496
Rate per 100,000 inhabitants		624.0	6.3	36.9	154.8	426.0	3,321.7	612.3	2,061.3	648.1
Monroe, LA M.S.A.	179,125									
Includes Ouachita and Union Parishes										
City of Monroe	49,677	1,493	11	52	248	1,182	4,646	1,025	3,397	224
Total area actually reporting	95.6%	2,092	19	64	319	1,690	8,592	2,179	5,965	448
Estimated total..	100.0%	2,126	20	66	324	1,716	8,884	2,229	6,193	462
Rate per 100,000 inhabitants		1,186.9	11.2	36.8	180.9	958.0	4,959.7	1,244.4	3,457.4	257.9
Montgomery, AL M.S.A.	372,661									
Includes Autauga, Elmore, Lowndes, and Montgomery Counties										
City of Montgomery	199,565	1,215	30	62	448	675	8,989	2,293	5,824	872
Total area actually reporting	99.3%	1,745	44	136	528	1,037	13,166	3,219	8,761	1,186
Estimated total..	100.0%	1,758	44	137	530	1,047	13,248	3,235	8,821	1,192
Rate per 100,000 inhabitants		471.7	11.8	36.8	142.2	281.0	3,555.0	868.1	2,367.0	319.9
Morgantown, WV M.S.A.	138,954									
Includes Monongalia and Preston Counties										
City of Morgantown	31,109	89	2	12	19	56	674	129	517	28
Total area actually reporting	88.4%	318	3	59	27	229	1,684	410	1,186	88
Estimated total..	100.0%	366	3	65	34	264	2,245	502	1,623	120
Rate per 100,000 inhabitants		263.4	2.2	46.8	24.5	190.0	1,615.6	361.3	1,168.0	86.4
Mount Vernon-Anacortes, WA M.S.A................................	123,317									
Includes Skagit County										
City of Mount Vernon..	34,521	88	0	16	28	44	1,324	197	1,014	113

(Number, percent, rate per 100,000 population.)

Area	Population	Violent crime	Murder and nonnegligent manslaughter	Rape[1]	Robbery	Aggravated assault	Property crime	Burglary	Larceny-theft	Motor vehicle theft
City of Anacortes	16,532	15	0	1	4	10	463	65	369	29
Total area actually reporting	100.0%	230	6	36	54	134	4,424	852	3,263	309
Rate per 100,000 inhabitants		186.5	4.9	29.2	43.8	108.7	3,587.5	690.9	2,646.0	250.6
Muncie, IN M.S.A.	116,443									
Includes Delaware County										
City of Muncie	70,065	252	6	29	95	122	2,755	475	2,083	197
Total area actually reporting	100.0%	304	9	37	99	159	3,429	650	2,533	246
Rate per 100,000 inhabitants		261.1	7.7	31.8	85.0	136.5	2,944.8	558.2	2,175.3	211.3
Muskegon, MI M.S.A.	172,890									
Includes Muskegon County										
City of Muskegon	38,442	273	5	39	62	167	1,468	285	1,094	89
Total area actually reporting	100.0%	754	9	144	142	459	5,211	813	4,148	250
Rate per 100,000 inhabitants		436.1	5.2	83.3	82.1	265.5	3,014.1	470.2	2,399.2	144.6
Myrtle Beach-Conway-North Myrtle Beach, SC-NC M.S.A.	444,122									
Includes Brunswick County, NC and Horry County, SC										
City of Myrtle Beach, SC	31,864	538	5	46	139	348	4,395	469	3,555	371
City of Conway, SC	21,874	174	3	20	24	127	1,016	138	805	73
City of North Myrtle Beach, SC	15,945	121	2	21	28	70	1,227	194	918	115
Total area actually reporting	97.4%	2,015	32	313	336	1,334	15,950	2,824	11,805	1,321
Estimated total	100.0%	2,046	32	315	345	1,354	16,308	2,892	12,082	1,334
Rate per 100,000 inhabitants		460.7	7.2	70.9	77.7	304.9	3,672.0	651.2	2,720.4	300.4
Napa, CA M.S.A.	142,635									
Includes Napa County										
City of Napa	81,115	296	1	38	47	210	1,579	437	1,013	129
Total area actually reporting	100.0%	598	1	62	72	463	2,524	655	1,647	222
Rate per 100,000 inhabitants		419.3	0.7	43.5	50.5	324.6	1,769.6	459.2	1,154.7	155.6
Naples-Immokalee-Marco Island, FL M.S.A.	365,390									
Includes Collier County										
City of Naples	21,917	19	3	4	3	9	408	52	339	17
City of Marco Island	17,947	2	0	1	0	1	94	13	76	5
Total area actually reporting	100.0%	962	10	70	169	713	4,496	807	3,443	246
Rate per 100,000 inhabitants		263.3	2.7	19.2	46.3	195.1	1,230.5	220.9	942.3	67.3
Nashville - Davidson - Murfreesboro - Franklin, TN M.S.A.	1,863,012									
Includes Cannon, Cheatham, Davidson, Dickson, Hickman, Macon, Maury, Robertson, Rutherford, Smith, Sumner, Trousdale, Williamson, and Wilson Counties										
City of Nashville Metropolitan	668,685	7,371	81	464	1,985	4,841	24,719	4,545	18,446	1,728
City of Murfreesboro	129,730	790	6	55	152	577	3,867	627	3,042	198
City of Franklin	74,771	154	0	21	19	114	1,085	84	968	33
Total area actually reporting	100.0%	11,580	115	839	2,435	8,191	46,171	8,320	34,747	3,104
Rate per 100,000 inhabitants		621.6	6.2	45.0	130.7	439.7	2,478.3	446.6	1,865.1	166.6
New Bern, NC M.S.A.	126,088									
Includes Craven, Jones, and Pamlico Counties										
City of New Bern	30,137	124	2	7	41	74	1,046	167	856	23
Total area actually reporting	91.0%	291	3	22	65	201	2,797	823	1,853	121
Estimated total	100.0%	310	3	23	69	215	3,001	885	1,984	132
Rate per 100,000 inhabitants		245.9	2.4	18.2	54.7	170.5	2,380.1	701.9	1,573.5	104.7
New Haven-Milford, CT M.S.A.[3]	804,612									
Includes New Haven County										
City of New Haven	130,425	1,219	13	66	400	740	5,492	832	3,925	735
City of Milford	53,752	34	0	0	27	7	1,215	126	1,001	88
Total area actually reporting	100.0%	2,597	30	185	885	1,497	20,370	3,269	14,656	2,445
Rate per 100,000 inhabitants		322.8	3.7	23.0	110.0	186.1	2,531.7	406.3	1,821.5	303.9
New Orleans-Metairie, LA M.S.A.	1,272,995									
Includes Jefferson, Orleans, Plaquemines, St. Bernard, St. Charles, St. James, St. John the Baptist, and St. Tammany Parishes										
City of New Orleans	397,208	4,249	174	537	1,445	2,093	15,571	2,561	10,583	2,427
Total area actually reporting	99.7%	7,099	240	712	2,060	4,087	38,082	5,940	28,488	3,654

Table 4. Crime, by Selected Metropolitan Statistical Area, 2016—*Continued*

(Number, percent, rate per 100,000 population.)

Area	Population	Violent crime	Murder and nonnegligent manslaughter	Rape[1]	Robbery	Aggravated assault	Property crime	Burglary	Larceny-theft	Motor vehicle theft
Estimated total...	100.0%	7,113	240	713	2,062	4,098	38,206	5,961	28,585	3,660
Rate per 100,000 inhabitants.............................		558.8	18.9	56.0	162.0	321.9	3,001.3	468.3	2,245.5	287.5
New York-Newark-Jersey City, NY-NJ-PA M.S.A...............	20,177,990									
Includes the Metropolitan Divisions of Dutchess County-Putnam County, NY; Nassau County-Suffolk County, NY; Newark, NJ-PA; and New York-Jersey City-White Plains, NY-NJ										
City of New York, NY..	8,566,917	49,124	335	2,372	15,544	30,873	125,278	12,041	106,868	6,369
City of Newark, NJ..	281,450	2,637	100	99	1,334	1,104	6,308	1,138	3,048	2,122
City of Jersey City, NJ.......................................	266,179	1,276	24	86	547	619	4,483	953	2,979	551
City of White Plains, NY....................................	58,767	121	0	10	30	81	931	53	854	24
City of New Brunswick, NJ.................................	57,158	392	1	38	211	142	1,252	319	859	74
City of Lakewood Township, NJ.........................	100,269	169	2	12	61	94	949	193	718	38
Total area actually reporting.............................	99.8%	71,541	655	3,940	24,435	42,511	273,117	33,416	221,694	18,007
Estimated total..	100.0%	71,614	656	3,949	24,456	42,553	273,749	33,494	222,225	18,030
Rate per 100,000 inhabitants.............................		354.9	3.3	19.6	121.2	210.9	1,356.7	166.0	1,101.3	89.4
Dutchess County-Putnam County, NY M.D.	391,642									
Includes Dutchess and Putnam Counties										
Total area actually reporting.............................	99.1%	601	4	120	119	358	4,079	565	3,414	100
Estimated total..	100.0%	607	4	121	121	361	4,130	571	3,457	102
Rate per 100,000 inhabitants.............................		155.0	1.0	30.9	30.9	92.2	1,054.5	145.8	882.7	26.0
Nassau County-Suffolk County, NY M.D.	2,849,237									
Includes Nassau and Suffolk Counties										
Total area actually reporting.............................	98.8%	3,611	53	201	1,294	2,063	33,727	3,530	28,346	1,851
Estimated total..	100.0%	3,673	54	208	1,312	2,099	34,264	3,597	28,797	1,870
Rate per 100,000 inhabitants.............................		128.9	1.9	7.3	46.0	73.7	1,202.6	126.2	1,010.7	65.6
Newark, NJ-PA M.D.	2,506,862									
Includes Essex, Hunterdon, Morris, Somerset, Sussex, and Union Counties, NJ and Pike County, PA										
Total area actually reporting.............................	100.0%	7,110	151	423	3,365	3,171	35,082	6,232	23,658	5,192
Rate per 100,000 inhabitants.............................		283.6	6.0	16.9	134.2	126.5	1,399.4	248.6	943.7	207.1
New York-Jersey City-White Plains, NY-NJ M.D.	14,430,249									
Includes Bergen, Hudson, Middlesex, Monmouth, Ocean, and Passaic Counties, NJ and Bronx, Kings, New York, Orange, Queens, Richmond, Rockland, and Westchester Counties, NY										
Total area actually reporting.............................	99.9%	60,219	447	3,196	19,657	36,919	200,229	23,089	166,276	10,864
Estimated total..	100.0%	60,224	447	3,197	19,658	36,922	200,273	23,094	166,313	10,866
Rate per 100,000 inhabitants.............................		417.3	3.1	22.2	136.2	255.9	1,387.9	160.0	1,152.5	75.3
Niles-Benton Harbor, MI M.S.A.	154,139									
Includes Berrien County										
City of Niles..	11,282	64	0	20	12	32	287	65	191	31
City of Benton Harbor......................................	9,963	179	1	15	41	122	438	137	258	43
Total area actually reporting.............................	100.0%	696	10	151	102	433	3,605	772	2,641	192
Rate per 100,000 inhabitants.............................		451.5	6.5	98.0	66.2	280.9	2,338.8	500.8	1,713.4	124.6
North Port-Sarasota-Bradenton, FL M.S.A.	784,372									
Includes Manatee and Sarasota Counties										
City of North Port	63,386	89	1	21	11	56	861	166	668	27
City of Sarasota	55,732	291	3	19	85	184	2,199	314	1,763	122
City of Bradenton	55,518	328	4	31	72	221	1,713	325	1,323	65
City of Venice	22,514	24	0	5	5	14	374	65	293	16
Total area actually reporting.............................	100.0%	2,678	32	241	428	1,977	15,870	2,822	12,238	810
Rate per 100,000 inhabitants.............................		341.4	4.1	30.7	54.6	252.0	2,023.3	359.8	1,560.2	103.3
Norwich-New London, CT M.S.A.	159,068									
Includes New London County										
City of Norwich...	39,771	121	1	15	21	84	621	152	419	50
City of New London...	27,092	193	1	11	30	151	743	130	532	81
Total area actually reporting.............................	100.0%	465	3	52	70	340	3,278	513	2,557	208
Rate per 100,000 inhabitants.............................		292.3	1.9	32.7	44.0	213.7	2,060.8	322.5	1,607.5	130.8
Ocala, FL M.S.A..	346,358									
Includes Marion County										

Table 4. Crime, by Selected Metropolitan Statistical Area, 2016—*Continued*

(Number, percent, rate per 100,000 population.)

Area	Population	Violent crime	Murder and nonnegligent manslaughter	Rape[1]	Robbery	Aggravated assault	Property crime	Burglary	Larceny-theft	Motor vehicle theft
City of Ocala...................................	58,596	463	10	29	111	313	3,174	443	2,600	131
Total area actually reporting	100.0%	1,174	18	90	213	853	7,923	1,926	5,384	613
Rate per 100,000 inhabitants...............		339.0	5.2	26.0	61.5	246.3	2,287.5	556.1	1,554.5	177.0
Ocean City, NJ M.S.A...........................	93,755									
Includes Cape May County										
City of Ocean City..............................	11,287	14	0	1	5	8	364	58	306	0
Total area actually reporting	100.0%	217	0	25	54	138	2,830	532	2,249	49
Rate per 100,000 inhabitants...............		231.5	0.0	26.7	57.6	147.2	3,018.5	567.4	2,398.8	52.3
Odessa, TX M.S.A................................	163,843									
Includes Ector County										
City of Odessa	123,209	996	4	75	136	781	4,118	791	2,890	437
Total area actually reporting	100.0%	1,169	7	98	170	894	6,137	1,157	4,300	680
Rate per 100,000 inhabitants...............		713.5	4.3	59.8	103.8	545.6	3,745.7	706.2	2,624.5	415.0
Ogden-Clearfield, UT M.S.A.[3]............	653,748									
Includes Box Elder, Davis, Morgan, and Weber Counties										
City of Ogden	85,930	450	3	65	108	274	3,808	614	2,843	351
City of Clearfield...............................	30,783	29	0	13	3	13	664	120	501	43
Total area actually reporting	98.1%	996	9	267	173	547	14,205	2,418	10,807	980
Estimated total..................................	100.0%	1,017	9	271	178	559	14,508	2,467	11,023	1,018
Rate per 100,000 inhabitants...............		155.6	1.4	41.5	27.2	85.5	2,219.2	377.4	1,686.1	155.7
Oklahoma City, OK M.S.A....................	1,372,721									
Includes Canadian, Cleveland, Grady, Lincoln, Logan, McClain, and Oklahoma Counties										
City of Oklahoma City.........................	641,681	5,027	70	445	1,144	3,368	25,032	5,545	16,582	2,905
Total area actually reporting	100.0%	6,737	92	752	1,433	4,460	42,683	9,427	28,735	4,521
Rate per 100,000 inhabitants...............		490.8	6.7	54.8	104.4	324.9	3,109.4	686.7	2,093.3	329.3
Olympia-Tumwater, WA M.S.A.	274,020									
Includes Thurston County										
City of Olympia..................................	50,972	200	0	21	47	132	2,491	378	1,889	224
City of Tumwater................................	19,569	78	0	12	7	59	843	169	585	89
Total area actually reporting	100.0%	668	6	74	108	480	8,060	1,606	5,721	733
Rate per 100,000 inhabitants...............		243.8	2.2	27.0	39.4	175.2	2,941.4	586.1	2,087.8	267.5
Omaha-Council Bluffs, NE-IA M.S.A.....	923,710									
Includes Harrison, Mills, and Pottawattamie Counties, IA and Cass, Douglas, Sarpy, Saunders, and Washington Counties, NE										
City of Omaha, NE..............................	446,163	2,531	29	245	610	1,647	16,807	2,111	11,571	3,125
City of Council Bluffs, IA	62,642	150	4	27	55	64	3,862	387	3,043	432
Total area actually reporting	99.9%	3,242	36	388	722	2,096	25,394	3,334	17,981	4,079
Estimated total..................................	100.0%	3,244	36	389	722	2,097	25,415	3,336	17,998	4,081
Rate per 100,000 inhabitants...............		351.2	3.9	42.1	78.2	227.0	2,751.4	361.2	1,948.4	441.8
Orlando-Kissimmee-Sanford, FL M.S.A.[6]	2,445,214									
Includes Lake, Orange, Osceola, and Seminole Counties										
City of Orlando[6]................................	277,719	2,328	84	211	504	1,529	14,498	3,637	9,621	1,240
City of Kissimmee	71,197	508	0	47	114	347	2,670	585	1,955	130
City of Sanford	59,027	542	6	48	138	350	2,812	466	2,165	181
Total area actually reporting	99.4%	12,275	196	1,222	2,412	8,445	72,038	16,639	50,171	5,228
Estimated total..................................	100.0%	12,331	197	1,226	2,428	8,480	72,464	16,703	50,500	5,261
Rate per 100,000 inhabitants...............		504.3	8.1	50.1	99.3	346.8	2,963.5	683.1	2,065.3	215.2
Oshkosh-Neenah, WI M.S.A.	169,773									
Includes Winnebago County										
City of Oshkosh..................................	66,654	141	0	7	28	106	1,471	194	1,209	68
City of Neenah....................................	25,850	52	0	9	10	33	491	50	420	21
Total area actually reporting	100.0%	281	0	21	45	215	2,857	410	2,313	134
Rate per 100,000 inhabitants...............		165.5	0.0	12.4	26.5	126.6	1,682.8	241.5	1,362.4	78.9
Owensboro, KY M.S.A.	117,893									
Includes Daviess, Hancock, and McLean Counties										
City of Owensboro..............................	59,359	136	1	34	49	52	2,658	486	1,937	235

Table 4. Crime, by Selected Metropolitan Statistical Area, 2016—*Continued*

(Number, percent, rate per 100,000 population.)

Area	Population	Violent crime	Murder and nonnegligent manslaughter	Rape[1]	Robbery	Aggravated assault	Property crime	Burglary	Larceny-theft	Motor vehicle theft
Total area actually reporting...........................	100.0%	169	2	46	52	69	3,196	636	2,289	271
Rate per 100,000 inhabitants............................		143.4	1.7	39.0	44.1	58.5	2,710.9	539.5	1,941.6	229.9
Oxnard-Thousand Oaks-Ventura, CA M.S.A.	849,851									
Includes Ventura County										
City of Oxnard	209,048	948	12	69	429	438	6,073	978	4,309	786
City of Thousand Oaks.....................................	129,853	164	0	30	33	101	1,686	272	1,302	112
City of Ventura	110,228	368	8	53	109	198	3,750	628	2,838	284
City of Camarillo	68,072	123	4	21	31	67	1,125	202	824	99
Total area actually reporting...........................	100.0%	2,192	31	269	725	1,167	16,415	2,910	11,855	1,650
Rate per 100,000 inhabitants............................		257.9	3.6	31.7	85.3	137.3	1,931.5	342.4	1,395.0	194.2
Palm Bay-Melbourne-Titusville, FL M.S.A.	574,187									
Includes Brevard County										
City of Palm Bay..	108,823	516	4	57	47	408	1,841	454	1,252	135
City of Melbourne..	80,900	667	3	65	126	473	3,308	686	2,439	183
City of Titusville	45,723	355	3	40	61	251	1,868	463	1,183	222
Total area actually reporting...........................	100.0%	2,870	20	255	451	2,144	14,857	3,249	10,454	1,154
Rate per 100,000 inhabitants............................		499.8	3.5	44.4	78.5	373.4	2,587.5	565.8	1,820.7	201.0
Panama City, FL M.S.A.	200,502									
Includes Bay and Gulf Counties										
City of Panama City	38,847	276	3	17	50	206	2,098	330	1,587	181
Total area actually reporting...........................	100.0%	957	9	90	136	722	6,776	1,208	5,136	432
Rate per 100,000 inhabitants............................		477.3	4.5	44.9	67.8	360.1	3,379.5	602.5	2,561.6	215.5
Parkersburg-Vienna, WV M.S.A.	91,681									
Includes Wirt and Wood Counties										
City of Parkersburg	30,913	206	4	27	19	156	1,373	371	923	79
City of Vienna...	10,537	20	0	4	1	15	447	29	415	3
Total area actually reporting...........................	100.0%	360	4	47	24	285	2,425	596	1,703	126
Rate per 100,000 inhabitants............................		392.7	4.4	51.3	26.2	310.9	2,645.0	650.1	1,857.5	137.4
Pensacola-Ferry Pass-Brent, FL M.S.A.	484,608									
Includes Escambia and Santa Rosa Counties										
City of Pensacola	53,424	348	7	27	64	250	2,184	341	1,741	102
Total area actually reporting...........................	100.0%	2,219	25	243	396	1,555	12,338	2,441	9,137	760
Rate per 100,000 inhabitants............................		457.9	5.2	50.1	81.7	320.9	2,546.0	503.7	1,885.4	156.8
Peoria, IL M.S.A.	375,999									
Includes Marshall, Peoria, Stark, Tazewell, and Woodford Counties										
City of Peoria..	115,099	875	10	70	305	490	4,429	1,089	3,116	224
Total area actually reporting...........................	95.7%	1,463	14	166	356	927	8,215	1,876	5,981	358
Estimated total..	100.0%	1,497	14	171	366	946	8,489	1,919	6,198	372
Rate per 100,000 inhabitants............................		398.1	3.7	45.5	97.3	251.6	2,257.7	510.4	1,648.4	98.9
Philadelphia-Camden-Wilmington, PA-NJ-DE-MD M.S.A.	6,068,767									
Includes the Metropolitan Divisions of Camden, NJ; Montgomery County-Bucks County-Chester County, PA; Philadelphia, PA; and Wilmington, DE-MD-NJ										
City of Philadelphia, PA	1,570,826	15,534	273	1,259	6,199	7,803	49,334	6,985	36,856	5,493
City of Wilmington, DE	72,183	1,285	26	35	438	786	3,544	812	2,232	500
Total area actually reporting...........................	99.9%	27,091	480	2,046	9,875	14,690	131,765	20,263	101,444	10,058
Estimated total..	100.0%	27,098	480	2,046	9,877	14,695	131,822	20,270	101,492	10,060
Rate per 100,000 inhabitants............................		446.5	7.9	33.7	162.8	242.1	2,172.1	334.0	1,672.4	165.8
Camden, NJ M.D.	1,246,564									
Includes Burlington, Camden, and Gloucester Counties										
Total area actually reporting...........................	100.0%	3,396	83	282	1,112	1,919	24,291	5,135	17,728	1,428
Rate per 100,000 inhabitants............................		272.4	6.7	22.6	89.2	153.9	1,948.6	411.9	1,422.1	114.6
Montgomery County-Bucks County-Chester County, PA M.D.........	1,964,200									
Includes Bucks, Chester, and Montgomery Counties										
Total area actually reporting...........................	99.9%	2,342	33	232	655	1,422	27,761	3,178	23,452	1,131
Estimated total..	100.0%	2,345	33	232	656	1,424	27,783	3,181	23,470	1,132
Rate per 100,000 inhabitants............................		119.4	1.7	11.8	33.4	72.5	1,414.5	161.9	1,194.9	57.6
Philadelphia, PA M.D.	2,134,060									
Includes Delaware and Philadelphia Counties										

(Number, percent, rate per 100,000 population.)

Area	Population	Violent crime	Murder and nonnegligent manslaughter	Rape[1]	Robbery	Aggravated assault	Property crime	Burglary	Larceny-theft	Motor vehicle theft
Total area actually reporting	99.9%	17,639	311	1,341	6,925	9,062	59,550	8,305	45,163	6,082
Estimated total	100.0%	17,643	311	1,341	6,926	9,065	59,585	8,309	45,193	6,083
Rate per 100,000 inhabitants		826.7	14.6	62.8	324.5	424.8	2,792.1	389.4	2,117.7	285.0
Wilmington, DE-MD-NJ M.D.	723,943									
Includes New Castle County, DE; Cecil County, MD; and Salem County, NJ										
Total area actually reporting	100.0%	3,714	53	191	1,183	2,287	20,163	3,645	15,101	1,417
Rate per 100,000 inhabitants		513.0	7.3	26.4	163.4	315.9	2,785.2	503.5	2,085.9	195.7
Phoenix-Mesa-Scottsdale, AZ M.S.A.	4,662,302									
Includes Maricopa and Pinal Counties										
City of Phoenix	1,586,611	10,700	146	1,019	3,272	6,263	58,552	13,024	37,568	7,960
City of Mesa	478,277	2,051	19	272	450	1,310	11,214	1,950	8,404	860
City of Scottsdale	240,885	369	4	90	112	163	5,698	768	4,681	249
City of Tempe	178,654	902	4	155	237	506	8,144	1,200	6,494	450
Total area actually reporting	99.8%	19,876	256	2,148	5,247	12,225	133,534	25,703	94,366	13,465
Estimated total	100.0%	19,904	256	2,151	5,253	12,244	133,812	25,748	94,580	13,484
Rate per 100,000 inhabitants		426.9	5.5	46.1	112.7	262.6	2,870.1	552.3	2,028.6	289.2
Pine Bluff, AR M.S.A	92,403									
Includes Cleveland, Jefferson, and Lincoln Counties										
City of Pine Bluff	43,976	705	9	38	130	528	2,786	1,062	1,488	236
Total area actually reporting	100.0%	840	10	60	139	631	3,594	1,340	1,944	310
Rate per 100,000 inhabitants		909.1	10.8	64.9	150.4	682.9	3,889.5	1,450.2	2,103.8	335.5
Pittsburgh, PA M.S.A.	2,345,496									
Includes Allegheny, Armstrong, Beaver, Butler, Fayette, Washington, and Westmoreland Counties										
City of Pittsburgh	302,443	2,366	57	100	1,000	1,209	9,868	1,828	7,222	818
Total area actually reporting	97.9%	6,694	118	529	1,924	4,123	40,207	7,165	31,025	2,017
Estimated total	100.0%	6,778	119	536	1,945	4,178	40,964	7,260	31,659	2,045
Rate per 100,000 inhabitants		289.0	5.1	22.9	82.9	178.1	1,746.5	309.5	1,349.8	87.2
Pittsfield, MA M.S.A.	126,594									
Includes Berkshire County										
City of Pittsfield	43,031	340	3	37	39	261	1,016	364	620	32
Total area actually reporting	91.2%	616	3	80	50	483	2,138	649	1,421	68
Estimated total	100.0%	649	3	83	55	508	2,292	676	1,537	79
Rate per 100,000 inhabitants		512.7	2.4	65.6	43.4	401.3	1,810.5	534.0	1,214.1	62.4
Pocatello, ID M.S.A.	84,414									
Includes Bannock County										
City of Pocatello	54,448	207	2	18	14	173	1,630	316	1,184	130
Total area actually reporting	100.0%	241	3	20	18	200	2,218	361	1,712	145
Rate per 100,000 inhabitants		285.5	3.6	23.7	21.3	236.9	2,627.5	427.7	2,028.1	171.8
Portland-South Portland, ME M.S.A.[3]	529,510									
Includes Cumberland, Sagadahoc, and York Counties										
City of Portland	67,041	196	2	36	59	99	1,795	236	1,485	74
City of South Portland	25,674	44	0	6	11	27	596	75	505	16
Total area actually reporting	100.0%	711	8	145	127	431	8,954	1,512	7,148	294
Rate per 100,000 inhabitants		134.3	1.5	27.4	24.0	81.4	1,691.0	285.5	1,349.9	55.5
Portland-Vancouver-Hillsboro, OR-WA M.S.A.	2,435,620									
Includes Clackamas, Columbia, Multnomah, Washington, and Yamhill Counties, OR and Clark and Skamania Counties, WA										
City of Portland, OR	642,129	3,163	14	389	986	1,774	33,087	4,064	24,099	4,924
City of Vancouver, WA	174,912	675	0	117	148	410	5,533	860	3,666	1,007
City of Hillsboro, OR	104,440	298	0	79	64	155	2,010	232	1,613	165
City of Beaverton, OR	97,907	133	0	25	30	78	1,403	124	1,176	103
Total area actually reporting	98.3%	6,635	41	1,181	1,647	3,766	66,937	8,901	48,646	9,390
Estimated total	100.0%	6,725	42	1,199	1,665	3,819	68,056	9,029	49,529	9,498
Rate per 100,000 inhabitants		276.1	1.7	49.2	68.4	156.8	2,794.2	370.7	2,033.5	390.0
Port St. Lucie, FL M.S.A.	461,932									
Includes Martin and St. Lucie Counties										
City of Port St. Lucie	182,365	270	3	22	48	197	2,419	400	1,934	85

Table 4. Crime, by Selected Metropolitan Statistical Area, 2016—*Continued*

(Number, percent, rate per 100,000 population.)

Area	Population	Violent crime	Murder and nonnegligent manslaughter	Rape[1]	Robbery	Aggravated assault	Property crime	Burglary	Larceny-theft	Motor vehicle theft
Total area actually reporting...	100.0%	1,196	19	132	216	829	8,119	1,523	6,224	372
Rate per 100,000 inhabitants..		258.9	4.1	28.6	46.8	179.5	1,757.6	329.7	1,347.4	80.5
Prescott, AZ M.S.A.	225,038									
Includes Yavapai County										
City of Prescott	42,321	170	0	10	18	142	924	175	720	29
Total area actually reporting...	100.0%	653	6	49	49	549	4,326	841	3,246	239
Rate per 100,000 inhabitants..		290.2	2.7	21.8	21.8	244.0	1,922.3	373.7	1,442.4	106.2
Providence-Warwick, RI-MA M.S.A.[3,5]	1,612,295									
Includes Bristol County, MA and Bristol, Kent, Newport, Providence, and Washington Counties, RI										
City of Providence, RI3	179,340	1,031	10	112	300	609		1,154	4,132	
City of Warwick, RI	81,481	61	1	17	11	32	1,625	158	1,392	75
Total area actually reporting...	100.0%	5,079	39	625	1,059	3,356		5,922		
Rate per 100,000 inhabitants..		315.0	2.4	38.8	65.7	208.2		367.3		
Provo-Orem, UT M.S.A...	599,314									
Includes Juab and Utah Counties										
City of Provo...	115,739	149	2	57	20	70	2,713	266	2,292	155
City of Orem..	95,640	65	0	26	18	21	2,447	209	2,116	122
Total area actually reporting...	100.0%	465	5	164	64	232	10,556	1,241	8,766	549
Rate per 100,000 inhabitants..		77.6	0.8	27.4	10.7	38.7	1,761.3	207.1	1,462.7	91.6
Pueblo, CO M.S.A....	164,337									
Includes Pueblo County										
City of Pueblo..	109,927	1,081	9	171	224	677	7,473	1,797	4,505	1,171
Total area actually reporting...	100.0%	1,117	11	172	230	704	8,784	2,089	5,364	1,331
Rate per 100,000 inhabitants..		679.7	6.7	104.7	140.0	428.4	5,345.1	1,271.2	3,264.0	809.9
Punta Gorda, FL M.S.A...	176,234									
Includes Charlotte County										
City of Punta Gorda..	18,466	12	1	0	1	10	212	24	177	11
Total area actually reporting...	100.0%	391	5	35	20	331	2,671	432	2,127	112
Rate per 100,000 inhabitants..		221.9	2.8	19.9	11.3	187.8	1,515.6	245.1	1,206.9	63.6
Racine, WI M.S.A.	194,692									
Includes Racine County										
City of Racine	77,536	367	6	16	133	212	2,287	677	1,510	100
Total area actually reporting...	100.0%	427	8	29	148	242	3,748	875	2,715	158
Rate per 100,000 inhabitants..		219.3	4.1	14.9	76.0	124.3	1,925.1	449.4	1,394.5	81.2
Rapid City, SD M.S.A.	145,700									
Includes Custer, Meade, and Pennington Counties										
City of Rapid City..	74,573	536	2	88	80	366	2,966	480	2,236	250
Total area actually reporting...	100.0%	721	5	151	87	478	3,806	635	2,861	310
Rate per 100,000 inhabitants..		494.9	3.4	103.6	59.7	328.1	2,612.2	435.8	1,963.6	212.8
Reading, PA M.S.A.	414,729									
Includes Berks County										
City of Reading...	87,834	597	10	47	233	307	2,292	685	1,417	190
Total area actually reporting...	99.1%	1,128	17	110	299	702	6,740	1,416	4,973	351
Estimated total...	100.0%	1,135	17	111	301	706	6,795	1,423	5,019	353
Rate per 100,000 inhabitants..		273.7	4.1	26.8	72.6	170.2	1,638.4	343.1	1,210.2	85.1
Redding, CA M.S.A...	178,755									
Includes Shasta County										
City of Redding..	91,918	720	5	84	143	488	3,837	710	2,608	519
Total area actually reporting...	100.0%	1,333	12	150	172	999	5,561	1,217	3,472	872
Rate per 100,000 inhabitants..		745.7	6.7	83.9	96.2	558.9	3,111.0	680.8	1,942.3	487.8
Reno, NV M.S.A.	457,558									
Includes Storey and Washoe Counties										
City of Reno..	244,554	1,717	9	139	393	1,176	7,933	1,208	5,381	1,344
Total area actually reporting...	100.0%	2,354	14	193	491	1,656	11,866	1,919	8,134	1,813
Rate per 100,000 inhabitants..		514.5	3.1	42.2	107.3	361.9	2,593.3	419.4	1,777.7	396.2
Riverside-San Bernardino-Ontario, CA M.S.A.	4,509,084									
Includes Riverside and San Bernardino Counties										
City of Riverside...	325,896	1,724	10	141	586	987	11,266	1,977	7,355	1,934

(Number, percent, rate per 100,000 population.)

Area	Population	Violent crime	Murder and nonnegligent manslaughter	Rape[1]	Robbery	Aggravated assault	Property crime	Burglary	Larceny-theft	Motor vehicle theft
City of San Bernardino	217,303	2,878	62	123	903	1,790	9,178	2,353	4,228	2,597
City of Ontario	172,606	602	8	32	227	335	4,718	885	2,764	1,069
City of Corona	166,534	185	3	39	74	69	3,693	741	2,236	716
City of Victorville	123,438	748	7	46	224	471	3,528	953	2,002	573
City of Temecula	114,381	145	2	4	55	84	2,587	341	1,940	306
City of Chino	87,081	207	1	13	52	141	2,151	439	1,407	305
City of Redlands	71,485	225	0	37	76	112	2,913	501	2,014	398
Total area actually reporting	100.0%	17,916	228	1,203	5,186	11,299	120,270	26,204	70,799	23,267
Rate per 100,000 inhabitants		397.3	5.1	26.7	115.0	250.6	2,667.3	581.1	1,570.1	516.0
Roanoke, VA M.S.A.	314,014									
Includes Botetourt, Craig, Franklin, and Roanoke Counties and Roanoke and Salem Cities										
City of Roanoke	99,978	413	13	36	117	247	4,195	423	3,549	223
Total area actually reporting	100.0%	763	16	106	148	493	7,110	771	5,961	378
Rate per 100,000 inhabitants		243.0	5.1	33.8	47.1	157.0	2,264.2	245.5	1,898.3	120.4
Rochester, MN M.S.A.	214,994									
Includes Dodge, Fillmore, Olmsted, and Wabasha Counties										
City of Rochester	113,306	242	0	76	49	117	2,479	375	1,972	132
Total area actually reporting	100.0%	296	0	91	53	152	3,138	526	2,418	194
Rate per 100,000 inhabitants		137.7	0.0	42.3	24.7	70.7	1,459.6	244.7	1,124.7	90.2
Rochester, NY M.S.A.	1,075,149									
Includes Livingston, Monroe, Ontario, Orleans, Wayne, and Yates Counties										
City of Rochester	209,643	1,845	43	161	670	971	7,812	1,475	5,673	664
Total area actually reporting	99.6%	3,012	51	458	913	1,590	21,396	3,539	16,745	1,112
Estimated total	100.0%	3,019	51	459	915	1,594	21,457	3,547	16,796	1,114
Rate per 100,000 inhabitants		280.8	4.7	42.7	85.1	148.3	1,995.7	329.9	1,562.2	103.6
Rockford, IL M.S.A.	337,323									
Includes Boone and Winnebago Counties										
City of Rockford	147,361	2,444	26	137	536	1,745	5,565	1,406	3,696	463
Total area actually reporting	99.0%	2,932	31	234	603	2,064	8,697	2,063	6,047	587
Estimated total	100.0%	2,939	31	235	605	2,068	8,756	2,072	6,094	590
Rate per 100,000 inhabitants		871.3	9.2	69.7	179.4	613.1	2,595.7	614.2	1,806.6	174.9
Rocky Mount, NC M.S.A.[4]	147,228									
Includes Edgecombe and Nash Counties										
City of Rocky Mount[3]	55,431	435	4	12	116	303		593		98
Total area actually reporting	93.9%	635	12	31	148	444		1,062		155
Estimated total	100.0%	660	12	33	155	460		1,114		165
Rate per 100,000 inhabitants		448.3	8.2	22.4	105.3	312.4		756.6		112.1
Rome, GA M.S.A.	96,420									
Includes Floyd County										
City of Rome	36,278	208	4	8	52	144	1,398	239	1,088	71
Total area actually reporting	100.0%	309	5	27	67	210	2,765	624	1,954	187
Rate per 100,000 inhabitants		320.5	5.2	28.0	69.5	217.8	2,867.7	647.2	2,026.6	193.9
Sacramento - Roseville - Arden - Arcade, CA M.S.A.	2,283,312									
Includes El Dorado, Placer, Sacramento, and Yolo Counties										
City of Sacramento	495,471	3,549	41	88	1,136	2,284	15,283	3,070	9,389	2,824
City of Roseville	132,566	199	0	21	95	83	3,316	393	2,596	327
City of Folsom	77,245	76	0	9	34	33	1,384	264	1,006	114
Total area actually reporting	100.0%	9,384	95	595	2,742	5,952	54,595	10,479	35,750	8,366
Rate per 100,000 inhabitants		411.0	4.2	26.1	120.1	260.7	2,391.0	458.9	1,565.7	366.4
Saginaw, MI M.S.A.	191,925									
Includes Saginaw County										
City of Saginaw	48,942	718	10	56	62	590	926	369	503	54
Total area actually reporting	100.0%	1,168	18	128	108	914	3,346	836	2,359	151
Rate per 100,000 inhabitants		608.6	9.4	66.7	56.3	476.2	1,743.4	435.6	1,229.1	78.7
Salem, OR M.S.A.	416,427									
Includes Marion and Polk Counties										
City of Salem	166,508	533	7	38	128	360	6,661	907	5,114	640

Table 4. Crime, by Selected Metropolitan Statistical Area, 2016—*Continued*

(Number, percent, rate per 100,000 population.)

Area	Population	Violent crime	Murder and nonnegligent manslaughter	Rape[1]	Robbery	Aggravated assault	Property crime	Burglary	Larceny-theft	Motor vehicle theft
Total area actually reporting	100.0%	952	19	94	189	650	11,947	1,769	8,976	1,202
Rate per 100,000 inhabitants		228.6	4.6	22.6	45.4	156.1	2,868.9	424.8	2,155.5	288.6
Salinas, CA M.S.A.	434,506									
Includes Monterey County										
City of Salinas	158,729	1,005	35	86	325	559	4,742	695	2,484	1,563
Total area actually reporting	100.0%	1,822	56	162	506	1,098	10,396	1,666	6,212	2,518
Rate per 100,000 inhabitants		419.3	12.9	37.3	116.5	252.7	2,392.6	383.4	1,429.7	579.5
Salisbury, MD-DE M.S.A.	397,778									
Includes Sussex County, DE and Somerset, Wicomico, and Worcester Counties, MD										
City of Salisbury, MD	33,417	297	2	11	103	181	1,695	234	1,410	51
Total area actually reporting	100.0%	1,609	15	156	352	1,086	10,755	2,533	7,939	283
Rate per 100,000 inhabitants		404.5	3.8	39.2	88.5	273.0	2,703.8	636.8	1,995.8	71.1
Salt Lake City, UT M.S.A.[3]	1,190,065									
Includes Salt Lake and Tooele Counties										
City of Salt Lake City	193,918	1,815	13	264	506	1,032	16,551	1,807	12,814	1,930
Total area actually reporting	99.9%	4,885	47	827	1,236	2,775	54,725	7,286	40,414	7,025
Estimated total	100.0%	4,885	47	827	1,236	2,775	54,736	7,288	40,422	7,026
Rate per 100,000 inhabitants		410.5	3.9	69.5	103.9	233.2	4,599.4	612.4	3,396.6	590.4
San Angelo, TX M.S.A.	120,833									
Includes Irion and Tom Green Counties										
City of San Angelo	101,870	371	6	58	54	253	4,991	875	3,839	277
Total area actually reporting	100.0%	403	6	78	58	261	5,484	1,081	4,095	308
Rate per 100,000 inhabitants		333.5	5.0	64.6	48.0	216.0	4,538.5	894.6	3,389.0	254.9
San Antonio-New Braunfels, TX M.S.A.[3]	2,426,076									
Includes Atascosa, Bandera, Bexar, Comal, Guadalupe, Kendall, Medina, and Wilson Counties										
City of San Antonio	1,498,642	10,754	149	1,190	2,232	7,183	77,786	12,235	58,318	7,233
City of New Braunfels	73,334	207	1	34	25	147	1,721	245	1,295	181
Total area actually reporting	99.9%	12,767	187	1,596	2,544	8,440	99,000	16,088	74,099	8,813
Estimated total	100.0%	12,771	187	1,597	2,545	8,442	99,029	16,093	74,121	8,815
Rate per 100,000 inhabitants		526.4	7.7	65.8	104.9	348.0	4,081.9	663.3	3,055.2	363.3
San Diego-Carlsbad, CA M.S.A.	3,317,259									
Includes San Diego County										
City of San Diego	1,413,414	5,332	50	572	1,387	3,323	28,624	4,743	18,042	5,839
City of Carlsbad	115,040	209	0	37	49	123	2,188	369	1,652	167
Total area actually reporting	100.0%	10,959	101	1,088	2,777	6,993	61,371	10,391	39,955	11,025
Rate per 100,000 inhabitants		330.4	3.0	32.8	83.7	210.8	1,850.1	313.2	1,204.5	332.4
San Francisco-Oakland-Hayward, CA M.S.A.	4,688,840									
Includes the Metropolitan Divisions of Oakland-Hayward-Berkeley, San Francisco-Redwood City-South San Francisco, and San Rafael										
City of San Francisco	871,155	6,190	57	342	3,175	2,616	47,402	4,978	36,991	5,433
City of Oakland	424,998	6,059	85	277	3,076	2,621	23,952	2,900	14,153	6,899
City of Hayward	161,122	631	13	66	348	204	4,641	707	2,308	1,626
City of Berkeley	122,651	602	2	54	361	185	5,420	805	3,965	650
City of San Leandro	91,870	487	3	31	280	173	3,530	499	2,070	961
City of Redwood City	87,046	164	0	43	44	77	1,503	260	1,087	156
City of San Ramon	76,901	39	0	9	12	18	823	140	616	67
City of Pleasanton	81,464	100	0	12	44	44	1,604	208	1,260	136
City of Walnut Creek	69,860	78	1	1	30	46	2,120	275	1,611	234
City of South San Francisco	67,995	149	1	25	43	80	1,416	307	902	207
City of San Rafael	59,435	249	0	28	111	110	1,713	255	1,186	272
Total area actually reporting	100.0%	22,400	239	1,589	10,467	10,105	156,988	21,502	107,276	28,210
Rate per 100,000 inhabitants		477.7	5.1	33.9	223.2	215.5	3,348.1	458.6	2,287.9	601.6
Oakland-Hayward-Berkeley, CA M.D.	2,787,325									
Includes Alameda and Contra Costa Counties										
Total area actually reporting	100.0%	14,022	169	937	6,613	6,303	88,683	12,410	55,717	20,556
Rate per 100,000 inhabitants		503.1	6.1	33.6	237.3	226.1	3,181.7	445.2	1,998.9	737.5
San Francisco-Redwood City-South San Francisco, CA M.D.	1,640,386									
Includes San Francisco and San Mateo Counties										

Table 4. Crime, by Selected Metropolitan Statistical Area, 2016—*Continued*

(Number, percent, rate per 100,000 population.)

Area	Population	Violent crime	Murder and nonnegligent manslaughter	Rape[1]	Robbery	Aggravated assault	Property crime	Burglary	Larceny-theft	Motor vehicle theft
Total area actually reporting	100.0%	7,903	67	600	3,686	3,550	63,330	8,101	48,115	7,114
Rate per 100,000 inhabitants.................................		481.8	4.1	36.6	224.7	216.4	3,860.7	493.8	2,933.2	433.7
San Rafael, CA M.D.	261,129									
Includes Marin County										
Total area actually reporting	100.0%	475	3	52	168	252	4,975	991	3,444	540
Rate per 100,000 inhabitants.................................		181.9	1.1	19.9	64.3	96.5	1,905.2	379.5	1,318.9	206.8
San Jose-Sunnyvale-Santa Clara, CA M.S.A.	1,991,233									
Includes San Benito and Santa Clara Counties										
City of San Jose...	1,041,844	3,887	47	451	1,214	2,175	24,749	4,260	12,786	7,703
City of Sunnyvale...	154,108	158	1	21	53	83	2,140	520	1,347	273
City of Santa Clara..	128,179	159	3	17	58	81	2,814	362	2,039	413
City of Mountain View..	81,726	132	0	9	29	94	1,776	280	1,377	119
City of Milpitas..	79,990	96	1	9	52	34	1,791	202	1,320	269
City of Palo Alto...	67,317	73	1	9	28	35	1,436	215	1,159	62
City of Cupertino..	60,948	71	0	7	16	48	997	268	661	68
Total area actually reporting	100.0%	5,578	58	658	1,645	3,217	43,340	7,661	25,613	10,066
Rate per 100,000 inhabitants.................................		280.1	2.9	33.0	82.6	161.6	2,176.5	384.7	1,286.3	505.5
San Luis Obispo-Paso Robles-Arroyo Grande, CA M.S.A.	281,827									
Includes San Luis Obispo County										
City of San Luis Obispo	47,774	178	0	39	21	118	2,076	251	1,730	95
City of Paso Robles	31,939	67	0	8	20	39	977	144	738	95
City of Arroyo Grande..	18,280	35	0	6	9	20	334	53	262	19
Total area actually reporting	100.0%	1,115	4	102	88	921	6,687	1,199	4,987	501
Rate per 100,000 inhabitants.................................		395.6	1.4	36.2	31.2	326.8	2,372.7	425.4	1,769.5	177.8
Santa Cruz-Watsonville, CA M.S.A........................	274,494									
Includes Santa Cruz County										
City of Santa Cruz...	64,969	521	4	45	106	366	3,610	354	2,874	382
City of Watsonville..	54,110	238	0	26	46	166	1,738	214	1,018	506
Total area actually reporting	100.0%	1,101	5	120	209	767	9,485	1,221	6,810	1,454
Rate per 100,000 inhabitants.................................		401.1	1.8	43.7	76.1	279.4	3,455.4	444.8	2,480.9	529.7
Santa Fe, NM M.S.A.	148,925									
Includes Santa Fe County										
City of Santa Fe..	84,663	324	1	30	84	209	3,234	1,123	1,870	241
Total area actually reporting	100.0%	555	2	42	107	404	4,267	1,629	2,354	284
Rate per 100,000 inhabitants.................................		372.7	1.3	28.2	71.8	271.3	2,865.2	1,093.8	1,580.7	190.7
Santa Maria-Santa Barbara, CA M.S.A.	445,908									
Includes Santa Barbara County										
City of Santa Maria..	106,200	506	9	45	168	284	2,638	521	1,452	665
City of Santa Barbara...	92,519	397	0	87	82	228	3,060	433	2,428	199
Total area actually reporting	100.0%	1,527	13	244	325	945	9,779	1,868	6,691	1,220
Rate per 100,000 inhabitants.................................		342.4	2.9	54.7	72.9	211.9	2,193.1	418.9	1,500.5	273.6
Santa Rosa, CA M.S.A.	502,249									
Includes Sonoma County										
City of Santa Rosa...	176,383	658	5	94	121	438	3,010	516	2,087	407
Total area actually reporting	100.0%	1,868	10	282	236	1,340	7,794	1,529	5,380	885
Rate per 100,000 inhabitants.................................		371.9	2.0	56.1	47.0	266.8	1,551.8	304.4	1,071.2	176.2
Savannah, GA M.S.A....	385,219									
Includes Bryan, Chatham, and Effingham Counties										
City of Savannah-Chatham Metropolitan	241,296	1,174	50	50	534	540	8,762	1,856	5,946	960
Total area actually reporting	100.0%	1,608	53	79	600	876	11,968	2,564	8,275	1,129
Rate per 100,000 inhabitants.................................		417.4	13.8	20.5	155.8	227.4	3,106.8	665.6	2,148.1	293.1
Seattle-Tacoma-Bellevue, WA M.S.A.	3,808,184									
Includes the Metropolitan Divisions of Seattle-Bellevue-Everett and Tacoma-Lakewood										
City of Seattle...	700,313	4,294	19	254	1,547	2,474	38,433	7,666	26,639	4,128
City of Tacoma..	209,914	2,000	13	159	540	1,288	13,749	2,420	8,710	2,619
City of Bellevue...	142,238	139	0	14	61	64	4,635	877	3,458	300
City of Everett...	108,988	490	1	64	148	277	5,608	949	3,701	958
City of Kent	128,604	372	6	66	165	135	7,527	1,060	5,034	1,433
City of Renton	101,908	341	4	36	146	155	5,767	834	3,872	1,061
City of Auburn..	78,400	329	6	49	98	176	3,618	732	2,188	698

Table 4. Crime, by Selected Metropolitan Statistical Area, 2016—*Continued*

(Number, percent, rate per 100,000 population.)

Area	Population	Violent crime	Murder and nonnegligent manslaughter	Rape[1]	Robbery	Aggravated assault	Property crime	Burglary	Larceny-theft	Motor vehicle theft
City of Lakewood............................	60,153	449	0	47	101	301	2,939	589	1,979	371
City of Redmond.............................	61,893	83	0	15	23	45	1,936	181	1,676	79
Total area actually reporting	100.0%	13,449	101	1,505	4,160	7,683	148,138	27,677	99,143	21,318
Rate per 100,000 inhabitants................		353.2	2.7	39.5	109.2	201.7	3,890.0	726.8	2,603.4	559.8
Seattle-Bellevue-Everett, WA M.D................	2,950,845									
Includes King and Snohomish Counties										
Total area actually reporting	100.0%	9,246	71	1,088	3,116	4,971	113,792	20,588	77,667	15,537
Rate per 100,000 inhabitants................		313.3	2.4	36.9	105.6	168.5	3,856.3	697.7	2,632.0	526.5
Tacoma-Lakewood, WA M.D.	857,339									
Includes Pierce County										
Total area actually reporting	100.0%	4,203	30	417	1,044	2,712	34,346	7,089	21,476	5,781
Rate per 100,000 inhabitants................		490.2	3.5	48.6	121.8	316.3	4,006.1	826.9	2,505.0	674.3
Sebastian-Vero Beach, FL M.S.A.....................	150,236									
Includes Indian River County										
City of Sebastian............................	24,441	42	0	4	7	31	467	69	376	22
City of Vero Beach	16,589	69	3	6	12	48	426	88	323	15
Total area actually reporting	100.0%	345	4	21	43	277	2,776	574	2,044	158
Rate per 100,000 inhabitants................		229.6	2.7	14.0	28.6	184.4	1,847.8	382.1	1,360.5	105.2
Sebring, FL M.S.A.................................	99,857									
Includes Highlands County										
City of Sebring...............................	10,516	45	3	4	7	31	499	110	369	20
Total area actually reporting	100.0%	327	7	27	49	244	2,667	674	1,873	120
Rate per 100,000 inhabitants................		327.5	7.0	27.0	49.1	244.3	2,670.8	675.0	1,875.7	120.2
Sheboygan, WI M.S.A.	115,401									
Includes Sheboygan County										
City of Sheboygan..........................	48,710	131	1	20	10	100	1,063	119	908	36
Total area actually reporting	100.0%	179	2	29	13	135	1,650	166	1,420	64
Rate per 100,000 inhabitants................		155.1	1.7	25.1	11.3	117.0	1,429.8	143.8	1,230.5	55.5
Sherman-Denison, TX M.S.A.	125,998									
Includes Grayson County										
City of Sherman.............................	41,139	127	4	20	23	80	1,251	297	866	88
City of Denison..............................	23,237	110	0	12	12	86	557	135	372	50
Total area actually reporting	97.1%	334	5	49	38	242	2,416	573	1,632	211
Estimated total..............................	100.0%	344	5	51	40	248	2,507	588	1,701	218
Rate per 100,000 inhabitants................		273.0	4.0	40.5	31.7	196.8	1,989.7	466.7	1,350.0	173.0
Shreveport-Bossier City, LA M.S.A.	442,787									
Includes Bossier, Caddo, De Soto, and Webster Parishes										
City of Shreveport...........................	196,467	1,865	42	157	492	1,174	10,721	2,318	7,646	757
City of Bossier City.........................	69,384	585	5	33	96	451	3,206	494	2,491	221
Total area actually reporting	99.7%	2,877	52	207	622	1,996	16,786	3,629	12,010	1,147
Estimated total..............................	100.0%	2,882	52	207	623	2,000	16,828	3,636	12,043	1,149
Rate per 100,000 inhabitants................		650.9	11.7	46.7	140.7	451.7	3,800.5	821.2	2,719.8	259.5
Sierra Vista-Douglas, AZ M.S.A.....................	125,652									
Includes Cochise County										
City of Sierra Vista	42,988	85	3	15	18	49	1,278	249	974	55
City of Douglas..............................	16,398	30	0	1	4	25	462	70	377	15
Total area actually reporting	89.6%	392	5	27	28	332	2,547	420	1,986	141
Estimated total..............................	100.0%	428	5	31	36	356	2,906	478	2,262	166
Rate per 100,000 inhabitants................		340.6	4.0	24.7	28.7	283.3	2,312.7	380.4	1,800.2	132.1
Sioux City, IA-NE-SD M.S.A........................	168,846									
Includes Plymouth and Woodbury Counties, IA; Dakota and Dixon Counties, NE; and Union County, SD										
City of Sioux City, IA	82,819	365	1	40	59	265	3,247	592	2,363	292
Total area actually reporting	98.5%	504	3	57	63	381	4,455	799	3,235	421
Estimated total..............................	100.0%	507	3	57	63	384	4,488	803	3,262	423
Rate per 100,000 inhabitants................		300.3	1.8	33.8	37.3	227.4	2,658.0	475.6	1,931.9	250.5
Sioux Falls, SD M.S.A.	256,120									
Includes Lincoln, McCook, Minnehaha, and Turner Counties										
City of Sioux Falls...........................	175,152	897	6	142	121	628	5,563	869	4,076	618

Table 4. Crime, by Selected Metropolitan Statistical Area, 2016—*Continued*

(Number, percent, rate per 100,000 population.)

Area	Population	Violent crime	Murder and nonnegligent manslaughter	Rape[1]	Robbery	Aggravated assault	Property crime	Burglary	Larceny-theft	Motor vehicle theft
Total area actually reporting	99.7%	993	10	153	124	706	6,429	1,154	4,595	680
Estimated total...	100.0%	994	10	153	124	707	6,439	1,155	4,603	681
Rate per 100,000 inhabitants............................		388.1	3.9	59.7	48.4	276.0	2,514.1	451.0	1,797.2	265.9
South Bend-Mishawaka, IN-MI M.S.A.[3]	319,742									
Includes St. Joseph County, IN and Cass County, MI										
City of South Bend, IN[2]	101,621	1,037	14	70	388	565	5,166	1,241	3,359	566
City of Mishawaka, IN....................................	48,267	165	1	35	69	60	2,523	283	2,034	206
Total area actually reporting	98.0%	1,463	16	172	489	786	9,644	2,214	6,523	907
Estimated total...	100.0%	1,481	16	175	492	798	9,767	2,233	6,618	916
Rate per 100,000 inhabitants............................		463.2	5.0	54.7	153.9	249.6	3,054.7	698.4	2,069.8	286.5
Spokane-Spokane Valley, WA M.S.A.[3]	553,915									
Includes Pend Oreille, Spokane,[2] and Stevens Counties										
City of Spokane[2]	214,028	1,279	8	185	306	780	16,455	2,648	11,815	1,992
City of Spokane Valley[2]	95,923	271	5	55	67	144	5,292	912	3,909	471
Total area actually reporting	99.9%	1,859	16	324	411	1,108	27,718	5,011	19,710	2,997
Estimated total...	100.0%	1,859	16	324	411	1,108	27,727	5,012	19,717	2,998
Rate per 100,000 inhabitants............................		335.6	2.9	58.5	74.2	200.0	5,005.6	904.8	3,559.6	541.2
Springfield, IL M.S.A.	210,256									
Includes Menard and Sangamon Counties										
City of Springfield..	116,563	1,301	6	99	249	947	5,158	1,250	3,681	227
Total area actually reporting	98.0%	1,547	8	146	276	1,117	6,339	1,575	4,446	318
Estimated total...	100.0%	1,556	8	147	279	1,122	6,411	1,586	4,503	322
Rate per 100,000 inhabitants............................		740.1	3.8	69.9	132.7	533.6	3,049.1	754.3	2,141.7	153.1
Springfield, MA M.S.A.	630,942									
Includes Hampden and Hampshire Counties										
City of Springfield..	154,102	1,588	12	81	522	973	5,073	1,486	3,000	587
Total area actually reporting	97.8%	3,351	18	319	775	2,239	14,257	3,313	9,846	1,098
Estimated total...	100.0%	3,393	18	323	782	2,270	14,451	3,348	9,991	1,112
Rate per 100,000 inhabitants............................		537.8	2.9	51.2	123.9	359.8	2,290.4	530.6	1,583.5	176.2
Springfield, MO M.S.A.	459,709									
Includes Christian, Dallas, Greene, Polk, and Webster Counties										
City of Springfield..	168,307	2,251	8	293	428	1,522	14,251	2,120	10,483	1,648
Total area actually reporting	100.0%	2,775	12	376	461	1,926	19,475	3,290	14,131	2,054
Rate per 100,000 inhabitants............................		603.6	2.6	81.8	100.3	419.0	4,236.4	715.7	3,073.9	446.8
Springfield, OH M.S.A.	135,331									
Includes Clark County										
City of Springfield..	59,503	411	5	34	184	188	4,040	963	2,817	260
Total area actually reporting	94.4%	460	5	44	193	218	5,259	1,272	3,660	327
Estimated total...	100.0%	471	5	46	197	223	5,428	1,300	3,794	334
Rate per 100,000 inhabitants............................		348.0	3.7	34.0	145.6	164.8	4,010.9	960.6	2,803.5	246.8
State College, PA M.S.A.	161,409									
Includes Centre County										
City of State College	58,119	39	0	8	10	21	491	35	447	9
Total area actually reporting	100.0%	152	2	65	19	66	1,719	238	1,452	29
Rate per 100,000 inhabitants............................		94.2	1.2	40.3	11.8	40.9	1,065.0	147.5	899.6	18.0
Staunton-Waynesboro, VA M.S.A.	119,934									
Includes Augusta County and Staunton and Waynesboro Cities										
City of Staunton	24,399	41	2	7	7	25	528	34	474	20
City of Waynesboro	21,464	40	1	12	6	21	486	40	424	22
Total area actually reporting	100.0%	159	7	33	16	103	1,746	281	1,377	88
Rate per 100,000 inhabitants............................		132.6	5.8	27.5	13.3	85.9	1,455.8	234.3	1,148.1	73.4
St. Cloud, MN M.S.A.	195,241									
Includes Benton and Stearns Counties										
City of St. Cloud	67,341	293	1	68	72	152	2,780	329	2,327	124
Total area actually reporting	100.0%	388	1	97	68	222	4,638	532	3,904	202
Rate per 100,000 inhabitants............................		198.7	0.5	49.7	34.8	113.7	2,375.5	272.5	1,999.6	103.5
St. George, UT M.S.A.	159,745									
Includes Washington County										

Table 4. Crime, by Selected Metropolitan Statistical Area, 2016—*Continued*

(Number, percent, rate per 100,000 population.)

Area	Population	Violent crime	Murder and nonnegligent manslaughter	Rape[1]	Robbery	Aggravated assault	Property crime	Burglary	Larceny-theft	Motor vehicle theft
City of St. George................................	81,755	160	0	54	14	92	1,465	350	995	120
Total area actually reporting.................	98.1%	265	0	78	18	169	2,676	571	1,916	189
Estimated total..................................	100.0%	270	0	79	19	172	2,757	583	1,977	197
Rate per 100,000 inhabitants................		169.0	0.0	49.5	11.9	107.7	1,725.9	365.0	1,237.6	123.3
St. Joseph, MO-KS M.S.A.........................	126,595									
Includes Doniphan County, KS and Andrew, Buchanan, and DeKalb Counties, MO										
City of St. Joseph, MO........................	76,577	428	7	49	104	268	4,546	749	3,221	576
Total area actually reporting.................	100.0%	532	10	60	110	352	5,141	920	3,580	641
Rate per 100,000 inhabitants................		420.2	7.9	47.4	86.9	278.1	4,061.0	726.7	2,827.9	506.3
St. Louis, MO-IL M.S.A.[2]........................	2,811,156									
Includes Bond, Calhoun, Clinton, Jersey, Macoupin, Madison, Monroe, and St. Clair Counties, IL and Franklin, Jefferson, Lincoln, St. Charles, St. Louis, and Warren Counties and St. Louis City, MO										
City of St. Louis, MO...........................	314,507	6,017	188	289	1,904	3,636	18,653	3,201	12,394	3,058
City of St. Charles, MO........................	69,364	138	0	22	35	81	1,756	155	1,472	129
Total area actually reporting.................	98.5%		312	1,058	3,419		69,303	12,322	50,093	6,888
Estimated total..................................	100.0%		313	1,070	3,443		70,004	12,438	50,642	6,924
Rate per 100,000 inhabitants................			11.1	38.1	122.5		2,490.2	442.5	1,801.5	246.3
Stockton-Lodi, CA M.S.A.........................	729,104									
Includes San Joaquin County										
City of Stockton.................................	308,348	4,381	49	128	1,185	3,019	11,634	2,251	7,550	1,833
City of Lodi......................................	65,067	351	5	9	84	253	1,935	438	1,189	308
Total area actually reporting.................	100.0%	6,005	62	220	1,624	4,099	22,629	4,239	14,848	3,542
Rate per 100,000 inhabitants................		823.6	8.5	30.2	222.7	562.2	3,103.7	581.4	2,036.5	485.8
Sumter, SC M.S.A.................................	107,671									
Includes Sumter County										
City of Sumter...................................	40,864	282	3	9	50	220	1,666	390	1,216	60
Total area actually reporting.................	100.0%	636	4	31	72	529	3,539	1,014	2,309	216
Rate per 100,000 inhabitants................		590.7	3.7	28.8	66.9	491.3	3,286.9	941.8	2,144.5	200.6
Syracuse, NY M.S.A..............................	655,589									
Includes Madison, Onondaga, and Oswego Counties										
City of Syracuse................................	143,925	1,063	30	68	329	636	4,651	1,021	3,290	340
Total area actually reporting.................	100.0%	1,812	35	336	430	1,011	12,838	2,281	9,941	616
Rate per 100,000 inhabitants................		276.4	5.3	51.3	65.6	154.2	1,958.2	347.9	1,516.3	94.0
Tallahassee, FL M.S.A............................	380,448									
Includes Gadsden, Jefferson, Leon, and Wakulla Counties										
City of Tallahassee.............................	191,564	1,686	11	207	405	1,063	11,073	2,120	7,854	1,099
Total area actually reporting.................	98.0%	2,373	17	282	476	1,598	15,347	3,279	10,734	1,334
Estimated total..................................	100.0%	2,403	17	284	485	1,617	15,581	3,314	10,915	1,352
Rate per 100,000 inhabitants................		631.6	4.5	74.6	127.5	425.0	4,095.4	871.1	2,869.0	355.4
Tampa-St. Petersburg-Clearwater, FL M.S.A.....................	3,020,266									
Includes Hernando, Hillsborough, Pasco, and Pinellas Counties										
City of Tampa..................................	375,904	1,906	29	80	488	1,309	7,800	1,477	5,695	628
City of St. Petersburg..........................	259,510	1,727	20	122	556	1,029	12,804	1,938	9,771	1,095
City of Clearwater..............................	113,904	636	5	89	145	397	3,755	555	2,968	232
City of Largo....................................	81,402	390	3	60	116	211	2,989	458	2,289	242
Total area actually reporting.................	100.0%	10,294	118	987	2,283	6,906	70,491	11,898	53,215	5,378
Rate per 100,000 inhabitants................		340.8	3.9	32.7	75.6	228.7	2,333.9	393.9	1,761.9	178.1
Texarkana, TX-AR M.S.A..........................	149,537									
Includes Little River and Miller Counties, AR and Bowie County, TX										
City of Texarkana, TX...........................	37,442	314	4	23	44	243	1,875	338	1,405	132
Total area actually reporting.................	100.0%	669	11	86	87	485	4,953	1,099	3,511	343
Rate per 100,000 inhabitants................		447.4	7.4	57.5	58.2	324.3	3,312.2	734.9	2,347.9	229.4
The Villages, FL M.S.A............................	124,785									
Includes Sumter County										

(Number, percent, rate per 100,000 population.)

Area	Population	Violent crime	Murder and nonnegligent manslaughter	Rape[1]	Robbery	Aggravated assault	Property crime	Burglary	Larceny-theft	Motor vehicle theft
Total area actually reporting	100.0%	292	1	25	12	254	1,093	277	763	53
Rate per 100,000 inhabitants...		234.0	0.8	20.0	9.6	203.6	875.9	222.0	611.5	42.5
Toledo, OH M.S.A.	604,373									
Includes Fulton, Lucas, and Wood Counties										
City of Toledo	278,366	3,319	37	316	803	2,163	11,191	3,381	7,081	729
Total area actually reporting	92.8%	3,662	42	419	880	2,321	16,577	4,268	11,358	951
Estimated total....................................	100.0%	3,728	43	433	902	2,350	17,540	4,427	12,122	991
Rate per 100,000 inhabitants...		616.8	7.1	71.6	149.2	388.8	2,902.2	732.5	2,005.7	164.0
Topeka, KS M.S.A.	232,459									
Includes Jackson, Jefferson, Osage, Shawnee, and										
Wabaunsee Counties										
City of Topeka..	127,166	711	17	54	248	392	7,148	1,114	5,227	807
Total area actually reporting	97.7%	899	21	74	252	552	8,878	1,497	6,407	974
Estimated total....................................	100.0%	910	21	76	253	560	8,984	1,512	6,489	983
Rate per 100,000 inhabitants...		391.5	9.0	32.7	108.8	240.9	3,864.8	650.4	2,791.5	422.9
Trenton, NJ M.S.A....	370,221									
Includes Mercer County										
City of Trenton..	83,644	1,127	21	59	427	620	2,186	883	930	373
Total area actually reporting	100.0%	1,490	25	107	587	771	6,585	1,590	4,454	541
Rate per 100,000 inhabitants...		402.5	6.8	28.9	158.6	208.3	1,778.7	429.5	1,203.1	146.1
Tucson, AZ M.S.A....	1,017,936									
Includes Pima County										
City of Tucson..	533,663	4,245	30	469	1,235	2,511	31,265	4,138	25,185	1,942
Total area actually reporting	99.4%	5,037	49	580	1,432	2,976	43,274	6,080	34,507	2,687
Estimated total....................................	100.0%	5,053	49	582	1,435	2,987	43,432	6,105	34,629	2,698
Rate per 100,000 inhabitants...		496.4	4.8	57.2	141.0	293.4	4,266.7	599.7	3,401.9	265.0
Tulsa, OK M.S.A....	984,554									
Includes Creek, Okmulgee, Osage, Pawnee, Rogers, Tulsa,										
and Wagoner Counties										
City of Tulsa..	405,748	4,444	72	439	1,088	2,845	23,956	5,780	14,516	3,660
Total area actually reporting	100.0%	5,798	91	670	1,244	3,793	35,669	8,761	22,107	4,801
Rate per 100,000 inhabitants...		588.9	9.2	68.1	126.4	385.3	3,622.9	889.8	2,245.4	487.6
Tuscaloosa, AL M.S.A.	241,294									
Includes Hale, Pickens, and Tuscaloosa Counties										
City of Tuscaloosa..	99,925	480	14	54	172	240	3,732	794	2,708	230
Total area actually reporting	100.0%	888	18	92	227	551	6,726	1,560	4,746	420
Rate per 100,000 inhabitants...		368.0	7.5	38.1	94.1	228.4	2,787.5	646.5	1,966.9	174.1
Tyler, TX M.S.A.[2,4]...	224,848									
Includes Smith County										
City of Tyler3..	105,044	429	5	64	106	254				159
Total area actually reporting	99.1%	731	7	83	150	491				429
Estimated total....................................	100.0%	736	7	84	151	494				432
Rate per 100,000 inhabitants...		327.3	3.1	37.4	67.2	219.7				192.1
Urban Honolulu, HI M.S.A.	995,572									
Includes Honolulu County										
Total area actually reporting	100.0%	3,331	16	382	836	2,097	30,592	3,758	22,488	4,346
Rate per 100,000 inhabitants...		334.6	1.6	38.4	84.0	210.6	3,072.8	377.5	2,258.8	436.5
Utica-Rome, NY M.S.A.	292,919									
Includes Herkimer and Oneida Counties										
City of Utica..	60,879	382	3	42	115	222	2,265	435	1,751	79
City of Rome..	32,345	52	0	13	14	25	619	128	463	28
Total area actually reporting	99.1%	774	4	186	151	433	5,495	1,005	4,316	174
Estimated total....................................	100.0%	779	4	187	152	436	5,534	1,010	4,349	175
Rate per 100,000 inhabitants...		265.9	1.4	63.8	51.9	148.8	1,889.3	344.8	1,484.7	59.7
Valdosta, GA M.S.A.	143,315									
Includes Brooks, Echols, Lanier, and Lowndes Counties										
City of Valdosta	55,880	205	6	17	65	117	3,057	581	2,333	143
Total area actually reporting	99.5%	456	7	29	95	325	4,693	1,022	3,424	247

Table 4. Crime, by Selected Metropolitan Statistical Area, 2016—*Continued*

(Number, percent, rate per 100,000 population.)

Area	Population	Violent crime	Murder and nonnegligent manslaughter	Rape[1]	Robbery	Aggravated assault	Property crime	Burglary	Larceny-theft	Motor vehicle theft
Estimated total...	100.0%	459	7	29	96	327	4,719	1,026	3,444	249
Rate per 100,000 inhabitants..............................		320.3	4.9	20.2	67.0	228.2	3,292.7	715.9	2,403.1	173.7
Vallejo-Fairfield, CA M.S.A.	437,638									
Includes Solano County										
City of Vallejo	122,293	1,053	15	111	353	574	4,810	2,366	1,321	1,123
City of Fairfield	114,521	476	7	56	147	266	2,845	420	1,888	537
Total area actually reporting	100.0%	2,022	24	204	647	1,147	11,719	3,397	6,158	2,164
Rate per 100,000 inhabitants..............................		462.0	5.5	46.6	147.8	262.1	2,677.8	776.2	1,407.1	494.5
Vineland-Bridgeton, NJ M.S.A......................	154,814									
Includes Cumberland County										
City of Vineland	60,823	297	1	15	128	153	2,412	559	1,779	74
City of Bridgeton	24,982	225	4	13	113	95	952	269	649	34
Total area actually reporting	100.0%	802	11	64	333	394	5,632	1,331	4,118	183
Rate per 100,000 inhabitants..............................		518.0	7.1	41.3	215.1	254.5	3,637.9	859.7	2,660.0	118.2
Virginia Beach-Norfolk-Newport News, VA-NC M.S.A.	1,724,733									
Includes Currituck and Gates Counties, NC and Gloucester, Isle of Wight, James City, Mathews, and York Counties and Chesapeake, Hampton, Newport News, Norfolk, Poquoson, Portsmouth, Suffolk, Virginia Beach, and Williamsburg Cities, VA										
City of Virginia Beach, VA	453,017	700	21	128	266	285	9,858	865	8,485	508
City of Norfolk, VA.................................	245,734	1,616	46	131	489	950	9,617	1,165	7,918	534
City of Newport News, VA	181,676	848	30	71	269	478	5,579	902	4,097	580
City of Hampton, VA..............................	135,504	442	24	40	180	198	4,650	589	3,741	320
City of Portsmouth, VA..........................	95,813	758	14	61	235	448	5,373	1,208	3,707	458
Total area actually reporting	99.3%	6,054	163	642	1,802	3,447	48,315	6,411	38,853	3,051
Estimated total.......................................	100.0%	6,072	164	643	1,805	3,460	48,481	6,471	38,949	3,061
Rate per 100,000 inhabitants..............................		352.1	9.5	37.3	104.7	200.6	2,810.9	375.2	2,258.3	177.5
Visalia-Porterville, CA M.S.A.	460,141									
Includes Tulare County										
City of Visalia	131,186	480	8	68	120	284	4,196	998	2,561	637
City of Porterville	56,421	215	0	16	52	147	1,315	280	771	264
Total area actually reporting	100.0%	1,624	33	135	329	1,127	11,608	2,692	6,805	2,111
Rate per 100,000 inhabitants..............................		352.9	7.2	29.3	71.5	244.9	2,522.7	585.0	1,478.9	458.8
Waco, TX M.S.A.......................................	263,878									
Includes Falls and McLennan Counties										
City of Waco...	133,790	695	4	126	156	409	4,882	1,087	3,648	147
Total area actually reporting	97.9%	1,104	7	205	185	707	7,216	1,556	5,364	296
Estimated total.......................................	100.0%	1,119	7	207	189	716	7,351	1,578	5,467	306
Rate per 100,000 inhabitants..............................		424.1	2.7	78.4	71.6	271.3	2,785.8	598.0	2,071.8	116.0
Walla Walla, WA M.S.A..............................	64,789									
Includes Columbia and Walla Walla Counties										
City of Walla Walla	32,326	122	2	23	17	80	1,372	233	1,041	98
Total area actually reporting	100.0%	162	2	36	20	104	2,050	365	1,525	160
Rate per 100,000 inhabitants..............................		250.0	3.1	55.6	30.9	160.5	3,164.1	563.4	2,353.8	247.0
Warner Robins, GA M.S.A.	189,578									
Includes Houston, Peach, and Pulaski Counties										
City of Warner Robins............................	74,419	494	6	31	143	314	4,111	768	3,125	218
Total area actually reporting	100.0%	857	9	45	191	612	6,711	1,315	5,030	366
Rate per 100,000 inhabitants..............................		452.1	4.7	23.7	100.8	322.8	3,540.0	693.6	2,653.3	193.1
Washington-Arlington-Alexandria, DC-VA-MD-WV M.S.A...	6,152,267									
Includes the Metropolitan Divisions of Silver Spring-Frederick-Rockville, MD and Washington-Arlington-Alexandria, DC-VA-MD-WV										
City of Washington, D.C.	681,170	7,711	138	527	3,149	3,897	31,661	2,360	26,402	2,899
City of Alexandria, VA............................	155,319	286	7	21	134	124	2,798	184	2,343	271
City of Frederick, MD	70,316	343	1	23	70	249	1,411	141	1,222	48
Total area actually reporting	88.6%	16,494	257	1,701	6,074	8,462	100,386	9,239	84,211	6,936

Table 4. Crime, by Selected Metropolitan Statistical Area, 2016—*Continued*

(Number, percent, rate per 100,000 population.)

Area	Population	Violent crime	Murder and nonnegligent manslaughter	Rape[1]	Robbery	Aggravated assault	Property crime	Burglary	Larceny-theft	Motor vehicle theft
Estimated total...	100.0%	18,535	275	1,888	6,663	9,709	113,381	11,316	94,312	7,753
Rate per 100,000 inhabitants...........................		301.3	4.5	30.7	108.3	157.8	1,842.9	183.9	1,533.0	126.0
Silver Spring-Frederick-Rockville, MD M.D.	1,293,480									
Includes Frederick and Montgomery Counties										
Total area actually reporting	100.0%	2,439	17	374	812	1,236	18,777	2,426	15,361	990
Rate per 100,000 inhabitants...........................		188.6	1.3	28.9	62.8	95.6	1,451.7	187.6	1,187.6	76.5
Washington-Arlington-Alexandria, DC-VA-MD-WV M.D.........	4,858,787									
Includes District of Columbia; Calvert, Charles, and Prince George's Counties, MD; Arlington, Clarke, Culpeper, Fairfax, Fauquier, Loudoun, Prince William, Rappahannock, Spotsylvania, Stafford, and Warren Counties and Alexandria, Fairfax, Falls Church, Fredericksburg, Manassas, and Manassas Park Cities, VA; and Jefferson County, WV										
Total area actually reporting	85.6%	14,055	240	1,327	5,262	7,226	81,609	6,813	68,850	5,946
Estimated total...	100.0%	16,096	258	1,514	5,851	8,473	94,604	8,890	78,951	6,763
Rate per 100,000 inhabitants...........................		331.3	5.3	31.2	120.4	174.4	1,947 1	183.0	1,624.9	139.2
Waterloo-Cedar Falls, IA M.S.A.	170,888									
Includes Black Hawk, Bremer, and Grundy Counties										
City of Waterloo	68,470	507	3	56	61	387	2,120	614	1,368	138
City of Cedar Falls...	41,651	66	0	20	9	37	708	118	559	31
Total area actually reporting	100.0%	756	3	92	72	589	3,386	898	2,288	200
Rate per 100,000 inhabitants...........................		442.4	1.8	53.8	42.1	344.7	1,981.4	525.5	1,338.9	117.0
Watertown-Fort Drum, NY M.S.A.	117,080									
Includes Jefferson County										
City of Watertown	26,765	181	1	41	15	124	1,171	194	953	24
Total area actually reporting	100.0%	281	2	92	17	170	2,079	349	1,681	49
Rate per 100,000 inhabitants...........................		240.0	1.7	78.6	14.5	145.2	1,775.7	298.1	1,435.8	41.9
Wausau, WI M.S.A.[3]	136,010									
Includes Marathon County										
City of Wausau	39,091	114	0	29	25	60	959	137	776	46
Total area actually reporting	100.0%	180	1	39	27	113	1,787	296	1,430	61
Rate per 100,000 inhabitants...........................		132.3	0.7	28.7	19.9	83.1	1,313.9	217.6	1,051.4	44.8
Weirton-Steubenville, WV-OH M.S.A.	119,362									
Includes Jefferson County, OH and Brooke and Hancock Counties, WV										
City of Weirton, WV	19,067	22	0	4	7	11	209	41	152	16
City of Steubenville, OH...................................	18,137	60	2	4	22	32	1,085	132	945	8
Total area actually reporting	86.3%	153	2	19	35	97	1,691	276	1,369	46
Estimated total...	100.0%	190	2	25	43	120	2,150	351	1,730	69
Rate per 100,000 inhabitants...........................		159.2	1.7	20.9	36.0	100.5	1,801.2	294.1	1,449.4	57.8
Wenatchee, WA M.S.A.	117,637									
Includes Chelan and Douglas Counties										
City of Wenatchee..	33,920	88	0	21	14	53	1,128	166	900	62
Total area actually reporting	100.0%	169	1	31	18	119	2,626	502	1,957	167
Rate per 100,000 inhabitants...........................		143.7	0.9	26.4	15.3	101.2	2,232.3	426.7	1,663.6	142.0
Wheeling, WV-OH M.S.A.	142,933									
Includes Belmont County, OH and Marshall and Ohio Counties, WV										
City of Wheeling, WV	27,486	266	1	12	30	223	669	183	453	33
Total area actually reporting	90.0%	475	4	55	36	380	1,878	481	1,295	102
Estimated total...	100.0%	500	4	60	43	393	2,223	538	1,568	117
Rate per 100,000 inhabitants...........................		349.8	2.8	42.0	30.1	275.0	1,555.3	376.4	1,097.0	81.9
Wichita, KS M.S.A.	643,764									
Includes Butler, Harvey, Kingman, Sedgwick, and Sumner Counties										
City of Wichita..	391,399	4,136	31	309	652	3,144	21,065	3,593	15,284	2,188
Total area actually reporting	99.2%	4,553	42	385	683	3,443			18,728	2,502

Table 4. Crime, by Selected Metropolitan Statistical Area, 2016—*Continued*

(Number, percent, rate per 100,000 population.)

Area	Population	Violent crime	Murder and nonnegligent manslaughter	Rape[1]	Robbery	Aggravated assault	Property crime	Burglary	Larceny-theft	Motor vehicle theft
Estimated total..................................	100.0%	4,563	42	387	684	3,450			18,806	2,510
Rate per 100,000 inhabitants.................		708.8	6.5	60.1	106.3	535.9			2,921.3	389.9
Wichita Falls, TX M.S.A.	150,165									
Includes Archer, Clay, and Wichita Counties										
City of Wichita Falls	104,685	445	9	124	123	189	3,734	825	2,646	263
Total area actually reporting	97.7%	535	12	134	127	262	4,493	1,022	3,139	332
Estimated total..................................	100.0%	544	12	135	129	268	4,576	1,035	3,203	338
Rate per 100,000 inhabitants.................		362.3	8.0	89.9	85.9	178.5	3,047.3	689.2	2,133.0	225.1
Williamsport, PA M.S.A.	115,682									
Includes Lycoming County										
City of Williamsport	29,163	104	5	8	39	52	792	101	668	23
Total area actually reporting	100.0%	238	7	32	58	141	1,752	248	1,452	52
Rate per 100,000 inhabitants.................		205.7	6.1	27.7	50.1	121.9	1,514.5	214.4	1,255.2	45.0
Wilmington, NC M.S.A.	282,695									
Includes New Hanover and Pender Counties										
City of Wilmington	117,852	759	15	44	204	496	4,771	1,277	3,219	275
Total area actually reporting	99.1%	1,021	17	81	268	655	8,270	2,081	5,771	418
Estimated total..................................	100.0%	1,028	17	82	270	659	8,348	2,096	5,831	421
Rate per 100,000 inhabitants.................		363.6	6.0	29.0	95.5	233.1	2,953.0	741.4	2,062.6	148.9
Winchester, VA-WV M.S.A.	134,144									
Includes Frederick County and Winchester City, VA and Hampshire County, WV										
City of Winchester, VA	27,363	61	1	27	16	17	776	122	638	16
Total area actually reporting	99.7%	185	7	67	26	85	1,964	341	1,535	88
Estimated total..................................	100.0%	186	7	67	26	86	1,977	343	1,545	89
Rate per 100,000 inhabitants.................		138.7	5.2	49.9	19.4	64.1	1,473.8	255.7	1,151.7	66.3
Worcester, MA-CT M.S.A.[5]	861,261									
Includes Windham County, CT and Worcester County, MA										
City of Worcester, MA..........................	184,595	1,642	8	63	394	1,177	5,358	1,366	3,473	519
Total area actually reporting	94.7%		12	282	584		13,153	2,815	9,422	916
Estimated total..................................	100.0%		12	295	606		13,782	2,927	9,893	962
Rate per 100,000 inhabitants.................			1.4	34.3	70.4		1,600.2	339.9	1,148.7	111.7
Yakima, WA M.S.A.	250,717									
Includes Yakima County										
City of Yakima	94,111	496	13	47	126	310	4,943	1,143	3,163	637
Total area actually reporting	100.0%	751	21	82	187	461	9,067	2,060	5,789	1,218
Rate per 100,000 inhabitants.................		299.5	8.4	32.7	74.6	183.9	3,616.4	821.6	2,309.0	485.8
York-Hanover, PA M.S.A.	443,062									
Includes York County										
City of York..........................	44,017	416	8	12	208	188	1,408	298	917	193
City of Hanover..........................	15,537	23	0	0	9	14	418	43	371	4
Total area actually reporting	100.0%	1,039	19	107	306	607	7,029	948	5,674	407
Rate per 100,000 inhabitants.................		234.5	4.3	24.2	69.1	137.0	1,586.5	214.0	1,280.6	91.9
Yuba City, CA M.S.A.	170,558									
Includes Sutter and Yuba Counties										
City of Yuba City..........................	67,198	272	8	24	76	164	2,030	406	1,389	235
Total area actually reporting	100.0%	678	13	50	137	478	4,635	1,097	2,800	738
Rate per 100,000 inhabitants.................		397.5	7.6	29.3	80.3	280.3	2,717.6	643.2	1,641.7	432.7
Aguadilla-Isabela, Puerto Rico M.S.A.	309,696									
Includes Aguada, Aguadilla, Anasco, Isabela, Lares, Moca, Rincon, San Sebastian, and Utuado Municipios										
Total area actually reporting	100.0%	424	22	12	86	304	2,030	703	1,253	74
Rate per 100,000 inhabitants.................		136.9	7.1	3.9	27.8	98.2	655.5	227.0	404.6	23.9
Arecibo, Puerto Rico M.S.A.	185,250									
Includes Arecibo, Camuy, Hatillo, and Quebradillas Municipios..........................										
Total area actually reporting	100.0%	314	10	4	96	204	1,633	393	1,121	119
Rate per 100,000 inhabitants.................		169.5	5.4	2.2	51.8	110.1	881.5	212.1	605.1	64.2
Guayama, Puerto Rico M.S.A.	77,771									
Includes Arroyo, Guayama, and Patillas Municipios										

Table 4. Crime, by Selected Metropolitan Statistical Area, 2016—*Continued*

(Number, percent, rate per 100,000 population.)

Area	Population	Violent crime	Murder and nonnegligent manslaughter	Rape[1]	Robbery	Aggravated assault	Property crime	Burglary	Larceny-theft	Motor vehicle theft
Total area actually reporting	100.0%	182	19	8	39	116	614	222	382	10
Rate per 100,000 inhabitants.........................		234.0	24.4	10.3	50.1	149.2	789.5	285.5	491.2	12.9
Mayaguez, Puerto Rico M.S.A..........................	94,038									
Includes Hormigueros and Mayaguez Municipios										
Total area actually reporting	100.0%	248	16	4	68	160	1,137	290	811	36
Rate per 100,000 inhabitants.........................		263.7	17.0	4.3	72.3	170.1	1,209.1	308.4	862.4	38.3
Ponce, Puerto Rico M.S.A.	309,512									
Includes Guanica, Guyanilla, Juana Diaz, Penuelas, Ponce, Villalba, and Yauco Municipios										
Total area actually reporting	100.0%	785	70	22	179	514	2,557	611	1,839	107
Rate per 100,000 inhabitants.........................		253.6	22.6	7.1	57.8	166.1	826.1	197.4	594.2	34.6
San German, Puerto Rico M.S.A..........................	128,279									
Includes Cabo Rojo, Lajas, Sabana Grande, and San German Municipios										
Total area actually reporting	100.0%	117	9	4	34	70	450	173	245	32
Rate per 100,000 inhabitants.........................		91.2	7.0	3.1	26.5	54.6	353.1	134.9	193.3	24.9
San Juan-Carolina-Caguas, Puerto Rico M.S.A..................	2,157,729									
Includes Aguas Buenas, Aibonito, Barceloneta, Barranquitas, Bayamon, Caguas, Canovanas, Carolina, Catano, Cayey, Ceiba, Ciales, Cidra, Comerio, Corozal, Dorado, Fajardo, Florida, Guaynabo, Gurabo, Humacao, Juncos, Las Piedras, Loiza, Luquillo, Manati, Maunabo, Morovis, Naguabo, Naranjito, Orocovis, Rio Grande, San Juan, San Lorenzo, Toa Alta, Toa Baja, Trujillo Alto, Vega Alta, Vega Baja, and Yabucoa Municipios										
Total area actually reporting	100.0%	5,292	504	106	2,653	2,029	25,686	5,515	16,802	3,369
Rate per 100,000 inhabitants.........................		245.3	23.4	4.9	123.0	94.0	1,190.4	255.6	778.7	156.1

[1] The rape figures in this table are an aggregate total of the data submitted using both the revised and legacy Uniform Crime Reporting (UCR) definitions.
[2] Because of changes in the state/local agency's reporting practices, figures are not comparable to previous years' data.
[3] The FBI determined that the agency's data were underreported. Consequently, those data are not included in this table.
[4] The FBI determined that the agency's data were overreported. Consequently, those data are not included in this table.
[5] The population for the city of Mobile, Alabama, includes 55,819 inhabitants from the jurisdiction of the Mobile County Sheriff's Department.
[6] The 2016 murder offenses include those victims of the Pulse Nightclub incident; therefore, figures are not comparable to previous years' data.

Table 5. Offense Analysis, United States, 2011–2016

(Number.)

Classification	2011	2012	2013[1]	2014	2015[1]	2016
Murder	14,661	14,856	14,319	14,164	15,883	17,250
Rape (revised definition)[2]	X	X	113,695	118,027	126,134	130,603
Rape (legacy definition)[3]	84,175	85,141	82,109	84,868	91,261	95,730
Robbery[4]	354,746	355,051	345,093	322,905	328,109	332,198
By location						
Street/highway	155,218	154,289	146,499	132,269	130,724	129,104
Commercial house	46,156	47,151	45,760	45,273	47,229	50,694
Gas or service station	8,539	8,660	8,354	8,072	8,916	9,690
Convenience store	18,108	18,180	17,103	17,380	18,661	20,619
Residence	60,138	59,979	57,372	54,120	54,142	55,002
Bank	7,038	6,666	6,512	5,939	5,691	5,903
Miscellaneous	59,549	60,126	63,495	59,853	62,747	61,185
Burglary[4]	2,185,140	2,109,932	1,932,139	1,713,153	1,587,564	1,515,096
By location						
Residence (dwelling)	1,628,656	1,571,635	1,428,448	1,253,915	1,136,664	1,053,559
Residence, night	442,390	429,662	395,604	349,441	328,736	311,536
Residence, day	859,299	832,944	756,617	669,364	594,668	543,461
Residence, unknown	326,967	309,028	276,227	235,111	213,260	198,563
Nonresidence (store, office, etc.)	556,484	538,297	503,691	459,238	450,900	461,537
Nonresidence, night	227,446	220,784	206,031	188,010	189,167	199,568
Nonresidence, day	196,461	192,963	183,380	167,749	159,177	159,493
Nonresidence, unknown	132,577	124,550	114,280	103,480	102,556	102,476
Larceny-theft (except motor vehicle theft)[4]	6,151,095	6,168,874	6,019,465	5,809,054	5,723,488	5,638,455
By type						
Pocket-picking	26,518	29,550	32,426	31,213	31,208	27,617
Purse-snatching	27,082	26,407	25,867	23,479	23,144	22,645
Shoplifting	1,077,791	1,147,679	1,199,157	1,247,199	1,276,575	1,177,804
From motor vehicles (except accessories)	1,523,950	1,480,790	1,405,858	1,332,924	1,373,720	1,475,917
Motor vehicle accessories	497,980	467,369	439,151	408,545	399,452	415,120
Bicycles	216,987	223,786	212,889	209,762	205,600	184,338
From buildings	728,050	745,238	740,092	712,073	664,381	605,080
From coin-operated machines	19,536	17,240	15,906	13,328	13,020	12,335
All others	2,033,200	2,030,815	1,948,120	1,830,531	1,736,388	1,717,599
By value						
Under $50	2,850,302	2,872,445	2,819,518	2,687,591	2,613,333	2,558,723
$50 to $200	1,399,484	1,398,870	1,342,473	1,306,350	1,278,027	1,219,866
Over $200	1,901,309	1,897,560	1,857,474	1,815,113	1,832,128	1,859,865
Motor vehicle theft	716,508	723,186	700,288	686,803	713,063	765,484

X = Not applicable.
[1] The crime figures have been adjusted.
[2] The figures shown in this column for the offense of rape were estimated using the revised Uniform Crime Reporting (UCR) definition of rape. See chapter notes for more detail.
[3] The figures shown in this column for the offense of rape were estimated using the legacy Uniform Crime Reporting (UCR) definition of rape. See chapter notes for more detail.
[4] Because of rounding, the number of offenses may not add to the total.

Table 6. Crime Trends, by Population Group, 2015–2016

(Number, percent change.)

Population group	Violent crime	Murder and nonnegligent manslaughter	Rape (revised definition)[1]	Rape (legacy definition)[2]	Robbery	Aggravated assault	Property crime	Burglary	Larceny-theft	Motor vehicle theft	Arson	Number of agencies	Estimated population, 2016
Total, All Agencies													
2015	1,173,095	15,181	108,930	6,310	315,137	727,537	7,538,827	1,482,228	5,375,095	681,504	42,259		
2016	1,217,400	16,459	112,470	6,616	319,826	762,029	7,440,034	1,413,294	5,296,630	730,110	43,249	15,623	305,431,251
Percent change	+3.8	+8.4	+3.2	+4.8	+1.5	+4.7	-1.3	-4.7	-1.5	+7.1	+2.3		
Total, Cities													
2015	938,136	11,826	81,231	4,191	276,513	564,375	5,983,208	1,087,800	4,347,725	547,683	32,487		
2016	978,267	12,863	84,460	4,272	282,000	594,672	5,923,615	1,042,326	4,292,416	588,873	33,104	11,158	208,061,722
Percent change	+4.3	+8.8	+4.0	+1.9	+2.0	+5.4	-1.0	-4.2	-1.3	+7.5	+1.9		
Group I (250,000 and over)													
2015	445,645	6,177	30,970	936	156,058	251,504	2,034,720	384,817	1,398,652	251,251	12,645		
2016	473,049	6,973	32,986	892	159,314	272,884	2,045,407	368,854	1,408,114	268,439	12,914	83	61,199,316
Percent change	+6.1	+12.9	+6.5	-4.7	+2.1	+8.5	+0.5	-4.1	+0.7	+6.8	+2.1		
1,000,000 and over (Group I subset)													
2015	188,327	2,234	13,138	-	69,293	103,662	727,139	131,821	501,813	93,505	3,923		
2016	201,825	2,688	13,972	-	71,652	113,513	742,200	125,303	517,051	99,846	4,229	11	27,658,777
Percent change	+7.2	+20.3	+6.3	-	+3.4	+9.5	+2.1	-4.9	+3.0	+6.8	+7.8		
500,000 to 999,999 (Group I subset)													
2015	139,003	2,092	9,109	620	46,953	80,229	703,775	133,644	487,061	83,070	4,125		
2016	147,007	2,228	9,603	600	47,395	87,181	699,498	128,981	482,417	88,100	4,116	23	16,781,999
Percent change	+5.8	+6.5	+5.4	-3.2	+0.9	+8.7	-0.6	-3.5	-1.0	+6.1	-0.2		
250,000 to 499,999 (Group I subset)													
2015	118,315	1,851	8,723	316	39,812	67,613	603,806	119,352	409,778	74,676	4,597		
2016	124,217	2,057	9,411	292	40,267	72,190	603,709	114,570	408,646	80,493	4,569	49	16,758,540
Percent change	+5.0	+11.1	+7.9	-7.6	+1.1	+6.8	*	-4.0	-0.3	+7.8	-0.6		
Group II (100,000 to 249,999)													
2015	151,098	1,992	13,776	627	44,621	90,082	1,053,444	198,316	745,157	109,971	4,997		
2016	157,638	2,118	14,186	624	45,659	95,051	1,044,575	188,685	737,743	118,147	5,165	219	32,521,418
Percent change	+4.3	+6.3	+3.0	-0.5	+2.3	+5.5	-0.8	-4.9	-1.0	+7.4	+3.4		
Group III (50,000 to 99,999)													
2015	109,770	1,201	10,405	551	29,904	67,709	868,445	153,641	640,351	74,453	4,268		
2016	112,649	1,210	11,041	603	30,509	69,286	866,392	148,627	637,330	80,435	4,228	477	33,071,956
Percent change	+2.6	+0.7	+6.1	+9.4	+2.0	+2.3	-0.2	-3.3	-0.5	+8.0	-0.9		
Group IV (25,000 to 49,999)													
2015	84,736	983	9,235	775	20,836	52,907	735,602	128,058	560,829	46,715	3,301		
2016	87,565	1,007	9,482	864	21,127	55,085	721,325	123,562	547,145	50,618	3,376	853	29,586,018
Percent change	+3.3	+2.4	+2.7	+11.5	+1.4	+4.1	-1.9	-3.5	-2.4	+8.4	+2.3		
Group V (10,000 to 24,999)													
2015	76,897	833	8,553	601	15,603	51,307	694,375	121,359	535,782	37,234	2,974		
2016	77,258	861	8,486	616	15,795	51,500	671,568	115,873	515,328	40,367	2,874	1,793	28,626,434
Percent change	+0.5	+3.4	-0.8	+2.5	+1.2	+0.4	-3.3	-4.5	-3.8	+8.4	-3.4		
Group VI (under 10,000)													
2015	69,990	640	8,292	701	9,491	50,866	596,622	101,609	466,954	28,059	4,302		
2016	70,108	694	8,279	673	9,596	50,866	574,348	96,725	446,756	30,867	4,547	7,733	23,056,580
Percent change	+0.2	+8.4	-0.2	-4.0	+1.1	0.0	-3.7	-4.8	-4.3	+10.0	+5.7		
Metropolitan Counties													
2015	187,976	2,453	19,865	1,606	35,981	128,071	1,250,091	297,579	842,845	109,667	7,305		
2016	191,384	2,754	20,068	1,828	35,054	131,680	1,226,478	280,397	828,604	117,477	7,637	2,010	73,068,087
Percent change	+1.8	+12.3	+1.0	+13.8	-2.6	+2.8	-1.9	-5.8	-1.7	+7.1	+4.5		
Nonmetropolitan Counties[3]													
2015	46,983	902	7,834	513	2,643	35,091	305,528	96,849	184,525	24,154	2,467		
2016	47,749	842	7,942	516	2,772	35,677	289,941	90,571	175,610	23,760	2,508	2,455	24,301,442
Percent change	+1.6	-6.7	+1.4	+0.6	+4.9	+1.7	-5.1	-6.5	-4.8	-1.6	+1.7		
Suburban Areas[4]													
2015	327,013	3,865	35,735	2,592	67,586	217,235	2,569,624	510,961	1,869,364	189,299	13,482		
2016	334,222	4,245	36,342	2,870	67,524	223,241	2,516,026	483,816	1,828,325	203,885	14,220	8,552	132,442,308
Percent change	+2.2	+9.8	+1.7	+10.7	-0.1	+2.8	-2.1	-5.3	-2.2	+7.7	+5.5		

Note: No agencies over 1,000,000 in population submitted rape data using the legacy UCR definition in 2016; therefore, the UCR Program could not provide a 2-year comparison for this agency group size.
* = Less than one-tenth of one percent.
[1]The figures shown in the rape (revised definition) column include only those reported by law enforcement agencies that used the revised Uniform Crime Reporting (UCR) definition of rape.
[2]The figures shown in the rape (legacy definition) column include only those reported by law enforcement agencies that used the legacy UCR definition of rape.
[3]Includes state police agencies that report aggregately for the entire state.
[4]Suburban areas include law enforcement agencies in cities with less than 50,000 inhabitants and county law enforcement agencies that are within a Metropolitan Statistical Area. Suburban areas exclude all metropolitan agencies associated with a principal city. The agencies associated with suburban areas also appear in other groups within this table.

Table 7. Rate: Number of Crimes Per 100,000 Population, by Population Group, 2016

(Number, rate.)

Population group	Violent crime		Murder and nonnegligent manslaughter		Rape (revised definition)[1]		Rape (legacy definition)[2]		Robbery	
	Number of offenses known	Rate	Number of offenses known	Rate	Number of offenses known	Rate	Number of offenses known	Rate	Number of offenses known	Rate
Total, All Agencies....................................	1,223,265	401.3	16,470	5.4	114,730	41.2	6,607	25.1	321,464	105.5
Total, Cities	979,579	471.6	12,802	6.2	86,015	44.4	4,268	31.0	282,459	136.0
Group I (250,000 and over).......................	472,814	771.4	6,928	11.3	33,385	56.7	981	41.3	159,106	259.6
1,000,000 and over (Group I subset)........	201,825	729.7	2,688	9.7	13,972	50.5	0	0.0	71,652	259.1
500,000 to 999,999 (Group I subset).......	150,170	861.9	2,242	12.9	9,992	62.6	600	41.2	48,381	277.7
250,000 to 499,999 (Group I subset).......	120,819	745.5	1,998	12.3	9,421	61.6	381	41.5	39,073	241.1
Group II (100,000 to 249,999)	156,588	485.3	2,098	6.5	14,459	47.1	526	34.1	45,431	140.8
Group III (50,000 to 99,999)	114,031	342.2	1,214	3.6	11,438	36.5	588	29.5	30,879	92.7
Group IV (25,000 to 49,999).......................	88,973	299.1	1,012	3.4	9,619	35.5	871	32.8	21,403	72.0
Group V (10,000 to 24,999)	78,120	272.6	880	3.1	8,723	33.7	632	22.9	16,079	56.1
Group VI (under 10,000).............................	69,053	307.9	670	3.0	8,391	42.0	670	27.3	9,561	42.6
Metropolitan Counties	195,630	267.3	2,807	3.8	20,618	32.3	1,819	19.6	36,227	49.5
Nonmetropolitan Counties[3]	48,056	200.6	861	3.6	8,097	39.1	520	16.1	2,778	11.6
Suburban Areas[4]	339,130	256.2	4,300	3.2	37,237	31.5	2,890	20.5	68,951	52.1

(Number, rate.)

Population group	Aggravated assault		Property crime		Burglary		Larceny-theft		Motor vehicle theft		Number of agencies	Estimated population, 2016
	Number of offenses known	Rate	Number of offenses known	Rate	Number of offenses known	Rate	Number of offenses known	Rate	Number of offenses known	Rate		
Total, All Agencies.............................	763,994	250.6	7,514,851	2,465.2	1,421,596	466.3	5,353,887	1,756.3	739,368	242.5	15,310	304,839,823
Total, Cities	594,035	286.0	5,969,716	2,874.1	1,045,176	503.2	4,328,750	2,084.1	595,790	286.8	10,831	207,707,230
Group I (250,000 and over).............................	272,414	444.5	2,061,132	3,363.0	368,632	601.5	1,420,247	2,317.3	272,253	444.2	82	61,289,111
1,000,000 and over (Group I subset).............	113,513	410.4	742,200	2,683.4	125,303	453.0	517,051	1,869.4	99,846	361.0	11	27,658,777
500,000 to 999,999 (Group I subset).............	88,955	510.5	732,585	4,204.4	133,045	763.6	506,516	2,907.0	93,024	533.9	24	17,424,128
250,000 to 499,999 (Group I subset).............	69,946	431.6	586,347	3,618.0	110,284	680.5	396,680	2,447.7	79,383	489.8	47	16,206,206
Group II (100,000 to 249,999).........................	94,074	291.6	1,036,660	3,212.9	186,189	577.1	731,555	2,267.3	118,916	368.6	218	32,265,177
Group III (50,000 to 99,999)...........................	69,912	209.8	881,257	2,644.6	151,264	453.9	648,625	1,946.5	81,368	244.2	480	33,323,383
Group IV (25,000 to 49,999)...........................	56,068	188.5	730,697	2,456.7	124,824	419.7	554,893	1,865.7	50,980	171.4	857	29,742,465
Group V (10,000 to 24,999)............................	51,806	180.8	685,091	2,390.3	118,082	412.0	525,509	1,833.5	41,500	144.8	1,794	28,661,210
Group VI (under 10,000).................................	49,761	221.9	574,879	2,563.5	96,185	428.9	447,921	1,997.3	30,773	137.2	7,400	22,425,884
Metropolitan Counties	134,159	183.3	1,254,279	1,713.9	285,709	390.4	848,805	1,159.9	119,765	163.7	2,010	73,181,004
Nonmetropolitan Counties[3]	35,800	149.5	290,856	1,214.3	90,711	378.7	176,332	736.2	23,813	99.4	2,469	23,951,589
Suburban Areas[4]	225,752	170.5	2,559,769	1,933.8	490,432	370.5	1,862,114	1,406.7	207,223	156.5	8,400	132,369,940

[1]The figures shown in the rape (revised definition) column include only those reported by law enforcement agencies that used the revised Uniform Crime Reporting (UCR) definition of rape.
[2]The figures shown in the rape (legacy definition) column include only those reported by law enforcement agencies that used the legacy UCR definition of rape.
[3]Includes state police agencies that report aggregately for the entire state.
[4]Suburban areas include law enforcement agencies in cities with less than 50,000 inhabitants and county law enforcement agencies that are within a Metropolitan Statistical Area. Suburban areas exclude all metropolitan agencies associated with a principal city. The agencies associated with suburban areas also appear in other groups within this table.

Table 8. Offense Analysis, Number and Percent Change, 2015–2016

(Number, percent, dollars; 14,554 agencies; 2016 estimated population 282,238,499.)

Classification	Number of offenses, 2016	Percent change from 2015	Percent distribution[1]	Average value (dollars)
Murder..	14,774	+7.8	NA	X
Rape[2]	100,373	NA	NA	X
Robbery...	280,357	+1.7	100.0	$1,400
By location..				
Street/highway..	108,957	-1.8	38.9	1,191
Commercial house...	42,783	+4.6	15.3	1,689
Gas or service station.....................................	8,178	+2.1	2.9	970
Convenience store	17,401	+6.7	6.2	732
Residence..	46,419	+2.3	16.6	1,758
Bank...	4,982	+0.8	1.8	3,531
Miscellaneous..	51,637	+5.0	18.4	1,367
Burglary	1,354,920	-4.4	100.0	2,361
By location..				
Residence (dwelling)	942,177	-7.1	69.5	2,273
Residence, night..	278,600	-4.5	20.6	1,913
Residence, day...	486,006	-8.6	35.9	2,258
Residence, unknown	177,571	-7.1	13.1	2,879
Nonresidence (store, office, etc.).....................	412,743	+2.6	30.5	2,562
Nonresidence, night	178,470	+6.0	13.2	2,585
Nonresidence, day	142,631	-0.1	10.5	2,182
Nonresidence, unknown.................................	91,642	+0.7	6.8	3,109
Larceny-theft (except motor vehicle theft)........................	4,971,925	-1.3	100.0	999
By type...				
Pocket-picking	24,352	-0.4	0.5	646
Purse-snatching	19,968	-1.6	0.4	475
Shoplifting...	1,038,574	-6.7	20.9	250
From motor vehicles (except accessories)............................	1,301,447	+6.5	26.2	869
Motor vehicle accessories...............................	366,048	+2.0	7.4	541
Bicycles..	162,547	-10.8	3.3	483
From buildings...	533,553	-6.3	10.7	1,449
From coin-operated machines..........................	10,877	-6.8	0.2	607
All others...	1,514,559	-1.4	30.5	1,649
By value..				
Over $200	2,256,253	-1.5	45.4	2,140
$50 to $200	1,075,664	-4.3	21.6	108
Under $50	1,640,008	+0.9	33.0	14
Motor Vehicle Theft..	700,143	+6.9	NA	7,680

NA = Not available.
X = Not applicable.
* = Less than one-tenth of one percent.
[1]Because of rounding, the percentages may not add to 100.0.
[2]The rape figure in this table is an aggregate total of the data submitted using both the revised and legacy Uniform Crime Reporting definitions.

Table 9. Property Stolen and Recovered, by Type and Value, 2016

(Dollars, percent; 13,981 agencies; 2016 estimated population 273,294,030.)

Type of property	Value of property (dollars)		Percent recovered
	Stolen	Recovered	
Total	$13,667,503,625	$3,776,517,466	27.6
Currency, notes, etc.	1,429,781,653	33,375,702	2.3
Jewelry and precious metals	1,362,002,838	55,751,909	4.1
Clothing and furs	362,025,765	38,980,936	10.8
Locally stolen motor vehicles	5,527,133,714	3,228,597,961	58.4
Office equipment	483,550,405	25,750,989	5.3
Televisions, radios, stereos, etc.	455,215,103	22,319,049	4.9
Firearms	155,186,427	14,794,219	9.5
Household goods	228,961,414	10,003,415	4.4
Consumable goods	139,167,892	15,512,495	11.1
Livestock	22,666,215	2,570,359	11.3
Miscellaneous	3,501,812,199	328,860,432	9.4

Table 10. Number and Percent of Offenses Cleared by Arrest or Exceptional Means, by Population Group, 2016

(Number, percent.)

Population group	Violent crime	Murder and nonnegligent manslaughter	Rape (revised definition)[1]	Rape (legacy definition)[2]	Robbery	Aggravated assault	Property crime	Burglary	Larceny-theft	Motor vehicle theft	Arson[3]	Number of agencies	Estimated population, 2016
Total, All Agencies													
Offenses known	1,183,933	15,566	111,241	6,822	306,172	744,132	7,319,177	1,393,570	5,211,566	714,041	42,131	15,336	297,593,825
Percent cleared by arrest	45.6	59.4	36.5	40.9	29.6	53.3	18.3	13.1	20.4	13.3	20.8		
Total Cities													
Offenses known	944,676	11,978	82,764	4,534	268,367	577,033	5,818,143	1,025,177	4,213,156	579,810	31,622	10,953	201,336,755
Percent cleared by arrest	43.7	57.1	34.7	43.3	29.1	51.6	18.2	12.4	20.5	12.2	20.1		
Group I (250,000 and over)													
Offenses known	446,513	6,229	31,796	1,137	148,440	258,911	1,992,102	358,785	1,371,236	262,081	12,563	83	59,116,292
Percent cleared by arrest	39.1	52.9	36.4	43.7	26.8	46.2	12.7	9.6	14.2	9.2	15.3		
1,000,000 and over (Group I subset)													
Offenses known	171,699	1,923	12,383	0	59,695	97,698	655,240	111,045	455,822	88,373	3,639	10	24,933,624
Percent cleared by arrest	44.4	60.2	37.6	0.0	31.1	53.0	12.4	9.6	13.9	8.3	14.1		
500,000 to 999,999 (Group I subset)													
Offenses known	150,170	2,242	9,992	600	48,381	88,955	732,585	133,045	506,516	93,024	4,350	24	17,424,128
Percent cleared by arrest	34.9	49.3	38.4	35.3	23.2	40.5	11.3	9.0	12.3	9.0	16.6		
250,000 to 499,999 (Group I subset)													
Offenses known	124,644	2,064	9,421	537	40,364	72,258	604,277	114,695	408,898	80,684	4,574	49	16,758,540
Percent cleared by arrest	37.1	50.1	32.6	53.1	24.6	44.2	14.8	10.3	16.9	10.5	14.9		
Group II (100,000 to 249,999)													
Offenses known	154,137	2,067	14,154	624	44,621	92,671	1,029,742	185,432	726,965	117,345	4,968	214	31,784,818
Percent cleared by arrest	42.0	59.5	33.2	42.1	27.7	49.8	16.6	11.6	18.7	11.8	20.2		
Group III (50,000 to 99,999)													
Offenses known	112,984	1,188	11,254	601	30,104	69,837	868,828	149,523	639,214	80,091	4,265	468	32,549,603
Percent cleared by arrest	49.2	63.5	35.5	43.1	33.7	57.9	19.9	13.0	22.4	12.5	21.3		
Group IV (25,000 to 49,999)													
Offenses known	84,913	949	9,055	856	20,613	53,440	703,177	120,839	532,352	49,986	3,232	813	28,308,217
Percent cleared by arrest	47.5	61.7	32.1	35.4	33.9	55.3	22.8	13.6	25.7	14.9	24.1		
Group V (10,000 to 24,999)													
Offenses known	75,496	848	8,180	632	15,109	50,727	654,670	113,344	501,960	39,366	2,839	1,702	27,155,943
Percent cleared by arrest	52.4	65.3	34.4	42.9	36.1	60.1	25.4	15.8	28.0	19.6	29.1		
Group VI (under 10,000)													
Offenses known	70,633	697	8,325	684	9,480	51,447	569,624	97,254	441,429	30,941	3,755	7,673	22,421,882
Percent cleared by arrest	54.0	60.4	32.5	54.2	36.2	60.6	24.1	17.7	25.6	24.0	24.8		
Metropolitan Counties													
Offenses known	191,881	2,736	20,192	1,716	35,096	132,141	1,214,788	278,245	825,554	110,989	7,842	1,997	72,365,974
Percent cleared by arrest	51.9	66.1	41.3	34.2	32.0	58.7	18.3	14.7	19.7	16.9	21.6		
Nonmetropolitan Counties													
Offenses known	47,376	852	8,285	572	2,709	34,958	286,246	90,148	172,856	23,242	2,667	2,386	23,891,096
Percent cleared by arrest	57.3	69.4	42.8	41.3	44.1	61.7	19.1	16.5	19.8	24.8	25.8		
Suburban Areas[4]													
Offenses known	329,716	4,147	35,781	2,790	66,051	220,947	2,461,511	475,833	1,790,558	195,120	13,728	8,314	128,677,778
Percent cleared by arrest	51.7	63.9	38.0	39.7	33.3	59.3	20.9	15.0	22.9	16.8	23.7		

[1] The figures shown in this column for the offense of rape were reported using the revised Uniform Crime Reporting (UCR) definition of rape. See chapter notes for more detail.
[2] The figures shown in this column for the offense of rape were reported using the legacy Uniform Crime Reporting (UCR) definition of rape. See chapter notes for more detail.
[3] Not all agencies submit reports for arson to the FBI. As a result, the number of reports the FBI uses to compute the percent of offenses cleared for arson is less than the number it uses to compute the percent of offenses cleared for all other offenses.
[4] Suburban area includes law enforcement agencies in cities with less than 50,000 inhabitants and county law enforcement agencies that are within a Metropolitan Statistical Area. Suburban area excludes all metropolitan agencies associated with a principal city. The agencies associated with suburban areas also appear in other groups within this table.

Table 11. Estimated Number of Arrests, 2016

(Number.)

Offense	Arrests
Total[1]	10,662,252
Violent crime[2]	515,151
Murder and nonnegligent manslaughter	11,788
Rape[3]	23,632
Robbery	95,754
Aggravated assault	383,977
Property crime[2]	1,353,283
Burglary	207,325
Larceny-theft	1,050,058
Motor vehicle theft	86,088
Arson	9,812
Other assaults	1,078,808
Forgery and counterfeiting	56,661
Fraud	128,531
Embezzlement	15,937
Stolen property; buying, receiving, possessing	93,981
Vandalism	195,951
Weapons; carrying, possessing, etc.	156,777
Prostitution and commercialized vice	38,306
Sex offenses (except forcible rape and prostitution)	51,063
Drug abuse violations	1,572,579
Gambling	3,705
Offenses against the family and children	88,748
Driving under the influence	1,017,808
Liquor laws	234,899
Drunkenness	376,433
Disorderly conduct	369,733
Vagrancy	24,851
All other offenses	3,254,871
Suspicion	576
Curfew and loitering law violations	34,176

[1] Does not include suspicion.
[2] Violent crimes are offenses of murder and nonnegligent manslaughter, rape, robbery, and aggravated assault. Property crimes are offenses of burglary, larceny-theft, motor vehicle theft, and arson.
[3] The rape figures in this table are an aggregate total of the data submitted using both the revised and legacy Uniform Crime Reporting definitions.

Table 12. Number and Rate of Arrests, by Geographic Region, 2016

(Number, rate per 100,000 inhabitants.)

Offense charged	United States total (13,055 agencies; population 257,118,573)		Northeast (3,130 agencies; population 45,162,860)		Midwest (3,222 agencies; population 50,287,054)		South (4,892 agencies; population 88,748,151)		West (1,811 agencies; population 72,920,508)	
	Total	Rate	Total	Rate	Total	Rate	Total	Rate	Total	Rate
Total[1]	8,481,162	3,298.5	1,263,318	2,797.2	1,619,069	3,219.7	3,204,603	3,610.9	2,394,172	3,283.3
Violent crime[2]	410,717	159.7	57,910	128.2	64,152	127.6	131,356	148.0	157,299	215.7
Murder and nonnegligent manslaughter	9,427	3.7	993	2.2	1,670	3.3	4,354	4.9	2,410	3.3
Rape[3]	18,802	7.3	3,247	7.2	4,200	8.4	6,303	7.1	5,052	6.9
Robbery	76,503	29.8	13,863	30.7	11,951	23.8	26,180	29.5	24,509	33.6
Aggravated assault	305,985	119.0	39,807	88.1	46,331	92.1	94,519	106.5	125,328	171.9
Property crime[2]	1,081,387	420.6	170,160	376.8	218,504	434.5	402,962	454.1	289,761	397.4
Burglary	165,376	64.3	22,105	48.9	22,747	45.2	59,811	67.4	60,713	83.3
Larceny-theft	839,617	326.5	140,326	310.7	180,355	358.7	321,813	362.6	197,123	270.3
Motor vehicle theft	68,567	26.7	6,584	14.6	13,951	27.7	19,158	21.6	28,874	39.6
Arson	7,827	3.0	1,145	2.5	1,451	2.9	2,180	2.5	3,051	4.2
Other assaults	859,316	334.2	143,394	317.5	166,385	330.9	340,331	383.5	209,206	286.9
Forgery and counterfeiting	45,067	17.5	7,719	17.1	7,783	15.5	19,319	21.8	10,246	14.1
Fraud	101,980	39.7	20,528	45.5	18,692	37.2	44,814	50.5	17,946	24.6
Embezzlement	12,688	4.9	1,494	3.3	2,302	4.6	6,617	7.5	2,275	3.1
Stolen property; buying, receiving, possessing	74,895	29.1	10,890	24.1	13,796	27.4	23,355	26.3	26,854	36.8
Vandalism	156,186	60.7	33,731	74.7	30,437	60.5	41,286	46.5	50,732	69.6
Weapons; carrying, possessing, etc.	124,741	48.5	15,560	34.5	25,195	50.1	43,243	48.7	40,743	55.9
Prostitution and commercialized vice	30,509	11.9	4,313	9.5	3,865	7.7	9,635	10.9	12,696	17.4
Sex offenses (except forcible rape and prostitution)	40,546	15.8	6,259	13.9	7,541	15.0	12,203	13.8	14,543	19.9
Drug abuse violations	1,250,650	486.4	215,838	477.9	229,151	455.7	462,354	521.0	343,307	470.8
Gambling	2,916	1.1	659	1.5	691	1.4	1,180	1.3	386	0.5
Offenses against the family and children	70,072	27.3	12,751	28.2	14,835	29.5	31,418	35.4	11,068	15.2
Driving under the influence	806,369	313.6	128,536	284.6	158,400	315.0	257,142	289.7	262,291	359.7
Liquor laws	186,047	72.4	21,718	48.1	63,418	126.1	50,259	56.6	50,652	69.5
Drunkenness	300,473	116.9	28,794	63.8	16,864	33.5	164,418	185.3	90,397	124.0
Disorderly conduct	294,345	114.5	73,545	162.8	91,602	182.2	80,286	90.5	48,912	67.1
Vagrancy	19,873	7.7	1,205	2.7	2,977	5.9	6,338	7.1	9,353	12.8
All other offenses (except traffic)	2,585,233	1,005.5	299,603	663.4	476,644	947.8	1,069,304	1,204.9	739,682	1,014.4
Suspicion	440	0.2	2	*	28	0.1	248	0.3	162	0.2
Curfew and loitering law violations	27,152	10.6	8,711	19.3	5,835	11.6	6,783	7.6	5,823	8.0

[1]Does not include suspicion.
[2]Violent crimes are offenses of murder and nonnegligent manslaughter, rape, robbery, and aggravated assault. Property crimes are offenses of burglary, larceny-theft, motor vehicle theft, and arson.
[3]The rape figures in this table are an aggregate total of the data submitted using both the revised and legacy Uniform Crime Reporting definitions.

Table 13. Arrests, by State, 2016

(Number.)

State	Total all classes	Violent crime	Property crime	Murder and nonnegligent manslaughter	Rape	Robbery	Aggravated assault	Burglary	Larceny-theft	Motor vehicle theft	Arson	Other assaults
ALABAMA												
Under 18	4,800	321	1,229	15	32	109	165	318	833	72	6	777
Total all ages	154,482	6,187	18,479	312	384	1,177	4,314	3,004	14,495	880	100	18,151
ALASKA												
Under 18	1,893	216	494	8	21	35	152	104	300	62	28	297
Total all ages	29,462	2,298	3,495	41	130	282	1,845	538	2,401	505	51	4,300
ARIZONA												
Under 18	22,997	1,020	5,113	15	53	336	616	759	3,968	341	45	3,667
Total all ages	263,699	11,145	37,592	242	344	1,849	8,710	3,957	31,907	1,551	177	26,150
ARKANSAS												
Under 18	8,045	424	1,801	10	44	91	279	414	1,308	74	5	1,433
Total all ages	132,165	4,860	13,791	143	289	561	3,867	2,174	11,084	488	45	11,849
CALIFORNIA												
Under 18	58,758	7,015	12,519	92	275	2,601	4,047	4,583	6,169	1,508	259	8,977
Total all ages	1,118,712	106,828	115,354	1,437	2,560	15,866	86,965	40,808	54,720	18,521	1,305	80,835
COLORADO												
Under 18	21,548	636	4,753	6	52	126	452	432	3,794	450	77	1,697
Total all ages	225,710	6,691	29,879	150	414	941	5,186	2,571	24,495	2,585	228	17,079
CONNECTICUT												
Under 18	8,264	416	1,902	5	28	161	222	261	1,330	275	36	1,974
Total all ages	100,280	3,741	14,845	62	222	1,016	2,441	1,935	11,971	842	97	17,935
DELAWARE												
Under 18	3,704	348	712	5	12	119	212	137	537	34	4	1,008
Total all ages	33,553	2,224	7,165	29	58	526	1,611	1,053	5,964	122	26	6,630
DISTRICT OF COLUMBIA												
Under 18	671	83	47	0	0	58	25	0	44	3	0	75
Total all ages	10,271	161	132	1	2	94	64	0	122	10	0	360
FLORIDA												
Under 18	57,843	3,861	17,688	45	248	1,541	2,027	4,817	10,005	2,810	56	8,670
Total all ages	726,396	35,807	102,639	642	1,747	6,521	26,897	18,037	76,139	8,211	252	76,450
GEORGIA												
Under 18	22,646	1,282	5,599	60	42	514	666	1,043	4,145	382	29	3,636
Total all ages	238,684	11,105	32,573	403	274	2,018	8,410	4,506	26,601	1,328	138	22,486
HAWAII												
Under 18	3,597	175	688	1	23	72	79	85	545	50	8	470
Total all ages	42,301	1,341	4,426	35	154	294	858	636	3,365	389	36	4,621
IDAHO												
Under 18	5,298	117	1,028	0	23	8	86	163	788	57	20	668
Total all ages	46,962	1,279	4,955	23	99	79	1,078	808	3,909	196	42	4,270
ILLINOIS												
Under 18	10,186	1,003	2,964	45	35	665	258	301	1,161	1,489	13	1,576
Total all ages	67,983	4,030	12,623	287	276	1,631	1,836	992	8,060	3,505	66	13,371
INDIANA												
Under 18	12,420	758	3,074	12	19	298	429	317	2,400	316	41	2,161
Total all ages	143,554	7,323	19,954	160	193	1,325	5,645	2,208	16,014	1,625	107	12,547
IOWA												
Under 18	10,671	558	2,556	3	34	110	411	391	1,978	152	35	1,560
Total all ages	95,962	4,876	13,033	55	154	396	4,271	1,585	10,839	525	84	7,790
KANSAS												
Under 18	4,081	170	910	6	25	33	106	84	738	69	19	643
Total all ages	53,823	1,948	4,899	50	126	205	1,567	579	3,907	363	50	7,741
KENTUCKY												
Under 18	5,639	402	1,466	17	32	223	130	340	853	263	10	1,039
Total all ages	210,586	3,487	18,219	185	236	1,122	1,944	2,994	14,286	886	53	11,703

Table 13. Arrests, by State, 2016—*Continued*

(Number.)

State	Total all classes	Violent crime	Property crime	Murder and nonnegligent manslaughter	Rape	Robbery	Aggravated assault	Burglary	Larceny-theft	Motor vehicle theft	Arson	Other assaults
LOUISIANA												
Under 18	19,018	1,328	4,669	28	112	333	855	1,211	3,085	353	20	3,061
Total all ages	191,920	11,372	32,355	339	499	1,646	8,888	5,422	25,436	1,388	109	23,075
MAINE												
Under 18	3,160	45	814	1	13	7	24	136	604	57	17	442
Total all ages	43,473	774	5,668	16	61	139	558	681	4,704	206	77	4,719
MARYLAND												
Under 18	19,506	1,935	4,862	11	74	1,067	783	932	3,169	620	141	4,630
Total all ages	182,631	9,737	25,715	270	403	3,223	5,841	4,777	19,083	1,502	353	21,522
MASSACHUSETTS												
Under 18	6,939	849	1,285	6	28	185	630	213	928	111	33	1,485
Total all ages	119,180	9,656	14,973	58	303	1,263	8,032	2,135	12,140	618	80	19,027
MICHIGAN												
Under 18	17,629	1,160	4,802	14	117	276	753	715	3,695	325	67	2,601
Total all ages	255,900	12,163	26,295	166	760	1,467	9,770	3,284	21,366	1,412	233	27,475
MINNESOTA												
Under 18	19,648	900	4,993	6	101	359	434	426	4,221	316	30	2,120
Total all ages	135,455	5,404	25,116	103	565	1,155	3,581	2,109	21,652	1,264	91	13,688
MISSISSIPPI												
Under 18	3,812	131	817	6	8	87	30	191	594	26	6	559
Total all ages	76,489	1,588	8,209	117	84	450	937	1,309	6,505	342	53	6,680
MISSOURI												
Under 18	19,416	966	4,265	18	101	339	508	493	3,439	270	63	3,253
Total all ages	240,878	10,223	34,373	339	516	1,926	7,442	4,153	27,668	2,344	208	23,578
MONTANA												
Under 18	4,263	78	859	0	9	8	61	83	704	56	16	504
Total all ages	30,550	1,114	4,883	14	48	69	983	326	4,229	293	35	4,092
NEBRASKA												
Under 18	8,921	168	2,377	5	59	54	50	102	2,133	115	27	1,351
Total all ages	68,310	1,912	10,124	40	259	296	1,317	582	9,070	416	56	8,242
NEVADA												
Under 18	8,441	1,047	1,408	5	52	372	618	264	995	137	12	1,444
Total all ages	125,932	8,351	10,450	166	257	1,905	6,023	2,519	6,978	900	53	14,022
NEW HAMPSHIRE												
Under 18	3,564	78	404	0	12	24	42	33	343	15	13	568
Total all ages	47,282	874	3,975	5	58	179	632	336	3,499	114	26	5,115
NEW JERSEY												
Under 18	17,784	1,409	2,794	13	69	637	690	615	2,029	88	62	1,633
Total all ages	294,972	10,001	26,736	198	396	3,000	6,407	4,334	21,723	499	180	22,348
NEW MEXICO												
Under 18	4,254	248	1,070	9	8	20	211	79	813	54	124	681
Total all ages	77,509	4,007	10,421	66	118	360	3,463	918	8,419	447	637	8,482
NEW YORK												
Under 18	20,322	1,692	5,312	16	193	693	790	851	3,998	392	71	2,767
Total all ages	271,780	13,238	49,196	255	1,091	3,280	8,612	5,780	41,354	1,820	242	29,532
NORTH CAROLINA												
Under 18	16,027	923	4,413	26	14	504	379	1,189	3,003	178	43	3,195
Total all ages	231,449	11,607	36,802	497	273	2,610	8,227	7,909	27,736	969	188	32,067
NORTH DAKOTA												
Under 18	3,788	53	626	0	4	6	43	31	540	48	7	391
Total all ages	34,817	743	3,563	14	45	76	608	281	2,894	234	154	2,789

Table 13. Arrests, by State, 2016—*Continued*

(Number.)

State	Total all classes	Violent crime	Property crime	Murder and nonnegligent manslaughter	Rape	Robbery	Aggravated assault	Burglary	Larceny-theft	Motor vehicle theft	Arson	Other assaults
OHIO												
Under 18	22,552	732	4,174	12	88	307	325	696	3,241	172	65	4,295
Total all ages	213,801	6,683	33,524	189	481	1,847	4,166	3,851	28,735	681	257	28,812
OKLAHOMA												
Under 18	9,236	449	2,272	17	30	118	284	356	1,772	102	42	964
Total all ages	112,401	4,653	15,856	183	207	649	3,614	2,056	12,965	623	212	8,195
OREGON												
Under 18	10,407	307	2,198	3	25	72	207	234	1,804	111	49	1,093
Total all ages	131,085	3,715	19,456	66	146	767	2,736	1,618	16,190	1,439	209	10,241
PENNSYLVANIA												
Under 18	40,826	2,678	5,563	22	202	1,045	1,409	868	4,120	450	125	4,811
Total all ages	350,797	18,416	50,837	377	1,003	4,820	12,216	6,158	41,938	2,340	401	39,904
RHODE ISLAND												
Under 18	2,489	109	494	0	17	38	54	92	365	20	17	411
Total all ages	27,494	896	2,881	18	85	143	650	592	2,126	127	36	4,002
SOUTH CAROLINA												
Under 18	12,987	682	3,308	35	63	258	326	614	2,527	145	22	2,116
Total all ages	158,298	6,929	24,138	293	411	1,200	5,025	3,385	19,664	968	121	16,445
SOUTH DAKOTA												
Under 18	5,016	106	1,000	0	3	11	92	103	770	122	5	492
Total all ages	47,214	1,291	3,554	23	44	57	1,167	352	2,897	289	16	4,447
TENNESSEE												
Under 18	22,110	1,401	4,060	21	42	364	974	815	2,766	421	58	4,106
Total all ages	339,280	16,142	37,897	301	291	1,936	13,614	5,322	29,785	2,606	184	29,825
TEXAS												
Under 18	65,539	3,938	14,953	62	375	1,422	2,079	2,590	11,155	1,101	107	12,047
Total all ages	820,979	31,989	95,012	889	2,311	7,056	21,733	12,201	76,604	5,795	412	94,190
UTAH												
Under 18	13,187	268	2,740	2	75	51	140	165	2,463	82	30	1,305
Total all ages	102,988	2,252	16,044	50	258	413	1,531	935	14,617	421	71	8,780
VERMONT												
Under 18	425	13	60	0	4	0	9	13	40	6	1	96
Total all ages	8,062	314	1,049	4	28	23	259	154	871	18	6	812
VIRGINIA												
Under 18	16,838	735	3,907	20	69	385	261	504	3,162	211	30	2,735
Total all ages	271,921	7,410	30,793	351	480	1,755	4,824	2,928	26,706	1,013	146	32,469
WASHINGTON												
Under 18	12,184	782	3,151	15	79	295	393	442	2,432	247	30	2,642
Total all ages	171,211	7,778	30,229	107	491	1,665	5,515	4,847	23,705	1,518	159	24,266
WEST VIRGINIA												
Under 18	1,050	48	152	2	5	6	35	24	110	13	5	249
Total all ages	39,742	1,905	5,826	41	101	157	1,606	771	4,777	238	40	4,684
WISCONSIN												
Under 18	41,813	1,111	6,135	7	149	434	521	655	4,900	532	48	2,570
Total all ages	261,400	7,556	31,446	244	781	1,570	4,961	2,771	27,253	1,293	129	15,905
WYOMING												
Under 18	3,332	22	558	0	2	3	17	46	476	27	9	419
Total all ages	28,213	500	2,577	13	33	19	435	232	2,188	109	48	2,068

Table 13. Arrests, by State, 2016—*Continued*

(Number.)

State	Forgery and counterfeiting	Fraud	Embezzlement	Stolen property; buying, receiving, possessing	Vandalism	Weapons; carrying, possessing, etc.	Prostitution and commercialized vice	Sex offenses (except rape and prostitution)	Drug abuse violations	Gambling	Offenses against the family and children
ALABAMA											
Under 18	20	24	1	121	190	93	0	29	191	0	44
Total all ages	1,382	3,774	190	2,020	1,583	1,681	1	706	10,193	0	982
ALASKA											
Under 18	1	10	8	5	135	24	0	33	207	0	1
Total all ages	96	236	81	82	1,024	311	13	281	1,006	0	195
ARIZONA											
Under 18	13	80	19	126	1,761	221	2	259	3,090	0	177
Total all ages	1,098	2,005	352	1,341	10,031	2,878	387	1,388	30,309	3	2,520
ARKANSAS											
Under 18	8	31	1	163	298	123	0	35	770	0	10
Total all ages	813	1,114	64	1,437	1,460	1,040	277	119	15,736	8	354
CALIFORNIA											
Under 18	62	180	15	982	3,050	3,379	112	1,123	6,291	3	3
Total all ages	5,000	6,324	955	16,500	17,202	27,707	7,601	9,222	219,016	266	236
COLORADO											
Under 18	6	63	7	32	833	294	1	102	2,440	0	52
Total all ages	679	2,512	101	456	5,354	2,363	510	437	14,790	3	2,849
CONNECTICUT											
Under 18	13	35	5	54	432	178	1	71	581	0	45
Total all ages	553	893	161	366	2,063	1,185	212	348	9,349	19	1,450
DELAWARE											
Under 18	3	70	2	119	207	98	0	33	340	0	0
Total all ages	290	1,769	198	468	886	388	89	128	4,289	1	195
DISTRICT OF COLUMBIA											
Under 18	0	0	0	14	20	35	0	0	19	0	0
Total all ages	1	9	0	22	43	83	0	5	328	0	2
FLORIDA											
Under 18	45	388	26	157	1,166	801	7	293	5,584	4	0
Total all ages	2,247	11,954	1,041	1,774	6,192	5,152	2,397	2,728	114,550	149	0
GEORGIA											
Under 18	65	112	8	373	620	551	12	418	2,402	7	133
Total all ages	2,379	3,323	223	2,819	3,643	3,141	455	2,783	39,593	76	2,944
HAWAII											
Under 18	2	8	0	21	121	15	3	42	454	0	1
Total all ages	140	265	32	130	570	297	159	218	2,574	76	17
IDAHO											
Under 18	1	33	1	30	247	77	0	60	730	0	40
Total all ages	111	252	40	243	761	306	11	209	8,031	0	724
ILLINOIS											
Under 18	9	4	0	39	294	738	0	17	1,343	44	6
Total all ages	128	183	0	87	2,072	3,234	187	302	12,958	456	254
INDIANA											
Under 18	18	68	3	83	447	255	2	105	1,100	1	171
Total all ages	1,351	1,670	204	547	1,419	2,386	309	776	18,041	21	1,042
IOWA											
Under 18	21	39	8	47	766	120	1	64	935	0	3
Total all ages	584	752	79	177	2,283	844	104	186	9,550	5	1,242
KANSAS											
Under 18	5	10	8	47	226	54	1	42	668	0	8
Total all ages	189	403	107	577	1,458	541	56	138	7,519	0	182

Table 13. Arrests, by State, 2016—*Continued*

(Number.)

State	Forgery and counterfeiting	Fraud	Embezzlement	Stolen property; buying, receiving, possessing	Vandalism	Weapons; carrying, possessing, etc.	Prostitution and commercialized vice	Sex offenses (except rape and prostitution)	Drug abuse violations	Gambling	Offenses against the family and children
KENTUCKY											
Under 18	20	13	7	464	184	95	0	33	501	0	5
Total all ages	1,021	1,003	441	2,628	1,132	891	252	297	23,308	9	4,547
LOUISIANA											
Under 18	10	38	4	372	600	452	11	172	1,475	14	42
Total all ages	731	1,473	172	2,283	3,739	3,777	521	1,355	27,529	79	1,538
MAINE											
Under 18	10	11	2	11	232	14	1	30	383	0	0
Total all ages	229	552	66	90	1,052	149	105	187	5,430	1	122
MARYLAND											
Under 18	26	42	1	22	929	636	8	144	2,167	19	10
Total all ages	582	896	115	144	2,721	3,181	584	687	30,692	133	1,972
MASSACHUSETTS											
Under 18	20	29	3	153	415	158	1	47	228	0	33
Total all ages	469	1,263	136	1,084	2,692	1,238	553	418	9,770	14	1,231
MICHIGAN											
Under 18	32	208	30	249	548	348	4	150	2,207	3	4
Total all ages	652	3,909	1,009	1,645	2,828	4,128	528	687	38,780	37	2,799
MINNESOTA											
Under 18	17	147	8	285	895	392	2	147	1,525	0	10
Total all ages	985	2,187	29	1,684	3,057	1,786	344	1,047	15,397	12	507
MISSISSIPPI											
Under 18	0	21	1	44	109	131	2	13	273	1	263
Total all ages	378	980	395	670	751	1,016	38	204	10,414	63	2,407
MISSOURI											
Under 18	21	98	18	370	816	294	7	254	2,452	3	45
Total all ages	1,351	2,454	369	3,195	4,076	3,706	415	1,289	41,674	75	2,596
MONTANA											
Under 18	2	12	2	4	245	6	0	38	360	0	271
Total all ages	112	258	32	62	952	112	3	126	2,638	0	442
NEBRASKA											
Under 18	7	77	15	80	654	93	0	95	1,304	0	27
Total all ages	274	1,374	98	619	2,210	1,103	131	453	11,878	0	1,257
NEVADA											
Under 18	10	37	3	144	282	167	70	42	837	2	29
Total all ages	605	1,635	331	1,584	1,482	1,893	2,892	714	13,770	33	963
NEW HAMPSHIRE											
Under 18	4	18	3	43	223	1	0	26	637	1	8
Total all ages	236	843	122	547	1,178	171	91	128	8,346	7	160
NEW JERSEY											
Under 18	40	64	10	415	693	667	9	107	3,574	31	37
Total all ages	1,047	3,896	320	2,693	3,858	4,054	849	963	61,579	421	7,426
NEW MEXICO											
Under 18	2	15	7	55	154	66	1	16	512	0	14
Total all ages	237	631	214	1,449	1,214	576	36	83	6,924	0	850
NEW YORK											
Under 18	102	159	1	485	2,075	395	16	296	3,331	1	29
Total all ages	2,801	4,419	62	3,441	14,798	3,624	627	1,970	65,379	74	595
NORTH CAROLINA											
Under 18	24	171	30	343	570	592	7	73	1,227	0	34
Total all ages	1,167	7,337	983	2,836	3,989	4,485	182	823	18,247	43	4,412

Table 13. Arrests, by State, 2016—*Continued*

(Number.)

State	Forgery and counterfeiting	Fraud	Embezzlement	Stolen property; buying, receiving, possessing	Vandalism	Weapons; carrying, possessing, etc.	Prostitution and commercialized vice	Sex offenses (except rape and prostitution)	Drug abuse violations	Gambling	Offenses against the family and children
NORTH DAKOTA											
Under 18	3	7	8	44	156	22	0	25	442	0	129
Total all ages	124	351	59	320	506	340	20	89	5,093	0	313
OHIO											
Under 18	30	134	0	521	1,034	318	10	157	1,811	1	184
Total all ages	1,002	2,086	21	3,202	3,599	3,211	1,308	558	32,324	41	1,622
OKLAHOMA											
Under 18	3	38	20	287	277	166	0	48	1,328	4	32
Total all ages	673	1,621	376	2,737	1,229	2,183	5	408	22,107	35	609
OREGON											
Under 18	9	54	1	27	1,040	106	0	67	1,854	0	6
Total all ages	558	1,752	44	558	4,012	1,660	284	519	13,639	0	335
PENNSYLVANIA											
Under 18	55	653	29	342	1,501	789	6	493	3,177	2	31
Total all ages	2,253	7,954	485	2,268	6,858	4,660	1,792	2,125	53,633	105	1,581
RHODE ISLAND											
Under 18	2	17	3	71	189	135	0	16	80	0	30
Total all ages	111	586	87	342	1,035	465	80	91	1,759	18	68
SOUTH CAROLINA											
Under 18	11	74	9	162	456	434	7	63	2,080	3	8
Total all ages	1,130	3,452	325	1,996	2,794	2,251	578	319	30,020	51	1,237
SOUTH DAKOTA											
Under 18	2	44	8	35	135	49	1	13	847	0	388
Total all ages	96	664	38	177	466	255	26	53	7,912	0	766
TENNESSEE											
Under 18	45	142	4	117	1,036	391	0	116	2,501	39	55
Total all ages	1,876	5,797	707	1,038	4,563	2,741	1,161	568	44,185	170	4,036
TEXAS											
Under 18	135	275	153	181	1,779	843	53	431	10,612	15	95
Total all ages	4,659	6,515	918	1,057	8,120	12,375	4,506	3,005	140,314	490	4,264
UTAH											
Under 18	7	30	0	94	694	205	16	214	1,786	0	36
Total all ages	680	886	21	1,053	2,631	844	191	600	15,111	4	1,297
VERMONT											
Under 18	0	2	2	4	37	7	0	10	23	0	8
Total all ages	20	122	55	59	197	14	4	29	593	0	118
VIRGINIA											
Under 18	36	129	37	177	753	328	3	122	2,068	0	55
Total all ages	1,905	5,240	1,405	917	4,021	3,562	913	692	39,132	20	1,780
WASHINGTON											
Under 18	10	28	1	210	756	237	9	133	1,360	0	9
Total all ages	881	994	60	3,354	4,973	1,711	553	637	11,017	0	280
WEST VIRGINIA											
Under 18	1	3	1	5	40	24	0	12	110	0	2
Total all ages	332	511	105	283	612	448	73	104	6,267	2	139
WISCONSIN											
Under 18	22	116	31	605	1,873	598	14	674	3,154	8	105
Total all ages	1,047	2,659	289	1,566	6,463	3,661	437	1,963	28,025	44	2,255
WYOMING											
Under 18	2	7	2	2	154	38	3	13	543	1	10
Total all ages	49	196	12	42	526	85	56	109	4,482	1	360

Table 13. Arrests, by State, 2016—*Continued*

(Number.)

State	Driving under the influence	Liquor laws	Drunkenness	Disorderly conduct	Vagrancy	All other offenses (except traffic)	Suspicion	Curfew and loitering law violations	Number of agencies	2016 estimated population
ALABAMA										
Under 18	28	225	31	378	2	1,096	0	0	240	3,800,629
Total all ages	8,126	2,496	7,283	2,129	67	69,052	0	0		
ALASKA										
Under 18	31	121	18	11	0	269	0	12	32	738,566
Total all ages	3,063	775	112	738	4	11,340	0	12		
ARIZONA										
Under 18	211	1,668	84	1,436	65	2,924	0	1,061	90	6,391,343
Total all ages	23,498	9,745	14,100	15,874	351	71,741	130	1,061		
ARKANSAS										
Under 18	44	219	87	470	0	1,765	0	363	271	2,786,173
Total all ages	6,703	1,769	6,589	2,425	890	60,504	0	363		
CALIFORNIA										
Under 18	493	1,210	880	1,264	101	9,645	0	1,454	613	39,012,007
Total all ages	129,752	8,857	69,869	3,906	6,597	285,231	0	1,454		
COLORADO										
Under 18	217	1,389	47	1,727	0	6,099	0	1,153	193	5,008,754
Total all ages	23,364	9,025	249	7,486	453	100,277	0	1,153		
CONNECTICUT										
Under 18	41	49	0	1,485	0	978	0	4	104	3,526,707
Total all ages	8,533	225	8	11,640	36	26,714	0	4		
DELAWARE										
Under 18	0	84	1	287	0	345	0	47	56	950,787
Total all ages	355	884	345	1,312	332	5,558	0	47		
DISTRICT OF COLUMBIA										
Under 18	0	0	0	39	0	338	0	1	2	0
Total all ages	11	1,024	89	172	30	7,798	0	1		
FLORIDA										
Under 18	109	496	0	0	0	18,548	0	0	668	20,566,240
Total all ages	35,042	14,280	0	0	0	313,994	0	0		
GEORGIA										
Under 18	89	326	20	2,184	99	4,380	0	330	402	8,150,300
Total all ages	18,939	4,262	1,442	14,886	1,574	69,708	0	330		
HAWAII										
Under 18	23	92	4	95	3	1,201	7	172	4	1,428,557
Total all ages	5,929	575	4	1,074	3	19,671	7	172		
IDAHO										
Under 18	61	324	30	237	0	1,557	0	57	101	1,324,720
Total all ages	6,195	1,324	254	1,458	10	16,472	0	57		
ILLINOIS										
Under 18	7	32	0	877	0	1,154	0	79	2	2,872,516
Total all ages	2,929	165	0	3,756	4	11,165	0	79		
INDIANA										
Under 18	61	745	38	697	33	2,374	8	218	204	4,305,899
Total all ages	13,492	3,665	4,316	3,517	81	50,656	19	218		
IOWA										
Under 18	71	689	99	1,211	0	1,519	0	404	206	2,810,823
Total all ages	9,836	3,943	6,983	4,104	9	29,178	0	404		
KANSAS										
Under 18	58	408	0	204	0	619	0	0	228	1,732,223
Total all ages	5,923	2,593	134	1,558	0	17,857	0	0		

Table 13. Arrests, by State, 2016—*Continued*

(Number.)

State	Driving under the influence	Liquor laws	Drunkenness	Disorderly conduct	Vagrancy	All other offenses (except traffic)	Suspicion	Curfew and loitering law violations	Number of agencies	2016 estimated population
KENTUCKY										
Under 18	66	26	57	230	0	1,028	0	3	419	4,424,357
Total all ages	16,901	94	14,259	4,095	137	106,159	0	3		
LOUISIANA										
Under 18	32	233	25	2,537	51	3,584	9	299	168	4,183,659
Total all ages	7,587	3,596	3,567	10,435	250	56,154	33	299		
MAINE										
Under 18	28	459	4	105	0	561	0	8	195	1,328,762
Total all ages	5,834	2,218	17	1,309	0	14,943	0	8		
MARYLAND										
Under 18	60	512	8	873	23	2,522	30	47	143	5,197,665
Total all ages	17,809	5,398	14	4,639	139	55,773	131	47		
MASSACHUSETTS										
Under 18	46	291	38	394	0	1,464	0	0	342	6,436,240
Total all ages	9,008	2,000	5,600	4,329	11	35,706	2	0		
MICHIGAN										
Under 18	194	1,371	4	666	0	2,723	0	325	606	9,696,514
Total all ages	27,571	10,690	367	6,536	241	87,235	0	325		
MINNESOTA										
Under 18	144	1,795	0	2,039	2	3,280	0	947	365	5,237,709
Total all ages	19,196	8,054	1	8,679	38	27,297	0	947		
MISSISSIPPI										
Under 18	66	29	23	511	15	709	4	90	63	1,383,530
Total all ages	7,160	983	3,721	3,790	41	26,836	75	90		
MISSOURI										
Under 18	182	877	16	1,325	6	3,333	0	815	375	5,768,437
Total all ages	19,729	5,280	330	8,158	1,222	75,970	0	815		
MONTANA										
Under 18	42	454	0	467	0	619	0	300	100	1,036,405
Total all ages	4,392	1,871	0	2,878	21	6,262	0	300		
NEBRASKA										
Under 18	109	682	0	427	0	1,311	0	144	153	1,721,852
Total all ages	6,948	4,862	0	2,714	16	13,951	0	144		
NEVADA										
Under 18	58	521	6	167	8	1,682	5	472	51	2,940,058
Total all ages	10,660	3,383	214	1,292	1,512	49,669	5	472		
NEW HAMPSHIRE										
Under 18	42	389	233	99	0	774	0	13	174	1,275,170
Total all ages	4,874	2,907	3,683	954	65	12,993	0	13		
NEW JERSEY										
Under 18	129	778	0	1,413	11	2,574	0	1,396	494	8,747,889
Total all ages	22,745	3,044	0	12,723	274	108,599	0	1,396		
NEW MEXICO										
Under 18	62	163	19	178	0	986	1	4	57	1,498,550
Total all ages	6,178	1,977	445	1,602	247	31,924	8	4		
NEW YORK										
Under 18	113	201	0	592	10	2,745	0	0	544	10,621,114
Total all ages	29,238	1,599	0	6,355	565	44,267	0	0		
NORTH CAROLINA										
Under 18	201	457	0	1,305	0	2,447	0	15	235	6,270,620
Total all ages	30,380	2,286	0	4,497	12	69,279	0	15		

Table 13. Arrests, by State, 2016—Continued

(Number.)

State	Driving under the influence	Liquor laws	Drunkenness	Disorderly conduct	Vagrancy	All other offenses (except traffic)	Suspicion	Curfew and loitering law violations	Number of agencies	2016 estimated population
NORTH DAKOTA										
Under 18	26	469	0	662	0	617	0	108	106	753,138
Total all ages	5,725	2,922	309	2,202	6	9,234	1	108		
OHIO										
Under 18	84	672	28	1,811	4	6,010	5	537	461	8,954,617
Total all ages	15,060	5,973	1,886	14,608	99	57,640	5	537		
OKLAHOMA										
Under 18	107	105	293	505	2	1,267	0	1,069	336	3,744,169
Total all ages	12,200	1,433	13,507	1,996	34	21,466	9	1,069		
OREGON										
Under 18	108	916	0	509	0	1,600	0	512	185	3,707,053
Total all ages	14,282	4,844	0	6,555	4	48,115	0	512		
PENNSYLVANIA										
Under 18	365	2,134	170	7,352	26	3,371	0	7,278	1,183	11,822,238
Total all ages	44,111	9,179	19,475	33,487	254	44,142	0	7,278		
RHODE ISLAND										
Under 18	11	48	1	452	0	408	0	12	48	1,056,426
Total all ages	2,719	486	10	2,239	0	9,607	0	12		
SOUTH CAROLINA										
Under 18	90	286	71	1,447	0	1,649	0	31	434	4,794,988
Total all ages	15,947	5,014	6,956	8,738	425	29,522	0	31		
SOUTH DAKOTA										
Under 18	77	569	14	330	0	786	0	120	107	789,651
Total all ages	7,196	2,596	2,538	2,454	436	12,126	3	120		
TENNESSEE										
Under 18	143	586	141	1,912	0	4,080	0	1,235	455	6,454,266
Total all ages	22,563	4,278	14,029	7,079	25	139,365	0	1,235		
TEXAS										
Under 18	421	1,596	1,104	1,836	61	12,532	0	2,479	973	27,089,093
Total all ages	67,950	10,928	71,819	10,520	2,194	247,675	0	2,479		
UTAH										
Under 18	196	675	80	807	27	3,538	2	467	109	2,801,231
Total all ages	8,713	3,860	2,909	2,809	40	33,791	5	467		
VERMONT										
Under 18	8	23	1	67	0	64	0	0	46	348,314
Total all ages	1,474	60	1	509	0	2,632	0	0		
VIRGINIA										
Under 18	97	620	112	490	0	3,667	0	767	404	8,266,632
Total all ages	20,084	5,223	20,125	2,965	157	92,341	0	767		
WASHINGTON										
Under 18	121	776	3	178	0	1,775	0	3	223	6,483,494
Total all ages	23,209	2,487	22	2,415	81	56,261	0	3		
WEST VIRGINIA										
Under 18	11	52	3	27	0	303	0	7	291	1,251,283
Total all ages	4,427	591	673	608	31	12,114	0	7		
WISCONSIN										
Under 18	235	2,266	0	7,876	61	12,221	0	2,138	409	5,643,675
Total all ages	24,795	12,675	0	33,316	825	84,335	0	2,138		
WYOMING										
Under 18	26	461	12	124	12	764	3	156	53	549,770
Total all ages	3,056	1,929	2,219	825	30	8,928	7	156		

Table 14. Long-Term Arrest Trends, 2006 and 2016

(Number, percent change; 13,055 agencies; 2016 estimated population 257,118,573; 2006 estimated population 186,371,331.)

Offense charged	Number of persons arrested								
	Total, all ages			Under 18 years of age			18 years of age and over		
	2006	2016	Percent change	2006	2016	Percent change	2006	2016	Percent change
Total[1]	8,676,456	8,481,602	-2.2	1,280,195	681,701	-46.8	7,396,261	7,799,901	+5.5
Violent crime[2]	361,401	410,717	+13.6	56,938	41,335	-27.4	304,463	369,382	+21.3
Murder and nonnegligent manslaughter ...	7,104	9,427	+32.7	642	682	+6.2	6,462	8,745	+35.3
Rape[3]	14,120	18,802	NA	2,111	2,952	NA	12,009	15,850	NA
Robbery	68,437	76,503	+11.8	18,201	15,339	-15.7	50,236	61,164	+21.8
Aggravated assault	271,740	305,985	+12.6	35,984	22,362	-37.9	235,756	283,623	+20.3
Property crime[2]	950,507	1,081,387	+13.8	255,450	147,350	-42.3	695,057	934,037	+34.4
Burglary	188,122	165,376	-12.1	51,953	25,513	-50.9	136,169	139,863	+2.7
Larceny-theft	679,290	839,617	+23.6	180,623	107,287	-40.6	498,667	732,330	+46.9
Motor vehicle theft	72,650	68,567	-5.6	17,651	12,520	-29.1	54,999	56,047	+1.9
Arson	10,445	7,827	-25.1	5,223	2,030	-61.1	5,222	5,797	+11.0
Other assaults	792,178	859,316	+8.5	152,396	102,694	-32.6	639,782	756,622	+18.3
Forgery and counterfeiting	68,319	45,067	-34.0	2,288	967	-57.7	66,031	44,100	-33.2
Fraud	181,863	101,980	-43.9	5,090	3,680	-27.7	176,773	98,300	-44.4
Embezzlement	13,008	12,688	-2.5	949	540	-43.1	12,059	12,148	+0.7
Stolen property; buying, receiving, possessing	79,077	74,895	-5.3	14,032	8,679	-38.1	65,045	66,216	+1.8
Vandalism	189,867	156,186	-17.7	76,202	31,181	-59.1	113,665	125,005	+10.0
Weapons; carrying, possessing, etc.	114,104	124,741	+9.3	27,707	15,452	-44.2	86,397	109,289	+26.5
Prostitution and commercialized vice	33,402	30,509	-8.7	733	396	-46.0	32,669	30,113	-7.8
Sex offenses (except forcible rape and prostitution)	50,656	40,546	-20.0	9,948	6,723	-32.4	40,708	33,823	-16.9
Drug abuse violations	1,078,156	1,250,650	+16.0	113,132	78,330	-30.8	965,024	1,172,320	+21.5
Gambling	2,807	2,916	+3.9	292	203	-30.5	2,515	2,713	+7.9
Offenses against the family and children ...	79,568	70,072	-11.9	3,348	2,738	-18.2	76,220	67,334	-11.7
Driving under the influence	925,818	806,369	-12.9	12,947	5,135	-60.3	912,871	801,234	-12.2
Liquor laws	408,511	186,047	-54.5	94,729	29,073	-69.3	313,782	156,974	-50.0
Drunkenness	368,271	300,473	-18.4	11,093	3,805	-65.7	357,178	296,668	-16.9
Disorderly conduct	422,187	294,345	-30.3	129,948	52,315	-59.7	292,239	242,030	-17.2
Vagrancy	18,106	19,873	+9.8	3,475	622	-82.1	14,631	19,251	+31.6
All other offenses (except traffic)	2,477,981	2,585,233	+4.3	248,829	123,257	-50.5	2,229,152	2,461,976	+10.4
Suspicion	1,125	440	-60.9	203	74	-63.5	922	366	-60.3
Curfew and loitering law violations	60,669	27,152	-55.2	60,669	27,152	-55.2	NA	NA	NA

NA = Not available.
[1]Does not include suspicion.
[2]Violent crimes are offenses of murder and nonnegligent manslaughter, rape, robbery, and aggravated assault. Property crimes are offenses of burglary, larceny-theft, motor vehicle theft, and arson.
[3]The 2006 rape figures are based on the legacy definition, and the 2016 rape figures are aggregate totals based on both the legacy and revised Uniform Crime Reporting definitions. For this reason, a percent change is not provided.

Table 15. Half-Decade Arrest Trends, by Age, 2011 and 2016

(Number, percent change; 13,055 agencies; 2016 estimated population 257,118,573; 2011 estimated population 211,166,146.)

Offense charged	Total, all ages			Under 18 years of age			18 years of age and over		
	2011	2016	Percent change	2011	2016	Percent change	2011	2016	Percent change
Total[1]	8,225,888	8,481,602	+3.1	991,398	681,701	-31.2	7,234,490	7,799,901	+7.8
Violent crime[2]	346,801	410,717	+18.4	43,914	41,335	-5.9	302,887	369,382	+22.0
Murder and nonnegligent manslaughter	6,968	9,427	+35.3	539	682	+26.5	6,429	8,745	+36.0
Rape[3]	13,168	18,802	NA	1,917	2,952	NA	11,251	15,850	NA
Robbery	67,650	76,503	+13.1	15,037	15,339	+2.0	52,613	61,164	+16.3
Aggravated assault	259,015	305,985	+18.1	26,421	22,362	-15.4	232,594	283,623	+21.9
Property crime[2]	1,105,151	1,081,387	-2.2	229,384	147,350	-35.8	875,767	934,037	+6.7
Burglary	197,756	165,376	-16.4	41,018	25,513	-37.8	156,738	139,863	-10.8
Larceny-theft	855,183	839,617	-1.8	175,433	107,287	-38.8	679,750	732,330	+7.7
Motor vehicle theft	44,336	68,567	+54.7	9,581	12,520	+30.7	34,755	56,047	+61.3
Arson	7,876	7,827	-0.6	3,352	2,030	-39.4	4,524	5,797	+28.1
Other assaults	827,577	859,316	+3.8	127,310	102,694	-19.3	700,267	756,622	+8.0
Forgery and counterfeiting	46,264	45,067	-2.6	1,065	967	-9.2	45,199	44,100	-2.4
Fraud	110,363	101,980	-7.6	3,583	3,680	+2.7	106,780	98,300	-7.9
Embezzlement	10,931	12,688	+16.1	301	540	+79.4	10,630	12,148	+14.3
Stolen property; buying, receiving, possessing	63,792	74,895	+17.4	9,127	8,679	-4.9	54,665	66,216	+21.1
Vandalism	160,380	156,186	-2.6	46,688	31,181	-33.2	113,692	125,005	+10.0
Weapons; carrying, possessing, etc.	99,115	124,741	+25.9	18,665	15,452	-17.2	80,450	109,289	+35.8
Prostitution and commercialized vice	26,777	30,509	+13.9	461	396	-14.1	26,316	30,113	+14.4
Sex offenses (except forcible rape and prostitution)	44,870	40,546	-9.6	8,482	6,723	-20.7	36,388	33,823	-7.0
Drug abuse violations	1,020,875	1,250,650	+22.5	101,191	78,330	-22.6	919,684	1,172,320	+27.5
Gambling	4,929	2,916	-40.8	618	203	-67.2	4,311	2,713	-37.1
Offenses against the family and children	76,387	70,072	-8.3	2,378	2,738	+15.1	74,009	67,334	-9.0
Driving under the influence	825,909	806,369	-2.4	7,013	5,135	-26.8	818,896	801,234	-2.2
Liquor laws	323,529	186,047	-42.5	63,622	29,073	-54.3	259,907	156,974	-39.6
Drunkenness	361,587	300,473	-16.9	8,185	3,805	-53.5	353,402	296,668	-16.1
Disorderly conduct	382,589	294,345	-23.1	91,752	52,315	-43.0	290,837	242,030	-16.8
Vagrancy	14,587	19,873	+36.2	641	622	-3.0	13,946	19,251	+38.0
All other offenses (except traffic)	2,325,288	2,585,233	+11.2	178,831	123,257	-31.1	2,146,457	2,461,976	+14.7
Suspicion	732	440	-39.9	78	74	-5.1	654	366	-44.0
Curfew and loitering law violations	48,187	27,152	-43.7	48,187	27,152	-43.7	NA	NA	NA

NA = Not available.
[1]Does not include suspicion.
[2]Violent crimes are offenses of murder and nonnegligent manslaughter, rape, robbery, and aggravated assault. Property crimes are offenses of burglary, larceny-theft, motor vehicle theft, and arson.
[3]The 2011 rape figures are based on the legacy definition, and the 2016 rape figures are aggregate totals based on both the legacy and revised Uniform Crime Reporting definitions. For this reason, a percent change is not provided.

Table 16. Year-to-Year Arrest Trends, by Age, 2015 and 2016

(Number, percent change; 13,055 agencies; 2016 estimated population 257,118,573; 2015 estimated population 217,039,923.)

Offense charged	Number of persons arrested								
	Total, all ages			Under 18 years of age			18 years of age and over		
	2015	2016	Percent change	2015	2016	Percent change	2015	2016	Percent change
Total[1]	7,213,389	8,481,602	+17.6	634,718	681,701	+7.4	6,578,671	7,799,901	+18.6
Violent crime[2]	328,454	410,717	+25.0	33,306	41,335	+24.1	295,148	369,382	+25.2
Murder and nonnegligent manslaughter ...	7,005	9,427	+34.6	493	682	+38.3	6,512	8,745	+34.3
Rape....................................	15,126	18,802	+24.3	2,401	2,952	+22.9	12,725	15,850	+24.6
Robbery.................................	60,085	76,503	+27.3	11,404	15,339	+34.5	48,681	61,164	+25.6
Aggravated assault	246,238	305,985	+24.3	19,008	22,362	+17.6	227,230	283,623	+24.8
Property crime[2]	1,001,386	1,081,387	+8.0	144,781	147,350	+1.8	856,605	934,037	+9.0
Burglary.................................	145,163	165,376	+13.9	23,887	25,513	+6.8	121,276	139,863	+15.3
Larceny-theft.................................	799,643	839,617	+5.0	109,356	107,287	-1.9	690,287	732,330	+6.1
Motor vehicle theft	50,447	68,567	+35.9	9,624	12,520	+30.1	40,823	56,047	+37.3
Arson.................................	6,133	7,827	+27.6	1,914	2,030	+6.1	4,219	5,797	+37.4
Other assaults.................................	727,435	859,316	+18.1	89,835	102,694	+14.3	637,600	756,622	+18.7
Forgery and counterfeiting........................	36,642	45,067	+23.0	694	967	+39.3	35,948	44,100	+22.7
Fraud.................................	90,590	101,980	+12.6	3,246	3,680	+13.4	87,344	98,300	+12.5
Embezzlement.................................	11,011	12,688	+15.2	426	540	+26.8	10,585	12,148	+14.8
Stolen property; buying, receiving, possessing	59,223	74,895	+26.5	6,715	8,679	+29.2	52,508	66,216	+26.1
Vandalism.................................	130,154	156,186	+20.0	29,227	31,181	+6.7	100,927	125,005	+23.9
Weapons; carrying, possessing, etc.	95,803	124,741	+30.2	13,078	15,452	+18.2	82,725	109,289	+32.1
Prostitution and commercialized vice.........	19,797	30,509	+54.1	292	396	+35.6	19,505	30,113	+54.4
Sex offenses (except forcible rape and prostitution).................................	34,420	40,546	+17.8	6,048	6,723	+11.2	28,372	33,823	+19.2
Drug abuse violations.............................	1,016,402	1,250,650	+23.0	69,355	78,330	+12.9	947,047	1,172,320	+23.8
Gambling.................................	3,055	2,916	-4.5	294	203	-31.0	2,761	2,713	-1.7
Offenses against the family and children ...	65,357	70,072	+7.2	2,335	2,738	+17.3	63,022	67,334	+6.8
Driving under the influence......................	676,560	806,369	+19.2	4,432	5,135	+15.9	672,128	801,234	+19.2
Liquor laws.................................	181,462	186,047	+2.5	30,876	29,073	-5.8	150,586	156,974	+4.2
Drunkenness.................................	268,115	300,473	+12.1	3,836	3,805	-0.8	264,279	296,668	+12.3
Disorderly conduct.................................	264,528	294,345	+11.3	49,315	52,315	+6.1	215,213	242,030	+12.5
Vagrancy.................................	15,495	19,873	+28.3	648	622	-4.0	14,847	19,251	+29.7
All other offenses (except traffic)..............	2,157,131	2,585,233	+19.8	115,610	123,257	+6.6	2,041,521	2,461,976	+20.6
Suspicion	573	440	-23.2	132	74	-43.9	441	366	-17.0
Curfew and loitering law violations..........	30,369	27,152	-10.6	30,369	27,152	-10.6	NA	NA	NA

NA = Not available.
[1]Does not include suspicion.
[2]Violent crimes are offenses of murder and nonnegligent manslaughter, rape, robbery, and aggravated assault. Property crimes are offenses of burglary, larceny-theft, motor vehicle theft, and arson.

Table 17. Full-Time Law Enforcement Employees,[1] by Region and Geographic Division and Population Group, 2016

(Number, rate per 1,000 inhabitants.)

Region/geographic division	Total (10,126 cities; population 192,569,624)	Group I (79 cities, 250,000 and over; population 59,221,977)	Group II (200 cities, 100,000 to 249,999; population 29,632,582)	Group III (433 cities, 50,000 to 99,999; population 30,220,472)	Group IV (773 cities, 25,000 to 49,999; population 26,885,069)	Group V (1,597 cities, 10,000 to 24,999; population 25,434,997)
Total						
Number of employees..	543,105	199,810	63,555	62,534	57,020	57,987
Average number of employees per 1,000 inhabitants	2.8	3.4	2.1	2.1	2.1	2.3
Northeast						
Number of employees..	150,352	66,610	8,428	15,399	18,309	18,553
Average number of employees per 1,000 inhabitants	3.3	5.6	2.9	2.4	2.2	2.1
New England						
Number of employees..	34,056	2,678	4,468	6,281	7,068	6,931
Average number of employees per 1,000 inhabitants	2.6	4.0	3.0	2.3	2.2	2.3
Middle Atlantic						
Number of employees..	116,296	63,932	3,960	9,118	11,241	11,622
Average number of employees per 1,000 inhabitants	3.6	5.7	2.9	2.4	2.1	2.0
Midwest						
Number of employees..	94,374	31,832	7,333	11,733	11,890	13,012
Average number of employees per 1,000 inhabitants	2.5	3.7	2.0	1.8	1.9	2.0
East North Central						
Number of employees..	60,559	24,326	3,669	7,089	8,645	7,761
Average number of employees per 1,000 inhabitants	2.6	4.0	2.0	1.9	1.9	2.0
West North Central						
Number of employees..	33,815	7,506	3,664	4,644	3,245	5,251
Average number of employees per 1,000 inhabitants	2.4	2.9	2.0	1.7	1.9	2.1
South						
Number of employees..	184,239	52,351	27,507	19,997	17,872	19,962
Average number of employees per 1,000 inhabitants	3.2	2.9	2.5	2.5	2.5	2.9
South Atlantic						
Number of employees..	89,129	23,469	12,958	10,855	9,079	9,520
Average number of employees per 1,000 inhabitants	3.6	3.7	2.6	2.6	2.7	3.0
East South Central						
Number of employees..	25,156	4,093	4,200	2,582	3,111	3,513
Average number of employees per 1,000 inhabitants	3.5	3.1	2.9	2.7	2.6	3.1
West South Central						
Number of employees..	69,954	24,789	10,349	6,560	5,682	6,929
Average number of employees per 1,000 inhabitants	2.7	2.4	2.2	2.3	2.3	2.6
West						
Number of employees..	114,140	49,017	20,287	15,405	8,949	6,460
Average number of employees per 1,000 inhabitants	2.2	2.4	1.7	1.6	1.7	2.0
Mountain						
Number of employees..	41,165	15,909	7,076	4,823	3,654	2,473
Average number of employees per 1,000 inhabitants	2.5	2.4	2.0	1.9	1.9	2.3
Pacific						
Number of employees..	72,975	33,108	13,211	10,582	5,295	3,987
Average number of employees per 1,000 inhabitants	2.0	2.3	1.6	1.5	1.6	1.9

[1] Full-time law enforcement employees include civilians.
[2] The designation county is a combination of both metropolitan and nonmetropolitan counties.
[3] Suburban areas include law enforcement agencies in cities with less than 50,000 inhabitants and county law enforcement agencies that are within a Metropolitan Statistical Area (see Data Declaration). Suburban areas exclude all metropolitan agencies associated with a principal city. The agencies associated with suburban areas also appear in other groups within this table.

Table 17. Full-Time Law Enforcement Employees,[1] by Region and Geographic Division and Population Group, 2016—Continued

(Number, rate per 1,000 inhabitants.)

Region/geographic division	Group VI (7,044 cities, under 10,000; population 21,174,527)	Total city agencies	2016 estimated city population	County[2] (3,091 agencies; population 85,069,134)	Total city and county agencies	2016 estimated total agency population	Suburban areas[3] (7,050 agencies; population 116,271,221)
Total							
Number of employees............................	102,199	10,126	192,569,624	390,037	13,217	277,638,758	434,964
Average number of employees per 1,000 inhabitants	4.8			4.6			3.7
Northeast							
Number of employees............................	23,053	2,628	45,116,740				
Average number of employees per 1,000 inhabitants	3.6						
New England							
Number of employees............................	6,630	795	12,871,266				
Average number of employees per 1,000 inhabitants	3.8						
Middle Atlantic							
Number of employees............................	16,423	1,833	32,245,474				
Average number of employees per 1,000 inhabitants	3.5						
Midwest							
Number of employees............................	18,574	2,537	37,123,846				
Average number of employees per 1,000 inhabitants	3.3						
East North Central							
Number of employees............................	9,069	1,309	23,081,262				
Average number of employees per 1,000 inhabitants	3.1						
West North Central							
Number of employees............................	9,505	1,228	14,042,584				
Average number of employees per 1,000 inhabitants	3.6						
South							
Number of employees............................	46,550	3,587	57,655,948				
Average number of employees per 1,000 inhabitants	6.9						
South Atlantic							
Number of employees............................	23,248	1,635	24,823,862				
Average number of employees per 1,000 inhabitants	8.0						
East South Central							
Number of employees............................	7,657	653	7,286,658				
Average number of employees per 1,000 inhabitants	6.3						
West South Central							
Number of employees............................	15,645	1,299	25,545,428				
Average number of employees per 1,000 inhabitants	5.9						
West							
Number of employees............................	14,022	1,374	52,673,090				
Average number of employees per 1,000 inhabitants	5.9						
Mountain							
Number of employees............................	7,230	614	16,789,215				
Average number of employees per 1,000 inhabitants	6.1						
Pacific							
Number of employees............................	6,792	760	35,883,875				
Average number of employees per 1,000 inhabitants	5.7						

[1] Full-time law enforcement employees include civilians.
[2] The designation county is a combination of both metropolitan and nonmetropolitan counties.
[3] Suburban areas include law enforcement agencies in cities with less than 50,000 inhabitants and county law enforcement agencies that are within a Metropolitan Statistical Area (see Data Declaration). Suburban areas exclude all metropolitan agencies associated with a principal city. The agencies associated with suburban areas also appear in other groups within this table.

Table 18. Full-Time Law Enforcement Officers, by Region and Geographic Division, and Population Group, 2016

(Number, rate per 1,000 inhabitants.)

Region/geographic division	Total (10,126 cities; population 192,569,624)	Group I (79 cities, 250,000 and over; population 59,221,977)	Group II (200 cities, 100,000 to 249,999; population 29,632,582)	Group III (433 cities, 50,000 to 99,999; population 30,220,472)	Group IV (773 cities, 25,000 to 49,999; population 26,885,069)	Group V (1,597 cities, 10,000 to 24,999; population 25,434,997)
Total						
Number of officers...	421,459	152,607	48,534	48,450	45,582	47,148
Average number of officers per 1,000 inhabitants	2.2	2.6	1.6	1.6	1.7	1.9
Northeast						
Number of officers...	118,398	48,245	7,103	12,744	15,469	15,777
Average number of officers per 1,000 inhabitants	2.6	4.0	2.5	1.9	1.8	1.8
New England						
Number of officers...	28,015	2,125	3,791	5,373	5,924	5,607
Average number of officers per 1,000 inhabitants	2.2	3.2	2.5	2.0	1.9	1.8
Middle Atlantic						
Number of officers...	90,383	46,120	3,312	7,371	9,545	10,170
Average number of officers per 1,000 inhabitants	2.8	4.1	2.4	1.9	1.8	1.7
Midwest						
Number of officers...	78,550	27,129	6,115	9,505	9,583	10,766
Average number of officers per 1,000 inhabitants	2.1	3.1	1.6	1.5	1.5	1.7
East North Central						
Number of officers...	51,479	21,368	3,156	5,810	7,007	6,492
Average number of officers per 1,000 inhabitants	2.2	3.5	1.7	1.6	1.5	1.7
West North Central						
Number of officers...	27,071	5,761	2,959	3,695	2,576	4,274
Average number of officers per 1,000 inhabitants	1.9	2.2	1.6	1.4	1.5	1.7
South						
Number of officers...	141,967	40,913	20,912	15,357	14,000	15,740
Average number of officers per 1,000 inhabitants	2.5	2.3	1.9	1.9	2.0	2.3
South Atlantic						
Number of officers...	69,077	17,848	10,036	8,421	7,253	7,664
Average number of officers per 1,000 inhabitants	2.8	2.8	2.0	2.0	2.2	2.4
East South Central						
Number of officers...	19,802	3,376	3,219	2,028	2,482	2,770
Average number of officers per 1,000 inhabitants	2.7	2.5	2.2	2.1	2.1	2.4
West South Central						
Number of officers...	53,088	19,689	7,657	4,908	4,265	5,306
Average number of officers per 1,000 inhabitants	2.1	1.9	1.6	1.7	1.7	2.0
West						
Number of officers...	82,544	36,320	14,404	10,844	6,530	4,865
Average number of officers per 1,000 inhabitants	1.6	1.8	1.2	1.2	1.2	1.5
Mountain						
Number of officers...	29,548	11,466	5,142	3,394	2,748	1,873
Average number of officers per 1,000 inhabitants	1.8	1.8	1.4	1.4	1.4	1.7
Pacific						
Number of officers...	52,996	24,854	9,262	7,450	3,782	2,992
Average number of officers per 1,000 inhabitants	1.5	1.8	1.1	1.1	1.2	1.4

[1] The designation county is a combination of both metropolitan and nonmetropolitan counties.
[2] Suburban areas include law enforcement agencies in cities with less than 50,000 inhabitants and county law enforcement agencies that are within a Metropolitan Statistical Area. Suburban areas exclude all metropolitan agencies associated with a principal city. The agencies associated with suburban areas also appear in other groups within this table.

Table 18. Full-Time Law Enforcement Officers, by Region and Geographic Division, and Population Group, 2016—Continued

(Number, rate per 1,000 inhabitants.)

Region/geographic division	Group VI (7,044 cities, under 10,000; population 21,174,527)	Total city agencies	2016 estimated city population	County[1] (3,091 agencies; population 85,069,134)	Total city and county agencies	2016 estimated total agency population	Suburban areas[2] (7,050 agencies; population 116,271,221)
Total							
Number of officers.............................	79,138	10,126	192,569,624	231,477	13,217	277,638,758	286,120
Average number of officers per 1,000 inhabitants	3.7			2.7			2.5
Northeast							
Number of officers.............................	19,060	2,628	45,116,740				
Average number of officers per 1,000 inhabitants	2.9						
New England							
Number of officers.............................	5,195	795	12,871,266				
Average number of officers per 1,000 inhabitants	3.0						
Middle Atlantic							
Number of officers.............................	13,865	1,833	32,245,474				
Average number of officers per 1,000 inhabitants	2.9						
Midwest							
Number of officers.............................	15,452	2,537	37,123,846				
Average number of officers per 1,000 inhabitants	2.8						
East North Central							
Number of officers.............................	7,646	1,309	23,081,262				
Average number of officers per 1,000 inhabitants	2.6						
West North Central							
Number of officers.............................	7,806	1,228	14,042,584				
Average number of officers per 1,000 inhabitants	3.0						
South							
Number of officers.............................	35,045	3,587	57,655,948				
Average number of officers per 1,000 inhabitants	5.2						
South Atlantic							
Number of officers.............................	17,855	1,635	24,823,862				
Average number of officers per 1,000 inhabitants	6.1						
East South Central							
Number of officers.............................	5,927	653	7,286,658				
Average number of officers per 1,000 inhabitants	4.9						
West South Central							
Number of officers.............................	11,263	1,299	25,545,428				
Average number of officers per 1,000 inhabitants	4.2						
West							
Number of officers.............................	9,581	1,374	52,673,090				
Average number of officers per 1,000 inhabitants	4.2						
Mountain							
Number of officers.............................	4,925	614	16,789,215				
Average number of officers per 1,000 inhabitants	4.2						
Pacific							
Number of officers.............................	4,656	760	35,883,875				
Average number of officers per 1,000 inhabitants	3.9						

[1] The designation county is a combination of both metropolitan and nonmetropolitan counties.
[2] Suburban areas include law enforcement agencies in cities with less than 50,000 inhabitants and county law enforcement agencies that are within a Metropolitan Statistical Area. Suburban areas exclude all metropolitan agencies associated with a principal city. The agencies associated with suburban areas also appear in other groups within this table.

Table 19. Full-Time Law Enforcement Employees, by Selected State and City, 2016

(Number.)

State/city	Population	Total law enforcement employees	Total officers	Total civilians
ALABAMA				
Abbeville	2,608	17	9	8
Alabaster	33,040	80	61	19
Albertville	21,525	69	45	24
Andalusia	9,071	36	25	11
Anniston	22,205	107	87	20
Arab	8,334	34	26	8
Ardmore	1,390	11	7	4
Ashford	2,161	6	5	1
Ashland	1,974	14	9	5
Athens	25,603	59	48	11
Atmore	10,021	27	22	5
Attalla	5,870	27	22	5
Auburn	63,871	116	110	6
Bay Minette	9,281	29	22	7
Bayou La Batre	2,607	18	13	5
Boaz	9,729	35	24	11
Brewton	5,441	32	24	8
Brighton	2,846	8	4	4
Brookwood	1,821	5	5	0
Brundidge	1,972	12	7	5
Butler	1,781	7	7	0
Camden	1,916	8	7	1
Centre	3,586	12	11	1
Centreville	2,691	6	6	0
Chatom	1,227	4	4	0
Chickasaw	5,927	26	21	5
Citronelle	3,884	12	8	4
Coaling	1,646	4	4	0
Collinsville	1,971	8	4	4
Creola	1,961	9	5	4
Crossville	1,845	5	5	0
Cullman	15,459	72	51	21
Dadeville	3,136	13	12	1
Daleville	5,109	27	16	11
Daphne	25,564	74	50	24
Decatur	55,374	148	133	15
Demopolis	7,089	30	24	6
Dora	1,947	12	7	5
Dothan	69,071	233	161	72
Douglas	761	4	4	0
Eclectic	1,034	8	8	0
Elba	3,894	24	14	10
Enterprise	28,227	70	52	18
Eufaula	12,503	51	31	20
Evergreen	3,742	25	19	6
Fairfield	10,869	30	21	9
Fairhope	19,470	59	36	23
Falkville	1,266	10	9	1
Fayette	4,465	12	12	0
Flomaton	1,405	13	8	5
Florala	1,971	3	3	0
Florence	40,160	130	105	25
Foley	17,639	90	61	29
Fort Payne	14,156	43	38	5
Fultondale	9,188	33	26	7
Gardendale	13,675	41	31	10
Georgiana	1,654	13	8	5
Glencoe	5,150	8	8	0
Goodwater	1,318	8	4	4
Gordo	1,675	4	4	0
Grove Hill	1,481	5	5	0
Gulf Shores	11,340	65	47	18
Guntersville	8,421	46	34	12
Haleyville	4,072	16	11	5
Hartford	2,651	13	8	5
Hartselle	14,540	29	28	1
Headland	4,778	19	11	8
Helena	18,525	27	22	5

Table 19. Full-Time Law Enforcement Employees, by Selected State and City, 2016—*Continued*

(Number.)

State/city	Population	Total law enforcement employees	Total officers	Total civilians
Hoover............	85,601	227	165	62
Hueytown..........	15,632	47	38	9
Huntsville.........	192,587	606	500	106
Irondale...........	12,439	43	35	8
Jacksons Gap.......	798	3	3	0
Killen	979	4	4	0
Kimberly	2,931	14	4	10
Lafayette..........	2,989	15	13	2
Lanett.............	6,451	27	25	2
Level Plains	2,012	4	4	0
Lexington..........	721	4	4	0
Lincoln............	6,579	19	17	2
Lineville...........	2,306	11	7	4
Loxley	1,817	18	13	5
Luverne...........	2,843	16	11	5
Madison	47,729	106	80	26
Maplesville........	703	5	5	0
Mentone..........	369	1	1	0
Millbrook	15,446	42	32	10
Mobile............	249,921	736	496	240
Montevallo	6,716	17	13	4
Montgomery........	199,565	614	503	111
Mountain Brook.....	20,737	69	56	13
Mount Vernon	1,508	6	6	0
Munford	1,253	1	1	0
Napier Field.......	346	2	2	0
Northport	25,045	77	59	18
Ohatchee..........	1,144	3	3	0
Oneonta	6,624	20	19	1
Opelika...........	30,180	104	84	20
Opp	6,657	30	21	9
Orange Beach......	5,932	67	47	20
Oxford............	21,234	72	61	11
Ozark.............	14,679	38	33	5
Pelham	23,162	84	69	15
Phenix City........	38,521	108	84	24
Pine Hill	910	4	4	0
Pleasant Grove.....	10,293	20	15	5
Powell............	957	1	1	0
Prattville..........	35,698	92	83	9
Priceville..........	3,291	5	5	0
Prichard	22,299	53	33	20
Rainbow City	9,573	33	23	10
Rainsville.........	5,047	16	12	4
Ranburne..........	410	2	2	0
Red Bay	3,125	12	8	4
Roanoke	5,993	29	22	7
Robertsdale........	6,019	25	14	11
Saraland	13,967	57	40	17
Sardis City.........	1,764	4	4	0
Scottsboro	14,711	68	44	24
Skyline............	837	2	1	1
Snead.............	844	4	4	0
Southside..........	8,602	19	13	6
Spanish Fort.......	8,312	24	20	4
Steele	1,085	3	3	0
St. Florian	475	2	2	0
Sumiton...........	2,400	15	7	8
Summerdale	1,181	7	7	0
Thomaston	395	1	1	0
Town Creek	1,058	3	3	0
Trinity............	2,170	7	7	0
Troy	18,985	78	55	23
Trussville	21,229	68	55	13
Tuscaloosa	99,925	352	274	78
Tuskegee	8,623	28	17	11
Uniontown.........	2,364	9	8	1
Valley.............	9,465	30	28	2
Vernon	1,876	8	8	0
Warrior...........	3,204	18	11	7

Table 19. Full-Time Law Enforcement Employees, by Selected State and City, 2016—*Continued*

(Number.)

State/city	Population	Total law enforcement employees	Total officers	Total civilians
Weaver	3,101	11	8	3
Wedowee	807	8	8	0
Wetumpka	8,280	38	30	8
ALASKA				
Anchorage	299,097	497	356	141
Bethel	6,522	19	9	10
Bristol Bay Borough	870	10	4	6
Cordova	2,186	11	6	5
Craig	1,256	11	5	6
Dillingham	2,419	19	7	12
Fairbanks	32,456	43	37	6
Haines	2,535	9	4	5
Homer	5,613	22	11	11
Hoonah	757	8	4	4
Juneau	32,964	82	50	32
Kenai	7,770	26	17	9
Ketchikan	8,221	32	20	12
Klawock	766	4	4	0
Kodiak	6,274	39	18	21
Kotzebue	3,290	19	11	8
Nome	3,846	15	8	7
North Pole	2,201	14	13	1
North Slope Borough	9,710	74	47	27
Palmer	6,959	28	13	15
Petersburg	3,162	11	7	4
Sand Point	1,080	5	4	1
Seward	2,813	23	9	14
Sitka	8,836	27	13	14
Skagway	1,075	11	4	7
Soldotna	4,619	15	13	2
St. Paul	512	10	4	6
Unalaska	4,517	28	12	16
Valdez	3,847	19	10	9
Wasilla	9,585	52	25	27
Whittier	213	4	4	0
Wrangell	2,380	13	6	7
ARIZONA				
Apache Junction	38,506	87	57	30
Avondale	81,605	183	122	61
Benson	4,851	20	11	9
Bisbee	5,132	14	11	3
Buckeye	64,563	112	86	26
Bullhead City	39,426	113	71	42
Camp Verde	11,213	28	19	9
Casa Grande	51,995	97	77	20
Chandler	265,922	497	329	168
Chino Valley	11,202	30	22	8
Clarkdale	4,271	9	8	1
Clifton	3,774	11	4	7
Colorado City	4,834	10	7	3
Coolidge	12,387	43	31	12
Cottonwood	11,932	54	31	23
Douglas	16,398	40	27	13
Eagar	4,863	8	6	2
El Mirage	34,376	54	40	14
Eloy	17,110	40	26	14
Flagstaff	71,179	150	102	48
Florence	31,130	37	29	8
Fredonia	1,320	3	3	0
Gilbert	255,899	341	227	114
Glendale	242,938	542	419	123
Globe	7,366	22	19	3
Goodyear	82,018	132	96	36
Hayden	993	6	6	0
Holbrook	5,012	15	13	2
Huachuca City	1,735	12	5	7
Jerome	458	4	4	0
Kearny	2,055	8	3	5

Table 19. Full-Time Law Enforcement Employees, by Selected State and City, 2016—*Continued*

(Number.)

State/city	Population	Total law enforcement employees	Total officers	Total civilians
Kingman	29,069	71	54	17
Lake Havasu City	53,746	103	68	35
Mammoth	1,499	5	3	2
Marana	42,808	116	88	28
Maricopa	49,627	86	65	21
Mesa	478,277	1,221	804	417
Miami	1,776	10	7	3
Nogales	20,143	68	53	15
Oro Valley	44,089	128	100	28
Page	7,516	28	17	11
Paradise Valley	14,155	40	32	8
Parker	3,045	13	10	3
Patagonia	886	3	3	0
Payson	15,351	47	26	21
Peoria	174,797	275	184	91
Phoenix	1,586,611	3,706	2,762	944
Pima	2,554	6	6	0
Pinetop-Lakeside	4,354	19	14	5
Prescott	42,321	81	68	13
Prescott Valley	42,900	81	61	20
Quartzsite	3,615	12	11	1
Safford	9,717	25	21	4
Sahuarita	25,792	50	43	7
San Luis	32,227	54	35	19
Scottsdale	240,885	633	401	232
Sedona	10,457	37	22	15
Show Low	10,892	40	28	12
Sierra Vista	42,988	94	70	24
Snowflake-Taylor	9,835	22	13	9
Somerton	15,196	27	19	8
South Tucson	5,727	20	18	2
Springerville	1,952	9	7	2
St. Johns	3,482	9	6	3
Superior	2,963	9	8	1
Surprise	130,679	181	127	54
Tempe	178,654	493	355	138
Thatcher	5,019	12	11	1
Tolleson	7,105	41	29	12
Tombstone	1,298	10	7	3
Tucson	533,663	1,168	870	298
Wellton	2,944	7	6	1
Wickenburg	6,835	23	16	7
Willcox	3,511	17	9	8
Williams	3,140	21	13	8
Winslow	9,581	31	21	10
Yuma	94,696	258	170	88
ARKANSAS				
Alexander	2,841	6	6	0
Alma	5,595	21	13	8
Arkadelphia	10,755	29	23	6
Ashdown	4,434	13	11	2
Ash Flat	1,060	4	4	0
Atkins	3,056	8	7	1
Augusta	2,024	6	6	0
Austin	3,723	4	4	0
Bald Knob	2,910	9	6	3
Barling	4,748	12	12	0
Batesville	10,732	24	23	1
Bay	1,815	3	3	0
Bearden	884	1	1	0
Beebe	8,269	27	18	9
Bella Vista	28,274	40	27	13
Benton	34,920	90	64	26
Bentonville	46,458	98	68	30
Berryville	5,386	14	12	2
Bethel Heights	2,512	7	6	1
Black Rock	618	1	1	0
Blytheville	14,523	49	37	12
Bono	2,257	4	4	0

(Number.)

State/city	Population	Total law enforcement employees	Total officers	Total civilians
Booneville	3,872	13	9	4
Bradford	760	2	2	0
Brinkley	2,837	15	10	5
Brookland	3,245	5	5	0
Bryant	20,687	48	39	9
Bull Shoals	1,929	3	3	0
Cabot	25,927	53	42	11
Caddo Valley	602	4	4	0
Camden	11,191	42	26	16
Cammack Village	744	4	4	0
Caraway	1,268	3	3	0
Carlisle	2,176	9	5	4
Cave City	1,861	4	4	0
Cave Springs	3,369	7	7	0
Centerton	12,584	22	20	2
Charleston	2,475	5	5	0
Cherokee Village	4,583	9	8	1
Clarendon	1,475	5	4	1
Clarksville	9,482	22	18	4
Clinton	2,526	8	7	1
Conway	66,104	166	126	40
Corning	3,122	12	8	4
Cotter	947	2	2	0
Crossett	5,166	27	17	10
Damascus	382	2	2	0
Danville	2,338	6	5	1
Dardanelle	4,642	17	10	7
Decatur	1,787	6	6	0
Dell	206	1	1	0
De Queen	6,724	16	14	2
Dermott	2,688	13	7	6
Des Arc	1,624	4	4	0
De Valls Bluff	581	1	1	0
De Witt	3,162	13	9	4
Diamond City	781	1	1	0
Diaz	1,235	2	2	0
Dierks	1,084	3	3	0
Dover	1,401	5	5	0
Dumas	4,253	20	11	9
Dyer	857	1	1	0
El Dorado	18,297	68	51	17
Elkins	3,005	6	6	0
England	2,752	15	11	4
Etowah	325	1	1	0
Eudora	2,070	6	4	2
Eureka Springs	2,084	16	12	4
Fairfield Bay	2,254	17	7	10
Farmington	6,852	12	11	1
Fayetteville	84,726	169	123	46
Flippin	1,331	7	6	1
Fordyce	3,979	14	9	5
Forrest City	14,544	42	32	10
Fort Smith	88,573	189	141	48
Gassville	2,144	4	4	0
Gentry	3,443	10	8	2
Glenwood	2,125	2	2	0
Gosnell	3,261	7	7	0
Gravette	3,253	10	9	1
Greenbrier	5,416	15	9	6
Green Forest	2,769	13	10	3
Greenland	1,406	4	4	0
Greenwood	9,372	21	20	1
Greers Ferry	867	4	3	1
Gurdon	2,132	5	4	1
Guy	721	2	2	0
Hamburg	2,772	6	5	1
Hampton	1,274	3	3	0
Hardy	756	3	3	0
Harrisburg	2,304	6	5	1
Harrison	13,178	43	31	12

Table 19. Full-Time Law Enforcement Employees, by Selected State and City, 2016—*Continued*

(Number.)

State/city	Population	Total law enforcement employees	Total officers	Total civilians
Hazen	1,392	6	5	1
Heber Springs	7,144	24	15	9
Helena-West Helena	10,898	33	21	12
Higginson	659	1	1	0
Highfill	641	3	3	0
Highland	1,056	3	3	0
Hope	9,852	31	25	6
Hot Springs	35,716	130	102	28
Hoxie	2,660	4	4	0
Hughes	1,302	3	3	0
Jacksonville	28,684	86	72	14
Jasper	446	1	1	0
Johnson	3,683	13	12	1
Jonesboro	75,230	182	155	27
Judsonia	2,028	4	3	1
Keiser	694	1	1	0
Kensett	1,650	3	3	0
Lake City	2,374	4	4	0
Lakeview	723	2	2	0
Lake Village	2,388	16	10	6
Lamar	1,680	3	3	0
Lavaca	2,425	3	3	0
Leachville	1,845	4	3	1
Lepanto	1,824	7	3	4
Lewisville	1,161	1	1	0
Lincoln	2,468	5	5	0
Little Flock	2,781	6	6	0
Little Rock	198,800	639	525	114
Lonoke	4,248	16	11	5
Lowell	8,812	24	18	6
Luxora	1,088	2	2	0
Magnolia	11,642	23	21	2
Malvern	11,016	24	22	2
Mammoth Spring	968	2	2	0
Mansfield	1,088	4	4	0
Marianna	3,701	24	12	12
Marion	12,270	30	27	3
Marked Tree	2,489	10	6	4
Marmaduke	1,238	4	4	0
Marvell	1,022	7	4	3
Maumelle	18,068	41	32	9
Mayflower	2,473	11	9	2
McCrory	1,577	5	5	0
McGehee	3,866	25	10	15
McRae	679	2	2	0
Mena	5,635	15	14	1
Menifee	306	1	1	0
Mineral Springs	1,152	2	2	0
Monette	1,533	3	3	0
Monticello	9,860	28	21	7
Morrilton	6,733	26	23	3
Mountain Home	12,305	34	26	8
Mountain View	2,856	11	10	1
Mulberry	1,630	3	3	0
Murfreesboro	1,569	3	3	0
Nashville	4,450	17	16	1
Newport	7,733	19	13	6
North Little Rock	67,344	215	178	37
Ola	1,246	4	3	1
Osceola	7,138	38	25	13
Ozark	3,572	11	9	2
Pangburn	602	2	2	0
Paragould	28,254	59	48	11
Paris	3,427	14	9	5
Parkin	1,047	2	2	0
Pea Ridge	5,331	15	14	1
Perryville	1,426	5	5	0
Piggott	3,619	8	8	0
Pine Bluff	43,976	173	143	30
Plainview	596	1	1	0

State/city	Population	Total law enforcement employees	Total officers	Total civilians
Plumerville	801	4	4	0
Pocahontas	6,405	15	14	1
Pottsville	3,131	9	7	2
Prairie Grove	5,345	10	10	0
Prescott	3,103	10	9	1
Quitman	738	4	4	0
Ravenden	446	1	1	0
Redfield	1,593	7	6	1
Rison	1,270	3	3	0
Rogers	64,616	139	98	41
Rose Bud	482	3	2	1
Russellville	29,366	57	51	6
Salem	1,635	3	3	0
Searcy	24,452	65	50	15
Shannon Hills	3,926	5	5	0
Sheridan	4,858	30	14	16
Sherwood	30,676	95	67	28
Siloam Springs	16,277	46	31	15
Springdale	79,288	200	142	58
Stamps	1,525	5	2	3
Star City	2,163	6	5	1
St. Charles	220	1	1	0
Stuttgart	9,002	29	22	7
Sulphur Springs	529	3	3	0
Swifton	748	1	1	0
Texarkana	30,429	104	80	24
Trumann	7,118	25	18	7
Tuckerman	1,739	5	4	1
Tyronza	741	2	2	0
Van Buren	23,133	57	44	13
Vilonia	4,568	9	9	0
Waldron	3,406	10	9	1
Walnut Ridge	4,630	8	8	0
Ward	4,835	11	10	1
Warren	5,767	19	12	7
Weiner	683	1	1	0
West Fork	2,587	5	5	0
West Memphis	24,818	96	76	20
White Hall	5,114	17	15	2
Wynne	8,161	20	18	2
CALIFORNIA				
Alameda	79,597	110	81	29
Albany	19,975	32	24	8
Alhambra	86,035	125	84	41
Alturas	2,549	7	7	0
Anaheim	353,504	562	408	154
Anderson	10,273	23	17	6
Angels Camp	3,755	7	6	1
Antioch	112,090	123	95	28
Arcadia	58,816	91	66	25
Arcata	17,913	38	25	13
Arroyo Grande	18,280	30	26	4
Arvin	21,195	30	22	8
Atascadero	30,108	38	28	10
Atherton	7,218	27	19	8
Atwater	29,437	34	27	7
Auburn	14,078	27	20	7
Avenal	12,941	17	15	2
Azusa	50,393	94	57	37
Bakersfield	378,788	530	390	140
Baldwin Park	77,400	98	65	33
Banning	31,191	43	27	16
Barstow	23,894	54	36	18
Bear Valley	5,464	12	6	6
Beaumont	45,249	56	38	18
Bell	36,347	45	33	12
Bell Gardens	43,316	72	50	22
Belmont	27,492	44	30	14
Belvedere	2,131	8	7	1

(Number.)

State/city	Population	Total law enforcement employees	Total officers	Total civilians
Benicia	28,400	49	33	16
Berkeley	122,651	263	175	88
Beverly Hills	35,018	184	117	67
Bishop	3,793	16	10	6
Blythe	18,961	31	21	10
Brawley	26,076	50	36	14
Brea	42,465	95	61	34
Brentwood	60,512	83	62	21
Brisbane	4,807	18	15	3
Broadmoor	4,411	11	10	1
Buena Park	83,768	121	81	40
Burbank	105,720	234	154	80
Burlingame	30,792	56	36	20
Calexico	40,336	35	23	12
California City	13,244	26	16	10
Calipatria	7,384	3	3	0
Calistoga	5,364	14	9	5
Campbell	41,457	67	42	25
Capitola	10,241	29	21	8
Carlsbad	115,040	150	103	47
Carmel	3,931	24	14	10
Cathedral City	54,317	74	49	25
Central Marin	35,265	46	41	5
Ceres	48,372	62	46	16
Chico	91,122	137	86	51
Chino	87,081	159	107	52
Chowchilla	18,487	24	16	8
Chula Vista	270,175	305	225	80
Citrus Heights	87,811	134	88	46
Claremont	36,553	61	37	24
Clayton	12,057	12	10	2
Clearlake	15,165	28	23	5
Cloverdale	8,848	22	15	7
Clovis	105,865	162	100	62
Coalinga	16,282	32	21	11
Colma	1,534	24	18	6
Colton	55,100	72	46	26
Colusa	5,926	9	8	1
Concord	129,903	201	150	51
Corcoran	22,111	29	17	12
Corning	7,522	19	12	7
Corona	166,534	225	158	67
Coronado	24,974	63	42	21
Costa Mesa	113,816	172	112	60
Cotati	7,479	15	10	5
Covina	49,222	87	59	28
Crescent City	6,622	10	9	1
Culver City	39,880	153	100	53
Cypress	49,557	69	53	16
Daly City	107,640	133	100	33
Davis	68,087	91	60	31
Delano	52,656	69	50	19
Del Rey Oaks	1,700	6	6	0
Desert Hot Springs	28,573	30	24	6
Dinuba	24,156	49	38	11
Dixon	19,592	24	19	5
Dos Palos	5,158	8	7	1
Downey	114,704	150	106	44
East Palo Alto	29,957	40	33	7
El Cajon	104,483	179	121	58
El Centro	44,213	71	48	23
El Cerrito	25,222	47	40	7
Elk Grove	169,742	211	128	83
El Monte	117,354	152	108	44
El Segundo	17,113	73	56	17
Emeryville	12,060	51	38	13
Escalon	7,601	11	10	1
Escondido	152,897	211	156	55
Etna	712	3	3	0
Eureka	26,981	71	47	24

Table 19. Full-Time Law Enforcement Employees, by Selected State and City, 2016—*Continued*

(Number.)

State/city	Population	Total law enforcement employees	Total officers	Total civilians
Exeter	10,589	18	16	2
Fairfax	7,662	16	11	5
Fairfield	114,521	169	114	55
Farmersville	10,812	15	13	2
Ferndale	1,368	4	4	0
Firebaugh	8,484	15	11	4
Folsom	77,245	95	70	25
Fontana	209,531	275	185	90
Fort Bragg	7,292	21	15	6
Fortuna	12,013	22	15	7
Foster City	34,081	50	36	14
Fountain Valley	57,291	80	59	21
Fowler	6,397	13	12	1
Fremont	235,881	282	180	102
Fresno	524,796	1,013	748	265
Fullerton	141,968	210	141	69
Galt	25,638	49	33	16
Gardena	60,770	119	95	24
Garden Grove	176,230	218	159	59
Gilroy	54,130	87	62	25
Glendale	202,903	328	232	96
Glendora	52,380	86	51	35
Gonzales	8,533	13	10	3
Grass Valley	12,961	24	21	3
Greenfield	17,343	21	18	3
Gridley	6,584	19	14	5
Grover Beach	13,686	26	18	8
Guadalupe	7,365	13	11	2
Gustine	5,801	12	10	2
Hanford	55,973	77	53	24
Hawthorne	89,299	136	88	48
Hayward	161,122	310	194	116
Healdsburg	11,830	26	17	9
Hemet	84,838	92	62	30
Hercules	25,553	22	20	2
Hermosa Beach	19,930	62	34	28
Hillsborough	11,575	33	25	8
Hollister	37,953	33	27	6
Huntington Beach	204,071	334	214	120
Huntington Park	59,692	86	51	35
Huron	6,852	17	10	7
Imperial	17,582	22	18	4
Indio	89,201	99	63	36
Inglewood	112,059	219	175	44
Ione	6,860	6	6	0
Irvine	266,663	301	213	88
Irwindale	1,440	35	28	7
Jackson	4,649	11	10	1
Kensington	5,364	10	10	0
Kerman	14,654	22	19	3
King City	14,111	17	13	4
Kingsburg	11,905	17	14	3
Laguna Beach	23,486	83	49	34
La Habra	62,483	99	69	30
Lakeport	4,817	13	12	1
Lake Shastina	2,546	3	3	0
La Mesa	60,681	97	68	29
La Palma	15,975	25	19	6
La Verne	33,011	60	40	20
Lemoore	25,875	38	31	7
Lincoln	47,206	27	20	7
Lindsay	13,533	19	14	5
Livermore	89,553	133	89	44
Livingston	14,076	25	17	8
Lodi	65,067	97	67	30
Lompoc	44,541	68	45	23
Long Beach	476,476	1,173	806	367
Los Alamitos	11,774	26	23	3
Los Altos	31,000	42	27	15
Los Angeles	4,007,905	12,692	9,850	2,842

Table 19. Full-Time Law Enforcement Employees, by Selected State and City, 2016—*Continued*

(Number.)

State/city	Population	Total law enforcement employees	Total officers	Total civilians
Los Banos	37,738	62	37	25
Los Gatos	30,947	54	37	17
Madera	64,753	78	60	18
Mammoth Lakes	7,891	13	10	3
Manhattan Beach	35,955	105	66	39
Manteca	77,104	86	59	27
Marina	21,539	35	28	7
Martinez	38,541	45	33	12
Marysville	12,241	25	18	7
McFarland	14,263	16	13	3
Mendota	11,481	16	14	2
Menlo Park	33,726	67	47	20
Merced	83,106	125	89	36
Mill Valley	14,491	26	20	6
Milpitas	79,990	109	85	24
Modesto	212,880	300	214	86
Monrovia	37,637	82	51	31
Montclair	39,085	68	47	21
Montebello	64,206	99	66	33
Monterey	28,506	61	43	18
Monterey Park	61,710	98	69	29
Moraga	17,505	12	11	1
Morgan Hill	44,015	59	39	20
Morro Bay	10,719	19	17	2
Mountain View	81,726	129	86	43
Mount Shasta	3,277	12	9	3
Murrieta	111,043	128	89	39
Napa	81,115	110	69	41
National City	61,550	120	86	34
Nevada City	3,167	12	10	2
Newark	45,893	77	55	22
Newman	11,037	15	12	3
Newport Beach	87,482	228	140	88
Novato	56,263	80	56	24
Oakdale	22,572	32	22	10
Oakland	424,998	1,046	750	296
Oceanside	177,340	278	204	74
Ontario	172,606	339	254	85
Orange	141,841	213	143	70
Orange Cove	9,706	12	11	1
Orland	7,587	13	11	2
Oroville	16,322	44	24	20
Oxnard	209,048	337	227	110
Pacifica	39,650	35	33	2
Pacific Grove	15,795	24	14	10
Palm Springs	47,909	127	88	39
Palo Alto	67,317	137	79	58
Palos Verdes Estates	13,730	35	29	6
Paradise	26,532	33	19	14
Parlier	15,262	11	10	1
Pasadena	143,288	357	234	123
Paso Robles	31,939	44	31	13
Petaluma	60,933	82	58	24
Piedmont	11,515	27	19	8
Pinole	19,451	33	22	11
Pismo Beach	8,264	31	19	12
Pittsburg	70,663	96	77	19
Placentia	52,800	68	45	23
Placerville	10,705	26	18	8
Pleasant Hill	35,140	57	41	16
Pleasanton	81,464	110	77	33
Pomona	154,109	261	154	107
Porterville	56,421	86	60	26
Port Hueneme	22,570	27	21	6
Red Bluff	14,138	38	24	14
Redding	91,918	131	98	33
Redlands	71,485	118	80	38
Redondo Beach	68,447	143	92	51
Redwood City	87,046	116	91	25
Reedley	25,828	40	27	13

Table 19. Full-Time Law Enforcement Employees, by Selected State and City, 2016—*Continued*

(Number.)

State/city	Population	Total law enforcement employees	Total officers	Total civilians
Rialto	103,893	142	105	37
Richmond	110,868	242	177	65
Ridgecrest	29,003	50	32	18
Rio Dell	3,390	5	5	0
Rio Vista	8,554	14	12	2
Ripon	15,318	31	22	9
Riverside	325,896	503	350	153
Rocklin	62,006	79	55	24
Rohnert Park	42,723	85	59	26
Roseville	132,566	183	125	58
Ross	2,492	8	8	0
Sacramento	495,471	954	652	302
Salinas	158,729	191	134	57
San Bernardino	217,303	360	215	145
San Bruno	43,613	65	49	16
Sand City	391	10	9	1
San Diego	1,413,414	2,522	1,815	707
San Fernando	25,194	41	27	14
San Francisco	871,155	2,892	2,296	596
San Gabriel	40,580	64	49	15
Sanger	25,078	37	33	4
San Jose	1,041,844	1,352	939	413
San Leandro	91,870	131	90	41
San Luis Obispo	47,774	78	55	23
San Marino	13,528	30	25	5
San Mateo	104,802	148	111	37
San Pablo	30,674	67	46	21
San Rafael	59,435	86	65	21
San Ramon	76,901	81	65	16
Santa Ana	337,419	523	310	213
Santa Barbara	92,519	205	140	65
Santa Clara	128,179	215	144	71
Santa Cruz	64,969	115	93	22
Santa Maria	106,200	166	111	55
Santa Monica	93,921	374	204	170
Santa Paula	30,784	38	30	8
Santa Rosa	176,383	251	172	79
Sausalito	7,198	24	19	5
Scotts Valley	12,016	26	19	7
Seal Beach	24,721	45	30	15
Seaside	34,827	46	37	9
Sebastopol	7,734	19	14	5
Selma	24,641	38	30	8
Shafter	18,608	38	26	12
Sierra Madre	11,212	18	15	3
Signal Hill	11,677	47	34	13
Simi Valley	127,252	177	122	55
Soledad	24,805	21	17	4
Sonora	4,802	17	10	7
South Gate	96,791	118	79	39
South Lake Tahoe	21,765	56	37	19
South Pasadena	26,256	49	35	14
South San Francisco	67,995	110	80	30
Stallion Springs	2,628	3	3	0
St. Helena	6,142	18	13	5
Stockton	308,348	610	412	198
Suisun City	29,768	33	21	12
Sunnyvale	154,108	278	209	69
Susanville	14,798	19	17	2
Sutter Creek	2,484	4	4	0
Taft	9,543	26	16	10
Tehachapi	12,770	24	15	9
Tiburon	9,263	16	13	3
Torrance	149,078	309	208	101
Tracy	87,844	126	85	41
Truckee	16,326	34	22	12
Tulare	62,902	109	72	37
Tulelake	990	1	1	0
Turlock	73,031	117	78	39
Tustin	81,642	131	87	44

Table 19. Full-Time Law Enforcement Employees, by Selected State and City, 2016—*Continued*

(Number.)

State/city	Population	Total law enforcement employees	Total officers	Total civilians
Ukiah	15,897	49	32	17
Union City	75,501	104	75	29
Upland	76,956	96	69	27
Vacaville	97,671	150	99	51
Vallejo	122,293	150	110	40
Ventura	110,228	165	125	40
Vernon	114	51	39	12
Visalia	131,186	200	135	65
Walnut Creek	69,860	118	85	33
Watsonville	54,110	86	68	18
Weed	2,479	13	8	5
West Covina	108,950	156	93	63
Westminster	92,582	115	79	36
Westmorland	2,275	5	5	0
West Sacramento	53,532	89	69	20
Wheatland	3,775	9	8	1
Whittier	87,860	167	120	47
Williams	5,208	9	7	2
Willits	4,856	16	11	5
Willows	6,053	10	9	1
Winters	7,120	13	11	2
Woodlake	7,727	9	8	1
Woodland	59,190	75	61	14
Yreka	7,559	20	14	6
Yuba City	67,198	78	52	26
COLORADO				
Alamosa	9,927	27	23	4
Arvada	117,186	215	158	57
Aspen	6,926	36	27	9
Ault	1,642	6	5	1
Aurora	366,477	810	670	140
Avon	6,532	19	17	2
Basalt	3,900	12	11	1
Bayfield	2,611	8	8	0
Black Hawk	126	34	23	11
Blue River	915	2	1	1
Boulder	109,189	267	176	91
Breckenridge	4,971	31	23	8
Brighton	38,363	88	63	25
Broomfield	66,953	209	108	101
Brush	5,456	14	11	3
Buena Vista	2,790	9	8	1
Burlington	3,624	8	7	1
Calhan	790	3	3	0
Campo	104	2	2	0
Canon City	16,390	40	32	8
Carbondale	6,728	17	15	2
Castle Rock	57,109	93	69	24
Cedaredge	2,170	8	6	2
Centennial	111,479	171	137	34
Center	2,196	14	8	6
Central City	736	2	2	0
Cherry Hills Village	6,649	28	23	5
Collbran	702	2	2	0
Colorado Springs	464,113	924	645	279
Columbine Valley	1,381	6	6	0
Commerce City	55,341	120	96	24
Cortez	8,761	49	29	20
Craig	8,724	26	21	5
Crested Butte	1,599	8	6	2
Cripple Creek	1,147	26	18	8
Dacono	4,925	13	10	3
De Beque	496	4	4	0
Del Norte	1,588	4	3	1
Delta	8,778	20	17	3
Denver	699,259	1,799	1,483	316
Dillon	972	9	8	1
Durango	18,248	65	55	10
Eagle	6,715	12	11	1

(Number.)

State/city	Population	Total law enforcement employees	Total officers	Total civilians
Eaton	5,045	10	8	2
Edgewater	5,330	18	17	1
Elizabeth	1,411	6	5	1
Englewood	33,657	100	71	29
Erie	22,115	27	25	2
Estes Park	6,335	30	19	11
Evans	21,975	38	35	3
Fairplay	681	3	3	0
Federal Heights	12,563	36	24	12
Firestone	12,375	26	21	5
Florence	3,861	12	11	1
Fort Collins	164,670	292	206	86
Fort Lupton	7,903	16	14	2
Fort Morgan	11,313	31	26	5
Fountain	28,115	62	51	11
Fowler	1,141	3	3	0
Fraser/Winter Park	2,205	10	9	1
Frederick	12,045	20	17	3
Frisco	3,108	15	10	5
Fruita	12,825	18	16	2
Georgetown	1,052	3	3	0
Glendale	5,396	36	25	11
Glenwood Springs	9,978	31	24	7
Golden	20,616	64	43	21
Granby	1,880	7	6	1
Grand Junction	60,628	197	111	86
Greeley	102,491	196	145	51
Greenwood Village	16,024	89	63	26
Gunnison	6,110	30	14	16
Gypsum	7,012	3	3	0
Haxtun	926	3	3	0
Hayden	1,847	6	4	2
Holyoke	2,237	3	3	0
Hotchkiss	895	3	3	0
Hudson	1,477	3	3	0
Hugo	737	2	2	0
Idaho Springs	1,730	8	7	1
Ignacio	723	7	6	1
Johnstown	16,143	20	18	2
Kersey	1,602	4	4	0
Kiowa	753	4	4	0
Kremmling	1,461	4	4	0
Lafayette	28,421	48	38	10
La Junta	6,919	17	10	7
Lakeside	8	7	6	1
Lakewood	154,553	417	263	154
Lamar	7,479	33	19	14
La Salle	2,070	8	8	0
La Veta	752	2	2	0
Leadville	2,656	10	9	1
Limon	1,917	6	5	1
Littleton	47,288	95	70	25
Lochbuie	5,516	10	9	1
Log Lane Village	873	2	2	0
Lone Tree	13,593	49	42	7
Longmont	93,268	204	137	67
Louisville	20,814	38	32	6
Loveland	76,936	149	103	46
Mancos	1,388	4	4	0
Manitou Springs	5,397	18	16	2
Manzanola	416	2	2	0
Meeker	2,344	6	6	0
Milliken	6,551	11	9	2
Monte Vista	4,262	17	14	3
Montrose	19,054	50	36	14
Monument	6,497	17	14	3
Morrison	436	10	9	1
Mountain View	532	8	8	0
Mountain Village	1,412	9	6	3
Mount Crested Butte	833	9	8	1

Table 19. Full-Time Law Enforcement Employees, by Selected State and City, 2016—*Continued*

(Number.)

State/city	Population	Total law enforcement employees	Total officers	Total civilians
Nederland...	1,534	6	5	1
New Castle	4,706	9	8	1
Northglenn	39,890	79	60	19
Oak Creek	894	3	3	0
Olathe	1,790	4	4	0
Ouray	1,008	6	6	0
Pagosa Springs.......................................	1,763	8	7	1
Palisade	2,654	10	8	2
Palmer Lake	2,621	2	2	0
Paonia	1,395	4	4	0
Parachute	1,110	5	4	1
Parker	50,409	113	72	41
Platteville	3,737	6	6	0
Pueblo	109,927	250	195	55
Rangely..	2,378	10	5	5
Ridgway..	987	3	3	0
Rifle	9,613	24	20	4
Rocky Ford	3,801	8	8	0
Salida...	5,516	17	15	2
Sanford..	846	1	1	0
Sheridan	6,113	34	31	3
Silt	3,069	6	6	0
Silverthorne	4,530	16	14	2
Simla	635	2	2	0
Snowmass Village	2,935	13	10	3
South Fork	359	2	2	0
Springfield	1,385	4	4	0
Steamboat Springs..................................	12,512	37	24	13
Sterling	14,087	25	20	5
Stratton	659	1	1	0
Telluride	2,434	15	10	5
Thornton	136,451	245	180	65
Timnath	3,234	7	6	1
Trinidad	7,990	31	22	9
Vail	5,496	61	29	32
Walsenburg	2,871	10	8	2
Walsh	512	1	1	0
Westminster	114,514	247	174	73
Wheat Ridge...	31,389	102	75	27
Wiggins..	893	2	2	0
Windsor..	22,404	27	23	4
Woodland Park	7,226	28	19	9
Wray..	2,382	7	6	1
Yuma	3,612	8	7	1
CONNECTICUT				
Ansonia	18,776	49	42	7
Avon..	18,464	41	32	9
Berlin	20,695	55	42	13
Bethel	19,712	50	37	13
Bloomfield	20,801	59	47	12
Branford	28,168	62	49	13
Bridgeport	148,180	433	376	57
Bristol	60,445	143	118	25
Brookfield	17,278	43	33	10
Canton	10,337	20	15	5
Cheshire	29,259	59	47	12
Clinton	13,008	36	27	9
Coventry	12,437	19	14	5
Cromwell	14,041	33	25	8
Danbury..	85,335	151	146	5
Darien..	21,995	57	49	8
Derby...	12,660	36	34	2
East Hampton	12,839	17	15	2
East Hartford	50,733	153	123	30
East Haven	28,879	56	52	4
Easton..	7,649	17	15	2
East Windsor	11,443	34	26	8
Enfield	44,258	114	94	20
Fairfield..	61,889	113	107	6
Farmington	25,684	61	45	16

(Number.)

State/city	Population	Total law enforcement employees	Total officers	Total civilians
Glastonbury	34,724	75	57	18
Granby	11,301	20	15	5
Greenwich	62,970	178	151	27
Groton	9,189	34	27	7
Groton Long Point	512	5	5	0
Groton Town	29,910	64	59	5
Guilford	22,343	40	33	7
Hamden	61,138	135	108	27
Hartford	123,736	430	398	32
Madison	18,212	41	27	14
Manchester	57,957	135	104	31
Meriden	59,812	125	113	12
Middlebury	7,645	13	11	2
Middletown	46,580	122	109	13
Milford	53,752	138	116	22
Monroe	19,898	56	43	13
Naugatuck	31,469	68	57	11
New Britain	72,720	169	161	8
New Canaan	20,509	51	45	6
New Haven	130,425	509	454	55
Newington	30,610	64	51	13
New London	27,092	92	77	15
New Milford	27,111	62	50	12
Newtown	28,105	48	44	4
North Branford	14,234	27	22	5
North Haven	23,777	58	49	9
Norwalk	88,989	217	177	40
Norwich	39,771	102	88	14
Old Saybrook	10,145	32	25	7
Orange	13,940	53	43	10
Plainfield	15,015	22	18	4
Plainville	17,782	45	37	8
Plymouth	11,731	30	24	6
Portland	9,369	12	11	1
Putnam	9,331	18	15	3
Redding	9,317	23	17	6
Ridgefield	25,358	48	42	6
Rocky Hill	20,085	48	36	12
Seymour	16,462	43	41	2
Shelton	41,638	61	52	9
Simsbury	24,519	47	37	10
Southington	43,948	89	68	21
South Windsor	25,803	52	38	14
Stamford	130,116	315	267	48
Stonington	18,337	48	37	11
Stratford	52,841	107	100	7
Suffield	15,641	22	17	5
Thomaston	7,570	28	16	12
Torrington	34,626	87	76	11
Trumbull	36,741	86	75	11
Vernon	28,915	64	49	15
Wallingford	44,840	90	69	21
Waterbury	108,491	316	272	44
Waterford	19,236	54	47	7
Watertown	21,792	48	39	9
West Hartford	62,979	146	128	18
West Haven	54,800	138	123	15
Weston	10,425	17	16	1
Westport	28,198	75	62	13
Wethersfield	26,306	61	48	13
Willimantic	17,766	48	43	5
Wilton	18,845	47	45	2
Winchester	10,750	24	19	5
Windsor	28,998	67	54	13
Windsor Locks	12,543	32	25	7
Wolcott	16,666	32	23	9
Woodbridge	8,864	31	23	8
DELAWARE				
Bethany Beach	1,193	11	9	2
Blades	1,377	3	3	0

Table 19. Full-Time Law Enforcement Employees, by Selected State and City, 2016—*Continued*

(Number.)

State/city	Population	Total law enforcement employees	Total officers	Total civilians
Bridgeville	2,297	8	5	3
Camden	3,512	9	8	1
Cheswold	1,424	3	3	0
Clayton	3,165	10	9	1
Dagsboro	875	4	4	0
Delaware City	1,750	5	4	1
Delmar	1,757	13	12	1
Dewey Beach	378	10	8	2
Dover	37,824	136	105	31
Ellendale	422	1	1	0
Elsmere	6,149	13	12	1
Felton	1,423	4	4	0
Fenwick Island	425	6	6	0
Frankford	950	1	1	0
Georgetown	7,177	20	18	2
Greenwood	1,086	5	4	1
Harrington	3,719	13	12	1
Laurel	4,150	16	15	1
Lewes	3,065	13	12	1
Middletown	20,666	35	31	4
Milford	10,392	40	30	10
Millsboro	4,286	13	12	1
Milton	2,875	8	8	0
Newark	34,297	88	71	17
New Castle	5,392	17	16	1
Newport	1,059	10	9	1
Ocean View	2,075	10	9	1
Rehoboth Beach	1,485	27	17	10
Seaford	7,725	35	22	13
Selbyville	2,440	7	6	1
Smyrna	11,573	29	22	7
South Bethany	507	8	7	1
Wilmington	72,183	360	302	58
Wyoming	1,497	4	4	0
DISTRICT OF COLUMBIA				
Washington	681,170	4,352	3,753	599
FLORIDA				
Alachua	9,900	31	22	9
Altamonte Springs	43,499	114	98	16
Apalachicola	2,291	8	7	1
Apopka	49,796	128	94	34
Arcadia	7,893	19	15	4
Astatula	1,938	6	6	0
Atlantic Beach	13,302	37	25	12
Atlantis	2,126	19	14	5
Auburndale	15,356	41	33	8
Aventura	38,009	119	80	39
Bal Harbour Village	2,955	36	24	12
Bartow	19,322	58	36	22
Bay Harbor Islands	6,117	29	22	7
Belleair	4,017	14	12	2
Belle Isle	6,835	16	15	1
Belleview	4,813	16	14	2
Biscayne Park	3,243	10	10	0
Blountstown	2,495	14	10	4
Boca Raton	94,931	287	182	105
Bonifay	2,712	6	6	0
Bowling Green	2,916	7	7	0
Boynton Beach	75,141	202	148	54
Bradenton	55,518	145	118	27
Bradenton Beach	1,257	10	10	0
Brooksville	7,881	26	23	3
Bunnell	2,856	11	9	2
Cape Coral	179,631	306	221	85
Casselberry	27,220	57	48	9
Cedar Key	703	3	3	0
Chattahoochee	3,059	11	10	1
Chiefland	2,213	14	12	2

State/city	Population	Total law enforcement employees	Total officers	Total civilians
Chipley	3,557	12	11	1
Clearwater	113,904	352	231	121
Clermont	33,158	71	65	6
Clewiston	7,579	25	17	8
Cocoa	17,825	87	63	24
Cocoa Beach	11,669	50	33	17
Coconut Creek	60,633	130	96	34
Cooper City	36,900	77	59	18
Coral Gables	51,980	229	160	69
Coral Springs	131,159	290	193	97
Cottondale	894	3	3	0
Crescent City	1,533	6	5	1
Crestview	23,749	60	48	12
Cross City	1,702	5	5	0
Dade City	7,061	29	22	7
Dania	31,806	75	68	7
Davenport	3,677	12	11	1
Davie	102,692	248	184	64
Daytona Beach	65,495	250	218	32
Daytona Beach Shores	4,417	36	28	8
Deerfield Beach	80,713	132	122	10
De Funiak Springs	5,927	27	20	7
DeLand	30,881	74	56	18
Delray Beach	67,400	213	155	58
Doral	58,309	158	118	40
Edgewater	21,729	35	30	5
Edgewood	2,856	16	13	3
El Portal	2,509	8	8	0
Eustis	20,292	51	38	13
Fernandina Beach	12,489	37	32	5
Flagler Beach	4,946	17	15	2
Fort Lauderdale	181,218	662	508	154
Fort Myers	76,579	238	179	59
Fort Pierce	44,987	133	108	25
Fort Walton Beach	22,314	54	40	14
Fruitland Park	4,548	15	14	1
Gainesville	131,242	360	299	61
Green Cove Springs	7,352	20	15	5
Groveland	12,192	33	26	7
Gulf Breeze	6,435	24	17	7
Gulfport	12,384	34	30	4
Gulf Stream	846	12	12	0
Haines City	23,278	57	44	13
Hallandale	39,960	129	92	37
Havana	1,674	13	9	4
Hialeah	239,451	324	260	64
Hialeah Gardens	24,370	54	38	16
Highland Beach	3,767	15	14	1
Holly Hill	12,002	31	27	4
Homestead	67,700	152	112	40
Howey-in-the-Hills	1,179	6	6	0
Indialantic	2,861	15	10	5
Indian Creek Village	92	14	10	4
Indian Harbour Beach	8,523	27	20	7
Indian River Shores	4,209	22	19	3
Interlachen	1,346	4	4	0
Jacksonville	880,557	2,947	1,758	1,189
Jacksonville Beach	23,418	81	62	19
Jasper	4,099	8	7	1
Jennings	869	2	2	0
Juno Beach	3,532	17	15	2
Jupiter	64,273	142	114	28
Jupiter Inlet Colony	454	6	6	0
Jupiter Island	901	24	16	8
Kenneth City	5,095	13	12	1
Key Biscayne	13,113	44	33	11
Key Colony Beach	862	5	5	0
Key West	25,976	118	92	26
Kissimmee	71,197	220	126	94
Lady Lake	14,877	34	27	7

Table 19. Full-Time Law Enforcement Employees, by Selected State and City, 2016—*Continued*

(Number.)

State/city	Population	Total law enforcement employees	Total officers	Total civilians
Lake Alfred	5,568	14	10	4
Lake City	12,186	54	38	16
Lake Clarke Shores	3,586	12	11	1
Lake Hamilton	1,370	7	6	1
Lake Helen	2,700	5	4	1
Lakeland	105,766	353	237	116
Lake Mary	16,506	59	42	17
Lake Placid	2,172	10	8	2
Lake Wales	15,819	48	43	5
Lantana	11,239	37	29	8
Largo	81,402	182	140	42
Lauderdale-by-the-Sea	6,541	26	24	2
Lauderdale Lakes	35,222	41	39	2
Lauderhill	72,504	123	98	25
Lawtey	717	2	2	0
Leesburg	22,313	82	58	24
Lighthouse Point	11,256	41	32	9
Live Oak	6,946	22	18	4
Longboat Key	7,343	26	18	8
Longwood	14,171	47	42	5
Lynn Haven	20,496	36	26	10
Madison	2,849	15	14	1
Maitland	17,824	51	44	7
Manalapan	458	12	10	2
Marco Island	17,947	37	34	3
Margate	58,030	140	105	35
Marianna	9,464	22	17	5
Mascotte	5,549	13	12	1
Melbourne	80,900	211	152	59
Melbourne Beach	3,243	11	10	1
Melbourne Village	697	5	5	0
Mexico Beach	1,187	8	7	1
Miami	449,469	1,559	1,201	358
Miami Beach	93,165	492	394	98
Miami Springs	14,620	53	41	12
Midway	3,325	5	5	0
Milton	9,788	25	19	6
Miramar	140,288	272	203	69
Monticello	2,393	13	9	4
Mount Dora	13,796	51	34	17
Naples	21,917	98	67	31
Neptune Beach	7,316	27	20	7
New Port Richey	16,038	58	41	17
New Smyrna Beach	24,658	57	44	13
Niceville	15,142	34	26	8
North Bay Village	8,552	36	26	10
North Lauderdale	44,229	58	51	7
North Miami	62,974	160	114	46
North Miami Beach	44,442	140	106	34
North Palm Beach	13,023	31	30	1
North Port	63,386	127	98	29
Oakland	2,890	12	11	1
Oakland Park	44,903	96	85	11
Ocala	58,596	231	159	72
Ocean Ridge	1,928	21	16	5
Ocoee	45,330	89	77	12
Orange City	11,262	28	23	5
Orange Park	8,763	29	21	8
Orlando	277,719	915	715	200
Ormond Beach	41,325	82	61	21
Palatka	10,362	38	30	8
Palm Bay	108,823	212	155	57
Palm Beach	8,702	93	62	31
Palm Beach Gardens	53,811	159	108	51
Palm Beach Shores	1,221	15	11	4
Palmetto	13,371	47	34	13
Palm Springs	22,581	68	44	24
Panama City	38,847	131	95	36
Panama City Beach	12,844	77	58	19
Parker	4,661	10	9	1

(Number.)

State/city	Population	Total law enforcement employees	Total officers	Total civilians
Parkland	31,571	45	40	5
Pembroke Pines	169,156	298	218	80
Pensacola	53,424	200	140	60
Perry	7,063	22	20	2
Pinellas Park	52,113	121	101	20
Plantation	94,075	252	165	87
Plant City	37,949	84	67	17
Ponce Inlet	3,183	14	12	2
Port Orange	60,546	99	85	14
Port Richey	2,779	19	13	6
Port St. Joe	3,441	8	8	0
Port St. Lucie	182,365	289	229	60
Punta Gorda	18,466	49	34	15
Quincy	7,760	33	25	8
Riviera Beach	34,304	150	107	43
Rockledge	26,967	71	50	21
Sanibel	7,395	39	25	14
Sarasota	55,732	209	163	46
Satellite Beach	10,737	30	21	9
Sea Ranch Lakes	739	11	7	4
Sebastian	24,441	52	34	18
Sebring	10,516	39	35	4
Sewall's Point	2,180	10	9	1
South Daytona	12,653	32	26	6
South Miami	12,354	55	50	5
South Palm Beach	1,437	8	8	0
Springfield	9,550	24	19	5
Starke	5,390	20	19	1
St. Augustine	14,359	62	49	13
St. Cloud	47,289	117	79	38
St. Petersburg	259,510	759	548	211
Stuart	16,640	70	44	26
Sunrise	94,400	231	175	56
Tallahassee	191,564	437	372	65
Tamarac	65,516	99	81	18
Tampa	375,904	1,212	951	261
Tarpon Springs	24,834	61	48	13
Tavares	15,741	28	25	3
Temple Terrace	25,972	66	50	16
Tequesta	6,003	23	18	5
Titusville	45,723	123	86	37
Trenton	2,079	4	3	1
Umatilla	3,751	9	8	1
Valparaiso	5,023	15	11	4
Venice	22,514	57	44	13
Vero Beach	16,589	71	52	19
Village of Pinecrest	19,692	78	54	24
Virginia Gardens	2,508	8	7	1
Wauchula	4,936	17	13	4
West Melbourne	21,156	44	37	7
West Miami	7,163	22	18	4
West Palm Beach	108,074	365	278	87
White Springs	773	10	10	0
Wildwood	6,788	43	33	10
Williston	2,741	18	11	7
Wilton Manors	12,535	48	33	15
Windermere	3,320	14	13	1
Winter Garden	41,556	100	71	29
Winter Haven	38,488	112	86	26
Winter Park	30,359	110	80	30
Winter Springs	35,100	65	51	14
Zephyrhills	14,833	45	30	15
GEORGIA				
Abbeville	2,796	5	5	0
Adairsville	4,804	18	16	2
Adel	5,313	23	21	2
Alamo	3,374	4	4	0
Alapaha	653	2	1	1
Albany	74,330	186	162	24

State/city	Population	Total law enforcement employees	Total officers	Total civilians
Alma	3,548	12	10	2
Alto	1,166	3	1	2
Americus	15,838	39	33	6
Aragon	1,241	4	3	1
Arcade	1,801	3	3	0
Ashburn	3,757	18	16	2
Athens-Clarke County	123,934	292	228	64
Atlanta	472,579	2,140	1,694	446
Auburn	7,621	23	16	7
Austell	7,204	32	23	9
Avondale Estates	3,175	11	11	0
Bainbridge	12,473	46	44	2
Baldwin	3,287	14	7	7
Barnesville	6,611	19	17	2
Baxley	4,452	12	11	1
Berlin	559	1	1	0
Blackshear	3,608	16	13	3
Blairsville	542	8	7	1
Bloomingdale	2,778	15	12	3
Blythe	697	1	1	0
Braselton	9,912	17	16	1
Bremen	6,380	22	20	2
Brookhaven	52,442	85	77	8
Brunswick	16,309	63	59	4
Byron	5,222	23	19	4
Cairo	9,772	24	21	3
Calhoun	16,439	49	42	7
Camilla	5,080	18	16	2
Canton	25,985	50	45	5
Carrollton	26,593	76	63	13
Centerville	7,657	18	15	3
Chatsworth	4,362	17	15	2
Claxton	2,324	9	8	1
Clayton	2,250	12	12	0
Cleveland	3,828	16	15	1
Cochran	4,234	14	13	1
College Park	14,724	117	91	26
Conyers	16,004	84	64	20
Coolidge	526	2	1	1
Cordele	10,907	35	26	9
Covington	14,077	66	55	11
Cumming	5,772	24	15	9
Dallas	13,135	29	20	9
Dalton	33,989	96	83	13
Danielsville	579	3	3	0
Darien	1,842	10	10	0
Davisboro	1,989	2	2	0
Dawson	4,315	23	16	7
Decatur	22,449	51	39	12
Doerun	772	4	4	0
Donalsonville	2,680	13	9	4
Douglasville	33,287	122	97	25
Dublin	16,195	63	57	6
Duluth	29,720	93	78	15
Dunwoody	49,232	64	54	10
Eastman	5,232	15	13	2
Eatonton	6,528	22	15	7
Elberton	4,432	22	20	2
Ellaville	1,892	6	6	0
Ellijay	1,691	10	10	0
Emerson	1,546	11	9	2
Enigma	1,285	3	3	0
Eton	902	3	3	0
Fairburn	14,151	44	37	7
Fairmount	739	6	5	1
Fayetteville	17,157	46	41	5
Fitzgerald	9,001	28	23	5
Flowery Branch	6,895	18	16	2
Folkston	5,349	7	6	1

(Number.)

State/city	Population	Total law enforcement employees	Total officers	Total civilians
Forest Park	19,570	89	68	21
Forsyth	4,042	18	13	5
Fort Oglethorpe	9,911	29	27	2
Fort Valley	8,374	29	23	6
Franklin	964	8	8	0
Franklin Springs	1,195	2	2	0
Gainesville	39,425	111	98	13
Glennville	5,068	15	13	2
Glenwood	737	2	2	0
Gordon	1,946	11	6	5
Gray	3,271	14	13	1
Greensboro	3,411	22	18	4
Grovetown	13,469	28	21	7
Guyton	1,891	4	4	0
Hahira	2,928	8	7	1
Hampton	7,451	18	16	2
Harlem	3,026	8	7	1
Hartwell	4,523	26	20	6
Hazlehurst	4,189	17	13	4
Helen	536	9	8	1
Hiram	3,840	18	15	3
Hoboken	531	2	1	1
Hogansville	3,126	21	14	7
Holly Springs	11,034	28	27	1
Homeland	861	7	7	0
Homerville	2,487	13	11	2
Jackson	4,966	14	12	2
Jesup	9,525	29	27	2
Johns Creek	84,629	81	72	9
Jonesboro	4,752	39	31	8
Kennesaw	34,204	75	58	17
Kingsland	16,597	35	33	2
Kingston	657	1	1	0
Lafayette	7,185	24	22	2
LaGrange	30,931	100	84	16
Lake City	2,752	20	19	1
Lakeland	3,314	7	5	2
Lake Park	729	4	4	0
Lawrenceville	30,913	94	70	24
Leary	583	2	1	1
Leslie	384	4	3	1
Lilburn	12,854	38	30	8
Locust Grove	5,862	23	20	3
Loganville	11,409	33	30	3
Lyons	4,372	20	18	2
Madison	4,034	17	15	2
Manchester	4,068	15	10	5
Marietta	59,516	175	137	38
McIntyre	615	5	5	0
McRae-Helena	8,786	12	11	1
Metter	4,107	11	10	1
Midville	262	1	1	0
Midway	1,992	6	6	0
Milledgeville	19,072	68	44	24
Millen	2,889	10	10	0
Milton	38,551	41	37	4
Montezuma	3,141	13	11	2
Mountain City	1,056	3	3	0
Mount Zion	1,743	4	4	0
Nashville	4,834	17	14	3
Newnan	38,137	93	79	14
Nicholls	3,378	3	2	1
Norcross	16,929	58	42	16
Norman Park	961	3	2	1
Oakwood	4,218	16	14	2
Oxford	2,210	4	4	0
Palmetto	4,780	17	15	2
Patterson	755	2	2	0
Peachtree City	35,387	68	63	5

Table 19. Full-Time Law Enforcement Employees, by Selected State and City, 2016—*Continued*

(Number.)

State/city	Population	Total law enforcement employees	Total officers	Total civilians
Pelham	3,669	13	12	1
Pine Mountain	1,368	10	8	2
Pooler	24,006	55	49	6
Porterdale	1,494	4	4	0
Port Wentworth	8,177	32	27	5
Poulan	793	6	5	1
Powder Springs	15,004	33	30	3
Quitman	3,863	18	16	2
Remerton	1,127	9	8	1
Reynolds	1,016	8	6	2
Richland	1,502	7	7	0
Richmond Hill	12,520	39	32	7
Ringgold	3,722	11	11	0
Riverdale	16,142	52	38	14
Rochelle	1,109	6	4	2
Rockmart	4,322	20	18	2
Rome	36,278	97	89	8
Roswell	95,684	196	141	55
Royston	2,574	15	13	2
Sandersville	5,724	21	18	3
Sandy Springs	107,685	144	127	17
Sardis	957	5	5	0
Savannah-Chatham Metropolitan	241,296	821	570	251
Senoia	4,233	17	15	2
Sky Valley	264	2	2	0
Smyrna	57,152	127	90	37
Snellville	20,025	56	44	12
Sparks	1,999	3	3	0
Sparta	1,275	10	4	6
Springfield	2,903	7	6	1
Statesboro	31,176	80	61	19
Statham	2,647	6	5	1
Stillmore	527	1	1	0
St. Marys	18,102	33	30	3
Stone Mountain	6,171	19	18	1
Summerville	4,442	17	16	1
Suwanee	19,432	45	36	9
Swainsboro	7,512	24	21	3
Sylvania	2,527	13	11	2
Sylvester	6,019	23	19	4
Talbotton	874	2	2	0
Tallapoosa	3,170	11	10	1
Tallulah Falls	168	2	2	0
Tennille	1,826	3	3	0
Thunderbolt	2,641	12	10	2
Tifton	16,799	46	38	8
Toccoa	8,252	28	27	1
Trenton	2,226	8	8	0
Tybee Island	3,124	33	24	9
Tyrone	7,243	19	17	2
Valdosta	55,880	157	135	22
Vidalia	10,721	43	29	14
Vienna	3,735	9	7	2
Villa Rica	15,095	48	40	8
Walthourville	3,957	6	5	1
Warner Robins	74,419	146	104	42
Warwick	404	6	5	1
Watkinsville	2,877	8	8	0
Waverly Hall	842	3	3	0
Waycross	13,934	62	52	10
West Point	3,785	23	15	8
Whigham	480	4	3	1
Willacoochee	1,395	6	5	1
Winder	15,652	42	37	5
Winterville	1,182	2	2	0
Woodland	361	1	1	0
Woodstock	31,243	55	50	5

Table 19. Full-Time Law Enforcement Employees, by Selected State and City, 2016—*Continued*

(Number.)

State/city	Population	Total law enforcement employees	Total officers	Total civilians
Wrens	2,026	8	7	1
Wrightsville	3,620	6	5	1
Zebulon	1,150	6	6	0
HAWAII				
Honolulu	995,572	2,537	2,042	495
IDAHO				
Aberdeen	1,915	7	4	3
American Falls	4,291	10	8	2
Bellevue	2,296	5	5	0
Blackfoot	11,700	30	27	3
Boise	220,749	363	272	91
Bonners Ferry	2,549	7	7	0
Buhl	4,305	9	8	1
Caldwell	52,792	78	64	14
Chubbuck	14,515	33	19	14
Coeur d'Alene	50,155	98	80	18
Cottonwood	925	1	1	0
Emmett	6,617	14	13	1
Filer	2,724	6	6	0
Fruitland	5,170	15	9	6
Garden City	11,667	35	27	8
Gooding	3,497	9	7	2
Grangeville	3,156	6	6	0
Hagerman	866	1	1	0
Hailey	8,175	14	13	1
Heyburn	3,250	8	7	1
Homedale	2,554	6	6	0
Idaho City	472	1	1	0
Idaho Falls	59,615	132	87	45
Jerome	11,234	21	18	3
Kamiah	1,269	4	4	0
Kellogg	2,061	7	7	0
Ketchum	2,732	15	11	4
Kimberly	3,680	9	8	1
Lewiston	32,665	63	41	22
McCall	3,139	14	12	2
Meridian	94,113	115	92	23
Montpelier	2,493	5	5	0
Moscow	25,307	43	35	8
Mountain Home	13,627	31	26	5
Nampa	91,520	167	112	55
Orofino	3,056	6	5	1
Osburn	1,503	2	2	0
Parma	2,101	4	4	0
Payette	7,360	16	14	2
Pinehurst	1,573	2	2	0
Pocatello	54,462	127	88	39
Ponderay	1,138	7	6	1
Post Falls	31,026	70	43	27
Preston	5,214	8	7	1
Priest River	1,761	7	5	2
Rathdrum	7,681	16	13	3
Rexburg	28,112	40	32	8
Rigby	4,040	8	7	1
Rupert	5,736	13	12	1
Salmon	3,019	8	8	0
Sandpoint	7,931	20	17	3
Shelley	4,321	8	8	0
Shoshone	1,492	5	5	0
Soda Springs	2,921	7	7	0
Spirit Lake	2,117	7	6	1
St. Anthony	3,423	6	5	1
St. Maries	2,310	4	4	0
Sun Valley	1,426	11	10	1

Table 19. Full-Time Law Enforcement Employees, by Selected State and City, 2016—*Continued*

(Number.)

State/city	Population	Total law enforcement employees	Total officers	Total civilians
Twin Falls	48,083	102	71	31
Weiser	5,281	15	12	3
Wilder	1,640	4	4	0
ILLINOIS				
Addison	37,246	119	66	53
Altamont	2,306	5	5	0
Alton	26,829	75	58	17
Annawan	854	1	1	0
Antioch	14,302	29	26	3
Arlington Heights	76,077	136	108	28
Arthur	2,288	6	6	0
Assumption	1,106	1	1	0
Athens	1,928	4	4	0
Auburn	4,788	9	5	4
Batavia	26,558	46	40	6
Berkeley	5,201	20	17	3
Bethalto	9,314	18	14	4
Bloomington	78,604	161	125	36
Bolingbrook	74,471	124	109	15
Bourbonnais	18,552	31	24	7
Braidwood	6,160	17	14	3
Brookfield	18,935	34	29	5
Buffalo Grove	41,511	74	63	11
Burnham	4,209	12	10	2
Burr Ridge	10,863	30	27	3
Byron	3,628	7	6	1
Cairo	2,402	12	7	5
Cambridge	2,104	1	1	0
Camp Point	1,123	1	1	0
Campton Hills	11,390	6	6	0
Canton	14,116	29	20	9
Carbondale	26,373	83	67	16
Carlinville	5,615	17	12	5
Carlyle	3,211	8	7	1
Carol Stream	40,473	82	60	22
Carthage	2,534	4	4	0
Cary	17,903	29	26	3
Caseyville	4,003	13	12	1
Centreville	4,970	10	10	0
Champaign	87,071	141	119	22
Charleston	21,067	34	31	3
Chenoa	3,199	5	5	0
Chester	8,590	11	8	3
Chicago	2,725,153	13,135	11,954	1,181
Chicago Ridge	14,383	35	31	4
Chillicothe	6,253	14	11	3
Christopher	2,771	6	6	0
Cicero	83,807	176	150	26
Clarendon Hills	8,724	15	14	1
Coal City	5,469	11	10	1
Cobden	1,136	3	3	0
Colfax	1,043	1	1	0
Columbia	10,288	22	16	6
Countryside	6,015	27	24	3
Crest Hill	21,211	30	28	2
Crete	8,171	18	17	1
Creve Coeur	5,235	10	8	2
Crystal Lake	40,374	69	60	9
Darien	22,285	40	34	6
Decatur	72,694	189	158	31
De Kalb	43,034	77	62	15
Delavan	1,622	3	3	0
De Pue	1,726	3	3	0
De Soto	1,571	4	3	1
Divernon	1,153	3	3	0
Dixon	15,246	34	30	4
Downers Grove	49,894	98	71	27
Dupo	3,881	6	6	0
Earlville	1,619	3	3	0

(Number.)

State/city	Population	Total law enforcement employees	Total officers	Total civilians
East Hazel Crest	1,545	11	9	2
East Peoria	23,008	60	48	12
Edwardsville	25,133	56	42	14
Effingham	12,660	35	21	14
Elgin	112,886	246	182	64
Elk Grove Village	33,255	105	89	16
Elmhurst	46,318	89	67	22
Elmwood	2,088	2	2	0
Elwood	2,253	11	10	1
Erie	1,543	2	2	0
Eureka	5,388	6	6	0
Evanston	75,716	227	166	61
Evergreen Park	19,836	80	62	18
Fairfield	5,019	13	9	4
Farmington	2,305	5	5	0
Fox Lake	10,495	25	22	3
Frankfort	18,822	32	28	4
Freeburg	4,218	11	10	1
Freeport	24,257	63	45	18
Galena	3,276	11	10	1
Genoa	5,197	8	7	1
Germantown	1,285	1	1	0
Gibson City	3,408	8	6	2
Gifford	1,117	1	1	0
Gilman	1,743	2	2	0
Glenview	48,008	74	69	5
Granite City	28,899	69	56	13
Greenfield	1,010	2	2	0
Gurnee	31,014	90	60	30
Hanover Park	38,402	81	56	25
Henry	2,301	5	4	1
Herrin	12,985	26	19	7
Herscher	1,547	3	3	0
Hickory Hills	14,134	32	25	7
Highland	9,827	26	19	7
Hillsboro	5,635	8	8	0
Hillsdale	509	1	1	0
Hinckley	2,056	3	3	0
Hinsdale	17,790	25	23	2
Hodgkins	1,862	23	21	2
Hoffman Estates	52,177	103	88	15
Homer	1,199	1	1	0
Hometown	4,340	4	1	3
Homewood	19,379	43	38	5
Hopedale	839	1	1	0
Ina	2,365	2	2	0
Island Lake	8,079	14	13	1
Itasca	8,825	24	21	3
Jacksonville	19,039	45	41	4
Johnsburg	6,303	12	10	2
Joliet	147,886	330	263	67
Kankakee	26,509	72	68	4
Kenilworth	2,563	12	9	3
Kewanee	12,460	29	22	7
Kincaid	1,424	3	2	1
Kingston	1,154	2	2	0
Kirkland	1,732	3	3	0
Ladd	1,231	2	2	0
La Grange	15,754	38	28	10
Lake Villa	8,849	18	17	1
Lake Zurich	20,051	51	34	17
La Salle	9,194	23	22	1
Lawrenceville	4,428	7	7	0
Lemont	16,927	30	27	3
Le Roy	3,585	7	7	0
Lexington	2,058	2	2	0
Lincolnwood	12,655	40	33	7
Lindenhurst	14,408	17	14	3
Lisle	23,063	41	32	9
Lombard	43,866	82	68	14

Table 19. Full-Time Law Enforcement Employees, by Selected State and City, 2016—*Continued*

(Number.)

State/city	Population	Total law enforcement employees	Total officers	Total civilians
Loves Park	23,349	37	34	3
Lovington	1,104	2	2	0
Lyons	10,719	19	13	6
Macomb	18,402	29	26	3
Marengo	7,467	15	13	2
Marissa	1,833	4	4	0
Maroa	1,727	3	3	0
Maryville	7,978	13	13	0
Mattoon	18,026	42	38	4
McHenry	26,581	57	46	11
Mendota	7,173	18	15	3
Metropolis	6,290	19	14	5
Milledgeville	973	2	2	0
Moline	42,517	98	79	19
Monee	5,068	15	13	2
Monmouth	9,261	28	17	11
Morris	14,507	28	25	3
Morrison	4,137	6	6	0
Morton	16,310	28	22	6
Mount Carmel	6,982	15	10	5
Mount Carroll	1,602	3	3	0
Mount Morris	2,854	5	4	1
Mount Prospect	54,839	102	82	20
Mount Zion	5,865	11	9	2
Moweaqua	1,736	2	2	0
Mundelein	31,685	70	51	19
Neoga	1,609	3	3	0
New Athens	1,930	4	4	0
New Lenox	26,085	41	37	4
Newton	2,807	7	6	1
Niles	29,886	68	55	13
Normal	54,727	93	81	12
Norridge	14,629	49	35	14
Oak Brook	8,130	43	40	3
Oakbrook Terrace	2,169	23	19	4
Oak Forest	28,088	52	41	11
Oak Lawn	56,791	124	108	16
Okawville	1,392	3	3	0
Olney	8,984	14	13	1
Orion	1,818	2	2	0
Orland Park	59,009	124	98	26
Ottawa	18,263	50	35	15
Palestine	1,324	2	2	0
Palos Hills	17,578	34	31	3
Park City	7,357	14	11	3
Park Forest	21,947	48	40	8
Park Ridge	37,805	66	54	12
Pawnee	2,707	6	6	0
Pekin	33,052	64	54	10
Peotone	4,114	10	9	1
Pingree Grove	7,162	7	6	1
Plano	11,358	18	16	2
Pontiac	11,771	18	17	1
Pontoon Beach	5,598	20	14	6
Posen	5,992	20	18	2
Princeton	7,534	19	17	2
Prophetstown	1,999	2	2	0
Quincy	40,799	83	70	13
Raleigh	348	1	1	0
Red Bud	3,564	6	6	0
Richmond	1,904	5	5	0
Riverwoods	3,639	8	8	0
Robinson	7,616	14	13	1
Rockdale	1,942	5	5	0
Rockford	147,363	323	288	35
Rolling Meadows	24,205	57	50	7
Roscoe	10,523	14	13	1
Roselle	23,037	36	29	7
Rosemont	4,206	99	77	22
Round Lake Beach	27,796	38	37	1

(Number.)

State/city	Population	Total law enforcement employees	Total officers	Total civilians
Round Lake Heights	2,713	5	5	0
Roxana	1,472	7	6	1
Royalton	1,135	3	3	0
Rushville	2,927	4	4	0
Salem	7,249	23	15	8
Sandoval	1,221	3	3	0
Sauget	151	11	11	0
Savanna	2,845	7	7	0
Schiller Park	11,807	39	32	7
Seneca	2,278	6	5	1
Shawneetown	1,150	3	3	0
Silvis	7,487	21	15	6
Sleepy Hollow	3,354	8	7	1
South Beloit	7,639	15	14	1
South Chicago Heights	4,137	10	9	1
South Elgin	22,436	35	31	4
South Jacksonville	3,248	6	5	1
South Pekin	1,115	2	2	0
Springfield	116,563	268	241	27
Spring Valley	5,269	12	10	2
St. Anne	1,213	3	3	0
St. Charles	33,556	63	52	11
Steger	9,502	19	15	4
St. Elmo	1,402	3	3	0
Stickney	6,785	23	16	7
Stonington	882	2	2	0
Streator	13,082	26	24	2
Tolono	3,483	2	2	0
Urbana	42,461	68	54	14
Vernon Hills	26,574	71	42	29
Vienna	1,696	3	3	0
Walnut	1,338	2	2	0
Warren	1,366	4	3	1
Wauconda	13,843	27	25	2
Waukegan	88,337	189	150	39
Wenona	975	2	2	0
West Chicago	27,490	51	46	5
West Dundee	7,406	18	16	2
Westmont	24,992	40	35	5
Wheaton	53,848	82	66	16
Wheeling	38,158	95	60	35
White Hall	2,389	7	5	2
Willow Springs	5,701	10	7	3
Winnebago	2,995	6	6	0
Wood Dale	13,943	44	35	9
Wood River	10,225	24	18	6
Worth	10,781	27	24	3
Zion	24,067	59	46	13
INDIANA				
Auburn	13,010	24	23	1
Avon	17,076	25	23	2
Bremen	4,561	17	12	5
Clinton	4,799	9	8	1
Columbia City	8,873	18	17	1
East Chicago	28,503	101	94	7
Edinburgh	4,560	13	12	1
Elkhart	52,505	142	120	22
Elwood	8,427	18	17	1
Evansville	119,908	305	281	24
Fairmount	2,832	6	5	1
Frankfort	15,987	33	31	2
Gas City	5,931	10	10	0
Greenwood	56,502	66	58	8
Hammond	77,005	234	207	27
Highland	22,783	45	38	7
Hobart	28,223	71	62	9
Indianapolis	866,351	1,806	1,612	194
Jeffersonville	47,327	87	82	5
Kendallville	9,942	24	19	5

Table 19. Full-Time Law Enforcement Employees, by Selected State and City, 2016—Continued

(Number.)

State/city	Population	Total law enforcement employees	Total officers	Total civilians
La Porte	21,891	49	43	6
Mishawaka	48,267	121	107	14
Mooresville	9,675	27	21	6
Munster	22,865	42	37	5
New Whiteland	5,991	7	6	1
North Vernon	6,599	19	16	3
Portage	36,715	74	67	7
Portland	6,183	16	12	4
Scottsburg	6,655	14	14	0
Sellersburg	8,723	18	16	2
Seymour	19,762	56	40	16
South Bend	101,621	284	240	44
Tell City	7,253	20	12	8
Valparaiso	32,796	55	50	5
Vincennes	17,937	42	38	4
Walkerton	2,289	10	6	4
Warsaw	14,657	43	37	6
Westfield	38,186	50	45	5
Whitestown	6,850	13	12	1
Whiting	4,848	20	18	2
Winchester	4,732	13	13	0
Zionsville	26,877	30	29	1
IOWA				
Adel	4,356	10	9	1
Albia	3,840	7	6	1
Algona	5,453	14	10	4
Altoona	17,503	29	26	3
Ames	66,333	76	52	24
Anamosa	5,454	9	8	1
Ankeny	59,236	62	54	8
Arnolds Park	1,255	6	5	1
Atlantic	6,781	13	12	1
Audubon	1,988	4	4	0
Belle Plaine	2,464	5	5	0
Belmond	2,303	5	5	0
Bettendorf	35,946	52	45	7
Bloomfield	2,611	7	6	1
Blue Grass	1,724	2	2	0
Boone	12,702	19	18	1
Buffalo	1,304	3	3	0
Burlington	25,376	47	43	4
Camanche	4,320	6	6	0
Carlisle	4,225	7	6	1
Carroll	9,940	16	15	1
Carter Lake	3,791	11	10	1
Cedar Falls	41,651	41	40	1
Cedar Rapids	131,181	280	214	66
Centerville	5,343	17	11	6
Chariton	4,194	5	4	1
Charles City	7,417	21	14	7
Cherokee	4,983	9	8	1
Clarinda	5,386	11	10	1
Clarion	2,752	7	6	1
Clear Lake	7,555	22	16	6
Clinton	25,906	46	40	6
Clive	17,836	27	24	3
Colfax	2,043	4	4	0
Coralville	20,957	37	33	4
Council Bluffs	62,642	129	109	20
Cresco	3,826	7	7	0
Creston	7,860	15	11	4
Davenport	103,118	178	158	20
Decorah	7,864	21	13	8
Denison	8,335	17	12	5
Des Moines	211,501	446	343	103
De Witt	5,226	12	11	1
Dubuque	59,026	108	101	7
Dyersville	4,231	6	6	0
Eagle Grove	3,389	7	7	0

State/city	Population	Total law enforcement employees	Total officers	Total civilians
Eldora	2,696	4	4	0
Eldridge	6,348	10	9	1
Emmetsburg	3,795	7	6	1
Estherville	5,947	12	12	0
Evansdale	4,824	8	7	1
Fairfield	9,982	21	14	7
Forest City	3,994	8	8	0
Fort Dodge	24,557	46	40	6
Fort Madison	10,654	21	19	2
Garner	3,104	5	5	0
Glenwood	5,250	11	10	1
Grinnell	9,127	17	15	2
Grundy Center	2,715	4	4	0
Hampton	4,256	8	7	1
Harlan	4,982	9	8	1
Hawarden	2,552	4	4	0
Hiawatha	7,235	14	14	0
Humboldt	4,579	6	6	0
Independence	6,041	12	11	1
Indianola	15,601	22	20	2
Iowa City	75,527	103	80	23
Iowa Falls	5,186	14	10	4
Jefferson	4,176	7	7	0
Johnston	21,635	29	27	2
Keokuk	10,577	27	24	3
Knoxville	7,239	15	14	1
Le Claire	4,029	8	7	1
Le Mars	9,750	15	14	1
Leon	1,890	4	3	1
Lisbon	2,212	1	1	0
Manchester	5,051	16	10	6
Maquoketa	5,961	18	11	7
Marengo	2,511	4	4	0
Marion	37,845	57	45	12
Marshalltown	27,628	58	41	17
Mason City	27,230	51	46	5
Missouri Valley	2,668	6	6	0
Monticello	3,832	7	6	1
Mount Pleasant	8,389	16	14	2
Mount Vernon	4,482	6	6	0
Muscatine	24,010	43	40	3
Nevada	6,836	10	8	2
New Hampton	3,430	6	6	0
New Sharon	1,290	1	1	0
Newton	15,102	27	22	5
North Liberty	16,458	21	20	1
Norwalk	10,371	14	13	1
Oelwein	6,104	15	10	5
Ogden	2,041	3	3	0
Onawa	2,859	6	6	0
Orange City	6,225	7	7	0
Osage	3,659	7	6	1
Osceola	4,976	12	11	1
Oskaloosa	11,626	18	16	2
Ottumwa	24,543	47	38	9
Pella	10,368	24	18	6
Perry	8,160	19	12	7
Pleasant Hill	9,415	20	18	2
Polk City	4,524	6	6	0
Prairie City	1,715	3	3	0
Princeton	937	1	1	0
Red Oak	5,424	11	9	2
Rock Valley	3,762	5	5	0
Sac City	2,129	4	4	0
Sergeant Bluff	4,579	9	8	1
Sheldon	5,067	7	7	0
Sigourney	1,995	3	3	0
Sioux Center	7,544	7	7	0
Sioux City	82,819	150	125	25
Spencer	11,211	28	18	10

(Number.)

State/city	Population	Total law enforcement employees	Total officers	Total civilians
Spirit Lake..	5,049	10	9	1
Storm Lake...	10,959	23	19	4
Story City...	3,439	6	6	0
Tama...	2,809	5	5	0
Tipton...	3,196	7	6	1
Toledo...	2,176	5	5	0
Urbandale..	45,012	59	51	8
Vinton...	5,128	9	8	1
Walcott..	1,639	3	3	0
Washington..	7,437	12	11	1
Waterloo..	68,470	133	124	9
Waukee..	20,186	22	20	2
Waukon..	3,701	7	7	0
Waverly..	10,104	17	16	1
Webster City...	7,768	17	12	5
West Burlington.......................................	3,055	10	9	1
West Des Moines......................................	65,631	78	63	15
Williamsburg...	3,221	6	6	0
Wilton...	2,808	4	4	0
Windsor Heights.......................................	4,893	11	10	1
Winterset...	5,170	8	8	0
KANSAS				
Abilene..	6,501	17	14	3
Altamont..	1,041	3	3	0
Andale...	1,004	2	2	0
Andover...	12,937	33	26	7
Anthony...	2,224	6	5	1
Argonia..	485	1	1	0
Arkansas City..	12,085	28	24	4
Arma...	1,445	5	5	0
Atchison...	10,654	24	23	1
Attica..	584	1	1	0
Atwood..	1,187	3	3	0
Augusta...	9,304	34	25	9
Baldwin City	4,698	11	10	1
Basehor...	5,563	13	11	2
Bel Aire...	7,574	13	12	1
Belle Plaine..	1,610	4	4	0
Belleville..	1,894	4	4	0
Beloit..	3,784	6	6	0
Benton..	875	2	2	0
Blue Rapids..	976	2	2	0
Bonner Springs..	7,625	27	25	2
Buhler...	1,330	3	3	0
Burlington..	2,604	9	7	2
Burrton..	894	2	2	0
Caldwell...	1,023	2	2	0
Caney..	2,054	11	6	5
Canton..	731	1	1	0
Carbondale...	1,388	2	2	0
Cawker City..	453	1	1	0
Cedar Vale..	525	1	1	0
Chanute...	9,279	20	18	2
Chapman..	1,372	2	2	0
Cheney..	2,170	7	7	0
Cherokee..	713	1	1	0
Cherryvale..	2,203	6	6	0
Chetopa...	1,074	4	4	0
Clay Center...	4,140	7	6	1
Clearwater..	2,547	6	5	1
Coffeyville..	9,555	30	21	9
Colby..	5,418	18	12	6
Coldwater..	802	1	1	0
Columbus...	3,116	9	8	1
Colwich...	1,388	3	3	0
Concordia...	5,183	16	9	7
Conway Springs.......................................	1,231	2	2	0
Council Grove..	2,068	8	7	1
Derby..	23,708	55	45	10

(Number.)

State/city	Population	Total law enforcement employees	Total officers	Total civilians
Dodge City	27,997	63	43	20
Eastborough	767	6	6	0
Edwardsville	4,377	18	17	1
El Dorado	12,913	28	27	1
Elkhart	2,011	2	2	0
Ellinwood	2,053	5	5	0
Ellis	2,065	5	5	0
Ellsworth	3,043	7	6	1
Elwood	1,181	2	2	0
Erie	1,097	5	4	1
Eudora	6,424	11	10	1
Fairway	3,987	11	9	2
Fort Scott	7,792	29	20	9
Fredonia	2,296	7	6	1
Frontenac	3,419	11	7	4
Galena	2,901	10	9	1
Galva	882	1	1	0
Garden City	27,038	91	62	29
Garden Plain	907	3	3	0
Garnett	3,229	8	8	0
Girard	2,754	7	6	1
Goddard	4,782	13	12	1
Goodland	4,450	10	9	1
Grandview Plaza	1,656	7	7	0
Greensburg	799	1	1	0
Halstead	2,094	6	5	1
Harper	1,383	3	3	0
Haven	1,221	3	3	0
Havensville	150	1	1	0
Hays	21,206	32	30	2
Haysville	11,288	32	25	7
Herington	2,371	7	6	1
Hesston	3,832	7	6	1
Hiawatha	3,080	9	8	1
Hill City	1,465	4	4	0
Hillsboro	2,845	5	5	0
Hoisington	2,607	7	6	1
Holcomb	2,167	4	3	1
Holton	3,250	7	7	0
Holyrood	430	1	1	0
Horton	1,711	10	6	4
Howard	609	1	1	0
Hugoton	3,974	8	6	2
Humboldt	1,838	5	4	1
Hutchinson	41,439	109	72	37
Independence	8,860	25	17	8
Inman	1,358	3	3	0
Iola	5,425	18	17	1
Junction City	24,780	66	45	21
Kansas City	151,623	425	339	86
Kechi	2,013	5	4	1
Kingman	3,070	7	7	0
Kiowa	1,009	2	2	0
La Cygne	1,104	2	2	0
La Harpe	536	2	1	1
Lake Quivira	941	1	1	0
Lansing	11,860	16	15	1
Larned	3,950	8	8	0
Lawrence	95,149	184	151	33
Leavenworth	36,100	75	52	23
Leawood	35,139	77	56	21
Lenexa	53,376	128	88	40
Liberal	20,785	51	36	15
Lindsborg	3,369	6	5	1
Linn Valley	806	3	3	0
Little River	541	1	1	0
Louisburg	4,266	11	10	1
Lyndon	1,016	2	2	0
Lyons	3,721	7	6	1
Macksville	536	1	1	0

Table 19. Full-Time Law Enforcement Employees, by Selected State and City, 2016—*Continued*

(Number.)

State/city	Population	Total law enforcement employees	Total officers	Total civilians
Maize	4,564	11	10	1
Maple Hill	622	1	1	0
Marion	1,825	6	5	1
Marquette	618	1	1	0
Marysville	3,329	9	8	1
McLouth	849	1	1	0
McPherson	13,146	36	31	5
Meade	1,605	4	3	1
Medicine Lodge	1,986	4	4	0
Melvern	361	1	1	0
Merriam	11,337	37	32	5
Minneapolis	1,996	5	5	0
Mission	9,523	31	29	2
Mission Hills	3,621	3	3	0
Moran	513	1	1	0
Mound City	677	1	1	0
Moundridge	1,689	4	4	0
Mulberry	504	1	1	0
Mulvane	6,347	19	14	5
Neodesha	2,333	8	7	1
Newton	19,226	41	36	5
North Newton	1,811	3	3	0
Norton	2,830	7	6	1
Oakley	2,104	11	6	5
Oberlin	1,758	5	5	0
Olathe	135,977	194	166	28
Osage City	2,825	7	7	0
Osawatomie	4,267	17	12	5
Osborne	1,358	3	3	0
Oswego	1,755	5	5	0
Ottawa	12,334	32	27	5
Overbrook	1,018	1	1	0
Overland Park	189,104	298	243	55
Oxford	1,019	3	3	0
Paola	5,509	21	15	6
Park City	7,671	16	14	2
Parsons	10,016	32	23	9
Peabody	1,131	2	2	0
Perry	905	1	1	0
Pittsburg	20,439	74	50	24
Plainville	1,893	5	5	0
Pleasanton	1,168	2	2	0
Prairie Village	21,958	54	41	13
Pratt	6,854	22	15	7
Protection	495	1	1	0
Quinter	955	1	1	0
Roeland Park	6,845	15	13	2
Rose Hill	4,007	9	8	1
Russell	4,537	8	8	0
Sabetha	2,589	9	4	5
Salina	47,805	98	73	25
Scott City	3,840	12	7	5
Sedgwick	1,709	2	2	0
Seneca	2,041	5	5	0
Shawnee	65,603	109	89	20
South Hutchinson	2,576	9	7	2
Spearville	811	1	1	0
Spring Hill	6,090	13	11	2
Stafford	976	3	3	0
Sterling	2,285	5	5	0
St. Francis	1,300	3	2	1
St. George	991	1	1	0
St. Marys	2,668	5	5	0
Stockton	1,321	6	6	0
Tonganoxie	5,295	13	12	1
Topeka	127,166	334	282	52
Troy	984	1	1	0
Udall	728	2	2	0
Valley Center	7,302	16	15	1
Valley Falls	1,150	3	3	0

(Number.)

State/city	Population	Total law enforcement employees	Total officers	Total civilians
Victoria	1,229	2	2	0
Wa Keeney	1,803	5	5	0
Wakefield	973	1	1	0
Waterville	646	1	1	0
Wathena	1,330	2	2	0
Wellington	7,954	20	17	3
Wellsville	1,810	4	4	0
Westwood	2,314	8	7	1
Wichita	391,399	794	612	182
Wilson	755	1	1	0
Winfield	12,176	31	25	6
Yates Center	1,315	3	3	0
KENTUCKY				
Adairville	888	1	1	0
Alexandria	9,112	19	16	3
Anchorage	2,434	14	10	4
Auburn	1,354	2	2	0
Beaver Dam	3,640	5	5	0
Benton	4,346	8	8	0
Berea	15,135	34	32	2
Booneville	75	1	1	0
Bowling Green	64,561	151	116	35
Brownsville	824	3	3	0
Burgin	966	2	2	0
Burkesville	1,511	6	6	0
Burnside	845	6	5	1
Butler	583	1	1	0
Campbellsville	11,357	22	20	2
Carrollton	3,877	17	10	7
Catlettsburg	1,798	8	8	0
Cave City	2,411	7	7	0
Central City	5,875	12	12	0
Clinton	1,306	5	5	0
Cold Spring	6,217	9	9	0
Covington	41,094	116	108	8
Crab Orchard	832	2	1	1
Cumberland	2,078	6	6	0
Dry Ridge	2,208	5	5	0
Eddyville	2,582	5	5	0
Edgewood	8,801	15	15	0
Edmonton	1,562	6	6	0
Elkhorn City	928	2	1	1
Elsmere	8,563	14	13	1
Erlanger	22,952	40	39	1
Ferguson	944	1	1	0
Flemingsburg	2,902	7	7	0
Fort Thomas	16,436	22	21	1
Fort Wright	5,801	13	13	0
Frankfort	27,926	59	56	3
Greensburg	2,116	5	5	0
Hardinsburg	2,332	5	5	0
Harrodsburg	8,399	30	19	11
Hawesville	1,006	1	1	0
Henderson	28,904	81	60	21
Highland Heights	7,216	11	10	1
Hillview	8,177	14	14	0
Hodgenville	3,259	7	7	0
Jackson	2,138	11	8	3
Jamestown	1,805	4	4	0
Jeffersontown	27,006	59	49	10
Jenkins	2,077	3	3	0
La Center	1,004	2	2	0
Lakeside Park-Crestview Hills	6,159	12	11	1
Lancaster	3,873	11	10	1
Lawrenceburg	11,140	22	14	8
Lebanon	5,710	24	15	9
Leitchfield	6,904	19	18	1
Louisa	2,452	6	6	0
Loyall	648	2	2	0

Table 19. Full-Time Law Enforcement Employees, by Selected State and City, 2016—*Continued*

(Number.)

State/city	Population	Total law enforcement employees	Total officers	Total civilians
Marion	2,976	11	6	5
Maysville	8,780	33	25	8
Middlesboro	9,615	28	24	4
Monticello	6,071	12	11	1
Morgantown	2,480	6	6	0
Mount Sterling	7,268	22	20	2
Mount Washington	14,162	19	18	1
New Haven	893	1	1	0
Owensboro	59,359	136	90	46
Paducah	24,836	79	71	8
Paris	9,883	23	22	1
Pioneer Village	2,866	5	5	0
Powderly	729	2	2	0
Princeton	6,142	15	14	1
Prospect	4,918	7	6	1
Radcliff	22,346	49	35	14
Richmond	33,965	61	47	14
Russell Springs	2,525	10	9	1
Russellville	7,073	21	20	1
Scottsville	4,446	26	18	8
Shepherdsville	12,098	31	29	2
Smiths Grove	740	1	1	0
Southgate	3,871	8	8	0
Springfield	3,093	13	8	5
Stanford	3,668	13	13	0
Taylor Mill	6,793	11	10	1
Taylorsville	1,035	5	4	1
Tompkinsville	2,277	13	10	3
Uniontown	960	2	2	0
Vanceburg	1,445	6	6	0
West Buechel	1,277	11	11	0
West Point	856	4	4	0
Wilder	3,099	12	12	0
Williamsburg	5,324	14	13	1
Woodburn	381	2	2	0
LOUISIANA				
Abbeville	12,471	39	37	2
Addis	4,808	12	11	1
Alexandria	47,936	190	157	33
Baker	13,655	28	24	4
Baldwin	2,328	14	6	8
Ball	3,989	9	7	2
Basile	1,815	13	7	6
Baton Rouge	228,389	814	641	173
Berwick	4,732	13	12	1
Blanchard	2,941	6	5	1
Bogalusa	11,882	51	34	17
Bossier City	69,384	200	161	39
Breaux Bridge	8,446	23	20	3
Broussard	11,998	32	28	4
Brusly	2,823	10	10	0
Bunkie	4,044	9	5	4
Carencro	8,763	26	24	2
Clarence	486	2	1	1
Clinton	1,564	9	7	2
Coushatta	1,832	8	7	1
Covington	10,178	44	36	8
Crowley	13,119	39	37	2
Denham Springs	10,107	36	27	9
De Quincy	3,147	12	12	0
De Ridder	10,939	30	24	6
Epps	834	2	1	1
Erath	2,106	11	7	4
Eunice	10,291	45	32	13
Farmerville	3,849	13	9	4
Ferriday	3,348	21	21	0
Fisher	225	1	1	0
Florien	628	3	3	0

(Number.)

State/city	Population	Total law enforcement employees	Total officers	Total civilians
Folsom	808	4	4	0
Franklinton	3,769	22	20	2
French Settlement	1,132	3	3	0
Golden Meadow	2,052	5	3	2
Gonzales	10,860	46	41	5
Gramercy	3,430	10	9	1
Greenwood	3,184	10	9	1
Gretna	17,908	133	100	33
Hammond	20,576	106	80	26
Harahan	9,364	25	22	3
Haughton	3,306	13	12	1
Houma	34,410	98	81	17
Ida	214	1	1	0
Independence	1,820	8	8	0
Iowa	3,266	17	13	4
Jena	3,420	7	7	0
Jennings	10,140	33	26	7
Kaplan	4,619	17	11	6
Kenner	67,164	232	167	65
Kentwood	2,368	10	10	0
Killian	1,324	4	3	1
Kinder	2,436	16	11	5
Krotz Springs	1,203	7	4	3
Lafayette	128,923	315	257	58
Lake Arthur	2,742	10	10	0
Lake Charles	76,864	186	183	3
Lake Providence	3,666	11	6	5
Leesville	6,270	28	26	2
Lutcher	3,341	3	3	0
Mamou	3,170	16	14	2
Mandeville	12,423	48	36	12
Mansfield	4,937	17	17	0
Many	2,778	13	13	0
Marion	753	1	1	0
Marksville	5,499	27	19	8
Monroe	49,677	180	137	43
Montgomery	721	3	3	0
Moreauville	899	5	4	1
Natchitoches	18,332	67	55	12
New Orleans	397,208	1,403	1,171	232
Oak Grove	1,650	6	6	0
Olla	1,385	2	2	0
Patterson	6,105	26	26	0
Pearl River	2,553	17	12	5
Pineville	14,379	72	72	0
Plaquemine	6,825	28	24	4
Ponchatoula	7,168	29	23	6
Port Allen	5,116	21	20	1
Port Vincent	750	3	3	0
Rayne	8,031	24	21	3
Rayville	3,658	16	14	2
Ringgold	1,420	5	5	0
Ruston	22,416	49	35	14
Scott	9,092	25	24	1
Shreveport	196,467	711	524	187
Slidell	28,107	99	67	32
Springhill	5,064	17	16	1
Sterlington	2,689	9	9	0
St. Francisville	1,689	8	8	0
St. Gabriel	7,183	19	12	7
Sulphur	20,142	62	41	21
Tallulah	6,930	14	14	0
Thibodaux	14,588	65	45	20
Vidalia	4,076	39	30	9
Ville Platte	7,234	46	31	15
Vinton	3,344	13	11	2
Walker	6,351	24	20	4
Welsh	3,226	20	18	2
Westlake	4,626	17	17	0
West Monroe	12,942	69	67	2

Table 19. Full-Time Law Enforcement Employees, by Selected State and City, 2016—*Continued*

(Number.)

State/city	Population	Total law enforcement employees	Total officers	Total civilians
White Castle	1,814	17	15	2
Wilson	571	4	4	0
Zachary	16,753	43	41	2
MAINE				
Ashland	1,222	2	2	0
Auburn	22,836	61	53	8
Augusta	18,347	58	43	15
Baileyville	1,444	4	4	0
Bangor	32,264	92	76	16
Bar Harbor	5,339	18	13	5
Bath	8,269	24	19	5
Belfast	6,685	16	15	1
Berwick	7,567	13	12	1
Biddeford	21,285	75	53	22
Boothbay Harbor	2,158	7	6	1
Brewer	9,185	22	20	2
Bridgton	5,405	8	8	0
Brownville	1,189	2	2	0
Brunswick	20,544	43	29	14
Bucksport	4,927	12	8	4
Buxton	8,171	10	5	5
Calais	2,953	5	5	0
Camden	4,863	12	10	2
Cape Elizabeth	9,364	14	13	1
Caribou	7,747	16	15	1
Carrabassett Valley	772	2	2	0
Clinton	3,291	2	2	0
Cumberland	7,821	13	11	2
Damariscotta	2,214	6	5	1
Dexter	3,775	4	4	0
Dixfield	2,462	2	2	0
Dover-Foxcroft	4,004	5	5	0
East Millinocket	2,986	2	2	0
Eastport	1,254	4	4	0
Eliot	6,362	9	8	1
Ellsworth	7,881	20	17	3
Fairfield	6,505	11	10	1
Falmouth	12,154	26	18	8
Farmington	7,401	14	13	1
Fort Fairfield	3,330	4	4	0
Fort Kent	3,940	9	5	4
Freeport	8,407	16	14	2
Fryeburg	3,385	5	5	0
Gardiner	5,558	13	12	1
Gorham	17,346	26	24	2
Gouldsboro	1,739	2	2	0
Greenville	1,582	3	2	1
Hallowell	2,303	5	5	0
Hampden	7,414	12	11	1
Holden	3,077	3	3	0
Houlton	5,835	17	11	6
Islesboro	567	1	1	0
Jay	4,750	8	7	1
Kennebunk	11,289	24	22	2
Kennebunkport	3,586	17	12	5
Kittery	9,686	24	18	6
Lewiston	36,126	91	80	11
Limestone	2,202	3	3	0
Lincoln	5,020	7	6	1
Lisbon	8,823	18	12	6
Livermore Falls	3,118	6	6	0
Machias	2,096	4	4	0
Madawaska	3,803	7	6	1
Mechanic Falls	2,990	5	5	0
Mexico	2,590	5	5	0
Milbridge	1,283	2	2	0
Millinocket	4,332	6	6	0
Milo	2,242	2	2	0
Monmouth	4,008	4	4	0

(Number.)

State/city	Population	Total law enforcement employees	Total officers	Total civilians
Mount Desert	2,074	10	6	4
Newport	3,224	6	6	0
North Berwick	4,672	9	8	1
Norway	4,911	10	9	1
Oakland	6,119	11	10	1
Ogunquit	916	11	10	1
Old Orchard Beach	8,807	23	21	2
Old Town	7,583	18	17	1
Orono	10,772	17	16	1
Oxford	4,034	9	8	1
Paris	5,085	8	7	1
Phippsburg	2,234	1	1	0
Pittsfield	4,051	5	5	0
Portland	67,041	216	157	59
Presque Isle	9,075	21	16	5
Rangeley	1,149	3	3	0
Richmond	3,394	4	4	0
Rockland	7,227	20	18	2
Rockport	3,392	7	6	1
Rumford	5,646	11	10	1
Sabattus	5,038	8	7	1
Saco	19,197	44	32	12
Sanford	20,914	43	39	4
Scarborough	19,851	58	40	18
Searsport	2,627	3	3	0
Skowhegan	8,454	13	13	0
South Berwick	7,454	13	9	4
South Portland	25,674	59	53	6
Southwest Harbor	1,774	9	5	4
Thomaston	2,776	5	5	0
Topsham	8,748	17	13	4
Van Buren	2,037	3	3	0
Veazie	1,855	4	4	0
Waldoboro	4,954	8	7	1
Washburn	1,578	2	2	0
Waterville	16,370	41	31	10
Wells	10,174	30	22	8
Westbrook	18,078	41	39	2
Wilton	3,922	6	6	0
Windham	17,983	29	26	3
Winslow	7,506	15	14	1
Winthrop	5,888	14	9	5
Wiscasset	3,638	5	4	1
Yarmouth	8,584	14	13	1
York	12,927	36	26	10
MARYLAND				
Aberdeen	15,704	51	41	10
Annapolis	39,703	153	109	44
Baltimore	618,385	2,908	2,512	396
Baltimore City Sheriff		201	156	45
Bel Air	10,200	42	32	10
Berlin	4,537	17	12	5
Berwyn Heights	3,311	9	8	1
Bladensburg	9,735	26	19	7
Boonsboro	3,457	6	5	1
Bowie	58,631	80	63	17
Brentwood	3,219	6	5	1
Brunswick	6,162	12	12	0
Cambridge	12,524	49	46	3
Capitol Heights	4,620	11	9	2
Centreville	4,696	12	12	0
Chestertown	5,067	15	14	1
Cheverly	6,546	15	12	3
Chevy Chase Village	2,080	17	11	6
Colmar Manor	1,482	4	3	1
Cottage City	1,383	3	3	0
Crisfield	2,642	14	11	3
Cumberland	19,995	54	50	4
Delmar	3,068	13	12	1

Table 19. Full-Time Law Enforcement Employees, by Selected State and City, 2016—*Continued*

(Number.)

State/city	Population	Total law enforcement employees	Total officers	Total civilians
Denton	4,337	13	12	1
District Heights	6,204	12	11	1
Easton	16,689	54	46	8
Edmonston	1,532	7	5	2
Elkton	15,837	45	40	5
Fairmount Heights	1,585	1	1	0
Federalsburg	2,646	7	7	0
Forest Heights	2,598	9	7	2
Frederick	70,316	186	148	38
Frostburg	8,601	20	15	5
Fruitland	5,287	20	19	1
Glenarden	6,390	14	12	2
Greenbelt	24,511	63	45	18
Greensboro	1,864	2	2	0
Hagerstown	40,567	114	101	13
Hampstead	6,365	11	10	1
Hancock	1,548	4	3	1
Havre de Grace	13,604	45	36	9
Hurlock	2,036	10	9	1
Hyattsville	18,666	50	38	12
Landover Hills	1,828	6	5	1
La Plata	9,201	19	18	1
Laurel	26,424	85	64	21
Luke	63	1	1	0
Manchester	4,820	6	6	0
Morningside	2,104	8	7	1
Mount Rainier	8,552	21	17	4
New Carrollton	12,914	27	21	6
North East	3,734	12	11	1
Oakland	1,868	2	2	0
Ocean City	7,045	126	96	30
Ocean Pines	12,207	18	14	4
Oxford	615	3	3	0
Perryville	4,451	13	12	1
Pocomoke City	4,124	23	16	7
Princess Anne	3,299	13	12	1
Ridgely	1,611	5	5	0
Rising Sun	2,860	6	6	0
Riverdale Park	7,373	28	19	9
Rock Hall	1,302	4	4	0
Salisbury	33,417	114	90	24
Seat Pleasant	4,826	17	13	4
Smithsburg	3,000	4	3	1
Snow Hill	2,082	6	6	0
St. Michaels	1,048	9	8	1
Sykesville	4,409	8	7	1
Takoma Park	17,905	58	40	18
Taneytown	6,749	15	14	1
Thurmont	6,507	15	13	2
Trappe	1,015	1	1	0
University Park	2,688	9	8	1
Upper Marlboro	671	3	3	0
Westminster	18,683	53	42	11
MASSACHUSETTS				
Abington	16,201	27	25	2
Acton	23,770	54	43	11
Acushnet	10,466	21	19	2
Adams	8,131	17	16	1
Agawam	28,844	57	47	10
Andover	35,558	71	51	20
Aquinnah	331	4	4	0
Arlington	45,004	84	66	18
Ashburnham	6,206	16	11	5
Ashby	3,242	9	5	4
Ashland	17,689	29	25	4
Attleboro	44,225	91	79	12
Auburn	16,508	46	35	11
Avon	4,505	15	11	4
Ayer	8,078	26	18	8

(Number.)

State/city	Population	Total law enforcement employees	Total officers	Total civilians
Barnstable	43,974	128	113	15
Barre	5,491	9	8	1
Becket	1,759	4	4	0
Bedford	14,280	38	29	9
Belchertown	14,985	22	18	4
Bellingham	16,922	40	33	7
Belmont	25,637	60	46	14
Berkley	6,678	8	8	0
Berlin	3,038	14	10	4
Bernardston	2,096	3	3	0
Beverly	41,303	72	68	4
Billerica	42,965	78	65	13
Blackstone	9,079	20	17	3
Bolton	5,210	13	12	1
Boston	673,880	2,678	2,125	553
Bourne	19,577	47	40	7
Boxborough	5,223	17	11	6
Boxford	8,271	11	11	0
Boylston	4,551	13	10	3
Braintree	37,673	92	77	15
Brewster	9,888	29	24	5
Brockton	95,189	208	187	21
Brookline	59,033	159	129	30
Buckland	1,857	2	2	0
Burlington	26,083	73	65	8
Cambridge	111,030	322	277	45
Canton	22,962	42	42	0
Carlisle	5,300	13	10	3
Carver	11,600	18	13	5
Charlton	13,430	22	18	4
Chatham	6,119	26	21	5
Chelmsford	35,251	64	52	12
Chelsea	40,096	119	110	9
Cheshire	3,143	1	1	0
Chicopee	56,887	136	132	4
Chilmark	926	5	5	0
Clinton	13,780	28	24	4
Cohasset	8,538	19	18	1
Concord	20,189	46	36	10
Dalton	6,642	11	10	1
Danvers	27,997	58	46	12
Dartmouth	34,630	88	70	18
Dedham	25,402	59	57	2
Deerfield	4,994	10	9	1
Dennis	13,905	52	45	7
Dighton	7,430	13	12	1
Douglas	8,741	19	15	4
Dover	6,008	17	16	1
Dracut	31,586	45	39	6
Dudley	11,558	15	14	1
Dunstable	3,471	9	8	1
East Bridgewater	14,390	23	21	2
Eastham	4,886	22	16	6
Easthampton	16,026	33	27	6
East Longmeadow	16,267	27	26	1
Easton	23,918	39	31	8
Egremont	1,207	3	3	0
Erving	1,771	5	5	0
Essex	3,675	10	9	1
Everett	46,754	110	101	9
Fairhaven	16,120	31	25	6
Fall River	88,371	265	218	47
Falmouth	31,382	59	55	4
Fitchburg	40,391	94	78	16
Foxborough	17,491	44	36	8
Framingham	71,422	158	144	14
Franklin	33,264	54	46	8
Freetown	9,199	18	18	0
Georgetown	8,623	16	12	4
Gloucester	29,836	52	47	5

Table 19. Full-Time Law Enforcement Employees, by Selected State and City, 2016—*Continued*

(Number.)

State/city	Population	Total law enforcement employees	Total officers	Total civilians
Goshen	1,073	2	2	0
Grafton	18,613	22	18	4
Granby	6,375	13	9	4
Granville	1,628	2	1	1
Great Barrington	6,870	16	15	1
Greenfield	17,456	44	34	10
Groton	11,372	25	19	6
Groveland	6,776	13	10	3
Hadley	5,372	15	11	4
Hamilton	8,181	18	13	5
Hampden	5,227	15	11	4
Hanson	10,666	25	20	5
Hardwick	4,019	4	4	0
Harwich	12,112	37	34	3
Hatfield	3,302	3	3	0
Haverhill	62,851	104	92	12
Hingham	23,204	52	50	2
Holbrook	11,047	22	21	1
Holland	2,505	2	2	0
Holliston	14,656	27	22	5
Holyoke	40,738	144	120	24
Hopedale	5,938	16	12	4
Hopkinton	16,960	32	23	9
Hudson	19,931	45	33	12
Ipswich	13,863	28	23	5
Kingston	13,378	31	24	7
Lakeville	11,417	22	17	5
Lancaster	8,150	12	11	1
Lanesboro	2,972	6	6	0
Lawrence	80,622	147	129	18
Leicester	11,355	23	18	5
Lenox	4,971	10	10	0
Leominster	41,547	83	67	16
Lexington	33,643	61	47	14
Lincoln	7,550	19	13	6
Littleton	10,074	24	18	6
Longmeadow	15,876	32	26	6
Lowell	111,027	336	239	97
Ludlow	21,484	44	38	6
Lunenburg	11,438	14	14	0
Lynn	92,443	200	181	19
Malden	61,102	114	101	13
Mansfield	23,681	48	35	13
Marblehead	20,563	39	30	9
Marion	5,098	16	16	0
Marlborough	39,899	77	65	12
Marshfield	25,696	49	46	3
Mashpee	14,122	42	35	7
Mattapoisett	6,282	19	19	0
Maynard	10,745	26	21	5
Medford	57,367	105	103	2
Medway	13,289	28	22	6
Melrose	28,070	47	47	0
Mendon	6,033	17	12	5
Merrimac	6,859	11	7	4
Methuen	49,912	111	93	18
Middleboro	24,490	47	41	6
Middleton	9,852	16	14	2
Milford	28,606	54	45	9
Millbury	13,532	24	19	5
Millville	3,228	6	5	1
Montague	8,242	16	16	0
Nahant	3,484	13	12	1
Nantucket	11,036	51	34	17
Natick	36,777	69	56	13
Needham	30,733	55	46	9
New Bedford	94,524	297	255	42
Newton	89,116	195	149	46
Norfolk	11,991	24	18	6
North Adams	13,162	34	29	5

Table 19. Full-Time Law Enforcement Employees, by Selected State and City, 2016—*Continued*

(Number.)

State/city	Population	Total law enforcement employees	Total officers	Total civilians
Northampton	28,521	69	63	6
North Andover	29,853	51	40	11
North Attleboro	29,013	58	44	14
Northborough	15,109	27	20	7
Northbridge	16,638	27	19	8
Northfield	2,984	4	4	0
North Reading	15,712	32	31	1
Norton	19,445	30	29	1
Norwell	11,030	26	21	5
Norwood	29,058	68	57	11
Orange	7,615	13	12	1
Orleans	5,810	27	22	5
Oxford	13,895	28	22	6
Palmer	12,171	26	19	7
Paxton	4,874	19	17	2
Peabody	52,501	111	92	19
Pelham	1,332	4	2	2
Pepperell	12,242	16	15	1
Petersham	1,243	2	2	0
Phillipston	1,751	2	2	0
Pittsfield	43,031	114	96	18
Plainville	9,178	24	19	5
Plymouth	59,088	134	119	15
Plympton	2,922	9	9	0
Princeton	3,465	7	6	1
Provincetown	2,959	25	19	6
Quincy	93,437	238	210	28
Randolph	33,807	61	59	2
Raynham	13,818	35	27	8
Reading	25,779	55	42	13
Rehoboth	12,033	28	23	5
Revere	53,514	107	98	9
Rochester	5,522	12	12	0
Rockport	7,222	20	16	4
Rowley	6,343	16	12	4
Royalston	1,271	1	1	0
Salem	42,888	106	100	6
Sandwich	20,312	45	35	10
Saugus	28,131	72	58	14
Scituate	18,462	38	33	5
Seekonk	15,159	39	37	2
Sharon	18,200	34	31	3
Sheffield	3,179	6	6	0
Sherborn	4,317	15	15	0
Shrewsbury	36,874	57	45	12
Somerset	18,223	37	30	7
Somerville	80,899	142	127	15
Southborough	10,048	22	17	5
Southbridge	16,819	42	36	6
South Hadley	17,748	30	25	5
Southwick	9,758	23	18	5
Spencer	11,782	21	17	4
Springfield	154,102	523	419	104
Sterling	7,993	14	13	1
Stockbridge	1,936	7	6	1
Stoneham	22,045	44	37	7
Stoughton	28,583	59	52	7
Stow	7,197	11	11	0
Sturbridge	9,520	25	19	6
Sudbury	19,035	34	25	9
Sunderland	3,652	5	5	0
Sutton	9,292	21	16	5
Swampscott	14,551	34	32	2
Swansea	16,418	36	30	6
Taunton	56,720	120	114	6
Templeton	8,169	14	9	5
Tewksbury	31,160	74	59	15
Tisbury	4,129	15	14	1
Topsfield	6,590	12	11	1
Townsend	9,585	16	15	1

Table 19. Full-Time Law Enforcement Employees, by Selected State and City, 2016—*Continued*

(Number.)

State/city	Population	Total law enforcement employees	Total officers	Total civilians
Truro	1,999	17	12	5
Tyngsboro	12,397	32	26	6
Uxbridge	13,916	23	18	5
Wakefield	27,080	46	45	1
Walpole	25,187	53	40	13
Waltham	63,613	170	143	27
Wareham	22,422	59	47	12
Watertown	34,655	71	67	4
Wayland	13,760	32	23	9
Webster	16,842	32	30	2
Wellesley	29,049	45	39	6
Wellfleet	2,737	19	13	6
Wenham	5,198	11	10	1
Westborough	18,984	31	29	2
West Brookfield	3,778	6	5	1
Westfield	41,700	88	81	7
Westford	24,103	49	45	4
Westminster	7,595	14	13	1
West Newbury	4,582	13	8	5
Weston	12,147	34	25	9
Westport	15,798	32	28	4
West Springfield	28,689	93	84	9
West Tisbury	2,927	10	9	1
Westwood	16,285	40	31	9
Weymouth	56,149	108	92	16
Whitman	14,852	27	26	1
Wilbraham	14,684	28	27	1
Williamsburg	2,466	1	1	0
Williamstown	7,591	14	11	3
Wilmington	23,667	50	48	2
Winchendon	10,727	19	14	5
Winchester	22,523	46	38	8
Winthrop	18,216	33	31	2
Woburn	39,638	80	75	5
Worcester	184,595	485	435	50
Wrentham	11,614	22	21	1
Yarmouth	23,299	73	61	12
MICHIGAN				
Adrian	20,600	30	28	2
Adrian Township	6,316	1	1	0
Akron	391	1	1	0
Albion	8,155	17	16	1
Allegan	5,086	10	9	1
Allen Park	27,284	43	40	3
Alma	9,159	16	15	1
Almont	2,734	7	6	1
Alpena	10,119	19	17	2
Ann Arbor	117,688	151	125	26
Argentine Township	6,591	6	5	1
Armada	1,747	2	2	0
Auburn Hills	22,933	53	48	5
Au Gres	853	1	1	0
Bad Axe	2,989	8	7	1
Bangor	1,843	5	5	0
Baraga	1,985	2	2	0
Baroda-Lake Township	3,774	4	4	0
Barry Township	3,413	2	2	0
Bath Township	12,552	13	12	1
Battle Creek	60,904	125	109	16
Bay City	33,725	53	49	4
Beaverton	1,044	2	2	0
Belding	5,772	8	8	0
Bellaire	1,062	3	3	0
Belleville	3,860	10	8	2
Bellevue	1,277	2	2	0
Benton Harbor	9,963	25	20	5
Benton Township	14,413	26	22	4
Berkley	15,328	34	27	7
Berrien Springs-Oronoko Township	9,085	9	8	1

Table 19. Full-Time Law Enforcement Employees, by Selected State and City, 2016—*Continued*

(Number.)

State/city	Population	Total law enforcement employees	Total officers	Total civilians
Beverly Hills	10,455	27	26	1
Big Rapids	10,389	17	16	1
Birch Run	1,465	6	5	1
Birmingham	21,012	42	32	10
Blackman Township	37,522	35	34	1
Blissfield	3,239	5	5	0
Bloomfield Hills	4,031	27	24	3
Bloomfield Township	42,313	74	54	20
Boyne City	3,785	8	7	1
Breckenridge	1,301	1	1	0
Bridgeport Township	9,993	11	10	1
Bridgman	2,251	5	5	0
Brighton	7,643	19	17	2
Bronson	2,333	4	4	0
Brown City	1,264	2	2	0
Brownstown Township	30,864	39	32	7
Buchanan	4,344	10	9	1
Buena Vista Township	8,158	10	9	1
Burton	28,563	43	40	3
Cadillac	10,372	17	15	2
Calumet	698	1	1	0
Cambridge Township	5,645	4	4	0
Canton Township	89,861	119	82	37
Capac	1,842	1	1	0
Carleton	2,335	3	2	1
Caro	4,074	7	7	0
Carrollton Township	5,781	6	6	0
Carson City	1,090	2	2	0
Caspian-Gaastra	1,190	1	1	0
Cass City	2,343	4	4	0
Cassopolis	1,721	5	5	0
Center Line	8,332	23	19	4
Central Lake	932	1	1	0
Charlevoix	2,546	8	7	1
Charlotte	9,051	18	16	2
Cheboygan	4,709	8	8	0
Chelsea	5,254	14	10	4
Chesterfield Township	44,963	55	41	14
Chikaming Township	3,090	5	5	0
Chocolay Township	5,952	5	4	1
Clare	3,071	8	8	0
Clawson	12,053	18	17	1
Clayton Township	7,156	4	4	0
Clay Township	8,844	19	16	3
Clinton	2,260	4	4	0
Clinton Township	100,514	102	93	9
Clio	2,516	4	4	0
Coldwater	10,827	20	17	3
Coleman	1,198	1	1	0
Coloma Township	6,388	10	7	3
Colon	1,156	3	3	0
Columbia Township	7,424	5	5	0
Constantine	2,062	3	3	0
Corunna	3,386	3	3	0
Covert Township	2,824	7	7	0
Croswell	2,318	6	6	0
Crystal Falls	1,404	2	2	0
Davison	4,927	7	6	1
Davison Township	19,029	20	18	2
Dearborn	94,646	246	189	57
Dearborn Heights	55,852	95	83	12
Decatur	1,759	4	4	0
Denton Township	5,358	6	6	0
Detroit	669,673	2,855	2,350	505
DeWitt Township	14,686	17	16	1
Dowagiac	5,849	15	14	1
Dryden Township	4,773	4	4	0
Dundee	4,004	2	2	0
Durand	3,317	6	6	0
East Grand Rapids	11,436	30	28	2

Part 4 — Crime in the United States, 2016 175

Table 19. Full-Time Law Enforcement Employees, by Selected State and City, 2016—*Continued*

(Number.)

State/city	Population	Total law enforcement employees	Total officers	Total civilians
East Jordan	2,376	4	4	0
East Lansing	48,451	67	54	13
Eastpointe	32,701	41	37	4
Eaton Rapids	5,226	9	8	1
Eau Claire	617	1	1	0
Ecorse	9,213	18	17	1
Elk Rapids	1,611	5	5	0
Elkton	774	2	2	0
Emmett Township	11,604	16	14	2
Erie Township	4,374	4	3	1
Escanaba	12,278	40	29	11
Essexville	3,381	8	8	0
Evart	1,853	2	2	0
Fair Haven Township	1,051	1	1	0
Farmington	10,553	24	23	1
Farmington Hills	81,649	137	100	37
Fennville	1,401	1	1	0
Fenton	11,383	18	14	4
Ferndale	20,232	48	38	10
Flat Rock	9,917	18	18	0
Flint	97,548	117	103	14
Flint Township	30,460	43	38	5
Flushing	8,028	10	10	0
Flushing Township	10,235	6	6	0
Forsyth Township	6,196	9	8	1
Fowlerville	2,898	7	6	1
Frankenmuth	5,037	7	7	0
Frankfort	1,283	3	3	0
Franklin	3,254	10	10	0
Fraser	14,667	48	37	11
Fremont	4,027	7	6	1
Fruitport Township	13,879	9	9	0
Gaines Township	6,177	1	1	0
Galesburg	2,050	4	4	0
Garden City	26,781	30	28	2
Gaylord	3,662	10	9	1
Genesee Township	20,393	14	12	2
Gerrish Township	2,922	7	7	0
Gibraltar	4,509	9	8	1
Gladstone	4,802	11	10	1
Gladwin	2,869	4	4	0
Grand Beach	278	4	4	0
Grand Blanc	7,940	19	16	3
Grand Blanc Township	36,598	46	39	7
Grand Haven	11,196	33	30	3
Grand Ledge	7,790	14	14	0
Grand Rapids	196,538	335	276	59
Grandville	16,070	26	24	2
Grant	880	1	1	0
Grayling	1,836	8	8	0
Green Oak Township	18,722	17	15	2
Greenville	8,438	19	17	2
Grosse Ile Township	10,123	23	17	6
Grosse Pointe	5,198	22	22	0
Grosse Pointe Farms	9,188	41	32	9
Grosse Pointe Park	11,160	38	33	5
Grosse Pointe Shores	2,920	17	17	0
Grosse Pointe Woods	15,699	32	27	5
Hamburg Township	21,714	18	17	1
Hampton Township	9,401	11	10	1
Hamtramck	21,929	35	30	5
Hancock	4,537	8	8	0
Harbor Beach	1,621	4	4	0
Harbor Springs	1,203	6	5	1
Harper Woods	13,764	32	28	4
Hart	2,093	4	4	0
Hartford	2,604	5	5	0
Hastings	7,274	15	13	2
Hazel Park	16,636	37	33	4
Hesperia	935	2	2	0

Table 19. Full-Time Law Enforcement Employees, by Selected State and City, 2016—*Continued*

(Number.)

State/city	Population	Total law enforcement employees	Total officers	Total civilians
Highland Park	10,810	8	7	1
Hillsdale	8,139	14	13	1
Holland	33,867	65	57	8
Holly	6,186	8	8	0
Home Township	1,350	1	1	0
Hopkins	608	1	1	0
Houghton	8,020	10	9	1
Howell	9,533	19	17	2
Hudson	2,229	2	2	0
Huntington Woods	6,360	18	16	2
Huron Township	15,622	24	18	6
Imlay City	3,569	8	8	0
Inkster	24,548	29	25	4
Ionia	11,370	18	16	2
Iron Mountain	7,482	12	12	0
Iron River	2,881	4	4	0
Ironwood	4,929	11	10	1
Ishpeming	6,485	10	9	1
Jackson	33,060	58	46	12
Jonesville	2,213	3	3	0
Kalamazoo	76,389	259	216	43
Kalamazoo Township	24,534	38	31	7
Kalkaska	2,042	4	3	1
Keego Harbor	3,040	4	4	0
Kentwood	51,897	81	68	13
Kingsford	5,057	17	17	0
Kinross Township	7,536	2	2	0
Lake Angelus	298	1	1	0
Lake Linden	985	1	1	0
Lake Odessa	2,032	3	3	0
Lake Orion	3,065	5	4	1
Lakeview	1,011	2	2	0
L'Anse	1,920	4	4	0
Lansing	115,199	213	188	25
Lansing Township	8,148	16	15	1
Lapeer	8,782	22	20	2
Lathrup Village	4,147	9	9	0
Laurium	1,933	4	4	0
Lawton	1,860	5	5	0
Lennon	499	1	1	0
Leslie	1,869	3	3	0
Lexington	1,119	3	3	0
Lincoln Park	36,808	46	40	6
Lincoln Township	14,500	12	11	1
Linden	3,811	5	5	0
Litchfield	1,343	2	2	0
Livonia	94,226	186	147	39
Lowell	3,931	6	5	1
Ludington	8,054	15	14	1
Luna Pier	1,380	2	2	0
Mackinac Island	479	5	5	0
Mackinaw City	802	6	6	0
Madison Heights	30,297	58	46	12
Madison Township	8,464	5	5	0
Mancelona	1,361	1	1	0
Manistee	6,057	12	12	0
Manistique	2,960	7	7	0
Manton	1,389	1	1	0
Marenisco Township	1,681	1	1	0
Marine City	4,124	4	4	0
Marlette	1,787	4	4	0
Marquette	21,283	37	33	4
Marshall	7,038	15	15	0
Marysville	9,722	16	14	2
Mason	8,461	13	12	1
Mattawan	1,938	5	5	0
Mayville	914	1	1	0
Melvindale	10,348	24	23	1
Mendon	859	2	2	0
Menominee	8,344	17	16	1

Table 19. Full-Time Law Enforcement Employees, by Selected State and City, 2016—*Continued*

(Number.)

State/city	Population	Total law enforcement employees	Total officers	Total civilians
Meridian Township	42,700	44	39	5
Metamora Township	4,241	4	4	0
Michiana	183	3	3	0
Midland	42,263	48	46	2
Milan	6,012	13	9	4
Milford	16,707	20	18	2
Millington	1,030	2	2	0
Monroe	19,971	43	38	5
Montague	2,362	5	5	0
Montrose Township	7,524	10	9	1
Morenci	2,181	2	2	0
Morrice	891	2	2	0
Mount Morris	2,941	4	4	0
Mount Morris Township	20,502	31	28	3
Mount Pleasant	26,069	35	29	6
Mundy Township	14,562	19	16	3
Munising	2,278	4	4	0
Muskegon	38,442	82	74	8
Muskegon Heights	10,785	23	20	3
Muskegon Township	17,791	15	14	1
Napoleon Township	6,764	12	12	0
Nashville	1,635	4	4	0
Negaunee	4,584	9	9	0
Newaygo	1,951	5	5	0
New Baltimore	12,409	18	17	1
New Buffalo	1,875	8	7	1
New Era	444	1	1	0
Niles	11,282	24	16	8
Northfield Township	8,617	11	10	1
North Muskegon	3,779	8	8	0
Northville	6,019	13	13	0
Northville Township	28,890	38	27	11
Norton Shores	24,256	31	29	2
Norway	2,789	6	6	0
Novi	59,441	84	62	22
Oak Park	29,838	61	49	12
Olivet	1,611	2	2	0
Ontwa Township-Edwardsburg	6,481	6	6	0
Orchard Lake	2,428	12	10	2
Oscoda Township	6,838	11	10	1
Otsego	3,998	7	6	1
Ovid	1,614	2	2	0
Owosso	14,605	18	17	1
Oxford	3,554	7	4	3
Paw Paw	3,441	9	8	1
Pentwater	843	3	3	0
Perry	2,088	4	4	0
Petoskey	5,731	20	19	1
Pigeon	1,158	1	1	0
Pinckney	2,439	6	6	0
Pinconning	1,264	1	1	0
Pittsfield Township	38,704	57	40	17
Plainwell	3,826	9	8	1
Pleasant Ridge	2,562	6	6	0
Plymouth	8,865	16	15	1
Plymouth Township	26,870	48	30	18
Portage	48,550	74	54	20
Port Austin	638	1	1	0
Port Huron	29,182	69	54	15
Portland	3,929	6	6	0
Potterville	2,619	4	4	0
Prairieville Township	3,409	3	2	1
Quincy	1,638	3	3	0
Raisin Township	7,577	6	5	1
Reading	1,052	1	1	0
Redford Township	47,218	65	56	9
Reed City	2,383	5	5	0
Richfield Township, Genesee County	8,315	11	9	2
Richfield Township, Roscommon County	3,628	5	4	1
Richland	793	3	3	0

(Number.)

State/city	Population	Total law enforcement employees	Total officers	Total civilians
Richland Township, Saginaw County	3,961	3	3	0
Richmond	5,882	11	9	2
River Rouge	7,480	20	18	2
Riverview	12,127	25	23	2
Rochester	13,050	28	21	7
Rockford	6,218	11	10	1
Rockwood	3,183	6	6	0
Rogers City	2,692	6	6	0
Romeo	3,630	11	8	3
Romulus	23,315	51	39	12
Roosevelt Park	3,820	5	5	0
Roseville	47,704	72	69	3
Royal Oak	59,367	93	78	15
Saginaw	48,942	61	53	8
Saginaw Township	39,421	46	41	5
Saline	9,158	17	13	4
Sandusky	2,580	6	5	1
Sault Ste. Marie	13,763	25	23	2
Schoolcraft	1,574	3	3	0
Scottville	1,213	2	2	0
Sebewaing	1,679	3	3	0
Shelby	2,010	3	3	0
Shelby Township	78,427	85	66	19
Shepherd	1,505	2	2	0
Somerset Township	4,580	3	3	0
Southfield	73,438	150	121	29
Southgate	29,158	40	36	4
South Haven	4,352	21	17	4
South Lyon	11,801	17	16	1
South Rockwood	1,635	2	2	0
Sparta	4,346	6	6	0
Spaulding Township	2,041	1	1	0
Spring Arbor Township	8,097	2	2	0
Springport Township	2,148	2	2	0
Standish	1,442	1	1	0
Stanton	1,414	1	1	0
St. Charles	1,940	2	2	0
St. Clair	5,368	7	7	0
St. Clair Shores	59,938	86	81	5
Sterling Heights	132,523	165	145	20
St. Ignace	2,376	6	5	1
St. Johns	7,916	11	10	1
St. Joseph	8,271	23	21	2
St. Joseph Township	9,850	12	11	1
St. Louis	7,212	7	6	1
Stockbridge	1,235	2	2	0
Sturgis	10,876	24	19	5
Sumpter Township	9,265	16	14	2
Swartz Creek	5,531	9	8	1
Sylvan Lake	1,798	4	4	0
Tawas	4,515	5	4	1
Taylor	61,290	90	74	16
Tecumseh	8,353	15	13	2
Thomas Township	11,505	7	7	0
Three Rivers	7,738	18	16	2
Tittabawassee Township	9,782	6	5	1
Traverse City	15,330	30	29	1
Trenton	18,294	34	33	1
Troy	83,743	149	102	47
Tuscarora Township	2,946	8	7	1
Ubly	822	1	1	0
Unadilla Township	3,405	3	3	0
Union City	1,581	5	5	0
Utica	4,980	18	14	4
Van Buren Township	28,090	55	40	15
Vassar	2,605	4	4	0
Vernon	753	1	1	0
Vicksburg	3,298	7	6	1
Walker	24,874	38	34	4
Walled Lake	7,132	6	6	0

Table 19. Full-Time Law Enforcement Employees, by Selected State and City, 2016—*Continued*

(Number.)

State/city	Population	Total law enforcement employees	Total officers	Total civilians
Warren	135,620	235	196	39
Waterford Township	73,308	70	53	17
Watervliet	1,684	3	3	0
Wayland	4,184	7	6	1
Wayne	16,989	21	21	0
West Bloomfield Township	66,123	103	70	33
West Branch	2,054	5	4	1
Westland	81,625	107	81	26
White Cloud	1,378	2	2	0
Whitehall	2,712	8	8	0
White Lake Township	31,135	36	26	10
White Pigeon	1,513	4	4	0
Williamston	3,888	6	6	0
Wixom	13,796	23	20	3
Wolverine Lake	4,397	6	6	0
Woodhaven	12,478	29	27	2
Wyandotte	25,029	46	32	14
Wyoming	75,917	102	87	15
Yale	1,896	3	3	0
Ypsilanti	20,019	34	29	5
Zeeland	5,650	11	10	1
Zilwaukee	1,562	2	2	0
MINNESOTA				
Aitkin	2,031	8	7	1
Akeley	431	1	1	0
Albany	2,661	5	4	1
Albert Lea	17,604	29	27	2
Alexandria	12,006	27	23	4
Annandale	3,317	5	5	0
Anoka	17,389	38	28	10
Appleton	1,328	3	3	0
Apple Valley	51,648	60	52	8
Arlington	2,157	3	2	1
Ashby	428	1	1	0
Atwater	1,122	2	2	0
Austin	24,529	36	33	3
Avon	1,481	4	3	1
Babbitt	1,528	4	4	0
Barnesville	2,581	5	5	0
Baudette	1,055	2	2	0
Baxter	7,993	15	14	1
Bayport	3,763	5	5	0
Becker	4,730	7	6	1
Belgrade/Brooten	1,504	2	2	0
Belle Plaine	6,968	11	9	2
Bemidji	14,690	35	33	2
Benson	3,045	8	7	1
Big Lake	10,421	14	12	2
Blackduck	778	2	2	0
Blaine	63,115	70	59	11
Blooming Prairie	1,993	3	3	0
Bloomington	87,134	148	118	30
Blue Earth	3,216	5	5	0
Bovey	813	2	2	0
Braham	1,765	3	3	0
Brainerd	13,327	29	23	6
Breckenridge	3,270	6	6	0
Breezy Point	2,356	7	6	1
Breitung Township	607	2	2	0
Brooklyn Center	30,893	60	48	12
Brooklyn Park	79,800	133	103	30
Brownton	734	1	1	0
Buffalo	16,134	21	18	3
Buffalo Lake	682	2	2	0
Burnsville	61,697	83	74	9
Caledonia	2,772	5	4	1
Cambridge	8,515	16	15	1
Canby	1,693	3	3	0
Cannon Falls	4,057	10	8	2

Table 19. Full-Time Law Enforcement Employees, by Selected State and City, 2016—*Continued*

(Number.)

State/city	Population	Total law enforcement employees	Total officers	Total civilians
Centennial Lakes	10,937	18	16	2
Champlin	24,048	31	26	5
Chaska	25,483	28	25	3
Chisholm	4,983	13	12	1
Clara City	1,312	2	2	0
Cloquet	12,064	24	22	2
Cold Spring/Richmond	5,547	10	9	1
Coleraine	2,005	2	2	0
Columbia Heights	19,754	32	26	6
Coon Rapids	62,380	70	63	7
Corcoran	5,586	9	8	1
Cottage Grove	36,164	48	41	7
Crookston	7,765	17	15	2
Crosby	2,336	7	7	0
Crosslake	2,222	5	5	0
Crystal	23,102	35	31	4
Danube	463	1	1	0
Dawson/Boyd	1,590	3	3	0
Dayton	5,185	7	6	1
Deephaven	3,880	8	7	1
Deer River	934	4	4	0
Detroit Lakes	9,075	17	15	2
Dilworth	4,437	7	6	1
Duluth	86,090	183	149	34
Eagan	66,698	83	70	13
Eagle Lake	2,933	2	2	0
East Grand Forks	8,649	25	23	2
East Range	3,665	8	8	0
Eden Prairie	64,037	93	67	26
Eden Valley	1,035	1	1	0
Edina	50,577	72	51	21
Elbow Lake	1,138	2	2	0
Elko New Market	4,831	4	4	0
Elk River	24,150	42	32	10
Elmore	632	1	1	0
Ely	3,398	8	7	1
Eveleth	3,665	11	10	1
Fairfax	1,160	2	2	0
Fairmont	10,137	19	16	3
Faribault	23,708	41	34	7
Farmington	23,060	27	24	3
Fergus Falls	13,312	28	23	5
Floodwood	521	4	3	1
Forest Lake	19,867	27	25	2
Fountain	408	1	1	0
Fridley	27,811	45	41	4
Fulda	1,229	2	2	0
Gaylord	2,233	4	4	0
Gilbert	1,791	7	7	0
Glencoe	5,495	9	8	1
Glenwood	2,571	6	5	1
Golden Valley	21,454	41	31	10
Goodview	4,168	5	4	1
Grand Rapids	11,181	23	20	3
Granite Falls	2,719	6	5	1
Hallock	948	1	1	0
Hastings	22,627	32	28	4
Hawley	2,203	4	4	0
Hector	1,062	2	2	0
Hermantown	9,761	19	16	3
Hibbing	16,176	29	26	3
Hill City	594	1	1	0
Hokah	556	1	1	0
Hopkins	18,169	36	27	9
Houston	964	2	2	0
Howard Lake	2,052	3	3	0
Hutchinson	13,867	34	22	12
International Falls	6,107	12	11	1
Inver Grove Heights	35,049	44	39	5
Isanti	5,493	10	9	1

Table 19. Full-Time Law Enforcement Employees, by Selected State and City, 2016—*Continued*

(Number.)

State/city	Population	Total law enforcement employees	Total officers	Total civilians
Isle	790	3	3	0
Janesville	2,253	3	3	0
Jordan	6,203	11	9	2
Kasson	6,157	9	8	1
Keewatin	1,046	2	2	0
Kimball	777	3	3	0
La Crescent	4,820	8	7	1
Lake City	5,021	11	10	1
Lake Crystal	2,522	3	3	0
Lakefield	1,648	3	3	0
Lakes Area	9,322	15	13	2
Lake Shore	1,026	2	2	0
Lakeville	61,581	64	55	9
Lamberton	785	1	1	0
Lester Prairie	1,678	3	3	0
Le Sueur	3,988	8	7	1
Lewiston	1,562	2	2	0
Lino Lakes	21,212	30	27	3
Litchfield	6,643	10	9	1
Little Falls	8,611	16	14	2
Long Prairie	3,325	6	6	0
Lonsdale	3,873	9	8	1
Madelia	2,240	4	4	0
Madison Lake	1,110	2	2	0
Mankato	41,300	65	56	9
Maple Grove	69,783	79	66	13
Mapleton	1,726	3	3	0
Maplewood	41,071	55	50	5
Marshall	13,645	25	21	4
Medina	6,216	11	10	1
Melrose	3,620	5	4	1
Menahga	1,346	3	3	0
Mendota Heights	11,252	18	17	1
Milaca	2,871	5	4	1
Minneapolis	416,751	1,018	847	171
Minneota	1,357	1	1	0
Minnesota Lake	654	1	1	0
Minnetonka	52,055	69	52	17
Minnetrista	9,675	15	13	2
Montevideo	5,184	11	10	1
Montgomery	2,907	5	4	1
Moorhead	42,507	72	56	16
Moose Lake	2,747	5	4	1
Morris	5,367	10	8	2
Mounds View	13,063	20	18	2
Mountain Lake	2,119	4	4	0
Nashwauk	965	3	3	0
New Brighton	22,521	33	28	5
New Hope	21,168	43	34	9
New Prague	7,631	12	10	2
New Richland	1,185	1	1	0
New Ulm	13,293	25	22	3
North Branch	10,233	13	11	2
Northfield	20,445	27	22	5
North Mankato	13,553	15	14	1
North St. Paul	12,495	19	17	2
Oakdale	28,211	38	32	6
Oak Park Heights	4,912	11	10	1
Olivia	2,333	4	4	0
Onamia	861	3	3	0
Orono	19,799	31	27	4
Ortonville	1,796	4	4	0
Osakis	1,715	3	3	0
Osseo	2,817	6	5	1
Ostrander	254	1	1	0
Owatonna	25,760	39	36	3
Park Rapids	3,963	10	9	1
Paynesville	2,434	5	5	0
Pequot Lakes	2,259	6	5	1
Pike Bay	1,635	3	3	0

(Number.)

State/city	Population	Total law enforcement employees	Total officers	Total civilians
Pine River	923	3	3	0
Plainview	3,217	8	7	1
Plymouth	76,996	88	72	16
Preston	1,294	3	3	0
Princeton	4,668	13	11	2
Prior Lake	25,767	28	25	3
Proctor	3,070	8	7	1
Ramsey	26,273	27	24	3
Red Wing	16,442	32	27	5
Redwood Falls	5,024	13	11	2
Renville	1,199	3	3	0
Richfield	36,410	50	42	8
Robbinsdale	14,510	28	24	4
Rochester	113,306	193	137	56
Rogers	12,847	21	18	3
Roseau	2,735	6	5	1
Rosemount	23,717	25	22	3
Roseville	35,954	56	48	8
Rushford	1,709	3	3	0
Sartell	16,943	21	18	3
Sauk Centre	4,367	7	6	1
Sauk Rapids	13,545	17	16	1
Savage	31,118	40	32	8
Shakopee	40,524	56	47	9
Silver Bay	1,799	5	5	0
Silver Lake	807	2	2	0
Slayton	2,035	4	4	0
Sleepy Eye	3,414	7	7	0
South Lake Minnetonka	12,247	16	13	3
South St. Paul	20,452	31	28	3
Springfield	2,052	5	5	0
Spring Grove	1,286	2	2	0
Spring Lake Park	6,484	13	11	2
St. Anthony	9,150	26	23	3
Staples	2,867	7	6	1
Starbuck	1,258	4	4	0
St. Charles	3,703	5	5	0
St. Cloud	67,341	132	105	27
St. Francis	7,442	12	10	2
Stillwater	19,051	24	20	4
St. James	4,441	8	7	1
St. Joseph	6,924	9	8	1
St. Louis Park	48,770	67	53	14
St. Paul	303,920	796	627	169
St. Paul Park	5,399	9	9	0
St. Peter	11,763	18	13	5
Thief River Falls	8,776	18	16	2
Tracy	2,108	3	3	0
Tri-City	1,425	3	3	0
Two Harbors	3,546	9	8	1
Virginia	8,564	21	21	0
Wabasha	2,437	8	7	1
Wadena	4,194	9	8	1
Waite Park	7,551	19	16	3
Walker	925	3	3	0
Warroad	1,804	5	4	1
Waseca	9,207	18	16	2
Wayzata	6,627	14	13	1
Wells	2,231	4	4	0
West Concord	772	1	1	0
West Hennepin	5,575	11	9	2
West St. Paul	19,762	32	29	3
Wheaton	1,351	3	3	0
White Bear Lake	25,484	37	28	9
Willmar	19,641	36	32	4
Windom	4,532	10	9	1
Winnebago	1,368	3	3	0
Winona	27,001	42	38	4
Winsted	2,285	4	4	0
Woodbury	69,032	79	67	12

Table 19. Full-Time Law Enforcement Employees, by Selected State and City, 2016—*Continued*

(Number.)

State/city	Population	Total law enforcement employees	Total officers	Total civilians
Worthington	13,151	34	22	12
Wyoming	7,816	11	10	1
Zumbrota	3,385	5	5	0
MISSISSIPPI				
Aberdeen	5,358	18	13	5
Ackerman	1,472	5	5	0
Amory	7,022	28	21	7
Biloxi	45,952	177	127	50
Byhalia	1,247	13	10	3
Byram	11,511	38	27	11
D'Iberville	11,795	38	36	2
Florence	4,407	23	15	8
Fulton	4,101	10	10	0
Gautier	18,566	47	36	11
Gulfport	72,668	207	153	54
Hernando	15,793	43	33	10
Horn Lake	27,077	67	50	17
Jackson	170,070	641	409	232
Laurel	18,894	73	51	22
Madison	26,119	86	67	19
McComb	12,632	57	33	24
Meridian	39,364	102	78	24
Ocean Springs	17,688	53	38	15
Oxford	23,052	81	68	13
Pascagoula	22,091	90	62	28
Pass Christian	5,690	23	20	3
Petal	10,747	31	26	5
Picayune	10,631	50	34	16
Ridgeland	24,406	89	62	27
Summit	1,677	8	7	1
Waveland	6,382	18	18	0
Wiggins	4,577	21	16	5
MISSOURI				
Adrian	1,611	3	3	0
Advance	1,369	3	3	0
Anderson	1,980	6	6	0
Annapolis	343	1	1	0
Arbyrd	482	1	1	0
Archie	1,205	3	3	0
Arnold	21,461	55	48	7
Ash Grove	1,465	5	5	0
Ashland	3,895	7	6	1
Aurora	7,471	24	17	7
Ava	2,924	12	7	5
Ballwin	30,609	59	48	11
Bates City	219	1	1	0
Battlefield	6,083	8	8	0
Bella Villa	739	4	4	0
Bellefontaine Neighbors	10,788	29	26	3
Bel-Nor	1,479	6	6	0
Bel-Ridge	2,719	13	12	1
Belton	23,170	58	41	17
Berkeley	9,063	35	27	8
Bertrand	786	1	1	0
Bethany	3,122	5	5	0
Billings	1,092	4	4	0
Birch Tree	658	1	1	0
Bismarck	1,491	3	3	0
Bloomfield	1,897	5	5	0
Blue Springs	54,445	141	98	43
Bolivar	10,790	27	21	6
Bonne Terre	7,175	11	11	0
Boonville	8,423	27	21	6
Bourbon	1,620	4	4	0
Bowling Green	5,400	11	8	3
Branson	11,593	58	43	15
Branson West	434	7	7	0
Braymer	842	1	1	0

Table 19. Full-Time Law Enforcement Employees, by Selected State and City, 2016—*Continued*

(Number.)

State/city	Population	Total law enforcement employees	Total officers	Total civilians
Breckenridge Hills	4,709	16	15	1
Brentwood	8,058	29	27	2
Bridgeton	11,835	60	49	11
Brookfield	4,324	17	10	7
Bucklin	442	1	1	0
Buckner	3,065	9	8	1
Buffalo	3,031	7	6	1
Butler	4,067	14	9	5
Butterfield Village	464	1	1	0
Cabool	2,126	11	7	4
California	4,415	9	8	1
Calverton Park	1,287	7	7	0
Camdenton	3,907	18	15	3
Cameron	9,817	23	16	7
Campbell	1,908	3	3	0
Canton	2,391	5	4	1
Cape Girardeau	39,738	118	81	37
Cardwell	682	2	2	0
Carl Junction	7,780	16	11	5
Carrollton	3,610	8	8	0
Carterville	1,843	5	5	0
Carthage	14,300	36	27	9
Caruthersville	5,887	19	19	0
Cassville	3,311	11	11	0
Center	505	1	1	0
Centralia	4,226	14	9	5
Charleston	5,797	19	14	5
Chesterfield	47,939	100	90	10
Chillicothe	9,495	22	14	8
Claycomo	1,475	9	9	0
Clayton	15,873	57	49	8
Cleveland	663	2	1	1
Clever	2,592	4	4	0
Clinton	8,878	23	22	1
Cole Camp	1,101	2	2	0
Columbia	121,143	182	150	32
Concordia	2,378	6	6	0
Conway	774	1	1	0
Cottleville	5,151	12	10	2
Country Club Village	2,465	2	2	0
Crane	1,337	1	1	0
Crestwood	11,977	32	26	6
Creve Coeur	18,367	54	48	6
Crocker	1,061	4	4	0
Crystal City	4,845	22	16	6
Crystal Lakes	346	2	1	1
Cuba	3,380	14	13	1
Delta	440	1	1	0
Desloge	4,916	11	11	0
De Soto	6,512	19	14	5
Des Peres	8,611	51	40	11
Dexter	8,014	23	18	5
Diamond	930	2	2	0
Dixon	1,486	10	6	4
Doniphan	1,990	11	8	3
Doolittle	600	1	1	0
Drexel	954	2	2	0
Duenweg	1,300	3	3	0
Duquesne	1,730	10	9	1
East Prairie	3,150	9	6	3
Edina	1,095	1	1	0
Edmundson	838	11	10	1
Eldon	4,646	15	14	1
El Dorado Springs	3,559	12	7	5
Ellisville	9,318	24	23	1
Ellsinore	448	2	2	0
Elsberry	1,996	3	3	0
Essex	457	1	1	0
Eureka	10,681	25	21	4
Excelsior Springs	11,562	35	24	11

Table 19. Full-Time Law Enforcement Employees, by Selected State and City, 2016—*Continued*

(Number.)

State/city	Population	Total law enforcement employees	Total officers	Total civilians
Exeter	775	1	1	0
Fair Grove	1,472	5	5	0
Fair Play	464	1	1	0
Farmington	18,564	34	26	8
Fayette	2,705	7	7	0
Ferguson	21,032	47	39	8
Ferrelview	464	1	1	0
Festus	12,157	35	25	10
Florissant	52,266	108	85	23
Fordland	818	2	2	0
Foristell	523	6	6	0
Forsyth	2,446	7	6	1
Fredericktown	4,097	13	11	2
Frontenac	3,872	21	20	1
Fulton	12,973	33	27	6
Gallatin	1,736	1	1	0
Garden City	1,621	4	4	0
Gerald	1,313	5	5	0
Gideon	1,031	2	2	0
Gladstone	27,138	58	43	15
Glendale	5,928	14	11	3
Goodman	1,230	2	2	0
Gower	1,496	3	3	0
Grain Valley	13,484	25	21	4
Granby	2,127	5	5	0
Grandview	25,412	60	51	9
Greenfield	1,306	4	4	0
Greenwood	5,641	9	9	0
Hamilton	1,692	4	4	0
Hannibal	17,825	48	37	11
Hardin	537	1	1	0
Harrisonville	9,975	29	21	8
Hartville	592	2	2	0
Hayti	2,759	10	9	1
Hazelwood	25,655	78	67	11
Herculaneum	4,030	12	11	1
Hermann	2,365	12	7	5
Higginsville	4,638	15	9	6
Highlandville	967	2	2	0
Hillsboro	3,121	9	7	2
Hillsdale	1,520	12	11	1
Holcomb	602	2	2	0
Holden	2,265	6	5	1
Hollister	4,515	19	13	6
Hornersville	630	3	3	0
Houston	2,081	6	6	0
Howardville	364	3	1	2
Humansville	1,036	1	1	0
Huntsville	1,516	1	1	0
Iberia	745	3	3	0
Independence	117,335	257	184	73
Indian Point	511	2	2	0
Iron Mountain Lake	713	1	1	0
Ironton	1,379	3	3	0
Jackson	15,092	31	23	8
Jasper	927	10	10	0
Jefferson City	43,171	125	88	37
Jonesburg	722	1	1	0
Joplin	52,001	146	102	44
Kahoka	2,013	3	3	0
Kansas City	478,364	1,875	1,356	519
Kearney	9,629	18	17	1
Kennett	10,610	30	22	8
Kimberling City	2,290	7	6	1
Kinloch	299	10	4	6
Kirksville	17,521	28	25	3
Kirkwood	27,793	75	61	14
Knob Noster	2,771	12	7	5
Laddonia	510	1	1	0
Ladue	8,612	32	26	6

State/city	Population	Total law enforcement employees	Total officers	Total civilians
La Grange	941	4	4	0
Lake Lotawana	2,029	8	6	2
Lake Ozark	1,795	17	11	6
Lakeshire	1,427	4	4	0
Lake St. Louis	15,534	40	31	9
Lake Tapawingo	723	3	3	0
Lake Waukomis	908	2	2	0
Lake Winnebago	1,146	5	5	0
Lamar	4,330	13	11	2
Lanagan	410	3	3	0
La Plata	1,330	3	3	0
Lathrop	2,042	10	10	0
Laurie	929	5	5	0
Lawson	2,397	6	5	1
Leadington	457	5	4	1
Leadwood	1,227	5	5	0
Lebanon	14,721	41	29	12
Lee's Summit	95,821	193	139	54
Leeton	562	1	1	0
Lexington	4,573	10	9	1
Liberal	714	1	1	0
Liberty	30,699	54	40	14
Licking	3,113	5	5	0
Lilbourn	1,126	2	2	0
Lincoln	1,169	3	3	0
Linn	1,423	4	4	0
Linn Creek	244	1	1	0
Lone Jack	1,139	6	6	0
Louisiana	3,284	11	5	6
Macon	5,427	12	10	2
Malden	4,092	16	14	2
Manchester	18,256	42	39	3
Mansfield	1,254	5	5	0
Maplewood	7,931	34	31	3
Marceline	2,139	8	7	1
Marionville	2,181	3	3	0
Marshall	13,031	33	26	7
Marshfield	7,230	11	10	1
Marston	472	1	1	0
Marthasville	1,155	2	2	0
Maryland Heights	27,374	95	78	17
Maryville	11,855	24	20	4
Matthews	628	2	2	0
Maysville	1,090	1	1	0
Memphis	1,831	3	3	0
Merriam Woods	1,764	2	2	0
Mexico	11,691	34	32	2
Milan	1,831	4	4	0
Miller	684	8	8	0
Miner	956	12	7	5
Moberly	13,900	38	27	11
Moline Acres	2,428	7	6	1
Monett	9,006	23	20	3
Monroe City	2,432	8	8	0
Montgomery City	2,714	5	5	0
Morehouse	916	2	2	0
Moscow Mills	2,585	5	5	0
Mound City	1,040	2	2	0
Mountain Grove	4,662	14	11	3
Mountain View	2,662	8	8	0
Mount Vernon	4,531	11	11	0
Neosho	12,218	27	25	2
Nevada	8,230	23	19	4
Newburg	448	2	2	0
New Florence	720	1	1	0
New Franklin	1,081	5	4	1
New Haven	2,097	7	7	0
New London	967	1	1	0
New Madrid	2,988	8	8	0
Nixa	21,377	35	29	6

Table 19. Full-Time Law Enforcement Employees, by Selected State and City, 2016—*Continued*

(Number.)

State/city	Population	Total law enforcement employees	Total officers	Total civilians
Noel	1,822	3	3	0
Normandy	7,618	32	31	1
North Kansas City	4,387	45	34	11
Northwoods	4,187	20	18	2
Oak Grove	7,956	16	15	1
Oakland	1,382	75	61	14
Oakview Village	394	3	3	0
O'Fallon	86,093	151	117	34
Olivette	7,893	24	22	2
Oregon	763	1	1	0
Oronogo	2,433	5	5	0
Orrick	804	3	3	0
Osage Beach	4,449	37	24	13
Osceola	909	3	3	0
Overland	15,940	58	42	16
Owensville	2,616	6	6	0
Ozark	19,366	37	33	4
Pacific	7,192	25	19	6
Pagedale	3,312	6	5	1
Palmyra	3,617	8	7	1
Park Hills	8,676	16	15	1
Parkville	6,450	18	17	1
Peculiar	4,937	10	9	1
Perry	696	1	1	0
Perryville	8,431	30	25	5
Pevely	5,682	20	14	6
Piedmont	1,976	7	7	0
Pierce City	1,277	4	4	0
Pilot Grove	760	1	1	0
Pilot Knob	707	2	2	0
Pineville	784	5	5	0
Platte City	4,859	11	10	1
Platte Woods	403	1	1	0
Plattsburg	2,286	6	6	0
Pleasant Hill	8,320	20	14	6
Pleasant Hope	614	1	1	0
Pleasant Valley	3,074	15	10	5
Polo	533	1	1	0
Poplar Bluff	17,309	63	48	15
Potosi	2,637	10	9	1
Purdy	1,103	2	2	0
Queen City	592	1	1	0
Qulin	452	1	1	0
Raymore	20,600	41	29	12
Raytown	29,377	72	53	19
Republic	16,219	27	22	5
Rich Hill	1,325	3	3	0
Richland	1,815	7	6	1
Richmond	5,558	13	11	2
Richmond Heights	8,466	40	39	1
Risco	325	1	1	0
Riverside	3,192	33	24	9
Riverview	2,831	10	10	0
Rockaway Beach	871	2	2	0
Rock Hill	4,648	11	10	1
Rock Port	1,217	3	3	0
Rogersville	3,436	8	7	1
Rolla	20,093	57	35	22
Salem	4,998	17	12	5
Salisbury	1,550	5	4	1
Savannah	5,115	7	6	1
Scott City	4,518	17	12	5
Sedalia	21,536	64	46	18
Seligman	838	3	2	1
Senath	1,700	3	3	0
Seneca	2,409	4	4	0
Seymour	1,975	3	3	0
Shelbina	1,627	6	5	1
Shrewsbury	6,197	22	20	2
Sikeston	16,455	75	63	12

(Number.)

State/city	Population	Total law enforcement employees	Total officers	Total civilians
Silex	309	1	1	0
Slater	1,827	5	4	1
Smithville	9,403	16	16	0
Southwest City	956	3	3	0
Sparta	1,798	1	1	0
Springfield	168,307	418	344	74
St. Ann	12,925	56	42	14
St. Charles	69,364	152	110	42
Steele	2,091	5	5	0
Steelville	1,711	6	6	0
Ste. Genevieve	4,486	10	10	0
St. James	4,130	10	9	1
St. John	6,454	24	22	2
St. Joseph	76,577	169	125	44
St. Louis	314,507	1,632	1,194	438
St. Marys	345	1	1	0
Stover	1,070	3	3	0
St. Peters	57,835	113	89	24
Strafford	2,366	7	7	0
St. Robert	6,112	22	16	6
Sturgeon	914	2	2	0
Sugar Creek	3,315	22	17	5
Sullivan	7,143	25	18	7
Summersville	500	2	2	0
Sunset Hills	8,548	33	26	7
Sweet Springs	1,463	3	3	0
Tarkio	1,459	3	3	0
Thayer	2,248	11	7	4
Town and Country	11,158	32	30	2
Trenton	5,874	16	10	6
Troy	11,730	26	24	2
Truesdale	730	1	1	0
Union	11,092	25	23	2
University City	35,002	96	68	28
Urbana	405	2	2	0
Velda City	1,400	11	10	1
Verona	601	1	1	0
Versailles	2,432	10	10	0
Viburnum	656	2	2	0
Vienna	594	1	1	0
Vinita Park	1,887	55	53	2
Walnut Grove	787	3	3	0
Warrensburg	20,136	38	35	3
Warrenton	8,147	22	20	2
Warsaw	2,093	7	7	0
Warson Woods	1,957	8	8	0
Washington	14,065	33	30	3
Waverly	819	1	1	0
Waynesville	5,467	13	12	1
Weatherby Lake	1,872	5	5	0
Webb City	11,192	26	22	4
Webster Groves	23,216	47	45	2
Wellsville	1,138	2	2	0
Wentzville	36,938	84	63	21
West Plains	12,334	32	28	4
Wheaton	699	2	2	0
Willard	5,485	13	12	1
Willow Springs	2,142	7	6	1
Winfield	1,439	3	3	0
Winona	1,305	8	4	4
Woodson Terrace	4,074	19	17	2
Wright City	3,511	12	11	1
MONTANA				
Baker	2,063	5	5	0
Belgrade	8,146	18	15	3
Billings	111,447	176	148	28
Boulder	1,213	3	3	0
Bozeman	44,739	70	62	8
Bridger	733	2	2	0

Table 19. Full-Time Law Enforcement Employees, by Selected State and City, 2016—*Continued*

(Number.)

State/city	Population	Total law enforcement employees	Total officers	Total civilians
Chinook	1,233	4	4	0
Colstrip	2,359	11	7	4
Columbia Falls	5,175	9	9	0
Columbus	2,072	5	4	1
Conrad	2,594	5	5	0
Cut Bank	3,023	8	7	1
Deer Lodge	2,938	7	6	1
Dillon	4,224	9	8	1
East Helena	2,065	5	5	0
Ennis	895	1	1	0
Fort Benton	1,459	4	4	0
Fromberg	445	1	1	0
Glasgow	3,442	11	8	3
Glendive	5,608	13	9	4
Great Falls	59,717	130	88	42
Hamilton	4,659	15	14	1
Havre	9,896	27	21	6
Helena	31,052	70	48	22
Hot Springs	548	2	2	0
Kalispell	22,470	48	38	10
Laurel	6,986	17	13	4
Libby	2,646	6	6	0
Livingston	7,364	12	12	0
Manhattan	1,656	3	3	0
Miles City	8,878	16	16	0
Missoula	71,860	130	104	26
Plains	1,053	3	3	0
Polson	4,744	16	15	1
Red Lodge	2,242	7	6	1
Ronan City	1,998	5	5	0
Sidney	7,190	11	11	0
Stevensville	1,940	3	3	0
Thompson Falls	1,334	4	4	0
Troy	876	4	4	0
West Yellowstone	1,353	12	6	6
Whitefish	7,226	19	16	3
Wolf Point	2,901	8	7	1
NEBRASKA				
Albion	1,577	3	3	0
Alliance	8,533	21	14	7
Ashland	2,577	5	4	1
Aurora	4,499	9	8	1
Bayard	1,136	4	4	0
Beatrice	12,340	35	22	13
Bellevue	56,294	108	92	16
Bennington	1,712	2	2	0
Blair	7,969	19	17	2
Broken Bow	3,551	6	5	1
Central City	2,876	6	5	1
Chadron	5,761	21	15	6
Columbus	22,911	49	33	16
Crete	7,047	13	12	1
Emerson	814	2	2	0
Fairbury	3,718	7	6	1
Falls City	4,173	13	9	4
Fremont	26,490	42	37	5
Gering	8,297	18	16	2
Gothenburg	3,503	6	5	1
Grand Island	51,980	102	85	17
Hastings	24,872	53	39	14
Holdrege	5,575	16	10	6
Imperial	2,054	4	4	0
Kearney	33,471	69	56	13
Kimball	2,388	4	4	0
La Vista	16,973	39	34	5
Lexington	10,044	23	21	2
Lincoln	281,138	465	327	138
Lyons	808	2	2	0
Madison	2,365	4	3	1

(Number.)

State/city	Population	Total law enforcement employees	Total officers	Total civilians
Milford	2,110	4	4	0
Minatare	796	2	2	0
Minden	3,023	5	5	0
Mitchell	1,658	4	4	0
Neligh	1,513	3	3	0
Norfolk	24,389	57	40	17
North Platte	24,092	65	40	25
Ogallala	4,538	10	9	1
Omaha	446,163	926	798	128
O'Neill	3,642	8	7	1
Ord	2,051	3	3	0
Plainview	1,216	3	3	0
Plattsmouth	6,454	17	14	3
Ralston	6,003	16	14	2
Randolph	916	1	1	0
Schuyler	6,160	10	8	2
Scottsbluff	14,747	35	30	5
Scribner	844	2	2	0
Sidney	6,983	16	14	2
St. Paul	2,369	4	4	0
Superior	1,869	4	4	0
Tekamah	1,727	4	4	0
Tilden	936	1	1	0
Valentine	2,857	6	5	1
Wahoo	4,508	6	6	0
Walthill	776	1	1	0
Waterloo	1,086	3	3	0
Wayne	5,549	11	7	4
West Point	3,367	7	6	1
Wilber	1,873	3	3	0
Wymore	1,406	3	3	0
York	7,885	22	16	6
NEVADA				
Boulder City	15,661	41	30	11
Carlin	2,291	7	6	1
Elko	20,687	44	37	7
Fallon	8,433	33	22	11
Henderson	291,584	588	350	238
Las Vegas Metropolitan Police Department	1,592,178	4,855	3,326	1,529
Lovelock	1,876	5	4	1
Mesquite	17,969	47	34	13
North Las Vegas	238,554	414	268	146
Reno	244,554	375	311	64
Sparks	97,269	156	110	46
West Wendover	4,271	23	13	10
Winnemucca	7,978	25	22	3
Yerington	3,067	6	5	1
NEW HAMPSHIRE				
Alexandria	1,625	2	2	0
Alstead	1,911	2	2	0
Alton	5,338	14	12	2
Amherst	11,272	24	18	6
Antrim	2,662	6	5	1
Ashland	2,055	5	5	0
Atkinson	6,817	7	6	1
Auburn	5,368	10	8	2
Barnstead	4,615	5	5	0
Barrington	8,894	11	10	1
Bedford	22,407	47	34	13
Belmont	7,315	19	16	3
Bennington	1,471	2	2	0
Berlin	9,241	31	22	9
Bethlehem	2,558	5	5	0
Boscawen	3,950	8	7	1
Bow	7,779	12	10	2
Bradford	1,664	3	3	0
Brentwood	4,786	6	6	0
Bristol	3,076	10	9	1

Table 19. Full-Time Law Enforcement Employees, by Selected State and City, 2016—*Continued*

(Number.)

State/city	Population	Total law enforcement employees	Total officers	Total civilians
Brookline	5,256	9	8	1
Campton	3,300	8	7	1
Candia	3,905	7	6	1
Canterbury	2,401	2	2	0
Carroll	745	4	4	0
Center Harbor	1,099	3	3	0
Charlestown	4,969	8	5	3
Chester	4,962	7	6	1
Claremont	12,913	24	19	5
Colebrook	2,167	5	5	0
Concord	42,610	89	78	11
Conway	9,915	33	23	10
Danville	4,466	7	6	1
Deerfield	4,436	7	6	1
Deering	1,924	2	2	0
Derry	33,249	64	51	13
Dover	31,054	73	50	23
Dublin	1,541	4	3	1
Dunbarton	2,799	4	4	0
Durham	17,078	23	20	3
Effingham	1,533	2	2	0
Enfield	4,544	8	7	1
Epping	6,927	17	16	1
Epsom	4,654	6	5	1
Exeter	14,635	36	27	9
Farmington	6,841	15	14	1
Fitzwilliam	2,328	3	3	0
Franconia	1,120	3	3	0
Franklin	8,446	27	19	8
Freedom	1,486	2	2	0
Fremont	4,648	5	4	1
Gilford	7,182	24	18	6
Gilmanton	3,780	6	5	1
Goffstown	18,000	41	29	12
Gorham	2,622	10	7	3
Grantham	2,953	5	4	1
Greenland	3,943	7	7	0
Hampstead	8,588	8	8	0
Hampton	15,358	43	34	9
Hampton Falls	2,303	4	4	0
Hancock	1,635	3	3	0
Hanover	11,430	30	19	11
Haverhill	4,641	9	8	1
Henniker	4,934	9	8	1
Hillsborough	5,974	19	13	6
Hinsdale	3,876	8	7	1
Holderness	2,095	5	5	0
Hollis	7,814	15	14	1
Hooksett	14,232	36	25	11
Hopkinton	5,614	7	7	0
Hudson	24,997	65	48	17
Jackson	814	1	1	0
Jaffrey	5,270	12	11	1
Keene	23,244	55	41	14
Kensington	2,133	5	4	1
Kingston	6,144	9	8	1
Laconia	16,300	48	38	10
Lancaster	3,322	9	7	2
Lebanon	13,668	44	31	13
Lee	4,403	8	7	1
Lincoln	1,721	14	9	5
Lisbon	1,569	3	3	0
Litchfield	8,482	13	11	2
Littleton	5,905	13	10	3
Londonderry	25,439	70	56	14
Loudon	5,455	8	7	1
Lyndeborough	1,706	1	1	0
Madison	2,521	4	4	0
Manchester	110,353	288	231	57
Marlborough	2,064	2	2	0

(Number.)

State/city	Population	Total law enforcement employees	Total officers	Total civilians
Meredith	6,396	18	14	4
Merrimack	25,675	52	40	12
Middleton	1,788	3	3	0
Milford	15,317	30	25	5
Milton	4,583	9	8	1
Mont Vernon	2,485	3	3	0
Moultonborough	4,008	10	10	0
Nashua	88,252	235	174	61
New Boston	5,524	8	7	1
Newbury	2,184	4	4	0
New Durham	2,662	4	4	0
Newfields	1,700	4	4	0
New Hampton	2,215	6	6	0
Newington	777	11	10	1
New Ipswich	5,212	6	5	1
New London	4,678	13	8	5
Newmarket	8,911	19	12	7
Newport	6,337	17	12	5
Newton	4,927	8	7	1
Northfield	4,805	10	9	1
North Hampton	4,435	12	11	1
Northumberland	2,145	3	3	0
Northwood	4,281	9	8	1
Nottingham	4,977	6	5	1
Orford	1,246	1	1	0
Ossipee	4,229	10	9	1
Pelham	13,384	28	20	8
Pembroke	7,118	11	9	2
Peterborough	6,469	13	11	2
Pittsfield	4,068	6	6	0
Plainfield	2,350	3	3	0
Plaistow	7,612	22	15	7
Plymouth	6,639	18	12	6
Portsmouth	21,612	79	60	19
Raymond	10,324	23	15	8
Rindge	5,822	8	7	1
Rochester	30,096	68	55	13
Rollinsford	2,527	4	4	0
Rye	5,396	10	9	1
Salem	28,949	77	63	14
Sanbornton	2,979	7	6	1
Sandown	6,348	7	7	0
Sandwich	1,307	2	2	0
Seabrook	8,804	34	27	7
Somersworth	11,757	32	26	6
South Hampton	809	2	2	0
Springfield	1,313	2	2	0
Strafford	4,090	5	5	0
Stratham	7,403	11	10	1
Sugar Hill	567	1	1	0
Sunapee	3,408	5	5	0
Thornton	2,491	4	3	1
Tilton	3,588	18	16	2
Troy	2,075	3	3	0
Wakefield	5,629	12	11	1
Warner	2,877	5	4	1
Waterville Valley	246	7	6	1
Weare	8,937	10	9	1
Webster	1,894	2	2	0
Wilton	3,692	8	7	1
Winchester	4,189	7	6	1
Windham	14,625	27	20	7
Wolfeboro	6,198	18	13	5
Woodstock	1,374	5	5	0
NEW JERSEY				
Aberdeen Township	18,562	42	35	7
Absecon	8,298	30	25	5
Allendale	6,849	20	15	5
Allenhurst	490	13	9	4

Table 19. Full-Time Law Enforcement Employees, by Selected State and City, 2016—*Continued*

(Number.)

State/city	Population	Total law enforcement employees	Total officers	Total civilians
Allentown	1,824	6	5	1
Alpine	1,918	12	12	0
Andover Township	5,979	17	12	5
Asbury Park	15,757	90	87	3
Atlantic City	39,202	397	278	119
Atlantic Highlands	4,297	19	14	5
Audubon	8,669	18	17	1
Avalon	1,273	29	21	8
Avon-by-the-Sea	1,774	11	11	0
Barnegat Township	22,272	51	49	2
Barrington	6,752	16	15	1
Bay Head	971	9	8	1
Bayonne	66,629	284	182	102
Beach Haven	1,168	13	11	2
Beachwood	11,219	20	18	2
Bedminster Township	8,239	17	15	2
Belleville	36,258	120	111	9
Bellmawr	11,380	23	21	2
Belmar	5,694	29	22	7
Belvidere	2,593	6	6	0
Bergenfield	27,646	52	49	3
Berkeley Heights Township	13,548	31	25	6
Berkeley Township	41,684	88	66	22
Berlin	7,544	18	17	1
Berlin Township	5,419	18	17	1
Bernards Township	27,024	43	38	5
Bernardsville	7,802	24	18	6
Beverly	2,555	7	7	0
Blairstown Township	5,791	6	6	0
Bloomfield	48,215	146	121	25
Bloomingdale	8,290	17	16	1
Bogota	8,397	20	15	5
Boonton	8,414	25	21	4
Boonton Township	4,359	13	13	0
Bordentown City	3,873	13	13	0
Bordentown Township	12,049	25	23	2
Bound Brook	10,494	29	24	5
Bradley Beach	4,261	21	18	3
Branchburg Township	14,676	27	26	1
Brick Township	74,818	196	134	62
Bridgeton	24,982	75	60	15
Bridgewater Township	45,251	82	74	8
Brielle	4,753	15	14	1
Brigantine	9,156	48	35	13
Brooklawn	1,919	6	6	0
Buena	4,520	11	9	2
Burlington City	9,785	33	30	3
Burlington Township	22,867	51	42	9
Butler	7,691	17	16	1
Byram Township	7,969	14	14	0
Caldwell	7,933	22	22	0
Cape May	3,496	26	21	5
Carlstadt	6,277	28	26	2
Carney's Point Township	7,809	18	17	1
Carteret	24,316	65	57	8
Cedar Grove Township	12,603	29	29	0
Chatham	8,954	23	19	4
Chatham Township	10,555	23	21	2
Cherry Hill Township	71,079	166	139	27
Chesilhurst	1,626	9	8	1
Chester	1,671	7	6	1
Chesterfield Township	7,534	11	10	1
Chester Township	7,940	17	16	1
Cinnaminson Township	16,871	24	24	0
Clark Township	15,609	51	40	11
Clayton	8,511	17	16	1
Clementon	4,913	13	12	1
Cliffside Park	24,977	50	48	2
Clifton	86,324	178	145	33
Clinton	2,645	10	10	0

Table 19. Full-Time Law Enforcement Employees, by Selected State and City, 2016—*Continued*

(Number.)

State/city	Population	Total law enforcement employees	Total officers	Total civilians
Clinton Township	12,933	23	22	1
Closter	8,674	19	19	0
Collingswood	13,943	27	23	4
Colts Neck Township	10,018	21	20	1
Cranbury Township	3,958	18	17	1
Cranford Township	24,324	68	53	15
Cresskill	8,815	26	22	4
Deal	735	22	18	4
Delanco Township	4,592	12	11	1
Delaware Township	4,478	8	7	1
Delran Township	16,739	34	30	4
Demarest	5,051	12	12	0
Denville Township	16,759	40	30	10
Deptford Township	30,400	69	64	5
Dover	18,290	37	33	4
Dumont	18,010	39	31	8
Dunellen	7,434	17	16	1
Eastampton Township	6,005	16	15	1
East Brunswick Township	49,016	110	84	26
East Greenwich Township	10,473	17	15	2
East Hanover Township	11,233	38	34	4
East Newark	2,707	8	8	0
East Orange	64,787	262	205	57
East Rutherford	9,166	38	37	1
East Windsor Township	27,537	49	43	6
Eatontown	12,264	45	37	8
Edgewater	12,079	33	30	3
Edgewater Park Township	8,769	15	14	1
Edison Township	102,679	226	177	49
Egg Harbor City	4,238	12	11	1
Egg Harbor Township	43,971	110	85	25
Elizabeth	129,096	388	293	95
Elk Township	4,122	13	12	1
Elmer	1,334	2	2	0
Elmwood Park	20,348	46	41	5
Emerson	7,716	23	20	3
Englewood	28,677	110	84	26
Englewood Cliffs	5,397	26	25	1
Englishtown	1,979	8	8	0
Essex Fells	2,157	13	13	0
Evesham Township	45,581	85	76	9
Ewing Township	36,435	94	75	19
Fairfield Township, Essex County	7,561	40	37	3
Fair Haven	6,010	13	13	0
Fair Lawn	33,646	72	59	13
Fairview	14,497	34	31	3
Fanwood	7,677	18	17	1
Far Hills	930	6	6	0
Flemington	4,654	14	13	1
Florence Township	12,805	27	25	2
Florham Park	11,794	38	32	6
Fort Lee	36,739	110	90	20
Franklin	4,814	17	16	1
Franklin Lakes	10,902	27	22	5
Franklin Township, Gloucester County	16,551	29	26	3
Franklin Township, Hunterdon County	3,237	6	6	0
Franklin Township, Somerset County	66,791	124	104	20
Freehold Borough	11,941	31	28	3
Freehold Township	35,736	69	65	4
Frenchtown	1,389	3	3	0
Galloway Township	37,280	81	59	22
Garfield	31,895	76	66	10
Garwood	4,352	20	16	4
Gibbsboro	2,228	10	10	0
Glassboro	19,245	50	45	5
Glen Ridge	7,647	34	23	11
Glen Rock	12,014	23	22	1
Gloucester City	11,247	31	29	2
Gloucester Township	63,484	147	125	22
Green Brook Township	7,266	24	23	1

Table 19. Full-Time Law Enforcement Employees, by Selected State and City, 2016—*Continued*

(Number.)

State/city	Population	Total law enforcement employees	Total officers	Total civilians
Greenwich Township, Gloucester County	4,824	21	19	2
Greenwich Township, Warren County	5,527	9	9	0
Guttenberg	11,701	28	26	2
Hackensack	44,968	138	119	19
Hackettstown	9,549	19	18	1
Haddonfield	11,323	23	21	2
Haddon Heights	7,482	16	15	1
Haddon Township	14,439	27	26	1
Haledon	8,432	18	18	0
Hamburg	3,131	10	8	2
Hamilton Township, Atlantic County	26,824	73	50	23
Hamilton Township, Mercer County	88,665	205	169	36
Hammonton	14,585	35	29	6
Hanover Township	14,468	37	30	7
Harding Township	3,900	12	11	1
Hardyston Township	7,991	24	18	6
Harrington Park	4,830	11	11	0
Harrison	15,788	46	35	11
Harrison Township	13,023	18	17	1
Harvey Cedars	340	8	8	0
Hasbrouck Heights	12,239	32	30	2
Haworth	3,469	13	12	1
Hawthorne	19,031	35	31	4
Hazlet Township	20,050	50	42	8
Helmetta	2,231	7	7	0
High Bridge	3,538	7	7	0
Highland Park	14,346	35	28	7
Highlands	4,838	19	16	3
Hightstown	5,491	14	13	1
Hillsborough Township	40,037	65	52	13
Hillsdale	10,569	22	19	3
Hillside Township	21,981	70	59	11
Hi-Nella	854	12	12	0
Hoboken	54,095	145	126	19
Ho-Ho-Kus	4,161	19	15	4
Holland Township	5,137	7	6	1
Holmdel Township	16,651	50	41	9
Hopatcong	14,388	31	24	7
Hopewell Township	18,570	38	30	8
Howell Township	52,306	102	86	16
Independence Township	5,502	10	9	1
Irvington	54,430	195	158	37
Island Heights	1,664	5	5	0
Jackson Township	56,563	105	87	18
Jamesburg	6,028	17	13	4
Jefferson Township	21,418	45	37	8
Jersey City	266,179	1,279	865	414
Keansburg	9,828	43	34	9
Kearny	42,208	115	109	6
Kenilworth	8,229	30	25	5
Keyport	7,126	23	17	6
Kinnelon	10,367	17	16	1
Lacey Township	28,540	57	43	14
Lakehurst	2,696	14	12	2
Lakewood Township	100,269	153	121	32
Lambertville	3,817	13	10	3
Laurel Springs	1,870	7	7	0
Lavallette	1,789	16	12	4
Lawnside	2,898	9	8	1
Lawrence Township, Mercer County	33,023	62	58	4
Lebanon Township	6,356	8	7	1
Leonia	9,224	20	17	3
Lincoln Park	10,327	29	23	6
Linden	42,100	153	127	26
Lindenwold	17,340	44	41	3
Linwood	6,950	17	16	1
Little Egg Harbor Township	20,686	59	43	16
Little Falls Township	14,478	30	26	4
Little Ferry	10,970	29	26	3
Little Silver	5,901	20	16	4

Table 19. Full-Time Law Enforcement Employees, by Selected State and City, 2016—*Continued*

(Number.)

State/city	Population	Total law enforcement employees	Total officers	Total civilians
Livingston Township	29,788	79	68	11
Lodi	24,841	47	44	3
Logan Township	5,939	19	18	1
Long Beach Township	3,015	49	37	12
Long Branch	30,959	103	82	21
Long Hill Township	8,749	25	23	2
Longport	884	12	12	0
Lopatcong Township	8,281	15	14	1
Lower Alloways Creek Township	1,702	13	11	2
Lower Township	21,982	57	44	13
Lumberton Township	12,400	20	18	2
Lyndhurst Township	22,530	54	51	3
Madison	16,098	36	28	8
Magnolia	4,267	11	11	0
Mahwah Township	26,588	60	52	8
Manalapan Township	40,407	57	54	3
Manasquan	5,798	21	16	5
Manchester Township	43,525	86	68	18
Mansfield Township, Burlington County	8,578	14	13	1
Mansfield Township, Warren County	7,461	15	14	1
Mantoloking	244	10	9	1
Mantua Township	14,939	28	26	2
Manville	10,424	27	24	3
Maple Shade Township	18,927	36	32	4
Maplewood Township	24,743	73	63	10
Margate City	6,214	37	27	10
Marlboro Township	40,764	103	73	30
Matawan	8,851	22	21	1
Maywood	9,804	26	22	4
Medford Lakes	4,072	10	9	1
Medford Township	23,481	34	30	4
Mendham	4,979	12	11	1
Mendham Township	5,846	15	14	1
Merchantville	3,751	15	13	2
Metuchen	13,879	33	28	5
Middlesex Borough	13,923	31	29	2
Middle Township	18,555	63	49	14
Middletown Township	65,919	135	112	23
Midland Park	7,330	16	15	1
Millburn Township	20,310	59	53	6
Milltown	7,044	19	16	3
Millville	28,177	85	74	11
Monmouth Beach	3,233	10	9	1
Monroe Township, Gloucester County	36,805	73	67	6
Monroe Township, Middlesex County	44,923	72	55	17
Montclair	38,108	121	104	17
Montgomery Township	23,160	35	29	6
Montvale	8,519	24	22	2
Montville Township	21,801	43	37	6
Moonachie	2,790	20	17	3
Moorestown Township	20,530	37	32	5
Morris Plains	5,615	19	17	2
Morristown	18,544	59	55	4
Morris Township	22,555	47	42	5
Mountain Lakes	4,291	14	13	1
Mountainside	6,887	27	22	5
Mount Arlington	5,324	15	14	1
Mount Ephraim	4,609	13	12	1
Mount Holly Township	9,483	24	21	3
Mount Laurel Township	41,828	69	61	8
Mount Olive Township	29,095	56	47	9
Mullica Township	6,089	13	12	1
Neptune City	4,790	19	17	2
Neptune Township	27,505	83	73	10
Netcong	3,240	9	9	0
Newark	281,450	1,383	1,113	270
New Brunswick	57,158	179	144	35
Newfield	1,522	5	5	0
New Hanover Township	8,218	3	3	0
New Milford	16,804	36	34	2

Table 19. Full-Time Law Enforcement Employees, by Selected State and City, 2016—*Continued*

(Number.)

State/city	Population	Total law enforcement employees	Total officers	Total civilians
New Providence	12,461	26	24	2
Newton	7,950	28	23	5
North Arlington	15,921	35	28	7
North Bergen Township	63,113	130	120	10
North Brunswick Township	42,777	98	81	17
North Caldwell	6,732	20	15	5
Northfield	8,502	21	20	1
North Haledon	8,529	21	17	4
North Hanover Township	7,594	11	10	1
North Plainfield	22,135	51	44	7
Northvale	4,876	13	13	0
North Wildwood	3,874	36	28	8
Norwood	5,869	16	15	1
Nutley Township	28,673	86	74	12
Oakland	13,176	27	23	4
Oaklyn	3,963	16	15	1
Ocean City	11,287	73	58	15
Ocean Gate	2,004	9	8	1
Oceanport	5,718	16	15	1
Ocean Township, Monmouth County	27,070	74	61	13
Ocean Township, Ocean County	8,927	26	18	8
Ogdensburg	2,266	6	6	0
Old Bridge Township	67,238	117	90	27
Old Tappan	6,039	14	13	1
Oradell	8,222	22	21	1
Orange	30,470	118	97	21
Palisades Park	20,861	40	32	8
Palmyra	7,296	19	18	1
Paramus	26,958	108	87	21
Park Ridge	8,927	20	19	1
Parsippany-Troy Hills Township	53,447	124	103	21
Passaic	70,972	180	154	26
Paterson	147,265	478	383	95
Paulsboro	5,937	20	18	2
Peapack and Gladstone	2,603	9	8	1
Pemberton Borough	1,378	7	6	1
Pemberton Township	27,739	43	38	5
Pennington	2,586	6	5	1
Pennsauken Township	35,402	81	73	8
Penns Grove	4,908	15	15	0
Pennsville Township	12,720	22	22	0
Pequannock Township	15,425	36	31	5
Perth Amboy	52,767	144	119	25
Phillipsburg	14,435	37	36	1
Pine Beach	2,149	8	7	1
Pine Hill	10,514	24	21	3
Pine Valley	12	6	6	0
Piscataway Township	58,181	105	85	20
Pitman	8,830	17	16	1
Plainfield	51,221	152	126	26
Plainsboro Township	23,621	47	35	12
Pleasantville	20,855	65	51	14
Plumsted Township	8,511	15	14	1
Pohatcong Township	3,224	13	12	1
Point Pleasant	18,502	43	33	10
Point Pleasant Beach	4,519	28	22	6
Pompton Lakes	11,164	24	20	4
Princeton	29,660	70	52	18
Prospect Park	5,940	18	17	1
Rahway	29,797	82	73	9
Ramsey	15,145	38	32	6
Randolph Township	25,877	41	36	5
Raritan	8,268	19	18	1
Raritan Township	22,011	36	33	3
Readington Township	15,893	25	23	2
Red Bank	12,187	47	40	7
Ridgefield	11,380	29	27	2
Ridgefield Park	13,107	35	28	7
Ridgewood	25,617	46	43	3
Ringwood	12,427	24	20	4

Table 19. Full-Time Law Enforcement Employees, by Selected State and City, 2016—*Continued*

(Number.)

State/city	Population	Total law enforcement employees	Total officers	Total civilians
Riverdale	4,409	20	16	4
River Edge	11,671	28	25	3
Riverside Township	7,980	14	14	0
Riverton	2,741	6	6	0
River Vale Township	10,053	21	19	2
Robbinsville Township	14,209	34	27	7
Rochelle Park Township	5,683	24	20	4
Rockaway	6,471	15	14	1
Rockaway Township	24,655	61	50	11
Roseland	5,857	24	24	0
Roselle	21,669	70	57	13
Roselle Park	13,669	40	34	6
Roxbury Township	23,425	45	42	3
Rumson	6,886	20	16	4
Runnemede	8,322	17	15	2
Rutherford	18,717	41	38	3
Saddle Brook Township	14,108	34	30	4
Saddle River	3,256	22	17	5
Salem	4,849	19	17	2
Sayreville	45,141	96	84	12
Scotch Plains Township	24,144	49	45	4
Sea Bright	1,331	11	11	0
Sea Girt	1,807	11	11	0
Sea Isle City	2,080	28	22	6
Seaside Heights	2,886	38	25	13
Seaside Park	1,541	15	13	2
Secaucus	19,528	76	65	11
Ship Bottom	1,128	12	11	1
Shrewsbury	4,199	21	16	5
Somerdale	5,496	15	14	1
Somers Point	10,667	37	30	7
Somerville	12,198	34	32	2
South Amboy	8,843	27	25	2
South Bound Brook	4,624	13	12	1
South Brunswick Township	45,862	106	80	26
South Hackensack Township	2,469	22	19	3
South Harrison Township	3,116	5	5	0
South Orange	16,332	51	44	7
South Plainfield	24,349	67	52	15
South River	16,391	70	34	36
South Toms River	3,737	12	11	1
Sparta Township	19,049	44	31	13
Spotswood	8,477	25	21	4
Springfield	17,764	46	42	4
Springfield Township	3,343	10	9	1
Spring Lake	2,959	13	13	0
Spring Lake Heights	4,648	12	12	0
Stafford Township	26,972	71	51	20
Stanhope	3,372	10	9	1
Stone Harbor	830	19	17	2
Stratford	6,974	17	15	2
Summit	22,078	51	46	5
Surf City	1,201	10	10	0
Teaneck Township	40,988	105	89	16
Tenafly	14,877	40	34	6
Tewksbury Township	5,862	11	10	1
Tinton Falls	17,747	42	41	1
Toms River Township	90,504	187	160	27
Totowa	10,948	32	28	4
Trenton	83,644	381	246	135
Tuckerton	3,374	12	11	1
Union Beach	5,476	18	15	3
Union City	69,345	249	162	87
Union Township	58,109	182	133	49
Upper Saddle River	8,369	21	17	4
Ventnor City	10,455	50	37	13
Vernon Township	22,359	38	30	8
Verona	13,523	35	30	5
Vineland	60,823	157	132	25
Voorhees Township	29,235	58	49	9

Table 19. Full-Time Law Enforcement Employees, by Selected State and City, 2016—*Continued*

(Number.)

State/city	Population	Total law enforcement employees	Total officers	Total civilians
Waldwick	10,134	24	19	5
Wallington	11,731	23	22	1
Wall Township	26,033	91	66	25
Wanaque	11,937	30	25	5
Warren Township	16,051	37	30	7
Washington Township, Bergen County	9,381	22	20	2
Washington Township, Gloucester County	47,477	84	77	7
Washington Township, Morris County	18,696	33	30	3
Washington Township, Warren County	6,430	28	27	1
Watchung	5,925	37	30	7
Waterford Township	10,720	26	23	3
Wayne Township	55,023	141	114	27
Weehawken Township	14,284	61	48	13
Wenonah	2,237	7	7	0
Westampton Township	8,707	25	22	3
West Amwell Township	2,767	7	7	0
West Caldwell Township	11,057	30	26	4
West Deptford Township	21,257	46	43	3
Westfield	30,427	71	58	13
West Long Branch	7,975	22	21	1
West Milford Township	26,734	51	44	7
West New York	53,813	119	109	10
West Orange	47,374	111	97	14
Westville	4,189	12	11	1
West Wildwood	566	5	5	0
West Windsor Township	28,482	59	47	12
Westwood	11,252	30	25	5
Wharton	6,593	22	20	2
Wildwood	5,115	49	39	10
Wildwood Crest	3,162	26	20	6
Willingboro Township	31,195	75	65	10
Winfield Township	1,509	8	8	0
Winslow Township	38,724	79	72	7
Woodbridge Township	102,124	252	194	58
Woodbury	9,937	32	29	3
Woodbury Heights	2,985	8	7	1
Woodcliff Lake	5,925	19	18	1
Woodland Park	12,594	28	25	3
Woodlynne	2,922	7	7	0
Wood-Ridge	8,335	27	22	5
Woodstown	3,529	11	9	2
Woolwich Township	12,675	24	23	1
Wyckoff Township	17,242	25	25	0
NEW MEXICO				
Alamogordo	30,768	76	56	20
Angel Fire	1,104	6	5	1
Artesia	12,180	46	27	19
Aztec	6,031	17	14	3
Belen	7,127	23	20	3
Bernalillo	8,946	23	21	2
Bloomfield	7,163	23	18	5
Bosque Farms	3,823	14	13	1
Capitan	1,373	3	3	0
Carlsbad	29,538	89	62	27
Carrizozo	931	4	3	1
Clayton	2,735	13	7	6
Cloudcroft	683	3	3	0
Clovis	39,725	79	54	25
Corrales	8,530	18	15	3
Cuba	736	5	4	1
Dexter	1,273	6	5	1
Edgewood	3,819	11	8	3
Espanola	10,030	36	23	13
Estancia	1,586	7	3	4
Eunice	3,182	13	8	5
Farmington	42,270	169	131	38
Gallup	23,528	70	56	14
Grants	9,245	22	19	3
Hatch	1,596	9	8	1

State/city	Population	Total law enforcement employees	Total officers	Total civilians
Hobbs	39,349	128	94	34
Hurley	1,249	5	3	2
Jal	2,234	14	7	7
Las Cruces	102,349	256	182	74
Las Vegas	13,256	53	33	20
Logan	951	4	4	0
Lordsburg	2,485	11	9	2
Los Alamos	17,667	70	33	37
Los Lunas	15,398	40	36	4
Magdalena	906	3	3	0
Mesilla	1,869	7	7	0
Milan	3,248	12	6	6
Moriarty	1,786	11	9	2
Portales	11,921	28	22	6
Questa	1,750	4	3	1
Raton	6,058	19	10	9
Red River	476	9	4	5
Rio Rancho	95,454	233	135	98
Roswell	48,556	103	79	24
Ruidoso	7,683	34	22	12
Ruidoso Downs	2,548	12	6	6
Santa Clara	1,629	5	4	1
Santa Fe	84,663	213	166	47
Santa Rosa	2,641	13	7	6
San Ysidro	195	2	2	0
Springer	924	3	3	0
Taos	5,746	23	17	6
Texico	1,114	2	2	0
Truth or Consequences	6,000	13	12	1
Tularosa	2,863	11	6	5
NEW YORK				
Addison Town and Village	2,541	3	3	0
Akron Village	2,840	1	1	0
Albany	98,617	433	336	97
Albion Village	5,984	11	11	0
Alfred Village	4,039	5	5	0
Allegany Village	1,726	3	2	1
Altamont Village	1,721	1	1	0
Amherst Town	120,436	179	149	30
Amity Town and Belmont Village	2,210	1	1	0
Amityville Village	9,477	23	22	1
Amsterdam	17,891	42	40	2
Arcade Village	1,971	5	5	0
Ardsley Village	4,674	19	19	0
Asharoken Village	653	3	3	0
Attica Village	2,457	3	3	0
Auburn	26,854	71	66	5
Avon Village	3,308	4	4	0
Baldwinsville Village	7,805	12	11	1
Ballston Spa Village	5,366	5	5	0
Batavia	14,931	33	30	3
Bath Village	5,605	11	9	2
Beacon	14,291	36	34	2
Bedford Town	18,063	44	39	5
Binghamton	45,780	145	131	14
Blooming Grove Town	11,907	14	12	2
Bolivar Village	998	1	1	0
Boonville Village	2,034	3	3	0
Brant Town	2,064	1	1	0
Briarcliff Manor Village	8,066	20	20	0
Brighton Town	36,889	44	38	6
Brockport Village	8,355	16	15	1
Bronxville Village	6,460	23	21	2
Buffalo	257,446	900	693	207
Cairo Town	6,437	1	1	0
Caledonia Village	2,136	3	3	0
Cambridge Village	1,822	6	6	0
Camden Village	2,196	2	2	0
Camillus Town and Village	24,622	26	24	2

(Number.)

State/city	Population	Total law enforcement employees	Total officers	Total civilians
Canajoharie Village	2,149	4	4	0
Canandaigua	10,407	24	22	2
Canastota Village	4,638	6	5	1
Canisteo Village	2,191	3	3	0
Canton Village	6,619	10	9	1
Carmel Town	34,355	38	31	7
Carthage Village	3,575	3	3	0
Catskill Village	3,840	14	13	1
Cayuga Heights Village	3,840	7	6	1
Cazenovia Village	2,861	5	4	1
Centre Island Village	409	7	7	0
Cheektowaga Town	78,100	162	126	36
Chester Town	7,941	14	14	0
Chester Village	3,907	14	13	1
Chittenango Village	4,855	3	1	2
Clarkstown Town	82,171	181	157	24
Clayton Village	1,950	3	3	0
Cobleskill Village	4,545	12	12	0
Coeymans Town	7,420	5	4	1
Cohoes	16,615	37	33	4
Colchester Town	2,015	1	1	0
Colonie Town	80,075	150	111	39
Cooperstown Village	1,780	5	4	1
Corning	10,841	24	20	4
Cornwall-on-Hudson Village	2,955	3	3	0
Cornwall Town	9,589	11	9	2
Cortland	18,856	46	43	3
Crawford Town	9,202	10	9	1
Croton-on-Hudson Village	8,308	22	20	2
Cuba Town	3,153	4	4	0
Dansville Village	4,525	5	5	0
Deerpark Town	7,749	3	3	0
Delhi Village	3,173	4	4	0
Depew Village	15,116	34	29	5
Deposit Village	1,586	1	1	0
DeWitt Town	25,616	48	44	4
Dobbs Ferry Village	11,180	28	26	2
Dolgeville Village	2,119	2	2	0
Dryden Village	2,137	4	4	0
Dunkirk	11,991	38	37	1
East Aurora-Aurora Town	13,823	20	15	5
Eastchester Town	20,150	48	46	2
East Fishkill Town	29,316	38	29	9
East Greenbush Town	16,483	31	22	9
East Hampton Town	19,950	92	68	24
East Hampton Village	1,130	27	23	4
Eden Town	7,670	5	4	1
Ellenville Village	4,070	12	11	1
Ellicott Town	5,140	12	12	0
Ellicottville	1,598	3	3	0
Elmira Heights Village	3,959	10	10	0
Elmira Town	5,786	4	4	0
Elmsford Village	4,838	19	19	0
Endicott Village	12,944	30	28	2
Evans Town	16,234	30	24	6
Fairport Village	5,350	11	10	1
Fallsburg Town	11,966	20	20	0
Floral Park Village	15,986	48	34	14
Florida Village	2,912	1	1	0
Fort Edward Village	3,258	5	5	0
Fort Plain Village	2,232	4	4	0
Frankfort Town	4,925	3	3	0
Frankfort Village	2,490	4	4	0
Franklinville Village	1,670	2	2	0
Fredonia Village	10,604	18	14	4
Freeport Village	43,419	115	98	17
Fulton City	11,483	34	33	1
Garden City Village	22,656	64	51	13
Gates Town	28,669	35	30	5
Geddes Town	10,349	17	15	2

(Number.)

State/city	Population	Total law enforcement employees	Total officers	Total civilians
Geneseo Village	8,199	8	8	0
Geneva	13,033	35	33	2
Glen Cove	27,480	54	50	4
Glens Falls	14,212	29	27	2
Glenville Town	21,754	24	22	2
Gloversville	14,908	30	28	2
Goshen Town	8,515	9	9	0
Goshen Village	5,384	20	17	3
Gouverneur Village	3,769	9	6	3
Gowanda Village	2,622	2	2	0
Granville Village	2,451	6	6	0
Great Neck Estates Village	2,839	15	12	3
Greece Town	96,975	105	99	6
Greenburgh Town	45,745	140	112	28
Greene Village	1,488	1	1	0
Greenwich Village	1,738	6	6	0
Greenwood Lake Village	3,104	6	5	1
Groton Village	2,402	1	1	0
Guilderland Town	34,405	48	35	13
Hamburg Town	46,028	78	61	17
Hamburg Village	9,608	14	13	1
Hamilton Village	4,166	5	5	0
Hancock Village	966	2	2	0
Harriman Village	2,486	7	7	0
Harrison Town	28,518	74	63	11
Hastings-on-Hudson Village	8,044	21	21	0
Haverstraw Town	37,756	69	64	5
Hempstead Village	55,870	140	118	22
Herkimer Village	7,478	19	19	0
Highland Falls Village	3,829	9	7	2
Holley Village	1,721	2	2	0
Hoosick Falls Village	3,419	1	1	0
Hornell	8,289	23	22	1
Horseheads Village	6,653	10	10	0
Hudson	6,381	29	25	4
Hudson Falls Village	7,170	14	14	0
Hunter Town	2,634	3	3	0
Huntington Bay Village	1,431	4	4	0
Ilion Village	7,877	20	18	2
Inlet Town	322	3	2	1
Interlaken Village	627	1	1	0
Irondequoit Town	50,874	60	49	11
Irvington Village	6,643	23	22	1
Ithaca	30,937	74	66	8
Jamestown	29,879	68	59	9
Johnson City Village	14,699	38	33	5
Johnstown	8,282	23	21	2
Kenmore Village	15,110	25	25	0
Kensington Village	1,189	6	6	0
Kent Town	13,274	25	20	5
Kingston	23,360	76	71	5
Kirkland Town	8,279	5	5	0
Lake Placid Village	2,453	15	12	3
Lake Success Village	3,072	25	22	3
Lakewood-Busti	4,509	13	12	1
Lancaster Town	37,418	64	49	15
Larchmont Village	6,186	28	25	3
Le Roy Village	4,269	7	7	0
Lewisboro Town	12,862	3	3	0
Lewiston Town and Village	16,009	11	10	1
Liberty Village	4,090	16	14	2
Little Falls	4,757	11	10	1
Liverpool Village	2,284	5	5	0
Lloyd Harbor Village	3,695	13	12	1
Lloyd Town	10,568	13	10	3
Long Beach	33,591	85	68	17
Lowville Village	3,406	6	6	0
Lynbrook Village	19,579	58	50	8
Macedon Town and Village	8,911	6	5	1
Malone Village	5,726	13	13	0

Table 19. Full-Time Law Enforcement Employees, by Selected State and City, 2016—*Continued*

(Number.)

State/city	Population	Total law enforcement employees	Total officers	Total civilians
Malverne Village	8,579	23	23	0
Mamaroneck Town	12,292	39	38	1
Mamaroneck Village	19,460	56	50	6
Marlborough Town	8,682	10	8	2
Massena Village	10,571	24	19	5
Maybrook Village	3,356	4	4	0
Mechanicville	5,160	12	10	2
Medina Village	5,781	12	11	1
Menands Village	4,000	14	11	3
Middleport Village	1,778	4	4	0
Middletown	27,752	75	64	11
Mohawk Village	2,611	4	4	0
Monroe Village	8,680	21	17	4
Montgomery Village	4,782	4	4	0
Monticello Village	6,438	25	23	2
Moriah Town	3,585	2	2	0
Mount Hope Town	6,899	4	4	0
Mount Morris Village	2,883	5	5	0
Mount Pleasant Town	26,903	47	41	6
Mount Vernon	68,881	261	192	69
Newark Village	8,786	18	17	1
New Berlin Town	1,548	2	2	0
Newburgh	28,171	99	86	13
Newburgh Town	30,933	56	46	10
New Castle Town	18,167	38	36	2
New Hartford Town and Village	20,441	24	20	4
New Paltz Town and Village	14,214	25	21	4
New Rochelle	80,389	211	152	59
New Windsor Town	26,835	48	38	10
New York	8,566,917	51,399	36,228	15,171
New York Mills Village	3,303	4	4	0
Niagara Falls	48,675	178	157	21
Niagara Town	8,080	6	5	1
Niskayuna Town	22,171	29	27	2
Nissequogue Village	1,762	2	2	0
North Castle Town	12,390	34	32	2
North Greenbush Town	12,232	19	17	2
Northport Village	7,387	21	17	4
North Syracuse Village	6,861	11	10	1
North Tonawanda	30,634	51	47	4
Norwich	6,929	20	20	0
Ocean Beach Village	81	4	4	0
Ogdensburg	10,840	30	25	5
Ogden Town	20,257	15	12	3
Old Brookville Village	2,230	33	25	8
Old Westbury Village	4,678	31	26	5
Olean	13,765	40	34	6
Olive Town	4,331	1	1	0
Oneonta City	13,857	28	23	5
Orangetown Town	37,962	86	82	4
Orchard Park Town	29,721	39	31	8
Oswego City	17,717	54	47	7
Owego Village	3,705	7	6	1
Oyster Bay Cove Village	4,313	14	14	0
Palmyra Village	3,390	6	5	1
Peekskill	24,129	64	54	10
Pelham Manor Village	5,614	22	21	1
Pelham Village	7,074	28	25	3
Penn Yan Village	4,988	13	12	1
Perry Village	3,487	3	3	0
Piermont Village	2,585	8	8	0
Plattsburgh City	19,765	58	51	7
Pleasantville Village	7,205	22	22	0
Port Chester Village	29,750	63	61	2
Port Dickinson Village	1,585	5	4	1
Port Jervis	8,565	31	30	1
Port Washington	19,272	63	55	8
Potsdam Village	9,744	16	13	3
Poughkeepsie	30,262	125	91	34
Poughkeepsie Town	39,222	91	80	11

State/city	Population	Total law enforcement employees	Total officers	Total civilians
Pound Ridge Town	5,275	2	1	1
Pulaski Village	2,299	1	1	0
Quogue Village	995	14	13	1
Ramapo Town	92,620	117	95	22
Rensselaer City	9,441	33	27	6
Riverhead Town	33,818	103	85	18
Rochester	209,643	864	747	117
Rockville Centre Village	24,229	64	55	9
Rome	32,345	76	74	2
Rosendale Town	5,927	2	1	1
Rotterdam Town	29,352	43	40	3
Rouses Point Village	2,161	1	1	0
Rye	16,108	41	36	5
Rye Brook Village	9,658	27	26	1
Sag Harbor Village	2,305	15	13	2
Salamanca	5,545	17	17	0
Sands Point Village	2,767	20	20	0
Saranac Lake Village	5,248	12	12	0
Saratoga Springs	28,005	86	73	13
Saugerties Town	19,128	28	24	4
Scarsdale Village	18,026	49	44	5
Schenectady	65,138	171	146	25
Schodack Town	11,730	11	10	1
Scotia Village	7,725	14	13	1
Seneca Falls Town	8,808	19	17	2
Shandaken Town	2,986	4	4	0
Shawangunk Town	14,098	4	4	0
Shelter Island Town	2,423	11	9	2
Sherrill	3,066	3	3	0
Sidney Village	3,729	8	7	1
Skaneateles Village	2,479	1	1	0
Sodus Village	1,743	1	1	0
Solvay Village	6,394	15	14	1
Southampton Town	51,191	126	94	32
Southampton Village	3,296	44	30	14
South Glens Falls Village	3,593	6	6	0
South Nyack Village	3,539	6	6	0
Southold Town	20,114	74	52	22
Spring Valley Village	32,844	58	51	7
St. Johnsville Village	1,687	1	1	0
Stony Point Town	15,599	26	25	1
Suffern Village	11,053	24	20	4
Syracuse	143,925	484	415	69
Tonawanda	14,864	33	27	6
Tonawanda Town	57,698	151	103	48
Troy	49,876	139	126	13
Tuckahoe Village	6,673	26	23	3
Tupper Lake Village	3,560	9	9	0
Tuxedo Park Village	605	5	4	1
Ulster Town	12,264	26	23	3
Utica	60,879	180	163	17
Vestal Town	28,253	37	34	3
Walden Village	6,810	16	13	3
Wallkill Town	28,540	40	39	1
Walton Village	2,901	5	5	0
Warsaw Village	3,357	5	5	0
Warwick Town	18,345	36	31	5
Washingtonville Village	5,765	16	14	2
Waterford Town and Village	8,439	11	8	3
Waterloo Village	5,012	8	7	1
Watertown	26,765	68	65	3
Watervliet	10,208	24	24	0
Watkins Glen Village	1,860	3	3	0
Waverly Village	4,231	11	10	1
Wayland Village	1,804	1	1	0
Webb Town	1,817	5	5	0
Webster Town and Village	44,487	36	32	4
Wellsville Village	4,506	11	10	1
Westfield Village	3,066	5	5	0
Westhampton Beach Village	1,790	18	15	3

Table 19. Full-Time Law Enforcement Employees, by Selected State and City, 2016—*Continued*

(Number.)

State/city	Population	Total law enforcement employees	Total officers	Total civilians
West Seneca Town	45,752	81	68	13
Whitehall Village	2,574	3	3	0
White Plains	58,767	201	191	10
Whitesboro Village	3,680	5	5	0
Whitestown Town	9,275	6	6	0
Windham Town	1,674	2	2	0
Woodbury Town	10,917	20	16	4
Woodstock Town	5,865	10	10	0
Yonkers	202,075	696	613	83
Yorktown Town	37,287	63	54	9
Yorkville Village	2,625	3	3	0
NORTH CAROLINA				
Aberdeen	7,549	30	28	2
Ahoskie	4,883	18	14	4
Albemarle	16,024	56	48	8
Andrews	1,746	6	5	1
Angier	5,097	14	14	0
Apex	47,324	91	74	17
Archdale	11,593	30	24	6
Asheboro	26,230	79	71	8
Asheville	89,546	263	200	63
Atlantic Beach	1,503	17	16	1
Aurora	522	1	1	0
Ayden	5,078	22	18	4
Badin	1,983	5	5	0
Bailey	564	2	2	0
Bakersville	450	1	1	0
Bald Head Island	174	19	18	1
Banner Elk	1,163	9	8	1
Beaufort	4,244	16	15	1
Beech Mountain	320	14	10	4
Belhaven	1,586	11	8	3
Belmont	10,593	39	30	9
Benson	3,648	14	13	1
Bessemer City	5,591	13	12	1
Bethel	1,628	5	5	0
Beulaville	1,335	3	3	0
Biltmore Forest	1,461	14	13	1
Biscoe	1,689	9	8	1
Black Creek	767	2	2	0
Black Mountain	8,368	22	18	4
Bladenboro	1,721	5	5	0
Blowing Rock	1,303	12	11	1
Boiling Spring Lakes	5,873	13	12	1
Boiling Springs	4,681	8	8	0
Boone	18,374	47	35	12
Boonville	1,204	5	5	0
Brevard	7,747	31	24	7
Bridgeton	437	1	1	0
Broadway	1,271	4	4	0
Brookford	374	1	1	0
Bryson City	1,466	9	8	1
Bunn	366	3	3	0
Burgaw	4,147	13	12	1
Burlington	52,760	161	121	40
Burnsville	1,653	8	8	0
Butner	7,781	39	32	7
Cameron	297	1	1	0
Candor	838	3	3	0
Canton	4,188	18	13	5
Cape Carteret	2,080	8	8	0
Carolina Beach	6,223	31	29	2
Carrboro	21,478	40	37	3
Carthage	2,416	11	10	1
Cary	164,835	223	185	38
Caswell Beach	428	4	4	0
Chadbourn	1,782	8	7	1
Chapel Hill	60,004	127	104	23
Charlotte-Mecklenburg[1]	896,379	2,302	1,743	559

(Number.)

State/city	Population	Total law enforcement employees	Total officers	Total civilians
Cherryville	6,018	19	14	5
China Grove	4,187	13	13	0
Chocowinity	821	3	3	0
Claremont	1,368	10	9	1
Clayton	19,968	46	43	3
Cleveland	874	5	5	0
Clinton	8,789	30	26	4
Clyde	1,247	4	4	0
Coats	2,467	6	6	0
Columbus	994	11	10	1
Concord	89,446	194	166	28
Conover	8,261	29	27	2
Conway	760	2	2	0
Cooleemee	974	3	3	0
Cornelius	28,756	77	62	15
Cramerton	4,361	15	15	0
Creedmoor	4,487	19	15	4
Dallas	4,656	17	13	4
Davidson	12,469	18	17	1
Dobson	1,570	7	7	0
Drexel	1,864	5	5	0
Duck	386	10	9	1
Dunn	9,804	42	37	5
Durham	263,716	679	490	189
East Bend	597	2	2	0
East Spencer	1,552	5	5	0
Eden	15,343	49	45	4
Edenton	4,822	21	19	2
Elizabeth City	17,852	68	56	12
Elizabethtown	3,577	18	17	1
Elkin	4,067	21	17	4
Elon	10,150	17	16	1
Emerald Isle	3,731	18	17	1
Enfield	2,407	10	9	1
Erwin	4,730	10	9	1
Fair Bluff	912	3	3	0
Fairmont	2,703	7	5	2
Farmville	4,776	22	18	4
Fayetteville	202,200	601	442	159
Fletcher	7,660	17	16	1
Forest City	7,246	33	31	2
Four Oaks	2,075	6	6	0
Foxfire Village	984	3	3	0
Franklin	3,947	18	17	1
Franklinton	2,156	8	8	0
Fremont	1,284	4	4	0
Fuquay-Varina	25,249	44	38	6
Garner	28,508	70	62	8
Garysburg	963	2	2	0
Gaston	1,051	3	3	0
Gastonia	75,118	192	170	22
Gibsonville	6,843	17	16	1
Glen Alpine	1,497	3	3	0
Goldsboro	35,871	101	89	12
Graham	14,712	40	37	3
Granite Falls	4,651	17	14	3
Granite Quarry	3,002	8	8	0
Greensboro	288,618	786	681	105
Greenville	91,766	222	178	44
Grifton	2,683	6	6	0
Hamlet	6,430	23	19	4
Havelock	20,283	30	24	6
Haw River	2,420	7	7	0
Henderson	15,249	54	45	9
Hendersonville	13,954	53	41	12
Hertford	2,148	9	8	1
Hickory	40,437	138	103	35
Highlands	939	14	13	1
High Point	111,435	268	222	46
Hillsborough	6,475	28	27	1

Table 19. Full-Time Law Enforcement Employees, by Selected State and City, 2016—*Continued*

(Number.)

State/city	Population	Total law enforcement employees	Total officers	Total civilians
Holden Beach	642	8	8	0
Holly Ridge	2,300	11	10	1
Holly Springs	32,862	60	49	11
Hope Mills	16,268	40	36	4
Hot Springs	562	1	1	0
Hudson	3,710	15	14	1
Huntersville	53,932	91	85	6
Indian Beach	115	5	5	0
Jackson	475	1	1	0
Jacksonville	66,686	143	115	28
Jefferson	1,605	4	4	0
Jonesville	2,251	11	10	1
Kannapolis	46,867	106	79	27
Kenansville	872	3	3	0
Kenly	1,472	8	8	0
Kernersville	23,943	87	68	19
Kill Devil Hills	7,132	35	29	6
King	7,091	23	20	3
Kings Mountain	10,785	40	32	8
Kinston	21,268	68	59	9
Kitty Hawk	3,482	18	16	2
Knightdale	14,875	29	27	2
Kure Beach	2,106	12	11	1
Lake Lure	1,182	10	9	1
Lake Royale	2,670	5	5	0
Lake Waccamaw	1,464	5	5	0
Landis	3,121	10	10	0
Laurel Park	2,341	7	7	0
Laurinburg	15,423	40	37	3
Leland	18,842	31	30	1
Lenoir	17,822	60	48	12
Lexington	19,407	62	55	7
Liberty	2,688	11	10	1
Lilesville	499	1	1	0
Lillington	3,532	13	12	1
Lincolnton	10,981	38	33	5
Littleton	641	3	3	0
Locust	2,973	12	12	0
Long View	4,901	16	16	0
Louisburg	3,582	13	12	1
Lowell	3,674	8	8	0
Lumberton	21,683	93	83	10
Madison	2,187	17	16	1
Maggie Valley	1,273	11	10	1
Magnolia	951	1	1	0
Maiden	3,379	15	14	1
Manteo	1,401	8	7	1
Marion	7,827	27	26	1
Marshall	876	3	3	0
Mars Hill	2,320	5	5	0
Marshville	2,684	8	8	0
Matthews	31,401	68	55	13
Maxton	2,454	13	9	4
Mayodan	2,469	14	14	0
Maysville	1,003	3	3	0
Mebane	14,201	34	30	4
Micro	493	1	1	0
Middlesex	812	4	4	0
Mint Hill	26,221	34	31	3
Misenheimer	715	5	5	0
Mocksville	5,170	22	21	1
Monroe	34,978	95	82	13
Montreat	723	5	5	0
Mooresville	36,482	98	79	19
Morehead City	9,477	45	40	5
Morganton	16,656	85	60	25
Morrisville	24,976	35	34	1
Mount Airy	10,345	47	36	11
Mount Gilead	1,180	7	7	0
Mount Holly	14,284	40	31	9

(Number.)

State/city	Population	Total law enforcement employees	Total officers	Total civilians
Mount Olive	4,752	21	19	2
Murfreesboro	3,038	7	6	1
Murphy	1,613	11	9	2
Nags Head	2,938	25	23	2
Nashville	5,459	16	15	1
Navassa	1,668	3	3	0
New Bern	30,137	103	81	22
Newland	684	5	5	0
Newport	4,841	9	9	0
Newton	13,049	43	36	7
Newton Grove	577	3	3	0
Norlina	1,074	5	5	0
North Topsail Beach	736	11	10	1
Northwest	776	2	2	0
North Wilkesboro	4,215	25	24	1
Norwood	2,397	8	7	1
Oakboro	1,877	5	5	0
Oak Island	7,651	23	21	2
Ocean Isle Beach	608	13	12	1
Old Fort	911	3	3	0
Oriental	882	1	1	0
Oxford	8,794	31	29	2
Parkton	440	1	1	0
Pembroke	3,009	18	14	4
Pikeville	695	4	4	0
Pilot Mountain	1,462	8	7	1
Pinebluff	1,467	3	3	0
Pinehurst	15,948	30	25	5
Pine Knoll Shores	1,368	7	7	0
Pine Level	1,893	5	5	0
Pinetops	1,308	4	4	0
Pineville	8,626	47	36	11
Pink Hill	538	2	2	0
Pittsboro	4,287	11	11	0
Plymouth	3,618	15	14	1
Polkton	3,526	2	2	0
Princeton	1,302	4	4	0
Raeford	4,907	18	17	1
Raleigh	460,593	875	729	146
Ramseur	1,703	6	6	0
Randleman	4,160	15	15	0
Ranlo	3,581	8	8	0
Red Springs	3,434	15	14	1
Reidsville	13,991	48	43	5
Richlands	1,720	8	8	0
Rich Square	891	1	1	0
River Bend	3,153	6	6	0
Roanoke Rapids	15,273	43	39	4
Robbins	1,195	3	3	0
Robersonville	1,412	8	8	0
Rockingham	9,155	39	34	5
Rockwell	2,148	6	6	0
Rocky Mount	55,431	202	160	42
Rolesville	6,962	20	19	1
Rose Hill	1,672	5	5	0
Rowland	1,052	7	6	1
Roxboro	8,331	35	31	4
Rutherfordton	4,173	15	14	1
Salisbury	34,121	76	69	7
Saluda	705	4	4	0
Sanford	29,347	105	82	23
Scotland Neck	1,948	7	6	1
Seagrove	229	1	1	0
Selma	6,351	26	24	2
Seven Devils	201	6	6	0
Shallotte	4,066	14	13	1
Sharpsburg	1,999	8	8	0
Shelby	20,168	85	72	13
Siler City	8,498	24	19	5
Smithfield	12,235	40	37	3

(Number.)

State/city	Population	Total law enforcement employees	Total officers	Total civilians
Snow Hill	1,570	6	6	0
Southern Pines	13,778	44	35	9
Southern Shores	2,897	13	12	1
Southport	3,617	11	11	0
Sparta	1,718	6	6	0
Spencer	3,296	14	13	1
Spindale	4,252	10	10	0
Spring Hope	1,311	6	6	0
Spring Lake	13,490	37	34	3
Spruce Pine	2,131	11	11	0
Stallings	15,569	26	21	5
Stanfield	1,491	5	4	1
Stanley	3,712	12	11	1
Stantonsburg	789	4	4	0
Star	874	4	4	0
Statesville	26,557	92	72	20
Stoneville	1,034	4	4	0
St. Pauls	2,422	18	13	5
Sugar Mountain	197	5	5	0
Sunset Beach	3,847	13	13	0
Surf City	2,256	20	19	1
Swansboro	3,250	11	10	1
Sylva	2,623	14	14	0
Tabor City	3,910	11	10	1
Tarboro	11,113	33	27	6
Taylorsville	2,078	11	11	0
Taylortown	825	3	3	0
Thomasville	27,117	72	66	6
Topsail Beach	424	9	8	1
Trent Woods	4,192	6	6	0
Troutman	2,576	14	14	0
Troy	3,411	12	11	1
Tryon	1,631	10	8	2
Valdese	4,455	13	12	1
Vanceboro	998	2	2	0
Vass	756	4	4	0
Wadesboro	5,541	26	20	6
Wagram	801	1	1	0
Wake Forest	39,996	83	68	15
Wallace	3,979	19	15	4
Walnut Creek	866	2	2	0
Warrenton	861	6	5	1
Warsaw	3,191	16	14	2
Washington	9,796	39	29	10
Waxhaw	14,367	26	24	2
Waynesville	9,801	42	34	8
Weaverville	3,988	15	14	1
Weldon	1,574	14	13	1
Wendell	6,368	17	16	1
West Jefferson	1,309	8	8	0
Whispering Pines	3,187	9	8	1
Whitakers	721	2	2	0
White Lake	778	6	6	0
Whiteville	5,635	24	22	2
Wilkesboro	3,527	23	21	2
Williamston	5,467	22	21	1
Wilmington	117,852	331	260	71
Wilson	49,734	124	109	15
Wilson's Mills	2,527	5	5	0
Windsor	3,819	9	9	0
Winfall	600	1	1	0
Wingate	3,930	7	7	0
Winston-Salem	243,507	699	536	163
Winterville	9,502	18	17	1
Woodfin	6,411	14	14	0
Woodland	733	1	1	0
Wrightsville Beach	2,581	25	23	2
Yadkinville	2,918	14	13	1

(Number.)

State/city	Population	Total law enforcement employees	Total officers	Total civilians
Youngsville..	1,228	11	10	1
Zebulon...	5,074	19	18	1
NORTH DAKOTA				
Arnegard...	129	2	2	0
Belfield...	1,115	3	2	1
Berthold..	510	1	1	0
Beulah..	3,450	7	6	1
Bismarck...	73,248	145	115	30
Bowman..	1,764	4	4	0
Burlington...	1,208	2	2	0
Carrington...	2,073	5	5	0
Cavalier...	1,233	4	4	0
Devils Lake..	7,394	18	16	2
Dickinson...	25,130	55	36	19
Ellendale...	1,281	2	2	0
Emerado..	434	1	1	0
Fargo..	121,217	183	160	23
Fessenden...	471	1	1	0
Grafton...	4,237	10	9	1
Grand Forks...	57,853	99	84	15
Harvey..	1,779	4	4	0
Hazen...	2,504	4	4	0
Hillsboro...	1,576	2	2	0
Jamestown..	15,417	36	31	5
Kenmare..	1,080	3	3	0
Killdeer...	1,392	5	5	0
Kulm..	342	1	1	0
Lamoure...	920	5	4	1
Lincoln..	3,776	4	4	0
Lisbon...	2,146	3	3	0
Mandan...	22,011	42	35	7
Medora...	138	3	3	0
Minot..	51,265	108	81	27
Napoleon...	785	2	2	0
New Town..	2,656	7	6	1
Northwood..	924	2	2	0
Oakes...	1,786	2	2	0
Powers Lake...	313	2	2	0
Rolla...	1,333	4	4	0
Rugby...	2,841	4	4	0
Sherwood..	253	1	1	0
South Heart...	459	3	3	0
Stanley..	3,079	5	5	0
Steele...	707	1	1	0
Surrey...	1,462	4	4	0
Thompson..	1,009	1	1	0
Tioga..	1,738	8	6	2
Valley City...	6,680	13	12	1
Wahpeton..	7,927	16	14	2
Watford City..	8,819	20	17	3
West Fargo...	35,389	61	51	10
Williston..	29,929	69	50	19
Wishek..	986	2	2	0
OHIO				
Ada..	5,782	9	8	1
Akron..	197,257	484	449	35
Alliance...	22,012	52	40	12
American Township..................................	12,254	1	1	0
Amherst..	12,156	26	20	6
Aurora...	15,897	36	28	8
Barberton..	26,172	44	42	2
Bath Township, Summit County..................	9,896	25	19	6
Bay Village...	15,346	27	23	4
Beavercreek...	46,490	61	47	14
Beaver Township......................................	6,492	14	11	3
Bedford...	12,678	36	31	5
Bellefontaine..	13,073	36	29	7
Bellville...	1,863	4	4	0

Table 19. Full-Time Law Enforcement Employees, by Selected State and City, 2016—*Continued*

(Number.)

State/city	Population	Total law enforcement employees	Total officers	Total civilians
Belpre	6,484	16	11	5
Bexley	13,775	36	30	6
Blanchester	4,249	7	7	0
Blue Ash	12,169	41	34	7
Bluffton	4,127	7	7	0
Bowling Green	31,404	52	37	15
Brecksville	13,390	38	30	8
Brooklyn	10,841	37	32	5
Brookville	5,902	12	11	1
Brunswick	34,774	53	40	13
Butler Township	7,856	14	14	0
Cambridge	10,341	27	22	5
Canal Fulton	5,489	11	10	1
Canfield	7,323	22	15	7
Carey	3,570	12	8	4
Catawba Island Township	3,539	4	4	0
Celina	10,383	21	16	5
Centerville	23,853	54	40	14
Chagrin Falls	4,003	12	11	1
Chester Township	10,371	12	12	0
Cincinnati	298,880	1,292	1,051	241
Circleville	13,930	27	21	6
Clearcreek Township	15,322	15	14	1
Cleveland	386,227	1,678	1,444	234
Cleveland Heights	44,696	104	95	9
Clyde	6,233	22	18	4
Coitsville Township	1,344	2	2	0
Coldwater	4,501	9	8	1
Columbiana	6,269	15	11	4
Conneaut	12,689	24	17	7
Copley Township	17,653	23	21	2
Cortland	6,894	9	9	0
Defiance	16,697	32	29	3
Delaware	38,658	59	52	7
Delhi Township	29,573	32	30	2
Dublin	45,860	91	63	28
East Cleveland	17,240	31	26	5
Eastlake	18,166	32	23	9
Elyria	53,633	94	79	15
Englewood	13,455	27	20	7
Euclid	47,416	98	92	6
Evendale	2,766	22	19	3
Fairborn	33,587	59	45	14
Fairfield	42,810	79	61	18
Fairfield Township	22,417	19	19	0
Fairport Harbor	3,093	6	5	1
Findlay	41,156	82	64	18
Forest Park	18,669	42	36	6
Fort Recovery	1,430	2	2	0
Fostoria	13,119	27	21	6
Gahanna	34,859	68	53	15
Genoa Township	26,415	26	24	2
Georgetown	4,436	7	7	0
Germantown	5,495	12	11	1
German Township, Montgomery County	2,893	4	4	0
Glenwillow	926	4	4	0
Grandview Heights	7,502	22	17	5
Gratis	855	2	2	0
Grove City	40,161	78	61	17
Groveport	5,813	24	23	1
Hamilton	62,423	120	111	9
Hamilton Township, Warren County	22,670	18	16	2
Harrison	10,819	24	21	3
Heath	10,528	25	18	7
Highland Heights	8,402	30	23	7
Hinckley Township	8,041	10	9	1
Hiram	1,238	2	2	0
Holland	1,698	9	9	0
Independence	7,132	44	31	13
Indian Hill	5,801	25	20	5

(Number.)

State/city	Population	Total law enforcement employees	Total officers	Total civilians
Jamestown	2,034	4	4	0
Kalida	1,566	1	1	0
Kent	29,995	56	42	14
Kettering	55,384	99	73	26
Lakewood	50,349	122	100	22
Lancaster	39,959	84	67	17
Lebanon	20,726	36	26	10
Lexington	4,715	13	9	4
Lima	37,715	102	84	18
Lithopolis	1,401	3	3	0
Lordstown	3,278	13	9	4
Louisville	9,115	12	11	1
Lyndhurst	13,624	35	27	8
Madison	3,182	5	4	1
Mansfield	46,656	116	82	34
Mariemont	3,431	11	10	1
Marysville	22,952	43	36	7
Mason	33,026	51	46	5
Maumee	13,875	56	42	14
Mechanicsburg	1,591	5	5	0
Medina	26,280	46	36	10
Mentor	46,852	110	81	29
Mentor-on-the-Lake	7,375	13	8	5
Miamisburg	20,000	37	34	3
Miami Township, Montgomery County	29,140	45	38	7
Middlefield	2,694	11	10	1
Middletown	48,768	103	68	35
Milan	1,343	3	3	0
Milford	6,910	19	17	2
Milton Township	2,470	5	5	0
Minerva	3,670	13	9	4
Minerva Park	1,327	7	6	1
Mingo Junction	3,299	4	4	0
Montgomery	10,558	22	20	2
Moreland Hills	3,303	16	15	1
Mount Vernon	16,685	33	30	3
Napoleon	8,566	19	14	5
New Albany	10,340	26	19	7
New Bremen	2,961	7	7	0
Newcomerstown	3,789	8	5	3
New Franklin	14,285	19	13	6
New London	2,366	5	5	0
Newton Falls	4,628	3	3	0
Niles	18,538	37	32	5
North Canton	17,435	29	22	7
North Ridgeville	33,095	47	38	9
Northwood	5,376	23	18	5
Norton	12,026	16	15	1
Norwalk	16,792	29	23	6
Oberlin	8,342	25	18	7
Olmsted Falls	8,859	10	10	0
Oregon	20,055	58	45	13
Ottawa	4,385	8	8	0
Perkins Township	11,844	23	22	1
Perrysburg Township	12,813	29	23	6
Pierce Township	11,559	16	15	1
Plain City	4,318	8	8	0
Port Clinton	5,939	18	13	5
Powell	13,273	21	19	2
Reynoldsburg	37,406	71	53	18
Richfield	3,713	24	17	7
Richmond Heights	10,445	25	19	6
Rittman	6,598	11	8	3
Rossford	6,547	16	15	1
Russell Township	5,250	10	9	1
Russellville	539	3	3	0
Sabina	2,530	5	5	0
Salem	11,943	21	21	0
Sandusky	25,078	49	47	2
Sebring	4,240	9	5	4

(Number.)

State/city	Population	Total law enforcement employees	Total officers	Total civilians
Seven Hills	11,661	17	16	1
Shaker Heights	27,478	82	60	22
Sharonville	13,819	48	40	8
Shawnee Hills	746	4	4	0
Shawnee Township	12,173	18	12	6
Sidney	20,797	46	36	10
Silver Lake	2,524	8	8	0
Solon	22,971	64	47	17
South Euclid	21,686	43	35	8
South Point	3,917	8	8	0
South Russell	3,827	9	9	0
Springboro	18,379	28	24	4
Springdale	11,175	39	33	6
Springfield	59,503	132	120	12
Springfield Township, Hamilton County	36,527	54	47	7
Springfield Township, Mahoning County	6,446	10	10	0
Steubenville	18,137	44	38	6
St. Henry	2,529	3	3	0
St. Marys	8,256	20	15	5
Stow	34,792	47	39	8
St. Paris	2,014	1	1	0
Streetsboro	16,364	37	29	8
Strongsville	44,626	85	71	14
Sugarcreek	2,236	6	6	0
Sugarcreek Township	8,283	18	17	1
Tallmadge	17,502	28	25	3
Thornville	997	1	1	0
Toledo	278,366	652	592	60
Troy	25,745	44	42	2
Uhrichsville	5,403	8	8	0
Union Township, Clermont County	47,933	62	48	14
University Heights	13,131	34	29	5
Utica	2,206	3	3	0
Valley View, Cuyahoga County	2,007	20	18	2
Vandalia	15,073	38	30	8
Van Wert	10,794	29	21	8
Walton Hills	2,236	18	13	5
Washington Court House	13,986	23	18	5
Waterville	5,511	12	11	1
West Carrollton	12,944	25	23	2
West Chester Township	61,080	106	83	23
Westerville	38,808	102	74	28
West Jefferson	4,291	15	11	4
West Salem	1,491	2	2	0
Whitehall	18,804	58	46	12
Whitehouse	4,528	10	10	0
Wickliffe	12,506	38	28	10
Wooster	26,883	43	40	3
Xenia	26,037	67	41	26
Youngstown	64,181	193	149	44
OKLAHOMA				
Achille	513	4	2	2
Ada	17,390	38	34	4
Allen	935	2	2	0
Altus	19,093	49	39	10
Alva	5,227	12	10	2
Anadarko	6,702	21	16	5
Antlers	2,336	9	4	5
Apache	1,426	3	3	0
Ardmore	25,315	70	51	19
Arkoma	1,912	5	3	2
Atoka	3,055	16	15	1
Barnsdall	1,203	2	2	0
Bartlesville	36,753	83	61	22
Beaver	1,442	2	2	0
Beggs	1,242	7	4	3
Bernice	561	2	2	0
Bethany	19,690	41	30	11
Big Cabin	261	5	4	1

State/city	Population	Total law enforcement employees	Total officers	Total civilians
Bixby	25,453	36	27	9
Blackwell	6,837	23	16	7
Blanchard	8,461	15	10	5
Boise City	1,103	2	2	0
Bristow	4,251	15	11	4
Broken Arrow	108,088	188	138	50
Broken Bow	4,133	19	14	5
Cache	2,944	6	6	0
Caddo	1,055	2	2	0
Calera	2,262	11	10	1
Caney	197	5	3	2
Canton	612	3	3	0
Carnegie	1,695	7	4	3
Carney	664	3	2	1
Cashion	857	3	3	0
Catoosa	7,145	16	15	1
Chandler	3,189	13	9	4
Checotah	3,246	13	9	4
Chelsea	1,970	3	3	0
Cherokee	1,574	3	3	0
Chickasha	16,579	40	30	10
Choctaw	12,382	19	18	1
Chouteau	2,088	9	8	1
Claremore	19,076	49	37	12
Clayton	790	5	5	0
Cleveland	3,209	7	7	0
Clinton	9,675	27	18	9
Coalgate	1,849	6	6	0
Colbert	1,191	5	2	3
Collinsville	6,678	15	11	4
Comanche	1,618	5	5	0
Cordell	2,917	6	5	1
Coweta	9,589	23	15	8
Crescent	1,550	8	4	4
Cushing	7,874	23	16	7
Davenport	822	1	1	0
Davis	2,816	11	9	2
Del City	22,152	45	35	10
Depew	483	2	2	0
Dewar	866	1	1	0
Dewey	3,511	12	11	1
Dibble	830	2	2	0
Drumright	2,874	5	5	0
Duncan	23,188	64	48	16
Durant	17,566	45	41	4
Edmond	91,869	158	119	39
Elgin	3,146	5	5	0
Elk City	12,939	41	27	14
El Reno	18,872	53	32	21
Enid	52,240	122	98	24
Eufaula	2,960	11	8	3
Fairfax	1,344	4	2	2
Fairview	2,672	9	6	3
Forest Park	1,089	6	4	2
Fort Gibson	4,068	11	10	1
Frederick	3,645	12	9	3
Geary	1,309	12	6	6
Glenpool	13,717	28	21	7
Goodwell	1,331	4	4	0
Grandfield	959	1	1	0
Grove	6,773	29	21	8
Guthrie	11,486	34	24	10
Guymon	12,001	22	15	7
Haileyville	773	3	3	0
Harrah	6,061	11	10	1
Hartshorne	1,997	5	5	0
Haskell	1,974	6	6	0
Healdton	2,774	6	5	1
Heavener	3,321	9	8	1
Hennessey	2,212	8	4	4

Table 19. Full-Time Law Enforcement Employees, by Selected State and City, 2016—*Continued*

(Number.)

State/city	Population	Total law enforcement employees	Total officers	Total civilians
Henryetta	5,732	18	12	6
Hinton	3,252	6	6	0
Hobart	3,596	13	7	6
Holdenville	5,743	14	9	5
Hollis	1,950	12	7	5
Hominy	3,499	8	4	4
Hooker	2,009	3	3	0
Howe	787	2	1	1
Hugo	5,206	23	16	7
Hulbert	605	3	3	0
Hydro	958	3	3	0
Idabel	7,006	25	19	6
Jay	2,479	12	8	4
Jenks	21,535	29	21	8
Jones	3,000	7	7	0
Kellyville	1,147	3	3	0
Kiefer	1,960	4	4	0
Kingfisher	4,912	13	11	2
Kingston	1,638	6	6	0
Krebs	1,958	8	6	2
Lahoma	659	2	2	0
Lamont	410	1	1	0
Lawton	96,420	235	167	68
Lexington	2,161	11	6	5
Lindsay	2,829	12	6	6
Locust Grove	1,403	8	4	4
Lone Grove	5,243	11	7	4
Luther	1,611	4	4	0
Madill	3,957	12	11	1
Mangum	2,894	16	6	10
Mannford	3,131	14	8	6
Marietta	2,750	7	6	1
Marlow	4,580	16	10	6
Maysville	1,234	4	3	1
McAlester	18,300	48	45	3
McLoud	4,633	10	9	1
Medicine Park	456	2	2	0
Meeker	1,177	6	5	1
Miami	13,620	38	29	9
Midwest City	57,797	125	92	33
Minco	1,661	4	4	0
Moore	61,511	93	88	5
Mooreland	1,298	2	2	0
Morris	1,458	3	3	0
Mounds	1,182	3	3	0
Mountain View	764	2	2	0
Muldrow	3,248	13	8	5
Muskogee	38,293	111	90	21
Mustang	20,813	33	23	10
Newcastle	9,816	18	17	1
Newkirk	2,242	5	5	0
Nichols Hills	3,921	20	16	4
Nicoma Park	2,483	5	5	0
Ninnekah	1,043	4	3	1
Noble	6,699	17	12	5
Norman	122,143	237	176	61
North Enid	938	4	4	0
Nowata	3,747	9	7	2
Oilton	1,015	2	2	0
Okemah	3,249	12	8	4
Oklahoma City	641,681	1,381	1,113	268
Okmulgee	12,177	26	24	2
Oologah	1,185	4	4	0
Owasso	35,551	73	55	18
Pauls Valley	6,163	18	13	5
Pawhuska	3,590	13	9	4
Pawnee	2,153	6	5	1
Perkins	2,862	8	8	0
Perry	5,091	20	12	8
Piedmont	7,420	11	9	2

(Number.)

State/city	Population	Total law enforcement employees	Total officers	Total civilians
Pocola	4,026	11	8	3
Ponca City	24,647	74	52	22
Porum	711	3	3	0
Poteau	8,770	31	25	6
Prague	2,466	17	8	9
Pryor Creek	9,455	27	22	5
Purcell	6,405	22	20	2
Ringling	996	2	2	0
Roland	3,604	10	7	3
Rush Springs	1,283	4	4	0
Salina	1,381	5	5	0
Sallisaw	8,530	28	20	8
Sand Springs	19,961	42	32	10
Sapulpa	20,667	53	40	13
Sawyer	316	3	3	0
Sayre	4,858	13	8	5
Seiling	887	2	2	0
Seminole	7,531	12	10	2
Shawnee	31,560	75	52	23
Skiatook	8,005	23	19	4
Snyder	1,336	3	3	0
South Coffeyville	771	7	5	2
Spencer	4,049	7	7	0
Sperry	1,281	2	2	0
Spiro	2,167	4	4	0
Stigler	2,783	13	9	4
Stillwater	49,637	111	72	39
Stilwell	4,026	17	12	5
Stonewall	475	2	2	0
Stratford	1,537	4	4	0
Stringtown	400	1	1	0
Stroud	2,782	15	8	7
Sulphur	5,130	12	10	2
Tahlequah	16,764	49	34	15
Talala	277	2	2	0
Talihina	1,091	10	5	5
Tecumseh	6,662	13	12	1
The Village	9,493	28	22	6
Tishomingo	3,080	8	7	1
Tonkawa	3,111	11	7	4
Tryon	504	1	1	0
Tulsa	405,748	912	747	165
Tushka	300	3	3	0
Tuttle	6,974	15	10	5
Union City	2,004	6	6	0
Valley Brook	784	14	8	6
Valliant	744	4	3	1
Verdigris	4,428	5	4	1
Vian	1,383	9	6	3
Vici	731	3	2	1
Vinita	5,621	22	15	7
Wagoner	8,787	20	15	5
Walters	2,486	4	4	0
Warner	1,619	3	3	0
Warr Acres	10,505	30	24	6
Washington	637	3	2	1
Watonga	3,002	10	8	2
Watts	308	3	2	1
Waukomis	1,381	4	4	0
Waurika	1,974	8	7	1
Waynoka	974	4	3	1
Weatherford	12,399	31	21	10
Webbers Falls	597	4	4	0
Weleetka	984	5	5	0
West Siloam Springs	839	9	9	0
Westville	1,554	9	5	4
Wetumka	1,238	5	4	1
Wewoka	3,449	8	7	1
Wilburton	2,653	7	6	1
Wilson	1,731	8	5	3

Table 19. Full-Time Law Enforcement Employees, by Selected State and City, 2016—*Continued*

(Number.)

State/city	Population	Total law enforcement employees	Total officers	Total civilians
Woodward	13,223	27	24	3
Wright City	741	3	2	1
Wyandotte	333	6	5	1
Wynnewood	2,226	6	5	1
Yale	1,222	6	3	3
Yukon	26,546	61	43	18
OREGON				
Albany	52,544	89	61	28
Ashland	21,017	42	29	13
Astoria	9,655	24	16	8
Aumsville	4,101	6	5	1
Baker City	9,741	18	15	3
Bandon	3,125	8	7	1
Beaverton	97,907	171	134	37
Bend	89,244	115	87	28
Black Butte		8	7	1
Boardman	3,378	11	10	1
Brookings	6,506	21	14	7
Burns	2,748	4	4	0
Canby	17,395	29	25	4
Cannon Beach	1,704	10	8	2
Carlton	2,080	4	3	1
Central Point	18,161	31	25	6
Clatskanie	1,761	5	4	1
Coburg	1,059	3	2	1
Columbia City	1,960	1	1	0
Condon	681	1	1	0
Coos Bay	16,224	37	24	13
Coquille	3,857	7	6	1
Corvallis	56,061	90	56	34
Cottage Grove	10,025	24	16	8
Dallas	15,411	20	17	3
Eagle Point	8,987	12	11	1
Enterprise	1,883	4	4	0
Eugene	164,883	323	188	135
Fairview	9,350	16	14	2
Florence	8,685	20	12	8
Forest Grove	24,433	36	31	5
Gearhart	1,536	3	3	0
Gervais	2,663	6	5	1
Gladstone	12,083	20	17	3
Gold Beach	2,284	7	6	1
Grants Pass	37,317	85	53	32
Gresham	111,491	153	122	31
Hermiston	17,280	38	27	11
Hillsboro	104,440	185	133	52
Hines	1,517	3	3	0
Hood River	7,719	16	14	2
Hubbard	3,323	6	5	1
Independence	9,355	18	14	4
Jacksonville	2,903	6	5	1
John Day	1,667	10	4	6
Junction City	5,935	14	8	6
Keizer	38,165	43	36	7
King City	3,804	7	6	1
Klamath Falls	22,296	41	36	5
La Grande	13,071	34	19	15
Lake Oswego	38,860	66	42	24
Lebanon	16,487	38	26	12
Lincoln City	8,588	32	21	11
Madras	6,735	11	10	1
Malin	804	7	7	0
Manzanita	627	4	4	0
McMinnville	34,242	43	37	6
Medford	80,794	137	100	37
Milton-Freewater	7,029	17	11	6
Milwaukie	20,935	42	38	4
Molalla	9,064	15	13	2
Monmouth	10,131	13	12	1

(Number.)

State/city	Population	Total law enforcement employees	Total officers	Total civilians
Mount Angel	3,448	9	7	2
Myrtle Creek	3,466	11	9	2
Myrtle Point	2,514	5	5	0
Newberg-Dundee	26,105	49	35	14
Newport	10,328	24	19	5
North Bend	9,669	25	16	9
North Plains	2,131	2	2	0
Oakridge	3,212	6	5	1
Ontario	10,925	25	22	3
Oregon City	36,485	52	45	7
Pendleton	16,927	27	23	4
Philomath	4,602	10	9	1
Phoenix	4,578	8	7	1
Pilot Rock	1,514	2	2	0
Portland	642,129	1,150	908	242
Prineville	9,595	29	16	13
Rainier	1,921	6	5	1
Redmond	29,164	45	36	9
Rockaway Beach	1,354	4	4	0
Rogue River	2,246	7	5	2
Roseburg	22,159	39	35	4
Salem	166,508	312	190	122
Sandy	14,104	21	17	4
Scappoose	7,005	11	10	1
Seaside	6,556	25	15	10
Sherwood	19,486	27	24	3
Silverton	9,860	18	17	1
Springfield	61,164	96	65	31
Stayton	8,028	15	13	2
St. Helens	13,184	15	13	2
Sutherlin	7,932	17	14	3
Sweet Home	9,337	22	15	7
Talent	6,483	10	8	2
The Dalles	15,413	25	22	3
Tigard	51,885	88	73	15
Tillamook	5,003	11	10	1
Toledo	3,521	12	7	5
Tualatin	27,370	45	37	8
Turner	2,010	2	2	0
Umatilla	7,026	13	11	2
Vernonia	2,139	5	4	1
Warrenton	5,340	12	11	1
West Linn	26,889	33	29	4
Winston	5,396	9	8	1
Woodburn	25,395	42	34	8
Yamhill	1,109	4	3	1
PENNSYLVANIA				
Abington Township, Montgomery County	55,623	114	92	22
Adams Township, Butler County	13,531	11	11	0
Adams Township, Cambria County	5,710	6	6	0
Akron	4,014	4	4	0
Albion	1,459	3	3	0
Alburtis	2,552	4	4	0
Aldan	4,168	5	5	0
Aleppo Township	1,903	17	14	3
Aliquippa	9,150	19	18	1
Allegheny Township, Blair County	6,652	8	7	1
Allegheny Township, Westmoreland County	8,213	10	9	1
Allentown	120,615	240	220	20
Altoona	45,158	69	61	8
Ambler	6,517	13	12	1
Ambridge	6,822	8	8	0
Amity Township	12,884	13	12	1
Annville Township	4,835	10	8	2
Archbald	6,951	18	18	0
Arnold	4,956	8	8	0
Ashland	2,718	2	2	0
Ashley	2,714	2	2	0
Aspinwall	2,756	7	6	1

Table 19. Full-Time Law Enforcement Employees, by Selected State and City, 2016—*Continued*

(Number.)

State/city	Population	Total law enforcement employees	Total officers	Total civilians
Aston Township	16,828	18	16	2
Athens	3,234	4	4	0
Athens Township	5,058	11	10	1
Avalon	4,630	6	5	1
Avoca	2,661	2	2	0
Avonmore Boro	976	1	1	0
Baden	4,018	3	3	0
Baldwin Borough	19,828	25	24	1
Baldwin Township	1,962	5	5	0
Bally	1,105	2	2	0
Bangor	5,189	11	10	1
Beaver	4,399	12	11	1
Beaver Falls	8,598	19	18	1
Beaver Meadows	837	1	1	0
Bedford	2,724	5	5	0
Bedminster Township	7,123	7	6	1
Bell Acres	1,396	3	3	0
Bellefonte	6,260	13	10	3
Bellevue	8,229	18	15	3
Bellwood	1,779	1	1	0
Ben Avon	1,776	17	14	3
Ben Avon Heights	377	17	14	3
Bensalem Township	60,362	122	99	23
Berlin	2,003	2	2	0
Bern Township	6,967	12	12	0
Bernville	950	1	1	0
Berwick	10,170	15	14	1
Bethel Park	32,077	44	38	6
Bethel Township, Berks County	4,136	3	3	0
Bethlehem	74,869	148	148	0
Bethlehem Township	23,869	36	35	1
Biglerville	1,211	2	2	0
Birdsboro	5,158	8	7	1
Birmingham Township	4,272	3	3	0
Blairsville	3,304	4	4	0
Blair Township	4,564	4	4	0
Blakely	6,289	6	6	0
Blawnox	1,413	3	3	0
Bloomsburg Town	14,532	20	16	4
Blossburg	1,512	2	2	0
Bonneauville	1,832	1	1	0
Boyertown	4,043	8	7	1
Brackenridge	3,201	4	4	0
Braddock Hills	1,857	2	2	0
Bradford	8,459	18	18	0
Bradford Township	4,814	5	5	0
Branch Township	1,774	2	2	0
Brecknock Township, Berks County	4,636	5	5	0
Brentwood	9,486	16	14	2
Briar Creek Township	3,005	4	4	0
Bridgeport	4,565	10	9	1
Bridgeville	5,081	9	8	1
Bridgewater	690	2	2	0
Brighton Township	8,434	8	8	0
Bristol	9,539	14	12	2
Bristol Township	53,978	68	61	7
Brockway	2,034	3	2	1
Brookhaven	8,090	8	7	1
Brookville	3,855	7	7	0
Brownsville	2,285	2	2	0
Bryn Athyn	1,397	5	5	0
Buckingham Township	20,440	22	20	2
Buffalo Township	7,258	5	5	0
Buffalo Valley Regional	12,284	16	15	1
Bushkill Township	8,430	17	16	1
Butler	13,198	24	23	1
Butler Township, Butler County	16,713	23	21	2
Butler Township, Luzerne County	9,713	11	10	1
Butler Township, Schuylkill County	5,657	4	4	0
Caernarvon Township, Berks County	4,074	8	7	1

Table 19. Full-Time Law Enforcement Employees, by Selected State and City, 2016—*Continued*

(Number.)

State/city	Population	Total law enforcement employees	Total officers	Total civilians
California...	7,004	8	7	1
Caln Township	14,167	21	20	1
Cambria Township	5,885	4	4	0
Cambridge Springs	2,528	3	3	0
Camp Hill..	7,929	13	12	1
Canonsburg	8,909	17	17	0
Canton	1,910	3	3	0
Carbondale	8,503	9	9	0
Carlisle..	19,225	33	30	3
Carnegie..	7,923	12	11	1
Carrolltown	810	2	2	0
Carroll Township, Washington County	5,539	2	2	0
Carroll Township, York County	6,309	11	11	0
Carroll Valley..	3,954	5	4	1
Castle Shannon...	8,219	16	15	1
Catasauqua	6,543	9	8	1
Catawissa	1,506	3	3	0
Cecil Township..	12,059	20	19	1
Center Township	11,750	15	14	1
Centerville	3,178	2	2	0
Central Berks Regional	9,458	15	14	1
Central Bucks Regional	15,380	30	27	3
Chambersburg...	20,770	36	33	3
Charleroi Regional	6,630	7	7	0
Chartiers Township	7,960	12	12	0
Cheltenham Township	37,064	78	70	8
Chester..	34,109	103	93	10
Chester Township	4,130	12	11	1
Cheswick..	1,727	1	1	0
Chippewa Township..	8,192	9	8	1
Churchill	2,973	10	10	0
Clairton	6,661	9	9	0
Clarion..	6,284	9	8	1
Clarks Summit	6,336	5	5	0
Claysville	806	3	3	0
Clearfield..	5,996	7	7	0
Cleona	2,146	4	4	0
Clifton Heights..	6,691	11	10	1
Clymer..	1,307	1	1	0
Coaldale	2,181	3	3	0
Coal Township	10,480	12	11	1
Coatesville..	13,157	33	29	4
Cochranton	1,104	2	2	0
Colebrookdale District...	6,007	11	9	2
Collegeville...	5,327	8	8	0
Collier Township	8,096	17	16	1
Collingdale	8,794	9	8	1
Colonial Regional...	20,361	26	24	2
Columbia..	10,385	20	17	3
Conemaugh Township, Cambria County................	1,910	2	2	0
Conemaugh Township, Somerset County...............	6,961	6	6	0
Conewago Township, Adams County.....................	7,200	10	9	1
Conewango Township	3,422	4	4	0
Conneaut Lake Regional	3,505	4	3	1
Connellsville..	7,492	15	14	1
Conoy Township	3,472	17	15	2
Conshohocken...	7,979	21	19	2
Conway...	2,145	4	4	0
Conyngham...	1,874	3	3	0
Coopersburg	2,428	7	7	0
Coplay..	3,236	4	4	0
Coraopolis	5,573	13	9	4
Cornwall..	4,249	7	6	1
Corry	6,384	12	11	1
Coudersport	2,469	4	4	0
Covington Township	2,265	3	3	0
Crafton..	6,316	10	9	1
Cranberry Township	30,940	31	27	4
Crescent Township...	2,601	2	2	0
Cresson	1,619	10	10	0

Table 19. Full-Time Law Enforcement Employees, by Selected State and City, 2016—*Continued*

(Number.)

State/city	Population	Total law enforcement employees	Total officers	Total civilians
Cresson Township	2,562	6	5	1
Croyle Township	2,274	1	1	0
Cumberland Township, Adams County	6,243	6	6	0
Cumberland Township, Greene County	6,385	3	3	0
Cumru Township	15,385	22	21	1
Curwensville	2,461	2	2	0
Dallas	2,779	4	4	0
Dallas Township	9,333	10	10	0
Dalton	1,204	2	2	0
Danville	4,686	8	6	2
Darby	10,687	18	17	1
Darby Township	9,329	14	13	1
Decatur Township	4,850	2	2	0
Delmont	2,631	4	4	0
Derry	2,576	2	2	0
Derry Township, Dauphin County	25,044	58	39	19
Dickson City	5,839	10	9	1
Donegal Township	2,432	3	3	0
Donora	4,641	6	6	0
Dormont	8,440	14	13	1
Douglass Township, Berks County	3,554	5	5	0
Douglass Township, Montgomery County	10,475	12	11	1
Downingtown	7,957	19	16	3
Doylestown Township	17,539	22	20	2
Dublin Borough	2,171	2	2	0
Du Bois	7,561	13	13	0
Duboistown	1,208	5	1	4
Dunbar	1,014	1	1	0
Duncansville	1,198	1	1	0
Dunmore	13,247	17	17	0
Duquesne	5,528	13	12	1
Duryea	4,935	4	4	0
East Bangor	1,655	1	1	0
East Berlin	1,537	1	1	0
East Bethlehem Township	2,288	1	1	0
East Brandywine Township	8,642	16	15	1
East Cocalico Township	10,502	15	14	1
East Coventry Township	6,767	8	7	1
East Deer Township	1,470	1	1	0
East Earl Township	6,848	8	8	0
Eastern Adams Regional	7,403	6	6	0
Eastern Pike Regional	4,614	11	10	1
East Fallowfield Township	7,590	7	7	0
East Franklin Township	3,949	1	1	0
East Hempfield Township	24,462	37	33	4
East Lampeter Township	17,090	38	35	3
East Lansdowne	2,665	5	3	2
East Marlborough Township	7,334	1	1	0
East McKeesport	2,671	3	3	0
East Norriton Township	14,171	30	28	2
Easton	26,938	66	62	4
East Pennsboro Township	21,712	22	21	1
East Penn Township	2,785	1	1	0
East Pikeland Township	7,411	8	8	0
East Pittsburgh	1,789	1	1	0
Easttown Township	10,644	14	13	1
East Union Township	1,591	2	2	0
East Whiteland Township	10,711	22	20	2
Ebensburg	3,175	4	4	0
Economy	9,389	13	12	1
Eddystone	2,407	10	9	1
Edgewood	3,059	9	9	0
Edgeworth	1,668	13	4	9
Edinboro	6,316	8	8	0
Edwardsville	4,716	13	12	1
Elizabeth	2,006	2	2	0
Elizabethtown	11,592	19	17	2
Elizabeth Township	13,216	12	12	0
Elkland	1,771	2	2	0
Ellwood City	7,561	12	10	2

(Number.)

State/city	Population	Total law enforcement employees	Total officers	Total civilians
Emmaus	11,398	21	19	2
Emporium	1,908	2	2	0
Emsworth	2,413	17	14	3
Ephrata	13,955	36	32	4
Erie	99,019	191	169	22
Etna	3,391	7	7	0
Evans City-Seven Fields Regional	4,599	3	3	0
Everett	1,745	3	3	0
Exeter	5,585	2	2	0
Exeter Township, Berks County	25,930	31	29	2
Exeter Township, Luzerne County	2,360	1	1	0
Fairchance	1,925	1	1	0
Fairview Township, Luzerne County	4,486	6	6	0
Fairview Township, York County	17,312	16	13	3
Falls Township, Bucks County	33,823	60	52	8
Fawn Township	2,348	1	1	0
Ferguson Township	19,222	24	22	2
Ferndale	1,544	1	1	0
Findlay Township	5,637	22	15	7
Fleetwood	4,085	5	5	0
Folcroft	6,643	12	11	1
Ford City	2,857	1	1	0
Forest City	1,789	2	2	0
Forest Hills	6,428	9	9	0
Forks Township	15,390	22	21	1
Forty Fort	4,109	4	4	0
Forward Township	3,336	1	1	0
Foster Township, McKean County	4,191	5	5	0
Fountain Hill	4,635	9	8	1
Fox Chapel	5,381	11	11	0
Frackville	3,715	5	5	0
Franconia Township	13,272	11	10	1
Franklin	6,255	23	17	6
Franklin Park	14,600	12	11	1
Franklin Township, Beaver County	3,970	3	3	0
Franklin Township, Carbon County	4,134	4	4	0
Franklin Township, Columbia County	588	4	4	0
Frazer Township	1,159	2	2	0
Freedom Township	3,418	3	3	0
Freeland	3,446	5	4	1
Freemansburg	2,611	2	2	0
Freeport	1,730	1	1	0
Galeton	1,119	1	1	0
Gallitzin	1,828	1	1	0
Geistown	2,353	3	3	0
Gettysburg	7,608	12	11	1
Girard	3,007	4	4	0
Glassport	4,408	5	5	0
Glenolden	7,177	11	10	1
Granville Township	5,046	10	8	2
Greencastle	4,051	5	4	1
Greenfield Township, Blair County	4,075	4	4	0
Greensburg	14,419	38	28	10
Green Tree	5,089	11	10	1
Greenville	5,794	8	7	1
Greenwood Township	1,912	1	1	0
Grove City	8,169	12	11	1
Hamburg	4,420	7	6	1
Hampden Township	29,684	26	25	1
Hampton Township	18,504	19	18	1
Hanover	15,537	28	25	3
Hanover Township, Luzerne County	10,901	16	16	0
Harmar Township	3,100	9	8	1
Harmony Township	3,100	5	5	0
Harrisburg	48,996	155	133	22
Harrison Township	10,448	21	18	3
Harveys Lake	2,763	3	3	0
Hastings	2,206	2	2	0
Hatboro	7,420	17	14	3
Hatfield Township	20,925	26	24	2

Table 19. Full-Time Law Enforcement Employees, by Selected State and City, 2016—*Continued*

(Number.)

State/city	Population	Total law enforcement employees	Total officers	Total civilians
Haverford Township	49,168	82	70	12
Hazleton	24,725	41	37	4
Hegins Township	3,457	2	2	0
Heidelberg	1,228	3	3	0
Heidelberg Township, Berks County	1,740	1	1	0
Hellam Township	8,666	10	8	2
Hellertown	5,809	11	10	1
Hemlock Township	2,266	6	6	0
Hempfield Township, Mercer County	3,705	7	6	1
Hermitage	15,958	32	29	3
Highspire	2,374	13	13	0
Hilltown Township	15,308	20	17	3
Hollidaysburg	5,782	9	7	2
Homer City	1,642	2	2	0
Homestead	3,104	12	11	1
Honesdale	4,185	5	5	0
Honey Brook	1,766	1	1	0
Hooversville	613	1	1	0
Hopewell Township	12,466	15	14	1
Horsham Township	26,669	47	40	7
Hughesville	2,093	3	3	0
Hummelstown	4,565	8	7	1
Huntingdon	7,017	12	12	0
Independence Township, Beaver County	2,442	1	1	0
Indiana	14,122	24	22	2
Indiana Township	7,267	10	10	0
Indian Lake	388	5	5	0
Ingram	3,271	4	4	0
Irwin	3,838	4	4	0
Ivyland	1,055	2	2	0
Jackson Township, Butler County	3,708	10	8	2
Jackson Township, Cambria County	4,180	2	2	0
Jackson Township, Luzerne County	4,648	2	2	0
Jeannette	9,274	17	14	3
Jefferson Hills Borough	11,505	17	16	1
Jefferson Township, Mercer County	1,875	2	2	0
Jenkins Township	4,453	3	3	0
Jermyn	2,082	1	1	0
Jessup	4,460	6	3	3
Jim Thorpe	4,614	8	7	1
Johnsonburg	2,351	2	2	0
Johnstown	21,227	41	38	3
Kane	3,588	3	3	0
Kennedy Township	8,211	10	8	2
Kennett Square	6,188	15	12	3
Kennett Township	8,294	6	5	1
Kidder Township	1,935	6	6	0
Kilbuck Township	689	17	14	3
Kingston	12,894	21	19	2
Kingston Township	6,963	11	11	0
Kiskiminetas Township	4,611	9	9	0
Kittanning	3,858	9	8	1
Kline Township	1,387	2	1	1
Knox	1,091	2	2	0
Koppel	739	2	2	0
Kulpmont	2,838	1	1	0
Kutztown	5,032	14	12	2
Lake City	2,952	3	3	0
Lancaster	59,340	148	124	24
Lancaster Township, Butler County	2,520	2	2	0
Langhorne Borough	1,594	1	1	0
Lansdale	16,558	32	23	9
Lansdowne	10,643	18	15	3
Lansford	3,771	5	5	0
Larksville	4,442	4	4	0
Laureldale	3,882	4	4	0
Lawrence Park Township	3,830	9	8	1
Lawrence Township, Clearfield County	7,489	9	8	1
Lebanon	25,549	44	41	3
Leechburg	2,055	3	3	0

State/city	Population	Total law enforcement employees	Total officers	Total civilians
Leetsdale	1,195	4	4	0
Leet Township	1,616	2	2	0
Lehighton	5,279	11	10	1
Lehigh Township, Northampton County	10,344	13	12	1
Lehman Township	3,474	3	3	0
Lewistown	8,260	15	14	1
Liberty	2,514	1	1	0
Ligonier	1,534	2	2	0
Ligonier Township	6,525	5	5	0
Limerick Township	18,939	27	25	2
Lincoln	1,059	4	2	2
Linesville	990	6	6	0
Lititz	9,232	17	14	3
Littlestown	4,486	9	8	1
Lock Haven	9,572	17	15	2
Locust Township	1,414	4	4	0
Logan Township	12,313	18	16	2
Lower Allen Township	19,206	23	20	3
Lower Burrell	11,408	18	17	1
Lower Frederick Township	4,901	3	3	0
Lower Gwynedd Township	11,574	19	18	1
Lower Heidelberg Township	6,059	11	10	1
Lower Makefield Township	32,793	42	38	4
Lower Merion Township	58,234	146	131	15
Lower Moreland Township	13,261	26	21	5
Lower Paxton Township	48,582	66	59	7
Lower Pottsgrove Township	12,194	19	17	2
Lower Providence Township	26,333	33	31	2
Lower Salford Township	15,415	20	18	2
Lower Saucon Township	10,764	17	15	2
Lower Southampton Township	19,185	33	30	3
Lower Swatara Township	8,881	16	14	2
Lower Windsor Township	7,486	10	9	1
Lykens	1,755	1	1	0
Macungie	3,146	5	5	0
Mahanoy City	4,053	3	3	0
Mahanoy Township	3,348	1	1	0
Mahoning Township, Carbon County	4,211	6	6	0
Mahoning Township, Lawrence County	2,943	2	2	0
Mahoning Township, Montour County	4,275	7	6	1
Malvern	3,527	6	5	1
Manheim	4,871	18	17	1
Manheim Township	39,930	75	63	12
Manor	3,310	3	3	0
Manor Township, Lancaster County	20,778	21	19	2
Mansfield	3,395	5	5	0
Marcus Hook	2,397	5	4	1
Marietta	2,612	17	15	2
Marion Township, Beaver County	899	2	2	0
Marlborough Township	3,332	3	3	0
Marple Township	23,805	32	29	3
Mars	1,650	1	1	0
Martinsburg	1,903	2	2	0
Marysville	2,535	2	2	0
Masontown	3,389	5	5	0
Mayfield	1,723	2	2	0
McAdoo	2,187	3	3	0
McCandless	28,902	30	28	2
McDonald Borough	2,085	5	5	0
McKeesport	21,156	55	52	3
McKees Rocks	5,992	10	9	1
McSherrystown	3,072	4	4	0
Meadville	12,999	28	22	6
Mechanicsburg	9,003	14	13	1
Media	5,370	22	14	8
Mercer	1,923	4	4	0
Mercersburg	1,557	2	2	0
Meshoppen	1,452	2	2	0
Meyersdale	2,063	6	6	0
Middleburg	1,313	3	2	1

Table 19. Full-Time Law Enforcement Employees, by Selected State and City, 2016—*Continued*

(Number.)

State/city	Population	Total law enforcement employees	Total officers	Total civilians
Middlesex Township, Butler County..	5,640	4	4	0
Middlesex Township, Cumberland County..................................	7,364	10	9	1
Middletown...	9,153	12	11	1
Middletown Township..	45,408	62	56	6
Midland..	2,552	3	3	0
Mifflinburg..	3,516	10	9	1
Mifflin County Regional..	16,889	14	14	0
Milford..	972	2	2	0
Millbourne..	1,162	1	1	0
Millcreek Township, Erie County...	54,089	78	62	16
Millcreek Township, Lebanon County......................................	5,600	2	2	0
Millersburg..	2,532	3	2	1
Millersville..	8,471	15	13	2
Millvale...	3,678	4	4	0
Milton...	6,908	9	8	1
Minersville..	4,232	5	5	0
Mohnton...	3,034	4	4	0
Monaca...	5,631	7	7	0
Monessen...	7,438	12	11	1
Monongahela..	4,172	11	8	3
Monroeville...	28,142	53	44	9
Montgomery..	1,553	1	1	0
Montgomery Township...	26,272	45	36	9
Montour Township...	1,314	3	3	0
Montrose..	1,509	1	1	0
Moon Township...	25,845	34	28	6
Moore Township..	9,235	11	10	1
Moosic..	5,758	10	10	0
Morris-Cooper Regional...	5,562	1	1	0
Morrisville...	8,581	13	11	2
Morton..	2,700	5	4	1
Moscow...	1,947	3	3	0
Mount Carmel...	5,698	8	8	0
Mount Carmel Township..	3,057	6	6	0
Mount Holly Springs..	2,038	2	2	0
Mount Joy...	8,204	13	12	1
Mount Lebanon...	32,692	54	45	9
Mount Oliver...	3,344	10	10	0
Mount Pleasant...	4,346	4	4	0
Mount Pleasant Township..	3,510	4	4	0
Mount Union...	2,387	5	5	0
Muhlenberg Township...	20,181	30	30	0
Muncy..	2,424	2	2	0
Muncy Township..	1,091	2	2	0
Munhall...	11,216	22	21	1
Murrysville..	20,142	23	21	2
Nanticoke...	10,218	15	14	1
Nanty Glo..	2,575	1	1	0
Narberth..	4,314	5	5	0
Neshannock Township...	9,319	8	8	0
Nether Providence Township..	13,827	15	14	1
Neville Township...	1,065	17	14	3
Newberry Township...	15,470	18	16	2
New Bethlehem..	2,741	2	2	0
New Brighton...	8,991	9	7	2
New Britain Township..	11,269	13	12	1
New Cumberland...	7,297	10	9	1
New Garden Township...	12,113	13	12	1
New Hanover Township..	12,814	10	9	1
New Holland..	5,439	15	14	1
New Hope...	2,507	11	9	2
New Kensington...	12,636	22	22	0
Newport Township...	5,399	2	2	0
New Sewickley Township..	7,454	9	9	0
Newtown...	2,217	5	5	0
Newtown Township, Bucks County..	22,914	32	28	4
Newtown Township, Delaware County...................................	12,864	19	17	2
New Wilmington..	2,190	5	5	0
Norristown..	34,425	82	67	15
Northampton...	9,846	14	12	2

Table 19. Full-Time Law Enforcement Employees, by Selected State and City, 2016—*Continued*

(Number.)

State/city	Population	Total law enforcement employees	Total officers	Total civilians
Northampton Township	39,559	47	41	6
North Belle Vernon	1,892	2	2	0
North Braddock	4,773	3	3	0
North Catasauqua	2,824	5	5	0
North Cornwall Township	7,811	9	9	0
North Coventry Township	8,054	12	11	1
North East, Erie County	4,148	7	7	0
Northeastern Regional	11,655	13	12	1
Northern Berks Regional	13,228	15	14	1
Northern Cambria Borough	3,625	2	2	0
Northern Lancaster County Regional	34,756	26	24	2
Northern Regional	34,787	31	29	2
Northern York Regional	68,894	53	49	4
North Fayette Township	14,733	24	19	5
North Franklin Township	4,601	10	10	0
North Hopewell Township	2,798	3	3	0
North Huntingdon Township	30,787	34	28	6
North Londonderry Township	8,420	10	9	1
North Middleton Township	11,542	11	10	1
North Sewickley Township	5,513	1	1	0
North Strabane Township	14,523	20	19	1
Northumberland	3,715	5	5	0
North Versailles Township	12,322	24	19	5
North Wales	3,254	4	4	0
Northwest Lancaster County Regional	19,732	18	16	2
Norwood	5,899	7	6	1
Oakmont	6,472	7	7	0
O'Hara Township	8,591	15	14	1
Ohio Township	6,401	17	14	3
Ohioville	3,461	2	2	0
Oil City	10,057	22	16	6
Old Forge	7,996	5	5	0
Old Lycoming Township	5,059	12	11	1
Oley Township	3,736	3	3	0
Olyphant	5,102	3	3	0
Orangeville Area	1,750	1	1	0
Orwigsburg	2,983	4	4	0
Overfield Township	2,847	1	1	0
Oxford	5,449	12	11	1
Paint Township	5,110	2	1	1
Palmerton	5,282	9	8	1
Palmer Township	21,492	36	34	2
Palmyra	7,476	9	8	1
Palo Alto	1,005	1	1	0
Parkesburg	3,705	9	8	1
Parkside	2,335	3	3	0
Parks Township	2,626	2	2	0
Patterson Township	2,962	4	4	0
Patton	1,665	2	2	0
Patton Township	16,027	20	18	2
Penbrook	2,968	7	7	0
Penndel	2,200	1	1	0
Penn Hills	41,841	53	50	3
Pennridge Regional	11,029	15	13	2
Penn Township, Butler County	4,941	4	3	1
Penn Township, Perry County	3,184	2	2	0
Penn Township, Westmoreland County	19,632	23	21	2
Penn Township, York County	16,243	24	22	2
Pequea Township	4,778	8	8	0
Perkasie	8,464	19	17	2
Perryopolis	1,717	2	2	0
Peters Township	22,274	23	21	2
Philadelphia	1,570,826	7,995	6,313	1,682
Phoenixville	16,695	31	30	1
Pine Creek Township	3,302	2	2	0
Pine Grove	2,134	2	2	0
Pitcairn	3,236	3	3	0
Pittsburgh	302,443	976	908	68
Pittston	7,635	9	9	0
Pittston Township	3,395	4	4	0

Table 19. Full-Time Law Enforcement Employees, by Selected State and City, 2016—*Continued*

(Number.)

State/city	Population	Total law enforcement employees	Total officers	Total civilians
Plains Township	9,743	19	18	1
Pleasant Hills	8,248	20	18	2
Plum	27,576	30	24	6
Plumstead Township	13,735	18	16	2
Plymouth	5,809	4	4	0
Plymouth Township, Montgomery County	17,887	51	45	6
Pocono Mountain Regional	42,284	46	41	5
Pocono Township	10,723	19	18	1
Point Township	3,695	5	5	0
Polk	790	2	2	0
Portage	2,484	2	2	0
Port Carbon	1,803	2	2	0
Portland	508	2	2	0
Port Vue	3,733	2	2	0
Pottstown	22,719	59	46	13
Pottsville	13,703	23	23	0
Pringle	967	20	19	1
Prospect Park	6,486	9	9	0
Pulaski Township, Lawrence County	3,323	2	2	0
Punxsutawney	5,841	12	9	3
Pymatuning Township	3,158	7	6	1
Quakertown	8,831	20	18	2
Quarryville	2,762	4	4	0
Raccoon Township	2,992	4	4	0
Radnor Township	31,625	46	42	4
Ralpho Township	4,301	6	6	0
Rankin	2,084	1	1	0
Reading	87,834	182	160	22
Reading Township	5,855	2	2	0
Redstone Township	5,425	3	3	0
Reilly Township	700	2	2	0
Renovo	1,229	1	1	0
Reserve Township	3,285	4	4	0
Reynoldsville	2,700	2	2	0
Rice Township	3,544	6	6	0
Richland Township, Bucks County	13,176	15	13	2
Richland Township, Cambria County	12,140	19	18	1
Ridgway	3,863	6	5	1
Ridley Park	7,041	12	10	2
Ridley Township	31,110	37	32	5
Riverside	1,909	3	3	0
Roaring Brook Township	1,936	1	1	0
Roaring Spring	2,528	3	3	0
Robeson Township	7,387	6	5	1
Robinson Township, Allegheny County	13,813	31	29	2
Rochester	3,551	7	6	1
Rochester Township	2,726	4	4	0
Rockledge	2,540	4	4	0
Ross Township	30,858	45	43	2
Rostraver Township	11,130	17	16	1
Royalton	1,048	5	5	0
Royersford	4,771	8	7	1
Rush Township	3,310	3	3	0
Sadsbury Township, Chester County	3,908	2	2	0
Salem Township, Luzerne County	4,197	5	5	0
Salisbury Township	13,762	19	17	2
Sandy Lake	651	1	1	0
Sandy Township	10,699	11	10	1
Saxonburg	1,485	1	1	0
Saxton	701	1	1	0
Sayre	6,418	13	10	3
Schuylkill Haven	5,189	8	8	0
Schuylkill Township, Chester County	8,587	13	11	2
Scottdale	4,226	6	6	0
Scott Township, Allegheny County	16,848	23	22	1
Scott Township, Columbia County	5,081	6	6	0
Scott Township, Lackawanna County	4,812	3	3	0
Scranton	77,332	170	150	20
Selinsgrove	5,820	7	6	1
Sewickley	4,364	9	8	1

(Number.)

State/city	Population	Total law enforcement employees	Total officers	Total civilians
Sewickley Heights	821	5	3	2
Shaler Township	28,467	28	26	2
Shamokin	7,124	11	10	1
Shamokin Dam	1,710	3	3	0
Sharon Hill	5,703	10	9	1
Sharpsburg	3,388	5	5	0
Shenandoah	4,835	4	4	0
Shenango Township, Lawrence County	7,323	7	7	0
Shenango Township, Mercer County	3,810	7	7	0
Shillington	5,263	8	7	1
Shinglehouse	1,086	1	1	0
Shippensburg	5,568	10	9	1
Shippingport	210	2	2	0
Shiremanstown	1,582	2	2	0
Shohola Township	2,332	1	1	0
Silver Spring Township	16,884	22	21	1
Sinking Spring	4,121	5	5	0
Slate Belt Regional	12,358	23	23	0
Slatington	4,285	6	6	0
Slippery Rock	3,605	4	4	0
Smethport	1,584	2	2	0
Smith Township	4,402	4	4	0
Solebury Township	8,628	16	14	2
Somerset	5,985	8	7	1
Souderton	6,771	6	5	1
South Abington Township	9,010	12	11	1
South Annville Township	2,939	2	2	0
South Beaver Township	2,656	4	4	0
South Buffalo Township	2,593	2	2	0
South Centre Township	4,197	4	4	0
South Coatesville	1,461	2	2	0
South Connellsville Borough	1,928	1	1	0
Southern Regional Lancaster County	3,863	8	8	0
Southern Regional York County	13,766	16	14	2
South Fayette Township	15,723	18	17	1
South Fork	866	1	1	0
South Greensburg	2,042	2	2	0
South Heidelberg Township	7,386	8	8	0
South Lebanon Township	9,796	8	7	1
South Londonderry Township	7,807	9	7	2
South Park Township	13,463	15	14	1
South Pymatuning Township	2,615	3	3	0
Southwestern Regional	17,774	15	14	1
Southwest Greensburg	2,073	2	2	0
Southwest Regional, Fayette County	7,688	4	4	0
South Whitehall Township	19,797	37	35	2
South Williamsport	6,261	9	7	2
Spring City	3,322	3	3	0
Springdale	3,369	3	3	0
Springdale Township	1,615	4	4	0
Springettsbury Township	26,931	35	32	3
Springfield Township, Bucks County	5,036	5	5	0
Springfield Township, Delaware County	24,438	37	32	5
Springfield Township, Montgomery County	19,603	30	28	2
Spring Garden Township	12,977	21	18	3
Spring Township, Berks County	27,517	30	29	1
Spring Township, Centre County	7,693	9	8	1
State College	58,119	65	55	10
St. Clair Boro	2,869	5	5	0
Steelton	5,921	12	11	1
St. Marys City	12,577	15	14	1
Stonycreek Township	2,695	3	3	0
Stowe Township	6,247	6	6	0
Strasburg	2,925	4	4	0
Stroud Area Regional	34,242	59	52	7
Sugarcreek	5,085	3	3	0
Sugarloaf Township, Luzerne County	4,111	5	5	0
Sugar Notch	970	7	1	6
Summerhill Township	2,354	2	2	0
Summit Hill	2,937	6	4	2

State/city	Population	Total law enforcement employees	Total officers	Total civilians
Sunbury	9,607	19	15	4
Susquehanna Regional	8,334	17	15	2
Susquehanna Township, Dauphin County	24,846	44	42	2
Swarthmore	6,214	9	9	0
Swatara Township	24,916	52	49	3
Sweden Township	853	1	1	0
Swissvale	8,829	15	15	0
Swoyersville	4,969	5	5	0
Sykesville	1,131	1	1	0
Tamaqua	6,777	7	6	1
Tarentum	4,449	8	7	1
Tatamy	1,128	1	1	0
Taylor	5,979	7	7	0
Telford	4,860	7	6	1
Throop	3,934	6	6	0
Tiadaghton Valley Regional	6,554	11	10	1
Tilden Township	3,591	3	3	0
Tinicum Township, Bucks County	3,957	5	5	0
Tinicum Township, Delaware County	4,113	19	17	2
Titusville	5,349	10	10	0
Towamencin Township	18,409	26	23	3
Towanda	2,792	7	7	0
Trafford	3,127	3	3	0
Trainer	1,847	4	4	0
Tredyffrin Township	29,601	47	42	5
Troy	1,259	2	2	0
Tullytown	1,856	7	6	1
Tulpehocken Township	3,309	3	3	0
Tunkhannock	1,770	3	3	0
Tunkhannock Township, Wyoming County	6,254	6	6	0
Turtle Creek	5,257	4	4	0
Tyrone	5,330	14	11	3
Union City	3,197	3	2	1
Uniontown	9,919	21	20	1
Union Township, Lawrence County	4,985	7	7	0
Upland	3,254	6	5	1
Upper Allen Township	19,815	23	22	1
Upper Burrell Township	2,260	2	2	0
Upper Chichester Township	17,054	23	22	1
Upper Darby Township	82,896	145	126	19
Upper Dublin Township	26,333	46	40	6
Upper Macungie Township	23,396	30	28	2
Upper Makefield Township	8,267	16	15	1
Upper Merion Township	28,661	80	64	16
Upper Moreland Township	24,270	41	35	6
Upper Nazareth Township	6,795	9	8	1
Upper Perkiomen	6,869	10	9	1
Upper Pottsgrove Township	5,511	9	8	1
Upper Providence Township, Delaware County	10,510	15	15	0
Upper Providence Township, Montgomery County	23,927	30	28	2
Upper Saucon Township	16,451	22	21	1
Upper Southampton Township	15,114	25	22	3
Upper St. Clair Township	19,726	36	29	7
Upper Uwchlan Township	11,603	11	11	0
Upper Yoder Township	5,210	13	13	0
Uwchlan Township	19,274	22	21	1
Valley Township	7,803	6	6	0
Vandergrift	4,999	9	8	1
Vandling	716	2	2	0
Vernon Township	5,449	2	2	0
Verona	2,436	4	3	1
Versailles	1,492	2	2	0
Walnutport	2,059	3	3	0
Warminster Township	32,577	48	43	5
Warren	9,264	21	15	6
Warrington Township	24,044	32	29	3
Warwick Township, Bucks County	14,741	18	17	1
Washington, Washington County	13,421	33	31	2
Washington Township, Fayette County	3,740	4	4	0
Washington Township, Franklin County	14,631	12	10	2

(Number.)

State/city	Population	Total law enforcement employees	Total officers	Total civilians
Washington Township, Northampton County..........................	5,180	5	5	0
Washington Township, Westmoreland County	7,216	7	7	0
Watsontown..........................	2,315	5	5	0
Waverly Township	1,708	3	3	0
Waynesboro..........................	10,902	18	16	2
Waynesburg..........................	4,021	11	8	3
Weatherly	2,450	4	4	0
Wellsboro	3,295	7	7	0
Wesleyville	3,204	8	7	1
West Brandywine Township	7,482	6	6	0
West Brownsville..........................	971	2	1	1
West Caln Township	9,097	2	2	0
West Carroll Township	1,234	2	2	0
West Chester..........................	20,129	60	47	13
West Conshohocken..........................	1,393	12	11	1
West Deer Township	11,975	12	11	1
West Earl Township	8,195	6	6	0
Western Berks Regional	2,549	6	5	1
West Fallowfield Township	2,602	2	2	0
Westfield	1,048	2	2	0
West Goshen Township..........................	23,398	34	30	4
West Grove Borough..........................	2,860	3	3	0
West Hazleton	4,485	4	3	1
West Hempfield Township..........................	16,538	23	20	3
West Hills Regional	10,302	12	11	1
West Homestead	1,917	7	6	1
West Lampeter Township	16,029	16	15	1
West Mahanoy Township	2,761	3	3	0
West Manchester Township	18,880	30	27	3
West Manheim Township..........................	8,371	9	9	0
West Mead Township	5,121	2	2	0
West Mifflin..........................	20,028	39	33	6
West Newton..........................	2,527	2	2	0
West Norriton Township..........................	15,799	30	27	3
West Penn Township	4,327	2	2	0
West Pikeland Township..........................	4,097	4	4	0
West Pike Run..........................	1,556	1	1	0
West Pittston	4,753	2	2	0
West Pottsgrove Township	3,885	9	8	1
West Reading	4,186	14	12	2
West Sadsbury Township..........................	2,481	5	5	0
West Salem Township	3,463	8	7	1
West Shore Regional	7,734	13	12	1
Westtown-East Goshen Regional	32,687	33	30	3
West View	6,668	13	11	2
West Vincent Township..........................	5,133	7	6	1
West Whiteland Township..........................	18,482	28	26	2
West York	4,560	8	8	0
Whitehall..........................	13,812	26	21	5
Whitehall Township..........................	27,426	50	45	5
Whitemarsh Township..........................	17,721	39	34	5
White Oak	7,758	13	12	1
Whitpain Township	19,237	38	30	8
Wiconisco Township	1,189	1	1	0
Wilkes-Barre	40,640	92	81	11
Wilkes-Barre Township..........................	2,921	15	14	1
Wilkinsburg	15,692	27	23	4
Wilkins Township	6,283	12	12	0
Williamsburg	1,216	1	1	0
Williamsport	29,163	55	51	4
Willistown Township	10,987	19	17	2
Wilson	7,758	13	12	1
Windber	3,938	3	2	1
Womelsdorf..........................	2,860	1	1	0
Woodward Township	2,408	2	2	0
Wrightsville	2,285	4	4	0
Wyoming..........................	3,038	4	4	0
Wyomissing	10,473	23	22	1
Yardley..........................	2,442	3	3	0
Yeadon..........................	11,537	14	13	1

Table 19. Full-Time Law Enforcement Employees, by Selected State and City, 2016—*Continued*

(Number.)

State/city	Population	Total law enforcement employees	Total officers	Total civilians
York	44,017	120	105	15
York Area Regional	55,292	48	44	4
Youngsville	1,653	2	2	0
Zelienople	3,689	10	9	1
RHODE ISLAND				
Barrington	16,218	30	23	7
Bristol	22,229	48	38	10
Burrillville	16,357	29	22	7
Central Falls	19,277	47	37	10
Charlestown	7,762	24	19	5
Coventry	34,967	69	55	14
Cranston	81,162	176	147	29
Cumberland	34,708	54	43	11
East Greenwich	13,120	42	34	8
East Providence	47,456	111	92	19
Foster	4,713	13	9	4
Glocester	10,037	20	15	5
Hopkinton	8,093	19	14	5
Jamestown	5,494	19	14	5
Johnston	29,322	80	67	13
Lincoln	21,770	42	34	8
Little Compton	3,505	13	9	4
Middletown	16,035	41	37	4
Narragansett	15,600	52	39	13
Newport	24,077	93	77	16
New Shoreham	1,046	8	4	4
North Kingstown	26,120	53	44	9
North Providence	32,540	78	61	17
North Smithfield	12,377	27	26	1
Pawtucket	71,640	170	138	32
Portsmouth	17,362	38	35	3
Providence	179,340	511	423	88
Richmond	7,621	18	13	5
Scituate	10,587	23	16	7
Smithfield	21,660	55	41	14
South Kingstown	30,872	70	52	18
Tiverton	15,768	41	29	12
Warren	10,460	27	22	5
Warwick	81,481	218	167	51
Westerly	22,675	60	49	11
West Greenwich	6,132	17	12	5
West Warwick	28,777	63	52	11
Woonsocket	41,511	114	92	22
SOUTH CAROLINA				
Abbeville	5,177	21	20	1
Aiken	30,800	114	86	28
Allendale	3,064	8	8	0
Anderson	27,522	128	91	37
Aynor	689	6	5	1
Bamberg	3,341	12	10	2
Barnwell	4,561	16	15	1
Batesburg-Leesville	5,457	24	20	4
Beaufort	13,477	55	48	7
Belton	4,374	12	12	0
Bennettsville	8,514	34	30	4
Bethune	347	1	1	0
Bishopville	3,237	13	11	2
Blacksburg	1,889	12	11	1
Blackville	2,273	6	5	1
Bluffton	17,498	56	50	6
Bonneau	508	4	2	2
Branchville	983	3	2	1
Briarcliffe Acres	544	1	1	0
Burnettown	2,795	2	2	0
Camden	7,132	33	25	8
Cameron	414	1	1	0
Cayce	13,729	74	57	17
Central	5,165	9	8	1

Table 19. Full-Time Law Enforcement Employees, by Selected State and City, 2016—Continued

(Number.)

State/city	Population	Total law enforcement employees	Total officers	Total civilians
Chapin	1,578	7	7	0
Charleston	135,153	530	430	100
Cheraw	5,766	27	25	2
Chesnee	907	5	5	0
Chester	5,462	22	20	2
Chesterfield	1,450	5	5	0
Clemson	15,767	39	29	10
Clinton	8,664	41	34	7
Clio	682	2	2	0
Clover	5,874	25	20	5
Columbia	134,489	424	338	86
Conway	21,874	53	49	4
Cottageville	733	6	6	0
Coward	749	1	1	0
Cowpens	2,288	7	5	2
Darlington	6,130	32	29	3
Denmark	3,274	11	10	1
Dillon	6,648	24	21	3
Due West	1,238	5	5	0
Duncan	3,350	19	17	2
Easley	20,911	55	44	11
Edgefield	4,762	9	9	0
Edisto Beach	415	7	7	0
Ehrhardt	499	3	2	1
Elgin	1,510	6	6	0
Elloree	677	3	3	0
Estill	1,933	10	9	1
Fairfax	1,787	7	6	1
Florence	38,382	120	92	28
Folly Beach	2,806	30	17	13
Forest Acres	10,654	33	26	7
Fort Lawn	862	3	2	1
Fort Mill	14,150	49	43	6
Fountain Inn	8,450	32	19	13
Gaffney	12,568	41	36	5
Gaston	1,662	3	3	0
Georgetown	9,044	39	35	4
Gifford	270	4	2	2
Goose Creek	41,540	90	63	27
Great Falls	1,923	5	5	0
Greeleyville	405	2	2	0
Greenville	65,686	230	182	48
Greenwood	23,250	60	56	4
Greer	28,927	72	54	18
Hampton	2,637	12	12	0
Hanahan	22,357	39	32	7
Hardeeville	5,893	22	20	2
Harleyville	699	4	4	0
Hartsville	7,837	37	33	4
Hemingway	427	4	3	1
Holly Hill	1,230	6	6	0
Honea Path	3,737	14	13	1
Inman	2,294	10	8	2
Irmo	12,240	26	23	3
Isle of Palms	4,419	24	17	7
Iva	1,288	10	10	0
Jackson	1,774	4	4	0
Jamestown	82	5	4	1
Johnsonville	1,509	6	5	1
Johnston	2,345	8	8	0
Jonesville	856	4	4	0
Kingstree	3,155	13	10	3
Lake City	6,809	23	19	4
Lamar	968	4	4	0
Lancaster	9,039	39	27	12
Lane	471	3	1	2
Latta	1,345	7	7	0
Laurens	9,173	31	27	4
Lexington	20,597	53	51	2
Liberty	3,242	15	10	5

Table 19. Full-Time Law Enforcement Employees, by Selected State and City, 2016—*Continued*

(Number.)

State/city	Population	Total law enforcement employees	Total officers	Total civilians
Loris	2,630	12	8	4
Lyman	3,456	10	9	1
Manning	4,023	17	16	1
Marion	6,674	21	18	3
Mauldin	25,540	60	49	11
McBee	853	1	1	0
McColl	2,049	7	7	0
McCormick	2,540	7	7	0
Moncks Corner	10,298	29	26	3
Mount Pleasant	84,277	167	146	21
Mullins	4,491	24	22	2
Myrtle Beach	31,864	300	219	81
Newberry	10,338	34	30	4
New Ellenton	2,134	4	3	1
Nichols	356	3	2	1
Ninety Six	2,050	7	5	2
North	737	3	3	0
North Augusta	22,755	88	62	26
North Charleston	110,490	394	327	67
North Myrtle Beach	15,945	103	73	30
Olanta	571	2	2	0
Olar	236	1	1	0
Orangeburg	13,365	84	58	26
Pacolet	2,373	7	7	0
Pamplico	1,249	2	2	0
Pawleys Island	108	5	5	0
Pelion	708	4	3	1
Pickens	3,183	13	13	0
Pine Ridge	2,263	7	3	4
Port Royal	12,417	23	22	1
Prosperity	1,204	3	3	0
Ridgeland	3,991	14	13	1
Ridgeville	1,811	2	2	0
Rock Hill	72,589	194	150	44
Salem	148	3	3	0
Salley	420	1	1	0
Saluda	3,603	13	11	2
Santee	930	6	6	0
Scranton	864	1	1	0
Seneca	8,308	50	37	13
Simpsonville	21,223	45	34	11
Society Hill	545	1	1	0
South Congaree	2,404	7	6	1
Spartanburg	38,083	138	115	23
Springdale	2,814	7	7	0
Springfield	499	1	1	0
St. George	2,197	10	10	0
St. Matthews	1,978	8	7	1
St. Stephen	1,829	6	6	0
Sullivans Island	1,940	11	10	1
Summerton	959	5	5	0
Summerville	50,154	115	94	21
Sumter	40,864	158	110	48
Surfside Beach	4,372	25	19	6
Swansea	904	3	2	1
Tega Cay	10,032	27	24	3
Travelers Rest	5,074	22	16	6
Turbeville	798	4	3	1
Union	7,981	34	31	3
Wagener	827	5	5	0
Walhalla	4,254	14	13	1
Walterboro	5,253	35	27	8
Ware Shoals	2,175	10	9	1
West Columbia	16,193	62	50	12
Westminster	2,493	11	11	0
West Pelzer	914	4	3	1
West Union	313	2	2	0
Whitmire	1,466	7	6	1
Williamston	4,161	17	16	1
Williston	3,007	11	10	1

(Number.)

State/city	Population	Total law enforcement employees	Total officers	Total civilians
Winnsboro	3,316	21	20	1
Woodruff	4,137	11	10	1
York	8,058	39	32	7
SOUTH DAKOTA				
Aberdeen	28,498	54	45	9
Alcester	752	2	2	0
Avon	567	1	1	0
Beresford	1,969	4	4	0
Box Elder	9,607	12	11	1
Brandon	10,042	13	12	1
Brookings	23,971	47	34	13
Canton	3,380	5	5	0
Clark	1,033	2	2	0
Deadwood	1,255	15	12	3
Eagle Butte	1,355	3	3	0
Elk Point	1,854	4	4	0
Faith	414	2	2	0
Flandreau	2,296	7	6	1
Freeman	1,284	2	2	0
Gregory	1,247	3	3	0
Groton	1,518	4	4	0
Hot Springs	3,507	8	7	1
Huron	13,459	36	26	10
Jefferson	511	1	1	0
Kadoka	718	1	1	0
Lead	2,974	6	5	1
Lennox	2,304	4	4	0
Leola	437	1	1	0
Madison	7,411	12	11	1
Menno	593	1	1	0
Milbank	3,162	7	7	0
Miller	1,427	4	4	0
Mitchell	15,749	30	27	3
Mobridge	3,465	16	8	8
North Sioux City	2,772	9	8	1
Parkston	1,483	3	3	0
Philip	747	2	2	0
Pierre	14,068	40	26	14
Rapid City	74,573	143	114	29
Scotland	816	1	1	0
Sioux Falls	175,152	276	239	37
Sisseton	2,451	7	7	0
Spearfish	11,429	31	21	10
Springfield	1,947	2	2	0
Sturgis	6,699	18	15	3
Summerset	2,329	3	3	0
Tea	5,064	6	6	0
Tripp	627	1	1	0
Tyndall	1,046	2	2	0
Vermillion	10,774	19	18	1
Wagner	1,593	5	5	0
Watertown	22,186	59	38	21
Webster	1,785	5	5	0
Winner	2,805	10	10	0
Yankton	14,575	29	26	3
TENNESSEE				
Adamsville	2,245	6	5	1
Alamo	2,486	5	5	0
Alcoa	9,503	49	41	8
Alexandria	978	3	3	0
Algood	3,770	14	14	0
Ardmore	1,213	11	7	4
Ashland City	4,650	13	11	2
Athens	13,717	31	29	2
Atoka	9,176	20	19	1
Baileyton	431	2	2	0
Baneberry	526	1	1	0
Bartlett	58,897	155	120	35

(Number.)

State/city	Population	Total law enforcement employees	Total officers	Total civilians
Baxter	1,388	6	6	0
Bean Station	3,085	7	7	0
Belle Meade	3,021	21	15	6
Bells	2,449	4	4	0
Benton	1,275	6	6	0
Berry Hill	549	18	14	4
Big Sandy	540	1	1	0
Blaine	1,869	2	2	0
Bluff City	1,719	8	8	0
Bolivar	5,032	24	22	2
Bradford	1,004	5	5	0
Brentwood	42,739	73	58	15
Brighton	3,018	6	6	0
Bristol	26,656	88	69	19
Brownsville	9,795	39	34	5
Bruceton	1,426	2	2	0
Burns	1,475	1	1	0
Calhoun	496	2	2	0
Camden	3,574	17	13	4
Carthage	2,273	12	8	4
Caryville	2,182	6	6	0
Celina	1,494	8	6	2
Centerville	3,574	23	13	10
Chapel Hill	1,471	6	6	0
Charleston	681	3	3	0
Chattanooga	177,801	523	434	89
Church Hill	6,714	11	10	1
Clarksville	152,526	348	282	66
Cleveland	44,423	103	85	18
Clifton	2,657	5	5	0
Clinton	10,091	40	33	7
Collegedale	11,245	22	22	0
Collierville	49,531	137	99	38
Collinwood	972	4	4	0
Columbia	37,219	97	85	12
Cookeville	32,292	90	70	20
Coopertown	4,426	4	3	1
Cornersville	1,227	2	2	0
Covington	9,039	36	35	1
Cowan	1,698	3	3	0
Cross Plains	1,725	2	2	0
Crossville	11,514	43	40	3
Crump	1,394	4	4	0
Cumberland City	300	2	2	0
Dandridge	2,949	12	11	1
Dayton	7,421	19	18	1
Decatur	1,571	6	6	0
Decaturville	869	1	1	0
Decherd	2,439	12	11	1
Dickson	15,501	48	43	5
Dover	1,465	5	5	0
Dresden	2,879	10	9	1
Dunlap	5,167	14	12	2
Dyer	2,262	7	6	1
Dyersburg	16,711	63	55	8
Eagleville	661	3	3	0
East Ridge	21,311	42	37	5
Elizabethton	13,672	40	36	4
Elkton	563	2	2	0
Englewood	1,529	6	5	1
Erin	1,288	5	5	0
Erwin	5,959	14	14	0
Estill Springs	2,043	6	6	0
Ethridge	476	1	1	0
Etowah	3,503	11	10	1
Fairview	8,440	19	18	1
Fayetteville	7,182	27	25	2
Franklin	74,771	139	128	11
Friendship	668	1	1	0
Gainesboro	954	5	4	1

State/city	Population	Total law enforcement employees	Total officers	Total civilians
Gallatin	35,154	92	71	21
Gallaway	654	1	1	0
Gatlinburg	4,229	53	44	9
Germantown	39,311	123	100	23
Gibson	370	4	3	1
Gleason	1,399	5	5	0
Goodlettsville	23,358	55	40	15
Gordonsville	1,203	6	6	0
Grand Junction	299	2	2	0
Graysville	1,517	5	4	1
Greenbrier	6,807	15	14	1
Greeneville	15,101	53	51	2
Greenfield	2,108	7	6	1
Halls	2,164	7	6	1
Harriman	6,195	17	16	1
Henderson	6,597	15	15	0
Hendersonville	56,965	132	105	27
Henry	467	1	1	0
Hohenwald	3,650	16	15	1
Hollow Rock	693	1	1	0
Hornbeak	406	1	1	0
Humboldt	8,287	35	29	6
Huntingdon	3,912	16	12	4
Huntland	852	5	5	0
Jacksboro	1,935	5	5	0
Jackson	66,990	256	212	44
Jamestown	1,945	9	9	0
Jasper	3,323	8	8	0
Jefferson City	8,549	29	27	2
Jellico	2,244	7	6	1
Johnson City	66,511	177	148	29
Jonesborough	5,338	21	17	4
Kenton	1,213	3	3	0
Kimball	1,398	9	9	0
Kingsport	53,059	153	113	40
Kingston	5,823	13	12	1
Kingston Springs	2,773	5	4	1
Knoxville	186,583	465	377	88
Lafayette	5,088	22	15	7
La Follette	6,977	30	21	9
La Vergne	35,228	66	53	13
Lawrenceburg	10,595	39	35	4
Lebanon	31,125	93	74	19
Lenoir City	9,175	24	22	2
Lewisburg	11,552	31	30	1
Lexington	7,859	32	27	5
Livingston	4,073	22	17	5
Lookout Mountain	1,887	21	16	5
Loretto	1,752	4	4	0
Loudon	5,800	15	14	1
Madisonville	4,823	20	17	3
Manchester	10,596	35	32	3
Martin	10,859	38	29	9
Maryville	28,661	56	50	6
Mason	1,594	4	3	1
Maynardville	2,343	4	4	0
McEwen	1,693	5	5	0
McKenzie	5,294	18	13	5
McMinnville	13,789	36	32	4
Memphis	656,434	2,385	1,978	407
Middleton	652	3	3	0
Milan	7,803	29	23	6
Millersville	6,748	16	12	4
Millington	11,002	41	30	11
Minor Hill	525	2	2	0
Monteagle	1,174	6	6	0
Monterey	2,858	7	6	1
Morristown	29,576	92	85	7
Moscow	528	4	4	0
Mountain City	2,463	8	8	0

(Number.)

State/city	Population	Total law enforcement employees	Total officers	Total civilians
Mount Carmel	5,424	4	4	0
Mount Juliet	33,048	70	55	15
Mount Pleasant	4,835	12	12	0
Munford	6,140	19	17	2
Murfreesboro	129,730	267	218	49
Nashville Metropolitan	668,685	1,708	1,398	310
Newbern	3,341	21	13	8
New Johnsonville	1,884	6	5	1
New Market	1,371	3	3	0
Newport	6,812	32	27	5
New Tazewell	2,943	9	9	0
Niota	718	4	3	1
Nolensville	7,164	6	6	0
Norris	1,655	11	7	4
Oakland	7,670	15	14	1
Oak Ridge	29,296	71	55	16
Obion	1,065	2	2	0
Oliver Springs	3,238	14	10	4
Oneida	3,701	17	12	5
Paris	10,143	37	26	11
Parsons	2,331	7	7	0
Petersburg	549	2	2	0
Pigeon Forge	6,230	69	57	12
Pikeville	1,642	3	3	0
Piperton	1,667	8	8	0
Pittman Center	578	3	3	0
Plainview	2,049	1	1	0
Pleasant View	4,327	5	5	0
Portland	12,502	36	27	9
Pulaski	7,572	28	26	2
Puryear	668	1	1	0
Red Bank	11,789	26	24	2
Red Boiling Springs	1,146	5	5	0
Ridgely	1,690	5	5	0
Ridgetop	2,021	6	6	0
Ripley	8,129	31	24	7
Rockwood	5,400	17	16	1
Rocky Top	1,764	9	6	3
Rogersville	4,374	13	12	1
Rossville	790	5	5	0
Rutherford	1,101	5	4	1
Rutledge	1,200	5	5	0
Savannah	7,035	20	18	2
Scotts Hill	985	2	2	0
Selmer	4,507	19	17	2
Sevierville	16,843	64	50	14
Sharon	911	1	1	0
Shelbyville	21,511	52	42	10
Signal Mountain	8,577	18	16	2
Smithville	4,662	15	14	1
Smyrna	48,016	100	77	23
Sneedville	1,338	1	1	0
Soddy-Daisy	13,215	36	29	7
Somerville	3,095	11	11	0
South Carthage	1,337	4	4	0
South Fulton	2,243	6	6	0
South Pittsburg	3,115	8	8	0
Sparta	5,131	15	14	1
Spencer	1,640	2	2	0
Spring City	1,998	9	9	0
Springfield	16,873	39	34	5
Spring Hill	37,599	52	48	4
Sunbright	544	2	2	0
Surgoinsville	1,785	1	1	0
Sweetwater	5,957	20	19	1
Tazewell	2,301	6	6	0
Tellico Plains	955	6	6	0
Tiptonville	4,331	7	7	0
Townsend	453	3	3	0
Tracy City	1,433	5	5	0

State/city	Population	Total law enforcement employees	Total officers	Total civilians
Trenton	4,108	20	15	5
Trezevant	838	1	1	0
Trimble	620	1	1	0
Troy	1,307	4	4	0
Tullahoma	19,229	42	37	5
Tusculum	2,667	2	2	0
Union City	10,506	42	34	8
Vonore	1,496	9	9	0
Wartburg	901	5	5	0
Wartrace	661	2	1	1
Watertown	1,524	5	5	0
Waverly	4,089	13	12	1
Waynesboro	2,380	6	6	0
Westmoreland	2,308	11	7	4
White Bluff	3,442	5	5	0
White House	11,419	25	22	3
White Pine	2,250	11	10	1
Whiteville	4,502	5	5	0
Whitwell	1,731	6	6	0
Winchester	8,545	25	23	2
Winfield	948	1	1	0
Woodbury	2,779	9	8	1
TEXAS				
Abernathy	2,728	5	5	0
Addison	16,067	68	59	9
Alamo	19,409	39	30	9
Alamo Heights	8,248	35	22	13
Alice	19,464	47	37	10
Allen	101,020	179	120	59
Alpine	5,939	16	11	5
Alton	16,137	21	16	5
Alvin	26,100	76	47	29
Amarillo	200,141	411	343	68
Andrews	14,428	20	19	1
Angleton	19,546	48	36	12
Anna	12,233	16	15	1
Anson	2,315	5	5	0
Aransas Pass	8,603	39	26	13
Arcola	1,679	6	6	0
Argyle	4,047	8	8	0
Athens	12,802	30	24	6
Atlanta	5,594	17	12	5
Aubrey	3,527	6	6	0
Austin	956,911	2,361	1,807	554
Azle	11,854	33	25	8
Baird	1,481	2	2	0
Balch Springs	25,474	53	36	17
Ballinger	3,767	9	7	2
Bangs	1,575	3	3	0
Bartonville	1,702	4	4	0
Bastrop	8,447	25	22	3
Bay City	17,595	63	41	22
Bayou Vista	1,603	6	6	0
Baytown	77,224	235	163	72
Beaumont	118,283	317	254	63
Bedford	49,803	126	76	50
Bee Cave	6,891	20	19	1
Beeville	13,362	34	25	9
Bellmead	10,212	31	20	11
Bellville	4,296	12	11	1
Belton	20,988	45	35	10
Benbrook	22,906	47	38	9
Bertram	1,398	3	3	0
Beverly Hills	2,034	13	9	4
Big Sandy	1,380	5	5	0
Big Spring	29,189	51	34	17
Bishop	3,154	10	6	4
Blanco	1,913	7	7	0
Blue Mound	2,509	11	7	4

Table 19. Full-Time Law Enforcement Employees, by Selected State and City, 2016—*Continued*

(Number.)

State/city	Population	Total law enforcement employees	Total officers	Total civilians
Boerne	14,368	51	38	13
Bogata	1,103	4	4	0
Bonham	10,070	27	18	9
Borger	12,894	29	27	2
Bovina	1,750	3	3	0
Bowie	5,108	20	15	5
Boyd	1,362	7	7	0
Brady	5,560	17	9	8
Brazoria	3,082	12	8	4
Breckenridge	5,556	19	12	7
Bremond	919	3	3	0
Brenham	16,736	38	33	5
Bridge City	7,959	21	15	6
Bridgeport	6,466	21	14	7
Brookshire	5,203	20	16	4
Brookside Village	1,577	4	4	0
Brownfield	9,750	24	19	5
Brownsville	185,583	354	244	110
Bryan	83,286	178	141	37
Buda	15,449	20	18	2
Bullard	2,906	11	10	1
Bulverde	4,999	16	15	1
Burkburnett	11,088	25	19	6
Burleson	45,116	82	61	21
Burnet	6,288	17	16	1
Cactus	3,198	10	8	2
Caddo Mills	1,497	5	5	0
Caldwell	4,318	11	10	1
Calvert	1,144	4	4	0
Cameron	5,445	16	11	5
Canyon	15,212	26	23	3
Carthage	6,858	23	17	6
Castle Hills	4,485	29	21	8
Castroville	2,960	10	9	1
Cedar Hill	49,215	87	64	23
Cedar Park	69,051	116	80	36
Celina	8,074	17	16	1
Center	5,218	25	18	7
Cibolo	28,077	37	32	5
Cisco	3,769	11	8	3
Clarksville	3,170	7	4	3
Cleburne	30,069	70	52	18
Cleveland	7,893	27	16	11
Clifton	3,344	8	7	1
Clute	11,490	30	22	8
Clyde	3,784	8	7	1
Cockrell Hill	4,340	21	15	6
Coleman	4,334	17	10	7
College Station	110,785	187	130	57
Colleyville	26,038	49	43	6
Collinsville	1,700	3	3	0
Colorado City	4,111	13	7	6
Columbus	3,625	12	11	1
Comanche	4,171	12	11	1
Combes	3,089	8	8	0
Commerce	9,062	23	17	6
Conroe	71,111	162	118	44
Converse	22,782	51	36	15
Coppell	41,654	69	62	7
Copperas Cove	33,237	67	45	22
Corpus Christi	327,948	625	444	181
Corrigan	1,529	19	13	6
Corsicana	23,974	45	36	9
Crandall	3,318	14	14	0
Crane	4,013	13	7	6
Crockett	6,480	16	14	2
Crosbyton	1,692	3	3	0
Crowell	850	1	1	0
Crowley	15,272	40	29	11
Crystal City	7,566	13	9	4

State/city	Population	Total law enforcement employees	Total officers	Total civilians
Cuero	7,167	16	15	1
Cumby	792	3	3	0
Daingerfield	2,432	8	7	1
Dalhart	8,455	19	15	4
Dallas	1,320,939	3,829	3,279	550
Dalworthington Gardens	2,395	17	12	5
Danbury	1,788	4	4	0
Decatur	6,621	30	25	5
Deer Park	34,156	83	56	27
De Kalb	1,653	5	5	0
Del Rio	36,177	76	60	16
Denison	23,237	58	44	14
Denton	134,054	217	161	56
Denver City	4,949	13	8	5
DeSoto	53,143	120	65	55
Devine	4,775	13	9	4
Diboll	5,399	19	14	5
Dickinson	20,131	44	29	15
Dilley	4,290	9	8	1
Dimmitt	4,153	9	7	2
Double Oak	3,118	8	8	0
Driscoll	754	5	4	1
Dublin	3,667	12	8	4
Dumas	15,051	30	24	6
Duncanville	40,075	66	54	12
Eagle Lake	3,652	11	10	1
Eagle Pass	29,257	78	63	15
Early	2,842	9	7	2
Eastland	3,799	12	10	2
Edgewood	1,452	4	4	0
Edinburg	86,535	195	141	54
Edna	5,855	12	10	2
El Campo	11,604	39	31	8
Electra	2,695	13	8	5
Elgin	9,229	26	20	6
El Paso	687,193	1,236	1,013	223
Elsa	6,861	23	17	6
Ennis	19,096	44	36	8
Euless	54,791	132	84	48
Everman	6,399	18	14	4
Fairfield	2,905	13	8	5
Fair Oaks Ranch	7,723	22	20	2
Fairview	8,685	15	15	0
Farmers Branch	33,571	100	68	32
Farmersville	3,474	12	10	2
Farwell	1,301	2	2	0
Ferris	2,552	15	10	5
Florence	1,249	2	2	0
Floresville	7,499	19	17	2
Flower Mound	72,600	121	81	40
Floydada	2,729	6	6	0
Forney	19,252	42	28	14
Fort Worth	851,849	2,007	1,566	441
Fredericksburg	11,205	34	30	4
Freer	2,718	10	6	4
Friendswood	39,402	78	58	20
Friona	3,849	10	6	4
Frisco	162,917	247	166	81
Fulton	1,580	1	1	0
Gainesville	16,349	56	42	14
Galena Park	11,209	23	18	5
Galveston	50,667	179	143	36
Ganado	2,116	3	3	0
Garden Ridge	3,971	13	12	1
Garland	238,859	454	326	128
Gatesville	15,717	26	17	9
Georgetown	67,436	117	80	37
George West	2,670	10	9	1
Giddings	5,102	16	12	4
Gilmer	5,246	19	15	4

Table 19. Full-Time Law Enforcement Employees, by Selected State and City, 2016—*Continued*

(Number.)

State/city	Population	Total law enforcement employees	Total officers	Total civilians
Gladewater	6,427	20	14	6
Glenn Heights	12,185	18	15	3
Godley	1,082	6	6	0
Gonzales	7,609	29	21	8
Gorman	1,045	2	2	0
Graham	8,857	25	23	2
Granbury	9,683	38	33	5
Grand Prairie	190,270	384	257	127
Grand Saline	3,130	7	7	0
Granger	1,536	2	2	0
Granite Shoals	5,104	9	9	0
Grapeland	1,404	3	3	0
Greenville	26,689	73	54	19
Gregory	2,012	5	5	0
Groesbeck	4,299	8	8	0
Groves	15,680	21	19	2
Gun Barrel City	6,048	19	13	6
Hallettsville	2,601	8	7	1
Haltom City	44,558	84	71	13
Hamilton	2,908	8	7	1
Hamlin	2,026	8	5	3
Harlingen	65,913	170	130	40
Hawkins	1,296	4	4	0
Hearne	4,459	18	12	6
Heath	8,400	20	19	1
Hedwig Village	2,724	23	17	6
Helotes	8,855	22	20	2
Hemphill	1,209	4	4	0
Hempstead	7,403	23	19	4
Hereford	14,941	33	27	6
Hewitt	14,384	35	23	12
Hidalgo	13,943	45	34	11
Highland Park	9,316	71	57	14
Highland Village	16,357	40	30	10
Hill Country Village	1,083	11	11	0
Hitchcock	7,753	26	19	7
Hollywood Park	3,338	13	12	1
Hondo	9,178	24	21	3
Hooks	2,739	7	7	0
Horizon City	19,808	40	23	17
Horseshoe Bay	3,585	21	19	2
Houston	2,334,348	6,632	5,182	1,450
Howe	2,840	6	6	0
Hubbard	1,359	5	5	0
Hughes Springs	1,780	9	9	0
Humble	15,770	80	57	23
Huntington	2,145	6	6	0
Huntsville	41,390	65	58	7
Hurst	39,345	121	75	46
Hutchins	5,809	23	17	6
Hutto	24,160	31	28	3
Idalou	2,343	4	4	0
Indian Lake	642	2	2	0
Ingleside	9,769	32	24	8
Ingram	1,828	7	6	1
Iowa Park	6,338	17	11	6
Irving	240,765	482	330	152
Italy	1,904	7	5	2
Itasca	1,621	6	6	0
Jacinto City	10,825	24	19	5
Jacksboro	4,410	9	8	1
Jacksonville	14,950	38	28	10
Jamaica Beach	1,059	6	6	0
Jarrell	1,209	3	3	0
Jasper	7,617	26	20	6
Jefferson	2,038	8	7	1
Jersey Village	7,954	28	26	2
Johnson City	2,021	5	5	0
Jones Creek	2,076	3	3	0
Jonestown	2,074	8	7	1

State/city	Population	Total law enforcement employees	Total officers	Total civilians
Joshua	6,101	14	12	2
Jourdanton	4,355	11	10	1
Junction	2,421	5	5	0
Karnes City	3,437	10	9	1
Katy	16,589	69	52	17
Kaufman	7,245	21	17	4
Keene	6,206	18	13	5
Keller	47,047	84	48	36
Kemah	2,028	20	16	4
Kenedy	3,444	12	11	1
Kennedale	7,910	22	20	2
Kermit	6,596	19	13	6
Kerrville	23,287	68	52	16
Kilgore	15,258	49	37	12
Killeen	143,248	353	252	101
Kingsville	26,227	67	47	20
Kirbyville	2,128	6	6	0
Knox City	1,194	2	2	0
Kress	681	1	1	0
Kyle	37,407	59	34	25
Lacy-Lakeview	6,629	26	17	9
La Feria	7,349	13	13	0
Lago Vista	6,643	23	16	7
La Grange	4,728	14	14	0
La Grulla	1,709	8	6	2
Laguna Vista	3,223	9	8	1
La Joya	4,350	16	11	5
Lake Dallas	8,053	19	14	5
Lake Jackson	27,676	59	44	15
Lakeside	1,401	3	3	0
Lakeview, Harrison County	6,454	16	12	4
Lakeway	14,771	45	31	14
Lake Worth	4,870	35	26	9
La Marque	16,191	35	29	6
Lamesa	9,429	24	18	6
Lampasas	7,898	31	18	13
Lancaster	39,219	57	48	9
La Porte	35,410	106	75	31
Laredo	259,325	546	473	73
La Vernia	1,312	7	7	0
La Villa	2,632	10	8	2
Lavon	3,045	10	9	1
League City	101,436	156	114	42
Leander	40,650	60	43	17
Levelland	13,997	33	22	11
Lewisville	105,762	219	149	70
Lexington	1,183	4	3	1
Liberty	9,169	26	18	8
Linden	1,978	6	5	1
Little Elm	41,421	51	47	4
Littlefield	6,033	19	12	7
Livingston	5,140	25	18	7
Llano	3,356	9	8	1
Lockhart	13,590	34	25	9
Lone Star	1,514	5	4	1
Longview	82,632	186	172	14
Lorena	1,745	6	5	1
Lubbock	252,900	526	392	134
Lufkin	36,581	99	75	24
Luling	5,838	19	12	7
Lumberton	12,500	20	17	3
Lyford	2,605	4	4	0
Lytle	2,946	8	7	1
Madisonville	4,681	15	13	2
Magnolia	1,932	17	15	2
Malakoff	2,292	6	6	0
Manor	8,200	28	24	4
Mansfield	65,882	225	95	130
Manvel	8,645	20	14	6
Marble Falls	6,323	32	19	13

State/city	Population	Total law enforcement employees	Total officers	Total civilians
Marlin	5,626	16	12	4
Marshall	23,876	67	47	20
Mathis	5,062	14	8	6
McAllen	142,227	408	262	146
McKinney	169,689	234	189	45
Melissa	8,132	11	11	0
Memorial Villages	12,282	45	32	13
Mercedes	16,830	38	31	7
Mesquite	145,786	300	218	82
Mexia	7,393	26	16	10
Midland	137,780	239	181	58
Midlothian	23,085	63	43	20
Mineola	4,649	19	13	6
Mineral Wells	14,391	37	28	9
Mission	84,380	193	148	45
Missouri City	75,607	131	102	29
Monahans	7,854	17	12	5
Mont Belvieu	5,482	18	11	7
Morgans Point Resort	4,257	9	8	1
Moulton	911	4	4	0
Mount Pleasant	16,058	45	32	13
Muleshoe	5,193	13	8	5
Munday	1,347	2	2	0
Murphy	21,175	34	23	11
Nacogdoches	34,079	87	63	24
Nash	3,177	8	8	0
Nassau Bay	4,118	12	12	0
Navasota	7,545	27	20	7
Nederland	17,240	38	24	14
Needville	3,088	7	7	0
New Boston	4,666	16	11	5
New Braunfels	73,334	142	117	25
New Deal	805	2	1	1
Nixon	2,482	7	5	2
Nolanville	4,876	10	10	0
Normangee	695	1	1	0
Northeast	2,535	8	8	0
Northlake	2,329	11	11	0
North Richland Hills	70,409	186	110	76
Oak Ridge	180	2	2	0
Oak Ridge North	3,181	17	17	0
Odessa	123,209	220	166	54
O'Donnell	803	1	1	0
Olmos Park	2,420	14	13	1
Olney	3,159	7	6	1
Olton	2,121	5	5	0
Omaha	986	2	2	0
Onalaska	1,770	8	8	0
Orange	19,493	56	40	16
Overton	2,532	12	7	5
Ovilla	3,933	10	9	1
Oyster Creek	1,136	11	7	4
Palacios	4,617	16	11	5
Palestine	18,194	54	37	17
Palmer	2,064	10	9	1
Palmhurst	2,714	18	13	5
Palm Valley	1,291	5	5	0
Palmview	5,763	37	27	10
Pampa	18,228	30	28	2
Panhandle	2,321	4	4	0
Pantego	2,558	16	11	5
Paris	24,706	86	61	25
Pasadena	154,648	345	268	77
Patton Village	1,632	18	17	1
Pearland	112,814	215	161	54
Pearsall	10,151	17	15	2
Pecos	9,669	41	19	22
Pelican Bay	1,653	4	4	0
Penitas	4,785	15	13	2
Perryton	9,354	24	14	10

State/city	Population	Total law enforcement employees	Total officers	Total civilians
Pflugerville	58,975	109	82	27
Pharr	77,744	164	125	39
Pilot Point	4,140	9	8	1
Pinehurst	2,078	8	6	2
Pittsburg	4,622	12	9	3
Plainview	20,667	40	33	7
Plano	288,242	512	350	162
Pleasanton	10,013	29	22	7
Port Aransas	4,055	30	19	11
Port Arthur	55,510	148	112	36
Port Isabel	5,015	25	18	7
Portland	16,340	42	27	15
Port Lavaca	12,458	23	17	6
Port Neches	12,741	22	19	3
Poteet	3,450	12	11	1
Pottsboro	2,267	9	8	1
Prairie View	6,538	7	6	1
Primera	4,743	9	8	1
Prosper	17,634	28	19	9
Queen City	1,466	6	6	0
Ralls	1,890	3	3	0
Rancho Viejo	2,502	8	8	0
Raymondville	11,104	23	14	9
Red Oak	12,278	26	24	2
Refugio	2,850	10	9	1
Reno	3,302	5	5	0
Richardson	113,216	248	155	93
Richland Hills	8,159	22	17	5
Richmond	12,245	38	28	10
Richwood	3,895	9	9	0
Riesel	1,021	3	3	0
Rio Bravo	4,819	1	1	0
Rio Grande City	14,518	39	28	11
Rio Hondo	2,453	7	7	0
River Oaks	7,782	22	17	5
Roanoke	7,707	40	29	11
Robinson	11,674	27	21	6
Robstown	11,596	32	24	8
Rockdale	5,619	16	10	6
Rockport	10,725	30	27	3
Rockwall	43,542	100	80	20
Rollingwood	1,570	9	9	0
Roma	10,310	36	28	8
Rosenberg	36,360	92	70	22
Round Rock	119,308	227	158	69
Rowlett	61,047	102	76	26
Royse City	11,914	17	16	1
Rusk	5,630	13	12	1
Sabinal	1,721	5	4	1
Sachse	25,467	42	28	14
Saginaw	22,540	42	34	8
Salado	2,140	5	5	0
San Angelo	101,870	193	162	31
San Antonio	1,498,642	2,819	2,152	667
San Augustine	1,989	8	7	1
San Benito	24,535	51	43	8
San Diego	4,350	8	7	1
Sanger	7,913	14	13	1
San Juan	37,075	58	47	11
San Marcos	64,380	143	103	40
San Saba	3,004	5	5	0
Sansom Park Village	4,892	14	13	1
Santa Anna	1,022	3	3	0
Santa Fe	13,172	26	21	5
Schertz	39,225	72	51	21
Schulenburg	2,941	9	8	1
Seagoville	16,085	29	20	9
Seagraves	2,836	7	5	2
Sealy	6,469	21	20	1
Seguin	28,319	78	56	22

Table 19. Full-Time Law Enforcement Employees, by Selected State and City, 2016—*Continued*

(Number.)

State/city	Population	Total law enforcement employees	Total officers	Total civilians
Selma	10,027	31	28	3
Seminole	7,656	14	12	2
Seven Points	1,447	12	8	4
Shamrock	2,007	7	3	4
Shavano Park	3,631	17	16	1
Shenandoah	2,914	24	23	1
Sherman	41,139	83	61	22
Shoreacres	1,624	6	6	0
Silsbee	6,693	21	15	6
Sinton	5,756	12	11	1
Smithville	4,159	18	11	7
Snyder	11,882	23	20	3
Socorro	33,447	41	29	12
Somerset	1,814	3	3	0
Sonora	2,841	7	5	2
Sour Lake	1,765	8	7	1
South Houston	17,650	40	29	11
Southlake	30,644	69	62	7
Southmayd	1,019	3	3	0
South Padre Island	2,895	34	25	9
Southside Place	1,859	13	8	5
Spearman	3,378	4	4	0
Springtown	2,841	15	11	4
Spring Valley	4,289	24	19	5
Spur	1,183	2	2	0
Stafford	18,602	65	48	17
Stagecoach	589	2	2	0
Stamford	2,944	7	6	1
Stanton	3,032	5	5	0
Stephenville	20,787	54	37	17
Stratford	2,085	3	3	0
Sugar Land	90,088	175	151	24
Sullivan City	4,223	12	8	4
Sulphur Springs	16,227	39	28	11
Sunrise Beach Village	734	5	5	0
Sunset Valley	708	14	13	1
Sweeny	3,780	8	8	0
Sweetwater	10,785	30	24	6
Taft	3,104	9	8	1
Tahoka	2,551	4	4	0
Taylor	16,979	36	25	11
Teague	3,575	8	8	0
Temple	73,411	178	144	34
Terrell	17,211	57	37	20
Texarkana	37,442	99	87	12
Texas City	48,095	82	61	21
The Colony	42,925	89	58	31
Thorndale	1,313	3	3	0
Thrall	936	3	3	0
Three Rivers	1,996	11	10	1
Tioga	874	2	2	0
Tool	2,274	11	7	4
Trinity	2,744	11	6	5
Trophy Club	12,645	20	16	4
Troup	1,986	9	8	1
Troy	1,883	6	6	0
Tulia	4,716	16	8	8
Tye	1,263	5	5	0
Tyler	105,044	238	190	48
University Park	25,103	53	39	14
Uvalde	16,619	54	38	16
Valley Mills	1,171	3	3	0
Van	2,695	8	8	0
Van Alstyne	3,406	14	9	5
Venus	3,366	10	9	1
Vernon	10,495	25	18	7
Victoria	68,603	142	107	35
Vidor	10,991	32	24	8
Waco	133,790	334	241	93
Waelder	1,115	4	4	0

State/city	Population	Total law enforcement employees	Total officers	Total civilians
Wake Village	5,466	8	7	1
Waller	2,559	11	10	1
Wallis	1,303	6	6	0
Waxahachie	34,152	76	59	17
Weimar	2,163	8	7	1
Weslaco	39,987	90	66	24
West	2,898	8	8	0
West Columbia	3,941	17	11	6
West Lake Hills	3,364	18	13	5
West Orange	3,459	11	9	2
Westover Hills	729	13	9	4
West Tawakoni	1,654	6	3	3
West University Place	15,932	33	24	9
Westworth	2,687	20	15	5
Wharton	8,706	33	24	9
Whitehouse	8,286	15	15	0
White Oak	6,317	20	16	4
Whitesboro	3,931	13	8	5
White Settlement	17,267	42	31	11
Whitewright	1,638	5	5	0
Whitney	2,103	8	7	1
Wichita Falls	104,685	284	199	85
Willis	6,401	18	16	2
Willow Park	5,130	13	12	1
Wills Point	3,551	10	10	0
Wilmer	3,978	17	12	5
Windcrest	5,877	36	26	10
Wink	1,087	2	2	0
Winnsboro	3,354	14	9	5
Winters	2,563	5	5	0
Wolfforth	4,371	12	11	1
Woodbranch	1,396	4	2	2
Woodville	2,457	10	9	1
Woodway	8,836	43	31	12
Wortham	1,019	4	4	0
Wylie	47,772	66	61	5
Yoakum	6,059	19	12	7
UTAH				
Alta	391	8	4	4
American Fork/Cedar Hills	39,028	42	35	7
Big Water	465	1	1	0
Blanding	3,876	5	5	0
Bluffdale	11,765	8	8	0
Bountiful	44,003	53	36	17
Brian Head	87	5	5	0
Brigham City	18,914	27	23	4
Cedar City	30,441	40	36	4
Centerfield	1,389	1	1	0
Centerville	17,204	23	18	5
Clearfield	30,783	42	31	11
Clinton	21,567	16	15	1
Cottonwood Heights	34,493	52	42	10
Draper	47,696	47	39	8
East Carbon	1,548	3	3	0
Enoch	6,348	8	4	4
Ephraim	7,009	5	5	0
Fairview	1,265	1	1	0
Farmington	23,505	20	17	3
Garland	2,449	3	3	0
Grantsville	10,253	15	13	2
Harrisville	6,347	10	9	1
Heber	14,954	24	19	5
Helper	2,094	6	5	1
Hildale	2,959	13	7	6
Hurricane	15,869	25	23	2
Kanab	4,406	7	6	1
Kaysville	31,055	29	26	3
La Verkin	4,220	4	4	0
Layton	75,482	107	75	32

(Number.)

State/city	Population	Total law enforcement employees	Total officers	Total civilians
Lehi	60,806	53	47	6
Lindon	10,958	17	15	2
Logan	50,767	84	55	29
Lone Peak	28,862	24	21	3
Mantua	741	5	5	0
Mapleton	9,479	9	8	1
Minersville	861	1	1	0
Moab	5,262	19	14	5
Monticello	2,085	3	3	0
Mount Pleasant	3,306	4	4	0
Murray	49,758	90	75	15
Myton	653	1	1	0
Naples	2,320	6	5	1
Nephi	5,594	12	10	2
North Ogden	18,654	22	19	3
North Park	15,088	12	10	2
North Salt Lake	20,572	25	20	5
Ogden	85,930	156	128	28
Orem	95,640	116	85	31
Park City	8,231	46	31	15
Parowan	2,951	5	5	0
Payson	19,738	21	20	1
Perry	4,739	8	7	1
Pleasant Grove	38,984	35	27	8
Pleasant View	9,548	10	8	2
Price	8,310	20	17	3
Provo	115,739	149	103	46
Richfield	7,597	17	15	2
Riverdale	8,699	22	19	3
Roosevelt	7,179	11	10	1
Roy	38,167	44	38	6
Salem	7,696	11	10	1
Salina	2,527	4	4	0
Salt Lake City	193,918	542	435	107
Sandy	94,601	143	109	34
Santa Clara/Ivins	15,107	17	15	2
Santaquin/Genola	12,289	12	11	1
Saratoga Springs	27,211	41	31	10
Smithfield	11,015	12	11	1
South Jordan	70,226	58	50	8
South Ogden	17,026	24	20	4
South Salt Lake	25,022	68	57	11
Spanish Fork	38,529	37	32	5
Springdale	561	5	5	0
Springville	32,825	35	25	10
St. George	81,755	155	107	48
Stockton	644	1	1	0
Sunset	5,191	9	8	1
Syracuse	28,011	23	21	2
Tooele	33,448	49	38	11
Tremonton	8,333	12	10	2
Vernal	11,687	25	22	3
Washington	25,564	26	24	2
Wellington	1,607	2	2	0
West Bountiful	5,559	10	9	1
West Jordan	113,595	146	112	34
West Valley	137,558	231	191	40
Willard	1,789	2	2	0
Woods Cross	11,600	19	16	3
VERMONT				
Barre	8,687	27	19	8
Barre Town	7,791	7	6	1
Bellows Falls	3,030	11	10	1
Bennington	15,265	31	23	8
Berlin	2,802	8	7	1
Bradford	2,760	2	2	0
Brandon	3,801	8	7	1
Brattleboro	11,607	37	22	15
Bristol	3,955	3	3	0

State/city	Population	Total law enforcement employees	Total officers	Total civilians
Burlington	42,454	134	96	38
Castleton	4,572	5	5	0
Chester	3,069	5	4	1
Colchester	17,437	35	27	8
Dover	1,095	7	6	1
Essex	21,217	31	25	6
Fair Haven	2,614	4	4	0
Hardwick	2,925	8	7	1
Hartford	9,747	30	22	8
Hinesburg	4,508	5	5	0
Killington	786	2	2	0
Ludlow	1,923	5	5	0
Lyndonville	1,187	3	3	0
Manchester	4,310	12	9	3
Middlebury	8,570	16	14	2
Milton	10,921	17	16	1
Montpelier	7,542	26	17	9
Morristown	5,452	11	11	0
Newport	4,415	14	12	2
Northfield	6,044	7	6	1
Norwich	3,369	5	4	1
Pittsford	2,858	1	1	0
Randolph	4,788	6	6	0
Richmond	4,134	6	6	0
Royalton	2,741	2	2	0
Rutland	15,698	46	34	12
Rutland Town	4,009	3	3	0
Shelburne	7,887	19	10	9
South Burlington	18,962	49	40	9
Springfield	9,132	21	16	5
St. Albans	6,799	28	22	6
St. Johnsbury	7,414	18	12	6
Stowe	4,474	11	11	0
Swanton	6,500	7	7	0
Thetford	2,603	2	2	0
Waterbury	5,120	2	2	0
Weathersfield	2,765	2	2	0
Williston	9,556	14	11	3
Wilmington	1,825	8	6	2
Windsor	3,447	10	10	0
Winhall	753	7	6	1
Winooski	7,178	20	16	4
Woodstock	2,971	8	5	3
VIRGINIA				
Abingdon	8,105	28	25	3
Alexandria	155,319	409	317	92
Altavista	3,478	13	13	0
Amherst	2,206	4	4	0
Appalachia	1,655	5	5	0
Ashland	7,559	28	25	3
Bedford	6,556	25	23	2
Berryville	4,323	8	7	1
Big Stone Gap	5,378	14	13	1
Blacksburg	44,528	71	61	10
Blackstone	3,467	12	9	3
Bloxom	384	1	1	0
Bluefield	5,247	22	17	5
Boykins	539	2	2	0
Bridgewater	5,939	9	9	0
Bristol	16,908	72	52	20
Broadway	3,831	5	5	0
Brookneal	1,120	2	2	0
Buena Vista	6,576	17	16	1
Burkeville	408	1	1	0
Cape Charles	1,019	3	3	0
Cedar Bluff	1,064	3	3	0
Charlottesville	46,979	157	124	33
Chase City	2,285	10	9	1
Chatham	1,482	3	3	0

Table 19. Full-Time Law Enforcement Employees, by Selected State and City, 2016—*Continued*

(Number.)

State/city	Population	Total law enforcement employees	Total officers	Total civilians
Chesapeake	236,570	501	387	114
Chilhowie	1,733	6	6	0
Chincoteague	2,909	14	10	4
Christiansburg	22,134	65	59	6
Clarksville	1,199	8	7	1
Clifton Forge	3,713	12	10	2
Clintwood	1,309	4	4	0
Coeburn	1,982	8	8	0
Colonial Beach	3,589	11	10	1
Colonial Heights	17,814	56	52	4
Covington	5,570	27	17	10
Crewe	2,225	6	5	1
Culpeper	17,733	52	44	8
Damascus	799	4	4	0
Danville	41,686	132	124	8
Dayton	1,598	7	6	1
Dublin	2,719	9	8	1
Dumfries	5,263	6	5	1
Elkton	2,826	7	6	1
Emporia	5,382	32	22	10
Exmore	1,443	6	6	0
Fairfax City	24,173	83	63	20
Falls Church	14,124	41	31	10
Farmville	8,159	28	26	2
Franklin	8,423	37	25	12
Fredericksburg	28,823	91	66	25
Front Royal	15,193	47	37	10
Galax	6,858	40	24	16
Gate City	1,937	5	5	0
Glade Spring	1,452	3	3	0
Glen Lyn	116	1	1	0
Gordonsville	1,595	7	7	0
Gretna	1,243	3	3	0
Grottoes	2,776	6	6	0
Grundy	970	6	6	0
Halifax	1,243	5	5	0
Hampton	135,504	393	271	122
Harrisonburg	52,972	113	95	18
Haymarket	2,019	7	6	1
Haysi	470	2	2	0
Herndon	24,806	70	55	15
Hillsville	2,666	14	13	1
Honaker	1,382	4	3	1
Hopewell	22,204	80	61	19
Hurt	1,269	2	2	0
Independence	923	2	2	0
Jonesville	968	4	4	0
Kenbridge	1,220	5	5	0
Kilmarnock	1,428	5	5	0
La Crosse	586	1	1	0
Lawrenceville	1,019	6	6	0
Lebanon	3,323	13	12	1
Leesburg	53,016	83	68	15
Lexington	7,264	19	17	2
Louisa	1,633	6	6	0
Luray	4,817	13	12	1
Lynchburg	80,215	198	172	26
Manassas	42,267	119	92	27
Manassas Park	15,912	43	34	9
Marion	5,956	22	20	2
Martinsville	13,553	51	46	5
Middleburg	835	6	6	0
Middletown	1,324	3	3	0
Mount Jackson	2,051	5	5	0
Narrows	1,940	5	5	0
New Market	2,220	5	5	0
Newport News	181,676	547	410	137
Norfolk	245,734	811	718	93
Norton	3,911	25	17	8
Occoquan	1,042	1	1	0

State/city	Population	Total law enforcement employees	Total officers	Total civilians
Onancock	1,260	5	5	0
Onley	516	5	5	0
Orange	4,992	16	14	2
Parksley	840	3	3	0
Pearisburg	2,655	7	7	0
Pembroke	1,073	3	3	0
Pennington Gap	1,793	9	8	1
Petersburg	32,293	120	93	27
Pocahontas	376	4	4	0
Poquoson	11,975	25	24	1
Portsmouth	95,813	312	231	81
Pound	957	5	5	0
Pulaski	8,855	31	27	4
Purcellville	9,547	16	14	2
Quantico	548	1	1	0
Radford	17,504	49	37	12
Remington	634	1	1	0
Rich Creek	744	1	1	0
Richlands	5,443	22	17	5
Richmond	222,430	802	680	122
Roanoke	99,978	292	245	47
Rocky Mount	4,803	23	21	2
Salem	25,396	85	62	23
Saltville	2,022	6	6	0
Shenandoah	2,334	6	5	1
Smithfield	8,418	25	21	4
South Boston	7,944	31	28	3
South Hill	4,503	18	16	2
Stanley	1,649	3	3	0
Staunton	24,399	62	46	16
Stephens City	1,962	3	3	0
St. Paul	910	6	6	0
Strasburg	6,622	19	17	2
Suffolk	88,342	243	182	61
Tangier	726	1	1	0
Tappahannock	2,387	10	9	1
Tazewell	4,378	17	15	2
Timberville	2,618	6	6	0
Victoria	1,668	4	4	0
Vienna	16,679	48	37	11
Vinton	8,266	25	23	2
Virginia Beach	453,017	951	779	172
Warrenton	9,953	26	24	2
Warsaw	1,492	4	4	0
Waverly	2,057	11	6	5
Waynesboro	21,464	53	42	11
Weber City	1,251	4	4	0
West Point	3,336	10	9	1
Williamsburg	15,256	40	37	3
Winchester	27,363	96	72	24
Windsor	2,681	6	6	0
Wise	3,093	13	12	1
Woodstock	5,277	18	16	2
Wytheville	8,097	39	29	10
WASHINGTON				
Aberdeen	16,155	48	35	13
Airway Heights	8,425	19	18	1
Algona	3,166	7	7	0
Anacortes	16,532	33	26	7
Arlington	19,142	28	23	5
Asotin	1,287	3	3	0
Auburn	78,400	128	108	20
Bainbridge Island	23,998	22	18	4
Battle Ground	19,734	26	22	4
Bellevue	142,238	215	175	40
Bellingham	86,005	174	113	61
Black Diamond	4,420	9	8	1
Blaine	5,130	13	11	2
Bonney Lake	20,449	32	27	5

(Number.)

State/city	Population	Total law enforcement employees	Total officers	Total civilians
Bothell	43,828	84	58	26
Bremerton	39,862	67	55	12
Brewster	2,350	6	5	1
Brier	6,753	8	7	1
Buckley	5,077	12	10	2
Burien	50,934	74	52	22
Burlington	8,680	32	27	5
Camas	22,350	29	26	3
Carnation	1,890	3	2	1
Castle Rock	2,197	6	5	1
Centralia	16,785	36	27	9
Chehalis	7,417	22	17	5
Cheney	11,703	21	15	6
Chewelah	2,607	6	5	1
Clarkston	7,330	15	14	1
Cle Elum	2,812	8	7	1
Clyde Hill	3,279	9	8	1
Colfax	2,883	6	6	0
College Place	9,114	13	10	3
Colville	4,728	12	10	2
Connell	5,747	6	6	0
Cosmopolis	1,583	6	5	1
Coulee Dam	1,092	3	3	0
Covington	19,529	24	18	6
Des Moines	31,523	43	32	11
Dupont	9,593	13	12	1
Duvall	7,876	13	12	1
East Wenatchee	13,746	24	21	3
Eatonville	2,930	5	4	1
Edgewood	9,918	9	8	1
Edmonds	41,705	63	54	9
Ellensburg	19,148	36	29	7
Elma	3,020	8	7	1
Enumclaw	11,709	30	17	13
Ephrata	8,116	18	15	3
Everett	108,988	226	187	39
Everson	4,128	7	6	1
Federal Way	96,338	159	130	29
Ferndale	13,338	22	19	3
Fife	10,134	40	30	10
Fircrest	6,728	8	8	0
Forks	3,787	12	5	7
Gig Harbor	9,124	18	16	2
Goldendale	3,439	8	7	1
Grand Coulee	2,064	7	7	0
Grandview	11,230	22	17	5
Granger	3,792	6	6	0
Hoquiam	8,342	24	23	1
Issaquah	37,308	61	33	28
Kalama	2,410	7	6	1
Kelso	11,897	31	27	4
Kenmore	22,340	18	14	4
Kennewick	79,837	106	91	15
Kent	128,604	188	139	49
Kettle Falls	1,596	4	3	1
Kirkland	88,627	130	94	36
Kittitas	1,439	3	3	0
La Center	3,159	10	8	2
Lacey	47,215	58	50	8
Lake Forest Park	13,369	23	19	4
Lake Stevens	31,440	33	27	6
Lakewood	60,153	112	96	16
Langley	1,085	4	4	0
Liberty Lake	9,187	12	11	1
Long Beach	1,359	7	6	1
Longview	36,854	69	58	11
Lynden	13,834	19	15	4
Lynnwood	37,217	102	70	32
Mabton	2,300	4	4	0
Maple Valley	26,304	24	19	5

(Number.)

State/city	Population	Total law enforcement employees	Total officers	Total civilians
Marysville	68,172	88	64	24
Mattawa	4,568	4	4	0
McCleary	1,612	3	3	0
Medina	3,278	9	8	1
Mercer Island	25,527	35	31	4
Mill Creek	20,419	27	22	5
Milton	7,785	14	13	1
Monroe	18,247	43	33	10
Montesano	3,875	9	8	1
Morton	1,129	3	3	0
Moses Lake	22,372	40	32	8
Mountlake Terrace	21,212	33	26	7
Mount Vernon	34,521	54	42	12
Moxee	3,911	5	5	0
Mukilteo	21,416	31	26	5
Napavine	1,794	2	2	0
Newcastle	11,576	12	9	3
Normandy Park	6,733	7	6	1
Oak Harbor	22,795	36	24	12
Ocean Shores	5,721	13	12	1
Odessa	864	2	2	0
Olympia	50,972	95	67	28
Omak	4,854	13	11	2
Oroville	1,674	6	5	1
Orting	7,594	11	11	0
Othello	7,893	21	14	7
Pacific	7,228	14	12	2
Palouse	1,027	3	3	0
Pasco	71,077	83	71	12
Pe Ell	634	1	1	0
Port Angeles	19,525	58	31	27
Port Orchard	13,897	25	23	2
Port Townsend	9,378	15	13	2
Poulsbo	10,199	20	17	3
Prosser	5,895	14	13	1
Pullman	33,456	40	29	11
Puyallup	40,167	77	56	21
Quincy	7,482	25	17	8
Raymond	2,804	7	6	1
Reardan	551	1	1	0
Redmond	61,893	123	79	44
Renton	101,908	146	117	29
Republic	1,072	2	2	0
Richland	55,475	76	62	14
Ridgefield	6,852	10	9	1
Ritzville	1,663	4	4	0
Roy	809	2	2	0
Royal City	2,234	3	3	0
Ruston	808	3	3	0
Sammamish	53,387	40	32	8
SeaTac	28,466	60	43	17
Seattle	700,313	1,946	1,384	562
Sedro Woolley	10,860	20	17	3
Selah	7,753	18	15	3
Sequim	6,868	22	19	3
Shelton	9,830	20	18	2
Shoreline	55,905	73	53	20
Snohomish	9,773	20	18	2
Snoqualmie	13,713	25	21	4
Soap Lake	1,586	5	4	1
South Bend	1,609	5	4	1
Spokane	214,028	400	307	93
Spokane Valley	95,923	102	101	1
Springdale	273	1	1	0
Stanwood	6,888	13	11	2
Steilacoom	6,257	10	9	1
Sumas	1,386	7	6	1
Sumner	9,753	23	19	4
Sunnyside	16,387	51	28	23
Tacoma	209,914	371	336	35

Table 19. Full-Time Law Enforcement Employees, by Selected State and City, 2016—*Continued*

(Number.)

State/city	Population	Total law enforcement employees	Total officers	Total civilians
Tenino...	1,761	3	2	1
Tieton..	1,264	3	2	1
Toledo...	727	5	4	1
Tonasket...	1,012	5	4	1
Toppenish...	8,997	22	13	9
Tukwila..	20,195	94	77	17
Tumwater..	19,569	33	28	5
Twisp...	946	2	2	0
Union Gap...	6,031	19	16	3
University Place.................................	33,196	16	15	1
Vancouver...	174,912	235	193	42
Walla Walla.......................................	32,326	71	46	25
Wapato..	5,067	18	15	3
Warden..	2,743	5	4	1
Washougal...	15,527	25	20	5
Wenatchee..	33,920	47	38	9
Westport..	2,011	8	7	1
West Richland....................................	14,127	21	18	3
White Salmon....................................	2,364	7	6	1
Winthrop...	425	2	1	1
Woodinville.......................................	11,953	19	15	4
Woodland..	5,902	12	10	2
Yakima..	94,111	183	140	43
Yelm...	8,780	14	12	2
Zillah..	3,157	8	7	1
WEST VIRGINIA				
Alderson..	1,181	3	3	0
Anmoore...	753	2	2	0
Ansted...	1,394	3	2	1
Athens...	933	1	1	0
Barboursville.....................................	4,091	22	20	2
Barrackville.......................................	1,324	3	2	1
Beckley..	16,940	73	54	19
Belington...	1,935	3	3	0
Belle...	1,202	4	4	0
Benwood...	1,350	6	6	0
Berkeley Springs...............................	606	2	2	0
Bethlehem...	2,410	4	4	0
Bluefield..	10,298	36	28	8
Bradshaw..	302	1	1	0
Bramwell...	362	2	2	0
Bridgeport...	8,402	33	29	4
Buckhannon......................................	5,662	11	10	1
Burnsville..	496	2	2	0
Cameron..	895	3	3	0
Capon Bridge....................................	363	3	2	1
Cedar Grove......................................	943	2	2	0
Ceredo..	1,377	9	5	4
Chapmanville....................................	1,199	3	3	0
Charleston...	49,429	187	163	24
Charles Town....................................	6,030	16	14	2
Chesapeake.......................................	1,492	3	3	0
Chester..	2,481	6	5	1
Clarksburg...	16,067	45	41	4
Clendenin..	1,179	3	3	0
Danville...	648	1	1	0
Davy...	378	1	1	0
Delbarton..	533	3	3	0
Dunbar..	7,612	16	15	1
Eleanor...	1,599	2	2	0
Elkins..	7,235	12	11	1
Fairmont...	18,733	40	34	6
Fairview..	415	1	1	0
Farmington..	377	2	1	1
Fayetteville.......................................	2,885	10	9	1
Follansbee...	2,870	7	7	0
Fort Gay..	678	3	3	0
Gary..	874	2	2	0
Gassaway..	901	1	1	0

State/city	Population	Total law enforcement employees	Total officers	Total civilians
Gauley Bridge	591	3	1	2
Gilbert	419	2	2	0
Glasgow	872	3	3	0
Glen Dale	1,452	11	6	5
Glenville	1,542	4	3	1
Grafton	5,145	7	6	1
Grantsville	546	3	3	0
Grant Town	619	1	1	0
Granville	3,362	13	13	0
Hamlin	1,120	2	2	0
Handley	339	1	1	0
Harpers Ferry/Bolivar	1,361	3	2	1
Harrisville	1,757	1	1	0
Hinton	2,500	6	5	1
Huntington	48,540	116	105	11
Hurricane	6,534	18	16	2
Iaeger	270	1	1	0
Kenova	3,058	13	8	5
Kermit	377	1	1	0
Keyser	5,212	14	9	5
Kimball	175	1	1	0
Kingwood	2,963	2	2	0
Lewisburg	3,971	14	12	2
Logan	1,625	9	8	1
Lumberport	861	2	2	0
Mabscott	1,365	3	3	0
Madison	2,900	6	6	0
Man	694	3	3	0
Mannington	2,079	4	4	0
Marmet	1,440	7	7	0
Martinsburg	17,789	51	44	7
Mason	937	3	3	0
Matewan	461	1	1	0
Matoaka	219	1	1	0
McMechen	1,826	3	3	0
Milton	2,683	8	7	1
Monongah	1,100	1	1	0
Montgomery	1,588	4	3	1
Moorefield	2,467	9	8	1
Morgantown	31,109	76	65	11
Moundsville	8,644	20	16	4
Mount Hope	1,371	5	4	1
Mullens	1,445	4	4	0
New Cumberland	1,055	2	2	0
New Haven	1,527	4	3	1
New Martinsville	5,190	15	11	4
Nitro	6,729	17	16	1
Nutter Fort	1,570	6	6	0
Oak Hill	8,104	19	15	4
Oceana	1,285	4	4	0
Paden City	2,483	5	4	1
Parkersburg	30,913	76	68	8
Parsons	1,424	1	1	0
Paw Paw	490	2	1	1
Pennsboro	1,068	1	1	0
Petersburg	2,543	2	2	0
Philippi	3,320	6	6	0
Piedmont	829	1	1	0
Pineville	621	3	3	0
Point Pleasant	4,262	10	9	1
Pratt	583	1	1	0
Princeton	6,017	23	21	2
Rainelle	1,480	5	4	1
Ranson	5,053	13	12	1
Ravenswood	3,837	12	11	1
Rhodell	169	2	1	1
Richwood	1,966	2	2	0
Ridgeley	637	2	1	1
Ripley	3,255	10	9	1
Rivesville	946	1	1	0

(Number.)

State/city	Population	Total law enforcement employees	Total officers	Total civilians
Romney	1,759	4	3	1
Ronceverte	1,749	6	6	0
Salem	1,544	3	3	0
Shepherdstown	2,064	6	5	1
Shinnston	2,164	7	7	0
Sistersville	1,361	4	4	0
Smithers	786	3	2	1
Sophia	1,313	4	4	0
South Charleston	12,957	45	42	3
Spencer	2,175	6	6	0
St. Albans	10,635	25	23	2
Star City	2,054	7	7	0
St. Marys	1,859	4	4	0
Stonewood	1,758	3	3	0
Summersville	3,459	17	16	1
Sutton	982	1	1	0
Sylvester	152	1	1	0
Terra Alta	1,496	2	2	0
Triadelphia	766	1	1	0
Vienna	10,537	20	17	3
War	760	2	2	0
Wayne	1,373	2	2	0
Webster Springs	725	5	4	1
Weirton	19,067	42	38	4
Welch	1,899	7	6	1
Wellsburg	2,685	8	7	1
West Logan	395	1	1	0
West Milford	616	2	2	0
Weston	4,078	7	5	2
Westover	4,267	7	7	0
Wheeling	27,486	77	68	9
White Hall	665	4	4	0
White Sulphur Springs	2,438	8	7	1
Whitesville	469	2	2	0
Williamson	2,968	10	8	2
Williamstown	2,977	8	7	1
Winfield	2,364	6	6	0
WISCONSIN				
Adams	1,879	5	5	0
Albany	1,018	3	3	0
Algoma	3,079	4	4	0
Alma	742	1	1	0
Altoona	7,446	14	13	1
Amery	2,816	6	6	0
Antigo	7,801	18	15	3
Appleton	74,439	137	110	27
Arcadia	3,004	4	4	0
Ashland	8,005	20	19	1
Ashwaubenon	17,219	60	54	6
Athens	1,094	1	1	0
Balsam Lake	988	1	1	0
Bangor	1,498	3	3	0
Baraboo	12,174	34	28	6
Barneveld	1,233	1	1	0
Barron	3,303	6	6	0
Bayfield	478	3	3	0
Bayside	4,417	14	13	1
Beaver Dam	16,640	35	31	4
Belleville	2,433	6	5	1
Beloit	36,878	77	65	12
Beloit Town	7,672	12	10	2
Berlin	5,400	13	12	1
Big Bend	1,318	3	3	0
Black River Falls	3,557	10	9	1
Blair	1,348	3	3	0
Blanchardville	817	1	1	0
Bloomer	3,515	7	6	1
Bloomfield	6,253	6	6	0
Blue Mounds	955	2	1	1

(Number.)

State/city	Population	Total law enforcement employees	Total officers	Total civilians
Boscobel	3,181	6	6	0
Boyceville	1,106	1	1	0
Brandon-Fairwater	1,221	2	1	1
Brillion	3,138	8	8	0
Brodhead	3,291	12	8	4
Brookfield	38,043	88	70	18
Brookfield Township	6,093	11	11	0
Brown Deer	12,101	35	32	3
Burlington	10,669	26	20	6
Butler	1,822	8	7	1
Caledonia	24,681	35	32	3
Campbellsport	1,970	2	2	0
Campbell Township	4,419	4	4	0
Cashton	1,095	4	2	2
Cedarburg	11,488	28	20	8
Chenequa	606	9	8	1
Chetek	2,185	6	5	1
Chilton	3,886	6	6	0
Chippewa Falls	14,109	26	23	3
Cleveland	1,464	3	2	1
Clinton	2,138	5	5	0
Clintonville	4,434	15	11	4
Colby-Abbotsford	4,078	7	6	1
Colfax	1,161	2	2	0
Columbus	4,996	12	10	2
Cornell	1,435	2	2	0
Cottage Grove	6,954	12	11	1
Crandon	1,852	4	3	1
Cross Plains	4,072	6	5	1
Cuba City	2,049	5	4	1
Cudahy	18,338	40	31	9
Cumberland	2,142	5	5	0
Dane	1,146	2	1	1
Darlington	2,397	5	5	0
Deforest	9,674	21	18	3
Delafield	7,194	16	14	2
Delavan	9,992	27	22	5
Delavan Town	5,337	12	11	1
De Pere	24,896	39	35	4
Dodgeville	4,645	10	10	0
Durand	1,831	3	3	0
Eagle River	1,356	6	6	0
Eagle Village	1,978	2	2	0
East Troy	4,298	7	7	0
Eau Claire	68,084	134	99	35
Edgar	1,459	1	1	0
Edgerton	5,554	11	10	1
Eleva	676	1	1	0
Elkhart Lake	962	3	3	0
Elkhorn	9,859	17	15	2
Ellsworth	3,180	5	5	0
Elm Grove	6,222	24	16	8
Elroy	1,359	3	3	0
Evansville	5,268	10	9	1
Everest Metropolitan	17,318	29	25	4
Fall Creek	1,315	2	2	0
Fall River	1,675	2	2	0
Fennimore	2,485	5	5	0
Fitchburg	28,588	61	49	12
Fond du Lac	42,907	80	73	7
Fontana	1,702	7	6	1
Fort Atkinson	12,433	25	19	6
Fox Lake	1,470	3	2	1
Fox Point	6,754	17	16	1
Fox Valley Metro	21,515	31	29	2
Franklin	36,313	75	59	16
Frederic	1,099	1	1	0
Freedom	6,098	2	2	0
Galesville	1,565	4	4	0
Geneva Town	5,050	8	7	1

Table 19. Full-Time Law Enforcement Employees, by Selected State and City, 2016—*Continued*

(Number.)

State/city	Population	Total law enforcement employees	Total officers	Total civilians
Genoa City	3,026	6	5	1
Germantown	20,042	43	33	10
Gillett	1,346	3	3	0
Gilman	395	2	1	1
Glendale	12,846	48	43	5
Grafton	11,532	29	22	7
Grand Chute	22,463	35	30	5
Grand Rapids	7,466	8	6	2
Grantsburg	1,279	3	3	0
Green Bay	105,452	228	189	39
Greendale	14,367	38	29	9
Greenfield	37,405	75	57	18
Green Lake	989	3	3	0
Hales Corners	7,758	19	16	3
Hartford	14,377	28	24	4
Hartland	9,239	18	16	2
Hayward	2,287	8	7	1
Hazel Green	1,245	4	2	2
Highland	843	1	1	0
Hillsboro	1,422	2	2	0
Hobart-Lawrence	13,793	9	8	1
Holmen	9,760	12	11	1
Horicon	3,697	8	7	1
Hortonville	2,714	6	5	1
Hudson	13,740	27	24	3
Hurley	1,484	7	6	1
Independence	1,342	3	3	0
Iron Ridge	899	1	1	0
Iron River	1,128	1	1	0
Jackson	6,877	12	11	1
Janesville	64,234	108	97	11
Jefferson	7,935	17	14	3
Juneau	2,669	5	4	1
Kaukauna	15,928	27	26	1
Kenosha	99,954	208	199	9
Kewaskum	4,117	8	8	0
Kewaunee	2,862	6	6	0
Kiel	3,720	7	7	0
Kohler	2,108	8	7	1
Kronenwetter	7,714	8	7	1
La Crosse	52,498	109	92	17
Ladysmith	3,147	9	8	1
La Farge	773	1	1	0
Lake Delton	2,975	22	20	2
Lake Geneva	7,803	32	23	9
Lake Hallie	6,546	9	8	1
Lake Mills	5,816	12	10	2
Lancaster	3,760	9	8	1
Linn Township	2,404	6	6	0
Lodi	3,052	6	5	1
Lomira	2,376	4	3	1
Luxemburg	2,562	2	2	0
Madison	252,136	580	476	104
Manawa	1,306	3	3	0
Manitowoc	32,877	73	63	10
Maple Bluff	1,344	5	5	0
Marathon City	1,513	2	2	0
Marinette	10,771	28	24	4
Marion	1,213	3	3	0
Markesan	1,406	3	3	0
Marshall Village	3,940	9	8	1
Marshfield	18,530	47	39	8
Mauston	4,365	9	8	1
Mayville	4,958	9	8	1
McFarland	8,290	18	16	2
Medford	4,335	10	9	1
Menasha	17,609	37	30	7
Menomonee Falls	36,218	73	57	16
Menomonie	16,308	34	27	7
Mequon	24,114	47	38	9

Table 19. Full-Time Law Enforcement Employees, by Selected State and City, 2016—*Continued*

(Number.)

State/city	Population	Total law enforcement employees	Total officers	Total civilians
Merrill	9,150	25	22	3
Middleton	19,263	48	38	10
Milton	5,601	13	11	2
Milwaukee	600,193	2,328	1,889	439
Mineral Point	2,496	5	5	0
Minocqua	4,438	16	11	5
Mishicot	1,401	2	2	0
Mondovi	2,631	4	4	0
Monona	8,288	24	20	4
Monroe	10,794	36	26	10
Montello	1,449	3	2	1
Mosinee	4,038	8	7	1
Mount Horeb	7,479	12	11	1
Mount Pleasant	26,286	53	48	5
Mukwonago	7,795	21	14	7
Mukwonago Town	8,147	7	6	1
Muscoda	1,259	3	3	0
Muskego	24,876	45	36	9
Neenah	25,850	51	41	10
Neillsville	2,399	7	6	1
New Berlin	39,873	78	67	11
New Glarus	2,170	4	4	0
New Holstein	3,213	7	6	1
New Lisbon	2,473	4	4	0
New London	7,148	19	17	2
New Richmond	8,913	17	16	1
Niagara	1,580	4	4	0
North Fond du Lac	5,003	10	9	1
North Hudson	3,832	5	4	1
Oak Creek	35,337	78	56	22
Oconomowoc	16,480	29	22	7
Oconomowoc Lake	615	7	6	1
Oconomowoc Town	8,662	11	10	1
Oconto	4,468	9	9	0
Oconto Falls	2,823	5	5	0
Omro	3,560	7	6	1
Onalaska	18,600	29	26	3
Oregon	10,189	17	15	2
Osceola	2,502	6	5	1
Oshkosh	66,654	112	98	14
Osseo	1,703	4	4	0
Owen	929	3	3	0
Palmyra	1,775	3	3	0
Park Falls	2,311	14	7	7
Pepin	787	1	1	0
Peshtigo	3,416	7	6	1
Pewaukee Village	8,207	20	18	2
Phillips	1,371	5	5	0
Plainfield	829	2	2	0
Platteville	12,859	26	20	6
Pleasant Prairie	20,928	37	33	4
Plover	12,360	22	19	3
Plymouth	8,518	15	15	0
Portage	10,394	26	22	4
Port Washington	11,633	25	20	5
Poynette	2,485	5	4	1
Prairie du Chien	5,731	13	12	1
Prescott	4,197	10	9	1
Princeton	1,180	3	3	0
Pulaski	3,552	8	7	1
Racine	77,536	215	191	24
Reedsburg	9,605	27	20	7
Rhinelander	7,477	19	16	3
Rib Lake	891	1	1	0
Rice Lake	8,391	17	17	0
Richland Center	4,980	13	11	2
Rio	1,041	2	2	0
Ripon	7,694	20	14	6
Ripon Town	1,392	1	1	0
River Falls	15,314	27	24	3

(Number.)

State/city	Population	Total law enforcement employees	Total officers	Total civilians
River Hills	1,606	11	11	0
Rome Town	2,692	7	6	1
Rosendale	1,038	1	1	0
Rothschild	5,342	12	10	2
Sauk Prairie	4,640	15	13	2
Saukville	4,465	13	11	2
Seymour	3,437	6	6	0
Shawano	9,095	22	20	2
Sheboygan	48,710	101	82	19
Sheboygan Falls	7,849	15	14	1
Shiocton	921	1	1	0
Shorewood	13,319	27	23	4
Shorewood Hills	2,149	8	6	2
Siren	773	3	2	1
Slinger	5,232	11	10	1
South Milwaukee	21,212	39	33	6
Sparta	9,708	21	19	2
Spencer	1,920	3	3	0
Spooner	2,565	8	7	1
Spring Green	1,655	4	3	1
Stanley	3,560	5	5	0
St. Croix Falls	2,048	6	5	1
Stevens Point	26,587	48	44	4
St. Francis	9,580	21	20	1
Stoughton	13,148	28	22	6
Strum	1,127	2	2	0
Sturgeon Bay	8,925	22	20	2
Sturtevant	6,958	9	8	1
Summit	4,828	10	10	0
Sun Prairie	32,943	69	52	17
Superior	26,451	61	56	5
Theresa	1,204	2	2	0
Thiensville	3,167	7	6	1
Three Lakes	2,124	5	5	0
Tomah	9,398	22	20	2
Tomahawk	3,189	9	8	1
Town of East Troy	4,094	12	6	6
Town of Madison	6,878	15	14	1
Town of Menasha	19,083	31	25	6
Trempealeau	1,632	2	2	0
Twin Lakes	6,119	18	13	5
Two Rivers	11,259	27	24	3
Verona	12,942	23	21	2
Viroqua	4,364	11	9	2
Walworth	2,843	7	6	1
Washburn	2,043	5	5	0
Waterloo	3,345	9	8	1
Watertown	23,816	51	38	13
Waukesha	72,223	150	118	32
Waunakee	13,556	21	19	2
Waupaca	6,001	15	14	1
Waupun	11,342	16	15	1
Wausau	39,091	81	72	9
Wautoma	2,120	6	5	1
Wauwatosa	47,771	113	87	26
West Allis	60,558	153	126	27
West Bend	31,791	70	53	17
Westby	2,276	3	3	0
Westfield	1,221	2	2	0
West Milwaukee	4,206	24	19	5
West Salem	5,055	8	7	1
Whitefish Bay	14,087	25	24	1
Whitehall	1,570	4	4	0
Whitewater	14,752	34	24	10
Wild Rose	694	2	2	0
Williams Bay	2,605	7	6	1
Winneconne	2,458	11	5	6
Wisconsin Dells	2,702	19	14	5

Table 19. Full-Time Law Enforcement Employees, by Selected State and City, 2016—*Continued*

(Number.)

State/city	Population	Total law enforcement employees	Total officers	Total civilians
Wisconsin Rapids	17,802	41	37	4
Woodruff	1,979	6	5	1
WYOMING				
Afton	1,983	4	4	0
Buffalo	4,640	22	13	9
Casper	61,343	129	93	36
Cheyenne	64,046	123	102	21
Cody	9,842	24	21	3
Diamondville	738	4	3	1
Douglas	6,617	25	17	8
Evanston	12,087	30	25	5
Evansville	2,999	10	8	2
Gillette	33,218	78	51	27
Glenrock	2,603	13	7	6
Green River	12,477	32	27	5
Greybull	1,886	6	5	1
Hanna	809	1	1	0
Jackson	10,713	37	30	7
Kemmerer	2,757	7	7	0
Lander	7,699	20	19	1
Laramie	32,411	71	46	25
Mills	3,854	17	13	4
Moorcroft	1,072	4	3	1
Newcastle	3,537	16	8	8
Pine Bluffs	1,149	1	1	0
Powell	6,491	24	17	7
Rawlins	9,004	28	18	10
Riverton	10,905	41	28	13
Rock Springs	24,161	58	46	12
Saratoga	1,675	9	4	5
Sheridan	17,956	44	28	16
Sundance	1,289	3	3	0
Thermopolis	2,967	11	6	5
Torrington	6,676	24	17	7
Wheatland	3,665	9	8	1
Worland	5,348	11	10	1

[1]The employee data presented in this table for Charlotte-Mecklenburg represent only Charlotte-Mecklenburg Police Department and exclude Mecklenburg County Sheriff's Office.

Table 20. Murder Victims, by Race, Ethnicity, and Sex, 2016

(Number.)

Race	Total	Sex		
		Male	Female	Unknown
Total	15,070	11,821	3,208	41
White	6,578	4,665	1,906	5
Black............................	7,881	6,749	1,126	6
Other race	400	266	133	1
Unknown race	213	141	43	29
Hispanic or Latino[1]	2,367	1,977	389	1
Not Hispanic or Latino[1]	9,725	7,600	2,120	5
Unknown[1].....................................	2,226	1,678	516	32

[1]Not all agencies provide ethnicity data, therefore the race and ethnicity totals do not equal the total number of victims.

Table 21. Murder Offenders, by Age, Sex, Race, and Ethnicity, 2016

(Number; percent; single victim/single offender.)

Age	Total	Sex			Race				Ethnicity[1]		
		Male	Female	Unknown	White	Black or African American	Other[2]	Unknown	Hispanic/ Latino	Not Hispanic/ Latino	Unknown
Total	16,964	10,310	1,295	5,359	5,004	6,095	291	5,574	1,533	5,566	5,447
Percent distribution[3].........................	100.0	60.8	7.6	31.6	29.5	35.9	1.7	32.9	12.2	44.4	43.4
Under 18[4].....................................	736	681	55	0	254	452	24	6	112	337	68
Under 22[4].....................................	2,905	2,632	270	3	1,002	1,798	68	37	456	1,364	295
18 and over[4].................................	10,180	8,938	1,216	26	4,653	5,124	263	140	1,364	4,993	1,089
Infant (under 1)...............................	0	0	0	0	0	0	0	0	0	0	0
1 to 4	0	0	0	0	0	0	0	0	0	0	0
5 to 8	0	0	0	0	0	0	0	0	0	0	0
9 to 12	10	10	0	0	3	7	0	0	0	6	1
13 to 16	374	343	31	0	130	228	14	2	56	174	39
17 to 19	1,413	1,289	122	2	478	882	35	18	213	680	131
20 to 24	2,593	2,288	301	4	913	1,587	55	38	387	1,251	280
25 to 29	1,941	1,726	212	3	808	1,070	39	24	285	944	209
30 to 34	1,339	1,156	176	7	649	627	45	18	182	609	151
35 to 39	931	805	124	2	490	402	24	15	126	483	90
40 to 44	643	555	88	0	359	258	19	7	96	320	70
45 to 49	509	432	75	2	294	195	16	4	56	249	49
50 to 54	440	381	58	1	277	146	11	6	41	229	47
55 to 59	276	234	42	0	185	80	10	1	17	141	32
60 to 64	190	173	16	1	124	55	9	2	6	104	22
65 to 69	114	101	13	0	77	24	7	6	7	65	14
70 to 74	51	46	5	0	39	10	2	0	0	28	7
75 and over	92	80	8	4	81	5	1	5	4	47	15
Unknown.......................................	6,048	691	24	5,333	97	519	4	5,428	57	236	4,290

[1]Not all agencies provide ethnicity data, therefore the race and ethnicity totals do not equal the total number of victims.
[2]Includes American Indian or Alaska Native, Asian, Native Hawaiian or Other Pacific Islander.
[3]Because of rounding, the percentages may not add to 100.0.
[4]Does not include unknown ages.

Table 22. Murder, by Victim/Offender Situations, 2015

(Number; percent; single victim/single offender.)

Situation	Total	Percent distribution (may not add to 100.0 due to rounding)
Total	13,455	100.0
Single victim/single offender	6,137	45.6
Single victim/unknown offender or offenders.................................	4,239	31.5
Single victim/multiple offenders..	1,551	11.5
Multiple victims/single offender..	835	6.2
Multiple victims/unknown offender or offenders............................	246	1.8
Multiple victims/multiple offenders..	447	3.3

Table 23. Murder Age of Victim, by Age of Offender, 2015

(Number; single victim/single offender.)

Age of victim	Total	Age of offender		
		Under 18 years	18 years and over	Unknown
Total	6,137	257	5,625	255
Under 18	520	86	419	15
18 and over	5,573	171	5,166	236
Unknown..	44	0	40	4

Note: This table is based on incidents where some information about the offender is known by law enforcement; therefore, when the offender age, sex, and race are all reported as unknown, these data are excluded from the table.

Table 24. Murder, Race, Ethnicity, and Sex of Victim by Race, Ethnicity, and Sex of Offender, 2016

(Number; single victim/single offender.)

Victim characteristic	Total	Sex			Race				Ethnicity		
		Male	Female	Unknown	White	Black or African American	Other[1]	Unknown	Hispanic/ Latino	Not Hispanic/ Latino	Unknown
Race..											
White	3,499	2,854	533	40	72	3,157	335	7	789	1,438	366
Black or African American......................	2,870	243	2,570	17	40	2,586	270	14	95	1,613	349
Other race[1]	221	56	37	123	5	185	35	1	14	132	24
Unknown..	86	43	16	4	23	75	11	0	12	24	17
Sex..											
Male	4,751	2,073	2,455	114	109	4,260	471	20	685	2,264	537
Female..	1,913	1,117	696	70	30	1,735	176	2	225	939	217
Unknown..	12	5	5	1	1	8	4	0	0	4	2
Ethnicity..											
Hispanic or Latino	985	792	142	10	41	907	63	15	661	205	39
Not Hispanic or Latino..........................	4,257	1,728	2,156	122	251	3,629	424	204	229	2,913	134
Unknown..	931	372	446	23	90	767	103	61	19	86	581

Note: This table is based on incidents where some information about the offender is known by law enforcement; therefore, when the offender age, sex, and race are all reported as unknown, these data are excluded from the table.
[1]Includes American Indian or Alaska Native, Asian, Native Hawaiian or Other Pacific Islander.

Table 25. Murder Victims, by Weapons, 2011–2016

(Number.)

Weapons	2011	2012	2013	2014	2015	2016
Total	12,795	12,888	12,253	12,270	13,750	15,070
Total firearms	8,653	8,897	8,454	8,312	9,778	11,004
Handguns	6,251	6,404	5,782	5,673	6,569	7,105
Rifles	332	298	285	258	258	374
Shotguns	362	310	308	264	272	262
Other guns	97	116	123	93	177	186
Firearms, type not stated	1,611	1,769	1,956	2,024	2,502	3,077
Knives or cutting instruments	1,716	1,604	1,490	1,595	1,589	1,604
Blunt objects (clubs, hammers, etc.)	502	522	428	446	450	472
Personal weapons (hands, fists, feet, etc.)[1]	751	707	687	682	659	656
Poison	5	13	11	10	8	11
Explosives	6	8	2	7	1	1
Fire	76	87	94	71	84	107
Narcotics	33	38	53	70	75	114
Drowning	15	14	4	14	14	9
Strangulation	88	90	85	89	99	98
Asphyxiation	92	106	95	102	120	91
Other weapons or weapons not stated	858	802	850	872	873	903

[1]Pushed is included in personal weapons.

Table 26. Murder, by State, Types of Weapon, 2016

(Number.)

State	Total murders[1]	Total firearms	Handguns	Rifles	Shotguns	Firearms (type unknown)	Knives or cutting instruments	Other weapons	Hands, feet, fists, etc.[2]
Alabama[3]	3	1	0	0	0	1	0	2	0
Alaska	52	43	12	4	1	26	3	6	0
Arizona	336	227	156	16	10	45	40	63	6
Arkansas	209	151	72	11	3	65	25	25	8
California	1,930	1,368	930	37	36	365	280	193	89
Colorado	202	136	87	4	4	41	27	28	11
Connecticut	76	48	24	0	1	23	12	13	3
Delaware	56	41	17	0	0	24	7	8	0
District of Columbia	136	105	105	0	0	0	19	6	6
Georgia	646	522	421	20	14	67	48	71	5
Hawaii	35	19	12	3	2	2	8	5	3
Idaho	47	17	13	1	0	3	5	21	4
Illinois[3]	941	799	728	14	5	52	61	62	19
Indiana	348	287	169	12	2	104	19	32	10
Iowa	71	43	25	2	1	15	12	10	6
Kansas	96	61	43	5	1	12	8	19	8
Kentucky	260	207	143	7	8	49	20	22	11
Louisiana	543	445	219	26	7	193	33	52	13
Maine	20	11	2	1	3	5	5	2	2
Maryland	430	328	309	2	3	14	52	29	21
Massachusetts	132	85	34	0	0	51	25	11	11
Michigan	597	443	191	15	12	225	45	89	20
Minnesota	99	60	42	2	1	15	12	19	8
Mississippi	154	128	101	4	6	17	4	14	8
Missouri	535	437	211	23	6	197	37	50	11
Montana	34	17	6	4	3	4	9	5	3
Nebraska	41	30	30	0	0	0	9	2	0
Nevada	209	141	21	2	0	118	20	42	6
New Hampshire	16	8	4	1	1	2	2	0	6
New Jersey	372	278	212	1	3	62	29	42	23
New Mexico	99	60	13	1	0	46	17	19	3
New York	628	367	305	2	9	51	130	99	32
North Carolina	595	421	262	20	22	117	50	80	44
North Dakota	14	8	5	2	0	1	3	1	2
Ohio	627	452	197	7	8	240	39	104	32
Oklahoma	243	171	135	9	9	18	31	23	18
Oregon	100	51	32	6	1	12	24	24	1
Pennsylvania	655	486	395	10	12	69	68	78	23
Rhode Island	29	12	5	0	0	7	9	6	2
South Carolina	363	281	172	7	9	93	29	36	17
South Dakota	21	7	7	0	0	0	5	4	5
Tennessee	486	356	202	10	7	137	49	69	12
Texas	1,459	1,066	630	51	31	354	175	136	82
Utah	71	42	31	1	0	10	6	20	3
Vermont	14	6	2	2	1	1	2	6	0
Virginia	482	352	151	10	10	181	33	67	30
Washington	195	127	69	11	5	42	19	38	11
West Virginia	76	47	30	2	0	15	4	21	4
Wisconsin	226	166	119	6	4	37	27	21	12
Wyoming	19	6	1	0	1	4	8	3	2
U.S. Virgin Islands	42	34	3	0	0	31	0	8	0

[1] Total number of murders for which supplemental homicide data were received.
[2] Pushed is included in hands, fists, feet, etc.
[3] Limited supplemental homicide data were received.

Table 27. Justifiable Homicide by Weapon, Law Enforcement,[1] 2011–2016

(Number.)

Year	Total	Total firearms	Handguns	Rifles	Shotguns	Firearms, type not stated	Knives or cutting instruments	Other dangerous weapons	Personal weapons
2011	404	401	305	36	11	49	2	0	1
2012	426	423	339	38	7	39	0	3	0
2013	471	467	334	46	9	78	0	3	1
2014	453	451	331	45	4	71	1	1	0
2015	459	458	315	43	7	93	0	1	0
2016	435	429	312	51	5	61	0	5	1

[1] The killing of a felon by a law enforcement officer in the line of duty.

Table 28. Justifiable Homicide by Weapon, Private Citizen,[1] 2012–2016

(Number.)

Year	Total	Total firearms	Handguns	Rifles	Shotguns	Firearms, type not stated	Knives or cutting instruments	Other dangerous weapons	Personal weapons
2012	270	209	156	13	11	29	49	9	3
2013	315	263	198	20	15	30	35	6	11
2014	286	227	174	6	11	36	35	13	11
2015	338	272	219	8	13	32	41	10	15
2016	331	276	197	12	10	57	34	7	14

[1] The killing of a felon, during the commission of a felony, by a private citizen.

Table 29. Robbery, by State, Types of Weapon, 2016

(Percent.)

State	Total[1]	Firearms	Knives or cutting instruments	Other weapons	Strong-arm	Agency count	Population
Alabama	4,415	2,876	143	369	1,027	264	4,392,449
Alaska	848	242	81	116	409	32	738,566
Arizona	6,882	3,002	802	716	2,362	90	6,514,042
Arkansas	2,045	1,096	120	176	653	272	2,827,056
California	54,762	15,489	5,207	6,063	28,003	732	39,209,622
Colorado	3,432	1,357	349	433	1,293	197	5,109,023
Connecticut	2,696	896	294	227	1,279	103	3,500,401
Delaware	1,359	648	99	101	511	56	950,787
District of Columbia	3,480	1,430	273	225	1,552	3	681,170
Florida	20,132	8,717	1,299	1,914	8,202	668	20,566,240
Georgia	11,935	7,409	425	931	3,170	504	9,639,636
Hawaii	994	162	93	135	604	4	1,428,557
Idaho	209	56	36	32	85	108	1,680,830
Illinois[2]	536	307	24	48	157	1	147,363
Indiana	6,883	3,420	360	586	2,517	217	4,663,407
Iowa	1,131	482	87	115	447	207	2,867,132
Kansas	1,248	607	98	97	446	227	2,211,329
Kentucky	3,369	1,664	238	330	1,137	420	4,424,357
Louisiana	5,514	2,976	238	419	1,881	187	4,553,790
Maine	266	59	40	34	133	197	1,331,479
Maryland	9,660	4,008	1,029	732	3,891	148	5,312,551
Massachusetts	5,247	1,357	977	930	1,983	346	6,477,104
Michigan	7,067	3,286	400	579	2,802	613	9,757,748
Minnesota	3,725	1,193	288	588	1,656	377	5,519,952
Mississippi	1,570	1,043	74	134	319	71	1,565,661
Missouri	6,481	3,508	323	440	2,210	576	5,939,159
Montana	266	70	32	49	115	106	1,036,405
Nebraska	940	477	68	70	325	224	1,820,419
Nevada	6,340	2,433	551	651	2,705	52	2,940,058
New Hampshire	415	83	75	41	216	174	1,275,170
New Jersey	8,934	3,157	782	579	4,416	569	8,944,469
New Mexico	2,697	1,171	379	304	843	104	1,906,995
New York	22,247	4,648	2,387	2,122	13,090	549	19,508,097
North Carolina	5,543	2,993	370	420	1,760	275	6,638,699
North Dakota	181	34	29	28	90	106	753,138
Ohio	11,576	3,497	517	766	6,796	472	9,736,188
Oklahoma	3,150	1,513	275	235	1,127	341	3,833,107
Oregon	2,194	521	220	251	1,202	180	3,681,279
Pennsylvania	11,764	5,077	786	780	5,121	1,241	11,691,589
Rhode Island	480	128	79	53	220	46	983,740
South Carolina	3,871	2,147	254	286	1,184	434	4,794,988
South Dakota	252	71	27	34	120	108	791,627
Tennessee	7,770	4,410	460	927	1,973	462	6,610,985
Texas	33,015	18,312	2,275	2,733	9,695	984	27,340,228
Utah	1,505	463	199	167	676	116	2,937,596
Vermont	48	16	6	4	22	46	348,314
Virginia	4,765	2,593	314	433	1,425	413	8,406,696
Washington	5,596	1,431	546	601	3,018	236	7,263,284
West Virginia	497	176	69	76	176	301	1,380,643
Wisconsin	4,698	2,557	222	393	1,526	413	5,730,771
Wyoming	58	21	2	13	22	55	556,446

[1] The number of robberies from agencies that submitted 12 months of data in 2016 for which breakdowns by type of weapon were included.
[2] Limited data were received.

Table 30. Aggravated Assault, by State, Types of Weapon, 2016

(Percent.)

State	Total[1]	Firearms	Knives or cutting instruments	Other weapons	Personal weapons	Agency count	Population
Alabama	17,364	3,994	1,762	10,068	1,540	264	4,392,449
Alaska	3,992	883	750	1,224	1,135	32	738,566
Arizona	19,232	5,024	2,822	4,559	6,827	90	6,514,042
Arkansas	11,385	3,884	1,662	2,564	3,275	272	2,827,056
California	104,295	20,633	17,156	36,031	30,475	732	39,209,622
Colorado	11,271	3,590	2,651	2,778	2,252	197	5,109,023
Connecticut	4,558	746	1,053	1,579	1,180	103	3,500,401
Delaware	3,120	1,054	596	1,095	375	56	950,787
District of Columbia	4,063	1,057	1,181	1,341	484	3	681,170
Florida	59,678	17,506	10,874	21,084	10,214	668	20,566,240
Georgia	22,896	8,329	3,204	5,867	5,496	504	9,639,636
Hawaii	2,769	180	424	1,074	1,091	4	1,428,557
Idaho	2,866	613	464	838	951	108	1,680,830
Illinois[2]	1,745	955	184	278	328	1	147,363
Indiana	14,225	3,233	1,506	3,876	5,610	217	4,663,407
Iowa	6,321	920	978	1,260	3,163	207	2,867,132
Kansas	6,441	2,223	1,282	1,652	1,284	227	2,211,329
Kentucky	5,035	1,714	662	1,829	830	420	4,424,357
Louisiana	18,173	5,284	2,803	4,958	5,128	187	4,553,790
Maine	948	74	160	218	496	197	1,331,479
Maryland	14,595	2,474	3,420	5,387	3,314	148	5,312,551
Massachusetts	17,289	1,940	3,935	7,504	3,910	346	6,477,104
Michigan	30,387	8,401	5,521	10,177	6,288	613	9,757,748
Minnesota	7,028	1,635	1,239	1,739	2,415	377	5,519,952
Mississippi	2,469	902	340	593	634	71	1,565,661
Missouri	21,610	7,914	2,563	5,792	5,341	576	5,939,159
Montana	2,948	477	399	964	1,108	106	1,036,405
Nebraska	3,409	763	641	1,077	928	224	1,820,419
Nevada	11,557	2,445	2,122	4,806	2,184	52	2,940,058
New Hampshire	1,546	302	375	323	546	174	1,275,170
New Jersey	11,075	2,196	2,313	3,741	2,825	569	8,944,469
New Mexico	9,104	2,092	1,627	2,775	2,610	104	1,906,995
New York	44,896	4,943	11,305	13,527	15,121	549	19,508,097
North Carolina	15,209	6,878	2,355	3,118	2,858	275	6,638,699
North Dakota	1,207	60	143	285	719	106	753,138
Ohio	14,648	5,339	2,608	4,218	2,483	472	9,736,188
Oklahoma	12,086	2,827	2,080	3,970	3,209	341	3,833,107
Oregon	6,061	904	1,095	1,981	2,081	180	3,681,279
Pennsylvania	20,817	4,731	3,033	4,977	8,076	1,241	11,691,589
Rhode Island	1,312	268	399	385	260	46	983,740
South Carolina	17,360	7,186	2,831	4,198	3,145	434	4,794,988
South Dakota	2,176	235	451	551	939	108	791,627
Tennessee	30,777	10,924	5,361	11,120	3,372	462	6,610,985
Texas	71,583	21,222	14,482	22,677	13,202	984	27,340,228
Utah	4,057	849	1,027	1,210	971	116	2,937,596
Vermont	302	39	59	53	151	46	348,314
Virginia	10,239	3,229	1,787	2,701	2,522	413	8,406,696
Washington	12,907	2,708	1,987	4,012	4,200	236	7,263,284
West Virginia	4,004	1,025	536	929	1,514	301	1,380,643
Wisconsin	10,729	2,824	1,175	2,324	4,406	413	5,730,771
Wyoming	1,087	90	159	257	581	55	556,446

[1]The number of robberies from agencies that submitted 12 months of data in 2016 for which breakdowns by type of weapon were included.
[2]Limited data were received.

Table 31. Property Stolen and Recovered, by Type and Value, 2016

(Dollars; percent; 13,981 agencies; 2016 estimated population 273,294,030.)

Type of property	Value of property		Percent recovered
	Stolen	Recovered	
Total	$13,667,503,625	$3,776,517,466	27.6
Currency, notes, etc.	1,429,781,653	33,375,702	2.3
Jewelry and precious metals........................	1,362,002,838	55,751,909	4.1
Clothing and furs..	362,025,765	38,980,936	10.8
Locally stolen motor vehicles......................	5,527,133,714	3,228,597,961	58.4
Office equipment..	483,550,405	25,750,989	5.3
Televisions, radios, stereos, etc.	455,215,103	22,319,049	4.9
Firearms..	155,186,427	14,794,219	9.5
Household goods...	228,961,414	10,003,415	4.4
Consumable goods......................................	139,167,892	15,512,495	11.1
Livestock...	22,666,215	2,570,359	11.3
Miscellaneous	3,501,812,199	328,860,432	9.4

Table 32. Crime Trends, by Population Group, 2015–2016

(Number; percent.)

Population group	Violent crime	Murder and nonnegligent manslaughter	Rape, revised definition[1]	Rape, legacy definition[2]	Robbery	Aggravated assault	Property crime	Burglary	Larceny-theft	Motor vehicle theft	Arson	Number of agencies	2016 estimated population
Total, all agencies													
2015	1,173,095	15,181	108,930	6,310	315,137	727,537	7,538,827	1,482,228	5,375,095	681,504	42,259		
2016	1,217,400	16,459	112,470	6,616	319,826	762,029	7,440,034	1,413,294	5,296,630	730,110	43,249	15,623	305,431,251
Percent change	+3.8	+8.4	+3.2	+4.8	+1.5	+4.7	-1.3	-4.7	-1.5	+7.1	+2.3		
Total, cities													
2015	938,136	11,826	81,231	4,191	276,513	564,375	5,983,208	1,087,800	4,347,725	547,683	32,487		
2016	978,267	12,863	84,460	4,272	282,000	594,672	5,923,615	1,042,326	4,292,416	588,873	33,104	11,158	208,061,722
Percent change	+4.3	+8.8	+4.0	+1.9	+2.0	+5.4		-4.2	-1.3	+7.5	+1.9		
Group I (250,000 and over)													
2015	445,645	6,177	30,970	936	156,058	251,504	2,034,720	384,817	1,398,652	251,251	12,645		
2016	473,049	6,973	32,986	892	159,314	272,884	2,045,407	368,854	1,408,114	268,439	12,914	83	61,199,316
Percent change	+6.1	+12.9	+6.5	-4.7	+2.1	+8.5	+0.5	-4.1	+0.7	+6.8	+2.1		
1,000,000 and over													
2015	188,327	2,234	13,138	-	69,293	103,662	727,139	131,821	501,813	93,505	3,923		
2016	201,825	2,688	13,972	-	71,652	113,513	742,200	125,303	517,051	99,846	4,229	11	27,658,777
Percent change	+7.2	+20.3	+6.3	-	+3.4	+9.5	+2.1	-4.9	+3.0	+6.8	+7.8		
500,000 to 999,999													
2015	139,003	2,092	9,109	620	46,953	80,229	703,775	133,644	487,061	83,070	4,125		
2016	147,007	2,228	9,603	600	47,395	87,181	699,498	128,981	482,417	88,100	4,116	23	16,781,999
Percent change	+5.8	+6.5	+5.4	-3.2	+0.9	+8.7	-0.6	-3.5		+6.1	-0.2		
250,000 to 499,999													
2015	118,315	1,851	8,723	316	39,812	67,613	603,806	119,352	409,778	74,676	4,597		
2016	124,217	2,057	9,411	292	40,267	72,190	603,709	114,570	408,646	80,493	4,569	49	16,758,540
Percent change	+5.0	+11.1	+7.9	-7.6	+1.1	+6.8	*	-4.0	-0.3	+7.8	-0.6		
Group II (100,000 to 249,999)													
2015	151,098	1,992	13,776	627	44,621	90,082	1,053,444	198,316	745,157	109,971	4,997		
2016	157,638	2,118	14,186	624	45,659	95,051	1,044,575	188,685	737,743	118,147	5,165	219	32,521,418
Percent change	+4.3	+6.3	+3.0	-0.5	+2.3	+5.5	-0.8	-4.9		+7.4	+3.4		
Group III (50,000 to 99,999)													
2015	109,770	1,201	10,405	551	29,904	67,709	868,445	153,641	640,351	74,453	4,268		
2016	112,649	1,210	11,041	603	30,509	69,286	866,392	148,627	637,330	80,435	4,228	477	33,071,956
Percent change	+2.6	+0.7	+6.1	+9.4	+2.0	+2.3	-0.2	-3.3	-0.5	+8.0	-0.9		
Group IV (25,000 to 49,999)													
2015	84,736	983	9,235	775	20,836	52,907	735,602	128,058	560,829	46,715	3,301		
2016	87,565	1,007	9,482	864	21,127	55,085	721,325	123,562	547,145	50,618	3,376	853	29,586,018
Percent change	+3.3	+2.4	+2.7	+11.5	+1.4	+4.1	-1.9	-3.5	-2.4	+8.4	+2.3		
Group V (10,000 to 24,999)													
2015	76,897	833	8,553	601	15,603	51,307	694,375	121,359	535,782	37,234	2,974		
2016	77,258	861	8,486	616	15,795	51,500	671,568	115,873	515,328	40,367	2,874	1,793	28,626,434
Percent change	+0.5	+3.4	-0.8	+2.5	+1.2	+0.4	-3.3	-4.5	-3.8	+8.4	-3.4		
Group VI (Under 10,000)													
2015	69,990	640	8,292	701	9,491	50,866	596,622	101,609	466,954	28,059	4,302		
2016	70,108	694	8,279	673	9,596	50,866	574,348	96,725	446,756	30,867	4,547	7,733	23,056,580
Percent change	+0.2	+8.4	-0.2	-4.0	+1.1	0.0	-3.7	-4.8	-4.3	+10.0	+5.7		
Metropolitan counties													
2015	187,976	2,453	19,865	1,606	35,981	128,071	1,250,091	297,579	842,845	109,667	7,305		
2016	191,384	2,754	20,068	1,828	35,054	131,680	1,226,478	280,397	828,604	117,477	7,637	2,010	73,068,087
Percent change	+1.8	+12.3	+1.0	+13.8	-2.6	+2.8	-1.9	-5.8	-1.7	+7.1	+4.5		

Table 32. Crime Trends, by Population Group, 2015–2016—*Continued*

(Number; percent.)

Population group	Violent crime	Murder and nonnegligent manslaughter	Rape, revised definition[1]	Rape, legacy definition[2]	Robbery	Aggravated assault	Property crime	Burglary	Larceny-theft	Motor vehicle theft	Arson	Number of agencies	2016 estimated population
Nonmetropolitan counties[3]													
2015................................	46,983	902	7,834	513	2,643	35,091	305,528	96,849	184,525	24,154	2,467		
2016................................	47,749	842	7,942	516	2,772	35,677	289,941	90,571	175,610	23,760	2,508	2,455	24,301,442
Percent change	+1.6	-6.7	+1.4	+0.6	+4.9	+1.7	-5.1	-6.5	-4.8	-1.6	+1.7		
Suburban areas[4]......................													
2015................................	327,013	3,865	35,735	2,592	67,586	217,235	2,569,624	510,961	1,869,364	189,299	13,482		
2016................................	334,222	4,245	36,342	2,870	67,524	223,241	2,516,026	483,816	1,828,325	203,885	14,220	8,552	132,442,308
Percent change	+2.2	+9.8	+1.7	+10.7	-0.1	+2.8	-2.1	-5.3	-2.2	+7.7	+5.5		

Note: No agencies over 1,000,000 in population submitted rape data using the legacy UCR definition in 2016; therefore, the UCR Program could not provide a 2-year comparison for this agency group size.
* = Less than one-tenth of 1 percent.
[1]The figures shown in this column for the offense of rape were reported using the revised Uniform Crime Reporting (UCR) definition of rape.
[2]The figures shown in this column for the offense of rape were reported using the legacy UCR definition of rape.
[3]Includes state police agencies that report aggregately for the entire state.
[4]Suburban areas include law enforcement agencies in cities with less than 50,000 inhabitants and county law enforcement agencies that are within a Metropolitan Statistical Area. Suburban areas exclude all metropolitan agencies associated with a principal city. The agencies associated with suburban areas also appear in other groups within this table.

Table 33. Crime Rates, by Population Group, 2015–2016

(Number; percent.)

Population group	Violent crime		Murder and nonnegligent manslaughter		Rape, revised definition[1]		Rape, legacy definition[2]		Robbery		Aggravated assault	
	Number of offenses known	Rate	Number of offenses known	Rate	Number of offenses known	Rate	Number of offenses known	Rate	Number of offenses known	Rate	Number of offenses known	Rate
Total, All Agencies........................	1,223,265	401.3	16,470	5.4	114,730	41.2	6,607	25.1	321,464	105.5	763,994	250.6
Total, cities...................................	979,579	471.6	12,802	6.2	86,015	44.4	4,268	31.0	282,459	136.0	594,035	286.0
Group I (250,000 and over)	472,814	771.4	6,928	11.3	33,385	56.7	981	41.3	159,106	259.6	272,414	444.5
1,000,000 and over.....................	201,825	729.7	2,688	9.7	13,972	50.5	0	0.0	71,652	259.1	113,513	410.4
500,000 to 999,999	150,170	861.9	2,242	12.9	9,992	62.6	600	41.2	48,381	277.7	88,955	510.5
250,000 to 499,999	120,819	745.5	1,998	12.3	9,421	61.6	381	41.5	39,073	241.1	69,946	431.6
Group II (100,000 to 249,999)........	156,588	485.3	2,098	6.5	14,459	47.1	526	34.1	45,431	140.8	94,074	291.6
Group III (50,000 to 99,999)...........	114,031	342.2	1,214	3.6	11,438	36.5	588	29.5	30,879	92.7	69,912	209.8
Group IV (25,000 to 49,999)...........	88,973	299.1	1,012	3.4	9,619	35.5	871	32.8	21,403	72.0	56,068	188.5
Group V (10,000 to 24,999)	78,120	272.6	880	3.1	8,723	33.7	632	22.9	16,079	56.1	51,806	180.8
Group VI (Under 10,000)	69,053	307.9	670	3.0	8,391	42.0	670	27.3	9,561	42.6	49,761	221.9
Metropolitan counties.....................	195,630	267.3	2,807	3.8	20,618	32.3	1,819	19.6	36,227	49.5	134,159	183.3
Nonmetropolitan counties[3]	48,056	200.6	861	3.6	8,097	39.1	520	16.1	2,778	11.6	35,800	149.5
Suburban areas[4]............................	339,130	256.2	4,300	3.2	37,237	31.5	2,890	20.5	68,951	52.1	225,752	170.5

[1] The figures shown in this column for the offense of rape were reported using the revised Uniform Crime Reporting (UCR) definition of rape.
[2] The figures shown in this column for the offense of rape were reported using the legacy UCR definition of rape.
[3] Includes state police agencies that report aggregately for the entire state.
[4] Suburban areas include law enforcement agencies in cities with less than 50,000 inhabitants and county law enforcement agencies that are within a Metropolitan Statistical Area. Suburban areas exclude all metropolitan agencies associated with a principal city. The agencies associated with suburban areas also appear in other groups within this table.

Table 33. Crime Rates, by Population Group, 2015–2016—*Continued*

(Number; percent.)

Population group	Property crime		Burglary		Larceny-theft		Motor vehicle theft		Number of agencies	2016 estimated population
	Number of offenses known	Rate	Number of offenses known	Rate	Number of offenses known	Rate	Number of offenses known	Rate		
Total, All Agencies........................	7,514,851	2,465.2	1,421,596	466.3	5,353,887	1,756.3	739,368	242.5	15,310	304,839,823
Total, cities..	5,969,716	2,874.1	1,045,176	503.2	4,328,750	2,084.1	595,790	286.8	10,831	207,707,230
Group I (250,000 and over)	2,061,132	3,363.0	368,632	601.5	1,420,247	2,317.3	272,253	444.2	82	61,289,111
1,000,000 and over....................	742,200	2,683.4	125,303	453.0	517,051	1,869.4	99,846	361.0	11	27,658,777
500,000 to 999,999...................	732,585	4,204.4	133,045	763.6	506,516	2,907.0	93,024	533.9	24	17,424,128
250,000 to 499,999...................	586,347	3,618.0	110,284	680.5	396,680	2,447.7	79,383	489.8	47	16,206,206
Group II (100,000 to 249,999).........	1,036,660	3,212.9	186,189	577.1	731,555	2,267.3	118,916	368.6	218	32,265,177
Group III (50,000 to 99,999)...........	881,257	2,644.6	151,264	453.9	648,625	1,946.5	81,368	244.2	480	33,323,383
Group IV (25,000 to 49,999)...........	730,697	2,456.7	124,824	419.7	554,893	1,865.7	50,980	171.4	857	29,742,465
Group V (10,000 to 24,999)...........	685,091	2,390.3	118,082	412.0	525,509	1,833.5	41,500	144.8	1,794	28,661,210
Group VI (Under 10,000)................	574,879	2,563.5	96,185	428.9	447,921	1,997.3	30,773	137.2	7,400	22,425,884
Metropolitan counties.....................	1,254,279	1,713.9	285,709	390.4	848,805	1,159.9	119,765	163.7	2,010	73,181,004
Nonmetropolitan counties[3].............	290,856	1,214.3	90,711	378.7	176,332	736.2	23,813	99.4	2,469	23,951,589
Suburban areas[4].............................	2,559,769	1,933.8	490,432	370.5	1,862,114	1,406.7	207,223	156.5	8,400	132,369,940

[1]The figures shown in this column for the offense of rape were reported using the revised Uniform Crime Reporting (UCR) definition of rape.
[2]The figures shown in this column for the offense of rape were reported using the legacy UCR definition of rape.
[3]Includes state police agencies that report aggregately for the entire state.
[4]Suburban areas include law enforcement agencies in cities with less than 50,000 inhabitants and county law enforcement agencies that are within a Metropolitan Statistical Area. Suburban areas exclude all metropolitan agencies associated with a principal city. The agencies associated with suburban areas also appear in other groups within this table.

Table 34. Offense Analysis, Number and Percent Change, 2015–2016

(Number; percent; dollars; 14,554 agencies; 2016 estimated population 282,238,499.)

Classification	Number of offenses, 2016	Percent change from 2015	Percent distribution[1]	Average value
Murder................................	14,774	+7.8	100.0	X
Rape[2]................................	100,373	X	100.0	X
Robbery................................	280,357	+1.7	100.0	$1,400
By location................................				
Street/highway................................	108,957	-1.8	38.9	1,191
Commercial house................................	42,783	+4.6	15.3	1,689
Gas or service station................................	8,178	+2.1	2.9	970
Convenience store................................	17,401	+6.7	6.2	732
Residence................................	46,419	+2.3	16.6	1,758
Bank................................	4,982	+0.8	1.8	3,531
Miscellaneous................................	51,637	+5.0	18.4	1,367
Burglary................................	1,354,920	-4.4	100.0	2,361
By location................................				
Residence (dwelling):	942,177	-7.1	69.5	2,273
Residence, night................................	278,600	-4.5	20.6	1,913
Residence, day................................	486,006	-8.6	35.9	2,258
Residence, unknown................................	177,571	-7.1	13.1	2,879
Nonresidence (store, office, etc.):	412,743	+2.6	30.5	2,562
Nonresidence, night................................	178,470	+6.0	13.2	2,585
Nonresidence, day................................	142,631	-0.1	10.5	2,182
Nonresidence, unknown................................	91,642	+0.7	6.8	3,109
Larceny-theft................................	4,971,925	-1.3	100.0	999
By type................................				
Pocket-picking................................	24,352	-0.4	0.5	646
Purse-snatching................................	19,968	-1.6	0.4	475
Shoplifting................................	1,038,574	-6.7	20.9	250
From motor vehicles (except accessories)..	1,301,447	+6.5	26.2	869
Motor vehicle accessories................................	366,048	+2.0	7.4	541
Bicycles................................	162,547	-10.8	3.3	483
From buildings................................	533,553	-6.3	10.7	1,449
From coin-operated machines................	10,877	-6.8	0.2	607
All others................................	1,514,559	-1.4	30.5	1,649
By value................................				
Over $200	2,256,253	-1.5	45.4	2,140
$50 to $200	1,075,664	-4.3	21.6	108
Under $50................................	1,640,008	+0.9	33.0	14
Motor vehicle theft................................	700,143	+6.9	100.0	7,680

X = Not applicable.
[1]Because of rounding, the percentages may not add to 100.0.
[2]The rape figure in this table is an aggregate total of the data submitted using both the revised and legacy Uniform Crime Reporting definitions.

Table 35. Offenses Known to Law Enforcement, by Selected Federal Agency, 2016

(Number.)

Agency and unit/office	Violent crime	Murder and nonnegligent manslaughter	Rape	Robbery	Aggravated assault	Property crime	Burglary	Larceny-theft	Motor vehicle theft	Arson
National Institutes of Health...................	0	0	0		0	70	0	70	0	0
United States Dept. of the Interior										
Bureau of Indian Affairs[1]										
Bureau of Land Management	14	1	0	1	12	583	14	544	25	0
Bureau of Reclamation......................	2	1	0	0	1	4	4	0	0	1
Fish and Wildlife Service...................	17	1	0	1	15	78	26	30	22	3
National Park Service	234	12	36	42	144	3,334	59	3,192	83	37

[1]The Bureau of Indian Affairs submits these statistics to the FBI Uniform Crime Reporting Program on a monthly basis throughout the calendar year and can be found at https://ucr.fbi.gov/crime-in-the-u.s/2016/crime-in-the-u.s.-2016/tables/table-9/table-9.xls/view

Table 36. Full-Time Law Enforcement Employees, by Selected Federal Agency, 2016

(Number.)

Agency and unit/office	Total law enforcement employees	Total officers	Total civilians
United States Dept. of the Interior			
Bureau of Indian Affairs[1]...............	771	341	430
Bureau of Land Management	297	277	20
Bureau of Reclamation................................	23	16	7
Fish and Wildlife Service..............................	789	661	128
National Park Service	2,409	2,010	399

[1]Tribal figures represented in the table at this URL (https://ucr.fbi.gov/crime-in-the-u.s/2016/crime-in-the-u.s.-2016/tables/table-29/table-29.xls/view) may be included in the aggregated totals listed under the Bureau of Indian Affairs data.

(Number.)

NIBRS offense code[1] NIBRS dffense description Field office	09A-09C Homicide offenses	11A-11D Sex offenses	13A-13C Assault offenses	23A-23H Larceny/theft offenses	26A-26E Fraud offenses	35A-35B Drug/narcotic offenses	39A-39D Gambling offenses	64A-64B Human trafficking	100 Kidnapping/abduction	120 Robbery	200 Arson	210 Extortion/blackmail	250 Counterfeiting/forgery	270 Embezzlement
Grand Total, All Field Offices	139	675	632	16	6,357	5,001	4	693	130	993	5	67	85	365
Albany	0	7	2	0	16	25	0	4	0	1	0	0	0	0
Albuquerque	19	19	35	1	5	50	0	2	2	17	0	0	1	1
Anchorage	0	0	5	0	12	9	0	2	1	7	0	0	0	1
Atlanta	0	8	3	0	231	116	0	7	3	15	0	0	0	6
Baltimore	3	23	4	0	52	50	0	11	0	20	0	1	0	1
Birmingham	0	5	0	0	91	43	0	4	0	1	0	0	0	2
Boston	1	2	7	0	83	111	0	9	0	63	0	20	0	0
Buffalo	0	14	3	0	120	182	0	6	0	11	0	1	0	1
Charlotte	2	18	17	0	83	179	0	13	8	16	0	0	1	42
Chicago	0	2	4	0	142	31	0	17	5	56	0	0	0	4
Cincinnati	0	10	3	0	16	63	0	8	2	6	0	0	0	0
Cleveland	0	4	3	0	51	77	0	12	2	20	0	1	0	0
Columbia	0	2	7	0	39	180	0	13	0	9	0	0	2	1
Dallas	0	7	2	0	87	67	0	19	1	29	0	0	0	14
Denver	3	15	16	0	37	17	0	16	3	27	0	0	21	0
Detroit	0	46	19	0	250	107	0	41	4	21	0	1	1	11
El Paso	0	10	7	0	44	71	0	4	1	2	0	2	1	3
Honolulu	0	0	7	0	170	25	0	3	0	4	0	0	0	0
Houston	0	6	2	0	227	15	0	22	1	37	0	0	0	75
Indianapolis	3	17	32	0	190	47	0	19	0	26	0	0	1	1
Jackson	0	6	5	0	57	15	0	2	0	2	0	0	1	9
Jacksonville	0	2	9	0	100	32	0	53	3	0	0	0	0	1
Kansas City	1	20	7	0	87	65	0	14	5	20	0	2	2	13
Knoxville	0	5	0	0	38	138	0	4	2	3	0	1	0	7
Las Vegas	0	5	14	0	84	65	0	6	0	15	0	0	2	1
Little Rock	0	9	4	0	191	59	0	7	0	9	0	2	0	1
Los Angeles	0	5	5	4	236	22	0	1	1	42	0	0	3	0
Louisville	0	33	1	0	211	76	0	10	0	9	0	11	1	0
Memphis	0	6	4	0	103	77	0	5	0	13	0	0	0	13
Miami	1	7	11	0	940	73	0	19	8	75	0	3	3	28
Milwaukee	0	6	4	0	16	63	0	5	0	10	0	0	4	1
Minneapolis	26	100	65	1	108	59	0	4	3	16	0	0	0	9
Mobile	1	1	1	0	56	87	0	5	2	6	0	0	0	1
New Haven	0	1	1	0	63	57	0	6	4	2	0	2	0	3
New Orleans	0	3	4	0	34	185	0	11	3	15	0	0	7	14
New York	0	9	5	0	349	160	0	25	5	41	0	2	14	12
Newark	0	12	2	0	22	43	0	73	4	32	0	0	4	1
Norfolk	0	5	0	0	31	14	0	28	0	9	0	0	7	3
Oklahoma City	0	1	8	0	381	66	0	0	0	22	0	5	0	9
Omaha	0	21	31	8	46	69	0	7	0	18	0	4	0	2
Philadelphia	0	20	15	0	356	129	0	39	2	67	0	1	0	4
Phoenix	70	78	139	0	37	52	0	36	19	20	1	0	0	5
Pittsburgh	0	3	0	0	34	182	0	4	0	17	0	0	0	0
Portland	0	13	9	0	41	58	0	7	0	7	0	1	0	2
Richmond	0	0	3	0	4	5	0	2	2	10	0	0	0	0
Sacramento	0	4	4	0	83	48	0	8	1	8	0	0	2	0
Salt Lake City	8	27	24	2	76	109	0	5	3	13	3	4	0	16
St. Louis	0	4	1	0	81	67	0	4	7	2	0	0	1	7
San Antonio	0	7	21	0	129	87	0	9	3	17	0	0	0	3
San Diego	0	1	12	0	23	34	4	5	1	4	0	0	0	0
San Francisco	0	2	3	0	94	38	0	7	1	9	0	0	0	1
San Juan[2]	0	1	14	0	42	546	0	0	4	31	0	2	2	10
Seattle	1	28	17	0	68	52	0	20	0	13	1	0	3	2
Springfield	0	1	2	0	29	48	0	2	0	3	0	0	0	0
Tampa	0	8	7	0	126	571	0	14	2	11	0	0	0	22
Washington, DC	0	6	2	0	35	85	0	14	12	14	0	0	1	2

[1]These arrests were for violations of one of the U.S. Code Sections listed. Arrests were not included for those made in a joint investigation with other agencies when a state or local code was used nor for fraud cases when a different provision of the U.S. Code was used for the basis of arrest.

[2]Population for the San Juan Field Office is a combination of the U.S. Census Bureau's estimated 2016 commonwealth total for Puerto Rico and the 2010 decennial census total for the U.S. Virgin Islands.

Table 37. Number of Arrestees by NIBRS Offense Code, by Selected FBI Field Office, 2016—*Continued*

(Number.)

NIBRS offense code[1] / NIBRS offense description Field office	280 Stolen property offenses	290 Destruction/ damage/ vandalism of property	370 Pornography/ obscene material	510 Bribery	520 Weapon law violations	720 Animal cruelty	Count of arrestees for Group A Offenses	90G Liquor law violations	90Z All other offenses	Count of arrestees for Group B Offenses	Total number of arrestees	Population per field office
Grand Total, All Field Offices.	141	19	1,446	42	2,719	34	19,563	4	2,992	2,996	22,559	332,826,009
Albany	0	0	32	0	7	0	55	0	11	11	66	4,266,252
Albuquerque	0	0	26	0	52	0	150	0	24	24	174	2,086,535
Anchorage	0	0	17	0	2	0	36	0	2	2	38	747,188
Atlanta	0	1	35	2	51	0	383	0	139	139	522	10,572,283
Baltimore	3	1	30	0	71	0	164	0	93	93	257	7,182,283
Birmingham	0	0	11	4	18	0	144	0	23	23	167	2,882,790
Boston	0	0	15	0	31	0	296	0	75	75	371	10,638,290
Buffalo	3	0	35	0	71	0	337	0	22	22	359	2,946,417
Charlotte	4	4	121	3	121	15	336	0	50	50	386	10,180,571
Chicago	0	0	7	1	43	0	257	0	28	28	285	9,348,926
Cincinnati	2	0	27	0	31	0	108	1	18	19	127	5,946,465
Cleveland	0	0	8	0	59	0	170	0	38	38	208	5,771,693
Columbia	7	0	13	0	63	0	250	0	15	15	265	4,984,808
Dallas	0	0	51	0	55	0	212	0	109	109	321	10,661,172
Denver	1	0	18	0	11	0	134	0	34	34	168	6,185,272
Detroit	1	0	71	1	100	0	489	0	88	88	577	10,327,259
El Paso	0	1	4	4	11	0	141	0	24	24	165	1,283,393
Honolulu	0	0	11	0	3	0	209	0	23	23	232	1,554,673
Houston	1	0	46	2	65	0	310	0	57	57	367	8,507,711
Indianapolis	16	0	37	0	69	0	334	0	26	26	360	6,644,024
Jackson	1	0	9	0	3	0	87	0	17	17	104	2,990,046
Jacksonville	0	0	11	0	9	0	199	0	18	18	217	5,220,065
Kansas City	3	0	55	1	61	0	221	0	135	135	356	6,181,702
Knoxville	0	0	22	0	48	0	191	0	19	19	210	2,610,893
Las Vegas	2	0	21	1	66	1	189	0	115	115	304	2,946,513
Little Rock	0	0	7	0	41	0	281	0	30	30	311	3,005,677
Los Angeles	11	0	20	0	25	0	316	0	167	167	483	19,439,492
Louisville	0	0	40	0	9	0	351	0	14	14	365	4,478,739
Memphis	3	0	7	0	77	0	208	0	26	26	234	4,058,290
Miami	12	0	31	0	65	0	1,137	0	366	366	1,503	6,954,954
Milwaukee	10	2	12	1	34	0	104	0	16	16	120	5,888,427
Minneapolis	0	2	61	0	32	0	382	0	40	40	422	7,523,153
Mobile	1	0	1	0	38	0	159	0	5	5	164	2,004,605
New Haven	9	0	2	0	32	0	136	0	19	19	155	3,653,221
New Orleans	0	0	4	1	38	0	255	0	24	24	279	4,817,513
New York	13	3	23	5	167	0	596	0	254	254	850	15,127,022
Newark	3	0	16	1	39	14	188	0	53	53	241	8,143,302
Norfolk	0	0	76	0	32	0	87	0	12	12	99	1,760,206
Oklahoma City	3	0	21	1	78	0	483	0	9	9	492	3,975,771
Omaha	3	0	20	0	30	0	204	0	29	29	233	5,142,056
Philadelphia	3	2	83	0	102	0	629	0	168	168	797	10,385,094
Phoenix	0	0	15	1	59	0	452	3	64	67	519	6,951,468
Pittsburgh	2	0	22	0	24	0	240	0	8	8	248	5,822,535
Portland	0	0	12	0	27	0	136	0	43	43	179	4,172,382
Richmond	0	0	7	0	14	2	26	0	7	7	33	4,114,051
Sacramento	0	0	5	0	55	0	156	0	24	24	180	8,017,308
Salt Lake City	0	0	24	0	67	0	274	0	25	25	299	6,104,020
St. Louis	9	0	36	0	42	0	166	0	23	23	189	2,993,533
San Antonio	0	1	38	5	62	0	273	0	44	44	317	7,496,195
San Diego	0	0	20	4	11	0	84	0	39	39	123	3,497,325
San Francisco	14	1	15	0	73	0	154	0	41	41	195	8,467,158
San Juan[2]	0	0	8	1	170	0	640	0	57	57	697	3,517,712
Seattle	0	0	21	0	57	0	200	0	23	23	223	7,331,183
Springfield	0	0	22	0	19	0	85	0	12	12	97	3,513,730
Tampa	0	0	21	0	32	0	739	0	53	53	792	8,575,658
Washington, DC	1	1	23	3	47	2	169	0	94	94	263	3,227,005

[1] These arrests were for violations of one of the U.S. Code Sections listed. Arrests were not included for those made in a joint investigation with other agencies when a state or local code was used nor for fraud cases when a different provision of the U.S. Code was used for the basis of arrest.
[2] Population for the San Juan Field Office is a combination of the U.S. Census Bureau's estimated 2016 commonwealth total for Puerto Rico and the 2010 decennial census total for the U.S. Virgin Islands.

Table 38. Number of Arrestees for Child Exploitation, by Selected FBI Field Office, 2016

(Number.)

Field office	Arrests[1]	Population per field office
Albany	43	4,266,252
Albuquerque	45	2,086,535
Anchorage	18	747,188
Atlanta	49	10,572,283
Baltimore	53	7,182,283
Birmingham	19	2,882,790
Boston	24	10,638,290
Buffalo	51	2,946,417
Charlotte	146	10,180,571
Chicago	18	9,348,926
Cincinnati	41	5,946,465
Cleveland	18	5,771,693
Columbia	24	4,984,808
Dallas	75	10,661,172
Denver	26	6,185,272
Detroit	137	10,327,259
El Paso	14	1,283,393
Honolulu	14	1,554,673
Houston	54	8,507,711
Indianapolis	61	6,644,024
Jackson	13	2,990,046
Jacksonville	37	5,220,065
Kansas City	86	6,181,702
Knoxville	29	2,610,893
Las Vegas	31	2,946,513
Little Rock	21	3,005,677
Los Angeles	26	19,439,492
Louisville	76	4,478,739
Memphis	16	4,058,290
Miami	44	6,954,954
Milwaukee	19	5,888,427
Minneapolis	122	7,523,153
Mobile	7	2,004,605
New Haven	4	3,653,221
New Orleans	11	4,817,513
New York	36	15,127,022
Newark	90	8,143,302
Norfolk	81	1,760,206
Oklahoma City	22	3,975,771
Omaha	40	5,142,056
Philadelphia	118	10,385,094
Phoenix	99	6,951,468
Pittsburgh	25	5,822,535
Portland	25	4,172,382
Richmond	7	4,114,051
Sacramento	13	8,017,308
Salt Lake City	53	6,104,020
St. Louis	44	2,993,533
San Antonio	48	7,496,195
San Diego	24	3,497,325
San Francisco	19	8,467,158
San Juan[2]	9	3,517,712
Seattle	49	7,331,183
Springfield	23	3,513,730
Tampa	39	8,575,658
Washington, DC	40	3,227,005

[1]Arrests were not included for those made in a joint investigation with other agencies when a local or state code was used nor for fraud cases when a different provision of the U.S. Code was used for the basis of arrest.
[2]Population for the San Juan Field Office is a combination of the U.S. Census Bureau's estimated 2016 commonwealth total for Puerto Rico and the 2010 decennial census total for the U.S. Virgin Islands.

This page intentionally left blank

Table 39. Number of Arrestees by NIBRS Offense Code, by Selected ATF Judicial District, 2016

(Number.)

NIBRS offense code[1] / NIBRS offense description Judicial district	09A Murder & nonnegligent manslaughter	13A Aggravated Assault	13C Intimidation	23H All other larceny	26A False pretenses/ swindle/ confidence game	26E Wire fraud	35A Drug/narcotic violations	35B Drug equipment violations	100 Kidnapping/ abduction	120 Robbery
Grand Total, All Judicial Districts	52	17	2	84	210	4	1,239	17	1	89
Alabama, Middle District	0	0	0	1	0	0	0	0	0	0
Alabama, Northern District	0	0	0	0	2	0	2	0	0	0
Alabama, Southern District	0	0	0	0	1	0	5	0	0	0
Alaska	0	0	0	0	2	0	2	0	0	0
Arizona	0	2	0	1	15	0	92	0	0	0
Arkansas, Eastern District	0	0	0	0	0	0	0	0	0	0
Arkansas, Western District	0	0	0	0	0	0	0	0	0	0
California, Central District	20	0	0	1	1	0	48	0	0	4
California, Eastern District	0	0	0	1	0	0	34	2	0	0
California, Northern District	0	0	0	0	1	0	14	0	0	0
California, Southern District	0	0	0	0	1	0	5	0	0	0
Colorado	6	0	0	3	1	0	4	0	0	3
Connecticut	0	0	0	0	0	0	17	0	0	0
Delaware	0	0	0	0	4	0	18	0	0	0
District of Columbia	0	0	0	0	0	0	9	6	0	1
Florida, Middle District	0	1	0	1	2	0	21	0	0	0
Florida, Northern District	0	0	0	0	2	0	13	0	0	1
Florida, Southern District	0	0	0	2	6	0	65	0	0	5
Georgia, Middle District	0	0	0	3	2	0	7	0	0	0
Georgia, Northern District	0	1	0	3	2	0	43	0	0	0
Georgia, Southern District	0	0	0	0	0	0	13	0	0	0
Guam[1]	0	0	0	0	0	0	1	0	0	0
Hawaii	0	0	0	0	0	0	0	0	0	2
Idaho	0	0	0	1	0	0	8	0	0	0
Illinois, Central District	1	0	0	0	1	0	9	0	0	0
Illinois, Northern District	0	1	1	5	3	0	18	0	0	0
Illinois, Southern District	0	0	0	2	0	0	10	0	0	0
Indiana, Northern District	1	0	0	4	5	1	29	0	0	0
Indiana, Southern District	0	0	0	2	1	0	6	0	0	8
Iowa, Northern District	0	0	0	0	2	0	2	0	0	0
Iowa, Southern District	1	0	1	1	3	0	7	0	0	3
Kansas	0	0	0	0	2	0	5	0	0	0
Kentucky, Eastern District	0	0	0	0	6	0	7	0	0	0
Kentucky, Western District	0	0	0	0	4	0	16	0	0	0
Louisiana, Eastern District	0	0	0	0	0	0	1	0	0	0
Louisiana, Middle District	0	0	0	0	0	0	0	0	0	0
Louisiana, Western District	0	0	0	1	0	0	1	0	0	0
Maine	0	0	0	0	1	0	0	0	0	0
Maryland	0	0	0	2	1	1	35	0	0	0
Massachusetts	0	0	0	0	5	0	53	3	0	0
Michigan, Eastern District	1	1	0	1	5	1	23	0	0	1
Michigan, Western District	0	0	0	1	4	0	7	0	0	5
Minnesota	0	0	0	4	0	0	7	1	0	4
Mississippi, Northern District	1	2	0	1	1	0	5	0	0	0
Mississippi, Southern District	0	0	0	2		0	0	0	0	2
Missouri, Eastern District	1	0	0	0	0	0	9	0	0	0
Missouri, Western District	1	0	0	4	6	1	26	0	0	0
Montana	0	0	0	0	1	0	0	0	0	0
Nebraska	0	0	0	0	2	0	14	0	0	0
Nevada	0	0	0	0	0	0	0	0	0	0
New Hampshire	0	0	0	0	3	0	0	0	0	0
New Jersey	0	0	0	0	1	0	2	0	0	0
New Mexico	0	0	0	1	0	0	54	0	0	0

(Number.)

NIBRS offense code[1]	200	250	270	280	520	Count of arrestees for Group A Offenses	90Z	Count of arrestees for Group B Offenses	Total number of arrestees	Population per judicial district
NIBRS offense description Judicial district	Arson	Counterfeiting/ forgery	Embezzlement	Stolen property offenses	Weapon law violations (includes firearms & explosives)		All other offenses (includes all alcohol & tobacco offenses)			
Grand Total, All Judicial Districts	90	0	6	54	6,170	8,035	588	588	8,623	338,635,594
Alabama, Middle District...........................	0	0	0	0	16	17	0	0	17	1,151,060
Alabama, Northern District.........................	1	0	0	1	92	98	0	0	98	2,867,854
Alabama, Southern District	0	0	0	0	47	53	0	0	53	844,386
Alaska..	0	0	0	0	38	42	1	1	43	741,894
Arizona...	0	0	0	3	109	222	12	12	234	6,931,071
Arkansas, Eastern District	1	0	0	1	24	26	0	0	26	1,640,011
Arkansas, Western District	0	0	0	0	14	14	0	0	14	1,348,237
California, Central District..........................	5	0	0	0	156	235	17	17	252	19,417,079
California, Eastern District..........................	1	0	0	0	59	97	11	11	108	8,005,253
California, Northern District	0	0	0	1	35	51	10	10	61	8,329,053
California, Southern District	7	0	0	0	33	46	2	2	48	3,498,632
Colorado	2	0	0	2	105	126	6	6	132	5,540,545
Connecticut	1	0	0	0	16	34	3	3	37	3,576,452
Delaware	1	0	0	1	34	58	0	0	58	952,065
District of Columbia	3	0	0	0	11	30	2	2	32	681,170
Florida, Middle District	0	0	0	0	173	198	2	2	200	11,863,843
Florida, Northern District...........................	1	0	0	1	61	79	1	1	80	1,845,130
Florida, Southern District...........................	1	0	0	0	210	289	13	13	302	6,903,466
Georgia, Middle District	0	0	0	5	23	40	1	1	41	2,008,453
Georgia, Northern District	7	0	0	3	47	106	4	4	110	6,725,416
Georgia, Southern District.........................	1	0	0	3	104	121	4	4	125	1,576,502
Guam[1]	0	0	0	0	5	6	0	0	6	159,358
Hawaii..	0	0	0	0	12	14	0	0	14	1,428,557
Idaho..	0	0	0	1	36	46	0	0	46	1,683,140
Illinois, Central District	0	0	0	0	60	71	0	0	71	2,220,575
Illinois, Northern District...........................	5	0	0	0	114	147	3	3	150	9,317,833
Illinois, Southern District...........................	0	0	0	1	50	63	7	7	70	1,263,131
Indiana, Northern District..........................	0	0	0	4	110	154	7	7	161	2,586,998
Indiana, Southern District..........................	3	0	0	0	62	82	4	4	86	4,046,055
Iowa, Northern District..............................	0	0	0	1	18	23	0	0	23	1,326,996
Iowa, Southern District...............................	1	0	0	0	40	57	4	4	61	1,807,697
Kansas..	2	0	0	0	81	90	3	3	93	2,907,289
Kentucky, Eastern District..........................	1	0	0	0	47	61	14	14	75	2,203,205
Kentucky, Western District	0	0	0	0	59	79	12	12	91	2,233,769
Louisiana, Eastern District..........................	0	0	0	0	15	16	1	1	17	1,680,123
Louisiana, Middle District	0	0	0	0	32	32	0	0	32	835,175
Louisiana, Western District	1	0	0	0	29	32	0	0	32	2,166,368
Maine..	0	0	0	0	27	28	0	0	28	1,331,479
Maryland...	1	0	0	1	110	151	33	33	184	6,016,447
Massachusetts	0	0	0	0	79	140	28	28	168	6,811,779
Michigan, Eastern District..........................	1	0	1	1	127	163	16	16	179	6,438,317
Michigan, Western District	2	0	4	2	58	83	8	8	91	3,489,983
Minnesota	0	0	0	4	53	73	1	1	74	5,519,952
Mississippi, Northern District.....................	0	0	0	2	20	32	4	4	36	1,115,684
Mississippi, Southern District.....................	0	0	0	0	34	38	1	1	39	1,873,042
Missouri, Eastern District...........................	3	0	0	0	138	151	15	15	166	2,930,503
Missouri, Western District	1	0	0	1	206	246	17	17	263	3,162,497
Montana..	0	0	0	0	70	71	2	2	73	1,042,520
Nebraska	0	0	0	0	18	34	3	3	37	1,907,116
Nevada	0	0	0	0	76	76	0	0	76	2,940,058
New Hampshire	0	0	0	1	13	17	3	3	20	1,334,795
New Jersey..	1	0	0	0	56	60	16	16	76	8,944,469
New Mexico..	0	0	0	0	70	125	0	0	125	2,081,015

Table 39. Number of Arrestees by NIBRS Offense Code, by Selected ATF Judicial District, 2016—*Continued*

(Number.)

NIBRS offense code[1]	09A	13A	13C	23H	26A	26E	35A	35B	100	120
NIBRS offense description Judicial district	Murder & nonnegligent manslaughter	Aggravated Assault	Intimidation	All other larceny	False pretenses/ swindle/ confidence game	Wire fraud	Drug/narcotic violations	Drug equipment violations	Kidnapping/ abduction	Robbery
New York, Eastern District	0	0	0	0	8	0	9	0	0	12
New York, Northern District	0	0	0	3	1	0	2	0	0	0
New York, Southern District	0	2	0	0	0	0	102	0	0	15
New York, Western District	3	0	0	1	1	0	24	0	0	0
North Carolina, Eastern District	0	0	0	0	0	0	26	0	0	4
North Carolina, Middle District	0	0	0	0	0	0	11	0	0	1
North Carolina, Western District	0	0	0	6	5	0	23	0	0	1
North Dakota	0	0	0	0	1	0	8	0	0	2
Northern Mariana Islands[1]	0	0	0	0	0	0	0	0	0	0
Ohio, Northern District	0	0	0	1	4	0	16	0	0	0
Ohio, Southern District	0	0	0	1	0	0	5	0	0	3
Oklahoma, Eastern District	0	0	0	5	0	0	0	0	0	0
Oklahoma, Northern District	0	0	0	0	0	0	2	0	1	0
Oklahoma, Western District	0	0	0	0	0	0	0	0	0	0
Oregon	0	0	0	0	0	0	2	0	0	0
Pennsylvania, Eastern District	0	0	0	3	11	0	1	0	0	0
Pennsylvania, Middle District	0	0	0	0	4	0	11	0	0	0
Pennsylvania, Western District	2	0	0	0	10	0	4	0	0	0
Puerto Rico	0	0	0	0	0	0	66	0	0	1
Rhode Island	0	0	0	0	0	0	7	0	0	0
South Carolina	0	0	0	7	3	0	20	0	0	0
South Dakota	0	0	0	0	0	0	4	1	0	2
Tennessee, Eastern District	0	0	0	0	1	0	5	0	0	1
Tennessee, Middle District	0	2	0	0	2	0	4	0	0	0
Tennessee, Western District	0	0	0	0	1	0	14	0	0	0
Texas, Eastern District	0	0	0	0	1	0	5	2	0	1
Texas, Northern District	0	0	0	0	0	0	6	0	0	0
Texas, Southern District	0	1	0	2	31	0	16	0	0	3
Texas, Western District	0	0	0	4	2	0	13	0	0	0
U. S. Virgin Islands[2]	0	0	0	0	0	0	2	0	0	0
Utah	0	0	0	1	0	0	3	0	0	0
Vermont	0	1	0	0	1	0	8	0	0	0
Virginia, Eastern District	9	1	0	0	7	0	14	0	0	1
Virginia, Western District	0	1	0	2	5	0	21	1	0	0
Washington, Eastern District	0	0	0	0	1	0	3	0	0	0
Washington, Western District	5	1	0	0	1	0	9	0	0	1
West Virginia, Northern District	0	0	0	0	5	0	0	1	0	0
West Virginia, Southern District	0	0	0	0	2	0	0	0	0	0
Wisconsin, Eastern District	0	0	0	0	3	0	4	0	0	0
Wisconsin, Western District	0	0	0	0	0	0	2	0	0	1
Wyoming	0	0	0	0	0	0	0	0	0	1

Table 39. Number of Arrestees by NIBRS Offense Code, by Selected ATF Judicial District, 2016—*Continued*

(Number.)

NIBRS offense code[1] NIBRS offense description Judicial district	200 Arson	250 Counterfeiting/ forgery	270 Embezzlement	280 Stolen property offenses	520 Weapon law violations (includes firearms & explosives)	Count of arrestees for Group A Offenses	90Z All other offenses (includes all alcohol & tobacco offenses)	Count of arrestees for Group B Offenses	Total number of arrestees	Population per judicial district
New York, Eastern District	0	0	0	0	75	104	6	6	110	8,292,302
New York, Northern District	2	0	0	0	37	45	3	3	48	3,403,475
New York, Southern District	2	0	0	0	178	299	51	51	350	5,248,160
New York, Western District	3	0	0	1	90	123	4	4	127	2,801,352
North Carolina, Eastern District	1	0	0	0	125	156	12	12	168	3,989,760
North Carolina, Middle District	0	0	0	0	114	126	3	3	129	2,951,033
North Carolina, Western District	0	0	0	0	76	111	6	6	117	3,205,995
North Dakota	1	0	0	0	62	74	0	0	74	757,952
Northern Mariana Islands[1]	0	0	0	0	1	1	0	0	1	53,883
Ohio, Northern District	0	0	0	1	66	88	0	0	88	17,502,937
Ohio, Southern District	0	0	0	0	66	75	1	1	76	5,888,564
Oklahoma, Eastern District	1	0	0	0	15	21	0	0	21	738,303
Oklahoma, Northern District	1	0	0	0	21	25	0	0	25	1,071,646
Oklahoma, Western District	0	0	0	0	14	14	0	0	14	2,113,612
Oregon	0	0	0	0	43	45	0	0	45	4,093,465
Pennsylvania, Eastern District	5	0	0	0	54	74	2	2	76	5,714,463
Pennsylvania, Middle District	0	0	0	1	39	55	0	0	55	3,322,992
Pennsylvania, Western District	2	0	0	0	58	76	5	5	81	3,746,772
Puerto Rico	0	0	0	1	216	284	7	7	291	3,411,307
Rhode Island	3	0	0	0	9	19	0	0	19	1,056,426
South Carolina	3	0	0	0	146	179	7	7	186	4,961,119
South Dakota	2	0	0	1	60	70	3	3	73	865,454
Tennessee, Eastern District	2	0	0	1	87	97	20	20	117	2,603,012
Tennessee, Middle District	0	0	1	0	40	49	4	4	53	2,478,759
Tennessee, Western District	0	0	0	0	88	103	9	9	112	1,569,423
Texas, Eastern District	0	0	0	1	104	114	19	19	133	3,917,463
Texas, Northern District	0	0	0	1	146	153	57	57	210	7,240,386
Texas, Southern District	1	0	0	1	193	248	3	3	251	9,610,367
Texas, Western District	0	0	0	1	148	168	3	3	171	7,094,380
U. S. Virgin Islands[2]	0	0	0	0	12	14	0	0	14	106,405
Utah	0	0	0	0	32	36	0	0	36	3,051,217
Vermont	0	0	0	0	12	22	2	2	24	624,594
Virginia, Eastern District	0	0	0	2	99	133	15	15	148	6,104,061
Virginia, Western District	1	0	0	0	43	74	43	43	117	2,307,747
Washington, Eastern District	0	0	0	0	40	44	0	0	44	1,583,932
Washington, Western District	2	0	0	1	68	88	4	4	92	5,704,068
West Virginia, Northern District	0	0	0	1	51	58	0	0	58	869,386
West Virginia, Southern District	4	0	0	0	22	28	1	1	29	961,716
Wisconsin, Eastern District	0	0	0	0	46	53	6	6	59	3,402,035
Wisconsin, Western District	0	0	0	0	8	11	1	1	12	2,376,673
Wyoming	0	0	0	0	34	35	0	0	35	585,501

[1] These arrests were for violations of one of the U.S. Code Sections listed. Arrests were not included for those made in a joint investigation with other agencies when a state or local code was used nor for fraud cases when a different provision of the U.S. Code was used for the basis of arrest.

[2] The population figures for Guam, Northern Mariana Island, and U.S. Virgin Islands were gathered from the 2010 U.S. Census.

Table 40. Number of Arrestees from Federally Issued Warrants by NIBRS Offense Code, by Selected U.S. Marshals Service Judicial District, 2016

(Number.)

NIBRS offense code	09A-09C	11A-11D	13A-13C	23A-23H	26A-26E	35A-35B	36A-36B	39A-39D	40A-40C	64A-64B	100	120	200	210	220	240
NIBRS offense description Judicial district	Homicide offenses	Sex offenses	Assault offenses	Larceny/theft offenses	Fraud offenses	Drug/narcotic offenses	Sex offenses, nonforcible	Gambling offenses	Prostitution offenses	Human trafficking	Kidnapping/abduction	Robbery	Arson	Extortion/blackmail	Burglary/breaking & entering	Motor vehicle theft
Grand Total, All Judicial Districts......	87	43	170	60	346	2,499	41	4	3	21	23	99	2	16	22	7
Alabama, Middle District.................	0	0	1	1	2	5	0	0	0	0	0	0	0	0	0	0
Alabama, Northern District.................	0	0	0	0	1	23	0	0	0	1	0	0	0	0	0	0
Alabama, Southern District.................	0	0	0	0	2	13	0	0	0	0	0	0	0	0	0	0
Alaska.................	0	0	5	0	2	2	0	0	0	0	0	0	0	0	0	0
Arizona.................	3	0	3	0	14	45	0	0	0	0	0	0	0	0	0	0
Arkansas, Eastern District.................	0	0	0	0	1	3	0	0	0	0	0	0	0	0	0	0
Arkansas, Western District.................	0	0	2	0	9	80	17	0	0	0	0	2	0	0	0	0
California, Central District.................	6	1	3	1	6	16	0	0	0	0	0	1	0	0	0	0
California, Eastern District.................	0	0	2	0	11	38	0	0	0	0	0	0	0	0	0	5
California, Northern District.................	1	1	0	0	1	23	0	0	0	0	0	0	0	0	0	0
California, Southern District............	1	2	1	0	3	40	0	0	0	3	0	0	0	0	0	0
Colorado	0	0	0	0	8	18	0	0	0	0	0	0	0	0	0	0
Connecticut...........	0	0	0	0	1	7	0	0	0	0	0	0	0	0	0	0
Delaware	0	0	2	0	0	3	0	0	0	1	0	0	0	0	0	0
District of Columbia	47	19	88	2	13	51	1	0	0	1	4	46	1	2	17	0
Florida, Middle District.................	1	1	2	2	6	31	0	0	0	2	0	0	0	0	0	0
Florida, Northern District.................	0	0	0	1	2	6	0	0	0	0	0	0	0	0	0	0
Florida, Southern District.................	0	1	3	2	22	72	1	0	0	0	0	1	0	0	0	0
Georgia, Middle District.................	0	0	0	0	2	54	0	0	0	0	0	0	0	0	0	0
Georgia, Northern District.................	1	1	0	0	6	10	0	0	0	0	0	0	0	1	0	0
Georgia, Southern District.................	0	0	0	1	1	14	0	0	0	0	0	0	0	0	0	0
Guam[1].................	0	0	0	0	0	0	0	0	0	0	0	0	0	0	0	0
Hawaii	0	0	0	0	4	40	3	0	0	0	0	0	0	1	0	0
Idaho.................	0	0	0	1	1	27	0	0	0	0	0	0	0	0	0	0
Illinois, Central District.................	0	0	0	0	0	1	0	0	0	0	0	0	0	0	0	0
Illinois, Northern District.................	2	0	0	0	2	24	0	0	0	0	0	0	0	0	0	0
Illinois, Southern District.................	0	0	0	0	0	18	0	0	0	0	0	0	0	0	0	0
Indiana, Northern District.................	0	0	2	0	2	9	0	0	0	0	0	0	0	0	0	0
Indiana, Southern District.................	0	0	0	0	0	6	0	0	0	0	0	0	0	0	0	0
Iowa, Northern District.................	0	0	0	0	1	82	1	0	0	3	0	3	0	0	0	0
Iowa, Southern District.................	0	0	0	0	0	8	0	0	0	0	0	0	0	0	0	0
Kansas.................	0	0	0	3	3	30	2	0	0	0	0	1	0	0	0	0
Kentucky, Eastern District.................	0	0	0	0	2	13	1	0	0	0	0	0	0	0	0	0

Table 40. Number of Arrestees from Federally Issued Warrants by NIBRS Offense Code, by Selected U.S. Marshals Service Judicial District, 2016—*Continued*

(Number.)

NIBRS offense code / NIBRS offense description Judicial district	250 Counterfeiting/ forgery	270 Embezzlement	280 Stolen property offenses	290 Destruction/ damage/ vandalism of property	370 Pornography/ obscene material	510 Bribery	520 Weapon law violations	720 Animal cruelty	Count of arrestees for Group A Offenses	90D Driving under the influence	90F Family offenses, nonviolent	90J Trespass of real property	90Z All other offenses	Count of arrestees for Group B Offenses	Total number of arrestees	Population per judicial district
Grand Total, All Judicial Districts......	19	8	36	4	66	10	737	2	4,325	1	17	3	30,545	30,566	34,891	338,635,594
Alabama, Middle District..................	0	0	0	0	1	0	17	0	9	0	0	0	71	71	80	1,151,060
Alabama, Northern District..................	0	0	0	1	2	0	27	0	25	0	0	0	163	163	188	2,867,854
Alabama, Southern District..................	0	0	0	0	0	0	16	0	15	0	0	0	242	242	257	844,386
Alaska..................	0	0	0	0	0	0	2	0	9	0	0	0	107	107	116	741,894
Arizona..................	0	0	1	0	1	0	6	0	65	0	0	0	1,991	1,991	2,056	6,931,071
Arkansas, Eastern District..................	0	0	0	0	0	0	4	0	4	0	0	0	127	127	131	1,640,011
Arkansas, Western District..................	3	1	0	0	0	0	25	0	110	0	0	0	62	62	172	1,348,237
California, Central District..................	1	0	0	0	0	0	2	0	34	0	1	0	518	519	553	19,417,079
California, Eastern District..................	0	0	1	0	0	0	5	0	56	0	0	0	284	284	340	8,005,253
California, Northern District..................	0	0	0	0	0	0	0	0	26	0	0	1	344	345	371	8,329,053
California, Southern District..................	0	0	0	1	12	0	4	0	50	0	1	0	963	964	1,014	3,498,632
Colorado	0	0	0	0	0	0	7	0	26	0	0	0	188	188	214	5,540,545
Connecticut..........	0	0	0	0	0	0	1	0	8	0	0	0	85	85	93	3,576,452
Delaware	0	0	0	0	0	0	4	0	6	0	0	0	21	21	27	952,065
District of Columbia	0	1	1	0	2	3	17	0	292	0	1	1	3,243	3,245	3,537	681,170
Florida, Middle District..................	0	0	0	0	0	0	9	0	45	0	0	0	534	534	579	11,863,843
Florida, Northern District..................	0	0	0	0	0	0	1	0	9	0	0	0	119	119	128	1,845,130
Florida, Southern District..................	0	1	0	0	0	2	14	0	102	0	0	0	499	499	601	6,903,466
Georgia, Middle District..................	0	0	0	0	3	0	22	1	56	0	0	0	97	97	153	2,008,453
Georgia, Northern District..................	2	0	0	0	0	0	4	0	19	0	0	0	229	229	248	6,725,416
Georgia, Southern District..................	0	0	0	0	0	0	4	0	16	0	0	0	145	145	161	1,576,502
Guam[1]..................	0	0	0	0	0	0	1	0	0	0	0	0	51	51	51	159,358
Hawaii	0	1	0	0	1	0	5	0	48	0	0	0	114	114	162	1,428,557
Idaho	0	0	0	0	0	0	1	0	29	0	0	0	157	157	186	1,683,140
Illinois, Central District..................	0	0	0	0	0	0	1	0	1	0	0	0	173	173	174	2,220,575
Illinois, Northern District..................	0	0	0	0	0	0	0	0	28	0	0	0	151	151	179	9,317,833
Illinois, Southern District..................	2	0	0	0	0	0	5	0	18	0	0	0	156	156	174	1,263,131
Indiana, Northern District..................	0	0	0	0	0	0	6	0	13	0	0	0	137	137	150	2,586,998
Indiana, Southern District..................	0	0	0	0	0	0	0	0	6	0	0	0	134	134	140	4,046,055
Iowa, Northern District..................	0	0	4	0	5	0	40	0	90	0	0	0	184	184	274	1,326,996
Iowa, Southern District..................	0	0	0	0	8	0	6	0	8	0	0	0	256	256	264	1,807,697
Kansas..................	0	0	0	0	0	0	19	0	39	0	0	0	318	318	357	2,907,289
Kentucky, Eastern District..................	0	0	0	0	0	0	1	0	16	0	0	0	262	262	278	2,203,205

(Number.)

NIBRS offense code / NIBRS offense description Judicial district	09A - 09C Homicide offenses	11A - 11D Sex offenses	13A - 13C Assault offenses	23A - 23H Larceny/ theft offenses	26A - 26E Fraud offenses	35A - 35B Drug/ narcotic offenses	36A - 36B Sex offenses, nonforcible	39A - 39 D Gambling offenses	40A - 40C Prostitution offenses	64A - 64B Human trafficking	100 Kidnapping/ abduction	120 Robbery	200 Arson	210 Extortion/ blackmail	220 Burglary/ breaking & entering	240 Motor vehicle theft
Kentucky, Western District	0	0	0	1	0	3	0	0	0	0	0	0	0	0	0	0
Louisiana, Eastern District	0	0	1	0	0	10	0	0	0	0	0	0	0	0	0	0
Louisiana, Middle District	0	0	0	0	0	3	0	0	0	0	0	0	0	0	0	0
Louisiana, Western District	2	0	0	1	1	5	0	0	0	0	0	1	0	0	0	0
Maine	0	0	0	0	2	3	0	0	0	0	0	0	0	0	0	0
Maryland	1	1	5	0	1	27	0	0	0	0	0	4	0	0	0	0
Massachusetts	0	0	1	0	1	19	0	0	0	0	0	4	0	0	0	0
Michigan, Eastern District	0	3	1	0	1	20	0	0	0	0	1	0	0	0	0	0
Michigan, Western District	0	0	1	0	2	9	0	0	0	1	0	0	0	0	0	0
Minnesota	0	0	0	0	4	15	0	0	1	0	0	0	0	0	0	0
Mississippi, Northern District	0	0	0	0	0	16	1	0	0	0	0	0	0	0	0	0
Mississippi, Southern District	0	0	0	0	4	5	0	0	0	0	0	0	0	0	0	0
Missouri, Eastern District	1	1	1	0	28	125	1	0	0	0	4	5	0	2	0	0
Missouri, Western District	0	0	0	1	1	40	0	0	0	0	0	0	0	0	0	0
Montana	0	1	1	0	0	23	1	0	0	0	0	0	0	0	0	0
Nebraska	1	0	1	0	1	42	0	0	0	0	0	0	0	0	0	0
Nevada	0	0	1	2	1	12	0	0	0	0	0	0	0	0	0	0
New Hampshire	0	0	0	0	2	5	0	0	0	0	0	0	0	0	0	0
New Jersey	1	0	2	0	5	7	0	0	0	0	0	0	0	0	0	0
New Mexico	1	0	4	0	4	55	0	0	0	1	0	0	0	0	3	2
New York, Eastern District	3	0	0	3	18	73	7	0	0	0	0	5	0	1	0	0
New York, Northern District	0	1	0	1	11	21	0	0	0	0	0	0	0	0	0	0
New York, Southern District	5	0	1	1	8	184	0	0	0	0	0	13	0	5	0	0
New York, Western District	0	0	4	0	0	5	0	0	0	0	1	2	0	0	1	0
North Carolina, Eastern District	0	0	0	0	3	7	0	0	0	0	1	0	0	0	0	0
North Carolina, Middle District	0	0	0	0	3	8	0	0	0	0	0	0	0	0	0	0
North Carolina, Western District	3	0	0	0	0	12	0	0	0	0	0	0	0	0	0	0
North Dakota	0	0	3	0	1	13	0	0	0	0	0	0	0	0	0	0
Northern Mariana Islands[1]	0	0	0	0	0	0	0	0	0	0	0	0	0	0	0	0
Ohio, Northern District	0	0	2	1	14	20	0	0	0	2	0	0	0	0	0	0
Ohio, Southern District	0	0	0	1	2	11	0	0	0	0	0	0	0	0	0	0
Oklahoma, Eastern District	1	0	0	0	0	1	0	0	0	0	0	0	0	0	0	0
Oklahoma, Northern District	0	0	0	0	1	1	0	0	0	0	0	1	0	0	0	0
Oklahoma, Western District	0	0	0	0	1	4	0	0	0	0	0	0	0	0	0	0
Oregon	2	1	0	0	2	17	0	0	0	1	0	0	0	2	0	0

(Number.)

NIBRS offense code / NIBRS offense description Judicial district	250 Counterfeiting/ forgery	270 Embezzlement	280 Stolen property offenses	290 Destruction/ damage/ vandalism of property	370 Pornography/ obscene material	510 Bribery	520 Weapon law violations	720 Animal cruelty	Count of arrestees for Group A Offenses	90D Driving under the influence	90F Family offenses, nonviolent	90J Trespass of real property	90Z All other offenses	Count of arrestees for Group B Offenses	Total number of arrestees	Population per judicial district
Kentucky, Western District	0	0	0	0	3	0	5	0	4	0	0	0	111	111	115	2,233,769
Louisiana, Eastern District	0	0	0	0	0	0	0	0	11	0	0	0	119	119	130	1,680,123
Louisiana, Middle District	0	0	0	0	0	0	7	0	3	0	0	0	55	55	58	835,175
Louisiana, Western District	0	0	0	0	1	0	3	0	10	0	0	0	86	86	96	2,166,368
Maine	0	0	0	0	0	0	0	0	5	0	0	0	101	101	106	1,331,479
Maryland	0	0	0	0	0	0	1	0	39	1	0	0	334	335	374	6,016,447
Massachusetts	0	0	0	0	0	0	2	0	25	0	0	0	265	265	290	6,811,779
Michigan, Eastern District	0	0	0	0	0	0	4	0	26	0	0	0	195	195	221	6,438,317
Michigan, Western District	0	0	0	0	0	0	0	0	13	0	0	0	190	190	203	3,489,983
Minnesota	0	0	0	0	0	0	4	0	20	0	0	0	218	218	238	5,519,952
Mississippi, Northern District	0	0	2	0	0	0	5	0	17	0	0	0	119	119	136	1,115,684
Mississippi, Southern District	0	0	0	0	0	0	6	0	9	0	0	0	151	151	160	1,873,042
Missouri, Eastern District	0	0	8	0	1	0	61	0	168	0	0	0	386	386	554	2,930,503
Missouri, Western District	0	0	0	0	1	0	13	0	42	0	0	0	428	428	470	3,162,497
Montana	0	0	0	0	0	0	9	0	26	0	0	0	368	368	394	1,042,520
Nebraska	0	0	0	0	4	0	9	0	45	0	0	0	338	338	383	1,907,116
Nevada	0	0	1	0	0	0	6	0	16	0	0	0	286	286	302	2,940,058
New Hampshire	0	0	0	0	0	0	2	0	7	0	0	0	99	99	106	1,334,795
New Jersey	0	0	0	0	0	0	0	1	15	0	0	0	218	218	233	8,944,469
New Mexico	0	0	0	0	0	0	10	0	70	0	0	0	805	805	875	2,081,015
New York, Eastern District	1	0	1	0	1	0	12	0	110	0	0	0	237	237	347	8,292,302
New York, Northern District	1	0	0	0	0	0	0	0	34	0	0	0	182	182	216	3,403,475
New York, Southern District	2	3	5	0	0	0	7	0	217	0	0	0	376	376	593	5,248,160
New York, Western District	0	0	0	0	0	0	0	0	13	0	0	0	295	295	308	2,801,352
North Carolina, Eastern District	0	0	0	0	0	0	1	0	11	0	0	0	239	239	250	3,989,760
North Carolina, Middle District	0	0	0	0	0	0	2	0	11	0	0	0	135	135	146	2,951,033
North Carolina, Western District	0	0	0	0	0	0	2	0	15	0	0	0	330	330	345	3,205,995
North Dakota	0	0	0	0	0	0	0	0	17	0	0	0	247	247	264	757,952
Northern Mariana Islands[1]	0	0	0	0	0	0	0	0	0	0	0	0	3	3	3	53,883
Ohio, Northern District	0	0	0	0	1	0	4	0	39	0	0	0	269	269	308	17,502,937
Ohio, Southern District	0	0	0	0	0	0	0	0	14	0	0	0	210	210	224	5,888,564
Oklahoma, Eastern District	0	0	0	0	0	0	2	0	2	0	0	0	48	48	50	738,303
Oklahoma, Northern District	0	0	0	0	0	0	1	0	3	0	0	0	165	165	168	1,071,646
Oklahoma, Western District	1	0	0	0	0	0	5	0	5	0	0	0	153	153	158	2,113,612
Oregon	0	0	0	1	0	0	3	0	25	0	0	0	483	483	508	4,093,465

(Number.)

NIBRS offense code / description / Judicial district	09A-09C Homicide offenses	11A-11D Sex offenses	13A-13C Assault offenses	23A-23H Larceny/theft offenses	26A-26E Fraud offenses	35A-35B Drug/narcotic offenses	36A-36B Sex offenses, nonforcible	39A-39D Gambling offenses	40A-40C Prostitution offenses	64A-64B Human trafficking	100 Kidnapping/abduction	120 Robbery	200 Arson	210 Extortion/blackmail	220 Burglary/breaking & entering	240 Motor vehicle theft
Pennsylvania, Eastern District.......	0	0	2	0	2	7	0	0	0	0	0	3	0	0	0	0
Pennsylvania, Middle District	0	0	0	0	1	18	0	0	0	0	0	0	0	0	0	0
Pennsylvania, Western District	0	0	1	0	2	5	0	0	0	0	0	0	0	0	0	0
Puerto Rico	0	0	0	4	7	68	0	0	0	0	0	0	0	0	0	0
Rhode Island	0	0	0	2	0	2	0	0	0	0	0	0	0	0	0	0
South Carolina.......	0	0	0	0	3	22	0	0	0	1	0	1	0	0	0	0
South Dakota.........	1	4	8	8	6	13	0	0	0	0	0	0	0	0	1	0
Tennessee, Eastern District..................	0	0	0	0	3	25	0	0	0	0	0	0	0	0	0	0
Tennessee, Middle District..................	0	0	0	0	0	4	0	0	0	0	0	1	0	0	0	0
Tennessee, Western District..................	0	0	0	1	3	6	0	4	0	0	0	0	0	0	0	0
Texas, Eastern District..................	0	1	1	0	2	42	0	0	0	0	1	1	0	0	0	0
Texas, Northern District..................	0	0	0	2	2	62	2	0	0	1	0	1	0	0	0	0
Texas, Southern District..................	1	0	6	1	17	143	0	0	0	1	9	1	0	0	0	0
Texas, Western District..................	0	2	3	12	3	94	1	0	2	0	0	0	0	1	0	0
U.S. Virgin Islands[1].	0	0	0	0	1	3	0	0	0	0	1	0	0	0	0	0
Utah	0	1	2	2	6	34	0	0	0	0	0	1	0	0	0	0
Vermont	0	0	0	0	2	16	0	0	0	0	0	0	0	0	0	0
Virginia, Eastern District..................	0	0	1	1	4	14	0	0	0	1	0	0	0	1	0	0
Virginia, Western District..................	0	0	2	1	17	100	0	0	0	1	0	0	1	0	0	0
Washington, Eastern District............	0	0	1	0	4	24	0	0	0	0	0	0	0	0	0	0
Washington, Western District............	1	1	0	0	4	21	1	0	0	0	0	1	0	0	0	0
West Virginia, Northern District	0	0	0	0	5	62	0	0	0	0	0	0	0	0	0	0
West Virginia, Southern District....	0	0	0	0	2	32	0	0	0	0	1	0	0	0	0	0
Wisconsin, Eastern District..................	1	0	0	0	0	6	0	0	0	0	0	0	0	0	0	0
Wisconsin, Western District..................	0	0	0	0	0	0	0	0	0	0	0	0	0	0	0	0
Wyoming...............	0	0	0	0	0	43	1	0	0	0	0	0	0	0	0	0

(Number.)

NIBRS offense code / NIBRS offense description Judicial district	250 Counter-feiting/ forgery	270 Embezzle-ment	280 Stolen property offenses	290 Destruction/ damage/ vandalism of property	370 Pornography/ obscene material	510 Bribery	520 Weapon law violations	720 Animal cruelty	Count of arrestees for Group A Offenses	90D Driving under the influence	90F Family offenses, nonviolent	90J Trespass of real property	90Z All other offenses	Count of arrestees for Group B Offenses	Total number of arrestees	Population per judicial district
Pennsylvania, Eastern District	0	0	0	0	0	0	1	0	14	0	0	1	248	249	263	5,714,463
Pennsylvania, Middle District	0	0	0	0	0	0	2	0	19	0	0	0	139	139	158	3,322,992
Pennsylvania, Western District	0	0	0	0	0	0	5	0	8	0	0	0	168	168	176	3,746,772
Puerto Rico	0	0	0	0	0	0	5	0	79	0	0	0	311	311	390	3,411,307
Rhode Island	0	0	0	0	0	0	0	0	4	0	0	0	64	64	68	1,056,426
South Carolina	0	1	0	0	2	0	7	0	27	0	0	0	421	421	448	4,961,119
South Dakota	0	0	0	0	5	0	5	0	41	0	0	14	496	510	551	865,454
Tennessee, Eastern District	0	0	0	0	0	0	13	0	28	0	0	0	379	379	407	2,603,012
Tennessee, Middle District	2	0	0	0	0	0	0	0	5	0	0	0	177	177	182	2,478,759
Tennessee, Western District	0	0	0	0	0	0	65	0	14	0	0	0	281	281	295	1,569,423
Texas, Eastern District	1	0	6	0	0	1	12	0	48	0	0	0	306	306	354	3,917,463
Texas, Northern District	0	0	0	0	1	2	19	0	70	0	0	0	489	489	559	7,240,386
Texas, Southern District	0	0	0	0	1	2	57	0	179	0	0	0	1,869	1,869	2,048	9,610,367
Texas, Western District	0	0	0	0	2	0	22	0	118	0	0	0	2,308	2,308	2,426	7,094,380
U.S. Virgin Islands[1]	0	0	0	0	0	0	5	0	5	0	0	0	43	43	48	106,405
Utah	0	0	1	1	0	0	11	0	46	0	0	0	398	398	444	3,051,217
Vermont	0	0	0	0	1	0	1	0	18	0	0	0	98	98	116	624,594
Virginia, Eastern District	0	0	0	0	0	0	2	0	22	0	0	0	314	314	336	6,104,061
Virginia, Western District	0	0	0	0	0	0	7	0	122	0	0	0	151	151	273	2,307,747
Washington, Eastern District	0	0	0	0	1	0	8	0	29	0	0	0	240	240	269	1,583,932
Washington, Western District	0	0	0	0	0	0	4	0	29	0	0	0	361	361	390	5,704,068
West Virginia, Northern District	1	0	5	0	0	0	13	0	67	0	0	0	303	303	370	869,386
West Virginia, Southern District	0	0	0	0	0	0	9	0	35	0	0	0	192	192	227	961,716
Wisconsin, Eastern District	0	0	0	0	0	0	0	0	7	0	0	0	259	259	266	3,402,035
Wisconsin, Western District	0	0	0	0	0	0	0	0	0	0	0	0	42	42	42	2,376,673
Wyoming	2	0	0	0	6	0	2	0	44	0	0	0	119	119	163	585,501

[1]Population for Guam, Northern Mariana Island, and U.S. Virgin Islands was gathered from the 2010 U.S. Census.

Table 41. Number of Arrestees from State-Issued Warrants by NIBRS Offense Code, by Selected U.S. Marshals Service Judicial District, 2016

(Number.)

NIBRS offense code / NIBRS offense description Judicial district	09A - 09C Homicide offenses	11A - 11D Sex offenses	13A - 13C Assault offenses	23A - 23H Larceny/theft offenses	26A - 26E Fraud offenses	35A - 35B Drug/ narcotic offenses	36A - 36B Sex offenses, nonforcible	39A - 39 D Gambling offenses	40A - 40C Prostitution offenses	64A - 64B Human trafficking	100 Kidnapping/ abduction	120 Robbery
Grand Total, All Judicial Districts	4,722	5,125	13,912	1,354	917	14,810	966	3	80	170	1,253	6,827
Alabama, Middle District........................	64	98	163	31	3	224	10	0	0	3	12	170
Alabama, Northern District......................	67	140	228	19	4	151	19	1	3	1	20	199
Alabama, Southern District	36	50	57	3	38	172	5	0	0	0	4	46
Alaska..	3	9	12	0	1	1	1	0	0	0	2	4
Arizona...	93	71	237	50	23	421	16	0	1	9	49	151
Arkansas, Eastern District......................	27	13	52	5	3	36	0	0	0	2	3	38
Arkansas, Western District	6	21	20	0	3	39	0	0	0	0	3	10
California, Central District......................	328	202	301	41	47	236	41	2	7	6	57	213
California, Eastern District......................	59	24	67	1	7	33	4	0	0	3	9	28
California, Northern District....................	105	37	57	2	5	57	7	0	1	3	4	44
California, Southern District....................	93	100	254	41	48	267	24	0	10	1	12	87
Colorado	4	13	10	1	4	28	1	0	2	0	3	5
Connecticut..	21	35	84	7	1	25	0	0	0	0	5	24
Delaware..	14	4	49	8	3	27	3	0	0	0	1	36
District of Columbia..............................	2	1	7	5	2	4	1	0	0	0	0	4
Florida, Middle District..........................	160	185	325	11	10	224	20	0	2	5	29	204
Florida, Northern District.......................	47	84	207	10	14	189	5	0	0	1	17	86
Florida, Southern District.......................	188	79	385	11	14	218	13	0	0	1	35	276
Georgia, Middle District	43	39	194	12	3	179	3	0	0	2	28	46
Georgia, Northern District......................	135	142	541	8	3	110	4	0	1	2	79	197
Georgia, Southern District......................	60	29	176	9	2	208	3	0	0	0	24	54
Guam[1]..	0	1	0	2	0	0	1	0	0	0	1	0
Hawaii..	9	17	36	9	5	73	2	0	0	0	3	18
Idaho...	15	27	61	0	0	2	2	0	0	1	4	14
Illinois, Central District	38	43	155	67	11	369	9	0	0	0	11	78
Illinois, Northern District........................	105	166	210	10	11	91	7	0	0	0	11	140
Illinois, Southern District........................	21	7	51	1	0	76	1	0	0	0	3	25
Indiana, Northern District.......................	47	75	105	10	16	150	19	0	0	0	13	74
Indiana, Southern District.......................	77	42	53	3	3	224	5	0	0	1	6	43
Iowa, Northern District..........................	8	12	24	3	1	35	1	0	0	1	0	9
Iowa, Southern District...........................	3	8	9	2	1	14	0	0	0	1	0	3
Kansas..	25	10	49	2	1	32	0	0	0	0	5	14
Kentucky, Eastern District.......................	24	13	48	0	2	121	10	0	0	0	2	24
Kentucky, Western District	8	6	20	1	1	27	3	0	0	0	3	13
Louisiana, Eastern District......................	133	58	157	6	6	83	7	0	0	3	18	122
Louisiana, Middle District	17	6	10	3	1	41	11	0	0	0	1	14
Louisiana, Western District	93	39	98	6	3	287	11	0	0	1	11	55
Maine...	2	7	21	0	0	22	0	0	0	0	0	10
Maryland..	159	66	406	21	13	273	27	0	3	1	14	226
Massachusetts.......................................	41	63	339	58	6	159	8	0	6	0	15	79
Michigan, Eastern District......................	46	95	353	92	142	451	21	0	5	1	12	131
Michigan, Western District	26	92	139	10	14	281	21	0	3	0	3	31
Minnesota..	12	13	36	0	1	22	4	0	2	1	2	26
Mississippi, Northern District..................	43	32	143	13	6	276	10	0	0	2	12	78
Mississippi, Southern District..................	52	26	115	27	21	204	12	0	2	1	16	83
Missouri, Eastern District.......................	22	21	34	0	1	75	4	0	0	0	2	30
Missouri, Western District	36	20	38	2	2	72	5	0	0	0	2	22
Montana...	3	30	59	33	5	170	5	0	0	0	6	6
Nebraska	17	43	248	75	31	283	6	0	1	0	6	51
Nevada...	8	9	17	11	15	99	6	0	1	0	1	7
New Hampshire	1	4	15	13	5	60	0	0	0	3	2	15
New Jersey..	100	79	356	37	20	368	4	0	2	0	13	188
New Mexico...	33	30	142	14	7	132	12	0	1	2	21	38

Table 41. Number of Arrestees from State-Issued Warrants by NIBRS Offense Code, by Selected U.S. Marshals Service Judicial District, 2016—*Continued*

(Number.)

NIBRS offense code NIBRS offense description Judicial district	09A - 09C Homicide offenses	11A - 11D Sex offenses	13A - 13C Assault offenses	23A - 23H Larceny/theft offenses	26A - 26E Fraud offenses	35A - 35B Drug/narcotic offenses	36A - 36B Sex offenses, nonforcible	39A - 39D Gambling offenses	40A - 40C Prostitution offenses	64A - 64B Human trafficking	100 Kidnapping/abduction	120 Robbery
New York, Eastern District	62	22	137	71	18	141	8	0	0	0	3	107
New York, Northern District	43	23	100	6	2	286	13	0	0	0	6	62
New York, Southern District	25	7	34	2	0	29	1	0	0	1	0	14
New York, Western District	34	19	123	3	1	156	10	0	0	2	8	94
North Carolina, Eastern District	77	60	150	22	34	175	38	0	0	3	35	140
North Carolina, Middle District	43	11	58	1	0	40	9	0	1	0	20	48
North Carolina, Western District	14	14	57	15	10	204	5	0	0	1	19	54
North Dakota	2	11	67	14	3	123	0	0	0	0	0	8
Northern Mariana Islands[1]	0	0	0	0	0	0	0	0	0	1	1	0
Ohio, Northern District	120	174	601	61	27	709	49	0	3	2	47	302
Ohio, Southern District	39	74	249	24	2	495	14	0	2	5	22	105
Oklahoma, Eastern District	15	46	202	5	1	149	18	0	0	1	27	39
Oklahoma, Northern District	23	16	37	3	6	66	2	0	0	0	3	26
Oklahoma, Western District	29	36	33	0	4	66	1	0	0	2	5	15
Oregon	38	40	45	1	1	93	38	0	2	0	3	15
Pennsylvania, Eastern District	69	60	240	9	13	110	7	0	1	0	4	128
Pennsylvania, Middle District	23	22	68	5	1	160	7	0	1	0	5	37
Pennsylvania, Western District	67	22	167	16	6	67	3	0	0	0	3	95
Puerto Rico	90	15	52	4	2	78	1	0	0	0	1	41
Rhode Island	11	14	51	15	6	31	1	0	0	0	1	12
South Carolina	230	65	245	11	6	285	42	0	0	8	117	178
South Dakota	6	27	68	9	5	239	9	0	1	5	7	11
Tennessee, Eastern District	38	32	199	6	2	244	3	0	1	3	32	71
Tennessee, Middle District	31	49	112	3	4	104	11	0	0	1	10	40
Tennessee, Western District	106	72	220	59	39	233	18	0	0	7	18	84
Texas, Eastern District	24	155	233	46	16	342	23	0	0	2	10	103
Texas, Northern District	130	435	784	14	30	263	34	0	7	14	14	292
Texas, Southern District	196	307	1,216	30	30	407	44	0	2	31	36	473
Texas, Western District	115	318	451	34	18	314	46	0	0	4	33	175
U.S. Virgin Islands[1]	0	0	0	0	0	0	0	0	0	0	0	0
Utah	19	65	209	5	10	96	12	0	0	8	24	68
Vermont	1	9	31	1	0	15	2	0	1	0	0	10
Virginia, Eastern District	91	104	199	6	0	130	18	0	0	0	63	127
Virginia, Western District	17	99	113	15	4	981	11	0	0	1	30	75
Washington, Eastern District	18	24	76	2	3	33	4	0	0	1	4	37
Washington, Western District	34	70	104	1	7	48	28	0	2	0	14	66
West Virginia, Northern District	15	24	35	4	0	271	3	0	0	4	2	15
West Virginia, Southern District	15	10	35	13	7	68	6	0	0	0	1	23
Wisconsin, Eastern District	32	13	36	3	2	42	7	0	3	1	4	30
Wisconsin, Western District	1	18	100	7	8	74	2	0	0	3	5	18
Wyoming	0	7	2	2	0	22	4	0	0	1	1	0

[1]Population for Guam, Northern Mariana Island, and U.S. Virgin Islands was gathered from the 2010 U.S. Census.

Table 41. Number of Arrestees from State-Issued Warrants by NIBRS Offense Code, by Selected U.S. Marshals Service Judicial District, 2016—*Continued*

(Number.)

NIBRS offense code	200	210	220	240	250	270	280	290	370	510	520	720
NIBRS offense description Judicial district	Arson	Extortion/ blackmail	Burglary/ breaking & entering	Motor vehicle theft	Counterfeiting/ forgery	Embezzlement	Stolen property offenses	Destruction/ damage/ vandalism of property	Pornography/ obscene material	Bribery	Weapon law violations	Animal cruelty
Grand Total, All Judicial Districts....................	255	53	4,450	628	361	55	373	114	350	8	4,930	5
Alabama, Middle District...............................	1	0	101	5	0	0	0	0	23	0	55	0
Alabama, Northern District............................	0	0	62	11	6	1	19	1	5	0	61	0
Alabama, Southern District	0	0	22	2	4	0	1	0	2	0	22	0
Alaska..	0	0	2	0	1	0	0	0	0	0	1	0
Arizona...	1	0	76	56	7	0	19	2	11	0	94	0
Arkansas, Eastern District..............................	0	0	22	0	1	0	2	2	0	0	19	0
Arkansas, Western District	0	0	6	0	1	0	3	0	0	0	7	0
California, Central District.............................	8	6	152	65	15	5	40	12	15	1	139	0
California, Eastern District.............................	0	0	13	17	0	1	5	0	1	0	47	0
California, Northern District...........................	0	0	25	0	1	1	6	1	0	0	41	0
California, Southern District...........................	3	1	69	23	6	0	9	6	6	0	83	0
Colorado	0	0	10	2	0	0	0	0	1	0	2	0
Connecticut...	4	0	12	0	1	0	0	0	0	0	15	0
Delaware	0	0	37	6	2	0	2	0	0	0	37	0
District of Columbia.....................................	0	0	1	2	0	0	0	0	0	0	1	0
Florida, Middle District	5	2	70	25	1	0	2	1	14	2	77	0
Florida, Northern District..............................	3	2	40	11	2	0	5	1	9	0	60	0
Florida, Southern District..............................	4	7	115	6	1	0	1	0	9	0	59	0
Georgia, Middle District	2	0	46	15	1	0	0	4	7	0	68	0
Georgia, Northern District............................	5	0	56	3	0	0	0	2	3	0	175	0
Georgia, Southern District............................	6	0	36	13	2	0	6	5	1	0	159	0
Guam[1]..	0	0	0	0	1	0	0	0	0	0	0	0
Hawaii..	1	0	5	6	0	0	0	0	0	0	13	0
Idaho...	0	0	2	0	0	0	0	0	4	0	3	0
Illinois, Central District	2	1	74	3	17	0	9	2	0	0	120	0
Illinois, Northern District...............................	3	0	94	3	5	0	0	0	6	0	38	0
Illinois, Southern District...............................	1	0	10	1	3	0	1	1	2	0	118	1
Indiana, Northern District..............................	2	1	59	4	5	0	2	0	3	1	37	1
Indiana, Southern District..............................	1	0	43	3	14	0	11	0	2	0	33	0
Iowa, Northern District.................................	1	0	14	0	2	0	0	0	0	0	9	0
Iowa, Southern District.................................	1	0	4	0	2	0	0	1	0	0	3	0
Kansas...	0	2	15	3	1	1	1	0	1	0	7	0
Kentucky, Eastern District..............................	2	0	18	0	1	0	0	0	4	0	19	0
Kentucky, Western District............................	0	0	8	4	2	0	1	0	1	0	17	0
Louisiana, Eastern District.............................	3	2	64	9	4	0	8	13	0	0	79	0
Louisiana, Middle District	0	1	15	0	0	0	0	0	2	0	7	0
Louisiana, Western District............................	1	1	69	3	4	0	1	1	6	0	139	0
Maine...	1	0	6	0	0	1	1	0	4	0	2	0
Maryland..	13	1	145	34	5	1	0	0	3	0	40	0
Massachusetts...	2	2	32	0	3	0	12	5	2	0	38	0
Michigan, Eastern District..............................	21	1	92	16	26	18	25	3	10	0	75	0
Michigan, Western District.............................	0	1	32	2	2	3	6	0	6	0	26	0
Minnesota...	0	0	6	0	1	0	0	0	2	0	40	0
Mississippi, Northern District..........................	1	0	47	1	3	0	9	1	2	1	28	0
Mississippi, Southern District.........................	8	1	88	19	6	7	10	1	2	0	48	0
Missouri, Eastern District...............................	0	0	9	5	0	1	0	0	3	0	72	0
Missouri, Western District..............................	2	1	14	2	3	0	3	2	1	0	21	0
Montana...	1	0	17	1	7	0	0	0	0	0	2	0
Nebraska	5	0	70	39	31	2	8	4	7	0	99	0
Nevada	0	0	16	4	3	0	7	0	0	0	6	0
New Hampshire	0	0	8	2	1	0	0	0	1	0	8	0
New Jersey..	10	1	149	3	4	0	6	0	0	0	220	0
New Mexico..	0	1	26	6	4	1	5	2	4	1	28	0
New York, Eastern District.............................	5	0	47	1	14	0	4	2	0	0	37	0
New York, Northern District...........................	1	0	95	0	3	0	0	0	0	0	74	0

Table 41. Number of Arrestees from State-Issued Warrants by NIBRS Offense Code, by Selected U.S. Marshals Service Judicial District, 2016—*Continued*

(Number.)

NIBRS offense code	200	210	220	240	250	270	280	290	370	510	520	720
NIBRS offense description Judicial district	Arson	Extortion/ blackmail	Burglary/ breaking & entering	Motor vehicle theft	Counterfeiting/ forgery	Embezzlement	Stolen property offenses	Destruction/ damage/ vandalism of property	Pornography/ obscene material	Bribery	Weapon law violations	Animal cruelty
New York, Southern District	0	0	8	0	0	0	0	1	0	0	26	0
New York, Western District	5	0	178	0	0	0	0	1	1	1	65	0
North Carolina, Eastern District	5	1	70	4	4	3	10	3	3	0	122	0
North Carolina, Middle District	0	0	6	0	0	0	0	0	1	0	55	0
North Carolina, Western District	0	0	27	3	0	0	5	0	2	0	38	0
North Dakota	0	0	13	5	2	0	1	0	8	0	10	0
Northern Mariana Islands[1]	0	0	0	0	0	0	0	0	0	0	0	0
Ohio, Northern District	19	0	313	17	13	2	20	4	10	0	145	0
Ohio, Southern District	10	1	217	4	4	0	12	0	3	0	134	0
Oklahoma, Eastern District	10	0	26	0	1	0	1	0	3	0	96	2
Oklahoma, Northern District	1	0	9	4	0	0	13	0	1	0	15	0
Oklahoma, Western District	0	1	8	1	0	0	2	0	1	0	15	0
Oregon	2	1	15	2	0	0	0	0	1	0	20	0
Pennsylvania, Eastern District	7	0	63	5	6	1	6	2	2	0	51	0
Pennsylvania, Middle District	1	0	19	0	2	0	1	0	1	0	39	0
Pennsylvania, Western District	0	0	49	3	3	0	3	0	0	0	35	0
Puerto Rico	1	0	24	10	0	0	0	2	0	0	58	0
Rhode Island	0	1	14	2	2	2	1	0	3	0	11	0
South Carolina	3	1	108	0	1	0	1	3	5	0	268	1
South Dakota	1	0	19	2	6	2	1	0	7	0	6	0
Tennessee, Eastern District	1	1	14	6	2	0	0	0	1	0	40	0
Tennessee, Middle District	3	2	14	1	0	0	2	0	3	0	26	0
Tennessee, Western District	1	1	75	14	13	0	3	13	0	0	93	0
Texas, Eastern District	7	0	79	5	14	0	1	1	4	1	40	0
Texas, Northern District	13	0	118	15	7	0	0	2	28	0	70	0
Texas, Southern District	2	0	180	25	15	0	4	4	26	0	122	0
Texas, Western District	15	0	107	17	14	1	19	0	8	0	69	0
U.S. Virgin Islands[1]	0	0	0	0	0	0	0	0	0	0	0	0
Utah	1	1	23	8	8	0	4	0	7	0	58	0
Vermont	1	0	14	0	0	0	1	0	0	0	0	0
Virginia, Eastern District	4	5	60	12	2	0	0	1	7	0	210	0
Virginia, Western District	4	1	80	19	0	0	0	2	18	0	153	0
Washington, Eastern District	1	0	36	1	0	0	1	0	0	0	18	0
Washington, Western District	3	0	12	1	2	0	5	0	3	0	21	0
West Virginia, Northern District	1	1	34	1	0	1	1	0	0	0	9	0
West Virginia, Southern District	0	0	27	0	1	0	4	0	0	0	24	0
Wisconsin, Eastern District	1	0	4	4	0	0	0	0	6	0	25	0
Wisconsin, Western District	1	0	20	1	3	0	1	0	1	0	14	0
Wyoming	1	0	1	0	7	0	0	0	1	0	1	0

[1]Population for Guam, Northern Mariana Island, and U.S. Virgin Islands was gathered from the 2010 U.S. Census.

Table 41. Number of Arrestees from State-Issued Warrants by NIBRS Offense Code, by Selected U.S. Marshals Service Judicial District, 2016—*Continued*

(Number.)

NIBRS offense code		90B	90C	90D	90F	90G	90H	90J	90Z			
NIBRS offense description Judicial district	Count of arrestees for Group A Offenses	Curfew/ loitering/ vagrancy violations	Disorderly conduct	Driving under the influence	Family offenses, nonviolent	Liquor law violations	Peeping tom	Trespass of real property	All other offenses	Count of arrestees for Group B Offenses	Total number of arrestees	Population per judicial district
Grand Total, All Judicial Districts....................	0	22	111	169	1,152	2	6	48	39,108	40,618	0	338,635,594
Alabama, Middle District.........	0	0	0	0	29	0	0	0	214	243	0	1,151,060
Alabama, Northern District.......	0	0	0	0	19	0	0	0	593	612	0	2,867,854
Alabama, Southern District	0	0	0	0	12	0	0	0	163	175	0	844,386
Alaska.....................................	0	0	0	0	0	0	0	0	35	35	0	741,894
Arizona...................................	0	0	3	4	20	0	1	0	1,890	1,918	0	6,931,071
Arkansas, Eastern District........	0	0	1	0	2	0	0	0	226	229	0	1,640,011
Arkansas, Western District	0	0	0	0	0	0	0	0	76	76	0	1,348,237
California, Central District.......	0	0	2	10	51	1	0	0	922	986	0	19,417,079
California, Eastern District........	0	0	0	0	8	0	0	0	293	301	0	8,005,253
California, Northern District	0	0	0	1	6	0	0	0	174	181	0	8,329,053
California, Southern District.....	0	0	2	40	60	0	0	0	2,967	3,069	0	3,498,632
Colorado	0	0	0	0	1	0	0	2	81	84	0	5,540,545
Connecticut............................	0	0	0	0	6	0	0	0	220	226	0	3,576,452
Delaware	0	0	0	0	0	0	0	0	205	205	0	952,065
District of Columbia................	0	0	0	0	0	0	0	0	11	11	0	681,170
Florida, Middle District	0	0	2	0	24	0	3	0	301	330	0	11,863,843
Florida, Northern District.........	0	0	0	0	16	0	0	1	428	445	0	1,845,130
Florida, Southern District.........	0	0	0	0	15	0	0	0	463	478	0	6,903,466
Georgia, Middle District	0	0	0	1	14	0	0	1	587	603	0	2,008,453
Georgia, Northern District........	0	0	0	0	10	0	0	0	489	499	0	6,725,416
Georgia, Southern District........	0	0	0	0	13	0	0	0	463	476	0	1,576,502
Guam[1]	0	0	0	0	0	0	0	0	231	231	0	159,358
Hawaii	0	0	0	0	7	0	0	0	242	249	0	1,428,557
Idaho......................................	0	0	0	0	1	0	0	0	60	61	0	1,683,140
Illinois, Central District	0	0	4	8	5	0	0	4	341	362	0	2,220,575
Illinois, Northern District..........	0	0	3	0	9	0	0	0	477	489	0	9,317,833
Illinois, Southern District..........	0	0	0	0	0	0	0	7	368	375	0	1,263,131
Indiana, Northern District.........	0	0	1	0	18	0	0	1	194	214	0	2,586,998
Indiana, Southern District........	0	0	1	0	4	0	0	0	251	256	0	4,046,055
Iowa, Northern District.............	0	0	2	0	0	0	0	0	142	144	0	1,326,996
Iowa, Southern District.............	0	0	0	0	4	0	0	0	194	198	0	1,807,697
Kansas....................................	0	0	0	0	4	0	0	0	1,685	1,689	0	2,907,289
Kentucky, Eastern District........	0	0	0	0	1	0	0	0	233	234	0	2,203,205
Kentucky, Western District	0	0	0	0	2	0	0	0	169	171	0	2,233,769
Louisiana, Eastern District........	0	0	1	1	10	0	0	0	289	301	0	1,680,123
Louisiana, Middle District	0	0	1	0	4	0	0	0	157	162	0	835,175
Louisiana, Western District.......	0	0	1	0	9	0	0	0	406	416	0	2,166,368
Maine......................................	0	0	0	0	0	0	0	0	38	38	0	1,331,479
Maryland	0	0	2	1	16	0	0	0	899	918	0	6,016,447
Massachusetts	0	0	1	3	2	0	0	2	168	176	0	6,811,779
Michigan, Eastern District........	0	0	5	18	24	0	0	1	1,354	1,402	0	6,438,317
Michigan, Western District.......	0	0	0	1	4	0	0	0	710	715	0	3,489,983
Minnesota	0	0	0	0	0	0	0	0	135	135	0	5,519,952
Mississippi, Northern District....	0	0	1	1	4	0	0	0	427	433	0	1,115,684
Mississippi, Southern District....	0	0	0	1	3	0	0	0	439	443	0	1,873,042
Missouri, Eastern District.........	0	0	0	0	4	0	0	0	121	125	0	2,930,503
Missouri, Western District	0	0	1	2	2	0	0	0	214	219	0	3,162,497
Montana..................................	0	0	1	0	5	0	0	0	919	925	0	1,042,520
Nebraska	0	0	0	19	15	0	0	1	232	267	0	1,907,116
Nevada....................................	0	0	0	6	8	0	0	0	140	154	0	2,940,058

Table 41. Number of Arrestees from State-Issued Warrants by NIBRS Offense Code, by Selected U.S. Marshals Service Judicial District, 2016—*Continued*

(Number.)

NIBRS offense description Judicial district	Count of arrestees for Group A Offenses	90B Curfew/ loitering/ vagrancy violations	90C Disorderly conduct	90D Driving under the influence	90F Family offenses, nonviolent	90G Liquor law violations	90H Peeping tom	90J Trespass of real property	90Z All other offenses	Count of arrestees for Group B Offenses	Total number of arrestees	Population per judicial district
New Hampshire	0	0	0	0	1	0	0	0	209	210	0	1,334,795
New Jersey	0	1	1	0	36	0	0	3	1,259	1,300	0	8,944,469
New Mexico	0	0	0	0	18	0	0	0	461	479	0	2,081,015
New York, Eastern District	0	0	1	5	0	0	0	2	213	221	0	8,292,302
New York, Northern District	0	13	0	0	2	0	0	0	482	497	0	3,403,475
New York, Southern District	0	0	0	1	1	0	0	0	106	108	0	5,248,160
New York, Western District	0	0	0	0	1	0	0	0	186	187	0	2,801,352
North Carolina, Eastern District	0	0	0	0	7	0	0	0	549	556	0	3,989,760
North Carolina, Middle District	0	0	0	0	1	0	0	0	152	153	0	2,951,033
North Carolina, Western District	0	0	2	2	0	0	0	0	269	273	0	3,205,995
North Dakota	0	0	0	2	22	0	0	1	169	194	0	757,952
Northern Mariana Islands[1]	0	0	0	0	0	0	0	0	0	0	0	53,883
Ohio, Northern District	0	6	3	4	85	0	0	4	1,387	1,489	0	17,502,937
Ohio, Southern District	0	0	2	6	21	0	0	1	476	506	0	5,888,564
Oklahoma, Eastern District	0	0	5	1	68	1	0	1	175	251	0	738,303
Oklahoma, Northern District	0	0	2	4	10	0	0	0	79	95	0	1,071,646
Oklahoma, Western District	0	0	2	0	5	0	0	0	134	141	0	2,113,612
Oregon	0	1	0	1	2	0	0	0	199	203	0	4,093,465
Pennsylvania, Eastern District	0	0	0	1	1	0	0	0	830	832	0	5,714,463
Pennsylvania, Middle District	0	0	0	0	2	0	0	0	442	444	0	3,322,992
Pennsylvania, Western District	0	0	4	2	13	0	0	1	632	652	0	3,746,772
Puerto Rico	0	0	0	0	3	0	0	1	42	46	0	3,411,307
Rhode Island	0	0	1	0	4	0	0	0	187	192	0	1,056,426
South Carolina	0	0	2	0	81	0	0	0	326	409	0	4,961,119
South Dakota	0	0	0	0	10	0	0	0	95	105	0	865,454
Tennessee, Eastern District	0	0	1	0	13	0	0	0	349	363	0	2,603,012
Tennessee, Middle District	0	0	0	0	3	0	0	0	417	420	0	2,478,759
Tennessee, Western District	0	0	0	0	17	0	0	9	360	386	0	1,569,423
Texas, Eastern District	0	0	2	10	27	0	1	0	443	483	0	3,917,463
Texas, Northern District	0	0	11	3	26	0	1	1	485	527	0	7,240,386
Texas, Southern District	0	0	32	5	38	0	0	1	2,246	2,322	0	9,610,367
Texas, Western District	0	0	1	1	62	0	0	3	907	974	0	7,094,380
U.S. Virgin Islands[1]	0	0	0	0	0	0	0	0	1	1	0	106,405
Utah	0	0	0	1	19	0	0	0	82	102	0	3,051,217
Vermont	0	0	0	0	1	0	0	0	13	14	0	624,594
Virginia, Eastern District	0	0	0	0	14	0	0	0	341	355	0	6,104,061
Virginia, Western District	0	0	2	0	34	0	0	0	471	507	0	2,307,747
Washington, Eastern District	0	0	0	0	0	0	0	0	483	483	0	1,583,932
Washington, Western District	0	0	0	0	7	0	0	0	411	418	0	5,704,068
West Virginia, Northern District	0	1	0	1	9	0	0	0	192	203	0	869,386
West Virginia, Southern District	0	0	0	0	4	0	0	0	112	116	0	961,716
Wisconsin, Eastern District	0	0	1	1	1	0	0	0	187	190	0	3,402,035
Wisconsin, Western District	0	0	1	1	10	0	0	0	472	484	0	2,376,673
Wyoming	0	0	0	0	2	0	0	0	41	43	0	585,501

[1]Population for Guam, Northern Mariana Island, and U.S. Virgin Islands was gathered from the 2010 U.S. Census.

Table 42. FBI Employment, by Gender, 2016

(Number.)

Employee	Male	Female	Total
Total	20,711	16,001	36,712
Special agents	11,014	2,707	13,721
Professional staff	9,497	13,255	22,752
Police officers	200	39	239

Table 43. ATF Employment, by Gender, 2016

(Number.)

Employee	Male	Female	Total
Total	7,006	3,328	10,334
Special agents	2,299	363	2,662
Professional staff	1,204	1,301	2,505
Police officers	3,503	1,664	5,167

Table 44. USMS Employment, by Gender, 2016

(Number.)

Employee	Male	Female	Total
Total	7,425	1,647	9,072
Deputy U.S. marshals	3,202	364	3,566
Professional staff	3,945	1,266	5,211
Police officers	278	17	295

Table 45. Human Trafficking, Offenses and Clearances by Participating State, 2016

(Number.)

State	Commercial sex acts			Involuntary servitude			Total		
	Offenses	Total cleared	Clearances under 18	Offenses	Total cleared	Clearances under 18	Offenses	Total cleared	Clearances under 18
Alaska	11	8	0	1	0	0	12	8	0
Arizona	19	5	0	0	0	0	19	5	0
Arkansas	4	4	0	2	0	0	6	4	0
Colorado	12	3	0	22	9	0	34	12	0
Connecticut	1	0	0	1	0	0	2	0	0
Delaware	0	0	0	0	0	0	0	0	0
Florida	98	50	0	7	4	0	105	54	0
Hawaii	2	0	0	0	0	0	2	0	0
Illinois	21	0	0	3	0	0	24	0	0
Indiana	4	2	2	0	0	0	4	2	2
Kansas	0	0	0	2	1	0	2	1	0
Louisiana	121	92	2	2	2	0	123	94	2
Maryland	17	15	0	0	0	0	17	15	0
Massachusetts	0	0	0	3	3	0	3	3	0
Michigan	1	1	0	2	0	0	3	1	0
Minnesota	235	191	1	0	0	0	235	191	1
Mississippi	0	0	0	0	0	0	0	0	0
Missouri	16	15	3	0	0	0	16	15	3
Montana	1	0	0	0	0	0	1	0	0
Nevada	140	58	35	0	0	0	140	58	35
North Dakota	4	0	0	1	1	0	5	1	0
Ohio	1	0	0	0	0	0	1	0	0
Oklahoma	42	37	1	4	3	0	46	40	1
Oregon	0	0	0	0	0	0	0	0	0
Puerto Rico	0	0	0	0	0	0	0	0	0
Rhode Island	5	2	0	1	0	0	6	2	0
South Carolina	15	9	2	7	7	0	22	16	2
South Dakota	0	0	0	0	0	0	0	0	0
Tennessee	55	26	0	0	0	0	55	26	0
Texas	130	51	2	127	27	0	257	78	2
U.S. Virgin Islands	0	0	0	0	0	0	0	0	0
Utah	0	0	0	0	0	0	0	0	0
Vermont	2	2	0	0	0	0	2	2	0
Washington	13	3	0	1	1	0	14	4	0
Wisconsin	34	19	1	1	0	0	35	19	1
Wyoming	3	2	0	2	1	0	5	3	0

Table 46. Human Trafficking Arrests, by Age and Participating State, 2016

(Number.)

State	Juvenile male	Juvenile male	Juvenile male	Juvenile male	Juvenile male	Juvenile female	Adult male					Adult female
Alaska												
Commercial sex acts	0					0	3					0
Involuntary servitude	0					0	0					0
Arizona												
Commercial sex acts	0					0	0					0
Involuntary servitude	0					0	20					14
Arkansas												
Commercial sex acts	0					0	1					0
Involuntary servitude	0					0	0					0
California^												
Commercial sex acts	0					0	1					0
Involuntary servitude	0					0	0					0
Colorado												
Commercial sex acts	0					0	1					0
Involuntary servitude	0					0	1					1
Connecticut												
Commercial sex acts	0					0	0					0
Involuntary servitude	0					0	10					4
Indiana												
Commercial sex acts	0					0	2					0
Involuntary servitude	0					0	0					0
Louisiana												
Commercial sex acts	0					0	6					1
Involuntary servitude	0					0	4					5
Maryland												
Commercial sex acts	0					0	12					1
Involuntary servitude	0					0	4					0
Massachusetts												
Commercial sex acts	0					0	2					0
Involuntary servitude	0					0	0					0
Michigan												
Commercial sex acts	0					0	1					0
Involuntary servitude	0					0	0					0
Minnesota												
Commercial sex acts	0					0	195					11
Involuntary servitude	0					0	0					0
Missouri												
Commercial sex acts	1					0	7					2
Involuntary servitude	0					0	1					1
Montana												
Commercial sex acts	0					0	1					0
Involuntary servitude	0					0	0					0
Nevada												
Commercial sex acts	0					1	27					5
Involuntary servitude	0					0	6					1
North Dakota												
Commercial sex acts	0					0	1					0
Involuntary servitude	0					0	0					0
Oklahoma												
Commercial sex acts	6					4	19					14
Involuntary servitude	0					0	1					0
Rhode Island												
Commercial sex acts	0					0	2					0

(Number.)

State	Juvenile						Adult					
	Juvenile male	Juvenile male	Juvenile male	Juvenile male	Juvenile male	Juvenile female	Adult male					Adult female
Involuntary servitude.............................	0					0	0					0
South Carolina												
Commercial sex acts	0					0	4					2
Involuntary servitude.............................	0					0	0					0
Tennessee												
Commercial sex acts	0					0	20					2
Involuntary servitude.............................	0					0	0					0
Texas												
Commercial sex acts	1					39	352					119
Involuntary servitude.............................	0					0	9					5
Washington												
Commercial sex acts	0					0	0					0
Involuntary servitude.............................	1					3	0					0
Wisconsin												
Commercial sex acts	0					0	9					4
Involuntary servitude.............................	0					0	0					0
Wyoming												
Commercial sex acts	0					0	1					1
Involuntary servitude.............................	0					0	1					0

^ = Data submitted through the Bureau of Indian Affairs.

Table 47. Human Trafficking Arrests, by Race and Participating State, 2016

(Number.)

State	Juvenile						Adult					
	White	Black or African American	American Indian/Alaska Native	Asian	Native Hawaiian/ Other Pacific Islander	Total	White	Black or African American	American Indian/Alaska Native	Asian	Native Hawaiian/ Other Pacific Islander	Total
Alaska												
Commercial sex acts	0	0	0	0	0	0	1	2	0	0	0	3
Involuntary servitude........	0	0	0	0	0	0	0	0	0	0	0	0
Arizona												
Commercial sex acts	0	0	0	0	0	0	0	0	0	0	0	0
Involuntary servitude........	0	0	0	0	0	0	21	13	0	0	0	34
Arkansas												
Commercial sex acts	0	0	0	0	0	0	0	1	0	0	0	1
Involuntary servitude........	0	0	0	0	0	0	0	0	0	0	0	0
California^												
Commercial sex acts	0	0	0	0	0	0	0	0	1	0	0	1
Involuntary servitude........	0	0	0	0	0	0	0	0	0	0	0	0
Colorado												
Commercial sex acts	0	0	0	0	0	0	1	0	0	0	0	1
Involuntary servitude........	0	0	0	0	0	0	0	1	1	0	0	2
Connecticut												
Commercial sex acts	0	0	0	0	0	0	0	0	0	0	0	0
Involuntary servitude........	0	0	0	0	0	0	7	4	0	3	0	14
Indiana												
Commercial sex acts	0	0	0	0	0	0	0	2	0	0	0	2
Involuntary servitude........	0	0	0	0	0	0	0	0	0	0	0	0
Louisiana												
Commercial sex acts	0	0	0	0	0	0	0	7	0	0	0	7
Involuntary servitude........	0	0	0	0	0	0	6	3	0	0	0	9
Maryland												
Commercial sex acts	0	0	0	0	0	0	3	8	0	2	0	13
Involuntary servitude........	0	0	0	0	0	0	0	4	0	0	0	4
Massachusetts												
Commercial sex acts	0	0	0	0	0	0	1	1	0	0	0	2
Involuntary servitude........	0	0	0	0	0	0	0	0	0	0	0	0
Michigan												
Commercial sex acts	0	0	0	0	0	0	0	1	0	0	0	1
Involuntary servitude........	0	0	0	0	0	0	0	0	0	0	0	0
Minnesota												
Commercial sex acts	0	0	0	0	0	0	142	39	5	19	1	206
Involuntary servitude........	0	0	0	0	0	0	0	0	0	0	0	0
Missouri												
Commercial sex acts	0	1	0	0	0	1	1	8	0	0	0	9
Involuntary servitude........	0	0	0	0	0	0	2	0	0	0	0	2
Montana												
Commercial sex acts	0	0	0	0	0	0	0	0	1	0	0	1
Involuntary servitude........	0	0	0	0	0	0	0	0	0	0	0	0
Nevada												
Commercial sex acts	1	0	0	0	0	1	3	29	0	0	0	32
Involuntary servitude........	0	0	0	0	0	0	1	6	0	0	0	7
North Dakota												
Commercial sex acts	0	0	0	0	0	0	1	0	0	0	0	1
Involuntary servitude........	0	0	0	0	0	0	0	0	0	0	0	0
Oklahoma												
Commercial sex acts	8	2	0	0	0	10	21	11	1	0	0	33
Involuntary servitude........	0	0	0	0	0	0	0	1	0	0	0	1

(Number.)

State	Juvenile						Adult					
	White	Black or African American	American Indian/Alaska Native	Asian	Native Hawaiian/ Other Pacific Islander	Total	White	Black or African American	American Indian/Alaska Native	Asian	Native Hawaiian/ Other Pacific Islander	Total
Rhode Island												
Commercial sex acts	0	0	0	0	0	0	1	0	0	0	0	1
Involuntary servitude........	0	0	0	0	0	0	0	0	0	0	0	0
South Carolina												
Commercial sex acts	0	0	0	0	0	0	1	5	0	0	0	6
Involuntary servitude........	0	0	0	0	0	0	0	0	0	0	0	0
Tennessee												
Commercial sex acts	0	0	0	0	0	0	10	10	0	2	0	22
Involuntary servitude........	0	0	0	0	0	0	0	0	0	0	0	0
Texas												
Commercial sex acts	20	20	0	0	0	40	386	82	2	1	0	471
Involuntary servitude........	0	0	0	0	0	0	13	1	0	0	0	14
Washington												
Commercial sex acts	0	0	0	0	0	0	0	0	0	0	0	0
Involuntary servitude........	0	0	4	0	0	4	0	0	0	0	0	0
Wisconsin												
Commercial sex acts	0	0	0	0	0	0	3	10	0	0	0	13
Involuntary servitude........	0	0	0	0	0	0	0	0	0	0	0	0
Wyoming												
Commercial sex acts	0	0	0	0	0	0	0	2	0	0	0	2
Involuntary servitude........	0	0	0	0	0	0	1	0	0	0	0	1

^ = Data submitted through the Bureau of Indian Affairs.

Table 48. Human Trafficking Arrests, by Ethnicity and Participating State, 2016

(Number.)

State	Juvenile			Adult		
	Asian	Native Hawaiian/Other Pacific Islander	Total	Asian	Native Hawaiian/Other Pacific Islander	Total
Arizona						
Commercial sex acts	0	0	0	0	0	0
Involuntary servitude	0	0	0	16	18	34
Arkansas						
Commercial sex acts	0	0	0	0	1	1
Involuntary servitude	0	0	0	0	0	0
California^						
Commercial sex acts	0	0	0	0	1	1
Involuntary servitude	0	0	0	0	0	0
Colorado						
Commercial sex acts	0	0	0	1	0	1
Involuntary servitude	0	0	0	0	2	2
Connecticut						
Commercial sex acts	0	0	0	0	0	0
Involuntary servitude	0	0	0	0	14	14
Indiana						
Commercial sex acts	0	0	0	0	2	2
Involuntary servitude	0	0	0	0	0	0
Maryland						
Commercial sex acts	0	0	0	0	13	13
Involuntary servitude	0	0	0	0	4	4
Minnesota						
Commercial sex acts	0	0	0	42	164	206
Involuntary servitude	0	0	0	0	0	0
Missouri						
Commercial sex acts	0	1	1	0	9	9
Involuntary servitude	0	0	0	0	2	2
Montana						
Commercial sex acts	0	0	0	0	1	1
Involuntary servitude	0	0	0	0	0	0
Nevada						
Commercial sex acts	1	0	1	2	30	32
Involuntary servitude	0	0	0	0	7	7
North Dakota						
Commercial sex acts	0	0	0	0	1	1
Involuntary servitude	0	0	0	0	0	0
Oklahoma						
Commercial sex acts	2	8	10	3	30	33
Involuntary servitude	0	0	0	0	1	1
Rhode Island						
Commercial sex acts	0	0	0	0	1	1
Involuntary servitude	0	0	0	0	0	0
South Carolina						
Commercial sex acts	0	0	0	0	6	6
Involuntary servitude	0	0	0	0	0	0
Tennessee						
Commercial sex acts	0	0	0	3	19	22
Involuntary servitude	0	0	0	0	0	0

Table 48. Human Trafficking Arrests, by Ethnicity and Participating State, 2016—*Continued*

(Number.)

State	Juvenile			Adult		
	Asian	Native Hawaiian/Other Pacific Islander	Total	Asian	Native Hawaiian/Other Pacific Islander	Total
Texas						
Commercial sex acts	9	31	40	119	352	471
Involuntary servitude	0	0	0	7	7	14
Wisconsin						
Commercial sex acts	0	0	0	0	13	13
Involuntary servitude	0	0	0	0	0	0
Wyoming						
Commercial sex acts	0	0	0	0	0	0
Involuntary servitude	0	0	0	0	1	1

Note: Not all agencies provide ethnicity data; therefore, the race and ethnicity totals will not equal.
^ = Data submitted through the Bureau of Indian Affairs.

Table 49. Cargo Theft by Participating State, by Incidents and Stolen/Recovered Values, 2016

(Number; dollars; percent.)

State	Number of agencies reporting an incident	Number of incidents reported	Value of property		Percent recovered
			Stolen	Recovered	
Total	147	692	$26,933,356	$8,449,949	31.4
Alaska..	1	3	331	0	0.0
Arkansas.....................................	2	3	169,212	30,000	17.7
Colorado	2	2	77,741	34,000	43.7
Delaware	3	6	695,564	530,566	76.3
Florida	10	26	3,080,534	497,070	16.1
Georgia	4	12	312,684	53,000	17.0
Indiana	1	1	700	0	0.0
Maine...	2	2	225	0	0.0
Michigan.....................................	22	45	1,005,058	454,024	45.2
Mississippi...................................	1	6	6,102	0	0.0
Montana.....................................	1	1	2,000	0	0.0
Nevada	2	3	283,001	104,901	37.1
New Hampshire	1	1	50,921	49,721	97.6
North Dakota...............................	1	1	15,269	0	0.0
Oklahoma...................................	1	1	21,657	0	0.0
South Carolina.............................	12	21	359,943	238,563	66.3
Tennessee	16	298	4,821,502	501,156	10.4
Texas..	56	249	15,140,787	5,881,948	38.8
Utah...	1	1	610	0	0.0
Virginia.......................................	8	10	889,515	75,000	8.4

Table 50. Cargo Theft Property Stolen and Recovered, by Type of Value, 2016

(Dollars; percent.)

Type of property	Value of property		Percent recovered
	Stolen	Recovered	
Total	$26,933,356	$8,449,949	31.4
Alcohol	826,360	1,029	0.1
Automobile	392,879	180,000	45.8
Bicycle	6,527	0	0.0
Building materials	1,262,488	441,583	35.0
Camping, hunting, fishing equipment, supplies	144	0	0.0
Chemicals	20,400	0	0.0
Clothes, furs	390,666	5,420	1.4
Computer hardware, software	530,772	515,925	97.2
Consumable goods	3,066,939	301,116	9.8
Credit,debit cards[1]	0	0	
Drugs, narcotics	50,081	0	0.0
Farm equipment	3,368	500	14.8
Firearm accessories	41,200	40,000	97.1
Firearms	15,550	3,650	23.5
Fuel	29,770	0	0.0
Household goods	1,557,553	112,920	7.2
Identity documents[1]	0	0	
Industrial equipment	371,693	52,183	14.0
Jewelry, precious metals	17,768	548	3.1
Lawn, yard, garden equipment	5,406	4,206	77.8
Livestock	120,000	0	0.0
Medical, medical lab equipment	702	0	0.0
Merchandise	732,734	27,568	3.8
Metals, nonprecious	1,126,825	952,500	84.5
Money	35,029	0	0.0
Musical instruments	9,000	0	0.0
Negotiable instrument	15	0	0.0
Nonnegotiable instrument[1]	0	0	
Office equipment	303,062	0	0.0
Other	6,770,506	1,021,466	15.1
Other motor vehicles	122,700	60,000	48.9
Pending inventory	10	0	0.0
Photographic, optical equipment	53,100	2,800	5.3
Portable electronic communications	1,262,051	18,185	1.4
Purse,wallet	959	0	0.0
Radio, TV, VCR	472,001	1,500	0.3
Recreational, sports equipment	100,500	0	0.0
Tools	379,657	21,850	5.8
Trailers	2,589,730	1,735,703	67.0
Trucks	3,919,445	2,879,963	73.5
Vehicle parts	345,766	69,334	20.1

[1]According to Uniform Crime Reporting guidelines, the value of property stolen and/or recovered must be zero for this property description.

Table 51. Cargo Theft, by Location, 2016

(Number.)

Type of property	Total locations
Air/bus/train terminal	2
Amusement park	1
Commercial office building	61
Construction site	1
Convenience store	46
Department/discount store	6
Dock/wharf/freight/modal terminal	51
Drug store/doctor's office/hospital	2
Government/public building	1
Grocery/supermarket	14
Highway/road/alley/street	90
Hotel/motel/etc.	7
Industrial site	21
Liquor store	1
Parking lot/garage	305
Park/playground	1
Rental storage facility	7
Residence/home	7
Rest area	2
Restaurant	2
School/college	1
Service/gas station	32
Shopping mall	1
Specialty store (TV, fur, etc.)	4
Other/unknown	48

Table 52. Cargo Theft, by Victim Type, 2016

(Number.)

Victim type	Total victims
Business	626
Government	3
Individual	89
Other	6

Table 53. Cargo Theft, by Offense, 2016

(Number.)

Type of property	Total locations
Grand total of offenses	730
Cargo theft applicable offenses	
All other larceny	168
Burglary	19
Embezzlement	29
False pretenses, swindle, confidence game	7
Motor vehicle theft	105
Robbery	6
Theft from building	14
Theft from vehicle	363
Total cargo theft applicable offenses	711
Other offenses occurring with cargo offenses	
Destruction of property	13
Shoplifting	1
Stolen property offense	5
Total other offenses occurring with cargo offense	19

Table 54. Highlights from the Uniform Crime Reporting Program's Supplemental Information, by Selected Characteristics, 2016

(Number.)

Characteristic	Total	Sex		
		Male	Female	Unknown
Murder Victims, Race and Ethnicity, 2016	15,070	11,821	3,208	41
White	6,576	4,665	1,906	5
Black	7,881	6,749	1,126	6
Other races	400	266	133	1
Unknown race	213	141	43	29
Hispanic or Latino	2,367	1,977	389	1
Not Hispanic or Latino	9,725	7,600	2,120	5
Unknown ethnicity	2,226	1,678	516	32
Agency Employment, FBI, ATF, and USMS				
FBI	36,712	20,711	16,001	X
Special agents	13,721	11,014	2,707	X
Professional staff	22,752	9,497	13,255	X
Police officers	239	200	39	X
ATF	36,712	20,711	16,001	X
Special agents	2,662	2,299	363	X
Professional staff	2,505	1,204	1,301	X
Police officers	5,167	3,503	1,664	X
USMS	10,334	7,006	3,328	X
Special agents	3,566	3,202	364	X
Professional staff	5,211	3,945	1,266	X
Police officers	295	278	17	X
Human Trafficking Arrests, by Ethnicity				
Juvenile				
Total, United States	52	X	X	X
Hispanic or Latino	12	X	X	X
Not Hispanic or Latino	40	X	X	X
Adult				
Total, United States	892	X	X	X
Hispanic or Latino	193	X	X	X
Not Hispanic or Latino	699	X	X	X
Total Cargo Theft, by Victim Type				
Business	626	X	X	X
Government	3	X	X	X
Individual	89	X	X	X
Other	6	X	X	X

Note: For the murder and human trafficking data, not all agencies provide ethnicity data; therefore, the ethnicity totals do not equal the total number of victims. These states provided human trafficking data: Arizona, Arkansas, California, Colorado, Connecticut, Indiana, Maryland, Minnesota, Missouri, Montana, Nevada, North Dakota, Oklahoma, Rhode Island, South Carolina, Tennessee, Texas, Wisconsin, Wyoming. California data was submitted through the Bureau of Indian Affairs.
X = Not applicable.

Methodology

Submitting Uniform Crime Reporting (UCR) program data to the Federal Bureau of Investigation (FBI) is a collective effort on the part of city, county, state, tribal, and federal law enforcement agencies to present a nationwide view of crime. Law enforcement agencies in 46 states and the District of Columbia voluntarily contribute crime data to the UCR program through their respective state UCR programs. For those states that do not have a state program, local agencies submit crime statistics directly to the FBI. The state UCR programs function as liaisons between local agencies and the FBI. Many states have mandatory reporting requirements, and many state programs collect data beyond the scope of the UCR program to address crime problems specific to their particular jurisdictions. In most cases, state programs also provide direct and frequent service to participating law enforcement agencies, make information readily available for statewide use, and help streamline the national program's operations.

A Note Regarding Rape

In 2013, the FBI UCR Program initiated collection of rape data under a revised definition within the Summary Reporting System. Previously, offense data for forcible rape was collected under the legacy UCR definition: the carnal knowledge of a female forcibly and against her will. Beginning with the 2013 data year, the term "forcible" was removed from the offense title, and the definition was changed. The revised UCR definition of rape is: Penetration, no matter how slight, of the vagina or anus with any body part or object, or oral penetration by a sex organ of another person, without the consent of the victim. Attempts or assaults to commit rape are also included; however, statutory rape and incest are excluded. For more information, please see https://www.fbi.gov/about-us/cjis/ucr/crime-in-the-u.s/2013/crime-in-the-u.s.-2013/rape-addendum/rape_addendum_final.

Criteria for State UCR Programs

The criteria established for state programs ensure consistency and comparability in the data submitted to the national program, as well as regular and timely reporting. These criteria are:

1. A UCR Program must conform to the FBI UCR Program's submission standards, definitions, specifications, and required deadlines.

2. A UCR Program must establish data integrity procedures and have personnel assigned to assist contributing agencies in quality assurance practices and crime reporting procedures. Data integrity procedures should include crime trend assessments, offense classification verification, and technical specification validation.

3. A UCR Program's submissions must cover more than 50 percent of the law enforcement agencies within its established reporting domain and be willing to cover any and all UCR-contributing agencies that wish to use the UCR Program from within its domain. (An agency wishing to become a UCR Program must be willing to report for all of the agencies within the state.)

4. A UCR Program must furnish the FBI UCR Program with all of the UCR data collected by the law enforcement agencies within its domain.

These requirements do not prohibit the state from gathering other statistical data beyond the national collection.

Data Completeness and Quality

National program staff members contact the state UCR program in connection with crime-reporting matters and, when necessary and approved by the state, they contact individual contributors within the state. To fulfill its responsibilities in connection with the UCR program, the FBI reviews and edits individual agency reports for completeness and quality. Upon request, they conduct training programs within the state on law enforcement record-keeping and crime-reporting procedures. The FBI conducts an audit of each state's UCR data collection procedures once every three years, in accordance with audit standards established by the federal government. Should circumstances develop in which the state program does not comply with the aforementioned requirements, the national program may institute a direct collection of data from law enforcement agencies within the state.

Reporting Procedures

Offenses known and value of property—Law enforcement agencies tabulate the number of Part I offenses reported based on records of all reports of crime received from victims, officers who discover infractions, or other sources, and submit these reports each month to the FBI directly or through their state UCR programs. Part I offenses include murder and non-negligent manslaughter, forcible rape, robbery, aggravated assault, burglary, larceny-theft, motor vehicle theft, and arson. Each month, law enforcement agencies also submit to the FBI the value of property stolen and recovered in connection with the offenses and detailed information pertaining to criminal homicide.

Unfounded offenses and clearances—When, through investigation, an agency determines that complaints of crimes are unfounded or false, the agency eliminates that offense from its crime tally through an entry on the monthly report. The report also provides the total number of actual Part I offenses, the number of offenses cleared, and the number of clearances that involve only offenders under the age of 18. (Law enforcement can clear crimes in one of two ways: by the arrest of at least one person who is charged and turned over to the court for prosecution or by exceptional means—when some element beyond law enforcement's control precludes the arrest of a known offender.)

Persons arrested—In addition to reporting Part I offenses each month, law enforcement agencies also provide data on the age, sex, and race of persons arrested for Part I and Part II offenses. Part II offenses encompass all crimes, except traffic violations, that are not classified as Part I offenses.

Officers killed or assaulted—Each month, law enforcement agencies also report information to the UCR program regarding law enforcement officers killed or assaulted, and each year they report the number of full-time sworn and civilian law enforcement personnel employed as of October 31.

Editing Procedures

The UCR program thoroughly examines each report it receives for arithmetical accuracy and for deviations in crime data from month to month and from present to past years that may indicate errors. UCR staff members compare an agency's monthly reports with its previous submissions and with reports from similar agencies to identify any unusual fluctuations in the agency's crime count. Considerable variations in crime levels may indicate modified records procedures, incomplete reporting, or changes in the jurisdiction's geopolitical structure.

Evaluation of trends—Data reliability is a high priority of the FBI, which brings any deviations or arithmetical adjustments to the attention of state UCR programs or the submitting agencies. Typically, FBI staff members study the monthly reports to evaluate periodic trends prepared for individual reporting units. Any significant increase or decrease becomes the subject of a special inquiry. Changes in crime reporting procedures or annexations that affect an agency's jurisdiction can influence the level of reported crime. When this occurs, the FBI excludes the figures for specific crime categories or totals, if necessary, from the trend tabulations.

Training for contributors—In addition to the evaluation of trends, the FBI provides training seminars and instructional materials on crime reporting procedures to assist contributors in complying with UCR standards. Throughout the country, representatives from the national program coordinate with representatives of state programs and law enforcement personnel and hold training sessions to explain the purpose of the program, the rules of uniform classification and scoring, and the methods of assembling the information for reporting. When an individual agency has specific problems with compiling its crime statistics and its remedial efforts are unsuccessful, personnel from the FBI's Criminal Justice Information Services Division may visit the contributor to aid in resolving the problems.

UCR Handbook—The national UCR program publishes the *Uniform Crime Reporting (UCR) Handbook* (revised 2004), which details procedures for classifying and scoring offenses and serves as the contributing agencies' basic resource for preparing reports. The national staff also produces letters to UCR contributors, state program bulletins, and UCR newsletters as needed. These publications provide policy updates and new information, as well as clarification of reporting issues.

The final responsibility for data submissions rests with the individual contributing law enforcement agency. Although the FBI makes every effort through its editing procedures, training practices, and correspondence to ensure the validity of the data it receives, the accuracy of the statistics depends primarily on the adherence of each contributor to the established standards of reporting. Deviations from these established standards that cannot be resolved by the national UCR program may be brought to the attention of the Criminal Justice Information Systems Committees of the International Association of Chiefs of Police and the National Sheriffs' Association.

NIBRS Conversion

Thirty-three state programs are certified to provide their UCR data in the expanded National Incident-Based Reporting System (NIBRS) format. For presentation in this book, the NIBRS data were converted to the historical Summary Reporting System data. The UCR program staff constructed the NIBRS database to allow for such conversion so that UCR's long-running time series could continue.

Crime Trends

By showing fluctuations from year to year, trend statistics offer the data user an added perspective from which to study crime. Percent change tabulations in this publication are computed only for reporting agencies that provided comparable data for the periods under consideration. The FBI excludes from the trend calculations all figures except those received for common months from common agencies. Also excluded are unusual fluctuations of data that the FBI determines are the result of such variables as improved records procedures, annexations, and so on.

Caution to Users

Data users should exercise care in making any direct comparison between data in this publication and those in prior issues of *Crime in the United States*. Because of differing levels of participation from year to year and reporting problems that require the FBI to estimate crime counts for certain contributors, some data may not be comparable. In addition, this publication may contain updates to data provided in prior years' publications.

For information about the FBI's caution against ranking, including warnings about variables affecting crime and characteristics of jurisdictions, please see http://www.fbi.gov/about-us/cjis/ucr/ucr-statistics-their-proper-use.

Offense Estimation

Some tables in this publication contain statistics for the entire United States. Because not all law enforcement agencies provide data for complete reporting periods, the FBI includes estimated crime numbers in these presentations. The FBI estimates data for three areas: Metropolitan Statistical Areas (MSAs), cities outside MSAs, and nonmetropolitan counties; and computes estimates for participating agencies that do not provide 12 months of complete data. For agencies supplying 3 to 11 months of data, the national UCR program estimates for the missing data by following a standard estimation procedure using the data provided by the agency. If an agency has supplied less than 3 months of data, the FBI computes estimates by using the known crime figures of similar areas within a state and assigning the same proportion of crime volumes to nonreporting agencies. The estimation process considers the following: population size covered by the agency; type of jurisdiction (for example, police department versus sheriff's office); and geographic location.

Estimation of State-Level Data

In response to various circumstances, the FBI calculates estimated offense totals for certain states. For example, some states do not provide forcible rape figures in accordance with UCR guidelines. In addition, problems at the state level have, at times, resulted in no useable data. Also, the conversion of the National Incident-Based Reporting System (NIBRS) data to summary data has contributed to the need for unique estimation procedures.

Expanded Offense Tables

Expanded offense data are the details of the various offenses that the Uniform Crime Reporting Program collects beyond the count of how many crimes law enforcement agencies report. These details may include the type of weapon used in a crime, the type or value of items stolen, and so forth. Expanded homicide data provide supplemental details about murders such as the age, sex, and race of both the victim and the offender, the weapon used in the homicide, the circumstances surrounding the offense, and the relationship of the victim to the offender. In addition, expanded data include trends (for example, 2-year comparisons) and rates per 100,000 inhabitants.

Expanded offense data, including expanded homicide data, are information collected in addition to the reports of the number of crimes known. As a result, law enforcement agencies can report an offense without providing the supplemental data about that offense.

Federal Crime Data

In past years, these agencies' data were included in various tables in *Crime in the United States*. *Federal Crime Data* signals the move to presenting federal data in a way more attuned with local, state, and tribal UCR data. Included are the federal agencies that have submitted traditional UCR data for some time.

A few agencies, such as the National Institutes of Health (NIH) and several agencies within the U.S. Department of the Interior (DOI), investigate and police in ways similar to local or state authorities. These federal agencies have long reported data to the UCR Program. However, other federal agencies, the FBI included, found it more difficult to fit into the UCR model. This annual report was originally designed as a stepping stone to finding ways to provide a similar transparency and access to federal crime data that the UCR Program has brought to local, state, and tribal crime data for nearly 90 years. The arrest data from the FBI, ATF, and USMS have all been mapped to correspond to the UCR's National Incident-Based Reporting System (NIBRS) offense codes. This makes the overlay of federal data with local and state data much easier.

Comparability of federal data to state and local data

The best approach to viewing the federal data offered is to use it to gain an overall impression of the intensity of certain types of offenses within a specific area by overlaying the federal arrests in conjunction with the local and state information. As developments in the data collection continue to occur, more details will become available from federal agencies, and these impressions will become more sharply focused.

Federal crime data are often different from local and state data, not only in their collection, but also in their generation. The UCR Program has built its traditional data collection on three triggering events that are common to local and state agencies. Offense information begins with either, first, a complaint of a victim/citizen or, second, the observation of a crime in progress by a law enforcement officer. A third trigger for data is when an arrest is made and information related to that occurrence is reported.

For federal agencies, the initiation of investigation may be prompted in different ways. Many crimes, such as human trafficking and hate crime and their associated data, are brought to the attention of the FBI in much the same fashion:

- Reports from victims

- Liaison with other law enforcement agencies

- Information about victims (e.g., human trafficking, hate crime) brought to the FBI by nongovernmental organizations

- Reports from the media

The decision to handle a crime as a federal investigation or as a local investigation is determined on a case-by-case basis. Some of the factors that enter into the decision for federal agencies to pursue an investigation are the available evidence, the availability of resources at the local level, and, in the case of hate crime, statutory provisions that determine whether the U.S. Attorney will accept the case as a federal one. In addition, some states do not have a hate crime statute under which to pursue a case.

Why federal numbers are smaller than those of other UCR agencies

As mentioned previously, federal investigations, by nature, often begin under different circumstances and proceed and conclude on different timeframes than investigations conducted by local and state agencies. Just as federal agencies often do not have traditional offenses known to report, they also typically do not have a number of offenses to report until a case has been built and an arrest or indictment has occurred. Perhaps most impactful on the federal numbers is the fact that federal agencies often play a collaborative role with local and state agencies in crime investigations. Because the UCR Program has the "most local reporting" rule, which specifies that the agency involved that is the most local jurisdiction should report the incident to the UCR Program, investigations and arrests that federal authorities have worked on often are reported by city, county, state, or tribal agencies.

The UCR Program defines law enforcement officers as individuals who ordinarily carry a firearm and a badge, have full arrest powers, and are paid from governmental funds set aside specifically to pay sworn law enforcement.

Civilian employees include full-time agency personnel such as clerks, radio dispatchers, meter attendants, stenographers, jailers, correctional officers, and mechanics.

Data were not included for arrests made in joint investigations with other agencies when local or state codes were used nor for Human Trafficking cases when different provisions of the U.S. Code were used for the basis of arrest.

These data include arrests by the FBI or task forces for the following:

09A – 09C Homicide Arrests

Section
1111 – Murder
1112 – Manslaughter
1114 – Protection of officers and employees of the United States
3592(c) – Aggravating factors for homicide

11A – 11D Sex Offense Arrests

13A – 13C Assault Arrests

Section
2241 – Aggravated sexual abuse
2242 – Sexual abuse
2243 – Sexual abuse of a minor or ward
2244C – Abusive sexual contact
2251 – Sexual exploitation of children

Section
111 – Assaulting, resisting, or impeding certain officers or employees
113 – Assaults within maritime and territorial jurisdiction
844(e) – Whoever, through the use of mail, telephone, telegraph, or other instrument of interstate or foreign commerce willfully makes any threat

871 – Threats against President and successors to the President
875 – Interstate communications
876 – Mailing threatening communications
879 – Threats against former Presidents and certain other persons
1389 – Prohibition on attacks on United States servicemen on account of service
1501 – Assault on process server
1503 – Influencing or injuring officer or juror generally
1512 – Tampering with a witness, victim, or an informant
1841 – Protection of unborn children
2231 – Assault or resistance
2237 – Criminal sanctions for failure to heave to, obstruction of boarding, or providing false information
7212 – Attempts to interfere with administration of internal revenue laws
46504 – Interference with flight crew members and attendants

23A – 23H Larceny and Theft Arrests

26A – 26E Fraud Arrests

Section
1167 – Theft from gaming establishments on Indian lands
1708 – Theft or receipt of stolen mail matter generally

Section
6 – Regulation of futures trading and foreign transactions
13 – Agriculture violations generally; punishment; costs of prosecution
2024 – Unauthorized use, transfer, acquisition, alteration, or possession of benefits
211 – Receiving or securing compensation for appointment of employees
305 – Unlawful export information activities
78 – Violation of consumer credit protection
24 – Definitions relating to federal health care fraud
152 – Concealment of assets; false oaths and claims; bribery
156 – Knowing disregard of bankruptcy law or rule
157 – Bankruptcy fraud
286 – Conspiracy to defraud the Government with respect to claims
287 – False, fictitious or fraudulent claims
669 – Theft or embezzlement in a connection with health care
704 – Military medals or decorations
912 – Officer or employee of the United States
913 – Impersonator making arrest or search
914 – Creditors of the United States
1001 – Statements of entries especially fraud and false statements
1002 – Possession of false papers to defraud United States
1003 – Demands against the United States

1005 – Bank entries, reports and transactions
1006 – Federal credit institutions entries, reports and transactions
1007 – Federal Deposit Insurance Corporation transactions
1012 – Department of Housing and Urban Development transactions
1014 – Loan and credit applications generally; renewals and discounts; crop insurance
1015 – Naturalization, citizenship or alien registry
1017 – Government seals wrongfully used and instruments wrongfully sealed
1027 – False statements and concealment of facts in relations to documents required by the Employee Retirement Income Security Act of 1974
1028 – Fraud and related activity in connection with identification documents, authentication features, and information
1029 – Fraud and related activity in connection with access devices
1031 – Major fraud against the United States
1033 – Crimes by or affecting person engaged in the business of insurance whose activities affect interstate commerce
1035 – False statements relating to health care
1036 – Entry by false pretense to any real property, vessel, or aircraft of the United States or secure area of any airport or seaport
1037 – Fraud and related activity in connection with electronic mail
1038 – False information and hoaxes
1341 – Frauds and swindles
1342 – Fictitious name or address
1343 – Fraud by wire, radio, or television
1344 – Bank fraud
1346 – Definition of "scheme or artifice to defraud"
1347 – Healthcare fraud
1348 – Securities and commodities fraud
1423 – Misuse of evidence of citizenship or naturalization
1518 – Obstruction of criminal investigations of health care offenses
1521 – Retaliating against a federal judge or federal law enforcement officer by false claim or slander of title
1542 – False statement in application and use of passport
3301 – Securities fraud
7206 – Fraud and false statements
1242 – Enrollment by Board; standards and qualifications; suspension or termination of enrollment
5324 – Structuring transactions to evade reporting requirement prohibited
1 – Patents; establishments
1320 – Criminal penalties for acts involving federal health care programs
7413 – Federal enforcement of the public health and welfare

35A – 35B Drug and Narcotics Arrests

Section
801 – Congressional findings and declarations: controlled substances
811 – Authority and criteria for classification of substances
812 – Schedules of controlled substances
821 – Rules and regulations for registration and control of manufacture, distribution, and dispensing of controlled substances
824 – Denial, revocation, or suspension of registration to manufacture, distribute, or dispense a controlled substance
841 – Prohibited acts to manufacture, distribute, or dispense, or possess with intent to manufacture, distribute, or dispense, a controlled substance
842 – Prohibited acts who is a registrant to distribute or dispense a controlled substance not authorized by his registration to another registrant or other authorized person or to manufacture a controlled substance not authorized by his registration
843 – Prohibited act to use in the course of the manufacture, distribution, or dispensing of a controlled substance, or to use for the purpose of acquiring or obtaining a controlled substance
844 – Penalties for any person knowingly or intentionally to possess a controlled substance unless such substance was obtained directly, or pursuant to a valid prescription
845 – Transferred to 859
848 – Continuing criminal enterprise drug abuse prevention and control
849 – Transportation safety offenses drug abuse prevention and control
853 – Criminal forfeitures drug abuse prevention and control
856 – Maintaining drug-involved premises
859 – Distribution to persons under the age of twenty-one
860 – Distribution or manufacturing in or near schools and colleges
862 – Denial of federal benefits to drug traffickers and possessors
864 – Anhydrous ammonia
881 – Forfeitures drug abuse prevention and control
952 – Importation of controlled substances
959 – Possession, manufacture, or distribution of controlled substance
960 – Unlawful for any person to knowingly or intentionally import or export a controlled substance
70503 – While on board a covered vessel, an individual my not knowingly or intentionally manufacture or distribute, or possess with intent to manufacture or distribute, a controlled substance
70506 – A person shall be punished under the Comprehensive Drug Abuse Prevention and Control Act of 1970

70507 – Seizure of property described in the Drug Abuse Prevention and Control Act

39A – 39D Gambling Offenses Arrests

64A – 64B Human Trafficking Arrests

Section
1324 – Bringing in and harboring certain aliens
1351 – Fraud in foreign labor contracting
1581 – Peonage; obstructing enforcement
1583 – Enticement into slavery
1584 – Sale into involuntary servitude
1589 – Forced labor
1591 – Sex trafficking of children or by force, fraud, or coercion
1592 – Unlawful conduct with respect to documents in furtherance of trafficking, peonage, slavery, involuntary servitude, or forced labor
1593A – Benefitting financially from peonage, slavery, and trafficking in persons
1594 – General provisions
1596 – Additional jurisdiction in certain trafficking offenses
1597 – Unlawful conduct with respect to immigration documents
2251A – Selling or buying children
2421 – Transportation generally
2422 – Coercion and enticement
2423 – Transportation of minors
2425 – Use of interstate facilities to transmit information about a minor

100 Kidnapping and Abduction Arrests

120 Robbery Arrests

200 Arson Arrests

Section
1201 – Kidnapping
1202 – Ransom money
1203 – Hostage taking
1204 – International parental kidnapping

Section
2113 – Bank robbery and incidental crimes

Section
81 – Arson within special maritime and territorial jurisdiction

210 Extortion and Blackmail Arrests

Section
875 – Interstate communications
892 – Making extortionate extensions of credit
893 – Financing extortionate extensions of credit
894 – Collection of extensions of credit by extortionate means

250 Counterfeiting and Forgery Arrests

Section
21 – Stolen or counterfeit nature of property for certain crimes
473 – Dealing in counterfeit obligations or securities
499 – Military, naval, or official passes
505 – Seals of courts; signatures of judges or court officers
514 – Fictitious obligations
642 – Tools and materials for counterfeiting purposes
1010 – Department of Housing and Urban Development and Federal Housing Administration transactions
1546 – Fraud and misuse of visas, permits, and other documents
2320 – Trafficking in counterfeit goods or services

270 Embezzlement Arrests

Section
153 – Embezzlement against estate
641 – Public money, property or records
654 – Officer or employee of United States converting property of another
656 – Theft, embezzlement, or misapplication by bank officer or employee
657 – Lending, credit and insurance institutions
659 – Interstate of foreign shipments by carrier; state prosecutions
664 – Theft or embezzlement from employee benefit plan
1163 – Embezzlement and theft from Indian tribal organizations
1168 – Theft by officers or employees of gaming establishments on Indian lands

280 Stolen Property Arrests

Section
2312 – Transportation of stolen vehicles
2314 – Transportation of stolen goods, securities, moneys, fraudulent state tax stamps, or articles used in counterfeiting
2315 – Sale or receipt of stolen goods, securities, moneys, or fraudulent state tax stamps
2321 – Trafficking in certain motor vehicles or motor vehicle parts

290 Destruction, Damage, and Vandalism of Property Arrests

Section
248 – Freedom of access to clinic entrances
1366 – Destruction of energy facility
1512(c) – Whoever corruptly alters, destroys, mutilates, or conceals a record, document, or other object, or attempts to do so, with the intent to impair the object's integrity or availability for use in an official proceeding
1703 – Delay or destruction of mail or newspapers
1705 – Destruction of letter boxes or mail

370 Pornography and Obscene Material Arrests

Section
1462 – Importation or transportation of obscene material
1465 – Production and transportation of obscene matters for sale or distribution
1466 – Engaging in the business of selling or transferring obscene matter
1470 – Transfer of obscene material to minors
2252 – Certain activities relating to material involving the sexual exploitation of minors
2252A – Activities relating to material constituting or containing child pornography
2260 – Production of sexually explicit depictions of a minor for importation into the United States
223 – Obscene or harassing telephone calls in the District of Columbia or in interstate or foreign communications

Section
201 – Bribery of public officials and witnesses
212 – Offer of loan or gratuity to financial institution examiner
215 – Receipt of commissions or gifts for procuring loans
224 – Bribery in sporting events
1510 – Obstruction of criminal investigation

Section
841 – "Person" means any individual, corporation, company, association, firm, partnership, society, or joint stock company
842 – Unlawful acts in explosive materials
843 – Licenses and user permits in explosive materials
844 – Penalties in explosive materials
846 – Additional powers of the Attorney General in explosive materials
847 – Rules and regulations in explosive materials
848 – Effect on State Law in explosive materials
921 – The term "firearm" means (A) any weapon (including a starter gun) which will or is designed to or may readily be

converted to expel a projectile by the action of an explosive; (B) the frame or receiver of any such weapon; (C) any firearm muffler or firearm silencer; or (D) any destructive device."

510 Bribery Arrests

520 Weapon Law Arrests

Section

922(a) – Unlawful for any person, other than a licensed importer, licensed manufacturer, licensed dealer, or licensed collector to transport into or receive in the state where he resides

922(c) – A licensed importer, licensed manufacturer, or licensed dealer may sell a firearm to a person who does not appear in person at the license's business premises only if transferee submits a sworn statement

922(d) – Unlawful for any person to sell or otherwise dispose of a firearm or ammunition to any person knowing or having reasonable cause to believe that a person under indictment, a fugitive from justice, unlawful user of or addicted to a controlled substance, has been adjudicated as a mental defective or committed to a mental institution, is illegally in the United States, discharged from the Armed Forces under dishonorable conditions, has renounced his citizenship, subject to a court order that restrains such person from harassing, stalking or threatening an intimate partner, and has been convicted in any court of a misdemeanor crime of domestic violence

922(e) – It shall be unlawful for any person knowingly to deliver or cause to be delivered to any common or contract carrier for transportation or shipment in interstate or foreign commerce, to person other than licensed importers, licensed manufacturers, license dealers, or licensed collectors, any package or other container in which there is any firearm

922(g) – Unlawful for any person who has been convicted in any court of, a crime punishable by imprisonment for a term exceeding one year

922(j) – It shall be unlawful for any person to receive, possess, conceal, store, barter, sell, or dispose of any stolen firearm or stolen ammunition, or pledge or accept as security for a loan any stolen firearm or stolen ammunition

922(k) – It shall be unlawful for any person knowingly to transport, ship, or receive, in interstate or foreign commerce, any firearm which has had the importer's or manufacturer's serial number removed, obliterated, altered

922(n) – It shall be unlawful for any person who is under indictment for a crime punishable by imprisonment for a term exceeding one year to ship or transport in interstate or foreign commerce

922(o) – It shall be unlawful for any person to transfer or possess a machinegun

923 – Licensing

924 - Penalties

928 – Separability

930 – Possession of firearms and dangerous weapons in federal facilities

3665 – Firearms possessed by convicted felons

5841 – Registration of firearms

5842 – Identification of firearms

5861 – Prohibited acts under machine guns, etc.

5861(c) – To receive or possess a firearm made in violation of the provisions of machine guns, etc.

5861(d) – To receive or possess a firearm which is not registered to him in the National Firearms Registration and Transfer Record

5861(f) – To make a firearm in violation of the provisions

5861(i) – To receive or possess a firearm which is not identified by a serial number as required

5861(l) – To make, or cause making of, a false entry on any application, return, or record required by this chapter, knowing such entry to be false

46505 – Carrying a weapon or explosive on an aircraft

720 Animal Cruelty Arrests

Section

2156 – Animal fighting venture prohibition

41 – Hunting, fishing, trapping; disturbance or injury on wildlife refuges

90G Liquor Law Arrests

Section

47 – Use of aircraft or motor vehicles to hunt certain wild horses or burros; pollution of watering holes

49 – Enforcement of animal fighting prohibitions

Section

1156 – Intoxicants possessed unlawfully

3113 – Liquor law violations in Indian country

90Z All Other Offenses Arrests

Section

1229 – Initiation of removal proceedings

1325 – Improper entry by alien

1325(a) – Improper time or place; avoidance of examination or inspection; misrepresentation and concealment of facts

1326 – Reentry of removed aliens

84 – Interference with aids to navigation; penalty

506(a) – Any person who willfully infringes a copyright shall be punished

4 – Misprision of felony

13 – Laws of States adopted for areas within federal jurisdiction

39(a) – Aiming a laser pointer at an aircraft

42 – Importation or shipment or injurious mammals, birds, fish (including mollusks and crustacea), amphibia, and reptiles; permits, specimens for museums; regulations

219 – Officers and employees acting as agents of foreign principals

228 – Failure to pay legal child support obligations

243(b) – Exclusion of jurors on account of race or color

371 – Conspiracy to commit offense or to defraud United States

372 – Conspiracy to impede or injure officer

373 – Solicitation to commit a crime of violence

402 – Contempts constituting crimes

513 – Securities of the states and private entities

545 – Smuggling goods into the United States

554 – Smuggling goods from the United States

751 – Prisoners in custody of institution or officer

793(e) – Gathering, transmitting or losing defense information

831 – Prohibited transactions involving nuclear material

842(p) – Distribution of Information Relating to Explosives, Destructive Devices, and Weapons of Mass Destruction

931 – Prohibition on purchase, ownership, or possession of body armor by violent felons

951 – Agents of foreign governments

951(a) – Whoever, other than a diplomatic or consular officer or attaché, acts in the United States as an agent of a foreign government without prior notification to the Attorney General if required

952 – Diplomatic codes and correspondence

955 – Financial transactions with foreign governments

956 – Conspiracy to kill, kidnap, main, or injure persons or damage property in a foreign country

960 – Expedition against friendly nation

981 – Civil forfeiture

1030 – Fraud and related activity in connection with computers

1071 – Concealing person from arrest

1073 – Flight to avoid prosecution or giving testimony

1083 – Transportation between shore and ship; penalties

1117 – Conspiracy to murder

Section

1349 – Attempt and conspiracy

1365 – Tampering with consumer products

1425 – Procurement of citizenship or naturalization unlawfully

1511 – Obstruction of state or local law enforcement

1512 – Tampering with a witness, victim, or an informant

1519 – Destruction, alteration, or falsification of records in federal investigations and bankruptcy

1621 – Perjury generally

1622 – Subornation of perjury

1623 – False declarations before grand jury or court

1651 – Piracy under law of nations

1692 – Foreign mail as United States mail

1791 – Providing or possessing contraband in prison

1801 – Video voyeurism

1831 – Economic espionage

1924 – Unauthorized removal and retention of classified documents or material

1960 – Prohibition of unlicensed money transmitting businesses

1992 – Terrorist attaches and other violence against railroad carriers and against mass transportation systems on land, on water, or through the air

2156 – Production of defective national-defense material, national-defense premises, or national defense utilities

2250 – Failure to register as a sex offender

2332 – Criminal penalties for terrorism

2332A – Use of weapons of mass destruction

2332B – Acts of terrorism transcending national boundaries

2332F – Bombings of places of public use, government facilities, public transportation systems and infrastructure facilities

2339 – Harboring or concealing terrorists

2339A – Providing material support to terrorists

2339B – Providing material support or resources to designated foreign terrorist organizations

2341 – Definitions for trafficking in contraband cigarettes and smokeless tobacco

2342 – Unlawful acts for trafficking in contraband cigarettes and smokeless tobacco

2342(a) – It shall be unlawful for any person knowingly to ship, transport, receive, possess, sell, distribute, or purchase contraband cigarettes or contraband smokeless tobacco

2344 – Penalties for trafficking in contraband cigarettes and smokeless tobacco

2401 – Renumbered 2441

2441 – War crimes

2442 – Recruitment or use of child soldiers

3062 – General arrest authority for violation of release conditions

3103 – Grounds for issuing search warrant

3122 – Application for an order for a pen register or a trap and trace device

3146 – Penalty for failure to appear

3184 – Fugitives from foreign country to United States

3290 – Fugitives from justice

3606 – Arrest and return of a probationer

3615 – Criminal default

7201 – Attempt to evade or defeat tax

7202 – Willful failure to collect or pay over tax

7203 – Willful failure to file return, supply information, or pay tax

5324 – Structuring transactions to evade reporting requirement prohibited

5332 – Bulk cash smuggling into or out of the United States

1311 – Effluent limitations

1319(c) – Enforcement of criminal penalties

2077 – Unauthorized dealings in special nuclear material

46312 – Transportation hazardous material

Child Exploitation Arrests

Section

1204 – International parental kidnapping

1462 – Importation or transportation of obscene matters

1466 – Engaging in the business of selling or transferring obscene matter

1470 – Transfer of obscene material to minors

2241 – Aggravated sexual abuse

2242 – Sexual abuse

2243 – Sexual abuse of a minor or ward

2244c – Sexual abuse offenses involving your children

2251 – Sexual exploitation of children

2252 – Certain activities relating to material involving the sexual exploitation of minors

2260 – Production of sexually explicit depictions of a minor for importation into the United States

2421 – Transportation generally

2422 – Coercion and enticement

2423 – Transportation of minors

Employee counts were as of December 2016 for both FBI and ATF.

Population Estimation

Population estimates used in this table are the U.S. Census Bureau's published resident population estimates for counties for 2015. The U.S. Census Bureau calculates estimates based on the decennial census of 2010 and by applying measures of population changes. See https://factfinder.census.gov/faces/tableservices/jsf/pages/productview.xhtml?pid=PEP_2016_PEPANNRES&src=pt for further information on county breakdowns for each state.

Human Trafficking

As state participation has grown, the UCR Program has seen an increase in human trafficking data submissions. The program will continue efforts to expand, gather, and make available information regarding human trafficking incidents.

Trafficking Victims Protection Act

In January 2013, the national UCR Program began collecting offense and arrest data regarding human trafficking as authorized by the William Wilberforce Trafficking Victims Protection Reauthorization Act of 2008. The act requires the FBI to collect human trafficking offense data and to make distinctions between prostitution, assisting or promoting prostitution, and purchasing prostitution.

To comply with the Wilberforce Act, the national UCR Program created two additional offenses in the Summary Reporting System (SRS) and the National Incident-Based Reporting System (NIBRS) through which the UCR Program collects both offense and arrest data. The definitions for these offenses are:

Human Trafficking/Commercial Sex Acts: inducing a person by force, fraud, or coercion to participate in commercial sex acts, or in which the person induced to perform such act(s) has not attained 18 years of age.

Human Trafficking/Involuntary Servitude: obtaining of a person(s) through recruitment, harboring, transportation, or provision, and subjecting such persons by force, fraud, or coercion into involuntary servitude, peonage, debt bondage, or slavery (not to include commercial sex acts).

The data in the tables included in this report reflect the offenses and arrests recorded by state and local law enforcement agencies (LEAs) that currently have the ability to report the data to the national UCR Program. As such, they should not be interpreted as a definitive statement of the level or characteristics of human trafficking as a whole. The data declaration pages, which will help the user better understand the data, and the methodology used for the four following tables are located in the Data Declarations and Methodology section near the end of this report. In addition, a Question and Answer section about human trafficking data is provided as a supplement to this report.

Note: Regarding the data reported to the UCR Program, it is important to note that these data represent only one view of a complex issue—the law enforcement perspective. However, due to the nature of human trafficking, many of these crimes are never reported to the local, state, tribal, and federal LEAs that investigate them. In addition to the law enforcement facet in fighting these crimes, there are victim service organizations whose mission it is to serve the needs of the victims of human trafficking. In order to have the complete picture of human trafficking, it would be necessary to gather information from all of these sources.

Tables include the states that have added human trafficking offenses to their data collection and the number of agencies per state participating in the UCR Program. Even though a state program included human trafficking, the individual agencies in that state may or may not have added it to their collections.

Indiana, Mississippi, and portions of Ohio have no UCR state program to manage the collection of UCR data within the state. Each law enforcement agency is responsible for reporting its crime data directly to the FBI.

For UCR purposes, juveniles are individuals under the age of 18 years. Adults are 18 years of age or older.

The data used in creating these tables were from law enforcement agencies submitting one or more human trafficking incidents for at least 1 month of the calendar year. Also included are zero data for states which have incorporated human trafficking offenses in their data collection where no 2016 human trafficking incidents were reported to the FBI UCR Program.

The published data, therefore, do not necessarily represent reports from each participating agency for all 12 months of the calendar year. When the FBI determines that an agency's data collection methodology does not comply with national UCR guidelines, the figure(s) for that agency's offense(s) will not be included in the table, and the discrepancy will be explained in a footnote.

Cargo Theft

The FBI's Uniform Crime Reporting (UCR) Program collects cargo theft data to inform the law enforcement community, state and federal legislators, academia, and the public at large about this particular crime. The data can be used to create awareness and to measure the impact cargo theft has on the economy and potential threats to national security. Often cargo theft offenses are part of larger criminal schemes and have been found to be components of organized crime rings, drug trafficking, and funding for terrorism. The UCR collection of cargo theft data is new with only 4 years of data published, but the number of agencies reporting cargo theft incidents has increased each year. As more agencies participate, future versions of this cargo theft report will depict a more complete account of the occurrences of cargo theft in the United States.

Due to the significant economic impact cargo theft has on the United States economy, and the potential for use by terrorist organizations, Congress mandated H.R. 3199, the USA Patriot Improvement and Reauthorization Act of 2005 on March 9, 2006. It required the Attorney General to "take the steps necessary to ensure that reports of cargo theft collected by Federal, State, and local officials are reflected as a separate category in the Uniform Crime Reporting System, or any successor system, by no later than December 31, 2006." In response to this mandate, the Criminal Justice Information Services (CJIS) Advisory Policy Board approved a definition for collecting cargo theft in December 2006. Creation of the data specifications required to capture cargo theft data in the UCR's Summary Reporting System as well as the National Incident-Based Reporting System were finalized in 2010 with the first publication of cargo theft data in 2013.

Cargo theft is defined as "The criminal taking of any cargo including, but not limited to, goods, chattels, money, or baggage that constitutes, in whole or in part, a commercial shipment of freight moving in commerce, from any pipeline system, railroad car, motor truck, or other vehicle, or from any tank or storage facility, station house, platform, or depot, or from any vessel or wharf, or from any aircraft, air terminal, airport, aircraft terminal or air navigation facility, or from any intermodal container, intermodal chassis, trailer, container freight station, warehouse, freight distribution facility, or freight consolidation facility. For purposes of this definition, cargo shall be deemed as moving in commerce at all points between the point of origin and the final destination, regardless of any temporary stop while awaiting transshipment or otherwise."

This definition was developed, not as a legal description for prosecutorial purposes, but to capture the essence of the national cargo theft problem in the United States. The legal elements of knowledge and intent were intentionally omitted.

Participation in the UCR Program is voluntary, and agencies or states may choose not to participate. In 2013, seven states participated in the first release of cargo theft data from the national UCR Program. In 2014, a total of 29 states and the Bureau of Indian Affairs submitted cargo theft data to the UCR Program. In 2015, a total of 31 states and the Bureau of Indian Affairs participated in submitting data to the UCR Program. In 2016, a total of 30 states, the Bureau of Indian Affairs, and the National Institute of Health submitted cargo theft data, although only 20 states had at least one cargo theft incident and were able to verify the submitted data as publishable. Participation in the cargo theft data has remained steady; however, several factors have been identified having a direct impact on this important data collection:

- States may not have the resources required to make the necessary technical changes or to align their local and state statutes with federal requirements.

- States may not have the necessary resources to conduct data quality checks on reported incidents associated with cargo theft, which could result in inaccurate data.

- States may not have adequate resources to train participants on how to recognize and properly record cargo theft incidents.

- States may not perceive cargo theft as a priority or a significant problem within their states and make decisions based on their immediate needs regarding resource allocation.

Quality data concerning cargo theft can help us better understand this crime and the threats associated with it. As more agencies choose to report their incidents, the FBI's UCR Program will be able to provide more information about cargo theft on a national scale. For additional information on the UCR Program's collection of cargo theft incidents, visit https://www.fbi.gov/about-us/cjis/ucr/ucr-program-data-collections.

Tables present by state the total number of agencies that submitted data about cargo theft incidents, the number of incidents reported, the reported value of stolen property, the value and percentage of recovered property for each submitting state.

Data used were from all law enforcement agencies submitting one or more cargo theft incidents for at least 1 month of the calendar year. The published data, therefore, do not necessarily represent reports from each participating agency for all 12 months of the calendar year. Based on UCR guidelines, the property descriptions of credit/debit cards, nonnegotiable instruments, documents/personal or business, and identity-intangible, must be submitted with zero value for stolen and/or

recovered. In the Cargo Theft Program, the victim of a cargo theft may be an individual, a business, an institution, or society as a whole. The UCR Program counted one for each victim type reported in an incident.

Because cargo theft has been defined as "the criminal **taking of** any cargo . . .," there are specific crimes against property that apply to cargo theft. The applicable crimes against property include:

120 = Robbery
23D = Theft from building
23F = Theft from motor vehicle
23H = All other larceny
26A = False pretenses, swindle, confidence game
26B = Credit card, automatic teller machine fraud
26C = Impersonation
26E = Wire fraud
210 = Extortion, blackmail
220 = Burglary, breaking & entering
240 = Motor vehicle theft
270 = Embezzlement
510 = Bribery

In addition, cargo theft is not considered an offense by itself; all offenses that happen within a cargo theft incident are to be reported. Cargo theft data are derived by capturing the additional element of "theft of cargo" in incidents that contain any of the applicable offenses.

PART 5

Criminal Victimization, 2016

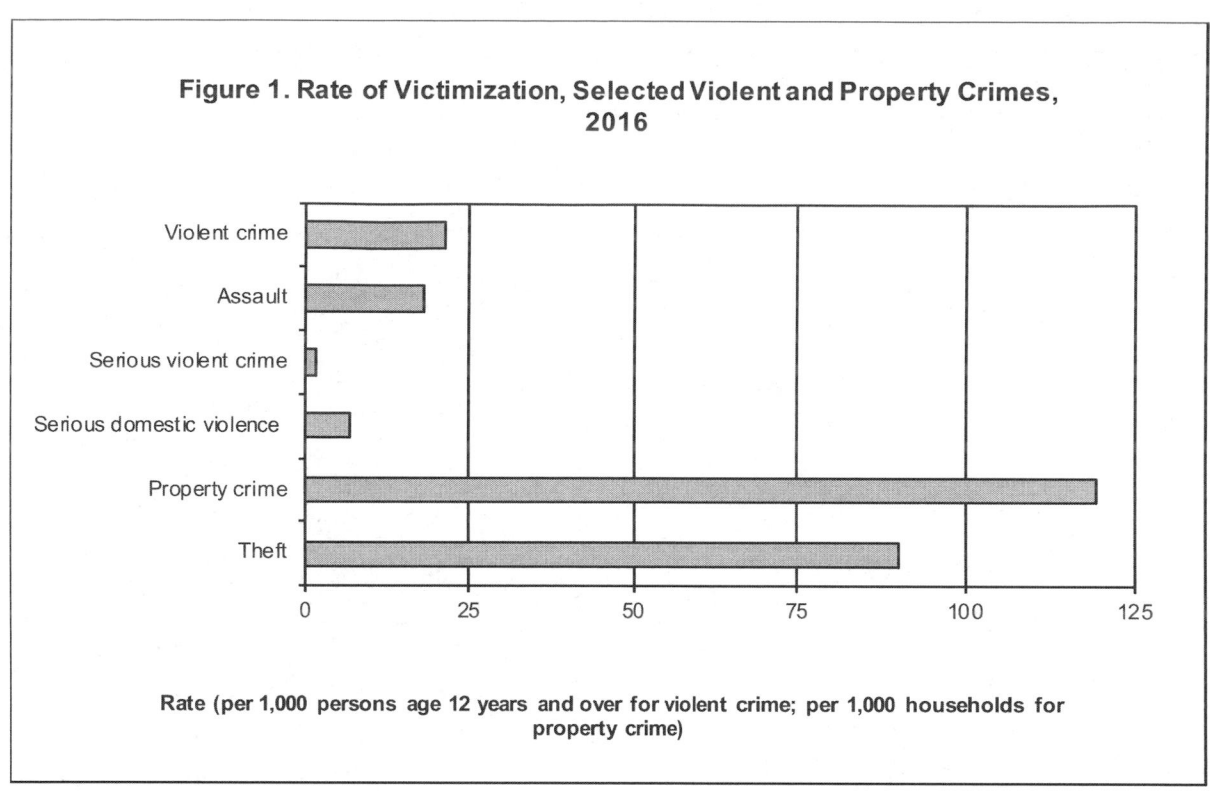

Figure 1. Rate of Victimization, Selected Violent and Property Crimes, 2016

Violent crime

Assault

Serious violent crime

Serious domestic violence

Property crime

Theft

0   25   50   75   100   125

Rate (per 1,000 persons age 12 years and over for violent crime; per 1,000 households for property crime)

- In 2016, U.S. residents age 12 years or older experienced approximately 5.7 million violent victimizations and 15.9 million property victimizations.

- Fewer than half (42 percent) of violent victimizations were reported to police.

- A total of 1.3 percent of all persons age 12 or older experienced one or more violent victimizations.

- The rate of stranger violence (8.2 per 1,000) was higher than the rate of intimate partner violence (2.2 per 1,000).

- Approximately 8.8 percent of all households experienced one property victimization in 2016.

- Motor vehicle thefts (80 percent) were the most likely crimes to be reported to police.

Note: The National Crime Victimization Survey (NCVS) underwent a routine redesign in 2016; consequently, the 2016 is generally not comparable to data from previous years. Among counties that remained in sample from the previous survey design, there was no measurable change in the rates of violent, serious violent, or property crime from 2015 to 2016. For more details, see the Methodology in the section or consult https://www.bjs.gov/index.cfm?ty=pbdetail&iid=6166.

Table 1. Victimization Rates in NCVS Continuing, Outgoing, and New Sample Counties, 2015 and 2016

(Rate per 1,000 persons age 12 years or older for violent crime; per 1,000 households for property crime.)

Type of crime	Continuing NCVS sample counties		Outgoing NCVS sample counties/New NCVS sample counties		Total sample counties, 2016
	2015*	2016	2015 outgoing**	2016 new	
Total violent crime[1]	18.7	19.5 A	18.3	24.2 A	21.1
Serious violent crime[2]	10.3	6.8	5.2	7.5 A	7.0
Total property crime[3]	108.1	113.9 A	118.6	130.0	119.4

* = Comparison year. 2015 continuing sample counties are compared to 2016 continuing sample counties.
** = Comparison year. 2015 outgoing sample counties are compared to 2016 new sample counties.
A = Significant difference from comparison year at the 95% confidence level.
[1]Includes rape or sexual assault, robbery, aggravated assault, and simple assault.
[2]In the NCVS, serious violent crime is a subset of violent crime and includes rape or sexual assault, robbery, and aggravated assault.
[3]Includes household burglary, theft, and motor vehicle theft.

Table 2. Violent and Property Victimization, by Type of Crime, 2016

(Number; rate.)

Type of crime	Number	Rate per 1,000[1]
Violent Crime[2]	5,749,330	21.1
Rape/sexual assault	323,450 A	1.2 A
Robbery	500,680 A	1.8 A
Assault	4,925,200	18.1
Aggravated assault	1,084,340 A	4.0 A
Simple assault*	3,840,860	14.1
Domestic violence[3]	1,109,610	4.1
Intimate partner violence[4]	597,740	2.2
Stranger violence	2,232,260	8.2
Violent crime involving injury	1,366,250	5.0
Serious Violent Crime[5]	1,908,470	7.0
Serious domestic violence[3]	402,430	1.5
Serious intimate partner violence[4]	272,380	1.0
Serious stranger violence	789,370	2.9
Serious violent crime involving weapons	1,267,810	4.7
Serious violent crime involving injury	746,850	2.7
Property Crime	15,917,430	119.4
Burglary	3,291,490 A	24.7 A
Motor vehicle theft	585,500 A	4.4 A
Theft**	12,040,440	90.3

Note: Violent crime classifications include rape or sexual assault, robbery, aggravated assault, and simple assault. Other violent crime categories in this table, including domestic violence and violent crime involving injury, are not mutually exclusive from these classifications. Detail may not sum to total due to rounding. Total population age 12 or older was 272,174,080 in 2016. Total number of households was 133,271,310 in 2016.
* = Comparison year for violent crime. Simple assault is compared to rape or sexual assault, robbery, and aggravated assault.
** = Comparison year for property crime.
A = Significant difference from comparison year at the 95% confidence level.
[1]For violent and serious violent crime, rate is per 1,000 persons age 12 or older. For property crime, rate is per 1,000 households.
[2]Excludes homicide because the NCVS is based on interviews with victims and cannot measure murder.
[3]Includes victimization committed by intimate partners and family members.
[4]Includes victimization committed by current or former spouses, boyfriends, or girlfriends.
[5]In the NCVS, serious violent crime includes rape or sexual assault, robbery, and aggravated assault.

Table 3. Firearm Violence, 2016

(Number; rate per 1,000 persons age 12 years or older; percent.)

Characteristic	Estimate
Firearm incidents	416,350
Firearm victimizations	480,940
Rate of firearm victimizations	1.8
Percent of firearms victimizations reported to police	60.5

Table 4. Rate of Crime Reported to Police in the Uniform Crime Reporting Program and National Crime Victimization Survey, 2016

(Rate.)

Type of crime	UCR rate per 1,000 residents[1]	NCVS rate per 1,000 persons age 12 or older (serious violent crime) or 1,000 households (property crime)
Serious Violent Crime[2]	3.9	3.6
Murder	0.1	X
Rape[3]	0.4	0.3
Robbery	1.0	1.0
Aggravated assault	2.5	2.3
Property Crime	24.5	119.4
Burglary	4.7	24.7 A
Motor vehicle theft	2.4	90.3

X = Not applicable.
A = Significant difference from comparison year at the 95% confidence level.
[1]Includes crimes against persons age 12 or younger, persons who are homeless, persons who are institutionalized, and crimes against commercial establishments. These populations are out of sample for the NCVS.
[2]In addition to rape, robbery, and aggravated assault, the NCVS includes sexual assault.
[3]The NCVS estimate includes sexual assault. See Methodology for details on the measurement of rape or sexual assault in the NCVS. The UCR estimate is based on the revised definition of rape.

Table 5. Percent of Victimizations Reported to Police, by Type of Crime, 2016

(Percent.)

Type of crime	2016
Violent Crime[1]	42.1
Rape/sexual assault[2]	22.9 A
Robbery	54.0 A
Assault	42.2
Aggravated assault	58.5 A
Simple assault*	37.5
Domestic violence[3]	49.1
Intimate partner violence[4]	46.9
Stranger violence	44.7
Violent crime involving injury	47.4
Serious Violent Crime[5]	51.3
Serious domestic violence[3]	52.6
Serious intimate partner violence[4]	51.9
Serious stranger violence	57.1
Serious violent crime involving weapons	60.1
Serious violent crime involving injury	50.2
Property Crime	35.7
Household burglary	49.7 A
Motor vehicle theft	79.9 A
Theft**	29.7

Note: Violent crime classifications include rape or sexual assault, robbery, aggravated assault, and simple assault. Other violent crime categories in this table, including domestic violence and violent crime involving injury, are not mutually exclusive from these classifications.
* = Comparison group for violent crime. Simple assault is compared to rape or sexual assault, robbery, and aggravated assault.
** = Comparison group for property crime.
A = Significant difference from comparison year at the 95% confidence level.
[1]Excludes homicide because the NCVS is based on interviews with victims and therefore cannot measure murder.
[2]For details on the measurement of rape and sexual assault in the NCVS, see https://www.bjs.gov/content/pub/pdf/cv16.pdf
[3]Includes victimization committed by intimate partners and family members.
[4]Includes victimization committed by current or former spouses, boyfriends, or girlfriends.
[5]In the NCVS, serious violent crime includes rape or sexual assault, robbery, and aggravated assault.

Table 6. Rate of Victimization Reported and Not Reported to the Police, by Type of Crime, 2016

(Rates per 1,000 persons age 12 or older for violent crime and per 1,000 households for property crime.)

Type of crime	Reported to police*	Not reported to police
Violent Crime[1]	8.9	11.8 [A]
Rape/sexual assault[2]	0.3	0.9 [A]
Robbery	1.0	0.7
Assault	7.6	10.2 [A]
Aggravated assault	2.3	1.6 [A]
Simple assault	5.3	8.6 [A]
Domestic violence[3]	2.0	1.9
Intimate partner violence[4]	1.0	1.1
Stranger violence	3.7	4.4
Violent crime involving injury	2.4	2.5
Serious Violent Crime[5]	3.6	3.2
Serious domestic violence[3]	0.8	0.6
Serious intimate partner violence[4]	0.5	0.5
Serious stranger violence	1.7	1.2 [B]
Serious violent crime involving weapons	2.8	1.7 [A]
Serious violent crime involving injury	1.4	1.3
Property Crime	42.6	75.2 [A]
Household burglary	12.3	12.1
Motor vehicle theft	3.5	0.8 [A]
Theft	26.9	62.3 [A]

Note: Violent crime classifications include rape or sexual assault, robbery, aggravated assault, and simple assault. Other violent crime categories in this table, including domestic violence and violent crime involving injury, are not mutually exclusive from these classifications. Victimization rates are per 1,000 persons age 12 or older for violent crime or per 1,000 households for property crime.
* = Comparison group.
A = Significant difference from comparison year at the 95% confidence level.
B = Significant difference from comparison year at the 90% confidence level.
[1]Excludes homicide because the NCVS is based on interviews with victims and therefore cannot measure murder.
[2]For details on the measurement of rape and sexual assault in the NCVS, see https://www.bjs.gov/content/pub/pdf/cv16.pdf
[3]Includes victimization committed by intimate partners and family members.
[4]Includes victimization committed by current or former spouses, boyfriends, or girlfriends.
[5]In the NCVS, serious violent crime includes rape or sexual assault, robbery, and aggravated assault.

Table 7. Percent of Violent Victimizations in Which Victims Received Assistance from a Victim Service Agency, by Type of Crime, 2016

(Percent.)

Type of crime	2015
Violent Crime[1]	9.5
Serious violent crime[2]*	12.2
Simple assault	8.1 [A]
Intimate partner violence[3]	25.5
Violent crime involving injury	12.7
Violent crime involving weapon	13.6

* = Comparison group. Serious violent crime is compared to simple assault.
A = Significant difference from comparison year at the 95% confidence level.
[1]Includes rape or sexual assault, robbery, aggravated assault, and simple assault. Excludes homicide because the NCVS is based on interviews with victims and therefore cannot measure murder.
[2]In the NCVS, serious violent crime includes rape or sexual assault, robbery, and aggravated assault.
[3]Includes victimization committed by current or former spouses, boyfriends, or girlfriends.

Table 8. Rate of Violent Victimization and Serious Violent Victimization and Percent Reported to Police, by Victim Demographic Characteristics, 2016

(Rate per 1,000 persons age 12 years or older; percent.)

Victim demographic characteristic	Rate of total violence per 1,000 persons age 12 or older		Percent of violence reported to police	
	Violent crime[1]	Serious violent crime[2]	Violent crime[1]	Serious violent crime[2]
Total	21.1	7.0	42.1	51.3
Sex..				
Male*	21.4	6.5 A	44.3	60.5
Female	20.8	7.5	40.0	43.7 A
Race/Hispanic Origin................				
White[3]	20.5	6.3	40.1	45.0 A
Black[3]*	24.1	8.2	39.8	59.8
Hispanic	20.2	8.2	51.6 A	64.8
Other[3,4]	23.0	8.5	42.9	47.8
Age...				
12–17 years	30.9	8.6	27.7	48.1
18–24 years*	30.9	11.0	35.7	51.5
25–34 years	31.8	12.8	38.9	37.8 B
35–49 years	22.9 A	6.8 A	49.8 A	58.6
50–64 years	16.1 A	5.2 A	49.1 A	65.2 B
65 years and over	4.4 A	1.1 A	60.4 A	62.0
Marital Status..........................				
Never married	29.8	10.7	33.5	45.8
Married....................................	12.4 A	3.3 A	50.8 A	62.9 A
Widowed..................................	10.7 A	2.6 A	48.1 B	60.5
Divorced..................................	30.1	11.9	53.8 A	56.0
Separated	675 A	20.0 A	43.2	39.7
Household Income....................				
$9,999 or less*	35.8	13.0	47.3	37.3
$10,000–$14,999.....................	35.6	13.9	50.2	54.8 B
$15,000–$24,999.....................	32.9	14.0	45.3	52.9 B
$25,000–$34,999.....................	21.0 A	6.3 A	44.2	57.9 A
$35,000–$49,999.....................	20.4 A	6.8 A	34.0 A	43.9
$50,000–$74,999.....................	17.6 A	5.8 A	42.4	57.1 A
$75,000 or more	15.7 A	4.1 A	39.4	54.3 A

Note: Victimization rates are per 1,000 persons age 12 or older.
* = Comparison group.
A = Significant difference from comparison year at the 95% confidence level.
B = Significant difference from comparison year at the 90% confidence level.
[1]Includes rape or sexual assault, robbery, aggravated assault, and simple assault. Excludes homicide because the NCVS is based on interviews with victims and therefore cannot measure murder.
[2]In the NCVS, serious violent crime includes rape or sexual assault, robbery, and aggravated assault.
[3]White, Black, and other race categories exclude persons of Hispanic or Latino origin.
[4]Includes American Indians and Alaska Natives; Asians, Native Hawaiians, and other Pacific Islanders; and persons of two or more races.

Table 9. Rate of Total Victimization and Percent of Victimizations Reported to Police, by Type of Crime and Household Location, 2016

(Rate per 1,000 persons age 12 years or older for violent crime; rate per 1,000 households for property crime; percent.)

Household location	Rate of total victimization			Percent of victimizations reported to police		
	Violent crime[1]	Serious violent crime[2]	Property crime[3]	Violent crime[1]	Serious violent crime[2]	Property crime[3]
Total	21.1	7.0	119.4	42.1	51.3	35.7
Region....................................						
Northeast*..............................	16.7	4.6	76.6	44.8	57.6	32.0
Midwest	27.0 A	9.7 A	114.1 A	34.6 A	45.2	33.7
South.......................................	16.3	6.2	115.5 A	48.1	57.7	40.3 A
West..	26.6 A	7.6 A	165.3 A	42.1	47.1	33.0
Location of Residence..............						
Urban*....................................	29.9	10.7	150.5	41.9	52.6	34.1
Suburban.................................	15.4 A	5.1 A	97.0 A	42.6	50.9	37.9 A
Rural.......................................	21.7 A	5.6 A	125.0 A	41.4	46.8	34.4

Note: Victimization rates are per 1,000 persons age 12 or older for violent crime and per 1,000 households for property crime.
* = Comparison group.
A = Significant difference from comparison group at the 95% confidence level.
[1]Includes rape or sexual assault, robbery, aggravated assault, and simple assault. Excludes homicide because the NCVS is based on interviews with victims and therefore cannot measure murder.
[2]In the NCVS, serious violent crime includes rape or sexual assault, robbery, and aggravated assault.
[3]Includes household burglary, motor vehicle theft, and theft.

Table 10. Number of Victims and Prevalence Rate, by Type of Crime, 2016

(Number; percent.)

Type of crime	Number[1]	Prevalence[2]
Violent Crime[3]	3,629,180	1.3
Rape/sexual assault	205,680 ᴬ	0.1 ᴬ
Robbery	417,190 ᴬ	0.2 ᴬ
Assault	3,136,760	1.2
Aggravated assault	784,600 ᴬ	0.3 ᴬ
Simple assault	2,450,840	0.9
Domestic violence[4]	630,720	0.2
Intimate partner violence[5]	309,030	0.1
Stranger violence	1,588,430	0.6
Violent crime involving injury	864,900	0.3
Serious Violent Crime[6]	1,354,370	0.5
Serious domestic violence[3]	246,360	0.1
Serious intimate partner violence[4]	146,310	0.1
Serious stranger violence	627,310	0.2
Serious violent crime involving weapons	896,350	0.3
Serious violent crime involving injury	509,680	0.2
Property Crime	11,715,650	8.8
Household burglary	2,569,980 ᴬ	1.9 ᴬ
Motor vehicle theft	546,180 ᴬ	0.4 ᴬ
Theft*	9,323,510	7.0

Note: Violent crime classifications include rape or sexual assault, robbery, aggravated assault, and simple assault. Other violent crime categories in this table, including domestic violence and violent crime involving injury, are not mutually exclusive from these classifications. Detail may not sum to total because a person or household may experience multiple types of crime.
* = Comparison group for property crime.
[1]Excludes homicide because the NCVS is based on interviews with victims and therefore cannot measure murder.
A = Significant difference from comparison year at the 95% confidence level.
[1]Number of persons age 12 or older who experienced at least one victimization during the year for violent crime, and number of households that experienced at least one victimization during the year for property crime.
[2]Percent of persons age 12 or older who experienced at least one victimization during the year for violent crime, and percent of households that experienced at least one victimization during the year for property crime.
[3]For details on the measurement of rape and sexual assault in the NCVS, see https://www.bjs.gov/content/pub/pdf/cv16.pdf
[3]Excludes homicide because the NCVS is based on interviews with victims and cannot measure murder.
[4]Includes victimization committed by intimate partners and family members.
[5]Includes victimization committed by current or former spouses, boyfriends, or girlfriends.
[6]In the NCVS, serious violent crime is a subset of violent crime and includes rape or sexual assault, robbery, and aggravated assault.

Table 11. Prevalence of Violent Crime, by Victim Demographic Characteristics, 2016

(Number; rate.)

Victim demographic characteristic	Number of persons victimized[1]	Prevalence rate[2]
Total	3,629,180	1.3
Sex		
Male*	1,872,700	1.4
Female	1,756,490	1.3 ᴬ
Race/Hispanic Origin		
White[3]	2,318,090 ᴬ	1.3
Black[3]*	485,670	1.4
Hispanic	540,690	1.2
Other[3,4]	284,730 ᴬ	1.3
Age		
12–17 years	469,490	1.9
18–24 years*	565,950	1.9
25–34 years	861,490 ᴬ	2.0
35–49 years	901,440 ᴬ	1.5 ᴬ
50–64 years	646,900	1.0 ᴬ
65 years and over	183,910 ᴬ	0.4 ᴬ
Marital Status		
Never married	1,822,230	1.9
Married	1,027,340 ᴬ	0.8 ᴬ
Widowed	96,920 ᴬ	0.6 ᴬ
Divorced	533,160 ᴬ	2.0
Separated	140,290 ᴬ	2.8 ᴬ

Note: Detail may not sum to total due to rounding.
* = Comparison group.
A = Significant difference from comparison year at the 95% confidence level.
[1]Number of persons age 12 or older who experienced at least one victimization during the year for violent crime.
[2]Percent of persons age 12 or older who experienced at least one victimization during the year for violent crime.
[3]White, Black, and other race categories exclude persons of Hispanic or Latino origin.
[4]Includes American Indians and Alaska Natives; Asians, Native Hawaiians, and Other Pacific Islanders; and persons of two or more races.

Methodology

Data are from the Bureau of Justice Statistics' (BJS) National Crime Victimization Survey (NCVS), which collects information on nonfatal crimes against persons age 12 or older from a nationally representative sample of U.S. households. The NCVS measures violent crimes, which include rape or sexual assault, robbery, aggravated assault, and simple assault. Property crimes include household burglary, motor vehicle theft, and theft. The survey also measures personal larceny, which includes pickpocketing and purse snatching. Unless otherwise noted, findings in this report are significant at the 95 percent confidence level. For additional estimates excluded from this report, see the NCVS Victimization Analysis Tool (NVAT) on the BJS Web site.

2016 NCVS Sample Redesign

To produce estimates on criminal victimization, the Bureau of Justice Statistics' (BJS) National Crime Victimization Survey (NCVS) collects information from a sample of U.S. households that represents the nation. The sample design is periodically changed to maintain the representativeness of the survey. In 2016, the NCVS sample was redesigned for two reasons:

1. To reflect changes in the U.S. population based on the 2010 Decennial Census

2. To make it possible to produce state- and local-level victimization estimates for the largest 22 states and specific metropolitan areas within those states

Every 10 years, the U.S. Census Bureau conducts the official population count of the United States. In 2016, a redesign of the NCVS sample was necessary to account for shifts in the population identified through the 2010 Decennial Census. From 2000 to 2010, the number of people residing in individual U.S. counties changed. Almost two-thirds of the nation's 3,143 counties gained population. Most counties along coastlines experienced population growth during this period, while others that lost population were clustered by region and were found in areas such as the Great Plains and Mississippi Delta.

The NCVS sampling process involves selecting primary sampling units (PSUs), which are counties, groups of counties, or large metropolitan areas identified through the Decennial Census and the U.S. Census Bureau's American Community Survey. Within the PSUs selected, the sampling process identifies addresses to be included in the sample and interviews are conducted with persons and households at those addresses.

Sampled households remain in the NCVS sample for seven waves (each wave is a 6-month period). The decennial sample update ensures that the sample reflects current population distributions. This process requires a phased shift of counties included in the 2000 sample design to those selected for the 2010 sample design, resulting in three types of counties in 2016: 1) continuing counties—those in both the 2000 and 2010 sample designs; 2) outgoing counties—those that were in the 2000 sample design, but not the 2010 sample design; and 3) new counties—those that were selected into the 2010 sample design, but were not in the 2000 sample design.

As part of ongoing efforts to enhance the usefulness and relevance of the NCVS, the sample also was expanded and redistributed to produce state and local estimates of victimization. Because the primary purpose of the NCVS has been to generate national estimates, the sample was initially designed to be representative of the United States as a whole and not individual states and local areas. To produce reliable estimates for the 22 most populous states and specific metropolitan areas within those states, it was necessary to change the NCVS sample design.

Implications of the 2016 Sample Redesign

When the 2016 NCVS data collection was complete, a comparison of the 2015 and 2016 victimization estimates showed that the violent and property crime rates had increased. Given recent patterns in NCVS data, these increases seemed too large to be a result of actual growth in crime, suggesting that the sample redesign may have affected the victimization rates. To better understand these results, the 2015 and 2016 victimization rates for new and continuing sample counties were examined separately. These comparisons showed that from 2015 to 2016 there were no statistically significant differences for continuing sample counties in the rates of total property crime, total violent crime, and total serious violent crime. In comparison, rates of total violent crime and total serious violent crime were higher in the new sample counties than in the outgoing sample counties.

Understanding the Increase in Victimization Estimates from 2015 to 2016

The NCVS sample redesign required a substantial addition of new counties to the sample. In 2016, the percentage of new sample counties (46 percent) was nearly double the percentage in typical survey cycle years, such as 2014 and 2015 (27 percent). Therefore, BJS needed additional interviewers to conduct interviews with the households in these new sample counties. Prior to the redesign, in typical years NCVS interviewers who were new to the survey conducted 3 percent to 4 percent of interviews. In 2016, new NCVS interviewers conducted about 11 percent of interviews.

Findings from the 2006 NCVS sample redesign, sample redesigns of other federal household surveys, and research on reporting patterns among respondents from the NCVS and other similar surveys were informative for understanding the potential impact of the 2016 NCVS redesign. This research shows that newer interviewers tend to collect more victimizations and generate higher rates of victimization than more experienced interviewers. The addition of new counties to the sample meant that more households were in the sample for the first time in 2016. For efficiency purposes, the new NCVS interviewers were also primarily assigned to households that were new to the sample. Prior research has demonstrated that NCVS respondents tend to report more victimizations during early interview waves. Thus, the effect of having a substantially higher percentage of new interviewers was combined with the effect of having a considerably larger share of new households. To better understand the increase in victimization rates, BJS and its contractors analyzed these and several other factors.

Even after conducting a thorough investigation, it was not possible to isolate the extent to which each factor contributed to the victimization rates, or the degree to which the change in rates from 2015 to 2016 resulted from the sample redesign rather than real changes in U.S. victimization levels. Therefore, data in this report focus primarily on the level and nature of violent and property crime victimization in 2016. Unless otherwise noted, 2016 estimates are based on the total NCVS sample. BJS will continue to monitor victimization estimates in future years to determine whether the impact of the sample redesign is limited to the 2016 estimates. Following the NCVS 2006 decennial redesign, BJS found that data since 2007 were comparable. For further information on the sample redesign and on the methodological changes to the NCVS in 2006, please consult https://www.bjs.gov/index.cfm?ty=pbdetail&iid=6166.

Differences in Rates of Reporting to Police in the UCR and NCVS

For 2016, the Federal Bureau of Investigation's (FBI) Uniform Crime Reporting (UCR) program showed that 3.9 serious violent crimes per 1,000 persons and 24.5 property crimes per 1,000 persons were known to law enforcement. According to the Bureau of Justice Statistics' (BJS) National Crime Victimization Survey (NCVS), 3.6 serious violent crimes per 1,000 persons age 12 or older and 42.6 property crimes per 1,000 households were reported to law enforcement during this same year.

Because the NCVS and UCR measure an overlapping, but not identical, set of offenses and use different methodologies, congruity is not expected between estimates from these two data sources. Restricting the NCVS to serious violence reported to police keeps the measures as similar as possible. However, significant methodological and definitional differences remain between serious violent crimes in the NCVS and the UCR:

- The UCR includes homicide and commercial crimes, while the NCVS excludes these crime types.

- The UCR excludes sexual assault, which the NCVS includes.

- NCVS estimates are based on interviews with a nationally representative sample of persons in U.S. households. UCR estimates are based on counts of crimes reported by an incomplete census of law enforcement agencies and are weighted to compensate for the incomplete reporting.

- The NCVS excludes crimes against children age 11 or younger and persons in institutions (e.g., nursing homes and correctional institutions). It may also exclude highly mobile populations and persons who are homeless. Victimizations against these persons are included in the UCR.

Given these differences, the two measures of crime should not be compared but should be viewed as complementary sources, which together provide a more comprehensive picture of crime in the United States. For additional information about the differences between the two programs, see *The Nation's Two Crime Measures* (NCJ 246832, BJS web, September 2014).

Prevalence of Crime

Annual estimates of a population's risk for criminal victimization may be examined using victimization or prevalence rates. Historically, Bureau of Justice Statistics (BJS) reports based on National Crime Victimization Survey (NCVS) data rely on victimization rates, which measure the extent to which victimizations occur in a specified population during a specific time. For crimes affecting persons, NCVS victimization rates are estimated by dividing the number of victimizations that occur during a specified time (T) by the population at risk for those victimizations and multiplying the rate by 1,000.

Prevalence rates also describe the level of victimization but are based on the number of unique persons (or households) in the population experiencing at least one victimization during a specified time. The key distinction between a victimization and prevalence rate is whether the numerator consists of the number of victimizations or victims. For example, a person who experienced two robberies on separate occasions within the past year would be counted twice in the victimization rate but once in the prevalence rate. Prevalence rates are estimated by dividing the number of victims in the specified population by the total number of persons in the population and multiplying the rate by 100. This is the percentage of the population victimized at least once in a given period.

Victimization and prevalence rates may also be produced for household crimes, such as burglary. In these instances, numerators and denominators are adjusted to reflect households rather than persons. To better understand the percentage of the population that is victimized at least once in a given period, prevalence rates are presented by type of crime and certain demographic characteristics. (For further information about measuring prevalence in the NCVS, see *Measuring the Prevalence of Crime with the National Crime Victimization Survey*, NCJ 241656, BJS web, September 2013.)

Survey Methodology

NCVS is an annual data collection conducted by the U.S. Census Bureau for the Bureau of Justice Statistics (BJS). The NCVS is a self-report survey in which interviewed persons are asked about the number and characteristics of victimizations experienced during the prior 6 months. The NCVS collects information on nonfatal personal crimes (rape or sexual assault, robbery, aggravated and simple assault, and personal larceny) and household property crimes (burglary, motor vehicle theft, and other theft) both reported and not reported to police. In addition to providing annual level and change estimates on criminal victimization, the NCVS is the primary source of information on the nature of criminal victimization incidents. *Criminal Victimization* can be found here: http://www.bjs.gov/index.cfm?ty=pbdetail&iid=5804

Survey respondents provide information about themselves (e.g., age, sex, race and Hispanic origin, marital status, education level, and income) and whether they experienced a victimization. The NCVS collects information for each victimization incident about the offender (e.g., age, race and Hispanic origin, sex, and victim–offender relationship), characteristics of the crime (including time and place of occurrence, use of weapons, nature of injury, and economic consequences), whether the crime was reported to police, reasons the crime was or was not reported, and victim experiences with the criminal justice system.

The NCVS is administered to persons age 12 or older from a nationally representative sample of households in the United States. The NCVS defines a household as a group of persons who all reside at a sampled address. Persons are considered household members when the sampled address is their usual place of residence at the time of the interview and when they

have no usual place of residence elsewhere. Once selected, households remain in the sample for 3 years, and eligible persons in these households are interviewed every 6 months either in person or over the phone for a total of 7 interviews.

All first interviews are conducted in person with subsequent interviews conducted either in person or by phone. New households rotate into the sample on an ongoing basis to replace outgoing households that have been in the sample for the 3-year period. The sample includes persons living in group quarters, such as dormitories, rooming houses, and religious group dwellings, and excludes persons living in military barracks and institutional settings such as correctional or hospital facilities, and persons who are homeless.

Nonresponse and Weighting Adjustments

In 2016, a total of 134,690 households and 224,520 persons age 12 or older were interviewed for the NCVS. In general, each household was interviewed twice during the year. The response rate was 78 percent for households and 84 percent for eligible persons.

Victimizations that occurred outside of the United States were excluded from this report. In 2016, fewer than 1 percent of the unweighted victimizations occurred outside of the United States.

Estimates in this report use data primarily from the 2016 NCVS data files. These data are weighted to produce annual estimates of victimization for persons age 12 or older living in U.S. households. Because the NCVS relies on a sample rather than a census of the entire U.S. population, weights are designed to adjust to known population totals and compensate for survey nonresponse and other aspects of the complex sample design.

NCVS data files include person, household, and victimization weights. Person weights provide an estimate of the population represented by each person in the sample. Household weights provide an estimate of the U.S. household population represented by each household in the sample. After proper adjustment, both household and person weights are also typically used to form the denominator in calculations of crime rates.

Victimization weights used in the analyses in this report account for the number of persons present during an incident and for high-frequency repeat victimizations (i.e., series victimizations). Series victimizations are similar in type but occur with such frequency that a victim is unable to recall each individual event or describe each event in detail. Survey procedures allow NCVS interviewers to identify and classify these similar victimizations as series victimizations and to collect detailed information on only the most recent incident in the series.

The weight counts series victimizations as the actual number of victimizations reported by the victim, up to a maximum of 10. Including series victimizations in national rates results in large increases in the level of violent victimization. However, trends in violent crime are generally similar, regardless of whether series victimizations are included. In 2016, series incidents accounted for fewer than 2 percent of all victimizations and fewer than 4 percent of all violent victimizations. Weighting series victimizations as the number of victimizations up to a maximum of 10 victimizations produces more reliable estimates of crime levels, while the cap at 10 minimizes the effect of extreme outliers on rates. Additional information on the enumeration of series victimizations is detailed in the report *Methods for Counting High-Frequency Repeat Victimizations in the National Crime Victimization Survey* (NCJ 237308, BJS web, April 2012).

Standard Error Computations

When national estimates are derived from a sample, as with the NCVS, caution must be used when comparing one estimate to another estimate or when comparing estimates over time.

Although one estimate may be larger than another, estimates based on a sample have some degree of sampling error. The sampling error of an estimate depends on several factors, including the amount of variation in the responses and the size of the sample. When the sampling error around an estimate is taken into account, the estimates that appear different may not be statistically different.

One measure of the sampling error associated with an estimate is the standard error. The standard error can vary from one estimate to the next. Generally, an estimate with a small standard error provides a more reliable approximation of the true value than an estimate with a large standard error. Estimates with relatively large standard errors are associated with less precision and reliability and should be interpreted with caution.

To generate standard errors around numbers and estimates from the NCVS, the Census Bureau produced generalized variance function (GVF) parameters for BJS. The GVFs take into account aspects of the NCVS complex sample design and represent the curve fitted to a selection of individual standard errors based on the Jackknife Repeated Replication technique. The GVF parameters were used to generate standard errors for each point estimate (e.g., counts, percentages, and rates).

BJS conducted tests to determine whether differences in estimated numbers, percentages, and rates in this report were statistically significant once sampling error was taken into account. Using statistical programs developed specifically for the NCVS, all comparisons in the text were tested for significance. The primary test procedure was the Student's t-statistic, which tests the difference between two sample estimates.

Differences described as higher, lower, or different passed a test at the 0.05 level of statistical significance (95 percent confidence level). Differences described as somewhat, slightly, or marginally different, or with some indication of difference, passed a test at the 0.10 level of statistical significance (90 percent confidence level). Caution is required when comparing estimates not explicitly discussed in this report.

Data users can use the estimates and the standard errors of the estimates provided in this report to generate a confidence interval around the estimate as a measure of the margin of error.

In this report, BJS also calculated a coefficient of variation (CV) for all estimates, representing the ratio of the standard error to the estimate. CVs provide a measure of reliability and a means for comparing the precision of estimates across measures with differing levels or metrics.

NCVS Measurement of Rape and Sexual Assault

Thee NCVS uses a two-stage measurement approach in the screening and classification of criminal victimization, including rape and sexual assault. In the first stage of screening, survey respondents are administered a series of "short-cue" screening questions designed to help respondents think about different experiences they may have had during the reference period (see NCVS-1 at https://www.bjs.gov/ content/pub/pdf/ncvs15_bsq.pdf).

This design improves respondent recall of events, particularly for incidents that may not immediately come to mind as crimes, such as those committed by family members and acquaintances. Respondents who answer affirmatively to any of the short-cue screening items are subsequently administered a crime incident report (CIR) designed to classify incidents into specific crime types (see NCVS-2 at https://www.bjs.gov/ content/pub/pdf/ncvs15_cir.pdf).

First stage of measurement. Two short-cue screening questions are specifically designed to target sexual violence:

1. Other than any incidents already mentioned, has anyone attacked or threatened you in any of these ways: (a) with any weapon, such as a gun or knife; (b) with anything like a baseball bat, frying pan, scissors, or stick; (c) by something thrown, such as a rock or bottle; (d) by grabbing, punching, or choking; (e) any rape, attempted rape, or other types of sexual attack; (f) any face-to-face threats; **or** (g) any attack or threat or use of force by anyone at all? Please mention it even if you are not certain it was a crime.

2. Incidents involving forced or unwanted sexual acts are often difficult to talk about. Other than any incidents already mentioned, have you been forced or coerced to engage in unwanted sexual activity by (a) someone you did not know; (b) a casual acquaintance; or (c) someone you knew well?

Respondents may screen into a CIR if they respond affirmatively to another short-cue screening question. For instance, a separate screening question cues respondents to think of attacks or threats that took place in specific locations, such as at home, work, or school. A respondent who recalled a sexual victimization that occurred at home, work, or school and answered affirmatively would be administered a CIR even if they did not respond affirmatively to the screening question targeting sexual violence.

Second stage of measurement. The CIR is used to collect information on the attributes of each incident. The key attributes of sexual violence that are used to classify a victimization as a rape or sexual assault are the type of attack and physical injury suffered. Victims are asked if "the offender hit you, knock[ed] you down, or actually attack[ed] you in any way"; if "the offender TR[IED] to attack you"; or if "the offender THREATEN[ED] you with harm in any way." The survey participant is classified as a victim of rape or sexual assault if he or she responds affirmatively to one of these three questions and then responds that the completed, attempted, or threatened attack was (a) rape; (b) attempted rape; (c) sexual assault; (d) verbal threat of rape; (e) verbal threat of sexual assault other than rape; (f) unwanted sexual contact with force (e.g., grabbing, fondling); or (g) unwanted sexual contact without force (e.g., grabbing, fondling).

Whether the victim selects one of these response options to describe the attack, he or she is also classified as a victim of rape or sexual assault if the injuries suffered as a result of the incident are described as: (a) rape; (b) attempted rape; or (c) sexual assault other than rape or attempted rape.

Coercion. Although the CIR does not ask respondents if psychological coercion was used, one screening question targeted to rape and sexual violence asks respondents if force or coercion was used to initiate unwanted sexual activity.

The final classification of incidents by the CIR results in the following definitions of rape and sexual assault used in the NCVS:

Rape. Coerced or forced sexual intercourse. Forced sexual intercourse means vaginal, anal, or oral penetration by the offender(s). This category could include incidents where the penetration was from a foreign object such as a bottle. Includes attempted rapes, male and female victims, and both heterosexual and same-sex rape. Attempted rape includes verbal threats of rape.

Sexual assault. A wide range of victimizations, separate from rape or attempted rape. These crimes include attacks or attempted attacks generally involving unwanted sexual contact between victim and offender. Sexual assaults may or may not involve force and include such things as grabbing or fondling. Sexual assault also includes verbal threats.

Comparison of NCVS Estimates to Other Survey Estimates

During the past several decades, a number of other surveys have also been used to study rape and sexual assault in the general population. BJS estimates of rape and sexual assault from the NCVS have typically been lower than estimates derived from other federal and private surveys. However, the NCVS methodology and definitions of rape and sexual assault differ from many of these surveys in important ways that contribute to the variation in estimates of the prevalence and incidence of these victimizations. Additional information about differences in self-report estimates of rape and sexual assault is available on the BJS website. BJS continues an active research program on the collection of rape and sexual assault data in an effort to improve the quality and accuracy of these estimates.

Despite the current differences in methods and estimates that exist between the NCVS and other surveys measuring rape and sexual assault, a strength of the NCVS is its capacity to be used to make comparisons between population subgroups and over time. Methodological differences that exist between the NCVS and the other surveys should not impact NCVS comparisons between groups or in trends over time.

PART 6

Hate Crime Statistics, 2016

HIGHLIGHTS

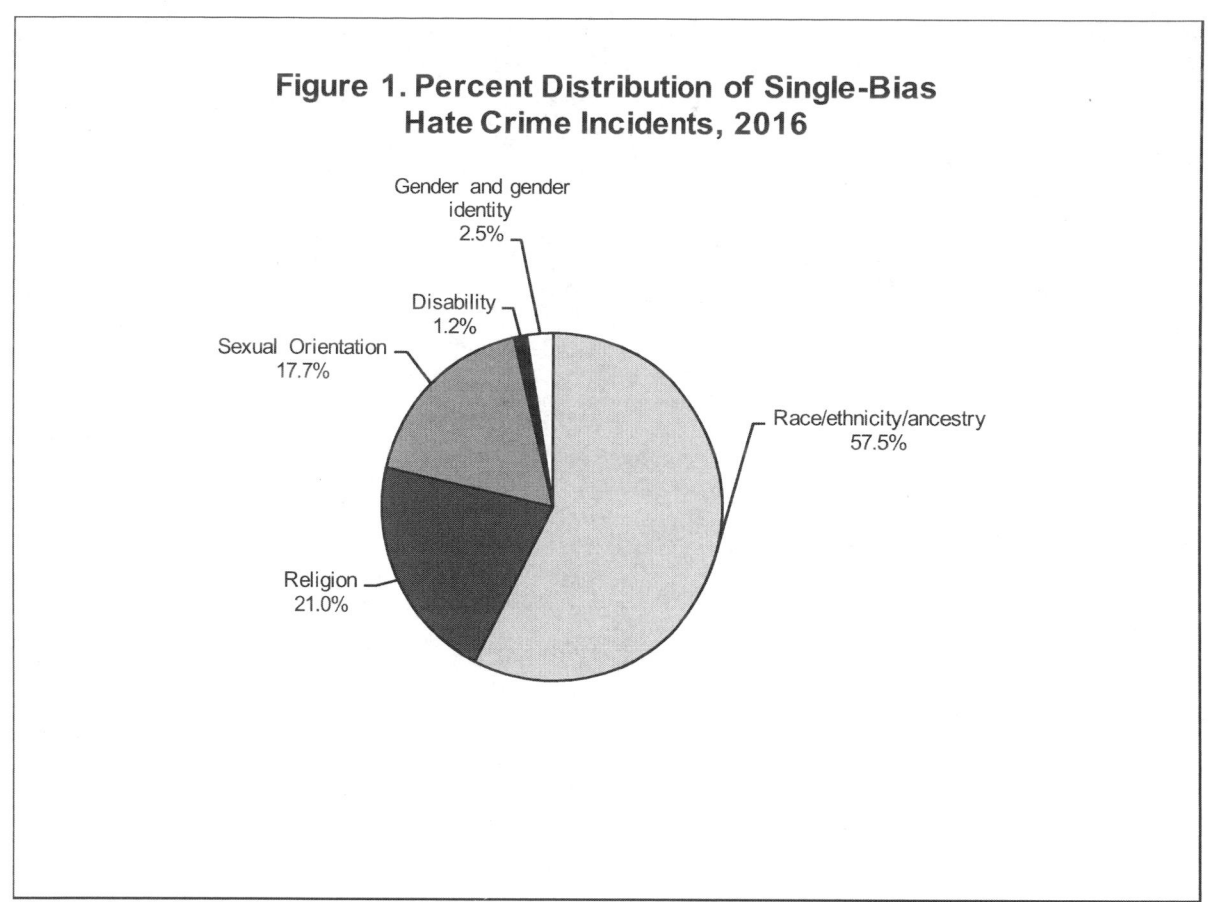

Figure 1. Percent Distribution of Single-Bias Hate Crime Incidents, 2016

Gender and gender identity
2.5%

Disability
1.2%

Sexual Orientation
17.7%

Race/ethnicity/ancestry
57.5%

Religion
21.0%

- In 2016, 15,254 law enforcement agencies participated in the Hate Crime Statistics Program. Of these agencies, 1,776 reported 6,121 hate crime incidents involving 7,321 offenses.

- There were 6,063 single-bias incidents that involved 7,227 offenses, 7,509 victims, and 5,727 known offenders. Among the 6,063 incidents, approximately 57.5 percent were racially/ethnically/ancestrally motivated, 17.7 percent resulted from sexual-orientation bias, 21.0 percent were motivated by religious bias, 2.0 percent were motivated by gender-identity bias, 1.2 percent were prompted by disability bias, and 0.5 percent (31 offenses) resulted from gender bias.

- The 58 multiple-bias incidents reported in 2015 involved 94 offenses, 106 victims, and 43 known offenders.

- The majority of the 2,519 hate crime offenses that were crimes against property (75.9 percent) were acts of destruction/damage/vandalism; the remaining crimes against property (24.1 percent) consisted of robbery, burglary, larceny-theft, motor vehicle theft, arson, and other crimes.

- There were 82 offenses defined as crimes against society (e.g., drug or narcotic offenses or prostitution).

Table 1. Incidents, Offenses, Victims, and Known Offenders, by Bias Motivation, 2016

(Number.)

Bias motivation	Incidents	Offenses	Victims[1]	Known offenders[2]
Total	6,121	7,321	7,615	5,770
Single-Bias Incidents	6,063	7,227	7,509	5,727
Race/Ethnicity/Ancestry	3,489	4,229	4,426	3,383
Anti-White	720	876	909	831
Anti-Black or African American................	1,739	2,122	2,220	1,588
Anti-American Indian or Alaska Native......	154	161	169	118
Anti-Asian	113	131	137	123
Anti-Native Hawaiian or Other Pacific Islander	9	9	9	8
Anti-Multiple Races, Group	136	178	190	104
Anti-Arab	51	56	57	60
Anti-Hispanic or Latino	344	449	483	380
Anti-Other Race/Ethnicity/Ancestry	223	247	252	171
Religion...	1,273	1,538	1,584	859
Anti-Jewish	684	834	862	421
Anti-Catholic...	62	63	65	45
Anti-Protestant..	15	20	22	12
Anti-Islamic (Muslim)...............................	307	381	388	243
Anti-Other Religion	74	90	91	53
Anti-Multiple Religions, Group	34	48	48	20
Anti-Mormon...	7	8	8	3
Anti-Jehovah's Witness............................	2	3	3	1
Anti-Eastern Orthodox (Russian, Greek, Other)	28	28	30	23
Anti-Other Christian	36	37	39	13
Anti-Buddhist...	1	1	1	0
Anti-Hindu	10	12	12	11
Anti-Sikh	7	7	8	10
Anti-Atheism/Agnosticism/etc..................	6	6	7	4
Sexual Orientation.................................	1,076	1,218	1,255	1,225
Anti-Gay (Male)..	675	765	787	806
Anti-Lesbian...	124	141	147	127
Anti-Lesbian, Gay, Bisexual, or Transgender (Mixed Group)	234	262	271	254
Anti-Heterosexual....................................	20	23	23	13
Anti-Bisexual	23	27	27	25
Disability..	70	76	77	67
Anti-Physical...	26	29	30	29
Anti-Mental...	44	47	47	38
Gender	31	36	36	28
Anti-Male...	7	10	10	7
Anti-Female...	24	26	26	21
Gender Identity	124	130	131	165
Anti-Transgender.....................................	105	111	111	149
Anti-Gender Non-Conforming.................	19	19	20	16
Multiple-Bias Incidents[3]	58	94	106	43

[1] The term *victim* may refer to an individual, business/financial institution, government entity, religious organization, or society/public as a whole.
[2] The term known offender does not imply that the identity of the suspect is known, but only that an attribute of the suspect has been identified, which distinguishes him/her from an unknown offender.
[3] A multiple-bias incident is an incident in which one or more offense types are motivated by two or more biases.

Table 2. Incidents, Offenses, Victims, and Known Offenders, by Offense Type, 2016

(Number.)

Offense type	Incidents[1]	Offenses	Victims[2]	Known offenders[3]
Total	6,121	7,321	7,615	5,770
Crimes against persons...........................	3,765	4,720	4,720	4,353
Murder and nonnegligent manslaughter	5	9	9	9
Rape (revised definition)[4]............................	24	24	24	29
Rape (legacy definition)[5]............................	0	0	0	0
Aggravated assault	684	873	873	1,031
Simple assault...	1,458	1,687	1,687	1,857
Intimidation..	1,577	2,109	2,109	1,409
Other[6]..	17	18	18	18
Crimes against property	2,519	2,519	2,813	1,618
Robbery..	134	134	163	249
Burglary..	123	123	138	87
Larceny-theft...	231	231	253	173
Motor vehicle theft	20	20	21	14
Arson..	39	39	51	33
Destruction/damage/vandalism	1,913	1,913	2,122	1,015
Other[6]..	59	59	65	47
Crimes against society[6]..........................	82	82	82	97

[1]The actual number of incidents is 6,121. However, the column figures will not add to the total because incidents may include more than one offense type, and these are counted in each appropriate offense type category.
[2]The term victim may refer to a person, business, institution, or society as a whole.
[3]The term known offender does not imply that the identity of the suspect is known, but only that an attribute of the suspect has been identified, which distinguishes him/her from an unknown offender. The actual number of known offenders is 5,770. However, the column figures will not add to the total because some offenders are responsible for more than one offense type, and are, therefore, counted more than once in this table.
[4]The figures shown in this row for the offense of rape include only those reported by law enforcement agencies that used the revised Uniform Crime Reporting (UCR) definition of rape.
[5]The figures shown in this row for the offense of rape include only those reported by law enforcement agencies that used the legacy UCR definition of rape.
[6]Includes additional offenses collected in the National Incident-Based Reporting System.

Table 3. Offenses, Known Offender's Race and Ethnicity, by Offense Type, 2016

(Number.)

Bias motivation	Total offenses	Known offender's race							Known offender's ethnicity[1]				Unknown offender
		White	Black or African American	American Indian or Alaska Native	Asian	Native Hawaiian or Other Pacific Islander	Group of multiple races	Unknown race	Hispanic or Latino	Not Hispanic or Latino	Group of multiple ethnicities	Unknown ethnicity	
Total	7,321	2,680	1,331	49	45	7	245	1,010	254	1,026	38	2,504	1,954
Crimes against persons	4,720	2,197	1,117	35	35	4	199	505	214	856	28	1,880	628
Murder and nonnegligent manslaughter............................	9	4	5	0	0	0	0	0	0	1	0	3	0
Rape (revised definition)[2]	24	9	6	2	0	0	0	3	2	2	1	14	4
Rape (legacy definition)[3].................	0	0	0	0	0	0	0	0	0	0	0	0	0
Aggravated assault.......................	873	395	268	9	7	1	63	56	69	179	9	313	74
Simple assault	1,687	764	513	17	9	3	93	184	90	377	14	654	104
Intimidation.................................	2,109	1,015	322	7	19	0	43	262	52	288	4	893	441
Other[4]...	18	10	3	0	0	0	0	0	1	9	0	3	5
Crimes against property	2,519	429	194	12	9	3	45	504	40	153	8	564	1,323
Robbery	134	25	67	3	0	0	13	11	10	30	1	47	15
Burglary	123	33	11	1	1	0	3	18	2	12	2	35	56
Larceny-theft...............................	231	69	33	1	1	0	2	33	1	21	1	101	92
Motor vehicle theft.......................	20	3	3	0	0	0	1	4	0	0	0	11	9
Arson...	39	13	5	0	0	0	2	4	3	3	1	7	15
Destruction/damage/vandalism.......	1,913	267	69	7	7	3	24	422	23	85	3	329	1,114
Other[4]...	59	19	6	0	0	0	0	12	1	2	0	34	22
Crimes against society[4]	82	54	20	2	1	0	1	1	0	17	2	60	3

[1]The sum of offenses by the known offender's ethnicity does not equal the sum of offenses by the known offender's race because not all law enforcement agencies that report offender race data also report offender ethnicity data.
[2]The figures shown in the rape (revised definition) row include only those reported by law enforcement agencies that used the revised Uniform Crime Reporting (UCR) definition of rape.
[3]The figures shown in the rape (legacy definition) row include only those reported by law enforcement agencies that used the legacy UCR definition of rape.
[4]Includes additional offenses collected in the National Incident-Based Reporting System.

Table 4. Offenses, Offense Type, by Bias Motivation, 2016

(Number.)

Bias motivation	Total offenses	Crimes against persons						
		Murder and nonnegligent manslaughter	Rape (revised definition)[1]	Rape (legacy definition)[2]	Aggravated assault	Simple assault	Intimidation	Other[3]
Total	7,321	9	24	0	873	1,687	2,109	18
Single-Bias Incidents..	7,227	9	23	0	866	1,677	2,074	17
Race/Ethnicity/Ancestry	4,229	7	10	0	548	1,002	1,320	5
Anti-White..	876	5	5	0	120	241	188	2
Anti-Black or African American...........................	2,122	2	2	0	273	455	782	2
Anti-American Indian or Alaska Native..............	161	0	1	0	8	17	36	0
Anti-Asian..	131	0	0	0	15	40	45	0
Anti-Native Hawaiian or Other Pacific Islander ...	9	0	0	0	0	4	3	0
Anti-Multiple Races, Group	178	0	0	0	17	36	49	0
Anti-Arab..	56	0	0	0	8	16	17	0
Anti-Hispanic or Latino.....................................	449	0	1	0	91	129	140	1
Anti-Other Race/Ethnicity/Ancestry	247	0	1	0	16	64	60	0
Religion..	1,538	0	1	0	85	168	433	1
Anti-Jewish..	834	0	0	0	12	61	238	0
Anti-Catholic..	63	0	0	0	1	5	6	0
Anti-Protestant...	20	0	0	0	1	3	1	0
Anti-Islamic (Muslim)...	381	0	0	0	52	75	144	0
Anti-Other Religion...	90	0	0	0	13	10	8	0
Anti-Multiple Religions, Group	48	0	0	0	2	4	21	0
Anti-Mormon..	8	0	0	0	0	0	2	0
Anti-Jehovah's Witness.......................................	3	0	0	0	0	0	2	0
Anti-Eastern Orthodox (Russian, Greek, Other)..	28	0	0	0	1	4	2	1
Anti-Other Christian...	37	0	0	0	1	3	2	0
Anti-Buddhist...	1	0	0	0	0	0	0	0
Anti-Hindu..	12	0	0	0	1	2	6	0
Anti-Sikh..	7	0	0	0	1	1	1	0
Anti-Atheism/Agnosticism/etc............................	6	0	1	0	0	0	0	0
Sexual Orientation..	1,218	1	9	0	197	414	289	4
Anti-Gay (Male)..	765	1	1	0	126	281	183	3
Anti-Lesbian...	141	0	4	0	23	46	37	0
Anti-Lesbian, Gay, Bisexual, or Transgender (Mixed Group)...................	262	0	4	0	45	71	59	1
Anti-Heterosexual..	23	0	0	0	1	2	7	0
Anti-Bisexual	27	0	0	0	2	14	3	0
Disability..	76	0	2	0	5	33	9	2
Anti-Physical...	29	0	0	0	2	15	4	1
Anti-Mental..	47	0	2	0	3	18	5	1
Gender	36	1	0	0	6	11	7	0
Anti-Male..	10	1	0	0	0	7	1	0
Anti-Female..	26	0	0	0	6	4	6	0
Gender Identity...	130	0	1	0	25	49	16	5
Anti-Transgender..	111	0	1	0	24	47	14	5
Anti-Gender Non-Conforming............................	19	0	0	0	1	2	2	0
Multiple-Bias Incidents[4]	94	0	1	0	7	10	35	1

[1] The figures shown in this column for the offense of rape include only those reported by law enforcement agencies that used the revised Uniform Crime Reporting (UCR) definition of rape.
[2] The figures shown in this column for the offense of rape include only those reported by law enforcement agencies that used the legacy UCR definition of rape.
[3] Includes additional offenses collected in the National Incident-Based Reporting System.
[4] A multiple-bias incident is an incident in which one or more offense types are motivated by two or more biases.

Table 4. Offenses, Offense Type, by Bias Motivation, 2016—*Continued*

(Number.)

Bias motivation	Total offenses	Crimes against property							Crimes against society[3]
		Robbery	Burglary	Larceny-theft	Motor vehicle theft	Arson	Destruction/ damage/ vandalism	Other[3]	
Total	7,321	134	123	231	20	39	1,913	59	82
Single-Bias Incidents	7,227	131	122	227	20	38	1,882	59	82
Race/Ethnicity/Ancestry	4,229	71	75	149	14	13	916	46	53
Anti-White	876	30	22	78	6	2	122	24	31
Anti-Black or African American	2,122	14	17	14	2	7	537	5	10
Anti-American Indian or Alaska Native	161	0	18	31	4	0	29	12	5
Anti-Asian	131	2	4	5	0	0	18	0	2
Anti-Native Hawaiian or Other Pacific Islander	9	0	0	0	0	0	2	0	0
Anti-Multiple Races, Group	178	4	5	0	1	2	62	2	0
Anti-Arab	56	1	0	0	0	1	13	0	0
Anti-Hispanic or Latino	449	19	2	5	0	0	57	0	4
Anti-Other Race/Ethnicity/Ancestry	247	1	7	16	1	1	76	3	1
Religion	1,538	10	29	47	4	18	720	6	16
Anti-Jewish	834	3	9	15	1	4	489	1	1
Anti-Catholic	63	0	3	10	1	1	31	1	4
Anti-Protestant	20	0	1	4	0	1	8	0	1
Anti-Islamic (Muslim)	381	4	2	3	0	5	92	0	4
Anti-Other Religion	90	1	6	1	0	0	49	1	1
Anti-Multiple Religions, Group	48	1	1	1	1	2	15	0	0
Anti-Mormon	8	0	0	1	0	1	2	0	2
Anti-Jehovah's Witness	3	0	0	1	0	0	0	0	0
Anti-Eastern Orthodox (Russian, Greek, Other)	28	0	3	8	1	0	5	1	2
Anti-Other Christian	37	1	3	2	0	3	22	0	0
Anti-Buddhist	1	0	0	0	0	0	1	0	0
Anti-Hindu	12	0	0	0	0	0	2	0	1
Anti-Sikh	7	0	1	0	0	0	2	1	0
Anti-Atheism/Agnosticism/etc.	6	0	0	1	0	1	2	1	0
Sexual Orientation	1,218	38	10	17	2	6	221	4	6
Anti-Gay (Male)	765	28	6	6	0	1	126	0	3
Anti-Lesbian	141	0	2	3	0	2	23	1	0
Anti-Lesbian, Gay, Bisexual, or Transgender (Mixed Group)	262	10	1	1	1	3	64	1	1
Anti-Heterosexual	23	0	0	5	0	0	6	0	2
Anti-Bisexual	27	0	1	2	1	0	2	2	0
Disability	76	1	3	8	0	0	6	2	5
Anti-Physical	29	0	2	2	0	0	1	1	1
Anti-Mental	47	1	1	6	0	0	5	1	4
Gender	36	0	3	0	0	0	7	1	0
Anti-Male	10	0	1	0	0	0	0	0	0
Anti-Female	26	0	2	0	0	0	7	1	0
Gender Identity	130	11	2	6	0	1	12	0	2
Anti-Transgender	111	11	1	2	0	1	5	0	0
Anti-Gender Non-Conforming	19	0	1	4	0	0	7	0	2
Multiple-Bias Incidents[4]	94	3	1	4	0	1	31	0	0

[1] The figures shown in this column for the offense of rape include only those reported by law enforcement agencies that used the revised Uniform Crime Reporting (UCR) definition of rape.
[2] The figures shown in this column for the offense of rape include only those reported by law enforcement agencies that used the legacy UCR definition of rape.
[3] Includes additional offenses collected in the National Incident-Based Reporting System.
[4] A multiple-bias incident is an incident in which one or more offense types are motivated by two or more biases.

Table 5. Offenses, Known Offender's Race, by Bias Motivation, 2016

(Number.)

Bias motivation	Total offenses	Known offender's race						
		White	Black or African American	American Indian or Alaska Native	Asian	Native Hawaiian or Other Pacific Islander	Group of multiple races	Unknown race
Total	7,321	2,680	1,331	49	45	7	245	1,010
Single-Bias Incidents	7,227	2,661	1,307	49	45	7	242	993
Race/Ethnicity/Ancestry	4,229	1,775	781	37	32	2	150	398
Anti-White	876	133	452	20	6	0	27	80
Anti-Black or African American	2,122	1,142	80	9	17	1	88	202
Anti-American Indian or Alaska Native	161	56	28	2	0	0	3	14
Anti-Asian	131	65	20	2	6	0	5	9
Anti-Native Hawaiian or Other Pacific Islander	9	4	4	0	0	0	0	0
Anti-Multiple Races, Group	178	54	33	0	1	0	9	17
Anti-Arab	56	32	6	0	1	0	3	6
Anti-Hispanic or Latino	449	228	114	2	0	1	12	24
Anti-Other Race/Ethnicity/Ancestry	247	61	44	2	1	0	3	46
Religion	1,538	389	118	5	5	2	32	410
Anti-Jewish	834	156	34	4	0	0	12	300
Anti-Catholic	63	9	3	0	2	0	3	22
Anti-Protestant	20	11	2	0	0	0	0	3
Anti-Islamic (Muslim)	381	135	49	1	2	0	9	66
Anti-Other Religion	90	20	20	0	1	2	1	7
Anti-Multiple Religions, Group	48	20	1	0	0	0	4	4
Anti-Mormon	8	2	2	0	0	0	0	0
Anti-Jehovah's Witness	3	2	0	0	0	0	0	0
Anti-Eastern Orthodox (Russian, Greek, Other)	28	15	3	0	0	0	0	1
Anti-Other Christian	37	4	2	0	0	0	1	6
Anti-Buddhist	1	0	0	0	0	0	0	0
Anti-Hindu	12	9	0	0	0	0	1	0
Anti-Sikh	7	4	1	0	0	0	1	1
Anti-Atheism/Agnosticism/etc.	6	2	1	0	0	0	0	0
Sexual Orientation	1,218	414	326	6	6	3	49	156
Anti-Gay (Male)	765	257	223	2	1	2	33	102
Anti-Lesbian	141	51	37	0	0	0	3	14
Anti-Lesbian, Gay, Bisexual, or Transgender (Mixed Group)	262	86	53	4	3	1	12	37
Anti-Heterosexual	23	12	1	0	2	0	1	0
Anti-Bisexual	27	8	12	0	0	0	0	3
Disability	76	35	16	1	1	0	1	6
Anti-Physical	29	14	8	0	1	0	1	2
Anti-Mental	47	21	8	1	0	0	0	4
Gender	36	18	9	0	0	0	1	4
Anti-Male	10	10	0	0	0	0	0	0
Anti-Female	26	8	9	0	0	0	1	4
Gender Identity	130	30	57	0	1	0	9	19
Anti-Transgender	111	27	54	0	0	0	9	14
Anti-Gender Non-Conforming	19	3	3	0	1	0	0	5
Multiple-Bias Incidents[2]	94	19	24	0	0	0	3	17

[1] The total number of offenses by the known offender's ethnicity do not equal the total number of offenses by the known offender's race because not all law enforcement agencies that report offender race data also report offender ethnicity data.

[2] A multiple-bias incident is an incident in which one or more offense types are motivated by two or more biases.

Table 5. Offenses, Known Offender's Race, by Bias Motivation, 2016—*Continued*

(Number.)

Bias motivation	Total offenses	Known offender's ethnicity[1]				Unknown offender
		Hispanic or Latino	Not Hispanic or Latino	Group of multiple ethnicities	Unknown ethnicity	
Total	7,321	254	1,026	38	2,504	1,954
Single-Bias Incidents	7,227	252	998	38	2,476	1,923
Race/Ethnicity/Ancestry	4,229	135	662	22	1,618	1,054
Anti-White	876	22	169	9	393	158
Anti-Black or African American..........................	2,122	82	267	5	808	583
Anti-American Indian or Alaska Native................	161	1	3	0	92	58
Anti-Asian...	131	6	28	3	40	24
Anti-Native Hawaiian or Other Pacific Islander	9	0	1	0	3	1
Anti-Multiple Races, Group	178	2	31	1	50	64
Anti-Arab	56	4	16	0	14	8
Anti-Hispanic or Latino	449	15	112	2	150	68
Anti-Other Race/Ethnicity/Ancestry	247	3	35	2	68	90
Religion..	1,538	23	100	9	364	577
Anti-Jewish	834	9	16	4	152	328
Anti-Catholic...	63	4	3	0	14	24
Anti-Protestant..	20	0	8	0	6	4
Anti-Islamic (Muslim).......................................	381	5	40	2	121	119
Anti-Other Religion	90	2	16	2	18	39
Anti-Multiple Religions, Group	48	0	4	0	21	19
Anti-Mormon...	8	0	4	0	0	4
Anti-Jehovah's Witness	3	0	0	0	0	1
Anti-Eastern Orthodox (Russian, Greek, Other)	28	0	4	0	15	9
Anti-Other Christian..	37	3	1	0	5	24
Anti-Buddhist..	1	0	0	0	0	1
Anti-Hindu..	12	0	2	0	5	2
Anti-Sikh..	7	0	2	1	4	0
Anti-Atheism/Agnosticism/etc...........................	6	0	0	0	3	3
Sexual Orientation..	1,218	80	177	7	406	258
Anti-Gay (Male)..	765	63	126	6	209	145
Anti-Lesbian..	141	6	24	0	34	36
Anti-Lesbian, Gay, Bisexual, or Transgender (Mixed Group)	262	10	20	1	140	66
Anti-Heterosexual...	23	1	1	0	9	7
Anti-Bisexual...	27	0	6	0	14	4
Disability	76	2	14	0	39	16
Anti-Physical..	29	0	7	0	14	3
Anti-Mental...	47	2	7	0	25	13
Gender	36	0	8	0	17	4
Anti-Male..	10	0	2	0	8	0
Anti-Female...	26	0	6	0	9	4
Gender Identity	130	12	37	0	32	14
Anti-Transgender..	111	12	33	0	30	7
Anti-Gender Non-Conforming............................	19	0	4	0	2	7
Multiple-Bias Incidents[2]	94	2	28	0	28	31

[1]The total number of offenses by the known offender's ethnicity do not equal the total number of offenses by the known offender's race because not all law enforcement agencies that report offender race data also report offender ethnicity data.

[2]A multiple-bias incident is an incident in which one or more offense types are motivated by two or more biases.

Table 6. Offenses, Victim Type, by Offense Type, 2016

(Number.)

Offense type	Total offenses	Victim type					
		Individual	Business/ financial institution	Government	Religious organization	Society/ public[1]	Other/ unknown/ multiple
Total	7,321	5,954	406	224	160	82	495
Crimes against persons[2]	4,720	4,720	NA	NA	NA	NA	NA
Crimes against property	2,519	1,234	406	224	160	0	495
Robbery	134	121	0	0	0	0	13
Burglary	123	79	18	1	10	0	15
Larceny-theft	231	148	61	4	6	0	12
Motor vehicle theft	20	18	2	0	0	0	0
Arson	39	18	3	2	10	0	6
Destruction/damage/vandalism	1,913	809	311	213	134	0	446
Other[2]	59	41	11	4	0	0	3
Crimes against society[2]	82	NA	NA	NA	NA	82	NA

NA = Not available.
[1]The victim type society/public is collected only in the National Incident-Based Reporting System (NIBRS).
[2]Includes additional offenses collected in the NIBRS.

Table 7. Victims, Offense Type, by Bias Motivation, 2016

(Number.)

Bias motivation	Total victims[1]	Total number of adult victims[2]	Total number of juvenile victims[2]	Crimes against persons						
				Murder and nonnegligent manslaughter	Rape (revised definition)[3]	Rape (legacy definition)[4]	Aggravated assault	Simple assault	Intimidation	Other[5]
Total	7,615	4,311	565	9	24	0	873	1,687	2,109	18
Single-Bias Incidents	7,509	4,254	558	9	23	0	866	1,677	2,074	17
Race/Ethnicity/Ancestry	4,426	2,685	384	7	10	0	548	1,002	1,320	5
Anti-White	909	586	41	5	5	0	120	241	188	2
Anti-Black or African American	2,220	1,297	261	2	2	0	273	455	782	2
Anti-American Indian or Alaska Native	169	120	6	0	1	0	8	17	36	0
Anti-Asian	137	83	5	0	0	0	15	40	45	0
Anti-Native Hawaiian or Other Pacific Islander	9	9	0	0	0	0	0	4	3	0
Anti-Multiple Races, Group	190	99	12	0	0	0	17	36	49	0
Anti-Arab	57	45	0	0	0	0	8	16	17	0
Anti-Hispanic or Latino	483	302	46	0	1	0	91	129	140	1
Anti-Other Race/Ethnicity/Ancestry	252	144	13	0	1	0	16	64	60	0
Religion	1,584	587	91	0	1	0	85	168	433	1
Anti-Jewish	862	264	60	0	0	0	12	61	238	0
Anti-Catholic	65	15	2	0	0	0	1	5	6	0
Anti-Protestant	22	9	0	0	0	0	1	3	1	0
Anti-Islamic (Muslim)	388	200	17	0	0	0	52	75	144	0
Anti-Other Religion	91	29	3	0	0	0	13	10	8	0
Anti-Multiple Religions, Group	48	26	4	0	0	0	2	4	21	0
Anti-Mormon	8	4	1	0	0	0	0	0	2	0
Anti-Jehovah's Witness	3	1	0	0	0	0	0	0	2	0
Anti-Eastern Orthodox (Russian, Greek, Other)	30	15	2	0	0	0	1	4	2	1
Anti-Other Christian	39	10	0	0	0	0	1	3	2	0
Anti-Buddhist	1	0	0	0	0	0	0	0	0	0
Anti-Hindu	12	4	2	0	0	0	1	2	6	0
Anti-Sikh	8	5	0	0	0	0	1	1	1	0
Anti-Atheism/Agnosticism/etc.	7	5	0	0	1	0	0	0	0	0
Sexual Orientation	1,255	819	65	1	9	0	197	414	289	4
Anti-Gay (Male)	787	508	36	1	1	0	126	281	183	3
Anti-Lesbian	147	87	7	0	4	0	23	46	37	0
Anti-Lesbian, Gay, Bisexual, or Transgender (Mixed Group)	271	192	18	0	4	0	45	71	59	1
Anti-Heterosexual	23	16	0	0	0	0	1	2	7	0
Anti-Bisexual	27	16	4	0	0	0	2	14	3	0
Disability	77	58	8	0	2	0	5	33	9	2
Anti-Physical	30	24	0	0	0	0	2	15	4	1
Anti-Mental	47	34	8	0	2	0	3	18	5	1
Gender	36	24	3	1	0	0	6	11	7	0
Anti-Male	10	7	3	1	0	0	0	7	1	0
Anti-Female	26	17	0	0	0	0	6	4	6	0
Gender Identity	131	81	7	0	1	0	25	49	16	5
Anti-Transgender	111	75	6	0	1	0	24	47	14	5
Anti-Gender Non-Conforming	20	6	1	0	0	0	1	2	2	0
Multiple-Bias Incidents[6]	106	57	7	0	1	0	7	10	35	1

Note: The aggregate of adult and juvenile individual victims does not equal the total number of victims because total victims include individuals, businesses, institutions, and society as a whole. In addition, the aggregate of adult and juvenile individual victims does not equal the aggregate of victims of crimes against persons because not all law enforcement agencies report the ages of individual victims.

[1] A victim can be an individual, a business, an institution, or society as a whole.
[2] The figures shown in this column are individual victims only.
[3] The figures shown in this column for the offense of rape include only those reported by law enforcement agencies that used the revised Uniform Crime Reporting (UCR) definition of rape.
[4] The figures shown in this column for the offense of rape include only those reported by law enforcement agencies that used the legacy UCR definition of rape.
[5] Includes additional offenses collected in the National Incident-Based Reporting System.
[6] A multiple-bias incident is an incident in which one or more offense types are motivated by two or more biases.

Table 7. Victims, Offense Type, by Bias Motivation, 2016—*Continued*

(Number.)

Bias motivation	Crimes against property							Crimes against society[5]
	Robbery	Burglary	Larceny-theft	Motor vehicle theft	Arson	Destruction/ damage/ vandalism	Other[5]	
Total	163	138	253	21	51	2,122	65	82
Single-Bias Incidents	160	135	249	21	49	2,082	65	82
Race/Ethnicity/Ancestry	92	83	164	15	24	1,051	52	53
Anti-White	39	25	87	6	4	129	27	31
Anti-Black or African American	16	17	16	3	13	624	5	10
Anti-American Indian or Alaska Native	0	20	34	4	0	29	15	5
Anti-Asian	2	6	5	0	0	22	0	2
Anti-Native Hawaiian or Other Pacific Islander	0	0	0	0	0	2	0	0
Anti-Multiple Races, Group	5	5	0	1	5	70	2	0
Anti-Arab	1	0	0	0	1	14	0	0
Anti-Hispanic or Latino	28	2	5	0	0	82	0	4
Anti-Other Race/Ethnicity/Ancestry	1	8	17	1	1	79	3	1
Religion	12	32	53	4	18	755	6	16
Anti-Jewish	3	10	18	1	4	513	1	1
Anti-Catholic	0	3	12	1	1	31	1	4
Anti-Protestant	0	1	4	0	1	10	0	1
Anti-Islamic (Muslim)	4	2	3	0	5	99	0	4
Anti-Other Religion	1	6	1	0	0	50	1	1
Anti-Multiple Religions, Group	1	1	1	1	2	15	0	0
Anti-Mormon	0	0	1	0	1	2	0	2
Anti-Jehovah's Witness	0	0	1	0	0	0	0	0
Anti-Eastern Orthodox (Russian, Greek, Other)	0	4	9	1	0	5	1	2
Anti-Other Christian	3	3	2	0	3	22	0	0
Anti-Buddhist	0	0	0	0	0	1	0	0
Anti-Hindu	0	0	0	0	0	2	0	1
Anti-Sikh	0	2	0	0	0	2	1	0
Anti-Atheism/Agnosticism/etc.	0	0	1	0	1	3	1	0
Sexual Orientation	44	10	18	2	6	251	4	6
Anti-Gay (Male)	32	6	7	0	1	143	0	3
Anti-Lesbian	0	2	3	0	2	29	1	0
Anti-Lesbian, Gay, Bisexual, or Transgender (Mixed Group)	12	1	1	1	3	71	1	1
Anti-Heterosexual	0	0	5	0	0	6	0	2
Anti-Bisexual	0	1	2	1	0	2	2	0
Disability	1	4	8	0	0	6	2	5
Anti-Physical	0	3	2	0	0	1	1	1
Anti-Mental	1	1	6	0	0	5	1	4
Gender	0	3	0	0	0	7	1	0
Anti-Male	0	1	0	0	0	0	0	0
Anti-Female	0	2	0	0	0	7	1	0
Gender Identity	11	3	6	0	1	12	0	2
Anti-Transgender	11	1	2	0	1	5	0	0
Anti-Gender Non-Conforming	0	2	4	0	0	7	0	2
Multiple-Bias Incidents[6]	3	3	4	0	2	40	0	0

Note: The aggregate of adult and juvenile individual victims does not equal the total number of victims because total victims include individuals, businesses, institutions, and society as a whole. In addition, the aggregate of adult and juvenile individual victims does not equal the aggregate of victims of crimes against persons because not all law enforcement agencies report the ages of individual victims.

[1] A victim can be an individual, a business, an institution, or society as a whole.
[2] The figures shown in this column are individual victims only.
[3] The figures shown in this column for the offense of rape include only those reported by law enforcement agencies that used the revised Uniform Crime Reporting (UCR) definition of rape.
[4] The figures shown in this column for the offense of rape include only those reported by law enforcement agencies that used the legacy UCR definition of rape.
[5] Includes additional offenses collected in the National Incident-Based Reporting System.
[6] A multiple-bias incident is an incident in which one or more offense types are motivated by two or more biases.

Table 8. Incidents, Victim Type, by Bias Motivation, 2016

(Number.)

Bias motivation	Total incidents	Victim type					
		Individual	Business/financial institution	Government	Religious organization	Society/public[1]	Other/unknown/multiple
Total	6,121	4,779	391	220	146	63	522
Single-Bias Incidents	6,063	4,740	385	214	145	63	516
Race/Ethnicity/Ancestry	3,489	2,906	211	131	21	37	183
Religion	1,273	641	144	66	118	14	290
Sexual Orientation	1,076	992	26	13	6	5	34
Disability	70	64	0	0	0	5	1
Gender	31	29	1	1	0	0	0
Gender Identity	124	108	3	3	0	2	8
Multiple-Bias Incidents[2]	58	39	6	6	1	0	6

[1]The victim type society/public is collected only in the National Incident-Based Reporting System.
[2]A multiple-bias incident is an incident in which one or more offense types are motivated by two or more biases.

Table 9. Known Offenders,[1] by Known Offender's Race, Ethnicity, and Age, 2016

(Number.)

Race/ethnicity/age	Total
Race	5,770
White	2,671
Black or African American	1,508
American Indian or Alaska Native	45
Asian	46
Native Hawaiian or Other Pacific Islander	7
Group of multiple races[2]	447
Unknown race	1,046
Ethnicity[3]	4,222
Hispanic or Latino	339
Not Hispanic or Latino	1,101
Group of multiple ethnicities[4]	97
Unknown ethnicity	2,685
Age[3]	4,100
Total known offenders 18 and over	3,435
Total known offenders under 18	664

[1]The term known offender does not imply that the identity of the suspect is known, but only that an attribute of the suspect has been identified, which distinguishes him/her from an unknown offender.
[2]The term group of multiple races is used to describe a group of offenders of varying races.
[3]The total number of known offenders by age and the total number of known offenders by ethnicity do not equal the total number of known offenders by race because not all law enforcement agencies report the age and/or ethnicity of the known offenders.
[4]The term group of multiple ethnicities is used to describe a group of offenders of varying ethnicities.

Table 10. Incidents, Bias Motivation, by Location, 2016

(Number.)

Location	Total incidents	Bias motivation						Multiple-bias incidents[1]
		Race	Religion	Sexual orientation	Disability	Gender	Gender Identity	
Total	6,121	3,489	1,273	1,076	70	31	124	58
Abandoned/condemned structure...............	5	2	3	0	0	0	0	0
Air/bus/train terminal	94	60	11	16	2	0	2	3
Amusement park	1	0	0	1	0	0	0	0
Arena/stadium/fairgrounds/coliseum	6	4	1	1	0	0	0	0
ATM separate from bank	1	1	0	0	0	0	0	0
Auto dealership new/used...........................	6	6	0	0	0	0	0	0
Bank/savings and loan................................	20	11	6	1	0	1	1	0
Bar/nightclub	96	49	3	43	0	0	0	1
Camp/campground......................................	3	2	0	1	0	0	0	0
Church/synagogue/temple/mosque..............	241	36	194	8	0	0	0	3
Commercial office building	117	63	29	20	1	0	3	1
Community center.......................................	11	5	4	2	0	0	0	0
Construction site...	19	12	7	0	0	0	0	0
Convenience store	88	57	16	11	0	1	3	0
Cyberspace...	4	3	0	1	0	0	0	0
Daycare facility...	2	2	0	0	0	0	0	0
Department/discount store..........................	72	45	11	13	2	0	1	0
Dock/wharf/freight/modal terminal	3	2	1	0	0	0	0	0
Drug store/doctor's office/hospital...............	64	49	11	2	2	0	0	0
Farm facility	0	0	0	0	0	0	0	0
Field/woods	31	19	7	2	0	0	3	0
Gambling facility/casino/race track	3	3	0	0	0	0	0	0
Government/public building........................	111	73	24	10	1	2	0	1
Grocery/supermarket	62	46	7	8	0	0	1	0
Highway/road/alley/street/sidewalk..............	1,128	718	117	241	7	1	35	9
Hotel/motel/etc.	44	32	3	8	0	0	1	0
Industrial site	12	10	1	1	0	0	0	0
Jail/prison/penitentiary/corrections facility.....	61	42	3	13	1	1	0	1
Lake/waterway/beach	6	2	0	4	0	0	0	0
Liquor store	15	12	2	1	0	0	0	0
Military installation.....................................	0	0	0	0	0	0	0	0
Park/playground...	98	66	13	12	2	1	2	2
Parking/drop lot/garage	351	222	50	68	3	0	5	3
Rental storage facility.................................	9	5	3	0	0	0	1	0
Residence/home..	1,670	1,008	249	327	32	11	24	19
Rest area..	4	3	0	1	0	0	0	0
Restaurant	143	92	14	29	3	2	3	0
School/college[2]	146	67	52	24	0	1	0	2
School—college/university..........................	210	107	61	36	1	0	5	0
School—elementary/secondary	248	155	48	29	6	1	2	7
Service/gas station	72	55	8	6	0	0	3	0
Shelter—mission/homeless..........................	16	10	2	2	0	0	2	0
Shopping mall..	8	6	2	0	0	0	0	0
Specialty store (TV, fur, etc.)	39	28	9	2	0	0	0	0
Other/unknown	777	297	301	132	7	8	27	5
Multiple locations	4	2	0	0	0	1	0	1

[1] A *multiple-bias incident* is an incident in which one or more offense types are motivated by two or more biases.
[2] The location designation *School/college* has been retained for agencies that have not updated their records management systems to include the new location designations of *School—college/university* and *School—elementary/secondary*, which allow for more specificity in reporting.

Table 11. Offenses, Offense Type, by Participating State, 2016

(Number.)

State	Total offenses	Crimes against persons						
		Murder and nonnegligent manslaughter	Rape (revised definition)[1]	Rape (legacy definition)[2]	Aggravated assault	Simple assault	Intimidation	Other[3]
Total	7,321	9	24	0	873	1,687	2,109	18
Alabama	17	0	0		0	2	11	0
Alaska	13	0	0		1	6	1	0
Arizona	291	0	0		41	65	112	0
Arkansas	15	0	0		1	5	2	0
California	1,142	0	1		191	240	308	0
Colorado	126	0	1		15	25	39	0
Connecticut	124	0	0		12	18	40	0
Delaware	19	0	0		1	7	5	1
District of Columbia	127	0	0		17	62	23	0
Florida	110	0	0		28	28	18	0
Georgia	46	0		0	6	16	12	0
Idaho	35	1	0		7	9	5	0
Illinois	122	0	1		23	32	31	0
Indiana	163	3	1	0	4	24	101	0
Iowa	21	0	0		4	2	8	0
Kansas	70	0	0		16	11	26	0
Kentucky	241	0	0		15	39	76	0
Louisiana	33	0	0		5	10	7	0
Maine	45	0	0		1	6	23	0
Maryland	40	0	0		11	11	0	0
Massachusetts	444	0	1		54	84	139	3
Michigan	459	0	3		62	96	179	2
Minnesota	165	0	0		28	52	47	0
Mississippi	10	0	0	0	0	3	0	0
Missouri	114	0	1		27	32	20	0
Montana	20	0	1		1	2	3	0
Nebraska	35	0	1	0	4	14	4	1
Nevada	49	0	1		13	18	3	0
New Hampshire	40	0	0		1	5	24	0
New Jersey	308	0	0		2	12	179	0
New Mexico	36	0	0	0	3	13	11	0
New York	598	0	1	0	61	209	0	0
North Carolina	208	0	0	0	27	47	70	0
North Dakota	8	0	0		1	4	3	0
Ohio	508	0	0	0	22	68	224	1
Oklahoma	35	0	2	0	2	7	15	0
Oregon	122	0	1	0	18	20	33	0
Pennsylvania	67	0	0		3	24	25	0
Rhode Island	13	0	0	0	0	4	0	0
South Carolina	23	0	0		4	5	4	0
South Dakota	21	0	0	0	1	9	2	0
Tennessee	190	0	0		18	62	44	1
Texas	224	5	0		42	57	53	5
Utah	72	0	2		2	22	2	1
Vermont	26	0	0		1	8	1	0
Virginia	150	0	2		10	52	31	0
Washington	482	0	2	0	52	111	133	3
West Virginia	48	0	2		10	16	2	0
Wisconsin	42	0	0	0	4	10	10	0
Wyoming	4	0	0		1	3	0	0
Guam	3	0	0		3	0	0	0

[1]The figures shown in this column for the offense of rape include only those reported by law enforcement agencies that used the revised Uniform Crime Reporting (UCR) definition of rape.
[2]The figures shown in this column for the offense of rape include only those reported by law enforcement agencies that used the legacy UCR definition of rape.
[3]Includes additional offenses collected in the National Incident-Based Reporting System.

(Number.)

State	Crimes against property							Crimes against society[3]
	Robbery	Burglary	Larceny-theft	Motor vehicle theft	Arson	Destruction/ damage/ vandalism	Other[3]	
Total	134	123	231	20	39	1,913	59	82
Alabama....................................	0	0	2	0	0	2	0	0
Alaska.......................................	1	0	0	0	1	3	0	0
Arizona.....................................	6	1	4	0	0	62	0	0
Arkansas...................................	0	1	1	0	1	3	0	1
California..................................	31	14	6	2	12	337	0	0
Colorado	4	1	1	0	1	39	0	0
Connecticut	1	1	7	0	0	39	1	5
Delaware	0	0	0	0	0	5	0	0
District of Columbia...................	6	0	2	0	0	17	0	0
Florida......................................	4	0	0	0	1	31	0	0
Georgia	1	1	0	0	0	10	0	0
Idaho..	0	0	0	0	0	13	0	0
Illinois......................................	1	0	1	0	1	32	0	0
Indiana.....................................	1	0	0	0	0	23	1	5
Iowa	0	0	0	0	1	5	0	1
Kansas......................................	0	2	4	0	0	9	2	0
Kentucky	4	11	20	4	2	61	7	2
Louisiana	0	2	3	0	0	4	0	2
Maine	0	0	1	0	0	14	0	0
Maryland	1	0	0	0	0	17	0	0
Massachusetts...........................	2	4	14	0	3	136	2	2
Michigan	2	6	10	1	1	75	6	16
Minnesota	4	0	1	0	1	32	0	0
Mississippi.................................	0	2	2	0	0	3	0	0
Missouri....................................	7	2	1	2	1	20	0	1
Montana....................................	0	2	4	1	0	4	1	1
Nebraska...................................	1	0	0	0	0	8	0	2
Nevada......................................	3	1	0	1	0	9	0	0
New Hampshire	0	0	0	0	0	10	0	0
New Jersey.................................	3	2	2	0	0	108	0	0
New Mexico................................	1	2	0	0	0	6	0	0
New York...................................	9	11	11	0	7	289	0	0
North Carolina	5	3	5	0	1	50	0	0
North Dakota	0	0	0	0	0	0	0	0
Ohio...	6	22	58	5	0	84	15	3
Oklahoma..................................	2	0	0	0	1	5	1	0
Oregon	1	2	1	0	0	43	1	2
Pennsylvania..............................	0	1	2	0	2	10	0	0
Rhode Island..............................	1	0	0	0	0	7	0	1
South Carolina...........................	0	0	2	0	0	8	0	0
South Dakota.............................	0	1	1	0	0	3	0	4
Tennessee	2	3	9	0	0	35	2	14
Texas..	9	3	8	0	0	42	0	0
Utah	1	3	6	0	0	18	2	13
Vermont	0	1	4	0	0	11	0	0
Virginia.....................................	2	1	4	0	1	42	4	1
Washington................................	11	13	22	4	1	113	12	5
West Virginia..............................	1	2	9	0	0	3	2	1
Wisconsin..................................	0	2	3	0	0	13	0	0
Wyoming...................................	0	0	0	0	0	0	0	0
Guam..	0	0	0	0	0	0	0	0

[1]The figures shown in this column for the offense of rape include only those reported by law enforcement agencies that used the revised Uniform Crime Reporting (UCR) definition of rape.
[2]The figures shown in this column for the offense of rape include only those reported by law enforcement agencies that used the legacy UCR definition of rape.
[3]Includes additional offenses collected in the National Incident-Based Reporting System.

Table 12. Agency Hate Crime Reporting, by Participating State and Territory, 2016

(Number.)

State	Number of participating agencies	Population covered	Agencies submitting incident reports	Total number of incidents reported
Total	15,254	289,814,003	1,776	6,121
Alabama	28	1,013,839	4	14
Alaska..	32	738,566	3	11
Arizona..	85	6,361,910	18	213
Arkansas..	288	2,853,645	5	12
California...	733	39,242,633	213	931
Colorado	229	5,519,770	37	104
Connecticut...	106	3,576,452	42	106
Delaware	63	952,065	8	15
District of Columbia	2	681,170	2	115
Florida	46	8,988,095	44	96
Georgia	493	8,216,137	6	39
Idaho...	111	1,683,140	14	27
Illinois...	738	12,373,460	42	111
Indiana	164	2,874,580	24	78
	241	3,113,786	12	17
Iowa	343	2,591,338	30	49
Kansas	405	4,427,530	79	206
Kentucky	139	3,560,451	10	26
Louisiana	199	1,331,479	14	40
Maine	154	6,016,447	10	37
Maryland				
Massachusetts	351	6,637,616	84	391
Michigan	625	9,847,710	166	399
Minnesota	331	5,178,985	34	119
Mississippi...	26	585,454	4	7
	612	6,089,857	24	88
Missouri...				
Montana...	109	1,042,048	10	20
Nebraska	235	1,846,626	7	31
Nevada	51	2,940,058	4	41
New Hampshire	174	1,275,170	19	28
	507	8,942,857	117	282
New Jersey...				
New Mexico...	18	576,958	2	26
New York...	584	19,738,790	72	595
North Carolina	528	10,145,637	41	148
North Dakota	108	757,493	6	8
	562	9,573,452	115	442
Ohio				
Oklahoma..	355	3,869,095	22	33
Oregon	170	3,547,910	28	104
Pennsylvania	1,463	12,644,372	20	61
Rhode Island	49	1,056,426	10	12
	440	4,936,962	21	23
South Carolina				
South Dakota...	112	787,337	12	18
Tennessee	463	6,651,194	55	142
Texas...	1,097	27,862,596	66	178
Utah	130	3,014,190	32	66
	90	624,594	15	25
Vermont				
Virginia	419	8,411,424	55	122
Washington	253	7,282,106	80	387
West Virginia	324	1,621,366	19	41
Wisconsin..	414	5,652,781	18	34
Wyoming...	55	556,446	1	3

Table 13. Hate Crime Incidents Per Bias Motivation and Quarter, by Selected State and Agency, 2016

(Number.)

State/agency	Number of incidents per bias motivation						Number of incidents per quarter				Population[1]
	Race/ Ethnicity/ Ancestry	Religion	Sexual orientation	Disability	Gender	Gender Identity	1st quarter	2nd quarter	3rd quarter	4th quarter	
ALABAMA											
Total	12	1	1	0	0	0					
Cities	12	1	1	0	0	0					
Birmingham	7	1	1	0	0	0	3	2	2	2	212,549
Florence	1	0	0	0	0	0	0	0	1	0	40,160
Foley	1	0	0	0	0	0	0	1	0	0	17,639
Hoover	3	0	0	0	0	0	1	0	1	1	85,601
ALASKA											
Total	11	0	0	0	0	0					
Cities	11	0	0	0	0	0					
Anchorage	4	0	0	0	0	0	1	0	2	1	299,097
Juneau	6	0	0	0	0	0	1	1	3	1	32,964
Wasilla	1	0	0	0	0	0	1	0	0	0	9,585
ARIZONA											
Total	110	50	53	1	0	0					
Cities	105	48	53	1	0	0					
Apache Junction	2	0	0	0	0	0	1	0	1	0	38,506
Chandler	2	2	0	0	0	0	1	0	1	2	265,922
Gilbert	1	0	0	0	0	0	1	0	0	0	255,899
Glendale	1	0	0	0	0	0	0	1	0	0	242,938
Mesa	3	0	2	0	0	0	3	0	0	2	478,277
Phoenix[2]	90	40	44	1	0	0	34	39	45	56	1,586,611
Prescott Valley	1	0	1	0	0	0	1	1			42,900
Sahuarita	1	0	0	0	0	0	0	0	0	1	25,792
Scottsdale	1	3	0	0	0	0	0		2	2	240,885
St. Johns	0	0	1	0	0	0	1	0	0	0	3,482
Tempe	0	0	1	0	0	0	1	0	0	0	178,654
Tucson	1	2	2	0	0	0	2	1	1	1	533,663
Williams	0	0	1	0	0	0	0	1	0	0	3,140
Yuma	2	1	1	0	0	0	1	1	2	0	94,696
Universities and Colleges	1	2	0	0	0	0					
Arizona State University, Main Campus	1	0	0	0	0	0	0	0	0	1	90,906
University of Arizona	0	2	0	0	0	0	0	2			42,595
Metropolitan Counties	4	0	0	0	0	0					
Maricopa	3	0	0	0	0	0		0	3	0	
Pima	1	0	0	0	0	0	0	1	0		
ARKANSAS											
Total	10	1	0	0	0	1					
Cities	5	1	0	0	0	1					
Fort Smith	3	1	0	0	0	0	2	0	0	2	88,573
Jacksonville	2	0	0	0	0	0	0	0	0	2	28,684
Little Rock	0	0	0	0	0	1	0	1	0	0	198,800
Metropolitan Counties	3	0	0	0	0	0					
Sebastian	3	0	0	0	0	0	0	1	0	2	
Nonmetropolitan Counties	2	0	0	0	0	0					
Sevier	2	0	0	0	0	0	0	0	2	0	
CALIFORNIA											
Total	522	171	208	2	3	27					
Cities	421	150	173	2	3	23					
Adelanto	1	0	1	0	0	0	0	1	1	0	33,479
Alameda	3	0	0	0	0	0	0	1	0	2	79,597
Alhambra	1	0	0	0	0	0	0	0	0	1	86,035
Anaheim	1	0	0	0	0	0	1	0	0	0	353,504
Antioch	2	0	0	0	0	0	0	0	2	0	112,090
Arcata	2	0	0	0	0	0	0	0	1	1	17,913
Azusa	2	0	0	0	0	0	2	0	0	0	50,393
Bakersfield	8	0	0	0	0	0	0	3	2	3	378,788
Baldwin Park	0	0	1	0	0	0	1	0	0	0	77,400
Bellflower	0	0	1	0	0	0	1	0	0	0	78,806
Berkeley	9	2	2	0	0	0	5	3	2	3	122,651
Beverly Hills	1	0	0	0	0	0	0	0	1	0	35,018
Brea	0	0	1	0	0	0	0	1	0	0	42,465
Buena Park	2	1	0	0	0	0	0	0	2	1	83,768
Burbank	1	0	0	0	0	0	0	0	1	0	105,720

Table 13. Hate Crime Incidents Per Bias Motivation and Quarter, by Selected State and Agency, 2016—*Continued*

(Number.)

State/agency	Race/ Ethnicity/ Ancestry	Religion	Sexual orientation	Disability	Gender	Gender Identity	1st quarter	2nd quarter	3rd quarter	4th quarter	Population[1]
Calabasas	3	0	0	0	0	0	1	0	2	0	24,492
Camarillo	1	0	0	0	0	0	0	1	0	0	68,072
Campbell	0	1	0	0	0	0	0	1	0	0	41,457
Capitola	1	0	0	0	0	0	0	0	0	1	10,241
Central Marin	2	0	0	0	0	0	0	1	1	0	35,265
Cerritos	0	0	1	0	0	0	0	0	1	0	50,159
Chico	3	0	0	0	0	0	0	1	0	2	91,122
Chino	2	0	1	0	0	0	0	1	1	1	87,081
Chino Hills	1	0	0	0	0	0	1	0	0	0	78,990
Chula Vista	1	2	2	0	0	0	1	1	3	0	270,175
Citrus Heights	1	0	1	0	0	0	1	0	0	1	87,811
Claremont	7	1	1	0	0	0	1	0	1	7	36,553
Clayton	0	0	2	0	0	0	0	2	0	0	12,057
Clearlake	1	0	0	0	0	0	0	0	0	1	15,165
Clovis	1	0	0	0	0	0	0	0	1	0	105,865
Coalinga	0	0	1	0	0	0	1	0	0	0	16,282
Compton	0	0	0	0	0	1	0	0	1	0	98,861
Concord	1	0	2	0	0	0	1	0	0	2	129,903
Culver City	0	0	1	0	0	0	0	1	0	0	39,880
Cupertino	2	1	0	0	0	0	0	0	3	0	60,948
Danville	0	1	0	0	0	0	1	0	0	0	44,897
Davis	5	1	1	0	0	1	2	0	1	5	68,087
Desert Hot Springs	0	0	1	0	0	0	0	1	0	0	28,573
Downey	1	0	0	0	0	0	0	1	0	0	114,704
East Palo Alto	0	0	1	0	0	0	0	0	0	1	29,957
Eastvale	0	1	0	0	0	0	0	1	0	0	60,115
Elk Grove	1	0	0	0	0	0	1	0	0	0	169,742
El Segundo	2	0	0	0	0	0	1	0	1	0	17,113
Encinitas	1	0	0	0	0	0	0	0	0	1	63,597
Escondido	1	0	0	0	0	0	0	1	0	0	152,897
Fairfield	1	1	1	0	0	0	2	0	1	0	114,521
Farmersville	0	1	0	0	0	0	0	0	1	0	10,812
Folsom	0	1	0	0	0	0	0	1	0	0	77,245
Fort Bragg	1	1	1	0	0	0	0	2	1	0	7,292
Fremont	1	0	0	0	0	0	1	0	0	0	235,881
Fresno	7	3	3	0	0	0	3	3	4	3	524,796
Fullerton	1	0	1	0	0	0	1	0	0	1	141,968
Garden Grove	1	1	0	0	0	0	1	0	0	1	176,230
Glendale	1	1	0	0	0	0	0	1	0	1	202,903
Hanford	0	1	0	0	0	0	0	1	0	0	55,973
Hawaiian Gardens	0	0	0	0	0	1	0	1	0	0	14,654
Hawthorne	0	1	0	0	0	0	0	0	0	1	89,299
Hayward	1	1	0	0	0	0	0	0	1	1	161,122
Highland	1	0	0	0	0	0	0	0	1	0	55,184
Hollister	0	0	1	0	0	0	0	0	1	0	37,953
Huntington Beach	3	3	0	0	0	0	1	1	3	1	204,071
Huntington Park	0	0	1	0	0	0	1	0	0	0	59,692
Irvine	2	0	0	0	0	0	1	0	0	1	266,663
Jurupa Valley	1	0	0	0	0	0	0	1	0	0	101,316
Kingsburg	1	0	0	0	0	0	1	0	0	0	11,905
Laguna Beach	1	0	0	0	0	0	0	0	0	1	23,486
La Habra	1	0	0	0	0	0	0	1	0	0	62,483
Lake Elsinore	1	0	1	0	0	0	1	1	0	0	63,907
Lakewood	3	0	1	0	0	0	2	0	1	1	81,921
La Mesa	2	1	0	0	0	0	0	0	1	2	60,681
La Mirada	0	2	0	0	0	0	0	2	0	0	49,715
Lancaster	5	0	2	0	0	1	1	4	1	2	161,963
La Puente	0	0	1	0	0	0	1	0	0	0	40,928
Loma Linda	1	0	0	0	0	0	0	1	0	0	24,190
Long Beach	2	2	3	0	0	1	2	0	3	3	476,476
Los Angeles	112	43	58	0	1	13	55	56	52	64	4,007,905
Malibu	2	0	0	0	0	0	1	0	0	1	13,030
Mammoth Lakes	1	0	0	0	0	0	0	1	0	0	7,891
Manteca	5	0	0	0	0	0	1	1	3	0	77,104
Merced	0	0	1	0	0	1	0	0	1	1	83,106
Modesto	6	4	1	0	0	0	2	4	2	3	212,880
Montclair	1	1	0	0	0	0	0	1	0	1	39,085

(Number.)

State/agency	Number of incidents per bias motivation						Number of incidents per quarter				Population[1]
	Race/ Ethnicity/ Ancestry	Religion	Sexual orientation	Disability	Gender	Gender Identity	1st quarter	2nd quarter	3rd quarter	4th quarter	
Monterey	1	0	0	0	0	0	0	0	0	1	28,506
Mountain View	0	1	0	0	0	0	1	0	0	0	81,726
Murrieta	0	0	0	0	1	0	0	0	0	1	111,043
Napa	0	0	1	0	0	0	0	0	0	1	81,115
National City	1	0	0	0	0	0	1	0	0	0	61,550
Newark	1	0	0	0	0	0	0	1	0	0	45,893
Norco	2	0	0	0	0	0	1	0	0	1	26,132
Norwalk	1	0	0	0	0	0	0	0	1	0	107,453
Novato	1	1	0	0	0	0	0	0	0	2	56,263
Oakland	3	3	3	0	0	0	3	2	2	2	424,998
Oceanside	2	2	3	0	0	0	1	3	1	2	177,340
Orange	1	0	0	0	0	0	0	1	0	0	141,841
Oxnard	4	1	1	0	0	0	2	1	1	2	209,048
Pacific Grove	1	0	0	0	0	0	0	1	0	0	15,795
Palmdale	6	2	0	0	0	0	5	0	2	1	159,441
Palm Springs	3	0	0	0	0	0	1	2	0	0	47,909
Palo Alto	3	1	0	0	0	0	1	2	1	0	67,317
Paradise	1	0	0	0	0	0	0	1	0	0	26,532
Parlier	0	0	1	0	0	0	0	1	0	0	15,262
Pasadena	1	1	0	0	0	0	1	0	1	0	143,288
Perris	0	1	0	0	0	0	0	0	0	1	76,260
Petaluma	1	0	0	0	0	0	1	0	0	0	60,933
Placentia	1	0	0	0	0	0	0	1	0	0	52,800
Pomona	2	1	2	0	0	0	2	1	2	0	154,109
Poway	0	0	1	0	0	0	0	0	0	1	50,606
Rancho Cucamonga	4	0	0	0	0	0	0	2	1	1	177,089
Rancho Palos Verdes	1	0	0	0	0	0	0	0	1	0	42,947
Redding	7	1	2	0	0	0	0	1	7	2	91,918
Redlands	4	0	2	0	0	0	1	2	3	0	71,485
Redwood City	2	0	2	0	0	0	0	0	1	3	87,046
Rialto	1	0	0	0	0	0	0	0	0	1	103,893
Richmond	4	0	0	0	0	0	0	1	1	2	110,868
Ridgecrest	1	0	0	0	0	0	0	1	0	0	29,003
Riverside	5	1	2	0	0	0	2	2	2	2	325,896
Roseville	7	4	0	0	0	0	0	1	4	6	132,566
Sacramento	2	0	4	0	0	0	4	1	1	0	495,471
Salinas	0	1	0	0	0	0	0	1	0	0	158,729
San Bernardino[2]	6	0	1	0	0	0	0	1	4	1	217,303
San Bruno	2	0	0	0	0	0	0	0	1	1	43,613
San Diego	16	7	12	0	0	0	7	10	6	12	1,413,414
San Fernando	0	1	1	0	0	0	1	0	0	1	25,194
San Francisco[2]	11	7	14	0	1	4	9	12	10	5	871,155
San Jose	10	7	2	0	0	0	5	1	4	9	1,041,844
San Leandro	15	3	3	1	0	0	4	5	5	8	91,870
San Luis Obispo	2	0	0	0	0	0	2	0	0	0	47,774
San Marcos	1	1	0	0	0	0	1	0	0	1	94,840
San Mateo	0	1	1	0	0	0	0	1	0	1	104,802
San Rafael	1	0	0	0	0	0	0	0	0	1	59,435
San Ramon	4	0	0	0	0	0	0	0	0	4	76,901
Santa Ana	2	3	1	0	0	0	3	2	0	1	337,419
Santa Clarita	6	4	0	0	0	0	3	1	2	4	219,611
Santa Cruz	7	3	2	0	0	0	4	1	2	5	64,969
Santa Monica	1	1	1	0	0	0	0	2	1	0	93,921
Santa Rosa	0	0	1	0	0	0	1	0	0	0	176,383
Santee	0	1	0	0	0	0	0	0	0	1	58,651
Sebastopol	1	0	0	0	0	0	0	1	0	0	7,734
Simi Valley	1	1	0	0	0	0	0	1	0	1	127,252
Solvang	0	0	1	0	0	0	0	0	1	0	5,844
Sonoma	1	0	0	0	0	0	1	0	0	0	11,113
Sonora	1	0	0	0	0	0	0	0	0	1	4,802
South Gate	0	1	1	0	0	0	0	0	1	1	96,791
South San Francisco	0	4	0	0	0	0	0	0	0	4	67,995
Stockton	2	0	0	1	0	0	0	0	2	1	308,348
Suisun City	1	0	0	0	0	0	0	1	0	0	29,768
Sunnyvale	0	1	0	0	0	0	0	0	1	0	154,108
Thousand Oaks	0	1	0	0	0	0	0	1	0	0	129,853
Torrance	0	1	0	0	0	0	0	0	1	0	149,078

Table 13. Hate Crime Incidents Per Bias Motivation and Quarter, by Selected State and Agency, 2016—*Continued*

(Number.)

State/agency	Race/ Ethnicity/ Ancestry	Religion	Sexual orientation	Disability	Gender	Gender Identity	1st quarter	2nd quarter	3rd quarter	4th quarter	Population[1]
Turlock	3	0	0	0	0	0	3	0	0	0	73,031
Twentynine Palms	1	0	0	0	0	0	0	0	0	1	26,213
Ukiah	0	0	1	0	0	0	0	1	0	0	15,897
Union City	0	0	1	0	0	0	0	1	0	0	75,501
Vacaville	1	0	0	0	0	0	1	0	0	0	97,671
Vallejo	2	0	0	0	0	0	0	0	1	1	122,293
Ventura	2	0	1	0	0	0	0	1	1	1	110,228
Victorville	1	0	1	0	0	0	0	1	0	1	123,438
Walnut Creek	1	1	1	0	0	0	0	1	1	1	69,860
Watsonville	0	1	0	0	0	0	1	0	0	0	54,110
West Covina	1	0	0	0	0	0	1	0	0	0	108,950
West Hollywood	2	0	5	0	0	0	0	2	2	3	36,594
Westminster	3	0	1	0	0	0	3	0	1	0	92,582
Wildomar	1	0	0	0	0	0	0	0	0	1	36,310
Windsor	2	0	0	0	0	0	1	0	0	1	27,594
Universities and Colleges	22	7	9	0	0	1					
California State Polytechnic University, San Luis Obispo	1	0	0	0	0	0	1	0	0	0	20,944
California State University:											
Dominguez Hills	4	0	0	0	0	0	2	0	0	2	14,635
Fullerton	0	0	1	0	0	0	0	1	0	0	38,948
Long Beach	2	0	0	0	0	0	0	0	2	0	37,446
San Jose	5	0	0	0	0	0	0	0	1	4	32,773
Stanislaus	0	0	1	0	0	0	1	0	0	0	9,282
Foothill-De Anza College	0	0	1	0	0	1	1	1	0	0	37,960
Humboldt State University	1	1	1	0	0	0	0	2	1	0	8,790
Riverside Community College	0	1	0	0	0	0	0	0	0	1	37,594
San Diego State University	3	0	0	0	0	0	1	1	0	1	34,254
University of California:											
Berkeley	1	2	1	0	0	0	1	1	0	2	38,189
Davis	1	0	0	0	0	0	1	0	0	0	35,186
Los Angeles	2	1	1	0	0	0	2	0	1	1	41,908
Riverside	0	1	0	0	0	0	1	0	0	0	21,385
San Diego	2	0	1	0	0	0	0	2	0	1	32,906
San Francisco	0	1	0	0	0	0	0	0	0	1	3,107
Santa Cruz	0	0	1	0	0	0	0	0	0	1	17,868
Ventura County Community College District	0	0	1	0	0	0	0	0	0	1	34,022
Metropolitan Counties	58	9	20	0	0	2					
Butte	0	0	1	0	0	0	0	0	1	0	
El Dorado	0	1	0	0	0	0	1	0	0	0	
Fresno	0	0	1	0	0	0	0	1	0	0	
Los Angeles	17	3	6	0	0	0	5	4	6	11	
Orange	2	0	0	0	0	0	2	0	0	0	
Riverside	3	0	1	0	0	1	0	1	3	1	
Sacramento	8	1	1	0	0	0	5	3	1	1	
San Bernardino	3	2	1	0	0	1	4	3	0	0	
San Diego	13	1	4	0	0	0	1	7	8	2	
San Mateo	1	1	1	0	0	0	1	1	1	0	
Santa Barbara	1	0	0	0	0	0	0	0	0	1	
Santa Clara	2	0	0	0	0	0	1	0	1	0	
Shasta	2	0	0	0	0	0	1	1	0	0	
Solano	1	0	0	0	0	0	0	0	1	0	
Sonoma	1	0	3	0	0	0	0	1	3	0	
Sutter	1	0	0	0	0	0	0	0	0	1	
Ventura	2	0	0	0	0	0	0	1	1	0	
Yuba	1	0	1	0	0	0	0	0	0	2	
Nonmetropolitan Counties	3	3	0	0	0	0					
Amador	0	1	0	0	0	0	0	0	1	0	
Humboldt	0	1	0	0	0	0	0	0	0	1	
Lake	1	0	0	0	0	0	0	1	0	0	
Mendocino	2	0	0	0	0	0	1	0	0	1	
Tuolumne	0	1	0	0	0	0	0	0	1	0	
Other Agencies	18	2	6	0	0	1					
California State Fair	1	0	0	0	0	0	0	0	1	0	
East Bay Regional Parks, Alameda County	0	1	0	0	0	0	0	0	0	1	
Fontana Unified School District	0	0	1	0	0	0	0	0	0	1	
Los Angeles Transportation Services Bureau[2]	10	0	4	0	0	1	7	2	3	3	

(Number.)

State/agency	Number of incidents per bias motivation						Number of incidents per quarter				Population[1]
	Race/ Ethnicity/ Ancestry	Religion	Sexual orientation	Disability	Gender	Gender Identity	1st quarter	2nd quarter	3rd quarter	4th quarter	
Port of San Diego Harbor	2	1	0	0	0	0	2	0	1	0	
San Francisco Bay Area Rapid Transit:											
Alameda County	2	0	0	0	0	0	1	0	0	1	
Contra Costa County	2	0	0	0	0	0	1	0	0	1	
Santa Clara Transit District	1	0	1	0	0	0	0	0	1	1	
COLORADO											
Total	67	19	23	0	0	0					
Cities	47	7	17	0	0	0					
Aspen	0	1	0	0	0	0	0	0	0	1	6,926
Aurora	15	0	3	0	0	0	1	3	6	8	366,477
Boulder	2	1	1	0	0	0	1	1	2	0	109,189
Breckenridge	0	0	1	0	0	0	0	0	1	0	4,971
Carbondale	1	0	0	0	0	0	0	1	0	0	6,728
Centennial	2	0	0	0	0	0	0	0	2	0	111,479
Colorado Springs	1	1	4	0	0	0	0	2	1	3	464,113
Delta	0	0	1	0	0	0	1	0	0	0	8,778
Denver	10	3	6	0	0	0	4	2	1	12	699,259
Dillon	0	1	0	0	0	0	0	0	0	1	972
Erie	1	0	0	0	0	0	0	0	1	0	22,115
Florence	1	0	0	0	0	0	0	0	1	0	3,861
Fort Collins	2	0	0	0	0	0	2	0	0	0	164,670
Fort Lupton	1	0	0	0	0	0	0	1	0	0	7,903
Fountain	0	0	1	0	0	0	0	0	0	1	28,115
Golden	1	0	0	0	0	0	0	0	1	0	20,616
Grand Junction	3	0	0	0	0	0	0	0	3	0	60,628
Longmont	3	0	0	0	0	0	0	0	1	2	93,268
Loveland	1	0	0	0	0	0	0	0	1	0	76,936
Nederland	1	0	0	0	0	0	0	0	1	0	1,534
Pueblo	1	0	0	0	0	0	0	0	0	1	109,927
Sterling	1	0	0	0	0	0	0	0	0	1	14,087
Universities and Colleges	2	3	3	0	0	0					
Auraria Higher Education Center[3]	0	0	1	0	0	0	0	1	0	0	
University of Colorado, Boulder	2	3	1	0	0	0	2	0	2	2	33,056
University of Northern Colorado	0	0	1	0	0	0	0	0	1	0	12,216
Metropolitan Counties	15	8	3	0	0	0					
Adams	1	0	0	0	0	0	0	0	1	0	
Arapahoe	2	1	2	0	0	0	0	3	1	1	
Boulder	1	1	0	0	0	0	0	0	0	2	
Douglas	2	0	0	0	0	0	0	0	1	1	
El Paso	1	0	0	0	0	0	1	0	0	0	
Larimer[2]	6	6	1	0	0	0	0	2	1	5	
Mesa	1	0	0	0	0	0	1	0	0	0	
Teller	1	0	0	0	0	0	0	1	0	0	
Nonmetropolitan Counties	3	1	0	0	0	0					
Custer	1	0	0	0	0	0	0	0	1	0	
Garfield	1	0	0	0	0	0	1	0	0	0	
San Juan	1	0	0	0	0	0	0	0	1	0	
Summit	0	1	0	0	0	0	0	0	0	1	
CONNECTICUT											
Total	62	30	14	0	0	0					
Cities	59	27	12	0	0	0					
Bloomfield	0	1	1	0	0	0	1	1	0	0	20,801
Bridgeport	5	1	0	0	0	0	0	4	2	0	148,180
Bristol	0	0	2	0	0	0	0	0	1	1	60,445
Clinton	1	0	0	0	0	0	0	0	1	0	13,008
Danbury	3	5	1	0	0	0	1	1	1	6	85,335
Darien	0	1	0	0	0	0	0	0	1	0	21,995
Greenwich	0	1	0	0	0	0	0	0	1	0	62,970
Groton	1	0	0	0	0	0	0	0	0	1	9,189
Groton Town	1	0	0	0	0	0	0	0	1	0	29,910
Guilford	1	0	0	0	0	0	1	0	0	0	22,343
Hartford	5	0	1	0	0	0	2	2	1	1	123,736
Ledyard	0	0	1	0	0	0	0	0	0	1	15,021
Madison	0	1	0	0	0	0	0	0	0	1	18,212
Manchester	6	0	1	0	0	0	1	2	1	3	57,957

(Number.)

State/agency	Number of incidents per bias motivation						Number of incidents per quarter				Population[1]
	Race/ Ethnicity/ Ancestry	Religion	Sexual orientation	Disability	Gender	Gender Identity	1st quarter	2nd quarter	3rd quarter	4th quarter	
Middletown	1	1	0	0	0	0	0	2	0	0	46,580
Naugatuck	1	0	0	0	0	0	0	1	0	0	31,469
New Haven	4	3	2	0	0	0	5	1	0	3	130,425
Newington	1	0	1	0	0	0	1	0	0	1	30,610
New London	0	2	0	0	0	0	2	0	0	0	27,092
Norwalk	5	2	0	0	0	0	1	5	0	1	88,989
Norwich	1	0	0	0	0	0	1	0	0	0	39,771
Old Saybrook	1	0	0	0	0	0	0	0	0	1	10,145
Ridgefield	0	1	0	0	0	0	0	0	0	1	25,358
Rocky Hill	0	1	0	0	0	0	0	0	0	1	20,085
Shelton	0	1	0	0	0	0	0	0	0	1	41,638
Southington	1	0	0	0	0	0	0	1	0	0	43,948
Stamford	5	1	2	0	0	0	4	2	1	1	130,116
Stratford	1	0	0	0	0	0	0	1	0	0	52,841
Torrington	1	2	0	0	0	0	0	1	1	1	34,626
Trumbull	1	0	0	0	0	0	1	0	0	0	36,741
Vernon	1	0	0	0	0	0	0	0	0	1	28,915
Wallingford	1	0	0	0	0	0	0	0	1	0	44,840
Waterbury	6	0	0	0	0	0	2	3	0	1	108,491
Waterford	0	1	0	0	0	0	0	0	1	0	19,236
West Hartford	1	1	0	0	0	0	0	0	0	2	62,979
Westport	2	0	0	0	0	0	0	2	0	0	28,198
Wethersfield	1	0	0	0	0	0	1	0	0	0	26,306
Willimantic	1	0	0	0	0	0	0	0	1	0	17,766
Woodbridge	0	1	0	0	0	0	0	0	1	0	8,864
Universities and Colleges	0	1	1	0	0	0					
Southern Connecticut State University	0	1	1	0	0	0	1	0	1	0	10,473
State Police Agencies	2	2	1	0	0	0					
Connecticut State Police	2	2	1	0	0	0	0	1	3	1	
Tribal Agencies	1	0	0	0	0	0					
Mashantucket Pequot Tribal	1	0	0	0	0	0	0	0	0	1	
DELAWARE											
Total	11	3	1	0	0	0					
Cities	3	1	0	0	0	0					
Camden	1	0	0	0	0	0	0	0	0	1	3,512
Newark	1	0	0	0	0	0	0	0	0	1	34,297
Rehoboth Beach	1	0	0	0	0	0	1	0	0	0	1,485
Smyrna	0	1	0	0	0	0	0	1	0	0	11,573
Metropolitan Counties	3	1	0	0	0	0					
New Castle County Police Department	3	1	0	0	0	0	1	0	2	1	
State Police Agencies	3	1	1	0	0	0					
State Police:											
Kent County	1	0	0	0	0	0	0	0	1	0	
New Castle County	2	1	1	0	0	0	1	2	0	1	
Other Agencies	2	0	0	0	0	0					
Park Rangers	2	0	0	0	0	0	0	0	0	2	
DISTRICT OF COLUMBIA											
Total	33	18	42	2	0	20					
Cities	26	18	40	1	0	19					
Washington	26	18	40	1	0	19	20	35	25	24	681,170
Other Agencies	7	0	2	1	0	1					
Metro Transit Police	7	0	2	1	0	1	0	4	3	4	
FLORIDA											
Total	43	19	32	1	0	1					
Cities	27	14	23	1	0	0					
Arcadia	1	0	0	0	0	0			1		7,893
Cape Coral	1	0	0	0	0	0				1	179,631
Casselberry	0	1	0	0	0	0			1		27,220
Cocoa	0	0	1	0	0	0	1				17,825
Coral Gables	1	0	0	0	0	0	1				51,980
Davie	3	1	1	0	0	0	2	3			102,692
Fort Myers	2	0	1	0	0	0	1		1	1	76,579
Gainesville	4	0	0	0	0	0	1			3	131,242
Homestead	1	0	1	0	0	0	2				67,700

Table 13. Hate Crime Incidents Per Bias Motivation and Quarter, by Selected State and Agency, 2016—Continued

(Number.)

State/agency	Number of incidents per bias motivation						Number of incidents per quarter				Population[1]
	Race/ Ethnicity/ Ancestry	Religion	Sexual orientation	Disability	Gender	Gender Identity	1st quarter	2nd quarter	3rd quarter	4th quarter	
Largo	1	0	1	0	0	0		1		1	81,402
Miami Beach	0	4	12	1	0	0	6	4	4	3	93,165
New Port Richey	2	0	0	0	0	0		2			16,038
North Miami	0	0	1	0	0	0		1			62,974
North Miami Beach	0	2	0	0	0	0		2			44,442
Oakland Park	0	0	1	0	0	0		1			44,903
Orlando	3	1	1	0	0	0		2	1	2	277,719
Palm Bay	3	1	0	0	0	0		2	1	1	108,823
Pinellas Park	1	0	0	0	0	0			1		52,113
Southwest Ranches	1	1	0	0	0	0	1		1		7,953
Sunrise	0	1	0	0	0	0			1		94,400
Tamarac	0	0	1	0	0	0	1				65,516
Tampa	2	0	1	0	0	0			2	1	375,904
Temple Terrace	0	0	1	0	0	0				1	25,972
Titusville	0	1	0	0	0	0	1				45,723
West Palm Beach	0	1	0	0	0	0			1		108,074
West Park	1	0	0	0	0	0	1				15,285
Universities and Colleges	1	0	0	0	0	0					
University of Florida	1	0	0	0	0	0			1		50,645
Metropolitan Counties	15	5	9	0	0	1					
Brevard	1	0	2	0	0	0		1	1	1	
Charlotte	1	0	0	0	0	0	1				
Clay	2	0	0	0	0	0	1			1	
Escambia	2	0	0	0	0	0	1	1			
Hillsborough	1	0	0	0	0	0			1		
Lake	1	0	0	0	0	0	1				
Lee	1	0	1	0	0	0	2				
Miami-Dade	0	1	0	0	0	0		1			
Orange	0	0	1	0	0	1	2			1	
Osceola	1	0	0	0	0	0	1				
Palm Beach	0	1	0	0	0	0				1	
Pasco	0	0	1	0	0	0				1	
Pinellas	1	0	1	0	0	0		2			
Seminole	0	1	0	0	0	0		1			
St. Johns	0	0	1	0	0	0			1		
St. Lucie	0	1	0	0	0	0			1		
Volusia	4	0	2	0	0	0		2	1	3	
GEORGIA											
Total	25	2	12	0	0	0					
Cities	1	0	5	0	0	0					
Atlanta	0	0	5	0	0	0	1	4	0	0	472,579
Conyers	1	0	0	0	0	0	0	0	0	1	16,004
Universities and Colleges	1	0	0	0	0	0					
University of Georgia	1	0	0	0	0	0	1	0	0	0	36,130
Metropolitan Counties	23	2	7	0	0	0					
Cobb County Police Department	19	2	4	0	0	0	6	7	12	0	
Fulton County Police Department	0	0	1	0	0	0	0	1	0	0	
Gwinnett County Police Department	4	0	2	0	0	0	2	1	3	0	
IDAHO											
Total	16	7	4	0	0	0					
Cities	13	6	3	0	0	0					
Blackfoot	0	0	1	0	0	0	0	0	1	0	11,700
Boise	0	2	1	0	0	0	1	1	1	0	220,749
Chubbuck	1	0	0	0	0	0	0	0	0	1	14,515
Coeur d'Alene	3	2	0	0	0	0	0	3	1	1	50,155
Meridian	1	1	0	0	0	0	0	0	0	2	94,113
Moscow	0	0	1	0	0	0	0	0	0	1	25,307
Mountain Home	1	0	0	0	0	0	0	0	0	1	13,627
Nampa	2	0	0	0	0	0	0	1	1	0	91,520
Payette	0	1	0	0	0	0	0	0	1	0	7,360
Pocatello	3	0	0	0	0	0	1	2	0	0	54,462
Twin Falls	2	0	0	0	0	0	0	2	0	0	48,083
Metropolitan Counties	2	1	1	0	0	0					
Ada	0	1	0	0	0	0	1	0	0	0	
Canyon	2	0	1	0	0	0	0	2	1	0	

(Number.)

State/agency	Number of incidents per bias motivation						Number of incidents per quarter				Population[1]
	Race/Ethnicity/Ancestry	Religion	Sexual orientation	Disability	Gender	Gender Identity	1st quarter	2nd quarter	3rd quarter	4th quarter	
Nonmetropolitan Counties	1	0	0	0	0	0					
Benewah	1	0	0	0	0	0	1	0	0	0	
ILLINOIS											
Total	73	13	21	0	1	3					
Cities	71	12	20	0	0	3					
Algonquin	2	0	0	0	0	0	0	1	1	0	30,673
Aurora	3	0	0	0	0	0	0	1	0	2	201,159
Berwyn	3	0	0	0	0	0	0	0	1	2	56,305
Bradley	3	0	0	0	0	0		1	1	1	15,561
Braidwood	1	0	0	0	0	0	0	0	1	0	6,160
Centralia	1	0	0	0	0	0	0	0	0	1	12,580
Champaign	1	0	1	0	0	0	0	0	1	1	87,071
Charleston	1	0	0	0	0	0	0	0	1	0	21,067
Chicago	26	9	14	0	0	2	5	19	10	17	2,725,153
Collinsville	1	0	0	0	0	0	0	0	0	1	24,599
Crete	0	0	1	0	0	0	0	0	0	1	8,171
Crystal Lake	1	0	0	0	0	0	1	0	0	0	40,374
De Kalb	1	0	0	0	0	0	0	0	1	0	43,034
Downers Grove	1	0	0	0	0	0	0	0	1	0	49,894
Effingham	1	1	0	0	0	0	0	0	0	2	12,660
Elk Grove Village	1	0	0	0	0	0	0	1	0	0	33,255
Flossmoor	1	0	0	0	0	0	0	0	1	0	9,479
Glenwood	1	0	0	0	0	0	0	0	1	0	8,996
Grayslake	1	0	0	0	0	0	1	0	0	0	20,916
Homewood	1	0	0	0	0	0	1	0	0	0	19,379
Joliet	1	0	1	0	0	0	0	0	1	1	147,886
Mokena	1	0	0	0	0	0	0	0	0	1	20,156
Monmouth	1	0	0	0	0	0	0	1	0	0	9,261
Morrison	0	0	1	0	0	0	0	1	0	0	4,137
New Lenox	1	0	0	0	0	0	0	0	0	1	26,085
Normal	3	0	0	0	0	0		0	2	1	54,727
Oak Lawn	1	0	0	0	0	0	1	0	0	0	56,791
Pekin	1	0	0	0	0	0	0	0	0	1	33,052
Peoria	1	0	0	0	0	0	1	0	0	0	115,099
Plainfield	1	1	0	0	0	0	0	0	0	2	43,063
Robinson	1	0	0	0	0	0	0	0	1	0	7,616
Rockford	3	0	2	0	0	0	1	2	1	1	147,363
Salem	1	0	0	0	0	0	0	1	0	0	7,249
Springfield	2	0	0	0	0	0	0	1	1	0	116,563
Urbana	0	1	0	0	0	0	0	0	0	1	42,461
West Chicago	1	0	0	0	0	0	0	0	1	0	27,490
Wheeling	0	0	0	0	0	1	1	0	0	0	38,158
Woodstock	1	0	0	0	0	0	0	0	0	1	25,259
Universities and Colleges	1	0	0	0	0	0					
Southern Illinois University, Carbondale	1	0	0	0	0	0	0	0	1	0	17,292
Metropolitan Counties	1	1	1	0	1	0					
Champaign	0	1	0	0	1	0	0	1	1	0	
Sangamon	1	0	0	0	0	0	0	0	0	1	
Will	0	0	1	0	0	0	0	1	0	0	
INDIANA											
Total	52	11	14	0	1	0					
Cities	42	5	11	0	0	0					
Anderson	0	0	1	0	0	0		1			55,134
Bloomington	7	0	2	0	0	0	3	1	1	4	84,772
Fort Wayne	2	0	2	0	0	0	1	1	1	1	261,642
Indianapolis	20	3	5	0	0	0	5	11	8	4	866,351
La Porte	2	0	0	0	0	0		2			21,891
Muncie	1	0	0	0	0	0	0	0	1	0	70,065
Munster	0	1	0	0	0	0	1				22,865
Plainfield	0	1	0	0	0	0	1	0	0		31,198
South Bend	10	0	0	0	0	0	3	2	5	0	101,621
Westville	0	0	1	0	0	0			1		5,641
Universities and Colleges	3	0	2	0	0	0					
Ball State University	1	0	0	0	0	0				1	21,196
Indiana University, Indianapolis	1	0	0	0	0	0		1			30,105

Table 13. Hate Crime Incidents Per Bias Motivation and Quarter, by Selected State and Agency, 2016—*Continued*

(Number.)

State/agency	Race/ Ethnicity/ Ancestry	Religion	Sexual orientation	Disability	Gender	Gender Identity	1st quarter	2nd quarter	3rd quarter	4th quarter	Population[1]
Purdue University	1	0	2	0	0	0	1	1	0	1	40,472
Metropolitan Counties	1	0	1	0	0	0					
Brown	0	0	1	0	0	0				1	
Porter	1	0	0	0	0	0			1		
Nonmetropolitan Counties	0	0	0	0	1	0					
Dubois	0	0	0	0	1	0	1				
State Police Agencies	6	6	0	0	0	0					
Indiana State Police	3	0	0	0	0	0			2	1	
State Police:											
Daviess County	0	1	0	0	0	0	0	0	0	1	
Marion County	1	1	0	0	0	0	0	1	0	1	
Monroe County	0	2	0	0	0	0	2	0	0	0	
Putnam County	1	0	0	0	0	0	0	0	1	0	
Scott County	1	0	0	0	0	0	0	1	0	0	
Vanderburgh County	0	1	0	0	0	0	0	0	1	0	
Washington County	0	1	0	0	0	0	0	1	0	0	
IOWA											
Total	13	2	2	0	0	0					
Cities	10	2	1	0	0	0					
Boone	1	0	0	0	0	0	0	0	1	0	12,702
Clinton	0	1	0	0	0	0	0	0	0	1	25,906
Des Moines	2	1	0	0	0	0	0	1	1	1	211,501
Dubuque	1	0	0	0	0	0	0	1	0	0	59,026
Iowa City	3	0	0	0	0	0	1	0	0	2	75,527
Newton	1	0	0	0	0	0	0	0	1	0	15,102
North Liberty	1	0	0	0	0	0	0	0	1	0	16,458
Oskaloosa	1	0	0	0	0	0	0	0	1	0	11,626
West Des Moines	0	0	1	0	0	0	0	0	0	1	65,631
Universities and Colleges	3	0	0	0	0	0					
Iowa State University	1	0	0	0	0	0	0	0	0	1	35,714
University of Iowa	2	0	0	0	0	0	0	0	0	2	30,844
Metropolitan Counties	0	0	1	0	0	0					
Linn	0	0	1	0	0	0	0	1	0	0	
KANSAS											
Total	36	5	5	3	0	0					
Cities	27	3	4	2	0	0					
Andover	1	0	0	0	0	0	0	0	0	1	12,937
Chanute	1	0	0	0	0	0	0	1	0	0	9,279
Coffeyville	0	0	0	1	0	0	0	0	1	0	9,555
Dodge City	2	0	0	1	0	0	1	1	1	0	27,997
Edwardsville	1	0	0	0	0	0	0	1	0	0	4,377
El Dorado	1	1	0	0	0	0	2	0	0	0	12,913
Elwood	1	0	0	0	0	0	0	0	1	0	1,181
Garden City	0	0	1	0	0	0	0	0	0	1	27,038
Hays	1	0	0	0	0	0	1	0	0	0	21,206
Hiawatha	1	0	0	0	0	0	0	1	0	0	3,080
Hutchinson	0	0	1	0	0	0	0	0	1	0	41,439
Independence	1	0	0	0	0	0	0	0	1	0	8,860
Lenexa	1	0	0	0	0	0	0	0	0	1	53,376
Newton	2	0	1	0	0	0	0	0	1	1	19,226
Oakley	1	0	0	0	0	0	0	1	0	0	2,104
Ottawa	1	0	0	0	0	0	0	0	0	1	12,334
Overland Park	2	2	0	0	0	0	2	0	1	1	189,104
Pittsburg	1	0	0	0	0	0	0	0	1	0	20,439
Pratt	1	0	0	0	0	0	0	1	0	0	6,854
Salina	3	0	0	0	0	0	0	0	1	2	47,805
Wichita	5	0	2	0	0	0	1	1	3	2	391,399
Universities and Colleges	3	0	0	0	0	0					
University of Kansas, Medical Center[3]	1	0	0	0	0	0	0	1	0	0	
Washburn University	1	0	0	0	0	0	0	0	0	1	6,615
Wichita State University	1	0	0	0	0	0	0	0	1	0	14,240
Metropolitan Counties	5	2	1	0	0	0					
Linn	1	0	0	0	0	0	0	0	0	1	
Riley County Police Department	2	1	1	0	0	0	2	1	1	0	
Shawnee	1	1	0	0	0	0	0	1	0	1	

(Number.)

State/agency	Number of incidents per bias motivation						Number of incidents per quarter				Population[1]
	Race/ Ethnicity/ Ancestry	Religion	Sexual orientation	Disability	Gender	Gender Identity	1st quarter	2nd quarter	3rd quarter	4th quarter	
Wabaunsee	1	0	0	0	0	0	0	0	1	0	
Nonmetropolitan Counties	1	0	0	1	0	0					
Greeley	0	0	0	1	0	0	0	0	1	0	
Reno	1	0	0	0	0	0	1	0	0		
KENTUCKY											
Total	135	43	22	2	1	3					
Cities	100	30	19	1	1	3					
Alexandria	1	0	0	0	0	0	0	1	0	0	9,112
Ashland	0	1	0	0	0	0	1	0	0	0	20,987
Audubon Park	1	0	0	0	0	0	1	0	0	0	1,515
Bellevue	1	0	1	0	0	0	0	0	0	2	5,879
Benton	0	1	1	0	0	0	0	0	0	2	4,346
Berea	2	1	0	0	0	0	1	0	1	1	15,135
Bowling Green	6	2	3	0	0	0	1	3	4	3	64,561
Cave City	1	0	0	0	0	0	0	1	0	0	2,411
Cloverport	1	0	0	0	0	0	0	0	1	0	1,157
Covington	4	3	3	0	0	0	2	3	3	2	41,094
Cynthiana	1	0	0	0	0	0	1	0	0	0	6,421
Elizabethtown	0	0	1	0	0	0	0	0	0	1	29,821
Elkton	0	1	0	0	0	0	1	0	0	0	2,181
Elsmere	2	0	1	0	0	0	1	1	0	1	8,563
Fort Mitchell	0	0	1	0	0	0	0	0	1	0	8,334
Frankfort	2	1	0	0	0	0	0	1	1	1	27,926
Franklin	2	0	0	0	0	0	0	0	1	1	8,852
Georgetown	3	0	0	0	0	0	1	1	1	0	33,007
Glasgow	1	0	1	0	0	0	0	1	1	0	14,560
Henderson	2	0	0	0	0	0	1	0	0	1	28,904
Highland Heights	0	1	0	0	0	0	0	0	0	1	7,216
Hopkinsville	5	0	0	0	0	0	3	1	0	1	32,222
Lakeside Park-Crestview Hills	0	0	1	0	0	0	0	0	0	1	6,159
Lancaster	1	0	0	0	0	0	1	0	0	0	3,873
Lexington	26	9	4	1	1	0	7	9	14	11	317,853
Louisville Metro	5	3	1	0	0	2	2	1	3	5	683,825
Loyall	1	0	0	0	0	0	0	0	0	1	648
Madisonville	2	2	0	0	0	0	4	0	0	0	19,467
Mayfield	2	0	0	0	0	0	1	0	1	0	10,086
Mount Washington	3	0	0	0	0	0	1	0	0	2	14,162
Murray	1	1	0	0	0	0	1	1	0	0	19,182
Nicholasville	5	1	0	0	0	0	2	0	3	1	30,093
Owensboro	4	0	0	0	0	0	1	0	0	3	59,359
Paducah	2	1	0	0	0	0	0	1	1	1	24,836
Paris	0	1	0	0	0	0	0	0	1	0	9,883
Radcliff	3	0	0	0	0	1	1	0	2	1	22,346
Richmond	1	0	0	0	0	0	0	0	0	1	33,965
Shelbyville	2	0	0	0	0	0	1	1	0	0	15,488
Shively	0	0	1	0	0	0	0	1	0	0	15,800
Stanton	0	1	0	0	0	0	0	0	1	0	2,651
St. Matthews	3	0	0	0	0	0	0	0	2	1	18,127
Versailles	1	0	0	0	0	0	0	1	0	0	25,923
Winchester	3	0	0	0	0	0	1	0	2	0	18,461
Universities and Colleges	3	1	2	0	0	0					
Eastern Kentucky University	1	0	0	0	0	0	0	1	0	0	16,844
Murray State University	0	1	0	0	0	0	0	0	0	1	10,998
University of Kentucky	1	0	0	0	0	0	0	0	0	1	29,727
University of Louisville	0	0	2	0	0	0	1	1	0	0	21,294
Western Kentucky University	1	0	0	0	0	0	0	0	1	0	20,063
Metropolitan Counties	14	4	1	1	0	0					
Boone	1	0	1	0	0	0	0	1	1	0	
Boyd	1	0	0	0	0	0	1	0	0	0	
Bracken	0	0	0	1	0	0	0	0	0	1	
Bullitt	4	0	0	0	0	0	0	2	2	0	
Campbell County Police Department	1	0	0	0	0	0	0	1	0	0	
Christian	1	0	0	0	0	0	0	0	1	0	
Daviess	1	1	0	0	0	0	0	0	0	2	
Hardin	1	0	0	0	0	0	1	0	0	0	
Jefferson	0	1	0	0	0	0	1	0	0	0	

(Number.)

State/agency	Number of incidents per bias motivation						Number of incidents per quarter				Population[1]
	Race/ Ethnicity/ Ancestry	Religion	Sexual orientation	Disability	Gender	Gender Identity	1st quarter	2nd quarter	3rd quarter	4th quarter	
Kenton	1	0	0	0	0	0	1	0	0	0	
Oldham County Police Department	1	0	0	0	0	0	0	0	1	0	
Pendleton	0	1	0	0	0	0	0	0	0	1	
Shelby	1	1	0	0	0	0	1	0	1	0	
Spencer	1	0	0	0	0	0	0	0	1	0	
Nonmetropolitan Counties	10	1	0	0	0	0					
Anderson	1	0	0	0	0	0	0	0	0	1	
Franklin	1	1	0	0	0	0	0	1	1	0	
Letcher	1	0	0	0	0	0	1	0	0	0	
Mason	1	0	0	0	0	0	0	0	0	1	
McCracken	1	0	0	0	0	0	1	0	0	0	
McCreary	1	0	0	0	0	0	0	1	0	0	
Muhlenberg County Police Department	2	0	0	0	0	0	2	0	0	0	
Nelson	1	0	0	0	0	0	0	0	1	0	
Wolfe	1	0	0	0	0	0	1	0	0	0	
State Police Agencies	5	6	0	0	0	0					
State Police:											
Bowling Green	1	3	0	0	0	0	0	0	2	2	
Harlan	0	1	0	0	0	0	0	1	0	0	
Hazard	2	0	0	0	0	0	0	0	1	1	
Henderson	1	1	0	0	0	0	0	0	2	0	
Mayfield	1	0	0	0	0	0	0	0	1	0	
Richmond	0	1	0	0	0	0	1	0	0	0	
Other Agencies	3	1	0	0	0	0					
Fayette County Schools	2	0	0	0	0	0	1	0	0	1	
Jefferson County School District	1	1	0	0	0	0	1	0	1	0	
LOUISIANA											
Total	20	3	4	0	0	0					
Cities	7	2	2	0	0	0					
Baton Rouge	2	0	1	0	0	0	0	0	1	2	228,389
New Orleans[2]	3	2	1	0	0	0	3	1	0	1	397,208
Thibodaux	1	0	0	0	0	0	0	0	1	0	14,588
Westlake	1	0	0	0	0	0	1	0	0	0	4,626
Metropolitan Counties	11	1	2	0	0	0					
Bossier	1	0	1	0	0	0	1	0	1	0	
Caddo	0	1	0	0	0	0	0	0	0	1	
St. Charles	6	0	0	0	0	0	0	0	6		
St. John the Baptist	4	0	1	0	0	0	0	3	2	0	
Nonmetropolitan Counties	2	0	0	0	0	0					
Avoyelles	1	0	0	0	0	0			1		
Madison	1	0	0	0	0	0	0	0	1	0	
MAINE											
Total	21	11	8	0	0	0					
Cities	16	10	6	0	0	0					
Augusta	0	1	1	0	0	0	1	0	1	0	18,347
Biddeford	0	1	0	0	0	0	0	0	1	0	21,285
Farmington	0	0	1	0	0	0	0	0	1	0	7,401
Lewiston	2	0	0	0	0	0	0	1	1	0	36,126
Lincoln	1	0	0	0	0	0	0	0	0	1	5,020
Old Orchard Beach	1	0	0	0	0	0	0	0	0	1	8,807
Portland	6	3	2	0	0	0	2	3	6	0	67,041
Saco	4	2	0	0	0	0	1	2	1	2	19,197
Sanford	1	0	1	0	0	0	0	1	0	1	20,914
Scarborough	0	1	0	0	0	0	0	1	0	0	19,851
South Portland	0	2	1	0	0	0	0	1	1	1	25,674
Waterville	1	0	0	0	0	0	0	0	0	1	16,370
Universities and Colleges	4	1	2	0	0	0					
University of Southern Maine	4	1	2	0	0	0	2	0	3	2	7,739
State Police Agencies	1	0	0	0	0	0					
State Police, Kennebec County	1	0	0	0	0	0	1	0	0	0	
MARYLAND											
Total	24	7	6	0	0	0					
Cities	2	0	3	0	0	0					
Baltimore	1	0	2	0	0	0	0	1	2	0	618,385

Table 13. Hate Crime Incidents Per Bias Motivation and Quarter, by Selected State and Agency, 2016—Continued

(Number.)

State/agency	Race/Ethnicity/Ancestry	Religion	Sexual orientation	Disability	Gender	Gender Identity	1st quarter	2nd quarter	3rd quarter	4th quarter	Population[1]
Laurel	1	0	1	0	0	0	0	2	0	0	26,424
Universities and Colleges	1	0	0	0	0	0					
University of Maryland, College Park	1	0	0	0	0	0	0	0	0	1	38,140
Metropolitan Counties	20	6	3	0	0	0					
Anne Arundel County Police Department	10	5	1	0	0	0	2	1	3	10	
Baltimore County Police Department	1	0	0	0	0	0	0	0	1	0	
Harford2	4	0	0	0	0	0	1	1	0	2	
Howard County Police Department	1	0	0	0	0	0	0		0	1	
Montgomery County Police Department	4	1	2	0	0	0	2		3	2	
State Police Agencies	0	1	0	0	0	0					
State Police, Anne Arundel County	0	1	0	0	0	0	0	0	0	1	
Other Agencies	1	0	0	0	0	0					
National Capitol Park Police, Montgomery County	1	0	0	0	0	0	0	1	0	0	
MASSACHUSETTS											
Total	212	94	76	8	8	16					
Cities	194	71	65	8	7	16					
Acton	2	0	0	0	0	1	1	2	0	0	23,770
Andover	2	1	0	0	0	0	1	2	0	0	35,558
Arlington2	9	1	0	1	0	0	2	4	3	1	45,004
Barnstable	0	0	3	1	0	0	1	0	3	0	43,974
Belmont	1	0	0	0	0	0	0	0	0	1	25,637
Beverly	2	1	0	0	0	0	1	1	1	0	41,303
Billerica	1	1	0	0	0	0	1	0	0	1	42,965
Boston2	75	16	28	1	0	9	29	34	27	30	673,880
Boxford	0	1	0	0	0	0	0	0	0	1	8,271
Braintree2	6	1	1	0	1	0	3	1	2	1	37,673
Cambridge2	16	6	4	0	0	0	5	7	3	10	111,030
Chelmsford	0	0	0	0	1	0	0	1	0	0	35,251
Chelsea	0	1	0	0	0	0	0	0	1	0	40,096
Chicopee	1	0	0	0	0	0	1	0	0	0	56,887
Cohasset	1	0	0	0	0	0	0	0	0	1	8,538
Danvers	0	3	0	0	0	0	0	0	1	2	27,997
Dartmouth	1	0	0	0	0	0	0	0	1	0	34,630
Dennis	2	0	0	0	0	0	0	0	1	1	13,905
Dudley	0	1	0	0	0	0	0	0	0	1	11,558
Everett2	7	1	0	0	0	0	1	0	4	3	46,754
Fitchburg	0	1	0	0	0	0	0	0	0	1	40,391
Framingham	3	0	0	0	0	0	1	1	1	0	71,422
Freetown	1	0	0	0	0	0	0	0	1	0	9,199
Greenfield	0	0	0	0	1	0	0	0	1	0	17,456
Haverhill2	3	1	2	0	0	0	0	1	1	3	62,851
Holliston	0	0	1	0	0	0	0	1	0	0	14,656
Hopkinton	0	2	1	0	0	0	1	2	0	0	16,960
Lancaster	0	0	1	0	0	0	1	0	0	0	8,150
Lawrence	0	0	1	0	0	0	0	0	0	1	80,622
Lenox	0	0	1	0	0	0	0	0	1	0	4,971
Lexington	1	1	0	0	0	0	0	0	2	0	33,643
Lowell	0	1	1	0	0	0	1	0	0	1	111,027
Lynn2	5	0	2	0	0	1	2	1	3	1	92,443
Malden	1	0	2	0	0	0	0	0	2	1	61,102
Manchester-by-the-Sea	0	0	0	1	0	0	0	0	1	0	5,387
Mansfield	1	0	0	0	0	0	0	0	0	1	23,681
Mattapoisett	1	0	0	0	0	0	0	1	0	0	6,282
Medford	3	0	0	0	0	0	0	0	1	2	57,367
Methuen2	2	1	0	0	0	0	0	0	2	0	49,912
Milford	1	0	0	0	0	0	0	0	0	1	28,606
Millbury	0	1	0	0	0	0	1	0	0	0	13,532
Milton	1	0	1	0	0	0	0	0	2	0	27,317
Nahant	1	0	1	0	0	0	1	1	0	0	3,484
Newburyport	1	0	0	0	0	0	0	1	0	0	18,011
Newton2	7	16	0	0	0	1	8	6	4	3	89,116
Northampton2	2	1	1	0	0	0	1	0	2	1	28,521
Pepperell	0	1	0	0	0	0	0	0	1	0	12,242
Pittsfield	1	0	0	0	0	0	0	0	0	1	43,031
Provincetown	0	0	1	0	0	0	0	1	0	0	2,959
Quincy	3	0	1	0	1	0	1	1	2	1	93,437

Table 13. Hate Crime Incidents Per Bias Motivation and Quarter, by Selected State and Agency, 2016—Continued

(Number.)

State/agency	Number of incidents per bias motivation						Number of incidents per quarter				Population[1]
	Race/ Ethnicity/ Ancestry	Religion	Sexual orientation	Disability	Gender	Gender Identity	1st quarter	2nd quarter	3rd quarter	4th quarter	
Randolph	3	0	0	0	0	0	0	1	2	0	33,807
Salem	1	1	3	0	0	0	0	2	3	0	42,888
Saugus	1	0	0	0	0	0	1	0	0	0	28,131
Sharon	0	0	0	0	1	0	0	0	0	1	18,200
Shelburne	0	0	0	1	0	0	0	0	0	1	1,839
Somerville	6	3	1	1	0	0	2	2	2	5	80,899
Southbridge	1	0	0	0	0	0	0	0	1	0	16,819
Springfield	7	0	3	0	0	0	3	1	4	2	154,102
Stoughton	0	1	0	0	0	0	0	0	1	0	28,583
Sturbridge	0	0	0	1	0	0	0	1	0	0	9,520
Sudbury	0	1	0	0	0	0	0	0	0	1	19,035
Swampscott	0	3	0	0	0	0	0	2	0	1	14,551
Taunton	3	0	1	0	1	0	2	1	2	0	56,720
Topsfield	1	0	0	0	0	0	1	0	0	0	6,590
Waltham	1	0	1	1	0	3	2	1	1	2	63,613
Watertown[2]	0	2	2	0	0	0	0	0	2	1	34,655
Westfield	0	0	1	0	0	0	0	1	0	0	41,700
West Tisbury	0	0	0	0	1	0	0	0	1	0	2,927
Williamstown	1	0	0	0	0	0	0	0	1	0	7,591
Worcester	5	0	0	0	0	1	0	1	2	3	184,595
Universities and Colleges	14	22	10	0	1	0					
Boston University[2]	5	11	4	0	1	0	3	3	9	4	32,158
Brandeis University	0	1	0	0	0	0	0	0	0	1	5,752
Bridgewater State University	0	0	1	0	0	0	1	0	0	0	11,089
Bristol Community College	1	0	0	0	0	0	0	0	0	1	8,761
Clark University	0	3	0	0	0	0	2	0	0	1	3,485
Hampshire College	1	0	0	0	0	0	0	0	0	1	1,410
Massachusetts Institute of Technology	0	1	0	0	0	0	1	0	0	0	11,331
Northeastern University	0	1	0	0	0	0		1			19,940
Salem State University	0	0	3	0	0	0	2	1	0	0	9,215
Tufts University, Suffolk[2]	0	1	0	0	0	0	0	1	0	0	
University of Massachusetts:											
Amherst[2]	6	4	2	0	0	0	6	4	1	0	29,269
Medical Center, Worcester	1	0	0	0	0	0	0	0	0	1	1,079
Other Agencies	4	1	1	0	0	0					
Massachusetts Bay Transportation Authority:											
Middlesex County	1	0	0	0	0	0	0	0	1		
Suffolk County	3	1	1	0	0	0	1	1	1	2	
MICHIGAN											
Total	282	47	59	6	5	0					
Cities	209	41	44	4	1	0					
Albion	2	1	0	0	0	0	0	0	0	3	8,155
Allegan	0	0	1	0	0	0	0	1	0	0	5,086
Ann Arbor	0	1	0	0	0	0	0	0	0	1	117,688
Auburn Hills	1	0	0	0	0	0	0	1	0	0	22,933
Battle Creek	3	0	0	0	0	0	0	1	1	1	60,904
Belleville	1	0	0	0	0	0	0	0	0	1	3,860
Benton Harbor	1	0	0	0	0	0	1	0	0	0	9,963
Benton Township	2	0	0	0	0	0	0	0	2	0	14,413
Berkley	1	0	0	0	0	0	0	0	1	0	15,328
Big Rapids	1	0	0	0	0	0	0	0	0	1	10,389
Birmingham	0	1	0	0	0	0	0	1	0	0	21,012
Blackman Township	3	0	0	0	0	0	0	0	2	1	37,522
Bloomfield Hills	1	1	0	0	0	0	0	1	0	1	4,031
Bloomfield Township	1	1	0	0	0	0	0	0	0	2	42,313
Buena Vista Township	2	0	0	0	0	0	0	1	1	0	8,158
Burton	1	0	0	0	0	0	0	0	1	0	28,563
Cadillac	1	0	0	0	0	0	0	0	0	1	10,372
Caro	1	0	0	0	0	0	0	0	0	1	4,074
Chesterfield Township	1	0	0	0	0	0	1	0	0	0	44,963
Clawson	2	0	0	0	0	0	0	0	1	1	12,053
Clinton Township	1	0	0	0	0	0	1	0	0	0	100,514
Clio	1	0	0	0	0	0	0	0	1	0	2,516
Coldwater	1	0	0	0	0	0	0	1	0	0	10,827
Commerce Township	1	0	0	0	0	0	0	0	1	0	38,218
Dearborn	7	4	3	0	0	0	3	5	5	1	94,646

Table 13. Hate Crime Incidents Per Bias Motivation and Quarter, by Selected State and Agency, 2016—*Continued*

(Number.)

State/agency	Number of incidents per bias motivation						Number of incidents per quarter				Population[1]
	Race/ Ethnicity/ Ancestry	Religion	Sexual orientation	Disability	Gender	Gender Identity	1st quarter	2nd quarter	3rd quarter	4th quarter	
Dearborn Heights	1	1	0	0	0	0	0	0	1	1	55,852
Detroit	16	1	13	2	0	0	6	6	7	13	669,673
East Lansing	2	1	0	0	0	0	2	0	0	1	48,451
Eastpointe	3	0	0	0	0	0	0	1	0	2	32,701
Eaton Rapids	1	0	0	0	0	0	0	0	1	0	5,226
Escanaba	1	0	0	0	1	0	0	0	2	0	12,278
Evart	1	0	0	0	0	0	0	0	1	0	1,853
Farmington	0	0	1	0	0	0	0	0	1	0	10,553
Ferndale	2	0	0	0	0	0	0	1	0	1	20,232
Flint	14	1	1	0	0	0	1	4	8	3	97,548
Flushing	0	0	1	0	0	0	0	1	0	0	8,028
Forsyth Township	1	0	0	0	0	0	1	0	0	0	6,196
Fruitport Township	1	0	0	0	0	0	0	0	1	0	13,879
Galesburg	2	0	0	0	0	0	0	1	0	1	2,050
Garden City	2	1	0	0	0	0	0	0	1	2	26,781
Gaylord	1	0	0	0	0	0	0	0	1	0	3,662
Genesee Township	0	0	1	0	0	0	1	0	0	0	20,393
Grand Rapids	2	0	0	0	0	0	0	1	0	1	196,538
Grandville	0	1	0	0	0	0	0	1	0	0	16,070
Grant	3	0	0	0	0	0	0	2	0	1	880
Grosse Pointe Park	1	0	1	0	0	0	0	0	1	1	11,160
Grosse Pointe Woods	1	0	0	0	0	0	0	1	0	0	15,699
Hampton Township	1	0	0	0	0	0	0	0	0	1	9,401
Hamtramck	3	2	0	0	0	0	2	2	1	0	21,929
Harper Woods	1	0	0	0	0	0	0	1	0	0	13,764
Hart	1	0	0	0	0	0	0	0	1	0	2,093
Hastings	1	0	0	0	0	0	0	1	0	0	7,274
Highland Park	5	1	1	0	0	0	1	0	3	3	10,810
Houghton	2	0	0	0	0	0	1	0	0	1	8,020
Huntington Woods	0	1	0	0	0	0	1	0	0	0	6,360
Huron Township	1	0	0	0	0	0	0	0	1	0	15,622
Independence Township	2	0	0	0	0	0	1	0	0	1	36,689
Inkster	3	2	1	0	0	0	2	1	2	1	24,548
Ishpeming	2	0	0	0	0	0	1	0	0	1	6,485
Kalamazoo	1	0	0	0	0	0	0	1	0	0	76,389
Lansing	1	1	0	0	0	0	2	0	0	0	115,199
Lapeer	1	0	1	0	0	0	1	0	1	0	8,782
Lawton	2	0	0	0	0	0	0	1	0	1	1,860
Leslie	1	0	0	0	0	0	0	1	0	0	1,869
Lincoln Park	1	0	0	0	0	0	0	1	0	0	36,808
Lincoln Township	2	0	0	0	0	0	0	0	0	2	14,500
Livonia	3	1	0	0	0	0	0	0	3	1	94,226
Ludington	3	0	0	0	0	0	0	2	1	0	8,054
Mackinac Island	0	0	1	0	0	0	0	1	0	0	479
Marysville	0	0	1	0	0	0	0	1	0	0	9,722
Mason	1	0	0	0	0	0	0	1	0	0	8,461
Melvindale	2	0	0	0	0	0	0	1	1	0	10,348
Meridian Township	4	1	1	0	0	0	2	0	0	4	42,700
Monroe	2	0	0	0	0	0	0	1	1	0	19,971
Montrose Township	0	1	1	0	0	0	0	2	0	0	7,524
Mount Pleasant	1	0	0	0	0	0	0	1	0	0	26,069
Muskegon	0	1	1	0	0	0	0	0	0	2	38,442
Muskegon Township	0	0	1	0	0	0	0	0	0	1	17,791
Niles	1	1	0	0	0	0	0	0	2	0	11,282
Norton Shores	3	0	0	0	0	0	0	1	1	1	24,256
Ontwa Township-Edwardsburg	0	0	1	0	0	0	0	0	1	0	6,481
Owosso	1	0	0	0	0	0	0	0	1	0	14,605
Oxford Township	1	0	0	0	0	0	1	0	0	0	18,164
Pittsfield Township	1	1	1	0	0	0	0	0	2	1	38,704
Plymouth	0	0	1	0	0	0	0	0	1	0	8,865
Plymouth Township	0	0	1	0	0	0	0	0	0	1	26,870
Pontiac	2	0	0	0	0	0	1	0	1	0	60,003
Portage	1	0	0	0	0	0	0	0	1	0	48,550
Port Huron	0	0	1	0	0	0	0	0	1	0	29,182
Redford Township	1	1	0	0	0	0	0	1	1	0	47,218
Richland	1	0	0	0	0	0	0	1	0	0	793
River Rouge	1	0	0	0	0	0	0	0	0	1	7,480

(Number.)

State/agency	Number of incidents per bias motivation						Number of incidents per quarter				Population[1]
	Race/ Ethnicity/ Ancestry	Religion	Sexual orientation	Disability	Gender	Gender Identity	1st quarter	2nd quarter	3rd quarter	4th quarter	
Rochester Hills	2	0	0	0	0	0	1	0	1	0	73,913
Romulus	4	0	0	0	0	0	0	2	1	1	23,315
Roseville	3	0	0	0	0	0	1	1	1	0	47,704
Royal Oak	1	0	0	0	0	0	1	0	0	0	59,367
Saginaw	3	1	1	0	0	0	2	2	0	1	48,942
Saginaw Township	2	0	0	0	0	0	0	1	1	0	39,421
Saline	1	0	0	0	0	0	0	0	1	0	9,158
Sault Ste. Marie	0	0	2	0	0	0	2	0	0	0	13,763
Shelby Township	3	0	1	0	0	0	0	1	1	2	78,427
Southfield	1	1	1	0	0	0	1	1	0	1	73,438
Southgate	3	0	1	0	0	0	1	2	1	0	29,158
South Lyon	2	0	0	0	0	0	0	1	1	0	11,801
St. Charles	1	1	0	0	0	0	0	0	2	0	1,940
St. Joseph Township	1	0	0	0	0	0	0	1	0	0	9,850
Sturgis	1	0	0	0	0	0	0	1	0	0	10,876
Taylor	3	0	0	0	0	0	0	1	1	1	61,290
Tittabawassee Township	1	0	0	0	0	0	0	0	1	0	9,782
Traverse City	4	3	0	0	0	0	0	2	2	3	15,330
Troy	7	0	0	0	0	0	0	1	3	3	83,743
Van Buren Township	2	0	2	0	0	0	0	0	2	2	28,090
Warren	7	1	0	2	0	0	2	2	2	4	135,620
Waterford Township	1	0	0	0	0	0	1	0	0	0	73,308
West Bloomfield Township	5	4	0	0	0	0	1	2	4	2	66,123
Wyoming	0	1	0	0	0	0	1	0	0	0	75,917
Universities and Colleges	16	4	3	0	0	0					
Eastern Michigan University	4	2	0	0	0	0	0	0	2	4	21,824
Grand Valley State University	0	0	1	0	0	0	0	0	1	0	25,325
Michigan State University	2	1	1	0	0	0	0	0	1	3	50,538
Mott Community College	1	0	0	0	0	0	0	0	1	0	8,617
Schoolcraft College	1	0	0	0	0	0	0	0	1	0	11,687
University of Michigan:											
Ann Arbor	6	1	1	0	0	0	2	2	1	3	43,651
Flint	1	0	0	0	0	0	0	0	0	1	8,470
Western Michigan University	1	0	0	0	0	0	0	0	1	0	23,529
Metropolitan Counties	24	0	8	1	1	0					
Barry	2	0	0	0	0	0	0	2	0	0	
Calhoun	1	0	1	0	0	0	0	0	2	0	
Eaton	1	0	0	0	0	0	0	0	1	0	
Genesee	1	0	0	0	0	0	0	0	0	1	
Ingham	2	0	0	0	0	0	0	2	0	0	
Jackson	3	0	0	0	0	0	0	0	3	0	
Kent	1	0	1	0	0	0	1	1	0	0	
Lapeer	2	0	1	0	0	0	2	0	0	1	
Livingston	0	0	0	1	1	0	1	0	0	1	
Macomb	1	0	0	0	0	0	0	1	0	0	
Monroe	3	0	0	0	0	0	0	1	1	1	
Montcalm	1	0	1	0	0	0	1	0	1	0	
Muskegon	1	0	0	0	0	0	0	0	1	0	
Oakland	0	0	2	0	0	0	1	0	1	0	
Saginaw	2	0	0	0	0	0	1	1	0	0	
St. Clair	0	0	1	0	0	0	0	0	0	1	
Van Buren	1	0	1	0	0	0	0	0	0	2	
Washtenaw	2	0	0	0	0	0	0	0	1	1	
Nonmetropolitan Counties	18	1	2	1	1	0					
Benzie	1	0	0	0	0	0	1	0	0	0	
Clare	1	0	0	0	0	0	0	0	1	0	
Emmet	1	0	0	0	0	0	0	1	0	0	
Gratiot	2	0	0	0	0	0	0	1	0	1	
Hillsdale	1	0	0	0	0	0	0	1	0	0	
Huron	1	0	0	0	0	0	0	0	0	1	
Ionia	1	0	0	0	0	0	0	0	1	0	
Luce	0	0	0	1	0	0	0	0	1	0	
Marquette	1	0	0	0	0	0	0	1	0	0	
Mason	1	0	0	0	0	0	0	0	0	1	
Mecosta	2	0	0	0	0	0	0	1	1	0	
Menominee	3	0	0	0	0	0	1	2	0	0	
Oceana	1	0	1	0	0	0	1	1	0	0	

Table 13. Hate Crime Incidents Per Bias Motivation and Quarter, by Selected State and Agency, 2016—Continued

(Number.)

State/agency	Number of incidents per bias motivation						Number of incidents per quarter				Population[1]
	Race/ Ethnicity/ Ancestry	Religion	Sexual orientation	Disability	Gender	Gender Identity	1st quarter	2nd quarter	3rd quarter	4th quarter	
Sanilac	1	0	0	0	0	0	0	0	1	0	
Tuscola	1	1	1	0	1	0	0	0	2	2	
State Police Agencies	14	1	2	0	2	0					
State Police:											
Ingham County	2	0	0	0	0	0	0	0	0	2	
Isabella County	3	0	2	0	0	0	1	1	2	1	
Jackson County	1	0	0	0	0	0	0	0	0	1	
Kent County	3	0	0	0	0	0	0	0	1	2	
Livingston County	0	1	0	0	1	0	0	0	0	2	
Mecosta County	1	0	0	0	0	0	0	1	0	0	
Muskegon County	0	0	0	0	1	0	1	0	0	0	
Oceana County	4	0	0	0	0	0	0	2	1	1	
Other Agencies	1	0	0	0	0	0					
Gerald R. Ford International Airport	1	0	0	0	0	0	0	0	1	0	
MINNESOTA											
Total	77	30	15	0	0	0					
Cities	71	28	15	0	0	0					
Blaine	2	0	0	0	0	0	1	0	0	1	63,115
Bloomington	1	0	0	0	0	0	0	0	0	1	87,134
Brooklyn Center	1	0	0	0	0	0	1	0	0	0	30,893
Brooklyn Park	8	1	1	0	0	0	4	2	2	2	79,800
Cottage Grove	2	0	0	0	0	0	1	1	0	0	36,164
Crystal	2	0	0	0	0	0	1	0	1	0	23,102
Eagan	2	0	0	0	0	0	0	0	0	2	66,698
Inver Grove Heights[2]	7	0	1	0	0	0	1	1	3	2	35,049
Little Falls	1	0	0	0	0	0	0	0	1	0	8,611
Mankato	3	0	2	0	0	0	0	0	2	3	41,300
Maplewood	2	0	0	0	0	0	1	0	0	1	41,071
Minneapolis	20	13	5	0	0	0	5	16	11	6	416,751
Minnetonka	0	2	0	0	0	0	1	1	0	0	52,055
Moorhead	0	0	1	0	0	0	1	0	0	0	42,507
New Hope	1	0	0	0	0	0	0	1	0	0	21,168
Oakdale[2]	1	1	0	0	0	0	0	1	0	0	28,211
Orono	0	1	0	0	0	0	0	1	0	0	19,799
Plymouth	4	1	1	0	0	0	2	1	2	1	76,996
Roseville[2]	1	1	1	0	0	0	0	1	1	0	35,954
Sauk Centre	0	1	0	0	0	0	0	1	0	0	4,367
Savage	0	1	0	0	0	0	0	1	0	0	31,118
South St. Paul	1	0	0	0	0	0	0	0	1	0	20,452
Spring Lake Park	1	0	0	0	0	0	0	0	0	1	6,484
St. Cloud	3	1	1	0	0	0	2	2	1		67,341
St. Louis Park	2	3	0	0	0	0	0	0	1	4	48,770
St. Paul	5	2	2	0	0	0	3	1	3	2	303,920
Wayzata	1	0	0	0	0	0	0	0	1	0	6,627
Universities and Colleges	0	1	0	0	0	0					
University of Minnesota, Twin Cities	0	1	0	0	0	0	0	0	0	1	50,678
Metropolitan Counties	5	0	0	0	0	0					
Carver	1	0	0	0	0	0	0	0	1	0	
Mille Lacs	1	0	0	0	0	0	1	0	0	0	
Ramsey	2	0	0	0	0	0	0	0	0	2	
Wright	1	0	0	0	0	0	0	1	0	0	
Nonmetropolitan Counties	1	0	0	0	0	0					
Crow Wing	1	0	0	0	0	0	1	0	0	0	
Other Agencies	0	1	0	0	0	0					
Minneapolis-St. Paul International Airport	0	1	0	0	0	0	0	1		0	
MISSISSIPPI											
Total	4	1	2	0	0	0					
Cities	3	1	1	0	0	0					
Biloxi	0	0	1	0	0	0	1	0	0	0	45,952
Olive Branch	3	1	0	0	0	0	1	0	0	3	36,513
Metropolitan Counties	0	0	1	0	0	0					
DeSoto	0	0	1	0	0	0	1	0	0	0	

Table 13. Hate Crime Incidents Per Bias Motivation and Quarter, by Selected State and Agency, 2016—Continued

(Number.)

State/agency	Race/ Ethnicity/ Ancestry	Religion	Sexual orientation	Disability	Gender	Gender Identity	1st quarter	2nd quarter	3rd quarter	4th quarter	Population[1]
Nonmetropolitan Counties................................	1	0	0	0	0	0					
Stone	1	0	0	0	0	0				1	
MISSOURI											
Total	65	13	10	0	1	0					
Cities	62	11	10	0	1	0					
Battlefield............................	1	0	0	0	0	0	0	0	1	0	6,083
Blue Springs	1	0	0	0	0	0	0	1	0	0	54,445
Bolivar	0	1	0	0	0	0	0	1	0	0	10,790
Branson............................	1	0	0	0	0	0	1	0	0	0	11,593
Bridgeton	0	0	1	0	0	0	0	0	0	1	11,835
Cameron	1	0	0	0	0	0	0	0	1	0	9,817
Chesterfield............................	1	1	0	0	0	0	2	0	0	0	47,939
Clayton	1	0	0	0	0	0	1	0	0	0	15,873
Columbia	5	0	2	0	0	0	0	1	5	1	121,143
Gladstone	1	0	0	0	0	0	0	0	1	0	27,138
Independence	1	0	1	0	0	0	1	1	0	0	117,335
Kansas City	33	6	4	0	0	0	7	7	16	13	478,364
Lee's Summit	1	0	0	0	1	0	0	1	1	0	95,821
Marionville	1	0	0	0	0	0	0	1	0	0	2,181
North Kansas City............................	1	0	0	0	0	0	0	0	0	1	4,387
Rolla............................	2	0	0	0	0	0	2	0	0	0	20,093
St. Charles............................	1	0	0	0	0	0	0	0	1	0	69,364
St. Joseph............................	0	0	1	0	0	0	0	1	0	0	76,577
St. Louis............................	8	1	0	0	0	0		3	3	3	314,507
St. Peters2............................	1	2	1	0	0	0	0	1	2	0	57,835
University City............................	1	0	0	0	0	0	1	0	0		35,002
Universities and Colleges	2	1	0	0	0	0					
University of Missouri:											
Kansas City	2	0	0	0	0	0	0	0	0	2	16,685
St. Louis	0	1	0	0	0	0	0	0	1	0	16,738
Metropolitan Counties	1	1	0	0	0	0					
St. Louis County Police Department....................	1	1	0	0	0	0	2	0	0	0	
MONTANA											
Total	10	5	4	0	1	0					
Cities	4	4	2	0	1	0					
Billings	2	1	1	0	0	0	3	0	0	1	111,447
Columbia Falls............................	0	0	0	0	1	0	1	0	0	0	5,175
Conrad............................	1	0	0	0	0	0	0	1	0	0	2,594
Havre............................	1	0	0	0	0	0	0	0	0	1	9,896
Helena............................	0	3	0	0	0	0	1	2	0	0	31,052
Whitefish............................	0	0	1	0	0	0	0	0	1	0	7,226
Nonmetropolitan Counties................................	6	1	2	0	0	0					
Big Horn............................	2	0	2	0	0	0	2	1	0	1	
Broadwater	1	0	0	0	0	0	0	0	1	0	
Lewis and Clark............................	3	0	0	0	0	0	0	0	3	0	
Richland............................	0	1	0	0	0	0	0	0	1	0	
NEBRASKA											
Total	23	4	3	0	1	0					
Cities	23	4	3	0	1	0					
Crete............................	2	0	0	0	0	0	2	0	0	0	7,047
Grand Island............................	2	0	0	0	0	0	1	1	0	0	51,980
Kearney............................	1	0	0	0	0	0	0	1	0	0	33,471
Lincoln............................	13	3	2	0	1	0	6	6	4	3	281,138
Norfolk............................	1	0	0	0	0	0	0	1	0	0	24,389
Omaha............................	4	1	0	0	0	0	3	0	2	0	446,163
Papillion............................	0	0	1	0	0	0	0	0	1	0	19,576
NEVADA											
Total	31	4	6	0	0	1					
Cities	31	4	6	0	0	1					
Henderson............................	9	1	1	0	0	0	2	4	3	2	291,584
Las Vegas Metropolitan Police Department[2].........	19	1	5	0	0	1	3	10	2	10	1,592,178

Table 13. Hate Crime Incidents Per Bias Motivation and Quarter, by Selected State and Agency, 2016—*Continued*

(Number.)

State/agency	Race/ Ethnicity/ Ancestry	Religion	Sexual orientation	Disability	Gender	Gender Identity	1st quarter	2nd quarter	3rd quarter	4th quarter	Population[1]
North Las Vegas	3	1	0	0	0	0	0	1	3	0	238,554
Reno	0	1	0	0	0	0	0	0	0	1	244,554
NEW HAMPSHIRE											
Total	15	6	5	2	0	0					
Cities	15	6	4	2	0	0					
Belmont	1	0	0	0	0	0	1	0	0	0	7,315
Boscawen	0	0	1	0	0	0	0	1	0	0	3,950
Bow	1	0	0	0	0	0	0	0	1	0	7,779
Brookline	0	1	0	0	0	0	0	1	0	0	5,256
Claremont	1	0	0	0	0	0	0	1	0	0	12,913
Concord	1	0	1	0	0	0	0	1	1	0	42,610
Derry	1	0	0	0	0	0	0	0	0	1	33,249
Dover	0	0	0	1	0	0	1	0	0	0	31,054
Durham	0	1	0	0	0	0	0	0	0	1	17,078
Exeter	2	1	0	0	0	0	1	1	1	0	14,635
Farmington	2	0	1	0	0	0	0	0	3	0	6,841
Hillsborough	1	0	0	0	0	0	0	0	0	1	5,974
Keene	1	2	0	0	0	0	0	0	1	2	23,244
Laconia	1	1	0	1	0	0	0	2	0	1	16,300
Manchester	0	0	1	0	0	0	0	0	0	1	110,353
Pembroke	1	0	0	0	0	0	1	0	0	0	7,118
Sandown	1	0	0	0	0	0	0	0	0	1	6,348
Troy	1	0	0	0	0	0	0	0	1	0	2,075
Universities and Colleges	0	0	1	0	0	0					
University of New Hampshire	0	0	1	0	0	0	1	0	0	0	15,351
NEW JERSEY											
Total	137	110	34	1	0	0					
Cities	130	110	33	1	0	0					
Aberdeen Township	1	1	0	0	0	0		0	1	1	18,562
Allendale	0	1	0	0	0	0	0	1	0	0	6,849
Atlantic City	1	0	0	0	0	0	0	0	1	0	39,202
Bergenfield	0	1	0	0	0	0	0	1	0	0	27,646
Blairstown Township	1	1	0	0	0	0	0	2	0	0	5,791
Bloomfield	1	0	0	0	0	0	0	1	0	0	48,215
Brick Township	0	1	1	0	0	0		1	1	0	74,818
Cinnaminson Township	1	0	0	0	0	0	0	1	0	0	16,871
Colts Neck Township	0	0	1	0	0	0		0	1	0	10,018
Cresskill	0	1	0	0	0	0	0	1	0	0	8,815
Dunellen	0	1	0	0	0	0		0	0	1	7,434
East Brunswick Township	6	2	1	0	0	0		6	2	1	49,016
East Hanover Township	1	0	0	0	0	0		0	0	1	11,233
East Orange	1	0	0	0	0	0	1	0	0	0	64,787
East Rutherford	0	1	0	0	0	0	0	1	0	0	9,166
East Windsor Township	2	0	0	0	0	0		1	0	1	27,537
Edgewater	0	1	0	0	0	0	0	0	0	1	12,079
Edison Township	2	1	0	0	0	0		2	0	1	102,679
Evesham Township	4	1	1	0	0	0	2	1	1	2	45,581
Ewing Township	0	1	0	0	0	0		0	1	0	36,435
Florence Township	0	0	1	0	0	0	0	1	0	0	12,805
Fort Lee	1	1	1	0	0	0	1	0	1	1	36,739
Freehold Borough	2	0	0	0	0	0		0	0	2	11,941
Freehold Township	2	0	0	0	0	0		1	1	0	35,736
Galloway Township	0	1	0	0	0	0	0	0	1	0	37,280
Glassboro	1	1	1	0	0	0		1	0	2	19,245
Hackensack	2	2	1	0	0	0	2	2	0	1	44,968
Hamilton Township, Mercer County	0	2	0	0	0	0		2	0	0	88,665
Hammonton	0	1	0	0	0	0	0	0	1	0	14,585
Hanover Township	1	0	0	0	0	0		0	0	1	14,468
Harrison Township	0	1	1	0	0	0		1	0	1	13,023
Highland Park	2	1	0	0	0	0		3	0	0	14,346
Highlands	1	0	0	0	0	0		0	1	0	4,838
Hillsborough Township	1	0	0	0	0	0		0	0	1	40,037
Hoboken	2	0	1	0	0	0		0	1	2	54,095
Holmdel Township	0	3	0	0	0	0		1	0	2	16,651
Hopewell Township	0	1	0	0	0	0		0	0	1	18,570

(Number.)

State/agency	Number of incidents per bias motivation						Number of incidents per quarter				Population[1]
	Race/ Ethnicity/ Ancestry	Religion	Sexual orientation	Disability	Gender	Gender Identity	1st quarter	2nd quarter	3rd quarter	4th quarter	
Howell Township	4	6	1	0	0	0		3	7	1	52,306
Jackson Township	1	1	0	0	0	0		2	0	0	56,563
Jersey City	3	1	0	0	0	0		0	1	3	266,179
Keansburg	5	0	0	0	0	0		1	2	2	9,828
Lacey Township	0	1	0	0	0	0		0	1	0	28,540
Lakewood Township	3	14	0	0	0	0	2	6	7	2	100,269
Lindenwold	0	1	0	0	0	0	0	0	1	0	17,340
Linwood	0	1	0	0	0	0	0	0	1	0	6,950
Little Falls Township	2	0	1	0	0	0		0	0	3	14,478
Livingston Township	1	1	0	0	0	0	1	0	0	1	29,788
Lodi	0	1	0	0	0	0	0	1	0	0	24,841
Long Branch	2	1	0	0	0	0		0	0	3	30,959
Madison	0	1	0	0	0	0		1	0	0	16,098
Magnolia	1	1	0	0	0	0	0	1	1	0	4,267
Manalapan Township	0	3	1	0	0	0		1	0	3	40,407
Manasquan	1	0	0	0	0	0		0	0	1	5,798
Manchester Township	1	0	0	0	0	0		0	0	1	43,525
Medford Township	2	1	0	0	0	0	0	0	3		23,481
Metuchen	0	1	0	0	0	0		0	0	1	13,879
Middletown Township	1	0	0	0	0	0		0	0	1	65,919
Monmouth Beach	1	0	0	1	0	0		2	0	0	3,233
Montclair	2	2	2	0	0	0	2	0	0	4	38,108
Montville Township	1	0	0	0	0	0		1	0	0	21,801
Moonachie	1	0	0	0	0	0	0	0	0	1	2,790
Moorestown Township	0	1	0	0	0	0	0	0	1	0	20,530
Mount Arlington	1	0	0	0	0	0		0	1	0	5,324
Mount Laurel Township	0	2	0	0	0	0	0	0	1	1	41,828
Mount Olive Township	1	0	0	0	0	0		1	0	0	29,095
Neptune Township	8	0	4	0	0	0		3	7	2	27,505
Newark	0	2	1	0	0	0	2	0	0	1	281,450
New Brunswick	5	2	2	0	0	0		1	5	3	57,158
New Providence	0	1	0	0	0	0	0	1	0	0	12,461
Newton	0	1	0	0	0	0		0	0	1	7,950
North Brunswick Township	0	1	0	0	0	0		1	0	0	42,777
Northfield	1	1	0	0	0	0	0	0	2	0	8,502
North Haledon	1	0	0	0	0	0		1	0	0	8,529
Nutley Township	1	0	0	0	0	0	0	0	0	1	28,673
Ocean Township, Monmouth County	3	3	3	0	0	0		1	5	3	27,070
Paramus	0	1	0	0	0	0	0	1	0	0	26,958
Passaic	1	0	0	0	0	0		0	1	0	70,972
Pemberton Township	3	0	0	0	0	0	0	1	1	1	27,739
Pequannock Township	1	0	0	0	0	0		1	0	0	15,425
Piscataway Township	0	1	0	0	0	0		0	1	0	58,181
Plainsboro Township	0	1	0	0	0	0		0	0	1	23,621
Point Pleasant Beach	0	1	0	0	0	0		0	1	0	4,519
Pompton Lakes	1	0	0	0	0	0		0	1	0	11,164
Princeton	1	2	1	0	0	0		2	2	0	29,660
Randolph Township	0	2	0	0	0	0		2	0	0	25,877
Raritan Township	0	0	1	0	0	0		0	1	0	22,011
Readington Township	1	0	0	0	0	0		1	0	0	15,893
Robbinsville Township	0	1	0	0	0	0		0	0	1	14,209
Rockaway Township	0	1	0	0	0	0		0	0	1	24,655
Saddle Brook Township	0	1	0	0	0	0	1	0	0	0	14,108
Scotch Plains Township	1	0	0	0	0	0	0	0	1	0	24,144
Sea Isle City	1	0	0	0	0	0	0	0	1	0	2,080
Secaucus	2	1	1	0	0	0		0	3	1	19,528
Somerville	0	0	1	0	0	0		0	1	0	12,198
South Brunswick Township	3	11	1	0	0	0		4	5	6	45,862
South Orange	2	0	1	0	0	0	1	0	0	2	16,332
South River	0	1	0	0	0	0		1	0	0	16,391
Spotswood	1	0	0	0	0	0		1	0	0	8,477
Toms River Township	0	2	0	0	0	0		0	2	0	90,504
Trenton	1	0	0	0	0	0		0	1	0	83,644
Union Township	0	1	0	0	0	0	0	0	0	1	58,109
Vineland	2	2	0	0	0	0	0	0	0	4	60,823
Voorhees Township	2	0	0	0	0	0	1	0	0	1	29,235
Washington	1	0	0	0	0	0	0	0	0	1	6,508

Table 13. Hate Crime Incidents Per Bias Motivation and Quarter, by Selected State and Agency, 2016—Continued

(Number.)

State/agency	Number of incidents per bias motivation						Number of incidents per quarter				
	Race/ Ethnicity/ Ancestry	Religion	Sexual orientation	Disability	Gender	Gender Identity	1st quarter	2nd quarter	3rd quarter	4th quarter	Population[1]
Washington Township, Gloucester County............	1	0	1	0	0	0		0	2	0	47,477
Washington Township, Warren County.................	1	0	0	0	0	0	0	0	0	1	6,430
West Deptford Township	1	0	0	0	0	0		1	0	0	21,257
West Long Branch	1	1	1	0	0	0		2	0	1	7,975
Winslow Township	1	0	0	0	0	0	0	0	0	1	38,724
Woodbridge Township	0	1	0	0	0	0		0	1	0	102,124
Woodbury............................	11	0	0	0	0	0		6	5		9,937
Woolwich Township	1	0	0	0	0	0		0	0	1	12,675
State Police Agencies..................................	7	0	1	0	0	0					
State Police:											
Burlington County...............	1	0	1	0	0	0	1	0	1	0	
Cumberland County.............	1	0	0	0	0	0	0	0	1	0	
Salem County..................	1	0	0	0	0	0		1	0	0	
Sussex County.................	3	0	0	0	0	0	3	0	0	0	
Warren County.................	1	0	0	0	0	0	0	0	1	0	
NEW MEXICO											
Total	8	9	9	0	0	0					
Cities	8	9	9	0	0	0					
Albuquerque......................	7	9	9	0	0	0	2	2	11	10	561,560
Los Lunas.......................	1	0	0	0	0	0		1			15,398
NEW YORK											
Total	155	311	99	1	5	24					
Cities	101	205	87	1	5	20					
Albany	1	0	0	0	0	0	0	1	0	0	98,617
Amherst Town......................	2	0	0	0	0	0	0	2	0	0	120,436
Auburn	0	1	0	0	0	0	0	0	1		26,854
Bedford Town	0	1	0	0	0	0	0	0	1	0	18,063
Binghamton	1	0	0	0	0	0	0	0	1	0	45,780
Brighton Town....................	1	0	0	0	0	0	0	1	0	0	36,889
Buffalo	5	0	1	0	0	1	1	1	4	1	257,446
Cheektowaga Town	1	0	0	0	0	0	0	0	0	1	78,100
Clarkstown Town	1	2	0	0	0	0	0	0	3	0	82,171
Colonie Town	0	1	0	0	0	0	0	0	1	0	80,075
Cooperstown Village...............	1	0	0	0	0	0	0	0	1	0	1,780
Crawford Town	1	0	0	0	0	0	0	0	0	1	9,202
Dobbs Ferry Village...............	0	1	0	0	0	0	0	1	0	0	11,180
Elmira..........................	1	0	0	0	0	0	0	1	0	0	27,995
Glen Cove.......................	0	0	1	0	0	0	0	1	0	0	27,480
Hamburg Town	1	0	0	0	0	0	1	0	0	0	46,028
Lake Placid Village................	1	0	0	0	0	0	0	1	0	0	2,453
Larchmont Village.................	0	2	0	0	0	0	0	1	0	1	6,186
Middletown	0	1	0	0	0	0	0	1	0	0	27,752
Monroe Village...................	0	3	0	0	0	0	1	1	1	0	8,680
New Rochelle	1	4	0	0	0	0	1	0	0	4	80,389
New York........................	74	183	79	1	5	19	66	85	85	125	8,566,917
Niagara Falls.....................	0	0	1	0	0	0	0	0	1	0	48,675
North Tonawanda.................	2	0	0	0	0	0	0	0	2	0	30,634
Norwich	1	0	0	0	0	0	0	0	0	1	6,929
Peekskill........................	0	0	1	0	0	0	1	0	0	0	24,129
Ramapo Town	1	1	1	0	0	0	1	1	1	0	92,620
Rochester.......................	1	0	1	0	0	0	0	1	0	1	209,643
Saratoga Springs	0	1	0	0	0	0	0	0	0	1	28,005
Schenectady.....................	0	1	0	0	0	0	0	0	0	1	65,138
Southampton Town................	1	0	0	0	0	0	1	0	0	0	51,191
Spring Valley Village..............	0	1	0	0	0	0	0	0	1	0	32,844
Utica...........................	0	0	1	0	0	0	0	1	0	0	60,879
Wellsville Village.................	1	0	0	0	0	0	0	0	0	1	4,506
Yonkers.........................	2	2	1	0	0	0	0	1	1	3	202,075
Universities and Colleges.....................................	15	10	4	0	0	3					
Cornell University	0	0	2	0	0	0	0	1	1	0	21,904
State University of New York:											
Binghamton	1	0	1	0	0	0	0	1	1	0	16,913
Buffalo	1	3	0	0	0	3	3	3	0	1	29,796
Downstate Medical Center...........	0	0	1	0	0	0	0	0	1	0	1,858
State University of New York Agricultural and Technical College, Morrisville...............	4	2	0	0	0	0	0	0	6	0	2,940

Table 13. Hate Crime Incidents Per Bias Motivation and Quarter, by Selected State and Agency, 2016—*Continued*

(Number.)

State/agency	Race/Ethnicity/Ancestry	Religion	Sexual orientation	Disability	Gender	Gender Identity	1st quarter	2nd quarter	3rd quarter	4th quarter	Population[1]
State University of New York College:											
Brockport	1	0	0	0	0	0	0	0	1	0	8,161
Buffalo	1	1	0	0	0	0	1	0	0	1	10,330
Geneseo	2	1	0	0	0	0	0	0	0	3	5,699
New Paltz	3	0	0	0	0	0	0	0	0	3	7,751
Plattsburgh	1	1	0	0	0	0	1	0	0	1	5,718
Potsdam	1	0	0	0	0	0	0	0	0	1	3,904
Purchase	0	2	0	0	0	0	1	1	0	0	4,169
Metropolitan Counties	17	79	4	0	0	1					
Albany	1	0	0	0	0	0	0	0	0	1	
Monroe	1	1	0	0	0	0	2	0	0	0	
Nassau	7	45	0	0	0	0	8	10	9	25	
Oswego	1	0	0	0	0	0	0	0	0	1	
Saratoga	0	1	0	0	0	0	0	1	0	0	
Schoharie	0	1	0	0	0	0	1	0	0	0	
Suffolk County Police Department	7	30	4	0	0	1	10	12	8	12	
Westchester Public Safety	0	1	0	0	0	0	0	0	1	0	
Nonmetropolitan Counties	1	0	0	0	0	0					
Chenango	1	0	0	0	0	0	0	1	0		
State Police Agencies	10	5	4	0	0	0					
State Police:											
Albany County	1	1	1	0	0	0	0	0	0	3	
Chemung County	0	1	0	0	0	0	1	0	0	0	
Dutchess County	0	1	0	0	0	0	0	0	0	1	
Franklin County	0	0	1	0	0	0	0	0	1	0	
Jefferson County	1	0	1	0	0	0	0	1	0	1	
Montgomery County	1	0	0	0	0	0	0	0	0	1	
New York County	2	1	0	0	0	0	0	0	0	3	
Niagara County	0	0	1	0	0	0	0	0	0	1	
Orange County	0	1	0	0	0	0	1	0	0	0	
Oswego County	1	0	0	0	0	0	1	0	0	0	
Rockland County	1	0	0	0	0	0	0	1	0	0	
Schoharie County	1	0	0	0	0	0	0	1	0	0	
Wayne County	1	0	0	0	0	0	0	1	0	0	
Westchester County	1	0	0	0	0	0	0	0	0	1	
Other Agencies	11	12	0	0	0	0					
New York City Metropolitan Transportation Authority	11	11	0	0	0	0	3	2	2	15	
State Park, Finger Lakes Region	0	1	0	0	0	0	0	0	1	0	
NORTH CAROLINA											
Total	99	21	26	0	1	2					
Cities	75	17	24	0	0	1					
Apex	3	0	0	0	0	0	0	1	1	1	47,324
Asheville	1	0	2	0	0	0	1	0	2	0	89,546
Boone	0	0	1	0	0	0	0	1	0	0	18,374
Charlotte-Mecklenburg	16	3	8	0	0	0	6	11	5	5	896,379
Concord	0	1	0	0	0	0	0	0	1	0	89,446
Durham	2	1	0	0	0	0	0	1	1	1	263,716
Fayetteville	7	0	0	0	0	0	0	1	4	2	202,200
Gastonia	3	0	0	0	0	0	0	0	2	1	75,118
Greensboro	1	4	1	0	0	0	0	1	4	1	288,618
Greenville	1	0	4	0	0	1	2	2	1	1	91,766
Hickory	1	0	0	0	0	0	0	0	0	1	40,437
High Point	5	0	0	0	0	0	1	1	0	3	111,435
Huntersville	1	0	0	0	0	0	1	0	0	0	53,932
Jacksonville	0	0	1	0	0	0	0	0	1	0	66,686
Littleton	1	0	0	0	0	0	0	1	0	0	641
Morganton	4	0	0	0	0	0	0	0	1	3	16,656
Raleigh	15	7	6	0	0	0	8	6	9	5	460,593
Roanoke Rapids2	4	0	0	0	0	0	1	1	2	0	15,273
Rockingham	1	0	0	0	0	0	0	0	0	1	9,155
Rocky Mount	1	0	0	0	0	0	0	0	1	0	55,431
Salisbury	3	0	0	0	0	0	0	1	0	2	34,121
Siler City	1	0	0	0	0	0	0	0	0	1	8,498
Wilmington	4	1	0	0	0	0	2	1	1	1	117,852
Wilson	0	0	1	0	0	0	0	0	1	0	49,734

Table 13. Hate Crime Incidents Per Bias Motivation and Quarter, by Selected State and Agency, 2016—*Continued*

(Number.)

State/agency	Number of incidents per bias motivation						Number of incidents per quarter				Population[1]
	Race/ Ethnicity/ Ancestry	Religion	Sexual orientation	Disability	Gender	Gender Identity	1st quarter	2nd quarter	3rd quarter	4th quarter	
Universities and Colleges	4	1	2	0	0	1					
Duke University	0	1	0	0	0	0	0	0	0	1	15,984
East Carolina University	1	0	0	0	0	0	1	0	0	0	28,289
North Carolina Central University	0	0	1	0	0	1	0	0	1	1	8,011
North Carolina School of the Arts	2	0	0	0	0	0	1	1	0	0	970
University of North Carolina, Greensboro	1	0	1	0	0	0	0	1	0	1	19,393
Metropolitan Counties	15	2	0	0	0	0					
Forsyth	6	0	0	0	0	0	1	3	1	1	
Franklin	4	0	0	0	0	0	2	1	0	1	
Gaston County Police Department	1	0	0	0	0	0	0	0	1	0	
Iredell	2	0	0	0	0	0	1	0	0	1	
New Hanover	1	0	0	0	0	0	0	0	0	1	
Randolph	0	1	0	0	0	0	0	0	1	0	
Yadkin	1	1	0	0	0	0	1	0	0	1	
Nonmetropolitan Counties	4	1	0	0	1	0					
Jackson[2]	1	1	0	0	0	0	0	0	0	1	
Moore	0	0	0	0	1	0	1	0	0	0	
Sampson[2]	2	0	0	0	0	0	0	0	0	2	
Surry	1	0	0	0	0	0	0	0	0	1	
Other Agencies	1	0	0	0	0	0					
University of North Carolina Hospitals	1	0	0	0	0	0	0	0	1	0	
NORTH DAKOTA											
Total	7	1	0	0	0	0					
Cities	5	1	0	0	0	0					
Bismarck	2	0	0	0	0	0	0	0	0	2	73,248
Grand Forks	0	1	0	0	0	0	0	0	1	0	57,853
Watford City	2	0	0	0	0	0	0	0	1	1	8,819
Williston	1	0	0	0	0	0	0	0	1	0	29,929
Universities and Colleges	1	0	0	0	0	0					
University of North Dakota	1	0	0	0	0	0	0	0	1	0	14,951
Nonmetropolitan Counties	1	0	0	0	0	0					
Hettinger	1	0	0	0	0	0	0	0	0	1	
OHIO											
Total	336	35	60	9	1	1					
Cities	308	28	56	8	1	0					
Akron	3	0	1	0	0	0	1	2	1	0	197,257
Albany	0	0	1	0	0	0	0	0	0	1	918
Athens	1	0	0	0	0	0	0	0	1	0	25,203
Aurora	2	0	1	0	0	0	0	1	1	1	15,897
Barberton	1	0	0	0	0	0	0	0	0	1	26,172
Beaver Township	0	0	1	0	0	0	0	1	0	0	6,492
Bellbrook	0	1	0	1	0	0	2	0	0	0	7,074
Bellefontaine	1	0	1	0	0	0	0	1	1	0	13,073
Bexley	0	1	0	0	0	0	0	0	1	0	13,775
Blue Ash	1	1	1	0	1	0	3	0	0	1	12,169
Boardman[2]	1	0	0	0	0	0	0	1	0	0	39,692
Canton	1	0	0	0	0	0	0	1	0	0	71,652
Chillicothe	1	0	0	0	0	0	0	0	1	0	21,692
Cincinnati	32	2	8	0	0	0	7	10	10	15	298,880
Circleville	1	0	0	0	0	0	0	0	1	0	13,930
Cleveland	8	0	0	0	0	0	2	5	1	0	386,227
Colerain Township	4	0	0	0	0	0	3	1	0	0	58,907
Columbus[2]	123	10	18	0	0	0	42	29	49	31	862,515
Dayton	5	0	0	0	0	0	0	4	0	1	140,260
Defiance	1	0	0	0	0	0	0	0	0	1	16,697
Delhi Township	3	0	0	0	0	0	1	1	1	0	29,573
East Palestine	2	0	0	0	0	0	0	1	1	0	4,548
Elyria	2	0	1	0	0	0	1	2	0	0	53,633
Fairborn	1	0	1	0	0	0	1	0	0	1	33,587
Fairview Park	1	0	0	0	0	0	0	0	0	1	16,318
Findlay	0	1	0	0	0	0	1	0			41,156
Gahanna	2	1	0	0	0	0	1	2	0	0	34,859
Garfield Heights	0	0	1	0	0	0	1			0	27,938
Green Township	0	0	1	0	0	0	0	0	0	1	58,764
Greenville	1	0	0	0	0	0	0	1	0	0	12,962

(Number.)

State/agency	Number of incidents per bias motivation						Number of incidents per quarter				Population[1]
	Race/ Ethnicity/ Ancestry	Religion	Sexual orientation	Disability	Gender	Gender Identity	1st quarter	2nd quarter	3rd quarter	4th quarter	
Grove City	5	0	0	0	0	0	1	2	1	1	40,161
Hamilton	9	0	0	0	0	0	1	3	3	2	62,423
Heath	1	0	0	0	0	0	0	0	1	0	10,528
Hilliard	2	0	1	0	0	0	0	2	1	0	34,832
Huber Heights	3	0	1	1	0	0	1	1	2	1	38,180
Independence	1	0	0	0	0	0	0	0	0	1	7,132
Jackson Township, Stark County	2	0	1	0	0	0	2	0	1	0	40,780
Lockland	1	0	0	0	0	0	1	0	0	0	3,422
Lyndhurst	1	1	1	0	0	0	0	1	1	1	13,624
Mansfield	1	2	0	0	0	0	2	1	0	0	46,656
Marietta	1	0	0	0	0	0	0	1	0		13,867
Massillon	3	0	0	0	0	0	1	2	0	0	32,268
Maumee	0	1	0	0	0	0	0	0	1	0	13,875
Mayfield Heights	1	0	0	0	0	0	0	1	0	0	18,770
Medina Township	1	0	0	0	0	0	1	0	0	0	9,015
Miamisburg	0	1	0	0	0	0	0	1	0	0	20,000
Miami Township, Montgomery County	1	0	0	0	0	0	0	0	0	1	29,140
Monroe	1	0	0	0	0	0	0	1	0	0	15,933
Montgomery	1	0	0	0	0	0	1	0	0	0	10,558
Montpelier	1	0	0	0	0	0	1	0	0	0	3,980
Montville Township	1	0	0	0	0	0	0	1	0	0	11,815
Moraine	3	0	0	0	0	0	1	0	1	1	6,385
Mount Healthy	1	0	0	0	0	0	0	0	1	0	6,028
Napoleon	2	0	2	0	0	0	2	0	1	1	8,566
New Franklin	1	0	0	0	0	0	0	1	0	0	14,285
Newton Falls	1	0	0	0	0	0	0	0	1	0	4,628
North College Hill	0	0	1	0	0	0	0	0	1	0	9,320
Oberlin	0	1	0	0	0	0	0	0	0	1	8,342
Parma	1	2	0	0	0	0	1	1	0	1	79,576
Portsmouth	1	0	0	0	0	0	0	1	0		20,442
Powell	1	0	0	0	0	0	0	1	0	0	13,273
Reynoldsburg	1	0	0	0	0	0	0	0	1	0	37,406
Salem	0	0	0	4	0	0	1	0	3	0	11,943
Shelby	1	0	1	0	0	0	0	1	1	0	9,012
Sidney	2	0	1	0	0	0	0	1	2	0	20,797
South Euclid	1	0	0	0	0	0	0	1	0	0	21,686
Springfield Township, Hamilton County	0	0	1	0	0	0	0	1	0	0	36,527
Springfield Township, Summit County	1	0	1	0	0	0	0	1	0	1	17,813
Steubenville	1	0	0	0	0	0		0	1	0	18,137
Streetsboro	0	0	0	1	0	0	0	0	0	1	16,364
Toledo	31	0	4	0	0	0	3	3	17	12	278,366
Troy	0	0	2	0	0	0	2	0	0	0	25,745
Upper Arlington	1	0	0	0	0	0	1	0	0	0	35,150
Upper Sandusky	1	0	0	0	0	0	0	0	1	0	6,515
Urbana	9	0	0	0	0	0	0	0	0	9	11,482
Vienna Township	1	0	0	0	0	0	0	0	0	1	3,817
Wadsworth	1	0	0	0	0	0	0	0	1	0	21,910
Wapakoneta	2	1	0	0	0	0	0	1	1	1	9,815
Warren	1	0	0	0	0	0	0	0	0	1	40,005
West Chester Township	1	0	0	0	0	0	0	1	0	0	61,080
West Jefferson	0	0	0	1	0	0	0	0	1	0	4,291
Wilmington	1	1	0	0	0	0	0	1	1	0	12,443
Wooster	1	0	0	0	0	0	1	0	0	0	26,883
Xenia	1	0	0	0	0	0	1	0	0	0	26,037
Yellow Springs	1	1	0	0	0	0	1	1	0	0	3,857
Youngstown	2	0	1	0	0	0	0	1	2	0	64,181
Zanesville	1	0	2	0	0	0	1	0	1	1	25,494
Universities and Colleges	5	0	1	0	0	0					
Capital University	0	0	1	0	0	0	0	0	0	1	3,465
Kent State University	1	0	0	0	0	0			1		30,067
Ohio State University, Columbus	2	0	0	0	0	0	0	0	0	2	58,663
Otterbein University	1	0	0	0	0	0	0	1	0	0	2,808
University of Akron	1	0	0	0	0	0	0	0	1	0	23,101
Metropolitan Counties	13	4	3	1	0	1					
Butler	1	1	0	0	0	0	1	0	1	0	
Clark	0	1	1	0	0	0	0	2	0	0	
Clermont	0	1	0	0	0	0	0	1	0	0	

Table 13. Hate Crime Incidents Per Bias Motivation and Quarter, by Selected State and Agency, 2016—Continued

(Number.)

State/agency	Number of incidents per bias motivation						Number of incidents per quarter				Population[1]
	Race/Ethnicity/Ancestry	Religion	Sexual orientation	Disability	Gender	Gender Identity	1st quarter	2nd quarter	3rd quarter	4th quarter	
Delaware	1	0	0	0	0	0	0	0	1	0	
Geauga	1	0	0	0	0	0	0	0	0	1	
Greene	6	1	0	0	0	0	2	1	2	2	
Lawrence	1	0	0	0	0	0	0	0	1	0	
Lorain	0	0	0	0	0	1	0	0	1	0	
Montgomery	1	0	1	0	0	0	0	0	2	0	
Summit	1	0	0	0	0	0	0	0	1	0	
Trumbull	1	0	0	1	0	0	1	0	1	0	
Warren	0	0	1	0	0	0	1	0	0	0	
Nonmetropolitan Counties	7	2	0	0	0	0					
Ashland	1	0	0	0	0	0	0	1	0	0	
Ashtabula	1	0	0	0	0	0	0	0	1	0	
Champaign	1	0	0	0	0	0	0	0	0	1	
Fayette	0	1	0	0	0	0	0	1	0	0	
Gallia	1	0	0	0	0	0	0	0	1	0	
Highland	1	0	0	0	0	0	1	0	0	0	
Mercer	0	1	0	0	0	0	0	1	0	0	
Pike	1	0	0	0	0	0	0	1	0	0	
Ross	1	0	0	0	0	0	0	1	0	0	
Other Agencies	3	1	0	0	0	0					
Cleveland Metropolitan Park District	2	1	0	0	0	0	1	1	1	0	
Ohio Department of Natural Resources	1	0	0	0	0	0	0	0	1	0	
OKLAHOMA											
Total	20	5	5	3	0	0					
Cities	9	4	4	0	0	0					
Anadarko	1	0	0	0	0	0	0	0	1	0	6,702
Blanchard	0	1	0	0	0	0	0	1	0	0	8,461
Collinsville	2	0	0	0	0	0	0	1	0	1	6,678
Cushing	1	1	0	0	0	0	0	0	0	2	7,874
Heavener	0	0	1	0	0	0	1	0	0	0	3,321
Norman	1	0	1	0	0	0	1	0	1	0	122,143
Nowata	0	1	0	0	0	0	0	0	0	1	3,747
Oklahoma City	3	0	0	0	0	0	1	0	0	2	641,681
Perry	0	0	1	0	0	0	1	0	0	0	5,091
Tulsa	0	1	0	0	0	0	0	1	0	0	405,748
Union City	1	0	0	0	0	0	0	0	0	1	2,004
Woodward	0	0	1	0	0	0	0	0	0	1	13,223
Metropolitan Counties	6	1	0	0	0	0					
Lincoln	1	0	0	0	0	0	0	0	1	0	
Okmulgee	1	0	0	0	0	0	0	1	0	0	
Wagoner	4	1	0	0	0	0	1	0	3	1	
Nonmetropolitan Counties	5	0	1	3	0	0					
Craig	0	0	0	1	0	0	0	0	1	0	
Delaware	2	0	0	1	0	0	0	1	2	0	
Garvin	1	0	0	0	0	0	1	0	0	0	
Kingfisher	1	0	0	0	0	0	1	0	0	0	
Payne	0	0	0	1	0	0	0	0	0	1	
Seminole	0	0	1	0	0	0	1	0	0	0	
Woodward	1	0	0	0	0	0	0	0	1	0	
OREGON											
Total	61	23	17	2	0	1					
Cities	57	19	13	1	0	1					
Ashland	1	0	1	0	0	0	1	0	0	1	21,017
Beaverton	2	0	0	0	0	0	0	0	0	2	97,907
Coos Bay	0	1	0	0	0	0	0	0	1	0	16,224
Cornelius	1	0	0	0	0	0	0	0	0	1	12,402
Corvallis	1	1	0	0	0	0	1	1	0	0	56,061
Eugene	27	5	4	1	0	1	2	12	11	13	164,883
Gervais	0	0	1	0	0	0	1	0	0	0	2,663
Gresham	4	1	1	0	0	0	2	1	1	2	111,491
Hood River	0	1	0	0	0	0	1	0			7,719
Lincoln City	0	3	0	0	0	0	0	0	0	3	8,588
Medford	0	0	1	0	0	0	0	1	0	0	80,794
Newberg-Dundee	1	0	0	0	0	0	0	1	0	0	26,105
Oregon City	2	0	0	0	0	0	1	1	0	0	36,485

(Number.)

State/agency	Number of incidents per bias motivation						Number of incidents per quarter				Population[1]
	Race/ Ethnicity/ Ancestry	Religion	Sexual orientation	Disability	Gender	Gender Identity	1st quarter	2nd quarter	3rd quarter	4th quarter	
Portland	5	3	2	0	0	0	2	2	4	2	642,129
Salem	4	2	2	0	0	0	3	1	2	2	166,508
Springfield	6	1	0	0	0	0	2	1	2	2	61,164
Talent	1	0	0	0	0	0	0	1	0	0	6,483
Tigard	2	1	0	0	0	0	0	1	0	2	51,885
Tualatin	0	0	1	0	0	0	0	1	0	0	27,370
Metropolitan Counties	1	1	1	0	0	0					
Jackson	0	1	0	0	0	0	0	0	1	0	
Lane	1	0	0	0	0	0	0	1	0	0	
Washington	0	0	1	0	0	0	0	0	0	1	
Nonmetropolitan Counties	3	3	3	1	0	0					
Crook	1	0	1	0	0	0	2	0	0	0	
Hood River	0	1	0	0	0	0	1	0	0	0	
Jefferson	0	0	1	0	0	0	0	0	1	0	
Morrow	1	1	0	0	0	0	0	0	2	0	
Umatilla	0	1	1	1	0	0	0	0	2	1	
Union	1	0	0	0	0	0	0	1	0	0	
PENNSYLVANIA											
Total	40	9	11	1	0	0					
Cities	32	8	9	1	0	0					
Abington Township, Montgomery County	1	1	0	0	0	0	0	2	0	0	55,623
Camp Hill	1	0	0	0	0	0	0	0	1	0	7,929
Carlisle	0	0	1	0	0	0	0	1	0	0	19,225
Ferguson Township	1	0	0	0	0	0	0	1	0	0	19,222
Hamburg	1	0	0	0	0	0	0	0	0	1	4,420
Johnstown	1	0	0	0	0	0	1	0	0	0	21,227
Lancaster	1	0	0	0	0	0	0	1	0	0	59,340
Mechanicsburg	2	0	0	0	0	0	0	0	0	2	9,003
Philadelphia	7	4	7	0	0	0	3	3	2	10	1,570,826
Pittsburgh	11	2	1	0	0	0	2	2	6	4	302,443
Reading	1	0	0	0	0	0	1	0	0	0	87,834
Scranton	1	1	0	0	0	0	0	1	1	0	77,332
State College	2	0	0	1	0	0	2	0	1	0	58,119
Washington Township, Franklin County	1	0	0	0	0	0	1	0	0	0	14,631
Whitemarsh Township	1	0	0	0	0	0	0	0	1	0	17,721
Universities and Colleges	4	0	2	0	0	0					
Pennsylvania State University, University Park	4	0	2	0	0	0	5	0	0	1	47,307
Metropolitan Counties	1	0	0	0	0	0					
Allegheny	1	0	0	0	0	0	0	1	0	0	
State Police Agencies	3	1	0	0	0	0					
State Police:											
Delaware County	1	0	0	0	0	0	0	0	0	1	
Monroe County	0	1	0	0	0	0	1	0	0	0	
Skippack	2	0	0	0	0	0	0	0	0	2	
RHODE ISLAND											
Total	2	6	3	1	0	0					
Cities	2	4	1	0	0	0					
Cranston	0	1	0	0	0	0	0	1	0	0	81,162
Pawtucket	1	1	0	0	0	0	0	1	0	1	71,640
Portsmouth	0	1	0	0	0	0	0	0	1	0	17,362
Providence	0	0	1	0	0	0	0	1	0	0	179,340
South Kingstown	0	1	0	0	0	0	0	0	1	0	30,872
Tiverton	1	0	0	0	0	0	0	0	0	1	15,768
Universities and Colleges	0	2	1	0	0	0					
Brown University	0	1	1	0	0	0	1	1	0	0	9,458
University of Rhode Island	0	1	0	0	0	0	1	0	0	0	16,613
State Police Agencies	0	0	1	1	0	0					
State Police:											
Chepachet	0	0	0	1	0	0	1	0	0	0	
Lincoln	0	0	1	0	0	0	0	1	0	0	
SOUTH CAROLINA											
Total	18	1	3	1	0	0					
Cities	10	1	1	0	0	0					
Andrews	1	0	0	0	0	0	0	0	0	1	2,894

(Number.)

State/agency	Race/Ethnicity/Ancestry	Religion	Sexual orientation	Disability	Gender	Gender Identity	1st quarter	2nd quarter	3rd quarter	4th quarter	Population[1]
	Number of incidents per bias motivation						**Number of incidents per quarter**				
Blackville	0	1	0	0	0	0	1	0	0	0	2,273
Chester	1	0	0	0	0	0	0	0	1	0	5,462
Cottageville	1	0	0	0	0	0	0	0	1	0	733
Florence	0	0	1	0	0	0	0	1	0	0	38,382
Folly Beach	2	0	0	0	0	0	0	1	1	0	2,806
Greer	1	0	0	0	0	0	0	1	0	0	28,927
Moncks Corner	1	0	0	0	0	0	0	1	0	0	10,298
North Myrtle Beach	1	0	0	0	0	0	0	0	0	1	15,945
Pageland	1	0	0	0	0	0	0	1	0	0	2,745
Simpsonville	1	0	0	0	0	0	0	1	0	0	21,223
Universities and Colleges	2	0	0	1	0	0					
Clemson University	1	0	0	0	0	0	0	0	0	1	22,698
Coastal Carolina University	0	0	0	1	0	0	0	0	0	1	10,263
Trident Technical College	1	0	0	0	0	0	0	0	0	1	15,043
Metropolitan Counties	4	0	2	0	0	0					
Anderson	1	0	0	0	0	0	0	1	0	0	
Darlington	0	0	1	0	0	0	0	1	0	0	
Greenville	1	0	0	0	0	0	0	0	1	0	
Horry County Police Department	2	0	0	0	0	0	0	2	0	0	
Sumter	0	0	1	0	0	0	0	1	0	0	
Nonmetropolitan Counties	2	0	0	0	0	0					
Abbeville	1	0	0	0	0	0	1	0	0	0	
Georgetown	1	0	0	0	0	0	1	0	0	0	
SOUTH DAKOTA											
Total	6	2	5	3	0	2					
Cities	4	2	3	2	0	1					
Aberdeen	0	0	0	0	0	1	0	0	0	1	28,498
Brandon	0	1	0	0	0	0	0	1	0	0	10,042
Brookings	0	0	0	1	0	0	0	1	0	0	23,971
Chamberlain	0	0	1	0	0	0	0	1	0	0	2,383
Madison	0	0	1	0	0	0	0	0	1	0	7,411
Rapid City	2	0	0	1	0	0	0	1	1	1	74,573
Sioux Falls	2	1	1	0	0	0	0	2	0	2	175,152
Metropolitan Counties	2	0	1	1	0	0					
Meade	1	0	0	0	0	0	0	0	1	0	
Minnehaha	1	0	1	0	0	0	0	1	1	0	
Union	0	0	0	1	0	0	1	0	0	0	
Nonmetropolitan Counties	0	0	1	0	0	1					
Hamlin	0	0	1	0	0	0	0	1	0	0	
Jerauld	0	0	0	0	0	1	1	0	0	0	
TENNESSEE											
Total	93	18	25	6	0	0					
Cities	50	12	20	3	0	0					
Alcoa	4	0	2	0	0	0	0	0	1	5	9,503
Alexandria	2	0	0	0	0	0	0	0	2	0	978
Bristol	1	0	0	0	0	0	0	0	1	0	26,656
Chattanooga	1	2	0	0	0	0	1	1	0	1	177,801
Clarksville	1	0	0	0	0	0	0	0	0	1	152,526
Cleveland	4	0	0	0	0	0	1	0	2	1	44,423
Coopertown	0	0	1	0	0	0	1	0	0	0	4,426
Covington	0	1	0	1	0	0	0	1	1	0	9,039
Cowan	0	0	0	1	0	0	0	1	0	0	1,698
Dyersburg	1	0	0	0	0	0	0	0	0	1	16,711
East Ridge	1	0	0	0	0	0	0	0	1	0	21,311
Franklin	0	1	0	0	0	0	0	0	1	0	74,771
Gallaway	2	0	0	0	0	0	2	0	0	0	654
Greenbrier	1	0	0	0	0	0	1	0	0	0	6,807
Hendersonville	1	0	0	0	0	0	0	0	1	0	56,965
Humboldt	1	0	0	0	0	0	0	0	1	0	8,287
Jackson	2	1	0	0	0	0	1	0	2	0	66,990
Jamestown	7	0	0	0	0	0	7	0	0	0	1,945
Jasper	0	0	1	0	0	0	0	0	1	0	3,323
Johnson City	0	0	1	1	0	0	1	0	0	1	66,511
Kingsport	1	0	0	0	0	0	0	0	0	1	53,059
Knoxville	0	1	0	0	0	0	0	1	0	0	186,583

(Number.)

State/agency	Number of incidents per bias motivation						Number of incidents per quarter				Population[1]
	Race/ Ethnicity/ Ancestry	Religion	Sexual orientation	Disability	Gender	Gender Identity	1st quarter	2nd quarter	3rd quarter	4th quarter	
Lebanon	2	1	0	0	0	0	2	0	0	1	31,125
Lenoir City	1	0	0	0	0	0	0	0	0	1	9,175
Livingston	1	0	0	0	0	0	0	0	1	0	4,073
Memphis	1	1	7	0	0	0	3	3	2	1	656,434
Milan	1	0	0	0	0	0	0	1	0	0	7,803
Millington	1	0	0	0	0	0	0	1	0	0	11,002
Morristown	1	0	0	0	0	0	1	0	0	0	29,576
Murfreesboro[2]	2	0	1	0	0	0	0	1	1	1	129,730
Nashville Metropolitan	5	2	5	0	0	0	3	4	5	0	668,685
Newport	1	0	0	0	0	0	0	0	1	0	6,812
Oak Ridge	0	0	1	0	0	0	0	1	0	0	29,296
Pigeon Forge	2	1	0	0	0	0	1	2	0	0	6,230
Portland	0	1	0	0	0	0	0	0	1	0	12,502
Spring Hill	2	0	0	0	0	0	1	0	0	1	37,599
White House	0	0	1	0	0	0	1	0	0	0	11,419
Universities and Colleges	3	1	1	0	0	0					
Pellissippi State Community College	0	1	0	0	0	0	0	0	0	1	10,325
Tennessee Technological University	2	0	0	0	0	0	0	0	2	0	10,900
University of Tennessee, Knoxville	0	0	1	0	0	0	0	0	1	0	27,845
University of the South	1	0	0	0	0	0	1	0	0	0	1,797
Metropolitan Counties	28	4	4	3	0	0					
Anderson	1	0	0	0	0	0	0	0	1	0	
Bradley	2	0	1	0	0	0	1	0	1	1	
Dickson	2	0	0	0	0	0	0	2	0	0	
Hamblen	1	0	0	0	0	0	0	0	0	1	
Hamilton	2	4	1	1	0	0	3	2	0	3	
Knox	1	0	0	0	0	0	0	0	1	0	
Montgomery	1	0	0	0	0	0	0	0	0	1	
Roane	0	0	1	0	0	0	0	0	1	0	
Rutherford	1	0	0	0	0	0	0	0	0	1	
Shelby	16	0	0	2	0	0	6	5	2	5	
Sullivan	1	0	1	0	0	0	0	2	0	0	
Nonmetropolitan Counties	1	1	0	0	0	0					
Lawrence	0	1	0	0	0	0	0	0	0	1	
Sevier	1	0	0	0	0	0	1	0	0	0	
Other Agencies	11	0	0	0	0	0					
Department of Safety	11	0	0	0	0	0	1	1	7	2	
TEXAS											
Total	104	23	37	5	1	8					
Cities	91	17	28	4	1	8					
Arlington	4	1	0	0	0	0	0	2	2	1	392,666
Austin	10	2	6	0	0	1	7	6	4	2	956,911
Beaumont	4	0	0	0	0	0	3	0	0	1	118,283
Bedford	1	0	0	0	0	5	0	0	0	6	49,803
Borger	1	0	0	0	0	0	0	0	1	0	12,894
Burleson	1	0	0	0	0	0	0	1	0	0	45,116
Cedar Hill	1	0	0	0	0	0	0	0	1	0	49,215
Cedar Park	1	0	1	0	0	0	0	2	0	0	69,051
Center	0	0	0	0	1	0	0	0	0	1	5,218
College Station	0	1	0	0	0	0	0	0	1	0	110,785
Converse	0	0	0	1	0	0	0	1	0	0	22,782
Dallas	7	2	2	0	0	0	1	5	4	1	1,320,939
Denison	0	0	1	0	0	0	0	1	0	0	23,237
Denton	2	0	1	0	0	0	1	1	1	0	134,054
El Paso	0	0	1	0	0	0	0	0	0	1	687,193
Fort Worth	11	3	5	1	0	0	7	5	3	5	851,849
Frankston	1	0	0	0	0	0	0	1	0	0	1,163
Galveston	5	0	1	0	0	0	1	1	3	1	50,667
Gilmer	1	0	0	0	0	0	0	1	0	0	5,246
Grand Prairie	1	0	0	0	0	0	0	1	0	0	190,270
Hedwig Village	0	1	0	0	0	0	0	1	0	0	2,724
Houston	3	1	2	0	0	2	1	1	3	3	2,334,348
League City	1	0	0	0	0	0	0	1	0	0	101,436
Levelland	2	0	0	0	0	0	0	0	1	1	13,997
Lewisville	2	0	0	0	0	0	1	0	0	1	105,762
Livingston	1	0	0	0	0	0	1	0	0	0	5,140

(Number.)

State/agency	Number of incidents per bias motivation						Number of incidents per quarter				Population[1]
	Race/ Ethnicity/ Ancestry	Religion	Sexual orientation	Disability	Gender	Gender Identity	1st quarter	2nd quarter	3rd quarter	4th quarter	
Longview	2	0	0	1	0	0	0	0	1	2	82,632
McKinney	5	0	2	0	0	0	0	3	2	2	169,689
Odessa	2	1	0	0	0	0	1	0	1	1	123,209
Plano	1	0	0	0	0	0	0	0	1	0	288,242
Pleasanton	1	0	0	0	0	0	0	0	1	0	10,013
Reno	0	1	0	0	0	0	0	0	1	0	3,302
Rockwall	1	0	0	0	0	0	0	1	0	0	43,542
Round Rock	0	1	1	0	0	0	0	1	1	0	119,308
San Angelo	0	0	1	0	0	0	0	0	0	1	101,870
San Antonio	6	2	1	0	0	0	2	1	4	2	1,498,642
San Marcos	0	0	1	0	0	0	0	0	0	1	64,380
Seabrook	1	0	0	0	0	0	0	1	0	0	14,091
Sealy	1	0	0	0	0	0	0	1	0	0	6,469
Sugar Land	1	0	0	0	0	0	0	0	0	1	90,088
Teague	1	0	0	0	0	0	0	0	1	0	3,575
Temple	1	0	0	0	0	0	0	0	0	1	73,411
Texas City	2	0	0	0	0	0	0	0	0	2	48,095
Tomball	1	0	0	0	0	0	0	0	0	1	11,700
Tyler	2	0	1	1	0	0	1	3	0	0	105,044
Weslaco	1	0	1	0	0	0	0	2	0	0	39,987
Wichita Falls	1	1	0	0	0	0	0	1	0	1	104,685
Willis	1	0	0	0	0	0	0	0	1	0	6,401
Universities and Colleges	3	3	3	0	0	0					
Amarillo College	1	0	0	0	0	0	1	0	0	0	9,936
Baylor University, Waco	1	0	0	0	0	0	0	0	0	1	16,787
Southwestern University	0	0	2	0	0	0	0	0	0	2	1,515
Texas State Technical College, West Texas[3]	0	0	1	0	0	0	1	0	0	0	
Texas Tech University, Lubbock	1	0	0	0	0	0	0	0	0	1	35,859
Tyler Junior College	0	1	0	0	0	0	0	1	0	0	10,934
University of Texas, Dallas	0	2	0	0	0	0	2	0	0	0	24,554
Metropolitan Counties	7	3	3	1	0	0					
Bexar	1	0	0	0	0	0	1	0	0	0	
Lubbock	1	0	0	0	0	0	0	0	0	1	
Parker	0	0	1	1	0	0	0	1	1	0	
Travis	3	2	2	0	0	0	1	4	1	1	
Williamson	2	1	0	0	0	0	1	1	0	1	
Nonmetropolitan Counties	2	0	1	0	0	0					
Brewster	0	0	1	0	0	0	1	0	0	0	
San Jacinto	1	0	0	0	0	0	1	0	0	0	
Zavala	1	0	0	0	0	0	0	0	1	0	
Other Agencies	1	0	2	0	0	0					
Dallas-Fort Worth International Airport	0	0	1	0	0	0	0	0	1	0	
Hospital District, Dallas County	1	0	0	0	0	0	0	0	1	0	
Independent School District, El Paso	0	0	1	0	0	0	0	0	0	1	
UTAH											
Total	47	8	9	2	0	0					
Cities	31	6	7	1	0	0					
Bountiful	3	0	0	0	0	0	0	0	0	3	44,003
Centerville	1	0	0	0	0	0	0	0	1	0	17,204
Draper	0	1	0	0	0	0	0	1	0	0	47,696
Farmington	0	1	0	0	0	0	0	1	0	0	23,505
Grantsville	2	0	0	0	0	0	0	2	0	0	10,253
Helper	1	0	0	0	0	0	1	0	0	0	2,094
Hurricane	1	0	0	0	0	0	0	0	1	0	15,869
Layton	1	0	0	0	0	0	0	0	1	0	75,482
Lindon	1	0	0	0	0	0	0	0	0	1	10,958
Moab	1	0	0	0	0	0	0	0	1	0	5,262
North Ogden	2	0	0	0	0	0	0	1	1	0	18,654
Ogden[2]	3	0	4	1	0	0	1	1	3	3	85,930
Payson	1	0	1	0	0	0	1	1	0	0	19,738
Pleasant View	1	0	0	0	0	0	0	1	0	0	9,548
Roosevelt	0	0	1	0	0	0	0	0	0	1	7,179
Salt Lake City	1	0	0	0	0	0	0	0	1	0	193,918
Santa Clara/Ivins	0	1	0	0	0	0	0	0	0	1	15,107
Saratoga Springs	0	2	0	0	0	0	0	2	0	0	27,211
South Jordan	1	0	0	0	0	0	0	1	0	0	70,226

Table 13. Hate Crime Incidents Per Bias Motivation and Quarter, by Selected State and Agency, 2016—*Continued*

(Number.)

State/agency	Race/ Ethnicity/ Ancestry	Religion	Sexual orientation	Disability	Gender	Gender Identity	1st quarter	2nd quarter	3rd quarter	4th quarter	Population[1]
South Ogden	1	0	0	0	0	0	0	1	0	0	17,026
South Salt Lake	1	0	0	0	0	0	0	0	1	0	25,022
St. George	2	0	0	0	0	0	0	0	0	2	81,755
Tooele	2	0	1	0	0	0	1	2	0	0	33,448
West Jordan	2	0	0	0	0	0	0	0	2	0	113,595
West Valley	3	1	0	0	0	0	3	0	0	1	137,558
Universities and Colleges	2	0	1	0	0	0					
Brigham Young University	2	0	0	0	0	0	0	0	1	1	33,469
Utah State University, Logan	0	0	1	0	0	0	0	0	0	1	28,622
Metropolitan Counties	1	2	0	0	0	0					
Salt Lake County Unified Police Department	0	1	0	0	0	0	1	0	0	0	
Utah	1	0	0	0	0	0	0	0	1	0	
Washington	0	1	0	0	0	0	0	0	1	0	
State Police Agencies	10	0	0	0	0	0					
Utah Highway Patrol	10	0	0	0	0	0	3	3	1	3	
Other Agencies	3	0	1	1	0	0					
Utah Transit Authority	3	0	1	1	0	0	2	0	2	1	
VERMONT											
Total	16	5	3	1	0	0					
Cities	15	3	3	1	0	0					
Barre	1	0	0	0	0	0	0	0	1	0	8,687
Barre Town	1	0	0	0	0	0	0	1	0	0	7,791
Brandon	1	0	0	0	0	0	1	0	0	0	3,801
Burlington	2	1	2	0	0	0	2	0	1	2	42,454
Chester	0	0	0	1	0	0	0	1	0	0	3,069
Colchester	1	0	0	0	0	0	0	1	0	0	17,437
Middlebury	0	1	0	0	0	0	0	0	0	1	8,570
Milton	1	0	1	0	0	0	0	1	1	0	10,921
Rutland	0	1	0	0	0	0	0	0	0	1	15,698
Springfield	1	0	0	0	0	0	0	0	0	1	9,132
St. Albans	2	0	0	0	0	0	0	2	0	0	6,799
St. Johnsbury	4	0	0	0	0	0	0	3	0	1	7,414
Williston	1	0	0	0	0	0	0	0	0	1	9,556
Universities and Colleges	0	2	0	0	0	0					
University of Vermont	0	2	0	0	0	0	0	0	2	0	12,815
Nonmetropolitan Counties	1	0	0	0	0	0					
Lamoille	1	0	0	0	0	0	1	0	0	0	
VIRGINIA											
Total	76	21	22	3	0	0					
Cities	23	6	8	1	0	0					
Alexandria	0	0	2	0	0	0	0	1	1	0	155,319
Chesapeake	2	1	0	1	0	0	2	1	1	0	236,570
Clifton Forge	1	0	0	0	0	0	1	0	0	0	3,713
Covington	0	1	0	0	0	0	0	0	1	0	5,570
Front Royal	1	0	2	0	0	0	1	0	1	1	15,193
Hampton	1	0	0	0	0	0	0	1	0	0	135,504
Harrisonburg	3	1	0	0	0	0	1	0	3	0	52,972
Herndon	0	1	0	0	0	0	0	0	1	0	24,806
Manassas	1	0	0	0	0	0	0	0	1	0	42,267
Newport News	3	0	1	0	0	0	0	1	2	1	181,676
Norfolk	0	1	0	0	0	0	0	0	1	0	245,734
Portsmouth	3	0	0	0	0	0	0	1	1	1	95,813
Purcellville	1	0	0	0	0	0	0	0	1	0	9,547
Radford	1	0	0	0	0	0	0	0	0	1	17,504
Richmond	0	1	0	0	0	0	1	0	0	0	222,430
Rocky Mount	1	0	0	0	0	0	1	0	0	0	4,803
Virginia Beach	2	0	3	0	0	0	0	0	3	2	453,017
Waynesboro	1	0	0	0	0	0	1	0	0	0	21,464
Williamsburg	1	0	0	0	0	0	0	0	0	1	15,256
Woodstock	1	0	0	0	0	0	0	1	0	0	5,277
Universities and Colleges	6	1	3	0	0	0					
College of William and Mary	0	0	1	0	0	0	1	0	0	0	8,484
Emory and Henry College	1	0	0	0	0	0	0	1	0	0	1,117
George Mason University	0	1	0	0	0	0	1	0	0	0	33,929
Hampton University	1	0	0	0	0	0	0	0	1		4,269

Table 13. Hate Crime Incidents Per Bias Motivation and Quarter, by Selected State and Agency, 2016—Continued

(Number.)

State/agency	Race/ Ethnicity/ Ancestry	Religion	Sexual orientation	Disability	Gender	Gender Identity	1st quarter	2nd quarter	3rd quarter	4th quarter	Population[1]
Old Dominion University	2	0	0	0	0	0	2	0	0	0	24,672
Radford University	1	0	0	0	0	0	1	0	0	0	9,743
University of Virginia	0	0	1	0	0	0	0	0	0	1	23,883
Virginia Commonwealth University	1	0	1	0	0	0	0	0	0	2	30,918
Metropolitan Counties	42	12	7	0	0	0					
Albemarle County Police Department	3	0	1	0	0	0	1	2	1	0	
Amelia	1	0	0	0	0	0	0	0	1	0	
Arlington County Police Department	2	1	0	0	0	0	0	0	1	2	
Fairfax County Police Department	14	6	4	0	0	0	7	7	3	7	
Franklin	0	1	0	0	0	0	0	0	0	1	
Frederick	1	0	0	0	0	0	0	0	0	1	
Hanover	1	0	0	0	0	0	0	0	0	1	
Henrico County Police Department	0	1	0	0	0	0	1	0	0	0	
Loudoun	5	1	2	0	0	0	0	0	1	7	
Mathews	1	0	0	0	0	0	0	0	1	0	
Montgomery	0	1	0	0	0	0	1	0	0	0	
Powhatan	1	0	0	0	0	0	0	0	1	0	
Prince William County Police Department	5	1	0	0	0	0	1	0	2	3	
Spotsylvania	1	0	0	0	0	0	0	0	0	1	
Stafford	4	0	0	0	0	0	0	2	0	2	
Washington	2	0	0	0	0	0	0	1	1	0	
York	1	0	0	0	0	0	0	0	0	1	
Nonmetropolitan Counties	3	0	1	2	0	0					
Accomack	0	0	0	2	0	0	0	0	2	0	
Grayson	1	0	0	0	0	0	0	0	0	1	
Louisa	1	0	1	0	0	0	0	1	1	0	
Shenandoah	1	0	0	0	0	0	0	1	0	0	
State Police Agencies	2	2	3	0	0	0					
State Police:											
Chesapeake	1	0	0	0	0	0	0	0	1	0	
Fairfax County	0	1	1	0	0	0	0	1	0	1	
Goochland County	0	0	1	0	0	0	0	0	0	1	
Newport News	1	0	0	0	0	0	0	0	0	1	
Rockingham County	0	0	1	0	0	0	0	0	1	0	
Surry County	0	1	0	0	0	0	0	0	0	1	
WASHINGTON											
Total	239	61	70	2	3	14					
Cities	190	51	59	2	2	11					
Aberdeen	1	0	1	0	0	0	2	0	0	0	16,155
Algona	1	0	0	0	0	0	0	0	1	0	3,166
Arlington	1	0	0	0	0	0	0	0	0	1	19,142
Auburn	4	1	0	0	0	0	1	2	1	1	78,400
Bainbridge Island	0	0	1	0	0	0	0	0	1	0	23,998
Battle Ground	1	0	0	0	0	0	0	0	0	1	19,734
Bellevue	2	13	3	0	0	0	6	5	3	4	142,238
Bellingham	7	0	1	0	0	0	3	0	1	4	86,005
Bothell	1	0	0	0	0	0	0	0	0	1	43,828
Brier	1	0	0	0	0	0	1	0	0	0	6,753
Centralia	4	1	0	0	0	0	1	0	4	0	16,785
Darrington	1	0	0	0	0	0	1	0	0	0	1,381
Des Moines	1	0	0	0	0	0	0	0	0	1	31,523
Edmonds	4	1	0	0	0	0	0	0	3	2	41,705
Enumclaw	1	0	0	0	0	0	0	0	1	0	11,709
Everett	4	1	0	0	0	0	2	0	0	3	108,988
Federal Way	2	0	0	0	0	0	1	0	0	1	96,338
Forks	1	0	0	0	1	0	0	1	1	0	3,787
Granite Falls	0	0	1	0	0	0	0	0	1	0	3,516
Kent	8	3	5	0	0	0	3	5	5	3	128,604
Kettle Falls	1	0	0	0	0	0	0	0	1	0	1,596
Kirkland	1	0	0	0	0	0	0	1	0	0	88,627
Lake Forest Park	0	1	0	0	0	0	0	0	0	1	13,369
Lake Stevens	2	0	0	0	0	0	0	1	1	0	31,440
Lakewood	2	0	1	0	0	0	0	0	1	2	60,153
Longview[2]	5	2	0	0	0	0	2	1	1	2	36,854
Lynnwood	2	0	0	0	0	0	0	0	1	1	37,217
Marysville	2	1	0	0	0	1	2	0	1	1	68,172

Table 13. Hate Crime Incidents Per Bias Motivation and Quarter, by Selected State and Agency, 2016—*Continued*

(Number.)

State/agency	Number of incidents per bias motivation						Number of incidents per quarter				Population[1]
	Race/ Ethnicity/ Ancestry	Religion	Sexual orientation	Disability	Gender	Gender Identity	1st quarter	2nd quarter	3rd quarter	4th quarter	
Mill Creek	0	0	1	0	0	0	0	0	0	1	20,419
Milton	1	0	0	0	0	0	0	1	0	0	7,785
Mountlake Terrace	1	0	0	0	0	0	0	0	1	0	21,212
Mount Vernon	0	0	0	0	0	1	0	1	0	0	34,521
Mukilteo	0	1	0	0	0	0	0	1	0	0	21,416
Oak Harbor	2	0	0	1	0	0	0	2	1	0	22,795
Olympia	1	0	0	0	0	0	0	0	1	0	50,972
Orting	3	0	0	0	0	0	0	1	2	0	7,594
Pasco	1	0	0	0	0	0	0	1	0	0	71,077
Port Angeles	4	0	1	0	0	0	0	2	2	1	19,525
Port Townsend	0	1	0	0	0	0	0	0	0	1	9,378
Pullman	0	1	1	0	0	0	1	0	1	0	33,456
Puyallup	2	1	0	0	0	0	1	2	0	0	40,167
Redmond[2]	2	5	0	0	0	0	0	1	0	5	61,893
Renton	5	1	2	0	0	0	0	4	2	2	101,908
Richland	2	0	0	0	0	0	0	0	1	1	55,475
Sammamish	5	1	0	0	1	0	0	0	6	1	53,387
Seattle	64	12	33	0	0	9	30	27	33	28	700,313
Snohomish	1	0	0	0	0	0	0	0	1	0	9,773
Spokane	6	1	1	0	0	0	1	2		5	214,028
Spokane Valley	8	1	1	0	0	0	2	1	1	6	95,923
Stanwood	1	0	0	0	0	0	0	0	0	1	6,888
Tacoma	4	0	5	0	0	0	2	2	3	2	209,914
Tenino	1	0	0	0	0	0	0	0	1	0	1,761
Tukwila	1	0	0	0	0	0	1	0	0	0	20,195
Vancouver	4	0	0	0	0	0	0	4	0	0	174,912
Walla Walla	6	0	0	1	0	0	4	2	0	1	32,326
White Salmon	2	0	0	0	0	0	1	1	0	0	2,364
Woodinville	0	1	0	0	0	0	0	0	1	0	11,953
Yakima	3	1	1	0	0	0	0	2	1	2	94,111
Universities and Colleges	3	1	4	0	1	1					
Eastern Washington University	0	0	1	0	0	0	1	0	0	0	12,361
Evergreen State College	0	0	1	0	0	1	1	1	0	0	4,190
University of Washington	1	1	1	0	1	0	0	2	1	1	45,408
Washington State University, Pullman	1	0	0	0	0	0	1	0	0	0	29,686
Western Washington University	1	0	1	0	0	0	0	0	0	2	15,332
Metropolitan Counties	41	8	7	0	0	1					
Clark	1	0	0	0	0	0	0	0	0	1	
Cowlitz	2	1	2	0	0	0	1	0	3	1	
King	11	2	1	0	0	0	2	4	4	4	
Pierce	10	0	1	0	0	0	3	2	0	6	
Skagit	0	0	0	0	0	1	0	1	0	0	
Snohomish	4	2	0	0	0	0	2	2	1	1	
Spokane	1	0	0	0	0	0	0	0	0	1	
Walla Walla	0	1	0	0	0	0	0	0	1	0	
Whatcom[2]	8	2	3	0	0	0	5	3	3	2	
Yakima	4	0	0	0	0	0	0	1	1	2	
Nonmetropolitan Counties	3	1	0	0	0	1					
Grays Harbor	1	0	0	0	0	0	1	0	0	0	
Island	1	0	0	0	0	0	0	0	0	1	
Lewis	1	0	0	0	0	0	0	0	1	0	
Mason	0	1	0	0	0	0	0	0	1	0	
San Juan	0	0	0	0	0	1	0	0	0	1	
Tribal Agencies	1	0	0	0	0	0					
Lummi Tribal	1	0	0	0	0	0	0	0	0	1	
Other Agencies	1	0	0	0	0	0					
Port of Seattle	1	0	0	0	0	0	1	0	0	0	
WEST VIRGINIA											
Total	30	1	7	3	0	0					
Cities	20	1	6	2	0	0					
Beckley	1	0	0	0	0	0	0	0	1	0	16,940
Buckhannon	1	0	0	0	0	0	0	0	0	1	5,662
Charleston	10	1	4	0	0	0	4	5	4	2	49,429
Fairmont	0	0	0	1	0	0	1	0	0	0	18,733
Fayetteville	2	0	0	0	0	0	1	1	0	0	2,885
Huntington	0	0	1	1	0	0	1	1	0	0	48,540

Table 13. Hate Crime Incidents Per Bias Motivation and Quarter, by Selected State and Agency, 2016—*Continued*

(Number.)

State/agency	Number of incidents per bias motivation						Number of incidents per quarter				Population[1]
	Race/ Ethnicity/ Ancestry	Religion	Sexual orientation	Disability	Gender	Gender Identity	1st quarter	2nd quarter	3rd quarter	4th quarter	
Moundsville	1	0	0	0	0	0	1	0	0	0	8,644
Oak Hill	2	0	0	0	0	0	0	1	1	0	8,104
Parkersburg	0	0	1	0	0	0	1	0	0	0	30,913
Philippi	1	0	0	0	0	0	0	0	1	0	3,320
Ranson	1	0	0	0	0	0	0	1	0		5,053
Wheeling	1	0	0	0	0	0	0	1	0	0	27,486
Metropolitan Counties	7	0	1	1	0	0					
Berkeley	1	0	0	0	0	0	0	0	1	0	
Brooke	1	0	0	0	0	0	0	0	0	1	
Cabell	1	0	0	0	0	0	0	0	0	1	
Hancock	2	0	0	0	0	0	1	1	0	1	
Jefferson	1	0	0	0	0	0	0	0	0	1	
Kanawha	1	0	1	1	0	0	1	1	1	0	
Nonmetropolitan Counties	3	0	0	0	0	0					
Mason	3	0	0	0	0	0	0	0	2	1	
WISCONSIN											
Total	22	8	3	0	0	1					
Cities	18	7	3	0	0	1					
Appleton	1	0	0	0	0	0	1	0	0	0	74,439
Cross Plains	0	0	1	0	0	0	1	0	0	0	4,072
Fox Valley Metro	1	0	0	0	0	0	0	0	1	0	21,515
Green Bay	1	0	0	0	0	0	1	0	0	0	105,452
Hudson	0	0	1	0	0	0	0	0	0	1	13,740
Janesville	1	0	0	0	0	0	0	1	0	0	64,234
La Crosse	1	0	0	0	0	0	0	1	0	0	52,498
Madison	8	7	0	0	0	0	0	8	2	5	252,136
Manitowoc	1	0	0	0	0	0	0	1	0	0	32,877
Milwaukee	0	0	1	0	0	1	0	1	1	0	600,193
New Richmond	1	0	0	0	0	0	0	0	1	0	8,913
Onalaska	1	0	0	0	0	0	0	1	0	0	18,600
Osceola	1	0	0	0	0	0	0	0	0	1	2,502
Stoughton	1	0	0	0	0	0	0	0	0	1	13,148
Metropolitan Counties	3	1	0	0	0	0					
Fond du Lac	2	0	0	0	0	0	1	0	0	1	
Outagamie	1	0	0	0	0	0	0	0	1	0	
St. Croix	0	1	0	0	0	0	0	0	0	1	
Nonmetropolitan Counties	1	0	0	0	0	0					
Rusk	1	0	0	0	0	0	0	0	1	0	
WYOMING											
Total	3	0	0	0	0	0					
Cities	3	0	0	0	0	0					
Gillette	3	0	0	0	0	0	0	2	0	1	33,218

[1]Population figures are published only for the cities. The figures listed for the universities and colleges are student enrollment and were provided by the United States Department of Education for the 2015 school year, the most recent available. The enrollment figures include full-time and part-time students.
[2]Includes one incident reported with more than one bias motivation.
[3]Student enrollment figures were not available.

Methodology

HATE CRIMES

The Federal Bureau of Investigation (FBI) began the procedures for implementing, collecting, and managing hate crime data after Congress passed the Hate Crime Statistics Act in 1990. This act required the collection of data "about crimes that manifest evidence of prejudice based on race, religion, sexual orientation, or ethnicity." Beginning in 2013, law enforcement agencies could submit hate crime data in accordance with a number of program modifications. In 1994, the Hate Crime Statistics Act was amended to include bias against persons with disabilities. The Church Arson Prevention Act, which was signed into law in July 1996, removed the sunset clause from the original statute and mandated that the collection of hate crime data become a permanent part of the UCR program. In 2009, Congress further amended the Hate Crime Statistics Act by passing the Matthew Shepard and James Byrd, Jr., Hate Crime Prevention Act. The amendment includes the collection of data for crimes motivated by bias against a particular gender and gender identity, as well as for crimes committed by, and crimes directed against, juveniles. In response to the Shepard/Byrd Act, the FBI modified its data collection so that reporting agencies could indicate whether hate crimes were committed by, or directed against, juveniles.

Definitions

Hate crimes include any crime motivated by bias against race, religion, sexual orientation, ethnicity/national origin, and/or disability. Because motivation is subjective, it is sometimes difficult to know with certainty whether a crime resulted from the offender's bias. Moreover, the presence of bias alone does not necessarily mean that a crime can be considered a hate crime. Only when law enforcement investigation reveals sufficient evidence to lead a reasonable and prudent person to conclude that the offender's actions were motivated, in whole or in part, by his or her bias should an incident be reported as a hate crime.

Starting with the 2015 data, incidents motivated by race and ethnicity are grouped in the new "Race/Ethnicity/Ancestry" single-bias category. New subcategories include anti-Arab, anti–Hispanic or Latino (the former ethnicity designation), and anti–other race/ethnicity/ancestry. Under "Anti-Religion," new subcategories include anti-Mormon, anti–Jehovah's Witness, anti–Eastern Orthodox (Russian/Greek/other), anti-Buddhist, anti-Hindu, and anti-Sikh.

Data Collection

The UCR (Uniform Crime Reporting) program collects data about both single-bias and multiple-bias hate crimes. A single-bias incident is defined as an incident in which one or more offense types are motivated by the same bias. A multiple-bias incident is defined as an incident in which more than one offense type occurs and at least two offense types are motivated by different biases.

A table enumerating selected places in the United States that did not report hate crimes in 2016 is available at https://ucr.fbi.gov/hate-crime/2016/tables/table-14/table_14_hate_crime_zero_data_submitted_per_quarter_by_state_and_agency_2016-.xls.xlsx/view.

Important Note: Rape

In 2013, the FBI UCR Program initiated the collection of rape data under a revised definition and removed the term "forcible" from the offense name. The changes bring uniformity to the offense in both the Summary Reporting System (SRS) and the National Incident-Based Reporting System (NIBRS) by capturing data (1) without regard to gender, (2) including penetration of any bodily orifice by any object or body part, and (3) including offenses where physical force is not involved. The UCR Program now defines rape as follows:

- **Rape (revised):** Penetration, no matter how slight, of the vagina or anus with any body part or object, or oral penetration by a sex organ of another person, without the consent of the victim. This includes the offenses of rape, sodomy, and sexual assault with an object.

- **Rape (legacy):** The carnal knowledge of a female forcibly and against her will.

The offenses of fondling, incest, and statutory rape are included in the Crimes Against Persons, Other category.

Beginning January 1, 2017, the UCR Program discontinued collecting rape data via the SRS according to the historical, legacy definition. Only rape data submitted under the revised definition will be published for 2017 and subsequent years. This change will not affect agencies that submit rape data via NIBRS.

Crimes Against Persons, Property, or Society

The UCR program's data collection guidelines stipulate that a hate crime may involve multiple offenses, victims, and offenders within one incident; therefore, the Hate Crime Statistics program is incident-based. According to UCR counting guidelines:

- One offense is counted for each victim in *crimes against persons*

- One offense is counted for each offense type in *crimes against property*

- One offense is counted for each offense type in *crimes against society*

Victims

In the UCR program, the victim of a hate crime may be an individual, a business, an institution, or society as a whole.

Offenders

According to the UCR program, the term *known offender* does not imply that the suspect's identity is known; rather, the term indicates that some aspect of the suspect was identified, thus distinguishing the suspect from an unknown offender. Law enforcement agencies specify the number of offenders, and when possible, the race of the offender or offenders as a group.

Race/Ethnicity

The UCR program uses the following racial designations in its Hate Crime Statistics program: White; Black; American Indian or Alaskan Native; Asian; Native Hawaiian or Other Pacific Islander; and Multiple Races, Group. In addition, the UCR program uses the ethnic designations of Hispanic or Latino and Not Hispanic or Latino.

The law enforcement agencies that voluntarily participate in the Hate Crime Statistics program collect details about an offender's bias motivation associated with 11 offense types already being reported to the UCR program: murder and nonnegligent manslaughter, rape, aggravated assault, simple assault, and intimidation (crimes against persons); and robbery, burglary, larceny-theft, motor vehicle theft, arson, and destruction/damage/vandalism (crimes against property). The law enforcement agencies that participate in the UCR program via the National Incident-Based Reporting System (NIBRS) collect data about additional offenses for *crimes against persons* and *crimes against property*. These data appear in the category of other. These agencies also collect hate crime data for the category called *crimes against society*, which includes drug or narcotic offenses, gambling offenses, prostitution offenses, and weapon law violations.

PART 7

Indicators of School Crime and Safety, 2015

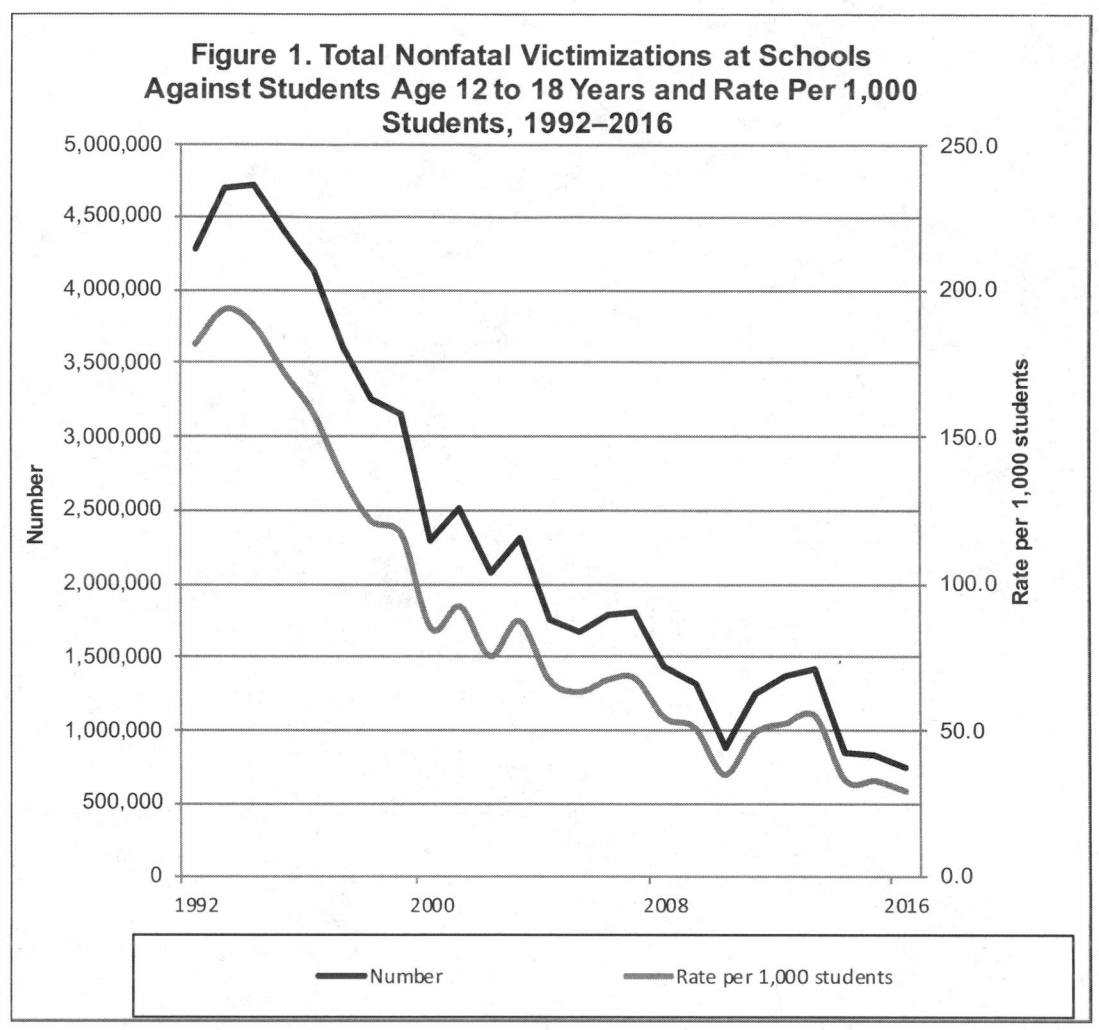

Figure 1. Total Nonfatal Victimizations at Schools Against Students Age 12 to 18 Years and Rate Per 1,000 Students, 1992–2016

- Approximately 749,000 nonfatal victimization incidents of students age 12 to 18 years occurred in schools in 2016; incidents included 294,000 theft victimizations and 455,400 violent victimizations (both simple assault and serious violent victimizations).

- The 2016 rate of nonfatal victimization incidents per 1,000 students age 12 to 18 years was 29.3 at school and 23.5 away from school; the at-school rate declined 83.9 percent from 1992 to 2014, while the away-from-school rate dropped 86.4 percent.

- Rural and urban-area students had higher rates of total victimization (36.8 and 36.7 per 1,000 students in the age group, respectively) than their suburban counterparts (23.6 victimizations per 1,000 students).

- During the 2014–2015 school year, the latest year for which data are available, there were 47 school-associated violent deaths of all connected persons (students, staff, and other nonstudents). Of these deaths, 28 were homicides, 17 were suicides, and 2 were due to legal interventions. That year, 20 of the homicides and 9 of the suicides occurred at school.

- In 2015, 20.8 percent of students age 12 to 18 years reported experiencing bullying. The greatest proportion of incidents came from mocking, name-calling, and insulting.

Table 1. School-Associated Violent Deaths of All Persons, Homicides and Suicides of Youth Ages 5 to 18 Years at School, and Total Homicides and Suicides of Youth Ages 5 to 18 Years, by Type of Violent Death: 1992–1993 to 2014–2015

(Number.)

Year	School-associated violent deaths[1] of all persons (includes students, staff, and other nonstudents)						Homicides of youth age 5 to 18 years		Suicides of youth age 5 to 18 years	
	Total	Homicides	Suicides	Legal interventions	Unintentional firearm-related deaths	Undetermined violent deaths	Homicides at school[2]	Total homicides	Suicides at school[2]	Total suicides[3]
1992–1993	57	47	10	0	0	0	34	2,721	6	1,680
1993–1994	48	38	10	0	0	0	29	2,932	7	1,723
1994–1995	48	39	8	0	1	0	28	2,696	7	1,767
1995–1996	53	46	6	1	0	0	32	2,545	6	1,725
1996–1997	48	45	2	1	0	0	28	2,221	1	1,633
1997–1998	57	47	9	1	0	0	34	2,100	6	1,626
1998–1999	47	38	6	2	1	0	33	1,777	4	1,597
1999–2000	37[4]	26[4]	11[4]	0[4]	0[4]	0[4]	14[4]	1,567	8[4]	1,415
2000–2001	34[4]	26[4]	7[4]	1[4]	0[4]	0[4]	14[4]	1,509	6[4]	1,493
2001–2002	36[4]	27[4]	8[4]	1[4]	0[4]	0[4]	16[4]	1,498	5[4]	1,400
2002–2003	36[4]	25[4]	11[4]	0[4]	0[4]	0[4]	18[4]	1,553	10[4]	1,331
2003–2004	45[4]	37[4]	7[4]	1[4]	0[4]	0[4]	23[4]	1,474	5[4]	1,285
2004–2005	52[4]	40[4]	10[4]	2[4]	0[4]	0[4]	22[4]	1,554	8[4]	1,471
2005–2006	44[4]	37[4]	6[4]	1[4]	0[4]	0[4]	21[4]	1,697	3[4]	1,408
2006–2007	63[4]	48[4]	13[4]	2[4]	0[4]	0[4]	32[4]	1,801	9[4]	1,296
2007–2008	44[4]	39[4]	7[4]	2[4]	0[4]	0[4]	21[4]	1,744	5[4]	1,231
2008–2009	44[4]	29[4]	15[4]	0[4]	0[4]	0[4]	18[4]	1,605	7[4]	1,344
2009–2010	35[4]	27[4]	5[4]	3[4]	0[4]	0[4]	19[4]	1,410	2[4]	1,467
2010–2011	32[4]	26[4]	6[4]	0[4]	0[4]	0[4]	11[4]	1,339	3[4]	1,456
2011–2012	45[4]	26[4]	14	5[4]	0[4]	0[4]	15[4]	1,201	5[4]	1,568
2012–2013	53[4]	41[4]	11[4]	1[4]	0[4]	0[4]	31[4]	1,186	6[4]	1,590
2013–2014.......	48[4]	26[4]	20[4]	1[4]	0[4]	0[4]	12[4]	1,050	8[4]	1,645
2014–2015.......	47[4]	28[4]	17[4]	2[4]	0[4]	0[4]	20[4]	1,168	9[4]	1,785

Note: Unless otherwise noted, data are reported for the school year, defined as July 1 through June 30. Some data have been revised from previously published figures. Violent deaths for which the manner was undetermined; that is, the information pointing to one manner of death was no more compelling than the information pointing to one or more other competing manners of death when all available information was considered.
[1] A school-associated violent death is defined as "a homicide, suicide, or legal intervention (involving a law enforcement officer), in which the fatal injury occurred on the campus of a functioning elementary or secondary school in the United States," while the victim was on the way to or from regular sessions at school, or while the victim was attending or traveling to or from an official school-sponsored event.
[2] "At school" includes on school property, on the way to or from regular sessions at school, and while attending or traveling to or from a school-sponsored event.
[3] Total youth suicides are reported for calendar years 1992 through 2012 (instead of school years 1992-93 through 2012-13).
[4] Data from 1999–2000 onward are subject to change until interviews with school and law enforcement officials have been completed. The details learned during the interviews can occasionally change the classification of a case.

Table 2. Number of Nonfatal Victimizations Against Students Ages 12 to 18 Years and Rate of Victimization Per 1,000 Students, by Type of Victimization and Location, 1992–2016

(Number; rate per 1,000 students.)

Location and year	Number of nonfatal victimizations				Rate of victimization per 1,000 students			
			Violent				Violent	
	Total	Theft	All violent	Serious violent[1]	Total	Theft	All violent	Serious violent[1]
At School[2]								
1992	4,281,200	2,679,400	1,601,800	197,600	181.5	113.6	67.9	8.4
1993	4,692,800	2,477,100	2,215,700	535,500	193.5	102.1	91.4	22.1
1994	4,721,000	2,474,100	2,246,900	459,100	187.7	98.4	89.3	18.3
1995	4,400,700	2,468,400	1,932,200	294,500	172.2	96.6	75.6	11.5
1996	4,130,400	2,205,200	1,925,300	371,900	158.4	84.5	73.8	14.3
1997	3,610,900	1,975,000	1,635,900	376,200	136.6	74.7	61.9	14.2
1998	3,247,300	1,635,100	1,612,200	314,500	121.3	61.1	60.2	11.7
1999	3,152,400	1,752,200	1,400,200	281,100	117.0	65.1	52.0	10.4
2000	2,301,000	1,331,500	969,500	214,200	84.9	49.1	35.8	7.9
2001	2,521,300	1,348,500	1,172,700	259,400	92.3	49.4	42.9	9.5
2002	2,082,600	1,088,800	993,800	173,500	75.4	39.4	36.0	6.3
2003	2,308,800	1,270,500	1,038,300	188,400	87.4	48.1	39.3	7.1
2004	1,762,200	1,065,400	696,800	107,300	67.2	40.6	26.6	4.1
2005	1,678,600	875,900	802,600	140,300	63.2	33.0	30.2	5.3
2006[3]	1,799,900	859,000	940,900	249,900	67.5	32.2	35.3	9.4
2007	1,801,200	896,700	904,400	116,100	67.8	33.7	34.0	4.4
2008	1,435,500	648,000	787,500	128,700	54.3	24.5	29.8	4.9
2009	1,322,800	594,500	728,300	233,700	51.0	22.9	28.1	9.0
2010	892,000	469,800	422,300	155,000	34.9	18.4	16.5	6.1
2011	1,246,200	647,700	598,600	89,500	49.3	25.6	23.7	3.5
2012	1,364,900	615,600	749,200	89,000	52.4	23.6	28.8	3.4
2013	1,420,900	454,900	966,000	125,500	55.0	17.6	37.4	4.9
2014	850,100	363,700	486,400	93,800	33.0	14.1	18.9	3.6
2015	841,100	309,100	531,900	99,000	32.9	12.1	20.8	3.9
2016[4]	749,900	294,000	455,000	71,700	29.3	11.5	17.8	2.8
Away from School								
1992	4,084,100	1,857,600	2,226,500	1,025,100	173.1	78.7	94.4	43.5
1993	3,835,900	1,731,100	2,104,800	1,004,300	158.2	71.4	86.8	41.4
1994	4,147,100	1,713,900	2,433,200	1,074,900	164.9	68.1	96.7	42.7
1995	3,626,600	1,604,800	2,021,800	829,700	141.9	62.8	79.1	32.5
1996	3,483,200	1,572,700	1,910,600	870,000	133.5	60.3	73.3	33.4
1997	3,717,600	1,710,700	2,006,900	853,300	140.7	64.7	75.9	32.3
1998	3,047,800	1,408,000	1,639,800	684,900	113.8	52.6	61.3	25.6
1999	2,713,800	1,129,200	1,584,500	675,400	100.8	41.9	58.8	25.1
2000	2,303,600	1,228,900	1,074,800	402,100	85.0	45.3	39.6	14.8
2001	1,780,300	961,400	819,000	314,800	65.2	35.2	30.0	11.5
2002	1,619,500	820,100	799,400	341,200	58.6	29.7	28.9	12.4
2003	1,824,100	780,900	1,043,200	412,800	69.1	29.6	39.5	15.6
2004	1,371,800	718,000	653,700	272,500	52.3	27.4	24.9	10.4
2005	1,429,000	637,700	791,300	257,100	53.8	24.0	29.8	9.7
2006[3]	1,413,100	714,200	698,900	263,600	53.0	26.8	26.2	9.9
2007	1,371,700	614,300	757,400	337,700	51.6	23.1	28.5	12.7
2008	1,132,600	498,500	634,100	258,600	42.8	18.9	24.0	9.8
2009	857,200	484,200	372,900	176,800	33.1	18.7	14.4	6.8
2010	689,900	378,800	311,200	167,300	27.0	14.8	12.2	6.5
2011	966,100	541,900	424,300	137,600	38.2	21.4	16.8	5.4
2012	991,200	470,800	520,400	169,900	38.0	18.1	20.0	6.5
2013	778,500	403,000	375,500	151,200	30.1	15.6	14.5	5.8
2014	621,300	288,900	332,400	165,000	24.1	11.2	12.9	6.4
2015	545,100	263,100	281,900	110,900	21.3	10.3	11.0	4.3
2016[4]	601,300	251,200	350,100	140,100	23.5	9.8	13.7	5.5

Note: "Serious violent victimization" includes the crimes of rape, sexual assault, robbery, and aggravated assault. "All violent victimization" includes serious violent crimes as well as simple assault. "Theft" includes attempted and completed purse-snatching, completed pickpocketing, and all attempted and completed thefts, with the exception of motor vehicle thefts. Theft does not include robbery, which involves the threat or use of force and is classified as a violent crime. "Total victimization" includes theft and violent crimes. Data in this table are from the National Crime Victimization Survey (NCVS); due to differences in time coverage and administration between the NCVS and the School Crime Supplement (SCS) to the NCVS, data in this table cannot be compared with data in tables that are based on the SCS. Detail may not sum to totals because of rounding.
[1]Serious violent victimization is also included in all violent victimization.
[2]"At school" includes inside the school building, on school property, and on the way to and from school.
[3]Every 10 years, the survey sample is redesigned to reflect changes in the population. Due to the sample redesign and other methodological changes implemented in 2006, use caution when comparing 2006 estimates to other years.
[4]Every 10 years, the survey sample is redesigned to reflect changes in the population. The sample redesign impacted the comparability of 2016 estimates to estimates for earlier years. Caution should be used when making comparisons to earlier years. For more information, see *Criminal Victimization*, 2016 (available at https://www.bjs.gov/index.cfm?ty=pbse&sid=6)

Table 3. Number of Nonfatal Victimizations Against Students Ages 12 to 18 Years and Rate of Victimization Per 1,000 Students, by Type of Victimization, Location, and Selected Student Characteristics, 2016

(Number; rate per 1,000 students.)

Location and year	Number of nonfatal victimizations		Violent		Rate of victimization per 1,000 students		Violent	
	Total	Theft	All violent	Serious violent[1]	Total	Theft	All violent	Serious violent[1]
At School[2]								
Total	749,400	294,000	455,400	71,700	29.3	11.5	17.8	2.8
Sex								
Male	500,900	171,800	329,100	36,600	38.1	13.1	25.0	2.8
Female	248,500	122,200	126,400	35,100	20.1	9.9	10.2	2.8
Age								
12 to 14 years	449,500	153,100	296,300	32,900	37.0	12.6	24.4	2.7
15 to 18 years	300,000	140,900	159,100	38,800	22.4	10.5	11.9	2.9
Race/ethnicity[3]								
White......................	353,800	172,600	181,200	34,400	27.3	13.3	14.0	2.6
Black	155,300	48,200	107,100	13,600 (!)	42.3	13.1	29.2	3.7 (!)
Hispanic	155,500	42,700	110,800	12,000 (!)	23.3	6.5	16.8	1.8 (!)
Other	86,800	30,500	56,300	11,700 (!)	37.5	13.2	24.3	5.1 (!)
Urbanicity[4]								
Urban......................	285,200	104,100	181,100	23,100 (!)	36.7	13.4	23.3	3.0 (!)
Suburban	337,900	130,800	207,100	26,900	23.6	9.1	14.4	1.9
Rural	126,400	59,200	67,200	21,700 (!)	36.8	17.2	19.6	6.3
Household income[5]								
Less than $15,000.................	109,300	43,900	65,400	10,600 (!)	46.0	18.5	27.5	4.5 (!)
$15,000 to $29,999..............	111,600	47,800	63,800	15,100 (!)	28.4	12.2	16.2	3.8 (!)
$30,000 to $49,999..............	118,300	41,400	76,900	NA	22.3	7.8	14.5	NA
$50,000 to $74,999..............	102,000	39,800	62,200	15,100 (!)	25.6	10.0	15.6	3.8 (!)
$75,000 or more..................	308,300	121,100	187,200	30,200	31.0	12.2	18.8	3.0
Away from School								
Total	601,300	251,200	350,100	140,100	23.5	9.8	13.7	5.5
Sex								
Male	345,200	145,400	199,700	56,100	26.2	11.1	15.2	4.3
Female	256,100	105,700	150,400	84,100	20.7	8.5	12.1	0.8
Age								
12 to 14 years	245,100	109,100	136,100	70,000	20.2	9.0	11.2	5.8
15 to 18 years	356,200	142,100	214,100	70,200	26.6	10.6	16.0	5.2
Race/ethnicity[3]								
White......................	305,000	129,700	175,400	70,500	23.5	10.0	13.5	5.4
Black	93,200	15,100	78,100	16,500 (!)	25.4	4.1	21.3	4.5 (!)
Hispanic	159,100	76,000	83,200	51,800	24.2	11.6	12.6	7.9
Other	43,900	30,400	13,500 (!)	NA	19.0	13.1	5.8 (!)	NA
Urban/city[4]								
Urban......................	230,900	73,900	157,000	59,700	29.7	9.5	20.2	7.7
Suburban	239,400	116,000	123,400	53,100	16.7	8.1	8.6	3.7
Rural	131,000	61,300	69,700	27,300 (!)	38.2	17.9	20.3	8.0 (!)
Household income[5]								
Less than $15,000.................	43,400	19,300	24,100	11,000 (!)	18.3	8.1	10.1	4.6 (!)
$15,000 to $29,999..............	183,300	60,200	123,100	33,900	46.7	15.3	31.4	8.6
$30,000 to $49,999..............	124,800	59,200	65,600	22,300 (!)	23.5	11.1	12.4	4.2 (!)
$50,000 to $74,999..............	80,800	43,400	37,400	20,100 (!)	20.3	10.9	9.4	5.1 (!)
$75,000 or more..................	168,900	69,100	99,900	52,800	17.0	6.9	10.0	5.3

Note: "Serious violent" victimization includes the crimes of rape, sexual assault, robbery, and aggravated assault. "All violent" victimization includes serious violent crimes as well as simple assault. "Theft" includes attempted and completed purse-snatching, completed pickpocketing, and all attempted and completed thefts, with the exception of motor vehicle thefts. Theft does not include robbery, which involves the threat or use of force and is classified as a violent crime. "Total victimization" includes theft and violent crimes. Data in this table are from the National Crime Victimization Survey (NCVS) and are reported in accordance with Bureau of Justice Statistics standards. Detail may not sum to totals because of rounding and missing data on student characteristics. The population size for students ages 12–18 was 25,546,100 in 2016. Every 10 years, the survey sample is redesigned to reflect changes in the population. The sample redesign impacted the comparability of 2016 estimates to estimates for earlier years. Caution should be used when making comparisons to earlier years. For more information, see Criminal Victimization, 2016 (available at https://www.bjs.gov/index.cfm?ty=pbse&sid=6).
Source: U.S. Department of Justice, Bureau of Justice Statistics, National Crime Victimization Survey (NCVS), 2016. (This table was prepared August 2017.)
NA = Not available.
(!) = Interpret data with caution. Estimate based on 10 or fewer sample cases, or the coefficient of variation is greater than 50 percent.
[1]Serious violent victimization is also included in all violent victimization.
[2]"At school" includes inside the school building, on school property, and on the way to and from school.
[3]Race categories exclude persons of Hispanic ethnicity. "Other" includes Asians, Pacific Islanders, American Indians/Alaska Natives, and persons of two or more races.
[4]Refers to the Standard Metropolitan Statistical Area (MSA) status of the respondent's household as defined by the U.S. Census Bureau. Categories include "central city of an MSA (Urban)," "in MSA but not in central city (Suburban)," and "not MSA (Rural)."
[5]Income data for 2016 were imputed. For more information, see Criminal Victimization, 2016 (available at https://www.bjs.gov/index.cfm?ty=pbse&sid=6).

Table 4. Percentage of Students in Grades 9 to 12 Who Reported Being Threatened or Injured with a Weapon on School Property During the Previous 12 Months, by Selected Student Characteristics and Number of Times Threatened or Injured: Selected Years, 1993–2015

(Percent.)

| Number of times and year | Total | Sex | | Race/ethnicity[1] | | | | | | | Grade | | | |
		Male	Female	White	Black	Hispanic	Asian[2]	Pacific Islander[2]	American Indian/ Alaska Native	Two or more races[2]	9th	10th	11th	12th
At Least Once														
1993	7.3	9.2	5.4	6.3	11.2	8.6	NA	NA	11.7	NA	9.4	7.3	7.3	5.5
1995	8.4	10.9	5.8	7.0	11.0	12.4	NA	NA	11.4 (!)	NA	9.6	9.6	7.7	6.7
1997	7.4	10.2	4.0	6.2	9.9	9.0	NA	NA	12.5 (!)	NA	10.1	7.9	5.9	5.8
1999	7.7	9.5	5.8	6.6	7.6	9.8	7.7	15.6	13.2 (!)	9.3	10.5	8.2	6.1	5.1
2001	8.9	11.5	6.5	8.5	9.3	8.9	11.3	24.8	15.2 (!)	10.3	12.7	9.1	6.9	5.3
2003	9.2	11.6	6.5	7.8	10.9	9.4	11.5	16.3	22.1	18.7	12.1	9.2	7.3	6.3
2005	7.9	9.7	6.1	7.2	8.1	9.8	4.6	14.5 (!)	9.8	10.7	10.5	8.8	5.5	5.8
2007	7.8	10.2	5.4	6.9	9.7	8.7	7.6 (!)	8.1 (!)	5.9	13.3	9.2	8.4	6.8	6.3
2009	7.7	9.6	5.5	6.4	9.4	9.1	5.5	12.5	16.5	9.2	8.7	8.4	7.9	5.2
2011	7.4	9.5	5.2	6.1	8.9	9.2	7.0	11.3	8.2	9.9	8.3	7.7	7.3	5.9
2013	6.9	7.7	6.1	5.8	8.4	8.5	5.3	8.7 (!)	18.5	7.7	8.5	7.0	6.8	4.9
2015	6.0	7.0	4.6	4.9	7.9	6.6	3.6 (!)	20.5 (!)	8.2 (!)	8.0	7.2	6.2	5.5	4.4
Number of Times, 2015														
0 times	94.0	93.0	95.4	95.1	92.1	93.4	96.4	79.5	91.8	92.0	92.8	93.8	94.5	95.6
1 time	2.7	3.1	2.3	2.4	4.1	2.6	X	X	X	3.8 (!)	3.5	2.9	2.5	1.8
2 or three times	1.5	1.6	1.3	1.5	1.6 (!)	1.4	0.5 (!)	X	3.1 (!)	1.7 (!)	2.1	1.3	1.1	1.3
4 to 11 times	1.0	1.3	0.6	0.6	1.4 (!)	1.4	X	X	X	1.2 (!)	0.9	1.3	1.1 (!)	0.7 (!)
12 or more times	0.8	1.0	0.4 (!)	0.4	0.9 (!)	1.2	X	X	X	1.3 (!)	0.6	0.7	0.8	0.6

Note: Survey respondents were asked about being threatened or injured "with a weapon such as a gun, knife, or club on schoolproperty." "On school property" was not defined for respondents. Detail may not sum to totals because of rounding.
NA = Not available.
X = Not applicable.
[1] Race categories exclude persons of Hispanic ethnicity.
[2] Before 1999, Asian students and Pacific Islander students were not categorized separately, and students could not be classified as two or more races. Because the response categories changed in 1999, caution should be used in comparing data on race from 1993, 1995, and 1997 with data from later years.

Table 5. Number and Percentage of Public and Private School Teachers Who Reported That They Were Threatened with Injury or Physically Attacked by a Student from School During the Previous 12 Months, by Selected Teacher and School Characteristics, Selected Years, 1993–1994 through 2011–2012

(Number; percent.)

Incident and year	Total	Sex		Race/ethnicity[1]				Instructional level[1]		Control of school	
		Male	Female	White	Black	Hispanic	Other[2]	Elementary	Secondary	Public[3]	Private
						Number of teachers					
Threatened with Injury											
1993–1994	342,700	115,900	226,800	295,700	23,900	15,900	7,300	135,200	207,500	326,800	15,900
1999–2000	304,900	95,100	209,800	252,500	28,300	17,200	7,000	148,100	156,900	287,400	17,500
2003–2004	252,800	78,400	174,400	198,900	32,500	12,400	9,000	113,600	139,200	242,100	10,700
2007–2008	289,900	88,300	201,600	234,700	28,700	17,900	8,600	130,000	160,000	276,600	13,300
2011–2012	352,900	84,500	268,400	279,900	34,200	27,100	11,800	189,800	163,200	338,400	14,500
Physically Attacked											
1993–1994	121,100	30,800	90,300	104,300	7,700	6,200	2,800	77,300	43,800	112,400	8,700
1999–2000	134,800	30,600	104,200	111,700	11,600	8,800	2,600	102,200	32,600	125,000	9,800
2003–2004	129,200	23,600	105,700	102,200	15,100	7,000	5,000	89,800	39,400	121,400	7,800
2007–2008	156,000	34,900	121,100	132,300	12,300	8,200	3,200 (!)	114,700	41,300	146,400	9,600
2011–2012	209,800	32,500	177,300	171,300	18,800	11,800	7,900	160,700	49,100	197,400	12,400
						Percent of teachers					
Threatened with Injury											
1993–1994	11.7	14.7	10.5	11.5	11.9	13.1	13.4	8.7	15.0	12.8	4.2
1999–2000	8.8	11.0	8.1	8.6	11.6	9.1	8.3	8.0	9.9	9.6	3.9
2003–2004	6.8	8.5	6.2	6.4	11.8	5.5	8.7	5.7	8.0	7.4	2.3
2007–2008	7.4	9.3	6.8	7.2	11.1	6.7	7.6	6.6	8.4	8.1	2.7
2011–2012	9.2	9.2	9.2	8.8	13.8	9.4	9.1	9.6	8.7	10.0	3.1
Physically Attacked											
1993–1994	4.1	3.9	4.2	4.1	3.9	5.2	5.2	5.0	3.2	4.4	2.3
1999–2000	3.9	3.5	4.0	3.8	4.8	4.6	3.1	5.5	2.1	4.2	2.2
2003–2004	3.5	2.6	3.8	3.3	5.5	3.1	4.8	4.5	2.3	3.7	1.7
2007–2008	4.0	3.7	4.1	4.1	4.7	3.1	2.8 (!)	5.8	2.2	4.3	2.0
2011–2012	5.4	3.5	6.0	5.4	7.6	4.1	6.1	8.2	2.6	5.8	2.7

Note: Teachers who taught only prekindergarten students are excluded. Instructional level divides teachers into elementary or secondary based on a combination of the grades taught, main teaching assignment, and the structure of the teachers' class(es). Race categories exclude persons of Hispanic ethnicity. Detail may not sum to totals because of rounding. Some data have been revised from previously published figures.
(!) = Interpret data with caution. The coefficient of variation (CV) for this estimate is between 30 and 50 percent.
[1]Teachers were classified as elementary or secondary on the basis of the grades they taught, rather than on the level of the school in which they taught. In general, elementary teachers include those teaching prekindergarten through grade 5 and those teaching multiple grades, with a preponderance of grades taught being kindergarten through grade 6. In general, secondary teachers include those teaching any of grades 7 through 12 and those teaching multiple grades, with a preponderance of grades taught being grades 7 through 12 and usually with no grade taught being lower than grade 5.
[2]Includes American Indians/Alaska Natives, Asians, and Pacific Islanders; for 2003–2004 and later years, also includes persons of two or more races.
[3]Includes traditional public and public charter schools.

Table 6. Percentage of Public Schools Recording Incidents of Crime at School and Reporting Incidents to Police, Number of Incidents, and Rate Per 1,000 Students, by Type of Crime, Selected Years, 1999–2000 through 2015–2016

(Percent; number; rate per 1,000 students.)

Type of crime recorded or reported to police	Percent of schools						2015–2016		
	1999–2000	2003–2004	2005–2006	2007–2008	2009–2010	2013–2014[1]	Percent of schools	Number of incidents	Rate per 1,000 students
Recorded Incidents									
Total	86.4	88.5	85.7	85.5	85.0	NA	78.9	1,381,200	28.0
Violent Incidents	71.4	81.4	77.7	75.5	73.8	65.0	68.9	864,900	17.5
Serious violent incidents	19.7	18.3	17.1	17.2	16.4	13.1	15.5	40,800	0.8
Rape or attempted rape	0.7	0.8	0.3	0.8	0.5	0.2 (!)	0.9	1,100	...
Sexual assault other than rape[2]	2.5	3.0	2.8	2.5	2.3	1.7	3.4	6,100	0.1
Physical attack or fight with a weapon	5.2	4.0	3.0	3.0	3.9	1.8	2.6	5,300	0.1
Threat of physical attack with a weapon	11.1	8.6	8.8	9.3	7.7	8.7	8.5	18,300	0.4
Robbery with a weapon	0.5 (!)	0.6	0.4	0.4 (!)	0.2	‡	0.5 (!)	600	...
Robbery without a weapon	5.3	6.3	6.4	5.2	4.4	2.5	2.7	9,500	0.2
Physical attack or fight without a weapon	63.7	76.7	74.3	72.7	70.5	57.5	64.9	567,000	11.5
Threat of physical attack without a weapon	52.2	53.0	52.2	47.8	46.4	47.1	39.4	257,000	5.2
Theft[3]	45.6	46.0	46.0	47.3	44.1	NA	38.7	166,000	3.4
Other Incidents[4]	72.7	64.0	68.2	67.4	68.1	NA	58.5	350,400	7.1
Possession of a firearm/explosive device	5.5	6.1	7.2	4.7	4.7	NA	4.0	10,500 (!)	0.2 (!)
Possession of a knife or sharp object	42.6	NA	42.8	40.6	39.7	NA	38.4	70,600	1.4
Distribution of illegal drugs[5]	12.3	12.9	NA	NA	NA	NA	NA	NA	NA
Possession or use of alcohol or illegal drugs[5]	26.6	29.3	NA	NA	NA	NA	NA	NA	NA
Distribution, possession, or use of illegal drugs[6]	NA	NA	25.9	23.2	24.6	NA	24.9	112,100	2.3
Inappropriate diistribution, possession, or use of prescription drugs[7]	NA	NA	NA	NA	12.1	NA	9.5	20,100	0.4
Distribution, possession, or use of alcohol[6]	NA	NA	16.2	14.9	14.1	NA	13.3	29,900	0.6
Sexual harassment	36.3	NA	NA	NA	NA	NA	NA	NA	NA
Vandalism	51.4	51.4	50.5	49.3	45.8	NA	33.4	107,200	2.2
Reported Incidents to Police									
Total	62.5	65.2	60.9	62.0	60.0	NA	47.4	448,900	9.1
Violent Incidents	36.0	43.6	37.7	37.8	39.9	NA	32.7	195,600	4.0
Serious violent incidents	14.8	13.3	12.6	12.6	10.4	NA	10.0	20,000	0.4
Rape or attempted rape	0.6	0.8	0.3	0.8	0.5	NA	0.7	900	...
Sexual assault other than rape[2]	2.3	2.6	2.6	2.1	1.4	NA	2.7	3,600	0.1
Physical attack or fight with a weapon	3.9	2.8	2.2	2.1	2.2	NA	1.3	2,500 (!)	0.1 (!)
Threat of physical attack with a weapon	8.5	6.0	5.9	5.7	4.5	NA	5.3	7,500	0.2
Robbery with a weapon	0.3 (!)	0.6	0.4	0.4	0.2	NA	0.3 (!)	400 (!)	...
Robbery without a weapon	3.4	4.2	4.9	4.1	3.5	NA	1.9	5,000	0.1
Physical attack or fight without a weapon	25.8	35.6	29.2	28.2	34.3	NA	25.1	121,500	2.5
Threat of physical attack without a weapon	18.9	21.0	19.7	19.5	15.2	NA	12.9	54,200	1.1
Theft[3]	28.5	30.5	27.9	31.0	25.4	NA	18.1	71,600	1.5
Other Incidents[4]	52.0	50.0	50.6	48.7	46.3	NA	33.5	181,700	3.7
Possession of a firearm/explosive device	4.5	4.9	5.5	3.6	3.1	NA	1.9	7,500 (!)	0.2 (!)
Possession of a knife or sharp object	23.0	NA	25.0	23.3	20.0	NA	15.8	27,700	0.6
Distribution of illegal drugs[5]	11.4	12.4	NA	NA	NA	NA	NA	NA	NA
Possession or use of alcohol or illegal drugs[5]	22.2	26.0	NA	NA	NA	NA	NA	NA	NA
Distribution, possession, or use of illegal drugs[6]	NA	NA	22.8	20.7	21.4	NA	19.9	82,200	1.7
Inappropriate diistribution, possession, or use of prescription drugs[7]	NA	NA	NA	NA	9.6	NA	7.4	15,100	0.3
Distribution, possession, or use of alcohol[6]	NA	NA	11.6	10.6	10.0	NA	8.6	17,800	0.4
Sexual harassment	14.7	NA	NA	NA	NA	NA	NA	NA	NA
Vandalism	32.7	34.3	31.9	30.8	26.8	NA	12.9	31,600	0.6

Note: Responses were provided by the principal or the person most knowledgeable about crime and safety issues at the school. "At school" was defined to include activities that happen in school buildings, on school grounds, on school buses, and at places that hold school-sponsored events or activities. Respondents were instructed to include incidents that occurred before, during, and after normal school hours or when school activities or events were in session. Detail may not sum to totals because of rounding and because schools that recorded or reported more than one type of crime incident were counted only once in the total percentage of schools recording or reporting incidents.

NA = Not available.

... = Rounds to zero.

(!) = Interpret data with caution. The coefficient of variation (CV) for this estimate is between 30 and 50 percent.

[1] Data for 2013–14 were collected using the Fast Response Survey System (FRSS), while data for all other years were collected using the School Survey on Crime and Safety (SSOCS). The 2013–14 FRSS survey was designed to allow comparisons with SSOCS data. However, respondents to the 2013–14 survey could choose either to complete the survey on paper (and mail it back) or to complete the survey online, whereas respondents to SSOCS did not have the option of completing the survey online. The 2013–14 survey also relied on a smaller sample. The smaller sample size and difference in survey administration may have impacted the 2013–14 results.

[2] Prior to 2015–2016, the wording of the survey item was "sexual battery other than rape."

[3] Theft/larceny (taking things worth over $10 without personal confrontation) was defined for respondents as "the unlawful taking of another person's property without personal confrontation, threat, violence, or bodily harm." This includes pocket picking, stealing a purse or backpack (if left unattended or no force was used to take it from owner), theft from a building, theft from a motor vehicle or motor vehicle parts or accessories, theft of a bicycle, theft from a vending machine, and all other types of thefts.

[4] Caution should be used when making direct comparisons of "Other incidents" between years because the survey questions about alcohol and drugs changed, as outlined in footnotes 5, 6, and 7.

[5] The survey items "Distribution of illegal drugs" and "Possession or use of alcohol or illegal drugs" appear only on the 1999–2000 and 2003–2004 questionnaires. Different alcohol- and drug-related survey items were used on the SSOCS questionnaires for later years.

[6] The survey items "Distribution, possession, or use of illegal drugs" and "Distribution, possession, or use of alcohol" appear only on the SSOCS questionnaires for 2005-2006 and later years.

[7] The survey item "Inappropriate distribution, possession, or use of prescription drugs" appears only on the 2009–2010 and 2015–2016 questionnaires.

Table 7. Percentage of Students Ages 12 to 18 Years Who Reported That Gangs Were Present at School During the School Year, by Selected Student and School Characteristics and Location, Selected Years, 2001–2015

(Percent.)

Year and location	Total	Sex		Race/ethnicity[1]					Grade							Control of school	
		Male	Female	White	Black	Hispanic	Asian	Other	6th	7th	8th	9th	10th	11th	12th	Public	Private
2001[2]																	
Total	20.1	21.4	18.8	15.5	28.6	32.0	NA	21.4	11.2	15.7	17.3	24.3	23.6	24.2	21.1	21.6	4.9
Urban	28.9	31.9	25.9	20.5	32.4	40.3	NA	27.0	14.9	23.7	24.0	35.3	33.1	34.2	34.1	31.9	5.0
Suburban	18.3	18.9	17.5	15.4	25.4	27.1	NA	20.0	9.0	13.7	16.6	20.8	22.3	22.7	18.6	19.5	4.3 (!)
Rural	13.3	14.0	12.5	12.1	22.5	16.8 (!)	NA	‡	11.0	8.9	10.1	18.9	14.4	15.8	11.5 (!)	13.7	‡
2003[2]																	
Total	20.9	22.3	19.5	14.2	29.5	37.2	NA	22.0	10.9	16.3	17.9	26.1	26.3	23.4	22.2	22.5	3.9
Urban	30.9	32.1	29.7	19.8	32.8	42.6	NA	30.6	21.6	25.5	25.2	38.2	35.3	34.6	34.8	33.7	6.0
Suburban	18.4	20.5	16.3	13.8	28.3	34.6	NA	18.2	7.5	13.2	16.2	24.3	24.1	20.4	19.3	19.9	2.4 (!)
Rural	12.3	12.2	12.4	10.7	21.8 (!)	12.7 (!)	NA	‡	‡	9.4	10.9 (!)	13.8	18.0	15.0	13.3	12.8	‡
2005[2]																	
Total	24.2	25.3	22.9	16.8	37.6	38.9	20.2	27.7	12.1	17.3	19.1	28.3	32.6	28.0	27.9	25.8	4.2
Urban	36.2	37.4	35.0	23.7	41.8	48.9	25.0	33.9	19.9	24.2	30.5	40.3	50.6	44.3	39.5	39.1	7.7
Suburban	20.8	22.4	19.1	16.0	36.2	32.1	18.1	29.0	8.9	14.9	14.6	24.8	27.9	25.5	25.1	22.3	3.0 (!)
Rural	16.4	16.1	16.7	14.1	24.4	26.2	19.0 (!)	‡	8.3	15.2	14.7	21.0	22.0	13.3 (!)	15.8 (!)	17.2	‡
2007																	
Total	23.2	25.1	21.3	16.0	37.6	36.1	17.4	26.4	15.3	17.4	20.6	28.0	28.1	25.9	24.4	24.9	5.2
Urban	32.3	35.3	29.2	23.4	39.7	40.4	18.4	31.9	17.8	24.1	25.9	41.1	38.6	34.7	38.4	35.6	7.3
Suburban	21.0	23.1	18.9	15.9	35.5	33.3	16.3	29.0	14.0	15.4	19.6	23.1	26.6	23.6	22.4	22.7	2.8 (!)
Rural	15.5	14.9	16.1	10.9	36.8	27.5 (!)	‡	14.3	15.6 (!)	13.1	14.7	21.7	15.2	18.7	7.6 (!)	15.6	11.8 (!)
2009																	
Total	20.4	20.9	19.9	14.1	31.4	33.0	17.2	15.3	11.0	14.8	15.9	24.9	27.7	22.6	21.9	22.0	2.3 (!)
Urban	30.7	32.8	28.6	19.4	40.0	38.9	18.9	23.2	14.5	21.0	24.4	34.2	44.8	34.9	36.0	33.7	4.1 (!)
Suburban	16.6	17.2	16.0	13.5	20.2	28.3	14.5	14.8	9.7	11.2	11.8	22.4	21.0	19.4	17.6	18.1	‡
Rural	16.0	13.7	18.1	11.8	35.4	27.3 (!)	‡	‡	8.3 (!)	16.5	14.2 (!)	18.8	19.6	13.4	17.3 (!)	16.2	‡
2011																	
Total	17.5	17.5	17.5	11.1	32.7	26.4	9.9	9.9	8.2	10.2	11.3	21.7	23.0	23.2	21.3	18.9	1.9 (!)
Urban	22.8	23.0	22.6	13.9	31.6	31.0	7.6 (!)	12.3	5.4 (!)	11.7	16.2	27.5	31.1	28.1	32.9	25.7	‡
Suburban	16.1	16.5	15.6	11.3	33.5	23.2	12.0 (!)	10.4	8.6	9.3	9.0	18.9	21.5	23.7	18.5	17.1	2.9 (!)
Rural	12.1	10.2	14.1	7.7	34.5	22.1 (!)	‡	‡	11.1	10.1	9.6 (!)	19.3	13.9	10.6	9.2 (!)	12.5	‡
2013																	
Total	12.4	12.9	12.0	7.5	18.6	20.1	9.4	14.3	5.0	7.7	7.8	13.9	17.7	17.1	14.6	13.3	2.3 (!)
Urban	18.3	18.6	18.0	14.3	20.6	22.6	10.4	17.9	9.6	12.0	13.2	19.6	24.8	26.7	18.2	19.9	4.6 (!)
Suburban	10.8	11.7	9.8	6.5	17.3	19.3	8.2 (!)	13.0	3.0 (!)	6.6	6.3	12.2	15.4	15.1	14.1	11.7	‡
Rural	6.8	5.7	7.9	4.1	16.1	9.4 (!)	‡	11.9	‡	4.2 (!)	‡	8.0 (!)	11.3	8.1 (!)	9.0 (!)	6.8	‡
2015																	
Total	10.7	10.9	10.4	7.4	17.1	15.3	4.1 (!)	12.7	5.7	6.8	7.2	13.3	13.3	13.3	13.1	11.3	2.4
Urban	15.3	14.8	15.8	12.3	19.3	17.8	5.9 (!)	17.5	6.4 (!)	9.0	10.9	19.5	19.8	21.9	17.3	16.4	4.4
Suburban	10.2	10.7	9.6	7.1	19.3	14.7	‡	11.4	6.0	5.8	6.3	13.4	12.1	12.1	13.3	10.7	‡
Rural	3.9	4.2	3.7	3.5	3.4 (!)	‡	‡	‡	‡	5.5	3.2 (!)	4.5 (!)	5.3 (!)	‡	‡	4.1	‡

Note: "Urbanicity" refers to the Standard Metropolitan Statistical Area (MSA) status of the respondent's household as defined by the U.S. Census Bureau. Categories include "central city of an MSA (Urban)," "in MSA but not in central city (Suburban)," and "not MSA (Rural)." All gangs, whether or not they are involved in violent or illegal activity, are included. "At school" includes in the school building, on school property, on a school bus, and going to and from school.

NA = Not available.

(!) = Interpret data with caution. The coefficient of variation (CV) for this estimate is between 30 and 50 percent.

‡ = Reporting standards not met. Either there are too few cases for a reliable estimate or the coefficient of variation (CV) is 50 percent or greater.

[1]Race categories exclude persons of Hispanic ethnicity. "Other" includes American Indians/Alaska Natives, Asians (prior to 2005), Pacific Islanders, and, from 2003 onward, persons of Two or more races. Due to changes in racial/ethnic categories, comparisons of race/ethnicity across years should be made with caution.

[2]In 2005 and prior years, the period covered by the survey question was "during the last 6 months," whereas the period was "during this school year" beginning in 2007. Cognitive testing showed that estimates for earlier years are comparable to those for 2007 and later years.

Table 8. Percentage of Students in Grades 9 to 12 Who Reported That Illegal Drugs Were Made Available to Them on School Property During the Previous 12 Months, by Selected Student Characteristics, Selected Years, 1993–2015

(Percent.)

Student characteristic	1993	1995	1997	1999	2001	2003	2005	2007	2009	2011	2013	2015
Total	24.0	32.1	31.7	30.2	28.5	28.7	25.4	22.3	22.7	25.6	22.1	21.7
Sex												
Male	28.5	38.8	37.4	34.7	34.6	31.9	28.8	25.7	25.9	29.2	24.5	24.2
Female	19.1	24.8	24.7	25.7	22.7	25.0	21.8	18.7	19.3	21.7	19.7	19.1
Race/ethnicity[1]												
White	24.1	31.7	31.0	28.8	28.3	27.5	23.6	20.8	19.8	22.7	20.4	19.8
Black	17.5	28.5	25.4	25.3	21.9	23.1	23.9	19.2	22.2	22.8	18.6	20.6
Hispanic	34.1	40.7	41.1	36.9	34.2	36.5	33.5	29.1	31.2	33.2	27.4	27.2
Asian[2]	NA	NA	NA	25.7	25.7	22.5	15.9	21.0	18.3	23.3	22.6	15.3
Pacific Islander[2]	NA	NA	NA	46.9	50.2	34.7	41.3	38.5	27.6	38.9	27.7	30.1 (!)
American Indian/Alaska Native	20.9	22.8	30.1	30.6	34.5	31.3	24.4	25.1	34.0	40.5	25.5	19.8
Two or more races[2]	NA	NA	NA	36.0	34.5	36.6	31.6	24.6	26.9	33.3	26.4	24.7
Grade												
9th	21.8	31.1	31.4	27.6	29.0	29.5	24.0	21.2	22.0	23.7	22.4	21.6
10th	23.7	35.0	33.4	32.1	29.0	29.2	27.5	25.3	23.7	27.8	23.2	21.9
11th	27.5	32.8	33.2	31.1	28.7	29.9	24.9	22.8	24.3	27.0	23.2	22.7
12th	23.0	29.1	29.0	30.5	26.9	24.9	24.9	19.6	20.6	23.8	18.8	20.3
Urban/city[3]												
Urban	NA	NA	31.2	30.3	32.0	31.1	NA	NA	NA	NA	NA	NA
Suburban	NA	NA	34.2	29.7	26.6	28.4	NA	NA	NA	NA	NA	NA
Rural	NA	NA	22.7	32.1	28.2	26.2	NA	NA	NA	NA	NA	NA

Note: "On school property" was not defined for survey respondents.
NA = Not available.
(!) = Interpret data with caution. The coefficient of variation (CV) for this estimate is between 30 and 50 percent.
[1]Race categories exclude persons of Hispanic ethnicity.
[2]Before 1999, Asian students and Pacific Islander students were not categorized separately, and students could not be classified as two or more races. Because the response categories changed in 1999, caution should be used in comparing data on race from 1993, 1995, and 1997 with data from later years.
[3]Refers to the Standard Metropolitan Statistical Area (MSA) status of the respondent's household as defined by the U.S. Census Bureau. Categories include "central city of an MSA (Urban)," "in MSA but not in central city (Suburban)," and "not MSA (Rural)."

Table 9. Percentage of Students Ages 12 to 18 Years Who Reported Being the Target of Hate-Related Words and Seeing Hate-Related Graffiti at School During the School Year by Selected Student and School Characteristics and Location, Selected Years, 1999–2015

(Percent.)

Student/school characteristic	1999[1]	2001[1]	2003[1]	2005[1]	2007	2009	2011	2013	2015
HATE-RELATED WORDS									
Total	NA	12.3	11.7	11.2	9.7	8.7	9.1	6.6	7.2
Sex									
Male	NA	12.8	12.0	11.7	9.9	8.5	9.0	6.6	7.8
Female	NA	11.7	11.3	10.7	9.6	8.9	9.1	6.7	6.7
Race/Ethnicity[2]									
White	NA	12.1	10.9	10.3	8.9	7.2	8.3	5.3	6.3
Black	NA	13.9	14.2	15.1	11.4	11.1	10.7	7.8	9.4
Hispanic	NA	11.0	11.4	10.5	10.6	11.2	9.8	7.4	6.5
Asian	NA	NA	NA	10.9	11.1	10.7	9.0	10.3	10.8
Other	NA	13.6	14.1	14.2	10.6	10.0	10.4	11.2	11.4
Grade									
6th	NA	12.1	11.9	11.1	12.1	8.3	9.0	6.7	10.1
7th	NA	14.1	12.5	13.1	10.7	9.6	9.9	7.5	7.0
8th	NA	13.0	12.8	11.2	11.0	10.9	8.4	7.4	9.2
9th	NA	12.1	13.5	12.8	10.9	8.0	10.2	6.6	7.4
10th	NA	13.1	11.6	10.9	9.0	9.7	9.6	6.4	6.5
11th	NA	12.7	8.3	9.0	8.6	8.4	8.7	7.5	6.0
12th	NA	7.9	10.8	9.7	6.0	5.8	7.5	4.1	5.4
Urban/City[3]									
Urban	NA	11.9	13.2	12.2	9.7	9.9	8.0	7.2	6.5
Suburban	NA	12.4	10.7	9.4	9.3	8.3	9.8	6.6	8.3
Rural	NA	12.4	12.2	15.5	11.0	8.1	8.5	5.7	4.9
Control of School									
Public	NA	12.7	11.9	11.6	10.1	8.9	9.3	6.6	7.6
Private	NA	8.2	9.7	6.8	6.1	6.6	6.9	6.7	2.8 (!)
HATE-RELATED GRAFFITI									
Total	36.3	35.5	36.3	38.4	34.9	29.2	28.4	24.6	27.2
Sex									
Male	33.8	34.9	35.0	37.7	34.4	29.0	28.6	24.1	26.3
Female	38.9	36.1	37.6	39.1	35.4	29.3	28.1	25.1	28.1
Race/Ethnicity[2]									
White	36.4	36.2	35.2	38.5	35.5	28.3	28.2	23.7	28.6
Black	37.6	33.6	38.1	38.0	33.7	29.0	28.1	26.3	24.9
Hispanic	35.6	35.1	40.3	38.0	34.8	32.2	29.1	25.6	26.7
Asian	NA	NA	NA	34.5	28.2	31.2	29.9	20.8	17.5
Other	32.2	32.1	31.4	46.9	38.7	25.8	25.9	28.4	29.7
Grade									
6th	30.3	34.9	35.7	34.0	35.5	28.1	25.9	21.9	30.0
7th	34.9	34.9	37.2	37.0	32.3	27.9	26.0	21.7	24.7
8th	35.6	36.7	34.2	35.7	33.5	30.8	25.9	24.0	27.2
9th	39.2	35.7	37.0	41.6	34.5	28.1	28.7	27.2	28.2
10th	38.9	36.2	40.7	40.7	36.4	31.0	33.3	26.0	28.6
11th	37.0	36.1	36.6	40.2	35.3	27.4	32.1	25.8	26.2
12th	35.6	33.0	32.2	37.8	37.7	30.4	25.7	24.2	26.1
Urban/City[3]									
Urban	37.0	35.7	38.6	40.9	34.4	31.1	27.5	27.8	26.4
Suburban	37.3	36.0	35.9	38.0	34.2	28.6	29.9	23.7	28.0
Rural	32.7	33.8	33.9	35.8	37.8	27.7	24.9	21.6	25.7
Control of School									
Public	38.0	37.3	37.9	40.0	36.4	30.7	29.7	25.6	28.3
Private	20.7	16.8	19.5	18.6	18.5	11.8	13.4	12.6	11.5

Note: "At school" includes in the school building, on school property, on a school bus, and, from 2001 onward, going to and from school. "Hate-related" refers to derogatory terms used by others in reference to students' personal characteristics.
NA = Not available.
(!) = Interpret data with caution. The coefficient of variation (CV) for this estimate is between 30 and 50 percent.
[1] In 2005 and prior years, the period covered by the survey question was "during the last 6 months," whereas the period was "during this school year" beginning in 2007. Cognitive testing showed that estimates for earlier years are comparable to those for 2007 and later years.
[2] Race categories exclude persons of Hispanic ethnicity. "Other" includes American Indians/Alaska Natives, Asians (prior to 2005), Pacific Islanders, and, from 2003 onward, persons of two or more races. Due to changes in racial/ethnic categories, comparisons of race/ethnicity across years should be made with caution.
[3] Refers to the Standard Metropolitan Statistical Area (MSA) status of the respondent's household as defined by the U.S. Census Bureau. Categories include "central city of an MSA (Urban)," "in MSA but not in central city (Suburban)," and "not MSA (Rural)."

Table 10. Percentage of Students Ages 12 to 18 Years Who Reported Being Bullied at School During the School Year, by Type of Bullying and Selected Student and School Characteristics, Selected Years, 2005–2015

(Percent.)

Student/school characteristic	Total bullied at school[1]	Type of bullying						
		Made fun of, called names, or insulted	Subject of rumors	Threatened with harm	Tried to make do things did not want to do	Excluded from activities on purpose	Property destroyed on purpose	Pushed, shoved, tripped, or spit on
2005[2]								
Total	28.1	18.7	14.7	4.8	3.5	4.6	3.4	9.0
Sex								
Male...............................	27.1	18.5	11.0	5.2	3.9	4.1	3.5	10.9
Female............................	29.2	19.0	18.5	4.4	3.1	5.2	3.3	7.1
Race/Ethnicity[3]								
White..............................	30.0	20.1	15.8	5.1	3.6	5.3	3.4	9.7
Black..............................	28.5	18.5	14.2	4.9	4.7	4.5	4.6	8.9
Hispanic..........................	22.3	14.7	12.4	4.6	2.6	3.0	2.7	7.6
Asian..............................	NA	NA	NA	NA	NA	NA	NA	NA
Other..............................	24.6	16.3	11.6	2.1	2.1 (!)	2.5	2.5 (!)	6.8
Grade								
6th.................................	36.6	26.3	16.4	6.4	4.4	7.4	3.9	15.1
7th.................................	35.0	25.2	18.9	6.3	4.7	7.1	4.6	15.4
8th.................................	30.4	20.4	14.3	4.3	3.8	5.4	4.5	11.3
9th.................................	28.1	18.9	13.8	5.3	3.2	3.8	2.7	8.2
10th...............................	24.9	15.5	13.6	4.9	3.6	3.6	2.9	6.8
11th...............................	23.0	14.7	13.4	3.2	2.8	3.3	2.6	4.2
12th...............................	19.9	11.3	12.5	3.5	1.8	2.2	2.4	2.9
Urban/City[4]								
Urban..............................	26.0	17.7	13.3	5.5	4.1	4.9	3.9	8.5
Suburban.........................	28.9	18.9	14.6	4.4	3.1	4.5	3.0	9.0
Rural..............................	29.0	19.8	17.2	5.0	3.7	4.5	3.8	9.9
Control of School[5]								
Public..............................	28.6	19.0	14.9	5.1	3.5	4.5	3.5	9.3
Private	22.7	15.3	12.4	0.9 (!)	3.0 (!)	6.2	2.0 (!)	5.5
2007								
Total	31.7	21.0	18.1	5.8	4.1	5.2	4.2	11.0
Sex								
Male...............................	30.3	20.3	13.5	6.0	4.8	4.6	4.0	12.2
Female............................	33.2	21.7	22.8	5.6	3.4	5.8	4.4	9.7
Race/Ethnicity[3]								
White..............................	34.1	23.5	20.3	6.3	4.8	6.1	4.2	11.5
Black..............................	30.4	19.5	15.7	5.8	3.2	3.7	5.6	11.3
Hispanic..........................	27.3	16.1	14.4	4.9	3.0	4.0	3.6	9.9
Asian..............................	18.1	10.6	8.2	‡	‡	‡	1.8	3.8 (!)
Other..............................	34.1	20.1	20.8	7.7	3.1	7.7	3.4	14.4
Grade								
6th.................................	42.7	31.2	21.3	7.0	5.4	7.4	5.2	17.6
7th.................................	35.6	27.6	20.2	7.4	4.1	7.7	6.0	15.8
8th.................................	36.9	25.1	19.7	6.9	3.6	5.4	4.6	14.2
9th.................................	30.6	20.3	18.1	4.6	5.1	4.5	3.5	11.4
10th...............................	27.7	17.7	15.0	5.8	4.6	4.6	3.4	8.6
11th...............................	28.5	15.3	18.7	4.9	4.2	3.9	4.4	6.5
12th...............................	23.0	12.1	14.1	4.3	2.1	3.5	2.4	4.1
Urban/City[4]								
Urban..............................	30.7	20.0	15.5	5.2	3.6	4.9	4.2	9.2
Suburban.........................	31.2	21.1	17.4	5.7	4.1	5.0	4.0	11.2
Rural..............................	35.2	22.1	24.1	7.0	5.1	6.3	4.9	13.1
Control of School[5]								
Public..............................	32.0	21.1	18.3	6.2	4.2	5.2	4.1	11.4
Private	29.1	20.1	16.0	1.3 (!)	3.6	5.9	5.0	6.5
2009								
Total	28.0	18.8	16.5	5.7	3.6	4.7	3.3	9.0

Table 10. Percentage of Students Age 12 to 18 Years Who Reported Being Bullied at School During the School Year, by Type of Bullying and Selected Student and School Characteristics, Selected Years, 2005–2015—Continued

(Percent.)

Student/school characteristic	Total bullied at school[1]	Type of bullying						
		Made fun of, called names, or insulted	Subject of rumors	Threatened with harm	Tried to make do things did not want to do	Excluded from activities on purpose	Property destroyed on purpose	Pushed, shoved, tripped, or spit on
Sex								
Male	26.6	18.4	12.8	5.6	4.0	3.8	3.4	10.1
Female	29.5	19.2	20.3	5.8	3.2	5.7	3.2	7.9
Race/Ethnicity[3]								
White	29.3	20.5	17.4	5.4	3.7	5.2	3.3	9.1
Black	29.1	18.4	17.7	7.8	4.8	4.6	4.6	9.9
Hispanic	25.5	15.8	14.8	5.8	2.7	3.6	2.6	9.1
Asian	17.3	9.6	8.1	‡	‡	3.4 (!)	‡	5.5 (!)
Other	26.7	17.4	12.9	9.7 (!)	4.5 (!)	4.5 (!)	3.8 (!)	7.1 (!)
Grade								
6th	39.4	30.6	21.4	9.3	4.2	6.6	4.0	14.5
7th	33.1	23.6	17.3	5.7	4.6	5.6	4.6	13.1
8th	31.7	22.8	18.1	6.8	5.4	6.9	6.1	12.8
9th	28.0	19.2	16.6	7.1	4.0	4.5	2.9	9.7
10th	26.6	15.0	17.0	5.8	3.1	4.0	2.9	7.3
11th	21.1	13.9	13.9	4.8	2.5	3.6	1.5 (!)	4.4
12th	20.4	11.1	13.1	2.0	1.7 (!)	2.6	1.3 (!)	3.0
Urban/City[4]								
Urban	27.4	17.0	16.5	6.6	4.2	4.0	4.2	9.0
Suburban	27.5	19.3	15.5	5.2	3.2	5.0	2.9	8.9
Rural	30.7	20.2	19.9	6.1	4.1	5.2	3.3	9.5
Control of School[5]								
Public	28.8	19.3	16.9	5.9	3.8	4.7	3.4	9.4
Private	18.9	13.3	11.6	4.4	1.9	4.9	1.8	4.5
2011								
Total	27.8	17.6	18.3	5.0	3.3	5.6	2.8	7.9
Sex								
Male	24.5	16.2	13.2	5.0	3.6	4.8	3.3	8.9
Female	31.4	19.1	23.8	5.1	3.0	6.4	2.3	6.8
Race/Ethnicity[3]								
White	31.5	20.6	20.3	5.8	3.3	7.1	3.1	8.6
Black	27.2	16.4	18.6	5.5	4.3	4.7	3.3	9.3
Hispanic	21.9	12.7	15.1	3.3	2.9	2.8	2.4	6.2
Asian	14.9	9.0	7.7	‡	2.7	2.9	‡	2.1
Other	23.7	15.0	17.0	6.5	‡	5.0	‡	7.2
Grade								
6th	37.0	27.0	23.1	4.9	3.9	6.6	3.7	12.7
7th	30.3	22.4	18.3	6.9	4.5	7.8	4.0	12.6
8th	30.7	20.7	19.0	5.3	2.9	6.4	4.0	10.8
9th	26.5	16.4	16.3	5.4	3.3	4.1	2.5	7.3
10th	28.0	16.9	19.6	5.1	3.9	5.3	2.2	6.7
11th	23.8	12.7	17.1	4.0	2.4	4.7	1.8	3.9
12th	22.0	10.6	16.7	3.5	2.3	4.3	1.9	2.7
Urban/City[4]								
Urban	24.8	15.9	16.1	4.4	3.1	4.6	2.5	7.6
Suburban	29.0	18.4	18.7	5.0	3.2	6.0	3.0	8.2
Rural	29.7	18.4	21.4	6.3	3.9	5.8	3.0	7.3
Control of School[5]								
Public	28.4	17.9	18.8	5.3	3.3	5.5	2.9	8.1
Private	21.5	13.9	12.6	1.6	2.9	5.6	2.1	4.7
2013								
Total	21.5	13.6	13.2	3.9	2.2	4.5	1.6	6.0
Sex								
Male	19.5	12.6	9.6	4.1	2.4	3.5	1.8	7.4
Female	23.7	14.7	17.0	3.7	1.9	5.5	1.3	4.6

Table 10. Percentage of Students Age 12 to 18 Years Who Reported Being Bullied at School During the School Year, by Type of Bullying and Selected Student and School Characteristics, Selected Years, 2005–2015—Continued

(Percent.)

Student/school characteristic	Total bullied at school[1]	Type of bullying						
		Made fun of, called names, or insulted	Subject of rumors	Threatened with harm	Tried to make do things did not want to do	Excluded from activities on purpose	Property destroyed on purpose	Pushed, shoved, tripped, or spit on
Race/Ethnicity[3]								
White	23.7	15.6	14.6	4.4	2.0	5.4	1.5	6.1
Black	20.3	10.5	12.7	3.2	2.7	2.7	2.0	6.0
Hispanic	19.2	12.1	11.5	4.0	1.6	3.5	1.4	6.3
Asian	9.2	7.5	3.7	‡	3.8 (!)	2.2	1.6 (!)	2.0 (!)
Other	25.2	16.5	17.3	4.3 (!)	4.0 (!)	6.5	2.1 (!)	8.5
Grade								
6th	27.8	21.3	16.1	5.9	3.4	6.5	3.1	11.0
7th	26.4	17.9	15.5	6.1	3.0	6.3	2.2	11.6
8th	21.7	14.5	12.7	3.9	2.3	5.2	1.5 (!)	6.5
9th	23.0	13.7	13.8	3.6	2.6	4.3	1.2 (!)	4.9
10th	19.5	12.9	12.9	4.3	1.7	4.6	1.3	3.7
11th	20.0	11.2	12.5	3.0	1.5	2.4	1.6 (!)	3.4
12th	14.1	6.4	9.7	1.0 (!)	1.3 (!)	2.5	0.7 (!)	3.0
Urban/City[4]								
Urban	20.7	12.8	12.7	3.9	2.7	4.1	1.4	5.6
Suburban	22.0	14.2	13.4	3.9	2.0	4.7	1.3	6.4
Rural	21.4	13.2	13.3	4.1	1.7	4.2	2.8	5.8
Control of School[5]								
Public	21.5	13.5	13.2	3.9	2.2	4.3	1.6	6.1
Private	22.4	15.3	13.4	3.9	2.7 (!)	6.7	1.3 (!)	5.2
2015								
Total	20.8	13.3	12.3	3.9	2.5	5.0	1.8	5.1
Sex								
Male	18.8	12.7	9.1	4.8	2.7	4.4	1.9	6.0
Female	22.8	13.9	15.5	2.9	2.3	5.7	1.8	4.2
Race/Ethnicity[3]								
White	21.6	14.2	12.8	3.9	2.1	5.6	1.6	5.3
Black	24.7	17.2	14.3	5.2	3.4 (!)	4.9	1.6 (!)	5.6
Hispanic	17.2	9.5	10.4	2.9	2.1 (!)	3.4	2.0 (!)	3.7
Asian	15.6	10.1 (!)	4.9 (!)	‡	‡	‡	‡	3.9 (!)
Other	25.9	16.4	18.6	8.9 (!)	9.1 (!)	9.8 (!)	‡	11.2 (!)
Grade								
6th	31.0	21.4	17.7	7.3	5.2	10.1	4.0 (!)	13.1
7th	25.1	18.6	12.9	3.8	2.9 (!)	6.4	2.7 (!)	7.8
8th	22.2	15.6	13.1	5.0	2.9 (!)	5.1	3.0 (!)	7.5
9th	19.0	12.5	10.6	2.8 (!)	2.7 (!)	4.4	1.3 (!)	4.4
10th	21.2	12.6	12.9	2.9 (!)	1.7 (!)	5.7	1.2 (!)	2.2 (!)
11th	15.8	8.8	10.2	4.2	‡	3.0	‡	2.1 (!)
12th	14.9	6.2	10.8	2.5 (!)	2.4 (!)	2.4	‡	1.6 (!)
Urban/City[4]								
Urban	21.5	14.5	11.4	3.9	2.9	5.1	2.4	5.6
Suburban	21.1	13.3	13.2	3.9	2.6	5.4	1.6	4.8
Rural	18.2	10.9	10.6	3.8 (!)	‡	3.7	‡	5.2
Control of School[5]								
Public	21.1	13.4	12.5	4.0	2.6	5.0 (!)	1.8	5.2
Private	16.1	11.5	8.6	‡	‡	5.0	‡	3.6 (!)

Note: "At school" includes the school building, on school property, on a school bus, and going to and from school.
NA = Not available.
(!) = Interpret data with caution. The coefficient of variation (CV) for this estimate is between 30 and 50 percent.
‡ = Reporting standards not met. Either there are too few cases for a reliable estimate or the coefficient of variation (CV) is 50 percent or greater.
[1]Students who reported experiencing more than one type of bullying at school were counted only once in the total for students bullied at school.
[2]In 2005 and prior years, the period covered by the survey question was "during the last 6 months," whereas the period was "during this school year" beginning in 2007. Cognitive testing showed that estimates for earlier years are comparable to those for 2007 and later years.
[3]Race categories exclude persons of Hispanic ethnicity. "Other" includes American Indians/Alaska Natives, Pacific Islanders, and persons of two or more races.
[4]Refers to the Standard Metropolitan Statistical Area (MSA) status of the respondent's household as defined by the U.S. Census Bureau. Categories include "central city of an MSA (Urban)," "in MSA but not in central city (Suburban)," and "not MSA (Rural)." These data by metropolitan status were based on the location of households and differ from those published in *Student Reports of Bullying and Cyber-Bullying: Results from the 2013 School Crime Supplement to the National Crime Victimization Survey,* which were based on the urban-centric measure of the location of the school that the child attended.
[5]Control of school as reported by the respondent. These data differ from those based on a matching of the respondent-reported school name to the Common Core of Data's Public Elementary/Secondary School Universe Survey or the Private School Survey, as reported in *Student Reports of Bullying and Cyber-Bullying: Results from the 2013 School Crime Supplement to the National Crime Victimization Survey.*

METHODOLOGY

This annual report, a joint effort by the Bureau of Justice Statistics and the National Center for Education Statistics (NCES), provides the most current statistical information on the nature of crime in schools. It presents data on crime and safety at school from the perspectives of students, teachers, and principals. This report contains 23 indicators of crime and safety at school from a number of sources, including the National Crime Victimization Survey (NCVS), the School Crime Supplement to the NCVS, the Youth Risk Behavior Survey, the School Survey on Crime and Safety, and the School and Staffing Survey. Topics covered include victimization at school, teacher injury, bullying and cyber-bullying, school conditions, fights, weapons, availability and student use of drugs and alcohol, student perceptions of personal safety at school, and crime at postsecondary institutions. For more information or to access the full report, please see https://nces.ed.gov/pubs2018/2018036.pdf.

Data

The Bureau of Justice Statistics' (BJS) **National Crime Victimization Survey (NCVS)** is the nation's primary source of information on criminal victimization. The survey underwent a sample redesign in 2016; information is available in the *Criminal Victimization chapter* and at https://www.bjs.gov/index.cfm?ty=pbdetail&iid=6166.

Nonresponse and Weighting Adjustments

In 2016, a total of 134,690 households and 224,520 persons age 12 or older were interviewed for the NCVS. In general, each household was interviewed twice during the year. The response rate was 78 percent for households and 84 percent for eligible persons.

Victimizations that occurred outside of the United States were excluded from this report. In 2016, fewer than 1 percent of the unweighted victimizations occurred outside of the United States.

Estimates in this report use data primarily from the 2016 NCVS data files. These data are weighted to produce annual estimates of victimization for persons age 12 or older living in U.S. households. Because the NCVS relies on a sample rather than a census of the entire U.S. population, weights are designed to adjust to known population totals and compensate for survey nonresponse and other aspects of the complex sample design.

NCVS data files include person, household, and victimization weights. Person weights provide an estimate of the population represented by each person in the sample. Household weights provide an estimate of the U.S. household population represented by each household in the sample. After proper adjustment, both household and person weights are also typically used to form the denominator in calculations of crime rates.

Victimization weights used in the analyses in this report account for the number of persons present during an incident and for high-frequency repeat victimizations (i.e., series victimizations). Series victimizations are similar in type but occur with such frequency that a victim is unable to recall each individual event or describe each event in detail. Survey procedures allow NCVS interviewers to identify and classify these similar victimizations as series victimizations and to collect detailed information on only the most recent incident in the series.

The weight counts series victimizations as the actual number of victimizations reported by the victim, up to a maximum of 10. Including series victimizations in national rates results in large increases in the level of violent victimization. However, trends in violent crime are generally similar, regardless of whether series victimizations are included. In 2016, series incidents accounted for fewer than 2 percent of all victimizations and fewer than 4 percent of all violent victimizations. Weighting series victimizations as the number of victimizations up to a maximum of 10 victimizations produces more reliable estimates of crime levels, while the cap at 10 minimizes the effect of extreme outliers on rates. Additional information on the enumeration of series victimizations is detailed in the report *Methods for Counting High-Frequency Repeat Victimizations in the National Crime Victimization Survey* (NCJ 237308, BJS web, April 2012).

The **School-Associated Violent Deaths Study (SAVD)** is an epidemiological study developed by the Centers for Disease Control and Prevention in conjunction with the U.S. Department of Education and the U.S. Department of Justice. SAVD seeks to describe the epidemiology of school-associated violent deaths, identify common features of these deaths, estimate the rate of school-associated violent deaths in the United States, and identify potential risk factors for these deaths. The study includes descriptive data on all school-associated violent deaths in the United States, including all homicides, suicides, or legal intervention deaths in which the fatal injury occurred on the campus of a functioning elementary or secondary school; while the victim was on the way to or from regular sessions at such a school; or while attending or on the way to or from an official school-sponsored event. Victims of such incidents include nonstudents, as well as students and staff members. SAVD includes descriptive information about the school, event, victim(s), and offender(s). The SAVD study has collected data from July 1, 1992, through the present.

SAVD uses a four-step process to identify and collect data on school-associated violent deaths. Cases are initially identified through a search of the LexisNexis newspaper and media database. Then law enforcement officials from the office that investigated the deaths are contacted to confirm the details of the case and to determine if the event meets the case definition. Once a case is confirmed, a law enforcement official and a school official are interviewed regarding details about the school, event, victim(s), and offender(s). A copy of the full law enforcement report is also sought for each case. The information obtained on schools includes school demographics, attendance/absentee rates, suspensions/expulsions and mobility, school history of weapon-carrying incidents, security measures, violence prevention activities, school response to the event, and school policies about weapon carrying. Event information includes the location of injury, the context of injury (while classes were being held, during break, etc.), motives for injury, method of injury, and school and community events happening around the time period. Information obtained on victim(s) and offender(s) includes demographics, circumstances of the event (date/time, alcohol or drug use, number of persons involved), types and origins of weapons, criminal history, psychological risk factors, school-related problems, extracurricular activities, and family history, including structure and stressors.

For several reasons, all data for years from 1999 to the present are flagged as preliminary. For some recent data, the interviews with school and law enforcement officials to verify case details have not been completed. The details learned during the interviews can occasionally change the classification of a case. Also, new cases may be identified because of the expansion of the scope of the media files used for case identification. Sometimes other cases not identified during earlier data years using the independent case finding efforts (which focus on nonmedia sources of information) will be discovered. Also, other cases may occasionally be identified while the law enforcement and school interviews are being conducted to verify known cases.

Created as a supplement to the NCVS and co-designed by the National Center for Education Statistics and Bureau of Justice Statistics, the School Crime Supplement (SCS) survey has been conducted in 1989, 1995, and biennially since 1999 to collect additional information about school-related victimizations on a national level. This report includes data from the 1995, 1999, 2001, 2003, 2005, 2007, 2009, 2011, and 2013 collections. The 1989 data are not included in this report as a result of methodological changes to the NCVS and SCS. The SCS was

designed to assist policymakers, as well as academic researchers and practitioners at federal, state, and local levels, to make informed decisions concerning crime in schools. The survey asks students a number of key questions about their experiences with and perceptions of crime and violence that occurred inside their school, on school grounds, on the school bus, or on the way to or from school. Students are asked additional questions about security measures used by their school, students' participation in after-school activities, students' perceptions of school rules, the presence of weapons and gangs in school, the presence of hate-related words and graffiti in school, student reports of bullying and reports of rejection at school, and the availability of drugs and alcohol in school. Students are also asked attitudinal questions relating to fear of victimization and avoidance behavior at school.

The SCS survey was conducted for a 6-month period from January through June in all households selected for the NCVS (see discussion above for information about the NCVS sampling design and changes to the race/ethnicity variable beginning in 2003). Within these households, the eligible respondents for the SCS were those household members who had attended school at any time during the 6 months preceding the interview, were enrolled in grades 6–12, and were not homeschooled. In 2007, the questionnaire was changed and household members who attended school sometime during the school year of the interview were included. The age range of students covered in this report is 12–18 years of age. Eligible respondents were asked the supplemental questions in the SCS only after completing their entire NCVS interview. It should be noted that the first or unbounded NCVS interview has always been included in analysis of the SCS data and may result in the reporting of events outside of the requested reference period.

A total of about 9,700 students participated in the 1995 SCS, 8,400 in 1999, 8,400 in 2001, 7,200 in 2003, 6,300 in 2005, 5,600 in 2007, 5,000 in 2009, 6,500 in 2011, and 5,700 in 2013. In the 2013 SCS, the household completion rate was 86 percent.

The **Youth Risk Behavior Surveillance System (YRBSS)** is an epidemiological surveillance system developed by the Centers for Disease Control and Prevention (CDC) to monitor the prevalence of youth behaviors that most influence health. The YRBSS focuses on priority health-risk behaviors established during youth that result in the most significant mortality, morbidity, disability, and social problems during both youth and adulthood. The YRBSS includes a national school-based Youth Risk Behavior Survey (YRBS) as well as surveys conducted in states and large urban school districts. This report uses 1993, 1995, 1997, 1999, 2001, 2003, 2005, 2007, 2009, 2011, and 2013 YRBSS data.

The national YRBS uses a three-stage cluster sampling design to produce a nationally representative sample of students in grades 9–12 in the United States. The target population consisted of all public and private school students in grades 9–12 in the 50 states and the District of Columbia. The first-stage sampling frame included selecting primary sampling units (PSUs) from strata formed on the basis of urbanization and the relative percentage of Black and Hispanic students in the PSU. These PSUs are either counties; subareas of large counties; or groups of smaller, adjacent counties. At the second stage, schools were selected with probability proportional to school enrollment size.

The final stage of sampling consisted of randomly selecting, in each chosen school and in each of grades 9–12, one or two classrooms from either a required subject, such as English or social studies, or a required period, such as homeroom or second period. All students in selected classes were eligible to participate. In surveys conducted before 2013, three strategies were used to oversample Black and Hispanic students: (1) larger sampling rates were used to select PSUs that are in high-Black and high- Hispanic strata; (2) a modified measure of size was used that increased the probability of selecting schools with a disproportionately high minority enrollment; and (3) two classes per grade, rather than one, were selected in schools with a high percentage of combined Black, Hispanic, Asian/Pacific Islander, or American Indian/Alaska Native enrollment. In 2013, only selection of two classes per grade was needed to achieve an adequate precision with minimum variance. Approximately 16,300 students participated in the 1993 survey, 10,900 students participated in the 1995 survey, 16,300 students participated in the 1997 survey, 15,300 students participated in the 1999 survey, 13,600 students participated in the 2001 survey, 15,200 students participated in the 2003 survey, 13,900 students participated in the 2005 survey, 14,000 students participated in the 2007 survey, 16,400 students participated in the 2009 survey, 15,400 participated in the 2011 survey, and 13,600 participated in the 2013 survey.

The overall response rate was 70 percent for the 1993 survey, 60 percent for the 1995 survey, 69 percent for the 1997 survey, 66 percent for the 1999 survey, 63 percent for the 2001 survey, 67 percent for the 2003 survey, 67 percent for the 2005 survey, 68 percent for the 2007 survey, 71 percent for the 2009 survey, 71 percent for the 2011 survey, and 68 percent for the 2013 survey. NCES standards call for response rates of 85 percent or better for cross-sectional surveys, and bias analyses are required by NCES when that percentage is not achieved. For YRBS data, a full nonresponse bias analysis has not been done because the data necessary to do the analysis are not available. The weights were developed to adjust for nonresponse and the oversampling of Black and Hispanic students in the sample. The final weights were constructed so that only weighted proportions of students (not weighted counts of students) in each grade matched national population projections.

The **School Survey on Crime and Safety (SSOCS)** is managed by the National Center for Education Statistics (NCES) on behalf of the U.S. Department of Education. SSOCS collects extensive crime and safety data from principals and school administrators of U.S. public schools. Data from this collection can be used to examine the relationship between school characteristics and violent and serious violent crimes in primary schools, middle schools, high schools, and combined schools. In addition, data from SSOCS can be used to assess what crime prevention programs, practices, and policies are used by schools. SSOCS has been conducted in school years 1999–2000, 2003–04, 2005–06, 2007–08, and 2009–10.

SSOCS was developed by NCES and is funded by the Office of Safe and Drug-Free Schools of the U.S. Department of Education. The 2009–10 SSOCS (SSOCS: 2010) was conducted by the U.S. Census Bureau. Data collection began on February 24, 2010, when questionnaire packets were mailed to sampled schools, and continued through June 11, 2010.

Definitions

General Terms

Crime—Any violation of a statute or regulation or any act that the government has determined is injurious to the public, including felonies and misdemeanors. Such violation may or may not involve violence, and it may affect individuals or property.

Incident—A specific criminal act or offense involving one or more victims and one or more offenders.

Multistage sampling—A survey sampling technique in which there is more than one wave of sampling. That is, one sample of units is drawn, and then another sample is drawn within that sample. For example, at the first stage, a number of Census blocks may be sampled out of all the Census blocks in the United States. At the second stage, households are sampled within the previously sampled Census blocks.

Prevalence—The percentage of the population directly affected by crime in a given period. This rate is based upon specific information elicited directly from the respondent regarding crimes committed against his or her person, against his or her property, or against an individual bearing a unique relationship to him or her. It is not based upon perceptions and beliefs about, or reactions to, criminal acts.

School—An education institution consisting of one or more of grades K–12.

School crime—Any criminal activity that is committed on school property.

School year—The 12-month period of time denoting the beginning and ending dates for school accounting purposes, usually from July 1 through June 30.

Stratification—A survey sampling technique in which the target population is divided into mutually exclusive groups or strata based on some variable or variables (e.g., metropolitan area) and sampling of units occurs separately within each stratum.

Unequal probabilities—A survey sampling technique in which sampled units do not have the same probability of selection into the sample. For example, the investigator may oversample rural students in order to increase the sample sizes of rural students. Rural students would then be more likely than other students to be sampled.

Specific Terms Used in Various Surveys

School-Associated Violent Deaths Study (SAVD)

Homicide—An act involving a killing of one person by another resulting from interpersonal violence.

Legal intervention death—An act involving the killing of one person by a law enforcement agent in the course of arresting or attempting to arrest a lawbreaker, suppressing a disturbance, maintaining order, or engaging in another legal action.

School-associated violent death—A homicide or suicide in which the fatal injury occurred on the campus of a functioning elementary or secondary school in the United States, while the victim was on the way to or from regular sessions at such a school, or while the victim was attending or traveling to or from an official school-sponsored event. Victims included nonstudents as well as students and staff members.

Suicide—An act of taking one's own life voluntarily and intentionally.

National Crime Victimization Survey (NCVS)

Aggravated assault—Attack or attempted attack with a weapon, regardless of whether or not an injury occurs, and attack without a weapon when serious injury results.

At school (students)—Inside the school building, on school property (school parking area, play area, school bus, etc.), or on the way to or from school.

Metropolitan Statistical Areas (MSAs)—Geographic entities defined by the U.S. Office of Management and Budget (OMB) for use by federal statistical agencies in collecting, tabulating, and publishing federal statistics.

Rape—Forced sexual intercourse including both psychological coercion as well as physical force. Forced sexual intercourse means vaginal, anal, or oral penetration by the offender(s). Includes attempts and verbal threats of rape. This category also includes incidents where the penetration is from a foreign object, such as a bottle.

Robbery—Completed or attempted theft, directly from a person, of property or cash by force or threat of force, with or without a weapon, and with or without injury.

Serious violent victimization—Rape, sexual assault, robbery, or aggravated assault.

Sexual assault—A wide range of victimizations, separate from rape or attempted rape. These crimes include attacks or attempted attacks generally involving unwanted sexual contact between the victim and offender. Sexual assault may or may not involve force and includes such things as grabbing or fondling. Sexual assault also includes verbal threats.

Simple assault—Attack without a weapon resulting either in no injury, minor injury, or an undetermined injury requiring less than 2 days of hospitalization. Also includes attempted assault without a weapon.

Theft—Completed or attempted theft of property or cash without personal contact.

Victimization—A crime as it affects one individual person or household. For personal crimes, the number of victimizations is equal to the number of victims involved. The number of victimizations may be greater than the number of incidents because more than one person may be victimized during an incident.

Victimization rate—A measure of the occurrence of victimizations among a specific population group. For personal crimes, the number of victimizations is equal to the number of victims involved. Each victimization that is reported by the respondents is counted, so there may be one incident with two victims, which would be counted as two victimizations. The number of victimizations may be greater than the number of incidents because more than one person may be victimized during an incident.

Violent victimization—Includes serious violent victimization, rape, sexual assault, robbery, aggravated assault, or simple assault.

School Crime Supplement (SCS)

At school—In the school building, on school property, on a school bus, or going to or from school.

Bullied—Students were asked if any student had bullied them at school in one or more ways during the school year. Specifically, students were asked if another student had made fun of them, called them names, or insulted them; spread rumors about them; threatened them with harm; pushed, shoved, tripped, or spit on them; tried to make them to do something they did not want to do; excluded them from activities on purpose; or destroyed their property on purpose.

Gang—Street gangs, fighting gangs, crews, or something else. Gangs may use common names, signs, symbols, or colors. All gangs, whether or not they are involved in violent or illegal activity, are included.

Hate-related graffiti—Hate-related words or symbols written in school classrooms, school bathrooms, school hallways, or on the outside of the school building.

Hate-related words—Students were asked if anyone called them an insulting or bad name at school having to do with their race, religion, ethnic background or national origin, disability, gender, or sexual orientation.

Serious violent victimization—Rape, sexual assault, robbery, or aggravated assault.

Total victimization—Combination of violent victimization and theft. If a student reported an incident of either type, he or she is counted as having experienced any victimization. If the student reported having experienced both, he or she is counted once under "total victimization."

Violent victimization—Includes serious violent victimization, rape, sexual assault, robbery, aggravated assault, or simple assault.

Youth Risk Behavior Survey (YRBS)

On school property—On school property is included in the question wording, but was not defined for respondents.

Rural school—A school located outside a Metropolitan Statistical Area (MSA).

Suburban school—A school located inside an MSA, but outside the "central city."

Urban school—A school located inside an MSA and inside the "central city."

Weapon—Examples of weapons appearing in the questionnaire include guns, knives, and clubs.

School Survey on Crime and Safety (SSOCS)

Gang—An ongoing loosely organized association of three or more persons, whether formal or informal, that has a common name, signs, symbols, or colors, whose members engage, either individually or collectively, in violent or other forms of illegal behavior.

Hate crime—A criminal offense or threat against a person, property, or society that is motivated, in whole or in part, by the offender's bias against a race, color, national origin, ethnicity, gender, religion, disability, or sexual orientation.

Intimidation—To frighten, compel, or deter by actual or implied threats. It includes bullying and sexual harassment. (Intimidation was not defined in the front of the questionnaire in 2005–06.)

Physical attack or fight—An actual and intentional touching or striking of another person against his or her will, or the intentional causing of bodily harm to an individual.

Rape—Forced sexual intercourse (vaginal, anal, or oral penetration). Includes penetration from a foreign object.

Robbery—The taking or attempting to take anything of value that is owned by another person or organization, under confrontational circumstances by force or threat of force or violence and/or by putting the victim in fear. A key difference between robbery and theft/larceny is that a threat or battery is involved in robbery.

Serious violent incidents—Include rape, sexual battery other than rape, physical attacks or fights with a weapon, threats of physical attack with a weapon, and robbery with or without a weapon.

Sexual battery—An incident that includes threatened rape, fondling, indecent liberties, child molestation, or sodomy. Principals were instructed that classification of these incidents should take into consideration the age and developmentally appropriate behavior of the offenders.

Sexual harassment—Unsolicited, offensive behavior that inappropriately asserts sexuality over another person. The behavior may be verbal or nonverbal.

Theft/larceny—Taking things valued at over $10 without personal confrontation. Specifically, the unlawful taking of another person's property without personal confrontation, threat, violence, or bodily harm. Included are pocket picking, stealing purse or backpack (if left unattended or no force was used to take it from owner), theft from a building, theft from a motor vehicle or motor vehicle parts or accessories, theft of bicycles, theft from vending machines, and all other types of thefts.

Vandalism—The willful damage or destruction of school property, including bombing, arson, graffiti, and other acts that cause property damage. Includes damage caused by computer hacking.

Violent incidents—Include rape, sexual battery other than rape, physical attacks or fights with or without a weapon, threats of physical attack with or without a weapon, and robbery with or without a weapon.

Weapon—Any instrument or object used with the intent to threaten, injure, or kill. Includes look-alikes if they are used to threaten others.

PART 8

Jail Inmates in 2016

HIGHLIGHTS

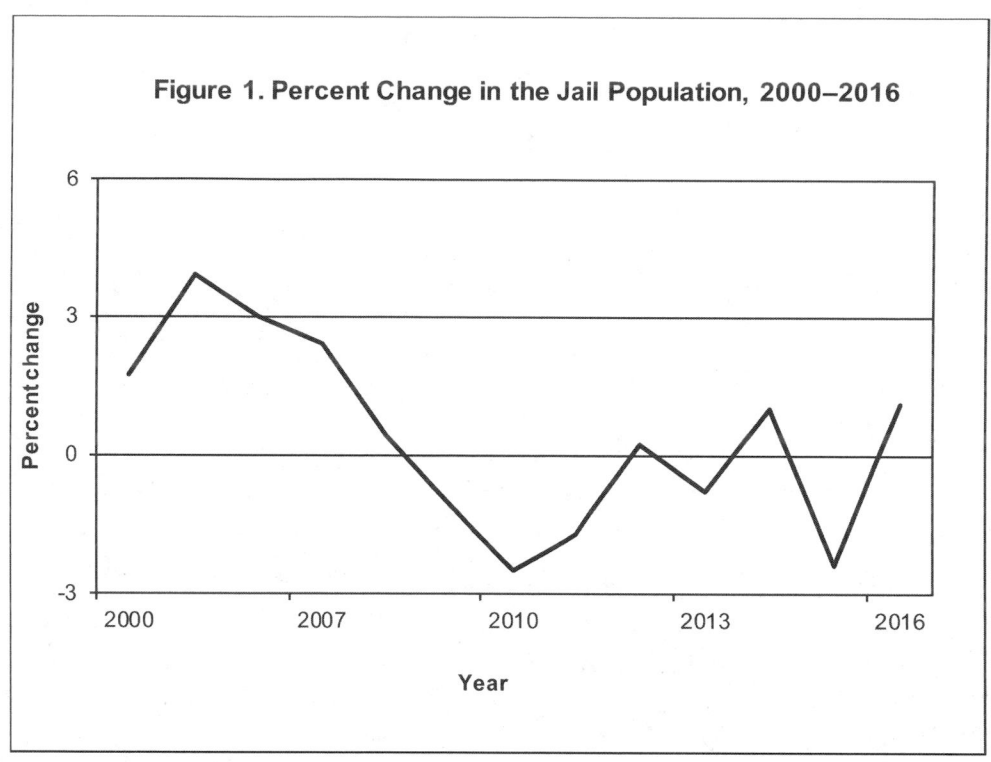

Figure 1. Percent Change in the Jail Population, 2000–2016

- The number of inmates confined in county and city jails was an estimated 740,700 at midyear 2016, lower than the peak of 776,600 inmates on an average day at midyear 2008.

- At midyear 2016, the jail incarceration rate had decreased from a peak of 259 per 100,000 U.S. residents at midyear to about 229 per 100,000 population.

- Approximately 10.6 million admissions to jail occurred in 2016, continuing the trend of steady decline that has been experienced since 2008.

- Fewer than 4,000 juveniles age 17 years or younger were held in local jails at midyear 2016; this was significantly below the peak of about 7,600 in 2000 and 2010.

- Approximately 80 percent of jail beds were occupied in 2016, down from 95 percent in 2007, while 17 percent of jails were operating at or above 100 percent of their operating capacity.

- At yearend 2016, non-Hispanic Blacks (599 per 100,000 Black residents) were incarcerated in jail at a rate 3.5 times that of non-Hispanic whites (171 per 100,000 White residents).

Table 1. Inmates Confined at Midyear, Average Daily Population and Incarceration Rates, 2000 and 2005–2016

(Number; percent.)

Year	Confined inmates[1]	Average daily population[2]	Annual admissions[3]	Jail incarceation rate[4]
2000...	621,100**	618,300**	11,200,000**	220**
2005...	747,500	733,400	12,100,000**	253**
2006...	765,800**	755,300**	12,200,000**	256**
2007...	780,200**	773,100**	13,100,000**	259**
2008...	785,500**	776,600**	13,600,000**	258**
2009...	767,400**	768,100**	12,800,000**	250**
2010...	748,700	748,600**	12,900,000**	242**
2011...	735,600	735,600	11,800,000**	236**
2012...	744,500	737,400	11,600,000**	237**
2013...	731,200	731,400	11,700,000	231
2014...	744,600	739,000	11,400,000**	234
2015...	727,400	719,500	10,700,000	227
2016*...	740,700	731,300	10,600,000	229
Average Annual Percent Change				
2000–2015...	1.1	1.0	-0.3	0.2
2015–2016...	1.8	1.6	-0.8	1.1

Note: Data are rounded to the nearest 100 for confined inmates and average daily population and to the nearest 100,000 for admissions. Results may differ from previous reports in the series due to data updates received from jails.
* = Comparison year.
** = Not compared because the jail population goes through seasonal variation, typically with fewer inmates at yearend than at midyear.
[1]Number of inmates held on the last weekday in June.
[2]Sum of all inmates in jail each day for a year divided by the number of days in the year. Prior to 2015, the average daily population was calculated for the 12-month period ending on the last weekday in June. The 2015 and 2016 average daily population were calculated for the calendar year ending on December 31.
[3]Annual admissions in 2005 and 2007 through 2014 were estimated based on admissions during a one week period in June. The 2000, 2006, 2015, and 2016 annual admissions were for the calendar year ending December 31.
[4]Number of confined inmates in local jails per 100,000 U.S. residents at midyear.

Table 2. Jail Incarceration Rates, by Sex, Race, and Hispanic Origin, Midyear 2000, 2005, and 2010–2014 and Yearend 2015–2016

(Number.)

Demographic characteristic	Midyear[1]							Yearend[2]	
	2000	2005	2010	2011	2012	2013	2014	2015	2016*
Total[3]...		253**	242**	236**	237**	231**	234**	215	217
Adults only[4]...	292**	334**	315**	307**	308**	299**	302**	277	280
Sex[3,4]									
Male...	397**	449**	432**	419**	418**	404**	405**	375	377
Female...	49**	63	59**	59**	62	64	67**	60	62
Race/Hispanic Origin[3,5]									
White...	133**	167	168	167	173	174	178**	169	171
Black/African American...	745**	804**	745**	720**	708**	668**	668**	607	599
Hispanic/Latino...	264**	263**	233**	219**	213**	200**	200**	174	185
American Indian/Alaska Native[4]...	261**	339**	436	411	402	438	442	357	359
Asian/Native Hawaiian/Other Pacific Islander[4]...	43**	43**	33**	34**	33	31	35**	32	30
Two or more races...	Ö	25	14**	21	25	26	16**	24	31

Note: Number of confined inmates in local jails per 100,000 U.S. residents at midyear or yearend. Results may differ from previous reports in the series due to data updates received from jails.
* = Comparison year for each characteristic.
** = Difference with comparison year is significant at the 95% confidence level.
Ö = Not collected.
[1]Based on the inmate population confined on the last weekday in June.
[2]Based on the inmate population confined on December 31. In 2015 and 2016, the Annual Survey of Jails collected demographic data on inmate population at yearend instead of midyear.
[3]Includes both adults and juveniles.
[4]Excludes persons age 17 or younger.
[5]Excludes persons of Hispanic or Latino origin, unless specified.

Table 3. Percent of Confined Inmates in Local Jails, by Characteristics, Midyear 2000, 2005, and 2010–2014 and Yearend 2015–2016

(Percent.)

Characteristic	Midyear[1]							Yearend[2]	
	2000	2005	2010	2011	2012	2013	2014*	2015	2016
Sex									
Male	88.6**	87.3**	87.7**	87.3**	86.8**	86.0**	85.3	85.7	85.5
Female	11.4**	12.7**	12.3**	12.7**	13.2**	14.0**	14.7	14.3	14.5
Adult	98.8**	99.1**	99.0**	99.2**	99.3**	99.4**	99.4**	99.5	99.5
Male	87.4**	86.5**	86.7**	86.6**	86.1**	85.4**	84.8	85.3	85.0
Female	11.3**	12.6**	12.3**	12.6**	13.2**	13.9**	14.6	14.2	14.5
Juvenile[3]	1.2**	0.9**	1.0**	0.8**	0.7**	0.6**	0.6	0.5	0.5
Held as adult[4]	1.0**	0.8**	0.8**	0.6**	0.6**	0.5**	0.5**	0.4	0.4
Held as juvenile	0.2**	0.1	0.3**	0.2**	0.1	0.1**	0.1**	0.1**	0.1
Race/Hispanic Origin[5]									
White...................................	41.9**	44.3**	44.3**	44.8**	45.8**	47.2	47.4	48.3	48.1
Black/African American	41.3**	38.9**	37.8**	37.6**	36.9**	35.8**	35.4	35.1	34.4
Hispanic/Latino.......................	15.2	15.0	15.8	15.5	15.1	14.8	14.9	14.3**	15.2
American Indian/Alaska Native	0.9**	1.0	1.3	1.3	1.2	1.4	1.4	1.2	1.2
Asian/Native Hawaiian/Other Pacific Islander......	0.8**	0.7	0.7**	0.7**	0.7	0.7**	0.8	0.8	0.8
Two or more races.....................	Ö	0.1	0.1**	0.2**	0.2**	0.2	0.1**	0.2	0.3
Conviction Status									
Convicted...............................	44.0**	38.0**	38.9**	39.4**	39.4**	38.0**	37.2**	37.5**	34.9
Unconvicted...........................	56.0**	62.0**	61.1**	60.6**	60.6**	62.0**	62.8**	62.5**	65.1
Most serious type of offense									
Felony	Ö	Ö	Ö	Ö	Ö	Ö	Ö	67.9**	69.7
Misdemeanor...........................	Ö	Ö	Ö	Ö	Ö	Ö	Ö	26.5**	25.4
Other...................................	Ö	Ö	Ö	Ö	Ö	Ö	Ö	5.5**	4.9

Note: Detail may not sum to 100% due to rounding. Results may differ from previous reports in the series due to data updates received from jails.
* = Comparison year.
** = Difference with comparison year is significant at the 95% confidence level.
Ö = Not collected.
[1]Based on the inmate population confined on the last weekday in June.
[2]Based on the inmate population confined on December 31. In 2015 and 2016, the Annual Survey of Jails collected demographic data on inmate population at yearend instead of midyear.
[3]Persons age 17 or younger.
[4]Includes juveniles who were tried or awaiting trial as adults.
[5]Excludes persons of Hispanic or Latino origin, unless specified.

Table 3A. Number of Confined Inmates in Local Jails, by Characteristics, Midyear 2000, 2005, and 2010–2014 and Yearend 2015–2016

(Number.)

Characteristic	Midyear							Yearend[1]	
	2000	2005	2010	2011	2012	2013	2014	2015	2016*
Total	621,100	747,500	748,700	735,600	744,500	731,200	744,600	692,500	704,500
Sex									
Male	550,200	653,000	656,400	642,300	645,900	628,900	635,500	593,700	602,200
Female	71,000	94,600	92,400	93,300	98,600	102,400	109,100	98,800**	102,300
Adult	613,500	740,800	741,200	729,700	739,100	726,600	740,400	689,100	700,800
Male	543,100	646,800	649,300	636,900	640,900	624,700	631,600	590,500	598,900
Female	70,400	94,000	91,900	92,800	98,100	101,900	108,800	98,500**	101,900
Juvenile[2]	7,600	6,800	7,600	5,900	5,400	4,600	4,200	3,500	3,700
Held as adult[3]	6,100	5,800	5,600	4,600	4,600	3,500	3,700	3,100	3,000
Held as juvenile	1,500	1,000	1,900	1,400	900	1,100	500	400**	700
Race/Hispanic Origin[4]									
White	260,500	331,000	331,600	329,400	341,100	344,900	352,800	334,700	338,700
Black/African American	256,300	290,500	283,200	276,400	274,600	261,500	263,800	243,000	242,200
Hispanic/Latino	94,100	111,900	118,100	113,900	112,700	107,900	110,600	98,900**	107,200
American Indian/Alaska Native	5,500	7,600	9,900	9,400	9,300	10,200	10,400	8,500	8,600
Asian/Native Hawaiian/Other Pacific Islander	4,700	5,400	5,100	5,300	5,400	5,100	6,000	5,800	5,600
Two or more races	Ö	1,000	800	1,200	1,500	1,600	1,000	1,600	2,100
Conviction Status[3]									
Convicted	271,300	284,400	291,300	289,600	293,100	278,000	277,100	259,900**	245,900
Unconvicted	349,800	463,200	457,400	446,000	451,400	453,200	467,500	432,600**	458,600
Most serious type of offense									
Felony	Ö	Ö	Ö	Ö	Ö	Ö	Ö	470,400**	491,200
Misdemeanor	Ö	Ö	Ö	Ö	Ö	Ö	Ö	183,800	178,800
Other	Ö	Ö	Ö	Ö	Ö	Ö	Ö	38,300	34,500

Note: Data adjusted for nonresponse and rounded to the nearest 100. Detail may not sum to total due to rounding. Results may differ from previous reports in the series due to data updates received from jails.
* = Comparison year. Midyear populations are not compared to yearend populations because the jail population goes through seasonal change, typically with fewer inmates at yearend than at midyear.
** = Difference with comparison year is significant at the 95% confidence level.
Ö = Not collected.
[1]Data are based on the number of inmates confined on December 31. Starting in 2015, the Annual Survey of Jails collected total counts at midyear and yearend, but characteristic data were collected only at yearend and no longer at midyear.
[2]Persons age 17 or younger.
[3]Includes juveniles who were tried or awaiting trial as adults.
[4]Excludes persons of Hispanic or Latino origin, unless specified.

Table 4. Average Daily Jail Population, by Size of Jurisdiction, 2016

(Number; percent.)

| Jail jurisdiction size | Jail jurisdictions | | Total average daily population[1] | | Mean average daily population |
	Number	Percent	Number	Percent	
Total	2,850	100.0	731,300	100.0	257
49 or fewer.............................	1,014	35.6	21,400	2.9	21
50 to 99	536	18.8	36,300	5.0	68
100 to 249	657	23.1	107,000	14.6	163
250 to 499	297	10.4	107,100	14.6	360
500 to 999	197	6.9	138,800	19.0	703
1,000 to 2,499	118	4.2	171,300	23.4	1,448
2,500 and over	30	1.1	149,500	20.4	4,958

Note: Detail may not sum to total due to rounding.
[1]The average daily population is the sum of all inmates in jail each day for the calendar year divided by the number of days in the year.

Table 5. Percent of Jail Capacity Occupied, by Size of Jurisdiction, 2016

(Number; percent.)

Jail jurisdiction size	Total average daily population[1]	Rated capacity[2]	Percent of capacity occupied[3]	Percent of jail jurisdictions operating at more than 100% of rated capacity
Total	731,300	915,400	79.9	16.5
49 or fewer.............................	21,400	38,400	55.6**	7.0**
50 to 99	36,300	51,400	70.7**	19.0
100 to 249	107,000	126,700	84.4**	25.6**
250 to 499	107,100	129,900	82.4**	21.9**
500 to 999	138,800	173,100	80.2	20.4**
1,000 to 2,499	171,300	209,100	81.9**	15.7
2,500 or more*	149,500	186,800	80.0	13.8

Note: Detail may not sum to total due to rounding.
* = Comparison group.
** = Difference with comparison group is significant at the 95% confidence level.
[1]Sum of all inmates in jail each day for the calendar year divided by the number of days in the year.
[2]Maximum number of beds or inmates assigned by a rating official to a facility, excluding separate temporary holding areas.
[3]The average daily population divided by the rated capacity.

Table 6. Inmate Turnover Rate and Expected Length of Stay, by Size of Jurisdiction, 2016

(Number; percent.)

Jail jurisdiction size	Average daily population[1]	Annual admissions	Weekly inmate turnover rate[2]	Expected length of stay in days[3]
Total	731,300	10,629,800	55	25.1
49 or fewer.............................	21,400	696,900	122.8**	11.2**
50 to 99	36,300	748,700	77.3**	17.7**
100 to 249	107,000	1,981,300	69.6**	19.7**
250 to 499	107,100	1,564,100	55.4**	25.0**
500 to 999	138,800	1,886,000	51.5**	26.9**
1,000 to 2,499	171,300	2,156,600	48.1**	29.0**
2,500 or more*	149,500	1,596,200	40.4	34.2

Note: Detail may not sum to total due to rounding.
* = Comparison group.
** = Difference with comparison group is significant at the 95% confidence level.
[1] Sum of all inmates in jail each day for the calendar year divided by the number of days in the year.
[2]The sum of weekly admissions and releases divided by the average daily population. Weekly admissions and releases are calculated as the annual admissions and releases divided by the number of weeks in the year.
[3]The average daily population multiplied by the number of days in a year divided by the number of annual admissions.

Table 7. Persons Under Jail Supervision, by Confinement Status, 2000 and 2006–2016

(Number.)

Year	Total	Held in jail	Supervised outside of a jail facility[1]
Midyear[2]			
2000	687,000	621,100	65,900
2006	826,000	765,800	60,200
2007	848,400	780,200	68,200
2008	858,400	785,500	72,900
2009	837,600	767,400	70,200
2010	809,400	748,700	60,600
2011	798,400	735,600	62,800
2012	808,600	744,500	64,100
2013	790,600	731,200	59,400
2014	808,100	744,600	63,500
Yearend[3]			
2015	747,400	692,500	54,900
2016	758,700	704,500	54,200

Note: Data are rounded to the nearest 100. Detail may not sum to total due to rounding. Differences between 2015 and 2016 were not statistically significant. Results may differ from previous reports in the series due to data updates received from jails.
* =Comparison year. Midyear populations are not compared to yearend populations because the jail population goes through seasonal change, typically with fewer inmates at yearend than at midyear.
[1]Excludes persons supervised by a probation or parole agency. Includes offenders who serve their sentence of confinement on weekends only (i.e., Friday to Sunday); persons under electronic monitoring; persons in work release programs, work gangs, and other alternative work programs; and persons in drug, alcohol, mental health, and other medical treatment.
[2]Based on population confined or supervised on the last weekday in June.
[3]Data are based on the number of persons under jail supervision on December 31.

Table 8. Staff Employed in Local Jails, by Sex, Yearend 2015 and 2016

(Number; percent.)

Job function	Number		Percent	
	2015	2016*	2015	2016*
Job Function				
Total	213,000**	226,300	100.0	100.0
Correctional Officers[1]	169,300**	178,800	79.5	79.0
Male	117,300**	124,300	55.1	54.9
Female	51,900	54,500	24.4	24.1
All Other Staff[2]	43,700**	47,500	20.5	21.0
Male	19,700	21,000	9.3	9.3
Female	24,000**	26,500	11.3	11.7
Inmate to Correctional Officer Ratio[3]	4.1**	3.9	X	X

Note: Data are adjusted for nonresponse and rounded to the nearest 100. Detail may not sum to total due to rounding. Italics indicate that the difference with comparison year is significant at the 95% confidence level.
X = Not applicable.
* = Comparison year.
**Difference with comparison year is significant at the 95% confidence level.
[1]Includes deputies, monitors, and other custody staff who spend more than 50% of their time with the incarcerated population.
[2]Includes administrators, clerical and maintenance staff, educational staff, professional and technical staff, and other unspecified staff who spend more than 50% of their time in the facility.
[3]Number of confined inmates per correctional officer.

METHODOLOGY

Sampling Design

In years between the complete censuses of jails, the Bureau of Justice Statistics (BJS) conducts the Annual Survey of Jails (ASJ) to estimate the number and characteristics of the jail population in the United States. The ASJ is a nationally representative survey of all county or city jail jurisdictions and all regional jails in the country. The federal jurisdiction and combined jail and prison systems in Alaska, Connecticut, Delaware, Hawaii, Rhode Island, and Vermont are not covered. These are included in BJS's prison collection. However, Alaska's 15 locally operated jails are covered.

A jail jurisdiction is a county (parish in Louisiana) or municipal government that administers one or more local jails and represents the entity responsible for managing jail facilities under its authority. Most jail jurisdictions consist of a single facility, but some have multiple facilities or multiple facility operators, called reporting units. For example, four reporting units in Allegheny County, Pennsylvania, represent a single jail jurisdiction. The ASJ sample is drawn at the jurisdiction level. When a jail jurisdiction with multiple reporting units is sampled, data are collected from all reporting units within that jail jurisdiction. BJS collapses the reporting units into jail jurisdictions and reports statistics at the jurisdiction level.

The ASJ uses a stratified probability sampling design based on jail population data collected through the most recent Census of Jails (2013). Jails in the ASJ sample are surveyed annually until the next sample refresh. The most recent sample refresh occurred in 2015. A sample of 876 jail jurisdictions were selected to represent the approximately 2,851 jail jurisdictions nationwide. In selecting the jails, all jurisdictions were grouped into 10 strata based on their average daily population (ADP) and presence of juveniles measured in the most recent Census of Jails. In 8 of the 10 strata, a random sample of jail jurisdictions was selected. The remaining two strata were certainty strata, where all jurisdictions were selected with a probability of 1. One certainty stratum consisted of all jails that were operated jointly by two or more jurisdictions (referred to as multijurisdictional jails). The other certainty stratum consisted of all jail jurisdictions that held juvenile inmates at the time of the 2013 Census of Jails and had an ADP of 500 or more inmates during the 12 months ending on December 31, 2013, held only adults and had an ADP of 750 or more, were located in California, or were known to be operating in 2015 and not included in the 2013 Census of Jails.

The ASJ sample includes all California jail jurisdictions. This sampling feature was introduced in 2013 in response to the enactment of California Assembly Bill (AB) 109 and AB 117, aimed to reduce the number of inmates housed in state prisons starting on October 1, 2011. After the enactment of these two laws, the jail population in California experienced an unusual increase that the rest of the United States did not experience. For this reason, the ASJ sampling design was modified to include all California jail jurisdictions in a certainty (self-representing) stratum. (See *Methodology* in *Jail Inmates at Midyear 2014*, NCJ 248629, BJS web, June 2015.) The inclusion of all California jail jurisdictions resulted in an additional 21 jurisdictions (California has 65 jurisdictions in total). The sample also includes in the certainty stratum six new jail jurisdictions that were known to be operating in 2015 and not represented in the sampling frame (2013 Census of Jails).

Nonresponse Weighting Adjustment

Nonresponse weighting was implemented to account for unit nonresponse. Jurisdictions were grouped into weighting classes based on sampling stratum and the 2013 inmate population. Using a simple weighting class method, a nonresponse weighting adjustment factor was calculated within each weighting class h as:

$$F_h = (\sum^{n_h} W_{hi} \times JURISA_{hi} \, F_h = i = 1) / (\sum^{n_h} W_{hi} \times JURISR_{hi} \, i = 1)$$

where

n_h = number of jurisdictions sampled in weighting class h,

W_{hi} = sampling weight for jurisdiction i in weighting class h,

$JURISA_{hi}$ = active status indicator for jurisdiction i in weighting class h (1 = active, 0 = out-of-scope), and

$JURISR_{hi}$ = response indicator of jurisdiction i in weighting class h (1 = respondent, 0 = nonrespondent).

Final Weight

The final weight FW_{hi} for each jail jurisdiction is calculated as the product of the sampling weight, the weighting class adjustment within each weighting class, and the jurisdiction's response factor.

$$FW_{hi} = W_{hi} \times F_h \times JURISR_{hi}$$

Item Nonresponse Imputation

Item response rates ranged from 94 percent to 100 percent. For responding jail jurisdictions that were unable to provide some requested items, a weighted sequential hot-deck/cold-deck imputation procedure was used to impute values. This procedure, implemented using the SUDAAN software package, substitutes current-year respondent and prior-year (2015 ASJ, cold-deck) data for missing values. The donor for each missing item was randomly selected from within a set of similar jails, sorted by related previous year population values. The resulting imputed values are generally similar to the reported values of the previous year but are not identical because of differences between each donor and item pairing and the year-to-year fluctuation in donor population values.

Midyear and Yearend Population Differences

Prior to 2015, the ASJ used midyear (last weekday in June) as the reference date in data collection. The 2015 ASJ changed the reference date to December 31. The 2016 ASJ continued to use the yearend reference date. Comparisons of yearend data with previous midyear data need to consider seasonal variations, as jails typically hold fewer inmates at yearend than at midyear.

Calculating Weekly Inmate Turnover Rates

The weekly jail inmate turnover rate is the sum of the average weekly admissions and releases divided by the ADP. The inmate turnover rate is an indicator of the fluctuation of the jail population.

Jail Functions

Jails in the ASJ include confinement facilities operated under the authority of a sheriff, police chief, or city or county administrator. They are intended for adults but may hold juveniles before or after they are adjudicated. Facilities include jails, detention centers, city or county correctional centers, special jail facilities (such as medical or treatment centers and pre-release centers) and temporary holding or lockup facilities that are part of the jail's combined function. Inmates sentenced to jail facilities usually have a sentence of 1 year or less.

Within the ASJ, jails:

- receive individuals pending arraignment and hold them awaiting trial, conviction, or sentencing
- re-admit probation, parole, and bail bond violators and absconders temporarily detain juveniles pending their transfer to juvenile authorities
- hold mentally ill persons pending their movement to appropriate mental health facilities
- hold individuals for the military, for protective custody, for contempt, and for the courts as witnesses
- release convicted inmates to the community on completion of sentence
- transfer inmates to federal, state, or other authorities house inmates for federal, state, or other authorities because of crowding of their facilities
- operate community-based programs as alternatives to incarceration

For more information, please see https://www.bjs.gov/content/pub/pdf/ji16.pdf.

Terms and Definitions

Admissions: Persons who are officially booked and housed in jails by formal legal document and the authority of the courts or some other official agency. Jail admissions include persons sentenced to weekend programs and those who are booked into the facility for the first time. Excluded from jail admissions are inmates re-entering the facility after an escape, work release, medical appointment or treatment facility appointment, and bail and court appearances. BJS collects jail admissions for the last 7 days in June.

Average daily population (ADP): The average is derived by the sum of inmates in jail each day for a year, divided by the number of days in the year.

Average annual change: The mean average change across a 12-month time period.

Calculating annual admissions: Annual jail admissions are calculated by multiplying weekly admissions by the sum of 365 days divided by 7 days.

Calculating weekly jail turnover rate: This rate is calculated by adding admissions and releases and dividing by the average daily population.

Inmates confined: The number of inmates held in custody.

Jail incarceration rate: The number of inmates held in the custody of local jails, per 100,000 U.S. residents.

Percent of capacity occupied: This percentage is calculated by taking the number of inmates, dividing by the rated capacity, and multiplying by 100.

Rated capacity: The number of beds or inmates assigned by a rating official to a facility, excluding separate temporary holding areas.

Releases: Persons released after a period of confinement (e.g., sentence completion, bail or bond releases, other pretrial releases, transfers to other jurisdictions, and deaths). Releases include those persons who have completed their weekend program and who are leaving the facility for the last time. Excluded from jail releases are temporary discharges including work release, medical appointment or treatment center, court appearance, furlough, day reporting, and transfers to other facilities within the jail's jurisdiction.

Standard errors and tests of significance: As with any survey, the ASJ estimates are subject to error arising from sampling rather than using a complete enumeration of the jail population. A common way to express this sampling variability is to construct a 95 percent confidence interval around each survey estimate. Typically, multiplying the standard error by 1.96 and then adding or subtracting the result from the estimate produces the confidence interval. This interval expresses the range of values that could result among 95 percent of the different samples that could be drawn.

Under jail supervision but not confined: This classification includes all persons in community-based programs operated by a jail facility. These programs include electronic monitoring, house arrest, community service, day reporting, and work programs. The classification excludes persons on pretrial release and who are not in a community-based program run by the jail, as well as persons under supervision of probation, parole, or other agencies; inmates on weekend programs; and inmates who participate in work release programs and return to the jail at night.

Weekend programs: Offenders in these programs are allowed to serve their sentences of confinement only on weekends (i.e., Friday to Sunday).

PART 9

Law Enforcement Officers Killed and Assaulted, 2017

HIGHLIGHTS

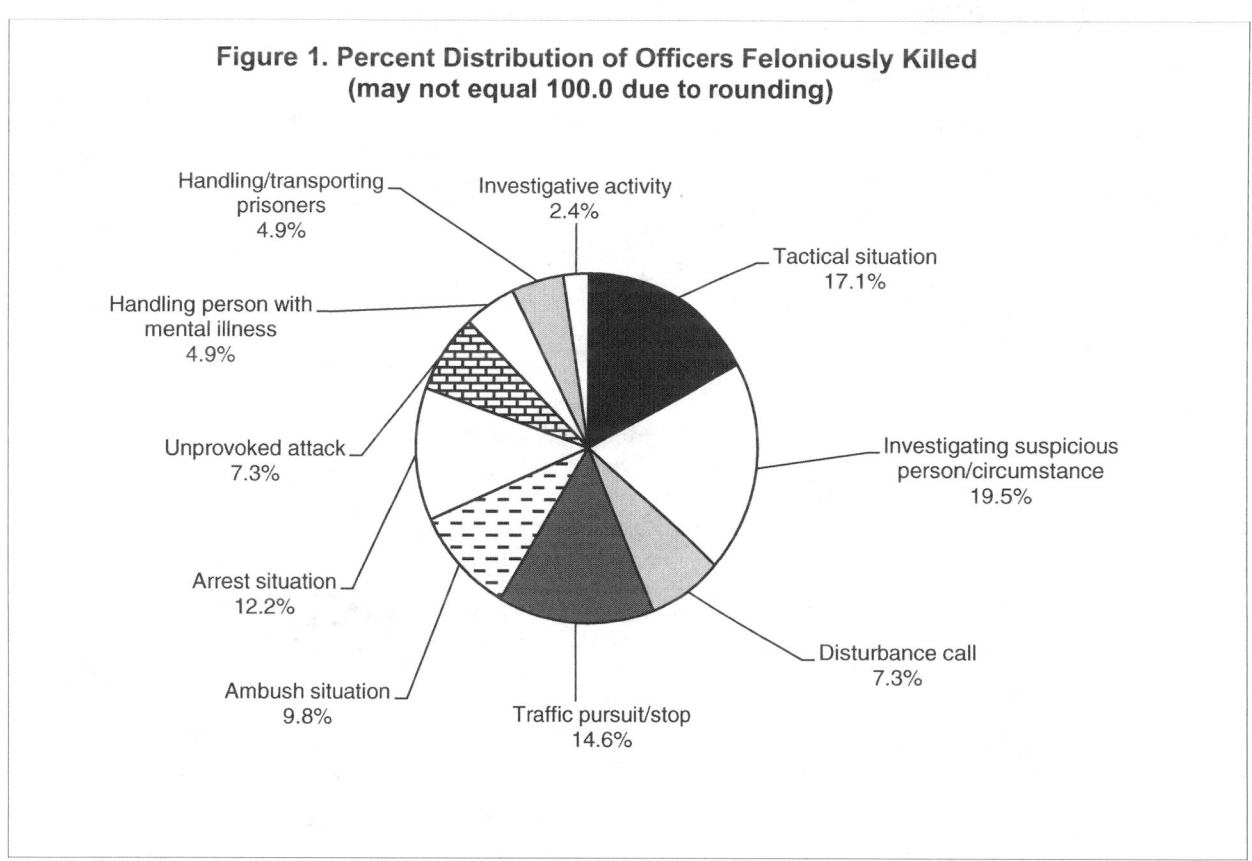

**Figure 1. Percent Distribution of Officers Feloniously Killed
(may not equal 100.0 due to rounding)**

Handling/transporting prisoners 4.9%

Investigative activity 2.4%

Tactical situation 17.1%

Handling person with mental illness 4.9%

Investigating suspicious person/circumstance 19.5%

Unprovoked attack 7.3%

Arrest situation 12.2%

Disturbance call 7.3%

Ambush situation 9.8%

Traffic pursuit/stop 14.6%

- In 2017, 46 law enforcement officers died from injuries incurred in the line of duty during felonious incidents. Of the officers feloniously killed, 26 were employed by city police departments, including 8 who were members of law enforcement agencies in cities with 250,000 or more inhabitants.

- Line-of-duty deaths in 2015 occurred in 25 states and Puerto Rico. By region, 24 officers were feloniously killed in the South, 11 officers in the Midwest, 6 officers in the West, 3 officers in the Northeast, and 2 officers in Puerto Rico.

- The average age of the officers who died in 2017 was 38 years old. The slain officers' average length of law enforcement service was 11 years. Of these officers, 43 were male and 3 were female.

- In 2017, 47 law enforcement officers died as the result of accidents that occurred in the line of duty. Accidental line-of-duty deaths of law enforcement officers occurred in 26 states.

- Participating federal law enforcement agencies reported that 1,784 officers were assaulted while performing their duties in 2017.

- No federal law enforcement officers were feloniously killed in 2017. Of the 1,784 reported assaulted, 426 were reported as injured.

Table 1. Law Enforcement Officers Feloniously Killed, by Region, Geographic Division, and State/Territory, 2008–2017

(Number.)

Area	Total	2008	2009	2010	2011	2012	2013	2014	2015	2016	2017
Number of Victim Officers	496	41	48	55	72	49	27	51	41	66	46
Northeast	50	3	7	3	10	6	2	8	4	4	3
New England	6	0	0	1	0	2	1	1	0	1	0
Connecticut	0	0	0	0	0	0	0	0	0	0	0
Maine	0	0	0	0	0	0	0	0	0	0	0
Massachusetts	4	0	0	1	0	1	1	0	0	1	0
New Hampshire	2	0	0	0	0	1	0	1	0	0	0
Rhode Island	0	0	0	0	0	0	0	0	0	0	0
Vermont	0	0	0	0	0	0	0	0	0	0	0
Middle Atlantic	44	3	7	2	10	4	1	7	4	3	3
New Jersey	4	0	1	0	2	0	0	1	0	0	0
New York	17	0	0	0	4	2	1	5	2	1	2
Pennsylvania	23	3	6	2	4	2	0	1	2	2	1
Midwest	92	9	5	10	21	6	4	8	5	13	11
East North Central	55	6	2	8	12	2	3	5	3	6	8
Illinois	14	3	2	4	1	0	1	0	1	0	2
Indiana	8	0	0	0	2	0	1	3	0	1	1
Michigan	14	1	0	3	4	1	1	0	0	2	2
Ohio	14	2	0	1	4	1	0	1	1	2	2
Wisconsin	5	0	0	0	1	0	0	1	1	1	1
West North Central	37	3	3	2	9	4	1	3	2	7	3
Iowa	5	0	0	0	1	0	1	0	0	2	1
Kansas	7	0	1	0	1	2	0	1	0	2	0
Minnesota	7	0	1	2	1	1	0	0	1	0	0
Missouri	11	3	0	0	3	1	0	1	0	2	1
Nebraska	1	0	0	0	0	0	0	0	1	0	0
North Dakota	3	0	0	0	1	0	0	0	0	1	1
South Dakota	3	0	1	0	2	0	0	0	0	0	0
South	219	20	21	22	29	22	15	17	19	30	24
South Atlantic	98	13	7	11	18	10	5	10	3	13	8
Delaware	4	0	1	0	1	0	0	0	0	0	2
District of Columbia	0	0	0	0	0	0	0	0	0	0	0
Florida	28	3	3	4	6	2	2	4	1	0	3
Georgia	22	2	0	5	3	1	0	2	1	7	1
Maryland	6	1	0	1	0	0	1	0	0	2	1
North Carolina	14	2	3	1	2	3	0	2	0	1	0
South Carolina	8	2	0	0	2	1	0	1	1	1	0
Virginia	11	3	0	0	3	0	1	1	0	2	1
West Virginia	5	0	0	0	1	3	1	0	0	0	0
East South Central	35	2	5	4	6	5	3	0	5	4	1
Alabama	8	0	4	1	1	2	0	0	0	0	0
Kentucky	5	1	0	0	0	1	1	0	2	0	0
Mississippi	11	0	0	3	1	1	2	0	2	1	1
Tennessee	11	1	1	0	4	1	0	0	1	3	0
West South Central	86	5	9	7	5	7	7	7	11	13	15
Arkansas	9	0	1	2	1	0	0	1	1	1	2
Louisiana	23	2	0	3	0	2	1	1	6	4	4
Oklahoma	4	0	2	0	0	0	0	0	0	0	2
Texas	50	3	6	2	4	5	6	5	4	8	7
West	110	9	13	17	10	9	6	14	9	17	6
Mountain	51	2	2	10	5	5	1	7	7	8	4
Arizona	17	2	0	4	3	2	0	3	0	2	1
Colorado	10	0	1	1	2	1	0	0	2	2	1
Idaho	1	0	0	0	0	0	0	0	1	0	0
Montana	4	0	0	2	0	0	0	1	0	0	1
Nevada	6	0	0	1	0	1	0	2	1	0	1
New Mexico	6	0	1	0	0	0	0	0	3	2	0
Utah	7	0	0	2	0	1	1	1	0	2	0
Wyoming	0	0	0	0	0	0	0	0	0	0	0
Pacific	59	7	11	7	5	4	5	7	2	9	2
Alaska	5	0	0	2	0	0	0	2	0	1	0
California	38	3	5	5	3	2	5	5	2	6	2
Hawaii	0	0	0	0	0	0	0	0	0	0	0
Oregon	5	2	0	0	2	0	0	0	0	1	0
Washington	11	2	6	0	0	2	0	0	0	1	0

(Number.)

Area	Total	2008	2009	2010	2011	2012	2013	2014	2015	2016	2017
Puerto Rico and other outlying areas.....	25	0	2	3	2	6	0	4	4	2	2
American Samoa.............................	0	0	0	0	0	0	0	0	0	0	0
Guam..	0	0	0	0	0	0	0	0	0	0	0
Mariana Islands.............................	0	0	0	0	0	0	0	0	0	0	0
Puerto Rico....................................	24	0	2	3	2	5	0	4	4	2	2
U.S. Virgin Islands.........................	1	0	0	0	0	1	0	0	0	0	0

Table 2. Law Enforcement Officers Feloniously Killed, by Population Group/Agency Type, 2008–2017

(Number.)

Area	Total	2008	2009	2010	2011	2012	2013	2014	2015	2016	2017
Number of Victim Officers........................	496	41	48	56	72	49	27	51	41	66	46
Group I (cities 250,000 and over)...................	100	12	15	13	13	6	4	8	10	12	8
Group II (cities 100,000–249,999)....................	40	1	3	3	9	4	2	6	2	8	2
Group III (cities 50,000–99,999)......................	30	1	4	3	9	2	2	2	1	2	4
Group IV (25,000–49,999).............................	35	5	1	6	4	2	3	2	4	6	2
Group V (cities 10,000–24,999).......................	31	3	3	2	5	3	2	4	2	5	2
Group VI (cities under 10,000)	54	0	6	5	10	4	3	5	5	8	8
Metropolitan counties....................................	95	9	8	9	14	11	6	11	5	15	7
Nonmetropolitan counties.............................	40	4	4	6	4	5	3	4	2	3	5
State agencies...	32	3	1	5	0	5	2	4	4	4	4
Federal agencies	14	3	1	1	2	1	0	1	2	1	2
Puerto Rico and other outlying areas..............	25	0	2	3	2	6	0	4	4	2	2

Table 3. Law Enforcement Officers Feloniously Killed, by Time of Incident, 2008–2017

(Number.)

Time of day	Total	2008	2009	2010	2011	2012	2013	2014	2015	2015	2016
Number of Victim Officers	496	41	48	56	72	49	27	51	41	66	46
Total A.M. hours	228	24	21	23	36	24	13	20	22	28	17
12:01 a.m.–2 a.m.	54	9	3	7	7	5	3	4	4	8	4
2:01 a.m.–4 a.m.	40	4	1	4	9	3	3	6	6	2	2
4:01 a.m.–6 a.m.	21	2	2	3	2	3	3	3	1	1	1
6:01 a.m.–8 a.m.	23	0	5	2	5	3	0	1	1	1	5
8:01 a.m.–10 a.m.	41	4	8	1	3	4	1	0	8	10	2
10:01 a.m.–noon	49	5	2	6	10	6	3	6	2	6	3
Total P.M. hours	264	17	27	33	36	23	14	31	18	37	29
12:01 p.m.–2 p.m.	37	0	5	2	5	2	3	7	1	10	2
2:01 p.m.–4 p.m.	47	4	3	4	6	3	3	9	2	8	5
4:01 p.m.–6 p.m.	37	2	3	4	8	3	1	6	2	3	5
6:01 p.m.–8 p.m.	36	4	3	4	5	6	2	1	5	2	4
8:01 p.m.–10 p.m.	57	2	10	10	3	6	2	4	7	9	4
10:01 p.m.–midnight	50	5	3	9	9	3	3	4	1		9
Not reported	4	0	0	0	0	2	0	0	1	1	0

Table 3A. Law Enforcement Officers Feloniously Killed, by Lighting and Weather/Environmental Conditions by Location of Incident, 2013–2017

(Number.)

Characteristic	Total	Commercial			Government		
		Inside of structure	Outside	Location not reported	Inside of structure	Outside	Location not reported
Number of Victim Officers.....................	231	10	24	0	6	3	0
Lighting							
Artificial	45	6	8	0	6	2	0
Dark...	58	1	6	0	0	0	0
Dawn...	3	0	2	0	0	0	0
Daylight	107	3	8	0	0	1	0
Dusk	11	0	0	0	0	0	0
Other	0	0	0	0	0	0	0
Not reported	7	0	0	0	0	0	0
Weather/environmental							
Blizzard	0	0	0	0	0	0	0
Blowing dirt/sand/soil	0	0	0	0	0	0	0
Clear..	157	0	20	0	0	3	0
Cloudy	10	0	2	0	0	0	0
Flooding..	0	0	0	0	0	0	0
Fog/smog/smoke.....................................	2	0	0	0	0	0	0
Hurricane	0	0	0	0	0	0	0
Rain	11	0	0	0	0	0	0
Severe crosswinds...................................	0	0	0	0	0	0	0
Sleet/hail	0	0	0	0	0	0	0
Snow	5	0	2	0	0	0	0
Tornado...	0	0	0	0	0	0	0
Other	1	0	0	0	0	0	0
Not reported	12	0	0	0	0	0	0
Not applicable (indoors).........................	33	10	0	0	6	0	0

Note: Ten years of data for the topics presented in this table are not available at this time. A 10-year table is expected to be available for the publication of 2020 data.
[1]Examples of public space include, but are not limited to, alleys, highways, lakes, parks, rivers, roads, and sidewalks.

Table 3A. Law Enforcement Officers Feloniously Killed, by Lighting and Weather/Environmental Conditions by Location of Incident, 2013–2017—Continued

(Number.)

Characteristic	Public space[1]			Residential			Other		
	Inside of structure	Outside	Location not reported	Inside of structure	Outside	Location not reported	Inside of structure	Outside	Location not reported
Number of Victim Officers	1	111	0	16	56	1	0	3	0
Lighting									
Artificial	0	14	0	2	7	0	0	0	0
Dark	0	31	0	7	12	0	0	1	0
Dawn	0	1	0	0	0	0	0	0	0
Daylight	1	52	0	4	35	1	0	2	0
Dusk	0	9	0	0	2	0	0	0	0
Other	0	0	0	0	0	0	0	0	0
Not reported	0	4	0	3	0	0	0	0	0
Weather/environmental									
Blizzard	0	0	0	0	0	0	0	0	0
Blowing dirt/sand/soil	0	0	0	0	0	0	0	0	0
Clear	0	84	0	0	47	0	0	3	0
Cloudy	0	5	0	0	3	0	0	0	0
Flooding	0	0	0	0	0	0	0	0	0
Fog/smog/smoke	0	2	0	0	0	0	0	0	0
Hurricane	0	0	0	0	0	0	0	0	0
Rain	0	6	0	0	5	0	0	0	0
Severe crosswinds	0	0	0	0	0	0	0	0	0
Sleet/hail	0	0	0	0	0	0	0	0	0
Snow	0	2	0	0	0	1	0	0	0
Tornado	0	0	0	0	0	0	0	0	0
Other	0	0	0	0	1	0	0	0	0
Not reported	0	12	0	0	0	0	0	0	0
Not applicable (indoors)	1	0	0	16	0	0	0	0	0

Note: Ten years of data for the topics presented in this table are not available at this time. A 10-year table is expected to be available for the publication of 2020 data.
[1]Examples of public space include, but are not limited to, alleys, highways, lakes, parks, rivers, roads, and sidewalks.

Table 4. Law Enforcement Officers Feloniously Killed, by Day of Incident, 2008–2017

(Number.)

Day of the week	Total	2008	2009	2010	2011	2012	2013	2014	2015	2016	2017
Number of Victim Officers......	496	41	48	56	72	49	27	51	41	66	46
Sunday	77	6	9	5	13	7	2	9	5	13	8
Monday	56	1	5	6	12	5	3	7	6	4	8
Tuesday	70	7	6	11	11	10	5	5	6	6	3
Wednesday	73	6	4	12	8	5	3	4	9	15	7
Thursday	77	7	7	11	9	9	6	7	3	12	6
Friday	67	8	4	6	11	5	5	8	4	7	9
Saturday	76	6	13	5	8	8	3	11	8	9	5

Table 5. Law Enforcement Officers Feloniously Killed, by Month of Incident, 2008–2017

(Number.)

Month	Total	2008	2009	2010	2011	2012	2013	2014	2015	2016	2017
Number of Victim Officers......	496	41	48	56	72	49	27	51	41	66	46
January	38	8	1	4	9	6	2	2	0	2	4
February	33	4	1	4	3	4	5	1	0	9	2
March	45	0	6	5	9	1	1	8	6	5	4
April	32	1	8	1	9	4	3	1	0	1	4
May	45	2	0	7	3	3	1	9	10	3	7
June	40	6	6	4	6	4	2	4	3	3	2
July	48	4	7	7	8	2	1	4	1	10	4
August	48	4	4	4	7	8	2	3	6	5	5
September	36	6	4	1	1	5	4	6	4	3	2
October	36	1	2	5	5	1	1	4	4	9	5
November	44	1	4	6	2	4	0	5	4	13	5
December	51	4	5	8	10	7	5	4	3	3	2

Table 6. Law Enforcement Officers Feloniously Killed, by Age Group of Victim Officer, 2008–2017

(Number.)

Age group	Total	2008	2009	2010	2011	2012	2013	2014	2015	2016	2017
Number of Victim Officers......	496	41	48	56	72	49	27	51	41	66	46
Under 25 years	20	2	1	3	2	2	0	5	2	2	1
25–30 years	84	7	9	12	17	8	2	3	5	10	11
31–35 years	101	7	8	13	11	12	9	11	9	14	8
36–40 years	82	11	11	9	12	8	7	7	2	8	7
41–45 years	87	3	13	7	10	8	4	12	9	12	9
46–50 years	66	4	3	5	13	6	1	9	10	9	6
51–55 years	33	5	0	1	4	5	2	3	2	9	2
56–60 years	16	2	3	4	3	0	1	0	1	0	2
Over 60 years	7	0	0	2	0	0	1	1	1	2	0
Average age (years)	39	39	38	38	38	38	39	39	40	40	38

Table 7. Law Enforcement Officers Feloniously Killed, by Years of Service of Victim Officer, 2008–2017

(Number.)

Years of service	Total	2008	2009	2010	2011	2012	2013	2014	2015	2016	2017
Number of Victim Officers	496	41	48	56	72	49	27	51	41	66	46
Less than 1	12	0	0	1	0	2	0	2	4	2	1
1–5	128	15	13	22	17	12	4	11	8	13	10
6–10	125	11	12	13	24	13	10	8	11	13	7
11–15	76	6	9	6	8	5	8	11	4	13	9
16–20	76	2	6	9	8	10	1	13	5	13	2
21–25	39	4	3	1	12	1	1	5	6	4	2
26–30	27	3	4	1	1	4	2	0	2	8	2
More than 30	8	0	0	3	2	1	1	1	0	0	0
Not reported	5	0	1	0	0	1	0	0	1	0	2
Average years of service	12	10	12	10	12	12	13	13	12	13	11

Table 8. Law Enforcement Officers Feloniously Killed, by Profile of Victim Officer, Averages, 1998–2017

(Number.)

Characteristic	2017	5-year averages		10-year averages	
		2008–2012	2013–2017	1998–2007	2008–2017
Age	38	38	39	37	39
Years of service	11	11	12	10	12
Height	5'10"	5'11"	5'10"	5'11"	5'10"
Weight	205	203	204	199	203

Note: The deaths of the 72 law enforcement officers that resulted from the events of September 11, 2001, are not included in this table.

Table 9. Law Enforcement Officers Feloniously Killed, by Race and Sex of Victim Officer, 2008–2017

(Number.)

Characteristic	Total	2008	2009	2010	2011	2012	2013	2014	2015	2016	2017
Number of Victim Officers	496	41	48	55	72	49	27	51	41	66	46
Race	427	30	42	47	68	43	25	47	29	61	35
White	54	10	3	7	3	6	2	2	8	4	9
Black/African American	8	1	2	0	1	0	0	0	2	0	2
American Indian/Alaska Native	2	0	1	1	—	—	—	—	—	—	—
Asian/Native Hawaiian/Other Pacific Islander[1]	5	—	—	—	0	0	0	2	2	1	0
Asian[1]	0	—	—	—	0	0	0	0	0	0	0
Ethnicity[2]											
Hispanic or Latino	46	—	—	—	7	9	2	11	4	7	6
Not Hispanic or Latino	293	—	—	—	65	35	24	39	36	57	37
Not reported	157	41	48	55	0	5	1	1	1	2	3
Sex											
Male	471	37	47	53	69	44	25	51	38	64	43
Female	25	4	1	2	3	5	2	0	3	2	3

NA = Not available.
[1] For 2008, 2009, and 2010, the race categories "Asian" and "Native Hawaiian/Other Pacific Islander" were combined.
[2] Beginning in 2011, ethnicity was added to the data collection.

Table 10. Law Enforcement Officers Feloniously Killed, by Use of Weapon by Victim Officer, Assisting Officer, and Offender During Incident, 2008–2017

(Number; percent.)

Characteristic	Total	2008	2009	2010	2011	2012	2013	2014	2015	2016	2017
Number of victim officers...	496	41	48	55	72	49	27	51	41	66	46
Average number of rounds fired by victim officers...	1.3	1.8	0.8	1.9	2.1	0.7	0.9	0.9	1.6	1.2	1.0
Average number of rounds fired by assisting officers[1]	10.2	4.9	8.6	6.7	11.6	9.6	3.6	16.1	10.0	15.7	9.4
Average number of rounds fired by offenders[2]	6.6	7.7	3.9	4.6	5.2	10.0	6.5	5.8	6.7	9.2	5.7
Number of victim officers who fired own weapon...	104	11	12	16	18	6	5	5	6	15	10
Average number of rounds fired by victim officers who fired own weapon...	7.1	7.0	4.1	7.5	9.7	6.0	5.8	9.6	11.2	6.1	4.4
Average number of victim officer's rounds that struck offenders	1.2	1.0	1.5	1.6	0.8	1.5	0.7	4.0	0.7	0.3	1.5
Percentage hit rate of victim officers' rounds striking offenders...	15.7	12.9	32.4	19.4	8.1	20.0	8.7	41.7	6.0	5.1	27.3
Average number of rounds fired by assisting officers...	6.4	6.4	3.6	3.2	9.2	14.7	2.7	2.5	2.0	6.8	6.0
Average number of rounds fired by offenders	7.2	7.1	4.0	7.3	9.8	8.2	6.7	4.4	10.0	5.2	8.4
Number of victim officers who attempted to (but did not) use own weapon...	72	4	9	7	11	2	3	8	7	11	10
Average number of rounds fired by assisting officers[3]	17.5	11.3	14.2	12.4	7.3		1.0	15.2	23.0	40.0	15.7
Average number of rounds fired by offenders	7.5	33.0	7.6	3.3	3.6	2.0	2.3	9.3	3.4	13.5	3.1
Number of victim officers who did not use and did not attempt to use own weapon...	279	14	18	20	41	39	18	36	28	39	26
Average number of rounds fired by assisting officers[1]	9.5	4.0	4.2	7.2	12.9	7.6	4.5	16.6	4.3	13.1	7.4
Average number of rounds fired by offenders[2]	6.4	4.5	2.5	4.1	4.3	10.5	7.3	4.6	6.7	10.0	5.5
Number of victim officers who did not use own weapon, but attempt to use own weapon information was not reported...	36	12	8	12	1	0	0	2	0	1	0
Average number of rounds fired by assisting officers[3]	9.2	1.2	17.8	4.8		0.0	0.0	41.0	0.0		0.0
Average number of rounds fired by offenders[3]	4.2	3.2	3.3	3.3		0.0	0.0	15.0	0.0	3.0	0.0
Number of victim officers in which victim officer's use of weapon was not reported...	5	0	1	0	1	2	1	0	0	0	0

Note: When calculating the averages presented in this table, the FBI's Law Enforcement Officers Killed and Assaulted Program used all available data for each incident. For example, in a specific incident, if the number of rounds fired by the victim officer is known, but the number of rounds fired by the offender is not known, the known number was included in the calculation for the average number of rounds fired by victim officers.
[1]The number of rounds fired during an incident in 2013 was excluded when calculating average number of rounds fired by assisting officers to provide more accurate statistics.
[2]The number of rounds fired during an incident in 2017 was excluded when calculating average number of rounds fired by offenders to provide more accurate statistics.
[3]For 2011, 2012 and 2015, number of rounds data were not available for inclusion in these averages.

Table 11. Law Enforcement Officers Feloniously Killed, by Victim Officer Killed with Own Weapon, Disarmed[1] of Weapon or Weapon Taken from Victim Officer, and Weapon Stolen[2] by Offender, 2008–2017

(Number.)

Characteristic	Total	2008	2009	2010	2011	2012	2013	2014	2015	2016	2017
Number of victim officers	496	41	48	55	72	49	27	51	41	66	46
Killed with own weapon	22	4	2	5	3	1	1	1	4	0	1
Disarmed of weapon/weapon taken from victim officer	21	3	2	5	3	1	1	1	4	0	1
Weapon stolen[3]	11	1	1	4	1	0	0	0	3	0	1
Weapon not stolen	10	2	1	1	2	1	1	1	1	0	0
Weapon stolen information not reported	0	0	0	0	0	0	0	0	0	0	0
Not disarmed of weapon/weapon not taken from victim officer	1	1	0	0	0	0	0	0	0	0	0
Weapon stolen	0	0	0	0	0	0	0	0	0	0	0
Weapon not stolen	1	1	0	0	0	0	0	0	0	0	0
Weapon stolen information not reported	0	0	0	0	0	0	0	0	0	0	0
Disarmed of weapon/weapon taken information not reported	0	0	0	0	0	0	0	0	0	0	0
Weapon stolen	0	0	0	0	0	0	0	0	0	0	0
Weapon not stolen	0	0	0	0	0	0	0	0	0	0	0
Weapon stolen information not reported	0	0	0	0	0	0	0	0	0	0	0
Killed with weapon other than own	473	37	45	50	69	48	26	50	37	66	45
Disarmed of weapon/weapon taken from victim officer	41	3	3	3	9	5	3	7	5	3	0
Weapon stolen	25	2	3	1	4	3	2	6	2	2	0
Weapon not stolen	16	1	0	2	5	2	1	1	3	1	0
Weapon stolen information not reported	0	0	0	0	0	0	0	0	0	0	0
Not disarmed of weapon/weapon not taken from victim officer	431	34	42	47	59	43	23	43	32	63	45
Weapon stolen	7	2	2	2	0	0	0	0	0	0	1
Weapon not stolen	423	32	40	44	59	43	23	43	32	63	44
Weapon stolen information not reported	1	0	0	1	0	0	0	0	0	0	0
Disarmed of weapon/weapon taken information not reported	1	0	0	0	1	0	0	0	0	0	0
Weapon stolen	0	0	0	0	0	0	0	0	0	0	0
Weapon not stolen	1	0	0	0	1	0	0	0	0	0	0
Weapon stolen information not reported	0	0	0	0	0	0	0	0	0	0	0
Killed with weapon information not reported	1	0	1	0	0	0	0	0	0	0	0
Disarmed of weapon/weapon taken from victim officer	1	0	1	0	0	0	0	0	0	0	0
Weapon stolen	1	0	1	0	0	0	0	0	0	0	0
Weapon not stolen	0	0	0	0	0	0	0	0	0	0	0
Weapon stolen information not reported	0	0	0	0	0	0	0	0	0	0	0
Not disarmed of weapon/weapon not taken from victim officer	0	0	0	0	0	0	0	0	0	0	0
Weapon stolen	0	0	0	0	0	0	0	0	0	0	0
Weapon not stolen	0	0	0	0	0	0	0	0	0	0	0
Weapon stolen information not reported	0	0	0	0	0	0	0	0	0	0	0
Disarmed of weapon/weapon taken information not reported	0	0	0	0	0	0	0	0	0	0	0
Weapon stolen	0	0	0	0	0	0	0	0	0	0	0
Weapon not stolen	0	0	0	0	0	0	0	0	0	0	0
Weapon stolen information not reported	0	0	0	0	0	0	0	0	0	0	0

Note: The term "weapon" includes all weapon types that may be issued to a law enforcement officer.
[1] The term "disarmed" indicates the victim officer was physically disarmed of one or more of his or her weapons by the offender(s) during the incident.
[2] The term "stolen" indicates a weapon issued to the victim officer was taken from the scene of the incident by the offender(s).
[3] One 2015 incident involved an offender(s) who commandeered the victim officer's patrol vehicle, fatally struck the victim officer with the patrol vehicle, and drove the patrol vehicle from the scene of the incident.

Table 12. Law Enforcement Officers Feloniously Killed with Own Weapons, by Victim Officer's Type of Weapon, 2008–2017

(Number.)

Type of weapon	Total	2008	2009	2010	2011	2012	2013	2014	2015	2016	2017
Number of Victim Officers Killed with Own Weapon	22	4	2	6	3	1	1	1	3	0	1
Total, handgun	21	4	2	5	3	1	1	1	3	0	1
.38 caliber	2	1	0	0	1	0	0	0	0	0	0
.40 caliber	10	3	1	1	2	0	0	1	1	0	1
.45 caliber	1	0	0	1	0	0	0	0	0	0	0
9 millimeter	6	0	1	3	0	0	1	0	1	0	0
Not reported	2	0	0	0	0	1	0	0	1	0	0
Rifle, total	0	0	0	0	0	0	0	0	0	0	0
Shotgun, total	0	0	0	1	0	0	0	0	0	0	0
12 gauge	1	0	0	1	0	0	0	0	0	0	0

Table 13. Law Enforcement Officers Feloniously Killed, Time of Incident, by Type of Assignment, 2017

(Number.)

Characteristic and time	Total	2-officer patrol	1-officer patrol		Investigative/detective		Tactical assignment (uniformed)		Plainclothes assignment	
			Alone	Assisted	Alone	Assisted	Alone	Assisted	Alone	Assisted
Number of Victim Officers	46	4	17	9	0	4	0	3	0	1
Total A.M. hours	17	1	6	4	0	1	0	0	0	0
12:01 a.m.–2 a.m.	4	1	1	1	0	0	0	0	0	0
2:01 a.m.–4 a.m.	2	0	1	0	0	0	0	0	0	0
4:01 a.m.–6 a.m.	1	0	0	1	0	0	0	0	0	0
6:01 a.m.–8 a.m.	5	0	3	0	0	0	0	0	0	0
8:01 a.m.–10 a.m.	2	0	1	1	0	0	0	0	0	0
10:01 a.m.–noon	3	0	0	1	0	1	0	0	0	0
Total P.M. hours	29	3	11	5	0	3	0	3	0	1
12:01 p.m.–2 p.m.	2	0	1	0	0	1	0	0	0	0
2:01 p.m.–4 p.m.	5	1	2	1	0	0	0	1	0	0
4:01 p.m.–6 p.m.	5	1	0	0	0	2	0	1	0	1
6:01 p.m.–8 p.m.	4	1	2	1	0	0	0	0	0	0
8:01 p.m.–10 p.m.	4	0	3	0	0	0	0	0	0	0
10:01 p.m.–midnight	9	0	3	3	0	0	0	1	0	0

Table 13. Law Enforcement Officers Feloniously Killed, Time of Incident, by Type of Assignment, 2017—Continued

(Number.)

Characteristic and time	Special assignment		Undercover		Court/prisoner security		Other[1]		Off duty
	Alone	Assisted	Alone	Assisted	Alone	Assisted	Alone	Assisted	
Number of Victim Officers	1	1	0	0	0	1	2	0	3
Total A.M. hours	1	0	0	0	0	1	2	0	1
12:01 a.m.–2 a.m.	1	0	0	0	0	0	0	0	0
2:01 a.m.–4 a.m.	0	0	0	0	0	0	0	0	1
4:01 a.m.–6 a.m.	0	0	0	0	0	0	0	0	0
6:01 a.m.–8 a.m.	0	0	0	0	0	0	2	0	0
8:01 a.m.–10 a.m.	0	0	0	0	0	0	0	0	0
10:01 a.m.–noon	0	0	0	0	0	1	0	0	0
Total P.M. hours	0	1	0	0	0	0	0	0	2
12:01 p.m.–2 p.m.	0	0	0	0	0	0	0	0	0
2:01 p.m.–4 p.m.	0	0	0	0	0	0	0	0	0
4:01 p.m.–6 p.m.	0	0	0	0	0	0	0	0	0
6:01 p.m.–8 p.m.	0	0	0	0	0	0	0	0	0
8:01 p.m.–10 p.m.	0	0	0	0	0	0	0	0	1
10:01 p.m.–midnight	0	1	0	0	0	0	0	0	1

[1]Includes officers on overtime/extra duty activities and other types of assignments not listed.

Table 14. Law Enforcement Officers Feloniously Killed, by Circumstance Encountered by Victim Officer Upon Arrival at Scene of Incident, 2013–2017[1]

(Number.)

Circumstance	Total	2013	2014	2015	2016	2017
Number of victim officers	231	27	51	41	66	46
Administrative assignment	2	0	0	1	0	1
Prisoner transport	2	0	0	1	0	1
Other administrative assignment	0	0	0	0	0	0
Ambush (entrapment/premeditation)	45	3	11	7	19	5
Arrest situation	11	1	0	2	4	4
Attempting to control/handcuff/restrain offender(s)	3	0	0	2	0	1
Verbal advisement only	8	1	0	0	4	3
Assist another law enforcement officer	12	0	4	2	4	2
Deploying/providing equipment (traffic cones, flares, etc.)	4	0	1	1	1	1
Foot pursuit	1	0	0	1	0	0
Officer down (requiring emergency assistance)	0	0	0	0	0	0
Officer requiring emergency assistance (not pursuit)	1	0	0	0	1	0
Vehicular pursuit	2	0	0	0	1	1
Other emergency circumstance	3	0	2	0	1	0
Other nonemergency circumstance	1	0	1	0	0	0
Assist motorist	2	0	1	1	0	0
Citizen complaint	0	0	0	0	0	0
Animal bite	0	0	0	0	0	0
Animal disturbance (barking dog, unleashed dog, etc.)	0	0	0	0	0	0
Business check	0	0	0	0	0	0
Check on welfare of citizen	0	0	0	0	0	0
Drug complaint	0	0	0	0	0	0
Traffic complaint	0	0	0	0	0	0
Verbal complaint of noncriminal violation	0	0	0	0	0	0
Disorder/disturbance	10	1	5	1	2	1
Civil disorder (mass disobedience, riot, etc.)	0	0	0	0	0	0
Disturbance call (disorderly subject, fight, etc.)	5	0	4	0	1	0
Domestic disturbance (family quarrel, no assault)	2	0	0	0	1	1
Domestic violence	3	1	1	1	0	0
Encounter or assist an emotionally disturbed person	2	0	1	0	0	1
Investigative/enforcement	99	13	20	17	28	21
Drug-related matter (drug bust, buy, etc.)	2	0	0	0	1	1
Handling person with mental illness	2	0	0	2	0	0
Investigate motor vehicle crash	1	0	0	0	0	1
Investigate possible DUI/DWI suspect (operating a vehicle)	1	0	1	0	0	0
Investigate suspicious person/circumstance	34	6	6	5	11	6
Investigative activity	13	2	2	1	6	2
Tactical situation	25	4	4	4	7	6
Traffic stop (felony traffic stop)	2	0	1	0	0	1
Traffic stop (traffic violation stop)	11	1	2	4	1	3
Undercover situation	2	0	2	0	0	0
Wanted person	6	0	2	1	2	1
Pursuit	19	1	4	4	4	6
Foot	11	0	1	2	4	4
Vehicular	8	1	3	2	0	2
Respond to alarm	0	0	0	0	0	0
Burglary	0	0	0	0	0	0
Robbery	0	0	0	0	0	0
Respond to crime in progress	10	2	3	1	2	2
Assault	1	0	1	0	0	0
Burglary	1	0	0	0	1	0
Larceny-theft	0	0	0	0	0	0
Motor vehicle theft	0	0	0	0	0	0
Person with firearm (no shots fired)	2	0	2	0	0	0
Robbery	3	1	0	0	1	1
Shooting/shots fired	3	1	0	1	0	1
Tampering with vehicle	0	0	0	0	0	0

Table 14. Law Enforcement Officers Feloniously Killed, by Circumstance Encountered by Victim Officer Upon Arrival at Scene of Incident, 2013–2017[1] —*Continued*

(Number.)

Circumstance	Total	2013	2014	2015	2016	2017
Other crime against person	0	0	0	0	0	0
Other crime against property	0	0	0	0	0	0
Respond to report of crime	1	0	1	0	0	0
Assault	0	0	0	0	0	0
Burglary	0	0	0	0	0	0
Homicide	0	0	0	0	0	0
Larceny-theft	0	0	0	0	0	0
Motor vehicle theft	0	0	0	0	0	0
Person with firearm (no shots fired)	1	0	1	0	0	0
Robbery	0	0	0	0	0	0
Shooting/shots fired	0	0	0	0	0	0
Tampering with vehicle	0	0	0	0	0	0
Other crime against person	0	0	0	0	0	0
Other crime against property	0	0	0	0	0	0
Traffic control (crash scene, directing traffic, etc.)	1	0	0	1	0	0
Unprovoked attack	16	6	1	3	3	3
Other	1	0	0	1	0	0

[1]Ten years of data for the topics presented in this table are not available at this time. A 10-year table is expected to be available for the publication of 2020 data.

Table 15. Law Enforcement Officers Feloniously Killed, by Specific Activity Being Performed by Victim Officer at Time of Attack, 2013–2017[1]

(Number.)

Circumstance	Total	2013	2014	2015	2016	2017
Number of victim officers..	231	27	51	41	66	46
Administrative assignment	5	0	0	4	0	1
Prisoner transport..	2	0	0	1	0	1
Other administrative assignment	3	0	0	3	0	0
Ambush (entrapment/premeditation)	0	0	0	0	0	0
Arrest situation	33	8	4	5	7	9
Attempting to control/handcuff/restrain offender(s).....................	20	4	2	5	4	5
Verbal advisement only..	13	4	2	0	3	4
Assist another law enforcement officer	9	1	3	1	2	2
Deploying/providing equipment (traffic cones, flares, etc.)...........	4	0	1	1	1	1
Foot pursuit..	0	0	0	0	0	0
Officer down (requiring emergency assistance)	0	0	0	0	0	0
Officer requiring emergency assistance (not pursuit).....................	1	1	0	0	0	0
Vehicular pursuit	0	0	0	0	0	0
Other emergency circumstance	3	0	2	0	1	0
Other nonemergency circumstance	1	0	0	0	0	1
Assist motorist	3	1	0	1	0	1
Citizen complaint...	1	0	0	1	0	0
Animal bite	0	0	0	0	0	0
Animal disturbance (barking dog, unleashed dog, etc.).................	0	0	0	0	0	0
Business check	0	0	0	0	0	0
Check on welfare of citizen	1	0	0	1	0	0
Drug complaint	0	0	0	0	0	0
Traffic complaint...	0	0	0	0	0	0
Verbal complaint of noncriminal violation	0	0	0	0	0	0
Disorder/disturbance...	9	0	4	1	4	0
Civil disorder (mass disobedience, riot, etc.).................................	0	0	0	0	0	0
Disturbance call (disorderly subject, fight, etc.)	4	0	3	0	1	0
Domestic disturbance (family quarrel, no assault).........................	2	0	1	0	1	0
Domestic violence	3	0	0	1	2	0
Encounter or assist an emotionally disturbed person	1	0	1	0	0	0
Investigative/enforcement	105	10	22	18	33	22
Drug-related matter (drug bust, buy, etc.).....................................	1	0	0	0	1	0
Handling person with mental illness	2	0	1	1	0	0
Investigate motor vehicle crash	1	0	0	0	0	1
Investigate possible DUI/DWI suspect (operating a vehicle)...........	1	0	0	0	1	0
Investigate suspicious person/circumstance...................................	35	6	6	6	12	5
Investigative activity...	14	0	2	1	6	5
Tactical situation...	29	3	4	6	9	7
Traffic stop (felony traffic stop)...	2	0	1	0	1	0
Traffic stop (traffic violation stop)..	15	1	4	3	3	4
Undercover situation	2	0	2	0	0	0
Wanted person...	3	0	2	1	0	0
Pursuit	24	2	7	2	8	5
Foot	17	0	5	1	7	4
Vehicular	7	2	2	1	1	1
Respond to alarm...	0	0	0	0	0	0
Burglary	0	0	0	0	0	0
Robbery	0	0	0	0	0	0
Respond to crime in progress	11	1	2	2	3	3
Assault..	0	0	0	0	0	0
Burglary	1	0	0	0	1	0
Larceny-theft...	0	0	0	0	0	0
Motor vehicle theft...	0	0	0	0	0	0
Person with firearm (no shots fired)	3	0	2	1	0	0
Robbery	4	1	0	1	1	1
Shooting/shots fired	3	0	0	0	1	2
Tampering with vehicle...	0	0	0	0	0	0

Table 15. Law Enforcement Officers Feloniously Killed, by Specific Activity Being Performed by Victim Officer at Time of Attack, 2013–2017[1] —*Continued*

(Number.)

Circumstance	Total	2013	2014	2015	2016	2017
Other crime against person	0	0	0	0	0	0
Other crime against property	0	0	0	0	0	0
Respond to report of crime	1	0	1	0	0	0
Assault	0	0	0	0	0	0
Burglary	0	0	0	0	0	0
Homicide	0	0	0	0	0	0
Larceny-theft	0	0	0	0	0	0
Motor vehicle theft	0	0	0	0	0	0
Person with firearm (no shots fired)	1	0	1	0	0	0
Robbery	0	0	0	0	0	0
Shooting/shots fired	0	0	0	0	0	0
Tampering with vehicle	0	0	0	0	0	0
Other crime against person	0	0	0	0	0	0
Other crime against property	0	0	0	0	0	0
Traffic control (crash scene, directing traffic, etc.)	5	0	0	1	4	0
Unprovoked attack	0	0	0	0	0	0
Other	24	4	7	5	5	3

[1]Ten years of data for the topics presented in this table are not available at this time. A 10-year table is expected to be available for the publication of 2020 data.

Table 16. Law Enforcement Officers Feloniously Killed During Traffic-Related Incidents,[1] by Circumstance at Scene of Incident, by Type of Assignment, 2013–2017[2]

(Number.)

Location of offender	Total	Approaching offender(s)	Approaching suspect vehicle		Returning to victim officer's vehicle	Seated in victim officer's vehicle	
			On driver's side	On passenger's side		Prior to approaching suspect vehicle	After obtaining contact with offenders
Number of victim officers killed during traffic-related incidents[1]	35	5	7	1	1	9	2
Prone..	0	0	0	0	0	0	0
On ground	0	0	0	0	0	0	0
On vehicle/object.................................	0	0	0	0	0	0	0
Seated	16	1	5	1	0	3	1
In suspect vehicle	16	1	5	1	0	3	1
In victim officer's vehicle....................	0	0	0	0	0	0	0
Seated outside in vicinity of suspect vehicle...........................	0	0	0	0	0	0	0
Front driver's side	0	0	0	0	0	0	0
Front passenger's side...........................	0	0	0	0	0	0	0
Rear driver's side....................................	0	0	0	0	0	0	0
Rear passenger's side.............................	0	0	0	0	0	0	0
Seated outside in vicinity of victim officer's vehicle	0	0	0	0	0	0	0
Front driver's side	0	0	0	0	0	0	0
Front passenger's side...........................	0	0	0	0	0	0	0
Rear driver's side....................................	0	0	0	0	0	0	0
Rear passenger's side.............................	0	0	0	0	0	0	0
Standing in vicinity of suspect vehicle	7	0	1	0	0	2	0
Front driver's side	3	0	1	0	0	1	0
Front passenger's side...........................	3	0	0	0	0	1	0
Rear driver's side....................................	0	0	0	0	0	0	0
Rear passenger's side.............................	1	0	0	0	0	0	0
Standing in vicinity of victim officer's vehicle	2	0	0	0	0	2	0
Front driver's side	0	0	0	0	0	0	0
Front passenger's side...........................	1	0	0	0	0	1	0
Rear driver's side....................................	0	0	0	0	0	0	0
Rear passenger's side.............................	1	0	0	0	0	1	0
Unrestricted movement..................................	3	0	0	0	1	2	0
Outside of suspect vehicle	1	0	0	0	1	0	0
Outside of victim officer's vehicle.......	2	0	0	0	0	2	0
Other..	4	2	1	0	0	0	0
Multiple locations due to multiple offenders	1	0	0	0	0	0	1
Not reported...	2	2	0	0	0	0	0

Note: For 2013 through 2017, 27 of the 35 victim officers who were feloniously killed during traffic-related incidents contacted radio dispatchers prior to or during the attack.
[1]Traffic-related incidents include traffic stops (felony traffic stops and traffic violation stops), investigating possible DUI/DWI suspects, and assisting motorists.
[2]Ten years of data for the topics presented in this table are not available at this time. A 10-year table is expected to be available for the publication of 2020 data.

Table 16. Law Enforcement Officers Feloniously Killed During Traffic-Related Incidents,[1] by Circumstance at Scene of Incident, by Type of Assignment, 2013–2017[2]—Continued

(Number.)

Location of offender	Standing in vicinity of suspect's vehicle				Standing in vicinity of victim officer's vehicle				Not reported
	Front driver's side	Front passenger's side	Rear driver's side	Rear passenger's side	Front driver's side	Front passenger's side	Rear driver's side	Rear passenger's side	
Number of victim officers killed during traffic-related incidents[1]	4	0	2	1	2	0	0	0	1
Prone.........................	0	0	0	0	0	0	0	0	0
On ground	0	0	0	0	0	0	0	0	0
On vehicle/object.......	0	0	0	0	0	0	0	0	0
Seated	4	0	0	0	0	0	0	0	1
In suspect vehicle	4	0	0	0	0	0	0	0	1
In victim officer's vehicle.........	0	0	0	0	0	0	0	0	0
Seated outside in vicinity of suspect vehicle.........	0	0	0	0	0	0	0	0	0
Front driver's side	0	0	0	0	0	0	0	0	0
Front passenger's side.........	0	0	0	0	0	0	0	0	0
Rear driver's side	0	0	0	0	0	0	0	0	0
Rear passenger's side.........	0	0	0	0	0	0	0	0	0
Seated outside in vicinity of victim officer's vehicle	0	0	0	0	0	0	0	0	0
Front driver's side	0	0	0	0	0	0	0	0	0
Front passenger's side.........	0	0	0	0	0	0	0	0	0
Rear driver's side	0	0	0	0	0	0	0	0	0
Rear passenger's side.........	0	0	0	0	0	0	0	0	0
Standing in vicinity of suspect vehicle.........	0	0	1	1	2	0	0	0	0
Front driver's side	0	0	0	0	1	0	0	0	0
Front passenger's side.........	0	0	1	1	0	0	0	0	0
Rear driver's side.........	0	0	0	0	0	0	0	0	0
Rear passenger's side.........	0	0	0	0	1	0	0	0	0
Standing in vicinity of victim officer's vehicle	0	0	0	0	0	0	0	0	0
Front driver's side	0	0	0	0	0	0	0	0	0
Front passenger's side.........	0	0	0	0	0	0	0	0	0
Rear driver's side.........	0	0	0	0	0	0	0	0	0
Rear passenger's side.........	0	0	0	0	0	0	0	0	0
Unrestricted movement.........	0	0	0	0	0	0	0	0	0
Outside of suspect vehicle.........	0	0	0	0	0	0	0	0	0
Outside of victim officer's vehicle.........	0	0	0	0	0	0	0	0	0
Other.........	0	0	1	0	0	0	0	0	0
Multiple locations due to multiple offenders	0	0	0	0	0	0	0	0	0
Not reported.........	0	0	0	0	0	0	0	0	0

Note: For 2013 through 2017, 27 of the 35 victim officers who were feloniously killed during traffic-related incidents contacted radio dispatchers prior to or during the attack.
[1] Traffic-related incidents include traffic stops (felony traffic stops and traffic violation stops), investigating possible DUI/DWI suspects, and assisting motorists.
[2] Ten years of data for the topics presented in this table are not available at this time. A 10-year table is expected to be available for the publication of 2020 data.

Table 17. Law Enforcement Officers Feloniously Killed, by Type of Weapon, 2008–2017

(Number.)

Type of weapon	Total	2008	2009	2010	2011	2012	2013	2014	2015	2016	2017
Number of Victim Officers	496	41	48	55	72	49	27	51	41	66	46
Total firearms	455	35	45	54	63	44	26	46	38	62	42
Handgun	323	25	28	38	49	34	18	33	29	37	32
Rifle	104	6	15	15	7	7	5	10	7	23	9
Shotgun	25	4	2	1	6	3	3	3	1	1	1
Multiple firearms used by offender(s), unable to determine which caused fatal injury[1]	2	NA	NA	NA	1	0	0	0	0	1	0
Type of firearm not reported	1	0	0	0	0	0	0	0	1	0	0
Knife or other cutting instrument[2]	0	0	0	0	NA	NA	NA	NA	NA	NA	NA
Knife[2]	3	NA	NA	NA	1	1	0	0	0	0	1
Other cutting instrument[2]	0	NA	NA	NA	0	0	0	0	0	0	0
Bomb	2	2	0	0	0	0	0	0	0	0	0
Blunt instrument	0	0	0	0	0	0	0	0	0	0	0
Personal weapons (hands, feet, fists, etc.)	5	0	0	0	2	2	0	1	0	0	0
Vehicle	31	4	3	1	6	2	1	4	3	4	3
Other	0	0	0	0	0	0	0	0	0	0	0
Number of Victim Officers Who Had Prior Knowledge That a Weapon Might Be Involved in the Incident	161	12	21	20	26	6	8	15	17	25	11

NA = Not available.

[1] Beginning in 2011, a new option was added: "Multiple firearms used by offender(s), unable to determine which caused fatal injury."
[2] For 2008, 2009, and 2010, the type of weapon categories "Knife" and "Other cutting instrument" were combined.

Table 18. Law Enforcement Officers Feloniously Killed, by Number of Victim Officers Wearing Uniform, Body Armor, or Holster, 2008–2017

(Number.)

Characteristic	Total	2008	2009	2010	2011	2012	2013	2014	2015	2016	2017
Number of Victim Officers	496	41	48	55	72	49	27	51	41	66	46
Wearing body armor	356	32	36	37	52	25	19	40	30	51	34
In uniform	332	26	32	34	47	25	18	40	28	50	32
Not in uniform	24	6	4	3	5	0	1	0	2	1	2
Wearing uniform not reported	0	0	0	0	0	0	0	0	0	0	0
Wearing holster	466	37	45	52	69	43	27	48	37	64	44
In uniform	409	30	39	45	61	38	20	43	35	59	39
Not in uniform	52	7	6	7	8	2	7	5	2	3	5
Wearing uniform not reported	5	0	0	0	0	3	0	0	0	2	0

Table 19. Law Enforcement Officers Feloniously Killed, Age Group of Known Offender, 2008–2017

(Number.)

Age group	Total	2008	2009	2010	2011	2012	2013	2014	2015	2016	2017
Number of Known Offenders	517	42	45	80	76	50	28	60	37	55	44
Under 18..........	19	3	2	1	5	1	0	3	0	3	1
18–24..........	120	8	14	24	20	14	9	13	4	11	3
25–30..........	127	10	6	23	19	14	7	18	14	6	10
31–35..........	88	4	9	12	9	6	6	10	10	10	12
36–40..........	52	5	5	8	7	4	2	9	1	6	5
41–45..........	39	7	5	6	3	5	0	1	1	5	6
46–50..........	28	3	1	0	5	2	3	3	2	6	3
51–55..........	19	1	2	3	4	1	1	1	3	2	1
56–60..........	13	1	0	2	4	0	0	2	2	2	0
Over 60..........	7	0	1	1	0	1	0	0	0	1	3
Not reported..........	5	0	0	0	0	2	0	0	0	3	0
Average age..........	32	32	31	31	32	31	31	31	34	34	36

Table 20. Law Enforcement Officers Feloniously Killed, by Profile of Known Offender, Averages, 1998–2017

(Number.)

Characteristic	2017	5-year averages		10-year averages	
		2008–2012	2013–2017	1998–2007	2008–2017
Age	36	31	33	29	32
Height	5'10"	5'10"	5'10"	5'10"	5'10"
Weight	184	181	185	177	182

Note: The 14 known offenders involved in the events of September 11, 2001, are not included in this table.

Table 21. Law Enforcement Officers Feloniously Killed, by Race and Sex of Known Offender, 2008–2017

(Number.)

Characteristic	Total	2008	2009	2010	2011	2012	2013	2014	2015	2016	2017
Number of Known Offenders	517	42	45	80	76	50	28	60	37	55	44
Race											
White..........	288	20	28	32	44	30	15	43	18	32	26
Black/African American	197	21	17	39	28	17	12	14	18	15	16
American Indian/Alaska Native	12	0	0	4	2	1	0	2	1	1	1
Asian/Native Hawaiian/Other Pacific Islander[1]..........	3	1	0	2	NA	NA	NA	NA	NA	NA	NA
Asian[1]..........	3	NA	NA	NA	1	0	0	1	0	0	1
Native Hawaiian/Other Pacific Islander[1]	1	NA	NA	NA	0	1	0	0	0	0	0
Not reported	13	0	0	3	1	1	1	0	0	7	0
Ethnicity[2]											
Hispanic or Latino..........	51	NA	NA	NA	7	6	3	19	3	8	5
Not Hispanic or Latino..........	280	NA	NA	NA	68	40	23	39	33	39	38
Not reported	186	42	45	80	1	4	2	2	1	8	1
Sex											
Male..........	501	40	43	78	74	49	27	55	37	54	44
Female	15	2	2	2	2	1	1	5	0	0	0
Not reported	1	0	0	0	0	0	0	0	0	1	0

NA = Not available.
[1] For 2008, 2009, and 2010, the race categories "Asian" and "Native Hawaiian/Other Pacific Islander" were combined.
[2] Beginning in 2011, ethnicity was added to the data collection.

Table 22. Law Enforcement Officers Feloniously Killed, by Status of Known Offender at Time of Incident, 2008–2017

(Number.)

Characteristic	Total	2008	2009	2010	2011	2012	2013	2014	2015	2016	2017
Number of Known Offenders	517	42	45	80	76	50	28	60	37	55	44
Under judicial supervision................................	137	12	13	19	19	12	6	12	11	15	18
Conditional release, pending criminal prosecution	24	3	3	1	5	2	2	1	3	1	3
Escapee from penal institution................................	1	0	0	1	0	0	0	0	0	0	0
Halfway house	2	0	0	0	1	0	0	0	0	0	1
Parole................................	42	5	3	8	4	4	2	5	3	3	5
Probation	58	4	7	9	7	5	2	5	4	10	5
Serving time in penal institution[1]	1	NA	NA	NA	0	0	0	0	0	0	1
Other judicial supervision[1]	9	NA	NA	NA	2	1	0	1	1	1	3
Known to agency as											
Controlled substance dealer	56	5	5	7	9	6	4	12	2	4	2
Controlled substance possessor	61	9	2	12	9	5	2	10	2	9	1
Controlled substance user	88	11	10	19	13	6	3	8	2	12	4
Known or suspected gang member[2]	32	NA	NA	NA	8	4	2	7	4	7	0
Known or suspected terrorist (domestic or international)[2]	2	NA	NA	NA	1	0	0	0	0	0	1
Other[2]	60	NA	NA	NA	11	2	7	6	7	12	15
Use of alcohol and/or controlled substance											
Under influence................................	101	5	3	17	12	13	4	13	13	15	6
Alcohol................................	28	2	2	7	4	3	3	2	3	1	1
Controlled substance[3]................................	14	3	1	10	NA	NA	NA	NA	NA	NA	NA
Amphetamines/methamphetamines................................	9	NA	NA	NA	0	0	1	3	0	4	1
Barbiturates	1	NA	NA	NA	0	0	0	1	0	0	0
Cocaine (all forms except Crack)	1	NA	NA	NA	0	1	0	0	0	0	0
Crack/cocaine	1	NA	NA	NA	0	0	0	1	0	0	0
Hashish................................	0	NA	NA	NA	0	0	0	0	0	0	0
Heroin	2	NA	NA	NA	0	0	0	0	2	0	0
LSD................................	0	NA	NA	NA	0	0	0	0	0	0	0
Marijuana	14	NA	NA	NA	2	2	0	3	2	3	2
Morphine	0	NA	NA	NA	0	0	0	0	0	0	0
Opium	0	NA	NA	NA	0	0	0	0	0	0	0
PCP	1	NA	NA	NA	0	0	0	1	0	0	0
Other depressants not listed	0	NA	NA	NA	0	0	0	0	0	0	0
Other hallucinogens not listed	0	NA	NA	NA	0	0	0	0	0	0	0
Other narcotics not listed................................	0	NA	NA	NA	0	0	0	0	0	0	0
Other stimulants not listed................................	0	NA	NA	NA	0	0	0	0	0	0	0
Other dangerous drug/substance	2	NA	NA	NA	1	0	0	0	0	1	0
Multiple forms of substances	28	NA	NA	NA	5	7	0	2	6	6	2
Not under influence	54	8	8	9	11	3	3	4	2	3	3
Use of alcohol/controlled substance not reported	362	29	34	54	53	34	21	43	22	37	35
Known to agency as having prior mental disorders........	26	2	3	2	7	2	2	1	3	2	2
Relationship between victim officer and offender..........											
Prior relationship through law enforcement (arrest, investigation, etc.)	54	5	3	8	11	4	3	3	4	10	3
Prior relationship through non-law enforcement (acquaintance, neighbor, relative, etc.)........................	3	0	0	1	0	0	2	0	0	0	0
No known relationship	443	37	33	66	65	46	23	57	33	43	40
Not reported	17	0	9	5	0	0	0	0	0	2	1

NA = Not available.
[1] Beginning in 2011, new options were added, including: "Serving time in penal institution" and "Other judicial supervision."
[2] Beginning in 2011, new options were added, including: "Known or suspected gang member" and "Known or suspected terrorist (domestic or international)."
[3] Beginning in 2011, new options were added to indicate "Type of controlled substance."

Table 23. Law Enforcement Officers Feloniously Killed, by Judicial History of Known Offender Prior to Incident, 2008–2017

(Number.)

Judicial history prior to incident	Total	2008	2009	2010	2011	2012	2013	2014	2015	2016	2017
Number of Known Offenders	517	42	45	80	76	50	28	60	37	55	44
Previously arrested	435	36	35	71	64	41	20	51	32	45	40
Convicted on prior criminal charge[1]	107	24	28	55	NA	NA	NA	NA	NA	NA	NA
Conviction as adult[2]	224	NA	NA	NA	48	29	13	35	28	37	34
Conviction as juvenile	93	6	8	10	18	6	2	10	9	13	11
Halfway house[3]	6	NA	NA	NA	1	1	0	2	0	1	1
House arrest[3]	0	NA	NA	NA	0	0	0	0	0	0	0
Incarceration in penal institution[3]	69	NA	NA	NA	19	4	4	9	10	11	12
Parole or probation[4]	85	18	26	41	NA	NA	NA	NA	NA	NA	NA
Parole[4]	71	NA	NA	NA	14	7	3	12	12	13	10
Probation[4]	158	NA	NA	NA	37	17	8	26	18	31	21
Prior arrest for:											
Assault on law enforcement officer/resisting arrest[5]	35	6	9	20	NA	NA	NA	NA	NA	NA	NA
Assault on law enforcement officer[5]	38	NA	NA	NA	10	1	1	7	5	7	7
Crime of violence (includes arrests for aggravated assault, murder, rape, and robbery)[6]	84	17	23	44	NA	NA	NA	NA	NA	NA	NA
Drug law violation	223	19	13	39	27	20	8	34	15	26	22
Murder	23	1	2	7	1	2	0	1	3	4	2
Other crime of violence (includes arrests for aggravated assault, rape, and robbery)[6]	179	NA	NA	NA	38	19	12	22	24	35	29
Resisting arrest[5]	84	NA	NA	NA	19	9	3	15	11	14	13
Weapons violation	208	14	18	40	32	15	7	26	19	21	16

NA = Not available.
[1]For 2008, 2009, and 2010, adult and juvenile convictions were combined into one category, "Convicted on prior criminal charge."
[2]In 2011, "Conviction as adult" was added as an option for judicial history.
[3]In 2011, new options for judicial history were added, including: "Halfway house," "House arrest," and "Incarceration in penal institution."
[4]For 2008, 2009, and 2010, the judicial history categories "Parole" and "Probation" were combined.
[5]For 2008, 2009, and 2010, the prior arrests categories "Assault on law enforcement officer" and "Resisting arrest" were combined.
[6]For 2008, 2009, and 2010, "Crime of violence" counts for prior arrests included prior murders. Beginning in 2011, "Crime of violence" was renamed to "Other crime of violence" since "Murder" is listed separately.

Table 24. Law Enforcement Officers Feloniously Killed, by Disposition of Known Offender, 2006–2015

(Number.)

Disposition	2006–2010	2011–2015	2006–2015
Number of Known Offenders	292	251	543
Fugitive	3	0	3
Arrested and charged	200	145	345
Guilty of murder	130	88	218
Received death sentence	25	11	36
Received life imprisonment	74	55	129
Received prison term (ranging from 5 years to 999 years)	31	20	51
Sentence not reported	0	2	2
Guilty of lesser offense related to murder	19	15	34
Guilty of crime other than murder	15	2	17
Acquitted/dismissed/nolle prosequi	25	3	28
Indeterminate charge and sentence	1	0	1
Committed to psychiatric institution	1	9	10
Case pending/disposition unknown	8	27	35
Died in custody prior to sentencing	1	1	2
Not arrested	87	101	188
Justifiably killed	58	57	115
Justifiably killed by victim officer	20	13	33
Justifiably killed by person(s) other than victim officer	38	44	82
Committed suicide	24	37	61
Killed by civilian(s)	0	2	2
Died under other circumstance	0	4	4
Other	3	0	3
Not repoted	2	1	3
Not reported	2	5	7

Table 25. Law Enforcement Officers Accidentally Killed, by Region, Geographic Division, and State/Territory, 2008–2017

(Number.)

Area	Total	2008	2009	2010	2011	2012	2013	2014	2015	2016	2017
Number of Victim Officers...............	527	68	48	72	53	48	49	45	45	52	47
Northeast.....................	70	11	6	8	8	9	5	8	5	5	5
New England..................	15	1	2	3	2	4	0	1	0	1	1
Connecticut...................	3	1	0	2	0	0	0	0	0	0	0
Maine............................	2	0	0	0	1	0	0	0	0	0	1
Massachusetts	9	0	2	1	1	3	0	1	0	1	0
New Hampshire	0	0	0	0	0	0	0	0	0	0	0
Rhode Island..................	1	0	0	0	0	1	0	0	0	0	0
Vermont	0	0	0	0	0	0	0	0	0	0	0
Middle Atlantic...............	55	10	4	5	6	5	5	7	5	4	4
New Jersey	15	2	0	4	1	1	0	2	3	2	0
New York.......................	25	3	3	1	5	2	3	3	0	2	3
Pennsylvania..................	15	5	1	0	0	2	2	2	2	0	1
Midwest	73	5	9	14	7	3	4	4	6	12	9
East North Central..........	49	5	6	7	3	3	4	3	4	8	6
Illinois	12	0	0	3	0	1	2	1	1	2	2
Indiana	7	2	2	2	0	0	0	1	0	0	0
Michigan	11	0	2	0	1	0	1	1	2	2	2
Ohio..............................	12	2	1	1	2	1	1	0	0	3	1
Wisconsin	7	1	1	1	0	1	0	0	1	1	1
West North Central	24	0	3	7	4	0	0	1	2	4	3
Iowa.............................	4	0	0	0	1	0	0	0	0	3	0
Kansas..........................	3	0	0	2	0	0	0	0	0	1	0
Minnesota	1	0	0	0	0	0	0	0	0	0	1
Missouri........................	13	0	2	4	3	0	0	1	2	0	1
Nebraska	2	0	1	0	0	0	0	0	0	0	1
North Dakota..................	0	0	0	0	0	0	0	0	0	0	0
South Dakota	1	0	0	1	0	0	0	0	0	0	0
South............................	277	32	21	39	27	28	31	19	29	24	27
South Atlantic	119	14	12	16	16	14	9	4	12	8	14
Delaware	0	0	0	0	0	0	0	0	0	0	0
District of Columbia........	1	0	0	1	0	0	0	0	0	0	0
Florida	23	4	1	4	1	2	1	1	1	4	4
Georgia	30	3	2	3	6	4	2	1	5	2	2
Maryland	15	3	0	3	2	3	0	0	3	1	0
North Carolina................	14	2	3	0	4	2	1	1	0	1	0
South Carolina................	14	1	2	2	1	0	2	0	2	0	4
Virginia	20	1	3	3	2	3	3	1	1	0	3
West Virginia	2	0	1	0	0	0	0	0	0	0	1
East South Central..........	49	4	4	6	3	3	7	7	9	1	5
Alabama........................	14	2	1	0	2	1	3	2	2	0	1
Kentucky	5	0	0	1	0	1	0	0	2	0	1
Mississippi	14	1	2	2	0	0	4	2	2	0	1
Tennessee	16	1	1	3	1	1	0	3	3	1	2
West South Central	109	14	5	17	8	11	15	8	8	15	8
Arkansas........................	9	2	1	0	0	0	4	0	0	1	1
Louisiana	21	0	1	3	3	2	3	1	2	5	1
Oklahoma......................	14	3	1	1	0	2	2	2	1	0	2
Texas	65	9	2	13	5	7	6	5	5	9	4
West.............................	100	17	12	11	10	8	9	13	5	9	6
Mountain.......................	45	6	8	4	4	6	4	4	2	5	2
Arizona..........................	13	2	1	1	2	1	2	2	0	2	0
Colorado........................	8	0	0	0	0	4	0	1	2	1	0
Idaho............................	2	0	2	0	0	0	0	0	0	0	0
Montana	3	1	1	0	1	0	0	0	0	0	0
Nevada	5	1	2	0	0	0	1	0	0	0	1
New Mexico	8	1	2	1	0	0	1	1	0	1	1
Utah..............................	5	1	0	2	0	1	0	0	0	1	0
Wyoming........................	1	0	0	0	1	0	0	0	0	0	0
Pacific	55	11	4	7	6	2	5	9	3	4	4
Alaska	1	0	0	0	0	0	1	0	0	0	0
California.......................	47	11	3	6	5	0	3	9	2	4	4
Hawaii	3	0	0	0	1	2	0	0	0	0	0
Oregon	1	0	0	0	0	0	0	0	1	0	0
Washington....................	3	0	1	1	0	0	1	0	0	0	0

Table 25. Law Enforcement Officers Accidentally Killed, by Region, Geographic Division, and State/Territory, 2008–2017—*Continued*

(Number.)

Area	Total	2008	2009	2010	2011	2012	2013	2014	2015	2016	2017
Puerto Rico and other outlying areas.....	7	3	0	0	1	0	0	1	0	2	0
American Samoa..............................	0	0	0	0	0	0	0	0	0	0	0
Guam...	0	0	0	0	0	0	0	0	0	0	0
Mariana Islands	0	0	0	0	0	0	0	0	0	0	0
Puerto Rico....................................	6	2	0	0	1	0	0	1	0	2	0
U.S. Virgin Islands..........................	1	1	0	0	0	0	0	0	0	0	0

Table 26. Law Enforcement Officers Accidentally Killed, by Population Group/Agency Type, 2008–2017

(Number.)

Area	Total	2008	2009	2010	2011	2012	2013	2014	2015	2016	2017
Number of Victim Officers......................	527	68	48	72	53	48	49	45	45	52	47
Group I (cities 250,000 and over)...............	60	10	4	9	5	9	5	6	4	4	4
Group II (cities 100,000–249,999)...............	30	5	3	3	3	3	4	1	3	3	2
Group III (cities 50,000–99,999)..............	27	4	3	2	5	1	5	2	3	2	0
Group IV (25,000–49,999)........................	24	2	1	6	3	6	1	2	1	1	1
Group V (cities 10,000–24,999)	17	3	1	2	0	1	3	2	1	1	3
Group VI (cities under 10,000)	62	8	4	4	7	2	6	7	7	10	7
Metropolitan counties............................	111	14	10	13	11	12	10	10	10	12	9
Nonmetropolitan counties........................	60	5	11	9	3	4	5	7	4	4	8
State agencies.....................................	107	13	10	19	12	6	8	5	12	9	13
Federal agencies	22	1	1	5	3	4	2	2	0	4	0
Puerto Rico and other outlying areas...........	7	3	0	0	1	0	0	1	0	2	0

Table 27. Law Enforcement Officers Accidentally Killed, by Time of Incident, 2008–2017

(Number.)

Time of day	Total	2008	2009	2010	2011	2012	2013	2014	2015	2016	2017
Number of Victim Officers......................	527	68	48	72	53	48	49	45	45	52	47
Total A.M. hours	249	32	23	39	22	25	16	26	17	25	24
12:01 a.m.–2 a.m................................	60	10	8	10	5	6	3	6	2	6	4
2:01 a.m.–4 a.m.................................	52	7	2	8	9	5	5	4	4	5	3
4:01 a.m.–6 a.m.................................	31	5	4	4	3	4	1	1	2	3	4
6:01 a.m.–8 a.m.................................	44	3	3	5	3	5	3	7	4	5	6
8:01 a.m.–10 a.m...............................	25	3	2	4	1	4	2	3	2	1	3
10:01 a.m.–noon	37	4	4	8	1	1	2	5	3	5	4
Total P.M. hours	269	36	25	32	31	23	30	19	27	24	22
12:01 p.m.–2 p.m...............................	42	6	4	4	6	3	3	4	4	6	2
2:01 p.m.–4 p.m................................	42	5	3	5	6	5	4	4	4	3	3
4:01 p.m.–6 p.m................................	40	4	3	3	7	2	4	3	5	5	4
6:01 p.m.–8 p.m................................	32	3	3	5	4	2	3	2	2	3	5
8:01 p.m.–10 p.m..............................	55	7	8	6	3	5	10	2	5	4	5
10:01 p.m.–midnight	58	11	4	9	5	6	6	4	7	3	3
Not reported......................................	9	0	0	1	0	0	3	0	1	3	1

Table 28. Law Enforcement Officers Accidentally Killed, by Day and Time of Incident, 2008–2017

(Number.)

Time of day	Total	Sunday	Monday	Tuesday	Wednesday	Thursday	Friday	Saturday
Number of Victim Officers	47	7	3	10	5	5	9	8
Total A.M. hours	24	4	2	6	3	3	5	1
12:01 a.m.–2 a.m.	4	1	0	2	0	1	0	0
2:01 a.m.–4 a.m.	3	1	0	0	1	0	1	0
4:01 a.m.–6 a.m.	4	1	0	2	0	1	0	0
6:01 a.m.–8 a.m.	6	1	0	2	2	0	1	0
8:01 a.m.–10 a.m.	3	0	1	0	0	1	0	1
10:01 a.m.–noon	4	0	1	0	0	0	3	0
Total P.M. hours	22	3	1	3	2	2	4	7
12:01 p.m.–2 p.m.	2	0	0	0	0	0	2	0
2:01 p.m.–4 p.m.	3	1	0	0	1	0	0	1
4:01 p.m.–6 p.m.	4	0	0	0	1	0	0	3
6:01 p.m.–8 p.m.	5	1	0	2	0	0	0	2
8:01 p.m.–10 p.m.	5	0	1	1	0	2	0	1
10:01 p.m.–midnight	3	1	0	0	0	0	2	0
Not reported	1	0	0	1	0	0	0	0

Table 29. Law Enforcement Officers Accidentally Killed, by Day of Incident, 2008–2017

(Number.)

Day of the week	Total	2008	2009	2010	2011	2012	2013	2014	2015	2016	2017
Number of Victim Officers	527	68	48	72	53	48	49	45	45	52	47
Sunday	77	10	5	11	7	6	6	9	6	10	7
Monday	75	12	8	8	7	7	6	5	12	7	3
Tuesday	70	8	5	7	10	5	7	9	3	6	10
Wednesday	53	7	7	8	2	2	6	4	5	7	5
Thursday	75	11	9	10	10	8	4	5	6	7	5
Friday	91	11	7	17	7	8	12	8	4	8	9
Saturday	86	9	7	11	10	12	8	5	9	7	8

Table 30. Law Enforcement Officers Accidentally Killed, by Month of Incident, 2008–2017

(Number.)

Month	Total	2008	2009	2010	2011	2012	2013	2014	2015	2016	2017
Number of Victim Officers	527	68	48	72	53	48	49	45	45	52	47
January	53	7	9	8	4	4	1	6	6	2	6
February	34	6	4	9	4	1	0	2	1	1	6
March	43	3	2	3	8	3	5	2	5	9	3
April	36	0	5	6	1	3	5	5	5	1	5
May	53	6	6	4	8	4	9	6	2	3	5
June	48	4	3	15	5	4	2	1	5	5	4
July	39	3	3	3	5	8	6	1	3	4	3
August	41	8	4	4	3	2	3	1	5	5	6
September	51	9	2	6	4	6	3	5	3	9	4
October	51	9	4	10	2	4	5	6	2	7	2
November	37	9	2	1	3	5	3	4	5	4	1
December	41	4	4	3	6	4	7	6	3	2	2

Table 31. Law Enforcement Officers Accidentally Killed, by Age Group of Victim Officer, 2008–2017

(Number.)

Age group	Total	2008	2009	2010	2011	2012	2013	2014	2015	2016	2017
Number of Victim Officers	527	68	48	72	53	48	49	45	45	52	47
Under 25	31	2	7	2	3	2	1	4	7	2	1
25–30	105	17	13	15	9	6	6	7	10	12	10
31–35	87	11	8	15	3	9	5	9	4	12	11
36–40	89	14	7	13	11	6	11	8	7	6	6
41–45	73	10	4	5	8	13	11	5	7	5	5
46–50	59	6	7	8	9	8	5	3	2	7	4
51–55	42	4	2	6	5	3	8	5	3	5	1
56–60	23	3	0	5	2	1	2	2	3	0	5
Over 60	15	1	0	2	3	0	0	2	1	2	4
Not reported	3	0	0	1	0	0	0	0	1	1	0
	39	38	35	39	41	40	41	39	37	38	40
Average age (years)	38	36	37	38	35	39	41	40	41	39	37

Table 32. Law Enforcement Officers Accidentally Killed, by Years of Service of Victim Officer, 2008–2017

(Number.)

Years of service	Total	2008	2009	2010	2011	2012	2013	2014	2015	2016	2017
Number of Victim Officers	527	68	48	72	53	48	49	45	45	52	47
Less than 1	32	3	2	4	2	2	2	5	4	6	2
1–5	157	19	20	24	13	9	9	14	18	14	17
6–10	121	18	12	18	13	14	12	13	3	9	9
11–15	70	9	4	8	7	9	8	3	7	8	7
16–20	62	9	4	8	6	8	7	3	9	5	3
21–25	27	3	2	2	5	3	5	0	2	2	3
26–30	33	3	4	4	3	3	3	5	2	5	1
More than 30	22	3	0	4	4	0	2	2	0	2	5
Not reported	3	1	0	0	0	0	1	0	0	1	0
Average years of service	11	11	9	11	13	12	13	10	9	11	12

Table 33. Law Enforcement Officers Accidentally Killed, by Profile of Victim Officer, Averages, 1998–2017

(Number.)

Characteristic	2017	5-year averages		10-year averages	
		2008–2012	2013–2017	1998–2007	2008–2017
Age	40	39	39	38	39
Years of service	12	11	11	10	11
Height	5'10"	5'11"	5'11"	5'10"	5'11"
Weight	218	205	213	196	209

Table 34. Law Enforcement Officers Accidentally Killed, by Race and Sex of Victim Officer, 2008–2017

(Number.)

Characteristic	Total	2008	2009	2010	2011	2012	2013	2014	2015	2016	2017
Number of Victim Officers......................	527	68	48	72	53	48	49	45	45	52	47
Race											
White..	444	59	44	60	45	36	43	43	33	40	41
Black/African American	63	7	4	8	7	10	6	0	9	9	3
American Indian/Alaska Native	5	0	0	2	0	0	0	0	0	1	2
Asian/Native Hawaiian/Other Pacific Islander[1]	2	1	0	1	NA	NA	NA	NA	NA	NA	NA
Asian[1]..	5	NA	NA	NA	0	2	0	2	0	0	1
Native Hawaiian/Other Pacific Islander[1]	2	NA	NA	NA	1	0	0	0	1	0	0
Not reported	6	1	0	1	0	0	0	0	2	2	0
Ethnicity[2]											
Hispanic or Latino......................................	32	NA	NA	NA	4	6	2	7	3	7	3
Not Hispanic or Latino	297	NA	NA	NA	46	40	47	38	40	43	43
Not reported	198	68	48	72	3	2	0	0	2	2	1
Sex											
Male	499	61	48	67	50	46	49	42	41	50	45
Not reported	28	7	0	5	3	2	0	3	4	2	2

NA = Not available.
[1] For 2008, 2009, and 2010, the race categories "Asian" and "Native Hawaiian/Other Pacific Islander" were combined.
[2] Beginning in 2011, ethnicity was added to the data collection.

Table 35. Law Enforcement Officers Accidentally Killed, Time of Incident, by Type of Assignment, 2017

(Number.)

Characteristic and time	Total	2-officer patrol	1-officer patrol		Investigative/detective		Tactical assignment (uniformed)		Plainclothes assignment	
			Alone	Assisted	Alone	Assisted	Alone	Assisted	Alone	Assisted
Number of Victim Officers..............	47	3	22	7	1	0	0	0	0	0
Total A.M. hours	24	2	11	3	0	0	0	0	0	0
12:01 a.m.–2 a.m.........................	4	0	3	1	0	0	0	0	0	0
2:01 a.m.–4 a.m............................	3	1	1	1	0	0	0	0	0	0
4:01 a.m.–6 a.m............................	4	0	3	1	0	0	0	0	0	0
6:01 a.m.–8 a.m............................	6	1	2	0	0	0	0	0	0	0
8:01 a.m.–10 a.m..........................	3	0	1	0	0	0	0	0	0	0
10:01 a.m.–noon	4	0	1	0	0	0	0	0	0	0
Total P.M. hours	22	1	10	4	1	0	0	0	0	0
12:01 p.m.–2 p.m.	2	0	1	0	1	0	0	0	0	0
2:01 p.m.–4 p.m...........................	3	0	2	1	0	0	0	0	0	0
4:01 p.m.–6 p.m...........................	4	0	1	0	0	0	0	0	0	0
6:01 p.m.–8 p.m.	5	0	2	1	0	0	0	0	0	0
8:01 p.m.–10 p.m.	5	0	3	1	0	0	0	0	0	0
10:01 p.m.–midnight	3	1	1	1	0	0	0	0	0	0
Not reported...................................	1	0	1	0	0	0	0	0	0	0

Table 35. Law Enforcement Officers Accidentally Killed, Time of Incident, by Type of Assignment, 2017—Continued

(Number.)

Characteristic and time	Special assignment		Undercover		Court/prisoner security		Other[1]		Off duty
	Alone	Assisted	Alone	Assisted	Alone	Assisted	Alone	Assisted	
Number of Victim Officers	1	6	0	0	0	0	3	1	3
Total A.M. hours	1	3	0	0	0	0	3	0	1
12:01 a.m.–2 a.m.	0	0	0	0	0	0	0	0	0
2:01 a.m.–4 a.m.	0	0	0	0	0	0	0	0	0
4:01 a.m.–6 a.m.	0	0	0	0	0	0	0	0	0
6:01 a.m.–8 a.m.	1	0	0	0	0	0	2	0	0
8:01 a.m.–10 a.m.	0	2	0	0	0	0	0	0	0
10:01 a.m.–noon	0	1	0	0	0	0	1	0	1
Total P.M. hours	0	3	0	0	0	0	0	1	2
12:01 p.m.–2 p.m.	0	0	0	0	0	0	0	0	0
2:01 p.m.–4 p.m.	0	0	0	0	0	0	0	0	0
4:01 p.m.–6 p.m.	0	3	0	0	0	0	0	0	0
6:01 p.m.–8 p.m.	0	0	0	0	0	0	0	1	1
8:01 p.m.–10 p.m.	0	0	0	0	0	0	0	0	1
10:01 p.m.–midnight	0	0	0	0	0	0	0	0	0
Not reported	0	0	0	0	0	0	0	0	0

[1] Includes officers on overtime/extra duty activities and other types of assignments not listed.

Table 36. Law Enforcement Officers Accidentally Killed, by Lighting and Weather/Environmental Conditions, by Location of Incident, 2013–2017

(Number.)

Characteristic	Total	Aircraft accident	Drowning	Fall	Firearm-related incident	Motor vehicle crash	Pedestrian officer struck by vehicle	Other
Number of Victim Officers	238	5	8	8	9	163	40	5
Lighting								
Artificial	13	0	0	1	3	6	3	0
Dark	102	2	5	2	1	73	16	3
Dawn	8	0	0	0	0	5	3	0
Daylight	94	3	3	3	5	64	15	1
Dusk	4	0	0	0	0	4	0	0
Other	0	0	0	0	0	0	0	0
Not reported	17	0	0	2	0	11	3	1
Weather/environmental								
Blizzard	0	0	0	0	0	0	0	0
Blowing dirt/sand/soil	0	0	0	0	0	0	0	0
Clear	159	3	4	3	6	114	27	2
Cloudy	18	0	0	2	0	12	4	0
Flooding	4	0	4	0	0	0	0	0
Fog/smog/smoke	4	0	0	0	0	3	0	1
Hurricane	1	0	0	0	0	1	0	0
Rain	22	1	0	0	0	18	3	0
Severe crosswinds	0	0	0	0	0	0	0	0
Sleet/hail	0	0	0	0	0	0	0	0
Snow	5	0	0	0	0	2	3	0
Tornado	0	0	0	0	0	0	0	0
Other	1	0	0	0	0	0	0	1
Not reported	19	1	0	2	0	13	3	0
Not applicable (indoors)	5	0	0	1	3	0	0	1

Note: Ten years of data for the topics presented in this table are not available at this time. A 10-year table is expected to be available for the publication of 2020 data.

Table 37. Federal Law Enforcement Officers Killed and Assaulted, Department and Agency, by Number of Victim Officers and Known Offenders, 2016–2017

(Number.)

Department and agency	Victim officers		Known offenders	
	2016	2017	2016	2017
Number of Victim Officers/Known Offenders	1,447	1,784	1,201	604
U.S. Capitol Police...	25	16	32	12
U.S. Department of Defense[1]		23		11
Department of the Air Force..		0		0
Department of the Army..		0		0
Department of the Navy..		23		11
National Security Agency..		0		0
Pentagon Force Protection Agency		0		0
U.S. Department of Homeland Security[2,3]	503	687	476	95
U.S. Customs and Border Protection (CBP)[2]...............................	484	506	457	
CBP, Office of Air and Marine	19	12	1	
CBP, Office of Border Patrol...............................	397	432	377	
CBP, Office of Field Operations...........................	68	62	79	
U.S. Immigration and Customs Enforcement[3]	0	159	0	76
U.S. Secret Service..	19	22	19	19
U.S. Department of the Interior[4,5]	621	724	520	311
Bureau of Indian Affairs...	504	609	474	307
Bureau of Land Management..	4	4	3	4
National Park Service[4]...	107	98	37	
U.S. Fish and Wildlife Service (FWS)[5]	6	13	6	0
FWS, Division of Refuge Law Enforcement[5]	6	13	6	
FWS, Office of Law Enforcement	0	0	0	0
U.S. Department of Justice[6]...	298	333	173	172
Bureau of Alcohol, Tobacco, Firearms and Explosives	11	18	11	16
Federal Bureau of Investigation...	16	16	9	13
U.S. Drug Enforcement Administration[6]	5	10	2	
U.S. Marshals Service..	266	289	151	143
U.S. Department of the Treasury	0	1	0	3
Internal Revenue Service..	0	1	0	3
Treasury Inspector General for Tax Administration......................	0	0	0	0
U.S. Postal Inspection Service	0	0	0	0

[1] For 2016, data were not reported by the U.S. Department of Defense.
[2] For 2017, known offender data were not reported by the U.S Customs and Border Protection.
[3] For 2016, data requests to the U.S. Immigration and Customs Enforcement (ICE) were inadvertently received and addressed by entities within ICE that did not possess the appropriate resources to provide comprehensive and complete data; therefore, caution must be taken when comparing 2016 data to 2017 data.
[4] For 2017, known offender data were not reported by the National Park Service.
[5] For 2017, known offender data were not reported by the FWS, Division of Refuge Law Enforcement.
[6] For 2017, known offender data were not reported by the U.S. Drug Enforcement Administration.

Table 38. Federal Law Enforcement Officers Killed and Assaulted, Department and Agency, by Number of Victim Officers Killed and Injured, 2016–2017

(Number.)

Department and agency	Killed		Injured	
	Firearms	Other weapons	Firearms	Other weapons
Number of Victim Officers/Known Offenders	0	0	8	418
U.S. Capitol Police..	0	0	2	7
U.S. Department of Defense	0	0	0	2
Department of the Air Force	0	0	0	0
Department of the Army	0	0	0	0
Department of the Navy	0	0	0	2
National Security Agency..	0	0	0	0
Pentagon Force Protection Agency	0	0	0	0
U.S. Department of Homeland Security	0	0	4	221
U.S. Customs and Border Protection (CBP)....................	0	0	4	133
CBP, Office of Air and Marine	0	0	1	4
CBP, Office of Border Patrol	0	0	2	101
CBP, Office of Field Operations................................	0	0	1	28
U.S. Immigration and Customs Enforcement	0	0	0	76
U.S. Secret Service...	0	0	0	12
U.S. Department of the Interior..	0	0	0	124
Bureau of Indian Affairs..	0	0	0	105
Bureau of Land Management	0	0	0	0
National Park Service	0	0	0	15
U.S. Fish and Wildlife Service (FWS)	0	0	0	4
FWS, Division of Refuge Law Enforcement	0	0	0	4
FWS, Office of Law Enforcement	0	0	0	0
U.S. Department of Justice	0	0	2	64
Bureau of Alcohol, Tobacco, Firearms and Explosives	0	0	0	0
Federal Bureau of Investigation.......................................	0	0	1	3
U.S. Drug Enforcement Administration	0	0	0	1
U.S. Marshals Service...	0	0	1	60
U.S. Department of the Treasury	0	0	0	0
Internal Revenue Service..	0	0	0	0
Treasury Inspector General for Tax Administration..........	0	0	0	0
U.S. Postal Inspection Service...	0	0	0	0

Table 39. Federal Law Enforcement Officers Killed and Assaulted, Department and Agency, by Extent of Injury of Victim Officer, 2013–2017

(Number.)

Department and agency	2013			2014			2015			2016			2017		
	Killed	Injured	Not injured	Killed	Injured	Not injured	Killed	Injured	Not injured	Killed	Injured	Not injured	Killed	Injured	Not injured
Number of Victim Officers/Known Offenders	4	292	1,478	0	170	867	1	176	814	1	324	1,122	0	426	1,358
U.S. Capitol Police	0	6	7	0	0	3	0	5	8	0	4	21	0	9	7
U.S. Department of Defense[1]													0	2	21
Department of the Air Force													0	0	0
Department of the Army													0	0	0
Department of the Navy													0	2	21
National Security Agency													0	0	0
Pentagon Force Protection Agency													0	0	0
U.S. Department of Homeland Security[2,3,4,5,6]	2	122	466	0	39	123	0	36	103	0	146	357	0	225	462
U.S. Customs and Border Protection (CBP)[2,3,4]	2	121	432	0	18	109	0	24	81	0	139	345	0	137	369
CBP, Office of Air and Marine	0	0	27	0	0	11	0	0	19	0	0	19	0	5	7
CBP, Office of Border Patrol[2,3,4]	2	98	368							0	132	265	0	103	329
CBP, Office of Field Operations	0	23	37	0	18	98	0	24	62	0	7	61	0	29	33
U.S. Immigration and Customs Enforcement[5,6]				0	7	1	0	4	4	0	0	0	0	76	83
U.S. Secret Service	0	1	34	0	14	13	0	8	18	0	7	12	0	12	10
U.S. Department of the Interior[7]	1	106	768	0	84	523	0	85	485	0	117	504	0	124	600
Bureau of Indian Affairs[7]	1	94	711	0	69	481	0	74	431	0	86	418	0	105	504
Bureau of Land Management	0	0	5	0	1	4	0	1	2	0	0	4	0	0	4
National Park Service	0	12	47	0	13	34	0	7	47	0	31	76	0	15	83
U.S. Fish and Wildlife Service (FWS)	0	0	5	0	1	4	0	3	5	0	0	6	0	4	9
FWS, Division of Refuge Law Enforcement	0	0	5	0	1	4	0	3	5	0	0	6	0	4	9
FWS, Office of Law Enforcement	0	0	0	0	0	0	0	0	0	0	0	0	0	0	0
U.S. Department of Justice[8]	1	58	234	0	46	211	1	49	214	1	57	240	0	66	267
Bureau of Alcohol, Tobacco, Firearms and Explosives	0	2	12	0	5	5	0	1	10	0	0	11	0	0	18
Federal Bureau of Investigation	0	11	20	0	3	8	0	9	17	0	5	11	0	4	12
U.S. Drug Enforcement Administration[8]	1	0	6	0	0	6	0	1	10	0	2	3	0	1	9
U.S. Marshals Service	0	45	196	0	38	192	1	38	177	1	50	215	0	61	228
U.S. Department of the Treasury	0	0	0	0	0	1	0	0	1	0	0	0	0	0	1
Internal Revenue Service	0	0	0	0	0	1	0	0	0	0	0	0	0	0	1
Treasury Inspector General for Tax Administration	0	0	0	0	0	0	0	0	1	0	0	0	0	0	0
U.S. Postal Inspection Service	0	0	3	0	1	6	0	1	3	0	0	0	0	0	0

[1] For 2013, 2014, 2015, and 2016, data were not reported by the U.S. Department of Defense.
[2] For 2013, detailed incident data were not reported by the CBP, Office of Border Patrol, for the 2 killed victim officers; therefore, the deaths were not represented in the feloniously killed section of this publication.
[3] For 2014, extent of injury data for 373 victim officers were not reported by the CBP, Office of Border Patrol.
[4] For 2015, extent of injury data for 349 victim officers were not reported by the CBP, Office of Border Patrol.
[5] For 2013, data were not reported by the U.S. Immigration and Customs Enforcement.
[6] For 2014, 2015, and 2016, data requests to the U.S. Immigration and Customs Enforcement (ICE) were inadvertently received and addressed by entities within ICE that did not possess the appropriate resources to provide comprehensive and complete data; therefore, caution must be taken when comparing prior years' data to 2017 data.
[7] For 2013, detailed incident data were not reported by the Bureau of Indian Affairs for the killed victim officer; therefore, the death was not represented in the feloniously killed section of this publication.
[8] For 2013, detailed incident data were not reported by the U.S. Drug Enforcement Administration for the killed victim officer; therefore, the death was not represented in the feloniously killed section of this publication.

Table 40. Federal Law Enforcement Officers Killed and Assaulted, by Region, Geographic Division, and State/Territory, 2017

(Number.)

Area	Total	Firearm	Knife or other cutting instrument	Bomb	Blunt instrument	Personal weapons	Vehicle	Other
Number of Victim Officers................................	1,769	116	19	0	21	676	142	795
Northeast..	111	1	0	0	1	48	4	57
New England.................................	29	1	0	0	0	13	1	14
Connecticut.............................	11	0	0	0	0	7	0	4
Maine......................................	0	0	0	0	0	0	0	0
Massachusetts.........................	10	1	0	0	0	4	0	5
New Hampshire........................	1	0	0	0	0	0	1	0
Rhode Island............................	3	0	0	0	0	0	0	3
Vermont..................................	4	0	0	0	0	2	0	2
Middle Atlantic............................	82	0	0	0	1	35	3	43
New Jersey..............................	17	0	0	0	1	9	1	6
New York.................................	40	0	0	0	0	15	1	24
Pennsylvania...........................	25	0	0	0	0	11	1	13
Midwest	278	8	4	0	11	25	9	221
East North Central........................	50	4	2	0	10	4	6	24
Illinois.....................................	8	2	0	0	0	2	1	3
Indiana....................................	8	0	0	0	4	0	0	4
Michigan.................................	7	0	1	0	0	2	2	2
Ohio..	17	1	1	0	6	0	1	8
Wisconsin................................	10	1	0	0	0	0	2	7
West North Central.......................	228	4	2	0	1	21	3	197
Iowa..	0	0	0	0	0	0	0	0
Kansas.....................................	2	1	0	0	0	1	0	0
Minnesota...............................	9	1	0	0	1	4	2	1
Missouri..................................	5	1	0	0	0	0	1	3
Nebraska.................................	8	0	0	0	0	4	0	4
North Dakota...........................	70	0	1	0	0	4	0	65
South Dakota	134	1	1	0	0	8	0	124
South..	570	39	5	0	5	201	44	276
South Atlantic.............................	239	22	3	0	4	80	12	118
Delaware.................................	0	0	0	0	0	0	0	0
District of Columbia.................	81	3	0	0	2	15	1	60
Florida....................................	64	8	3	0	2	34	4	13
Georgia	38	9	0	0	0	19	4	6
Maryland.................................	3	2	0	0	0	0	0	1
North Carolina.........................	3	0	0	0	0	1	0	2
South Carolina.........................	3	0	0	0	0	0	3	0
Virginia...................................	42	0	0	0	0	11	0	31
West Virginia...........................	5	0	0	0	0	0	0	5
East South Central.......................	37	1	0	0	0	3	8	25
Alabama..................................	5	0	0	0	0	0	0	5
Kentucky.................................	7	0	0	0	0	0	0	7
Mississippi..............................	4	1	0	0	0	0	0	3
Tennessee...............................	21	0	0	0	0	3	8	10
West South Central......................	294	16	2	0	1	118	24	133
Arkansas.................................	9	0	0	0	0	0	0	9
Louisiana................................	6	4	0	0	0	0	0	2
Oklahoma...............................	12	0	0	0	0	4	2	6
Texas......................................	267	12	2	0	1	114	22	116
West...	801	66	10	0	4	400	83	238
Mountain....................................	562	63	7	0	1	296	61	134
Arizona...................................	273	32	6	0	1	141	10	83
Colorado.................................	23	1	1	0	0	16	0	5
Idaho......................................	92	0	0	0	0	46	46	0
Montana..................................	30	1	0	0	0	23	3	3
Nevada....................................	11	0	0	0	0	9	0	2
New Mexico	101	27	0	0	0	52	1	21
Utah.......................................	7	2	0	0	0	3	0	2
Wyoming.................................	25	0	0	0	0	6	1	18
Pacific..	239	3	3	0	3	104	22	104
Alaska.....................................	0	0	0	0	0	0	0	0
California................................	185	2	3	0	3	90	14	73
Hawaii.....................................	1	0	0	0	0	1	0	0
Oregon....................................	32	0	0	0	0	3	5	24
Washington.............................	21	1	0	0	0	10	3	7

Table 40. Federal Law Enforcement Officers Killed and Assaulted, by Region, Geographic Division, and State/Territory, 2017—*Continued*

(Number.)

Area	Total	Firearm	Knife or other cutting instrument	Bomb	Blunt instrument	Personal weapons	Vehicle	Other
Puerto Rico and other outlying areas......................	9	2	0	0	0	2	2	3
American Samoa...	0	0	0	0	0	0	0	0
Guam..	0	0	0	0	0	0	0	0
Mariana Islands	0	0	0	0	0	0	0	0
Puerto Rico...	8	2	0	0	0	1	2	3
U.S. Virgin Islands...	1	0	0	0	0	1	0	0

Note: Location data for 15 victim officers who were assaulted with "Other" weapons were not reported by the National Park Service.

METHODOLOGY

Survey Coverage

This year, the LEOKA program is releasing the 2017 publication on a new schedule. Also, due to a technical refresh, this year's publication includes additional details about incidents in which officers are killed and assaulted.

Officers Killed

When an officer is killed in the line of duty, the FBI gathers data about circumstances pertaining to the death. The data come from various sources:

- City, university and college, county, state, tribal, and federal law enforcement agencies participating in the Uniform Crime Reporting Program may report line-of-duty deaths that occur in their jurisdictions

- FBI field offices report line-of-duty deaths of law enforcement officers that occur in the United States and its outlying areas

- Several nonprofit organizations, such as the Concerns of Police Survivors and the National Law Enforcement Officers Memorial Fund, which provide various services to the families of fallen officers, also furnish information about line-of-duty deaths

When the FBI receives notification of a line-of-duty death, the Law Enforcement Officers Killed and Assaulted (LEOKA) Program's staff works with FBI field offices to contact the fallen officer's employing agency and request additional details about the fatal incident. The LEOKA staff also obtains criminal history data from the FBI's Interstate Identification Index about individuals who are identified in connection with line-of-duty felonious deaths.

Officers Assaulted

The Uniform Crime Reporting (UCR) Program collects information monthly about assaults on duly sworn city, university and college, county, state, and tribal law enforcement officers. The agencies that employ these officers collect and submit data either through their state UCR Programs or, for non-Program states, directly to the FBI. For assault data to be included in this publication, law enforcement agencies must have submitted information for all 12 months of 2015 regarding their sworn officers who were assaulted as well as the number of officers

and civilians their agencies employed full time for the reporting year.

Law enforcement agencies report to the UCR Program the number of assaults resulting in injuries to their officers or instances in which an offender used a weapon that could have caused injury or death. Law enforcement agencies report other assaults (i.e., those not causing injury) if they involved more than verbal abuse or minor resistance to an arrest.

The data in this report pertain to felonious deaths, accidental deaths, and assaults of duly sworn law enforcement officers who, at the time of the incident, met the following criteria. These law enforcement officers:

- Wore/carried a badge (ordinarily).

- Carried a firearm (ordinarily).

- Were duly sworn and had full arrest powers.

- Were members of a law enforcement agency.

- Were acting in an official capacity, whether on or off duty, at the time of incident.

- If killed, the deaths were directly related to the injuries received during the incident.

An exception to the above criteria includes individuals who were killed or assaulted while acting in a law enforcement capacity at the request of a law enforcement agency whose officers meet the LEOKA criteria. (See below for further explanation in reference to this exception.)

Exclusions from the LEOKA Program's Data Collection

Deaths resulting from the following are not included in the LEOKA Program's statistics:

- Natural causes, such as, heart attack, stroke, aneurism, etc.

- On duty, but death is attributed to their own personal situation, such as, domestic violence, neighbor conflict, etc.

- Suicide

Examples of job positions not typically included in the LEOKA Program's statistics (unless they meet the above exception):

- Corrections/correctional officers

- Bailiffs

- Probation/parole officers

- Federal judges

- U.S. and Assistant U.S. Attorneys

- Bureau of Prison Officers

- Private Security Officers

In September 2014, the LEOKA Program expanded its collection criteria to include the data of individuals who are killed or assaulted while temporarily serving as a law enforcement officer at the request of a law enforcement agency whose officers meet the general current collection criteria. These individuals must be under the supervision of a certified law enforcement officer from the requesting agency at the time of the incident, but they are not required to be in the physical presence of the supervisory officer while they are working an assigned duty. The data of individuals who met this exception and were submitted in 2015 are included in this publication.

Example of permitted exception: An unpaid reserve officer responded to a structure fire along with a law enforcement officer. As the reserve officer exited the patrol unit, he was immediately confronted in an ambush-style attack and was fatally shot by the offender.

Example of permitted exception: A correctional officer was fatally shot while assisting local law enforcement agencies who were tracking a man wanted for murdering his parents. The officer was a canine handler at a local correctional facility and was asked to assist during the incident based on the need for the canine. (If the correctional officer was working in his/her normal capacity as a correctional officer when killed, that correctional officer would not be counted in the LEOKA Program's statistics.)

Federal Law Enforcement Officers Killed and Assaulted

Data published by the FBI concerning federal officers who were killed or assaulted in the line of duty are provided by the following six federal departments:

- U.S. Capitol Police

- U.S. Department of Defense

- U.S. Department of Homeland Security

- U.S. Department of the Interior

- U.S. Department of Justice

- U.S. Department of the Treasury

- U.S. Postal Inspection Service

Within these departments are the agencies, bureaus, and services that employ most of the personnel who are responsible for protecting government officials and enforcing and investigating violations of federal law. Every year, the FBI contacts these agencies and requests information about the officers who were killed or assaulted in the line of duty.

The information concerning federal officers differs slightly from the data regarding assaults on city, university and college, county, state, and tribal law enforcement officers. First, the data regarding federal officers include all reports of assaults regardless of the extent (or the absence) of personal injury. Second, the circumstance categories are tailored to represent the unique duties of federal law enforcement personnel.

Data Considerations

When reviewing the tables, charts, and summaries presented in this publication, readers should be aware of certain features of the LEOKA data collection process that could affect their interpretation of the information.

- The data in the tables and charts reflect the number of victim officers, not the number of incidents or weapons used.

- The UCR Program considers any parts of the body that can be used as weapons (such as hands, fists, or feet) to be personal weapons and designates them as such in its data.

- Law enforcement agencies use a different methodology for collecting and reporting data about officers who were killed than the methodology used for those who were assaulted. As a result, information about officers killed and information about officers assaulted reside in two separate databases, and the data are not comparable.

- Because the information in the tables of this publication is updated each year, the FBI cautions readers against making comparisons between the data in this publication and those in prior editions.

Caution Against Comparisons with Data from Other Organizations

The FBI's LEOKA Program is one of a number of entities that report information concerning line-of-duty deaths and/or assaults of law enforcement officers in the United States. Each organization has its own purpose and may use different methods to collect and report information or focus on somewhat different aspects of these important topics. Therefore, care should be taken not to compare LEOKA data to data provided by other entities, such as the Officer Down Memorial Page, National Law Enforcement Officers Memorial Fund, and others. More information about the LEOKA Program's mission and history is included at https://ucr.fbi.gov/leoka/2017/home.

History

Beginning in 1937, the FBI's UCR Program collected and published statistics on law enforcement officers killed in the line of duty in its annual publication, *Crime in the United States*. Statistics regarding assaults on officers were added in 1960. In June 1971, executives from the law enforcement conference, "Prevention of Police Killings," called for an increase in the FBI's involvement in preventing and investigating officers' deaths. In response to this directive, the UCR Program expanded its collection of data to include more details about the incidents in which law enforcement officers were killed and assaulted.

Using this comprehensive set of data, the FBI began in 1972 to produce two reports annually, the *Law Enforcement Officers Killed Summary* and the *Analysis of Assaults on Federal Officers*. These two reports were combined in 1982 to create the annual publication, *Law Enforcement Officers Killed and Assaulted*.

Definitions

Type of Incident

Feloniously Killed – Incident type in which an officer, while engaged in or on account of the performance of their official duties, was fatally injured as a direct result of a willful and intentional act by an offender.

Accidentally Killed – Incident type in which an officer was fatally injured as a result of an accident or negligence that occurred while the officer was acting in an official capacity. Due to the hazardous nature of the law enforcement profession, deaths of law enforcement officers are considered accidental if the act causing the death is found not to be willful and intentional.

Assaulted – An unlawful attack by one person upon another for the purpose of inflicting severe or aggravated bodily injury. This type of assault is accompanied by the use of a weapon or by a means likely to produce death or great bodily injury.

Detailed Assault Data – The detailed data collection is limited to officers who are assaulted and injured with firearms or knives/other cutting instruments. – Incident type in which an officer, while engaged in or on account of the performance of their official duties, received nonfatal injuries as a direct result of a willful and intentional act by an offender.

Race

White – A person having origins in any of the original peoples of Europe, the Middle East, or North Africa.

Black/African American – A person having origins in any of the black racial groups of Africa. Terms such as "Haitian" or "Negro" can be used in addition to "Black or African American."

Asian – Included within "Asian/Pacific Islander" in LEOKA publication tables referring to Race – A person having origins in any of the original peoples of the Far East, Southeast Asia, or the Indian subcontinent, including, for example, Cambodia, China, India, Japan, Korea, Malaysia, Pakistan, the Philippine Islands, Thailand, and Vietnam.

Native Hawaiian/Other Pacific Islands – Included within "Asian/Pacific Islander" in LEOKA publication tables referring to Race – A person having origins in any of the original peoples of Hawaii, Guam, Samoa, or other Pacific Islands, e.g., individuals who are Carolinian, Fijian, Kosraean, Melanesian, Micronesian, Northern Mariana Islander, Palauan, Papua New Guinean, Ponapean (Pohnpelan), Polynesian, Solomon Islander, Tahitian, Tarawa Islander, Tokelauan, Tongan, Trukese (Chuukese), and Yapese. (*Note*: The term "Native Hawaiian" does not include individuals who are native to the state of Hawaii simply by virtue of being born there.)

American Indian/Alaska Native – A person having origins in any of the original peoples of North and South America (including Central America), and who maintains tribal affiliation or community attachment.

Type of Assignment

2-Officer vehicle – An assignment where the officer is on patrol and is accompanied by another law enforcement officer(s) in the agency's marked patrol vehicle.

1-Officer vehicle – An assignment where the officer is on patrol and is not accompanied by another officer in the agency's marked patrol vehicle.

Foot patrol – An assignment where the officer is patrolling a designated route on foot.

Administrative – Included within "Other" in LEOKA publication tables referring to Type of Assignment – An assignment in which an officer is working management, performance, or executive duties of the local, state, or federal jurisdiction. Examples include, but are not limited to:

- handling, transporting, or maintaining custody of persons who are in the custodial care of a law enforcement agency subsequent to an arrest and/or while dealing with persons who are being detained in accordance with the law;

- attending community meetings, crime preventive programs, or other organized functions as an official representative of a law enforcement agency;

- performing duties and recreational activities associated with agency sanctioned programs such as D.A.R.E., Boys and Girls Clubs, or other youth programs; or

- serving of writs, notices, summonses, subpoenas, hearing notices, notifications, and other civil processes; and transporting of papers, equipment, or persons associated with official agency sanctioned activities, functions, and programs.

Investigative/detective – Included within "Other" in LEOKA publication tables referring to Type of Assignment – An officer whose occupation is mainly to investigate and solve crimes.

Plainclothes assignment – Included within "Other" in LEOKA publication tables referring to Type of Assignment – A non-uniformed assignment where the officer's role and identity as a sworn law enforcement officer is not intended to be confidential or clandestine.

Tactical assignment (uniformed) – Included within "Other" in LEOKA publication tables referring to Type of Assignment – A uniformed assignment where an officer is strategically deployed in order to achieve a specific goal or objective. These are typically high-risk assignments.

Undercover – Included within "Other" in LEOKA publication tables referring to Type of Assignment – A non-uniformed assignment where the officer requires anonymity or blending into a group or environment to gather evidence or intelligence. The disclosure of the officer's identity would pose a significant safety risk.

Off duty – An officer who is off duty at the time of incident, but is acting in such a way which is sanctioned by, recognized by, or derived from authority.

Circumstances at Scene of Incident

Disturbance (bar fight, person with firearm, etc.) – A breach of the peace type of circumstance resulting in a call for law enforcement to respond. Examples include, but are not limited to: curfew violations, disorderly persons, drinking in public, fights, fireworks violations, gambling in public space, persons under the influence, landlord/tenant disputes, loitering, loud noise of any type (excluding animal disturbance complaints by a citizen), littering, nuisance complaints, prostitution offenses, trespassing or unwanted guests, vagrancy violations, and verbal altercations.

Domestic disturbance (family quarrel, etc.) – A breach of the peace or crime against a person occurring within a family, families, or other relatives or members of the household. Examples include, but are not limited to: family disputes, family intimidations, family arguments, and assisting citizens with the removal of legally owned possessions at locations where prior domestic disturbances or other related offenses have occurred. (Family includes a current or former spouse, parent, or guardian of the victim; a person with whom the victim shares a child in common; a person who is or has been in a social relationship of a romantic or intimate nature with the victim; a person who is cohabiting with or has cohabited with the victim as a spouse, parent, or guardian; or by a person who is or has been similarly situated to a spouse, parent, or guardian of the victim.)

Domestic violence – Included within "Domestic disturbance (family quarrels, etc.)" in LEOKA publication tables referring to Circumstance at Scene of Incident – The use, attempted use, or threatened use of physical force, or a weapon; or the use of coercion or intimidation; or committing a crime against property by a current or former spouse, parent, or guardian of the victim; a person with whom the victim shares a child in common; a person who is or has been in a social relationship of a romantic or intimate nature with the victim; a person who is cohabiting with or has cohabited with the victim as a spouse, parent, or guardian; or by a person who is or has been similarly situated to a spouse, parent, or guardian of the victim.

Burglary – The unlawful entry of a structure with the intent to commit a felony or a theft.

Burglary in progress/pursuing burglary suspect – Situation where an officer is pursuing, arresting, or attempting to arrest an offender involved in a burglary.

Robbery – The taking, or attempting to take, anything of value under confrontational circumstances from the care, custody, or control of a person by force, threat of force, or violence and/or by putting the victim in fear of immediate harm.

Robbery in progress/pursuing robbery suspect – Situation where an officer is pursuing, arresting, or attempting to arrest an offender involved in a robbery.

Drug-related matter – Situation where an officer is pursuing, arresting, or attempting to arrest an offender involved in a drug-related matter, such as, drug busts, buys, etc.

Drug complaint – Included within "Drug-related matter" in LEOKA publication tables referring to Circumstance at Scene of Incident – Incident where a citizen reports the use or presence of illegal drugs or drug paraphernalia. Examples include, but are not limited to, the possession, buying, or selling of illegal drugs or drug paraphernalia.

Attempting other arrest – Situation where an officer is arresting or attempting to arrest an offender either through verbal advisement or through physical contact, such as, attempting to restrain, control, or handcuff the offender.

Civil disorder (mass disobedience, riot, etc.) – An activity where an officer is to control, disperse, or terminate a riot or mass disobedience.

Handling, transporting, custody of prisoner – Situation where an officer is handling, transporting, or maintaining custody of persons who are in the custodial care of a law enforcement agency subsequent to an arrest and/or while dealing with persons who are being detained in accordance with the law.

Investigating suspicious person/circumstance – An activity where an officer's intent is to investigate an unusual occurrence, an out-of-the-ordinary condition, or a suspicious person or circumstance.

Ambush – Situation where an officer is assaulted, unexpectedly, as the result of premeditated design by the perpetrator.

Ambush (entrapment/premeditation) – Situation where an unsuspecting officer was targeted or lured into danger as the result of conscious consideration and planning by the offender.

Unprovoked attack – An attack on an officer not prompted by official contact at the time of the incident between the officer and the offender.

Investigative activity (surveillance, search, interview, etc.) – An activity where an officer is making official inquiries relating to prior criminal offenses and/or perpetrators. Examples include, but are not limited to, obtaining follow-up information or additional information relating to any crime (excluding drug offense complaints) or interviewing a citizen relating to any criminal matter (excluding drug offenses).

Handling person with mental illness – Situation where an officer is handling a person who is known or suspected to be suffering from a mental illness that impairs judgment, behavior, perceptions of reality, or their ability to cope with the ordinary demands of life. Examples include, but are not limited to: mental patients, suicidal persons, service of commitment orders, and calls to investigate persons or activities where it is suspected that a person is suffering from a mental illness.

Felony vehicle stop – A vehicle stop made by an officer that is considered to be high-risk in nature.

Traffic violation stop – A vehicle stop made by an officer due to a motorist's violation of traffic rules and regulations.

Tactical situation (barricaded offender, hostage taking, high-risk entry, etc.) – Situation where an officer is strategically deployed in order to achieve a specific goal or objective. Examples include, but are not limited to: serving search warrants, hostage situations, barricaded offenders, search warrants for drug violations, and any other situations that could be deemed "high-risk," such as, serving an arrest warrant on a known armed felon.

PART 10

Probation and Parole, 2016

PAR.

HIGHLIGHTS

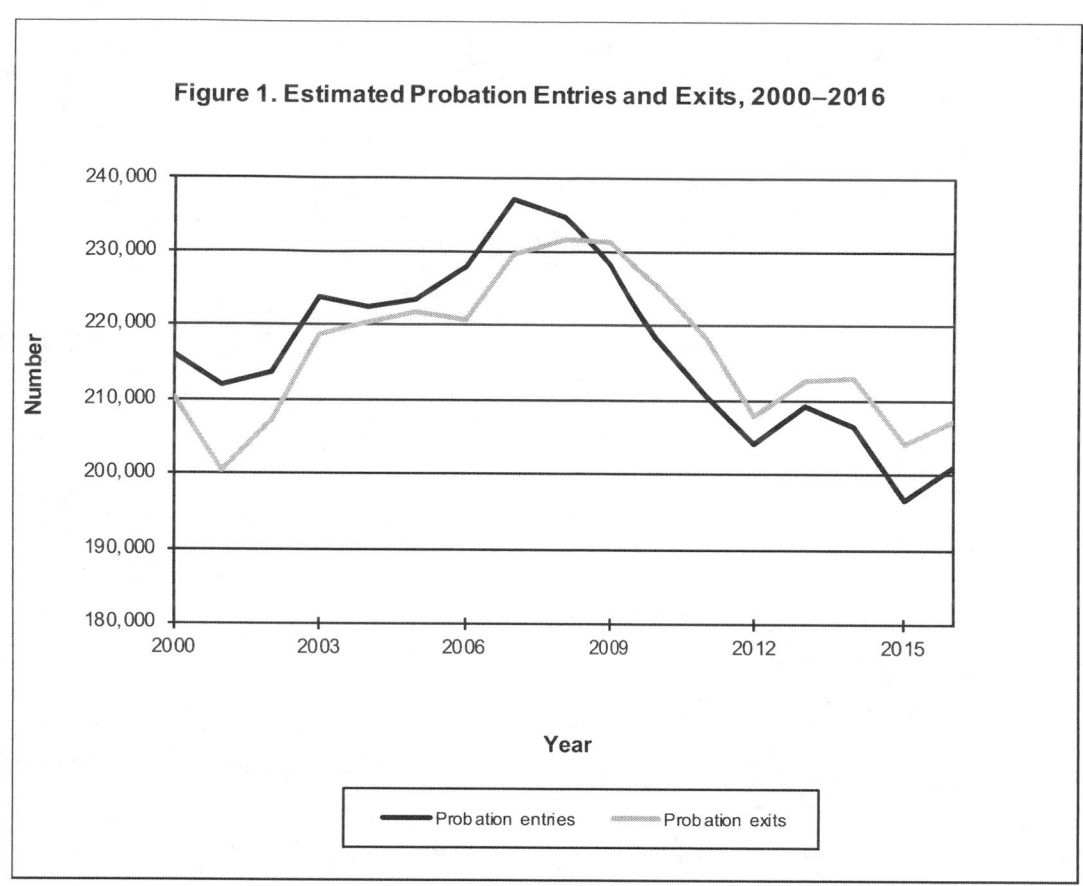

Figure 1. Estimated Probation Entries and Exits, 2000–2016

- At yearend 2016, an estimated 4,537,100 adults were under community supervision, down by about 49,800 offenders (1.1 percent) from January 1, 2016; the total community supervision population in 2016 was at its lowest level since 1999.

- Approximately 1 in 55 adults in the United States was under community supervision at yearend 2016.

- Between yearend 2015 and 2016, the adult probation population declined by approximately 1.4 percent (about 52,500 offenders), dropping to an estimated 3,673,100 offenders at yearend 2015.

- The adult parole population increased by 0.5 percent (4,300 offenders) between yearend 2015 and 2016 to an estimated 874,800 offenders.

- Parole exits decreased from an estimated 463,700 in 2015 to 456,000 in 2016, while probation exits increased from 2,043,200 in 2015 to 2,071,400 in 2016.

Table 1. Adults Under Community Supervision on Probation or Parole, 2000–2016

(Number; percent.)

Year	Total	Probation	Parole
2000	4,564,900	3,839,400	725,500
2001	4,665,700	3,934,500	731,100
2002	4,748,100	3,995,000	753,100
2003	4,847,300	4,073,800	773,500
2004	4,916,300	4,140,400	775,900
2005	4,946,600	4,162,300	784,400
2006	5,035,000	4,236,800	798,200
2007	5,119,000	4,293,000	826,100
2008	5,093,400	4,271,200	826,100
2009	5,019,900	4,199,800	824,600
2010	4,888,500	4,055,900	840,800
2011	4,818,300	3,973,800	855,500
2012	4,790,700	3,944,900	858,400
2013	4,749,800	3,912,900	849,500
2014	4,713,200	3,868,400	857,700
2015	4,650,900	3,789,800	870,500
2016			
January 1, 2016	4,586,900	3,725,600	870,700
December 31, 2016	4,537,100	3,673,100	874,800
Percent change, 2000–2016	-0.6	-4.3	-20.6
Percent change, 1/1/16–12/31/16	-1.1	-1.4	-0.5

Note: Counts are rounded to the nearest 100. Detail may not sum to total due to rounding. Estimates are based on most recent data and may differ from previously published statistics. Reporting methods for some probation agencies changed over time. From 2008 to 2016, detail may not sum to total because total was adjusted to exclude parolees who were also on probation.

Table 2. Rates of U.S. Adult Residents on Community Supervision, Probation, and Parole, 2000, 2005, 2010–2015

(Number; rate.)

Year	Number per 100,000 U.S. adult residents			U.S. adult residents on:		
	Community supervision[1,2]	Probation	Parole	Community supervision[1]	Probation	Parole
2000	2,162	1,818	344	1 in 46	1 in 53	1 in 285
2005	2,215	1,864	351	1 in 45	1 in 54	1 in 285
2010	2,067	1,715	356	1 in 48	1 in 58	1 in 281
2011	2,017	1,663	358	1 in 50	1 in 60	1 in 279
2012	1,984	1,634	356	1 in 50	1 in 61	1 in 281
2013	1,946	1,603	348	1 in 51	1 in 62	1 in 287
2014	1,911	1,568	348	1 in 52	1 in 64	1 in 288
2015	1,872	1,526	350	1 in 53	1 in 66	1 in 285
2016	1,811	1,467	349	1 in 55	1 in 68	1 in 287

Note: Rates are based on most recent data available and may di er from previously published statistics. Rates are based on the total community supervision, probation, and parole population counts as of December 31 of the reporting year and were computed using the estimates of the U.S. resident population of persons age 18 or older from the U.S. Census Bureau for January 1 of the following year.
[1] Includes adults on probation and adults on parole.
[2] For 2008 to 2016, detail may not sum to total because the community supervision rate was adjusted to exclude parolees who were also on probation.

Table 3. Parolees on Probation Excluded from the January 1 and December 31 Community Supervision Populations, 2008–2016

(Number.)

Year	January 1	December 31
2008	3,562	3,905
2009	3,905	4,959
2010	8,259	8,259
2011	8,259	10,958
2012	10,958	12,672
2013	12,672	12,511
2014	12,511	12,919
2015	12,919	9,375
2016	9,375	10,822

Note: Counts are based on most recent data and may differ from previously published statistics. Individuals being supervised on both probation and parole are excluded from community supervision population to avoid double counting. For 2011 through 2016, data are based on the December 31 count of the prior reporting year. For 2010, the December 31, 2010, count was used as a proxy because additional states reported these data in 2010.

Table 4. One-Day Difference Based on Reporting Changes for Probation and Parole, 2000–2015

(Number.)

Year	Probation population difference from December 31 to January 1 of the following year	Parole population difference from December 31 to January 1 of the following year
2000	-13,320	-1,630
2001	-2,980	1,190
2002	28,900	-2,210
2003	18,860	23,610
2004	3,150	-4,020
2005	4,260	-3,740
2006	-21,660	1,670
2007	-59,280	-4,920
2008	-33,670	1,390
2009	-73,120	13,700
2010	-2,400	-80
2011	9,770	-2,830
2012	2,960	-23,640
2013	20,980	540
2014	9,750	170
2015	-64,150	130

Note: Counts are rounded to the nearest 10. Calculated as the difference between December 31 of the year displayed and January 1 of the following year.

Table 5. Adults Under Community Supervision, 2016

(Number; percent; rate.)

Jurisdiction	Community supervision population[1]		Entries		Exits		Community supervision population, 12/31/16[1]	Change, 2016		Number under community supervision per 100,000 adult residents, 12/31/16[3]
	December 31, 2015	January 1, 2016	Reported	Estimated[2]	Reported	Estimated[2]		Number	Percent	
U.S. Total....................	4,650,900	4,586,900	1,997,600	2,469,300	2,356,700	2,527,400	4,537,100	-49,800	-1.1	1,810
Federal.......................	132,800	133,100	53,700	53,700	57,300	57,300	131,700	-1,400		53
State........................	4,518,100	4,453,900	1,943,900	2,415,600	2,299,400	2,470,100	4,405,400	-48,400	-1.1	1,758
Alabama......................	64,600	59,600	17,000	17,000	16,100	16,100	60,700	1,200	2	1,609
Alaska..........................	U	8,600	7,700	7,700	7,800	7,800	8,400	-200	-2	1,520
Arizona........................	83,300	83,300	35,600	35,600	34,100	34,100	84,800	1,500	2	1,587
Arkansas[4]...................	51,500	51,400	22,200	22,200	19,400	19,400	51,500	100	0	2,246
California[4]..................	349,600	325,000	164,900	192,000	159,400	181,700	333,300	8,300	1	1,100
Colorado[4]..................	89,200	88,800	63,200	63,600	61,100	61,600	90,900	2,200	2	2,106
Connecticut	45,300	45,000	24,100	24,100	23,100	23,100	44,700	-300		1,580
Delaware	16,100	16,100	12,600	12,600	12,900	12,900	15,800	-300	-2	2,101
District of Columbia.......	9,900	9,900	5,900	5,900	6,100	6,100	9,600	-200	-3	1,709
Florida[4]......................	225,400	226,100	134,300	150,200	142,600	156,300	218,600	-7,400	-3.3	1,315
Georgia[4]	451,800	430,800	U	U	U	U	U	U	U	U
Hawaii	22,500	22,400	5,000	5,000	5,600	5,600	21,900	-500	-2	1,949
Idaho...........................	37,800	37,800	15,500	15,500	15,800	15,800	37,500	-300		2,980
Illinois	151,300	151,800	66,900	66,900	76,200	76,200	143,400	-8,300	-6	1,451
Indiana	122,500	121,100	84,700	84,700	89,100	89,100	116,700	-4,400	-4	2,300
Iowa	35,600	35,500	19,300	19,300	19,700	19,700	35,100	-400	-1.2	1,456
Kansas	20,900	20,900	26,000	26,000	25,400	25,400	21,500	600	3	978
Kentucky	70,600	68,800	27,900	35,900	29,700	40,800	63,800	-5,000	-7	1,858
Louisiana	71,900	72,000	28,800	28,800	29,800	29,800	71,000	-1,100	-1.5	1,985
Maine..........................	6,700	6,700	3,300	3,300	3,300	3,300	6,800	100	2	634
Maryland	87,400	87,400	37,800	37,800	42,300	42,300	82,800	-4,600	-5	1,770
Massachusetts	66,900	66,900	67,900	67,900	71,200	71,200	63,600	-3,300	-4.9	1,167
Michigan[4]....................	193,900	192,200	U	U	U	U	U	U	U	U
Minnesota	105,100	105,000	54,400	54,400	55,400	55,400	103,900	-1,000		2,447
Mississippi[4]	44,800	44,800	16,400	16,400	23,400	23,400	37,700	-7,000	-16	1,660
Missouri[4].....................	62,600	62,400	38,400	38,400	39,200	39,300	61,600	-800		1,305
Montana.......................	9,700	9,900	5,000	5,000	4,700	4,700	10,200	300	3	1,247
Nebraska	13,700	13,700	11,500	11,500	13,900	13,900	14,600	900	6.6	1,013
Nevada	19,200	19,200	9,400	9,400	9,300	9,300	19,000	-200	-1.3	831
New Hampshire	6,300	6,300	4,000	4,000	3,900	3,900	6,400	100	1	592
New Jersey....................	151,300	151,300	38,000	38,000	33,600	33,600	155,700	4,400	2.9	2,231
New Mexico..................	16,800	15,400	8,700	14,900	16,000	16,000	15,500	100	0.8	973
New York......................	145,600	146,400	46,900	46,900	50,900	50,900	142,400	-4,000	-3	913
North Carolina	97,400	97,400	62,600	62,600	64,600	64,600	95,200	-2,200	-2	1,205
North Dakota................	6,900	7,000	6,100	6,100	6,000	6,000	7,100	200	2	1,228
Ohio[4]..........................	262,000	254,700	130,400	143,900	130,200	144,500	256,400	1,700	1	2,842
Oklahoma....................	33,400	33,400	13,400	13,400	11,300	11,300	35,500	2,100	6	1,193
Oregon	U	60,000	37,600	37,600	36,200	36,200	61,400	1,400	2	1,887
Pennsylvania	296,200	296,200	155,300	155,300	159,900	159,900	291,600	-4,600	-2	2,880
Rhode Island	24,400	24,400	200	4,900	200	6,000	23,200	-1,100	-4.6	2,735
South Carolina..............	38,500	38,300	15,900	15,900	17,600	17,600	36,700	-1,600	-4	944
South Dakota................	9,800	9,600	5,100	5,100	5,400	5,400	9,300	-300	-4	1,420
Tennessee	75,400	75,900	27,100	27,100	27,800	27,800	74,700	-1,200	-2	1,443
Texas...........................	488,800	488,400	179,500	179,500	184,300	184,300	482,900	-5,500	-1.1	2,328
Utah	15,700	15,700	8,300	8,300	8,000	8,000	15,900	300	2	740
Vermont	6,300	6,200	U	3,500	U	3,900	5,800	-400	-6.5	1,153
Virginia	57,000	57,000	34,600	34,600	38,100	38,100	62,500	5,400	10	952
Washington[4]..................	104,700	105,100	43,800	47,300	42,700	51,600	100,600	-4,400	-4.2	1,763
West Virginia	10,100	10,100	2,100	3,200	3,200	3,200	10,100	-100		692
Wisconsin[4,5]..................	65,600	66,400	U	29,500	7,800	31,000	64,900	-1,500	-2	1,442
Wyoming	5,900	5,600	3,300	3,300	3,400	3,400	5,500	-100	-2.4	1,235

Note: Counts are rounded to the nearest 100. Detail may not sum to total due to rounding. Data quality may vary across jurisdictions for counts of entries and exits; therefore, the population on December 31, 2016, does not equal the population on January 1, 2016, plus entries, minus exits.
U = Not known.
[1]The December 31, 2015, and January 1, 2016, population excludes 9,375 offenders and the December 31, 2016, population excludes 10,822 offenders under community supervision who were on both probation and parole. See Methodology for more detail on dual status.
[2]Reported data will equal estimated data in cases where no imputation was required.
[3]Rates were computed using the estimated U.S. adult resident population in each jurisdiction on January 1, 2017.
[4]See Methodology for more detail.
[5]Exits reported were deaths and absconders.

Table 6. Adults on Probation, 2016

(Number; percent; rate.)

Jurisdiction	Probation population		Entries		Exits		Probation population, 12/31/16	Change, 2016		Number on probation per 100,000 adult residents, 12/31/16[2]
	December 31, 2015	January 1, 2016	Reported	Imputed[1]	Reported	Imputed[1]		Number	Percent	
U.S. Total	3,789,785	3,725,638	1,574,587	2,012,200	1,928,687	2,071,400	3,673,120	-52,518	-1.4	1,466
Federal	18,368	18,320	8,240	8,240	9,155	9,155	17,284	-1,036	-5.7	7
State	3,771,417	3,707,318	1,566,347	2,003,900	1,919,532	2,062,300	3,655,836	-51,482	-1.4	1,459
Alabama	56,700	51,694	14,477	14,477	13,994	13,994	52,177	483	0.9	1,382
Alaska	U	6,513	6,942	6,900	6,834	6,800	6,621	108	1.7	1,193
Arizona	76,005	76,005	24,136	24,136	22,768	22,768	77,373	1,368	1.8	1,447
Arkansas	28,900	29,003	11,328	11,328	9,450	9,450	30,881	1,878	6.5	1,347
California[3,4]	263,531	238,911	138,876	138,876	136,166	136,166	239,735	824	1	791
Colorado[4]	78,883	78,810	55,501	56,000	53,701	54,200	80,740	1,930	2.4	1,870
Connecticut	42,346	42,064	21,483	21,483	20,920	20,920	41,311	-753	-1.8	1,461
Delaware	15,646	15,646	12,463	12,463	12,714	12,714	15,395	-251	-1.6	2,049
District of Columbia	5,536	5,546	4,576	4,576	4,284	4,284	5,838	292	5.3	1,034
Florida[4]	220,769	221,446	128,167	144,100	136,484	150,100	214,066	-7,380	-3.3	1,288
Georgia[4,5]	432,235	410,964	U	U	U	U	U	U	U	U
Hawaii	20,912	20,912	4,400	4,400	4,796	4,796	20,516	-396	-1.9	1,828
Idaho	32,898	32,898	12,480	12,480	12,969	12,969	32,409	-489	-1.5	2,578
Illinois	122,125	122,125	42,970	43,000	51,106	51,100	113,989	-8,136	-6.7	1,154
Indiana	113,076	111,709	77,640	77,640	81,047	81,047	108,302	-3,407	-3	2,135
Iowa	29,875	29,819	15,502	15,502	16,067	16,067	29,254	-565	-1.9	1,213
Kansas	16,588	16,588	21,493	21,493	21,427	21,427	16,654	66	0.4	758
Kentucky	54,049	52,266	17,125	25,100	17,834	28,900	48,457	-3,809	-7.3	1,411
Louisiana	40,764	40,959	12,875	12,875	13,660	13,660	40,174	-785	-1.9	1,124
Maine	6,708	6,702	3,290	3,290	3,307	3,307	6,817	115	1.7	632
Maryland	76,505	76,505	33,494	33,494	37,470	37,470	72,529	-3,976	-5.2	1,550
Massachusetts	64,934	64,934	65,772	65,772	68,917	68,917	61,789	-3,145	-4.8	1,133
Michigan[4]	175,965	175,189	U	U	U	U	U	U	U	U
Minnesota	98,258	98,165	47,266	47,266	48,579	48,579	96,852	-1,313	-1.3	2,280
Mississippi[4]	36,333	36,333	9,753	9,753	17,019	17,019	29,067	-7,266	-20	1,280
Missouri[4]	44,876	44,762	25,127	25,200	26,090	26,100	43,799	-963	-2.2	928
Montana	8,610	8,818	4,444	4,444	4,143	4,143	9,132	314	3.6	1,115
Nebraska	12,626	12,626	9,951	9,951	12,425	12,425	13,489	863	6.8	937
Nevada	13,724	13,724	5,724	5,724	5,414	5,414	13,724	0	...	601
New Hampshire	3,861	3,861	2,508	2,508	2,430	2,430	3,939	78	2	366
New Jersey	136,137	136,137	32,456	32,456	28,004	28,004	140,589	4,452	3.3	2,015
New Mexico	15,048	13,778	6,288	12,600	13,615	13,615	12,714	-1,064	-7.7	798
New York	100,996	101,789	26,494	26,494	30,355	30,355	97,928	-3,861	-3.8	628
North Carolina	85,634	85,634	48,995	48,995	52,163	52,163	82,466	-3,168	-3.7	1,044
North Dakota	6,303	6,343	4,591	4,591	4,593	4,593	6,341	-2	...	1,090
Ohio[4]	243,710	236,375	122,295	135,800	123,450	137,800	236,754	379	0.2	2,624
Oklahoma	31,281	31,281	13,004	13,004	10,723	10,723	33,562	2,281	7.3	1,129
Oregon	U	35,938	28,028	28,000	27,308	27,300	36,658	720	2	1,127
Pennsylvania	183,868	183,868	94,091	94,091	97,467	97,467	180,492	-3,376	-1.8	1,783
Rhode Island	23,920	23,920	U	4,700	U	5,800	22,781	-1,139	-4.8	2,680
South Carolina	33,843	33,652	13,483	13,483	14,501	14,501	32,634	-1,018	-3	839
South Dakota	7,118	6,959	3,311	3,311	3,660	3,660	6,610	-349	-5	1,009
Tennessee	62,325	62,829	23,703	23,703	23,431	23,431	62,609	-220	-0.4	1,209
Texas	378,937	378,514	144,055	144,055	148,284	148,284	374,285	-4,229	-1.1	1,805
Utah	12,181	12,164	5,616	5,616	5,551	5,551	12,229	65	0.5	568
Vermont	5,170	5,164	U	2,900	U	3,200	4,904	-260	-5	969
Virginia	55,472	55,472	33,897	33,897	37,532	37,532	60,821	5,349	9.6	927
Washington[4]	93,535	93,953	37,969	41,600	37,108	46,000	89,317	-4,636	-4.9	1,565
West Virginia	7,008	7,008	U	1,100	1,539	1,539	6,523	-485	-6.9	448
Wisconsin[4,6]	46,144	46,183	U	22,900	6,351	24,600	44,489	-1,694	-3.7	988
Wyoming	5,113	4,860	2,564	2,564	2,758	2,758	4,666	-194	-4	1,046

Note: Data quality may vary across jurisdictions for counts of entries and exits; therefore, the population on December, 31, 2016, does not equal the population on January 1, 2016, plus entries, minus exits. Counts may not be actual as reporting agencies may provide estimates on some or all detailed data.

... = Less than 0.05%.

U = Not known.

[1]Reported data will equal estimated data in cases where no imputation was required.

[2]Rates were computed using the estimated U.S. adult resident population in each jurisdiction on January 1, 2017.

[3]January 1, 2016, reflects a reporting change resulting in a decrease of 24,650 from the population reported for December 31, 2015.

[4]See Probation: Explanatory Notes in Methodology for more detail.

[5]January 1, 2016, reflects a reporting change resulting in a decrease of 21,271 from the population reported for December 31, 2015.

[6]Exits reported were deaths and absconders.

Table 7. Adults Exiting Probation, by Type of Exit, 2016

(Number.)

Jurisdiction	Total reported	Completion	Incarcerated				Absconder	Discharged to warrant or detainer	Other unsatisfactory	Death	Other[1]	Unknown or not reported
			With new sentence	Under current sentence	To receive treatment	Other/ unknown						
U.S. Total..................	1,928,687	971,498	64,177	98,698	4,678	65,650	49,159	11,958	262,418	12,367	80,106	307,978
Federal	9,155	7,714	0	800	0	0	0	0	118	90	0	433
State........................	1,919,532	963,784	64,177	97,898	4,678	65,650	49,159	11,958	262,300	12,277	80,106	307,545
Alabama*	13,994	10,880	1,603	486	0	0	0	1	0	322	2	700
Alaska*......................	6,834	1,300	1,936	2,201	U	U	630	U	U	55	U	712
Arizona*....................	22,768	16,176	U	4,893	X	0	U	U	1,268	331	100	0
Arkansas*..................	9,450	5,150	449	1,802	567	0	0	24	1,269	183	6	0
California*.................	136,166	58,090	0	0	0	0	0	0	53,388	0	24,688	0
Colorado*	53,701	34,115	256	927	0	6,589	5,065	0	165	394	5,007	1,183
Connecticut*	20,920	15,985	U	U	U	U	371	4,564	U	U	U	0
Delaware*..................	12,714	7,720	337	976	U	U	U	U	1,634	119	1,928	0
District of Columbia....	4,284	3,345	0	0	0	725	0	0	94	45	75	0
Florida*.....................	136,484	72,412	13,236	19,974	17	132	304	1,308	3,134	1,017	81	24,869
Georgia*	294,357	137,526	U	U	U	U	U	U	156,831	U	U	0
Hawaii*......................	4,796	3,502	236	533	U	453	U	U	U	68	4	0
Idaho*.......................	12,969	3,123	U	19	1,203	26	6	3	U	60	U	8,529
Illinois*.....................	51,106	37,435	427	6,090	X	X	X	X	7,154	X	X	0
Indiana*....................	81,047	50,271	8,287	9,452	U	U	7,077	U	U	U	5,960	0
Iowa	16,067	11,014	1,431	258	0	0	15	0	3,193	125	31	0
Kansas*.....................	21,427	13,363	X	X	X	130	2,472	U	2,970	U	2,492	0
Kentucky*..................	17,834	9,969	1,502	3,699	0	1,974	88	0	37	384	181	0
Louisiana*	13,660	8,187	1,394	2,708	X	16	X	X	1,085	221	49	0
Maine........................	3,307	2,532	U	U	U	589	U	U	U	U	U	186
Maryland	37,470	23,736	3,533	3,231	U	X	U	U	4,949	550	1,063	408
Massachusetts*	68,917	U	U	U	U	U	U	U	U	U	U	68,917
Michigan*..................	94,767	39,203	1,831	2,677	208	204	155	716	4,295	229	1,764	43,485
Minnesota	48,579	U	U	U	U	U	U	U	U	U	U	48,579
Mississippi.................	17,019	12,855	889	2,017	0	585	0	0	0	70	573	30
Missouri.....................	26,090	11,102	935	3,701	939	18	8,766	U	U	431	U	198
Montana*...................	4,143	1,570	310	753	4	54	17	0	0	56	188	1,191
Nebraska	12,425	9,727	1,694	10	0	0	0	0	789	56	148	1
Nevada*	5,414	2,794	0	0	0	0	14	0	2,201	405	0	0
New Hampshire	2,430	2,242	U	170	X	X	U	U	X	18	U	0
New Jersey.................	28,004	U	U	U	U	U	6	U	U	20	U	27,978
New Mexico*..............	13,615	8,585	U	732	U	U	2,907	1,092	U	73	4	222
New York....................	30,355	17,973	U	U	U	U	U	U	U	447	U	11,935
North Carolina	52,163	27,407	3,015	3,825	X	X	8,275	X	8,078	656	X	907
North Dakota..............	4,593	2,304	736	1,156	U	U	314	0	U	69	0	14
Ohio*........................	123,450	53,984	3,033	8,290	1,722	1,125	3,849	2,288	5,380	958	5,880	36,941
Oklahoma*.................	10,723	8,458	463	785	U	U	125	U	109	146	U	762
Oregon*	27,308	7,391	479	4,010	0	0	125	0	134	142	1,373	13,654
Pennsylvania*	97,467	73,891	10,954	3,390	0	0	1,127	35	619	1,122	6,329	0
Rhode Island..............	U	U	U	U	U	U	U	U	U	U	U	U
South Carolina...........	14,501	10,856	478	2,876	0	0	0	0	0	227	64	0
South Dakota*...........	3,660	1,922	U	U	U	735	U	U	U	U	U	1,003
Tennessee*................	23,431	15,055	3,051	4,216	0	0	325	0	0	457	327	0
Texas*.......................	148,284	96,279	U	U	U	44,697	U	U	X	1,727	5,581	0
Utah	5,551	2,097	381	362	0	0	8	0	1,636	112	955	0
Vermont	U	U	U	U	U	U	U	U	U	U	U	U
Virginia	37,532	15,584	0	0	0	7,414	0	80	0	589	13,691	174
Washington*..............	37,108	15,211	811	589	18	184	11	1,847	1,740	185	1,545	14,967
West Virginia*	1,539	U	323	558	U	U	658	U	U	U	U	0
Wisconsin[2].................	6,351	U	U	U	U	U	6,176	U	U	175	U	0
Wyoming	2,758	1,463	167	532	0	0	398	0	148	33	17	0

Note: Based on reported data only.
* = Some or all data were estimates.
U = Not known.
X = Not applicable.
[1]Includes 21,578 probationers who transferred to another jurisdiction and 58,528 probationers who exited supervision for other reasons.
[2]Exits reported were deaths and absconders.

Table 8. Characteristics of Adults on Probation, 2000, 2015, and 2016

(Percent.)

Characteristic	2000	2015	2016
Total	100.0	100.0	100.0
Sex	100.0	100.0	100.0
Male	78.0	75.0	75.0
Female	22.0	25.0	25.0
Race/Hispanic origin[1]	100.0	100.0	100.0
White	54.0	55.0	55.0
Black/African American	31.0	30.0	28.0
Hispanic/Latino	13.0	13.0	14.0
American Indian/Alaska Native	1.0	1.0	1.0
Asian/Native Hawaiian/Other Pacific Islander	1.0	1.0	1.0
Two or more races	NA	...	...
Status of supervision	100.0	100.0	100.0
Active	76.0	76.0	75.0
Residential/other treatment program	NA	1.0	1.0
Financial conditions remaining	NA	2.0	2.0
Inactive	9.0	4.0	4.0
Absconder	9.0	7.0	7.0
Supervised out of jurisdiction	3.0	2.0	2.0
Warrant status	NA	5.0	5.0
Other	3.0	4.0	4.0
Type of offense	100.0	100.0	100.0
Felony	52.0	57.0	59.0
Misdemeanor	46.0	41.0	40.0
Other infractions	2.0	2.0	2.0
Most serious offense	100.0	100.0	100.0
Violent	NA	20.0	20.0
Domestic violence	NA	4.0	4.0
Sex offense	NA	4.0	4.0
Other violent offense	NA	13.0	13.0
	NA		
Property	NA	28.0	26.0
Drug	24.0	25.0	24.0
Public order	24.0	15.0	17.0
DWI/DUI	18.0	13.0	14.0
Other traffic offense	6.0	2.0	2.0
Other[2]	52.0	12.0	13.0

Note: Characteristics are based on probationers with a known status. Detail may not sum to total due to rounding.
... = Less than 0.5%.
NA = Not available.
[1]Excludes persons of Hispanic or Latino origin, unless specified.
[2]Includes violent and property offenses in 2000 because those data were not collected separately.

Table 9. Adults on Parole, 2016

(Number; percent; rate.)

Jurisdiction	Parole population December 31, 2015	Parole population January 1, 2016	Entries Reported	Entries Estimated[1]	Exits Reported	Exits Estimated[1]	Parole population, 12/31/16	Change, 2016 Number	Change, 2016 Percent	Number on parole per 100,000 adult residents, 12/31/16[2]
U.S. Total......................	870,526	870,657	422,975	457,100	428,022	456,000	874,777	4,120	0.5	349
Federal..........................	114,471	114,746	45,469	45,469	48,108	48,108	114,385	-361	-0.3	46
State..............................	756,055	755,911	377,506	411,700	379,914	407,900	760,392	4,481	0.6	303
Alabama	8,138	8,150	2,515	2,515	2,103	2,103	8,562	412	5.1	227
Alaska	U	2,100	717	700	1,005	1,000	1,812	-288	-13.7	326
Arizona	7,379	7,379	11,481	11,481	11,360	11,360	7,500	121	1.6	140
Arkansas	23,093	22,910	10,868	10,868	9,902	9,902	23,792	882	3.8	1,038
California[3]	86,053	86,053	26,007	53,100	23,212	45,600	93,598	7,545	8.8	309
Colorado..................	10,269	9,953	7,657	7,657	7,424	7,424	10,186	233	2.3	236
Connecticut	2,939	2,939	2,591	2,591	2,151	2,151	3,379	440	15	119
Delaware....................	425	425	129	129	167	167	387	-38	-8.9	52
District of Columbia	4,594	4,548	1,330	1,330	1,853	1,853	4,025	-523	-11.5	713
Florida......................	4,611	4,611	6,110	6,110	6,155	6,155	4,566	-45	...	27
Georgia....................	24,130	24,413	9,434	9,434	11,461	11,461	22,386	-2,027	-8.3	285
Hawaii	1,540	1,479	629	629	822	822	1,367	-112	-7.6	122
Idaho	4,875	4,875	3,055	3,055	2,876	2,876	5,054	179	3.7	402
Illinois	29,146	29,629	23,889	23,889	25,083	25,083	29,428	-201	-0.7	298
Indiana....................	9,434	9,420	7,056	7,056	8,091	8,091	8,385	-1,035	-11	165
Iowa	5,918	5,901	3,810	3,810	3,660	3,660	6,051	150	2.5	251
Kansas	4,331	4,331	4,465	4,465	3,966	3,966	4,830	499	11.5	220
Kentucky..................	16,563	16,536	10,757	10,757	11,910	11,910	15,383	-1,153	-7	448
Louisiana..................	31,187	31,187	15,888	15,888	16,168	16,168	30,907	-280	-0.9	864
Maine	21	21	1	1	1	1	21	0	...	2
Maryland..................	10,887	10,887	4,295	4,295	4,877	4,877	10,305	-582	-5.3	220
Massachusetts..............	1,978	1,995	2,111	2,111	2,255	2,255	1,851	-144	-7.2	34
Michigan....................	17,909	U	U	U	U	U	U	U	U	216
Minnesota..................	6,808	6,810	7,129	7,129	6,864	6,864	7,075	265	3.9	167
Mississippi..................	8,424	8,424	6,597	6,597	6,376	6,376	8,645	221	2.6	381
Missouri	17,694	17,657	13,255	13,255	13,120	13,120	17,792	135	0.8	377
Montana....................	1,092	1,092	533	533	551	551	1,074	-18	-1.6	131
Nebraska....................	1,043	1,050	1,537	1,537	1,499	1,499	1,088	38	3.6	76
Nevada......................	5,507	5,507	3,635	3,635	3,881	3,881	5,261	-246	-4.5	230
New Hampshire..............	2,451	2,451	1,461	1,461	1,476	1,476	2,436	-15	-0.6	226
New Jersey..................	15,180	15,180	5,539	5,539	5,591	5,591	15,128	-52	-0.3	217
New Mexico	2,888	2,763	2,384	2,384	2,367	2,367	2,780	17	0.6	175
New York	44,562	44,562	20,443	20,443	20,579	20,579	44,426	-136	-0.3	285
North Carolina	11,744	11,744	13,647	13,647	12,388	12,388	12,726	982	8.4	161
North Dakota	644	634	1,545	1,545	1,375	1,375	804	170	26.8	138
Ohio........................	18,284	18,284	8,085	8,085	6,735	6,735	19,634	1,350	7.4	218
Oklahoma	2,116	2,116	383	383	604	604	1,895	-221	-10.4	64
Oregon	U	24,077	9,561	9,600	8,927	8,900	24,711	634	2.6	760
Pennsylvania	112,351	112,351	61,179	61,179	62,443	62,443	111,087	-1,264	-1.1	1,097
Rhode Island	433	441	239	239	220	220	460	19	4.3	54
South Carolina	5,021	4,963	2,460	2,460	3,076	3,076	4,347	-616	-12.4	112
South Dakota..............	2,652	2,673	1,788	1,788	1,774	1,774	2,687	14	0.5	410
Tennessee..................	13,093	13,063	3,353	3,353	4,324	4,324	12,092	-971	-7.4	234
Texas......................	111,892	111,892	35,398	35,398	36,003	36,003	111,287	-605	-0.5	537
Utah........................	3,506	3,502	2,640	2,640	2,435	2,435	3,707	205	5.9	172
Vermont....................	1,090	1,083	U	600	U	700	935	-148	-13.7	185
Virginia	1,576	1,576	711	711	601	601	1,650	74	4.7	25
Washington................	11,198	11,131	5,782	5,782	5,591	5,591	11,322	191	1.7	198
West Virginia................	3,123	3,123	2,113	2,113	1,686	1,686	3,550	427	13.7	244
Wisconsin[4]	19,453	20,241	U	6,500	1,450	6,400	20,401	160	0.8	453
Wyoming	812	783	691	691	632	632	842	59	7.5	189

Note: Data quality may vary across jurisdictions for counts of entries and exits; therefore, the population on December, 31, 2016, does not equal the population on January 1, 2016, plus entries, minus exits. Counts may not be actual as reporting agencies may provide estimates on some or all detailed data.
... = Less than 0.05%.
U = Not known.
[1]Reported data will equal estimated data in cases where no imputation was required.
[2]Rates were computed using the estimated U.S. adult resident population in each jurisdiction on January 1, 2017.
[3]Includes Post-Release Community Supervision and Mandatory Supervision parolees: 44,687 parolees on January 1, 2016; and 27,093 entries, 22,343 exits, and 49,437 parolees on December 31, 2016.
[4]Exits reported were deaths and absconders.

Table 10. Adults Entering Parole, by Type of Entry, 2016

(Number.)

Jurisdiction	Total reported	Discretionary[1]	Mandatory[2]	Reinstatement[3]	Term of supervised release[4]	Other[5]	Unknown or not reported
U.S. Total..................................	422,975	187,341	116,303	11,575	75,974	5,026	26,756
Federal	45,469	289	0	0	45,180	0	0
State..	377,506	187,052	116,303	11,575	30,794	5,026	26,756
Alabama*....................................	2,515	2,506	9	U	U	0	0
Alaska*.......................................	717	143	325	249	X	0	0
Arizona.......................................	11,481	27	11,374	80	0	0	0
Arkansas*...................................	10,868	9,085	1,783	0	0	0	0
California*..................................	26,007	U	U	U	U	0	26,007
Colorado	7,657	2,727	3,305	1,475	0	150	0
Connecticut................................	2,591	1,235	0	0	1,356	0	0
Delaware*...................................	129	U	U	U	U	0	129
District of Columbia...................	1,330	199	0	0	1,131	0	0
Florida	6,110	34	5,363	0	700	13	0
Georgia*.....................................	9,434	9,434	0	0	0	0	0
Hawaii*.......................................	629	629	0	0	X	0	0
Idaho*..	3,055	1,701	U	1,347	U	7	0
Illinois*......................................	23,889	18	23,006	90	X	559	216
Indiana	7,056	0	7,056	0	0	0	0
Iowa	3,810	3,810	0	0	0	0	0
Kansas..	4,465	0	3	153	4,215	34	60
Kentucky*...................................	10,757	6,618	4,138	0	0	1	0
Louisiana	15,888	575	14,974	285	26	28	0
Maine*..	1	0	0	1	0	0	0
Maryland*...................................	4,295	1,962	2,333	U	U	0	0
Massachusetts	2,111	1,998	0	113	0	0	0
Michigan	U	U	U	U	U	U	U
Minnesota*.................................	7,129	2	6,659	0	0	468	0
Mississippi..................................	6,597	4,770	621	0	0	862	344
Missouri*....................................	13,255	10,142	837	1,248	X	1,028	0
Montana......................................	533	533	0	0	0	0	0
Nebraska*...................................	1,537	1,320	0	211	X	6	0
Nevada*......................................	3,635	2,271	1,209	155	X	0	0
New Hampshire*.........................	1,461	785	0	573	X	103	0
New Jersey..................................	5,539	3,339	2,200	X	0	0	0
New Mexico*...............................	2,384	U	U	U	2,133	251	0
New York....................................	20,443	5,272	6,439	0	7,867	865	0
North Carolina*..........................	13,647	31	281	X	13,335	0	0
North Dakota..............................	1,545	1,545	0	0	0	0	0
Ohio...	8,085	72	7,809	204	0	0	0
Oklahoma*..................................	383	383	X	X	X	0	0
Oregon.......................................	9,561	2,294	7,186	4	11	66	0
Pennsylvania*.............................	61,179	57,542	0	3,637	0	0	0
Rhode Island*.............................	239	239	X	X	X	0	0
South Carolina............................	2,460	809	1,651	0	0	0	0
South Dakota*............................	1,788	500	1,175	U	20	93	0
Tennessee	3,353	3,267	6	75	0	5	0
Texas..	35,398	34,110	403	509	X	376	0
Utah...	2,640	2,452	0	77	0	111	0
Vermont	U	U	U	U	U	U	U
Virginia	711	258	453	0	0	0	0
Washington................................	5,782	224	5,134	424	0	0	0
West Virginia*.............................	2,113	2,071	42	0	0	0	0
Wisconsin	U	U	U	U	U	U	U
Wyoming	691	615	0	76	0	0	0

* = Some or all data were estimates.
U = Not known.
X = Not applicable.
[1]Includes persons entering due to a parole board decision.
[2]Includes persons whose release from prison was not decided by a parole board and persons entering due to determinate sentencing, good-time provisions, or emergency releases.
[3]Includes persons returned to parole after serving time in a prison due to a parole violation. Depending on the reporting jurisdiction, reinstatement entries may include only parolees who were originally released from prison through a discretionary release, mandatory release, or a combination of both types. May also include those originally released through a term of supervised release.
[4]Includes persons sentenced by a judge to a fixed period of incarceration based on a determinate statute immediately followed by a period of supervised release in the community.
[5]See https://www.bjs.gov/content/pub/pdf/ppus16.pdf for examples of commonly provided categories.

Table 11. Adults Exiting Parole, by Type of Exit, 2016

(Number.)

| Jurisdiction | Total reported | Completion | Returned to incarceration | | | | Absconder | Other unsatisfactory | Death | Other[1] | Unknown or not reported |
			With new sentence	With revocation	To receive treatment	Other/ unknown					
U.S. Total..................	428,022	242,154	31,831	69,855	2,757	11,982	7,925	5,395	6,214	17,760	32,149
Federal...................	48,108	28,906	0	11,276	0	0	0	285	801	0	6,840
State........................	379,914	213,248	31,831	58,579	2,757	11,982	7,925	5,110	5,413	17,760	25,309
Alabama*.....................	2,103	1,513	415	58	U	U	U	U	90	27	0
Alaska*.......................	1,005	446	190	369	U	U	U	U	U	U	0
Arizona*......................	11,360	7,682	16	2,472	0	0	37	1,094	59	0	0
Arkansas*....................	9,902	3,665	262	5,741	0	0	0	0	196	38	0
California*...................	23,212	U	U	U	U	U	U	U	U	U	23,212
Colorado	7,424	4,027	827	2,397	0	2	0	0	104	67	0
Connecticut.................	2,151	1,094	0	0	0	878	179	0	0	0	0
Delaware*....................	167	54	2	6	U	U	U	6	2	97	0
District of Columbia.................	1,853	789	0	0	0	653	0	198	54	159	0
Florida	6,155	3,957	337	764	0	0	0	0	1	791	305
Georgia*......................	11,461	8,675	304	22	U	2,235	0	0	120	0	105
Hawaii*.......................	822	293	0	336	0	0	75	0	7	111	0
Idaho*.........................	2,876	748	373	U	6	U	186	U	33	154	1,376
Illinois*.......................	25,083	15,533	1,770	6,570	X	X	50	9	297	854	0
Indiana*......................	8,091	3,830	389	1,985	0	0	1,491	0	65	331	0
Iowa	3,660	1,967	713	789	0	0	4	145	41	1	0
Kansas........................	3,966	3,201	162	0	0	0	404	0	32	167	0
Kentucky*....................	11,910	5,513	486	2,093	X	3,631	X	X	187	X	0
Louisiana*...................	16,168	7,059	1,439	1,232	X	1,396	X	1,539	245	3,258	0
Maine.........................	1	0	1	0	0	0	0	0	0	0	0
Maryland	4,877	2,990	493	516	U	X	U	614	119	44	101
Massachusetts*............	2,255	1,749	68	408	0	14	0	0	16	0	0
Michigan	U	U	U	U	U	U	U	U	U	U	U
Minnesota*..................	6,864	3,646	299	2,883	0	0	0	0	36	0	0
Mississippi*.................	6,376	1,142	1,621	0	0	392	0	0	51	3,170	0
Missouri......................	13,120	4,982	1,004	3,439	692	1,478	1,266	X	238	X	21
Montana......................	551	306	22	206	0	0	0	0	14	3	0
Nebraska*....................	1,499	1,063	X	416	X	13	X	X	7	X	0
Nevada*......................	3,881	2,574	304	525	X	390	35	0	53	0	0
New Hampshire	1,476	679	U	797	X	X	U	U	U	U	0
New Jersey..................	5,591	3,961	98	1,387	X	0	~	0	113	32	0
New Mexico*................	2,367	672	196	1,172	0	276	0	0	42	9	0
New York.....................	20,579	10,571	1,318	6,362	2,056	0	0	X	272	X	0
North Carolina*............	12,388	9,184	931	397	X	0	1,590	163	123	X	0
North Dakota................	1,375	1,011	72	239	U	0	40	U	13	0	0
Ohio...........................	6,735	4,251	1,595	127	0	0	275	0	224	263	0
Oklahoma*...................	604	555	14	10	X	X	X	X	25	X	0
Oregon........................	8,927	4,661	862	2,041	3	0	5	885	163	172	135
Pennsylvania*..............	62,443	41,664	6,293	5,302	0	0	765	299	793	7,327	0
Rhode Island...............	220	167	8	41	0	0	0	0	4	0	0
South Carolina.............	3,076	2,740	32	212	0	0	0	0	40	52	0
South Dakota*..............	1,774	916	172	583	X	79	0	X	24	X	0
Tennessee	4,324	2,603	887	704	0	0	0	0	130	0	0
Texas..........................	36,003	27,855	5,400	1,273	X	469	X	X	941	16	49
Utah...........................	2,435	425	274	1,547	0	0	0	142	34	13	0
Vermont	U	U	U	U	U	U	U	U	U	U	U
Virginia	601	101	105	35	0	0	0	0	8	349	3
Washington	5,591	3,799	892	760	0	76	0	0	64	0	0
West Virginia*..............	1,686	1,172	58	272	0	0	152	0	32	0	0
Wisconsin[2].................	1,450	U	U	U	U	U	1,339	U	111	U	U
Wyoming	632	417	27	133	0	0	32	16	4	1	2

* = Some or all data were estimates.
U = Not known.
X = Not applicable.
[1]Includes 2,239 parolees who were transferred to another state and 15,521 parolees who exited for other reasons.
[2]Exits reported were deaths and absconders.

Table 12. Characteristics of Adults on Parole, 2000, 2015, and 2016

(Percent.)

Characteristic	2005	2014	2015
Total	100.0	100.0	100.0
Sex	100.0	100.0	100.0
Male	88.0	87.0	87.0
Female	12.0	13.0	13.0
Race/Hispanic origin[1]	100.0	100.0	100.0
White	38.0	44.0	45.0
Black/African American	40.0	38.0	38.0
Hispanic/Latino	21.0	16.0	15.0
American Indian/Alaska Native	1.0	1.0	1.0
Asian/Native Hawaiian/other Pacific Islander	...	1.0	1.0
Two or more races	NA	...	...
Status of supervision	100.0	100.0	100.0
Active	83.0	83.0	82.0
Inactive	4.0	5.0	5.0
Absconder	7.0	6.0	7.0
Supervised out of state	5.0	4.0	4.0
Financial conditions remaining	...	...	...
Other	1.0	3.0	2.0
Maximum sentence to incarceration	100.0	100.0	100.0
Less than 1 year	3.0	6.0	6.0
1 year or more	97.0	94.0	94.0
Most serious offense	100.0	100.0	100.0
Violent	NA	32.0	30.0
Sex offense	NA	8.0	8.0
Other violent offense	NA	24.0	22.0
Property	NA	21.0	21.0
Drug	NA	31.0	31.0
Weapon	NA	4.0	4.0
Other[2]	NA	13.0	13.0

... = Less than 0.5%.
NA = Not available.
[1]Excludes persons of Hispanic or Latino origin, unless specified.
[2]Includes public order offenses.

METHODOLOGY

About the Data

The Bureau of Justice Statistics' (BJS) Annual Probation Survey and Annual Parole Survey began in 1980 and collect data from probation and parole agencies in the United States that supervise adults. In these data, adults are persons subject to the jurisdiction of an adult court or correctional agency. Juveniles prosecuted as adults in a criminal court are considered adults. Juveniles under the jurisdiction of a juvenile court or correctional agency are excluded from these data.

The National Criminal Justice Information and Statistics Service of the Law Enforcement Assistance Administration, BJS's predecessor agency, began a statistical series on parole in 1976 and on probation in 1979. The two surveys collect data on the total number of adults supervised in the community on January 1 and December 31 each year, the number of entries and exits to supervision during the reporting year, and characteristics of the population at yearend.

Both surveys cover all 50 states, the District of Columbia, and the federal system. BJS depends on the voluntary participation of state central reporters and separate state, county, and court agencies for these data. During 2016, RTI International served as BJS's collection agent for the 50 states and the District of Columbia. Data for the federal system were provided directly to BJS from the Office of Probation and Pretrial Services, Administrative Office of the United States Courts, through the Federal Justice Statistics Program.

Probation

The 2016 Annual Probation Survey was sent to 456 agencies, four fewer than on the 2015 population frame. Because two local Michigan probation agencies merged, their individual listings were removed from the 2016 population frame. Also, one local Michigan probation agency was added based on a review of the list of supervising agencies. In addition, three local Ohio probation agencies were removed due to consolidation of agency reporting. One local Florida probation agency changed from being privately run to county run.

The 456 respondents included 42 central state agencies and the District of Columbia; 414 separate state, county, or court agencies; and the federal system. States with multiple state agencies included Alabama (3), Colorado (8), Florida (42), Georgia (2), Idaho (2), Kentucky (3), Michigan (129), Missouri (2), Montana (4), New Mexico (2), Ohio (181), Oklahoma (3), Pennsylvania (2), Tennessee (3), and Washington (32). Pennsylvania

and Georgia are both included as central state agencies, but each provides data from two departments within the state government. Of the 456 agencies in the population frame, 1 locality in Colorado, 5 in Florida, 17 in Michigan, 1 in Missouri, 11 in Ohio, and 4 in Washington did not provide data for the 2016 collection. The final response rate was 91 percent.

The Michigan Department of Corrections was unable to provide data for 2016 because of staffing changes. At the state's request, the December 31, 2015, population count for Michigan was used as an estimate for both January 1, 2016, and December 31, 2016. Estimates for December 31, 2016, have been included in national and state totals. The Georgia Department of Community Supervision, Adult Felony Probation Supervision, requested that the December 31, 2015, population count be used as an estimate for the January 1, 2016, count. They provided the total population count for December 31, 2016, but did not provide any additional data for 2016.

Probation: Explanatory Notes

Probation agencies vary in their ability to provide counts consistent with Bureau of Justice Statistics (BJS) definitions on an annual basis. Some agencies report the number of cases, while others report the number of individuals they supervise. Because an individual can have multiple probation sentences, counting cases can artificially inflate probation totals. BJS requests that agencies report the number of individuals under supervision, and each year some agencies make the conversion, resulting in what appears to be a large decrease from previous years' data. BJS documents these and other reporting anomalies below:

Alabama—The Alabama Board of Pardons and Paroles, in preparation for a new data management system, found many errors in older records that required reconciliation.

California—Reporting changes from 2015 to 2016—data are not comparable to those reported in previous years, most likely as the result of one county changing from reporting the number of probation cases to individuals. Other counties made minor adjustments at yearend; however, those changes are small in comparison to the major correction from reporting cases to individuals. is change resulted in a decrease of 24,650 probationers on January 1, 2016 (238,911), compared to December 31, 2015 (263,561).

Colorado—Nonreporting agencies in 2016—one local agency did not report data. The most recently available December 31 population count for this agency was used to estimate January

1, 2016, and December 31, 2016. Another agency was unable to report the January 1, 2016, and December 31, 2016, population but was able to provide other data for 2016.*

Florida—Nonreporting agencies in 2016—five local agencies did not report data. The most recently available December 31 population count was used to estimate January 1, 2016, and December 31, 2016, counts for this agency.* Data cleanup by local agencies resulted in an increase of 3,666 probationers on January 1, 2016 (221,446), compared to December 31, 2015 (217,780).

Georgia—Nonreporting agency in 2016—a state agency in Georgia requested that the December 31, 2015, population count be used as an estimate for the January 1, 2016, count. They provided the total population count for December 31, 2016 but did not provide additional data for 2016. Counts for December 31, 2016, have been included in national and combined state totals.*

Reporting changes between 2015 and 2016—data are not comparable to those reported in previous years as the result of one reporter. The Georgia Department of Community Supervision provided counts based on summary counts submitted by independent local probation agencies. It switched from reporting cases to individuals in 2016, resulting in a decrease of 21,271 on January 1, 2016 (410,964), compared to December 31, 2015 (432,235).

Kentucky—One agency was required to estimate their population due to an update in computer systems.

Michigan—Nonreporting agencies in 2016—the Michigan DOC was unable to provide data for 2016 because of staffing changes. At the state's request, the December 31, 2015, population count was used as an estimate for January 1, 2016, and December 31, 2016. Estimates for December 31, 2016, have been included in national and "all state" totals.*

Mississippi—Reporting changes between 2015 and 2016—the state agency closed the records of individuals who had been on inactive supervision. This change resulted in an increase of 4,019 offenders exiting probation in 2016.

Missouri—Nonreporting agency—one agency that made up fewer than 0.5 percent of the state's population total did not report. For the nonreporting agency, December 31, 2015, population counts were used to estimate January 1, 2016, and December 31, 2016, populations.*

New Mexico—One agency updated their estimates due to a new case-management system.

Ohio—Nonreporting agencies in 2016—eleven local agencies did not report data. The most recently available December 31

population count was used to estimate January 1, 2016, and December 31, 2016, populations for these agencies.*

Washington—Nonreporting agencies in 2016—four local agencies did not report data. December 31, 2015, population counts were used to estimate January 1, 2016, and December 31, 2016, populations for these agencies.*

Wisconsin—The state probation agency, overseeing the entire state probation population, was able to report the number of probationers who died or absconded, but it was not able to report the total number of exits or entries to probation during 2016. Total entries and exits were imputed for 2016.*

(* = See https://www.bjs.gov/content/pub/pdf/ppus16.pdf for more information.)

The number of probation agencies included in the survey expanded in 1998 and continued to expand through 1999 to include misdemeanor probation agencies in a few states that fell within the scope of this survey. For a discussion of this expansion, see *Probation and Parole in the United States, 2010* (NCJ 236019, BJS web, November 2011).

Parole

The 2016 Annual Parole Survey was sent to 53 agencies: 50 central state reporters, which included the state parole agency in Pennsylvania (which also provided data for its 65 counties), the District of Columbia, and the federal system. In this report, federal parole includes a term of supervised release from prison, mandatory release, parole, military parole, or special parole. A federal judge orders a term of supervised release at the time of sentencing, and it is served after release from a federal prison sentence.

The California Department of Corrections and Rehabilitation did not provide data on the parole population for 2016. To produce the national yearend population estimates, data for December 31, 2016, reported on the California Department of Corrections and Rehabilitation Website were used to estimate the December 31, 2016, state parole population. Additional information about the data collection instruments is available on the BJS website.

Parole: Explanatory Notes

Each year, changes in legislation or o ender management systems require states to alter previously submitted data or the data they can currently submit. The Bureau of Justice Statistics documents these changes as reported by the data respondents:

Arkansas—Reporting changes from 2015 to 2016—legislation changes in July 2015 required Arkansas Community

Corrections to track suspended imposition of sentence (SIS) cases, resulting in a substantial increase in the number of SIS cases under parole supervision. This is reflected in the total number of dual parole and SIS cases. It includes 2,641 dual parole and SIS, 546 dual parole and probation, and 6 dual boot camp and probation cases.

California— The state agency was not able to provide data on the 2016 parole population. To produce the national yearend population estimates, data for December 31, 2016, reported in *Parole Counts for Parole Statuses by Parole Region, District, and Units for December 31, 2016* (http://www.cdcr.ca.gov/Reports_Research/Offender_Information_Services_Branch/Monthly/PAROLE/PAROLEd1612.pdf) were used to estimate the December 31, 2016, state parole population. Estimates of state entries and exits were based on data reported by the state on the 2015 Annual Parole Survey, using the reported December 31, 2015, counts and data from *Parole Counts for Parole Statuses by Parole Region, District, and Units for December 31, 2016.*

Colorado—Reporting changes between 2015 and 2016— the Department of Corrections (DOC) noted the 2015 submission included interstate compact cases supervised by the DOC for another state. They corrected this for 2016, and data no longer include these cases. These changes resulted in a decrease of 1,600 parolees from 2015. Data may not be comparable to previous years.

Wisconsin— The state probation agency, overseeing the entire state probation population, was able to report the number of probationers who died or absconded but was not able to report the total number of exits or entries to probation during 2016. Entries and exits were imputed for 2016.*

(* = See https://www.bjs.gov/content/pub/pdf/ppus16.pdf for more information.)

Estimating change in population counts

Technically, the change in the probation and parole populations from the beginning of the year to the end of the year should equal the difference between entries and exits during the year. However, those numbers may not be equal. Some probation and parole information systems track the number of cases that enter and exit community supervision, not the number of offenders. This means that entries and exits may include case counts as opposed to counts of individuals, while the beginning and yearend population counts represent individuals. Some individuals are being supervised for more than one charge or case simultaneously. Additionally, all of the data on entries and exits may not have been logged into the information systems, or the information systems may not have fully processed all of the data before the data were submitted to BJS.

As a result, the January 1, 2016, population, plus entries, minus exits, is 6,682 persons less than the published December 31 population at the national level. For parolees, the calculated total is 3,020 fewer persons than the published December 31 population. (Estimates of annual change reported in appendix tables 1,2, and 4 were calculated as the difference between the January 1 and December 31 populations within the reporting year.)

Jurisdiction counts reported for January 1 may differ from December 31 counts reported in the previous year. As a result, the direction of change based on yearend data could be in the opposite direction of the within-year change.

For more information on the imputation of probation and parole entries, as well as on the changes made in 2016, please see https://www.bjs.gov/content/pub/pdf/ppus16.pdf.

Types of Federal Offenders Under Community Supervision

Since the Sentencing Reform Act of 1984 was enacted on November 1, 1987, offenders sentenced to federal prison are no longer eligible for parole but are required to serve a term of supervised release following release from prison. Those sentenced to prison prior to November 1, 1987, continue to be eligible for parole, as do persons violating laws of the District of Columbia, military offenders, and foreign treaty transfer offenders. (See http://www.uscourts.gov/news/TheThirdBranch/11-05-01/Parole_in_the_Federal_ Probation_System.aspx.)

In 2008, the Annual Parole Survey included a new type of entry-to-parole category—term of supervised release—to better classify the large majority of entries to parole reported by the federal system. It is a fixed period of release to the community that follows a fixed period of incarceration based on a determinate sentencing statute. Both are determined by a judge at the time of sentencing. For details about estimating methods used to analyze national trends for all types of entry to parole, see *Probation and Parole in the United States, 2010* (NCJ 236019, BJS web, November 2011).

The Sentencing Reform Act also required the adoption and use of sentencing guidelines, which took effect on the same day. Many offenses for which probation had been the typical sentence prior to this date, particularly property and regulatory offenses, subsequently resulted in sentences to prison. Changes in how federal o enders are supervised in the community were first described in the BJS report *Federal Offenders Under Community Supervision, 1987-96* (NCJ 168636, BJS web, August 1998) and updated in *Federal Criminal Case Processing, 2002: With Trends 1982-2002, Reconciled Data* (NCJ 207447, BJS web, January 2005).

PART 11

2018 Update on Prisoner Recidivism: A 9-Year Follow-Up Period (2005–2014)

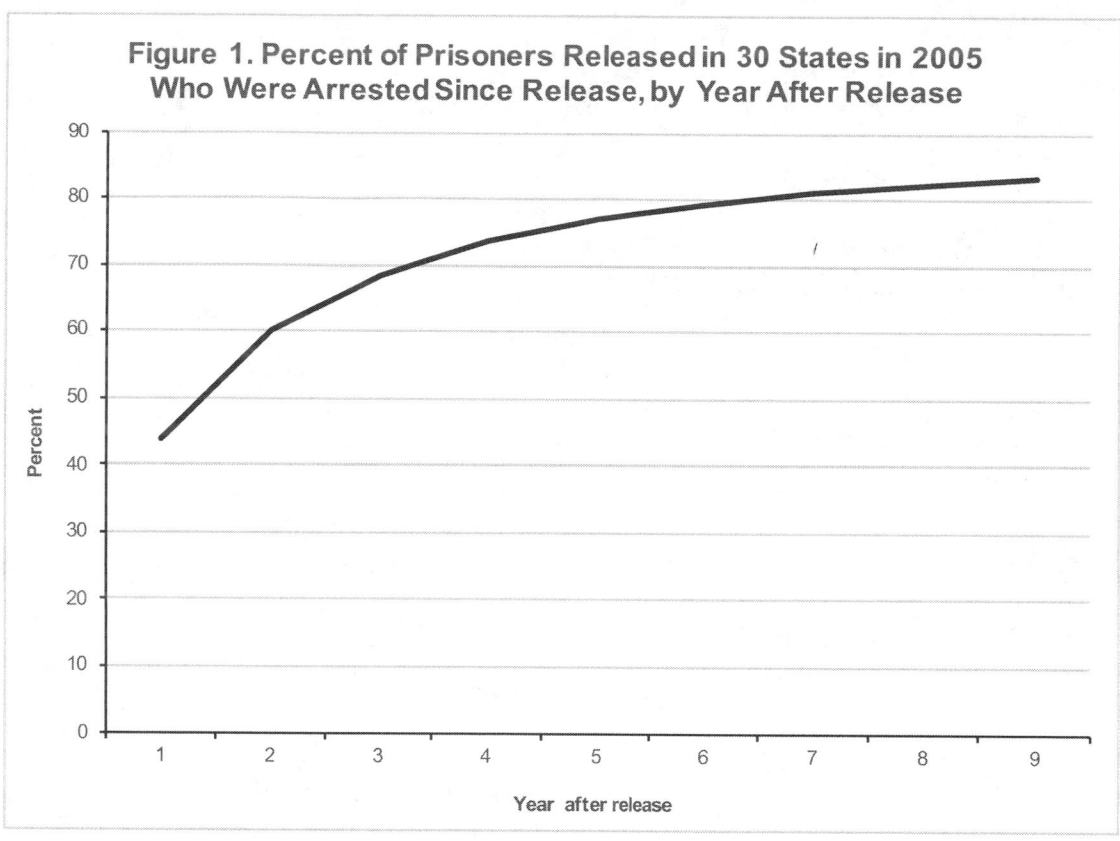

Figure 1. Percent of Prisoners Released in 30 States in 2005 Who Were Arrested Since Release, by Year After Release

- The 401,288 state prisoners released in 2005 had an estimated 1,994,000 arrests during the 9-year period, an average of 5 arrests per released prisoner. Sixty percent of these arrests occurred during years 4 through 9.

- An estimated 68 percent of released prisoners were arrested within 3 years, 79 percent within 6 years, and 83 percent within 9 years. Almost half (47 percent) of prisoners who did not have an arrest within 3 years of release were arrested during years 4 through 9.

- Approximately 82 percent of prisoners arrested during the 9-year period were arrested within the first 3 years; 42 percent of prisoners were arrested during the first year following release, while 24 percent were arrested during year 9.

- During each year and cumulatively in the 9-year follow-up period, released property offenders were more likely to be arrested than released violent offenders.

- More than three-quarters (77 percent) of released drug offenders were arrested for a non-drug crime within 9 years.

- Eight percent of prisoners arrested during the rst year after release were arrested outside the state that released them, compared to 14 percent of prisoners arrested during year 9.

Table 1. Characteristics of Prisoners Released in 30 States in 2005

(Percent; number.)

Characteristic	Percent
Total	100.0
Sex	
Male	89.3
Female	10.7
Race/Hispanic origin[1]	
White..	39.7
Black/African American	40.1
Hispanic/Latino	17.7
Other[2]	2.4
American Indian or Alaska Native..	1.2
Asian, Native Hawaiian, or Other Pacific Islander.........................	0.8
Age at release	
24 or younger	17.7
25–29	19.4
30–34	16.0
35–39	15.7
40 or older	31.2
Most serious commitment offense	
Violent	25.7
Propert	29.7
Drug	31.9
Public order[3]..	12.7
Number of released prisoners..	401,288

Note: Data on prisoners' sex and age at release were known for 100% of cases and race and Hispanic origin for nearly 100%. Detail may not sum to total due to rounding.
[1]Excludes persons of Hispanic or Latino origin, unless specified.
[2]Includes persons of two or more races or other unspecified races.
[3]Includes 0.8% of cases in which the prisoner's most serious offense was unspecified.

Table 2. Cumulative Percent of Prisoners Released in 30 States in 2005 Who Were Arrested Within or Outside the State of Release, by Year After Release

(Percent.)

Year after release	Within or outside the state of release			Outside the state of release*		
	Total	Percent arrested	Percent not arrested	Total	Percent arrested	Percent not arrested
1..	100.0	43.9	56.1	100.0	3.3	96.7
2..	100.0	60.1	39.9	100.0	5.7	94.3
3..	100.0	68.4	31.6	100.0	7.7	92.3
4..	100.0	73.5	26.5	100.0	9.3	90.7
5..	100.0	77.0	23.0	100.0	10.9	89.1
6..	100.0	79.4	20.6	100.0	12.2	87.8
7..	100.0	81.1	18.9	100.0	13.4	86.6
8..	100.0	82.4	17.6	100.0	14.4	85.6
9..	100.0	83.4	16.6	100.0	15.4	84.6

Note: Detail may not sum to total due to rounding.
* = Prisoners arrested outside the state of release could have also been arrested within the state of release.

Table 3. Percent of Prisoners Released in 30 States in 2005 Who Were Arrested After Release, by Prisoner Characteristics and Year of First Arrest

(Percent.)

Characteristic	Total arrested within 9 years	Year 1	Year 2	Year 3	Year 4	Year 5	Year 6	Year 7	Year 8	Year 9
All released prisoners	83.4	43.9	16.2	8.3	5.1	3.5	2.3	1.7	1.3	1.0
Sex										
Male	84.2	44.9	16.3	8.3	5.1	3.4	2.3	1.7	1.3	0.9
Female	76.8	35.1	15.7	8.5	5.5	4.2	2.5	2.2	1.7	1.4
Age at release										
24 or younger	90.1	51.8	17.0	7.7	4.8	3.4	2.0	1.7	1.0	0.7
25–39	85.3	44.9	16.7	8.6	5.2	3.6	2.3	1.7	1.4	0.9
25–29	87.0	45.9	16.8	8.8	5.5	3.8	2.5	1.5	1.3	0.9
30–34	84.3	43.9	16.5	8.2	5.3	3.5	2.3	1.9	1.7	1.0
35–39	84.3	44.6	16.8	8.7	4.9	3.4	2.2	1.7	1.2	0.9
40 or older	76.5	37.8	15.1	8.1	5.1	3.5	2.5	1.9	1.4	1.2
Race/Hispanic origin[1]										
White	80.9	40.2	15.8	8.4	5.2	3.8	2.6	2.2	1.5	1.2
Black/African American	86.9	46.0	17.4	8.6	5.5	3.4	2.3	1.6	1.2	0.9
Hispanic/Latino	81.3	47.3	14.3	7.2	4.2	3.1	2.2	0.9	1.3	0.7
Other[2]	82.4	44.1	16.4	8.8	4.5	3.0	1.3	2.1	1.3	1.1
American Indian or Alaska Native	85.0	43.5	16.3	9.5	4.8	3.6	1.6	2.7	1.6	1.4
Asian, Native Hawaiian, or Other Pacific Islander	79.4	45.0	16.0	8.3	4.0	1.3	1.3	1.3	1.2	1.0

Note: Data on prisoners' sex and age at release were known for 100% of cases and race and Hispanic origin for nearly 100%. Detail may not sum to total due to rounding.
[1] Excludes persons of Hispanic or Latino origin, unless specified.
[2] Includes persons of two or more races or other unspecified races.

Table 4. Post-Release Arrests of Prisoners Released in 30 States in 2005, by Year After Arrest

(Number; percent.)

Year after	Number of arrests during year/period	Percent of arrests during year/period	Cumulative number of all arrests since release	Cumulative percent of all arrests since release
Total	1,994,000	100.0	X	X
Years 1 to 3	804,000	40.3	X	X
1	306,000	15.4	306,000	15.4
2	260,000	13.0	567,000	28.4
3	238,000	11.9	804,000	40.3
Years 4 to 6	620,000	31.1	X	X
4	219,000	11.0	1,024,000	51.3
5	210,000	10.6	1,234,000	61.9
6	190,000	9.6	1,425,000	71.4
Years 7 to 9	570,000	28.6	X	X
7	196,000	9.8	1,620,000	81.2
8	194,000	9.7	1,814,000	91.0
9	180,000	9.0	1,994,000	100.0

Note: Number of post-release arrests was rounded to the nearest 1,000. Detail may not sum to total due to rounding.
X = Not applicable.

Table 5. Annual Arrest Percentage of Prisoners Released in 30 States in 2005, by Prisoner Characteristics

(Percent.)

Characteristic	Year 1	Year 2	Year 3	Year 4	Year 5	Year 6	Year 7	Year 8	Year 9
All released prisoners	43.9	37.7	34.3	31.9	30.1	28.0	27.4	25.9	24.0
Sex									
Male	44.9	38.2	34.7	32.3	30.5	28.4	27.8	26.4	24.3
Female	35.1	33.2	30.7	28.0	26.6	24.3	23.8	21.9	21.3
Age at release									
24 or younger	51.8	42.3	36.7	34.4	34.3	31.3	31.9	30.3	27.6
25–39	44.9	38.9	35.7	33.4	31.1	29.3	28.9	27.5	25.6
25–29	45.9	39.2	36.3	33.2	31.7	30.3	29.3	28.3	26.4
30–34	43.9	38.1	34.4	32.8	30.3	28.2	28.1	27.2	24.1
35–39	44.6	39.3	36.3	34.1	31.3	29.3	29.4	27.1	26.1
40 or older	37.8	33.1	30.5	28.1	25.9	23.8	22.2	20.7	19.4
Race/Hispanic origin[1]									
White	40.2	35.0	32.2	29.9	28.7	26.8	26.2	25.0	22.9
Black/African American	46.0	40.6	36.5	34.1	31.9	29.5	29.1	27.3	25.3
Hispanic/Latino..............................	47.3	36.9	33.6	31.4	29.3	26.8	25.7	24.0	23.4
Other[2]	44.1	37.8	35.3	32.0	27.8	28.7	29.9	29.2	24.6
American Indian or Alaska Native....	43.5	37.8	38.8	32.3	29.9	31.3	34.7	31.0	26.0
Asian, Native Hawaiian, or Other Pacific Islander..........................	45.0	39.1	29.7	31.3	25.2	25.4	26.2	27.5	21.2

Note: Data on prisoners' sex and age at release were known for 100% of cases, and race and Hispanic origin were known for nearly 100% of cases.
[1]Excludes persons of Hispanic or Latino origin, unless specified.
[2]Includes persons of two or more races or other unspecified races.

Table 6. Annual Arrest Percentage of Prisoners Released in 30 States in 2005, by Most Serious Commitment Offense and Type of Post-Release Arrest Offense

(Percent.)

Most serious commitment offense	Year 1	Year 2	Year 3	Year 4	Year 5	Year 6	Year 7	Year 8	Year 9
Any arrest after release									
All released prisoners	43.9	37.7	34.3	31.9	30.1	28.0	27.4	25.9	24.0
Violent*	38.9	33.7	30.4	28.1	27.2	25.0	25.2	24.1	21.4
Property	50.8^	41.6^	38.3^	36.5^	33.2^	31.3^	30.6^	29.3^	27.6^
Drug	42.8^	38.5^	34.9^	31.8^	30.2^	37.6^	26.7^	25.0	23.4^
Public order.......................................	40.5	34.3	31.2	28.9	28.0	27.0^	25.8	23.8	22.5
Violent arrest after release									
All released prisoners	9.0	8.3	7.6	7.6	7.2	6.5	6.6	6.0	5.2
Violent*	11.0	10.2	8.4	8.8	8.9	6.8	6.9	6.5	5.8
Property	9.3^	7.8^	7.7	7.8^	6.9^	7.1	7.2	6.2	5.7
Drug	6.8^	7.2^	6.7^	6.2^	6.2^	5.3^	5.7^	5.4^	4.4^
Public order.......................................	9.7	8.6 A	8.3	8.1	7.3 A	7.2	6.6	6.4	5.3
Arrest after release for same type as most serious commitment offense[1]									
All released prisoners	21.0	18.0	15.6	14.5	13.7	12.2	11.8	11.5	10.6
Violent	11.0	10.2	8.4	8.8	8.9	6.8	6.9	6.5	5.8
Property	25.0	20.6	17.6	16.9	15.6	14.2	14.1	13.9	12.6
Drug	22.0	19.6	17.2	15.0	13.8	12.2	11.5	11.4	11.0
Public order.......................................	29.2	23.8	21.1	19.2	18.4	18.2	17.0	16.0	14.5
Arrest after release for different type as most serious commitment offense[1]									
All released prisoners	36.1	30.9	28.0	26.3	24.6	23.1	22.8	21.5	20.0
Violent	35.2	30.4	27.6	25.1	23.9	22.7	22.8	22.0	19.5
Property	42.4	34.4	31.6	30.6	27.6	26.0	25.6	24.1	23.0
Drug	34.8	31.3	27.9	26.0	24.6	22.7	22.2	20.7	19.1
Public order.......................................	26.3	22.6	20.7	19.8	18.7	17.9	18.0	16.6	16.0

Note: Persons could have been in prison for more than one offense; the most serious one is reported in this table. Each arrest may include more than one type of offense. "Type of offense" refers to the categories of violent, property, drug, and public order. Public order includes 0.8% of cases in which prisoners' most serious offense was unspecified.
* = Comparison group.
^ = Difference with comparison group is significant at the 95% confidence level.
[1]Percentages in these two categories do not sum to the "any arrest after release" category because categories overlap.

Table 7. Cumulative Percent of Prisoners Released in 30 States in 2005 Who Were Arrested Following Release, by Most Serious Commitment Offense and Type of Post-Release Arrest Offense

(Percent.)

Most serious commitment offense	Year 1	Year 2	Year 3	Year 4	Year 5	Year 6	Year 7	Year 8	Year 9
Any arrest after release									
All released prisoners	43.9	60.1	68.4	73.5	77.0	79.4	81.1	82.4	83.4
Violent*	38.9	54.2	62.2	67.6	71.6	74.2	76.1	77.7	78.7
Property	50.8 A	67.1 A	75.0 A	79.6 A	82.4 A	84.4 A	85.8 A	86.9 A	87.8 A
Drug	42.8 A	59.9 A	68.6 A	73.9 A	77.5 A	79.8 A	81.5 A	82.7 A	83.8 A
Public order	40.5	55.9	65.0 A	70.2 A	74.1 A	76.9 A	79.2 A	80.6 A	81.9 A
Violent arrest after release									
All released prisoners	9.0	15.8	20.9	25.4	29.3	32.3	35.0	37.3	39.1
Violent*	11.0	19.1	24.5	29.6	34.0	36.9	39.5	41.7	43.4
Property	9.3 A	15.8 A	20.9 A	25.7 A	29.3 A	32.9 A	36.0 A	38.5 A	40.4 A
Drug	6.8 A	12.7 A	17.5 A	21.3 A	25.1 A	27.7 A	30.1 A	32.1 A	34.0 A
Public order	9.7	16.4 A	21.8 A	26.6 A	30.0 A	32.9 A	35.7 A	38.1 A	39.8 A
Arrest after release for same type as most serious commitment offense[1]									
All released prisoners	21.0	32.5	39.6	45.0	49.1	52.1	54.5	56.5	58.2
Violent	11.0	19.1	24.5	29.6	34.0	36.9	39.5	41.7	43.4
Property	25.0	37.5	45.0	50.4	54.6	57.6	60.0	61.9	63.5
Drug	22.0	34.7	42.5	47.9	51.8	54.4	56.7	58.6	60.4
Public order	29.2	42.4	50.4	56.1	60.3	63.8	66.6	68.6	70.3
Arrest after release for different type as most serious commitment offense[1]									
All released prisoners	36.1	51.0	59.4	65.0	68.9	71.7	73.9	75.6	76.9
Violent	35.2	49.6	57.5	63.0	67.1	69.9	72.1	73.7	74.8
Property	42.4	58.0	66.4	71.8	75.3	77.9	79.8	81.4	82.6
Drug	34.8	50.2	58.8	64.6	68.6	71.4	73.6	75.3	76.7
Public order	26.3	39.7	48.2	54.3	58.4	61.6	64.6	66.5	68.2

Note: Persons could have been in prison for more than one offense; the most serious one is reported in this table. Each arrest may include more than one type of offense. "Type of offense" refers to the categories of violent, property, drug, and public order. Public order includes 0.8% of cases in which prisoners' most serious offense was unspecified.
* = Comparison group.
A = Difference with comparison group is significant at the 95% confidence level.
[1]Percentages in these two categories do not sum to the "any arrest after release" category because categories overlap.

Table 8. Annual Arrest Percentage of Prisoners Released in 30 States in 2005, by Whether Arrested Within or Outside the State of Release

(Percent.)

Year after release	All released prisoners		Among released prisoners arrested during the year, percent arrested outside state of release
	Outside state of release	Within or outside state of release	
1	3.3	43.9	7.5
2	3.4	37.7	9.0
3	3.4	34.3	10.0
4	3.5	31.9	10.9
5	3.6	30.1	12.0
6	3.5	28.0	12.6
7	3.6	27.4	13.3
8	3.5	25.9	13.6
9	3.4	24.0	14.2
Arrested anytime in follow-up period	15.4	83.4	X

Note: Detail may not sum to total due to rounding.
X = Not applicable.

Table 9. Number of Prisoners Released in 30 States in 2005

(Number; percent.)

State	Number of released prisoners[1]	Number of sample cases	Released prisoners included in the study[2]		Criminal history record collected	
			Weighted total	Sample size	Number	Percent
Total released	412,731	70,878	401,288	68,701	67,966	98.9
Alaska..	1,827	1,158	1,707	1,082	1,062	98.2
Arkansas.......................................	10,844	2,785	10,426	2,675	2,618	97.9
California......................................	107,633	4,604	105,392	4,511	4,510	100.0
Colorado	8,277	2,351	7,942	2,254	2,247	99.7
Florida	31,537	3,350	30,636	3,253	3,240	99.6
Georgia	12,321	2,763	12,011	2,687	2,592	96.5
Hawaii..	1,041	793	1,016	774	767	99.1
Iowa...	4,607	1,897	4,406	1,816	1,810	99.7
Louisiana	12,876	2,806	12,422	2,712	2,697	99.4
Maryland	10,200	2,597	9,769	2,488	2,468	99.2
Michigan.......................................	12,177	2,603	11,633	2,490	2,471	99.2
Minnesota.....................................	4,619	1,897	4,570	1,877	1,873	99.8
Missouri..	15,997	2,919	15,404	2,810	2,805	99.8
Nebraska	1,386	966	1,364	951	951	100.0
Nevada	5,022	1,973	4,930	1,935	1,787	92.4
New Jersey.....................................	13,097	2,697	12,964	2,666	2,622	98.3
New York.......................................	23,963	3,532	23,226	3,433	3,433	100.0
North Carolina	11,743	2,748	11,229	2,626	2,616	99.6
North Dakota.................................	884	686	865	671	663	98.8
Ohio...	15,832	3,070	15,555	3,015	2,927	97.1
Oklahoma......................................	7,768	2,345	7,424	2,240	2,169	96.8
Oregon...	4,731	1,955	4,595	1,900	1,898	99.9
Pennsylvania..................................	12,452	2,840	11,884	2,712	2,685	99.0
South Carolina...............................	10,046	2,537	9,971	2,516	2,500	99.4
South Dakota.................................	2,159	1,285	2,142	1,275	1,268	99.5
Texas..	43,532	3,779	42,770	3,713	3,713	100.0
Utah	3,000	1,569	2,951	1,543	1,534	99.4
Virginia...	12,776	2,719	12,148	2,585	2,574	99.6
Washington...................................	8,439	2,443	8,093	2,343	2,341	99.9
West Virginia.................................	1,945	1,211	1,842	1,148	1,125	98.0

[1]Excludes released prisoners whose sentence was less than one year; releases to custody, detainer, or warrant; releases due to death; escapes or absent without leave; transfers; administrative releases; and releases on appeal. The first release was selected for persons released multiple times during 2005.
[2]Percentages in these two categories do not sum to the "any arrest after release" category because categories overlap.

METHODOLOGY

Measuring Recidivism

Recidivism measures require three characteristics:

1. a starting event, such as a release from prison

2. a measure of failure following the starting event, such as a subsequent arrest, conviction, or return to prison

3. an observation or follow-up period that generally extends from the date of the starting event toa predefined end date (e.g., 6 months, 1 year, 3 years, 5 years, or 9 years)

This study used four outcome measures to examine the recidivism patterns of former state prisoners. Arrest data were used because they provided the offense details needed to produce these four measures for prisoners from all 30 states in the study.

1. Cumulative arrest percentage is the percentage of prisoners who had been arrested at least once at various points in the follow-up period. For example, the cumulative arrest percentage for year 5 is the percentage of all released prisoners who had at least one arrest during the 5-year period. BJS previously examined the cumulative percentage of prisoners who had a subsequent conviction or returned to prison within 5 years following release. The return-to-prison analysis for the 5-year follow-up study was limited to 23 of the study's 30 states with the data needed to identify returns to prison during the entire observation period.

2. Annual percentage of first arrests is the percentage of prisoners who had their first arrest following release during a specific year in the follow-up period. The denominator for each annual first-arrest percentage from years 1 through 9 is the total number of prisoners released in the 30 states during 2005. The numerators are the number of prisoners arrested for the first time during each of those years (i.e., they had not been arrested during a prior year in the follow-up period). The sum of the annual first-arrest percentages during a follow-up period equals the cumulative arrest percentage for the same period.

3. Annual arrest percentage of released prisoners includes those who were arrested at least once during a particular year within the follow-up period. The denominator for each percentage from years 1 through 9 is the total number of prisoners released in the 30 states during 2005. The numerators are the number of prisoners arrested during the particular year, regardless of whether they had been arrested during a prior year.

4. Annual volume of arrests is the total number of arrests of released prisoners during a particular year in the follow-up period. The total volume of arrests is the sum of each annual volume of arrests during the entire follow-up period. A prisoner may have had multiple arrests during a year or in the follow-up period, and a single arrest may have involved charges for more than one crime.

Measuring Desistance

Desistance is measured as the percentage of prisoners who, after a particular year, had no subsequent arrests during the remainder of the 9-year follow-up period. For example, if a prisoner was arrested during year 3 but was not arrested during years 4 through 9, the prisoner would be classified as having desisted during year 3. While recidivism is a measure of arrest at any point during the follow-up period, desistance is a measure of the absence of arrest between a particular point within the follow-up period and the end of the follow-up period.

Importance of Recidivism and Desistance Measures

Measures of recidivism and desistance provide information relevant to a deeper understanding of criminal behavior and the administration of justice in a wide range of policy areas. For example, law enforcement officials interested in the amount of crime committed by released prisoners can turn to statistics on the annual volume of arrests. Parole and probation agencies interested in the involvement of various types of former prisoners in criminal activities after release may focus on variations in cumulative arrest percentages. Treatment providers looking for measures of program effectiveness will be interested in desistance patterns. Additionally, task forces and policymakers examining the movement of criminals across state borders will be interested in the types of released prisoners most likely to commit new crimes (i.e., recidivate) in other states.

Sampling

This study estimates the recidivism patterns of persons released in 2005 from state prisons in 30 states. States were included in this study if the state departments of corrections could provide the prisoner records and the FBI or state identification numbers on persons released from prison during 2005. The fingerprint-based identification numbers were required to obtain the criminal history records on released prisoners. The prisoner records—obtained from the state departments of corrections through the Bureau of Justice Statistics' (BJS) National Corrections Reporting Program (NCRP)—also included each prisoner's sex, race, Hispanic origin, date of birth, confinement offenses, sentence length, type of prison release, and date of release. The 30 states whose departments of corrections submitted the NCRP data on prisoners released in 2005 included Alaska, Arkansas, California, Colorado, Florida, Georgia, Hawaii, Iowa, Louisiana, Maryland, Michigan, Minnesota, Missouri, Nebraska, Nevada, New Jersey, New York, North Carolina, North Dakota, Ohio, Oklahoma, Oregon, Pennsylvania, South Carolina, South Dakota, Texas, Utah, Virginia, Washington, and West Virginia.

Across the 30 states in 2005, a total of 412,731 prisoners were released and were eligible for this study. That number excludes 131,997 prisoners (for a total of 544,728) who were sentenced to less than one year, transferred to the custody of another authority, died in prison, were released on bond, were released to seek or participate in an appeal of a case, or escaped from prison or were absent without official leave. The first release during 2005 was used for those prisoners released multiple times during the year.

From the universe of persons released from prison in the 30 states in 2005 in this study, all males and females who were in prison for homicide were selected with certainty into the study. Analyses were done to determine the number of non-homicide prisoners that would be needed from each state's universe of released prisoners to yield a statistically sound estimate of that state's recidivism and desistance rates. As a result, states contributed different numbers of records to the final sample. To achieve the desired state-level samples, lists of all males and females imprisoned for a non-homicide offense were sorted separately by the county in which the sentence was imposed, race, Hispanic origin, age, and most serious commitment offense. The within-state sampling rate for female prisoners was double that of males to improve the precision of female recidivism and desistance estimates. The combined number of persons in the 30 state samples totaled 70,878 individuals who were representative of all state prisoners released in those states during 2005. (This number dropped to 67,966 after accounting for those who died during the subsequent 9 years, lacked criminal history records, or had invalid release records.) Each prisoner in the sample was assigned a weight based on the probability of selection within the state.

Collecting and Processing Criminal Records for Recidivism Research

In 2008, BJS entered into a data-sharing agreement with the FBI's Criminal Justice Information Services Division and the International Justice and Public Safety Network (Nlets) to allow BJS access to criminal history records through the FBI's Interstate Identification Index (III). Additionally, a data

security agreement was executed between BJS, the FBI, and Nlets to define the operational and technical practices used to protect the confidentiality and integrity of the criminal history data during data exchange, processing, and storage.

The FBI's III is an automated pointer system that allows authorized agencies to determine whether any state repository has criminal history records on an individual. Nlets is a computer-based network that is responsible for interstate transmissions of federal and state criminal history records. It allows authorized users to query III and send requests to states holding criminal history records on an individual. The FBI also maintains criminal history records for which it has sole responsibility for disseminating, such as information on federal arrests. The identification bureaus that operate the central repositories in each state respond automatically to requests over the Nlets network with an individual's criminal history record. Put together, these requests represent the individual's national criminal history record.

Once BJS received approval from the FBI's Institutional Review Board to conduct this recidivism study on prisoners released in 2005, Nlets transmitted the state and FBI identification numbers on the sampled prisoners to the FBI's III system to collect the criminal history records on behalf of BJS. The criminal history records include information from the state of release and all other states in which the sampled prisoners had been arrested both prior to the release in 2005 and afterward.

Nlets parsed the fields from individual criminal history records into a relational database consisting of state- and federal-specific numeric codes and text descriptions (e.g., criminal statutes and case outcome information) into a uniform record layout. NORC at the University of Chicago assisted BJS with standardizing the content of the relational database into a uniform coding structure to support national-level recidivism research.

BJS conducted a series of data-quality checks on the criminal history records to assess the accuracy and completeness of the information, including an examination of the response messages and the identification numbers that failed to match a record in III. To ensure that the correct records were received on the released prisoners using their fingerprint-based identification numbers, BJS compared other individual identifiers in the NCRP data to those reported in the criminal history records. For 98 percent of cases, a released prisoner's date of birth in the NCRP data exactly matched the prisoner's birthdate in the criminal history records. Nearly 100 percent (99.9 percent) of the NCRP and criminal history records matched prisoner sex, race, and Hispanic origin.

BJS reviewed the criminal history records for differences and inconsistencies in reporting practices and noticed some variations across states. During data processing and analysis, steps were taken to standardize the information and to minimize the impact these variations had on the overall recidivism and desistance estimates. For example, administrative (e.g., a criminal registration or the issuance of a warrant) and procedural (e.g., transferring a suspect to another jurisdiction) records embedded in the criminal history data that did not refer to an actual arrest were identified and removed. Traffic offenses (except for vehicular manslaughter, driving while intoxicated, and hit-and-run) were also excluded because the reporting of these events in the criminal history records varied widely by state.

Deaths During the Follow-Up Period

BJS documented that 2,173 of the 70,878 sampled prisoners died during the 9-year follow-up period, and BJS removed these cases from the recidivism and desistance analysis along with four additional cases that were determined to be invalid release records. The fingerprint-verified death notices obtained through the FBI's III system were used to identify some of the sampled prisoners who died within the 9 years following release in 2005. Additional deaths were identified through the Social Security Administration's (SSA) public Death Master File (DMF). While the public DMF provided a more complete source of death information than the FBI's III system, the public DMF provided death information only for the years 2005 to 2011. Therefore, the identification of those who died between 2012 and 2014 was limited to the FBI's III data, which included only fingerprint-verified deaths. The number of released prisoners who were identified as dead between 2005 and 2011 in the public DMF is an undercount of the actual number of deaths within the sample. Due to state disclosure laws, the public DMF does not include information on certain protected state death records received via SSA's contracts with the states. Beginning in 2011, the SSA removed more than 4 million state-reported death records from the public DMF and began adding fewer records to the public DMF. As a result, the public DMF contains an undercount of annual deaths.

The extent to which the public DMF undercounts the annual number of deaths is not exactly known. Analyses of deaths in the public DMF compared to those reported by the Centers for Disease Control and Prevention's (CDC) mortality counts suggest that the public DMF undercounted the overall number of deaths in the United States by about 10 percent in 2005. The undercount increased during succeeding years, and as of 2010, the public DMF contained less than half (45 percent) of the deaths reported by the CDC. If the number of released prisoners who died during the follow-up period and were removed from the recidivism and desistance analysis were adjusted to account for this undercount, the estimated cumulative recidivism rate would likely increase by about one percentage point.

Missing Criminal History Records

Among the 68,701 sampled prisoners not identified as deceased during the follow-up period, BJS did not receive criminal history records on 735 prisoners, either because the state departments of correction were unable to provide their FBI or state identification number or because the prisoner had an identification number that did not link to a criminal history record either in the FBI or state record repositories. To account for the missing criminal history records and to ensure the recidivism and desistance statistics were representative of all 68,701 prisoners in the analysis, BJS developed weighting class adjustments to account for those prisoners without criminal history information to reduce nonresponse bias.

To create the statistical adjustments, the 68,701 sampled prisoners were stratified into groups by crossing the two categories of sex (male or female), five categories of age at release (24 or younger, 25 to 29, 30 to 34, 35 to 39, or 40 or older), four categories of race/Hispanic origin (non-Hispanic White, non-Hispanic Black, Hispanic, or other race), and four categories of the most serious commitment offense (violent, property, drug, or public order). Within each of the subgroups, statistical weights were applied to the data of the 67,966 prisoners with criminal history information to allow their data to represent the 735 prisoners without criminal history information.

Conducting Tests of Statistical Significance

This study was based on a sample, not a complete enumeration, so the estimates are subject to sampling error. One measure of the sampling error associated with an estimate is the standard error. The standard error can vary from one estimate to the next. In general, an estimate with a smaller standard error provides a more reliable approximation of the true value than an estimate with a larger standard error. Estimates with relatively large standard errors should be interpreted with caution. BJS conducted tests to determine whether differences in the estimates were statistically significant once sampling error was taken into account.

All differences discussed in this report are statistically significant at the 95 percent confidence interval level. Standard errors were generated using Stata, a statistical so ware package that calculates sampling errors for data from complex sample surveys.

Offense Definitions

Violent offenses include homicide, rape or sexual assault, robbery, assault, and other miscellaneous or unspecified violent offenses.

Property offenses include burglary, fraud or forgery, larceny, motor vehicle the, and other miscellaneous or unspecified property offenses.

Drug offenses include possession, trafficking, and other miscellaneous or unspecified drug offenses.

Public order offenses include violations of the peace or order of the community or threats to the public health or safety through unacceptable conduct, interference with a governmental authority, or the violation of civil rights or liberties. This category includes weapons offenses, driving under the influence, probation and parole violation, obstruction of justice, commercialized vice, disorderly conduct, and other miscellaneous or unspecified offenses.

Arrests for Probation and Parole Violations

In this report, arrests for probation and parole violations were included as public order offenses. Excluding arrests for probation and parole violations from the analysis would have had only a small impact on the recidivism rates. Excluding probation and parole violations from the annual arrest percentages, 39.5 percent of prisoners released in 30 states in 2005 were arrested in year 1, 34.3 percent were arrested in year 2, 31.5 percent in year 3, 29.7 percent in year 4, 28.2 percent in year 5, 25.9 percent in year 6, 25.9 percent in year 7, 24.6 percent in year 8, and 23.0 percent in year 9. Overall, excluding probation and parole violations, 82.4 percent of prisoners released in 30 states in 2005 were arrested within 9 years. In other words, 99 percent of prisoners who were arrested during the 9-year follow-up period were arrested for an offense other than a probation or parole violation.

APPENDIX: SOURCES FOR TABLES

Part 1. Capital Punishment, 2016

1   Bureau of Justice Statistics, National Prisoner Statistics program (NPS-8), 2016
2   Bureau of Justice Statistics, National Prisoner Statistics program (NPS-8), 2016
3   Bureau of Justice Statistics, National Prisoner Statistics program (NPS-8), 2016
4   Bureau of Justice Statistics, National Prisoner Statistics program (NPS-8), 2016
5   Bureau of Justice Statistics, National Prisoner Statistics program (NPS-8), 2016
6   Bureau of Justice Statistics, National Prisoner Statistics program (NPS-8), 2016
7   Bureau of Justice Statistics, National Prisoner Statistics program (NPS-8), 1930–2016
8   Bureau of Justice Statistics, National Prisoner Statistics program (NPS-8), 1953–2016
9   Bureau of Justice Statistics, National Prisoner Statistics program (NPS-8), 1973–2016
10   Bureau of Justice Statistics, National Prisoner Statistics program (NPS-8), 1968–2016

Part 2. Correctional Populations in the United States, 2016

1   Bureau of Justice Statistics, Annual Probation Survey, Annual Parole Survey, Annual Survey of Jails, and National Prisoner Statistics program, 2000 and 2006–2016
2   Bureau of Justice Statistics, Annual Probation Survey, Annual Parole Survey, Annual Survey of Jails, and National Prisoner Statistics program, 2000 and 2006–2016; and U.S. Census Bureau, postcensal resident populations for January of the following year 2001 and 2006–2016
3   Bureau of Justice Statistics, Annual Probation Survey, Annual Parole Survey, Annual Survey of Jails, and National Prisoner Statistics program, 2007 and 2016
4   Bureau of Justice Statistics, Annual Probation Survey, Annual Parole Survey, Annual Survey of Jails, and National Prisoner Statistics program, 2007–2016
5   Bureau of Justice Statistics, Annual Probation Survey, Annual Parole Survey, Deaths in Custody Reporting Program, and National Prisoner Statistics program, 2014; and U.S. Census Bureau, unpublished U.S. resident population estimates within jurisdiction on January 1, 2015
6   Bureau of Justice Statistics, Annual Probation Survey, Annual Parole Survey, and National Prisoner Statistics program, 2000–2016
7   Bureau of Justice Statistics, Annual Surveys of Probation and Parole, Deaths in Custody Reporting Program, and National Prisoner Statistics program, 2016; and U.S. Census Bureau, unpublished U.S. resident population estimates within jurisdiction on January 1, 2017
8   Bureau of Justice Statistics, Annual Survey of Jails and National Prisoner Statistics program, 2000, 2010, and 2015–2016; and U.S. Census Bureau, postcensal estimated resident populations for January 1 of the following year, 2001, 2011, 2016, and 2017
9   Bureau of Justice Statistics, National Prisoner Statistics program and Survey of Jails in Indian Country, 2000, 2010, and 2015–2016

Part 3. Crimes Against Persons with Disabilities, 2009–2015

1   Bureau of Justice Statistics, National Crime Victimization Survey, 2011–2015; and U.S. Census Bureau, American Community Survey, 2011–2015
2   Bureau of Justice Statistics, National Crime Victimization Survey, 2011–2015; and U.S. Census Bureau, American Community Survey, 2011–2015
3   Bureau of Justice Statistics, National Crime Victimization Survey, 2011–2015; and U.S. Census Bureau, American Community Survey, 2011–2015
4   Bureau of Justice Statistics, National Crime Victimization Survey, 2011–2015; and U.S. Census Bureau, American Community Survey, 2011–2015
5   Bureau of Justice Statistics, National Crime Victimization Survey, 2011–2015; and U.S. Census Bureau, American Community Survey, 2011–2015

6   Bureau of Justice Statistics, National Crime Victimization Survey, 2011–2015

7   Bureau of Justice Statistics, National Crime Victimization Survey, 2011–2015; and U.S. Census Bureau, American Community Survey, 2011–2015

8   Bureau of Justice Statistics, National Crime Victimization Survey, 2011–2015

9   Bureau of Justice Statistics, National Crime Victimization Survey, 2011–2015

10   Bureau of Justice Statistics, National Crime Victimization Survey, 2011–2015

11   Bureau of Justice Statistics, National Crime Victimization Survey, 2011–2015

12   Bureau of Justice Statistics, National Crime Victimization Survey, 2011–2015

13   Bureau of Justice Statistics, National Crime Victimization Survey, 2011–2015

Part 4. Crime in the United States, 2016

1   United States Department of Justice, Federal Bureau of Investigation, Uniform Crime Reports, 2016

2   United States Department of Justice, Federal Bureau of Investigation, Uniform Crime Reports, 2016

3   United States Department of Justice, Federal Bureau of Investigation, Uniform Crime Reports, 2016

4   United States Department of Justice, Federal Bureau of Investigation, Uniform Crime Reports, 2016

5   United States Department of Justice, Federal Bureau of Investigation, Uniform Crime Reports, 2016

6   United States Department of Justice, Federal Bureau of Investigation, Uniform Crime Reports, 2016

7   United States Department of Justice, Federal Bureau of Investigation, Uniform Crime Reports, 2016

8   United States Department of Justice, Federal Bureau of Investigation, Uniform Crime Reports, 2016

9   United States Department of Justice, Federal Bureau of Investigation, Uniform Crime Reports, 2016

10   United States Department of Justice, Federal Bureau of Investigation, Uniform Crime Reports, 2016

11   United States Department of Justice, Federal Bureau of Investigation, Uniform Crime Reports, 2016

12   United States Department of Justice, Federal Bureau of Investigation, Uniform Crime Reports, 2016

13   United States Department of Justice, Federal Bureau of Investigation, Uniform Crime Reports, 2016

14   United States Department of Justice, Federal Bureau of Investigation, Uniform Crime Reports, 2016

15   United States Department of Justice, Federal Bureau of Investigation, Uniform Crime Reports, 2016

16   United States Department of Justice, Federal Bureau of Investigation, Uniform Crime Reports, 2016

17   United States Department of Justice, Federal Bureau of Investigation, Uniform Crime Reports, 2016

18   United States Department of Justice, Federal Bureau of Investigation, Uniform Crime Reports, 2016

19   United States Department of Justice, Federal Bureau of Investigation, Uniform Crime Reports, 2016

20   United States Department of Justice, Federal Bureau of Investigation, Uniform Crime Reports, 2016

21   United States Department of Justice, Federal Bureau of Investigation, Uniform Crime Reports, 2016

22   United States Department of Justice, Federal Bureau of Investigation, Uniform Crime Reports, 2016

23   United States Department of Justice, Federal Bureau of Investigation, Uniform Crime Reports, 2016

24   United States Department of Justice, Federal Bureau of Investigation, Uniform Crime Reports, 2016

25   United States Department of Justice, Federal Bureau of Investigation, Uniform Crime Reports, 2016

26   United States Department of Justice, Federal Bureau of Investigation, Uniform Crime Reports, 2016

27   United States Department of Justice, Federal Bureau of Investigation, Uniform Crime Reports, 2016

28   United States Department of Justice, Federal Bureau of Investigation, Uniform Crime Reports, 2016

29   United States Department of Justice, Federal Bureau of Investigation, Uniform Crime Reports, 2016

30   United States Department of Justice, Federal Bureau of Investigation, Uniform Crime Reports, 2016

31   United States Department of Justice, Federal Bureau of Investigation, Uniform Crime Reports, 2016

32   United States Department of Justice, Federal Bureau of Investigation, Uniform Crime Reports, 2016

33   United States Department of Justice, Federal Bureau of Investigation, Uniform Crime Reports, 2016

34   United States Department of Justice, Federal Bureau of Investigation, Uniform Crime Reports, 2016

35   United States Department of Justice, Federal Bureau of Investigation, Uniform Crime Reports, 2016

36   United States Department of Justice, Federal Bureau of Investigation, Uniform Crime Reports, 2016

37   United States Department of Justice, Federal Bureau of Investigation, Uniform Crime Reports, 2016

38   United States Department of Justice, Federal Bureau of Investigation, Uniform Crime Reports, 2016

39   United States Department of Justice, Federal Bureau of Investigation, Uniform Crime Reports, 2016

40   United States Department of Justice, Federal Bureau of Investigation, Uniform Crime Reports, 2016

41   United States Department of Justice, Federal Bureau of Investigation, Uniform Crime Reports, 2016

42   United States Department of Justice, Federal Bureau of Investigation, Uniform Crime Reports, 2016

43   United States Department of Justice, Federal Bureau of Investigation, Uniform Crime Reports, 2016

44	United States Department of Justice, Federal Bureau of Investigation, Uniform Crime Reports, 2016
45	United States Department of Justice, Federal Bureau of Investigation, Uniform Crime Reports, 2016
46	United States Department of Justice, Federal Bureau of Investigation, Uniform Crime Reports, 2016
47	United States Department of Justice, Federal Bureau of Investigation, Uniform Crime Reports, 2016
48	United States Department of Justice, Federal Bureau of Investigation, Uniform Crime Reports, 2016
49	United States Department of Justice, Federal Bureau of Investigation, Uniform Crime Reports, 2016
50	United States Department of Justice, Federal Bureau of Investigation, Uniform Crime Reports, 2016
51	United States Department of Justice, Federal Bureau of Investigation, Uniform Crime Reports, 2016
52	United States Department of Justice, Federal Bureau of Investigation, Uniform Crime Reports, 2016
53	United States Department of Justice, Federal Bureau of Investigation, Uniform Crime Reports, 2016
54	United States Department of Justice, Federal Bureau of Investigation, Uniform Crime Reports, 2016

Part 5. Criminal Victimization, 2016

1. Bureau of Justice Statistics, based on internal data from the U.S. Census Bureau, National Crime Victimization Survey (NCVS), 2015–2016
2. Bureau of Justice Statistics, National Crime Victimization Survey (NCVS), 2016
3. Bureau of Justice Statistics, National Crime Victimization Survey (NCVS), 2016
4. Bureau of Justice Statistics, National Crime Victimization Survey (NCVS), 2016; and FBI, *Crime in the United States, 2016*, https://ucr.fbi.gov/crime-in-the- u.s/2016/crime-in-the-u.s.-2016/topic-pages/tables/table-1
5. Bureau of Justice Statistics, National Crime Victimization Survey (NCVS), 2016
6. Bureau of Justice Statistics, National Crime Victimization Survey (NCVS), 2016
7. Bureau of Justice Statistics, National Crime Victimization Survey (NCVS), 2016
8. Bureau of Justice Statistics, National Crime Victimization Survey (NCVS), 2016
9. Bureau of Justice Statistics, National Crime Victimization Survey (NCVS), 2016
10. Bureau of Justice Statistics, National Crime Victimization Survey (NCVS), 2016
11. Bureau of Justice Statistics, National Crime Victimization Survey (NCVS), 2016

Part 6. Hate Crime Statistics, 2016

1. Federal Bureau of Investigation, Hate Crime Statistics, 2016
2. Federal Bureau of Investigation, Hate Crime Statistics, 2016
3. Federal Bureau of Investigation, Hate Crime Statistics, 2016
4. Federal Bureau of Investigation, Hate Crime Statistics, 2016
5. Federal Bureau of Investigation, Hate Crime Statistics, 2016
6. Federal Bureau of Investigation, Hate Crime Statistics, 2016
7. Federal Bureau of Investigation, Hate Crime Statistics, 2016
8. Federal Bureau of Investigation, Hate Crime Statistics, 2016
9. Federal Bureau of Investigation, Hate Crime Statistics, 2016
10. Federal Bureau of Investigation, Hate Crime Statistics, 2016
11. Federal Bureau of Investigation, Hate Crime Statistics, 2016
12. Federal Bureau of Investigation, Hate Crime Statistics, 2016
13. Federal Bureau of Investigation, Hate Crime Statistics, 2016

Part 7. Indicators of School Crime and Safety, 2015

1. Centers for Disease Control and Prevention (CDC), 1992–2015 School-Associated Violent Death Surveillance System (SAVD-SS) (partially funded by the U.S. Department of Education, Office of Safe and Healthy Students), previously un-published tabulation (June 2017); CDC, National Center for Injury Prevention and Control, Web-based Injury Statistics Query and Reporting System Fatal (WISQARSTM Fatal), 1992–2014, retrieved June 2017 from http://www.cdc.gov/injury/wisqars/index.html; and Federal Bureau of Investigation and Bureau of Justice Statistics, Supplementary Homicide Reports (SHR), preliminary data (September 2017)
2. U.S. Department of Justice, Bureau of Justice Statistics, National Crime Victimization Survey (NCVS), 1992 through 2016
3. U.S. Department of Justice, Bureau of Justice Statistics, National Crime Victimization Survey (NCVS), 2015

4   Centers for Disease Control and Prevention, Division of Adolescent and School Health, Youth Risk Behavior Surveillance System (YRBSS), 1993 through 2015

5   U.S. Department of Education, National Center for Education Statistics, Schools and Staffing Survey (SASS), "Public School Teacher Data File" and "Private School Teacher Data File," 1993–94, 1999–2000, 2003–04, 2007–08, and 2011–12; and "Charter School Teacher Data File," 1999–2000

6   U.S. Department of Education, National Center for Education Statistics, 1999–2000, 2003–04, 2005–06, 2007–08, 2009–10, and 2015–16 School Survey on Crime and Safety (SSOCS), 2000, 2004, 2006, 2008, 2010, and 2016; and Fast Response Survey System (FRSS), "School Safety and Discipline: 2013–14," FRSS 106, 2014

7   U.S. Department of Justice, Bureau of Justice Statistics, School Crime Supplement (SCS) to the National Crime Victimization Survey, 2001 through 2016

8   Centers for Disease Control and Prevention, Division of Adolescent and School Health, Youth Risk Behavior Surveillance System (YRBSS), 1993 through 2015

9   U.S. Department of Justice, Bureau of Justice Statistics, School Crime Supplement (SCS) to the National Crime Victimization Survey, 1999 through 2015

10   U.S. Department of Justice, Bureau of Justice Statistics, School Crime Supplement (SCS) to the National Crime Victimization Survey, selected years, 2005 through 2015

Part 8. Jail Inmates in 2016

1   Bureau of Justice Statistics, Annual Survey of Jails, 2000 and 2006–2016; Census of Jail Inmates, midyear 2005; and Deaths in Custody Reporting Program, 2000 and 2006 (admissions only)

2   Bureau of Justice Statistics, Annual Survey of Jails, 2000 and 2010–2016; and Census of Jail Inmates, midyear 2005

3   Bureau of Justice Statistics, Annual Survey of Jails, 2000 and 2010–2016; and Census of Jail Inmates, midyear 2005

3A   Bureau of Justice Statistics, Annual Survey of Jails, 2000 and 2006–2016; and Census of Jail Inmates, midyear 2005

4   Bureau of Justice Statistics, Annual Survey of Jails, 2016

5   Bureau of Justice Statistics, Annual Survey of Jails, 2016

6   Bureau of Justice Statistics, Annual Survey of Jails, 2016

7   Bureau of Justice Statistics, Annual Survey of Jails, 2000 and 2006–2016

8   Bureau of Justice Statistics, Annual Survey of Jails, 2016

Part 9. Law Enforcement Officers Killed and Assaulted, 2017

1   United States Department of Justice, Federal Bureau of Investigation, Uniform Crime Reports, 2017
2   United States Department of Justice, Federal Bureau of Investigation, Uniform Crime Reports, 2017
3   United States Department of Justice, Federal Bureau of Investigation, Uniform Crime Reports, 2017
4   United States Department of Justice, Federal Bureau of Investigation, Uniform Crime Reports, 2017
5   United States Department of Justice, Federal Bureau of Investigation, Uniform Crime Reports, 2017
6   United States Department of Justice, Federal Bureau of Investigation, Uniform Crime Reports, 2017
7   United States Department of Justice, Federal Bureau of Investigation, Uniform Crime Reports, 2017
8   United States Department of Justice, Federal Bureau of Investigation, Uniform Crime Reports, 2017
9   United States Department of Justice, Federal Bureau of Investigation, Uniform Crime Reports, 2017
10   United States Department of Justice, Federal Bureau of Investigation, Uniform Crime Reports, 2017
11   United States Department of Justice, Federal Bureau of Investigation, Uniform Crime Reports, 2017
12   United States Department of Justice, Federal Bureau of Investigation, Uniform Crime Reports, 2017
13   United States Department of Justice, Federal Bureau of Investigation, Uniform Crime Reports, 2017
14   United States Department of Justice, Federal Bureau of Investigation, Uniform Crime Reports, 2017
15   United States Department of Justice, Federal Bureau of Investigation, Uniform Crime Reports, 2017
16   United States Department of Justice, Federal Bureau of Investigation, Uniform Crime Reports, 2017
17   United States Department of Justice, Federal Bureau of Investigation, Uniform Crime Reports, 2017
18   United States Department of Justice, Federal Bureau of Investigation, Uniform Crime Reports, 2017
19   United States Department of Justice, Federal Bureau of Investigation, Uniform Crime Reports, 2017
20   United States Department of Justice, Federal Bureau of Investigation, Uniform Crime Reports, 2017
21   United States Department of Justice, Federal Bureau of Investigation, Uniform Crime Reports, 2017
22   United States Department of Justice, Federal Bureau of Investigation, Uniform Crime Reports, 2017
23   United States Department of Justice, Federal Bureau of Investigation, Uniform Crime Reports, 2017

24   United States Department of Justice, Federal Bureau of Investigation, Uniform Crime Reports, 2017
25   United States Department of Justice, Federal Bureau of Investigation, Uniform Crime Reports, 2017
26   United States Department of Justice, Federal Bureau of Investigation, Uniform Crime Reports, 2017
27   United States Department of Justice, Federal Bureau of Investigation, Uniform Crime Reports, 2017
28   United States Department of Justice, Federal Bureau of Investigation, Uniform Crime Reports, 2017
29   United States Department of Justice, Federal Bureau of Investigation, Uniform Crime Reports, 2017
30   United States Department of Justice, Federal Bureau of Investigation, Uniform Crime Reports, 2017
31   United States Department of Justice, Federal Bureau of Investigation, Uniform Crime Reports, 2017
32   United States Department of Justice, Federal Bureau of Investigation, Uniform Crime Reports, 2017
33   United States Department of Justice, Federal Bureau of Investigation, Uniform Crime Reports, 2017
34   United States Department of Justice, Federal Bureau of Investigation, Uniform Crime Reports, 2017
35   United States Department of Justice, Federal Bureau of Investigation, Uniform Crime Reports, 2017
36   United States Department of Justice, Federal Bureau of Investigation, Uniform Crime Reports, 2017
37   United States Department of Justice, Federal Bureau of Investigation, Uniform Crime Reports, 2017
38   United States Department of Justice, Federal Bureau of Investigation, Uniform Crime Reports, 2017
39   United States Department of Justice, Federal Bureau of Investigation, Uniform Crime Reports, 2017
40   United States Department of Justice, Federal Bureau of Investigation, Uniform Crime Reports, 2017

Part 10. Probation and Parole, 2016

1   Bureau of Justice Statistics, Annual Probation Survey and Annual Parole Survey, 2000–2016
2   Bureau of Justice Statistics, Annual Probation Survey and Annual Parole Survey, 2000, 2005, 2010–2016; and U.S. Census Bureau, National Intercensal Estimates, 2001, 2006, and 2011–2017
3   Bureau of Justice Statistics, Annual Probation Survey and Annual Parole Survey, 2000–2016
4   Bureau of Justice Statistics, Annual Probation Survey and Annual Parole Survey, 2000–2016
5   Bureau of Justice Statistics, Annual Probation Survey and Annual Parole Survey, 2016
6   Bureau of Justice Statistics, Annual Probation Survey and Annual Parole Survey, 2016
7   Bureau of Justice Statistics, Annual Probation Survey, 2016
8   Bureau of Justice Statistics, Annual Probation Survey, 2000, 2015, and 2016
9   Bureau of Justice Statistics, Annual Parole Survey, 2016
10   Bureau of Justice Statistics, Annual Parole Survey, 2016
11   Bureau of Justice Statistics, Annual Parole Survey, 2016
12   Bureau of Justice Statistics, Annual Parole Survey, 2000, 2015, and 2016

Part 11. 2018 Update on Prisoner Recidivism: A 9-Year Follow-Up Period (2005–2014)

1   Bureau of Justice Statistics, Recidivism of State Prisoners Released in 2005 data collection, 2005–2014
2   Bureau of Justice Statistics, Recidivism of State Prisoners Released in 2005 data collection, 2005–2014
3   Bureau of Justice Statistics, Recidivism of State Prisoners Released in 2005 data collection, 2005–2014
4   Bureau of Justice Statistics, Recidivism of State Prisoners Released in 2005 data collection, 2005–2014
5   Bureau of Justice Statistics, Recidivism of State Prisoners Released in 2005 data collection, 2005–2014
6   Bureau of Justice Statistics, Recidivism of State Prisoners Released in 2005 data collection, 2005–2014
7   Bureau of Justice Statistics, Recidivism of State Prisoners Released in 2005 data collection, 2005–2014
8   Bureau of Justice Statistics, Recidivism of State Prisoners Released in 2005 data collection, 2005–2014
9   Bureau of Justice Statistics, Recidivism of State Prisoners Released in 2005 data collection, 2005–2014

INDEX

H

HANGING
Method of execution, by state, 9

HATE CRIMES
Age
known offender's age, 350
Ancestry
incidents, offenses, victims, and known offenders, 341, 343, 345
victims, offense type, by bias motivation, 348
Bias motivation
incidents, by motivation and location, 351
incidents, offenses, victims, and known offenders, 341
incidents, victim type, by bias motivation, 350
incidents per bias motivation and quarter, selected state, 355
offense type, by bias motivation, 343, 345
victims, offense type, by bias motivation, 348
Cities
incidents per bias motivation and quarter, 355
Counties
incidents per bias motivation and quarter, 355
Crimes against persons
incidents, offenses, victims, and known offenders, 342
offenses, offense type, by participating state, 352
offenses, victim type, by offense type, 347
Crimes against property
incidents, offenses, victims, and known offenders, 342
offenses, offense type, by participating state, 352
offenses, victim type, by offense type, 347
Crimes against society
incidents, offenses, victims, and known offenders, 342
Disabled persons
incidents, offenses, victims, and known offenders, 341, 343, 345
victims, offense type, by bias motivation, 348
Ethnicity
incidents, offenses, victims, and known offenders, 341, 343, 345
known offender's ethnicity, 350
known offender's ethnicity, by offense type, 342
victims, offense type, by bias motivation, 348
Gender identity
incidents, offenses, victims, and known offenders, 341, 343, 345
victims, offense type, by bias motivation, 348
Metropolitan statistical areas
incidents per bias motivation and quarter, 355
Multiple-bias incidents, 341-350
Race
bias motivation, 341, 343, 345
known offender's race, 350
known offender's race, by offense type, 342
victims, offense type, by bias motivation, 348
Religion
incidents, offenses, victims, and known offenders, 341, 343, 345
victims, offense type, by bias motivation, 348
School crime and safety
percentage of students reporting hate crimes, 401

Sex
incidents, offenses, victims, and known offenders, 341, 343, 345
victims, offense type, by bias motivation, 348
Sexual orientation
incidents, offenses, victims, and known offenders, 341, 343, 345
victims, offense type, by bias motivation, 348
Single-bias incidents, 341-350
States
agency hate crime reporting by participating state, 354
incidents per bias motivation and quarter, 355
offenses, offense type, by participating state, 352
Territories
offenses, offense type, by participating territory, 352
Universities and colleges
incidents per bias motivation and quarter, 355

HISPANIC ORIGIN
Capital punishment
demographic of prisoners under sentence of death, 8
number of persons under sentence of death, by race, 13
Criminal victimization
prevalence of violent crime, by victim demographics, 329
rate of violent victimization and percent reported, 328
Jail inmates
confined inmates in local jails, 416
incarceration rates, by Hispanic origin, 415
number of confined inmates in local jails, 417
Law enforcement officers accidentally killed
victim officer, 453
Law enforcement officers feloniously killed
profile of known offender, 446
victim officer, 435
Murder offenders, 262, 263
Murder victims, 262, 263
Prisoner recidivism
annual arrest percentage of prisoners released, by characteristics, 491
percent of prisoners released who were arrested after release, 490
School crime and safety
bullying, 402
gang activity, 399
hate crimes, 401
illegal drugs, 400
percent of students reporting weapons threats, 396
teachers reporting threats, 397

HOMICIDES
Justifiable homicide by weapon, law enforcement, 266
Justifiable homicide by weapon, private citizens, 266
Murder offenders
see **MURDER OFFENDERS**
Murder victims
see **MURDER VICTIMS**
School crime and safety, 393

HUMAN TRAFFICKING
Age
arrests, by age and participating state, 298
Arrests
age and participating state, 298